The 30th North Carolina
Infantry in the Civil War:
A History and Roster

ALSO BY WILLIAM THOMAS VENNER

*The 11th North Carolina Infantry in the Civil War:
A History and Roster* (McFarland, 2015)

*The 7th Tennessee Infantry in the Civil War:
A History and Roster* (McFarland, 2013)

The 30th North Carolina Infantry in the Civil War
A History and Roster

William Thomas Venner

McFarland & Company, Inc., Publishers
Jefferson, North Carolina

LIBRARY OF CONGRESS CATALOGUING-IN-PUBLICATION DATA

Names: Venner, William Thomas, 1950– author.
Title: The 30th North Carolina Infantry in the Civil War : a history and roster / William Thomas Venner.
Description: Jefferson, North Carolina : McFarland & Company, Inc., Publishers, 2018. | Includes bibliographical references and index.
Identifiers: LCCN 2017048372 | ISBN 9781476662404 (softcover : acid free paper) ∞
Subjects: LCSH: Confederate States of America. Army. North Carolina Infantry Regiment, 30th. | North Carolina—History—Civil War, 1861–1865—Regimental histories. | United States—History—Civil War, 1861–1865—Regimental histories. | United States—History—Civil War, 1861–1865—Campaigns.
Classification: LCC E573.5 30th .V46 2018 | DDC 973.7/456—dc23
LC record available at https://lccn.loc.gov/2017048372

BRITISH LIBRARY CATALOGUING DATA ARE AVAILABLE

ISBN (print) 978-1-4766-6240-4
ISBN (ebook) 978-1-4766-2790-8

© 2018 William Thomas Venner. All rights reserved

No part of this book may be reproduced or transmitted in any form or by any means, electronic or mechanical, including photocopying or recording, or by any information storage and retrieval system, without permission in writing from the publisher.

Front cover: *inset* unidentified Confederate soldiers; *background* Confederate entrenchments near Petersburg, Virginia (both photographs from Library of Congress)

Printed in the United States of America

McFarland & Company, Inc., Publishers
Box 611, Jefferson, North Carolina 28640
www.mcfarlandpub.com

To the men of the 30th North Carolina
Infantry and their families.
We must not let their memories fade.

Table of Contents

Preface   1

1. The 30th North Carolina Infantry Is Formed   3
2. Lost Innocence at Gaines' Mill   18
3. The Realities of War—Malvern Hill   30
4. Summer 1862—The Road to Sharpsburg   41
5. The Sunken Road at Sharpsburg   51
6. Winter 1862–1863: Rebuilding the Regiment   66
7. Chancellorsville—Fighting for Stonewall Jackson   83
8. The Road to Gettysburg   98
9. Gettysburg   108
10. Disaster at Kelly's Ford   125
11. Winter 1863–1864   139
12. Slaughter at Spotsylvania   151
13. The Killing Continues—Harris Farm to Cold Harbor   171
14. Campaigning with the Army of the Valley District   187
15. September 1864—Disaster in the Shenandoah Valley   207
16. Cedar Creek: Jubal Early Is Flanked Again   222
17. Winter Near Petersburg, 1864–1865   234
18. The End at Appomattox   246

Appendix 1. 30th North Carolina Infantry Casualties   263
Appendix 2. 30th North Carolina Infantry Roster   304
Chapter Notes   391
Bibliography   419
Index   423

Preface

On September 13, 1861, a 22-year-old student interrupted his studies at Davidson College, NC, and took a train to Raleigh. Later that evening, this youth, William Erskine Ardrey, scribbled onto the first page of a just purchased journal, "Entered on pay roll of 30th N.C. Regt." Forty-three months later, on April 13, 1865, Captain Ardrey dashed a hurried sentence into his weathered and crowded-with-entrees register, "On our way home. With light hearts and weary limbs." William Ardrey, just like two million other American young men, had taken part in our nation's civil war, and in April 1865, as one of the fortunate ones, returned home to begin rebuilding the world shattered by his country's horrendous conflict.

Ardrey enlisted into the 30th North Carolina Infantry as a naïve young man and four years later came home a changed and broken, combat veteran. He wrote in December 1865, "Nothing to drink and no money, poor as the devil, and feel so mean I can taste it." William Ardrey though, along with being lucky in war, was also blessed in love; he soon married the girl whose letters sustained him throughout that strife—Margaret "Maggie" Robinson. His bride, a 23-year-old woman, believed in her guy and was able to put this shattered ex-soldier's life together again. Maggie and William had six children over the next ten years. Sadly though, she died in 1879, but not before molding their children's future and reviving her man to his pre-war vigor and attitude. Later, William Ardrey would marry again, this time to Mary Howie, and they also would have six children. The now-restored William Ardrey supported his large family by farming, and even served terms in North Carolina's legislature, before passing away in 1907 at the age of sixty-seven.

William Ardrey's wartime experiences are not unique; at first he was a gullible youth-turned-soldier, like so many others. Though he may have been better educated than most, and survived the dangers of camp life and the horrors of battle, his story is not much different from the vast multitude of others in his generation who signed their names to enlistment papers. Then, when he returned home and underwent the healing a supportive and loving woman could provide, his life again mirrored what tens of thousands of other Civil War veterans experienced. He was a civilian, then a soldier, and once again a civilian. American had been at peace, went to war, and once again was at peace.

Today, William Ardrey's journal is archived at Davidson College, and is available for study. His daily thoughts and observations present us with a snapshot of what happened to him. Ardrey, and tens of thousands like him, whether wearing gray or blue, scratched their thoughts and feelings onto paper by pencil or quill. They have presented us with a glimpse of what their world was like, as well as give us a way to acknowledge their experiences. Their war occurred so long ago and is difficult to conceive how they lived, and why things happened the way they did. And in our hurried world today, sadly, their stories are fading into the shadowy mists of the past, slipping from our consciousness and melting from our memories.

How can I write about men like William Ardrey? I did not serve in the military and thus have not had the occasion to be in harm's way—so I cannot tell you what it feels like to be in battle. I did not grow up in the South, so I possess little experience with the Southern life style. Right now I sit at a desk writing on a computer, bathed by LCD lighting, cooled by air conditioning, and satiated from a pleasant and filling breakfast—so I have no understanding what it is like to survive in a tent, to have no recourse from freezing cold or sweltering heat, and to try to subsist on a handful of cornmeal and a rancid chunk of salt pork.

I freely admit these limitations to you as I write this regimental history of the 30th North Carolina Infantry. My goal, since I know little about what it feels like to be a mid-nineteenth century Southerner, or what it was like to stand with comrades on a Civil War battle line, is to remain as quiet as possible. But if I'm not going to speak, who is? To me, it is pretty obvious—let William Ardrey and his companions talk. I believe the history of our Civil War becomes much more valuable if we listen to those men who were there. It is their voices we most need to hear.

The 30th North Carolina Infantry in the Civil War contains more than two thousand quotes from William Ardrey and others like him. William Ardrey and his comrades, as well as the men they sought to kill, were linked in a close fraternity of combat soldiers. These spokesmen for their generation stood in the rain, shivered in the cold, and sweated in the heat. They withstood bad, or limited food, and were terrorized by the horrible effects of disease. These men tolerated poor leadership, mindless hours of drill, as well as the ghastly consequences of battle. They wrote letters to loved ones, chronicled events in journals and diaries, composed after-action reports, newspaper articles, reminiscences, and years later, regimental histories and battle discussions, leaving us with a treasure trove of personally experienced narratives. Their stories are interwoven and immensely powerful. *The 30th North Carolina Infantry in the Civil War* is this account; a story created by those who served under the Thirtieth's banner, their comrades, and the men they faced against, across so many lethal fields of battle. Together, they are the ones who write this history.

Chapter 1

The 30th North Carolina Infantry Is Formed

As Col. Francis "Frank" Parker surveyed his regiment, he turned to his adjutant, Lt. Frederick Philips and said, "They're ready." Lieutenant Philips nodded as the 30th North Carolina's senior officer continued, "I think the men are all anxious to be sent forward; they seem to be desirous to meet the invaders and drive them from our soil."[1] Lieutenant Fred Philips shuddered as the sounds of artillery rumbled through the trees sheltering over eight hundred Carolinian soldiers.[2] A near deafening burst from a close-by explosion caused some of the men to flinch. Parker's volunteers had not been in a battle before, but today, June 27, 1862, with the regiment not far from Gaines' Mill, there was little doubt Parker's men would suffer the cruel effects of artillery and musketry. Frank Parker gazed proudly at his Tar Heels and proclaimed, "[This is] not a fine dressed, nor finely equipped Regiment, but I have one which will do good fighting."[3] Fred Philips, Parker's brother-in-law, had never been close enough to the Yankees to have even seen a single enemy soldier. He glanced at his younger sister's husband and wished he had the older man's battle experience. The 25-year-old lieutenant's impression of war involved drill, parades, and marching.[4] Philips felt like a number of the riflemen in the 30th NC's ranks, much like Pvt. John Bone (Co. I), who wrote, "We had now spent about nine months as soldiers, but only knew ... very little of the life of a soldier or the art of war."[5]

In April 1861, Frank Parker had answered North Carolina's Governor John Ellis' call to defend the Old North State by immediately assisting in the bringing-in of a company of volunteers (the Enfield Blues) to Raleigh. His formation mustered into the 1st North Carolina Infantry with Parker serving as a lieutenant. Two months later he was in command of the Enfield Blues when the regiment met Union forces at Big Bethel on June 10, 1861. That scrap was not much more than a prolonged skirmish, but to the neophyte citizen-soldiers, and the war-naïve nation, the conflict was of immense proportion. The fight also resulted in the Confederacy's first soldier killed in battle, Pvt. Henry Wyatt. Also, Frank Parker came out of the fight knowing he could lead men under dire conditions, as well as the troops in the 30th North Carolina who knew their leader had been in combat, regarded him with awe. However, Parker did not inform them the fact that "four companies of [the 1st NC] did not fire a single shot in the fight, and [he was] ... sorry that the Enfield Blues [were] one of them." Parker wrote to his wife, explaining that "the attack was made on the side opposite to our lines, ... at least one fourth of a mile from us ... we did not even see a Yankee the whole day."[6]

Regardless of Parker's battle inexperience, the 1st North Carolina was only a six-months' formation and by the time it was mustered out of service, he, like most of the regiment's ambitious officers, had secured other infantry commands. Frank Parker was no different, though his promotion came in an unusual manner; North Carolina's Governor, John Ellis, who had been ailing with respiratory problems, "[died] … at Red Sulfur Springs in Virginia … [of] asthma or consumption, or a combination of both."[7] Ellis' replacement, Interim Governor Henry T. Clark, was Frank Parker's first cousin. Henry Clark found a new position for Parker, Colonel of the just mustered-in 30th North Carolina Infantry.[8]

Francis Marion Parker, born in 1827, was the eighth of nine children. His father, a successful merchant and devout member of the Episcopal Church, believed bestowing the name of a renowned Revolutionary War hero (Francis Marion, the Swamp Fox) upon his son would guide him with noble virtues.[9] Parker's mother, the daughter from a family with a deep pedigree of influential figures, assured the household would never lack for finances. Together, they raised Frank, as they called him, and his other siblings to respect God and honor one's responsibilities. The young Parker attended a number of fine schools and academies, and grew into adulthood, well educated, and "deeply imbued with the principles of the Democratic Party."[10]

Frank Parker's father died in 1849, leaving the 22-year-old in charge of the family plantation. At the time, the estate had 600 acres of land and 28 slaves, producing 27 bales of cotton, 3,500 bushels of corn, 300 bushels of peas, and 75 bushels of sweet potatoes.[11] The young farmer relished his new responsibilities, and two years later, married 16-year-old Sarah "Sally" Tartt Philips, the daughter of a prominent Edgecombe County physician.[12] They prospered and in 1853, purchased their own plantation near Enfield, NC. By the eve of the war, the couple had four children, and an estate valued at over $24,000. Their twenty-one slaves produced 1,000 bushels of corn, 120 bushels of oats, 200 bushels of peas, 300 bushels of sweet potatoes, and 27 bales of cotton.[13] Then, in 1861, when Frank Parker marched off to Raleigh as 2nd Lieutenant of the Enfield Blues, he left the management of the plantation's fields to Hilliard Parker, one of his slaves.[14] And now, barely six months later, he was awarded a commission as Colonel of the 30th North Carolina.

Francis M. Parker was 34 when he assumed command of the 30th NC (Clark, 1901).

The 30th North Carolina Infantry entered into Confederate service on September 26, 1861, formed from ten companies of volunteers coming primarily from the state's Piedmont and Inner Coastal Plain.[15] Colonel Frank Parker took command of nearly nine hundred newly recruited Tar Heels, assisted by Lt. Col. Walter Draughan and Maj. James Kell. Both of Parker's field officers were prominent men, the 50-year-old Walter Draughan owned a plantation in Cumberland County, NC, worth $67,000, and the 26-year-old James T. Kell, was a rising physician from Charlotte.[16] Frank Parker was immediately impressed with Walter Draughan, writing Sally, "The Lieut. Col. is a very clever man, but a very silent one. I think he will be a first rate officer."[17] Parker continued, "The [Lt.] Col. is a ... gentleman; very polite, and a great stickler for etiquette; he likes every thing done in proper form."[18] Strangely, he had little to say about the younger officer, though rapidly accepted his assistance, and often had the major tackle battalion drill. In November, Parker admitted to Sally, "I have not drilled them [the regiment] in Battalion drill yet."[19]

30th North Carolina Infantry[20]
October 10, 1861

Unit			Strength
Field & Staff		Col. Parker, Francis M. Lt. Col. Draughan, Walter F. Maj. Kell, James T.	11
Co. A	Sampson Rangers Sampson Co.	Cpt. Holmes, James C. 1st Lt. Sillers, William W. 2nd Lt. Patrick, Cornelius	119
Co. B	Nat Macon Guards Warren Co.	Cpt. Drake, William C. 1st Lt. Williams, Buckner D. 2nd Lt. Brame, John M.	86
Co. C	Brunswick Double-Quicks Brunswick Co.	Cpt. Green, Joseph 1st Lt. Allen, David C. 2nd Lt. Tharp, Samuel P.	92
Co. D	Neuse River Guards Wake & Granville Co.	Cpt. Grissom, Eugene 1st Lt. Allen, Solomon J. 2nd Lt. Bailey, Allen	90
Co. E	Duplin Turpentine Boys Duplin Co.	Cpt. McMillan, John C. 1st Lt. Johnson, Cornelius 2nd Lt. Boney, William J.	83
Co. F	Sparta Band Edgecombe Co.	Cpt. Pitt, Franklin G. 1st Lt. Moore, Willis M. 2nd Lt. Pitt, James W.	91
Co. G	Granville Rangers Granville Co.	Cpt. Taylor, Richard P. 1st Lt. Mitchell, Rush J. 2nd Lt. Barnett, James A.	72
Co. H	Moore County Rifles Moore Co.	Cpt. Swann, William M. 1st Lt. McIntosh, Archibald A. 2nd Lt. McIntosh, Daniel W.	83
Co. I	Ladies' Guards Nash Co.	Cpt. Arrington, William T. 1st Lt. Bunn, Elias 2nd Lt. Harris, James J.	87
Co. K	Mecklenburg Beauregards Mecklenburg Co.	Cpt. Morrow, Benjamin F. 1st Lt. Bell, Charles E. 3rd Lt. Witherspoon, John G.	72
			886

The regiment's rambunctious volunteers waited impatiently among the hastily built structures of Camp Mangum, a few miles from Raleigh. They were anxious to be sent to Virginia and defeat the Linconites. Colonel Parker recorded their feelings, writing, "we will whip them back, or give them a right to a small part of our soil, say 2 feet by 6 feet."[21]

The Thirtieth's volunteers had come from large cities such as Raleigh and Charlotte, small towns like Clinton, Warrenton, Chinquapin, and Tarboro, and isolated villages barely larger than a general store and a post office. Some recruits were sons of wealthy planters, like Thomas Lee (Co. A), whose father's estate topped $80,000, while scores and scores of others owned nothing and could not even sign their names.[22]

While a number of volunteers could not read or write, most had simple, grade-school educations. Even so, there also was a sprinkling of fellows with college education, such as Maj. James Kell, who had earned a medical degree from New York University; Pvt. Monroe McKinney (Co. K), a professor of French at Charlotte's North Carolina Military Institute; and Pvt. William Ardrey (Co. K), a student at Davidson College. There were teachers, Sgt. Archibald Lawhorn (Co. A) and 3rd Lt. Lorenzo Cain (Co. C), as well as plantation overseers like Cpl. John Wescott (Co. C). Others joining the regiment were blacksmiths; Pvt. Benjamin Butler (Co. E); butchers, Pvt. Alford Poland (Co. I); millers, Cpl. Louis Wells (Co. F); well diggers, Pvt. James Deaton (Co. H); shoe makers, Jefferson Thomas (Co. H); turpentine laborers, Pvt. James Joyner (Co. I); and tobacconists, Pvt. George Reams (Co. G).[23]

The oldest recruit was 53: Pvt. Frederick Crenshaw (Co. D), who hurried to Raleigh to enlist, leaving behind his carpenter's shop. Another advanced-in-age volunteer, Pvt. Joseph Norris (Co. E). was a 51-year-old farmer, hailing from Magnolia, NC. And the regiment's youngest soldier, 13-year-old Pvt. Samuel Davis had fast-talked his little, 4-foot-10 self into Company D. When Davis' commander, Cpt. Eugene Grissom discovered just how young the small fellow was, he immediately assigned him to drummer duty.[24]

The Thirtieth's ranks were filled with many young men who came by themselves, as well as by large clans of men-folk, all enlisting together. The largest family representation came from Warren County, NC, the Shearin clan. Eight Shearin's volunteered into Company B: Thomas G. (aged 18), John L. (19), Moses and Thomas G. (22), Gardiner (23), John R. (30), Jacob (36), and Richard (37). And finally, there were hundreds and hundreds of farmers and farm boys, including at least two pairs of father-son sets, such as Pvt. William Howey (Co. K) and John Howey (Co. K) and Archibald Kelly, Sr. (Co. H), and his son Archibald Kelly, Jr. (Co. H).

The Thirtieth's citizen-soldiers had flocked to Camp Mangum, inspired by the rhetoric of ardent politicians, and combined with inflamed feelings of patriotism many of the young men demanded immediate action. An ardent Tar Heel wrote, "[My] conscience was clear in the conviction that [we] ... had the right and law on [our] ... side to fight in the defense of the reserved right of the States." He also remarked, "[Our] cause was just, God was just and would not suffer wrong to prevail over right."[25] Private John Bone (Co. I) wrote, "How well I have remembered it.... I was sworn in with three others, all strong able-bodied men." He continued, "we were waiting at the depot, many of the men had their canteens filled with whiskey."[26] A third young man added, "it is hard for me to leave ... but I consider I am doing rightly.... I think my first duties are to my country."[27] And finally, a spirited fellow, not concerned with politics, stated proudly, "volunteering was a passport into the favor of his best girl, who hailed him as the defender of her country and herself."[28]

Regardless of why the young men rushed to Camp Mangum, once they set foot into the facility's grounds they entered into a world of commotion and confusion. One of the Thirtieth's volunteers, 1st Sgt. John Witherspoon (Co. K) remarked, "[This] camp is nothing but a large crowd of men."²⁹ Thousands of citizen-volunteers had already arrived. These earlier-appearing men had been equipped, organized into regiments, and shipped off to Virginia or eastern North Carolina. What equipment remained behind in the camp's storerooms was either broken or so antiquated it could have been, as one Tar Heel complained, "if not used in the Crusades, certainly ... in the wars of Queen Anne."³⁰ There were no uniforms, accouterments, or muskets left for the Thirtieth's volunteers. To drill, the men were armed with pikes. A volunteer griped, "[We] trained with a spear, called the 'Confederate Pike,' which had a ten-foot wooden handle with a steel dagger-shaped blade."³¹ Colonel Parker grumbled about the State's preparations for his regiment, writing, "everything is raw and in confusion."³²

Fortunately, Frank Parker's regiment did not remain long at Camp Mangum. He received orders to move the regiment just two days after the unit mustered into service.

The father-son combination of 42-year-old William Howey and 17-year-old John Howey joined Co. K (Weymouth, 1981).

He loaded his exhilarated Tar Heels onto train cars, amid the cacophony of cheering crowds and sobbing loved ones. One soldier noted, "The [boys] were looking to the glory of tempestuous war ... [and] were in fine spirits, and judging from the actions of some, spirits were in them." He also admitted, "The mothers and sisters and sweethearts saw beyond—the hardships, the suffering, the wounds, the dying."³³

The next morning, September 29, 1861, the regiment's train arrived at their destination. Private John Bone (Co. I) recorded, "On Sunday morning about nine o'clock, we were pulled into Wilmington, N.C, and got off under the big car shed at the bank of the Cape Fear river.... We were sleepy, tired and hungry." The 19-year-old from Nash County, NC, also wrote, "We ... were given quarters that night in a long building."³⁴ The following day Parker led his men to a location he called Camp Lamb.³⁵ Private Bone (Co. I) noted, "we marched out near Oakdale Cemetery, and cleaned up a camp ground and stretched tents.... We now came down to squad and company drill and guarding camps. It was here that we drew our arms and ammunition."³⁶

Barely a week later, on October 9, 1861, the Thirtieth marched to the Cape Fear River and boarded steamboats. A Tar Heel recorded, "[We] traveled by steamboat to Smithville [now Southport] and camped at Camp Walker on the outskirts of town."³⁷ Colonel Frank Parker described their location, writing, "it is a pleasant encampment, high and dry, and very sandy. We use water from Smithville."³⁸ Here, the regiment began a schedule of training and guard duty, and protecting the coastal defenses. Private John Bone (Co. I) wrote, "We were stationed here to guard the inlet from the main ocean to the river." He also added, "We cleaned up [a] drill ground near the edge of the little town and began to get down to business."[39]

Colonel Parker oversaw the training, though he did not actually participate, instead allowing Maj. James Kell to lead the battalion evolutions. He remarked, "I think there is material in [the regiment] ... out of which a first rate Regt. can be made. The officers, by a very large majority, are very clever gentlemen."[40] Parker's riflemen, naturally, were not as delighted by the drill as their commander. One Carolinian groused, "Squad, company and regimental drill [went on] continually.... No let up. The boys would fume, fuss and complain, but to no avail." He continued, "[We] could see no use in this everlasting drill ... in the hot sun, under great fatigue."[41] Another complained, "[The] purposes for ... drill—To keep the men from enjoying a little rest ... [and] to exasperate the men beyond ... endurance."[42] Private John Bone (Co. I), who stoically endured the exercises, recalled, "We could now begin to keep step with a drum and began to feel like we were soldiers."[43]

No matter how fed up with the drill, the riflemen, on the other hand, were happy to perform guard mount, and they pressured their company commanders for that duty assignment. First Sergeant John Witherspoon (Co. K) wrote, "It is indeed grand to [view] ... the sea coast and see the large breakers and waves lashing against the shore."[44] Another rifleman added, "I am here ... enjoying ... the pretty bay ... [with] thousands of fishes jumping about."[45] Colonel Parker, taking advantage of his "rank-has-its-privileges" position, explored the countryside and wrote to his wife, "Smithville is ... on the Cape Fear River; here a great number of the families of Wilmington spend their summers, having private residences here." He also added, "All night long, the roar of the old ocean may be heard; it sounds grand."[46]

While Parker's officers hustled to transform nine hundred Tar Heels into soldiers, Col. Parker struggled to obtain equipment, uniforms, and weapons. He wrote Sally, "I hope I am getting matters straight and if the Yankees will let me alone a little longer, I may have a Regt. which will be able to do good service."[47] Unfortunately, just as Parker began to feel confident his regiment was becoming battle-ready, sickness riddled the ranks. Private John Bone (Co. I) remarked, "Disease ... set in on us, such as measles, mumps,

John G. Witherspoon (Co. K), 23 years old, was promoted to third lieutenant on September 27, 1861 (courtesy Living History Association of North Carolina).

yellow jaundice, and many other things due to camp life."[48] Doctors Henry Joyner and Charles Gregory soon found their aid station swamped with sick soldiers, with the first patients coming from Cpt. Joseph Green's Company C. Sadly, on October 11, 1861, two young men died from pneumonia: 20-year-old William Maltsby (Co. C) and 22-year-old John C. Simmons (Co. C). Two days later, a third Company C rifleman succumbed to his illness, 17-year-old Michael Chimis.[49] A few days later, the newly promoted, 3rd Lt. John Witherspoon (Co. K) recorded, "more than ½ of the Regt. are not fit for duty."[50] Colonel Parker, shaken by this spreading calamity, wrote to his wife, "There is a good deal of sickness in the Regt. now, mostly from mumps and measles, with a little typhoid fever. There have been a few deaths."[51]

The Thirtieth's surgeons quickly gave orders for the most critical cases to be transported to the military hospital in Wilmington. One of these patients, Pvt. John Bone (Co. I), was shipped to this hospital, afflicted with a serious case of the measles. The young soldier recorded, "The hospital had been some kind of hotel, being about two stories high and the rooms about twelve feet square. The floor, with a blanket or two spread down, and our knapsacks for a heads, was our bed, with a blanket or two laid over us." He also noted, "We had [a] few nurses, one or two to the room and they were sent from camp and did not want to stay. Our doctor would come around once or twice during the day and night."[52] Fortunately, the medical staff in Wilmington, along with the facility's better health conditions put a halt to what could have been a disastrous epidemic. Even though over 330 of Parker's men would spend time in Wilmington's Military hospital in the next six months, just a little over a dozen patients would die.[53] Though each of these deaths represented a tragedy for those men and their families, the Thirtieth would be spared the horrible losses crippling other North Carolina units in the Wilmington area during the summer of 1862. Nonetheless, in time, the Thirtieth would also be devastated by disease, but for now, Parker's men were spared most of the lethal sickness's consequences.

During the first week of November 1861, the Thirtieth was ordered to relieve the 18th NC. Parker marched his companies back to the wharf, but his men were forced to wait because the ships were not ready. Lieutenant John Witherspoon (Co. K) growled, "all is confusion ... our regt. has been at the wharf ... at Smithville ever since yesterday morning." Finally, after considerable frustration, the men boarded transports and were shipped to a location not far from Fort Fisher. Colonel Parker then recorded, "The name of the camp was taken from the poor fellow who was killed at the battle of Bethel, Henry L. Wyatt."[54]

Private John Bone (Co. I) described Camp Wyatt, writing, "The camp and drill ground was already cleaned here, we only had to stretch tents." He added, once he and his comrades had established their canvas homes, "The camp [is] lying between the Atlantic Ocean and the Cape Fear river on a strip of land about one mile wide, with Fort Fisher at the end near the inlet." Later, once he knew more about their locality, Bone noted, "the wind has a fair sweep here and [is] nearly all the time blowing ... [and] The soil [is] ... a sandy desert, so our situation here [is] not a very pleasant one."[55] Parker immediately ordered his men to resume their training. He bragged to Sally, "I have just commenced.... Battalion drill, and the men seem to like it."[56] His riflemen though, refused to see any value in this exercise. One unhappy rifleman groused, "he could not understand the necessity of being trained by an officer in the manual of arms and being drilled into a machine. [He] could whip the Yankees anyhow, without all this damn foolishness."[57]

Besides drill, the Thirtieth's riflemen were also besieged by another perplexity—lice. A Tar Heel wrote, "We had been here not many days when scratching was in order. Search found lice, body lice! Horror of horrors!" He continued, "The boys kept it hid as long as they could. They would sneak off by themselves, disrobe and [a] slaughter would commence." This soldier had more to add, "[Later] there was no more retiring out of sight. The boys would strip off and go to killing in the camp.... Building a blaze, holding the garment over it and scraping them off we found was the best method.... They would pop like salt."[58] Colonel Parker, following his surgeons' recommendations, ordered his men to wash. Colonel Parker recorded, "I allow ... [the men] to wash their clothes, and clean up generally on Saturdays; so that they can come out clean at inspection on Sunday morning."[59]

When not drilling, or attending to personal matters, the men of the Thirtieth protected the Confederate forts guarding the entrance to the Cape Fear River. The regiment was a short march from Fort Fisher, a defensive structure consisting of a series of sand-mounded palisades extending for nearly a mile and containing at least thirty heavy artillery pieces. These guns were capable of shelling any enemy ship attempting to enter the Cape Fear River.[60] Though guard duty was monotonous and dull, most Carolinians preferred this task. Private John Bone (Co. I) wrote, "I was detailed as a guard and sent down to this fort to help protect it. I had to walk the beach to and fro for a hundred yards or so. At night, when not on post, my place for sleep was in the magazine with the ammunition."[61] A few days later, on November 18, 1861, a blockade ship approached Fort Fisher and shelled its defenses. Captain Benjamin Morrow's Company K was performing fort duty that day, and an excited Lt. Witherspoon scribbled to his family, "[Our gunners] exchanged 7 shots with the blockade this morning. We had 4 shots and they 3. No damage to us. We opened fire and had the last shot."[62]

Back in Camp Wyatt, once the excitement faded away, the tedious business of drill and military life protecting Fort Fisher's guns continued. One soldier wrote his family, "Reveille sounds, up we'd rise, rubbing our eyes for lack of water to wash them, sleeping in our clothes, did not have to dress, not even to put on shoes, for we slept in them too. Fall in for roll call! Oh, joy!"[63] Private John Bone (Co. I) also recorded, "There was a tall pole planted near Camp Wyatt, the height being sixty or seventy feet high, with attachments, so that it could be climbed. Every morning a boy would ascend to the top, with a spyglass and view the ocean ... [for] blockade vessel[s]."[64] On November 15, 1861, the soldiers watched a blockade runner slip past Lincoln's screen of Federal ships. Frank Parker described the ship, writing, "Our whole camp witnessed a very interesting sight this morning; it was a large vessel, which had run the blockade, and was coming up the

Fort Fisher consisted of a series of dirt-mounded gun emplacements (*Photographic History of the Civil War*, 1911).

river to Wilmington." The colonel continued, "she was sailing beautifully before a fine breeze, with all sails set; [and] her canvas seemed to swell with pride at having eluded the blockading steamer off the bar."[65]

The Thirtieth's young soldiers believed their activities were important, and as their drilling competence improved, their morale increased. A visit by the paymaster also enhanced the Tar Heel's attitudes, with one rifleman joyfully writing home, "Crisp new bills from the mint of the Confederacy made our eyes dance and filled our hearts with joy."[66] Colonel Parker, noticing his troops' spirit, added, "the men ... are in better spirits generally. They have just been paid off too, this may affect their feelings."[67]

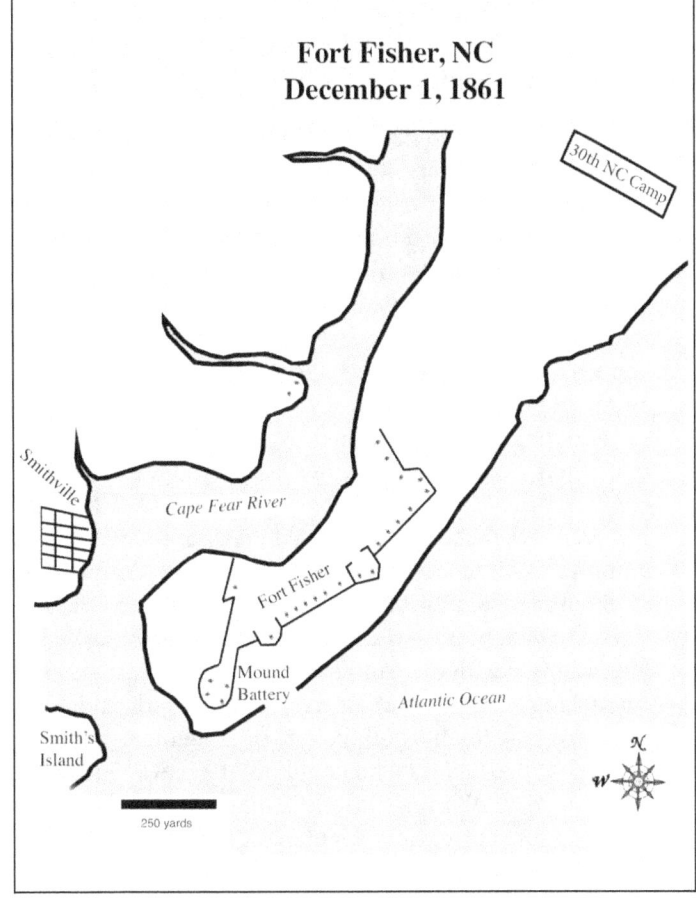

As fall gave way to winter, the weather degraded from pleasant to cold, wet, and windy. The Thirtieth's quartermasters, led by Cpt. Buckner Williams, a 28-year-old merchant from Warrenton, NC, struggled to protect their men from the elements.[68] Frank Parker wrote, "Our tents are getting rather airy. The Quarter Master has commenced on the winter quarters, and I suppose will have them completed by the first of Jan."[69]

Confederate Military Pay[70]

Rank	Monthly Pay
Private	$11
Corporal	$13
Sergeant	$17
1st Sergeant	$20
2nd Lieutenant	$80
1st Lieutenant	$90
Adjutant	$100
Captain	$130
Major	$150
Lieutenant Col.	$170
Colonel	$195

The colonel conferred with the Confederate high command and received confirmation his regiment would not be moved during the winter. Parker then gave the orders for the construction of a permanent camp.[71] Private John Bone (Co. I) recorded, "We ... built winter quarters of sawed lumber large enough for a company of one hundred to a house, and went into them by companies." Bone added a quick complaint, "We spent the winter here in drilling."[72]

When the winter rains limited outside activities, the men were crowded together in a closely packed concentration, a condition most had never before experienced. Friction between individuals erupted, forcing Col. Parker to record, "So far I have ... two very bad cases in the guard house; one of these, I shall have to punish severely."[73] Parker dealt with these isolated disturbances, however, in another matter—alcohol, his provost guards fought a losing battle. The colonel griped to his wife in frustration, "I have not only had men of the Regt. in the guard house for drinking, but I have arrested and confined ... citizen[s] of the county, for selling whiskey to the men."[74] Private William Ardrey (Co. K) admitted he and some of his Company K messmates, "[Nathan] Orr, [William] Williamson and [he] missed battalion drill ... [and were] confined to Camp for one month."[75] Lieutenant John Witherspoon (Co. K) observed his colonel's efforts and penned a note to his family, stating, "Great effort is ... [being expended] to turn all the volunteers into regulars."[76]

Winter's inactivity convinced many of the volunteers this was the perfect time to go home and visit family. At first, the men applied for furloughs, which Col. Parker granted as much as regulations allowed. Unfortunately, so many men petitioned for leave he was forced to turn hundreds down. Parker confessed to Sally, "I am placed just now in a very unenviable position; I suppose there are at least six or eight men coming to me every day, asking for leave of absence." He continued, explaining his decisions, writing, "I have made it a rule to allow all the married men to go home first."[77]

For those fellows who could not get leave to travel home, some were able to finagle passes to visit Wilmington, while others just took off, promising to return at their own leisure before springtime. Lieutenant John Witherspoon (Co. K) wrote, "The authorities want rigid discipline enforced.... We had 20 men to desert this week."[78] For those lucky enough to spend time in Wilmington, they found a welcoming environment for their freshly printed Confederate money. Wilmington, with a population of nearly 11,000 citizens, was experienced at providing diversions; after all, the city was a seaport and had been entertaining sailors for over a hundred years. The town's merchants were experts at providing ways to separate young men from their hard-earned cash. Wilmington boasted a dozen saloons, as well as many restaurants, tattoo parlors, and brothels.[79] One such well-visited hotspot, Manatgue's Billiard and Eating Saloon, advertised, "the best of everything is kept at this house."[80] The young soldiers quickly discovered where to go, and one bragged, "I have been enjoying myself with the ladies."[81] Another proclaimed, "Some of the boys were smitten by the elegant forms and beautiful faces of the girls."[82]

In early February 1862, United States infantry commanded by Brig. Gen. Ambrose Burnside attacked the Carolina coast near Roanoke, NC and defeated the Confederate forces guarding the State's Outer Banks.[83] Burnside then shifted his forces towards New Bern, NC. Colonel Parker received orders to get his regiment ready to join the fight against Burnside's invaders. The Thirtieth's riflemen boarded transports, excited about the prospects of the coming battle and were hauled back to Camp Lamb, outside Wilmington. Here, the Tar Heels waited impatiently for several days before learning their orders to march had been cancelled—the battle at New Bern had already been lost. Brigadier General Lawrence Branch, in charge of the Confederate troops defending that town, wrote, "the enemy had 13 regiments ... [I] had seven regiments in defense." He continued, reporting the Union struck his right center, a portion of his held by militia: "[When] the militia ... abandoned their post ... the 35th NC very quickly followed ... in utmost disorder.... This laid open ... [the 7th NC], and a large portion of the breastwork was left vacant." More Union troops poured into this gap, forcing Branch to record, "The enemy column ... attack[ed] what remained of ... [the 7th NC] ... and drove them ... inflicting heavy loss." Brigadier General Branch concluded his report, writing, "my next care was to secure the retreat."[84]

Colonel Parker's disappointed soldiers loitered in Camp Lamb for several days as other North Carolina formations drifted into the area. Parker detached company K, assigning them picket duty in Wilmington, and then marched the rest of the regiment to a location near the Masonboro Sound.[85] The Thirtieth's commander wrote, "Our Regt. is in good health, and is getting in good fighting order ... as regard drill and strength, we now number nine hundred and twenty nine." He also added, "We are at another new encampment [Camp Holmes].... It is a beautiful location for a camp; on a hill, and very near to a large branch of good running water, and about 2 miles from the ocean, within sound of its roar." Parker continued, "we are right among the long leaf pines.... This is so pleasant a place."[86] However, for the soldiers left behind to guard Wilmington, since they were not allowed to visit the city when not on duty, there was little to do. Private William Ardrey (Co. K) scribbled in his diary, simply, "on picket guard ... cleaned my gun."[87]

A week later, Col. Parker heard that Northern sympathizers in Onslow County, NC, encouraged by the Yankee success at New Bern, were raiding Southern towns and plantations. He received word to move his regiment into Onslow County and prevent this destruction. Parker, on April 18, 1862, ordered Companies A, D, and H, "under Col. Draughan ... to Onslow County, to check the marauding parties of the enemy."[88] He then sent Company E to relieve Cpt. Morrow's boys in Wilmington, and once Company K rejoined the regiment at Camp Lamb, the Thirtieth set out for Onslow County.

The march to Onslow County took the men north, along dirt roads through an unpopulated area. The novice soldiers floundered beneath the weight of their gear. Private John Bone (Co. I) recalled, "This was the first march of any considerable distance that we had been called on to perform.... We started off in fine spirits, each one loaded with baggage.... The next morning we were all sore all over."[89] Private William Ardrey (Co. K) added, "[We] marched through the most barren and desolate country of long leaf pines I ever saw ... [and, I] saw an alligator."[90] Lieutenant John Witherspoon (Co. K) penned a note, reviewing their hike, writing, "50 miles in this sand is equal to 100 miles in our country."[91] And finally, rifleman Bone summed up this initial trek, stating, "We reached Onslow County in a few days, very sore, worried and jaded."[92] The Thirtieth remained at Hatchet Mills, not far from Jacksonville, Onslow County, NC, for the next few weeks, chasing rumors but never apprehending any looters or plunderers.

Meanwhile, the Confederate government, which now had come to the realization President Abraham Lincoln was serious about fighting a prolonged war, passed the Furlough and Bounty Act. This legislation guaranteed Confederate commanders they would not lose their short-term, enlisted troops. One writer noted, "This extraordinary law ... assur[ed] the re-enlistment of the twelve-months' volunteers whose terms expired in the late winter of early spring. A bounty of fifty dollars and a furlough of thirty days were promised to all enlisted men and noncommissioned officers who agreed to serve for the duration of the war to a maximum of three years."[93] When Lt. John Witherspoon (Co.

K) learned this news he remarked, "It seems that every man will have to go into service from the Pres[ident's] message."⁹⁴ Private John Bone (Co. I) also noted this statute, writing, "They passed a law, asking all men to re-enlist for three years in the war, with the promise of fifty dollars bounty and thirty days furlough."⁹⁵ Another rifleman, not believing the government would actually pay him a bounty, wrote to his wife in disgust, "I hered [sic.] yesterday that I would have to stay twelve months, and if I do I want you to send me a pair of shoes."⁹⁶

The Confederate leadership, wise to the ambitions of its forces' officers, also stipulated that "When the reorganization of the Army was effected through re-enlistment … the men could elect their own company and field officers."⁹⁷ Knowing this, officers immediately began drumming up support for re-enlistment. Colonel Parker sweetened the enticement by letting his aspiring captains know the first company to completely re-enlist would be sent home on furlough as a unit. The competition was fierce. Private John Bone (Co. I) proclaimed, "[Cpt. William Arrington] … went to work and with this inducement soon had every man re-enlisted. We soon packed … and bade farewell to our comrades … no other company was allowed to all go home at a time."⁹⁸ Frank Parker added, "Capt. Arrington … I assure you, he is very proud of it … [and his men] are happy fellows tonight."⁹⁹

Once the companies had re-enlisted, each formation then went about the business of re-electing officers. Many of the companies had officers who had demonstrated poor, or little leadership ability, and the enlisted men used this opportunity to replace them with popular fellows. Colonel Parker, who won his re-election, wrote, "Maj. James T. Kell defeated Lt. Col. Draughan for lieutenant colonel … [and] 1st Lt. William W. Sillers (Co. A) was elected major." Frank Parker, saddened to see Draughan go, wrote to his wife, "I am sorry to say that Lt. Col. Draughan was not re-elected…. The Thirtieth lost a worthy officer." He continued: "[1st Lt. William Sillers] is a very nice man, a capital selection, and … will make a good officer; you may probably have heard me speak of him very favorably."¹⁰⁰

In a few of the units, some of the men were so well liked the event was little more than a formality. One Tar Heel wrote, "[To] assure the desired outcome of an election with a directness that others dared not emulate … [our first sergeant] had the company fall in … with arms; then he read the order for the elections of a Second Lieutenant, and said briskly, 'Men, there are but two candidates for the office, and there is but one of them worth a damn. I nominate him. All who are in favor … come to a shoulder' … [he then ordered] … 'Company, Shoulder arms.'" With that, the men, complying with their first sergeant's command, shouldered arms. The NCO counted all the shouldered rifles and proclaimed the election's outcome. Following this, the first sergeant turned to the newly promoted officer and said, "[Sir] … take charge of the company and dismiss them."¹⁰¹

In all, among the Thirtieth's ten companies, four captains, five first lieutenants, and seven junior lieutenants were replaced. The just-elected leaders were usually lower ranking officers or sergeants, nevertheless, enlisted men were also elevated to officer status: Ephraim Greer, a 29-yer-old teacher from Lockwood's Folly, NC went from private to first lieutenant in Company C; the 23-year-old Pvt. Robert Clairborne of Granville Co., NC, became Company G's second lieutenant; and in Company K, the 23-year-old William Ardrey was surprised by his advancement to second lieutenant, and the 33-year-old merchant, Pvt. J. Thomas Downs earned a third lieutenant's position.¹⁰² Colonel Frank Parker then met with his new officers; one of them, Cpt. John Witherspoon (Co. K), wrote proudly to his parents, "I am now captain of the old company which was unexpected on my part."[103]

A week later, on May 9, 1862, the regiment received orders to return to Wilmington. The soldiers gathered up their equipment and hiked back to the city, and from there, to the Wrightsville Sound, arriving on May 15, 1862.[104] Then, six days later the Thirtieth was shifted back to Masonboro Sound. Colonel Parker noted this move to his wife, writing, "we have moved again…. We are now on an elevated spot, with good water near, and such a delightful breeze!" He continued, "We also have the benefit of bathing in salt water…. It is such a pleasant camp, that I am afraid something will turn up to take us away from it soon."[105] Parker, once again, commenced a routine of heavy drilling, forcing Cpt. John Witherspoon (Co. K) to write, "We are all trying to soldier to the best of our ability…. The weather is getting quite warm. We occasionally have men to faint."[106] His lieutenant, William Ardrey (Co. K) noted, "Company K [was] furnished with canteens and haversacks." He also remarked happily, "Strawberry pies for dinner."[107]

Colonel Frank Parker conferred with his second-in-command, James Kell, and Maj. William Sillers and they discussed the strengths and weaknesses of each of their companies. They determined the regiment was better served by changing its skirmish companies. Parker issued new orders, defining new, first and tenth companies. Lieutenant Ardrey wrote, "The Regt. was rearranged. Captain Grissom [Co. D] on the right [and] Capt. Wicker [Co. H] on the left."[108] Frank Parker also discovered one of his volunteers to be much younger than expected. Walter Turner (Co. I) had enlisted, saying he was eighteen, but in reality he was fourteen. His captain shifted the youth to the band, however, the boy's talents were elsewhere. Frank Parker took Walter Turner under his wing and made him his orderly.[109]

The Thirtieth was ordered away from their luxurious location and back to Wilmington and Camp Lamb. Rumors swept the regiment—there was electrifying hints the Thirtieth had been chosen to join the Confederate army in Virginia. The new officers hustled to acquire new coats, causing a surprising situation, as there were not enough tailors to meet their demands. Captain John Witherspoon (Co. K) wrote home, pleading, "I am waiting to hear something of the uniform. I sent directions in your letter to Phillips how to make it. Confederate style of Capt." He added, "All the officers are getting new suits. A Captain's uniform in Wilmington is worth $110."[110]

William E. Ardrey (Co. K), 23 years old, was elected second lieutenant on May 1, 1862 (courtesy Davidson College Archives).

The scuttlebutt proved true and on June 13, 1862, the Thirtieth's enthusiastic riflemen boarded trains for Virginia.[111] Colonel Frank Parker recorded, "[We] left from Wilmington on the evening of the 13th."[112] Unfortunately, things did not go according to plans; half of the regiment's train cars were not coupled properly and became disengaged. They were left behind at the station while the engine and the first part of the train headed for Virginia. It took the engineers several miles of travel before they realized their locomotive was not pulled a full load. They reversed direction and returned to Wilmington and retrieved all the missing cars.[113] Lieutenant William Ardrey (Co. K) chronicled their journey, writing, "set out at 9 o'clock that night.... Passed through Goldsboro at sunset without halting ... [and] arrived at Weldon at 11 o'clock a.m." He continued, "[We] took dinner at 65 cents ... [and then] Set out for Petersburg at 2 o'clock p.m." Ardrey noted, "As we passed through Jarnet's depot the ladies sent water to the cars and made several loyal demonstrations." He completed the chronology, writing that "[We] arrived at Petersburg at 4 p.m. ... [and] took up quarters in the market house."[114] The 30th North Carolina had successfully completed its duties guarding the State's coastline; now the regiment was in Virginia, and within a few miles of tens of thousands of Federal soldiers. Now, Col. Frank Parker and his nine hundred Carolinians would be tested in battle.

Walter Turner (Co. I), 14 years old, was made Col. Parker's orderly (Clark, 1901).

30th North Carolina Infantry[115]
June 1, 1862

Unit		Strength
Field & Staff	Col. Parker, Francis M. Lt. Col. Kell, James T. Maj. Sillers, William W. Sgt. Maj. Lawhorn, Archibald F.	4
Co. A	Cpt. Holmes, James C. 1st Lt. Williams, Gary 2nd Lt. Stevens, Charles T.	100
Co. B	Cpt. Drake, William C. 1st Lt. Davis, Weldon E. 2nd Lt. Nicholson, John H.	79
Co. C	Cpt. Allen, David C. 1st Lt. Greer, Ephraim J. 2nd Lt. Bennett, Solomon W.	74
Co. D	Cpt. Grissom, Eugene 1st Lt. Allen, Charles N. 2nd Lt. Rogers, Charles M.	92

Unit		Strength
Co. E	Cpt. McMillan, John C. 1st Lt. Johnson, Ira J. 2nd Lt. McMillan, Daniel T.	98
Co. F	Cpt. Moore, Willis M. 1st Lt. Harrell, George K. 2nd Lt. Pitt, James W.	102
Co. G	Cpt. Barnett, James A. 1st Lt. Badgett, James W. 2nd Lt. Claireborne, Robert F.	73
Co. H	Cpt. Wicker, Jesse J. 1st Lt. McNeil, Henry J. 2nd Lt. Jackson, Archibald J.	88
Co. I	Cpt. Arrington, William T. 1st Lt. Harris, James J. 2nd Lt. Williford, Burton B.	101
Co. K	Cpt. Witherspoon, John G. 1st Lt. Orr, Nathan D. 2nd Lt. Ardrey, William E.	69
		880

Chapter 2

Lost Innocence at Gaines' Mill

Once Col. Frank Parker learned which brigade his regiment had been assigned, he and his second-in-command, Lt. Col. James Kell made a call upon their new boss, Brig. Gen. George B. Anderson. At first, Parker had been informed his formation was slotted to join a brigade commanded by Brig. Gen. Samuel Garland; however, even before the orders could be finalized, the Confederate high command decided to create an all-North Carolina brigade, including the Thirtieth, and awarded the brigade to George Anderson. Parker and Kell met Gen. Anderson and immediately felt confident their leader would serve the regiment well. As a fellow officer remarked, "He was a six footer of fine figure with specially good legs which gave him a very graceful seat on horseback and his face was as attractive as his figure, with brown hair, blue eyes and general good nature in every feature."[1]

Brigadier General George B. Anderson was a fighter and his reputation as a fearless soldier widely known. He was 31 years old, and a native of Hillsboro, NC, as well as an 1852 West Point graduate. Upon earning his commission as a lieutenant, Anderson served out on the western frontier, but when the shelling of Fort Sumter occurred, he resigned his position and joined the Confederacy. George Anderson secured a posting as colonel of the 4th NC Infantry, and was able to get his Tar Heel regiment immediately transferred to Virginia. President Jefferson Davis noticed George Anderson's courageous actions in the fights around Williamsburg and promoted him to brigadier general on June 9, 1862. Then, just a couple days later, Anderson's brigade was assembled: four infantry regiments from North Carolina.[2]

Colonel Frank Parker's 30th NC was combined with three other regiments, the 2nd, 4th, and 14th NC. One of these formations had no battle experience, while another just a little, and the third quite a lot. The 2nd NC, commanded by Col. Charles C. Tew had been in existence for just over a year, but had seen no combat. Upon organization, the Second was shifted to Virginia but missed the fight at Manassas. Tew's men then spent the next six months doing picket duty along the Potomac River. However, when Burnside invaded North Carolina's east coast, the Second was rushed back to the Old North State. Colonel Charles Tew's troops did not arrive in time to fight at New Bern, so the regiment was sent to Camp Wyatt, where, as one of the men in the Second wrote, "[We] drilled and threw up walls of sand and at night patrolled the beach and fought fleas."[3] The 4th NC Infantry, the regiment originally led by George Anderson, was now commanded by Major Bryan Grimes. This Tar Heel unit had been badly bloodied, both by disease during the summer and fall of 1861, and in the fights about Williamsburg, and the conflict at Seven Pines. Now, Maj. Grimes' companies could not muster two hundred men to answer at roll call, but as one noted, "they had the appearance and bearing of regular troops."[4]

And the 14th NC, led by Lt. Col. William A. Johnston, had also seen what lead and steel could do to a Carolina lad. The Fourteen lost 17 men in the battle of Williamsburg, and just over a dozen at Seven Pines. Therefore, even though Johnston's regiment had been in two battles, his men emerged from both conflicts with minimal casualties. Johnston's men were proud of the fact they had "seen the elephant," but the regiment had not been badly stung by its dangers. Thus, the Fourteenth's soldiers walked about with the air of confident soldiers who believed they knew what war was all about. One wrote, "There is always a certain *cachet* about great men ... they carry their great air ... more fairly than the timid shufflers, who only dare to look up at them through blinkers."[6]

30th North Carolina Infantry[5]
June 20, 1862

Unit		Strength
Field & Staff	Col. Parker, Francis M. Lt. Col. Kell, James T. Maj. Sillers, William W.	5
Co. A	Cpt. Holmes, James C. 1st Lt. Williams, Gary 2nd Lt. Stevens, Charles T.	91
Co. B	Cpt. Drake, William C. 1st Lt. Davis, Weldon E. nd Lt. Nicholson, John H.	73
Co. C	Cpt. Allen, David C. 1st Lt. Greer, Ephraim J. 2nd Lt. Bennett, Solomon W.	66
Co. D	Cpt. Grissom, Eugene 1st Lt. Allen, Charles N. 2nd Rogers, Charles M.	94
Co. E	Cpt. McMillan, John C. 1st Lt. Johnson, Ira J. 2nd Lt. McMillan, Daniel T.	105
Co. F	Cpt. Moore, Willis M. 1st Lt. Harrell, George K. 2nd Lt. Pitt, James W.	107
Co. G	Cpt. Bennett, James A. 2nd Lt. Clairborne, Robert F. 3rd Lt. Crews, Alexander	73
Co. H	Cpt. Wicker, Jesse J. 1st Lt. McNeil, Henry J. 2nd Lt. Jackson, Archibald J.	90
Co. I	Cpt. Arrington, William T. 1st Lt. Harris, James J. 2nd Lt. Williford, Burton B.	111
Co. K	1st Lt. Orr, Nathan D. 2nd Lt. Ardrey, William E. 3rd Lt. Downs, John T.	65
		880

Colonel Frank Parker's regiment marched to a camp ground five miles from Richmond and the men pitched their tents. The Thirtieth was large, almost nine hundred strong, as many of the companies had aggressively recruited more volunteers. Nonetheless, no one had been part of anything larger than what they experienced within their own regiment. Private John Bone (Co. I), astounded by the massive numbers of men, animals and equipment packed together in Anderson's brigade, wrote, "It was now tents, men, guns, artillery, and horses everywhere, drums beating, bands playing, and cannon firing ... both day and night."[7] Private John Bone, along with his fellow riflemen, gawked at the Confederacy's preparations for war, and worried about how they would act when Yankee bullets came at them.

General Anderson immediately employed Parker's companies. Lieutenant William Ardrey (Co. D) noted this, writing, "Went out to work on the fortifications."[8] Other companies were armed with new Enfield rifles and sent to the picket line, tasked with guarding the Confederate camp. Private John Bone (Co. I), along with the rest of the men in his company, felt uneasy about this new duty. He remarked, "our Regiment was ... placed on picket duty at Seven Pines, near the enemy, this being the first time we had been close to the enemy." He admitted, they did not know what to do, and when they queried their veteran Carolina brothers, received but a smidgen of help. John Bone wrote, [We] ... would [ask] ... our questions in regard to our situation. They would tell us that it was nothing but a picket line in front of us ... this gave us some relief."[9]

On June 21, 1862, several of Col. Parker's companies were sent out as pickets. Lieutenant William Ardrey (Co. D) wrote, "The 30th Regt. went out on picket duty on the lines six miles from Richmond and one-fourth of a mile of the enemy's lines." Ardrey continued,

The 31-year-old Brig. Gen. George B. Anderson commanded the brigade that included the 30th NC (1862 woodcut).

"[We were] so near that we could see their balloons and see them on trees watching us and when we would climb trees we could see them in camp." The wide-eyed Tar Heels took their posting seriously, trying to accustom themselves to being within artillery range of their enemy. The day went by quietly, until, as Lt. Ardrey noted, "[that] evening when we were ordered to advance our lines."[10]

Companies A, D, I, and K spread out in a long, thin skirmish line, creeping one hundred yards toward the Union pickets, closing the distance between the two forces to just over three hundred yards. Then, because of jumbled messages between the neophyte officers, the Carolinians became confused and they scampered back to their original position. However, once everyone calmed down, the embarrassed officers regained control of themselves and their men, and pushed forward again, closing to within one hundred yards of the blue coats. Private John Bone (Co. I) recalled, "We were ordered ... to advance upon the line, which we did in very good order ... although great excitement prevailed with many."[11] Lieutenant Ardrey (Co. D) reported, "the second time we advanced some 300 yards and opened fire upon the enemy, and they replied promptly."[12] Yankee bullets buzzed among the Tar Heels and they all dropped to the ground. More Federal musketry continued to rip through the air, accompanied by an occasional artillery round. William Ardrey wrote, "The shot and shell were flying around all the time."[13]

Captain Eugene Grissom (Co. D), the 31-year-old physician from Tranquility, NC, darted about, reassuring his novice riflemen, encouraging them to stay calm and take deliberate aim at the Federals, some of them completely visible barely one hundred yards away. Grissom's men were lying down or sheltered behind trees while the captain stood, unruffled by the minié balls zipping past. Suddenly, a bullet ripped through Grissom's upper chest, shattering his clavicle and knocking him to the ground.[14] Private Bone (Co. I) wrote, "Captain Grissom got shot through the shoulder and he was the first man to get wounded in the Regiment by the enemy."[15] Several Neuse River Guards hurried to their commander's side and carried Grissom to safety. A few moments later, Yank lead mangled Pvt. Archibald Lewis' (Co. A) arm.[16] Meanwhile, the Carolinians continued firing at the blue coats, though as twilight overtook the fight, it became impossible to determine their musketry's effectiveness. The battle-rattled Southerners fell back to their original position once darkness put an end to the shooting.

The Thirtieth's surgeons, Drs. Henry Joyner and Charles Gregory quickly went to work on the regiment's casualties, sadly both soldiers' injuries were severe. Eugene Grissom would never return to his company. A Carolinian wrote, "Eugene Grissom['s] ... disabling for the balance of the war ... was a serious loss to the regiment. Captain Grissom was an officer of superior talent."[17] Later that evening, the Thirtieth's regimental chaplain, Alexander Betts, a 31-year-old Methodist minister from Elizabeth, NC, visited the wounded men and was horrified by their injuries. He scribbled, "I saw the first wounded of my regiment, A. A. Lewis [Co. A] ... and [Cpt.] Grissom [Co. D]."[18] The Reverend Betts, whose political philosophies and approach sometimes frustrated Col. Parker, had not been a supporter of secession, but once North Carolina withdrew from the Union, he offered his services. Betts would remain with the Thirtieth throughout the conflict, supporting the Thirtieth's men and their families, though he never got over the fact his State had gone to war. Alexander Betts wrote, "The day ... that President Lincoln had called upon the State troops to force the seceding States back into the Union. That was one of the saddest days of my life."[19] Regardless of his feelings, Alexander Betts was of much help to the men, however, his methods forced Frank Parker to complain to his wife, "I do not fancy the Chaplain.... He is altogether too sanctimonious [and] uses too many extravagant expressions,"[20]

The next day, June 22, 1862, different North Carolina companies assumed picket duty, enabling the Thirtieth's Company D's stunned men to recover from the shock of losing their company commander. Colonel Parker notified 1st Lt. Charles Allen (Co. D), he now was in charge of the company, causing a ripple effect among the unit's lieutenants and sergeants. Meanwhile, for the rest of the regiment, which was filled with youthful Tar Heels, the loss of two of their members did not create a lasting impression. Lieutenant William Ardrey (Co. K) remarked, "We climbed trees and looked over at the enemy."[21]

The Thirtieth went back out on the picket line that evening, the riflemen primed for revenge. Private John Bone (Co. I) recorded, "We were held on picket line that night, with orders that if we saw or heard the enemy to fire on them. As soon as it began to get dark the men began to fire and it was kept up through the night ... and yet the enemy did not approach nor return fire."[22] The next morning, a staff member from Gen. Anderson's headquarters chastised Col. Parker, notifying him his men would remain out on picket until they learned some discipline. John Bone noted, "We were told next morning that we had to stay on that picket line until we learned to keep less fuss.... The next night there was scarcely a gun fired, and the next morning [June 24, 1862] we were relieved [by the 14th NC] and went back to camp very glad to get off picket duty."[23]

Two days later, June 26, 1862, the Confederate army went into action, causing Alexander Betts to write, "Everything in motion, troops, troops, wagons, wagons, artillery, artillery."[24] Brigadier General George Anderson ordered his brigade out of camp. The Tar Heels hiked along the Mechanicsville turnpike until reaching the bridge spanning the Chickahominy River.[25] The structure had been damaged and a work crew scurried about, trying to repair the destruction. General Anderson's regiments deployed, facing toward the east, with the 2nd and 4th NC forming the first line and the 30th and 14th NC behind them. A Southerner noted, "[The 30th] halted in a beautiful grove of trees near the ruined Mechanicsville Bridge across the Chickahominy."[26] The brigade remained here several hours, all-the-while everyone listened to the throaty rumble of artillery and the rattle of musketry. The soldiers were deluged by rumors sweeping up and down the lines, telling of a great battle. Lieutenant William Ardrey (Co. K) wrote, "We were halted on a high hill and the cannonading was grand and terrific."[27]

Lieutenant Ardrey also noted, "Pres. Davis, Gens. Lee, Hill ... and a number of other distinguished men were out to witness the scene."[28] Though most of the soldiers had not seen these men before, they were well aware of them, especially Gen. Daniel H. Hill, their state's highest-ranking officer. They also were familiar with President Jefferson Davis, as many had viewed photographs of their nation's leader, but few knew Robert E. Lee. One rifleman remarked, "When General Lee took command, to the army at large he was simply a name—we knew nothing of him."[29] Nonetheless, regardless of each soldier's recognition of their senior commanders, they were impressed to be in close proximity of these leaders. Lieutenant Ardrey (Co. K) noted, "it was one of the grandest and most exciting scenes to see." He also added, as they listened to the sounds of the distant battle, "[We could] hear our troops driving the enemy from their strongholds, [and] see the shells exploding and to see the smoke in the distance."[30] Ardrey did mention, "[There was] considerable firing on the lines, but we could hear [no facts about] ... the fight."[31]

Once the bridge was ready for traffic, the brigade formed up and crossed, with, as a member of the 2nd NC bragging, "we were the first troops to cross the bridge (just repaired by the pioneers) leading up to the town."[32] From here, the brigade turned northward, following a road taking them through Mechanicsville, and then for another mile, before redeploying his brigade, again facing east, with the 2nd and 4th NC in front. Anderson's brigade now supported a Confederate artillery battery. When Col. Parker's men straggled into position behind the 2nd NC their movement was hampered by mud, as heavy rains had turned the countryside into a bottomless morass. Soon though, once the regiment was posted, the men could see they were on a broad ridge, overlooking a mud-choked, vegetation-lined watercourse called Beaver Dam Creek.

As Anderson's Tar Heels settled in, the battery commenced shelling Union locations on the eastern side of the creek. Lieutenant William Ardrey (Co. K) recorded, "We took our position on the side of a big hill in an open field to support batteries that had been placed [there].... They opened fire on the enemy and soon it was returned." At first, the Union shells appeared harmless but as the Yank gunners continued to fire at the Confederates their aim improved. Ardrey remarked, "the shells were falling and exploding all around us and we lay close to the ground."[33] Rifleman John Bone (Co. I) described the bombardment, writing, "[we] were shelled very heavy ... many shells ... burst around us." He added, "I recollect very well about dark one shell struck the ground just in front of me, throwing dust all over me, passing betwixt me and the man on my left."[34] While Pvt. Bone was lucky, another shell detonated near Company B and shrapnel slashed through the flesh and bone of Pvt. Robert Pegram's (Co. B) left thigh. Stretcher-bearers whisked the wounded 24-year-old from Warrenton, NC away and hurried him to their regimental surgeons. Robert Pegram would need over three months to recover.[35]

The 31-year-old Alexander Betts was the 30th NC's chaplain for the entire war (Clark, 1901).

The artillery duel lasted for several hours before firing ceased around 10:00 p.m.[36] Then, as darkness stilled the entire landscape, Pvt. John Bone (Co. I) recalled, "We bivouacked on the field that night ... expecting to be called up at any time, so we slept with our outfit on and upon our muskets."[37] This was their first night away from camp, and in the proximity of the enemy. Lieutenant William Ardrey (Co. K) wrote, "We lay on our arms all night."[38]

Few men slept well, and most were ready to shake off their blankets when commands came to form up. Lieutenant Ardrey noted, "Before daylight we ... started out." The past days' rain swelled the Chickahominy River, cresting its banks, and spilling water out into the low-lying areas. There was so much standing water that a mile on each side of the river was inundated. The Southerners now had to negotiate this terrain. The Thirtieth stumbled its way through the Beaver Dam Creek portion of the Chickahominy swamp, slogging eastward. Ardrey reported, "we moved ... very cautiously ... through thick woods and waded meadows knee-deep."[39]

General Anderson's four regiments slopped through the swamp, working their way southward before eventually climbing up out of the muck, just in time to see a Yank formation retreat. Though the soaked and mud-splattered Tar Heel riflemen had no way of knowing, their brigade, as well as Brig. Gen. Samuel Garland's North Carolinians had been sent to flank a blue coat position. One Confederate reported, "At daylight, General

[D. H.] Hill found his route blocked and sent Garland's and Anderson's brigades to the left to turn the enemy."[40] The Federals, realizing their predicament, fled. Lieutenant William Ardrey (Co. K) wrote, "Arrived at a Yankee camp ... the camp was neatly arranged and they left all their property there.... We captured several prisoners and ambulances and tore down the telegraph posts."[41] Following this, Col. Parker received orders to reform his companies and move forward with the brigade.

The Tar Heels pushed their way southeasterly for several miles before reaching the flooded lowlands of the Powhite River. A Southerner described the area, writing, "All the cleared ground visible to the Confederates led down to a boggy little stream.... This was bordered widely by almost impenetrable underbrush and by large trees and small."[42] General Anderson ordered his Tar Heels to deploy; again the 30th NC was placed in the brigade's second line. When the formation advanced against a screen of Union troops, the Tar Heels stumbled forward slowly in short surges, followed by exasperating delays. Frank Parker's men only had to keep their heads down, and move in support. One Tar Heel rifleman scribbled to his family, "We pushed through a swamp, through the dense underwood, on through the trees cut down and limbs sharpened to delay our progress."[43] The leading regiments clashed with Union skirmishers and a Southerner noted, "Anderson's brigade ... met the enemy in the woods on the edge of the swamp. After a bloody contest, the woods [were] cleared of the enemy."[44] Trailing along in the second line, a battle untested Carolinian remarked, "You never heard bullets whistle so in your life."[45] Countless stray bullets buzzed past the Tar Heels, and smacked into the trees. However, one minié bullet slammed into Sgt. Andrew Steel (Co. K), killing him.[46] Private John Bone (Co. I) recalled, "As we advanced ... [I saw] two dead men and a fine horse, with one hind foot shot off. These were the first dead people that I had ever seen that were killed." The alarmed John Bone added, "This was a sad looking scene to me and I felt then that I would be the next."[47]

The 30th NC passed through the Chickahominy swamp as they approached the Gaines' Mill battlefield (Johnson and Buel, 1887).

The Tar Heels emerged from the swamp, soaked, mud-coated, mosquito-bitten, and completely frustrated. This was not how Parker's riflemen had envisioned war to be. One wrote, "They had been reared on stories of Napoleon's great victories; but instead of an assured march, with flapping flags, to a described position, they had ... that day [experienced] ... groping, floundering, halts, confusion, [and] uncertainty." Parker's riflemen, believing they knew about war and its difficulties, were dismayed by how long it had taken their brigade to fight its way through the swampy underbrush. The Southerner noted, "In place of swift movement, there was ... delay that seemed endless to those who waited for the command to advance. Through it all, maddening and ceaseless, was the ear-splitting din of conflict."[48] Now, the Confederates' ranks were jumbled and they faced an unknown force mostly hidden in the tangle of underbrush. Some of the rattled troops opened fire. Lieutenant William Ardrey (Co. K) recorded, "We got in sight of Gen. Ewell's division and thought it was the enemy ... [we] soon discovered our mistake."[49]

General Anderson got his regimental commanders to sort out their overlapping and mixed ranks, and by 4:00 p.m. he was able to form his brigade for battle. The Tar Heels moved beyond a ragged stand of trees. Here, at the edge of the vegetation, Anderson halted his men. The novice soldiers studied the grounds before them. One wrote, "It was now past 4 o'clock. Over the field hung the smoke. Dim and red shone the June sun."[50] Another recorded, "Between the edge of the wooded swamp and the Federal position was an open [field] some 400 yards wide.[51] The sharp-eyed men in Parker's regiment could see a strong line of Yank riflemen posted near the top of the plateau, protecting a six-gun battery. One gray-coated soldier remarked, "The Federals had their infantry and their artillery ... at a good elevation, most of it open farm land."[52]

The Union gunners, experienced red-legs commanded by Cpt. John Tidball opened fire upon the Confederates. Explosions erupted along the Thirtieth's line of battle, spewing flame and shrapnel into Carolina flesh. First Sergeant Robert Crumpler (Co. A) was knocked to the ground as chunks of sizzling steel sliced into his thigh. Moments later, a close-by detonation wounded Pvt. Samuel Williams (Co. D), shoving him to the ground, causing, "deafness in [his] left ear."[53] More shells impacted near Parker's men. Private William Everett (Co. F) was killed by shrapnel, and Pvt. William Dew (Co. F) severely injured with wounds to his chest and face.[54] Artillery rounds continued to explode among the Carolinians. Lieutenant William Ardrey (Co. K) wrote, "Col. James T. Kell was wounded and [Sgt.] Abner B. Hood [Co. K] ... killed."[55] Colonel Frank Parker wrote, "Lt. Col. Kell was disabled by wounds from a fragment of shell to such an extent as to render him unfit for active duty for the rest of the war."[56] Private Bone noted sadly, "[Soldiers] were killed while others were wounded ... it seemed that they [US artillery] would kill every one of us."[57]

General Anderson called his regimental commanders together and told them to ready their regiments for an attack on the Union position. Major Grimes Brian Grimes (4th NC) warned the general his unit might be unable to respond to an order to charge. Grimes reported the 4th NC was, "only a mere skeleton of a regiment, as ... there were not more than 150 men and officers for duty."[58] George Anderson ordered Maj. Grimes to move his battered regiment out of the line and to hold them in readiness as support. Frank Parker hurried back to his officers and passed the message; then the line officers rushed to their men, admonishing them it was time to be brave. The riflemen gritted their teeth and stood shoulder-to-should, each man being more afraid to show fear to his comrades than of whatever was coming next. General George Anderson gave the command and his brigade moved forward.

Captain John Tidball's gunners manning their 3-inch rifles trained their weapons on the advancing Confederate formation. John Tidball wrote, "The rebels started coming, and kept coming."⁵⁹ The Yank cannon were about six hundred yards away; their fire should have been destructive. However, Tidball's gunners had been working much of the day, firing at distant targets, and shelling the infantry hidden in the woods. This meant their caissons were close to empty, resulting in a slow and limited firing. Even so, their rounds were cruelly effective. Among Col. Parker's men, Pvt. William Strickland (Co. E) was killed, Pvt. Isaac Hunt (Co. G) severely wounded, and Pvt. James Boney (Co. E) killed.⁶⁰ Private John Bone (Co. I) wrote, "shell, grapeshot and canister shot ... were poured down upon us from the enemy's batteries."⁶¹

Four hundred yards away from Anderson's gray coats three regiments of U.S. Regulars manned a battle line: the 3rd, 4th, and the 12th U.S., commanded by Lt. Col. Robert Buchanan. He wrote, "[I saw] a considerable force of the enemy coming up from the ravine to [our front].... [We prepared] ... to repel [them]."⁶² Colonel Parker gave the order to fire when his Tar Heels got within two hundred yards of the blue coats. Private John Bone (Co. I) wrote, "we were ordered to [shoot] ... here was our first fire in regular line of battle, and it was a heavy one too."⁶³ An officer in the 3rd U.S. remarked, "The enemy suddenly appeared in front of the Twelfth ... and almost decimated the regiment at a volley."⁶⁴

Then, the experienced veterans in the 3rd and 4th U.S. opened upon the Confederate line. Minié bullets slammed into the Carolinians. Private James Goodrich (Co. A) was killed, as was Pvt. John McCall (Co. C), and Pvt. Mathew Parrish (Co. G).⁶⁵ Private James McMullen's (Co. K) shoulder was destroyed by a bullet while Pvt. Montgomery Edwards (Co. F) received, "a gunshot wound in [his] side."⁶⁶ The Thirtieth's advanced staggered as Northern lead tossed more Carolinians to the ground. Lieutenant William Ardrey (Co. K) remarked, "the scene was awful to see our fellow soldiers and friends falling around us."⁶⁷ Private John Bone (Co. K) wrote, "we had a commission officer and some others ... stop and not go any further."⁶⁸ The Thirtieth's color sergeant, Hardy Royal (Co. A) lurched backward, wounded. ⁶⁹ The regiment's flag fell to the ground. A mounted staff officer rode by and snatched up the ensign. He waved it above his head. Lieutenant William Ar-

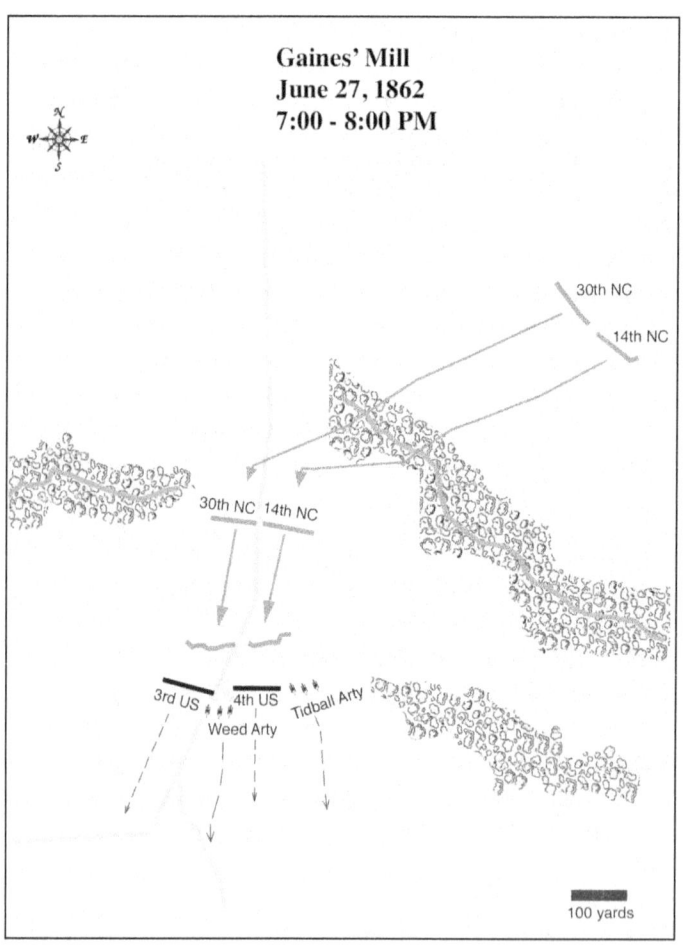

Gaines' Mill
June 27, 1862
7:00 - 8:00 PM

drey (Co. K) wrote, "Capt. [Thomas] Blunt, Gen. Anderson's aide, rode up and took our flag and loped off with it and we yelled and followed him, but the brave fellow fell dead from his horse."[70]

The Thirtieth's line officers got their men moving forward again, and they advanced, firing as they closed the distance with the Yanks. Private John Bone (Co. I) recalled, "I continued to load and fire."[71] But the Northerners fought back ferociously; Lt. Col. Buchanan wrote, "[my] two battalions ... [fought] in as handsome a line of battle as I ever saw on drill ... killing many of them."[72] Private Blackman Tew (Co. A) was killed, Pvt. John Thompson (Co. B) suffered a badly shattered arm, Cpl. James Hunt's (Co. G) leg was fractured, Pvt. William C. Peed (Co. D) struck in his left side, and 3rd Lt. Lorenzo Eagles (Co. F) severely wounded.[73] But the rest of the Tar Heels ignored their fallen comrades and pressed forward. Lieutenant Ardrey (Co. K) wrote, "it was the most exciting scene imaginable, so much so that we forgot all fear and danger."[74].

As the Confederates pushed to within one hundred yards of the Federal position the blue coats' resolve began to unravel. An officer in the 4th U.S. wrote, "As soon as the enemy opened fire ... [our commander] left the field.... Without informing any one of his intentions, and [was] not heard of since."[75] Leaderless, the unit began to waver, especially when the Northern riflemen realized the Confederate attack was not faltering. And for the Yanks in the 3rd U.S., they could see the gray line was long enough to lap around their left flank. An officer in the 3rd U.S. wrote, "I found [our] ... whole left wing exposed to a murderous fire."[76] The 3rd U.S. began to back up, the veterans not panicking, but remaining in line and firing as they gave ground. Private James Williamson (Co. A) was hit in the right hip, Pvt. Abram Danford (Co. C) struck in the face, and Pvt. Martin Wiggins (Co. F) downed by a minié ball through his thigh.[77] And Pvt. James Dickson (Co. E) also went down, "a bullet lodged in his shoulder."[78]

General Anderson's riflemen were now close enough to the Yank artillery for effective shooting. Captain John Tidball's gunners began taking casualties from Tar Heel bullets, causing and him to report, "[We were] being exposed to a sharp fire of musketry ... [and] the ammunition of my limbers, with the exception of a few rounds ... was exhausted.... I thought it prudent to withdraw."[79] Thus, with the 3rd U.S. slowly backing up, and with the withdrawal of the artillery, the jittery 4th U.S. line collapsed. Lieutenant William Ardrey (Co. K) wrote, "We raised a yell and soon the Yankees ran like turkeys."[80]

30th North Carolina Infantry[81]
Gaines' Mill Casualties
June 27, 1862

Unit	Commander	Loss
Field & Staff	Col. Parker, Francis M.	1
Co. A	Cpt. Holmes, James C.	6
Co. B	Cpt. Drake, William C.	7
Co. C	Cpt. Allen, David C.	6
Co. D	1st Lt. Allen, Charles N.	8
Co. E	Cpt. McMillan John C.	11
Co. F	Cpt. Moore, Willis M.	11
Co. G	Cpt. Bennett, James A.	6

Unit	Commander	Loss
Co. H	Cpt. Wicker, Jesse J.	11
Co. I	Cpt. Arrington, William T.	1
Co. K	1st Lt. Orr, Nathan D.	6
		74

The Carolinians swarmed over the just-vacated Federal position, now a stretch of ground covered by dozens of wounded and dead, and littered with the debris of a fleeing infantry force. Lieutenant Ardrey noted, "they left all their knapsacks, guns and everything."[82] The jubilant Tar Heels milled around, staring at the blue coats left behind and rifling through abandoned gear. Colonel Parker hollered at his captains to regain control of their companies and within a few minutes the Thirtieth was again a combat force. But their energies had been spent; this race across a quarter mile of open ground had sapped everything the novice soldiers possessed. William Ardrey added, "[we] were very much fatigued."[83]

General Anderson ordered his brigade off the hillcrest to a location protecting it from Yank artillery. Pickets were posted, and the regiments told to "stand down." It was now time to assess the cost. Colonel Frank Parker informed his company commanders he wanted an accounting, as well as details sent out to locate the regiment's casualties. The Thirtieth's weary soldiers spent the rest of the evening tracking down their missing comrades and compiling muster rolls, a most sobering task. Lieutenant Ardrey recalled, "To see the wounded ... [on] the fields was an awful sight to see."[84] The neophyte soldiers shuddered when they considered their casualties. Burial teams dug graves for sixteen comrades, while almost five-dozen men were carried to the regimental field hospital. Doctors Henry Joyner and Charles Gregory toiled all night, patching wounds, amputating limbs, and struggling to save each man's life. Unfortunately, within the next month or so, eleven severely injured young Tar Heels died from this day's wounds.[85]

Later that evening new guards were posted to relieve the pickets and these soldiers protected the brigade during the night. One of these riflemen wrote, "We were lying on the rear side of a hill and the exploding shells did us but little damage and left us liberty to view with awe the fiery balls 'comin' and agoying' [sic]." He continued, "I think as pretty sight as I ever beheld was here after nightfall—seeing the shells leaving the gun's muzzle, a great ball of fire rising higher and higher in the heavens, the burning fuse making a flame distinctly marking its course, then slowly descending in a curve ... and bursting into a thousand fragments with a loud explosion."[86]

Next morning, June 28, 1862, the battered men in the Thirtieth struggled to their feet, relieved to learn from Col. Parker they would not be immediately moving. Then, enterprising foragers scattered about to raid the abandoned Yanks' equipment. One Carolinian remarked, "The knapsacks of our enemy, picked up here and there, supplied some of the boys with food, which was shared as far as it went with others."[87] Lieutenant William Ardrey (Co. K) wrote, "Next morning we feasted on the Yankee crackers and coffee [and] ... butter ... coffee, hams, beef tongue and whiskey." Ardrey also noted, "[We] looked over the battlefield and saw the dead and wounded and the field was totally covered with captured artillery, horses, guns, knapsacks and clothing of every description."[88]

Later, the men were ordered to fall in, and soon, the Thirtieth followed the rest of the brigade as it trudged south and east for several miles before coming to Grapevine Bridge. This bridge spanned the Chickahominy River, but had been destroyed by the retreating Northerners. One butternut soldier wrote, "In the morning [June 28, 1862] our division in the lead, we struck out for the grapevine bridge in pursuit of the retreating enemy to find the bridge destroyed and no crossing till it could be repaired."[89] Colonel Parker was ordered to deploy his companies and the riflemen slogged onto the saturated low-land, grumbling about their condition. Lieutenant Ardrey (Co. K) complained, "[we] pursued them to the Chickahominy swamp where we remained on picket duty all day in mud shoe-deep." He also noticed, "We were near the Yankee hospital where there were 200 or 300 killed and wounded, and hearing of the groans all day."[90]

That evening a severe thunderstorm rolled over the area, soaking the soldiers and necessitating a miserable, sleepless night. One of the riflemen described the deluge, writing, "The night after the battle of Gaines Mill thunder rolled and lightning flashed ... nearer and nearer the storm drew on, long flashes of vivid lightning lit up the darkness, ear-splitting claps of thunder followed ... [and finally] ... rain hurled by [a] forceful wind."[91] Another wrote, "[There was] drowning rain of the night of June 28–29."[92] The next morning, with the bridge still not repaired, and the Chickahominy swamp's waters deeper and more expansive, the Confederate army could not move. Lieutenant William Ardrey (Co. K) wrote, "Remained in the swamp and feasted on the spoils of the enemy." He also mentioned, "The surgeons were amputating limbs off the enemy's wounded, all day which was very unpleasant."[93]

CHAPTER 3

The Realities of War— Malvern Hill

30th North Carolina Infantry[1]
July 1, 1862

Unit		Strength
Field & Staff	Col. Parker, Francis M. Maj. Sillers, William W. Cpt. Holmes, James C.	4
Co. A	1st Lt. Williams, Gary 2nd Lt. Stevens, Charles T.	79
Co. B	1st Lt. Davis, Weldon E. 2nd Lt. Nicholson, John H. 1st Sgt. Loughlin, James H.	63
Co. C	Cpt. Allen, David C. 1st Lt. Greer, Ephraim J. 2nd Lt. Bennett, Solomon W.	56
Co. D	1st Lt. Allen, Charles N. 2nd Rogers, Charles M. 3rd Lt. Gill, William J.	81
Co. E	Cpt. McMillan, John C. 1st Lt. Johnson, Ira J. 2nd Lt. McMillan, Daniel T.	89
Co. F	Cpt. Moore, Willis M. 1st Lt. Harrell, George K. 2nd Lt. Pitt, James W.	91
Co. G	Cpt. Barnett, James A. 2nd Lt. Clairborne, Robert F. 3rd Lt. Crews, Alexander	64
Co. H	Cpt. Wicker, Jesse J. 1st Lt. McNeil, Henry J. 2nd Lt. Jackson, Archibald J.	76
Co. I	Cpt. Arrington, William T. 1st Lt. Harris, James J. 2nd Lt. Williford, Burton B.	104
Co. K	1st Lt. Orr, Nathan D. 2nd Lt. Ardrey, William E. 3rd Lt. Downs, John T.	56
		763

The pioneers reconstructing the bridge across the Chickahominy River had not completed their task by nightfall on June 29, 1862, frustrating the Southerners' high command's plans of adding Jackson's divisions to the Confederate forces pressing the Union army. The Chickahominy was an impassible barrier; without a bridge there could be no movement. A Confederate officer wrote, "A forbidding place the swamp was ... the stream itself was shallow and little scarped ... the sole difficulty in crossing it was offered by the underbrush and briers along the banks. Deciduous trees and pines so shaded the lower growth that it had lush, entangling thickness ... the forest and the wide-spreading branches baffled the adventurer half a mile, even a mile, from the little stream ... and set a barrier almost impassible"[2]

Colonel Frank Parker and his brother-in-law, 25-year-old Frederick Philips, the regiment's newly appointed adjutant worked with the company officers to rebuild each unit's chain of command. The loss of sergeants and corporals meant each company commander was forced to temporarily promote riflemen to fill empty slots. Three companies no longer had captains, and a fourth captain, Company A's James Holmes, now acted as an interim wing commander. Holmes had assumed the field command responsibilities created by Lt. Col. James Kell's loss. Captain Holmes turned over his company to 1st Lt. Gary Williams. James Holmes meshed easily with Maj. William Sillers, after all the two men had organized and recruited Company A.[3] Meanwhile, for the Carolinian soldiers, the new realities of their military adventure had horribly changed—war was not a game. One rifleman wrote his wife, "I am in for the war, [w]hole hope or none."[4] Chaplain Alexander Betts, saddled the responsibility of dealing with the casualties, wrote his wife, "[I must] write to Mrs. Tedder [Pvt. Sidney Tedder (Co. K)] and Mrs. Hood [Pvt. Abner Hood (Co. K)], whose husbands ha[ve] fallen."[5]

That afternoon (June 30, 1862) Confederate engineers completed a bridge over the Chickahominy River and the Southerners marched across. General Anderson led his brigade as they hiked to another choke point, the White Oak Bridge, also destroyed by the retreating Yankees. Several blue coat batteries shelled the leading Southern units and Gen. Thomas "Stonewell" Jackson assembled a force of artillery to counter this threat. Jackson's gunners bombarded the Yank batteries, forcing the Northerners to withdraw their pieces. However, when Confederate work crews advanced to rebuild the bridge a brigade of Union troops occupying the opposite bank of the White Oak River opened fire. The construction crews scampered to safety, and the two sides faced each other, separated by this thin band of impassible water. A Tar Heel wrote, "[A] Federal force prevented the Confederates from rebuilding the bridge and thus kept Jackson's men at bay while the battle of Fraser's Farm was raging."[6] This fight at Frayer's Farm lasted for several hours, meanwhile a good portion of the Confederate army sat idly, unable to come to their brothers' aid. Eventually the conflict subsided and the Yanks withdrew, enabling the Confederate pioneers to safely approach the damaged bridge spans.

The Southerners waited while crews cobbled together a passage, a job requiring hours, and then, when it was repaired, the infantry marched again, heading south. The Carolina riflemen followed as their division's column trekked past the Frayser's Farm battlefield. Lieutenant William Ardrey (Co. K) wrote, "The ground was covered with dead and wounded of the enemy and every house we passed was crowded with their wounded."[7] Another Tar Heel, staggered by what he saw, wrote, "Passing over the battlefield of Frayser's farm we had to remove the dead from the road, and came to a Yankee field hospital. It was ghastly beyond description.... Piles of arms, feet, hands, torn, lacerated and amputated from wounded human bodies." The horrified rifleman continued: "men's bodies ... thinly covered in haste with earth, sometimes a hand or foot sticking out.... Dead horses, poor innocent beasts slaughtered and torn by shot and exploding shell, scattered over the field.... The stench, the deadly effluvia, had attracted the scavenger of the country."[8]

Brigadier General George Anderson's brigade filed past hundreds of sullen blue coats huddling together, captured in the fight. The brigade was halted and Gen. Anderson called his regimental commanders together. When they assembled, Anderson informed Maj. Brian Grimes (4th NC) he was to remove his small command from the brigade and guard the Yankees. One of that regiment's officers wrote, "[The 4th NC] was detached to guard more than 1,000 captured prisoners and a large quantity of supplies."[9] Following this short break, the Tar Heels continued their march to the south and east.

They covered five miles before bumping to a halt, the column's leading regiments running into Union defenses. Lieutenant William Ardrey (Co. K) reported, "In the evening we approached near the enemy and our batteries opened fire on them. They returned it furiously and it lasted several hours, when the Yankees retreated." Ardrey also noted, "We lay on the field, [cooked] our meat on a stick and feasted on beef and crackers."[10] As the Carolinians rested in the cooling evening's air, Col. Frank Parker received an order to send a detachment back to Frayser's battlefield. Private John Bone (Co. I), a member of one of the companies selected for this job, wrote, "That evening there was a detail made ... to go back on the battlefield and bury the dead.... We were furnished shovels and ... as we would come to the dead men, we would dig a hole by their side and lay them in. If we could get a blanket we would spread it over them and then cover it with dirt." Bone commented, writing, "This seemed very bad to us."[11] These Tar Heels returned to their regiment, subdued by their experience. First Lieutenant Ephraim Greer (Co. C), depressed by what he had just seen, sought out the Thirtieth's chaplain. Alexander Betts wrote of their meeting, "Bro. E. J. Greer ... left his pocket book containing $42.21 with me."[12]

The soldiers were rousted from their bedrolls early the next morning, July 1, 1862. They ate the last of their captured rations, causing one Southerner to write, "[we] feasted on Yankee spoils,"—and prepared to march.[13] Rumors informed the Tar Heel riflemen a large force of blue coats occupied a ridge, barely a mile from where their column stood. Frank Parker's men went quiet, silenced by the possibility of impending danger. Jackson deployed his brigades with the men of Gen. Anderson's three-regiment brigade positioned in the front. As the Carolina formation moved forward distant Union artillery began firing at them. General Daniel Hill wrote, "We had to advance across an open field and ford a creek before getting under cover of the woods."[14] In Anderson's brigade, Col. Parker's men raced forward, enduring the shelling, and then entered the protection provided by a stand of trees and underbrush. But they weren't safe; a screen of Northern skirmishers open fire upon them. Colonel Parker's riflemen took cover behind tree trunks and fallen limbs, and returned fire. The thicket crackled with the sounds of a brisk skirmish. One soldier wrote, "The woods were full of smoke, and bullets buzzed round our heads like a swarm of angry bees."[15] Colonel Parker reported, "we went ... at the double quick and drove the cowardly rascals ... [from] the woods."[16] The Thirtieth pushed the Federals without loss, though resistance to the Confederate advance was tougher for its brother regiments; both the 2nd and 14th NC to suffered casualties. Colonel Frank Parker also learned that "Brigadier General Anderson, on the extreme left ... had ... been wounded and carried off the field."[17] Colonel Charles Tew (2nd NC) assumed brigade command.

The Tar Heels advanced cautiously through the vegetation until being ordered to halt as they neared the wood's edge. Colonel Parker sent skirmishers to the tree line, and stood down the rest of his regiment. Water details were organized; meanwhile, NCOs made sure everyone's cartridge boxes were refilled with ammunition. Some of the men prepared coffee. No one knew how long they would be sitting beneath the shade of these trees, but the Tar Heels were becoming experts at using what time they had available. Some of the men napped, while others smoked, though most of the men sat around in small groups, pondering what would happen next. They tried to relax but few were able to, because, as one Confederate complained, "the flies bit as viciously as the mosquitoes stung."[18]

Col. Charles C. Tew, 34 years old, assumed command of the brigade when Gen. George Anderson was wounded (courtesy North Carolina Museum of History).

The riflemen on the skirmish line had a much better view of their situation. They could see their position clearly; the Confederates occupied the base of a long, sloping ridge, and the Yankees held the crest. The ground between them and the blue coats was open, a space of nearly a thousand yards of pasture, wheat, corn, and barley. Rifleman John Bone (Co. I) recalled, "Our Brigade was placed [at the base of] ... the center of the hill. It was high with a long slope; and a broad field below."[19] Another soldier wrote, "It offered the Federals a perfect field of fire for 300 or 400 yards."[20] Even the youngest rifleman, with only the experience of the Thirtieth's brief assault at Gaines' Mill could see an attack up this slope would be suicide.

Division level staff officers shouldered their way up, beside the skirmishers and examined the foreboding heights. They studied the blue coats' position and grumbled among themselves. Major General Daniel Hill wrote, "The Yankees were found to be strongly posted on a commanding hill, all the approaches to which could be swept by artillery, and were guarded by swarms of infantry securely sheltered by fences, ditches, and ravines." He dourly continued, "Tier after tier of batteries were grimly visible on the plateau."[21] Another officer observed, "Every part of this position was crowned with guns ... [and] powerful lines of infantry were in support."[22] General Hill returned from his reconnaissance, shaking his head in dismay, concluding, "An examination now satisfied me that an attack could not but be hazardous to our arms."[23]

One of the Union batteries was positioned closer to the Confederates than others. The Carolinian marksmen sought permission to shoot. When given approval, they began to fire upon the Northern gunners. The commander of the Federal artillery unit noted, "the enemy's sharpshooters drew up in a wooded ravine and annoyed us ... wounding two of my men.... I ... fired canister into the ravine to silence the enemy's sharpshooters."[24] The Yanks' shells crashed into the woods, forcing the Tar Heels to seek cover. One rifleman wrote, "[We were] lying for hours in line, exposed to bursting shells and falling limbs of trees."[25] Private John Bone (Co. I) added, "Many shells exploded over us, cutting off tree branches and their tops, killing and wounding men; it was an awful situation."[26]

The Confederate high command ordered artillery forward to silence the Yank cannons, however, only one battery was shifted into position. The Union gunners all along the ridge crest aimed their pieces at these four cannons. One of the Yank artillerymen wrote, "the enemy succeeded in placing a field battery about 1,200 yards ... from our front."[27] Another gunner added, "the enemy opened fire upon us from a battery in a field of wheat ... well masked by stacked and standing grain."[28] The Confederate cannoneers served their pieces effectively, causing one of the Northern artillerymen to write, "The rebel battery ... was worked with much speed and some skill, occasionally doing some little injury within our lines ... [but] not worthy of any notice."[29] Then, the entire Federal artillery force volleyed. A blue coat remarked, "[Our] batter[ies] at once opened fire upon them with fine effect, the spherical case shot doing good execution on their teams and among their artillerymen." This officer then observed, "The enemy's batter[y] ... discontinued [its] fire."[30] General Daniel Hill, irate at this uneven and humiliating artillery duel, wrote Jackson, "A single battery ... was ordered up and knocked to pieces in a few minutes." He continued: "the firing from our batteries was of the most farcical character."[31] However, for Colonel Parker's men, and the rest of the North Carolina infantry hiding in the woods, this entire exchange of artillery meant, as one scribbled, "shattered branches and fragments of shells ... fell ... around [us]."[32]

An eruption of musketry off to the Tar Heels' right told Parker's riflemen a force of Confederates had begun an attack. Frank Parker's men, as one noted, "loitered in the thickets ... listen[ing]," and were not able to view what was happening, but they all guessed it would not be long before they, too, received word to advance.[33] The Carolinians shuddered at this prospect as rumors swept the formation, telling of Southerners being chopped to pieces by musketry and cannon. Brigadier General Lewis Armistead, commanding the Confederate regiments in this action, wrote, "About 3 p.m. ... the enemy approached with a heavy body of skirmishers. I ordered ... my brigade to drive them back, which they did." Armistead continued, "In their ardor [my men] went too far ... it was folly ... to withdraw ... [or] charge."[34] An hour later, five Confederate brigades were added to Armistead's regiments and they all crashed against the Union positions, only to suffer ghastly casualties.

Meanwhile, Gen. Daniel Hill argued with his superior, attempting to convince him an assault was futile, but Jackson was adamant, and finally, bluntly ordered him to attack. Hill recorded Jackson's command: "Press forward on the right, the enemy is retreating."[35] Daniel Hill questioned Jackson, hoping an error had been made. He described their situation, writing, "We could only reach the first line of batteries by traversing an open space of from 300 to 400 yards, exposed to a murderous fire of grape and canister from the artillery and musketry from the infantry."[36] But the aggressive commander insisted Gen. Hill carry out the attack, and make it immediately. General Hill reluctantly ordered his brigades forward. A Tar Heel rifleman in the 2nd NC remarked, "Soon the word was passed, 'Up, Second, and at them,' and our Brigade ... sprang forward through the woods with a shout." He continued, "We crossed one fence, went through another piece of woods, then over another fence, into an open field on the other side of which was a long line of Yankees."[37] Another added, "With trailing arms we shot forward up the incline, reached the rail fence, threw it down, realigned ... and struck out with a yell."[38]

It was 6:30 p.m., and as Colonel Charles Tew's three regiments moved forward, with the 2nd NC on the left, the Thirtieth in the center, and the 14th NC on the right. The brigade's battle line covered a front of over a quarter mile.[39] The Tar Heels marched shoulder-to-shoulder, colors and senior officers out in front, followed by twin ranks of riflemen, and file closers immediately behind, every man moving as drilled, marching at, "direct step of 28 inches, [at a] common time rate of 90 steps per minute."[40] The Carolina brigade was a massed target advancing at a rate of approximately one hundred yards each minute, an opportunity exciting the Federal artillerymen. One Northerner wrote, "In front of our line of battle the ground was open and admitted easy passage of any troops ... [open] within some 500 yards of our front."[41]

Private John Bone (Co. I) described the first part of their advance, writing, "We were then ordered to charge up the slope which we did the best we could; the 30th Regiment got through in very good order. We were now almost at the top of the hill, in a broad open field."[42] Another Carolinian recalled, "[The] troops advanced across an open field with the enemy batteries some 700–800 yards distant."[43] But now the Confederates were within easy range of the artillery, and the veteran Union gunners anxiously awaited the order to pull their lanyards. When they order came, Pvt. Richard Brooks (Co. G) noted, "the Federal Army fired point blank cannon fire into the charging Confederates."[44] A blue coat bragged, "Sixty cannon, all trained on the advancing column, vomited forth their storm of iron hail."[45] In all probability, nor more than two-dozen artillery pieces were sighted to cover the three-regiments' quarter-mile wide battlefront. The Union cannoneers served their weapons efficiently, firing each piece approximately one round every sixty seconds.

A storm of death slashed into the Tar Heels. Colonel Frank Parker's regiment shuddered as deadly steel ripped into the Tar Heels, striking a portion of the Thirtieth's ranks with lethal ordnance erupting every seven or eight seconds. Among those falling, in Company A, a well-directed blast sent grape-shot ripping through the men, killing Pvt. James Baggot, slashing Pvt. Thomas Howard's head, crashing into Pvt. Alexander Pope's chest, and slicing Pvt. Wiley Pope's head and knee. Company D staggered when a shell detonated among its ranks, killing Cpl. James Allen, Pvt. Arrington Davis and Pvt. James R. Davis, as well as spewing shrapnel into Pvt. Calvin Mangun's hip and foot, and shattering Pvt. Joseph Mason's left leg. And in Company I, an explosion killed Cpt. William Arrington, and sent molten steel ripping into Pvt. Joel Price's head and Pvt. George Sherwood's shoulder and jaw.[46] Moments later, another shell chewed through Parker's men, reducing strong Carolina lads into mangled flesh and shattered bone.

The Yank infantry watched as more grape shot, solid shell, and shrapnel exploded among the Confederate ranks. One Northerner noted with amazement that their guns caused "large rents, which were filled up." He added, writing in awe, "shoulder to shoulder, seemingly irresistible, they continued to advance."[47] The Carolina riflemen stumbled forward, howling, trying to ignore the destruction shredding their comrades. One wrote, "The thunder blast from the artillery changed from solid shot to a thick storm of grape, canister and shrapnel ... falling like a flail in the hands of a giant upon the unresisting grain."[48] Dozens more of Parker's boys were tossed to the ground by the Federal onslaught. A blast savaged Company I. Private John Bone (Co. I) wrote, "a shell burst over my head and a piece struck.... Singleton Langley and shattered his thigh. I went to him and straightened out his leg and put a blanket under his head."[49] Not far from Pvt. Langley, Cpl. Exum Vick (Co. I) lie, having had his "leg nearly blown off."[50] A shocked rifleman would scribble later, "such volleys of grape and shrapnel as we had never met before."[51]

Colonel Frank Parker's resolute riflemen pushed forward, his farm boys and shop keepers having covered two hundred yards during 120 seconds of devastating fire and steel. An observer noted, "The brigade moved with alacrity about half way ... when the terrible fire of artillery and the opening fire of the infantry induced it to halt."[52] More Tar Heels went down; grape shot had sliced through Company K, shattering Pvt. George Jennings' thigh, mangling Pvt. John Black's left arm, and killing Pvt. James Robinson. Company C was hit; 1st Lt. Ephraim Greer's "left leg was cut off below the knee" by a chunk of steel, Sgt. John Tharp had three fingers sliced away from his hand, and Pvt. George Washington Harris' knee joint was splintered.[53] A blue coat remarked how the Union shells ripped through the Confederate line, writing, "grape and canister ... cut mercilessly and cruelly ... [one round] lifted a whole platoon."[54]

The Confederates staggered up the deadly slope as all the Union artillerymen shif-ted to canister. A Northern gunner wrote, "When they got within 400 yards we closed our case shot and opened on them with canister; and such destruction I never elsewhere witnessed. At each discharge great gaps were made in their ranks."[55] These huge shot-gun-like explosions of tore huge holes in the Tar Heel line. In Company B, Pvt. Nicholas Shearin was killed, Pvt. Dudley Neal struck in the leg, Pvt. Robert Duke's body pierced completely through, and Cpl. John Newson was downed with a shredded right thigh. Private Philip Gill was stuck in the face and, "suffer[ed] total loss of vision in the left eye ... and impairment ... of the other."[56] One embattled rifleman wrote, "[A comrade] "was instantly killed by a grape shot passing through his body. He never knew what killed him." The horrified soldier continued, "I took a testament from his pocket to ... [give] to his father.... This was the only time I ever put my hand into the pocket of a friend or foe during the war."[57] Another wrote, "The enemy mowed us down by fifties."[58]

The Southerners' advance had lasted four minutes and now the courageous Tar Heels had closed to within three hundred yards. They were almost close enough for the Union troops to hear their yells above the artillery's thunder. An appreciative Yank noted, "Nearer and nearer it came, and the wild Southern yell was heard."[59] Another admitted, "The attack [was] desperate and determined."[60] This Carolina courage still did not waver; another sixty seconds of marching put their battered ranks at 200-yards' range—within lethal rifle shooting distance. A blue-coated infantryman wrote, "When the attacking force came within range of our arms our whole line sprang to their feet and poured into the enemy a withering fire."[61] Now, volleys of 58-caliber minié bullets pummeled the Confederate lines. Corporal Lewis Pipkin (Co. A) was killed, as was Pvt. Isham Jones (Co. D) and Cpl. William Rivenbark (Co. E). Captain Willis Moore (Co. F) fell wounded, along with Cpl. William Kittrell (Co. G), Pvt. John Younts (Co. K) and Pvt. John Woodward (Co. I).[62] A stunned Southerner groaned, "[We were] mowed down like grain before the sickle and swept away like chaff by the wind."[63]

Colonel Frank Parker's men could go no farther. A Yank wrote respectfully, "Human endurance had reached it utmost limits."[64] The Thirtieth may have stopped advancing, but the Union musketry and artillery did not cease. The regimental formation fell apart. One soldier wrote, "It was astonishing how soon ... disintegration began."[65] Corporal Sherman Royal (Co. A) was struck in the head, Pvt. John Cox (Co. H) hit in the right arm, Pvt. James Morgan (Co. F) shot through the shoulder, Cpl. Samuel Leonard (Co. C) injured by a bullet to his chest, and Pvt. John Manellis (Co. E), suffered a, "fracture of his 5th right rib, the ball passing out [between] the 7–8 ... left side ... ribs near the spine."⁶⁶ Captain John Witherspoon (Co. K) wrote, "I was struck on the shoulder but was not hurt."⁶⁷ Private John Bone (Co. I) recalled, "just as I reached the edge of the filed, I heard a ball hit my left hand companion and he fell dead."⁶⁸

The Tar Heels could move no farther, it was almost as if the incoming minié bullets and canister were so thick they made an impenetrable wall. One Carolinian noted, "[We] reached within 200 yards of the enemy ... before halting."⁶⁹ Another wrote, "[The men began] to lie down, and commenced shooting"⁷⁰ Private John Bone (Co. I) recorded, "We stopped and opened fire; it was a hot place, with lead and iron."⁷¹ Sadly, these tenacious Tar Heel riflemen who returned fire failed to cause much damage. One Northerner added, "the fire of the enemy, being generally too high, did us com-

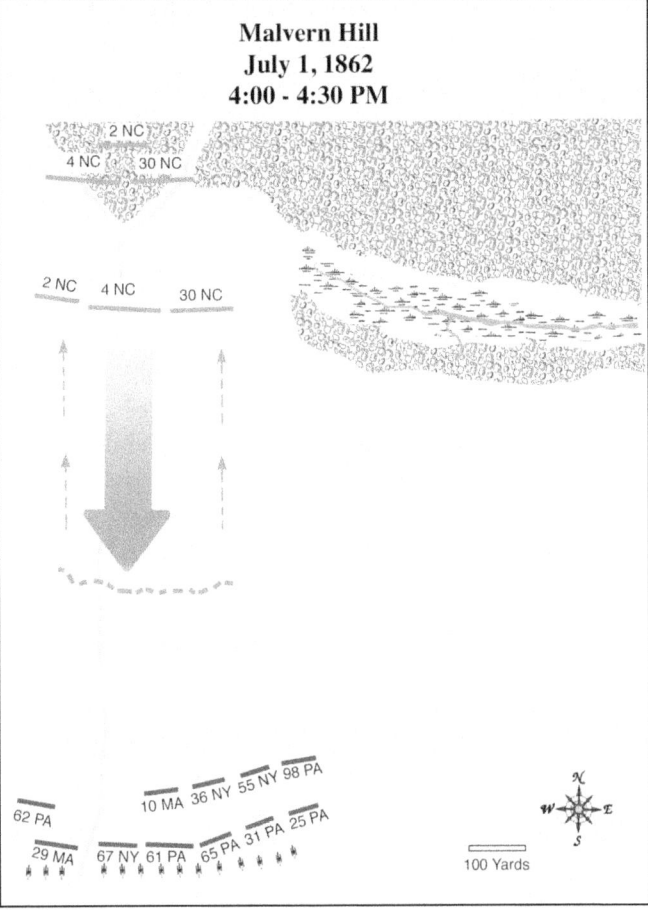

paratively little injury."⁷² The Federals riflemen, little bothered by the scattered Southern musketry, poured death into the Confederates. A gray-coated officer admitted, "It was not war; it was mass murder."⁷³ The Thirtieth's ranks no longer resembled a solid battle line; instead, little groups of men clustered together, shooting tenaciously, others knelt or lie prone, some firing, while the rest hugged the ground. John Bone noted, "As I loaded and fired I could see the men fall and hear them halloo all around me."⁷⁴

A Federal artilleryman wrote, "well-directed discharges of shrapnel ... soon silenced the musketry."⁷⁵ A canister round ripped through Company D, its dozens of round, molten shot killing Pvt. James Wheeler and Pvt. Almond White, and wounding Hardy O'Neal (right arm), Pvt. George Pierce (right knee), and Pvt. James White (stomach).⁷⁶ Lieutenant William Ardrey (Co. K) scrawled a note, writing, "we were repulsed by their batteries."⁷⁷ Private John Bone (Co. I) wrote, "Finally I was wounded in the hand."⁷⁸ Colonel Frank Parker lamented, "my Regt. suffered severely."⁷⁹ Another Confederate added, "Our whole division was cut to pieces."⁸⁰ Distraught riflemen began to crawl backwards, away from the disaster. An officer remarked, "my men began to give way, and ... many ceased to respond to my efforts to hold them in line and maintain the position."⁸¹ Private John Bone (Co. I) confessed, "I made my way down the hill the best I could, expecting to be hit by a ball or piece of shell."⁸² Another Confederate added, "[we] slipped back down the hill."⁸³ The Union infantry ceased shooting, shocked by the devastation they had caused. One stunned but triumph officer wrote, "after a sharp contest, last[ing] only a few minutes, the enemy broke and fled."[84] Their assault was over in no more than ten to fifteen minutes, and now, as a Northerner bragged, "The ground over which they [had] passed was covered with their dead and dying."[85] Regretfully, considering the heavy Confederate casualties, they barely harmed the Union infantry. One blue coat gloated, "the loss in my brigade was small."[86] Another reported, "The attack and repulse had been so rapid ... very few casualties had occurred on our side."[87]

Once back among the safety of the woods Col. Frank Parker assisted his surviving company officers as they struggled to reorganize their units. Frank Parker wrote, "I withdrew [the 30th NC], and rallied for another attempt, but ... [the regiment was] very much scattered."[88] Private John Bone (Co. I) added, "Col. Parker got as many of his Regiment together as he could; it was getting dark and they were scattered from the retreat. We assembled back in a forest of trees, near the place where we had formed our line of battle before we made the charge."[89] Colonel Parker then surveyed the battlefield, horrified by the Thirtieth's destruction. One Tar Heel wrote, "The fight was over, the wounded began crawling away to find friends and the litter-bearer[s]."[90] Hardly a half hour had passed since Col. Charles Tew unwillingly gave the order for their three regiments to advance. Now, their formations were shattered and barely capable of mounting a feeble defense. A Southern officer reported, "[we] set to work ... to collect our commands together, and bivouacked them in a place of security."[91] Among the Thirtieth's ranks, the survivors shook their heads in consternation. One moaned, "roll call ... was the saddest ever. Silence was the only response to many names ... as the sergeant continued the roll call down the list, some messmate would falter out, 'Dead.'"[92] Afterwards, Cpt. John Witherspoon (Co. K) recorded simply, "We have been engaged ... [I am] safe."[93]

The Federal troops, exultant in their easy victory, fanned out among the abandoned Confederates, rounding up prisoners, helping wounded, and searching for souvenirs. A Bay State officer added, "The ground was covered with their dead and wounded, and for more than an hour, prisoners kept coming in, some severely wounded, while a large number were entirely unhurt."[94] Another officer boasted, "The [Rebels] left a battle-flag behind."[95] This Confederate flag belonged to the 14th NC, which had suffered the loss of so many color-guards, the emblem was forgotten when the demolished regiment fell back. Though the 14th NC's flag had symbolic value, a practical Massachusetts officer, understanding the war's realities, recorded, "The enemy were armed with Enfield rifles, of a later and better manufacture than our own, and many of our men changed muskets advantageously, on the battlefield."[96]

Later that evening Lt. William Ardrey (Co. K) scribbled in his diary, "we were completely exhausted.... We lay in the woods, shells bursting around us all the time. The firing ceased about 10 o'clock that night."[97] Private John Bone (Co. I) added, "We remained in the forest all night ... the artillery ... ceased, it commenced raining, and rained the rest of the night."[98] Colonel Frank Parker, protected from the rain beneath a makeshift shelter, wrote his wife, "thanks to a kind protecting Providence, I am safe ... my men fell around me thick and fast, and not a hair of my head was touched." He continued, "we had 16 killed, 94 wounded, 30 missing.... I fear a great many of the wounded will die yet."[99] Frank Parker's initial count would change in the coming hours as stragglers made their way back to the regiment, and the Thirtieth's surgeons had the time to make more accurate reports—the 30th NC lost just over 130 men in the ten-minute attack on Malvern Hill.

30th North Carolina Infantry[100]
Malvern Hill Casualties
July 1, 1862

Unit	Commander	Loss
Field & Staff	Col. Parker, Francis M.	-
Co. A	1st Lt. Williams, Gary	12
Co. B	1st Lt. Davis, Weldon E.	11
Co. C	Cpt. Allen, David C.	17
Co. D	1st Lt. Allen, Charles N.	15
Co. E	Cpt. McMillan, John C.	10
Co. F	Cpt. Moore, Willis M.	15
Co. G	Cpt. Barnett, James A.	11
Co. H	Cpt. Wicker, Jesse J.	16
Co. I	Cpt. Arrington, William T.	17
Co. K	1st Lt. Orr, Nathan D.	7
		131

The Carolinians awoke the next morning, soaked by the night's rain, and despondent from the number of missing friends and relatives. Private John Bone (Co. I) wrote, "Next morning everything was wet.... It was a sad morning to those that were living for we were in a sad condition."[101] Colonel Parker ordered his morose men to assemble for another fight, as confused brigade staffers were telling him they had reports of Federal units forming to attack. The colonel met with his company commanders and told them to be prepared, but he had no solid information. Captain John Witherspoon (Co. K) passed on this message to his lieutenants and NCOs, stating, "I don't know what moves we will take this morning."[102] Lieutenant William Ardrey (Co. K), recording the rumors the boys in his platoon told him, wrote, "Rained all morning and we were expecting an attack all the time."[103] Fortunately, the Yanks did not attack, nor did Col. Charles Tew receive orders from Gen. Daniel Hill to form for a charge. Instead, as Pvt. John Bone (Co. I) recalled how the elements continued to pummel the soldiers and wrote, "It rained all day.... I was as wet as if I had been dipped in water." He added, "I was about as wet as I could be ... and hungry."[104]

Later that afternoon, the Thirtieth did form up, but not for another fight. Instead, they followed the 2nd and 14th NC away from their bivouac and to a new camping ground. A Carolinian wrote, "After ... enduring rain all morning, the regiment marched through ankle-deep mud to a hill east of the battle ground and [made] camp."[105] General Hill informed his regimental commanders the Federals had fallen back; the threat of another battle was over. Daniel Hill reported, "The [Yankees] retreated in the night, leaving their dead unburied, their wounded on the ground ... and thousands of superior rifles thrown away." Hill added, "Arms accouterments, knapsacks, overcoats, and clothing of every description were wildly strewn on the road side."[106]

The exhausted Carolinians fixed meals above smoky fires and quietly considered yesterday's horrific events. Captain John Witherspoon (Co. K), shocked by his close brush with death, wrote his wife, "May God still continue to protect me until I shall see my family again." He then ended his letter with a plea, "I hope and pray to meet you once more on earth."[107] Lieutenant William Ardrey (Co. K), once he had tended to his platoon, noted in his diary, "The dead [are] buried and the wounds dressed ... [I am] completely worn out."[108] And Colonel Parker, after strolling through his regiment's solemn company streets, shared with his wife, "What can make people go to war? To witness the destruction of life on a battle field is enough to put a stop to all such arguments for its future."[109]

Chapter 4

Summer 1862—The Road to Sharpsburg

The Thirtieth's riflemen rose from their bedrolls on July 3, 1862, to the good news they would not be falling in for battle, nor would they be marching. The war-weary soldiers stumbled about camp, carrying out fatigue duties and guard mount, relieved to know the Yanks had backed far enough away there no longer was danger. Colonel Parker met with his officers and they discussed refilling missing leadership positions, as well as replacing lost NCOs. The Thirtieth was now a different regiment than it had been a week earlier. The two fights at Gaines' Mill and Malvern Hill had ripped away over a third of the unit's strength, while sickness, accidents, and exhaustion had sapped off another quarter—the regiment's strength now was barely four hundred.[1] Frank Parker had many issues to fix: morale was low, weapons needed repair and replacement, and the men had not received sufficient rations in some time. He immediately located the regiment's sutler and commissary wagons, and sent out a detail to escort these much-needed wagons bearing highly prized goods to their camp. Lieutenant William Ardrey (Co. K) recorded, "Our commissary and sutler wagons came down and brought us a supply of provisions and we were never so rejoiced to see something to eat." He continued, "Our sutler ... brought us some good butter, sausage, and baker's bread ... some of the boys made themselves sick eating."[2]

Sensing how quickly rations, fruit, and fresh bread had improved his men's spirits, Col. Frank Parker instantly put them back to work, commencing drill and picket duty. A few days later, on July 8, 1862, Parker received permission to shift the regiment's camp a half mile closer to the river, thus making it easier for his troops to wash their clothes. He also found another way to increase his Carolinians' attitudes. Lieutenant Ardrey scribbled in his journal, "Drew rations of whiskey, about half of Company E was tight, climbing trees, etc." Ardrey added, "Took a good wash and took off a shirt that I had been wearing three weeks."[3]

On July 9, 1862, Col. Parker ordered his men to break down their camp; he had received orders from Col. Charles Tew that the brigade was moving. Then, the troops of the 2nd, 14th, and 30th NC fell into line and hiked to Harrison's Landing, within fifteen miles of Richmond.[4] Lieutenant Ardrey wrote, "After a long, tiresome march ... we arrived at our old camp ... the quarter master brought us our tents [and] knapsacks.... We soon raised our tents and fixed up."[5] Also at this time, the brigade's detached regiment, the 4th NC, rejoined the formation.[6] The Carolinians remained at this new camp for the next week, relaxing as much as soldiers could. William Ardrey noted, "All quiet in camp, feasted on loaf, sausage and butter." He also confessed, "Capt. John Witherspoon went to Richmond [and] brought us some candy and whiskey."[7]

Now, with all the regiments present, Col. Charles Tew drilled the brigade.[8] Afterwards, Col. Tew called his regimental commanders together and they spoke about their brigade's most serious difficulty—the soldiers' health. The summer's heat, combined with mosquitoes, flies, and inadequate health practices had begun to ravage the men. Colonel Parker then called his company commanders together and they talked about the problem. Captain John Witherspoon (Co. K) recorded their concerns, writing, "Our entire Regt. has the diarrhea."[9] That evening, Col. Parker penned to his wife, "I am sorry to report the bad health of my Regt. There are more than 250 … sick; besides a good many in the Hospitals, in and around Richmond; [there] are only about 300 present for duty."[10] The regiment's sickest men ended up among Richmond's military hospitals, where most succumbed to typhoid fever: nine died in July and another fifteen in August. One of these victims falling to typhoid fever was the 33-year-old teacher from Bladen, NC, 3rd Lt. Lorenzo Cain (Co. C).[11] Among others who did not survive, 30-year-old Pvt. George Pegram (Co. B), died of tonsillitis, while Pvt. Samuel Graham (Co. H) was killed by tuberculosis.[12] Another Thirtieth soldier who was buried at this time, though not from illness, was a 36-year-old itinerate farmer who volunteered from Ararat, VA. Private Thomas Winn (Co. G) died, "suddenly of mysterious causes." When the medical staff attended to his body they reported, "Received of Capt. C. Monfit, A.Q.M., $1,391.60 [in] the effects of T. Winn, deceased."[13] No one was able to determine how Thomas Winn, a man arriving from civilian life with no savings, had acquired such as large amount of cash, nor was anyone able to learn why he had died.

Frank Parker, following the advice of his surgeon, Dr. Charles Gregory, ordered the men to eat vegetable, wash their uniforms and bedding, and clean the camp. Lieutenant William Ardrey (Co. K) wrote of these dictates, "[We] police[d] the camp and buil[t] arbors in front of the tent … the camp [is] very much improved, in fact a very nice camp [with] fine water." He added, "Inspection at 9 o'clock…. All the Company had on clean shirts of their own washing."[14] Then Cpt. John Witherspoon (Co. K) happily recorded, "We are due two months' pay."[15]

On July 17, 1862, the brigade was formed, along with its brother units in Maj. Gen. Daniel H. Hill's division and their commander informed them he was being transferred back to North Carolina. General Hill complimented his men, saying, "The Southern soldier is so remarkable … [he] has endeared to [his] commander by [his] uniform good conduct in the camp as well as in the field. The troops have ever shown by their quiet and conservative character, their orderly behavior and prompt obedience." Daniel Hill finished his speech, admonishing the men, "May you ever rebuke with proper scorn the wretches who desert your colors in battle."[16]

The Tar Heels faced another change in leadership soon after Gen. Hill relinquished command of his division—North Carolina needed a new governor. The State's temporary governor, Henry Clark, completed the departed John Ellis's term and now new elections were required. Two candidates contended for the position: William J. Johnston and Zebulon Vance. William Johnston, the Democrat, wholeheartedly supported Jefferson Davis's policies and argued North Carolina should give up some of its state's rights in defense of the Confederate cause. Zebulon Vance, on the other hand, championed the belief that all the state's civil liberties should be protected.[17] However, neither man campaigned, as both remained at their current positions; Vance was colonel of the 26th NC, and Johnston president of the Charlotte and South Carolina Railroad.[18] Lieutenant William Ardrey (Co. K) recorded the Thirtieth's vote, writing, "Election day for the North Carolina Soldiers. Our Regt ... gave Col. Wm. Johnston of Charlotte a large majority over Col. Vance for Gov."[19] Though Colonel Parker's men supported William Johnston, the majority of North Carolina's voters cast their ballots for Zebulon Vance. The election results were not close; Vance collected over 54,000 votes to Johnston's 24,500.[20]

On August 1, 1862, Col. Parker ordered a large detail composed of half the regiment to leave their muskets in camp, and shoulder picks and shovels for a work duty. He wrote, "sen[t] off ... 250 ... men ... from the Regt. ... down the James River, to throw up breastworks." Parker admitted as the noise from his griping Tar Heels melted away as they shuffled out of camp, "Our boys have an aversion to breastworks; they admire the manner of Jackson's fighting, and are all anxious to be under his command.... But good breastworks save many a man; I have seen and felt their great utility."[21]

Col. Zebulon Vance became North Carolina's governor in September 1862 (Library of Congress).

These Tar Heels labored among the earthen fortifications for the next several days, until, on August 5, 1862, Lt. Ardrey noted, "Received orders to go to camp and get our guns and be ready, that the enemy were advancing at Malvern Hill."[22] Once the men had retrieved their weapons, they hustled toward that old battleground. A Carolinian officer recorded simply, "marched to Malvern Hill." Lieutenant William Ardrey wrote, "we set out for Malvern Hill, very hot and hard marching. Arrived at Malvern Hill in the middle of the evening. Informed by the cavalry that the enemy held the hill."[23] The Tar Heels stumbled around the field, gawking at war's destruction, and the numerous shallow graves. Colonel Frank Parker lamented, "I was over the identical ground which we occupied that day, over which we charged, and from which we were forced to retire." He continued, "I saw the spot where Capt. Arrington fell; saw the graves of many of my brave men, and I assure you it gave me no pleasure to visit them. Poor fellows ... [they] deserve a more appropriate resting place, than the road side." Shaking his head in dismay, Parker finished his note to his wife, "It is pronounced by good military authority to be a very strong position, sad experience teaches us that this is so."[24] The Thirtieth's men dragged themselves back to camp once the threat dissipated.

During the next week, two officers resigned, both men frustrated by their continual poor health, and devastated by the regiment's casualties. First Lieutenant Nathan Orr (Co. K) wrote, "Having been in bad health for a long time, and as no material improvement has taken place yet, I consider that I will not be doing justice to the government or myself to remain in service.... I do most respectfully tender my resignation as first lieutenant."[25] And Lt. Col. James Kell, whose fractured hip refused to properly heal, penned, "I respectfully resign my commission as Lt. Col. ... I regret to do this exceedingly, and I assure you that nothing but physical inability could induce me to resign."[26] Finally, a third officer stepped down, the 41-year-old surgeon, Dr. Henry Joyner. Colonel Parker wrote of Joyner's leaving and replacement, "Dr. F. M. Garret, of Edgecombe, was commissioned Surgeon ... in [his] place."[27]

On August 18, 1862, Col. Parker gave the order, "prepare three days' rations," causing everyone to ponder what would happen next.[28] This directive, along with the news Maj. Gen. Daniel Hill had returned to command their division aided those soldiers who argued the Army of Northern Virginia was headed for a fight somewhere in northern Virginia. The next day, Lt. William Ardrey (Co. K) wrote, "Left camp, marched through Richmond. Got a feast of fruit, watermelons, etc. Marched up the Brook turnpike through Henrico and Hanover counties." On August 20, 1862, Ardrey added, "Crossed the South Anna River and encamped on the North Anna near Hanover Junction in a spruce pine grove."[29] Then, their brigade began receiving conflicting travel orders, commands sending the Tar Heels marching in one direction, and then hiking back to where they had just been. Colonel Parker wrote in frustration, "The Division ... took up the line of march for Gordonsville.... We marched one day in that direction [but] during the first night; our orders were countermanded; and the direction of the march changed to this part of the country instead of Gordonsville." Frantic commands ordering the Carolinians to hurry, caused added problems. Frank Parker complained, "We reached our encampment for the second day, about dark, very much fatigued, in fact almost broken down; [when] we [had] been in camp probably about two hours ... the order came to get the men in ranks, ready to move at a moments notice ... the men were exhausted already." Parker continued, "We marched off with the expectation of going only two miles, but marched at least six; and it being ... the night, and dark at that, made the march much more fatiguing."[30]

Major General Daniel Hill's division ended up near Gordonsville, VA, while most of Robert E. Lee's army shifted towards the Manassas area. Frenzied messages now arrived, commanding the Tar Heels to hurry eastward. They hiked to Orange Court House, in what Chaplain Alexander Betts called, "a long hard march on our men," moving so rapidly they outstripped their supplies, forcing the men to forage for food along the way. Lieutenant William Ardrey (Co. K) recorded, "Out of rations, subsisted on green corn and apples. He noted, "the soldiers stripped a 40 acre corn field."[31]

Then, fortunately for the footsore soldiers, they received orders to rest. There no longer was any need to hurry; they would not be able to reach the fighting the papers were calling Second Manassas. The brigade shifted northward and on August 29, 1862, as one Carolinian recorded, "they camped on the south side of the Rapidan River."[32] The next morning the men crossed the river and reached the Cedar Mountain battlefield. From there, they continued north until reaching Culpepper Court House. Here, the soldiers splashed across the Rapidan and made their way toward Warrenton. Alexander Betts starkly scribbled in his journal, "Men wade Rapidan.... Pass Culpepper C. H. ... Town and country around desolated by war. Sick and wounded Federals in town."[33] They marched relentlessly, crossing the North Fork of the Rappahannock, ever closing the gap between their brigade and Gen. Lee.

The next morning, August 31, 1862, the trek resumed, under moisture-laden skies. A Tar Heel wrote, "it began to rain at dawn. The 30th crossed the Rappahannock and marched all day in the mud, passing the damaged resort of Warrenton, Sulphur Springs."[34] On September 1, 1862, the Thirtieth paused briefly for a muster roll to be taken, recording the regiment's strength at 550 troops. Then, the men loaded their gear onto their shoulders and set out. Chaplain Betts wrote, "It began to rain before daylight. ... We needed rest, and were hoping we could enjoy that Sabbath in the woods."[35] Lieutenant William Ardrey (Co. K) added, "Set out still on scanty rations ... Passed through Warrenton, a beautiful town, saw a great many pretty young ladies, a very patriotic place. Marched up the Blue Ridge, the scenery grand and sublime."[37]

30th North Carolina Infantry[36]
September 1, 1862

Unit		Strength
Field & Staff	Col. Parker, Francis M. Maj. Sillers, William W.	4
Co. A	Cpt. Holmes, James C. 1st Lt. Williams, Gary 2nd Lt. Stevens, Charles T.	57
Co. B	1st Lt. Davis, Weldon E. 2nd Lt. Nicholson, John H.	48
Co. C	Cpt. Allen, David C. 2nd Lt. Bennett, Solomon W.	42
Co. D	1st Lt. Allen, Charles N. 2nd Rogers, Charles M. 3rd Lt. Gill, William J.	58
Co. E	Cpt. McMillan, John C. 2nd Lt. McMillan, Daniel T. 3rd Lt. Carr, Jacob O.	53
Co. F	Cpt. Moore, Willis M. 1st Lt. Harrell, George K.	77
Co. G	Cpt. Barnett, James A. 2nd Lt. Clairborne, Robert F. 3rd Lt. Crews, Alexander	51
Co. H	Cpt. Wicker, Jesse J. 1st Lt. McNeil, Henry J. 2nd Lt. Jackson, Archibald J.	54
Co. I	Cpt. Harris, James J. 1st Lt. Williford, Burton B.	64
Co. K	2nd Lt. Ardrey, William E. 3rd Lt. Downs, John T.	42
		550

The next day they reached the Manassas battlefield, viewing scenes which horrified the Tar Heels. Private John Bone (Co. I) recalled, "Our men were buried, but the Yankees were not; this was an awful scene. There were so many dead men lying stretched on the field that we could tell where their line of battle was formed." Lieutenant William Ardrey noted, "it was the most heart-rending scene that I ever witnessed, to see the field strewn with dead that had been lying five days unburied and perfectly black." Alexander Betts contributed, "Horrid scenes! Many dead Federals still on the field, though a squad of men, under flag of truce, has been some days caring for wounded and burying dead."[38]

That night the season's first frost chilled the Carolinians and made many wish they were at home. Chaplain Betts recorded, "Sle[pt] cold.... Frost next morning.... Call at a farm house to buy corn. A ... woman upbraids me."[39]

The Thirtieth's morale was elevated on September 3, 1862, when they passed through Leesburg, just before sunset. One rifleman recalled, "[we were] cheered incessantly by ladies."[40] The regiment camped just north of the town that evening. They rested for a day and on September 5, 1862, marched fifteen miles north from Leesburg to Lovettsville. The next day's hike took them to the south side of the Potomac River near Cheek's Ford. Lieutenant William Ardrey (Co. K), impressed by the countryside, wrote, "A very fertile country, the finest milk and butter I ever saw."[41]

By now, as the Tar Heels rested in the bivouac, they gazed across the Potomac onto Yankee land, waiting their turn to cross that span of water and invade the North. Most of the soldiers were excited by this prospect of carrying the war to their enemy, however, others shook their heads in disagreement and argued they had enlisted to defend their homes, not invade their neighbors. One such soldier wrote, "they had volunteered to resist invasion and not to invade; some did not believe it right to invade Northern territory."[42] Nonetheless, on September 7, 1862, the Thirtieth crossed. Lieutenant William Ardrey (Co. K) recorded, "Waded the Potomac in our shirts. Great rejoicing when we got to Maryland." Another Confederate wrote, "The soldiers were naïve in their half-nakedness, fully conscious of their prowess, and interested above all in the prospect of seeing pretty girls and of getting something to eat besides green corn."[43] Others though, were not interested in the women; the poor rations, heat, and forced marches had worn them down. Private John Bone (Co. I) muttered, "I got so sick that I could not keep time in ranks. We were required to make good time. They gave me permission to march in the rear."[44]

Pvt. William A. King (Co. B), 22 years old, died of typhoid fever on September 8, 1862 (Taylor, 1998).

Once in Maryland, the brigade rested. Second Lieutenant William Ardrey (Co. K), now in command of his company, wrote, "Rested all day. Made a requisition for shoes."[45] During this pause energetic Confederates visited nearby farms and were surprised to discover the locals were not interested in joining their cause. Colonel Parker remarked, "You may wish to know how we were received upon entering Maryland; the people are not very enthusiastic in their demonstrations of joy or pleasure." Frank Parker also brought his company commanders together and they worried about their regiment's high numbers of stragglers. He wrote his wife, "I suppose we will be kept in our present position until our stragglers, which were left behind, shall come up. We have had a terrible march from Richmond; a great many men have been made sick, some have broken down on the road, some have given out from sore feet." He finished his letter, writing, "our ranks have been somewhat thinned."[46] Another officer recorded, "[there was] straggling of a magnitude so appalling.... Thousands of men fell behind or disappeared.... Extortion, orders, threats, penalties alike failed ... the weak soldier fell away with the indifferent until ... none but the heroes remained."[47] So many soldiers had fallen out of the column their numbers caused many problems for the Confederate Provost Guards, who then treated them harshly. One such straggler, Pvt. John Bone (Co. I) groused, "When we reached the Potomac river at Leesburg, where the army had crossed into Maryland, we were stopped by an officer placed there, with orders to let none cross that were sick or barefooted."[48]

Brigadier General George Anderson rejoined the brigade, sending Col. Charles Tew back to the 2nd NC. General Anderson led the Tar Heels out of their bivouac on September 10, 1862, one of the last units to march. They followed the National Pike, with their trek taking them through Middletown in the Catoctin Mountains, and into Turner's Gap, on South Mountain. The march was long and difficult and more men fell out of the column. Private James Griffin (Co. I) scrawled a note, "[a friend] has bin [sic.] sick and was not well.... He was barfooted [sic.] and broke down. Put on a new par [sic.] of sockes [sic.] and war [sic.] them out and then put on some more."[49] Another rifleman added, "We had a hard march ... and were weary and footsore, in poor condition to meet the enemy, barely rations sufficient to keep soul and body together."[50] And company commander, 2nd Lt. William Ardrey (Co. K) wrote, "Marched through Frederick.... Passed through Middletown.... Left John Squires, John Howey, Orren L. Pierce, and John Hall sick."[51]

The march continued early the next morning, with the Southerners hiking, "through a hard rain," and not halting until they were eighteen miles from Frederick. The riflemen received no military rations so they foraged as they marched. One such hungry soldier confessed, "Corn from fields and apples from nearby trees were snatched and eaten as the men pushed on."[52] An officer, discouraged by the army's inability to supply its men with food, wrote, "they had little ... food. They added potatoes where they could, and they devoured almost anything the commissary issued, but they had green corn, meal after meal, as their basal diet." He summed up their condition, writing, "Many of those who ate too freely of the corn developed a serious diarrhea." Another officer remarked, "We call[ed] this ... the green corn campaign."[53]

When the brigade got within a few miles of Hagerstown, MD, the men could go no further. On September 12, 1862, the column did not move. The men were famished, exhausted, and many without proper foot-ware. Straggling troops and soldiers drifting away from the column in search of food had reached such proportions unit strengths were decimated. A soldier grumbled, "One-fifth of Lee's army were barefooted, one-half in rags and the whole of them half famished."[54] Lieutenant William Ardrey (Co. K) recorded, "Lay in camp 5 miles from Hagerstown.... Details sent for green corn for rations."[55] General Daniel Hill noted his five brigades were, "much depleted by straggling on the march into Maryland ... [his] entire division ... mustered less than 5,000 effectives."[56] Hill added, "The order excusing barefooted men from marching into Maryland had sent thousands to the rear. Divisions had become smaller than brigades ... brigades had become smaller than regiments, and regiments had become smaller than companies."[57]

The next day, Maj. Gen. Daniel Hill shifted his division to the western base of South Mountain, not far from Boonsboro, MD. The hungry soldiers fanned out, hunting food. That evening Brig. Gen. George Anderson met with his regimental commanders. Colonel Parker learned Hill's division had been tasked with defending the roads crossing South Mountain; the Yankees were not to be allowed to pass over South Mountain and march toward Sharpsburg. Hill dispatched two of his brigades, Garland's and Colquitt's, to block the two mountain passes. The other three brigades, Rodes, Ripley, and Anderson, were positioned in support. General Hill did not think his three-brigade reserve would be needed, but he wanted everyone to be able to move quickly if called.

General Anderson's messengers fanned out among his four regiments hours before dawn on September 14, 1862, ordering the Tar Heels to their feet. The sleepy riflemen formed up and moved onto the Old Sharpsburg Road by 4:30 a.m. Daniel Hill had changed his mind; he needed more than two brigades to hold the mountain passes. General Hill recorded, "An examination of the pass, very early on the morning of the 14th, satisfied me that it could only be held by a large force, and was wholly indefensible by a small one. I accordingly ordered up Anderson's brigade."[58] Brigadier General George Anderson slotted the 14th NC to lead the march, with the 30th NC following them, trailed by the 4th NC and the 2nd NC.

The Tar Heels hustled, struggling to move quickly up the steeply inclined road. By 7:00 a.m. the mountain pass rattled with musketry. Couriers soon notified the Carolinians; Garland's brigade was being attacked by an overwhelming force. More messengers thundered by on sweating horses, describing how Brig. Gen. Samuel Garland had been shot down and his regiments routed. An officer in Garland's brigade wrote, "Upon the fall of Garland ... the 12th NC, a badly trained regiment ... now broke in confusion and retreated."[59] This exposed the brigade's other regiments to flanking pressure, forcing them to fall back. Then, the entire line collapsed. General Hill recorded, "By 10 o'clock Garland had been killed and his brigade routed.[60]

General Hill admonished George Anderson to get his brigade into position to halt the Union advance. Anderson's Tar Heels raced to cover the gap Garland's men had exposed. Their climb was difficult; the road winding and steep, and quickly exhausted the hurrying Tar Heels. Colonel Bryan Grimes' 14th NC rushed up the road, now becoming clogged by fleeing soldiers. Grimes' men pushed the remnants of Garland's brigade aside and formed into line of battle. Colonel Grimes reported, "Upon arriving at the [Fox Gap] summit ... we filed on a left-hand road, which overlooked the enemy's approach."[61] The Thirtieth moved to a position to the left of the 14th NC, Parker's riflemen spreading out and taking cover amid the thick underbrush. When General Anderson arrived at the battle line he immediately saw there was no room for the 4th NC and 2nd NC, so he detached those two units and send them farther to the right. Suddenly, the mountaintop grew quiet. Anderson's regiments were now ready to defend the pass, but strangely, no blue coats could be seen.

Colonel Frank Parker ordered out a screen of skirmishers, placing them under the command of 24-year-old Cpt. Jesse Wicker (Co. H). The skirmishers pushed forward through the dense vegetation, searching for the Yanks. A Tar Heel officer wrote, "we moved down the mountainside ... [the] men concealed ... behind trees, rocks, and bushes." He continued, "We could see the enemy in two lines of battle.... We awaited with beating hearts the sure and steady approach." The soldier added, "[Our] guns were almost simultaneously emptied with deadly effect, and the [Yanks] rushed back pell-mell."[62] The Union line pushed forward, firing at Cpt. Wicker's skirmishers, wounding Pvt. Elsberry Edwards (Co. F). The Carolinians continued shooting at the Northerners but slowly retreated, being pushed by superior numbers. Private William Morgan (Co. H) was wounded a few minutes later. Then, Cpt. Jesse Wicker went down, severely wounded. Nearby skirmishers rushed to the fallen leader and carried him back to the regimental line. A lieutenant now led the skirmishers, and he worked to pull them back to safety.[63] Fortunately, the Union troops did not aggressively pursue, however, they managed to flank a number of Tar Heels and capture a dozen of them, including Pvt. Henry Baker (Co. H), who could not escape because of a serious gunshot wound.[64] The hillside grew quiet, save an occasional gunshot. The Thirtieth's riflemen waited, expecting the Federal assault, but the attack did not come. The men were tired, worn out by lack of sleep and the race up the mountainside. A Confederate wrote, "[they were] ... road weary ... after their all day struggle with the heat and thirst and dust."[65] As the morning's calm continued and the day's heat increased, many slumped down to the ground and napped. Colonel Parker's NCOs struggled with their men, as, "some of [the] wearied men slipped off in the woods to sleep."[66]

Later, a force of blue coats pushed against the 4th NC and 2nd NC. Swarms of Yanks rushed the thin, Confederate line, flanking the Tar Heels in places, and even getting behind their position. An officer in the 2nd NC wrote, "The Second was hotly engaged ... and fought in so many directions that no one knew which way was front." Brigadier General George Anderson hurried to the position and rallied the rattled men. A soldier recalled, "[when he was] informed some of the men who were getting excited, [and] seeing the blue coats in the rear, [he told them] ... the front was where the enemy appeared, and [their] muskets would carry as well in one direction as another."[67] Anderson sent from reinforcements from the 30th NC and 14th NC, creating a series of rushed movement surges. One Tar Heel wrote, "After remaining in this position for perhaps half an hour ... an order was received to flank to the [right], which was done. After remaining in our new position nearly an hour, we were ordered to move ... to our left."[68] Parker's fatigued soldiers struggled to adjust to this shifting. The Thirtieth's commander watched in dismay because, as he noted, "he could hardly keep his men awake as the deadly missiles were flying among them."[69]

30th North Carolina Infantry[70]
South Mountain Casualties
September 14, 1862

Unit	Commander	Loss
Field & Staff	Col. Parker, Francis M.	-
Co. A	Cpt. Holmes, James C.	-
Co. B	1st Lt. Davis, Weldon E.	-
Co. C	Cpt. Allen, David C.	-
Co. D	1st Lt. Allen, Charles N.	3
Co. E	Cpt. McMillan, John C.	-
Co. F	Cpt. Moore, Willis M.	5
Co. G	Cpt. Barnett, James A.	-

Unit	Commander	Loss
Co. H	Cpt. Wicker, Jesse J.	5
Co. I	Cpt. Harris, James J.	2
Co. K	2nd Lt. Ardrey, William E.	-
		15

The 2nd NC and 4th NC, their riflemen protected behind rocks, trees, and fallen timbers, drove back the Federals. General Hill noted, "The lack of complete [Union] success south of the pike was owing to the thick woods.... Thus it was that a thin line of men extending for miles along the crest of the mountain could ... for so many hours ... delay the Federal advance."[71] The Yanks fell back into the thickets covering the hillside, leaving behind a screen of sharpshooters. The next several hours went by without serious fighting, though gray and blue skirmishers dueled against each other. Major William Sillers wrote, "The regiment, except ... it skirmishers, was not actually engaged with any visible portion of the enemy's forces."[72] Later that evening, troops from Brig. Gen. David R. Jones's division slipped into the Tar Heels' positions and the Carolina soldiers trudged down from Fox Gap's heights, to return to their early morning's bivouac. Once the Thirtieth was settled down for the night, Adj. Fred Phillips completed a muster and notified Col. Parker, the regiment had lost fifteen men.[73] His regiment now could barely put 150 men on the battle line.

Chapter 5

The Sunken Road at Sharpsburg

The sounds of heavy musketry woke the Tar Heels even before the sun had risen. The weary Carolinians clustered around campfires, fighting off the night's damp coldness. Hardly anyone had slept well; a light rain chilled them most of the night, especially since few had their knapsacks and bedrolls. Captain John Witherspoon (Co. K) recalled, "Our baggage [had fallen] into the hands of the enemy."[1] A rifleman explained, "Our brigade had piled their knapsacks on the mountain and in retreating at night, all was lost." Another complained, "Our brigade had piled their knapsacks on [South Mountain] … and in retreating at night, all was lost." He continued, "So we lay on the earth with nothing but the blue heavens for a covering."[2] Not only did the troops lose their clothing and blankets, they also lost their rations. Lieutenant William Ardrey (Co. K) grumbled, "[we] subsisted four days on one day's ration."[3]

30th North Carolina Infantry[4]
September 17, 1862

Unit		Strength
Field & Staff	Col. Parker, Francis M. Maj. Sillers, William W. Adj. Philips, Frederick	4
Co. A	Cpt. Holmes, James 1st Lt. Williams, Gary	27
Co. B	1st Lt. Davis, Weldon 2nd Lt. Nicholson, John	22
Co. C	Cpt. Allen, David 1st Lt. Bennett, Solomon	24
Co. D	1st Lt. Allen, Charles 2nd Lt. Rogers, Charles	23
Co. E	Cpt. McMillan, John 2nd Lt. McMillan, Daniel	14
Co. F	Cpt. Moore, Willis 1st Lt. Harrell, George	27
Co. G	Cpt. Barnett, James 2nd Lt. Clairborne Robert	23
Co. H	1st Lt. McNeil, Henry 2nd Lt. Jackson, Archibald	30
Co. I	Cpt. Harris, James	

Unit		Strength
Co. I	1st Lt. Williford, Burton	31
Co. K	2nd Lt. Ardrey, William	
	3rd Lt. Downs, John T.	29
		254

Colonel Frank Parker ordered his adjutant, Fred Philips to assemble the morning reports as he met with his second-in-command, Maj. William Sillers. Parker instructed Sillers to get the regiment ready to move; the severity of the fighting north of them would soon draw them in, and Parker wanted the Thirtieth to be ready when Gen. Anderson called. Lieutenant Philips hustled back to his colonel and reported the regiment numbered just over one hundred seventy officers and riflemen ready for combat.[5] Colonel Parker was frustrated; he knew his formation totaled almost two hundred more, but soldiers had been lost when the Thirtieth crossed the Potomac into Maryland and in the hike from South Mountain, plus, a number of men did not possess proper footwear.

A brigade runner told Col. Parker to report to a brigade officers' meeting and the 35-year-old from Tarboro, NC, strapped on his sword and joined the other regimental commanders and Brig. Gen. George Anderson. The officers reported their battle strengths and George Anderson nodded; his brigade numbered just over 1,150.[6] General Anderson summarized the fighting north of them: a strong Yankee formation had struck Ewell's Division of Jackson's Corps and the two forces were pounding each other just north of a small church. Anderson surprised his brigade officers when he told them they would not be joining that fight; instead, Anderson's boss, Brig. Gen. Daniel Hill was sending them, and Robert Rodes' brigade to the east of the conflict in anticipation of the blue coats trying to flank Jackson's infantry. Daniel Hill wrote, "It was now apparent that the Yankees were massing [on] our [right]."[7] Anderson's and Rodes' men were all that Hill had left. His division was small, and he already had committed much of his force into the maelstrom north of the Dunker Church. One of Hill's officers recorded, "The division of D. H. Hill was by this time reduced to three thousand.... Hunger, sickness, forced marches, and the havoc of the field had done their worst."[8]

Just after 8:00 a.m., Col. Frank Parker's regiment led the way, with 1st Lt. Charles Allen's Company D in the lead.[9] They followed a guide who directed them onto a farmer's lane which was eroded below the surrounding fields. Parker's two hundred fifty men were followed by the 4th NC, a tiny unit numbering eighty, led by Cpt. William Marsh; then the large 14th NC, its 520 troops commanded by Col. Risden Bennett; and the 2nd NC, three hundred Tar Heels directed by Col. Charles Tew.[10] Behind Anderson's column, Brig. Gen. Robert Rodes' battle-weary riflemen shouldered their weapons and trailed into the sunken road. Robert Rodes' brigade had been mauled two days earlier on the slopes of South Mountain. He reported, "[My] brigade held [a] ... whole division at bay without assistance during four and a half hours' fighting, losing in that time ... 422." Rodes' continued, "My force [on September 17, 1862] did not amount to over 700."[11] And finally, a small collection of riflemen from Col. Alfred Colquitt's brigade joined in, behind Rodes' men. At 8:30 a.m., this force of Confederates halted in the sunken road, and fronted to the north, covering a battle front of just over nine hundred yards.[12]

Colonel Parker ordered 1st Lt. Henry McNeil's Company H to deploy as skirmishers north of the road, and then directed his Tar Heels to fortify their position.[13] General Robert Rodes' noted, "the men were [soon] busy improving their position by piling rails

Sunken Road, looking east (Page, 1907).

along their front."[14] Fortunately, the sunken road provided the Southerners with an immediately defensible location; Maj. William Sillers remarked, "Our line was formed in a road which, by wear of travel, had been let down to the depth of a foot or more into the earth."[15] Another officer noted, "At some points, the surrounding farm land stood three to six feet above the road bed."[16]

By 9:00 a.m., the Carolinians' improvements met their officers' expectations, just in time as General Robert E. Lee and division commander, Brig. Gen. Daniel Hill arrived, to inspect their defensive position. The soldiers cheered their general, and Col. John Gordon (6th AL) bragged, "These men are going to stay here, General, till the sun goes down or victory is won."[17] Colonel Parker and Maj. Sillers were not quite as optimistic as Col. Gordon. Frank Parker wrote, "[Our regiment] was much exposed by reason of our position [by] the crest of a hill."[18] William Sillers detailed their situation, recording, "In front of the right wing of our regiment, and at a distance of nor more than 50 paces, there was a ravine which, extending diagonally to the left, gradually narrowed down the level space in front until in front of the extreme left of the 30th there was not more than 30 paces of level ground."[19] In effect, as Col. Parker remarked, "The terrain to the regiment's north allowed the enemy to get within a short distance before coming into sight."[20]

The skirmishers in front of Rodes' brigade began shooting at targets just moments after Lee and Hill had completed their tour. Frank Parker walked among his riflemen, cautioning patience: the Thirtieth's skirmish line was deployed beyond the crest of the ridge arising fifty yards away from the sunken road. Parker could not see who Rodes' Alabamians were shooting at, and he did not know if there were Yankees close by. Frank

Parker had to rely on Lt. McNeil's (Co. H) skirmishers, now positioned out of sight. Colonel Parker noticed that the rest of the brigade's riflemen had been ordered to lie down—he directed his men to do the same. An officer remarked, "Colonel Tew (2nd NC) ordered his men to lie down and the other regiments followed suit."[21]

Seeing that other regimental officers were creeping forward to the broad ridge's crest to view what was happening, Col. Parker, accompanied by his adjutant, 1st Lt. Fred Philips walked out in front of the Thirtieth's position and made their way to the ridge top. They were stunned by what they saw; Yankee soldiers, three battle lines in depth, and at close intervals, stretched as far as could be seen to either side of the Roulette farm. Three massive Union brigades marched towards them, with each formation large enough to cover the Southerner's entire battle front. A Confederate officer checked his time piece; it was 9:15 a.m.[22]

The nearest Federal brigade, led by Brig. Gen. Max Weber, contained three regiments, the far right unit, the 1st DE, with its seven hundred troops festooned in bright blue uniforms and white gaiters, advanced, the front rank at charge bayonet and the rear rank at right shoulder shift.[23] These soldiers pushed aside the screen of gray-clad skirmishers, crashed through a cornfield, and appeared atop the low ridge-top barely fifty yards away from the Alabamians. Colonel John Gordon (6th AL) recalled, "What a pity ... to spoil with bullets such a scene of martial beauty."[24]

To the left of the 1st DE, and of more concern to Col. Frank Parker's Tar Heels, were the 5th MD, and then the 540 men of the 4th NY. Lieutenant McNeil's (Co. H) skirmishers slunk back to the ridge top, turning and firing at the approaching New Yorkers. Frank Parker returned to his men in the sunken road and cautioned patience. When Henry McNeil's company rejoined the Thirtieth, Col. Parker had his entire fighting force with, as 2nd Lt. William Ardrey (Co. K) recorded, "Captain Grissom [Co. D] on the right [and] Capt. Wicker [Co. H] on the left."[25]

Moments later, the Federal colors could be seen, and then the blue coats appeared on the slope's crest. Parker waited as the Yanks descended the slope, his company officers watching him for the command to fire. He noted, "I cautioned my men to hold their fire until I should give the command, and then to take deliberate, cool aim; that I would not give the command to fire until I could see the belt of the cartridge boxes of the enemy, and to aim at these."[26] When the Northerners were sixty feet away he gave the signal. The effect of that first volley was devastating. One Southerner wrote, "Through the tremendous cloud of smoke and flame they could see Yankee soldiers getting lifted off their feet and slammed to the ground."[27] Colonel Frank Parker recorded, "They [30th NC] obeyed my orders, gave a fine volley, which brought down the enemy as grain falls before a reaper.... I have never witnessed a more deliberate nor more destructive firing."[28] A Federal officer recorded, "[We] sallied gallantly to the front under a terrible tornado of shot."[29]

A Federal officer among the second line of Union troops approaching the sunken road wrote, "The Confederate volley sounded like shot rattling against a tin plate ... or the tearing of heavy canvas ... as it struck down soldiers in the first brigade. Men collapsed by the squads on the brow of the ridge."[30] The survivors of the three Union regiments lurched backwards, crushed by these initial volleys. One blue coat wrote, "[we] staggered and recoiled, and the right of our regiment was forced back to the edge of the cornfield."[31] Another wrote, "[we] suffered severely in killed and wounded."[32] Most of the dazed Federal soldiers offered little resistance as the stunned survivors retreated. Others fired several volleys into the Confederates sheltered behind their makeshift defense protecting the sunken road. A couple men in Col. Parker's regiment were struck, including Sgt. James Wells (Co. E), who went down with a serious injury, and 34-year-old Pvt. Andrew Dunn (Co. K) who was killed.[33]

It took less than fifteen minutes of well-aimed Confederate musketry to destroy all semblance of Union resolve. Then the Union assault collapsed and the men in Weber's three regiments fled from the Southerners' deadly fire, having suffered over eight hundred casualties.[34] The 4th New York, in those brief, lethal moments, lost 187 men killed or wounded.[35] One Federal wrote, "On the ground, a few yards in advance [of the ridge's crest] … lay a large number of our men, killed or wounded."[36] Frank Parker's exuberant Tar Heels refilled their cartridge boxes, ecstatic about their easy victory. A number of excited Confederates shouted out, "Go away, you black devils! Go home!"[37] However, within moments, word came from the Alabamians that another wave of Yankees approached. The men in the Thirtieth North Carolina quieted down and awaited this next charge, confident they could thrash these troops as well.

This second line of Federal soldiers was commanded by Col. Dwight Morris, and consisted of the 14th CT, 108th NY, and 130th PA, a force of nearly 2,500 men. They passed through Weber's shattered men and approached the ridge protecting them from the Confederates in the sunken road; the 14th CT or the right, the 130th PA in the center, and the 108th NY on the left. The 14th CT was huge, numbering over a thousand soldiers was led by Lt. Col. Sanford Perkins.[38] He maneuvered his massive regiment towards Rodes' entire brigade. When they reached the ridge and came within fifty yards of the

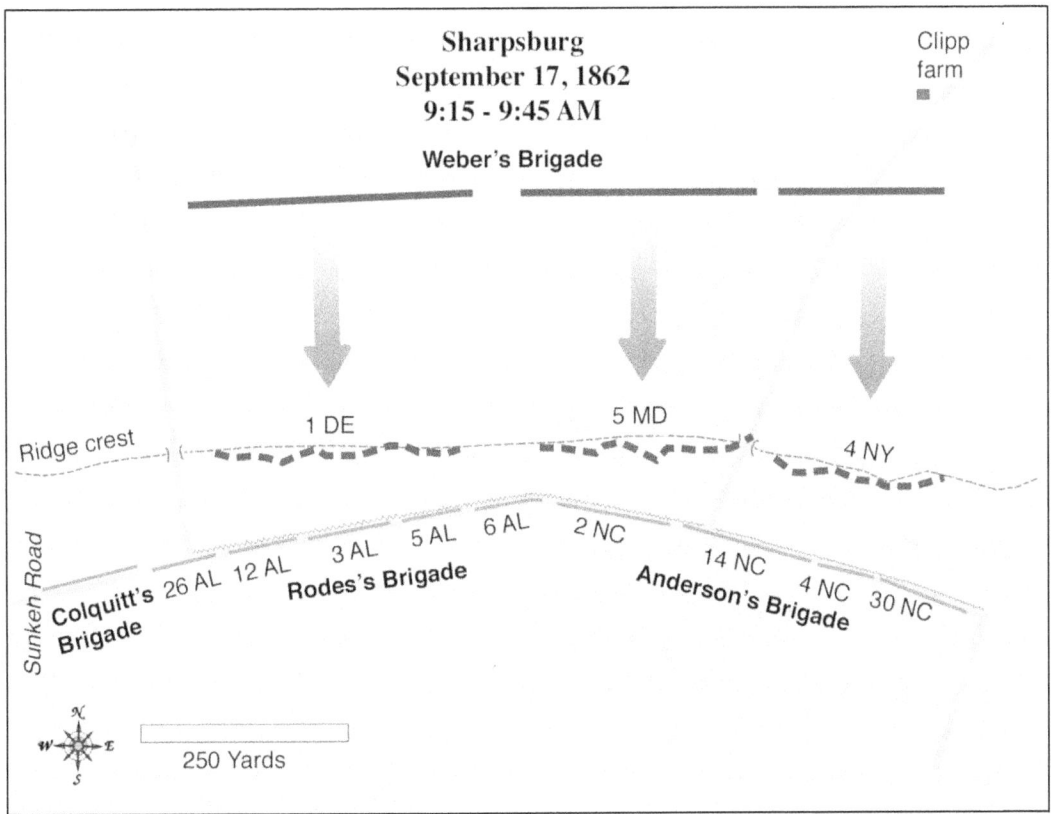

Alabamians, the Southerners unleashed a terrific volley. A Connecticut officer wrote, "[Our] line of troops ... seemed to melt under the enemy's fire."³⁹

Meanwhile, the 130th PA moved against Rodes' right-most regiment, and the 2nd and 14th NC. The Tar Heels' volleys immediately chopped into the Pennsylvanian ranks. The 108th NY, which squared off against the 4th and 30th NC, had lagged behind its brother regiments. The 108th NY was a brand new formation, with the men together for barely a month. Its officers and men had completed very little training, and possessed hardly any shooting experience. Their commander, Col. Oliver Palmer struggled to shift his thousand-man formation from a road column to a battle line.⁴⁰ Many of his men were complaining about wet uniforms, as they had been forced to cross Antietam Creek without being able to remove their shoes or roll up their pants.⁴¹

Colonel Frank Parker's Carolinians waited for the blue coats to reach the top of the slope, and then they pounded the Yanks with a volley. A soldier in the 108th NY remarked, "This was the most terrible slaughter seen during the war."⁴² Another wrote, "Along the eastern edge of this Sunken Road was a low wall which assisted in making it a natural and formidable rifle-pit from which the Confederates could not be seen ... their presence only being detected by the puffs of smoke from their numerous rifle fire or the tops of their butternut hats."⁴³ The hill crest was quickly covered with dead and wounded; first by the 4th NY, and now added to by the 108th NY. A New Yorker recalled, "the men faced the galling storm of iron hail, and constantly falling until their numbers were so severely decimated, that they withdrew to the meadow over which they had advanced."⁴⁴ The battered 108th NY fell back several hundred yards before its officers attempted to regain control of their shaken troops, but this proved quite difficult due to a well-observed artillery strike. The regimental historian noted, "In the efforts to reform the line ... a young man ... had his head taken off by a round shot."⁴⁵ In time though, a number of captains were able to rally the more resolute soldiers and these small groups of men crept back to the ridge and lie down just below the crest. They began a pesky fire upon the Tar Heels. Major William Sillers wrote, "The enemy continued to make his appearance, first on one hill, than another, but [now] always at long range.... Here a hot fire was kept up for a few minutes."⁴⁶ A few more Carolinians were struck; Pvt. John Holland (Co. A) was hit in the head, Pvt. Lemuel Warren (Co. F) also injured in the head, and Pvt. Edward Lewis (Co. I) killed.⁴⁷ The two sides shot at each other for thirty minutes before the 14th CT and

Sgt. James Wells (Co .E), 23, was severely wounded on September 17, 1862 (Taylor, 1998).

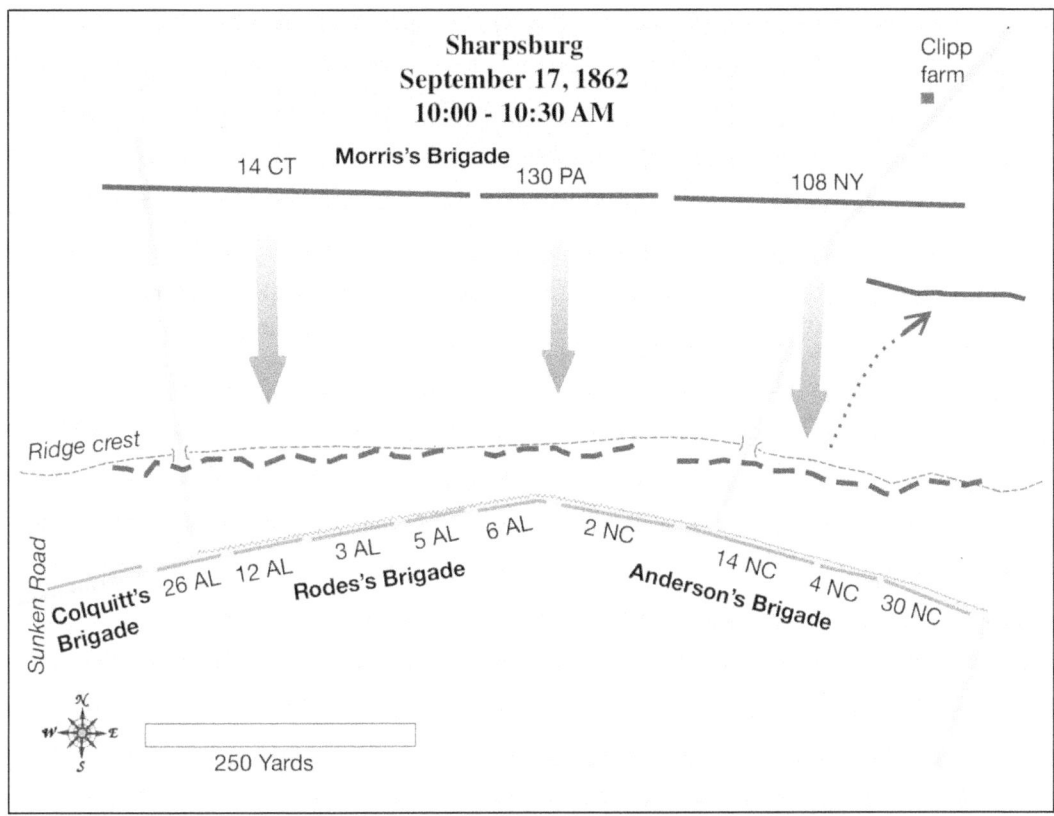

130th PA had suffered enough, and retreated. The fighters among the 108th NY did the same. This second assault on the sunken road had been another disaster. Colonel Dwight Morris reported his brigade lost 529 men. Colonel Oliver Palmer recorded the 108th NY's casualties as 295.[48]

Around 10:45 a.m., as Morris' survivors drifted away from danger, a third Union brigade advanced, regiments led by Brig. Gen. Nathan Kimball: the 14th IN, the 8th OH, the 132nd PA, and the 7th WV. Kimball's soldiers pushed aside Morris' mob and moved towards the sunken road, the 14th IN on the far right, the 8th OH and 132nd PA next, and the 7th WV on the left. Again, as had occurred with the first two brigades, Kimball's troops could not see what they faced until on top of the slope, and by that time, the Confederate riflemen were able to shatter the front ranks with devastating volleys. As Kimball's fresh soldiers, nearly 1,800 strong marched up the backside of the hill, scores of wounded cried out, warning their brothers of the dangers. Kimball's men lowered their heads, kept advancing, and crested the ridge. General Nathan Kimball recorded, "As my line advanced to the crest of a hill.... I found the enemy ... [and] a murderous fire was opened upon [us]."[49] The carnage stunned the blue coats, one wrote, "Hundreds of men dropped in the soft, white speckled clover north of the lane."[50] Nathan Kimball added, "My advance ... was checked."[51]

On the Federal's far left, the three hundred men in the 7th WV were hit just as hard.[52] Colonel Joseph Snider, who commanded this formation from the western part of Virginia, remarked, "The fighting was terrific."[53] The blue-coated Virginians retreated behind the crest and lay down among the dead and wounded, and began returning fire.

Snider wrote, "we engaged the enemy ... [and] our colors were shot down three times."[54] Both sides blazed away at each other for the next few minutes and more Tar Heels went down. Pvt. William Cooper (Co. D) was struck in the right arm, Pvt. James Brown (Co. H) killed, Pvt. Augustus Hathaway (Co. F) hit in the shoulder, and Pvt. Jeptha Baker (Co. K) mortally wounded with a bullet to his head.[55]

Then a mass of Confederates crashed out of the cornfield, south of the sunken road and slammed into the backs of the Tar Heels, men from Brig. Gen. Ambrose Wright's brigade. These newly arrived Georgians and Alabamians pushed at the North Carolinians and shouted for them to attack, causing confusion. General Wright demanded George Anderson send the 4th NC and 30th NC forward and assault the Yankees. But Anderson, who determined Wright was drunk, would have none of Wright's ultimatums, and refused to comply.[56] However, before the two generals could fight for domination, Ambrose Wright was hit by minié bullets, first in the leg, and then the chest.[57] His troops crowded in behind the Carolinians, or remained near the edge of the cornfield, south of the sunken road.

Colonel Snider's Virginians, protected by the ridge's crest, directed their fire into the masses of Confederates from a position which was to their advantage; they were above the gray-coats, firing down into the Southerners' closely packed ranks. Carolinians began to fall in much larger numbers. Sergeant William Edwards (Co. C) was killed, Pvt. Neill McDonald (Co. H) struck in the shoulder, and Pvt. Lorenzo Vick (Co. F) killed.[58] Moments later, off to the 30th NC's left flank, Brig. Gen. George Anderson went down,

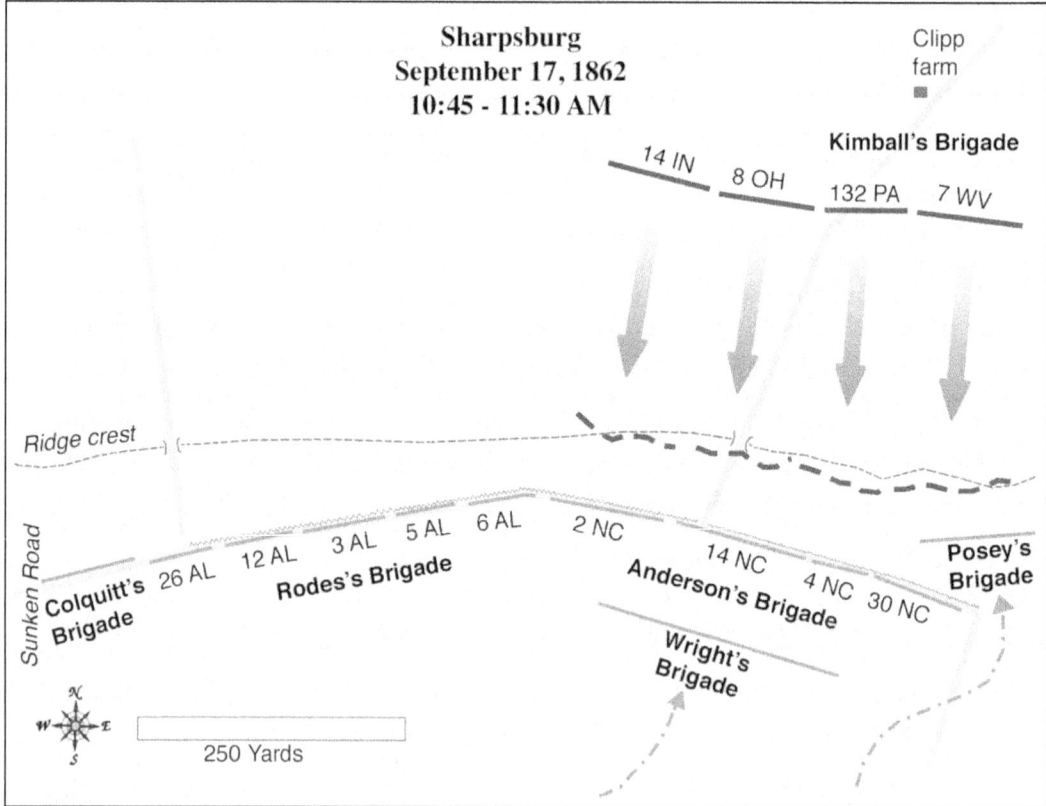

5. The Sunken Road at Sharpsburg

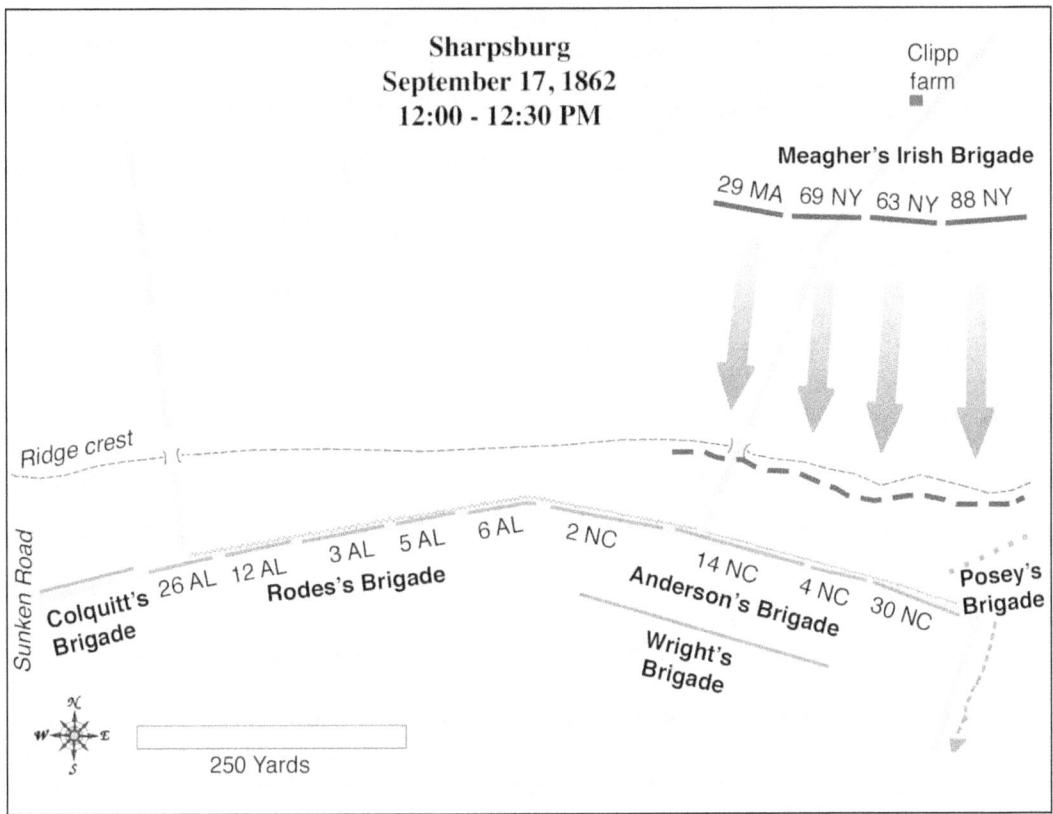

a minié bullet shattering his ankle. Anderson believed his wound was minor, saying, "[he was] slightly wounded in the foot," but his aides hustled him from the fight.[59] The senior regimental commander, Col. Charles Tew (2nd NC), was next in line to lead the brigade; unfortunately though, Anderson's staff could not locate him. A brigade runner, John Bagarly, did find Col. Frank Parker and notified him of Anderson's injury.[60]

Frank Parker called to his adjutant, 1st Lt. Fred Philips and instructed him to find Col. Tew. Lieutenant Philips worked his way west in the sunken road, passing the 4th NC and the 14th NC. When Philips reached the 2nd NC, he was directed to the colonel and quickly gave him the report. Fred Philips recalled, "Colonel Tew, who was standing erect, lifted his hat, gave [me] a polite bow, and fell immediately from a ... wound [to the temple]."[61] Lieutenant Philips left the fallen officer and attempted to make his way back towards the Thirtieth.

Colonel Parker noticed the time, it was now 11:00 a.m. His Tar Heels were holding their position, dealing out death to the men of the 7th WV, but also taking severe punishment in return. He soon received word Lt. Fred Philips had gone down. Parker wrote, "Adjutant Philips fell with a head wound himself on his return journey to the 30th's position."[62] The distraught colonel gazed at his regiment and shivered at the sight of so many men piled up in the bottom of the sunken road amid the growing pools of blood. He was not sure how long they could continue to take this pounding.

Fortunately, just at this moment, another Confederate formation pushed into the Carolinians' rear, the Mississippians of Col. Carnot Posey. One of their officers recorded, "[we] came on ... a brigade of North Carolina troops ... in a road.... [Our] regiment, as did the brigade, passed over these troops and confronted the enemy ... who were drawn up ... [and] pouring a destructive fire [onto] our ranks."[63] The Mississippians shifted to the right of the 30th NC and struck the 7th WV across its front and left flank. The Virginians, having now lost nearly half their strength, backed away from the fight.[64] Their commanded, Col. Joseph Snider, made light of their retreat, reporting, "we held them until our ammunition was exhausted."[65] When the 7th WV gave ground, the other regiments in Kimball's brigade also succumbed to the massive casualties they had received and withdrew. General Kimball noted, "I need not tell you how terrible was the conflict. The loss in my command is a lasting testimony of the sanguinary nature of the conflict." He reported his brigade suffered 640 casualties.[66] The 7th WV had lost 145.[67]

But there were more Federals to attack the sunken road position: another 1,300 New Englanders stepped forward, the men of Brig. Gen. Thomas Meagher's Irish brigade.[68] General Meagher's four regiments advanced towards the Confederates, the 29th MA on the far right, the 69th NY to its left, then the 63rd NY, and finally, on the far left, the 88th NY. He remarked, "Deploying from column into line of battle on the edge of [a] cornfield, [we] marched through it steadily and displayed ... admirable regularity ... [reaching] the fence, a few hundred paces from which the enemy were drawn up ... with ... battle flags defiantly displayed."[69] The 88th NY caught Posey's men by surprise and flanked them, nearly annihilating the 16th MS and sending that brigade reeling.[70] A Mississippian wrote, "A murderous fire ... played on us ... [and] we retired ... [in] a scene of great confusion."[71]

Thomas Meagher recalled, "My orders were, that, after the first and second volleys delivered in line of battle ... the brigade should charge with fixed bayonets on the enemy."[72] The North Carolinians allowed the Irish brigade to top the body-strewn ridge crest and descend a few yards before unleashing a massive volley. One New Yorker recorded, "A single volley decimated the brigade's front rank and sent every regimental color to the ground."[73] The blue coats stood on the ridge top and returned fire for several minutes, and then made a courageous though reckless charge. General Meagher bragged, "I permitted them to deliver their five or six volleys, and then personally ordered them to charge upon the rebel columns ... with fixed bayonets."[74] His soldiers advanced, "[fighting] in grand style—upright as if on parade."[75] The impetuous general wrote, "despite [the] fire of musketry ... literally cut lanes through our approaching line, the brigade advanced ... within 30 paces of the enemy."[76] The Tar Heel riflemen knocked Meagher from his horse and shot his brigade to pieces.

But the men in the Irish brigade would not quit; they fired ragged volleys into the Confederates, their buck-and-ball loads taking their toll.[77] Private James Black (Co. K) was killed, Pvt. William Wicker (Co. H) hit in the right forearm, and Pvt. Ephraim Dickens (Co. F) took a musket ball in his left thigh.[78] Even though the number of bodies covering the sunken road's surface continued to increase, the Confederate fire did not slacken. The Southern musketry pummeled the Federals, destroying each regiment. Brigadier General Daniel H. Hill wrote, "[The Federals were] met with a galling fire ... recoiled, and fell back ... and finally lay down behind the crest of the hill."[79] An officer in the 88th NY remarked, "I know not exactly how long we were in action, but we were long enough there to lose ... one third of our men."[80] Finally, the courageous New Englanders could take no more; they retreated to the shelter behind the ridge top. General Meagher scribbled, "my brigade, after having been reduced to 500 men, retired."[81]

It was now 12:15 PM, and another Federal brigade pushed forward through the crowd of dazed Yank survivors, this one led by Brig. Gen. John Caldwell, who directed the 7th NY, 61st NY, 64th NY, 81st PA, and 5th NH, another 1,200 soldiers.[82] General Caldwell wrote, "I ... arrang[ed] my line in the following manner; On the right, the 61st and 64th NY Vol. consolidated ... on the left, the 5th NH Vols. The 7th NY Vols. occupied the right center, and the 81st PA Vols. the left center."[83] His regiments moved up into the hollow behind the ridge and lay down.[84] Then, they crept up to the military crest and, while still in the prone position, opened fire upon the Confederates. One Southerner noted, "They were so close [we] had to hug the northern bank of the road to keep from getting hit."[85]

The slow and steady fire from Caldwell's men began to take effect upon the Tar Heels; more Carolinians were hit, as Federal bullets knocked the wounded and dead back into the sunken road. Major William Sillers recalled, "A desultory fire was kept up for some time."[86] Colonel Frank Parker urged his tired riflemen to keep shooting at the Yankees, but for the first time, they were taking casualties from a sheltered enemy that refused to stay out in the open and get slaughtered. William Sillers added, "Our fire at this point was not very effective."[87] Moments later, a messenger reached Parker and informed him of serious confusion along some of the regiments to their left. Frank Parker began making his way in that direction, but only made a few steps before a minié bullet struck him in the head. The 30th's chaplain, the Reverend Alexander Betts described Parker's wound, writing, "A rifle ball passed over Colonel Parker's head, cutting away a narrow strip of skin and plowing a nice little furrow in the skull, leaving the membrane that covers the brain visible but uninjured."[88] He fell, bleeding badly. Shocked aides rushed to his side and hustled their injured colonel from danger.

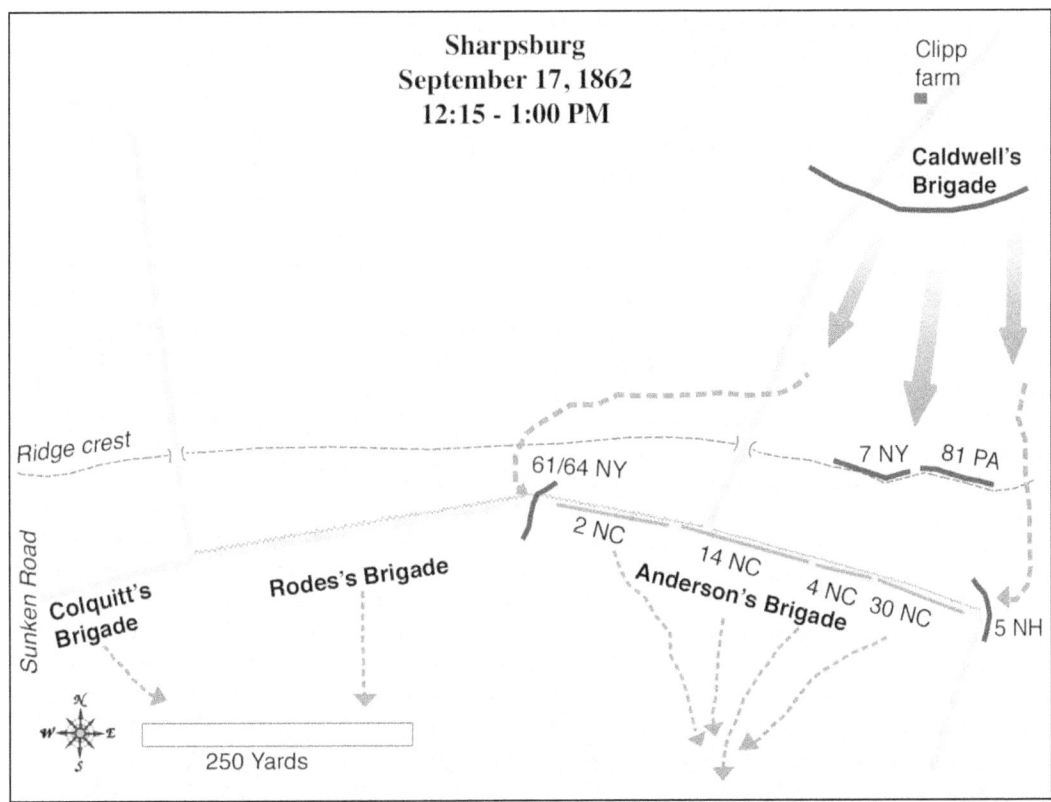

The 30th North Carolina was now in Maj. William Sillers' hands. He noted, "Colonel Parker [was] ... seriously wounded ... about [12:30] ... the regiment was [now] under my command."[89] Sillers sent a captain to the left to find out what was happening, and this officer discovered a growing disaster. A misinterpreted order had caused the 6th AL to withdraw, a movement which resulted in the other formations also abandoning the sunken road. General Robert Rodes lamented, "I did not see their retrograde movement until it was too late for me to rally them ... and immediately the other troops ... retreated ... in confusion."[90] The Carolina brigade now had no protection on their left flank.

Colonel Francis Barlow (61st NY) who commanded the combined 61st-64th NY battalion, a force of three hundred fifty troops, saw the Confederates' mistake and responded. He sent his riflemen forward into the gap and wheeled them to flank the 2nd NC. Barlow remarked, "My regiments at once advanced over the crest of the hill, and bravely engaged the enemy."[91] They punched into the Tar Heels and the Carolinians could not resist. The 2nd NC was short leaders, especially since Col. Charles Tew had been "shot through the head and placed in the sunken road," along with more of his officers, also casualties.[92] The Second North Carolina disintegrated and its survivors streamed southward, away from the New Yorkers' threat.

The men of the 14th NC watched their brothers flee and many of the regiment's left wing companies joined the retreat. The Fourteenth's center companies attempted to resist Barlow's riflemen but the Yanks had completely flanked them and were able to fire down the length of the Southern position. An officer in Barlow's command wrote, "[Our] regiment ... [broke] the center of the enemy's line, and killing or wounding nearly all that left the ditch to make their escape through the cornfield."[93] The Fourteenth collapsed. Colonel Barlow noted, "my regiments ... obtained an enfilading fire upon the enemy ... and the enemy ... seeing the uselessness of further resistance ... in accordance with our demands, threw down their guns."[94]

Third Lt. Alexander Crews (Co. G), 22 years old, was severely wounded at Sharpsburg (Clark, 1901).

Meanwhile, the 5th NH, whose line extended beyond the right of the Maj. Sillers' Tar Heels, was also led by a quick-thinking officer. Their commander, Col. Edward Cross brought his three hundred troops through the shattered remnants of the Irish brigade and realized a frontal assault would only result in his regiment's destruction. One of his officers noted, "in a twinkling we found ourselves opposed to the enemy and under a severe fire."[95] Colonel Cross knew repeated charges had done little more than litter the ground with dead and wounded so he wheeled his left wing and moved those companies to flank the Thirtieth's right. An officer in his command recorded, "We were fresh, and opened a withering ... fire on the rebels."⁹⁶ An embattled Confederate added, "we were flanked at that point."⁹⁷

Major William Sillers had been relying on his captains and senior lieutenants to keep the regiment's companies intact but now as Federal minié bullets began to plow into his men, more of the Thirtieth's leaders fell. First Lieutenant George Harrell (Co. F) dropped, ripped by lead coming from their right, as did 3rd Lt. William Gill (Co. D), who fell mortally wounded. Third Lieutenant Alexander Crews (Co. G) was knocked to the ground, "a minie ball pass[ing] through his chest," and 2nd Lt. Charles Rogers (Co. D) was killed.⁹⁸ William Sillers recalled in horror, "my attention was called to our right, which was again unsupported ... the situation deteriorated rapidly."⁹⁹ Sergeant Loren Griffin (Co. I) described their situation simply, "Our men got cut all to peces [sic]."¹⁰⁰ Sillers hollered at his company officers and most struggled to rally their men, though one captain, John McMillan (Co. E), could not be found; his sergeants said he had left the field.¹⁰¹

30th North Carolina Infantry
Sharpsburg Casualties¹⁰²
September 17, 1862

Unit	Commander	Loss
Field & Staff	Col. Parker, Francis	6
Co. A	Cpt. Holmes, James	6
Co. B	1st Lt. Davis, Weldon	4
Co. C	Cpt. Allen, David	6
Co. D	1st Lt. Allen, Charles	5
Co. E	Cpt. McMillan, John	5
Co. F	Cpt. Moore, Willis	14
Co. G	Cpt. Barnett, James	5
Co. H	1st Lt. McNeil, Henry	12
Co. I	Cpt. Harris, James	7
Co. K	2nd Lt. Ardrey, William	13
		79

More Tar Heels fell: Pvt. John Best (Co. E) had a bullet slash through his leg, Pvt. Aley Culp (Co. K) was hit in the thigh, Pvt. James Griffin (Co. I) suffered a shattered ankle, and Pvt. Rufus Weeks (Co. K) was struck in the shoulder.¹⁰³ Major William Sillers remarked, "I sent a captain to the left to see if anyone was there ... and he reported ... [the 4th NC] was uncovered as far as I could see."¹⁰⁴ A rifleman in the 4th NC added, "The minié balls, shot & shell rained down upon us from every direction except the rear."¹⁰⁵ As more Thirtieth riflemen fell before the Union flanking fire, there was nothing Sillers could do. He finally, "gave the order to fall back."¹⁰⁶ His men fled to the south. A soldier in the 5th NH bragged, "The 5th's ... volley[s] sent them rearward."¹⁰⁷

The battered Tar Heels slunk back into the cornfield and retreated without any semblance of order. A Southerner remarked, "[they were] broken beyond the power of rallying ... [and] retreat[ed] in [a] stampede."¹⁰⁸ The exuberant Yanks from New York and New Hampshire swept along the sunken road, the New Yorkers coming from the west, and the Granite State men from the east, gobbling up trapped Confederates. One crowed, "when I called out to them to surrender ... they at once threw down their arms.... I think ... we captured 275 or 300 prisoners."[109] The Carolinians ran until they were out of danger. Major William Sillers recorded, "We retired about 300 yards. Here we made a stand ... we remained until after nightfall."[110] Second Lieutenant William Ardrey (Co. K) wrote, "I considered myself extremely fortunate in escaping, unhurt."[111] The blue coats stumbled among the dead in the sunken road, shocked by what they saw. One described the scene, "On looking about me I found that we were in an old sunken road and that the bed of it lay from one to three feet below the surface of the crest along which it ran. In this road there lay so many dead rebels that there formed a line which one might have walked on as far as I could see."[112]

It was now just past 1:00 p.m., and the Thirtieth North Carolina's fighting was done. They, along with the other three Tar Heel regiments and the brigade from Alabama had

Bloody Lane (Gardner photo, Library of Congress).

held off several Union divisions for over three hours. The Confederates, though outnumbered at least three-to-one, shattered three major assaults and inflicted tremendous casualties, but in the end, they were outflanked and driven from the field. Federal losses in the attacks on the sunken road were nearly 2,900, more than the entire number of riflemen in Rodes' and Anderson's brigades.[113] Confederate casualties totaled 670.[114] Later that evening, once darkness silenced the killing, the survivors gathered around campfires and mourned their losses. One rifleman wrote, "The excitement of battle comes in the day of it, but the horrors of it two or three days after."[115]

Chapter 6

Winter 1862–1863: Rebuilding the Regiment

The battle-weary Carolinians arose on September 18, 1862, and formed for roll call. A few stragglers had joined the regiment during the night, but even so, since so few men answered their sergeants' calls the count was shockingly quick. Major William Sillers, the only surviving field officer took the Thirtieth's report to the brigade officers' meeting, where he learned the brigade's other units had suffered as badly as his. The senior brigade officer, Col. Risden Bennett (14th NC) informed the assembled officers to ready their men for whatever would happen, but as the experienced men gazed out at the quiet battlefield, they felt the Yanks did not want to continue the fight. Major Sillers returned to his small formation, and at 9:30 a.m. ration wagons arrived. Soon after this, Maj. Gen. Daniel Hill made his way among the troops. Their division commander spoke briefly, calling the men "the faithful few," and commending them for their fortitude and bravery.[1] Then, the troops were released to rest, and be ready if danger approached.

A cold drizzle dampened the field and soaked the Tar Heels, however, even more important to the traumatized men, the daylight hours passed with the Federals showing no signs of aggressive behavior. Alexander Betts recorded simply, "No fighting.... Rainy, damp."[2] Later, once the sun had set, Maj. Sillers received word the brigade would be moving; the army was going to leave Maryland. A few hours later, Lt. William Ardrey (Co. K) scribbled in his journal, "We left the field at midnight and recrossed the river without molestation."[3] The next morning, Chaplain Betts remarked, "Cross [the Potomac] at daybreak. Yesterday I bathed in this stream. Today dead bodies will be bathing in it."[4] The men silently trudged onto Virginian soil, having lost the exuberance they'd possessed when they had stepped onto Maryland's turf. The column hiked several hours and ended up a couple miles west of Shepherdstown, VA. The next day, September 20, 1862, the Southerners shifted eight miles farther west and bivouacked near Martinsburg. Again, the army commissary department could not support the men. Lieutenant William Ardrey noted, "Out of rations, ate three ears of green corn for dinner."[5]

The battered regiment received reinforcements, over a hundred men who had not been able to keep up with the army when it advanced towards Maryland, they had been corralled along the Virginia side of the Potomac. The Sharpsburg battle survivors welcomed these stragglers as they filtered back into the Thirtieth's ranks, and acknowledged the stunned looks from the newcomers when they reacted to the fact so many comrades were missing. What once had been a fine-looking regiment now was but a shadow of itself. Private John Bone (Co. I) summed up their situation, writing, "We were a very hard looking set of soldiers, the men had lost, thrown away and worn out about all that they started from Richmond with."[6] Major William Sillers also wrote about the regiment, noting, "Since the battle of the 17th, when Col. Parker was severely wounded in the head, I have been in command of the Regiment. I haven't had the heart to speak of the condition of our brigade after the fight." He finished his letter to his sister, writing, "God spare me the sight of ever again seeing it so much disorganized."[7]

The Tar Heels remained near Martinsburg for the next week, slowly recovering from their Maryland fight. Commissary wagons arrived, enabling the riflemen to eat something other than green corn. Lieutenant Ardrey wrote, "Bill of fare for breakfast, corn, roasted apples, beef and coffee." This food, along with days of inactivity, helped restore the exhausted men's morale. William Ardrey also noted, "Gen. Jackson passed the camp on his cream horse. Everybody hollering, his presence always greatly revived the troops."[8] Then, on September 27, 1862, the brigade moved away from Martinsburg, the men marching south ten miles to the Bunker Hill area. Lieutenant Ardrey recorded, "Left our camp.... Passed through Martinsburg ... a very ancient and dilapidated appearance.... Encamped near Bunkerville."[9]

Major William Sillers received word the brigade would be camping in this location for an extended period of time. The regiment's supply wagons were brought up and unloaded, company streets laid out, and canvas shelters and tents set up. The soldiers immediately spread out, foraging for more food. William Ardrey (Co. K) noted, "The boys [are] shooting squirrels all day."[10] Lieutenant Ardrey also recorded, "Capt. John G. Witherspoon [Co. K] and Lt. John T. Downs [Co. K] returned. I was much rejoiced to see them."[11] Ardrey's company increased in strength, as did others as well, however, some units also saw reductions in their numbers. Private Benjamin Bunn (Co. I), an 18-year-old student from Rocky Mount, NC, had mustered into his company as a rifleman, and quickly been promoted to first sergeant. Unfortunately, his leadership abilities had not proven adequate, so his officers removed his stripes and returned him to the ranks. The ambitious Benjamin Bunn then began a campaign for advancement, and on September 24, 1862, was transferred to the 47th NC.[12]

The regiment remained in camp as September turned to October, while the high command tried to figure out what strategy they would pursue. Supplies again ran out, leaving the Carolinians to fend for themselves. Lieutenant Ardrey grumbled, "Nothing to eat but beef without salt."[13] Two weeks later, on October 16, 1862, the

Benjamin Bunn (Co. I), 18 years old, was transferred to the 47th NC Infantry on September 24, 1862 (Clark, 1901).

Tar Heels were saddened by the news their commander, Brig. Gen. George B. Anderson, had died from the wounds he received at Sharpsburg. At first, Gen. Anderson's foot wound had not appeared to be serious, but his injury refused to improve. He was transported, first to a residence in Shepherdstown, and from there, to Staunton, VA. Anderson's condition deteriorated, so he was shipped to Raleigh, NC, where doctors amputated his foot. But by now infection had weakened his health, and the shock from the surgery worsened his condition to the point no recovery was possible. The Tar Heel brigade's leader died, and was buried in Raleigh, leaving the formation without an official commander.[14]

Major General Daniel Hill placed Col. Bryan Grimes (4th NC) in temporary command of the brigade. Bryan Grimes was hurt deeply by Anderson's death. Grimes had turned down a colonel's position in order to take a major's slot under George Anderson when Anderson was colonel of the 4th NC. Bryan Grimes recalled, "I felt my deficiency of a knowledge of military tactics and Col. Geo. B. Anderson [was] a graduate of West Point.... I preferred a subordinate position with an efficient officer."[15] Grimes had not been present for the Sharpsburg campaign, having suffered an unusual injury two weeks before the Confederates entered Maryland. Colonel Grimes recorded, "I received a very severe hurt from the kick of a horse, which incapacitated me from active duty, not being able to either walk or ride ... the serious nature of the injury ... an indentation in the bone ... [caused] amputation ... [to] seriously be talked about."[16] Fortunately amputation was not necessary and now, the 33-year-old planter from Pitt County, NC, was able to resume military duties. On October 25, 1862, Col. Grimes led the brigade away from their camp and toward Charlestown. Here, once the troops had established a camp, he passed on Gen. Hill's orders: they were to destroy the railroad tracks. Chaplain Alexander Betts recorded, "[The] Division moves and begins to tear up track of W[inchester] and Harper's Ferry R.R. Our Brigade operates on track below Charlestown during the night in a cold rain."[17] Captain John Witherspoon (Co. K) added, "we marched from six o'clock until 12 o'clock in the night and then worked alternate hours from [then] till morning in tearing up R.R. beyond Charlestown.... We burned away every stick that is connected with the R.R."[18] Colonel Bryan Grimes wrote, "The work was done effectually at night by

Col. Bryan Grimes (4th NC), 33 years old, assumed temporary command of the brigade following Brig. Gen. George Anderson's death (Library of Congress).

tearing up the cross-ties and putting them in large piles of twenty to thirty, and then crossing the iron rails over them and piling a few ties on top of each end of the rails, and just before day-light setting fire to them ... the fire so warping the rails as to unfit them for use."[19] The soldiers continued their destruction the next day as well, leaving Chaplain Betts with little to do. The curious minister traveled to Charlestown. He wrote, "[We] ride [to Charlestown] the spot of John Brown's execution, and see the prison in which he was confined. Lovely little town."[20] Bryan Grimes also remarked, "Charlestown, the site of the execution of the notorious Kansas Ruffian, John Brown."[21]

The Confederate high command gave new orders, and soon the riflemen were heading south, hiking through Berryville, VA, from there, to Millwood, VA, and then eastward. Lieutenant William Ardrey (Co. K) recorded, "Waded the Shenandoah.... Encamped near Paris in Ashby's Gap, right at the foot of the Blue Ridge."[22] Then, following an inspection and payroll muster, the Tar Heels marched farther south, arriving at Front Royal at 10:00 a.m. on November 4, 1862.[23] Here, the Thirtieth's riflemen laid out their company streets and settled down for what they thought would be an extended stay, comforted by the fact they were close to the supplies being transported by trains along the Manassas Gap Railroad's tracks. Unfortunately, before the Tar Heels could benefit from Confederate stockpiles, Maj. Sillers' men were told to move. The Thirtieth's leader wrote, "we were ordered to fall back across the Shenandoah River. It was very cold.... The poor men had to wade the river." William Sillers continued, "I was left in charge of the picket. We crossed after everyone else had gone over about eleven or twelve o'clock at night. We picketed the river banks, and the next morning it began snowing, and snowed briskly all that day, and part of the night."[24] Chaplain Alexander Betts added, "Move across river after night. Very cold. Men wade and walk a mile to camp, some without shoes. Water freezes by my side as I lie on the ground."[25] The riflemen were frustrated by a command from division which caused considerable discomfort. Colonel Grimes wrote, "there was the order forbidding the men [from] removing their pants, or shoes, which I thought ought to be done so as to enable the men to be dry after crossing."[26] That night, as the men huddled around smoky campfires, a discouraged Cpt. John Witherspoon (Co. K) scratched a letter to his wife, writing, "I think often of you and the babies.... No day ever passes without me thinking often of you and home." He continued, "[There is] no prospect of the war ending soon that I can see ... [and] Nothing has been said about my going home. I would like to get home Christmas if I could."[27]

The weather turned quite cold, punishing the poorly outfitted soldiers. Soon, dozens of Maj. Sillers' men were sick. There was little the regiment's surgeons could do, as there was no place to shelter the ailing Tar Heels. The Grim Reaper moved in among the sick, claiming victims. Alexander Betts morosely recorded, "[We] Bury H[ugh] Y. Kirkpatrick [Co. K] at night in Presbyterian cemetery. He enlisted at nineteen, from Mecklenburg County. Lovely Christian. Died in the house of Mrs. Davis ... 10:30 p.m." Chaplain Betts continued, "How sad the sight! How tenderly a few of his comrades raked away the snow, dug the grave and laid the noble youth away."[28] Captain John Witherspoon (Co. K) also noted Sgt. Kirkpatrick's death, writing, "I and four men buried Kirkpatrick last night by candlelight—he was only sick a few days."[29] More Tar Heels succumbed to illness, most dying in overcrowded military hospitals, fourteen died in September and October, and another eighteen in November.[30]

The Confederates marched westward as the weather turned vicious. One soldier noted, "It was raining, then commenced sleeting, and afterward went to snowing, covering the ground about six inches." He continued, "The mud was deep and partially frozen."[31] The Southerners slogged their way through the snow and frozen mud, suffering due to their lack of shoes and winter clothing. Alexander Betts watched as the Thirtieth's riflemen staggered along the road and recorded, "Snow begins to fall at 10 a.m. Bad day on bare feet."[32] Private John Bone (Co. I) struggled alongside his comrades and then wrote, "many of the men were barefooted, with large cracks in their feet, and when we would get up in the mornings and start on those turnpike roads, the blood would run out of their feet."[33] The column of shivering men reached Strasburg, VA on November 9, 1862. A melancholy Cpt. John Witherspoon (Co. K) grumbled, "This war has no appearance of coming to a close. When our country is sufficiently humbled it will cease and not before."[34]

The chilled Tar Heels set up camp and scrounged for firewood and food. Meanwhile, the Confederate high command settled the problem of what to do with Gen. Anderson's replacement—Col. Stephen Dodson Ramseur (49th NC) was promoted to brigadier general and assigned to lead their formation. Dodson Ramseur, as he was called, had been a student of Daniel H. Hill, who had helped him transfer from Davidson College to West Point. Ramseur graduated from the Academy in 1860 but did not receive the opportunity of military assignment before the war broke out. The 24-year-old quickly took a Confederate artillery command and served with this battery in the battle of Yorktown, before being awarded colonel of the 49th NC. Though Ramseur was a little guy, he impressed everyone with his fierce aggressiveness. One Southerner wrote, "Dodson's small stature and mild demeanor belied his willingness to confront bullies."[35] No one doubted Dodson Ramseur would lead from the front. Of course this courageous behavior was quite dangerous: "At Malvern Hill, on the 1st of July.... He was shot through the right arm, above the elbow."[36] Though Ramseur now had title to the Carolina brigade, his wound kept him from active duty, forcing Col. Bryan Grimes to remain in command.

Brig. Gen. Stephen Dodson Ramseur, 26 years old, took command of the North Carolina brigade (Library of Congress).

Major William Sillers' riflemen did not care who sat atop their brigade's leadership pyramid. They struggled to combat the elements, as well as the paltry army commissary, and had to make do with what they could get from home. The soldiers patched their clothes and washed when they found the time. Alexander Betts mentioned, "Wash day ... [The] bank of [the river] ... lined some distance with men half naked, some washing pants and drawers, others washing shirts and some picking their clothing. Some half naked hold their wet shirts to the fire to dry." He finished his writing, noting, "Sad sight! Would make wives, mothers and sisters weep."[37]

Major William Sillers led the Thirtieth out of their encampment on November 17, 1862, as his riflemen headed southward. The Tar Heels still did not possess adequate foot ware, and this deficiency hampered their movements. Major General Daniel Hill, frustrated by this shortcoming as well as dissatisfied because his regimental commanders had not been able to solve the problem, reacted harshly. Captain Matt Manly (2nd NC) wrote in disgust, "It was on this march, late one evening, that General Hill issued his memorable order that threw consternation among the company officers. It was to the effect that should any man be seen on the march next day without shoes the officer commanding the company should be 'placed in arrest and recommended to be dropped.'"[38] Major William Sillers scrambled his officers, because, as he knew in his regiment, "It is not one or two who are without shoes and half-clad; but it is the greater part of every company in our regiment who are in this condition."[39] Private John Bone (Co. I) recorded what happened, "There were orders sent to each regiment ... while we were on this march for every soldier that was barefooted to go to the butcher's pen ... and cut off some pieces of the raw hides, make holes in them, take some strings and tie them to our feet."[40] Captain Manly (2nd NC) wrote, "the skins of the newly-killed beeves were to be made into moccasins. All night was consumed in the work, as there were nearly one hundred men of the regiment without shoes." The Tar Heel continued, writing derisively of this knee-jerk order, "The next day the regiment appeared like a lot of cripples, the raw hide having curled and shrunk in the most uncomfortable way."[41]

30th North Carolina Infantry[42]
December 1, 1862

Unit		Strength
Field & Staff	Maj. Sillers, William Adj. Philips, Frederick	3
Co. A	Cpt. Holmes, James 1st Lt. Williams, Gary	54
Co. B	Cpt. Davis Weldon E. 1st Lt. Nicholson, John	42
Co. C	Cpt. Allen, David C. 1st Lt. Bennett, Solomon	48
Co. D	1st Lt. Allen, Charles N. 2nd Lt. Abernathy, Sidney	48
Co. E	1st Lt. Johnson, Ira 2nd Lt. Newton, Samuel	42
Co. F	Cpt. Moore, Willis B. 1st Lt. Harrell, George K.	54
Co. G	1st Lt. Badgett, James W. 1st Sgt. O'Brien, Alfred	54
Co. H	Cpt. Wicker, Jesse J. 1st Lt. McNeil, Henry J.	54
Co. I	Cpt. Harris, James J. 1st Lt. Williford, Burton B.	82

Unit		Strength
Co. K	Cpt. Witherspoon, John G.	
	2nd Lt. Downs, John T.	44
		525

The brigade arrived in the Gordonsville, VA area on November 24, 1862, and from there hiked eastward towards Port Royal, twelve miles below Fredericksburg. Again, lack of shoes caused many of the men to fall behind their units. General Stonewall Jackson, upset by this straggling, issued his own decree. A Southerner reported, "[Jackson] instructed his Provost Marshall to prevent all straggling of the sort that had so dangerously weakened the Army in the Maryland operations.... Jackson's orders were explicit: The Provost Marshall Guard was to shoot, first, all stragglers who refused to go to the front, and second, all soldiers who were said by two witnesses to be straggling for the second time."[43]

Once the sun set, December 12, 1862, Col. Grimes called the brigade's regimental commanders together and told them the formation had been ordered to march to Fredericksburg; news had come the Yanks were crossing the Rappahannock River. Major Sillers returned to his regiment and gave the word, "strike camp and prepare to march." The Thirtieth now mustered over five hundred men. William Sillers remained the only field officer present, and now relied on the regiment's senior captain, James Holmes (Co. A) as right wing commander, and Cpt. Willis Moore (Co. F) to lead the left wing, meaning five companies were commanded by lieutenants. The Thirtieth's riflemen were well-equipped with modern Enfields and possessed a good supply of ammunition, but the Tar Heels lacked foot ware, warm clothing, and sufficient tenting materials. The men were led by experienced officers, had been decently trained, and had a good reputation for courage in battle, however, everything else was in disarray.

The Carolinians formed in column and began hiking, their regiment one of many as Maj. Gen. Daniel Hill's entire division moved north. General Hill recorded, "Just before sundown on the 12th.... I received an order to march that night to Fredericksburg ... we began our march immediately."[44] One Southerner wrote, "That night was cold and clear and the soldiers were treated to a display of the aurora borealis." He continued, "Though this sight thrilled some, others were frightened.... Some of the soldiers believed [this] ... prophesied something horrible.... Tomorrow would bring the bloodiest day the world ever saw."[45] Hours later, the column bumped to a halt, caused by a traffic jam of soldiers. An officer noted, "we were stopped by encountering General Early's column some 3 miles from Hamilton's Crossing. We waited until daylight."[46] The sleepy soldiers slumped down upon the frozen road and napped while officers sorted out the confusion. Then, the Tar Heels were directed up into a stand of trees on a ridge near Hamilton's Crossing. The riflemen soon learned their brigade was part of the third line; they were safely positioned in the rear. Colonel Bryan Grimes wrote, "we marched all night and reached Hamilton's Crossing about day, and were placed in the reserve on the extreme right of Jackson's line."[47]

The Carolinians huddled around fires as morning overtook their position. An officer wrote, "The 13th of December dawned cold ... [the] hills were damp with the fog that covered the valley."[48] The winter sun struggled with the fog and eventually burned the mists away sometime after 10:00 a.m., however, due to their location, the men in the Thirtieth could see little of the battlefield. A few enterprising officers slipped away from the regiment and made their way to the front. They were astounded by the panorama before them. One wrote, "this was the grandest martial scene of the war.... Here was a vast plain, now peopled with an army worthy of its grand dimensions [with] ... fifty thousand gleaming bayonets." He continued, "Officers, on restless horses, rushed from point to point in gay uniforms. Field artillery was whisked into position.... Rank and file, foot and horse, small arms and field ordnance, presented so magnificent a pageant as to call forth the unbounded admiration of [our] adversaries."[49] Another officer added, "Could you beat this? ... It's splendid."[50]

The Union forces moved forward, aimed at Confederates posted to the north of where the Carolinians rested. A Federal officer reported, "the column of Meade's division advanc[ed] in fine order and with gallant determination ... directed into the point of wood ... on the extreme point of the ridge."[51] The Northerners rushed toward the Confederates, only to be swept by concentrated fire. A Confederate recalled, "Jackson's right and right-center poured into these sturdy ranks a most deadly volley from small arms. Spaces, gaps, and wide chasms instantly told the tale of a most fatal encounter." He continued, "Volley after volley of small arms continued the work of destruction, while Jackson's artillery ... kept up a withering fire on the lessening ranks."[52] But the Yanks refused to quit; more regiments surged forward, ignoring the casualties littering the ground. These waves of blue coats crashed into the Southern lines, smashing into Brig. Gen. James Archer's brigade, and into the gap between Archer's Tennesseans and the Virginians of Brig. Gen. Elisha Paxton's brigade. A Northerner wrote, "Meade's division successfully ... charged up the slope ... and gained the road and edge of the wood, driving the enemy."[53]

Sgt. John Wells (Co. E), 25 years old, was mortally wounded at Fredericksburg. He died of his wounds a week later (Taylor, 1998).

The Confederates reacted when the blue coats broke through between Archer and Paxton. General Daniel Hill noted, "We remained in ... position until noon, when the division was ordered to the extreme right to meet a ... movement of Yankees."[54] Colonel Grimes quickly shifted his Carolinians to the south, the second formation in a column of brigades. They left the cover provided by the trees, moving down out of the heights, and crossed a set of railroad tracks. Then, the column wheeled to the left in anticipation of flanking the Union assault. Meanwhile, other Confederate brigades, riflemen commanded by Maj. Gen. Jubal Early crashed headlong into the Northerner's advance. A Federal wrote, "The infantry combat was ... kept up a short time ... and after a severe contest, forced back."[55]

Union artillerymen, seeing General Daniel Hill's massed brigades opened fire upon the column. Most of the rounds impacted amid the Southerners of the leading brigade, though a few landed amongst the North Carolinians. Private John Hanchey (Co. E) and Pvt. John Pickett (Co. E) were both injured by shrapnel as the Thirtieth moved forward, as was Sgt. John Wells (Co. E), who fell, his body badly mangled. Another shell exploded near Company D, shattering both of Pvt. Elias Allen's thighs, as well as taking down Pvt. William L. Lumbley and Pvt. Elijah Wilkins.[56] General Daniel Hill sought permission to protect his men from the Federal artillery. The threat of a break-through had been averted, his men were not needed, and he saw no point in standing his troops out in the open to be shot at by Union artillery. He noted simply, "We were … soon ordered back."[57] Hill quickly turned his five brigades around and hustled them out of danger but not before shrapnel nearly blew off both of Pvt. Donald McDougald's (Co. H) legs, and injured, Pvt. Jesse Little (Co. F) and Pvt. James Mayo (Co. F).[58] The Carolinians scampered back into the woods, content to be protected from the artillery, and to let someone else do the fighting. One wrote, "[We] were subjected to artillery fire…. The 30th … suffered the loss of nine men wounded from artillery fire."[59]

The fighting north of the Tar Heel position stuttered to a stop and their area of the Fredericksburg battlefield quieted down, save for artillery duels and the scatterings of skirmish fire. Private John Bone (Co. I) wrote, "We remained in this position all day and night … it being very cold we suffered a great deal on account of being very thinly clothed and shoed."[60] The Thirtieth's surgeons, Drs. Charles Gregory and Francis Garrett worked to save Sgt. John Wells' (Co. E) life. They patched him up as best as they could, but his wounds were critical. He would succumb to his injuries a week later. Charles Gregory and Francis Garrett operated on Pvt. Donald McDougald (Co. H), and were forced to amputate one of his legs. His condition remained in poor health for several weeks, eventually though, the 25-year-old would recover.[61] The other soldiers' wounds were not as serious, and by nightfall, all had been tended to, and plans made to transport them to Richmond. Unfortunately, as the sun set and the winter's chill set in, the doctors were soon ambushed by a swarm of Carolinians felled by the elements. One of these Tar Heels, 37-year-old Pvt. Marley Woods (Co. E), contracted pneumonia and never recovered. He was taken to a hospital in Gordonsville, VA, where he died.[62]

30th North Carolina Infantry[63]
Fredericksburg Casualties
December 13–14, 1862

Unit	Commander	Loss
Field & Staff	Maj. Sillers, William.	-
Co. A	Cpt. Holmes, James.	1
Co. B	Cpt. Davis Weldon E.	-
Co. C	Cpt. Allen, David C.	2
Co. D	1st Lt. Allen, Charles N.	3
Co. E	1st Lt. Johnson, Ira	3
Co. F	Cpt. Moore, Willis B.	2
Co. G	1st Lt. Badgett, James W.	1
Co. H	Cpt. Wicker, Jesse J.	1

Unit	Commander	Loss
Co. I	Cpt. Harris, James J.	1
Co. K	Cpt. Witherspoon, John G.	2
		16

The Carolinians survived the frigid night, huddled around campfires, and snatching sleep when they could. One rifleman wrote, "We sit [it] very hard.... We have had some very cold weather.... We have no tents."[64] The men may have been cold and miserable, but they knew their condition was much better than the wounded laying untended, out on the battlefield. Colonel Bryan Grimes wrote, "The cries [from] the wounded in the hedged old field in our front ... was heart-rending and sickening ... and continued all night."[65] The chilled soldiers faced the new morning, "every man at his post, awaiting the expected charge." Bryan Grimes noted, "The fog hung low, and we waited impatiently for it to rise and show us the plain below."[66] Colonel Grimes called for skirmishers from each regiment, and the Thirtieth sent forward at least two dozen. General Daniel Hill recorded, "[Grimes'] brigade also furnished 100 sharpshooters ... and these were constantly skirmishing with the Yankees during the 14th and 15th."[67]

The brigade skirmishers moved forward and collided with Federal pickets, some of them, men from the Iron Brigade, a tough-fighting unit that had earned its nickname in the battles on South Mountain. These blue-coated soldiers were distinctive because they all wore large, black hats. One of these Yanks, a rifleman from Wisconsin wrote, "All that day ... the picket-firing was intense."[68] As the day slowly passed, several Thirtieth riflemen were wounded. Private Aaron DeArmond (Co. K) recalled, "I was struck by a [bullet] which cracked my arm ... 4 inches from my shoulder."[69] Another Tar Heel rifleman, Pvt. John Butler (Co. C), was struck in the face, and by late afternoon, several more Carolinians were slightly wounded.[70]

Fortunately, a truce was arranged between the two picket lines, otherwise it is possible more of Maj. William Sillers' men may have become casualties. A Yank recorded, "about 4 o'clock ... the picket-firing ... was abruptly ended by a Confederate challenging a 6th Wisconsin man to a fist fight in the middle.... The combatants got the attention of both picket-lines, who declared the fight a draw." The Northerner continued, "They ended the matter with a coffee and tobacco trade and an agreement to do no more firing ... unless an advance should be ordered."[71]

On December 15, 1862, once there was enough light to see, Col. Grimes received orders to send out his skirmishers again. The resolute Tar Heels pushed forward into the thick fog, calling out to their Northern counterparts that they were coming, in hopes the truce would hold. But the Yanks did not answer. A Southerner wrote, "At daylight our pickets were thrown forward and the enemy found gone." Word was immediately passed back to brigade headquarters and Col. Grimes ordered his Carolina regiments to advance. They moved forward and encountered the debris of a departed army. General Daniel Hill noted, "We captured 292 of the Yankee pickets and stragglers, and gathered up between 3,000 and 4,000 excellent rifles and muskets."[72] The battle of Fredericksburg had ended— Maj. Sillers' Thirtieth suffered sixteen casualties, as well as scores felled by pneumonia.[73]

The brigade moved two days later, marching south to Guinea Station, where the men were ordered to prepare for winter quarters, but told not to build anything until the Confederate high command made final decisions. Here, not far from the Richmond and Potomac Railroad tracks, the Tar Heels waited for permission to build their cold-season shelters, all the while, having to endure the December weather. Private John Bone (Co. I) complained, "we remained in position, it rained and froze, turning bitter cold, and we suffered awfully, the army being in worse shape at that time."[74] A chilled, Cpt. John Witherspoon (Co. K) grumbled, "we know nothing of what the army is doing.... We are wishing for winter quarters but don't know whether we will be gratified or not."[75] And another Carolinian considered their situation, writing satirically, "Our improvised quarters were so open we had the privilege of breathing God's pure, invigorating air."[76]

Finally, orders came to erect winter quarters. The men immediately began building cabins and huts in a frenzy of construction. A Confederate noted, "Some of the soldiers built log huts, and some dug themselves homes, which they covered with tent flies. Chimneys of many patterns rose ... chimneys were erected of mud and wood or of stone and plastered earth."[77] Private Aaron DeArmond (Co. K) wrote proudly of his home, "you should see our houses that we live in.... I have a tent to stay in and a chimney built to my tent.... I can live very comfortably in it."[78]

The brigade's winter schedule centered around drill when the weather allowed, fatigue duties, and picket responsibilities along the Rappahannock River. Major William Sillers' company officers organized their platoons, separating their men into cooking teams. One rifleman wrote, "The company was divided up into messes of five or more men for the convenience of drawing rations." He continued, "[We] took turns in duties alternate weeks. One would draw the commissary appointment, one would gather up the wood, one would bring water and make fires, another would cook ... then a change would be made."[79] Later, when the Thirtieth took its turn on the picket line, they would hike back to the Rappahannock and stand along its riverbanks, guarding against a Yank attack. On one of these rotations, Cpt. John Witherspoon (Co. K) remarked, "We are down near the picket-line with the balance of our Brigade ... we will be on picket tomorrow. The river is all that is between our picket and theirs."[80] Then, when their responsibility ended, William Sillers' men hurried back to the warmth of their winter huts.

As 1862 passed to 1863, the soldiers' needs to keep warm began to impact the surrounding countryside. Private John Bone noticed this, writing, "It was very cold most of the time ... most of the timber was cut off the land, and this gave the wind a very fair sweep at us."[81] Another Tar Heel observed, "We encamped in the woods, thick with small pine and oak. Day by day the trees were felled and used for necessary fires." He continued, "Day by day we had to bear the logs and limbs for fires from a greater distance. Finally the distance became so great we were driven to use the stumps dug out of the frozen ground."[82] And an officer also seeing this destruction, recalled, "to feed the avid fires, forests disappeared from the ridges." He added, "Houses ... that never looked at each other in almost the century they had been standing, stare at each other, impudently, in the face—having barely the trees that surround them."[83]

The young men, now with little to do, dreamed about home and the loved ones they missed. They all tried to secure furloughs, a wish fulfilled by only a few. Private Aaron DeArmond (Co. K) pleaded, "let all the poor soldiers return hoam [sic.] to their familys [sic]."[84] Even Maj. William Sillers received a rejection to his home-bound petition. He sadly wrote his sister, upon hearing of the death of a younger sister, "The news that my dear Annie Belle was dead came like a thunderbolt upon me—so sudden and unexpected." He continued, "I hardly know how to write you, since the news.... Oh if my furlough had been granted, I should have reached home just in time to have pressed her dear lips once more on earth!"[85]

6. Winter 1862–1863

The winter's grip on the countryside forced the Confederates to limit their activities. Private Aaron DeArmond (Co. K) scribbled, "all is quiet in camp at present and I hope it will remain so."[86] The soldiers spent their free time searching for distraction. A Tar Heel noted, "Books, passed from hand to hand, were devoured with avidity. Chess, backgammon, checkers, games of chance with cards and dice, beguiled the inclement days and long nights."[87] Unfortunately, when the homesick boys had nothing to do they worried about home. One young man bemoaned, "I am jealous of my best girl, and have a right to be, for an old widower with a spanking pair of horses and a light buggy is paying too much attention to her to suit me."[88] Captain John Witherspoon (Co. K) wrote his wife, concerned about a land purchase, mentioning, "I ... bought the land and.... Charlie had my note for $1200 with a credit of $500 ... If he don't settle it I want to do so myself so that you may have the benefit of the note you hold for your use."[89] Private Aaron DeArmond (Co. K) replied to a loved one's letter, writing, "You have no idea how glad it makes me feel when I get a letter from you."[90] And Chaplain Alexander Betts mentioned a rifleman's concern, repeating to his wife what the Tar Heel had told him: "I never can forget how tenderly he spoke of his wife, saying he did not know how to appreciate her till the war took him from her."[91]

Supplies remained short, forcing the men to scrounge for food, shelter materials, shoes, and clothing. A frustrated Lt. William Ardrey (Co. K) grumbled, "Rations very scarce."[92] Another Carolinian complained about their lack of canvas, writing, " The government could not furnish tents. Those we had captured from the Yankees were given to the officers and the remaining few to the rank and file." He continued, "The Yankees were well supplied ... with duck canvas about five feet square, with buttons and buttonholes ... which, when joined, would make a good tent. Many of these duck squares were now in the possession of our boys."[93] And Cpt. John Witherspoon sent a uniform home, requesting it be altered, growling, "I drew ... a coat and a pair of pants.... The pants didn't fit me and the pockets don't suit me.... I have not had them on."[94]

Then, smallpox swept through the Tar Heel regiments, swelling the field hospitals and overwhelming the regimental surgeons' attempts to stave off a disaster. Doctor Charles Gregory instituted a program to vaccinate the Thirtieth's men. Captain John Witherspoon (Co. K) wrote, "We have all been vaccinated and I hope there will be no danger of us taking the small pox.... The small pox I am afraid will almost ruin our army this winter. It

Cpt. William Drake (Co. B), 30 years old, resigned his commission on January 5, 1863 (Clark, 1901).

seems to be all over the Army."⁹⁵ Charles Gregory's action spared many, however, before the epidemic ended, a dozen young Tar Heels died, including the 24-year-old, 3rd Lt. Edward Ruark (Co. K). The young lieutenant was able to finagle a furlough and as he boarded the train for his home in Smithville, NC, he knew he did not feel well. By the time Ruark reached home he had an advanced case of smallpox. Edward Ruark died in early January 1863, after infecting his 56-year-old mother, and several others, who also succumbed to the illness.⁹⁶ Captain John Witherspoon wrote about the sickness among his company, mentioning one of his riflemen, also befouled by the disease: "John Black [Co. K] left here the other day with the small pox. All ... [who] were with him I have off in a tent to themselves. This precaution may possibly prevent it from spreading."⁹⁷ Sadly, Pvt. John Black died in early January 1863.

30th North Carolina Infantry
Deaths due to Disease
December 1862—April 1863

Unit	Commander	Loss
Field & Staff	Maj. Sillers, William.	-
Co. A	Cpt. Holmes, James.	14
Co. B	Cpt. Davis Weldon E.	5
Co. C	Cpt. Allen, David C.	9
Co. D	1st Lt. Allen, Charles N.	6
Co. E	1st Lt. Johnson, Ira	13
Co. F	Cpt. Moore, Willis B.	8
Co. G	1st Lt. Badgett, James W.	5
Co. H	Cpt. Wicker, Jesse J.	8
Co. I	Cpt. Harris, James J.	8
Co. K	Cpt. Witherspoon, John G.	10
		86

The smallpox epidemic subsided by the end of January 1863, only to be replaced by an onslaught of soldiers suffering from the ill-effects of living outdoors, especially since they were so poorly clothed and equipped. Doctor Charles Gregory found himself sending sick soldiers to the train depot for transport to Richmond's hospitals in large batches, all victims of pneumonia. This illness killed mercilessly, burying six men in January, ten in February, ten in March, and another eight in April.⁹⁸ Dysentery and chronic diarrhea also flourished, striking many of the immune-weakened Carolinians and killing another ten, making these winter months in Guinea Station horribly costly. The Thirtieth North Carolina was losing young Tar Heels at such a terrible rate these numbers easily doubled the killed-in-action figures of all the 1862 battles the regiment had participated in. Federal bullets may have been dangerous, but disease was far more lethal.

Though most of the dying men passed away in Richmond hospitals, or at home, when news reached their comrades, the men in the Thirtieth took each loss heavily. Their morale suffered. Major William Sillers wrote his sister, mentioning a lament many of his riflemen shared: "There is no dreaming here.... Dreadful reality is too near, and ever present."⁹⁹ Captain Witherspoon (Co. K) remarked, "We know not what awaits us. We know not what pain and suffering is in store for us." He continued, "I don't see any prospects of the war. Will another January find us under arms for the defense of our firesides? Time will only tell."[100]

The heartsick enlisted men clamored for furloughs to go home, while lonely officers contemplated their rank-endowed privilege of resigning. Captain Witherspoon considered turning in his commission and mentioned this to his wife, writing, "If I could keep out of the war I would almost be tempted to resign and go home. I have thought about it often."[101] Other officers did more than think about leaving: some did resign, such as Cpt. William Drake (Co. B), whose wound at Gaines' Mill had rendered him weak and ineffective. He left the Thirtieth in early January 1863.

Major William Sillers' men struggled to survive during what, as Pvt. Richard Brooks (Co. G) described, "a long, cold, and arduous winter."[102] The regiment tottered, the men's spirits a shadow from what it had been a year earlier. William Sillers wrote, "Death was once terrible to me.... But familiarity with battle-fields has hardened my feelings very much. Dead men are only less common than live ones." He continued, "A poor Soldier dies, is buried by the road-side or under the spreading branches of some tree in the midst of a field. No tear is shed. His name is forgotten. This is the last of him. There is a home-circle somewhere broken; somewhere there are tearful eyes and broken hearts. These are not here."[103]

The homesick and forlorn young Tar Heels began to slip out of camp at night, heading for home. Lieutenant William Ardrey (Co. K) recorded in his journal, "[January 11, 1863] ... ten men deserted from Co. I ... [January 27, 1863] 16 men deserted from the Regt."[104] The Thirtieth was not the only unit suffering from desertions; this plague swept throughout the Confederate army, creating a crisis among the high command. Floggings, and even executions were commenced in an attempt to discourage this flight. A Southern rifleman, observing these actions, wrote his family, "I have [seen] several men whipped for going home without leave."[105] Other brigades were forced to watch firing squads shoot hard-core deserters. Fortunately the men in the Thirtieth did not suffer that experience.

February's weather turned brutal, forcing the men to stay hunkered down in their huts. Major Sillers wrote, "The whole earth is white with snow that has been falling since the middle of last night. The weather is very cold."[106] Chaplain Alexander Betts recorded, "the snow is nearly knee deep.... [It is] exceedingly cold ... my ink ... freezes."[107] The men, imprisoned in their crudely made shelters, did little but strive to keep warm. One rifleman scribbled to his sweetheart, "The reason that I write so much is becas [sic.] I can't do any thang [sic.] else to satisfy my mind."[108] Another young Carolinian, lonely and wistful, wrote his girl, "I had much rather see you now than any body on the earth."[109]

The Thirtieth's men were rousted from their huts and sent out on picket in mid–February 1863. They trekked away from their camp and hiked to the Hamilton Crossing area, south of Fredericksburg. Major Sillers recorded, "We are here on picket duty—serving three days and resting three.... We have had snow on the ground for nearly two weeks." He also added, "The roads are terrible beyond description."[110] Private John Bone (Co. I) described their situation: "Our duty was to walk on the bank of the river for two hours at a time ... and then be off under our shelter four and then go back again for two hours."[111] Another Confederate added, "Some of the boys got in a canoe and crossed the river and made some exchanges with the Yankees; tobacco for coffee."[112] Later, once the sun went down and the winter's night clamped freezing temperatures upon the soldiers, they had to hustle to stay warm. One wrote, "[We] made big log fires to sleep by [to] thaw the ground around the fire to go to sleep. [The] fire would go down and [our] clothes would freeze to the ground."[113] And Cpt. John Witherspoon (Co. K) noted, "Sleeping on the ground goes harder on me than ever before."[114]

The Thirtieth served its time along the Rappahannock and then was replaced by one of its brother regiments. The men hurried back to their shelters, just in time to receive a shipment of boxes and packages from home. Captain Witherspoon happily wrote his wife, "Your eatables have been appreciated by the boys. All the sweet cakes and pies are eaten up. I am going to save the cheese. Mitty [Witherspoon (Co. K)] is very thankful for his candy."[115]

The weathered warmed slightly as February 1863 turned into March. The punishing freezes and smothering snows changed to chilled rain and fields of mud. An occasional sunny day enabled the Confederates to move about more easily, however, it also hinted to the veterans that another season of war was not far off. The Thirtieth's new recruits required training, and all the old hands needed refresher drill sessions. Captain Witherspoon remarked, "We have to drill from 7 to 8 in the AM, 11 to 12 and from 4 to 5 PM."[116] This resumption of drill also coincided with Brig. Gen. Dodson Ramseur's arrival. General Ramseur immediately inspected his four Tar Heel regiments and quickly ordered more drill. Captain Witherspoon wrote, "General Ramseur is quite strict in regard to drilling and sees to it himself."[117] General Stephen Dodson Ramseur rode about the camp, "his arm in a sling," insisting his junior officers be trained to handle the responsibilities of the men above them.[118] Since he now was one of the more-senior officers, Witherspoon also found himself assuming field-level responsibilities in the Thirtieth. He wrote, "I am on duty ... there being only four captains for duty to do the part of ten." Witherspoon added, "I had to drill the battalion the other day which has never been done by a captain in our Regt. That embarrassed me considerably at first.... I got along much better than I expected."[119]

Ramseur also organized a permanent brigade skirmishing unit. An officer in the 2nd NC wrote, "A most valuable corps of sharpshooters was created for the brigade by taking forty men from each regiment. This corps, [was] under Major D. W. Hurtt."[120]

Not long after Ramseur assumed command, the Thirtieth's men were heartened by Col. Frank Parker's return. Lieutenant William Ardrey (Co. K) wrote, "Col. F. M. Parker returned to the command, we were greatly rejoiced to see him and serenaded him with the 4th Regt. band."[121] Colonel Parker strolled through his regiment's company streets, inspecting the men, and evaluating their morale and appearance. His Tar Heels were quick to notice, as one recalled, "he now wore a sponge on the crease across his skull."[122] Frank Parker reviewed the men before writing in a letter to his wife, "Rations are rather scarce; but the men manage to get along on them; I am sorry to say that we have a good many desertions."[123] Parker, once he had an understanding of his regiment's condition, met with his new boss, Brig. Gen. Dodson Ramseur. Parker came away from their meeting and noted, "Our Brig. Genl. is quite a young man, not more than twenty-seven; he is a very strict disciplinarian. Drills very hard."[124]

Frank Parker worked diligently to rebuild the Thirtieth. Dozens of new recruits had been added to the regiment's rolls; they had to be equipped and trained. These men were different from the Boys of 61, as they lacked the patriotic fire the original volunteers had possessed. Most of the new men had not volunteered; they had been conscripted. Some were in camp against their will, and others came because of the signing-bonuses. One of these new recruits, Pvt. William Ragland (Co. G), was a soldier purely because of the money. Ragland admitted, "he was exempt from conscription due to the number of minor children (12) at home. [Ragland] was asked by a wealthy neighbor ... to go in his place. He was paid $500 to do so and used the money to pay off the mortgage on their farm."[125] Frank Parker though, believed he could mold these new fellows into effective soldiers.

Colonel Parker also reviewed his company command structures and ordered all officers on leave to report to their units. He attempted to promote officers, however, promotion among North Carolina troops was hampered by a State regulation requiring units to retain all officers on their muster rolls, regardless of whether or not the man was healthy enough to perform his duties. This regulation prevented Maj. William Sillers from advancement, even though he had been leading the regiment for months. The Thirtieth's second-in-command, Lt. Col. James Kell continued to be absent, as his badly damaged hip prevented him from walking or riding, but since he still remained on the rolls, Maj. Sillers could not be promoted. This was also the case among the line officers; several captains' absences meant lieutenants commanded, but these junior officers could not be promoted to the rank, commensurate with their responsibilities. And finally, because William Sillers could not be promoted, the senior captain, James Holmes, who had been Sillers' second-in-command since the day after Sharpsburg, also was prevented from advancement. However, Col. Parker was able to promote one officer—Kearny Arrington (Co. I). Parker recorded, "Kearny [W.] Arrington ... was elected a Lieut. in [Co. I]. He seems to be a very clever young man. [Arrington] is rather shy."[126]

By the last week in April 1863, Col. Parker's Thirtieth North Carolina had regained the fighting edge it had possessed a year earlier. Frank Parker now commanded a regiment led by experienced officers and battle-tested NCOs. He now had nearly five hundred riflemen; a mix of veterans and new recruits, who he felt were now adequately trained, effectively equipped, and their morale restored enough to make them a dependable fighting force. Colonel Parker believed the Thirtieth was ready for the coming campaigns.

Dodson Ramseur moved the brigade to the picket line on April 23, 1862. His Tar Heels moved crisply from camp, conforming to General Stonewall Jackson's new marching regulations. General Jackson required that "The troops were to rest ten minutes of every hour and unless specifically ordered, were not to cover more than one mile in twenty-five minutes. When they halted they must not break ranks till they stacked their arms."[127] They reached the area near Hamilton's Crossing, bivouacked, and soon were given picket duty along the Rappahannock River. Since the weather was seasonally pleasant, the men enjoyed being away from the smells and congestion of their winter camp. The Carolinians' past efforts to survive the winter had destroyed the area around Guinea Station. General Ramseur, who had been away from the brigade nearly all winter, described their winter quarters' locality, writing, "Broad forest had disappeared before soldiers' axes; earthworks and rifle pits scarred untended fields; horses trampled once-lovely grounds of mansions."[128]

Fortunately, along the Rappahannock, the Confederates found themselves amongst an area in much better condition. Lieutenant William Ardrey (Co. K) wrote, "On picket below Fredericksburg on the Rappahannock.... The scenery around is grand and magnificent ... enjoyed ourselves fishing on the river."[129] The Tar Heels also discovered a peaceful military arrangement: the Yankees on the other side of the Rappahannock were content to trade coffee for tobacco, and showed no signs of aggression. Colonel Frank Parker, while inspecting the picket positions remarked, "[The Federals] picket on one side of the river, and we on the other. Until recently, the pickets on both sides were allowed to talk to each other."[130]

Of course this ideal situation did not continue. Brigadier Gen. Robert Rodes, the temporary division command in place of the absent Maj. Gen. Daniel Hill, issued orders preventing the intercourse between pickets. The displeased Confederates pondered this command only briefly; soon rumors swept the Southern positions that Union forces were crossing the Rappahannock River, north of Fredericksburg. On April 29, 1863, Gen. Rodes ordered Ramseur to move his four regiments in response to a Yank threat near Massaponax Creek, about ten miles south of Fredericksburg. Here, the creek joined with the Rappahannock River and shallow waters enabled easy crossing. Robert Rodes wrote, "[I] ordered [Ramseur] with the whole of his brigade, to occupy the south side of the creek, guarding the ford near its mouth."[131]

The Thirtieth moved into position, Col. Parker laying out company placements, reserve locations, and picket postings. Union troops moved about on the eastern side of the Rappahannock, and within an hour, Federal batteries appeared, unlimbered, and began to bombard the Tar Heels. Dodson Ramseur recorded, "The brigade was placed below Massaponax Creek to dispute the enemy's crossing ... annoyed by their artillery." He added, "The brigade was shelled, with no one being able to expose himself without being fired at and a few men were lost."[132] General Ramseur ordered his sharpshooter corps forward and they began dueling with Union marksmen occupying the opposite riverbank. Ramseur noted, "The sharpshooters were placed in rifle pits along the river bank and a brisk fire was exchanged with the enemy's sharpshooters."[133]

Darkness halted the desultory artillery and sniper fire and Col. Parker's men rested, though few slept. A Carolinian wrote, "The small portion of the night allowed for rest was passed sleeping in the bushes on wet blankets."[134] Lieutenant William Ardrey (Co. K) scribbled in his journal, "[We] lay in line of battle all day in our entrenchments, considerable shelling all day from the enemy and our batteries did not reply much."[135] Everyone, veterans and new recruits alike, knew winter's peace and inactivity had ended—war had returned.

CHAPTER 7

Chancellorsville—Fighting for Stonewall Jackson

Colonel Frank Parker's regiment awoke on April 30, 1862, to a cool and misty morning. General Ramseur sent word the brigade would be marching, and Parker quickly notified his company commanders. The men prepared their gear and waited for the command to move, but the word did not come. Instead, as Lt. William Ardrey (Co. K) recorded, "[We] lay in line of battle all day in our entrenchments, [with] considerable shelling all day from the enemy." He also grumbled, "our batteries did not reply much."[1] Then, in late afternoon, Gen. Ramseur notified his regimental commanders he wanted the brigade to slip away from their position; it was important the Yanks did not know they were leaving. A Tar Heel remarked, "the brigade marched toward Fredericksburg, attempting to keep out of sight." He noted, they were, "spotted twice and shelled."[2] The Thirtieth arrived at its familiar position, on the heights near Hamilton's Crossing, and set up camp not long after the sun had set.

30th North Carolina Infantry[3]
May 1, 1863

Unit		Strength
Field & Staff	Col. Parker, Francis M. Maj. Sillers, William Cpt. Holmes, James C.	5
Co. A	1st Lt. Williams, Gary 3rd Lt. White, Lassiter M.	46
Co. B	Cpt. Davis Weldon E. 1st Lt. Nicholson, John	44
Co. C	Cpt. Allen, David C. 1st Lt. Bennett, Solomon	42
Co. D	1st Lt. Allen, Charles N. 2nd Lt. Abernathy, Sidney	49
Co. E	Cpt. McMillan, John C. 1st Lt. Johnson, Ira	50
Co. F	Cpt. Moore, Willis B. 1st Lt. Harrell, George K.	49
Co. G	1st Lt. Badgett, James W. 1st Sgt. O'Brien, Alfred	52

83

Unit		Strength
Co. H	Cpt. Wicker, Jesse J.	
	1st Lt. McNeil, Henry J.	50
Co. I	Cpt. Harris, James J.	
	1st Lt. Williford, Burton B.	74
Co. K	Cpt. Witherspoon, John G.	
	1st Lt. Ardrey, William E.	42
		503

The Thirtieth's riflemen buzzed with energy. They had heard the news Union troops were massing south of the Rappahannock River, west of Fredericksburg; the next day orders would come to move against these invaders. Colonel Parker commanded just over five hundred men, fit for duty. He had nearly all his officers back, though Lt. Col. James Kell was still absent. His riflemen were as rested as could be expected, and they all had faith Robert E. Lee would lead them to victory. The Carolinians arose on May 1, 1863, and formed into a marching column, and as one soldier wrote, "With Ramseur's Brigade in the van, Rodes' troops went off in the highest spirits."[4]

The Confederates moved quickly, heading west on the Orange Plank Road, covering nearly seven miles in less than four hours. The Southerners began hearing the thumping of artillery during the last hour of their trek, and as one Tar Heel remarked, "The men sensed a fight, and prenatal adrenaline put spring into their steps."[5]

The column was halted not far from the Tabernacle Church a little after 11:00 a.m.[6] Here, beneath a clear sky, the riflemen at the front of the long line of Southerners watched a knot of senior Confederate officers discussing their tactics. Lieutenant William Ardrey wiped the sweat from his forehead and glanced about. He noted in his journal, "The sun was warm and oppressive, the country ... poor and ... covered with dense forest."[7]

Brigadier General Robert Rodes, still in temporary command of Daniel Hill's division, met with Lt. Gen. Thomas "Stonewall" Jackson, who urgently ordered an aggressive assault.[8] Jackson informed Rodes that Brig. Gen. Carnot Posey's four regiments of Mississippians had made contact with blue-coated skirmishers a mile west of the church, and he needed reinforcements. Stonewall Jackson told Rodes to turn his first brigade over to Posey's boss, Maj. Gen. Richard Anderson. Robert Rodes called for Dodson Ramseur and gave him orders to go and support Posey. General Rodes recorded, "the column was halted by Gen. Jackson, and Gen. Ramseur's brigade detached."[9] Dodson Ramseur's Tar Heel riflemen shouldered their weapons and marched away from the division. One Carolinian in the 2nd NC studied Stonewall Jackson as his regiment moved past and recalled, "[He] seemed to be anxious to cast his eyes at every soldier ... as if to say, 'There is heavy work ahead.'"[10]

Brigadier General Dodson Ramseur hustled his regiments westward along the Orange Plank Road for the next hour before making contact with the Mississippians. General Anderson told Ramseur to slide to Posey's left, send out a regiment as skirmishers, keep abreast with Posey, and move forward. Ramseur assigned his regimental commanders their responsibilities: the 30th to be the brigade's right with the task of remaining in contact with Posey's brigade; the 14th NC in the center; and the 2nd NC on the left flank. Colonel Bryan Grimes (4th NC) recorded, "My regiment and a Mississippi command were detailed for the purpose of feeling the enemy, and were deployed to drive them."[11] Once his brigade was in position, Dodson Ramseur called for his brigade sharpshooters to move forward and reinforce Grimes' 4th NC. Major Daniel Hurtt (2nd NC), commanding the brigade's special unit, formed his selected men in front of the Carolina regiments.[12] Then, Ramseur advanced with the sharpshooters. A Confederate wrote, "Brig. Gen. Ramseur handled his own skirmishers, and with great skill and gallantry."[13] With these preparations complete, the two Confederate brigades moved towards the Yank skirmish line. It was now about 3:00 p.m.[14]

The fighting between skirmish lines proved brisk, however, the Yanks seemed disinclined to hold their ground. Bryan Grimes' Tar Heels, Posey's 12th MS, and Ramseur's brigade sharpshooters continually pressed forward, shoving the Northerners backwards. Private John Bone (Co. I) wrote, "There was a call for a corp of sharpshooters to meet the enemy. I was one, and we met them near the cedar road [and fought] through the day."[15] The tactics were simple: the Confederates pushed against the Yanks, face-to-face, and whenever the Federals got stubborn, artillery would be brought up to, as one Southerner recorded, "feel the woods," and then Ramseur sent parties to flank the Northern right.[16] The plan worked. A Federal officer grumbled, "Anderson gave [Brig. Gen. Thomas Rugar; XII Corps, 1st Div.] a lively fight and succeeded in getting in on his flanks."[17] Eventually, the blue-coats could resist no longer, and they scampered away. A Confederate recalled, "the enemy was encountered and driven back in great disorder by Ramseur's brigade, with General Posey on its right."[18]

The Confederates shoved the Federals backward nearly two miles, causing Pvt. John Bone (Co. I) to recall, "We ... advanced on the enemy driving them back and fighting until dark."[19] Then, as night's darkness hampered the fighting, the Southerners encountered newly built fortifications packed with fresh Yankees. One of these Federals reported, "As the enemy were gaining the advantage [we] fell back behind Hancock, who came to the front and took [our] place."[20] Northern artillery studded the emplacements, and these guns opened upon the gray-coats. General Dodson Ramseur, still dangerously out front with his brigade skirmishers, wrote, "About 6 p.m. we found the foe in force upon our front, and supported by batteries that poured grape unsparingly into the woods through which we were advancing."[21] Rifleman John Bone (Co. I) scribbled, "The fighting nearly ceased, only the sharpshooters keeping up a fire at times through the night."[22]

Colonel Parker's companies, the men having remained safely in the second line all afternoon, were ordered to protect themselves, but remain vigilant in case of a sudden attack. Stray bullets and an occasional artillery shell crashed through the trees above their heads. One Carolinian officer recorded, "I ... ordered [the men] to 'lie down' as we were [sheltered]."[23] Frank Parker relieved his regiment's sharpshooters, replacing the soldiers who had been in combat all afternoon with a fresh contingent. One of these tired skirmishers, Pvt. John Bone recorded, "We ... marched back to the rear ... through a thick wilderness of undergrowth, over brushes, logs, branches, and everything else."[24] The Tar Heels, once freed of the thought of further dangers, scrambled about, harvesting the bounty of having driven the well-supplied Federals from the battlefield. General Ramseur remarked, "as ... the enemy ... fell back in confusion before our sharpshooters for several miles, [they] strew[ed] the way with their arms and baggage."[25] Another Southerner added, "The Federals ... litter[ed] their [retreat] with knapsacks, canteens, haversacks, guns and accouterments."[26]

The battlefield grew quiet, silenced by night's full darkness. The Confederates were now within a mile of the Chancellor House, with its outbuildings setting just 1,500 yards north of their position.[27] The two armies' movements diminished and the exhausted men attempted sleep. However, newly arriving Northern troops labored in the dark, constructing fortifications. Meanwhile, both sides' pickets remained on post, struggling to stay awake. One wrote, "[We] were so near the Union lines that orders were given in the lowest tones ... the brigade employed the sign and countersign—'Liberty' was the challenge, and 'Independence,' the response." He continued, "Up the road a few hundred yards the axes of Union pioneers rang as they labored to strengthen Hooker's position."[28] Private Bone wrote, "We laid down in line of battle ... and slumbered on our muskets ... for we were exhausted and could rest almost anywhere."[29] Another added, "we slept on our arms, with a strong picket line on the outposts."[30]

On May 2, 1863, staff officers from Brig. Gen. Alfred Iverson's brigade awoke Dodson Ramseur hours before dawn and gave him instructions; he was to pull his brigade back. The Tar Heels were quietly awakened and by 5:30 a.m., filed away from their nighttime battle line, passing Iverson's men who were tasked to resume the defense. Brigadier General Ramseur's riflemen returned to their division. General Rodes recorded, "At an early hour.... Iverson's brigade was ordered to relieve Ramseur's, still on duty with Anderson in front."[31] When Ramseur's four regiments reached the Orange Plank Road the men were surprised to find the entire division forming up to march. The Tar Heels shifted into formation, once again at the head of the column, ready for Stonewall Jackson's aggressive commands. When word flashed down the column, the riflemen shouldered their rifles, strangely though, as Pvt. John Bone (Co. I) recalled, "we were expecting to be ordered forward, but to our surprise we were ordered to the rear."[32]

The column moved at about 8:00 a.m., crossing the Plank road, heading toward the Furnace road, and then turning south for Welford. The morning was cool, the roads moist. A foot-sore soldier observed, "Fortunately, the dirt roads were just wet enough to be easy on the feet and free from dust."[33] The Confederates marched quickly, guides directing the Tar Heels in what was becoming a quickly moving pace. A Carolinian in the 14th NC wrote, "The men marched much of the way in silence." He added, "The heavy woodland through which the route lay concealed our development."[34] Noon came and General Jackson ordered a halt, the men stacked arms and fixed a meal, many of Col. Parker's men feasting on spoils taken from captured haversacks. Then, sixty minutes later, the command came to resume the hike. They marched for another hour, took a short break, before receiving word to increase their speed. The Confederates hustled for two more hours, until, around 4:00 p.m., their column came in contact with other gray-clad units arrayed in a battle line.[35] Dodson Ramseur summed up their trek, recording, "[The division] marched by a circuitous route to the rear of the enemy."[36]

General Ramseur was ordered to shift his brigade into a support position, and to do this quickly. One of his men wrote, "As rapidly now as men could cover the mile and a half between the Plank Road and the old turnpike, Rodes' Brigades tramped northward ... and when they reached the turnpike, they headed eastward." He continued, "Unopposed, unobserved even, Rodes led them almost a mile to a long, low ridge."[37] Dodson Ramseur moved his four regiments into position facing southeast; his brigade part of a reserve line, slotted to support Brig. Gen. Alfred Colquitt's Georgians. Ramseur's formation occupied the far right flank of the Confederate second line, with Col. Parker's 30th NC astraddle the Germanna road; the 14th NC rested on the 30th's left, then the 2nd NC, and finally the 4th NC—all part of Stonewall Jackson's massive flanking maneuver.

The Confederates advanced at 5:15 p.m., and gunfire immediately punctuated the afternoon quiet.[38] Jackson's first line smashed into the unsuspecting men of Maj. Gen.

Oliver Howard's XI Corps. The Federal divisions were all facing south, unaware the Southerners had massed ten brigades directly west of their unsupported right flank. General Oliver Howard admitted, "the woods were so dense that [the Confederates] were able to mass a large force ... and outflanking my right."[39] The Yank right flank collapsed within minutes of the assault, and the blue coats fled from their positions. Major General Howard recorded, "the enemy ... enveloped my right, and the First Division ... gave up." He continued, "the whole front on the north of the Plank road gave way ... there was a blind panic and great confusion."[40]

Colonel Parker's Thirtieth patiently remained in position with its brother regiments, trailing behind Colquitt's men, just a hundred yards in its rear. There was little Parker's men could see, as the vegetation was so dense. One soldier noted, "[We were] amid the underbrush and in the woods where one could not see the length of a regiment."[41] For Frank Parker's Tar Heels, this battle was little more than a noisy ramble through thick foliage. General Ramseur wrote, "Brisk firing was ... heard upon our front and left."[42]

Then, unexpectedly, Ramseur's four regiments crashed into the rear of Iverson's brigade. Dodson Ramseur ordered his command to halt, and immediately Col. Parker told his men to lie down. Frank Parker hurried to his boss's side, and found him in a heated discussion with Alfred Iverson. The Georgia officer had halted his brigade and maneuvered it to face south rather than east so that it no longer aligned with the direction of Jackson's attack. This flank movement blocked the Tar Heels, and dropped both of the Confederate battle lines' right flanks out of alignment with the rest of Jackson's line. Parker watched silently as the two generals argued. Ramseur later would write, "[Iverson] told me ... by an officer of his staff that the enemy was attempting to turn his right." Ramseur replied there was nothing on their right, but Iverson would not agree. Finally, Dodson Ramseur acceded to Iverson's demands. He returned to his Tar Heels, and "immediately moved by the right flank, but heard no firing in this quarter." The Thirtieth pushed through the dense underbrush but could not find the threat that terrified Iverson. Ramseur stopped his brigade's movement and informed Iverson of this fact, but the Georgian refused to move his men. The North Carolina general continued his report, "Again [Iverson] sent his staff officer to inform me that the enemy was passing by his right flank.... I [told him] I would take care of his right flank."[43] With this, Iverson reluctantly refaced three of his regiments in compliance with Jackson's assault, leaving one to guard his right.

Colonel Frank Parker's Tar Heels remained the brigade's right flank, only now they were facing south, making his riflemen probably the farthest unit away from danger on the entire battle front. The Thirtieth moved southwards, the men struggling through the thick underbrush. One Tar Heel, instinctively knowing he was not in peril, wrote, "I recall one thing in that advance through tangled vines ... undergrowth, [and] shadowed by great trees: a turkey-gobbler ... arose in distracted flight and escaped without hue or cry in his pursuit."[44] General Ramseur led his four regiments southward nearly a thousand yards before halting the brigade. Ramseur wrote, "I then pressed on by the right flank ... and prosecuted the search for half a mile ... but not a solitary Yankee was to be seen." The Carolinian officer turned his brigade eastward and, "came up to the division line, and moved by the left flank to the support of Gen. Colquitt."[45]

By now the XI Corps had been driven back to the vicinity of the Chancellor house, where additional Northern brigades reinforced the shattered blue coat units. These forces, along with a backbone of artillery welded together a fighting force capable of slowing Jackson's tiring soldiers. Then, darkness descended over the battlefield, ending meaningful maneuvers, but not before some Confederates blundered through the thick underbrush and were ambushed by vigilant Federal units. General Rodes reported, "Pushing forward as rapidly as possible, the troops ... bec[ame] entangled in an abatis near the enemy's first line of fortifications." He continued, [This] caused the line to halt, and such was the confusion and darkness that it was not deemed advisable to make a farther advance."[46] Following this, the two sides hunkered down for the night, a reprieve in the fighting that benefitted the Yanks. A Carolinian grumbled, "Night proved the best ally of the enemy. Under cover of darkness he pushed fresh soldiers into positions and made new alignments of his forces."[47] The Union troops now had time to fortify. A Tar Heel noted, "the enemy [was] ... not idle. They felled trees in the woods, ... and built breastworks of logs."[48] One of these blue-coats wrote, "As soon as we were ... [on] the new line we commenced to cut the timber in our front to make a barricade ... trees as far as fifty feet or more were cut to fall parallel to our front. This formed an abatis." He continued, "By three in the morning we had a strong protection."[49]

The Confederates' mad rush against the Northerners, and the total rout that followed, left Jackson's formations tangled about in a confused jumble. The thick foliage, along with the night's blindness, prevented Jackson from determining where his brigades were positioned. He sent out staff officers to identify commands and ascertain fields of fire, but they achieved little coherency; the Confederate alignment was a mess. General Jackson, frustrated by his staff's inability to provide him with accurate information, personally set out to determine his formation's distribution.

Meanwhile, in the reserve battle line, Gen. Ramseur consolidated his brigade, shifting his regiments to construct a stronger position. Once the Tar Heels were in place, Ramseur turned the detailed work over to his regimental commanders, tasking them with making sure they were interlocked in a self-supporting defensive posture. On the brigade's far right flank, Col. Frank Parker, along with Maj. William Sillers and Cpt. James Holmes (Co. A), made sure all ten companies were intact. He sent out a layer of night guards, and ordered his battle line troops to stand down. Parker's regiment now rested within a thick grove of trees and undergrowth, about five hundred yards south of the Orange Plank road. His pickets heard a sudden outburst of musketry, which quickly died away. This flare-up woke some of the weary Carolinians but they soon relaxed, figuring it was frightened soldiers shooting at shadows; little did they know what had actually occurred.

Colonel Bryan Grimes (4th NC), whose regiment held the brigade's left flank, was out with his pickets when the firing erupted. He soon heard a disturbance and went exploring. Grimes recorded, "I met a party bearing a litter off the field, and enquired who it was. Someone said 'Lieutenant Sumter.'" The Fourteenth's colonel continued, "upon going a step or two further I encountered Gen. Rodes, who informed me that the wounded officer was none other than Gen. Jackson, but he thought it advisable that it should be concealed from the troops for fear of disheartening them."[50] Though this attempt to hide the truth was made but there was no way to conceal what had happened to the Confederate Second Corps commander; word quickly spread of his shooting. Private John Bone (Co. I) recalled, "Jackson was investigating the front [and] as he returned, he and his staff were mistaken for the enemy and fired upon by our own men." John Bone continued, "We were about two hundred yards [away]."[51] And Lt. William Ardrey (Co. K) also noted in his journal, "Gen. Stonewall Jackson was wounded in the arm by our own skirmishers in the night."[52] Ultimately it would be discovered pickets from the 18th North Carolina shot Jackson.

Brisk fighting resumed on May 3, 1863, at about 5:30 a.m., when riflemen from Brig. Gen. Joseph Archer's brigade moved forward. This advance was not planned, but occurred because exhausted officers misinterpreted orders. A lieutenant in the 7th TN wrote, "We reached our position just before day break.... So tired and exhausted were the men that a moment after being halted many ... were asleep. Just after dawn the brigade on our left began to move slightly to correct its alignment." He continued, "The officer on the extreme left of the Seventh, mistaking this for an advance, gave the order, 'Forward: the brigade on the left is advancing.' This order was immediately passed up the line and the Tennessee Brigade, by this mistake, moved forward at once."[53] This unplanned advance caught the Federals completely by surprise. A Northern commander on the heights above the Tennessee brigade's position wrote, "About 5:30 a.m. our pickets were driven in, and the enemy ... vigorously attacked our lines. In a few minutes the battle raged with great fury."[54] This fight did not last long, before as one senior Confederate officer noted, "Archer took four guns and 100 men ... [and] Hazel Grove."[55]

Major General J.E.B. Stuart, now in command of Jackson's corps, was quick to take advantage of this lucky break at Hazel Grove, and he ordered several more brigades to advance and push the startled Yanks before they could recover. He immediately saw Hazel Grove's benefits and called for Confederate artillery. Within an hour there were thirty Southern guns unlimbering on these heights, and they opened fire upon the bluecoats' positions. Thus, by the time Stuart's brigades commenced their attack, his infantry was supported by a massive artillery fist. The assault began just after 7:00 a.m. One rifleman wrote, "The attack was preceded by a hellish rain of shot and shell."[56]

Colonel Frank Parker and the Thirtieth waited in their reserve position, listening to the thunder of artillery and rattle of musketry. His riflemen were ready to enter the battle, though content to allow others to do the fighting. Fragments of news reached the Tar Heels; all good—the Yankees were being driven back. However, even though the Northerners were being shoved from their positions, back-up, blue-coated units rushed into the battle. Their counterattacks stalled the Confederate's progress. Stuart then called for his reserve brigades, including Ramseur's, sending word to advance a little after 9:00 a.m. Brigadier General Dodson Ramseur ordered his Carolinians to move forward; the 4th NC on his brigade-left, the 30th NC covering the right flank, and the 2nd NC and 14th NC occupying the two center positions, a total of fifteen hundred men.[57] The Tar Heels advanced proudly, because as one bragged, "The charge of the brigade upon the last stronghold of the enemy was made in view of Maj. Gen. J.E.B. Stuart."[58]

At first, the Tar Heels' only opposition was the vegetation. One Carolinian remarked, "[We moved] forward steadily, with no material stoppage except that occasioned by the tangled undergrowth."[59] The four regiments pushed ahead, moving slowly and steadily, each regiment maintaining contact with its brother units. They advanced four hundred yards before reaching a location in which Brig Gen. Ramseur could view the rising clouds of smoke ascending from the fight up ahead. He halted the brigade when he saw riders approach. Dodson Ramseur recorded, "After proceeding about one-fourth of a mile, I was applied to by Maj. Pegram for a support to his battery." He continued, "I detached Col. Parker, 30th NC for this purpose."[60]

Colonel Frank Parker led the Thirtieth away from the brigade, trailing behind the artillery staff officers. The regiment followed a trail through the woods that wound to the top of the heights called Hazel Grove, and emerged onto a ridge overlooking a broad field spreading out to the north. Confederate artillery studded the high ground, several batteries of Napoleons, and Parrot Rifles. Guides motioned Parker to place his riflemen out in front of the guns, part way down a sloping field. The Tar Heels filed past the sweating gunners and took their posting, ready to drive off any Yank infantry with the notion of trying to capture the Southern cannons. Private John Bone (Co. I) wrote, "Colonel Parker ordered his regiment to lie down, which we did."[61] The artillery resumed its shelling of Federal positions hidden in the woods, sending their rounds into a stand of woods a thousand yards away. Parker's men rested, watching the explosions shatter the distant trees, a scene they found quite interesting.

Meanwhile, Brig. Gen. Dodson Ramseur and his three regiments worked their way eastward, three-quarters of a mile north of Hazel Grove, moving forward with instructions to press the attack. They passed over the battlefield of the morning's conflicts, the Tar Heels ignoring the casualties as they scavenged among the Federal gear left behind in abandoned entrenchments. Ramseur's men came up behind a mass of Confederates huddling behind a line of captured breastworks. Brigadier General Robert Rodes recorded Ramseur's movements, writing, "Ramseur ... pushed forward on the right, passed the first line of entrenchments, which had already been carried, [and encountered] the first and second lines of our troops."[62] But now, there were so many soldiers bunched together, Ramseur's riflemen were forced to halt.

General Ramseur sought out the officers of the men hiding in the trenches and discovered their commander had been killed, and no one knew who was in charge. The weary, smoke-smudged riflemen told tales of fierce fighting and heavy casualties. One of these soldiers later recorded, his regiment, "went into the fight with 350 muskets, and in less than ten minutes had 160 men killed and wounded."[63] When Ramseur reminded the unnerved officers they were supposed to attack his words were met with disagreement and hostility. An officer in the 4th NC, who overheard his brigade commander's exchange with these rattled officers, noted, "Ramseur's brigade was formed in the rear of [Jones'] brigade that held a line of breastworks which we had captured.... This brigade was ordered to advance and charge the enemy in front, but they failed to comply with the order."[64] Another officer added, "In a few minute, Ramseur's line was moving into the crowded works. Sternly he ordered the troops who were crouching there to advance.... Not a man moved.... Again Ramseur gave the order; again the men in the earthwork ignored it."[65]

Seeing these troops were useless, Dodson Ramseur hurried back to Maj. Gen. J.E.B. Stuart and secured permission to pass over the frightened men and continue the attack. Stuart immediately agreed. Dodson Ramseur wrote, "I ... hurried back to [my] waiting line, which was disgusted with the behavior of the men in front. Loudly, ... commanded, 'Forward, march!' Without hesitation, the North Carolinians broke through the mob."[66] Colonel Bryan Grimes (4th NC) added, "Our men were entirely disgusted at their cowardly conduct, and I, myself, put my foot on the back and head of an officer of high rank in mounting the work, and ... ground his face in the earth."[67] Dodson Ramseur bragged, "At the command 'Forward' my brigade, with a shout, cleared the breastworks, and charged the enemy."[68] His three Tar Heel regiments, the 4th NC on the left, the 2nd NC in the center, and the 14th NC on the right, stomped their way forward and brushed back a line of blue-coated skirmishers. One Southerner scribbled, "Pushing through jungle-like foliage ... [we] wrestled the position from the Federals and found [our]-selves on the edge of a marshy area."[69] Another officer remarked, "Into the heavy timber, over breastworks occupied by disordered and broken troops of different commands, we went forward." He continued, "it reminded me of an advance through a wide gate-way along an avenue peopled with every agency of death and destruction."[70]

Ramseur's Tar Heels collided with Yanks holding a line of breastworks. Lieutenant William Ardrey (Co. K) recorded, "[the brigade] charged over the [stalled] brigade and drove the enemy from its breastworks and repulsed them with heavy slaughter."[71] Another Carolinian added, "We ... made a dash for the second line of breastworks, which we carried."[72] An officer in one of these retreating Northern units wrote, "we lost the field, and had to leave the noble fallen to the tender mercies of the enemy."[73] However, as the defeated blue coats fell back they were replaced by new formations, fresh and un-bloodied troops ready to fight. Now, both sides slugged away, firing as quickly as the riflemen could load their muskets, and as one Southerner proclaimed, "The struggle at this point was long and obstinate."[74] The Tar Heels pushed forward, but now much slower, and at a horrible cost. A soldier in the 14th NC described this fight, "Shot and shell, buck and ball rained upon us." He continued, "exploding missiles broke off the overhead limbs of trees and discharged them in great loads upon those who in search of cover crouched at their roots."[75]

Another Federal force crashed its way through the thick vegetation and began to threaten Ramseur's right flank. The Tar Heels in the 4th NC could not see this new danger and continued to shove forward, supported on the right by most of the 2nd NC. Dodson Ramseur wrote of their movements, "The 4th NC and seven companies of the 2nd NC drove the enemy before them until they had taken the last line of his works." But the situation on the right began to deteriorate; Ramseur recorded this: "The 14th NC and three companies of the 2nd NC were compelled to halt some 150 to 200 yards in rear of the [4th and 2nd NC], for the reason that ... the enemy was in heavy force on my right flank. Had Col. Bennett advanced, the enemy could easily have turned my right."[76] More Union troops stormed into the attack, striking the 4th NC and 2nd NC head-on, and pressuring the brigade's right, firing upon the 2nd NC's detached companies, and the 14th NC. An officer in the 7th NJ, one of these Union formations hitting the Tar Heels on their

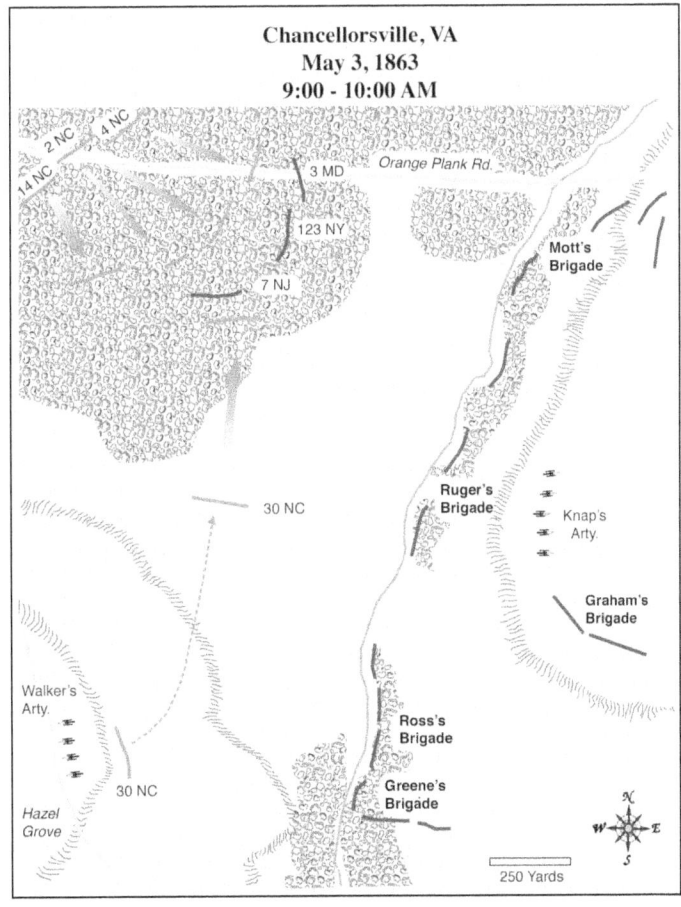

right, recorded, "my regiment advanced into the woods … and … maintain[ed] a flanking position."[77] Federal lead ravaged the Tar Heels, killing dozens and wounding scores more. An officer in the 14th NC recalled, "I remember [a rifleman] … coming in from the lines with his arm shattered by a ball and blood spurting from his wound.… I tied a gallows-string around his arm and he walked to the surgeon's knife with unruffled patience."[78] Ramseur summed up his brigade's struggle, writing, "my line was subjected to a horrible enfilade fire, by which I lost severely."[79]

The 4th NC and its contingent of 2nd NC could go no farther, as Yank units pressed against them, forcing the desperate Confederates to fight from behind any form of shelter they could find. Some of them were fortunate enough to get into a hastily constructed gun emplacement. One of these riflemen wrote, "The breastworks were not high enough to stand behind. We had to get down on our knees and then hold our heads down to keep the bullets from hitting them."[80] The New Jersey troops closed upon the 14th NC, firing as they approached. Dodson Ramseur went down, struck by a piece of shrapnel. A Tar Heel noted, "he was wounded in the [shin] by a shell."[81] When Ramseur's aides came to him, ready to remove the general from the battle, he refused. Major General J.E.B. Stuart recorded, "though painfully wounded, [Ramseur] persisted in retaining command."[82]

Regardless of Dodson Ramseur's inspiration, his Tar Heels staggered backward, driven by the relentless Union counterattack. His left flank troops, the 4th NC and most of the 2nd NC began a slow and controlled withdrawal. Dodson Ramseur recorded, "The enemy … pushed a brigade to the right and rear of Col. Grimes [4th NC], and seven companies of Col. Cox [2nd NC], with the intention of capturing their commands.… The move necessitated a retrograde movement on the part of Colonels Grimes and Cox, which was executed … with the loss of some prisoners who did not hear the command to retire."[83] Unfortunately, on the right, the situation quickly became catastrophic. An officer in the 2nd NC acknowledged, "the enfilading fire was most disastrous. The regiment … lost three-fourths of those present within about fifteen minutes."[84] Ramseur, hobbling badly on his injured leg, was worried about the severe casualties. One of his officers recorded, "His thinned ranks left Dodson Ramseur distraught. 'Is this all that is left of the Second?' he asked. 'This is all,' came the reply."[85]

The 7th NJ pressed forward, closing on the 14th NC and 2nd NC companies. The 14th NC's dead and wounded piled up quickly, and the regiment collapsed. One frightened rifleman admitted, "it was every man for himself."[86] As the 14th NC's battle line dissolved and its soldiers fled, this exposed the three, 2nd NC companies. The 7th NJ swarmed over this small group of Carolinians. A Confederate officer described the ensuing melee: "In the Second NC the color bearer was killed; the corporal who next took the colors was also killed, and all the color-guard (four corporals) present were wounded." He added, "The regiment was forced back by the enemy, and most of the officers and men near the colors were captured or disabled."[87] The commander of the 7th NJ, Col. Louis Francine, boasted, "my regiment … closed upon the Second North Carolina … charged, and captured their colors and themselves almost wholly."[88] Within minutes, nearly four dozen, 2nd NC troops were pinned down and captured. Ramseur's aggressive assault was moments away from turning into a complete disaster.

Meanwhile, Col. Frank Parker and his riflemen were spread out in front of Maj. William Pegram's guns as the artillerymen pounded the distant tree line. No Federal infantry had appeared, though Yank artillery had begun to fire at the Confederate guns and some of their shells fell among Parker's men. Private John Bone (Co. I) recalled, "a man who was lying very near to me, and all at once a cannon ball or shell struck his head and knocked it from his body."[89] Colonel Parker could heard the roar of musketry in the woods off to their left, and he surmised their brigade was fighting there. Frank Parker was desperate to end this baby-sitting responsibility and go to the support of his Tar Heel brothers. One Southerner wrote, "Parker was not about to sit this fight out."[90] He met with Maj. Pegram and they rapidly discussed the evolving situation—Pegram's guns were not in danger—but it was quite possible Ramseur needed help. William Pegram agreed, it was time for Parker to go. Frank Parker noted, "[We] remain[ed] in support of Pegram until that officer thought the danger had passed."[91]

Private John Bone wrote, "Colonel Parker ... ordered us to arise and go forward."[92] The Tar Heels stood up and formed into line of battle, a force of nearly four hundred riflemen, led by another hundred NCOs and officers. Parker had Maj. William Sillers in command of the right wing, composed of Companies A, B, F, H, and K, while Cpt. James Holmes led the other five formations in the left wing. In all, as the Thirtieth's riflemen stood shoulder-to-shoulder in a two-rank battle line, with file closers to the rear, the regiment formed a long front, just over 125 yards in width.[93] Frank Parker led the way; the regiment had to cross nearly a thousand yards of open ground before reaching the tangle of woods where heavy musketry told of a fierce infantry fight. Parker wrote, "the Thirtieth ... moved in the direction of heavy firing."[94]

A thousand yards' distance would take the Carolinians ten minutes, a long time to march in battle formation across an open field. Union gunners on the heights near the Fairview cemetery, just southwest of the Chancellor house observed this lone unit and trained their guns upon the unprotected regiment. The Yank artillery was firing at a distance of nearly 1,200 yards, and their target, though large, was also moving. Federal projectiles would take between three and five seconds to reach their destination.[95] This was not an easy-to-strike objective, but the gunners were well-trained and experienced. Their first shots were wide, but succeeding shells closed in on the Tar Heels.

An shrieking round exploded among Company I, killing Pvt. Jacob Odom, Pvt. John B. Griffin, and Pvt. George T. Winstead, as well as wounding several more. Moments later, another shell erupted near Company K, killing Cpl. Wilson L. Hartis and Pvt. Robert Barnett. This detonation also sent shrapnel ripping into Pvt. Benjamin C. Glover's hip, "destroying a large surface," and wounded two others.[96] The right wing staggered briefly, but grim-faced NCOs rallied the men, filled the gaps, and kept the line moving forward. By now they were half way to the safety of the trees, but also had shortened the distance for the artillerymen. The gunners adjusted their fuses, re-aimed their cannons, and blasted the resolute line of soldiers from North Carolina. A direct hit amongst Company B killed Pvt. Samuel D. Bishop, and the two Brack brothers, Baker B., and George W. This round also wounded, 1st Sgt. John G. Newsom in the right side, struck Pvt. George J. Duke in the arm and side, and mangled Pvt. Burwell B. Bobbitt's left hip.[97]

The Thirtieth's men gritted their teeth and hunched their shoulders, enduring this bombardment that killed and maimed. The shell-ravaged men gazed at the tree line, seeking its promise of safety, but knowing danger lurked hidden within that foliage. They had nowhere to go, except forward, moving from one type of lethal peril to another. Another shell impacted among Parker's ranks, spewing blood and Carolina flesh, this time in Company A. The regimental color sergeant, Hardy S. Royal was knocked to the earth, shrapnel and flame ripping into his thigh and knee. Other chunks of searing metal sliced into Cpl. James M. Crumpler's jaw, and shredded both of Pvt. Edward N Butler's thighs. And not far from these bleeding Tar Heels, Pvt. Ransom Naylor was killed, while Pvt. William J. Taylor was struck in the back and left shoulder.[98] Private John Bone (Co. I), who moved forward, shoulder-to-shoulder with his embattled brothers, simply wrote, "There was a battery in our front shelling us with all the force that it had."[99] Lieutenant William Ardrey (Co. K), marching with the file closers, and able to see the clumps of bloody men left behind each time a round struck somewhere among the riflemen, recorded in his journal, "They shelled us with grape, canister, and our men fell thick and fast."[100] Another projectile hit among the Carolinians, this time striking Company G. Private James M. Hobgood was severely mangled and his shattered body tossed to the ground. Private Richard D. Brooks, was hit, "by shell fragments resulting in a broken shoulder." And just feet away, Brooks' older brother, Henry, was also wounded.[101]

As Col. Frank Parker's determined Carolinians marched the last remaining yards across the open field, a couple more explosive shells spewed flame and scorching metal into more riflemen, leaving the Thirtieth's regimental surgeons with a full day's medical toil. Now though, the Thirtieth was free of the Union artillery's torment, but in no way were the men safe. Brigadier General Dodson Ramseur had rallied his embattled Tar Heels and they desperately held back a vigorous Northern assault. A Southerner wrote, "Ramseur's men clung doggedly to their foothold ... they could not hold much longer without support." This frantic defense had lasted a quarter of an hour and during this time the Tar Heel riflemen had used up most of their ammunition; the writer continued, "his men nearly out of ammunition. They held off their obstinate foe only by taking cartridges from the dead."[102]

Frank Parker's officers and NCOs patched together battle lines, moving riflemen to fill the holes caused by the artillery's carnage, and then Parker led his riflemen moved deeper into the woods, aiming straight for the heaviest sounds of battle. They crashed into a Yank formation, catching the blue coats completely by surprise. A Federal commander noted, "Ramseur's [regiment] ... managed to pass up the ravine ... and gain [our] right and rear."[103] Another wrote, "[Our] advance ... was checked by a charge made by the 30th North Carolina, as it came ... from Hazel Grove."[104]

Colonel Parker's Tar Heels surged through the underbrush, lashing into the Yank rear, cutting dozens down with close-range volleys. The blue coats could not respond; many just ran away. The rest fought back briefly and then threw down

Mitty "Jake" Witherspoon (Co. K), 18 years old, was mortally wounded on May 3, 1863 (Library of Congress).

their rifles. The fight was over in less than ten minutes, however, because it was at such close range, the Northerners who did fire their rifles downed Tar Heels, killing Pvt. Lewis T. Greer (Co. C) and Pvt. William T. Wallace (Co. E). First Sergeant Robert M. Crumpler (Co. A) was wounded, as Cpl. George W. Hundley (Co. B) and 2nd Lt. James E. Ferrell (Co. D). Private Ellis Johnson (Co. F) was struck in the head, Pvt. Henry H. Batchelor (Co. I) suffered a shattered right arm, and Pvt. Mitty T. Witherspoon's (Co. K) thigh was shattered.[105] Private John Bone (Co. I) recalled, "On getting near the works, the enemy left in great confusion.... We then turned our fire upon them and they fled."[106] Another rifleman remarked, "The [Yankees] immediately in our front were cut to pieces and swept off like a tidal wave sweeps the coast."[107] Colonel Parker added, "we drove [the Federals] from the field, capturing many prisoners, thus relieving our comrades."[108] A relieved Dodson Ramseur reported, "the 30th NC, approaching my position from the battery on the right, suddenly fell upon the flank and handsomely repulsed a heavy column of the enemy who were moving to get in my rear by my right flank, some 300 or 400 of them surrendering to him."[109] Ramseur's crisis melted away. The assuaged general recorded, "The charge of the [30th NC] ... made at a critical moment, when the enemy had broken and was hotly pressing the center of the line in our front with apparently overwhelming numbers, not only checked his advance, but threw him back in disorder, and pushed him with heavy loss."[110]

Frank Parker met up with Dodson Ramseur and the wounded general greeted the colonel with great emotion. One soldier observed, "Ramseur wept like a child."[111] Then, Ramseur regained his composure and demanded assessments from each of his regimental officers, and once he understood his brigade's battle readiness and strength, ordered an advance. Colonel Frank Parker wrote, "Proceeding about half a mile the regiment received the fire of the enemy from behind breastworks constructed of heavy timber, which we charged."[112] Again, Northern lead ripped through Carolina youths. Private William Pennington (Co. A) was wounded by a bullet glancing off his head, Jacob W. Shew (Co. C) was downed when a projectile ripped through his right leg, Pvt. Robert B. Pegram (Co. B) took a minié ball in his shoulder, and Pvt. John W. Wheeler (Co. D) was killed. Colonel Parker shouted at his men to persist, and they did, moving forward steadily. Frank Parker remarked, "I called my own color bearer ... it was not long before he too was shot down, and has since had a leg amputated. A second man took the flag, he too was struck down; but not killed; the third one bore it safely through the remainder of the day, but ... had a ball through the top of his hat."[113] Sadly, more were butchered by Federal lead: 1st Lt. Solomon W. Bennett (Co. C) suffered a shattered elbow, Pvt. Martin W. Wiggins' (Co. F) right arm was nearly ripped from his shoulder, and Pvt. Douglas C. Shaw's (Co. H) skull was fractured.[114] And 1st Lt. Burton B. Williford (Co. I) fell, a bullet smashing his thigh and slashing, "into the pubic region."[115]

The Federals abandoned their position. Colonel Risden Bennett (14th NC) was unhappy the blue coats did not stay and fight. Lieutenant William Ardrey (Co. K) wrote, "Col. Bennett ... leaped upon the breastworks and with his gigantic voice yelled out, "Go, you flop-eared puppies."[116] The yelling Tar Heels chased after the blue coats and suddenly found themselves out in an open field. Artillery immediately opened fire upon the Southerners, wounding and killing many. William Ardrey (Co. K) scribbled into his journal, "We charged the batteries at the Chancellorsville Hotel, that was strongly supported by their infantry."[117] The Confederates ceased their pursuit and scampered back to the last line of entrenchments they had captured. The trench was filled with bodies.

Private Archibald Jackson (Co. H) wrote, "we had to move the ded [*sic*.] back to have room up at the works."[118] Then, Frank Parker's Carolinians slouched down within the earthworks, gulping water from their canteens, and struggling to regain composure. Most everyone sagged down, weak with relief; their last sixty minutes under fire had shredded their ranks, it was now 10:00 a.m. Every soldier looked to his comrades and saw missing relatives and friends. Suddenly, they were exhausted. A Tar Heel noted, "When the exhilaration of the moment passed and the numbed men grasped the extent of their losses, many broke down."[119]

30th North Carolina Infantry[120]
Chancellorsville Casualties
May 3, 1863

Unit	Commander	Loss
Field & Staff	Col. Parker, Francis M. Maj. Sillers, William.	-
Co. A	1st Lt. Williams, Gary	15
Co. B	Cpt. Davis Weldon E.	15
Co. C	Cpt. Allen, David C.	9
Co. D	1st Lt. Allen, Charles N.	11
Co. E	Cpt. McMillan, John C.	7
Co. F	Cpt. Moore, Willis B.	8
Co. G	1st Lt. Badgett, James W.	12
Co. H	Cpt. Wicker, Jesse J.	5
Co. I	Cpt. Harris, James J.	20
Co. K	Cpt. Witherspoon, John G.	12
		115

Though the struggle to drive the Yanks from the area around Chancellorsville raged on, Dodson Ramseur and his four North Carolina regiments were fought out. He called for a casualty report and surviving sergeants quickly conducted roll calls within their companies. The toll had been bloody: the 2nd NC lost over 250; the 4th NC, 270; the 14th NC, over 140; and the 30th NC, 115.[121] Ramseur's brigade had lost half its strength in sixty minutes.

Later that afternoon, Brig. Gen. Ramseur received orders to move his battered brigade. He recorded, "afterward I was moved to a position on the Plank road, which was entrenched, and which we occupied until the division was ordered back to camp near Hamilton's Crossing."[122] Unfortunately, the weary men were not allowed to rest; a forest fire erupted not far from their position, threatening the wounded soldiers who could not move. A horrified Pvt. John Bone (Co. I) wrote, "We were now on the East side of the plank road, the West side was a forest of timber, and it was then on fire. We were ordered to go at once and put out the fire, there being many of our dead and wounded subject to being burned." He continued, "We moved our wounded and stopped the fire, but many of the dead bodies on both sides got burned."[123] Another rifleman added, "The burning of the deep, dry leaves had heated up the dead bodies and caused them to burn…. They were like lamps lighting up the woods."[124]

Once the exhausted Tar Heels had time to recover from the battle's physical demands, they moved about the area, searching among the Yank haversacks and backpacks, as well as looking for shoes. Lieutenant William Ardrey (Co. K) noted this fact, writing, "The fields were literally covered with the dead and dying."[125] Another Carolinian wrote, "[Jim] Smith marched to this battlefield barefooted. He said ... that he would get himself shoes from the first dead Yankee he saw. Here was his opportunity. The Yankee was lying on his back. Smith attempted to pull off his boots—a good pair." The rifleman continued his story: "The Yankee opened his eyes and said, 'Wait a minute, friend, and you can have them; I will not need them any more.' Jim dropped the Yankee's foot and said, 'I will go barefooted the rest of my life rather than wake another dead Yankee.'"[126]

That night, once darkness had stopped the killing, the war-weary soldiers huddled together around small campfires. The Ta Heels said little, the day's events and horrid scenes smothered their emotions. A rifleman observed, "Everything and everybody seemed changed, sad and dejected."[127] An officer recalled, "All the units ... now seemed to be 'fought out.'"[128] Private John Bone (Co. I) remembered, "Among the number killed was a very moral young man and a good soldier.... In the morning before he started from our bivouac he wanted to give his brother his pocketbook and rations, for he said that he thought he would be killed that day."[129] Colonel Frank Parker wrote his wife, "I have never seen so great [a] slaughter, as I saw on the field of Sunday. At the breastworks the enemy would be lying on one side, and our men on the other; some dead, some dying, others badly wounded." He continued, "Our loss is 25 killed, 99 wounded, only one missing; there are a number of slightly wounded, who are now on duty again; these we take no account of." Frank Parker finished his letter, writing simply, "How thankful I feel that I was not struck."[130] Not far from the exhausted colonel, a brooding Cpt. John Witherspoon (Co. K) penned a note to his wife, stating, "We have had a hard fight.... I have lost 2 men killed and 11 wounded. Sam [Boyce, Co. K] and me still safe." He continued, "Mitty [Witherspoon, Co. K] was wounded yesterday in the leg. The Doctor did not know this morning whether it will have to be amputated or not." The tired company commander ended his message, "Thank Heaven that I am saved thus far.... Pray for my preservation."[131]

As the dark hours continued, the men tried to sleep. Some slept soundly, their day's actions consuming all their energy. Others, though, slept very little. Private John Bone (Co. I) recalled, "men began to think more about their spiritual condition ... as they were beginning to see more of the evils of war, the certainty of death, and the uncertainty of life."[132] Another of these soldiers later admitted, "I could not sleep much that night ... for the moment my eyes closed I imagined I could see soldiers falling all around me, and their dying groans rang in my ears."[133]

Chapter 8

The Road to Gettysburg

The battle-weary Tar Heels woke on May 4, 1863, uneasy with the thought they would be going into combat again. They cooked their breakfast, filled canteens, and made sure their cartridge boxes were filled. Colonel Frank Parker replaced the night-time pickets with a fresh group, and then met with his company officers. As of yet, there was no word about movements, or assault plans. Lieutenant William Ardrey (Co. K), acting as one of the Thirtieth's officers on the picket line, soon realized the Yanks did not seem inclined to want to start anything. Instead, the two opposing skirmish forces lay within lethal shooting distance of each other, but neither did much shooting. The hours went by slowly, though peacefully; the pickets kept watch on each other while the soldiers within the entrenchments worked continuously to strengthen their fortifications. Later in the day, the two picket lines took to yelling insults at each—they were substituting words for bullets. William Ardrey wrote, "While lying in line of battle the soldiers commenced yelling and shouting and some droll fellow asked if Jackson was coming or if he was a rabbit."[1] Fortunately nothing came of the shouted ridicule, enabling Ardrey to also record, "[We] lay in our entrenchments all day, artillery firing and skirmishing all day … alleviating the suffering of the wounded and making entrenchments."[2]

Night's darkness took away combat possibilities and the Tar Heels settled down for a much more secure rest than the night before. The Thirtieth and its brother regiments in Ramseur's brigade were now well dug in along the Orange Plank road. Twenty-four hours of inactivity had refreshed the men, and the return of a few missing fellows, as well as some who were slightly wounded helped rebuild the young men's morale. May 5, 1863, was a repeat of the previous day. Lieutenant Ardrey penned in his journal, "lay in our entrenchments all day, very quiet, could hear the enemy fortifying; rained very hard."[3] The next morning, when Parker changed out the pickets, they came into the lines with the news they believed the Federals had retreated. General Dodson Ramseur, upon hearing this report, ordered his brigade skirmish corps to advance. Major Hurtt (2nd NC), commanding the sharpshooters, soon sent back word: "my outposts reported that the enemy had retired … the entire force had retreated during the night."[4] The Tar Heels could now relax, and for a change, the rain was not as much of a problem, many of the Confederates had collected Yankee shelter halves. They buttoned these five-foot-square pieces of canvas together and created protection from the continual downpour.

On May 7, 1863, Gen. Ramseur ordered the troops to break camp, form into a marching column and then, he led them away from the Chancellorsville battleground. They hiked all day, heading east, enduring the constant rain. Lieutenant William Ardrey recorded, "Raining very hard…. Took up a line of march for our camp at Hamilton's

Crossing, the hardest march I ever experienced, we were in mud and water knee deep. Arrived at camp entirely exhausted."[5] Though the weather and bottomless mud produced most of the Carolinians' misery, the men, themselves, were better protected from the rain than before the battle. General Robert Rodes noted this, writing, "It is worthy of remark that the enemy abandoned such a large number of knapsacks in retreating ... that when this division began its homeward march in the rain it was thoroughly equipped with oil-cloths and shelter-tents of the best quality."[6]

The next morning, "dawned cool and misty," a dismal setting for the gloom hovering over the war-weary soldiers, because, "among the camps, there was profound concern."[7] Rumors told of Stonewall Jackson's amputated arm, and his inability to recover. Everyone realized Jackson's brilliant tactics had enabled them to whip the blue coats, but his wounding, along with the damaging casualties pummeling each regiment spoke of the horrendous cost. William Ardrey (Co. K) recalled, "Perfect silence reigned throughout camp, everybody resting, sleeping and seemingly mourning the loss of their dead comrades.[8] The Thirtieth no longer could muster four hundred men, as so many friends, neighbors, and relatives were missing. Chaplain Alexander Betts, who had been home on a short leave, returned and wrote in shock; "[Found] my regiment. So [many] are gone forever! ... Many husbands left widows and orphans [behind]."[9] William Ardrey scribbled his thoughts that evening, reflecting a feeling common among the heavy-hearted Tar Heels, "Would God that this human slaughter was ended." He then finished, "I feel greatly thankful to the Almighty Protector that my life has been spared."[10] Two days later, May 10, 1863, the Confederates received the news Gen. Stonewall Jackson had died. Alexander Betts wrote, "The 'victory' cost many lives.... Gen. Jackson die[d] at 3 p.m."[11] Lieutenant William Ardrey added, "Gen. Jackson, the hero of the South, died. We deeply mourn his loss.... We hope that there are other Jackson's in the South and that God will continued to bless our glorious cause."[12]

General Dodson Ramseur left the brigade to tend to his injury, leaving Col. Frank Parker in command of the four Carolina regiments, and Maj. William Sillers in charge of the Thirtieth. Parker met with the other colonels and they discussed ... rebuilding their battered regiments. Colonel Bryan Grimes (4th NC) wrote, "we returned to near Hamilton's Crossing and [worked] ... to recover from our severe trials of the several previous days, and re-organized ... examined, and recommended for appointment ... our new officers to command. Here we passed the time in drilling."[13] Their riflemen, tired of endless duties, and exhausted with the war, did as little as possible. One soldier noted, "[we were] mourning [our] dead and writing letters."[14] One young farm boy-turned-soldier, lamented, "The gals has all quit writing to me. I can't hear from none of them."[15] Lieutenant Ardrey remarked, "Very quiet in camp, everybody seems to be lonely."[16] Everyone wanted to leave, and a few, including 2nd Lt. Robert Clairborne (Co. G) were able to find a way to go home. Lieutenant Clairborne wrote, "In consequence of disability from rheumatism and numerous disability cause from protracted sickness, and feeling myself unable of a service I do most respectfully tender my resignation as second lieutenant."[17] The vast majority of homesick men, though, realized they were trapped in a situation with no escape. A despondent youth groaned, "I think I never will get home any more."[18]

The Confederate high command realized their soldiers were restless. On May 16, 1863, the troops were paid, and Maj. Gen. Robert Rodes (he had been promoted on May 7, 1863) called the entire division together for a grand review. Two days later, Brig. Gen.

Dodson Ramseur returned, sending Col. Parker back to regimental command. Ramseur also came back to the brigade with rumors his men might be sent back to North Carolina, a dream energizing the homesick men. Lieutenant William Ardrey (Co. K) wrote, "Great deal of excitement about our brigade going to the 'Old North State.' We all thought the prospects very good."[19] Colonel Frank Parker wrote his wife, "It is reported that Genrl. D. H. Hill had made a request that our Brigade be sent to N. C."[20] But General Ramseur had no intentions of leaving the Army of Northern Virginia; he was adamant his legacy was connected to General Lee. Ramseur's response soon filtered down to his Tar Heels and they complained vigorously. Colonel Parker summed up their feelings: "Genrl. Ramseur was opposed to leaving this army.... There is a great dissatisfaction in the Brigade."[21] Captain John Witherspoon (Co. K) noted, "We will not be the fortunate Brig[ade]."[22] And William Ardrey added, "all our bright hopes were blasted."[23]

Meanwhile, General Robert E. Lee met with President Jefferson Davis and senior military leaders and they re-organized the Army of Northern Virginia. Initially, Lee's army had consisted of two corps: the First, commanded by Lt. Gen. James Longstreet, and the Second under Stonewall Jackson. But now, Lee was faced with trying to replace Jackson, and he was not able to find an adequate successor. Robert E. Lee's best option was to promote two men to lieutenant general and assign one (Richard S. Ewell) to the Second Corps, and create a Third Corps, to be commanded by another new promotion, Lt. Gen. Ambrose P. Hill.[24] Each Corps was to be composed of three large divisions; Maj. Gen. Robert Rodes' division now belonged to Ewell's Corps, and consisted of five infantry brigades (Daniel's, Iverson's, Doles,' Ramseur's, and O'Neal's).[25] Lee immediately sent out orders to increase drill, and to penalize those officers who slacked in their responsibilities. Lieutenant William Ardrey was caught by this new regulation and grumbled, "Lt. [John] Downs [Co. K] and myself reported to the Capt. for missing drill."[26]

On May 29, 1863, General Lee called for a grand review of Rodes' division, and he, along with Gen. Longstreet and Gen. Ewell attended. Captain James Harris (Co. I) described the event, "there was a grand Review of the army by General Lee. Our Division was drawn up on the large open flat below Dickerson's House.... The Division was drawn up in their columns, Daniel's Brigade being in the front line and occupying a space equal to the front of two of our Old Brigades." He continued, "Everything was in nice time and to older eyes than ours in the service it would have proved a scene of much interest.... The men with shoulders square, with pieces resting in the hollow of their right shoulder, eyes to the front ... marched steady to the cadence step, wheeling at the turning point, with as much grace and firmness of step as Napoleon's men would have done." The 28-year-old eligible bachelor-turned-company commander added, "Many ladies graced the occasion with their presence, who with long feathers in their caps and long skirts reaching almost to the ground sat their spirited chargers as if they too know 'something of war.'" He confessed, "I held myself erect neither looking to the right or left until I got opposite the ladies when an irresistible attraction drew my head round ... and my eyes rest[ed] on Su-per-la-tin beauty.... I was smitten."[27]

Later that afternoon, Col. Frank Parker, along with the division's other senior officers met with their new Corps commander. Richard Ewell was forty-six, a graduate of West Point, and a hero from the Mexican War.

Parker came away from the meeting and wrote, "Our corps [Jackson's] is now commanded by Genrl. Ewell; he is a fine officer; what to us, is a good recommendation.... Genrl. Ewell lost a leg at the second battle of Manassas. He has an artificial leg, and rides very well. I hope he may fill the place made vacant by the loss of the great, the noble Jackson."[28] Unfortunately, the Richard Ewell that Frank Parker met was not the same officer who had accumulated martial laurels. Ewell's leg had been shattered at Second Manassas and surgeons forced to amputate. He recovered from his wound at the home of his first cousin, Lizinka Campbell Brown, and during the ten months of convalescence the two fell in love. Richard Ewell married the 42-year-old widow in May 1863. These events changed him; people who knew Ewell before Second Manassas were amazed at the difference. One surmised, "Before his wedding, Ewell was known to be a habitual swearer, but [this] quickly ceased."[29]

On June 3, 1863, Brig. Gen. Dodson Ramseur called his regimental commanders together and passed down Lee's orders; the Army of Northern Virginia was going on the offensive. Colonel Frank Parker met with his company officers; Cpt. James Harris (Co. I) came away from the meeting, recalling, "[Here] came the order to Comdg. Offis. of Cos. To reduce baggage to a mere change of clothing and ... to prepare ... for a long march."[30] Lieutenant William Ardrey (Co. K) added, "Received orders to prepare for a long march and Company Commanders to make requisitions for four months' supply of clothing for their Companies."[31] The next morning, hours before dawn, the troops broke camp and formed on the road, ready to march toward the west. William Ardrey jotted in his journal, "set out at 4 o'clock a.m. Had a very warm [and] tiresome march."[32] The Tar Heels hiked sixteen miles before bivouacking near the Spotsylvania Court House.

Their march had begun. The Carolina riflemen did not know where they were going, but they knew Gen. Lee did; that was all that mattered. On June 5, 1863, their trek took them twenty-miles farther west. They camped not far from Old Verdierville. Ardrey recorded, "Very warm and nothing to interest the weary soldiers as they performed their tiresome duties."[33] The Confederates turned northward on June 6, 1863, and under rainy skies made their way toward the Rapidan River. That night Chaplain Alexander Betts scribbled, "Rain. I sit under the wagon, as my tent was left. I sleep on wet leaves."[34] The next day was spent crossing the Rapidan River at Summerville Ford and tramping past the Culpepper Court House. They covered nineteen miles.

On June 8, 1863, Maj. Gen. Robert Rodes issued new orders, as General Lee had concerns about supplies. Rodes wrote, "I ordered all the baggage, tents, etc., that could be spared to be sent to the rear ... each brigade was now enabled to transport three days' rations in its train, in addition to an equal amount in the division commissary train, [and] the men also carrying three days' rations in his haversack ... [we had] fully nine days' rations."[35] The Confederates resumed their march the next morning, hustling eastward along the Orange and Alexandria Railroad tracks, with the prospect of fighting a Yank cavalry force near Brandy Station, VA. The foot-sore troops did not arrive in time; the blue coats had already fled. On June 10, 1863, the Southerners retraced their steps back to Culpepper, and then turned northwest, ending up not far from the Hazel River. The troops were awakened before sunrise the next morning and soon took to the march. General Rodes remarked, "the route was resumed at an early hour, and, without exception, on the worst road I ever seen troops and trains pass over."[36] Lieutenant William Ardrey (Co. K), as he bedded down that evening, noted, "marched [fifteen] miles; arrived at Flint Hill, a village in the mountains; still a very fatiguing and monotonous march."[37]

The trek continued; on June 12, 1863, the Tar Heels hiked through Chester Gap in the Blue Ridge Mountains and made their way to Front Royal, where they were met by admiring crowds. William Ardrey (Co. K) scribbled, "Passed through Front Royal in the

Shenandoah Valley, enthusiastic shouts of applause went up from the citizens and the waving of white handkerchiefs expressed the emotions of joy ... the young ladies ... were handing out refreshments to the wearied soldiers."[38] Exasperatingly though, just as the young men were getting to know these adoring supporters, orders came to keep moving. The Tar Heels, as an officer recorded, "passed through Front Royal, forded both forks of the Shenandoah River, and halted for a few hours near Cedarville, VA."[39] Then, the tired riflemen shouldered their muskets and journeyed to Stonebridge, having covered seventeen miles by the time word came to make camp.

With dawn on June 13, 1863, the men arose and continued their march northward, staying on the main road running along the west banks of the Shenandoah River. Than, just before noon, word reached Gen. Rodes a force of Yankees had slipped in and taken Berryville, VA. He immediately ordered his brigades to capture the town. Captain James Harris (Co. I) recorded, "At about 11 or 12 o'clock we had arrived within a mile of town, our advance had been [seen] ... and our salutation received was a loud boom from a cannon ... which exploded about 200 or 300 yards in our front." He continued, "The attack was now planned and our Brigade selected to flank the town and approach it by way of the pike leading toward Charlestown. It was excessively warm and we marched in quick time about 5 miles before we halted. We were [now] ... within about 600 yards of the town. I don't believe that I ever was so near exhausted before." The Confederates advanced, prepared to rush the blue coats' position. James Harris remarked, "[We were] summoned forward and came in sight of their fortifications ... [but].... The cowards had deserted the place and given bail."[40] The Carolinians moved in and scavenged items from the blue coats' abandoned camp. Lieutenant William Ardrey noted, "All their tents, quarter-master supplies and stores, with dinners on the fire they left in utmost confusion."[41] Regrettably the troops were not allowed to stay; soon, commands came, forcing the tired men back onto the road. They trudged northwest, halting after dark, having covered twenty miles.

Sunrise brought the men to their feet and heading northwest towards Martinsburg, VA. Colonel Frank Parker's Tar Heels passed through several small villages and his men were greeted by cheering young women. Captain James Harris (Co. I), who had an eye for the ladies, wrote, "On we went never failing to be greeted at every house by the wayside, by any number of the fair sex who seemed much delighted to see us and who every house by the wayside, by any number of the fair sex who seemed much delighted to see us and who seemed as if they would lose their arms in waving their handkerchiefs."[42] Lieutenant William Ardrey added, "The ladies were so rejoiced in Smithfield that they crowded the streets with water and all kinds of eatables."[43] Another Tar Heel remarked, "As we threaded the streets ... a young lady of many personal charms, rushing to our head,

seized my reins and told me in moving tones of the oppression endured by the citizens."[44] But then, Gen. Rodes received word Union troops occupied Martinsville, and he wanted to bag them. He ordered his troops to hustle. The sweating riflemen hurried toward the town and reached its outskirts late that afternoon. General Rodes recorded, "Notwithstanding their fatiguing march ... [and] without halting, the infantry was put in a position for a direct attack—the Alabama brigade on the right.... Ramseur on the left, Doles and Iverson in the center, Daniels in reserve."[45] Captain James Harris (Co. I) recalled, "as had been the case at Berryville our plan was to attack at two or three different points at once. Our brigade when within one mile of the town moved off to the left of the turnpike while Iverson's moved to the right and occupied the heights." He continued. "By sunset our line of battle was formed and we advanced into town rapidly."[46] Another Tar Heel rifleman commented, "[We] formed in line of battle, raised the Rebel yell and charged."[47] And then, just as had occurred at Berryville, the Federals retreated. Harris noted, "Before we got halfway the black rows of Yankees [were] plainly seen on the heights beyond the town. It was their backs that we saw, for they were getting away as fast as their legs could carry them."[48] The Tar Heels closed in on the abandoned camp and harvested Union supplies. A Carolina officer wrote, "Our whole brigade partook of a hot dinner of beans and pork, baked beef, and fresh loaf bread ... by our accommodating Yankee friends. Every soldier filled his haversack with pure bean coffee, sugar, and other camp delicacies."[49] Another wrote, "They were preparing a meal, not scant rations we were accustomed to but pots, plenty of pots, full of stewed beef, loaf bread piled in stacks, with other edibles.... We ate all we could ... filled our haversacks and marched on greatly refreshed."[50] Unfortunately, the riflemen were not allowed to linger; soon the march continued. The Tar Heels finished the day having covered twenty miles.

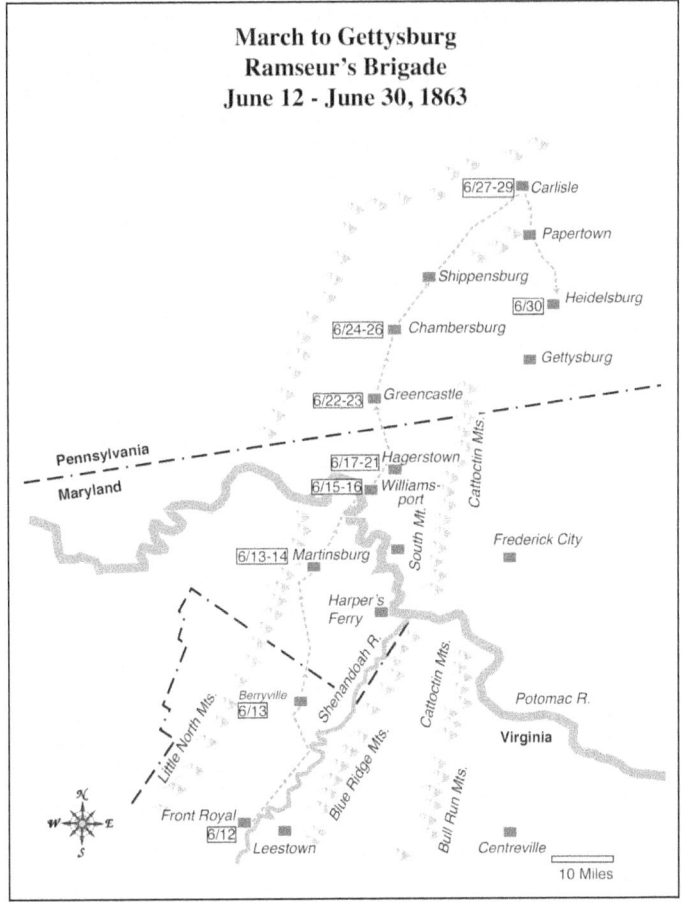

General Rodes allowed his tired men to sleep past sunrise on June 15, 1863. He wrote, "the troops were [permitted] to rest until 10:00 a.m."[51] He realized the continual marching was wearing down his infantry, and grinding through their foot ware. The division's general added, "these gallant fellows were still marching in ranks, with feet bruised, bleeding, and swollen."[52] Nonetheless, Rodes gave the order and his infantry formed into its marching formation. Robert Rodes added, "I put the division in motion for Williamsport, and arrived there by dark, after the most trying march we had yet had; most trying because of the intense heat, the character of the road, and the increased number of barefooted men in the command." He continued, "It was not until this day that the troops began to exhibit unmistakable signs of exhaustion, and that stragglers could be found in the line of march."[53]

Dodson Ramseur's Tar Heels were among the first troops to reach the Potomac. An advance guard was immediately sent splashing across the river and then the Carolinians quickly followed. Captain James Harris (Co. I) bragged, "Our brigade was the first to cross the Potomac."[54] A Southerner noted, "The river was almost 200 yards wide at this point, possessing a firm, rocky bottom, and from knee to armpit in depth. Most of the men took their clothes off and strung all they owned on their rifles, which they held above their heads.... They laughed and shouted as they struggled against the water's current."[55] Another Confederate noted, "Taking off our shoes, socks, pants, and drawers, we made a comical looking set of men."[56] Ramseur's four regiments were posted to cover the crossing, and then Iverson's Carolinians came across, trailed behind by Doles' Georgians. James Harris remarked, "this [being first to cross] created some jealously in the other brigades and it was not uncommon to hear … 'if there is any advance given, Ramseur's Brigade will get it.'"[57] Later, once the three brigades had solidified the Confederate beachhead on the Maryland side of the Potomac, the veteran soldiers began to contemplate their future. Lieutenant William Ardrey (Co. K) wrote into his journal what many thought, "The wish of all was that they be spared to re-cross the river."[58]

The Tar Heels moved through Williamsport and took up positions east and north of the town. They would remain here for two days while the rest of the Second Corps crossed the Potomac. General Ramseur told his regimental commanders to keep tight control over their men, as General Lee's orders emphasized limited damage to property. Regardless of these dictates, the enterprising Carolinians slipped out of camp and into Williamsport. Nearly all their interactions with the townsfolk went well. Lieutenant William Ardrey (Co. K) wrote, "Encamped at Williamsport.... Drew rations of whiskey, bought boots, shoes, hats and a great many articles at old prices."[59] However, not all exchanges were friendly; one such instance occurred with an officer in the 14th NC. The Carolinian recalled, "a Dutch woman of strong Union brawn drew a paddling-stick on Captain Gorman and began railing at the hungry Confederates generally: 'You eats up everything' … Gorman's situation was relieved by the arrival of Lieutenant Harney … who told the woman … if she did not behave herself he would pull every hair out of her head."[60]

The Confederates moved to Hagerstown, MD, on June 17, 1863. Here, Brig. Gen. Ramseur established his headquarters in the female seminary. The young Tar Heel riflemen noticed this and quickly were anxious to volunteer for headquarters guard duty. William Ardrey remarked, "Our camp was visited by some ladies."[61] Remarkably, few soldiers attained that posting, so most, when able, explored Hagerstown's streets and stores. Ardrey noted, "Hagerstown … we found there many sympathizers … with the South. White handkerchiefs floating from every window."[62] Chaplain Alexander Betts wrote, "Dr. J. V. Simmons in Hagerstown, fills a tooth for me and will not charge a 'rebel.'"[63] Then, returning to camp, the Tar Heels relaxed and wrote letters. A Carolinian recalled, "The men are in good spirits."[64] And finally, at night, they slept where they could. Alexander Betts recorded, "sleep in a barn near Hagerstown."[65]

The Confederates resumed their march on June 22, 1863. General Robert Rodes reported, "penetrated into the enemy's country … [with] Iverson's brigade … the first to touch Pennsylvania soil. After a march of thirteen miles, we bivouacked at Greencastle."[66] At first, the Pennsylvanians seemed surprised to see the long columns of gray-clad soldiers, however, as the Confederate moved farther north into the Keystone State, the locals' attitudes changed. Southern cavalry squads roamed the countryside, collecting livestock and horses, brusquely taking them without recourse. General Rodes noted, "some 2,000 or 3,000 head of cattle were taken … [and] 1,200 or 1,500 [horses]."[67] A Confederate added, "As the [Second] Corps moved deeper into the enemy's country and took sleek horses and fat cattle, faces grew sullen and words were sharp.... Some of the natives ... would look very sour at us."[68] Ramseur's brigade remained near Greencastle for another day, the Tar Heels spreading out in search of food. One Southerner admitted, "The soldiers ignored orders and slipped out of their camps, fanning out to strip nearby farms of poultry and fresh vegetables."[69] Lieutenant William Ardrey recorded, "went out and got a fine dinner and a mess of cherries with a Dutch family."[70]

The Confederates marched away from Greencastle on June 24, 1864, tramping northward. Robert Rodes recorded, "the division made 14 miles, passing through Chambersburg ... and bivouacked on the Conococheague, 2 miles beyond town."[71] The Carolina farm boys gawked at the Pennsylvania landscape. One rifleman wrote with amazement, "The rich, fertile land is covered with fine growing wheat, the finest ever."[72] Another commented, "Stretching before [us] were seemingly endless fields of wheat, oats, and hay ... cornfields, apple orchards, vegetable gardens and trees with ripened cherries."[73] Another added, "I have never yet seen any country in such a high state of cultivation."[74] And even Col. Frank Parker was impressed. He wrote his wife, "we have passed through the most magnificent country I have ever seen ... such fields of wheat and clover, I have never looked at, and such cattle too; these people certainly must have lived like lords."[75]

Again, as had happened at the end of each day's march, the Confederates fanned out from their bivouac and raided nearby farms. The jubilant young men brought their spoils back to camp, causing one soldier to write, "The boys certainly lived high now.... To have heard the squealing of pigs, the cackling of chickens, and the quacking of ducks ... one for the instant might have supposed himself on some market square."[76] Another remarked, "Dinners included 'confiscated chicken,' along with ... other stolen delectables, which were washed down ... [because] we succeeded in getting our canteens filled with cherry wine."[77] And an old veteran recollected, "The fatness of the land is amaz[ing].... It's like a hole full of blubber." He added, "It is like a renewal of Mexican times to enter a captured town. The people look as sour as vinegar."[78]

The Southerners' incursion into Pennsylvania did not set well with the locals. Captain James Harris (Co. I) observed, "when we arrived in Chambersburg Pa, man, woman, and children looked as sullen as an opossum ... or sour as a crab apple."[79] Another officer related an exchanged between a citizen and gray-coated soldiers, writing, "A woman standing by the roadside, seeing our uniforms were worn, dirty and ragged, asked ... why we did not wear better clothes? [A Tar Heel answered] 'We always put on our old clothes in which to kill hogs (Yankees).'"[80] And later, when a Pennsylvanian militia attempted to block a unit of Confederate scouts, these local troops were surrounded and forced to surrender. A Southern officer recorded, "En route to Carlisle, [Maj. Gen. Edward] Johnson had lined up his captured Pennsylvanian militiamen in their new Federal uniforms and had relieved them of their shoes and socks."[81] None of this helped to make for friendly interchanges. Lieutenant William Ardrey (Co. K) wrote, "The citizens did not seem delighted at our presence.... All the citizens looked upon us with scorn and contempt."[82]

General Robert Doles kept his division motionless on June 26, 1863, as Maj. Gen. Edward Johnson's division arrived, joining the two formations together. They now had a formidable force, mustering nearly thirteen thousand infantry soldiers, all who were enjoying this foray into Pennsylvania. Generals Doles and Johnson put their riflemen back on the road the next morning. Lieutenant William Ardrey recorded, "Rained very hard. Passed through the little village of Leesburg, Jackson, Hockensville ... though nothing of interest to attract our attention but the fear and stiffness of the citizens."[83] Chaplain Alexander Betts added, "Hard march. Mud! Mud!"[84] The Confederates moved through the town of Carlisle, and then that evening, after fifteen miles' march, Col. Frank Parker proudly proclaimed, "Ramseur's Brigade occupied Carlisle barracks."[85]

The next morning, June 28, 1863, Lieutenant William Ardrey (Co. K) wrote, "Encamped in the United States garrison at Carlisle, Penn. It is well improved and a beautiful and wealthy town."[86] Ardrey's observation was echoed by all the Tar Heels; indeed, the institution was a great place to stash their bedrolls. Captain James Harris (Co. I) crowed, "we reached Carlisle ... had plenty of ice and fared finely."[87] Major William Sillers bragged, "We drank ... claret with plenty of ice in it."[88] The foot-sore soldiers relaxed all day, doing as little as possible. They continued to eat well; Ardrey noted, "We had plenty of good things to eat and letters from home."[89] The next day the troops formed in front of the barracks and a large Confederate flag was raised. William Ardrey recorded, "Hoisted the Confederate flag upon the mast pole of the United States garrison ... speeches were made by Generals Trumbell, Rodes and Daniels; they complimented the North Carolina troops."[90] Then the Confederates broke ranks and the riflemen returned to an afternoon of cleaning weapons, fixing uniforms, cobbling together shoes, and sleeping. But as evening approached, rumors began to filter through the company groupings; something was amiss. Colonel Frank Parker wrote his wife, "we are only a few miles in Penn. what our object is, or how far in this direction we will go, I can not say.... We are entirely destitute of any news of the operations of the balance of the army."[91]

Late that night General Robert E. Lee sent Maj. Gen. Robert Rodes instructions to move his division. Rodes recorded, "have received orders to move toward the balance of the army ... supposed to be at or near Cashtown, we set out for that place."[92] He had his five brigades moving early on June 30, 1863, with the lead regiments following roads heading southward. The Tar Heels hiked through Papertown, Petersburg, and after covering twenty-two miles, bivouacked near Heidlersburg. Captain James Harris (Co. I)

The Carlisle Barracks were occupied by Ramseur's Brigade June 27–29, 1863 (*Frank Leslie's Illustrated Newspaper*, July 16, 1863, courtesy Archives and Special Collections, Dickinson College, Carlisle, PA).

wrote, "At an early hour on … the 30th of June we left Carlisle bearing to the left and crossing the Cumberland Mountains at Mount Holly Gap, issuing from the mountains at a little place called Paper Town."[93] Captain Harris observed, "If you wish to … see a show of babies just go to Pennsylvania. I am glad I have … to fight this generation for I should be afraid to risk it [against] the next." He continued, "I suggest that they should change the name of one little village through which we passed, Babytown."[94] As evidenced by Harris's comments, the men were in good spirits; an officer noticed this, writing, "Our march had been admirably conducted. We were always on the road at an early hour and, without hurry or the usual halts caused by troops crowding on one another, we made good distances each day and were in campy by sunset. I never before or afterward saw the men so buoyant."[95] The Thirtieth's chaplain agreed. Alexander Betts added, "[The] soldiers sleep among the rocks around me…. Thank God! I am happy. Happiness does not depend so much on our surroundings as some may think."[96]

Chapter 9

Gettysburg

30th North Carolina Infantry[1]
July 1, 1863

Unit		Strength
Field & Staff	Col. Parker, Francis M. Maj. Sillers, William Cpt. Holmes, James C.	4
Co. A	1st Lt. Williams, Gary 3rd Lt. White, Lassiter M.	22
Co. B	1st Lt. Davis, Weldon 1st Lt. Nicholson, John H.	17
Co. C	Cpt. Allen, David 2nd Lt. Swain, John R.	21
Co. D	Cpt. Allen, Charles 1st Lt. Abernathy, Sidney S.	22
Co. E	Cpt. McMillan, John 1st Lt. Johnson, Ira	29
Co. F	Cpt. Moore, Willis M. 1st Lt. Harrell, George	35
Co. G	1st Lt. Badgett, James W. 3rd Lt. Connell, Ira T.	22
Co. H	Cpt. Wicker, Jess J. 1st Lt. McNeil, Henry J.	26
Co. I	Cpt. Harris, James 2nd Lt. Arrington, Kearney	37
Co. K	Cpt. Witherspoon, John G. 2nd Lt. Downs, John T.	21
		258

Colonel Frank Parker's Tar Heels were up before sunrise, his veterans boiling coffee and eating from their Pennsylvania stores. The still-dark skies were overcast and hinting of rain showers, though the July air promised to reach punishing afternoon temperatures. Sergeants moved about the platoons, making sure their riflemen had ammunition, as well as full canteens. Roll calls were taken and morning reports completed. Adjutant Frederick Philips compiled the numbers and submitted the muster to Parker. The regimental commander was unhappy with these results; his formation continued to dwindle in strength. The past weeks' trek had stripped away scores of Carolinians, most falling away due to sickness and exhaustion, though some with injury, and at least a half dozen identified as deserters. On June 1, 1863, the Thirtieth numbered over four hundred. This morning, a month later, the regiment could not reach three hundred, and of that total, at least a quarter lacked foot ware.[2] Parker knew today's march would peel off additional Tar Heels, fellows who wanted to keep up but whose feet were so badly abused they would be unable to march.

Orders came to fall in. Frank Parker's captains assembled their companies and the Thirtieth formed on the road, ready to move. He did not know where they were headed; Gen. Ramseur's officers' call had only instructed the regimental leaders to have their troops ready to march, and prepared to fight. As one officer noted, "General Lee knows what he is about. This is certainly a grand move of his and if any man can carry it out successfully he can."[3] When Dodson Ramseur's command came to march an officer in the 4th NC recorded, "[We] were under arms and on the march by sunrise."[4]

The Thirtieth was the third regiment in Ramseur's column, following the 2nd NC and the 4th NC, with the 14th NC last. General Ramseur's brigade, numbering just over 1,100 men, were the tail end of Maj. Gen. Robert Rodes' division.[5] Dodson Ramseur remarked, "[We were] in rear of the division train, as a guard on the march from Heidlersburg to Gettysburg."[6] The men in the Thirtieth headed west toward Cashtown, moving slowly, at least a mile or two behind the lead brigade in Rodes' division. The July sun burned off the morning clouds and the summer's heat bore down on the Carolinians. One Southerner wrote, "The day was warm. Water was scarce."[7]

Several hours later rumors flashed down the long column: Yankees were occupying Gettysburg and Rodes was sending his brigades towards that town. General Rodes recorded, "upon arriving at Middletown, and hearing that Lt. Gen. Hill's Corps was moving upon Gettysburg, by order of Gen. Ewell, the head of the column was turned in that direction."[8] The leisurely march changed to "hurry-up." Captain James Harris (Co. I) noted this, writing, "our march ... was increased in speed."[9] Another Tar Heel added, "we resumed our march [and] ... we passed our wagons."[10] By now though, they were moving with haste. Rumors told the sweating Carolinians, Rodes' first brigades were already going into the attack. One rifleman wrote, "[We were] almost marching at a double quick for 7 miles."[11] And Cpt. James Harris (Co. I) noted, "we never halted until we got almost [to] the edge of the battlefield."[12] The Tar Heels hustled southward, their worn-out boots and bare feet churning up clouds of dust as the soldiers neared Gettysburg. Soon, the unmistakable thunder of artillery rumbled over the gray column. Captain James Harris recorded, "When about [four] miles from Gettysburg the boom of the cannon began to burst upon the ear & our march hitherto pretty rapid was increased."[13]

At about 1:00 p.m., Col. Parker's Thirtieth halted, still third in the brigade line, and was shifted to a battle front; the 4th NC on the left, then the 2nd NC, the 30th NC, and the 14th NC. General Ramseur wrote, "My brigade arrived on the field after the division had formed line of battle. I was then held in reserve."[14] A Tar Heel scribbled to his family, "We were ordered to lie down and wait [for] ... Ramseur to reconnoiter the ground."[15] The tired Carolinians reclined on the north side of a hill beneath the shade of a stand of trees, a high spot someone identified as Oak Hill.[16] Here, though safe from danger, the soldiers could hear the thumps from cannon and the rattle of musketry. They all guessed it would not be long before they would go forward into the fight. One veteran wrote,

"There we lay looking around upon our comrades and wondering who would be the ones who would be taken from us and in full health." He also added, "The loved ones at home were not forgotten at this moment."[17]

The men in the Thirtieth watched Brig. Gen. Ramseur return from his reconnaissance and order the 4th NC and 2nd NC forward. Dodson Ramseur reported, "After resting about fifteen minutes, I received orders to send two regiments to support Col. O'Neal.... I immediately detached the 2nd and 4th NC troops."[18] Surprisingly, stories filtered back to Parker's men describing a horrible disaster. One rifleman recorded, "We were astounded to get news from stragglers and thinking that our division was being driven back with heavy loss."[19] General Robert Rodes had committed Daniel's, Iverson's, and O'Neal's brigades in an ill-conceived assault on Union positions north of Gettysburg. Rodes' five thousand infantrymen had been crushed by the hard-fighting troops of Brig. Gen. Henry Baxter's brigade (I Corps). A Southerner later would analyze Rodes' tactics and remark, "[Rodes'] deployment probably was unavoidable, but it was far from ideal. It left the well-tested Brigadiers, Ramseur and Doles, out of the first attack and put the direction of the assault on O'Neal and on Iverson, who had not distinguished themselves in the battles of May."[20]

Brigadier General Alfred Iverson's Tar Heel brigade walked into a trap and was nearly annihilated. A Confederate wrote, "his line of battle had come under a decimating fire from Federals who were concealed behind a low stone wall."[21] Iverson's Tar Heels lost eight hundred men out of fifteen hundred in less than ten minutes. General Rodes, shocked by this debacle, wrote, "Iverson's ... dead lay in a distinctly marked line of battle. His left was overpowered, and many of his men, being surrounded, were captured."[22] A Federal recorded, There were, in a few feet of us, by actual count, 79 North Carolinians laying dead in a straight line. I stood on their right and looked down their line. It was perfectly dressed. Three had fallen to the front, the rest had fallen backward, yet the feet of all these dead men were in a perfectly straight line." He added, "Great God! When will this horrid war stop?"[23] Meanwhile, on Iverson's left, Col. Edward O'Neal's Alabama brigade had pushed forward and, though they were not decimated, were repulsed by Baxter's tenacious blue coats. And to Iverson's right, Brig. Gen. Junius Daniel and his North Carolina troops moved cautiously forward, swinging farther south, and avoiding serious casualties.

Robert Rodes rushed the 4th NC and 2nd NC to bolster O'Neal's men as that line crumbled and the defeated troops shuffled backwards. A soldier in the 4th NC wrote, "After waiting a few minutes, were ordered to advance in line of battle ... [Then] ... after proceeding a few hundred yards, this Regiment, together with the 2nd Regiment were recalled by Maj. Gen. Rodes and fronted on a hill to repel any attack from that quarter."[24] General Rodes hunted about for more reserves and settled upon the rest of Ramseur's men. Dodson Ramseur recorded, "The 14th and 30th NC [were] hastened to the support of Iverson."[25]

Colonel Frank Parker's Thirtieth numbered two hundred fifty men as they pushed through the stand of trees on Oak Hill. He had Maj. William Sillers commanding the right wing and Cpt. James Holmes the left. Also in line with the Thirtieth, Col. Risden Bennett's 14th NC marched forward; together they formed a two-regiment front covering about one hundred fifty yards. As the formation approached the battlefield a rifleman noted, "It was only a few minutes until we could hear the whistling of the bullets over our heads and every now and then one would strike in our ranks."[26] One such minié bullet struck Pvt. Wylie (Willie) Vick (Co. I), who fell, seriously wounded.[27] Once off Oak Hill's slopes the Tar Heels were joined by the 3rd AL, a regiment from O'Neal's brigade that had not been part of the destructive assault. Captain James Harris (Co. I) wrote, "as we were entering the field the 3rd Alabama Regt. joined our brigade ... this Regt. by some means was cut off ... [from] Rodes' old brigade." He added, "Our line of battle was formed about 2:30 p.m. [and] about 600 yards from that of the enemy. When within about 300 yards of them we came in full view."[28] As the Confederates emerged from the woods, Lt. William Ardrey (Co. K) was able to study the scene before him. Ardrey wrote, "The fields were literally strewn with the dead and dying."[29]

The Tar Heels could now see what lie before them—a strong defensive held by several Yank regiments. Captain Harris observed, "They occupied a position behind a Rock Wall which ran in a diagonal direction from our lines."[30] The Northerners were troops from Brig. Gen. Gabriel Paul's brigade (I Corps), the 104th NY and 13th MA. These blue coats were part of the force that had driven O'Neal's regiments backwards, however, when they saw the Tar Heels arrive, one Yank remarked, "we now began to have our hands full."[31] The Southerners gave out a holler and following Brig. Gen. Dodson Ramseur, advanced toward the Union position. The Carolinians marched shoulder-to-shoulder, grim-faced and steady. One recalled, "Our orders were to drive the enemy from behind this rock wall."[32]

The Federal skirmish line immediately evaporated, the blue coats scampering back to the protection of the stonewall. An officer in the 14th NC reported, "the command was moved to the front and engaged the enemy, driving in their sharpshooters and skirmishers, and advanced on the strong positions behind stone walls."[33] A soldier among the Union riflemen wrote, "The only thing we could do was stand and fire."[34] Their first volley struck the Carolinians at a range of about two hundred and fifty yards; however, even at this distance, Northern lead slammed into Carolina youth. Private Lewis Wicker (Co. H) was killed, while right beside him, his older brother, Pvt. Thomas Wicker (Co. H) suffered an, "arm broken by [a Minié] ball."[35] Sergeant Isaac Merrit (Co. A) was struck in the side and left arm, Pvt. James Southerland (Co. E) suffered a

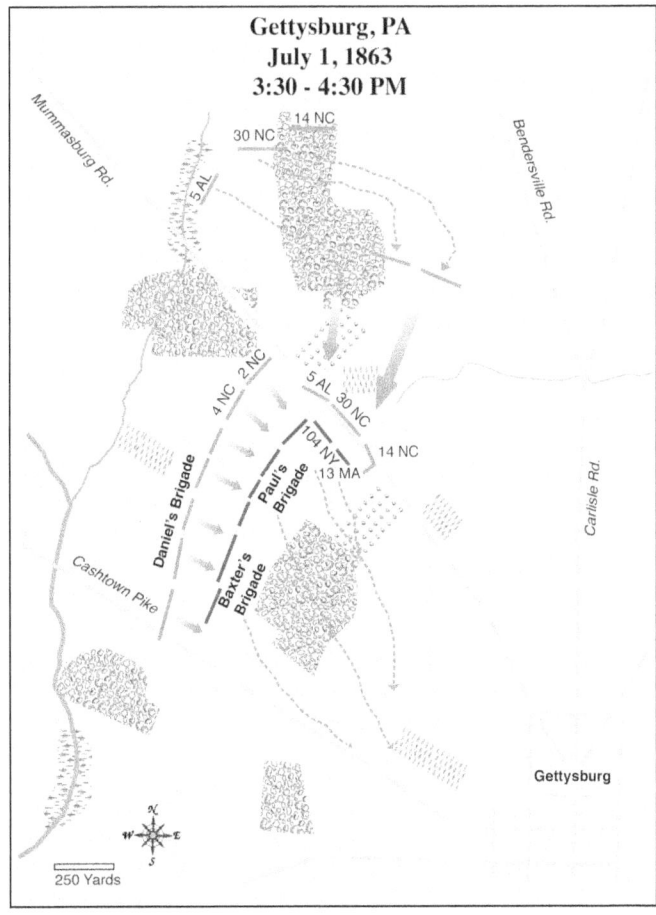

flesh wound to his thigh, and Pvt. Archibald Westray's (Co. I) right leg was shattered just below the knee.[36] More Tar Heels fell as the determined blue coats continued to put out a destructive fire. Captain Charles Allen's (Co. D) left arm, "was so broken up that it had to be amputated." Corporal D. Thomas Cheatham (Co. G) was, "wounded badly through the thigh," Pvt. William McAulay (Co. H) struck in the neck, and Pvt. Samuel Hewett (Co. C) killed.[37]

The Confederates closed to within one hundred yards of the stonewall during the next couple minutes. More Carolinians dropped to the ground as bullets struck Tar Heels: Sgt. Robert Williams' (Co. B) scalp was sliced open, Pvt. John Barker (Co. D) struck in the right arm and hand, and Pvt. Levi Crisp (Co. F) hurt, "badly in the mouth."[38] Colonel Parker wrote, "The fighting was of a desperate character."[39] The resolute Southerners inched to within seventy-five yards of the Yanks, and their own musketry ripped into the blue coats' riflemen. One Federal remarked, "we were in the thickest of the fight, and were badly cut up ... our colors fell twice, but the boys rallied and prevented their falling into the hands of the enemy."[40]

Colonel Frank Parker shuddered when he saw Dodson Ramseur's horse stagger and fall, but within seconds, the brigade commander climbed to his feet, raised his sword and continued forward. Another officer wrote, "General Ramseur led the charge and he was the only officer in the field who had a horse under him. The fine gray mare upon which he rode fell from bullet wounds within a few yards of the stone fence."[41] The Southerners' three regiments slogged forward, the Carolinian riflemen firing as they advanced. The 3rd AL, stepping forward on the Thirtieth's right was the farthest away from the Union position, as the Yank's stonewall angled sharply to the southeast, thus the Alabama troops sustained few losses. Colonel Parker's men, though, were parallel with the angled wall, and dozens had been hit. Fortunately, the 14th NC, advancing on the Thirtieth's left, extended beyond the Northerners' formation. They suffered few casualties and as Col. Risden Bennett (14th NC) recorded, "We assailed in front, the Fourteenth Regiment lapping their right."[42] Another Tar Heel added, "One wing of the enemy gave way when overlapped by our 14th North Carolina Regiment ... and their whole line fell back."[43]

The Tar Heels closed upon the Union position, more Carolina boys falling. Captain James Harris (Co. I) wrote, "Just before we got to the road Bob [Theophilus] Winstead's [Co. I] left was shattered by a mini ball; he fell at my side saying, 'Ah! Lord my leg is broken to pieces,' and fell over on his side."[44] Corporal Benjamin Smith (Co. C) had his jaw broken by a bullet; Cpl. Joseph Hight (Co. H), suffered "a flesh wound through [his] thigh; Pvt. Jolley B. Whitley (Co. I) was killed; and 3rd Lt. Alexander Brown (Co. H) fell, his left thigh ripped open.[45] Private Aaron DeArmond (Co. K) noted, "Ely Griffith [Co. K] was wounded in the hip."[46] And then, Frank Parker was hit. Chaplain Alexander Betts wrote, "Col. Parker's wound was in the face. The ball entered just below one eye and came just below the other, cutting the nasal tubes." Betts continued, writing, "When I knelt by him ... he seemed about to strangle with the blood."[47]

Fortunately, as the Thirtieth closed within fifty yards of the Federal riflemen, the Northerners' musketry slackened. General Ramseur recorded, "The enemy, seeing his right flank turned, made feeble resistance to the front attack."[48] One of these Yanks in the 104th NY admitted, "we saw the end was near and fell back towards the hills, each man for himself."[49] The Thirtieth's riflemen crowded near the stonewall as the blue coats fled. Colonel Parker, though, "wounded painfully through [the] face," turned command over to Maj. William Sillers, and as Lt. William Ardrey (Co. K) remarked, "Not withstanding the shock of his wound, he ordered his Reg. to reform and go ahead in the charge."[50] Moments later, the Thirtieth reached the wall. Captain James Harris (Co. I) wrote, "we were all mixed up. I called to my company.... I left and ran down the stone fence 60 yards ... the regiments seemed mixed up without any regularity or order among them. It was not panic—for no one appeared excited—the enemy was running, but it was created simply because the line was not preserved but a general massing at one point."[51]

The 14th NC, their battle line still in effective combat position, raced in behind the Federal position and cut off those resilient soldiers who resisted to the last. A Northerner in the 13th MA wrote, "some of us were gobbled up to rot in rebel prisons." He added, "[we lost] 195 casualties our of 285."[52] An officer in the 104th NY noted, "Suffice it that we lost heavily."[53] Another added, "25 officers and privates killed; 86 wounded; 94 prisoners and missing ... [out of] 250 troops."[54] There were other Federal regiments to the left of the 13th MA and 104th NY, these troops facing to the west to deal with Daniel's brigade, as well as other Confederate formations advancing from that direction. These Yanks were also caught in the vice created by the 14th NC's sweep. Eventually, Gen. Ramseur would be able to report, "[The Federals] ran off the field in confusion, leaving [their] killed and wounded, and between 800 and 900 prisoners in our hands."[55]

Major William Sillers and the Thirtieth's company commanders struggled to reform the regiment. Their riflemen milled about, gawking at the crowds of Federal prisoners—there were more prisoners than Confederates. Then, the 2nd NC and 4th NC slammed into the mob, arriving from the west, further adding to the confusion. General Ramseur shouted at his officers to sort out the mess, and after a few more minutes of disorder, Cpt. James Harris (Co. I) was able to state, "a new line was formed along the edge of the stone wall."[56] General Dodson Ramseur, now on foot, ordered the brigade sharpshooters to move south beyond the stonewall. He then let his regimental commanders know they were going to be attacking the retreating blue coats. Major William Sillers called to his company commanders, insisting they prepare their units; they would move as the sharpshooters cleared the way. Sillers gazed southward; the outer-most buildings of Gettysburg were a half-mile away. Captain James Harris (Co. I) noted, "We were now on a plain and in 600 or 800 yards of Gettysburg."[57]

First Lieutenant Frank Harney (14th NC) commanded the brigade sharpshooters. He spread out his hand-picked force numbering no more than sixty men, including at least a dozen from the Thirtieth, and they advanced. Harney's riflemen closed on the retreating Union mobs. The sharpshooters' movement was steady, as few Union formations remained with soldiers willing to stand and fight. Nonetheless, not all of the Federal units had been completely broken; there were a few battalions still with fight left in them. Colonel Risden Bennett (14th NC) remarked, "the enemy was retreating in some order."[58] Lieutenant Harney's marksmen took on these clumps of resistance; a Southerner recorded, "some blue units fought valiantly to cover the retreat."[59] Another Confederate added, "their whole line fell back. Not in a panic of defeat, but in one heroic stand after another till we drove them back ... to the town of Gettysburg."[60]

Major William Sillers kept his Tar Heel regiment in battle-line formation as it slowly trailed behind the brigade sharpshooters, though there was nothing for his Tar Heels to do. One Carolinian wrote, "Our sharpshooters being in front of the regiment, prevented our firing upon the enemy in his retreat."[61] William Sillers' riflemen were exhausted. Their fourteen-mile hike from last night's bivouac had been hurried, with the last four miles at the double-quick. Then, the Tar Heel charge to take the rock wall had been a frantic fifteen-minute rush, leaving everyone drained and worn out. Now, the July sun sapped at their remaining reserves. The temperature did not turn out to be as hot as many veterans had predicted, as a cloud layer covered the sky, which kept the heat from building. A scientist in Gettysburg recorded the 2:00 p.m. temperature at 86°F, but the humidity was high, punishing the soldiers.[62] Ultimately, Maj. Sillers could see many of his Carolinians on the verge of collapse, and even though the Thirtieth's file closers did all they could to prevent soldiers from falling out of the battle line, Sillers watched as exhausted men dribbled away. Colonel Bryan Grimes (4th NC) also noticed this situation, and reported, "[Because] of the fatiguing and exhausting march of the day ... the troops were too exhausted to move rapidly, as they otherwise would have done."[63]

A flurry of musketry erupted between the Lt. Harney's sharpshooters and a group of blue coats, causing the soldiers in the brigade line to take cover. General Ramseur sent forward reinforcements to support the unexpected flare-up but it ended quickly. Dodson Ramseur wrote, "Lieutenant [F. M.] Harney, 14th NC troops, command[ed] the sharpshooters ... [and] whipped a Yankee regiment (150th PA) ... and took their regimental colors from them with his own hands."[64] A member of the 150th PA confessed, "The [150th's] colors were held by Corporal [Joseph] Gutelius, of company D, who carried them to the town, and insisted on keeping them, although he was slightly wounded. Stopping a moment to rest, the rebels were on him, and he was shot dead with the colors clasped in his arms." This Federal writer continued, "it was alleged, with a handful of sharp-shooters."[65]

The blue coats scuttled into Gettysburg, leaving the tired Confederates to collect the hundreds of men left behind. Captain James Harris (Co. I) noted, "We took a great many prisoners, but halted when we got into Gettysburg."[66] It was now close to 4:00 p.m., and the assault's momentum melted away. One Tar Heel officer wrote, "It was a hot day and our men were much distressed by the heat and work. We straggled into town and then formed as quick as possible. Many of our command were overcome by the heat."[67] Major General Robert Rodes joined the gray formations as they cautiously approached Gettysburg's buildings, and reported, "The troops, being greatly exhausted by their march and somewhat disorganized by the hot engagement and rapid pursuit, were halted and prepared for further action."[68] The Confederates' move to crush the scattered Union forces had now come to an end.

Major William Sillers had his company commanders take control over their winded men, and then gave orders for everyone to rest. He joined the brigade's other regimental commanders at Ramseur's headquarters and learned everyone was waiting for direction from Gen. Ewell. Dodson Ramseur was adamant; the blue coats were beaten and on the run, one more well-placed assault could finish them off. An officer in his staff recalled, "With the eye of a born soldier [Dodson Ramseur] discerned the necessities of the situation at a glance ... [and] insisted that the pursuit be continued and Cemetery Heights be captured."[69] But Lt. Gen. Richard Ewell did not order an attack. Eventually Dodson Ramseur "received an order to ... form [a] line of battle in a street in Gettysburg running east and west."[70] Ramseur unhappily ordered his regiments to move. A Tar Heel officer grumbled, "We were the first to enter the town of Gettysburg ... [but] halted to rest on the road leading to Fairfield [Hagerstown]."[71] Another Carolinian complained, "it was 6 o'clock, and here was when the failure was made (and if Jackson had been with us it would not have been done.) We ought to have marched right into the heights that night."[72]

Brigadier General Ramseur led his four regiments out of Gettysburg, heading west on the Hagerstown road as division commander Robert Rodes positioned his brigades—Doles' men occupied central Gettysburg, Iverson's men the western outskirts, and Ramseur beyond the town's limits, facing southward. General Rodes griped, "receiving no orders to advance.... I ... placed my lines and skirmishers in a defensive attitude." He continued, "My skirmishers were promptly thrown out so as to cover more than half the town and the front of the division, which was drawn up in two lines, Doles,' Iverson's, and Ramseur's brigades making the front line, and extending from the left of the center of the town along one of its principal streets and out on the road to Fairfield."[73] An officer in the 14th NC recorded, "The command ... occupp[ied] an old road entering town on the southwest side."[74]

As darkness overtook the battlefield, Maj. Sillers worked with Adj. Frederick Philips to determine the regiment's losses. They determined three-dozen Tar Heels were absent, including their colonel, who now struggled for his life in a field hospital. As the men settled down for the night Sillers sent a detail back over the afternoon's battlefield in an attempt to locate their missing comrades. Then, a night guard was posted and the exhausted men bedded down. General Rodes wrote, "In this position we remained quietly, but with considerable annoyance from the enemy's sharpshooters and artillery, until morning of the next day."[75] Other Confederates observed, "That night the Yankees [worked] hard all night fortifying the heights."[76] Captain James Harris (Co. I) recorded, "During the night and early part of the next day (the 2nd) the other divisions of our army came up and got into position. Everything was a dead calm save an occasional shot from a picket."[77]

Major William Sillers was up before dawn on July 2, 1863. He and several officers studied the landscape, taking in Gettysburg and the hills south of the town. One Carolinian wrote, "The morning of the 2d of July showed these heights occupied by the host of the enemy, bristling with guns and protected by breastworks impregnable to assault in front."[78] Sillers shuddered at the thought of advancing across the open fields against that position. An attack now, as Gen. Rodes quickly surmised, "would have been absurd."[79] Providentially, the only orders coming to the Thirtieth were minor positional adjustments; an officer in the 14th NC recorded, "The [brigade] moved forward the second day of the battle and occupied a road running through farms."[80] Then, once pickets were posted, the Tar Heels did little. Sergeants made sure weapons were cleaned, cartridge boxes supplied, and canteens filled. After that, the Carolinians lounged about, keeping low and out of sight of Yank snipers. The hours went by slowly; pickets were changed frequently, but the battlefield remained strangely quiet. Later that afternoon, far to the south, massive formations battled, but for the men in the Thirtieth, this was someone else's fight.

Major Sillers was called to brigade headquarters after sunset; Gen. Ramseur had orders for a night assault. He explained the plan to the surprised officers, stating, "I received an order ... to advance in line of battle on the enemy's position on the Cemetery Hill."[81] General Ewell wanted two divisions to strike simultaneously; Early's men from the north and Rodes from the west. Richard Ewell hoped darkness would enable the Confederate infantry to approach and strike the Union lines with minimal losses. The Confederates were uneasy with Ewell's scenario, to attack at night was filled with danger; the odds of success were poor. The unhappy Dodson Ramseur laid out how he wanted his regiments positioned: the 4th NC on the left, then the 2nd NC, the 14th NC, and the 30th NC on the right flank. The brigade would have Iverson's men to their left, and

Daniel's people behind. Ramseur gave more instructions and then released his commanders to their units.

Captain James Harris (Co. I) recalled, "By this time, dusk had set in and 'attention' rang among our lines." The company commander continued, "[We were to] storm ... the enemy's batteries on their stronghold was the order of the night."[82] The Thirtieth's riflemen formed, the battle-veterans apprehensive and fretful; no one thought this tactic had merit. James Harris remarked, "It was cloudy and the moon had not risen, consequently it was quite dark." He added, "I cautioned my men to stick together and to pay attention to orders, not to fire, but to make for the enemy with all possible haste as soon as so ordered."[83] Then, Brig. Gen. Dodson Ramseur put the brigade into column-of-fours and striding up to the Thirtieth's position, led the Carolinians southward.

The Thirtieth moved as quietly as possible for five hundred yards before Ramseur halted the brigade. He right-faced his nine hundred riflemen, forming a battle line facing east, towards Cemetery Hill. Captain Harris reported, "In our front was a gentle rise of some eminence, just beyond a ravine down which ran a road leading out of town and now about parallel with our lines ... after this another small hill was to cross and yet another narrow ravine before the hill—on which was planted the enemy's batteries ... and a stone wall behind which was posted Yankee infantry."[84] General Ramseur ordered the brigade's sharpshooters forward. They eased eastward, slipping silently toward the Union lines, hidden in the darkness. Whispered commands instructed the Tar Heels they were to advance without firing; tonight the bayonet would be their weapon.

Major William Sillers quietly moved forward, checking to see that his regiment's battle line remained intact. The Thirtieth's riflemen crept forward, hunched down, peering into the night's darkness, fearing what lie ahead, as well as who followed behind. Captain James Harris admitted, "Daniel was in our rear to support us. To tell the truth, I dreaded his men equally as much or more than I did the Yankees, for the day before was the first engagement they had ever been in, and you know how much men become excited under fire in the day, much less in the night."[85]

Ramseur's sharpshooters pushed forward, the experienced riflemen maintaining a skirmish line. Finally, the Confederates' advance was discovered by Union pickets, who opened fire; their musket flashes defining their position. Dodson Ramseur noted, "[We advanced] within 200 yards of the enemy's position, where batteries were discovered in position to pour upon our lines direct, cross, and enfilade fires. Two lines of infantry behind stone walls and breastworks were supporting these batteries."[86] The Tar Heel sharpshooters returned fire and crept forward, scattering the Union skirmish line. But the Yanks did not retreat far; they were immediately supported by additional troops. Volleys rang out in the night's darkness, sending hundreds of minié bullets buzzing towards the Tar Heels. Private James Cheatham (Co. B), one of the Thirtieth's riflemen in the sharpshooter unit, was struck. He fell, crying for help. Several of his fellow comrades rushed to his side and carried him back to the main line.[87] The heavy Northern fire forced the Confederates to drop and take cover. General Robert Rodes wrote, "After driving in the enemy's skirmishers, the advance line was halted."[88]

A battery of Union artillery opened fire, their muzzle flashes bright in the night's obscurity. Captain James Harris (Co. I) recalled, "The enemy as if aware of our intention commenced bombing us, but fortunately throwing their shells too high."[89] The Confederate riflemen, knowing the Yankee gunners would soon find them, and fearing Daniel's nervous men might start shooting, all took to the ground, not knowing which was worse—being killed by Northern steel or Southern lead. James Harris stated, "We had now reached the top of the [first] hill.... Our movements on that memorable night—memorable ... from the deep emotions it called up in every man's bosom."[90]

Whispered commands passed along the sharpshooters' lines, ordering no more shooting, and once the firing stopped, the Federals also quit. Harris noted, "Cease firing!' was sung out by the Yankee commander of skirmishers on the opposite hill. I was glad to hear that command, for the bullets had already for some time been coming uncomfortably near."[91] Brigadier General Dodson Ramseur crept forward to his skirmish line to examine the Union positions. One of his sharpshooter officers pointed out where the Union main lines were, and the locations of artillery, based on what they had revealed by their musket and cannon flashes. Dodson Ramseur reported, "The strength and position of the enemy's batteries and their supports induced me to halt and confer with Gen. [Rodes]."[92] The division commander replied, "These facts ... convinced me that it would be a useless sacrifice of life to go on, and a recall was ordered."[93] However, as Ramseur and Rodes revised their battle plan the Tar Heel riflemen who lie on the night-dampened ground, figured they were planning a new attack strategy. Captain Harris wrote, "Halt, lie down,' is whispered along down our lines ... [we] could ... hear the enemy speaking [in] a low tone and officers telling their men to 'cover their files' [and] 'let them come.'"[94]

Finally, messengers crept along the battle line, informing the Thirtieth's officers the assault had been cancelled. James Harris remarked, "Suddenly, 'attention, about face, and forward march' is whispered ... what a relief ... many a heart was made glad."[95] But Maj. Gen. Rodes did not want to give up some of the ground his Tar Heels had gained that night. He recorded, "instead of falling back to the original line, I caused the front line to assume a strong position in the plain to the right of the town, along the hollow of an old roadbed. This position was much nearer the enemy, was clear of the town, and was one from which I could readily attack [in daylight] without confusion."[96] Captain James Harris (Co. I) wrote, "We dropped back about 150 yards to a small or narrow road running parallel with our lines. Here, we halted, lay down on our arms, and rested for the remainder of the night."[97] Major William Sillers had his company commanders assess their units; besides one man lost on the skirmish line, another rifleman, Pvt. John Utley (Co. H) was missing. His platoon mates scoffed, "He skulked off somewhere."[98]

Few men in the Thirtieth got much rest during the dark hours, and as the predawn began to lighten the eastern sky on July 3, 1863, an eruption of heavy musketry to the east of Gettysburg jolted awake those few who were asleep. Soon, rumors swept the anxious riflemen telling of a massive attempt to take the heights called Culp's Hill. Some of Maj. Sillers' more observant soldiers had noticed movement behind them during the night—the brigades of Daniel and O'Neil had marched away. Now, these two brigades, along with Maj. Gen. Edward Johnson's entire division were attempting the drive the Yanks from their hilltop perch. This assault, the Thirtieth's veterans concluded, would include Ramseur's troops, who would make an assault on the blue coat lines directly ahead. They shivered in the early morning's chill, though not from the cold.

Captain David Allen (Co. C) received the order to take command of the brigade's sharpshooters. He took the Thirtieth's picked men forward and relieved those who had spent the night hours out in front of the brigade. Meanwhile, the regiment got itself ready for a frontal assault; something the battle-experienced Tar Heels realized would be suicidal. The Thirtieth's adjutant, Frederick Philips wrote, "The morning light revealed the perilous position in which the brigade was left during the night.... We were much nearer the enemy than our friends."[99] Surprisingly, no order came for an attack. In fact, when Maj. Sillers inquired about the assault's status he was told there would not be any. When Cpt. James Harris heard this news he exclaimed, "The next day [July 3] ... dawned beautifully."[100] The Carolinians were content to hunker down behind a Pennsylvania farmer's stone fence and let others get killed.

Unfortunately the Northerners did not accept the brigade sharpshooters' close proximity, and reinforced skirmish lines pushed forward. Captain Harris recorded, "By 9:00 o'clock the skirmishing had become pretty heavy. The Yankees ... charged our picket line—our pickets gave way—the Yankees advanced to the top of the hill and have a commanding view of our position." He added, "Capt. Allen (Co. C) is in our front rallying his skirmishers for the charge.... Forward is the word, and, at a double quick with loud yells our men drive the enemy in confusion back down the hill, capturing several prisoners. This caused the enemy to open on us with their batteries, throwing ball, shell, canister and grape in rapid succession."[101] During this fight, Pvt. William Hood (Co. K) was, "wounded in the left hand ... on the skirmish line."[102] Major Sillers noted, "We sustained some losses during Thursday and Friday, chiefly among the sharpshooters."[103] Another Carolinian wrote, "We were exposed for sometime to the enemy's sharpshooters, who had friendly lodgment in houses around the town."[104]

The Thirtieth's riflemen hid behind the stonewall, with no one risking the hazards of poking his head above the rock fence—knowing what was going on was not worth the peril of getting killed by a Yank marksman. In time, the two skirmish lines ceased their pot shots at each other, and with the exception of a few individual duels between opposing sharpshooters, their part of the battleground grew quiet. Devoid of shooting it may have been, however, the Tar Heels soon were swamped by rumors of preparations for a massive infantry charge. The Carolinians heard these stories, as well as the fabulous news their brigade was not to be included, and wondered what would occur.

The peaceful interlude lasted until a couple minutes past 1:00 p.m., when two Confederate artillery pieces fired in close succession, and then the entire Southern artillery force erupted in a mighty cannonade.[105] Concussion swept over the Tar Heels, as well as the "whooshing" sounds as shells passed over their heads. Then, the entire Union position seemed to explode into a fiendish scene of flame, smoke and dust. Captain James Harris (Co. I) recorded, "more than 100 field pieces opened their thunder and sent forth hissing and screaming through the air their missiles of destruction."[106] Another recalled, "It seemed as if all the Demons in Hell were let loose, and were howling through the air."[107] Union artillery quickly responded and within minutes the entire countryside was filled with destruction. The ground shook, the air quivered, and smoke and dust blotted out both forces' lines. General Robert Rodes noted, "My troops lay about half way between the artillery of the Second Corps and that of the enemy on Cemetery Hill, and directly under the line of fire of fully 100 guns."[108] An anguished Tar Heel wrote, "Seventy cannon ... were pouring forth upon our devoted ranks every missile that human ingenuity could invent for our destruction."[109]

Ordnance began to land close to where Maj. Siller's men huddled behind their stone fence; not many, as the Yank artillery was directed against the Confederate guns, but enough to increase fear and cause damage. Captain Harris wrote, "the enemy continued to shell us ... [striking] Blount Walker ... [tearing] the whole covering off his shoulder ... and the bone so badly shivered as to show the marrow." Harris added, "It is a bad looking sight, but he bears it like a true shoulder and goes on unsupported to the Hospital."¹¹⁰ Another explosion mangled 3rd Lt. Ira Connell (Co. G), causing him to bleed to death. Moments later, another projectile sent chunks of burning steel ripping into Pvt. Henry Hathaway's (Co. F) jaw, and slicing into his shoulder. And not long after Hathaway was carried back to the field hospital, Pvt. Major Johnson (Co E) was felled by shrapnel; the metallic pieces smashing into his head, fracturing his skull.¹¹¹ Later, Brig. Gen. Dodson Ramseur would grumble, "[We] remained in line ... exposed to the artillery of the enemy and our own short-range guns, by the careless use of imperfect ammunition."¹¹²

The Carolinians huddled in terror; it was just as likely a poorly manufactured Confederate shell could strike as a well-made one from the blue coats. There was nothing the frightened Tar Heels could do but endure the bombardment. One soldier noted, "Most of the men were extremely tired ... [and] their nerves were worn down. Many of them simply settled the matter of what to do by going to sleep."¹¹³ Nonetheless, asleep or not, more Carolina boys were harmed. Private Abraham Brewer (Co. A) was injured when jagged-steel fragments mutilated his back, and shattered his left hand. Another explosion of shrapnel lacerated Pvt. George Madra's (Co. F) hand and hacked his knee into splintered fragments.¹¹⁴ Finally though, the cannon-fire ceased. Captain James Harris (Co. I) wrote, "stillness reigned supreme. The awful storm with all its attendant thunder had passed and now nothing disturbed the deep calm save for the stray shot of a picket or the deep rumbling of the distant thunder of a cannon far away to our right as it echoed and re-echoed among surrounding hills." He continued, "[Then] ... as far as the eye can reach on the right, long rows of infantry clear the woods and enter the field and move down towards the line occupied by us but to the right of us. It was a grand sight, never did men move in better lines—never did a flag wave over a braver set of man." Harris also added, "We ... were completely out of danger. Consequently we were ... mere spectators.... It was the grandest scene that I ever witnessed or ever expect to."¹¹⁵

The Tar Heels rose up from their hiding places and gawked at the massive wall of Confederate infantry moving across the open fields, the Southern riflemen covering nearly a mile of front.¹¹⁶ Captain Harris remarked, "The Yankees saw them as plainly as we did, and all the way down the inclined plane they throw shell into their lines with as much precision as if in 100 yards. But still undaunted, they move steadily forward. I expected when they got on the line with us that we would move forward with them, but I was mistaken; on they went, and we retained our position."¹¹⁷ A Confederate wrote, "Then the rebel yell sounded over the roar of the battle and [they] surged beyond the [Emmitsburg road] fences." Another scribbled later, "Many of the soldiers marched in a half-stoop with their head bowed, as if walking in a storm." And another recorded, "Volley after volley of crashing musket balls swept through the line and mowed [the Confederates] down like wheat before the scythe.... Half the flags went down.... Then the flags came up again."¹¹⁸ The Tar Heels' admiration turned to dismay, and then to shock. The assault was destroyed in less than twenty minutes; over five thousand Southern veterans were slaughtered.¹¹⁹

Major William Sillers' men were stunned as they tried to fathom what had just occurred. One Tar Heel wrote, "It was a second Fredericksburg, only the wrong way." Another added, "How painful indeed it must be to the parents and friends of [those] so young and promising, to hear that life's brittle thread has been cut."¹²⁰ Commands rolled down the Tar Heel line to prepare for an expected Federal counter attack. Sillers' troops turned their focus away from the huge field littered with devastated Southern manhood and readied their weapons and gear. The hours slowly ground by, with each additional minute adding to the soldiers' tension; but the Yankees did not come. Small units did creep forward cautiously, but none made aggressive moves. Most of the activity was by Northerners who went about the Confederate casualties, collecting wounded, gathering up prisoners, and burying the dead. One Yank reported, "Five hundred and twenty-two Confederates ... [were] buried in a mass grave in the field that extended from the angle area to the Emmitsburg Road."[121] Finally though, the sun settled below the western horizon, allowing the Confederates to set aside their muskets.

Meanwhile, during those last daylight hours of July 3, 1863, Maj. William Sillers' two surgeons, Dr. Charles Gregory and Dr. George Briggs struggled to save their injured Tar Heels' lives. The Thirtieth's field hospital was part of a much large medical center, a place of unimaginable horror. The entire facility was described by a horrified Gettysburg resident, who wrote, "Nothing before in my experience had ever paralleled the sight we see.... The [soldiers] were groaning and crying, the struggling and dying, crowded side-by-side, while attendants sought to aid and relieve them."[122] Surgeons Gregory and Briggs had forty-two wounded Carolina boys under their care. Some men were seriously injured, like Col. Frank Parker and Pvt. George Swain (Co. C); others were lightly hurt, like Pvt. James Southerland (Co. E), who now was able to limp about with bandages covering his injury, and Cpl. Elijah Bales (Co. K), who also weathered a flesh wound.[123]

Also, during these night hours, General Lee repositioned his battered forces. Major General Robert Rodes recorded, "During the night of the 3rd, my division fell back to the ridge which had been wrestled from the enemy in the first day's attack."[124] For the boys in the Thirtieth, this shift meant, as Cpt. James Harris (Co. I) noted, "That night at 12 o'clock we were waked up and marched back to the hill and on the turnpike road ... taking position just to the right of it and just against a Yankee Hospital."[125]

General Lee, within hours of the Pickett's Charge debacle, decided his army should no longer fight at Gettysburg and issued orders to create plans to move everyone back to Virginia. His staff quickly developed marching orders for the infantry, artillery, and cavalry; however, their major concern arose when they determined the army had over nineteen thousand wounded. While a number of these injured fellows could walk, most were incapable of movement—they had to be transported. Unfortunately, the Army of Northern Virginia only had 1,200 wagons available for hauling wounded soldiers; there were just too many casualties.[126] The Confederate planners faced the ugly truth; people would have to be left behind.

This horrible news was passed down the chain of command and reached Surgeons Charles Gregory and George Briggs. The two Carolina doctors now faced a terrible dilemma, the Thirtieth had enough vehicles to transport about half of their wounded; they would have to choose who would be abandoned. Sadly, two of the young men in their care had died from their injuries, Pvt. George T. Swain (Co. C) and Pvt. Aaron E. Griffith (Co. K) late on July 3, 1863. A small squad quickly buried them. Then Gregory and Briggs, with Chaplain Alexander Bett's assistance, sorted through their patients, determining who was healthy enough to travel, and who must remain behind. In all, they were able to find transport for twenty-one. The other nineteen Carolinians would be deserted and turned over to Northern mercies. Alexander Betts was so distraught, he admitted, "[I was so over-wrought] ... riding over the fields from one hospital to another, when I fell from my horse ... [and] not knowing I had fallen, and remain[ed] unconscious for an hour."[127]

With sunrise on July 4, 1863, the Confederate army had two tasks: prepare the wounded for transport, and fight off any Federal assaults before retreating back to Virginia. Captain Harris wrote, "A little after daybreak we had thrown up a pretty good breastwork and now stood prepared to receive the shock if the enemy felt prepared to give it."[128] An officer in the 14th NC commented, "On the morning of the 4th, our position was changed to a more formidable one."[129] However, even as the Carolinians manned their defensive position, gossip had already informed everyone many of their friends and relatives were going to be left behind. General Rodes noted, "During the day of the 4th, all the wounded who could walk or be transported in wagons and ambulances were sent to the rear."[130] Everyone was miserable. One soldier wrote, "[We] had done very hard fighting, lost a lot of men, and yet … failed to accomplish anything."[131]

Major William Sillers gathered his company commanders together. The regiment numbered just over two hundred riflemen and officers. Captain James Holmes (Co. A) was now second in command, though Cpt. John McMillan (Co. E) was actually more senior in rank than Holmes. However, following McMillan's court martial after Sharpsburg, no one looked to him for dependable leadership. Thus, the third in command slot fell to Cpt. Willis Moore (Co. F). Therefore, Sillers looked to Holmes and Moore to guide his regimental wings. They waited for something to happen, but the morning went by quietly. A Southerner wrote, "Noon came and passed. Not a gun was fired…. In another hour, rain began to fall."[132] At first the precipitation was light, but this did not last long. Soon, a deluge washed over the countryside. A Confederate remarked, "The very windows of heaven seem to have opened."[133]

The rain continued, pounding the Confederates, and impeded the formation of the wounded soldiers' wagon train. In time, medical personnel had loaded over twelve thousand injured Southerners into the vehicles and the lead wagons, those of Gen. Pettigrew's brigade (Third Corps), began to move, heading west. The immense convoy, once rolling, stretched out in a procession nearly seventeen miles in length. Brigadier General John Imboden, the cavalry commander tasked with protecting the wagons, wrote, "By 4 p.m. … the wagon train was in motion … it was after dark when the last wagons rolled out."[134]

Meanwhile, the Tar Heel riflemen watched as their wounded comrades disappeared down the saturated roads leading west, while glancing over their shoulders, checking to see that Union troops were not moving to attack. The afternoon hours went by slowly before the darkness fell over the soggy landscape. Then they received word to march. One Carolinian wrote, "A terrific downpour of rain fell which so hindered the movement that [our] rearguard did not start before early morning of the 5th [July]."[135] General Robert Rodes reported, "On the night of the 4th, we began to fall back toward Hagerstown, by way of Fairfield."[136] Captain James Harris (Co. I) added, "About midnight commenced falling back toward Hagerstown—marched very slowly, marching only about six miles the first day."[137] The Carolinians, now designated as part of the army's rearguard, slogged westward, continually scanning their rear for approaching blue coats. That evening Maj. Gen. Rodes noted, "[we] bivouacked on the night of the 5th, after a most wearisome march in mud and rain, 2 miles west of Fairfield."[138]

On July 6, 1863, division commander Robert Rodes spread out his brigades, Daniels to the north of the Fairfield road, Doles to the south, and Ramseur as their support. A Tar Heel in the 2nd NC recorded, "On the morning of July 6 … [as] the rear guard of the army … was engaged in several brief skirmishes on that day."[139] The Northerners' attack were made by cavalry units, though they did not push against the Confederates aggressively, and soon backed off, content to remain just out of dangerous range. The blue coats were satisfied to trail behind the Southerners, able to monitor the Confederates' retreat as well as pressure the rearguard reserves into maintaining a strong defensive force. General Rodes wrote, "at 3:30 p.m. we resumed the marched, and proceeded without annoyance or delay across the mountain, by Monterey Springs, to Waynesboro."[140] A Tar Heel rifleman grumbled, "I don't mind marching through the mud, 'tis soft; I don't mind being hungry, I can draw my belt tighter; but I do mind lack of sleep. I [hate] sleep walking—falling down in the mud and such wakes me."[141]

The next morning, July 7, 1863, Maj. Sillers studied the morning report tallies and was horrified to learn his regiment had lost almost twenty men during the past day-and-half's march.[142] He sought out his company commanders and first sergeants and discovered they were dismayed to learn that every company except K had experienced losses. The NCOs, in conversations with their platoons, learned most of the absent fellows were exhausted, sick, or completely discouraged. Two of these absent men, Sgt. Isaac Merritt (Co. A) and Pvt. Abraham Brewer (Co. A) had both been wounded, and when they did not get wagon transport, had attempted to march with the regiment, rather than be left behind at Gettysburg. Both could go no farther than the pass at South Mountain.[143] Others like Pvt. Nicholas Rackley (Co. I), had developed such a severe illness, they could not keep up. And finally, there were some simply identified as deserters.

Major Sillers, aware he regiment's strength now numbered less than two hundred, would later learn of one more disaster occurring while they retreated. On July 5, 1863, Federal cavalry units caught up with the wagon train carrying the Confederate army's wounded and attacked at several locations. The blue coats captured dozens of wagons and nearly one hundred wounded prisoners, including the colonel of the 11th North Carolina, Collett Leventhorpe. One such Yank raid struck among the 30th NC's supply wagons, and though no Tar Heels were taken, gear and equipment was captured. William Sillers recorded later, "In our retreat the Yankee Cavalry attacked our wagon-train. I don't know how many wagons were lost; but among those destroyed was our Regimental Headquarters wagon. I lost my trunk and bed-clothes—everything in fact but the clothes I had on and a change of underclothing ... which were in my saddle bags."[144]

General Ramseur's brigade straggled into Hagerstown. Captain James Harris recorded, "Arrived at Hagerstown ... about 1 o'clock. Camped there for three days just on the picket part of the time. Fared first rate—changed position and formed line of battle."[145] The exhausted Carolinians rested, scrounged for food, and warily watched Union horseman roam about, just out of artillery range. The blue coats attempted a few advances against the Confederate line, but these forays were half-hearted and never put Maj. Sillers' men in any danger. The Tar Heels occupied their position until July 11, 1863, along with the rest of the brigades in Rodes' division. Then, they were shifted to entrenchments near Williamsport. Ramseur's brigade was posted on the far left of Rodes' division, making them the left flank of the Confederate army.[146] The Federals did nothing more than harass the Southerners. The only problem facing the Carolinians was the rain. Chaplain Alexander Betts recorded, "Rain and wind for five days."[147]

The nearly continual rain soaking the soldiers and the countryside, also added so much runoff to the Potomac River, its waters swelled. The fords across the river no longer could be used, trapping Lee's army on the Maryland side. Confederate engineers hustled to construct a pontoon bridge near the community of Falling Waters, but in the meantime, the Southerners were forced to wait. Eventually the rains subsided and the Potomac's flood began to fall. Then, Gen. Lee was able to give orders for his soldiers to begin crossing. First, the wagon train of wounded crossed the pontoon bridge; this was followed by the supply convoy, artillery, and the soldiers of the First and Third Corps. The Second Corps remained in their entrenchments until commands came for them to move. A traffic jam remained at the Falling Waters bridge, so Ewell's men were told to wade across the still-swollen waters at a ford near Williamsport.

On July 13, 1863, the Carolinians moved. Major General Robert Rodes reported, "My division waded the river just above the aqueduct over the mouth of the Conococheague; the operation was a perilous one. It was very dark, raining, and excessively muddy. The men had to wade through the aqueduct, down the steep bank of soft and slippery mud, in which numbers lost their shoes and down which many fell." He continued, "The water was cold, deep, and rising; the lights on either side of the river were dim, just affording enough light to mark the places of entrance and exit; the cartridge-boxes of the men had to be placed around their necks: some small men had to be carried over by their comrades; the water was up to the armpits of a full-sized man."[148] Lieutenant William Ardrey (Co. D) scribbled in his journal, "Left our entrenchments and moved in the direction of Williamsport, Md. Arrived after dark, raining very hard, the Potomac very much swollen." He continued, "commenced re-crossing the river at 10 o'clock in the night; it was neck deep to a low man. We waded with our clothes on; order to swing our cartridge boxes around our necks ... the mud was nearly knee deep." Captain James Harris (Co. I) added, "Arrived there [Williamsport] after dark [and] remained until nearly 12 midnight. Commenced crossing—had to wade mud knee deep 3 or 4 hundred yards before we got to the river. This was rough & tough; waded the river striking us to our armpits; crossed without incident."[149] General Rodes completed his report on the crossing, writing, "We crossed without the loss of a single man, but I regret to say with the loss of some 25,000 or 30,000 rounds of ammunition, which were unavoidably wetted and spoiled."[150]

Once across the Potomac, and safely on the Virginia side, the water logged Confederates stumbled onto a road and shuffled forward in the dark. Captain Harris noted, "Marched about 3 miles through the rain—lay down perfectly drenched and slept about two hours. Waked up as wet and mangy as a huntsman's dog.[151] The worn-out and wet soldiers returned to the march not long after sunrise, and hiked to Darkesville. Here, the miserable men stacked arms and fell to the ground in exhaustion. Robert Rodes remarked, "When the division reached Darkesville, nearly one-half of the men and many officers were barefooted."[152] The next day Maj. Sillers received word Brig. Gen. James Pettigrew had been mortally wounded in the fight at Falling Waters. Pettigrew had been commanding the Confederate defenses as Falling Waters, buying time so the final cannons and infantry could get across the pontoon bridge and escape the Northerners' pincer movements. Major William Sillers penned a letter, writing, "Genl. Pettigrew ... was mortally wounded day before yesterday just before re-crossing the Potomac. Genl. Pettigrew was not dead yesterday at 12 o'clock but it is thought he will certainly die."[153] James Pettigrew's death saddened many men in the Thirtieth; he had been a very popular Tar Heel from the Old North State.

The Confederates remained in the Darkesville area for the next week; the men recuperating, fixing what gear could be repaired, bringing in new supplies, and attempting to scrounge foot ware. A number of Thirtieth soldiers who had missed the Gettysburg campaign marched into camp, adding to the regiment's shriveled strength. These new men may have added more numbers to the formation, but they did nothing for the unit's morale. The Gettysburg veterans all shared a melancholy the new men could not change.

One Tar Heel grumbled, "General Lee made a bad trip going into Maryland. Has got lots of men killed and no good done on our side." He added, "it looks like this war is going against us, but it is just as it is, and it can't stop.... They are going to overpower us for they can do it because they have so many more men than us."[154] Major William Sillers, alarmed at his regiment's morale, and yet powerless to change it, wrote, "Our campaign on the other side of the Potomac was not as successful as we could have wished."[155]

30th North Carolina Infantry[156]
Casualties: Gettysburg Campaign
June—July 1863

Unit	Commander	Loss
Field & Staff	Col. Parker, Francis	1
Co. A	1st Lt. Williams, Gary	5
Co. B	1st Lt. Davis, Weldon	5
Co. C	Cpt. Allen, David	7
Co. D	Cpt. Allen, Charles	13
Co. E	Cpt. McMillan, John	4
Co. F	Cpt. Moore, Willis M.	7
Co. G	1st Lt. Badgett, James W.	6
Co. H	Cpt. Wicker, Jess J.	15
Co. I	Cpt. Harris, James	14
Co. K	Cpt. Witherspoon, John G.	4
		76

CHAPTER 10

Disaster at Kelly's Ford

Brigadier General Dodson Ramseur ordered his Tar Heels to break camp before sunrise on July 22, 1863. He put his four regiments onto the road heading south, following the other brigades in Maj. Gen. Robert Rodes' division. The Confederates hiked all day, passing through Leetown, Smithfield, and nearly reaching Winchester before halting for the night. From there, the Carolinians trekked farther south, and when orders came to move up in support of Southern units facing off against blue coats, they hustled to Front Royal and then to Manassas Gap. General Rodes wrote, "the ... afternoon found us, after a march of 23 miles, facing nearly the whole Federal Army in the vicinity of Manassas Gap." Northerners exchanged musketry with troops from Brig. Gen. Ambrose Wright's brigade (Third Corps). Robert Rodes noted, "My division was ordered there to relieve Wright's brigade.... All my sharpshooters (about 250) men were ... sent to strengthen Wright's line."[1] The fight never developed much beyond skirmish fire, and then the Yanks withdrew. The Carolinians bivouacked not far from the pass, worn out by covering thirty-seven miles in two days beneath the scorching summer sun. The men were also concerned by the inability of the army to supply them with their logistical needs. Private Aaron DeArmond (Co. D), who had hobbled along that entire distance on worn-out shoes, scribbled to his wife, "Well, my dear.... I am nearly bare footed and if I don't get a pair of shoes I do not know what I will do."[2]

The next day, July 24, 1863, the Tar Heels turned around and marched back to Front Royal. They turned south and hiked along the western side of the Blue Ridge, before trekking up into the mountains, passing through Thorton's Gap. The Thirtieth's chaplain, Alexander Betts recorded; "Cross mountain at Thorton's Gap. Cool springs all the way up the mountains. Four miles up and four miles down."[3] Again, news reached the Southerners; blue coats were moving to attack. Major William Sillers remarked, "we [marched] through Front Royal by the Lauray Road, and crossed the Blue Ridge at Thorton's Gap. We are now here awaiting ... the enemy's advance." He added, "[The Federals'] ... great successes have in no doubt inspired him with renewed confidence in his ability to finally subdue us ... the disaster has come upon us, and it is now too late to repine."[4] And yet again, the Northerners backed off when Confederate infantry deployed for battle. The Carolinians resumed their march, arriving in the Madison Court House area on July 29, 1863. Lieutenant Archibald Jackson (Co. H) wrote, "Arrived yesterday. I have bin marching nearly all the time sense ... the 2nd of June but I have held out finley [sic.].... We have 26 men present for duty. We get plenty to eat if we could get more salt."[5]

The brigade rested for a couple days before moving to the Orange Court House area. Here, the soldiers, once again tethered to a railroad, rested while the army commenced the process of replenishing the equipment and supplies worn out or lost during the Gettysburg campaign. Meanwhile, as the barefoot men acquired shoes, Maj. Sillers received the first of several large shipments of replacements. Alexander Betts recorded on July 30, 1863, "Conscripts, thirty-five or forty arrive for our Regiment."[6] Private Aaron DeArmond (Co. K) mentioned, "we just had 16 men in the company until yesterday; we got 11 more conscripts to recruit our camp up again." He also added, "My dear, I am getting grey very fast; my beard is nearly white and.... I expect my head will be right white before this war is ended."[7]

Ramseur's brigade, along with their fellow Confederates in Rodes' division, divided time between rebuilding the debilitated regiments, and picket duty along the Rapidan river. More conscripts were added to the Thirtieth's ranks; by the end of August, ninety-three new faces had been added to the regiment, increasing the formation's strength by over a third.[8] Lieutenant William Ardrey (Co. K) noted, "The company had been recruited by its conscripts and now we have a large company in numbers."[9] Major William Sillers immediately put his company commanders and NCOs to work, drilling these men. But these replacements did not have the attitude of the original volunteers; almost every man now mustering into the Thirtieth was a conscript, and few wanted to be a part in the crusade to defend the Confederacy. William Sillers' training program was also hampered by a punishing heat wave. The frustrated major grumbled, "The last week has been a succession of about seven [very hot] days as I have felt for a long time. We have been doing nothing within three or four days. Previously we had commenced drilling; but it is really inhuman to drill anyone [in] such weather as this."[10] Nonetheless, even though the commander of the Thirtieth called off training because of the weather, Brig. Gen. Dodson Ramseur ignored the heat. Captain James Harris (Co. I) noted, "[We] have brigade drill two or three times a week and invariably drill twice a day, Saturdays and Sundays excepted."[11]

General Robert E. Lee, concerned by Gettysburg's non-replaceable loss of valuable veterans, attempted various schemes to replenish his army's numbers with these troops. A Southerner wrote, "Lee ... on the 11th of August offered a general pardon to deserters who would return to their commands. All soldiers who were under trial or were serving sentence for desertion were released."[12] Lee's program may have brought in some troops in other regiments, but for the Thirtieth, the returns were nil. Captain James Harris reported, "Not one of the deserters from my company have returned under the President's Proclamation." He wrote further, "[I] have had 5 conscripts added to my Company.... I was opposed to it, but they preferred my Co. to any other & I hated to refuse them. One has since departed [deserted] ... he [James B. Borrows] is a rare specimen of human depravity."[13]

Confederate morale remained dismal, forcing the high command to seek measures to stem the increasing number of desertions. Private Aaron DeArmond (Co. K) wrote, "I hope this war is very near to a close ... if it don't before long we will not have an army. Men are deserting every day. Men are getting tied of the war."[14] Major William Sillers did what he could to keep his company commanders and NCOs vigilant against deserters, and yet, four Carolinians slipped away in August 1863.[15] Finally, in desperation, the frustrated high command sought extreme measures. General Dodson Ramseur remarked, "a deserter from one of [my] regiments [4th NC] was executed by firing squad, after which the entire brigade marched past the corpse ... it was a sad sight."[16]

The Thirtieth also lost officers. Lieutenant William Ardrey (Co. K) recorded, "I presented Lieut. Col. T. J. Kell's and Lieut. N. D. Orr's resignations upon certificates of disability. Both of which were approved."[17] Lieutenant Colonel James Kell's hip wound had failed to heal properly, and he realized he could never return to active duty, and 1st Lt. Nathan Orr's (Co. K) health problems rendered him unable to withstand rigorous military activities; therefore both men resigned. Of course, once these two resignations were logged into the regiment's books, their empty positions meant advancement. Major William Sillers was promoted to lieutenant colonel, and William Ardrey earned his first lieutenant bars on September 1, 1863. Then, Cpt. James Holmes (Co. A), was elevated to assume Sillers' old rank—major.[18]

General Lee, also on September first, ordered a grand review of Lt. Gen. Ewell's Second Corps. The newly minted Company K first lieutenant recorded, "The three divisions arrived on the field about 9 o'clock and were formed in order according to the rank of the Lieut. Generals; Gen. Early's division in front, Gen. Johnson's in rear, and Gen. Rodes in the center. Each line was about three miles long." He continued, "We opened ranks, presented arms. The drums were beating, the bands playing while Gen. Lee and his staff passed up and down the lines. Then he took his position in front and three divisions passed in review.... It was one of the grandest sights that we had ever witnessed in our lives. The army was in fine condition and made a fine appearance. We felt proud of ourselves and our country." The young officer also added, "a great many ladies are present, which is very fine and a treat to the Soldiers."[19] Not far from Lt. Ardrey, Cpt. James Harris (Co. I), also noticed the women; he bragged to an acquaintance, "Tell Miss Lucy that I am the one she ought to have sent her love to.... I think that I am the greatest appreciator of female beauty and intelligence living."[20]

Several weeks passed peacefully; Lt. William Ardrey (Co. K) recorded, "We are having a quiet time in camp, drilling and preparing for action." Then, on September 14, 1863, the Thirtieth was moved. Ardrey noted, "We marched to Morton's Ford and went on picket duty."[21] The regiment built defenses and patrolled the south side of the Rappahannock river. The Thirtieth carried out these responsibilities for several days before being relieved by a brother regiment from Ramseur's brigade. They then went into camp. The Tar Heels' spirits remained poor; even Lt. Col. William Sillers was affected by this malaise. He wrote his wife, "How I wish I were tonight [at home].... All is quiet now; but whether it will remain so many days I cannot tell." He finished his letter, scribbling, "Kiss the dear children all."[22]

William Sillers' regiment grew in numbers as more conscripts were added to the company rolls. Over seventy more men arrived in September, to be distributed among the companies.[23] Lieutenant William Ardrey noted, "Co. K was reinforced by nine new conscripts."[24] Few of these draftees made decent riflemen. Some slipped away from the regiment as soon as they could, and one, Daniel Hinshaw (Co. D) was eventually discharged because of his religion—he "was a member of the Society of Friends [Quakers]."[25] The Thirtieth's numbers closed in on five hundred troops, but Lt. Col. William Sillers had little confidence he commanded a dependable fighting force.

A Northern troop movement brought the Confederates out of their morose complacency. General Ramseur led his brigade out of camp before sunrise on October 9, 1863. The Southerners marched northwest to Madison Court House, and from there, waded the Robertson river and hiked sixteen miles towards Warrenton. The troops bivouacked near the Culpepper Court House before arising the next morning and pushing on to Warrenton Springs. Here, the gray-clad soldiers encountered blue coats. A Tar Heel rifleman wrote, "[The brigade] sharpshooters sent to the front, and our line of battle was formed under fire of the enemy's artillery."[26] Private Morrison Webb (Co. F), a member of the sharpshooters' force, was wounded.[27]

A mass of Federals had separated itself from the main force and its commanders feared capture. The Northerners hastily withdrew, and the Confederate high command urged a rapid response to chase them down. A Carolinian remarked, "the brigade marched 10 miles, camping on the Sperryville Pike, 5 miles from Culpepper Court House ... the brigade crossed the Hazel R. at the burnt bridge and overtook the enemy at Warrantor Springs at 3 in the afternoon." He continued, "Sharpshooters were called to the front, but after a brief skirmish, the Federals retreated, and Ramseur's men crossed the Rappahannock and encamped at 9 p.m."[28] Another added, "[We] formed in line of battle. The enemy continued to retreat."[29] In this frantic exchange of musketry, Pvt. Marion Jackson's (Co. B) foot was shattered by a minié bullet, and Pvt. Richard Harris (Co. G) suffered a serious thigh wound.[30]

The Union formation fled and the Confederates hustled right after them. A Tar Heel described the chase, writing that the highway was littered "with the articles retreating soldiers throw away, knapsacks, blankets, [and] guns even." Another added, "The eyes of the Southerners lighted.... It was ... almost like boys chasing a hare."[31] But now Gen. Ramseur's infantrymen were no longer in the lead; this honor went to soldiers in the Third Corps. This meant Ramseur's men saw little of the spoils abandoned by the fleeing Yanks, instead, all that was left for them was stories of treasure acquired by others, and dust. Lieutenant William Ardrey (Co. K) wrote, "[It was] ... a warm and tiresome march."[32]

The Confederates at the front of the Southern column caught up with the Yanks at Bristoe Station in the afternoon of October 13, 1863. Several brigades in the Third Corps attacked Union troops protected behind a railroad bed and suffered horribly, losing over thirteen hundred men, many of them North Carolinians. A disgruntled Southerner wrote, "I consider every man killed and wounded ... an unnecessary sacrifice, and ... am fully convinced that somebody, high in command, is greatly to be blamed, and if justice were done, would be cashiered."[33] An officer in the 4th NC recorded, "Failure to coordinate the attack resulted in heavy casualties to troops in A.P. Hill's Corps and in the escape of the Federal rear guard."[34] When General Lee inspected the disaster and quietly said, "Bury these poor men and let us say no more about it."[35]

The next morning, October 14, 1863, Ramseur's brigade moved past the shattered Third Corps brigades and pushed against the Federal rear guard. Lieutenant William Ardrey recorded, "Arrived after night and found Gens. Cooke's and Kirkland's brigades badly cut up and disorganized.... We were marching leisurely along in the morning and the enemy's pickets fired into the front of our column. Gen. Ramseur was in front." He continued, "Soon we were forced into line of battle and repulsed the enemy, skirmishing with them all day."[36] Lieutenant Colonel William Sillers deployed his regiment and they faced off against Northerners spread out along the Rappahannock river's opposite banks. Federal minié bullets buzzed into the Tar Heels, wounding Pvt. James Bradshaw (Co. E). Sillers' men fired back at the blue coats, though it was hard to tell if their lead was doing any damage. Another Tar Heel fell; Pvt. John Grady's (Co. E) femur was shattered, forcing Dr. George Briggs to amputate his leg." And moments later, Pvt. Charles Ruffin (Co. I) was severely wounded.[37] The wounded farm boy was carried back to the surgeon, who could only shake his head. Chaplain Alexander Betts was called to tend to the dying youth. Betts recalled, "Charlie H. Ruffin ... wounded yesterday. Dies in my arms—in perfect peace. Charlie enlisted at 17, and perhaps, was the wildest boy in his Regiment."[38] Then, the Yanks fell back, leaving the Southerners holding their own side of the river, and having nothing else beside mangled men. A discouraged rifleman wrote, "we had quite a toilsome march.... I am sorry to say it was a fruitless one according to my opinion."[39]

Ramseur's brigade shifted several miles to the 37th mile-post on the Orange and Alexandria Railroad. Here, orders went out to the regiments; the commander of the 4th NC wrote, "Now tearing up bridges and destroying railroads."[40] A Tar Heel rifleman described their labors, writing, "[We were] ... [o]rdered to destroy the railroad by tearing up the rails, piling them on a heap made of cross-ties, [and] setting the cross-ties on fire."[41] Lieutenant William Ardrey (Co. K) also remarked, "It is very hard and laborious work."[42] The Carolinians completed this task and left the area on October 18, 1863. Lieutenant Ardrey wrote, "[We] marched to the Rappahannock river, raining in perfect torrents. We started out in the morning in the rain. Set out at 4 o'clock a.m., crossed the river on pontoon bridges near the R.R. crossing." He continued "We camped [near] Kelly's Ford, had a beautiful camp arranged by Gen. Rodes in perfect order. We commenced building winter quarters or log cabins to sleep in, we have a beautiful camp."[43] Alexander Betts, pleased to know the regiment was not going anywhere for the winter, happily described his shelter: "Build my log cabin—5 feet wide and 6 feet long—nice stick chimney—oil cloth roof. Nice place to read and write.... Sat on my bed (canvas on two poles) and put my feet to the fire, and wrote on a little box desk."[44]

Brigadier General Dodson Ramseur took furlough from the brigade, temporarily turning over command of his Carolinians to Col. Ridsen Bennett (14th NC). Ramseur's leave of absence was a happy one; he returned to the Old North State and married Ellen "Ellie" Richmond in a ceremony in Woodson, NC.[45] The brigade's interim commander, 23-year-old Risden Bennett, was from Wadesboro, NC. His neighbors described him as an energetic and adventurous fellow. At age seventeen, the young Bennett traveled from North Carolina to the Rocky Mountains, where he spent a summer living with a Plains Indian tribe. Bennett returned to the Southeast and enrolled at Davidson College, and then Cumberland University in Lebanon, TN. He earned a law degree and was a lawyer when the war began. Now, two years into the war, he had just returned to his regiment, having recovered from a wound received at Gettysburg. No one in Ramseur's brigade doubted his courage, though some wondered if he had the maturity to command an entire brigade.

Colonel Bennett worked out a rotating duty assignment; the brigade was charged with guarding the ford across the Rappahannock near the town of Kellysville. He assigned one regiment to man the defenses at Kelly's Ford, with a second a mile away in reserve. These two formations would hold this posting for several days, and then the brigade's other two regiments would replace them. The Rappahannock river at this location split the countryside, running from north to south; thus the Federals were on the east side while the Confederates occupied the west. The ford was easy to cross. A Yank on the east bank wrote, "the ford ... runs nearly south, the water is of a red, muddy color ... the stream ... is generally from 75 to 150 feet in width ... the water is nearly waist deep."[46] The little settlement of Kellysville resided next to the ford. Kellysville was no more than a dozen or so buildings, with the most prominent structure a solidly constructed brick building standing four or five stories. The blue coat soldier described the village, writing, "by the ford is a large brick mill, a store, a blacksmith's shop and various other buildings."[47]

The terrain surrounding Kelly's Ford favored the Union side of the river; there were high bluffs on the east bank overlooking the entire area. A Confederate wrote, "the ground on the [east] bank so fully commanded the [western] side that Confederates ... could not prevent the passage of the river by a strong Federal force at any time."[48] The gray-clad soldiers guarding the west bank dug rifle pits along the shore, and between the buildings as protection. But they knew once the Yanks opened fire with artillery from the towering heights, there was little to be done to resist. Fortunately, the Northerners seemed content to occupy the commanding ground, and showed little sign of wanting to attack. General Robert Rodes inspected his troops' defenses and saw how shaky the position would be once the Federals chose to attack. Rodes posted an artillery battery about a thousand yards west of Kellysville, to support the infantry pickets. Rodes though, was concerned. He wrote, "the bluffs are on the enemy's side, close to the river ... encircle the ground which my outpost force was compelled to occupy."[49]

30th North Carolina Infantry[50]
November 7, 1863

Unit		Strength
Field & Staff	Lt. Col. Sillers, William Maj. Holmes, James Cpt. Moore, Willis M.	5
Co. A	Cpt. Williams, Gary 1st Lt. White, Lallister M..	55
Co. B	Cpt. Davis, Weldon E. 1st Lt. Nicholson, John H.	41
Co. C	Cpt. Allen, David C. 2nd Lt. Swain, John R.	42
Co. D	1st Lt. Abernathy, Sidney S. 2nd Lt. Ferrell, James E.	44
Co. E	1st Lt. Johnson, Ira J. 2nd Lt. Newton, Samuel B.	57
Co. F	1st Lt. Harrell, George 2nd Lt. Eagles, Lorenzo D.	60
Co. G	1st Lt. Badgett, James W. 2nd Lt. Crews, Alexander	50
Co. H	Cpt. Wicker, Jesse J. 1st Lt. McNeil, Henry J.	59
Co. I	Cpt. Harris, James C. 2nd Lt. Arrington, Kearney	58
Co. K	Cpt. Witherspoon, John G. 2nd Lt. Downs, John T.	43
		514

On November 7, 1863, three hundred men of the 2nd North Carolina occupied the rifle pits along the shoreline, with the Thirtieth resting in support, just behind the artillery pieces.[51] Lieutenant Colonel William Sillers led just over five hundred riflemen and officers. His second-in-command, Maj. James Holmes commanded the right wing, composed of Companies C, E, F, H, and K. William Sillers' next-senior officer, Cpt. Willis Moore (Co. F) tended to the left wing, Companies A, B, D, G, and I. The morning dawned misty and chilled. The evening before, a Northerner wrote, "The fog settled down again at night." He added, "The water dashed over the mill [and] soon lulled me to sleep, as I had made a soft bed on a pile of meal bags."[52] William Sillers' men arose, fixed their scanty meals; one Tar Heel grumbled, "the men [were] short of rations and would have to eat roasted corn and acorns. They were so hungry it seems to me there was nothing but what they could eat."[53]

Lieutenant Colonel Sillers received word from Col. Charles Tew (2nd NC) describing worrisome Yankee activities; they were posting more artillery on the heights overlooking the town. The Federal artillery commander on site noted, "I placed Sleeper's (10th MA) battery ... on the heights close to the Rappahannock.... Battery E, 1st RI ... on the bluff ... overlooking Kellysville.... McKnight's battery (12th NY) ... in rear and on the right of.... Battery E."[54] Anticipating the Thirtieth might soon be needed, Sillers called an officers' meeting and told his company commanders to prepare their men.

Colonel Tew reacted to the growing threat by pushing three companies across the Rappahannock and fanning them out as skirmishers. These men squinted into the fog cloaking the low-lying areas. They heard the movement of infantry, but could not see anything. Then, the activity quieted down and nothing happened. Eventually the morning sun melted away the night's fog, revealing a Federal force arrayed at the base of the hills. One of the Yanks in this formation wrote, "At half-past one in the afternoon the two regiments [1st and 2nd USSS] deployed out in a skirmish line, and advancing over the open plain in front."[55] The Yanks came within musket ranks of Tew's three companies and rifle fire erupted. At first, the Confederates were not sure if the Yanks were infantry or cavalry, as the slowly advancing soldiers wore unusual green uniforms, not the normal blue. Their gunshots were not the distinctive thud-noises of muskets; instead they were sharp, cracking-popping sounds, much more characteristics of cavalry weapons.

The attacking Northerners moved like infantry skirmishers, small units advancing while others provided a base of fire. However, the assaulting green-coated soldiers, once completing a short dash forward, would then drop to the ground and open fire from a prone position, more an action typical of dismounted cavalry. The Union troops' rate of fire from this position—lying flat on one's belly—should have resulted in a slow fire, as a normal infantryman firing from the prone position was able to get off about a shot per minute. But these Yanks were firing five or six times each minute; an unheard of rate of fire for infantry. The Northerners' shooting quickly overwhelmed the Carolinians. An officer in the 2nd NC recorded, "Companies B, F, and K were on picket duty, and not receiving timely support, were the heaviest losers."[56] There were less than a hundred Tar Heels; the Yanks had six times that number. The Confederates were firing two times a minute, per soldier, while the Federals were shooting five or six in the same time interval. The Carolinians would eventually learn they were facing infantrymen armed with Sharps rifles, a modern, quick-firing, breach-loading weapon extremely accurate at distances far beyond the Enfields the Confederates used. One Federal rifleman bragged, "the rebel pickets ... could not stand the Sharps rife, which fires so fast and accurate ... [they] immediately fell back across the river to their rifle pits."[57] Another Northerner crowed, "The order to double-quick being given, away [we] went, driving the rebels pell-mell over the river."[58]

As his pickets frantically splashed across the ford and sought shelter in the 2nd NC's entrenchments Col. Charles Tew sent word he needed reinforcements. William Sillers called for his companies to fall into marching order. The Thirtieth's sergeant major, Peter

Arrington recorded, "[Our] regiment being the reserve picket at the ford supporting the 2nd N.C.T. was ordered to the front as the enemy had advanced in heavy force and was about to cross the river."⁵⁹ It took longer than Sillers wanted, but the Thirtieth's ten companies were finally in formation. He gave the command and the Thirtieth moved out of its reserve bivouac and passed the four Confederate cannons, now firing at the greencoated Yanks approaching the Rappahannock's eastern shore. General Robert Rodes recorded, "The Thirtieth North Carolina … was in reserve, protecting the solitary battery (Napoleon) … about three-quarters of a mile from the river in the edge of the nearest woods to the ford."⁶⁰ The Thirtieth was only a quarter of an hour away from the fight.

The Second North Carolina needed to hold out for fifteen minutes. Colonel Tew's rifleman hunkered down in their entrenchments and unleashed volleys upon their greencoated assailants. The Yanks dropped to their bellies along the riverbank and rapidly returned fire. The range between the two forces was less than one hundred yards. A Yank officer remarked, "It was now 'blaze away' on both sides in good earnest."⁶¹ However, at the same time a Northern battery, barely a half-mile away, began to sweep the Confederates' trenches. A Northern artilleryman wrote, "Captain Sleeper … opened on the brick mill at the ford, where the enemy's picket was stationed."⁶² The Tar Heels were forced to seek cover.

William Sillers' five hundred troops crossed the crest of the hill and emerged onto a flat, open field that sloped gently down to Kellysville. Sillers ordered his men forward at the double-quick; they increased their strides and quickened their pace. The Northern gunners immediately saw this solitary, 175-yard-wide formation moving towards them at a distance of less than two thousand yards. One Yank remarked, "After some sharp exchanges reinforcements were observed coming down on a run towards a large brick building."⁶³ Another blue coat wrote, "a [brigade] of infantry came out of the woods on the left of the ford on the opposite side, and, facing to the right, rushed at double-quick for the entrenchments on the river bank. A cross fire of artillery was brought to bear on them."⁶⁴ The three Northern batteries, nearly eighteen guns, adjusted their ranges and began to shell the Thirtieth. Private John Bone (Co. I) recalled, "The [enemy had] placed some artillery on an elevated place on the other side where they had a great advantage

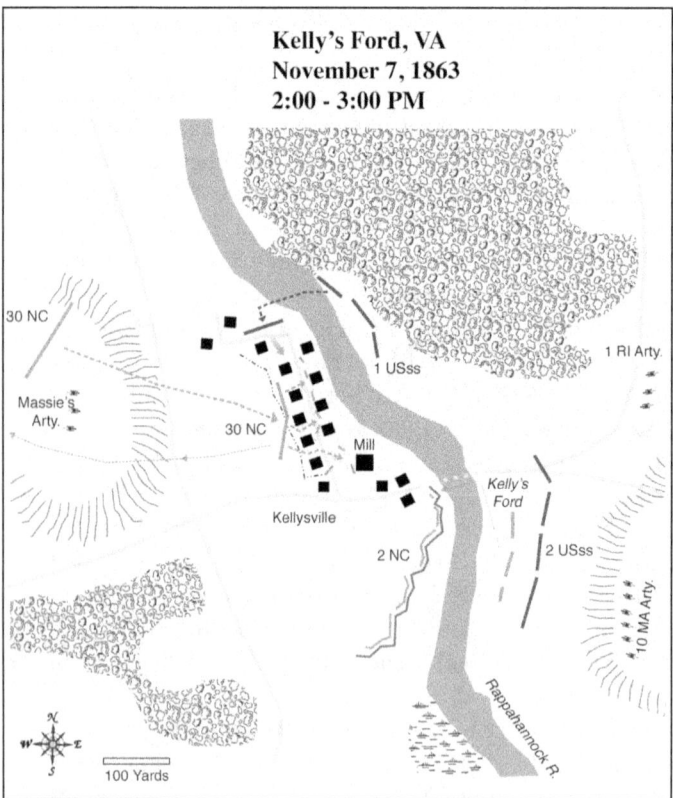

over our men ... they opened their artillery down on us, with grape shot and canister shell ... we had but little protection."[65]

The first shells missed the hustling Tar Heels, the short-targeted rounds exploding in bursts of flame, smoke, and dust, and those over-shooting, screamed by, to detonate somewhere behind. With all three batteries firing as fast as the gunners worked their guns, a shell struck almost every second, filling the Tar Heels' world with smoke, dust, fire, and terror. Unfortunately it did not take the Yank gunners long to adjust their range and score direct hits on Carolina flesh. Corporal William Batchelor (Co. I) was killed and Private Drewry Pridgen (Co. I) had one of his arms nearly blown off by a blast. Moments later, a round erupted among Company K, shredding Pvt. Thomas McLane's right eye, "the ball remaining in his head," and killing Pvt. Lovett Rayner. Another explosion sent shrapnel slicing through Adj. Frederick Philips' left thigh, and fracturing Sgt. Teachy Rivenbark's (Co. E) femur.[66] These blasts horrified the inexperienced conscripts, obliterating their courage. And for the veterans, again, just like at Malvern Hill and Chancellorsville, they found themselves advancing across an open field under direct artillery fire—they knew the deadly peril facing them.

Lieutenant Colonel William Sillers urged his men forward, and the Tar Heels hurried, many seeing the solid brick buildings of Kellysville as a refuge. More Carolinians fell; rounds struck among Company A, killing Pvt. William Boswell, mangling Pvt. Monroe Dove's thigh with sizzling chunks of shrapnel, chopping to shreds Pvt. James Williamson's right arm, and severely wounding Pvt. James Kelly. Another explosion sent metal slivers into Pvt. David Wortman's (Co. G) right eye, and burning steel into Pvt. Hampton Pruitt's (Co. G) chest.[67] More detonations wracked the Thirtieth, knocking down Tar Heels and breaking the regiment into mobs of men. A Union soldier remarked, "the place became too hot for them, causing them to scatter about—like so many bees from a hive."[68] General Rodes later wrote, "The Thirtieth North Carolina ... was speedily broken and demoralized under the concentrated artillery fire which swept the ground over which it had to march."[69]

Meanwhile, Col. Risden Bennett (14th NC) arrived at the Confederate artillery emplacement and quickly analyzed the situation. Bennett could see there was no way the 2nd NC could hold their position against the Union infantry, and he watched in horror as the Thirtieth was being blown to pieces trying to support this futile endeavor. Colonel Bennett realized once the Thirtieth reached the Second's position, they also would not be able to withstand a Federal assault. In effect, the Confederates were throwing away two regiments if they remained at their posts. He sent a messenger racing forward, ordering both regiments to withdraw.

The Thirtieth's frantic soldiers had reached Kellyville's outskirts, a couple houses, their properties outlined by stoutly made wooden fences. One such barrier forced the Thirtieth to halt its advance as the men climbed over the fence boards. Sergeant Major Peter Arrington recorded, "In advancing we had to cross a fence that ran obliquely to our line of battle which kept the Regt. very much broken, and together with the fact of there being a residence immediately in our front encircled by railings ... of the same kind ... which ... necessarily separated the men."[70] The regiment's companies reached the barricade at different times, as the fence was at a diagonal to the riflemen's advance. The frenzied men of Cpt. Willis Moore's left wing reached the mortise and post-construction first and clambered over it, each Carolinian rifleman acting individually. Then, once across, they rushed toward the safety of the town's buildings. The right wing reached the fence line, one company at a time, with each unit struggling to cross the stout barrier. Meanwhile, the Union artillery continued to pummel the Tar Heels. Private Alexander McFatter (Co. H) was knocked to the ground, fragments of scorching steel slicing into his shoulder and back; Pvt. Samuel Aycock (Co. B) was killed; Pvt. John Lewis's (Co. F) arm was nearly ripped from his body by a blast; and 1st Lt. Ira Johnson (Co. E) fell, shrapnel chopping into his hip.[71] A Federal artilleryman wrote, "[my artillery] having by a well-directed fire ... checked [the Confederate] advance."[72]

The messenger reached Lt. Col. William Sillers as he was struggling to keep his regiment's two wings together. Sergeant Major Peter Arrington, who was trying to assist his commander in re-directing the Thirtieth's men, wrote, "The Lt. Col. after passing the obstructions found it necessary to halt and reform but before he had time to accomplish his purpose, he received orders to withdraw."[73] Sillers gave the command to those men in the right wing who had not crossed the fence, ordering them to withdraw. Major James Holmes took charge of these men and hurried them back across the body-strewn field. William Sillers remained, emphatically calling to his soldiers who had rushed into the town. Colonel Frank Parker would later write, "Lt. Co. Sellers ... acted with his wonted coolness and courage."[74] Unfortunately, by now several hundred had already made their way into Kellysville. General Rodes noted, "[the 30th] deliberately [broke] ranks and fle[d] to the houses ... about the mill."[75]

Capt. Weldon Davis' (Co. B), 24 years old, leg was amputated following the fight at Kelly's Ford. He died two weeks later (courtesy Living History Association of North Carolina).

William Sillers shouted at Cpt. John Witherspoon (Co. K), who along with Sgt. Samuel Boyce (Co. K), had already clambered over the fence, and was attempting to corral men and turn them away from entering the town. Unfortunately, before Witherspoon could hear Sillers' words, a near-by explosion sent chunks of molten steel crashing into William Sillers' chest. The Thirtieth's commander fell: Cpt. Gary Williams (Co. A) recorded that "[Sillers] was wounded through the right lung" by the lethal shrapnel.[76] Captain Witherspoon did not see Sillers fall; instead, he worked his way to a clump of confused soldiers milling behind a brick house and convinced them to leave. These fellows scampered back across the dangerous, body-strewn pasture. Some were struck; Pvt. Andrew Thompson (Co. C) was killed, and Pvt. John Patterson (Co. C) injured when shrapnel ripped into his wrist.[77] Others survived; one such rifleman, Pvt. Richard "R. D." Brooks (Co. G), "showed bravery by falling back through the intense fire when ordered to do so."[78] Captain John Witherspoon found Cpt. Willis Moore and together they got another group of men to retreat, this group following Moore to safety. Again, as these Carolinians scurried across the dust and smoke shrouded open field, Union artillery preyed upon them. One such Northern round struck among a cluster of Company F's troops, wounding Sgt. James House, Pvt. William Spencer Barnes, and Pvt. Arthur Forbes.[79]

When the number of retreating Tar Heels diminished to paltry handfuls the Union gunners turned their cannons onto the town. One artilleryman recalled, "these three batteries ... concentrate[d] their fire upon the important positions of the enemy."[80] Private John Vuncannon (Co. C) went down, bleeding from wounds to his chest, hip, and hands. Another Tar Heel badly injured by these artillery shells was Pvt. William Daniel (Co. G), who was raked by shrapnel along his left thigh.[81] The Thirtieth's riflemen, seeing the Federal artillery bombard their hiding spots, sought better shelter within the town's brick structures. One wrote, "The [mill] house cellar and yard was filled with soldiers and behind the building, all in confusion."[82] Some took refuge in the large mill house, its thick brick walls providing some protection. A few Tar Heels went to the upper story windows and began shooting at the Yanks. A Northerner wrote, "One of [their] fellows began shooting at our men from a [mill] window above ... when he put his gun and head out again, Thorp pulled on him ... the reb's gun dropped to the ground outside, while the Johnny fell inside."[83] An artilleryman added, "I shelled the brick houses at the ford in which the enemy's [infantry] were."[84]

Now that the 2nd NC's soldiers were pinned down in their entrenchments by the artillery, and the Thirtieth's men trying to find hiding places within the houses, the Federal infantry commanders saw this as the perfect time to attack. The green-clad soldiers of the 1st and 2nd U.S. Infantry, known as Berdans' Sharpshooters, crossed the river north of the town in three places. Captain John Witherspoon tried to organize a defense and the riflemen he was able to command fired a volley at the advancing green coats. One of these Northerner noted, "[we] rushed down the slope headlong ... through the rapid water—waist deep ... under the galling fire from the enemy ... these were vicious fellows [who] fired to kill."[85] Sadly, Witherspoon did not have a large enough force, and their shooting was limited. Another Yank added, "[we] ran forward ... and when within ten feet of the first pit in their front, the enemy rising up, fired a volley, but being above, fortunately shot too high."[86]

The Berdan sharpshooters swarmed forward, shooting rapidly with their breech-loading weapons, overwhelming the Tar Heels' fire. A green coat wrote, "the Sharps rifle, which was [used] with such effect that completely surprised and bewildered them—some skedaddling or lying down in the pits, not daring to show their heads."[87] Captain John Witherspoon (Co. K), leading the Carolina defense, assembled another small force within the confines of a vegetable garden, but his efforts failed. Private Aaron DeArmond (Co. K) wrote, "Capt. J. G. Witherspoon was shot through the breast."[88] Captain Weldon Davis (Co. B), also with Witherspoon in the garden, fell, his right leg shattered by a minié bullet. And one of the Thirtieth's color guard, Cpl. Elias Allen (Co. D), was shot through the left lung. The small cluster of Carolinians remaining in the garden continued fighting back, but they were soon subdued, including Sgt. Samuel Boyce (Co. K), who fell, his right thigh shattered.[89] Aaron DeArmond recorded, "Sergt. S. J. Boyce was wounded in the right leg; the bone was broken ... six inches above the knee."[90] A triumphant Yank wrote, "Corp. James then rushed straight ahead through the splashing water, over a sand bar to the redoubt near the river. Mounting the same he received the surrender and sword of a North Carolina [officer] ... [Another green coat] fired ... just as the inmates had commenced waving their hats to surrender. The ball passed through one man's head and into another's shoulders, killing both."[91] The rest of the Southerners tossed down their Enfields and raised their hands. One of these riflemen to surrender was Cpl. Lawson Knott (Co. G).

The remaining Tar Heels huddled inside the various houses, some still thinking of resistance, though most just seeking hiding spots. The Federals moved from location to location, rousting out the crestfallen Carolinians. A Northerner described one such capture, writing, "Those in the building ... were considerably surprised by Lieut. Judkins, who, approaching the house noiselessly, suddenly burst in the door, [armed] ... with an axe ... demanded ... their immediate surrender, which was at once granted."[92] In some houses, the Tar Heels resisted, but their single-shot weapons were no match for the Sharps the Northerners possessed. First Sergeant John Newsom (Co. B) was shot in the head trying to hold his position; Pvt. Zachariah Dickey (Co. D), fell with a bullet through his right lung; and Pvt. John Pender (Co. I), received a wound to his left thigh.[93] Nearly all the rest just gave up and surrendered during the next thirty minutes of confusion. Private John Bone (Co. I) recalled, "Our men were compelled to give way and surrender."[94] A Southerner remarked, "Nearly [200] members of the 30th had taken shelter in a cluster of buildings, refused to abandon them when ordered to fall back across ground subject to enemy fire, and meekly surrendered to advancing Federals."[95] Colonel Frank Parker later noted, "the regiment was badly cut to pieces."[96] Chaplain Alexander Betts added, "the 2nd and 30th suffer sadly. Lieut. Col. Sillers is mortally wounded. Some are wounded and many captured."[97]

Meanwhile, Maj. James Holmes assembled his shattered companies in a hollow, just behind the four Napoleon cannons. Colonel Ridsen Bennett moved the Thirtieth away from the guns as he brought up another Tar Heel regiment—one he could depend upon—to protect the guns. Sergeant Major Peter Arrington recalled, "We fell back a short distance, deployed as skirmishers for the protection of our artillery but in a short time Col. Bennett of the 14th N.C.T. commanding Brigade ordered the Regt. to be deployed on a line farther to the right ... we held [the enemy] in check until night came to our relief."[98] A member of the 14th NC, who had been called up to bolster the shaky Thirtieth, wrote, "we ... awaited the charge of the Yankees till nightfall and then were withdrawn to the south bank of the Rapidan."[99]

The Union now held Kellysville, and more importantly, both sides of the ford. Reinforcements crossed the river and solidified the Federals' position, however, little thought was given to pressing the attack. The artillery men cleaned their cannons and called for ammunition resupply; they had fired an incredible number of shells during this fight. One battery commander reported his cannon firing over one thousand rounds of case shot, percussion shell, and canister.[100] Another noted, one of his sections, "fired 150 rounds of solid shot and spherical case."[101]

30th North Carolina Infantry[102]
Casualties
November 7, 1863

Unit	Commander	Loss
Field & Staff	Lt. Col. Sillers, William	2
Co. A	Cpt. Williams, Gary	21

Unit	Commander	Loss
Co. B	Cpt. Davis, Weldon E.	20
Co. C	Cpt. Allen, David C.	15
Co. D	1st Lt. Abernathy, Sidney S.	28
Co. E	1st Lt. Johnson, Ira J.	10
Co. F	1st Lt. Harrell, George	14
Co. G	1st Lt. Badgett, James W.	17
Co. H	Cpt. Wicker, Jesse J.	14
Co. I	Cpt. Harris, James C.	30
Co. K	Cpt. Witherspoon, John G.	14
		185

Once darkness removed the possibilities of more combat, Col. Bennett ordered the Thirtieth to withdraw from its position. Major James Holmes led his rattled regiment south, away from the scene of their disaster. The men stumbled into the brigade's winter camp area, sullen and morose. The Tar Heels spread out to their company locations, quietly, the conscripts who remained were completely shaken; the veterans burned with anger and shame. Major Holmes had his surviving company officers take roll. Their tallies confirmed what everyone knew—the regiment had lost almost two hundred men.[103] One Carolinian moaned, "we were unfortunate enough to lose many of our best men by wounds and capture."[104] Everyone lamented the loss of close friends, as well as relatives. However, they also mourned the death of Lt. Col. William Sillers, who would die two days later. Colonel Frank Parker summed up how the Carolinians felt about William Sillers, when he wrote, "[Sillers] commanded the respect and love of the entire command … [he was] as brave as the bravest, his loss was a sad one … to his regiment."[105] Lieutenant William Ardrey (Co. K) concurred, writing Sillers was, "a brave, good man."[106] Captain Gary Williams (Co. F) added, "[Sillers] is dead, and we can not bring him back.… I hope God will give Mis. Fannie and yourself strength to [?] this sad news."[107]

The Federals in Kellysville now had over 150 prisoners from the Thirtieth, twelve of whom were wounded. Northern surgeons did what they could for the injured soldiers, while provost guards marched the rest off to a holding pen, as preparations were made to ship the prisoners off to interment. Most were sent to the prisoner of war facility at Point Lookout, MD. However, Cpt. John Witherspoon (Co. K) and Cpt. Weldon Davis (Co. B) were sheltered in one of the houses in Kellysville. The owner of the home, John Kelly, wrote, "[Witherspoon and Davis] … were put in the room adjoining my room and I made them as comfortable as I could. The poor creatures suffering greatly all night.… I had buckets of cold water brought and gave it frequently all night to keep them from fainting." Mister Kelly added, "They expressed a great wish to be at home with their family."[108] John Witherspoon died from his wounds the next morning. Weldon Davis recovered enough to be shipped to a hospital in Washington, D.C. Here, surgeons amputated what remained of his leg. However, infection set in and he died from tetanus two weeks later.[109]

The day had been a disaster for Col. Risden Bennett's brigade. The 2nd NC and the 30th NC, a force of nearly eight hundred men had lost close to three hundred; and out of these numbers less than fifty were wounded or killed. The Federal losses were insignificant, three killed and a dozen wounded.[110] When Dodson Ramseur returned to his formation he wrote, "this affair was rather badly managed by the [officers] in command."[111] Not long after this, Gen. Rodes ordered the brigade to move. Alexander Betts grumbled, "Army falls back. I tear down my little house to get my cot out. Had occupied the sweet little home one week." He continued, "Sleep a little on the road, and get to Brandy Station at 2 a.m."[112] Sergeant Major Peter Arrington added, "The Regt. withdrew on the night of the 7th from Kelly's Ford and on the night of the 8th reached their old camp at Morton's Ford."[113] A few weeks later, Lt. William Ardrey (Co. K), who would soon be promoted to assume Cpt. John Witherspoon's responsibilities, wrote, "The true history of the past year can never be written. Thousands of our brave soldiers have poured their life's blood and left their bones to bleach on the battlefield, and their names will pass into oblivion." He continued, "We trust the war cloud will soon pass off and peace will soon be restored, and we all can return to our dear homes and our loved ones, never to hear of wars again."[114]

Chapter 11

Winter 1863–1864

On November 12, 1863, the brigade marched seven miles southwest to Stevensburg, and turned south, hiking another nine miles to the Rappahannock River. The Tar Heels waded across the river at Morton's Ford and set up camp on the south side. Captain John McMillan now led the Thirtieth, as Maj. James Holmes had been given temporary command of the brigade. With Brig. Gen. Dodson Ramseur on leave, James Holmes was the brigade's highest-ranking officer. The formation's other senior officers were all absent; Col. Risden Bennett (14th NC) had taken ill immediately after Kelly's Ford with such severity he was given a sixty-day medical furlough; Col. William Cox (2nd NC) had suffered a disabling wound to his face as his regiment tried to defend Kellysville; and the 4th NC's commanding officer, Col. Bryan Grimes was also on leave, at his Grimesland plantation, in Pitt County, NC.[1]

Major Holmes laid out brigade camping locations and then established regimental picket duty assignments at Morton's Ford. As the Thirtieth's men put up their shelters they lamented their losses, and worried about Lt. Col. William Sillers' plight. Alexander Betts' apprehensions showed when he wrote, "Anxious to hear from Col. Sillers ... but heard ... he died at Gordonsville at 9 a.m. yesterday." The Thirtieth's chaplain continued, "Shall I see him on earth no more? Telegraph[ed] to learn his body ha[d] been sent home."[2] Alexander Betts obtained permission to leave the regiment so he could check on Sillers. Betts recorded, "T[ook] cars to Gordonsville and found [Sillers'] body nicely packed in charcoal."[3] Meanwhile, the Thirtieth's Tar Heels settled into camp, with the tired soldiers remaining dispirited. Lieutenant William Ardrey (Co. K) noted, "the company and Regiment is in low spirits, ha[ve] not recovered from the battle of Kelly's Ford." He also remarked, "Capt. J. C. McMillan was in command of the Reg. ... all drills were suspended, and the men were building winter quarters."[4] Private John Bone (Co. I) noticed this erosion of discipline, writing, "They would let us sleep until sunrise in the morning."[5]

The Thirtieth's turn at river-guard duty came a week later. Chaplain Alexander Betts scribbled in his journal, "Regiment on picket."[6] A few days later, Lt. William Ardrey wrote, "Snow and bitter cold in camp ... on river." On November 26, 1863, Ardrey recorded, "the enemy crossed the river with their entire force at Germania Ford ... our troops were called out [of] the entrenchments."[7] Masses of Federal units splashed across the Rappahannock a dozen miles east of the Tar Heels' position, forcing the Confederate's Second Corps temporary leader, Maj. Gen. Jubal Early to scramble the formation's divisions. The Carolinians were awakened just after midnight, and hustled eastward, "under a 'lunar halo' and in bitter cold ... on the frozen road to Zoar Church."[8] Lieutenant Ardrey wrote, "Our army moved down the river to Mine Run, near Locust Grove, [a] very hard and rapid march."⁹ Once the Southerners arrived, division commander Maj. Gen. Robert Rodes assigned brigade positions. Brigadier General Dodson Ramseur, who had returned to the brigade on November 23, 1863, put the four Tar Heel regiments into battle formation, and pushed forward the brigade's sharpshooters.¹⁰ A few hours later, once the sun had burned away the morning's "foggy atmosphere," the brigade sharpshooters brushed up against blue coats from Brig. Gen. Henry Prince's (II Corps) division.¹¹ Major General Robert Rodes recorded, "my skirmishers were advanced several hundred yards, driving the enemy with ease."¹² A Federal officer reported, "General Prince's ... skirmishers soon encounter[ed] the enemy ... [who] opened a warm fire, and ... his line fell back a short distance ... the action ceasing."¹³ A Confederate officer added, "nothing could be accomplished."¹⁴ The two sides glared at each other, both cautiously waiting for the other to advance. Lieutenant William Ardrey wrote, "The weather was very cold and we lying in ... line of battle all day and constantly expecting the enemy to attack." He also noted, "[It] Rained very hard."¹⁵

That evening, once darkness hid movement, Maj. Gen. Early ordered his men to fall back about two miles to a position just west of Mine Run. The divisions peeled off from their battle line, one brigade at a time, with Rodes's men being the last to move. When Robert Rodes gave the order for his brigades to retreat, the formations shifted, individually, with Dodson Ramseur's Tar Heels being the final Southern force to move. Later, Dodson Ramseur would write, "About 12 o'clock at night the division fell back from its advanced position near Locust Grove.... My brigade was left to cover the movement."¹⁶ Major James Holmes, now leading the Thirtieth's Carolinians, finally received the word to pull back several hours after midnight. He struggled to get the message to his riflemen out on the skirmish line, and in the darkness, not all the men got the word; Pvt. William Pope (Co. A) was left behind and eventually captured.¹⁷ Ramseur's brigade, with Maj. Holmes leading the way, reached its new position at 4:00 a.m.¹⁸

General Ramseur's Tar Heels tried to catch a couple hours' sleep before sunrise, but once the sun was up orders came from division to fortify their position. General Rodes noted, "After a few hours rest on the morning of the 28th, the division was placed in line of battle ... occupying a commanding ridge which overlooked ... the valley of Mine Run."¹⁹ The Confederate riflemen examined their new ground and immediately liked what they saw. A Northern officer described their location, writing, "the enemy's position ... [was on] the western bank of Mine Run, with an elevation of over 100 feet, had a gentle and smooth slope to the creek, averaging over 1,000 yards of cleared ground.... The creek itself was a considerable obstacle, in many places swampy and impassable."²⁰ Robert Rodes continued, "The whole position was so much exposed to the enemy's artillery that the troops were ordered to entrench." When a few Union shells landed close by, the Confederates dug, "with great energy and success."²¹

A few hours later a cold rain drenched the Southerners, followed by a stiff breeze that pushed the clouds aside and the temperature dropped horribly. The only protection against the cold was the warmth produced by physical exertion; the troops continued to construct their entrenchments. General Ramseur recalled, "[Our] line was strongly and rapidly fortified."²² Federal skirmishers cautiously moved towards the Confederate breastworks and exchanged gunfire with gray-coated skirmishers, but the Yanks had little enthusiasm for pressing the attack. A Northern officer remarked, "A severe storm of rain had set in, delaying the march of the troops, particularly the artillery, and preventing the position being [attacked]."²³

Darkness ended any thought of a Union assault, however, rumors spread among the Confederates that the Yanks were going to try a night attack. This news kept the Southerners on edge, and as one rifleman noted, "Constant expectation of a Federal assault racked nerves." He continued, "having to keep all our things on all the time and one-half of the men up all night, in case of an attack [was exhausting]."[24] Major James Holmes's Carolinians had now gone three nights in a row with little sleep; their morale plummeted, they were hungry, cold, and now sleep-deprived. But after all they had done, the Northerners did not attack.

Once the sun ate away at the morning's mists on November 29, 1863, the Confederates expected the blue coats to strike. Federal artillery units opened upon the Southern positions, forcing the gray coats to hunker down. The chilled riflemen kept to their posts, knowing, as their Corps commander noted, "[when] fire was opened from his batteries, a general advance was looked for."[25] Union skirmishers crept forward and engaged the Southern picket line, and the morning's air resonated with the sounds of the scattered poppings of musketry. But that was all that happened; the hours slowly went by with nothing else occurring.

James Holmes exchanged pickets that night, sending out riflemen from Company B. They endured the cold and further lack of sleep and were on duty when the sun arose on November 30, 1863. Union artillery opened fire at 8:00 a.m. A heavy line of skirmishers advanced, threatening the Confederate pickets. McMillan's Tar Heels scurried back to the regiment's entrenchments, however, one rifleman, Pvt. Richard E. Shearin (Co. B), did not return safely. Somehow, he remained behind, to be captured.[26]

The Confederates waited impatiently for the blue coats to get within the killing zone. They looked forward to the coming fight with anticipation, as they were strongly entrenched and the Yankees were out in the open. An officer in the 4th NC proclaimed, "Our men had never felt more confident of victory than on [this] occasion. Our position was equally as strong, if not more so, than that at Fredericksburg, which ... [was] almost impregnable."[27] The Northern riflemen also realized what a horrible situation their generals had created. One Pennsylvanian groused, "Our orders were to charge right through Mine Run. The Run ... was four and a half feet deep and eight or ten feet wide." He continued, "The morning was bitter cold and I knew if I escaped the bullets I would freeze to death after going through the run."[28] A Tar Heel noted, "after a short time and a few volleys of musketry they did not move on quite so expeditiously and confidently."[29] Not surprisingly, the Union attackers backed away. The Federal commander announced, "A reconnaissance of the enemy's position showed it extremely formidable ... [this] careful

The Mine Run defenses (Alfred Ward sketch, 1863, Library of Congress).

examination ... convinced me there was no probability of success ... at about ten minutes of nine ... it was decided ... it was hopeless to make any attack."[30]

The Northern formations quickly withdrew, backing out of danger, leaving behind a thin screen of skirmishers, who immediately took to hiding places and did little to disturb the peace. The day went by quietly, though the men were tortured by the cold. Nothing happened that night, or the next day. On December 2, 1863, once daylight permitted activity, the Confederate pickets sent word back their blue-coated counterparts were gone, they had retreated. General Rodes ordered Brig. Gen. Ramseur to send his brigade forward. The Carolinians crept across the river and pushed forward the two miles to Locust Grove. The jubilant Tar Heels saw plenty of evidence the blue coats had fled; abandoned gear, trash, still smoldering fires, and despondent, broken men who had been left behind. Dodson Ramseur recorded, "my brigade ... followed the retreating enemy as far as the river, picking up some 50 or 60 stragglers."[31] Lieutenant William Ardrey (Co. K) wrote, "We were so much rejoiced ... [at] the news the enemy was recrossing the river."[32]

General Jubal Early sent the Second Corps back to their winter camps. Ramseur led the Tar Heel brigade in their return to the area near Morton's Ford, and then the Southerners settled down, hoping winter's weather had brought an end to the year's fighting. One battle-weary Carolinian, now that he was safely within his winter shelter, grumbled, "[The campaign was] one of hard marching, [and] day after day preparations for battles that did not materialize." Another complained it was "hard work and loss of sleep."[33]

The Confederates settled into a winter schedule, though the men had not received permission to construct permanent quarters. Even as the troops complained about their lack of shelter from the December cold, Maj. James Holmes met with his company commanders and worked out a schedule they hoped would improve morale. Another handful of conscripts arrived and these men were placed in various companies.[34] These new troops had to outfitted and trained. Lieutenant William Ardrey (Co. K) noted, "[at] Morton's Ford, Va. in camp drilling." He also mentioned, "Private [Mitchell] Pegram elected Lieut. in Co. B. He treated the Co. to a barrel of apples and invited me over to enjoy them with the company. They had been under my command during the time they had no officer."[35] Strangely, Pegram's election was never confirmed by Maj. Holmes; Pvt. Mitchel Pegram, an 18-year-old stock clerk from Warrenton, NC, would remain a rifleman for as long as he was with the regiment.

A wave of sickness swept through the Tar Heels, frustrating Holmes's efforts to improve the regiment's spirit. The young soldiers, living in tattered tent shelters and wearing worn-out cotton clothing, were unable to escape the constant exposure to the winter's cruelties. They began to succumb to illness in frightening numbers. Twenty-eight died in November and December 1863.[36] Lieutenant William Ardrey lamented the death of a soldier in his company, writing, "James Thompson of Co. K. died in the hospital, leaving a wife and three little children. O! the sadness it is to hear from the home of this cruel war. He was buried in the field near the camp and I wrote to his wife communicating the sad intelligence."[37] Private James Thompson, one of these twenty-eight to be buried before the New Year, was a 33-year-old carpenter who had been conscripted into the regiment in June 1863. Kelly's Ford had been his first fight.

Major James Holmes also suffered from poor health, though the cold affected the 37-year-old from Sampson County, NC, differently than most of the Tar Heels; for some reason his nervous system began to fail him whenever he remained out in the cold for long hours—his arm would go numb to the point of paralysis.[38] This unusual condition forced Holmes to turn the regiment over to someone else. In mid–December, Lt. Ardrey jotted in his journal, "Capt. J. C. McMillan ... [again] commanding regiment."[39]

Finally, on December 20, 1863, the Confederate high command gave the orders for permanent winter quarters. William Ardrey (Co. K) noted, "We moved near Orange Court House ... and went into camp, between the plank and pike roads. The Regt. was rearranged according to the rank of the captains. Building winter quarters and preparing for winter."[40] The Tar Heels hustled to cut down trees and collect lumber for their shelters. They barely completed their constructions before a brutal cold wave descended over Virginia. Alexander Betts recorded, "December 23rd–Snow and very cold.... December 24th—Very Cold." He also protested, "No chimney to my tent."[41]

Once the men were housed within their hastily built, canvas-roofed shacks, they began to think about Christmas. Now that the men were protected from the worst of the cold, the pain of being away from home and family afflicted them with merciless torment. Lieutenant Ardrey wrote, "Christmas day ... in camp and God grant it will be my last. We can not help but think of the good times we had spent at home on Christmas in former days." He continued, "Sergts. Taylor Lee and John Black went out in the country and bought us some brandy, apples, cakes and other luxuries and we had a big time of it." Then, the homesick officer considered all that had occurred in 1863, and wrote, "During this year many dear homes have been dissolved, many wives made widows, and thousands of children made orphans. All for the hope of our Liberty and the independence of the South, but it will be dearly bought if ever achieved."[42] A week later, Chaplain Alexander Betts recorded on New Year's Eve, "A New Year begins! Oh, may it be a good year! May it bring peace to my land! May it carry me and my fellow soldiers to our several homes."[43] The next morning, Ardrey added, "We welcome the New Year ... and all wishing for the independence of our Southern Confederacy, and praying that our Southern soil may not be so drenched with blood as it was last year, and that we may survive and return home to our loved ones."[44]

Regardless of what the lonesome soldiers wanted, the war continued. On January 2, 1864, Maj. James Holmes led the Thirtieth out of their winter quarters to Morton's Ford, as it was their regiment's turn to man the picket lines along the Rapidan River. The thermometers barely registered above freezing, and the Virginia air seeped with dampness. The biting cold punished the shivering Southerners. Lieutenant Ardrey scribbled, "On picket at Morton's Ford.... Capt. [Willis B.] Moore in command of the regiment, and Major Holmes ... [at] brigade. He was stricken with paralysis."[45] The Thirtieth's leadership position remained fluid. Major James Holmes's disabling infirmity had removed him from the regiment, and Cpt. John McMillan was granted a leave of absence, placing the regiment's next-senior captain, Willis Moore, a 24-year-old farm boy from a prosperous farming family in Edgecombe County, NC, in command.[46]

Just as the Thirtieth took up guard mount another band of polar air swept over them, bringing with it a fierce snow storm, causing Chaplain Alexander Betts to write, "Snowing all day."[47] The tempest continued for nearly forty-eight hours before subsiding. Lieutenant Ardrey recorded, "Heavy snow, about 8 inches deep."[48] The miserable Carolinians trudged around in the moist, white mess for another four days before being relieved by Brig. Gen. Cullen Battle's Alabamians. Then, the Tar Heels hiked back to their winter camp.

The Confederate army's logistical system failed, forcing commissary officers to limit the soldiers' rations. An unhappy Carolinian rifleman grumbled, "Our meat has been cut down to a quarter of a pound and they give us sugar, coffee, rice and sometimes dried fruit. When they only give us a quarter of a pound of meat and a tin cupful of flour, it is not enough for a hearty man."[49] Another wrote, "Cush is our principal diet."[50] Deplorably, as the winter deepened, the food situation worsened. An officer in the brigade commented, "Ramseur's soldiers subsisted for … most of January on a daily ration of ⅛–¼ pound of meat and 1⅛ pound of flour … which together with a pint of cornmeal, kept men alive but left them vulnerable to scurvy."[51] These privations brought a specter of starvation to the soldiers, along with poor health and an increase in disease. Nineteen more young Tar Heels died in January. Lieutenant William Ardrey (Co. K) sadly noted one of these deaths, writing, "T. A. Black died at Orange Court House. He was a good man and a brave soldier. We deeply feel the loss of such men."[52] Private Thomas A. Black (Co. K), a 43-year-old farmer from the eastern side of Charlotte, NC, had been conscripted into the Thirtieth in October 1863. He left behind a widow and 6-year-old son.[53]

The regiment's morale plummeted even lower, and the number of desertions crept upwards. One such AWOL Carolinian, Pvt. James Woods (Co. D), left his company and when Confederate provost guards cornered him, fought back, and he was, "killed while resisting guards in the woods."[54] Unfortunately, desertions were not the only expression of poor morale; Pvt. William Hood (Co. K), "was stabbed in the back by a member of the Fourth Regiment."[55]

Colonel Frank Parker returned to the regiment on January 21, 1864. His arrival, even though his face wound retained a ghastly look, was the first event to buoy the Carolinians' attitude. Lieutenant William Ardrey noted, "Col. F. M. Parker returned to the regiment and resumed command. We were glad to see him, he had been absent a long time."[56] Parker's appearance also enabled Maj. James Holmes permission to leave the Thirtieth with a medical furlough. Colonel Parker's first impression of his regiment's condition was one of dismay. He wrote his wife, "There is nothing doing in camp now, but the ordinary camp duties…. Our rations are short; we eat only two meals per day…. I take breakfast about 9 o'clock a.m., and the other meal about 3 p.m." He immediately began issuing leave to his men. Parker recorded, "The men are being furloughed now very liberally; twelve from every hundred arms bearing men are allowed to go home. The poor fellows appreciate it, and they richly deserve it."[57] Colonel Parker, also in an attempt to increase morale, promoted his brother-in-law, Frederick Philips to captain and assigned him to be the regimental quartermaster to supersede the regiment's quartermaster, Sgt. Theo Stallings. Parker hoped a captain's rank would get better results than what an NCO could achieve.[58]

The regiment Col. Parker now led was vastly different than the one he commanded on July 1, 1863. The Thirtieth's strength was just under four hundred officers and men, with at least a quarter of these conscripts. Frank Parker's staff consisted of 1st Lt. John Downs (Co. K) who acted as adjutant, and two of the regiment's senior captains as wing commanders. Parker did not include the Thirtieth's highest-ranking captain, John McMillan as part of the regiment's staff. Instead, he sent McMillan back to lead Company E. Parker remembered McMillan's problems during the battle of Sharpsburg and held that against him. Parker refused to allow McMillan an advance to field command, even though the captain had been in charge of the regiment for several months. Colonel Parker selected Cpt. Willis Moore (Co. F) for the right wing and Cpt. Jesse Wicker (Co. H) the left, the two, next-senior captains. The Thirtieth's sergeant major remained Peter Arrington, a 24-year-old who impressed Frank Parker. The colonel wrote, "I find Peter Arrington here as Serge. Major of the Regt., his is one of the cleverest young men I know of and a fine businessman."[59]

30th North Carolina Infantry[60]
February 1, 1864

Unit		Strength
Field & Staff	Col. Parker, Francis M. Cpt. Moore, Willis M.	5
Co. A	Cpt. Williams, Gary 1st Lt. White, Lallister M..	55
Co. B	Sgt. Shearin, John D.	23
Co. C	Cpt. Allen, David C. 2nd Lt. Swain, John R.	37
Co. D	3rd Lt. Rodgers, Martin L.	26
Co. E	Cpt. McMillan, John C. 1st Lt. Johnson, Ira J.	57
Co. F	1st Lt. Harrell, George 2nd Lt. Eagles, Lorenzo D.	47
Co. G	1st Lt. Badgett, James W. 3rd Lt. Fulford, John T.	40
Co. H	Cpt. Wicker, Jesse J. 1st Lt. McNeil, Henry J.	49
Co. I	Cpt. Harris, James C. 1st Lt. Arrington, Kearney	35
Co. K	1st Lt. Ardrey, William E. 2nd Lt. Downs, John T.	40
		393

The Thirtieth's men experienced a religious revival during the winter's cold months, an event Chaplain Alexander Betts found tremendously gratifying. He moved from company to company, conducting services and baptizing converts. Betts recorded his activities; his journal entries often reading as "Jan. 17—Preach in chapel in a.m. Bible class in p.m. Prayer meeting in Co. I at night.... Mar. 13—Preach to Daniels' Brigade in church in a.m. Return to ... chapel in time for communion.... Bible class in my chapel in p.m. I preach at night.... Prayer meeting in Company K."[61] The men in Alexander Betts's Thirtieth North Carolina, like soldiers form nearly all the regiments in the Confederate army, had experienced the ugly effects of war. They had seen comrades mutilated and killed, as well as die from disease. Very few Southerners now believed this war would end gently, and even fewer individuals felt they would emerge unscathed. The weary soldiers turned to God for protection in massive numbers. One historian noted, "Many of the soldiers even became convinced that God would intervene on their army's behalf."[62] Colonel Parker supported Betts in these endeavors, writing, "The religious state of feeling in the [regiment] is very good. Our Chaplain has erected a very comfortable chapel in which to worship; he holds services several times during the week; [the] men seem very attentive and much in earnest."[63] Alexander Betts did all he could to lead his Carolinians to God.

He summed up the revival, writing, "Prayer meeting in some Co., every night. In Co. G tonight ... every night, everywhere—All good men."[64]

Unfortunately not all the Tar Heels were acting as "good men." Colonel Parker dealt with those soldiers who refused to do their duty, or worse, carried out unlawful acts, or violence. He wrote of one such incident: "the Pitt boys; two [of] them Jack [John Pitt—Co. I] and Buck [Fred Pitt—Co. I] with [Joel] Price [Co. I], are sentenced to working on the defenses around Richmond and to wear a ball and chain during the war, and for the first seven days of each month, to be placed in stocks. Buck Pitt, for gallant conduct at Sharpsburg, is released and restored to his company."[65]

Colonel Parker led the Thirtieth away from winter camp on January 30, 1864. The following night, Lt. William Ardrey (Co. K) recorded, "Morton's Ford.... Our regiment on picket duty on the Rapidan River." Happily, the weather's cold grip on the countryside subsided, enabling the Confederates to enjoy themselves. Ardrey continued, "Very warm for the season.... I am tenting with Capt. McMillan and Dr. Lawson, having a lively time of it, as they are full of fun."[66] One of the Tar Heel riflemen added, "Picket duty along the banks of the river was frequently lazy because of truces entered into by the pickets.... A fair exchange of sugar and tobacco would be made. The Yankees had genuine coffee, ground and sweetened with sugar, and when possible coffee was always included in the exchange."[67]

The Federals took advantage of this sudden warm interlude by executing plans to send troops across the Rapidan, early on the morning of February 6, 1864. The blue coats of Brig. Gen. Joshua Owen (II Corps) advanced to the river, their movements hidden by a thick layer of fog shrouding the valley. The passage across the river at Morton's Ford was not easy; a Union officer in the three hundred-man assault force wrote, "the column moved forward and effected a crossing with considerable difficulty, owing to the strong current and depth of water which reached the waists of the men."[68] They reached the Confederate side of the river and struck the picket line held by the 2nd NC. A Northerner wrote, "A landing on the other side was effected, and the rifle-pits immediately attacked.... The enemy retreated in confusion, leaving in our hands as prisoners 28 privates and 2 lieutenants."[69] The surviving Carolinians scattered, fleeing away from the river. Meanwhile, more Union forces splashed across the river and assembled, to continue the attack.

This musketry and supporting artillery fire alerted Col. Parker and he called the Thirtieth to arms. He quickly formed the regiment and moved them towards the sounds of fighting. The Thirtieth was about a mile away and it took twenty minutes to reach the area where the 2nd NC's reserve engaged the advancing Yankees. Confederate cannons were rushed to the scene and began shelling the blue coats. The artillery commander remarked, "[we] opened fire ... upon them. This served to halt their advance."[70] The Thirtieth's battle line reinforced the 2nd NC near a collection of buildings locally known as Dr. Morton's residence, and here, Parker's riflemen took possession of a line of well-made entrenchments. A Yank noted this movement, "the enemy advanced a stronger line of skirmishers, and began rapidly to concentrate his troops immediately in my front."[71] The two Tar Heel regiments' fire stopped the Northerners.

Moments later, units from Brig. Gen. George Steuart's brigade arrived. They had been scheduled to replace the Carolinians on the picket line; instead, they appeared just in time to triple the Southerners' battle strength. More gray-coated forces were added, allowing William Ardrey to write, "Soon the corps was in line of battle. Gen. Early on the left, Gen. Johnston on the right, Gen. Rodes in the center." The Confederates counter-attacked that afternoon, using other brigades besides the Tar Heels. Lieutenant Ardrey scribbled, "In the evening about 6 o'clock, our skirmishers charged theirs, and drove them beyond the Morton house, until they encountered their line of battle.... The charge was in full view of our works, it was very exciting and loud cheers went up from our side for our brave soldiers."[72] The Union soldiers withdrew that night and the next day the two forces glared at each other, but did not continue fighting. Lieutenant Ardrey remarked, "In the morning Gen. Lee's army was on the south side, Gen. Meade's on the north side of the river, in full view of each other, and all quiet. It was certainly a grand sight. Gen. Lee rode up and down our lines several times."[73] Later that day, once the Confederate high command was certain the threat had ended, the Tar Heels hiked back to their winter camp. Ardrey added, "The enemy disappeared from our front and we marched back to our fortifications, into our camp. We were very tired and needed rest."[74]

Winter weather again dominated the soldiers' world. The next couple weeks in February were frigid, with more snow and exceedingly cold temperatures. Alexander Betts noted in his journal, "February 16—Snow on the ground.... February 17—Bitter cold.... February 18—Still bitter cold."[75] For the soldiers, still poorly dressed, inadequately housed, and eating substandard rations, this weather ate at their health. More Carolinians wasted away with disease, including 43-year-old Moses Penninger (Co. C), who died of septic pneumonia. Private Penninger had been conscripted in September 1863 from his farm in Cabarrus County, NC, leaving behind a wife and six children.[76]

Colonel Frank Parker's efforts to improve the regiment's morale had done little more than halt its decline. There was not much he could do to upgrade their conditions—the entire Confederate army was faring poorly—and many of his Tar Heels, especially those who had been conscripted into service against their will, no longer wished to take part in the Southern crusade for independence. Desertion sapped at the Thirtieth's numbers as individuals, and sometimes even small groups, slipped away. Private James L. Green (Co. H) grumbled, "When we were down on picket, five of our men ... went over to the Yankees.... One of them was my best friend.... Hunter and Branch were the men's names."[77] James Green, a 43-year-old farmer from Cleveland County, NC, along with his two pards, 42-year-old John S. Hunter and 48-year-old Everett L. Branch, had been conscripted in September 1863. These three farmers, all with wives and children just wanted to go home to their families.[78]

On February 18, 1864, Lt. William Ardrey (Co. K) was called to regimental headquarters by Col. Parker, and, as Ardrey succinctly noted in his journal, "I ... was promoted to the captaincy of the company."[79] His commission was long overdue, as he had been leading the company since Cpt. John Witherspoon's death at Kelly's Ford. The regiment then marched to the Rapidan River for a stint of picket duty. The new captain noted, "The 14th and 30th went on picket at Raccoon's Ford.... Lt. Downs and I slept in [a] corncrib."[80] A week later, regiments from Brig. Gen. Cullen Battle's brigade arrived and relieved the Tar Heels, allowing them to return to camp. However, just as the Carolinians arrived back at winter camp, the brigade received news the Yanks were again causing problems. Captain Ardrey recorded, "Received orders to prepare rations, that the enemy were making some demonstrations on the river. Gen. Kilpatrick's cavalry commenced crossing in the night at Ely's Ford. Estimated to be five thousand strong."[81]

Brigadier General Dodson Ramseur led his brigade as it chased after the raiders. Private James Green (Co. H) wrote, "I had to go on a March some twenty or more [miles]. It was a rain[in]g and a-freezing when I started. It rained all day long & at knight. It

[was] a pretty smart snow & we had to lie out and take it. I suffered a good deal with the cold."[82] Foot soldiers, especially the poorly shod men in the Confederate infantry, had no chance in chasing down decently mounted and well-equipped Federal cavalry. Captain Ardrey scribbled in frustration, "Gen. Kilpatrick made a raid around our army.... He cut the Va. Central Railroad in our rear and attacked our troops in the fortifications near Richmond.... Our division ... attempted to intercept him, but he escaped." Ardrey added, "We returned to our camp after a tiresome march. It was extremely cold and we were badly exposed to the bad weather."[83]

The regiment stayed in winter quarters for the next couple weeks. Captain William Ardrey recorded, "Our camp seems like home to us."[84] Their ration supply improved, though just barely. A Tar Heel rifleman noted, "Our meat is very slim, though we make out very well. As for bread we get more than we can eat.... We draw as much sugar and coffee as we could wish for. Meat is the only thing we are stinted with. We have not drawn any beef or ham in a month or two."[85]

A massive snow storm buried the Virginia countryside on March 22, 1864; Alexander Betts noted his tempest, writing, "Snow falls about 18 inches."[86] The young men soon were out in the drifts throwing snowballs at each other. General Dodson Ramseur and Brig. Gen. George Dole challenged each other to a snowball fight, and soon both had their brigades formed in battle lines and the Tar Heels fought Georgians until both sides were exhausted, wet, cold, and a number were injured. Both brigades claimed victory. Dodson Ramseur recorded the fracas, writing, "Heavy snowfall permitted snowball fights, the grandest of which took place on 23 March 1864, between Ramseur's and Dole's bri-

On March 23, 1864, Ramseur's Brigade battled Doles's Brigade in a massive snowball fight (Johnson & Buel, 1887).

gades of Rodes division and the Stonewall and Louisiana brigades of Edward Johnson's division. For the better part of a day the mock battle raged."[87]

This cold snap was immediately followed by a surge of warmer weather, resulting in a rapid snowmelt and the landscape transforming into a gruesome mud-bowl. The roads quickly became deeply rutted bogs and nearly all transport ceased. Colonel Frank Parker remarked, "we have had rain, which causes the roads to be very muddy. I think there is a probability of having more rain or snow soon; so the weather will keep every thing quiet for some time to come." Parker continued, noting that General Lee, concerned his troops were not getting any supplies by wagon, "issued an order forbidding all leaves of absence ... the reason given for this, is that the rail roads are needed for transportation."[88] However, even though the soldiers could not go home on leave, North Carolina's governor, Zebulon Vance arrived. He reviewed the Tar Heel brigade and gave a four-hour speech. A Carolinian rifleman recorded, "[Vance] has the whole assembly in an uproar in less than two minutes.... He said it did not sound right to ... address us as 'Fellow soldiers,' because he was not one of us—he used to be until he shirked out of the service for a little office down in North Carolina, so he would address us as 'Fellow Tar Heels,' as we always stick."[89]

Colonel Frank Parker, now that winter's icy grip had subsided, began efforts to drill his new conscripts, and retrain his veterans. He was especially sensitive to the criticism Dodson Ramseur cast his way. General Ramseur was furious at the Thirtieth's behavior at Kelly's Ford, and vowed none of his regiments would ever fail him again. He wrote his new bride, "I will proceed against some of my officers in the most rigorous manner unless they very speedily and decidedly mend their ways ... [some are] careless and inattentive to the strict performance of duty."[90] A Southerner wrote, "[Ramseur] drilled the soldiers hard, often twice a day. Conscripts faced thrice-daily sessions. The 30th, guilty of losing many prisoners at Kelly's Ford, received special attention, as on a late April day when it was drilled for two hours by Ramseur himself before an evening brigade drill that lasted two and one-half hours."[91] Colonel Parker, who was unhappy with Maj. James Holmes's performance at Kelly's Ford, saw this as a good time to slide Maj. James Holmes out of the regiment. He accepted without question, Holmes's bid to resign when he received a letter from Dr. W. S. Mitchell, who wrote, "we find the said Major [James C. Holmes] ... unfit for duty in the field on account of partial paralysis of the left side, principally affecting the arm ... we think he can perform light duty. We therefore recommend that he be retired to some post."[92]

Not long after Governor Vance's visit the Carolinian riflemen were jolted by the reality of military obligation when they were forced to watch an execution. A dismayed Pvt. James Green (Co. H) wrote, "I witnessed a scene yesterday that I never saw before. I saw three men tied to a stake and shot for desertion. They was marched to the stake by a band of music." He continued, "The preacher then prayed and they got on their knees and lent their backs against the stake and was tied fast, and they pulled off their hats and they blind folded them, and when the guns fired their heads dropped." Private Green finished, writing, "I never want to see such a sight again."[93] The sullen soldiers returned to their winter quarters, subdued by the execution, and completely cognizant of the consequences of not performing their duty to the Confederate army.

A springtime sun warmed the days and dried out the countryside. The trees added new leaves, and the farmers' plantings began to sprout. The soldiers longed to return home and tend to agricultural activities, but sadly, they knew the warming temperatures and firming roads meant another season of war. Colonel Parker led the Thirtieth back to the Rapidan River in the last week of April 1864 for picket duty. His veterans and conscripts enjoyed a couple pleasant days before, as one rifleman noted, "The 30th Regiment ... was on picket duty at Raccoon Ford when word came that the enemy was crossing the river on May 3."[94] Captain Fred Philips rushed supplies and rations to the Thirtieth. One officer noted, "So sure were some of the Confederate commanders of an advance with the dawn of the 4th [May] that they ordered the men to prepare three days' rations."[95] Private John Bone (Co. I) added, "Every preparation was made that could be for the coming campaign, and we looked forward to it with a solemn dread."[96] Colonel Parker walked among his riflemen as they gathered their things together. He observed, as did other officers, "Although the old, cheerful banter was audible, as the troops made ready to start their march, [many] ... thought the Army worse equipped and not in as good spirits as it had been before Gettysburg."[97]

Chapter 12

Slaughter at Spotsylvania

On May 4, 1864, Col. Frank Parker kept his regiment's riflemen vigilant on picket duty, guarding the crossing at Raccoon Ford. His Carolinians were well aware the Yankees had moved; Cpt. William Ardrey (Co. K) noted in his journal, "Gen. Grant's Grand Army of the Potomac crossed the river at Germanna and Ely's Fords."[1] Colonel Parker met with Brig. Gen. Dodson Ramseur and learned the Tar Heel brigade, along with a handful of other Confederate formations had been ordered to remain on picket while the rest of General Lee's army rushed eastward to meet the Federal attack. Dodson Ramseur recorded, "I was on outpost duty with my brigade at Raccoon Ford.... I was left with my own brigade, three regiments of Pegram's brigade, and three regiments from Johnson's division, to resist any crossing the enemy might attempt on my front."[2] Parker's veterans and conscripts all waited, content to hold Raccoon Ford, but also, anxious about the coming fight. They knew General Lee could not win without them.

30th North Carolina Infantry[3]
May 5, 1864

Unit		Strength
Field & Staff	Col. Parker, Francis M. Adj. Arrington, Peter W.	2
Co. A	Cpt. Williams, Gary 1st Lt. White, Lallister M..	40
Co. B	Sgt. Shearin, John D.	21
Co. C	Cpt. Allen, David C. 2nd Lt. Swain, John R.	34
Co. D	3rd Lt. Rodgers, Martin L.	30
Co. E	Cpt. McMillan, John C. 1st Lt. Johnson, Ira J.	57
Co. F	Cpt. Moore, Willis M. 1st Lt. Harrell, George	50
Co. G	1st Lt. Badgett, James W. 2nd Lt. Crews, Alexander	42
Co. H	Cpt. Wicker, Jesse J. 1st Lt. McNeil, Henry J.	42
Co. I	Cpt. Harris, James C. 1st Lt. Arrington, Kearney	40

Unit		Strength
Co. K	Cpt. Ardrey, William E.	
	1st Lt. Downs, John T.	44
		404

The call to rejoin the Army of Northern Virginia came the next day. The Carolinians took one last look at what had become a familiar setting, before marching southeast, heading toward an area of dense forest the locals called "The Wilderness." The column entered the region, which one Tar Heel described by writing, "Imagine a great, dismal forest containing 120 square miles—the worst kind of thicket of second-growth trees ... so thick with small pines and scrub oak, cedar, dogwood and other growth common to the country, with little ravines and hollows between the little hills ... with its tangled vines, where one could see barely ten paces."[4]

Dodson Ramseur's men moved quickly, as rumors swept through the ranks telling of heavy fighting. A rifleman remarked, "The message that always made hearts beat faster was passed down the files: Federals were ahead."[5] They hiked all day, covering three or four miles every hour, and as the afternoon deepened, the gray coats began to hear the rumble of artillery and the continuous rattle of musketry. Finally, not long after sunset, the Carolinians reached Lt. Gen. Richard Ewell's corps and nestled in, "moving to a position in the rear of Ewell's right."[6]

Colonel Frank Parker's formation numbered just over four hundred officers and men. He did not have another field-grade officer, just Adj. Peter Arrington. Parker elevated two of his senior captains, Jesse Wicker (Co. H) and David Allen (Co. C) to wing command; with Wicker in charge of the right wing, composed of Companies A, B, C, G, and H, and Allen taking the other units in the left. Frank Parker had relegated the regiment's most-senior captain, John McMillan (Co. E) to company command, as that formation was the largest in the Thirtieth, and, as before, Parker did not trust the officer. The Tar Heel colonel knew his troops were adequately equipped, decently trained, and with its melding of veterans and conscripts, he hoped they were properly prepared for the fighting lying ahead of them.

Gunfire woke the Carolinians just as soon as the pre-dawn's light enabled sufficient vision, when, as one Southerner noted, "At five o'clock ... the Federals advanced along the length of the line."[7] Parker's men scrambled to their feet, quickly cooking their breakfasts and tending to their weapons; they knew it would not long before they would be going into the fight. An order came to move and the riflemen formed up, ready to enter the fracas. Instead, their column filed to the right, away from the fight. A Tar Heel wrote, "Ramseur was ordered to the Confederate [right] arriving on the right of Daniel's brigade near the Chewing Farm."[8] They were still being held in reserve, several hundred yards behind the main Confederate position. Parker's riflemen stacked their arms and waited; meanwhile, the sounds of war intensified as blue coats from Brig. Gen. James Rickett's Division (VI Corps) slammed into Ewell's left flank brigades. The fighting raged for hours, but the Tar Heels were never called to move toward the sound of the guns; in fact, the Carolinians sat in their new position nearly all day long, waiting and fretting.

Finally, a couple hours before sunset, they got the word to advance. General Ramseur sent forward his sharpshooters, who pushed forward, past the Confederate breastworks, and into dense foliage, hunting for the Yanks' battle line. Frank Parker's regiment moved forward as Ramseur's far-right regiment until he received instructions to shift further to the right. Colonel Parker aimed his regiment in that direction and extended his line by spreading the companies' battlefronts. Private John Bone (Co. I) wrote, "In the evening we attacked ... by [a] flank move."[9] The Thirtieth advanced nearly eight hundred yards before bullets swept its skirmish line. Luckily, nearly all of these shots impacted harmlessly among the trees sheltering the regiment's skirmish line. Soon though, a minié ball slammed into Pvt. Bryant Bostick's (Co. E) left thigh, shattering his tibia. Moments later, and a lead projectile crashed into Cpl. William Sizemore's (Co. G) chest.[10] The Tar Heels pushed past their fallen brothers and fired at the soldiers hidden before them.

Surprisingly, the woods began to trill with the sounds of Indian war cries; a noise that halted the Carolina advance, and then fiercely painted warriors emerged from their hiding places. The Confederates recoiled back in surprise. Federal bullets struck more Carolina youths; Pvt. George Cole (Co. H) fell with a wound to his leg, and Pvt. William Pickett (Co. E) also suffered a serious injury.[11] Frank Parker's riflemen hunkered down, confounded by the forces resisting their advance. Who were these screaming heathens shooting at them? A Northerner wrote, "[Ojibwa] Indians of the Seventh Wisconsin regiment took an active part in the skirmishing. They covered their bodies very ingeniously with pine boughs to conceal themselves in the woods. When [the] skirmishers advanced from [their] lines ... the Indians would give a shout or war whoop."[12] Parker's NCOs and line officers steadied the skirmishers and with additional rifles added to this forward line, the Carolinians pressed against the warriors, slowly pushing them. Suddenly, the Ojibwa force collapsed. A Tar Heel noted, "the Indians fought 'bravely' in the wood but when driven into the open they did not again fire on us, but ran like deer."[13]

The Tar Heels chased after the retreating warriors, emerging from the heavy vegetation, and out onto an open field. Parker hurried his men across the pasture, worried they might get ambushed by other blue coats hiding in the trees at the field's edge. Fortunately, there were no Union troops patrolling the tree line, however, there were more Yanks, farther back in the woods. A Southerner noted, "Moving at the double-quick across Jones' field, Ramseur crashed into the leading elements of the IX Corps."[14] These Northerners were not prepared for a Confederate attack, and any resistance they attempted was immediately punished. The blue coats fled, falling back over nine hundred yards, leaving behind a nicely established camp with all its equipment and supplies. A Tar Heel recorded, "[We] whipped them badly. Burnside's Corps ... stampeded like sheep."[15] Dodson Ramseur recorded, "I turned the enemy's line, and by a ... charge with my skirmishers, under.... Maj. Osborne [4th NC], drove not only the enemy's skirmishers, but his line of battle, back fully half a mile, capturing some prisoners and the knapsacks and shelter-tents of an entire regiment."[16] Captain William Ardrey (Co. K) added, "[We] ... Captur[ed] all their baggage."[17] The Confederate riflemen picked through the gear, scrounging for equipment they needed. They also collected some strange items, including, as Col. Risden Bennett (14th NC) noted, "Among the captured [gear] were copies of the Bible in the Ojibwa language."[18]

Brigadier General Dodson Ramseur gave orders to his regimental commanders to collect their scattered troops and set them to digging entrenchments; they had done enough. Colonel Parker called to his company commanders as they gathered their formations, and the Tar Heels began fortifying a defensive position. The Thirtieth's surgeon, Dr. George Briggs established a medical station, while the regiment's wounded were assembled. The push against the Ojibwa skirmishers had resulted in seven wounded; though one, Cpl. William Sizemore (Co. G) was mortally injured. His neighbors gathered around him. One recalled, "a few friends in the company carried [Sizemore] to safety where, before he died asked his cousin, Richard David Brooks, to look after his wife ... and their daughter ... after the war."[19] Fortunately, the 23-year-old Pvt. Richard "R.D." Brooks did survive the war. He returned home to Granville County, NC, and eventually married William Sizemore's widow.[20]

The next morning, May 7, 1864, dawned warm and dry. The Tar Heel pickets reported little aggressive blue coat activity. The commander of the 4th NC wrote, "6 o'clock Saturday morning.–Enemy are moving.... Sharp shooters feeling to see if they [remain] in position, but hear nothing from them." He continued, "Enemy active, but nothing accomplished by them; [they are] regarded as badly whipped and demoralized."[21] This information was passed up to brigade headquarters, enabling Dodson Ramseur to note, "Before much of a dusty, warm Saturday ... had passed, it became clear ... that Grant would not renew the contest on the same ground."[22] Colonel Grimes [4th NC] added, "Spoils immense—looks bright for Confederacy."[23] The Carolina riflemen relaxed; the Yankees had been badly bloodied in the past two days' combat, and rumors abounded telling of a horrible tragedy befalling the Northerners. Captain William Ardrey (Co. K) recorded, "It was passed down the lines that Gen. Grant was captured and I never heard such enthusiasm and applause."[24] The veterans smiled at each other, past experiences suggested the blue coats would tuck their tails between the legs and limp away to lick their wounds.

General Robert Rodes ordered Ramseur to move his regiments. Dodson Ramseur wrote, "On the morning of the 7th I was moved in rear of our center as a reserve."[25] The Carolinian riflemen trudged a mile southwest of their night's position before orders came to stack arms and stand down. The day's temperature grew increasingly hot, and the humidity thickened, distressing the soldiers even more than the flies and mosquitoes. The sounds of combat had stilled, to be broken only by scattered rifle fire, or an occasional cannon report. But unsettling rumors slowly crept through the inactive Carolinians; the Union army was not retreating, it was shifting southward. As the day's hours crept by this news shifted from unsupported gossip to solid fact, and confirmed by the information General Ulysses Grant remained in command, and had vowed to, "fight it out on this line if it takes all summer." The brigade shifted southward that evening, hiking some distance before bivouacking.

General Ramseur had his Tar Heels up early on May 8, 1864. He informed his regimental commanders they would be required to hustle today, as they had to rejoin their Confederate brothers already sent ahead to counter Grant's quick slide to the south. The gray-coated riflemen formed into column and filed away from their position. They soon reached the battlefield where the Third Corps had fought for two days before collapsing just as Longstreet's First Corps arrived to drive the Yanks backward. Dodson Ramseur described the scene his troops marched past, writing, "The day was terribly hot and dusty. Partially buried corpses and dead horses littered the woods. Smoke from burning trees and undergrowth mingled with the gases steaming up through the thin covering of the graves' to create a suffocating stench in the hot, close air of the forest."[26] General Richard Ewell added to Ramseur's depiction, noting, "[It was] a very distressing march through intense heat amid thick dust and smoke from burning woods."[27]

Colonel Parker's riflemen shrugged off the horrible scenes and shuffled through the dust, more bothered by the heat and humidity. They were tired from their last couple nights' limited sleep, and as the day's temperatures scorched their skin and sucked away their bodies' moisture, their trek grew long and wearisome. A Carolinian enlisted man grumbled, "We were almost worn out with fatigue from marching or loss of sleep when we started from this place.... I don't think I ever saw a hotter day in all my life. The men were fainting by the dozens." The rifleman continued, "I threw away everything I had but my gun and accouterments, including three days' rations."[28] Private John Bone (Co. I) added, "a very, very warm day for this time of year.... We started and made quick time, stopping a few minutes in every two hours. Many men threw their baggage away, keeping only their guns, cartridge boxes and canteens." He continued, "Some of the best soldiers had to give up, owing to the hot weather, and were left beside the road."[29]

The column plodded southeast, passing Parker's Store and then turned east toward Shady Grove Court House, and from there; again east, aiming for Spotsylvania Court House. The torrid sun and smothering humidity was relentless; Dodson Ramseur wrote, "the heat took a high toll. Dozens of men fainted. Heatstroke claimed its victims."[30] However, as the exhausted men neared their destination orders came to increase their pace. They struggled to comply, now hearing the sounds of artillery, but many could no longer keep up and scores of stragglers fell away at the road's side. One soldier noted, "[The men] "were so tired and worn out they could hardly halloo."[31]

The brigade reached an area of high ground northeast of the courthouse and not far from the Alsop farmstead just before sunset. The Carolinians had been hearing fighting for the last hour and knew danger was near. The men were so exhausted they could barely stand, and yet, they prepared to fight. Captain William Ardrey (Co. K) recorded, "[It was] a very warm and fatiguing march.... [We] arrived on the field at 5:30 p.m.... [We were] hardly formed in line before," orders came to attack.[32] Private John Bone (Co. I) recorded, "We reached the place in the evening and formed line of battle, and advanced forward. We did not go far before we were upon the enemy."[33] Brigadier General Dodson Ramseur sent the brigade sharpshooters forward and they immediately came under a heavy fire. Ramseur reinforced the line. Lieutenant Colonel Edwin Osborne (4th NC) wrote, "two companies of the [4th] regiment were detailed to strengthen the line of sharpshooters commanded by Maj. Osborne, now numbering, so reinforced, some three hundred men."[34] Ramseur's four regiments followed close behind, Col. Parker's Thirtieth advancing in its normal position on the brigade's right flank.

Federal resistance forced Ramseur to throw his main battle line into the fight. The Tar Heels surged forward, crashing into the Union infantry's V Corps. The blue coats did not retreat; instead, their volleys raked the Carolinians. First sergeant Thomas Whitehurst (Co. F) tumbled backwards, "shot through the head." Private Joseph Butler (Co. A) dropped, his left leg shattered by a minié bullet, and Pvt. Sandy Johnston (Co. K) fell, his chest punctured.[35] The Carolinians inched forward, firing as they advanced. The Yanks began to step backwards. Edwin Osborne remarked, "The men ... cross[ed] a field some two hundred and fifty yards wide, and drove the enemy's sharpshooters before us." He continued, "[we] pushed forward ... [against] a line of battle on top of [a] ridge."[36] More young Carolinians fell, including Cpt. Willis Moore (Co. F), who was shot through his left breast. Also, Sgt. Horace Morrison (Co. H) was killed, and Pvt. Joshua North (Co. B) wounded.[37] General Ramseur noted, "[We] arrived just in time to prevent, by a vigorous charge, the Fifth Corps from turning General Humphrey's right flank."[38]

The Tar Heels closed on the Northerners, taking more casualties but inflicting them as well. Then, after an intense exchange of musketry, the blue coats broke. The Federals scattered, fleeing like wild animals from a forest fire. Dodson Ramseur proclaimed, "[We] exchanged fire with Federals for twenty minutes ... [and] drove the enemy back half a mile to his entrenchments ... eras[ing] the threat to Anderson's [Third Corps] flank."[39] Other Yank formations let the defeated troops file past, but had the advantage of hastily dug entrenchments. The worn-out Confederates shied away from a frontal assault on well-defended breastworks and the advance ended. The Southerners rifled through the abandoned Yankee gear until darkness put an end to their treasure hunting. A Carolinian rifleman noted, "We drove the enemy about a half mile, taking several prisoners, lots of provisions and the tents belonging to a Federal regiment."[40]

General Ramseur pulled his men back several hundred yards and established a brigade defensive line. He turned to his colonels, telling them to control their units. Frank Parker's company commanders gathered their troops together, took muster rolls to determine their losses, and then everyone began digging a line of entrenchments. Dodson Ramseur recorded, "My brigade was then withdrawn and constructed entrenchments on the right of Kershaw's division."[41] Once a defensive position had been constructed the exhausted men sank to the ground. Night-time picket duty was established, and as one soldier noted, "we lay with our arms on us, one or two men of each company standing up and peering into the darkness."[42] Meanwhile, Surgeon George Briggs gathered the regiment's casualties together and did what he could to ease the men's suffering. The Thirtieth had lost nine, however, another fourteen were missing.[43] These fellows were stragglers left behind in the frantic march to Spotsylvania and were lost to the regiment when a Federal cavalry patrol swept in and captured them.

Sunrise on May 9, 1864, enabled Gen. Ramseur to realize his brigade's entrenchments were out of line with adjoining units. He pulled his Carolinians out of their last night's work and shifted the regiments to better align with Brig. Gen. Junius Daniel's Tar Heels on the right, and Brig. Gen. Cullen Battle's Alabamians to the left. A Southerner noted this movement, writing, "Ramseur's brigade took position on the eastern face of the Mule Shoe salient."[44] Private John Bone (Co. I) remarked, "We now got a [new] location and made breastworks ... and held this position."[45] Dodson Ramseur put out a strong screen of skirmishers, who dueled with their blue-coated counterparts. Ramseur recorded, "Troops labored all day improving their trenches ... [while] skirmishing erupted."[46] Captain William Ardrey (Co. K) added, "Fortifying all day."[47] Ramseur, as he oversaw his Carolinians construct their breastworks, also noted, "the heat [was] ... unrelenting."[48]

May 10, 1864, went by slowly; Col. Parker inspected the regiment's fortification and ordered a few additional improvements. He also rotated different shifts of riflemen to man the skirmish line. But for the most part, his men took shelter within their works and quietly endured the punishing heat and humidity, and bothersome flies and mosquitoes. Parker's men watched as other units repositioned their lines and excavated new entrenchments. Some of these troops ripped the timbers out of the abandoned works and haphazardly refilled those trenches. Dodson Ramseur recalled, "Entrenchment continued ... [and] musketry crackled here and there."[49]

That evening, just as the shadows lengthened and Ramseur's Confederates were beginning to believe they had survived another day, the Yanks attacked the trenches to their right. Colonel Risden Bennett (14th NC) wrote, "[Upton] of the enemy, penetrating the thick cover of old field pines and other growth between us, suddenly emerged from cover in broken order and came upon us at the double-quick. They struck the Georgia brigade and mounting the works and flowed over into the trenches."[50] Colonel Emery Upton (VI Corps) led fifteen regiments arrayed in column formation across the two hundred yards of open ground just after 6:00 p.m., striking Brig. Gen. George Doles' Georgians. One of the Yanks in the 96th PA, a regiment in Upton's assault, wrote, "We started on the full run with cheers."[51] Ramseur's Tar Heels poked their heads above their breastworks and fired upon the right flank of the attacking force, downing a number of the Yanks, as well as slowing that column's advance. A Carolinian recorded, "Our brigade was immediately to the Georgian's left and took care of the enemy's extreme right, which never reached the works."[52] The Federal rifleman recalled, "Many a poor fellow fell pierced with rebel bullets before we reached the rifle pits."[53] The Northerner's rectangle of infantry punched through Doles' entrenchments and quickly swarmed beyond. The blue coat remarked, "They were very stubborn and the bayonet and clubbed muskets were used freely before the pit was fully in our possession. We captured, killed or wounded the big majority of the first pit."[54] Quick-thinking Southern officers immediately responded and threw their gray-clad riflemen against Upton's troops, who, surprised by their success, had begun to flounder within the maze of abandoned earthworks. Captain William Ardrey (Co. K) wrote, "The enemy assaulted our works occupied by Gen. Doles' and Daniels' Brigades, broke the lines capturing some prisoners. Gen. Gordon soon went up to their assistance. The enemy was repulsed with great slaughter."[55] Then, as darkness covered the fields, the noise fell away, leaving the soldiers hearing the cries of the wounded. The weary men settled down inside their trenches. One Carolinian scribbled to his wife, "By grace of God I am still spared. The Yankees have been punished severely. We now have good breastworks."[56]

The morning's sun arose on May 11, 1864, accompanied by hot, muggy air. The soldiers moved about slowly, cooking rations, brewing captured Yankee coffee, and scratching at mosquito bites. Picket duty was rotated as the night guard's tired men filed into the trenches, and others went out to assume their responsibilities. The hours went by slowly, and as the sun climbed into the sky the heat increased and the humidity became sweltering. The Tar Heel riflemen did little. One Carolinian wrote, "the [brigade] kept in line of battle most of the time."[57] Another Confederate added, "no fighting took place."[58] The most important activity, as far as the soldiers were concerned, was watching massive thunderheads grow on the horizon. A writer noted, "The regiment's farm boys, accustomed to reading the sky, predicted rain."[59] Precipitation began to fall a few hours before sunset, at first just lightly enough to dampen the soldiers' uniforms.[60] These first showers ended, to soon be followed by heavy rain; Dodson Ramseur recorded, "Thunderstorms ... drenched the field during the night."[61] Private John Bone (Co. I) groused, "We had a heavy rain most of the night, which kept me from getting much sleep."[62]

All the soldiers' rest was hindered by the rain, and by the streams of water draining into the entrenchments. At the same time though, the brigade's senior officers were also awake, trying to make sense of the reports being passed to them from the forward pickets—the Union troops were making movement noises. No one could determine if the Yanks were falling back, shifting to new positions, or massing for an assault. As the hours passed midnight the consensus began to lean toward, as Pvt. John Bone recalled, "There was an attack expected somewhere ... but we were not certain at what place."[63] The Confederate high command issued orders: "Lee ... instructed Ewell to remove 22 guns posted in the salient." The artillerymen began moving the cannon. However, once the pieces had been extracted, Lt. Gen. Richard Ewell, who was growing increasingly nervous, wrote, "Soon after midnight Maj. Gen. Johnson reported the enemy massing."[64] Ewell then ordered the guns be returned, and by four o'clock in the morning, the exasperated gunners were dragging their guns back to their emplacements.[65]

Dodson Ramseur did not sleep as he and his staff struggled with the conflicting reports coming from division and corps. Finally, sometime after 3:30 a.m., he decided to take measures to protect his brigade. Ramseur analyzed what Upton's men had been able to accomplish and knew that once a strong Yankee force broke through the entrenchments, there was little beyond that line to save the situation. The brigadier general did not want his brigade surprised, so he ordered the 2nd NC out of the brigade's trenches and posted this regiment behind the other Tar Heel formations, to act as a brigade reserve. The general recorded, "In anticipation of an attack on my front.... I had my brigade under arms at early dawn."[66] By 4:30 a.m., the rain had given way to a fine mist, creating a thick fog that smothered the countryside, limiting vision to almost nothing. The best form of observation was by ear, and the Tar Heels could hear the sounds of troop movements.

The Confederate entrenchments to Ramseur's right arched forward in the shape of an upside-down "U," the trenches twisting and turning as the Southerners sought fields of fire, creating a large salient, punching outwards nearly three-quarters of a mile, and spanning a distance (east to west) of just less than a mile. General Lee had positioned parts of two divisions to occupy these works; four brigades from Maj. Gen. Edward Johnson's Division, and a brigade from Robert Rodes' formation. The Salient's left flank was covered by Battle's and Ramseur's Brigades, while troops from Maj. Gen. Cadmus Wilcox's Division (Third Corps) manned the right.

Just after 4:30 a.m., there no longer any doubt about what was going to occur—a massive eruption of gunfire shattered the early morning's stillness—the Federals were attacking. Captain William Ardrey (Co. K) described the attack, writing, "The enemy assailed the works at daylight in the morning, having massed their forces under cover of the night and attacked before Gen Johnston had his artillery in position."[67] Brigadier General Dodson Ramseur listened as the musketry clattered, not more than a thousand yards to his right. His regimental commanders cautioned their troops to remain vigilant, but everyone was sneaking glances into the morning mists to their right. Ramseur recalled, "about five o'clock cheering and gunfire echoed from the right ... [and] swelled ... to a terrible assault coming from the northern end of the salient."[68] His brigade was safe for the moment, but as Ramseur listened to the fight's roar he could detect its proximity creeping closer to his men. Meanwhile, at the Salient's angle, blue and gray soldiers battled each other in frantic desperation. The Union high command was throwing five divisions into the fight; a dozen brigades totaling nearly eighteen thousand men. They crashed into the Confederate entrenchments. One of these Northerners proclaimed, "A fierce and bloody fight ensued in the works with bayonets and clubbed muskets."[69]

The Virginians in Col. William Witcher's brigade were quickly overwhelmed, as were many of the regiments in the combined Carolinian-Virginia brigade led by Brig. Gen. George Steuart. The two Virginian brigades commanded by Col. William Monaghan and Brig. Gen. James Walker resisted with limited success, but soon were driven from their portions of the trenches. A Federal wrote, "[Our] regiment ... moved rapidly forward over the first line of the enemy's works ... under heavy fire, capturing 150 prisoners."[70] Another added, "I pushed my brigade forward during the advance and assisted in driving the enemy from his line of works."[71] Captain William Ardrey recorded in alarm, "They succeeded in breaking the lines, capturing Gen Johnston and Gen Stewart with 2500 of the Division."[72] And, Pvt. John Bone scribbled, "about sunrise the enemy massed their troops in front of the Horse Shoe, and attacked and drove the men out."[73]

Dodson Ramseur struggled to learn more about this rapidly deteriorating situation but his attempts garnered little solid information. A Confederate noted this difficulty, writing, "The smoke of the guns and the mist kept the air dark until a comparatively late hour."[74] Frustrated by this failure, he turned his apprehensions into action, ordering the 2nd NC to redeploy. Ramseur remarked, "I soon discovered the enemy was gaining ground. I therefore moved the 2nd North Carolina which I had in reserve, to a position on the right, perpendicular to my line of battle."[75] The Carolinian general also notified his remaining three colonels to ready their men for instant reaction. Moments later he received orders from Gen. Rodes to shift his troops and counter attack. He directed Col. William Cox to right face his 2nd NC regiment and march farther east. Cox's formation moved a hundred yards before once again, facing north, towards the sounds of the fighting. Ramseur then told Col. Bryan Grimes to remove his 4th NC from their breastworks and form to the left of the 2nd NC. When Grimes' men were in position, the 14th NC was ordered to move alongside the 4th NC. Finally, Col. Frank Parker got the word to file his unit behind the three-regiment formation and take its usual position on the brigade's far right flank. Dodson Ramseur reported, "I formed my brigade in a line parallel to the two lines of works."[76] A Tar Heel then noted, "The men were ordered to lie down as Ramseur prepared his men to retake the fallen positions."[77]

Meanwhile, the killing within the Salient's angle continued, and spread south as the blue-coated soldiers pushed their way forward, capturing more trench line, and gobbling up Confederates. They also advanced into the trees behind the entrenchments, shooting into the woods, firing at the retreating Southerners. A Northerner boasted, "The enemy

The McCoull farmhouse, not far from Spotsylvania Court House (Johnson & Buel, 1887).

fled in great confusion and disorder ... [and] Our troops ... pursued the ... enemy ... until [we] encountered a second formidable line of earthworks, the existence of which was unknown to us."[78]

Captain Jesse Wicker (Co. H) led the 30th NC's right wing past the far right flank of the 2nd NC and onto a cleared patch of ground belonging to a farmer named McCoull. Bullets began to zip over the Tar Heels' heads and a couple soldiers collapsed, struck by these lethal chunks of lead. Wicker kept moving east until the last man in Cpt. David Allen's (Co. C) left wing had passed beyond the 2nd NC. Then, Col. Parker halted the regiment and fronted the unit. He ordered his Tar Heels to lie down. The Carolinians quickly sought the protection of the ground, though a number of officers and NCOs remained standing, or walked about behind their platoons and companies. More Yank bullets zipped out of the woods and a few of these missiles struck among the men not lying down, hitting 2nd Lt. Archibald Jackson (Co. H), who tumbled to the muddy ground, seriously wounded.[79] A Southerner wrote, "Now that he had orders to reinforce Daniel, Ramseur withdrew his regiments behind their works, forming a line which faced north and which extended a short distance out into the McCoull field."[80] Captain William Ardrey (Co. K) added, "Our brigade formed under the most terrific fire."[81] Private John Bone also remarked, "We were exposed very much while forming line of battle. Many were wounded at this point."[82]

Dodson Ramseur called to his Tar Heels, explaining the dire situation their army was in, and exhorted them to do their duty. He recalled, "Before ordering the charge I cautioned the men to keep the alignment, not to fire, to move slowly until the command to charge, and then to move forward at the run ... and not to pause until both lines of works were ours."[83] He also noted, "This was a serious time with us ... and would have been more so, if we could really realize our position."[84]

The Tar Heel riflemen remaining lying on their bellies, peering at the trees ahead of them, searching for blue coats. Bullets continued to buzz overhead, though now nearly all the officers and NCOs were also hunched down. General Ramseur approached Frank Parker and in a loud voice stated, "'Colonel we have got to charge those works, and get them back,' and [Parker] answered, 'We can do it.'"[85] Colonel Parker ordered his men to rise, and as Pvt. John Bone (Co. I) remembered, "the men were ordered to 'use our bayonets' before the charge ... [and] every

Second Lt. Archibald Jackson (Co. H), 29 years old, was mortally wounded on May 12, 1864. He died a week later (Taylor, 1998).

soldier knew what that meant."[86] The riflemen in the brigade's other three regiments also arose from the muddy ground and fixed their bayonets. Then, they waited anxiously, wiping at the water dripping in their eyes, as the rain once again was falling in heavy torrents. Ramseur recalled, "Tense minutes passed before the shouted order to charge rang out."[87]

Dodson Ramseur gave the order to half-wheel to the left and advance, and the Carolinians surged forward. One of Ramseur's riflemen remarked, "Soon the order came for the 14th to wheel to the left and ... charge the enemy."[88] Another wrote, "they dashed ahead with a yell."[89] Northern musketry began striking Tar Heels; Sgt. Thomas Howard (Co. A) fell backwards, dead; Pvt. Peter Buff (Co. B), dropped, wounded; Pvt. Wyatt Cornell (Co. G) tumbled sideways, his right elbow shattered; and Pvt. Hardy Burgess (Co. F) was knocked back, wounded in the hand.[90] The brigade pushed forward, the men howling as they advanced, and more riflemen dropped, some dead and many more wounded. General Dodson Ramseur twisted backwards off his horse, a bullet splashing through the flesh of his right arm, below the elbow. His aides rushed to him but he refused to leave his brigade. They bandaged his arm and he continued forward with his Carolinians.[91] The Confederates kept slogging ahead, through the mud, leaning forward as if pressing against a strong wind. Captain William Ardrey (Co. K) recalled, "After advancing near ½ mile while our fellow soldiers were falling thick and fast around us until our ranks were very much depleted."[92]

By now Union forces had worked their way through the first set of earthworks and discovered a second line. These ditches were mostly abandoned, as they had been dug in the past couple days of frantic entrenching, before officers realized their units needed to be shifted elsewhere. The blue coats swarmed over this excavated location and pushed farther southward. One soldier mentioned this advance, noting, "The victorious Federals ... fought their way down the salient to the clearing around the McCoull house."[93] But now, other Confederates had joined the fight, men from Brig. Gen. John Gordon's Brigade. His troops slowed the Union onslaught, and when Ramseur's Tar Heels reinforced Gordon's Georgians, the blue coats' attack stalled.[94] A Carolinian recorded, "Ramseur's men, who had had neither breakfast nor an opportunity to fill their canteens, could see Union flags fluttering above the captured works."[95]

Colonel Parker's riflemen unleashed a volley, and the Union troops responded with one of their own. Private Wiley Cress (Co. C) fell, a bullet mangling his right thigh; Pvt. John Saintsing (Co. B) took a lead ball in his right shoulder; 3rd Lt. John Fulford (Co. G) suffered a hit to his left arm; and Sgt. Brantly Henderson (Co. E) was killed.[96] A Northerner wrote, "The fire at this point was maintained but a short time, our whole line falling back to the enemy's first line of works."[97] A Southerner remarked, "When the command to charge [at the double-quick] was given, the entire brigade moved forward and drove the enemy out of the captured works."[98] A Northerner added, "The enemy ... threw heavy re-enforcements into the second line opposite to the point of my attack." He continued, "They now advanced against our troops, who had been checked by their second line of entrenchments."[99] Another blue coat added, "the enemy concentrating his whole fire upon [us], the works so gallantly won had to be abandoned, and the regiment fell back to the first line of rebel works captured."[100]

The Tar Heels jumped into the trench and from its chest-deep safety fired at the retreating Yanks. A Federal officer recorded, "they rolled the tide of battle back on us, [and] we fell back into and behind their first line of works."[101] Another remarked, "The loss of the regiment both in [our] officers and men was heavy."[102] General Ramseur's riflemen rounded up scores of Union soldiers left behind and hustled them away from the entrenchment. Colonel Grimes (4th NC) noted, "the very boldness of the move recovered the entire works ... capturing many prisoners and killing more Yankees than the Brigade numbered men."[103] The Carolinians' advance stopped, the men sucked at their canteens, stuffed more ammunition into their cartridge boxes, and fought to regain their wind. Musicians flitted among the wounded and helped get them back to safety. For a moment, the Tar Heels found themselves in a peaceful vortex, while to their left, right, and straight ahead, heavy musketry filled the rain-saturated air with noise and gun smoke. A number of riflemen fired into the fog of smoke rolling toward them, but most stood motionless, gasping for breath and content to remain within the breastwork's safety. The Carolina counterattack had broken down, far from its objective.

Colonel Bryan Grimes (4th NC) looked around for Gen. Ramseur and when he could not find him, consulted with Frank Parker and William Cox. Grimes recalled, "[We] rested a few minutes, and Ramseur having been shot in his right arm and not able to keep up, and seeing no one to apply to, and seeing the necessity for speedy action, I ordered a second charge, myself leading."[104] One of his riflemen remarked, "We drove them and recovered the [rear] line of our works, paused a moment and made a dash for the next and stronger line."[105] The Carolinians climbed out of the works and followed Col. Grimes. The Tar Heel riflemen, though, slid more to the left as they moved forward, half-wheeling to parallel the first line of entrenchments. However, as the Confederates advanced, Federal musketry proved again to be lethal. Private John Bone (Co. I) recorded, "We moved forward and many, oh many, made their last charge here."[106] Private James Squires (Co. K) was killed, as was 2nd Lt. James Lee (Co. K) and Pvt. Burgess Jackson (Co. F). Private James Pitt's (Co. I) left leg was torn open by a minié ball, Cpl. John Underwood (Co. H) fell, his right ankle shattered, and Pvt. John Bone (Co. I) was wounded.[107] Private John Bone recalled, "Just before we reached the first line of works, I was mortally wounded by a ball striking me in the right breast passing through my lungs and coming out beside my backbone."[108]

The brigade's left-flank regiment, the 14th NC smashed into the Salient's westernmost trench line and Col. Risden Bennett's Confederates grappled with the blue coats occupying this position. The 4th NC lapped around the 14th NC's right and crashed into the fortification's next hundred yards. The 14th's and 4th's riflemen fought at close quarters against the Yanks, often resorting to bayonets and fists. A Tar Heel officer recorded, "We reached the near side of these works while the enemy received us on the other side."[109] Another officer stated, "The 4th and 14th [became] jumbled together."[110] Meanwhile, more Union troops poured into the fight, crowding into the trench line's outer portion. One Northerner recorded, "[Our] regiment advanced steadily, crossed the first line of the enemy's works, and ... then engaged with the enemy."[111] A member of the 4th NC recalled, "The desperate character of the struggle ... was told by the rapidity of its musketry. So close was the fighting at the time, that the fire of friend and foe rose up rattling in a common roar.... [Our men] dropped thick and fast."[112]

In Colonel Parker's Thirtieth, the regiment farthest from the Salient's western side, their advance was mostly straight ahead. Captain David Allen's left wing drifted to the left as it attempted to keep abreast with the 2nd NC, which had also shifted left. Frank Parker's right wing continued forward, taking heavy fire from the Yanks holding the Mule Shoe's northern breastworks, and from a new force appearing from the east, their bullets hitting the formation from the right. Private Charles Riggan (Co. B) was knocked down, his right arm ripped open; Cpl. Thomas Shearin (Co. B) dropped, his right thigh shredded; 1st Lt. Lallister White (Co. A) was killed; Pvt. William Burgess (Co. H) killed; and Pvt. William Wanett (Co. C) killed.[113] Captain William Ardrey (Co. K) recorded, "[We were] under a most deadly fire.... Their missiles were coming so thick that scarcely a single man went through untouched."[114]

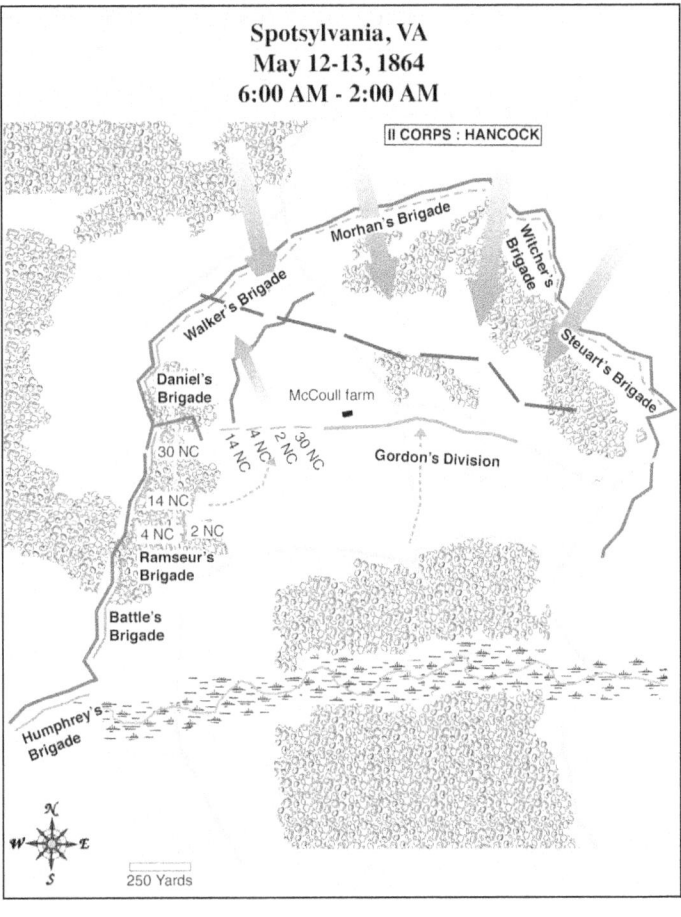

The battle between the brigade's left two regiments and the Federals trying to hold the trench line was desperate, often involving hand-to-hand fighting. One Confederate noted, "Ramseur's Carolinians ... were received by the enemy with a stubborn resistance."[115] Another wrote, "it was the only instance during the entire war in which any number of Ramseur's men used their bayonets."[116] The breastworks in this portion of the line did not exist as a single, long trench; instead, the works had been constructed by connecting a series of transverse, box-like rifle pits. One Southerner described the works, writing, "These traverses ... [were] log pens each of which served as a small fortress and became a miniature but extremely bloody battlefield."[117] The Confederate riflemen pushed forward, attacking the blue coats occupying a transverse, and in a melee of bayonets, fists, knives, and rifles swung as clubs, either killed or captured anyone who resisted. This was a slow and costly advance, slaughtering both Confederate and Yank. One Southerner grimly wrote, "From traverse to traverse [we] grimly moved on, clearing Federals from the ... works."[118] Another added, "the regiment ... went down the line and drove into the traverses by a front of fours. Out of there we expelled the enemy, giving him cold steel."[119] A Northerner reported, "The interior of the entrenchments presented a terrible and ghastly spectacle of dead, most of whom were killed by our men with the bayonet. So thickly lay the dead at this point, that at many places the bodies were touching and piled upon each other."[120] Another blue coat noted, "The [fighting in] these works was kept up for an hour or more when [our troops in] all that portion of the line on the right ... fell back and the enemy took possession of the works."[121] A Confederate described this local success, writing, "The pits at the breastworks were filled with water from [the] recent rain, many dead and wounded from both sides were lying in the pits when we reached them. The water was red with human gore. He continued, "In the traverse-lined pit men lay four deep ... limbs interlaced and intertwined."[122] The bodies of the dead were dragged out, and the men took shelter in their places."[123] Meanwhile, as the 14th and 4th NC recaptured several hundred yards of trenches, the 2nd NC also struck the next section of breastworks and, after another face-to-face scuffle, pushed the blue coats out of the works. A Yank recorded this loss, penning, "the enemy retook the works to our right and [seemed] determined to dislodge us."[124] Finally, Col. Bennett (14th NC) was able to record, "The enemy was driven out at 7:30 a.m."[125]

Unfortunately, Col. Parker's Thirtieth was in trouble. Fresh Union troops flooded over the eastern side of the Mule Shoe's fortifications and advanced upon the regiment's right flank. One of Ramseur's staff recorded, "[The] brigade did not extend far enough to the right to be able to retake the toe of the salient, and the Union troops holding the elevated knoll at the apex of the ... [Bloody Angle] were well positioned to pour a destructive fire down upon [Col. Parker's] men."[126] Private William McLemore (Co. A) was severely injured by a musket ball; Pvt. William Pilgreen (Co. C) and Pvt. John Bailey Williamson (Co. C) killed; 2nd Lt. Lorenzo Eagles (Co. F) fell, a bullet shattering his leg above the knee, and his brother, Pvt. Theodore Eagles (Co. F), also went down, his arm ripped open.[127] Dodson Ramseur reported, "The enemy still held the breastworks on my

The Mule Shoe's trenches often consisted of a series of connected transverse entrenchments (Johnson & Buel, 1887).

right, enfilading my line with a destructive fire."[128] Another Tar Heel remarked, "The 30th regiment on the right was in desperate peril."[129]

Northern regiments rushed at Parker's right flank, shooting rapidly, knocking down many of the unprotected riflemen, and causing some of the company formations to dissolve. Colonel Parker rushed to the area, attempting to rally his men, and was immediately grazed by a minié bullet. The Thirtieth's right wing began to drift backward as the embattled riflemen sought safety. However, in other locations, dozens of resolute Carolinians clustered around their leaders and refused to retreat. They were eventually overwhelmed by the blue coats and captured, including Cpt. Gary Williams (Co. A), 2nd Lt. John Swain (Co. C), and the right wing's commander, Cpt. Jesse Wicker (Co. H).[130] Captain William Ardrey (Co. K) recorded, "The enemy marched against the flanks of the 30th Regt and a hand-to-hand engagement ensued. About one third of the 30th were prisoners."[131] Private John Bone (Co. I) added, "our men were having a very hard time."[132]

Second Lt. Lorenzo Dow Eagles (Co. F), 27 years old, was severely wounded on May 12, 1864. He died twelve days later (courtesy Living History Association of North Carolina).

In another location, a group of Frank Parker's strong-willed Tar Heels manned an body-strewn section of breastworks, tenaciously resolved to protect the Thirtieth's battle flag. First Lieutenant Peter Arrington, the regimental adjutant, now carried the colors. He maintained a prominent posture, using the stars and bars as a rallying marker for Tar Heels who had become detached from their companies. A mob of Yanks closed on Arrington's position and suddenly the blue and gray soldiers found themselves right next to each other, only separated by a wall of piled logs. A Carolinian wrote, "the enemy pulled the Adjutant of the Thirtieth Regiment over the works by the hair of his head and captured him." The Southerner continued, "The colors ... were pulled out of the color-bearer's hands and carried off."[133] The aggressive Yank who took possession of the Thirtieth's flag is not known, as he was quickly killed. But then, the emblem was passed from man to man until it ended up in Pvt. Robert W. Ammerman's (14th PA) hands. Ammerman received credit for grabbing the flag and safely carrying out it out of the fight.[134]

As the Thirtieth's battle line melted away, observant Tar Heels in Ramseur's brigade recognized their comrades' plight. Colonel Risden Bennett (14th NC) noted, "[I] became concerned about the precarious position of the 30th on the brigade's right flank." Since Bennett's troops were now holding a secure portion of the trench line, he figured his men could help. Bennett continued, "[I] offered to take [my] regiment from left to right ... and drive back the growing masses of the enemy on our right."[135] Colonel Bennett posted a line of skirmishers to hold the breastworks and then ordered his regiment to right face and form a column-of-fours. One of his riflemen wrote, "Changing from the left to the right ... [and] With a Rebel yell we rushed down the line in column."[136] The 14th NC raced towards the Union masses, Risden Bennett leading a spearhead-shaped formation forward—a single regimental column attack, reminiscent of what Upton had done with fifteen regiments, and Grant with an entire corps. The Northerners gave up trying to destroy the rest of Col. Parker's formation and concentrated their fire upon Bennett's troops. A Tar Heel rifleman noted, "[We attacked] by a front of fours ... in the face of a galling fire, [at] a hazardous, tremendous risk."[137] The Fourteenth punched into the Yank masses, knocking their formations backwards. General Ramseur recalled, "Colonel Bennett, 14th NC ... [took] his regiment from left to right under severe fire and ... secured the right flank by giving the Federals cold steel."[138] One of Bennett's soldiers added, "[We] drove into the traverses ... [and] expelled the enemy."[139] Frank Parker's veterans rallied and joined with the 14th NC, attacking the retreating blue coats, riddling them with musketry. A Carolinian observed, "our ... men, closing up their rapidly thinning ranks, poured a continuous storm of leaden hail into the enemy's ranks, as he slowly, but stubbornly retired."[140] A Northerner wrote, "[We] lost the entrenchments to our right [and] we formed a line in an obtuse angle, but line after line melted away before the enemy's fire.... [We] lost heavily."[141]

The Tar Heels did not advance beyond this area of traverses; instead, the riflemen hunkered down within the earthworks' confines. This reprieve enabled the Union troops to occupy an outer line of the Mule Shoe's trenches. Both forces were less than a hundred feet away, the frantic riflemen firing their muskets as fast as they could load. A Carolinian scribbled, "though [we] crouched close to the slopes under an enfilade from the guns of the salient, their musketry rattled in ... deadly fire on the enemy."[142] Private John Bone (Co. I) remembered, "Here we were, one line of men, with two ranks (front and rear), and in front of us were two lines of breastworks, filled with men."[143] It was now about 9:00 a.m.

Ramseur's men realized it was safer to hold the works they had recaptured than to retreat So, they stayed hidden and only raised themselves up to fire, before quickly dropping down into their trenches. Amazingly, the Union soldiers were doing exactly the same thing; thus, the men from both sides remained below ground and only surfaced briefly to shoot. A Federal wrote, "We stood perhaps one hundred feet from the enemy's line, and so long as we maintained a continual fire they remained hidden in their entrenchments. But if an attempt to advance was made, an order would be given and they would rise up together and fire a volley at us."[144] The Tar Heel riflemen now understood their best chance for survival was to remain hidden within the breastworks, but if they left these protections, injury or death was almost certain. A soldier remarked, "If one advanced, there was little effective shelter against the hail of bullets."[145] Knowing this simple fact, everyone worked to improve his portion of the works. One grimly recorded, "The trenches ... ran with blood and had to be cleared of dead bodies."[146]

The Carolinians held their position for the next hour. More Confederates endured the slaughter as they hurried across the body-littered ground and joined Ramseur's men. General Richard Ewell noted the first unit to arrive, writing, "Harris' (Mississippi) brigade, which came to [our] assistance about 9 a.m., was sent to Ramseur's right, but it still failed to fill the trenches."[147] Then, General Lee was able to push more troops into the gap; Mississippians from Brig. Gen. William Mahone's Brigade (Third Corps) and South Carolinians commanded by Brig. Gen. Samuel McGowan (Third Corps). The Federals attempted to drive the Southerners from their position, but this assault was a disaster. Colonel Bryan Grimes (4th NC) recorded, "They made repeated efforts to retake our works but we successfully repulsed every attack."[148] Risden Bennett (14th NC) added, "We beat the enemy, a re-enforcement coming to his aid being almost annihilated."[149] A Federal commander sadly admitted, "The dense woods through which a portion of our troops had charged was the scene of a most fearful [slaughter]."[150] Colonel Bennett then noted, "It was midday by this time."[151]

Once the Confederates had shot this Federal blunder to pieces, neither side made any more attacks. Instead, the battle-weary men from both sides just kept up a continual fire, aimed not at enemy soldiers, but rather at the trenches in which they hid. A Southerner noted, "The wooden parts of the works fell prey to the storm, splinter[ing] like brush-brooms."[152] This constant, interdictory shooting prevented either force from attacking, retreating, or changing positions. And, as the men sadly learned, to show one's head meant death. First Lieutenant George Harrell (Co. F) was killed, "a ball passing though his head." Then another Confederate died in similar fashion; a Carolinian rifleman wrote, "The breastworks, made of logs, had cracks between the logs which would have been filled with earth if we had had spades and shovels…. Ed was looking through the crack when smitten by a minié ball."[153] Another recalled, "[A soldier] was looking … through a small crack below the top log of the works … [when] a ball penetrated the space [and] pierced his jugular vein."[154] And a third remarked, "When I raised up a bullet extracted my front teeth."[155] More of Frank Parker's Tar Heels went down, including Pvt. Thomas Price (Co. F), who was also killed, "shot through the head."[156]

The fighting at Spotsylvania was one of the few times the 30th's soldiers were forced to fight with their bayonets (Johnson & Buel, 1887).

Another hour went by, sixty agonizing minutes of continual rain, constant musketry, and more deaths. A Southerner recalled, "Rain continued to pelt them ... [and] The enemy did not let up."[157] Private Young Bailey (Co. D) was killed, and Pvt. Carleton Malpass (Co. E) shot through the right hip.[158] Another Tar Heel was slightly hurt, though his injury could have been much more serious; a soldier in the 4th NC wrote, "[One soldier] "received a painful contusion from a ball that passed through a heavy canteen of water which he carried, and which no doubt saved his life."[159]

The rain deluged the battlefield, the water cascading onto the combatants in near-blinding torrents. Muddy water drained into the trenches, turning each traverse and rifle pit into muck-filled wallows, saturating each man with a coating of slime and sludge. For the men though, no matter how grime-coated they were, they had to continue loading and shooting their weapons. A much-suffering soldier wrote, "During the day a heavy rain-storm prevailed, but notwithstanding the uncomfortableness [sic.] of the situation the men ... kept up a steady fire all day."[160] The shooting continued without let-up, the mud-covered soldiers hiding within their watery hideouts and then quickly raising up to fire, before immediately dropping back down into the gunk floating within their traverses. Captain John McMillan (Co. E) was knocked down into the muddy ooze, a bullet having drilled through his shoulder and right arm; Pvt. William Harris (Co. G) was killed, and Pvt. Charles Center (Co. H) fell, a bullet cracking his skull.[161] Private John Bone (Co. I) recalled, "the enemy had located themselves so that they had a crossfire on a part of the works, and killed many of our men during the day."[162]

The shooting persisted, the men moving almost like machines, loading and firing, and loading and firing. Anything above ground was hit by the storm of lead. Wounded men who could not find cover were soon struck again and again, and bodies lying out in the open were butchered beyond human acknowledgment. A horrified Southerner wrote, "Torrents of lead killed any wounded not under cover, then riddled beyond recognition their corpses."[163] Pvt. John Brown's (Co. E) jaw was fractured by a minié bullet. Private Wesley Skipper (Co. C) was struck in the head, and then a second ball ripped through his neck. And Third Lieutenant Samuel Moore (Co. F) had a bullet punch through his stomach, and as he lay in the mud, another projectile smacked into his back.[164] A Tar Heel recorded, "The wounded bled and groaned, stretched or huddled in every attitude of pain."[165]

The shooting continued, hour after hour. A soldier remarked, "Guns would become foul, when we would order the men back to wash them out and then return to fight on."[166] Another added, "I shot away 120 rounds of cartridges myself."[167] Ammunition supplies grew low. An officer reported, "About 3 o'clock in the afternoon word came.... Send us ammunition, or we must surrender." He continued, "A call for volunteers was answered ... [they] swung two boxes of cartridges on rails and delivered them."[168] The constant musketry, noise, and gore began to affect the men. One soldier observed, "fighting and exhausted, amidst blood and mud and brains, [the men] would sit on the bodies of their fallen comrades for rest." He also added, "During the long and fierce struggle I saw soldiers place the arms of their comrades who had fallen in such position as when they stiffened they would hold the cartridges we were using."[169] Another observed, "the trees were literally cut down by minie-balls from the enemy guns."[170] Colonel Risden Bennett (14th NC) observed, "About the middle of the afternoon a red oak many inches in diameter yielded to the storm of missiles and fell to the ground."[171]

Finally, the sun dropped below the horizon, plunging the rain-and-mud-soaked battlefield into darkness. But this did not stop the shooting; the worn-out soldiers continued firing, having now been rendered witless by the constant horror. A Federal officer recalled, "The rain poured down, the mud became almost impassable, men became exhausted, night closed on us."[172] Another soldier wrote, "Nightfall brought no slackening of the slaughter, it only served to increase the awful terror of the scene."[173] By 8:00 p.m., Col. Frank Parker's men were at the breaking point; they had been under constant fire for over fourteen hours, a longer span of time than all the accumulated hours of fighting for the entire war. And yet the shooting and killing did not stop; Pvt. William Crisp (Co. F) was shot through the shoulder, the bullet shattering bones and ripping flesh and lung tissue, and Cpt. James Harris (Co. I) was killed.[174]

But there was no one to take the Tar Heels' place, and even if there were reinforcements, Parker's men could not safely retire from the field; to climb up out of their mud-filled havens remained a death sentence. One Confederate noted, "The searching balls … sounded like humming bees; some like cats in the depths of night; others cut through the air with only a zip-like noise."[175] The Thirtieth's survivors did receive news, informing them Gen. Lee's engineers were building a new defensive line, and just as soon as it was completely, they would be given permission to fall back to this position. A senior Second Corps officer remarked, "a new line was laid out during the day by General Lee's chief engineer some 800 yards in rear of the [Salient] and constructed at night."[176] Nonetheless, for the next several hours, the Tar Heels could not move. The Carolinians wallowed around in the muck, some still firing at the muzzles flashes barely thirty yards away. Most of the exhausted men slumped down in the mud- and blood-oozing sludge and just waited out the final hours. Fewer and fewer soldiers on either side had the energy to keep shooting, and as the hours dragged past midnight, the battle's roar dwindled to desultory musketry.

30th North Carolina Infantry[177]
The Wilderness and Spotsylvania
Casualties:
May 5–12, 1864

Unit	Commander	Loss
Field & Staff	Col. Parker, Francis M.	2
Co. A	Cpt. Williams, Gary	26
Co. B	Sgt. Shearin, John D.	8
Co. C	Cpt. Allen, David C.	21
Co. D	3rd Lt. Rodgers, Martin L.	7
Co. E	Cpt. McMillan, John C.	19
Co. F	Cpt. Moore, Willis M.	25
Co. G	1st Lt. Badgett, James W.	16
Co. H	Cpt. Wicker, Jesse J.	22
Co. I	Cpt. Harris, James C.	10
Co. K	Cpt. Ardrey, William E.	14
		170

Finally, the word came to pull out. Frank Parker's remaining officers and NCOs gathered their battered companies together and the weary men slipped out of their muddy traverses and stumbled away. A Tar Heel wrote, "The savage fighting … went on without pause for 22 hours until 3:00 a.m. on May 13. At that time the Confederates withdrew to a new line at the base of the salient."[178] Dodson Ramseur's survivors silently filed into the new line, some eight hundred yards south of the Mule Shoe, and one recorded, "[We] held possession until 4 o'clock A. M. Friday, when we were ordered to move out, which we did just before day[light]."[179] The Thirtieth's officers called roll as their troops dropped to the ground, already asleep. Nearly every officer, whether blue or gray, would later write, "Our losses in killed and wounded were quite heavy."[180] The Tar Heel officers also realized, comrades had been left behind when their regiments abandoned the corpse-filled trenches. Colonel Bennett (14th NC) admitted a sad fact apparent to each regimental commander, "We left a number of our wounded men under the range of the enemy's fire."[181] Captain William Ardrey (Co. K), one of the Thirtieth's few senior officers remaining, recorded, "The loss in the 30th Regt was 25 killed 75 wounded and 72 prisoners."[182] One of the Tar Heel riflemen added, "[We] did some of the hardest fighting that day and night that has been done during the war."[183]

CHAPTER 13

The Killing Continues— Harris Farm to Cold Harbor

The exhausted Tar Heels staggered to their feet not long after sunrise on May 13, 1864. The morning was damp, misty, and smoky; however, most importantly, quiet. The Thirtieth's bone-tired pickets peered towards the Union positions, bleary-eyed, as they scanned a field covered, as one rifleman observed, "[With] dead men ... on the surface of the ground and in pools of water." He added, "The wounded bled and groaned ... [and there were] abandoned knapsacks, guns, accouterments were scattered all around."[1] Inside the Confederate's new entrenchments, the worn-out men tended to minor wounds, cuts, and bruises, and scrounged for dry firewood. One battle-weary rifleman exclaimed, "You would hardly recognize any of us at present. Every one looks as if he had passed through a hard spell of sickness, black and muddy as hogs."[2] Sergeant James Fuller (Co. G) exclaimed, "[We were] begrimed with smoke and mud."[3] And Brig. Gen. Dodson Ramseur, walking among his men, noted they were "black and muddy as hogs, and hollow-eyed as though recovering from a serious illness."[4] The Thirtieth's soldiers spoke little, stunned by what they had experienced. Yesterday's terror had lasted so long, and the horror was so overwhelming, many had become incapable of function. One tired soldier remarked, "many of the soldiers were so weary that they went through the motions of combat and scarcely knew what they were doing." He added, "Old soldiers stared and looked blank, as if the fury of the fight had driven them mad."[5]

The hours passed slowly; though mostly quiet, except for skirmishers and pickets who occasionally dueled with each other, and every now and then a cannon would probe a position. Captain William Ardrey (Co. K) recorded, "Some artillery and skirmishing ... during the day."[6] Colonel Frank Parker's riflemen did not venture far from their breastworks, though they could hear countless cries for help coming from their wounded brothers laying where they had fought yesterday. One of these injured Tar Heels was Pvt. John Bone (Co. I), who though seriously wounded, remained not far from the Mule Shoe's apex. He recalled, "It continued to rain in small showers all through the day." The 22-year-old added, "The day passed away, each line held their position." Then, as the afternoon hours waned into evening John Bone realized he needed help but was terrified by the thought of Yankees finding him if he called out. So, he slowly began to crawl towards the Confederate lines, moving cautiously during the darkened hours. John Bone was weak from his wound, and his journey took nearly all night, but finally he got within hailing distance of the Southern position. Bone stated, "I must now make myself known to our men before it got light enough for the enemy to see me, and I took a white handkerchief

... and put it on a stick and shook it. I was soon told to come on."[7] Moments later, the wounded rifleman was rescued by a Tar Heel officer. John Bone recalled, "No one can realize the relief that I felt in getting delivered to my companions."[8]

With morning's light on May 14, 1864, Col. Frank Parker finally had an accurate count of effectives remaining in the Thirtieth. His formation had gained a few soldiers who had been left behind when the brigade fell back, and, like Pvt. John Bone, had used the darkness to sneak back to safety. Parker began re-organizing his battered regiment, now numbering barely over two hundred fifty. The slaughter in the Mule Shoe had decimated the Thirtieth's leaders: Captain Gary Williams (Co. A) was missing, presumed captured; 1st Lt. Lallister White (Co. A) dead; 1st Lt. George Harrell (Co. F) dead; 3rd Lt. John Fulford (Co. G) wounded; Cpt. Jesse Wicker (Co. H) captured; 2nd Lt. Archibald Jackson (Co. H) seriously hurt; Cpt. James Harris (Co. I) dead; and 1st Lt. Kearney Arrington (Co. I) wounded and missing. The Thirtieth's commander had only two captains remaining; David Allen (Co. C) and William Ardrey (Co. K), and just nine lieutenants. This meant one company was now being led by a corporal, while another by a first sergeant. Frank Parker grouped his shriveled units into two wings, with both units not much larger than early war companies; the right to be commanded by Cpt. David Allen, and the left by Cpt. William Ardrey.[9] He combined officer-less companies with ones containing surviving lieutenants, and shifted the remaining officers in order to evenly distribute leadership. It was the best he could do.

The day went by quietly, though, as one rifleman admitted, "it seemed that the enemy was going to make an attack upon our line."[10] Colonel Parker rotated forward pickets throughout the day, and the mud-coated soldiers grimly endured their postings. Everyone else hunkered down within their section of the defensive line, waiting out the daylight hours, praying for darkness to remove the threat of battle. The Carolinians' morale was poor; so many comrades were missing, and yet nothing had been accomplished, except now they held a mud-clogged ditch a thousand yards behind another gore-and-water filled trench in which they had fought, and so many had been killed. They also were saddened by the news their beloved general, J.E.B. Stuart had been killed. A soldier wrote, "[Stuart's death] caused indescribable feeling in the Army."[11] The Confederates mourned Stuart's death, and pondered their own mortality. One wrote, "My escapes are regarded as miraculous."[12]

Early the next morning, May 15, 1864, pickets sent messages to Col. Parker, informing him the Yankees were no longer holding their fortifications. General Ramseur sent a strengthened skirmish line forward and they clashed with blue coats, but the Northerners exhibited no enthusiasm for holding their position. Captain William Ardrey scribbled into his diary, "Skirmishing all day.... The enemy retired from our front, the center of the line moving towards Fredericksburg." He noted, once the Yanks had fallen back, "Div dead ... buried and ... wounded ... removed."[13] Medical personnel now found it safe enough to explore the battlefield grounds and retrieve any remaining wounded. Then, the seriously injured were designated for shipment to Richmond. Private John Bone (Co. I) wrote, "All the wounded that were able they took to the railroad, so that they could be carried to a hospital for treatment and those that were not they took to a large grove to remain until they improved or died."[14]

Colonel Frank Parker was called to a senior officers' meeting and learned from Maj. Gen. Robert Rodes a good portion of Maj. Gen. Edward Johnson's Division was being re-organized, as three of his brigades had been destroyed. General Lee was now consolidating these battered brigades into one, and in this process, two North Carolina regiments, the 1st NC and the 3rd NC were being shifted to Ramseur's brigade. Frank Parker welcomed the thought of added strength to their brigade, but was soon disappointed, as both of the transferred regiments numbered less than an early-war platoon. An officer in the 1st NC recorded, "All but thirty of the whole regiment were captured ... [including] the colonel."[15] In total, the 1st NC and 3rd NC added sixty men to Ramseur's brigade.[16]

The brigade remained in their trenches for the next three days, the Tar Heels relishing the sensation of not being under lethal threat. The weather also changed; the rains giving way to hot, sun-filled days, enabling the men to dry out their equipment and wash their clothing. One Confederate wrote, "Now, after ten days of constant service, [the men were] ... unwashed—for I do not think a single soldier ... who was fit for duty had time to take his shoes off or wash his face."[17] Another noted, "On May 17, sunshine and a brisk wind dried clothing and brightened spirits."[18] Never-the-less, even as the Carolinians happily cleaned themselves, they knew, as one noted, "the roads began to dry."[19] The veterans understood what this fact meant; either Lee or Grant would move soldiers and cannons on the hardened roads, and danger would return.

Early in the morning of May 18, 1864, Col. Parker's pickets scampered back to the regiment's breastworks, bringing word of Yanks massing for an attack. Frank Parker put his troops on alert, and his Tar Heels, along with the rest of the Carolinians in Ramseur's brigade, primed their muskets and waited for an assault. The advance came just after 8:00 a.m., with blue coats from II and VI Corps moving forward. The Southern riflemen watched in shock as the Union lines shuffled towards them. Parker's men were well-protected in their fortification, and they knew General Ewell had posted nearly three dozen artillery pieces to cover their front. One soldier noted, "[They] scarcely could believe their eyes or realize that a frontal assault on the line was to be made by the enemy."[20] Another added, "This infantry in column formations ... stepped out rapidly, with their muskets at a 'right shoulder shift,' in successive lines, apparently several brigades deep, well aligned and steady, without bands, but with flags flying."[21] And a third Confederate recorded, "[Our] gunners could see the Federals in the abandoned works like fish in a barrel and gleefully began shooting."[22] Dodson Ramseur recorded, "the Federals advanced several brigades ... [we] directed a fire against the attackers that quickly drove them back in confusion. Several times the blue infantry regrouped and came on, only to be rebuffed ... their repulse was so easy ... [it was] dismissed ... as feeble."[23] The attacks were quickly shot to pieces and by 10:00 a.m., the front was again quiet, save for the cries of the wounded.

Brigadier General Ramseur sent out the brigade's pickets and as the rest of the hours slowly went by, messages were sent to brigade headquarters telling of a Yankee withdrawal. By nightfall, further probes revealed a full-scale retreat; the Northerners had shifted to the east, completely away from the Mule Shoe's Angle, and were miles away. The Tar Heels relaxed; maybe, the optimistic soldiers hoped, General Grant had finally given up. However, the veterans saw this situation differently; if Grant was retreating, then Lee would pursue. The fight was not over.

Sunrise on May 19, 1864, found the Tar Heels resting contentedly within their breastworks. One soldier wrote, "They had passed the morning quiet in the ditch, as they called their mud-caked entrenchments." He continued, "Marching orders came as a surprise."[24] The riflemen were issued extra ammunition and told to fall in. Soon, Brig. Gen. Dodson

Ramseur led the column towards the northwest, his brigade leading Rodes' Division. By 2:00 p.m. they reached the Spindle farm and viewed a battle's aftermath. A dismayed Confederate recalled, "the Spindle farm ... was criss-crossed with rows of corpses from earlier fighting. Grave diggers had thrown dirt over the bodies, but recent rains had left heads and feet protruding from the ground." He continued, "It was an awful sight and the stench was horrible ... [and] a dense sea of corrupted atmosphere filled the hollows."[25] They passed beyond the battlefield and an hour later marched across a bridge spanning the Ny River. Dodson Ramseur recorded, "About 3 p.m. ... the corps moved across the Ny River.... My brigade in front."[26] The column then turned southeast, passing the Armstrong house and the Stevens farm.

By now the afternoon's temperature was burning hot and the men sweated in the thick humidity. However, relief was on the way, the soldiers could see a line of tall thunderheads drifting towards them. Dodson Ramseur urged his Confederates forward; he had been informed the Northerners had assembled a large supply train near the Fredericksburg Road, and it was unprotected. One such report indicated, "The Fredericksburg road, as it leaves Spotsylvania Courthouse, runs northeast ... [and] a mile farther ... many of the supply trains were parked."[27] Ramseur wanted to capture those wagons, and the thought of breaking into those Yankee stores filled the Tar Heels with enthusiasm. Captain William Ardrey (Co. K) agreed, writing, "[We] moved around the right flank of the enemy to feel his strength and to capture his wagon train."[28] The Carolinians raced ahead and soon brigade guides informed Col. Frank Parker the next landmark was the

The Harris farmstead was owned by Susan Alsop (Library of Congress).

13. The Killing Continues   175

Harris place. The Harris homestead consisted of a small cluster of structures and outbuildings. A soldier described the farmstead, writing, "the Harris house is on an open field, a quarter to three-eights of a mile in length and a quarter of a mile in width."[29] Another noted, "The center of the line was in front of two log-houses.... Beyond us was an open meadow, probably [100 yards] ... wide, then timber."[30]

The Harris farm was also the focal point of a line of Union skirmishers; troops from the 4th NY Heavy Artillery. These were men had served some of the artillery pieces protecting Washington, D.C., but now General Grant had decided they were no longer needed as cannoneers. He ordered the soldiers be given muskets and sent them to join the Army of the Potomac as infantrymen. Three companies of the 4th NYHA protected the Federal's right flank, a battalion totaling substantially more than what Col. Parker commanded in the Thirtieth. One of these soldiers recorded, "Our battalion went into the fight with 394 men." He continued, "Cos. D, H, and K ... were sent forward.... Our line was against a rail fence just at the edge of a very thick woods." He added, "Our men were deployed as skirmishers thirty feet apart."[31]

Brigadier General Ramseur's advance scouts stumbled onto the New Yorkers and following the initial burst of musketry, the brigade commander halted his column and deployed the regiments into a battle line. Colonel Frank Parker had just over two hundred fifty officers and riflemen. His Thirtieth moved into its normal position within the brigade, on the right flank. Ramseur sent his sharpshooter corps forward through a dense stand of foliage that masked a low, swampy area clogged with tall cat tails, and then came up against the blue coats. A writer noted, "Rain began falling, lightly at first, then in torrents.... Just as the skies opened ... the Tar Heels ran headlong into the forward pickets of.... Co. K, 4th NYHA."[32] Surprisingly, the New Yorkers were not ready for the Tar Heels. One Yank rifleman wrote, "we were startled by the sudden firing of our videttes."[33]

30th North Carolina Infantry[34]
May 19, 1864

Unit		Strength
Field & Staff	Col. Parker, Francis M. Cpt. Allen, David C. Cpt. Ardrey, William E	3
Co. A	1st Sgt. Crumpler, Robert M.	15
Co. B	Cpl. Bell, William	13
Co. C	Sgt. Wescott, John W.	16
Co. D	3rd Lt. Rodgers, Martin L.	21
Co. E	1st Lt. Johnson, Ira J. 2nd Lt. Newton, Samuel B.	40
Co. F	2nd Lt. House, James W. 3rd Lt. Moore, Samuel R.	37
Co. G	1st Lt. Badgett, James W.	27
Co. H	1st Lt. McNeil, Henry J.	23
Co. I	3rd Lt. Perry, Sidney R.	30
Co. K	1st Lt. Downs, John T.	31
		257

Dodson Ramseur immediately gave the order for his regiments to advance and engage the Federals. He reported, "after the enemy discovered our movement, and when further delay, as I thought, would cause disaster, I [ordered the] attack with my brigade."[35] His Carolinians pressed forward, firing as they advanced, their first shots impacting among the riflemen of Company K. An astonished Yank wrote, "we saw the rebels coming from the woods in column, and a minute after they came into line and fired a volley at the house."[36] The Confederates closed upon the New Yorkers, engulfing Company K and then the men of Company H. These two blue formations equaled the entire Thirtieth's numbers but completely lacked battle experience. The Northerners recoiled and staggered backwards. The 4th NYHA's third company, another one hundred fifty men, had been posted in reserve. This unit was brought forward to bolster the Union line. One of these soldiers stated, "Soon the woods about the houses ... were alive with rebel skirmishers, pouring their fire from front and flank.... Co. D immediately came to [in] support."[37] This third unit crashed into the Tar Heels, and a blue-coated rifleman remarked, "Scarcely had [Co. D arrived] ... when the rebels advanced in two lines of battle in splendid order from the woods upon our simple picket lines."[38] Another added, "At 5 p.m., heavy musketry was heard."[39]

Ramseur's regiments advanced, firing as they moved, their deployment impressing the ex-artillerymen. One New York officer exclaimed, "It was a magnificent sight ... for the lines moved as steadily as if on parade, and if ever I longed for a battery with guns shotted with grape and canister ... it was then and there."[40] The Carolinians pushed forward, crowding the New Yorkers. A Tar Heel recorded, "Our skirmishers attacked their skirmishers ... and drove them back half a mile, when we came in contact with their ... line of battle."[41] But now, the Northerners' line steadied and the inexperienced riflemen scrambled to receive the Confederate assault. One wrote, "Retiring from the houses, we formed line behind an old rail fence back of the swamp. The rebels came on in quick time, and when they were in easy range we set up ... a hurrah and gave them such a fire that their line staggered."[42] First Lieutenant James Badgett (Co. G) twisted and fell, "a ball passing though [his] neck ... from behind the right ear to the mouth."[43] And not far from Badgett, Pvt. John McIver (Co. H) dropped, wounded, and 1st Sgt. James Wells (Co. E) was killed.[44] A Southerner remarked, "we met the enemy in the open field, without breastworks on either side. Both sides were determined to do their best."[45]

The veteran Tar Heels pushed forward, firing rapidly, riddling the New Yorkers, who stood parade ground tall. One Yank noted, "The enemy's fire was simply terrible; the ground which was brown and bare when we formed the line, was soon covered with a carpet of green leaves and foliage, cut from the limbs of the young pine trees."[46] But the Northerners refused to retreat; instead they directed lethal fire upon the Carolinians. A New Yorker wrote, "The enemy's skirmishers had reached the log-houses formally in our vidette line ... we opened fire.... I aimed at a man in a door—possibly some one else did the same. At any rate, I saw him drop."[47] The two forces, experienced Confederates and neophyte Yanks, battled for several minutes before the blue coats slowly gave ground. Then, a battery of Northern artillery opened upon the Tar Heels. A Federal recorded, "The action of the artillery was of no slight importance. The Confederates ... were forcing our lines back when the batteries opened."[48] Explosive shells erupted among the Carolinians, spewing jagged steel. Captain William Ardrey (Co. K) noted in his journal, "Sgt. Rufus B. Weeks was [struck] in the head and killed instantly."[49] Private William Adams (Co. K) was also downed, seriously wounded, and moments later, Col. Frank Parker "was shot through the stomach on [his] right side." Private Ephraim Dickens (Co. F) was killed, and 1st Lt. Henry McNeil (Co. H) dropped, his right tibia shattered.[50] The Tar Heels stumbled backwards, stunned by the shelling, leaving behind several of their wounded; including Cpl. William Burroughs (Co. G), who had fallen, his hip shattered, and Pvt. James Pierce (Co. K), who also was seriously hurt.[51] A relieved Northerner wrote, "after a sharp action, in which the batteries rendered good, service, the enemy was repulsed."[52]

The Thirtieth no longer had a senior commander, nonetheless Cpt. David Allen (Co. C) and Cpt. William Ardrey (Co. K) hustled to reform the regiment, once the Tar Heels had fallen back into the shelter of a stand of trees. The Carolinians hunkered down behind trees, stumps, logs, and a split rail fence. Their defensive position was noted by a Yank, who wrote, "[The] Confederate infantry held a strong position in the woods that skirted an open field, through which ran a crooked Virginia fence, three or four rails high."[53] The New Yorkers did not pursue, giving the Confederates a moment to recover, but this respite did not last long. A massive wall of Northerners pushed past the Fourth New York and advanced upon the Tar Heels. A comforted New Yorker wrote, "Shortly after six o'clock ... a battalion of the First Massachusetts Heavy Artillery came to our assistance."[54] The 1st MAHA, another artillery unit turned into infantry, advanced against Ramseur's riflemen with a force larger than the entire Carolina brigade. An officer in the 1st MAHA recorded, "The regiment went into action with 1,617 officers and men."[55]

The 1st MAHA attacked a battalion at a time, with the first formation to attack numbering three hundred sixty men. A Bay Stater described their advance, "As if on parade, we marched, touching elbows, to the edge of the wood.... We had proceeded but a short distance when we received a volley from Ramseur's brigade.... It was like a stroke of lightning from clear skies.... Fully a half of the ... men were dead or disabled." He added, "The cries of pain from loved comrades, wounded or dying; the rattle of musketry; the sound of leaden missiles tearing through the trees and the dull thud of bullets that reached their human marks produced a feeling of horror among those whose ears could hear."[56]

The 1st MAHA's second and third battalions moved forward, passing over the bodies of their comrades and assaulted the Confederates, who raked them viciously with accurate rifle fire. A Massachusetts fellow wrote, "As the battalions entered the young growth of timbers they had to ford a sluggish stream that lazily made its way among the alders. It was here while charging up the slope that the battalions suffered considerable loss."[57] The Federals shuffled to a stop and unleashed a tremendous volley. Most of their bullets shredded the tree branches above the Tar Heels' heads, but some did strike Carolina bodies, including Sgt. Burgess Nichols (Co. K), who was knocked down, wounded.[58] Then, the two forces blazed away at each other, the sweating riflemen firing as quickly as they could reload. Fortunately the gray-clad soldiers were protected while the Yanks stood out in the open. A Northerner admitted, "At times the smoke was so thick we could not see ten feet away; we could not see the Rebs but we knew they were there for the bullets came thickly. The boys were dropping all around me."[59] Thousands of rounds were fired in the next thirty minutes, with neither side advancing or retreating. The result was disastrous for the ex-artillery boys. A Federal confessed, "The ground was literally covered with the dead and wounded of the heavy artillery regiments." He continued, "Not having experience in fighting, they had neglected the precautions that veterans take, and instead of lying down, or taking advantage of the ground, they had taken their position on the crest of a hill, where they stood erect and furnished most admirable targets for the enemy, who fought as usual in the woods and behind fences."[60]

More Union forces joined the fight, additional troops from V Corps, and these infantry units extended the Northerner's flanks until they lapped around the Confederates' end. A jubilant heavy artilleryman proclaimed, "At 6:15, reinforcements from Birney arrived on the field and were quickly followed by the Maryland brigade."[61] These reinforcements enabled the Yanks to take control of the fight, and as Federal regiments inched around the Southerners' flanks, the Confederate commanders knew they were in trouble. Brigadier General Dodson Ramseur, now bleeding from another wound, remarked, "[When] my flanks were both partially enveloped I then retired about 200 yards and reformed my line."[62] This was not a calm movement but one carried out in haste, and especially for the units actually covering the Confederate's flanks, accompanied by frantic confusion. A Northerner bragged, "On finding so powerful a body in position to meet him, Ewell's leading troops recoiled, broken, from the encounter."[63] One Tar Heel griped, "We had a stiff fight.... Some of our men were so badly hurt that we had to leave them."[64] In the Thirtieth, once the blue coats began sweeping around their end, the situation deteriorated into a wild scramble. At least a dozen Carolinians were trapped and did not escape the Federal onslaught.

The inexperienced Northerners did not pursue the beaten Confederates; instead, they rounded up the Southerners left behind. A Yank confirmed their movements, writing, "we saw the Confederates hurled back in disorder ... we captured over four hundred prisoners." He also added, "Many of the captured Confederates ... seemed completely worn out with ... fatigue."[65] The blue coats then wasted valuable minutes reforming their lines,

Timothy O'Sullivan photo of North Carolinians killed near Harris farm. These men could have been from the 30th NC (Library of Congress).

and at this critical moment, a force of Confederates arrived, giving Dodson Ramseur an anchor on which to rally his men." Ramseur wrote, "Fortunately Pegram's gallant brigade came in on my left ... and we were able to hold."[66] The veteran Southerner riflemen clustered together and found a way to create a hasty defensive line. One of Ramseur's riflemen scribbled, "We lay there ... in mud and water, behind our little mounds of earth thrown up with our bayonets and hands."[67] Moments later, a Confederate battery was added to the defense, firming up their position. An appreciative Confederate acknowledged, "Fortunately General Hampton ... with his horse artillery ... did good service relieving the difficulties."[68]

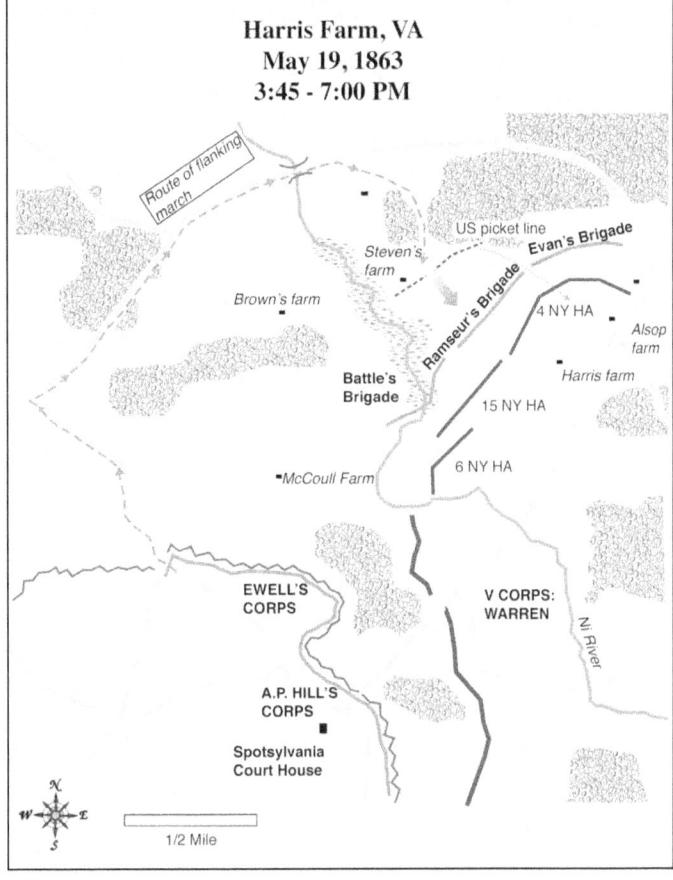

The Federals pushed against the Confederate's new defensive line and were driven back. A second, and a third advance was also resisted before the Northerners settled down to a static position that kept heavy pressure on the Southerners. Dodson Ramseur reported, "Several attacks of the enemy were repulsed, and we were able to hold our position until night."[69] Major General Winfield Hancock agreed, writing, "The fighting continued obstinately until about 9 o'clock."[70] Then, once darkness stilled the fighting, the two forces slumped down to the ground, though grimly not trusting the other. At 10:00 p.m., Richard Ewell gave the order to withdraw. One of his staff officers wrote, "we quietly retired under cover of an Egyptian darkness, regaining our original lines, wet and exhausted, at midnight, when we threw ourselves on the cold, damp ground and slept until morning."[71]

Colonel Bryan Grimes (4th NC) directed the weary Tar Heel brigade back to their ditches near Spotsylvania, as Dodson Ramseur had been forced to seek treatment for his wounds. Ramseur's brigade had suffered serious losses again, including Col. Frank Parker and Lt. Col. Edwin Osborne (4th NC). Dodson Ramseur's regiments had lost over one hundred veterans, though the Federals suffered much worse. A member of the 4th NYHA recorded, "Our battalion ... lost nearly 100," and an officer in the 1st MAHA wrote, "[Our] regiment ... lost ... 394."[72] Captain David Allen (Co. C), a 28-year-old farmer from Black Rock, NC now led the Thirtieth, his exhausted soldiers stumbling after him. They were distraught and angry at General Ewell. One grumbled, "we certainly accomplished very little, whilst we lost some good men."⁷³ Another wrote, "[We are] nearly all ... fagged out and need rest."⁷⁴

The next morning, May 20, 1864, Cpt. David Allen and Cpt. William Ardrey examined the regiment's battered leadership corps and made adjustments. Company G's commander, 1st Lt. James Badgett was now on his way to a Richmond hospital. His replacement now leading the company was his cousin, Sgt. Sandy Badgett. First lieutenant Henry McNeil (Co. H), also wounded, was succeeded by Sgt. Ard Harrington, who was one of the regiment's eldest volunteers, at forty-four years old. Captain William Ardrey became the regiment's right wing commander, and the unit's most-senior lieutenant; Ira Johnson (Co. E) was forced to assume left wing leadership. Frank Parker's injury was more serious than any of the other wounds he had suffered. He, along with Lt. Col. Edwin Osborne (4th NC) had been loaded into an ambulance and were on their way to Richmond.

30th North Carolina Infantry[75]
Harris Farm Casualties
May 19, 1864

Unit	Commander	Loss
Field & Staff	Col. Parker, Francis M.	1
Co. A	1st Sgt. Crumpler, Robert M.	-
Co. B	Cpl. Bell, William	1
Co. C	Sgt. Wescott, John W.	1
Co. D	3rd Lt. Rodgers, Martin L.	1
Co. E	1st Lt. Johnson, Ira J.	5
Co. F	2nd Lt. House, James W.	3
Co. G	1st Lt. Badgett, James W.	3
Co. H	1st Lt. McNeil, Henry J.	5
Co. I	3rd Lt. Perry, Sidney R.	1
Co. K	1st Lt. Downs, John T.	5
		26

Edwin Osborne wrote of Cpt. Fred Philips, who was in charge of the brigade wagon train, "The day was hot and we were parched with fever and thirst; but he supplied us from time to time with refreshing draughts of buttermilk and ice which the good people of the country gave him. It was served in a horse bucket."⁷⁶ Frank Parker would remain in Richmond for only a couple weeks before securing transportation home. He never returned to the regiment and later recorded, "[I had] received a wound which disqualified [me] for active service."⁷⁷

The brigade, now commanded by Col. Bryan Grimes (4th NC), shouldered their gear and marched away from the Spotsylvania trenches on May 21, 1864. A Tar Heel wrote, "Setting out on a pleasantly cool afternoon.... Ewell's Second Corps marched until eleven o'clock that night ... [and then] Lee posted the Second Corps on his right, astride the Richmond, Fredericksburg, and Potomac Railroad."⁷⁸ Captain William Ardrey (Co. K) added, "Marched all day ... crossing the small rivers Ny and Po ... arrived at Hanover Junction."⁷⁹ Again, the Confederates were hearing that Grant was not retreating; instead, the news told of the Union army slipping east and shunting farther south. Colonel Bryan Grimes noted, "Hanover Junction.–We reached here today after a most fatiguing jaunt. The enemy attempting to flank us as we moved down."[80] The Southerners immediately dug rifle pits and trenches, the experienced fighters convinced entrenchments were the only way to increase their odds of surviving. Of course, once their fortifications were satisfactory, the Tar Heels were ordered to move. The brigade shifted to a position overlooking the North Anna River, and then the men quickly set about creating new defenses. Captain Ardrey noted, "Formed our lines and preparing to meet the enemy.... We are strongly entrenched.... Rained very hard." He continued, "The enemy ... on the opposite side of the North Anna River."[81]

Colonel Bryan Grimes posted a thin picket line of riflemen overlooking the North Anna not far from the remains of a railroad bridge. Captain David Allen included a platoon of selected Tar Heels from the Thirtieth in this defense. These pickets reported Union forces moving forward early on May 24, 1864. The commander of these blue coats, Col. Thomas Smythe, recorded, "At 7 a.m. May 24, I received an order from General Gibbon [II Corps] to construct a rough bridge and cross a regiment of skirmishers."[82] One of his regimental commanders noted, "Ten volunteers were called for from each regiment ... to act as pioneer corps in construction of a rough bridge of felled trees across the river."[83] These hard-working Yanks completed their task in three hours and the first Union regiment rushed across the span at 10:15 a.m. The Federal brigade commander remarked, "the 8th Ohio Volunteers moved to the opposite side, deployed, and advanced to the enemy's earthworks, which they occupied, the enemy having fallen back."[84] The rest of the thousand-man brigade hustled across the makeshift bridge and deployed in line of battle.

The Tar Heel pickets had fallen back nearly a thousand yards to a line of rifle pits entrenched just inside a stand of trees. This was a solid position with an expansive field of fire. They waited for the Federal onslaught, but it did not come. Hours later, the blue coats moved; a Union officer writing, "At 3 p.m. I was ordered to advance and ascertain the position of the enemy. The 1st DE and 108th NY Volunteers were deployed as skirmishers and advanced half mile."[85] The Carolinian pickets opened fire and the Yanks dropped to the ground, searching for cover. The Northerner reported, "the enemy was posted in rifle-pits in the edge of the woods, while my skirmishers were obliged to pass on an elevated plowed field, the line was again brought to a halt."[86] The Federal commander ordered the 12th NJ to attack, and the blue coats raced across the open field in a wild rush, driving the thin Confederate line from its defenses, and in this confusion, Pvt. Laban Dudley (Co. H) and Pvt. Joseph Williams (Co. I) were captured.[87] The Tar Heels scampered back eight hundred yards before reaching a new defensive line. A Northern described this action, writing, "Our line advanced and drove the rebel skirmishers about a half mile across a wheat field ... and through the woods."[88]

Captain David Allen rotated his pickets out of the skirmish line with fresh riflemen and they joined the battle. The Union troops had sought shelter and the two forces fired away at each other, making a lot of noise but doing little to change the situation. The 12th NJ had suffered enough casualties to make the rest of the men cautious. Colonel Bryan Grimes remarked, "[The] Yankees still continue obstinate and still continue to rush on to their doom."[89] The Union commander re-enforced his line with five more of his small-sized regiments and they began to shoot at the Confederates. This desultory fire lasted for several hours, forcing one Federal officer to write, "Our line was engaged most of the [afternoon] in a severe skirmish with the enemy."⁹⁰ Unfortunately, though the battle's intensity was low, one Yank minié bullet hit Pvt. Samuel Lee (Co. K), shattering his pelvis. Captain William Ardrey recorded, "Nothing but artillery and skirmish firing.... Privt. S B Lee, my Co. mortally wounded on the skirmish line."⁹¹ Private Sam Lee, a 22-year-old farm boy from the eastern Charlotte area, did not recover from his injury; he died a month later.⁹² Moments later, another bullet struck Pvt. James McLure (Co. K), shattering his right wrist.⁹³

Colonel Bryan Grimes received orders to deploy his entire brigade outside the Confederate fortifications, slip through the woods to the left of the Union line, and strike the blue coats' flank. Grimes assembled his Tar Heels and they crept through the woods and crashed into the Yanks. The Carolinians hit the 69th NY, the 170th NY, and the 19th ME. These regiments resisted briefly, and in this exchange, Pvt. William Hood (Co. K) was wounded in the right hand.⁹⁴ A blue coat wrote, "[Our] men faced a storm of shot and shell, in the face of which no line of battle could live long. Here the Regiment lost heavily and fell back over the brow of a hill."⁹⁵ Then, the Yanks' courage shriveled and the Northern riflemen broke. Colonel Thomas Smythe wrote, "Just at dark a vigorous attack was made by the enemy on my left, which threw the 69th NY and 170th NY Volunteers into considerable disorder, which resulted in their falling back."⁹⁶ Bryan Grimes reported, "We drove them with considerable slaughter, losing but few."⁹⁷ The Tar Heels did not pursue the fleeing blue coats as darkness, and an intense thunderstorm put an end to the shooting. One soaked soldier remarked, "How it did rain."⁹⁸ General Ewell shifted Brig. Gen. John Hoffman's Virginian brigade out in front of the Carolinians, posting them to keep guard as advance pickets. The Virginians staggered out into what had become a swamp, with one of their soldiers gripping, they were, "half a leg deep in mud and water."⁹⁹

The next day the Confederates remained within their fortifications and the Yanks exhibited no intentions of assaulting; so, the two armies' pickets sniped at each other. Then, on the morning of May 26, 1864, the gray-clad videttes reported their counterparts were gone. A force was pushed forward and learned, as one officer noted, "The Army of the Potomac had withdrawn."¹⁰⁰ On May 27, 1864, as the Carolinian riflemen enjoyed a day without having to worry about danger, the Confederate high command made several leadership changes. Dodson Ramseur was promoted to major general and given command of their division; Bryan Grimes received a brigadier general's star, and removed from leading the Tar Heel brigade, to be given authority over what had been Brig. Gen. Junius Daniels' brigade.

The Tar Heels' new brigade commander was William R. Cox, a 32-yea-old lawyer-turned politician from Halifax County, NC. William Cox, before the war, had been an attorney in Tennessee, however, when the war began, he raised his own battery of artillery, the Ellis Artillery Company, and later an infantry company. Then Cox secured the major's position with the 2nd NC, and eventually earned promotion to colonel. He had suffered a number of wounds, as he was always up front, standing among his riflemen in their battle line. No one doubted his courage. Cox's conspicuous leadership in the maelstrom of Spotsylvania garnered him notice among the Second Corps' senior leadership, and when this brigade's command was opened, he was immediately selected.¹⁰¹

The Carolina brigade was a shadow of what it once had been. Even with the addition of the 1st NC and 3rd NC, the formation's entire strength was less than eight hundred soldiers. Besides William Cox, only two field-grade officers remained to lead; the rest of the regiments were commanded by captains. The 1st and 3rd NC were led by Cpt. William

Thompson; the 2nd NC by Lt. Col Walter Stallings; the 4th NC, Col. James Woods; the 14th NC, Cpt. Joseph Jones; and the 30th NC, Cpt. David Allen.

General Cox's first responsibility was to take his formation eastward, as the brigade marched twenty-four miles.[102] One of Cox's riflemen noted, "Col. W.R. Cox promoted to brigadier general and was placed in command of our brigade. On that day we marched toward Richmond and took position on the Totopotomoy, near Pole Green church."[103] The next day they continued their march, ending up on the road to the Bethesda Church. Captain William Ardrey wrote, "Bethesda Church and Mechanicsville.... Took position and fortified on the right of Mechanicsville Road 8 miles from Richmond."[104] The Tar Heels dug in on a low ridge, overlooking a swampy section of Beaver Dam Creek. Once pickets were posted, they could view the Union positions, also on an elevated area near the Bethesda Church, just over a mile away. A picket line of blue coats occupied the watery lowlands east of the creek. On

Brig. Gen. William R. Cox was 32 when he assumed command of the brigade (Library of Congress).

May 29, 1864, Cpt. Ardrey recorded, "All quiet on the lines."[105] A Yank officer agreed with Ardrey, writing, "Although [our] regiment was within 100 yards of the enemy's fortifications not a shot was fired."[106]

On May 30, 1864, the Thirtieth's riflemen learned their corps commander, Lt. Gen. Richard Ewell had been replaced by Lt. Gen. Jubal Early. Dodson Ramseur wrote, "Gen. Ewell's wound caused him to receive leave of absence.... Early succeeded him in command."[107] They also discovered their brigade's new leader was indisposed and Col. Risden Bennett (14th NC) had assumed leadership responsibilities. Colonel Bennett received word from Maj. Gen. Dodson Ramseur to prepare the Tar Heel brigade for a fight, the Confederate high command believed they had identified an isolated Union division and felt this formation could be flanked and crushed. The Carolinians slipped out of their works just after 2:00 p.m. and advanced into a dense stand of vegetation. Soon, they could hear gunfire as the brigade to their right as Brig. Gen. Bryan Grimes' men had collided with the Yankees. One blue coat grumbled, "the dirty scoundrels had two line of [troops] at right angles, so that they got a cross fire upon us."[108]

The Tar Heel regiments struggled to maintain their battle formations as they followed after their brigade's sharpshooters. Suddenly, gunfire flashed at their front and a few Carolinians went down. The Southerners leaned forward and pushed through the foliage as bullets thudded into tree trunks and stripped leaves and small branches from the vegetation above their heads. Private Morrison Langley (Co. F) staggered, fell, and died moments later.[109] The Tar Heels returned fire, shooting blindly into the thick brush, and a few minutes later, the Yank's musketry diminished. Then, they encountered the abandoned Northerners' position. Dodson Ramseur recorded, "[The men] moved forward, whereupon the Union [troops] retired to a line of works."[110] Colonel Bennett reformed the brigade and waited for more orders, but none came. He sent out a strong picket force in front of his battle line, but nothing else occurred. Risden Bennett, frustrated by this inactivity, complained, "We drove [the enemy] and but for the fall of darkness we might have scored a great success."[111] That night, once darkness stilled the battlefield, Bennett directed his brigade to return to their entrenchments. Unfortunately, some of the riflemen out on picket became separated and moved in the wrong direct. The Thirtieth lost Pvt. John Brigman (Co. E), Pvt. Felix Brown (Co. E), and Pvt. Robert Massingil (Co. K)—all captured.[112]

The next day was spent fortifying their position and rotating pickets in front of the Confederate position. Little happened on June 1, 1864, except the Tar Heels heard massive musketry and artillery fire in the distance, coming from their right. Captain William Ardrey noted in his journal, "The enemy attacked ... on the right and were repulsed with heavy loss."[113] Little else happened, and the Carolinians not out on picket remained within their entrenchments, resting.

June 2, 1864, began much as the previous day, with the Tar Heels loitering within their defenses, listening to others fight. Then, late in the morning, the pickets brought in word the Union troops in front of them were moving about and might be withdrawing. Captain William Ardrey noted, "It was discovered about 12 p.m. that the enemy was retiring from our front."[114] Major General Robert Rodes sent orders to Risden Bennett and Cullen Battle to push their brigades forward and find out if the blue coats were falling back. The Southerners advanced through a stand of underbrush and pressed against the Yankee skirmish line, which quickly dissolved. The Confederates continued forward and encountered the Federal fortifications, as well as a confused Union situation. One of these Northern officers grumbled, "[We] commenced at 4 o'clock in the afternoon to withdraw and while executing the movement the enemy made an attack."[115] Another officer added, "[There was] an interval being made in [our] line by withdrawing.... Bartlett's brigade without notice." The Federals could not counter the Confederates and the blue coats fled in disorder. The frustrated Yank officer noted, "The enemy appeared and captured those that remained."[116]

The Carolinian riflemen rounded up the frazzled Federals and details marched the blue-coated prisoners to the rear. Captain William Ardrey recorded, "We found their works to be vacated. All but a line of skirmishers, which was captured."[117] Then the brigade's regimental commanders re-organized their battle lines and once the Tar Heel formations were again under control, they continued pushing east. They advanced another eight hundred yards before reaching the edge of the wooded area. The veteran Southern riflemen paused, seeing an open field they must cross if they were to continue to pursue the fragmented Union troops. Risden Bennett and Cullen Battle made the decision—keep pushing.

The two Confederate brigades advanced, moving toward the Yanks, who now were clustering behind fences bordering a road. One of these blue coats recorded, "[Our] line was obliged to fall back and take up a new line across the Mechanicsville Road."[118] Captain William Ardrey observed, "After pursuing them for 1½ miles we found them in line on

... [a] road. A sharp engagement [followed]."[119] There were enough Yanks under officer control to enable the Northerners to open fire upon the Confederates. Federal lead was once again humming through the air, and striking Carolinians. Private James Johnston (Co. K) fell, wounded, as did Pvt. Silas Crisp (Co. F), who tumbled backwards, shot through the arm.[120] The Tar Heels' advance slowed as they returned fire.

The Tar Heels were in a poor position; they were out in the open, their advance stalled, and taking fire from a force that was growing stronger with each passing minute. More Southerners went down; Pvt. Bennett Webb (Co. F) was struck in the right leg, and Pvt. Shadrach Blevins (Co. G) dropped, his left arm ripped open.[121] Then, their situation went from not good to horrible; a Union battery rolled into position and unlimbered. These guns, barely five hundred yards away, opened up, their first canister rounds catching the Carolinians standing in close order, tearing large gaps in their lines. Private Henry Butler (Co. E) was killed, Pvt. Jesse Dean (Co. G) was struck in the head, and Cpt. William Ardrey went down, wounded. He later wrote, "a fragment of shell [struck] my head."[122] A jubilant blue coat remarked, "the rebels ... came up in three lines.... They were terribly slaughtered by canister, and went back in disorder."[123]

30th North Carolina Infantry[124]
Cold Harbor Casualties
May 31—June 4, 1864

Unit	Commander	Loss
Field & Staff	Cpt. Allen, David C.	1
Co. A	1st Sgt. Crumpler, Robert M.	1
Co. B	Cpl. Bell, William	-
Co. C	Sgt. Wescott, John W.	-
Co. D	3rd Lt. Rodgers, Martin L.	2
Co. E	2nd Lt. Newton, Samuel	4
Co. F	2nd Lt. House, James W.	3
Co. G	Sgt. Badgett, Sandy	4
Co. H	Sgt. Harvington, Ard	1
Co. I	3rd Lt. Perry, Sidney R.	2
Co. K	1st Lt. Downs, John T.	3
		21

The Carolinian line fragmented, the survivors fleeing for the safety of the trees. But the Union gunners did not stop shooting; more canister rounds swept through the Thirtieth. Private John Lawrence (Co. H) was tossed backwards, his face and jaw mangled, Cpl. William Burroughs' (Co. G) hip was pulverized, Henry Brooks (Co. G) was injured in the leg, and Pvt. Jacob Lanier (Co. E) had canister rip through his "bladder and bowels."[125] The survivors fled into the trees and continued running until they reached the Union trenches they had captured just a few minutes before. Fortunately the Northerners did not chase after them. The Thirtieth's veteran NCOs and remaining officers regained control of their panicked men, sorted out company organizations, made sure everyone had ammunition, and prepared for Yankee counter attacks. A Carolinian rifleman noted,

"We entrenched as best we could with the material at hand."[126] The Federals did attack, but with caution, and without much enthusiasm. They fell back, with one Northerner writing, "A portion of [our] old works was [now] occupied by the enemy."[127] Darkness put an end to the threat of more assaults, and the weary riflemen slumped down within their fortifications, exhausted. Captain William Ardrey, who now was being transported back to Richmond, wrote, "[Last night] I had a remarkable dream I was wounded in the head and it came to pass in the evening."[128]

The Union forces attacked in massive formations on June 3, 1864, and this assault was mercilessly slaughtered by concentrated Confederate musketry and artillery. One Tar Heel officer remarked, "This was one of the bloodiest fights of the campaign, and the enemy's loss was very heavy."[129] The Carolinians were not involved in this Federal disaster; instead, they manned their captured trenches, and rotated pickets out in front of their line. With their portion of the battlefield quiet, the war-weary Tar Heel riflemen worried more about their living conditions. One wrote, "In the trenches at Cold Harbor ... the water was scarce and bad ... [and] the hot sunshine during the day without protection and the biting, stinging mosquitoes at night." He also added, "June 4 and 5–held our position without being interrupted."[130]

A few days later the brigade was shifted to an area not far from Gaines Mill, where the Carolina regiments remained for the next several days in comparative safety. It was at this time Cpt. David Allen was able to assess the Thirtieth's battle-readiness. His report was similar to what many other regimental commanders were reporting, "A ... condition that ... [would] impair efficiency was the fact that about half the infantry, including even company officers, were without shoes."[131] Then, on June 12, 1864, the Carolinians received orders to prepare to march, their division was being sent west to the Shenandoah Valley.

Chapter 14

Campaigning with the Army of the Valley District

The Thirtieth's men awoke at 3:00 a.m. on June 13, 1864, and broke camp. Once everything was packed and the regiment ready, Cpt. David Allen ordered his two hundred men to move into position on the road to Charlottesville, VA, and not long after this, Brig. Gen. William Cox gave the command to march.[1] The Carolinians hiked all day, suffering from a blistering sun and sweltering humidity. That night the exhausted troops slumped to the ground, having covered almost twenty miles. Chaplain Alexander Betts noted in his journal, "What a tramp."[2] The Confederates trekked westward for the next two days, averaging nearly twenty miles each day. One foot-sore rifleman wrote, "[June] 15th the sun rose on the moving column; passed through Louisa and bivouacked 9 miles beyond. Weather very warm, roads dusty and hot to our naked feet."[3] The weary Southerners staggered into Charlottesville on June 16, 1864, having covered eighty miles in four days, with one officer remarking, "[It was] a most fatiguing and oppressive march."[4] The Confederates waited in Charlottesville for trains to move them farther away from the Spotsylvania slaughter-pens. Three days later, the Tar Heels climbed onto train cars and relished the breezes provided by their moving train. A windblown Pvt. Richard Brooks (Co. G) exclaimed, "[we] rode railroad flatcars ... to Lynchburg."[5] Another Carolinian added, "[We] took the train to Lynchburg. Oh, but this was better than toiling over long stretches of road."[6]

The men in the Thirtieth now knew their destination—they were headed to the Shenandoah Valley; their entire Corps, now led by Lt. Gen. Jubal A. Early, was going to rescue the South's valuable bread basket. The Carolinians' new Corps commander, Jubal Early was well known; the men called him "Old Jube" or "Old Granny," and everyone respected him as a tough fighter and a solid leader. Jubal Early was 47 years old and a Virginian with a military background. Early had graduated from West Point in 1837, ranked 18th out of fifty cadets. He had served in Florida's Seminole Indian War, but then resigned his commission, saying he, "was not a very exemplary soldier ... [with no] taste for scrubbing brass."[7] Early returned home, studied law, and became a successful lawyer. He practiced law until the outbreak of the Mexican War, when he served as a major in a Virginia Militia unit. This took him to Mexico, where he became afflicted with rheumatoid arthritis, an adversity that hampered him for the rest of his life.

Jubal Early returned to his life as an attorney once the Mexican War ended, and remained in his hometown until the Civil War began. Then, he received a commission as colonel of the 24th VA infantry and led this regiment until his promotion to brigadier general in July 1861. Early served as a brigade commander and was wounded in the Peninsula Campaign of 1862. He recovered quickly from his injury and at Sharpsburg, ascended to divisional leadership when his commander fell, and by Fredericksburg, General Lee had given him a permanent division to lead. Then, in November 1863, Early assumed temporary command of Lt. Gen. Richard Ewell's Second Corps when that officer became incapacitated. However, when Ewell recovered, Early resumed his role as division commander, but in May 1864, when Lt. Gen. A. P. Hill grew ill, General Lee elevated Early to lead the Third Corps. Jubal Early again demonstrated his ability to command. Nevertheless, when Hill regained his health, Early once again went back to his division. Later, Ewell's health failed him, Lee once again, moved Maj. Gen. Jubal Early to lead the Second Corps. By now General Lee was quite satisfied with Early's abilities and promoted him to lieutenant general, and when Ewell's health returned, Lee shifted Ewell to another position, leaving Early to lead the Second Corps.[8]

Now, in mid–June 1864, Jubal Early was taking his entire Corps west, to the Shenandoah Valley. He stood nearly six feet tall and weighed 170 pounds, though his arthritis left him bent and stooped, and coupled with a raspy voice, unkempt beard, and gray hair, everyone thought of him as an old man. Even Robert E. Lee, who was ten years older than Early, referred to him as, "his Bad Old Man."[9] Regardless though, what ever Lee called Jubal Early, the South's commanding general had complete confidence him, and hoped his eight thousand infantrymen would secure the Shenandoah Valley as well as tie up large numbers of Federal soldiers. The Carolinians in the Thirtieth had other nicknames for their general; one rifleman described their gruff and cantankerous leader: "[as] a ... malignant and very hairy old spider."[10] But, they were willing to fight for this tough Virginia.

Lt. Gen. Jubal Early was 47 when he led the Second Corps into the Shenandoah Valley (Library of Con-

The Thirtieth North Carolina was no longer the battle-ready formation it had been in April 1864. The continuous fighting in May 1864 had bled away half of the regiment's riflemen and officers, leaving behind a battered and shocked group of survivors. Captain David Allen (Co. C) was seconded by Cpt. William Ardrey (Co. K), who was absent, home on medical leave. Beneath Ardrey, the regiment had three first lieutenants, two second lieutenants, and three junior lieutenants. David Allen, along with Sgt. Maj. Frank Fitts, had been forced to combine some of the shriveled and officer-less companies into amalgamated units. Captain Allen then grouped these small companies into two, 100-man wings, with each organization led by a first lieutenant.[11] The Thirtieth would never again have a field grade officer; those leaders were gone, and even though Col. Frank Parker petitioned the Confederate high command to promote Cpt. Allen to a field-grade position, this action was never taken.[12]

The Thirtieth's riflemen, and their brothers from the other Carolina regiments in Brig. Gen. William Cox's brigade clambered off the train cars and formed into columns for more marching. One rifleman noted, "Arrived in Lynchburg 5 p.m. Pushed through this town of high, mountainous hills just in time to save the city. Bivouacked at the fair grounds."[13] The next morning's sunrise found the Tar Heels hiking westward, towards Liberty, VA, two-dozen miles away. That night a tired Carolinian scribbled, "Made 25 miles over very rough roads."[14] The Confederate foot soldiers covered another twenty miles on June 20, 1864, and bivouacked in Buford's Gap that evening. They rested only briefly and were again on the road before sunrise the next morning, trekking to Big Lick, VA, and from there, to Hanging Rock Pass, another twenty-plus mile march. The tired Southerners stumbled into their bivouac positions, exhausted and hungry. Many grumbled, "[We] had been without rations for two days."[15] Brigade commander Bryan Grimes recorded, "Been almost without rations—hard marching, and nothing to eat. Start before day, not stop till dark, except to rest for ten minutes." He added, "For the duration of forty-eight hours my Brigade did not have a mouthful of bread, and but little flesh.... Occasionally, when Gen. Rodes or Early passed the line, the cry was, 'Bread, bread, bread.'"[16]

The sun greeted the sleeping men the next morning, June 22, 1864, as no marching orders had been handed down to the weary infantrymen. The sore-footed men lounged all day in the mountain's cool air, scrounging for food, patching up worn-out shoes, and tending to blisters and tender muscles. But once again, hours before sunrise on the twenty-third, the men were roused from their slumbers and formed in column, ready for another day's journey. They were now west of the Blue Ridge Mountains, heading north to Buchanan and the southern reaches of the Shenandoah Valley. Confederate cavalry brushed aside Federal parties trying to slow the hiking rifle brigades. One Tar Heel rifleman recalled, "[June] 23rd—marched 21 miles toward Staunton. The enemy burned stacks of wheat in front that we needed so badly." He continued, "The raw wheat would have been a feast…. Two days without rations except the little we could flank."[17]

The Carolinians passed through Lexington, VA, two days later, with many men remarking about seeing General Stonewall Jackson's grave. Sergeant Aaron DeArmond (Co. K) wrote, "Came to Lexington … went through the graveyard whair [sic.] Jeneral [sic.] Jackson lay and honored his grave by coming to reverse armes [sic.] and passed out through the graveyard [holding] the position till we came out in the street. Then to a rite [sic.] shoulder shift arms."[18] Their march continued; the Tar Heels passed through Brownsburg and reached Middlebrook on June 25, 1864, after another two-dozen-plus mile walk. Then, they staggered into Strasburg late the next day.[19] The weary men received orders to set up camp. The Yankees had abandoned the region and many of Early's men they believed they had saved the Shenandoah Valley. An officer on Gen. Early's staff recorded, "[Our] army had reached Staunton, where [we] stopped to rest and refit."[20] Ration and baggage trains caught up with the winded soldiers, as well as mail. The men washed their sweat-stained clothing in a branch of the Shenandoah River and did what they could to repair their foot ware, but most of all; they scrambled for eats, and rested. One wrote, "Our hungry boys had a good time eating the sutler's stores, drinking their Champaign, wines and other liquors."[21]

The Tar Heels reformed on the road a week later, much refreshed, and filled with a determination to drive the blue coats from the last part of the Shenandoah Valley. They reached Winchester on July 2, 1864, and Leetown the next day, after trudging northward another grueling forty-plus miles. A Carolinian grumbled, "[We] resumed march at 4:30 a.m., made 24 miles. A very trying day. Passed through Winchester.... Water is scarce and sun very hot."[22] The next day, July 4, 1864, the Confederates pushed into Harper's Ferry and drove away the Union forces holding the town. The Tar Heels took possession of a huge Fourth of July meal. A jubilant Carolinian bragged, "The enemy had prepared a sumptuous feast, and was celebrating the day, when our men made the attack, drove him out of town, and captured everything just as he was about to begin the feast. Of course our hungry and thirsty men enjoyed the booty to the fullest."[23] And fortunately, as the men were being fed, quartermasters discovered a store of Federal brogans. One wrote, "By ... night ... the needed shoes had been ... distributed."[24]

The Southerners took to the road once the days' heat had begun to abate on July 5, 1864, and they bivouacked on the southern side of the Potomac River at Shepherdstown that night. They crossed the river into Maryland the next day; and for the Thirtieth's remaining veterans, this was the third time they had left Southern soil and invaded the North. Brigadier General William Cox gathered his regimental leaders together that evening and informed them their commander's plans—"Early [had] decided to bypass [Union commander] Siegel [at Maryland Heights overlooking Harper's Ferry] and move to threaten Baltimore and Washington."[25] Then, Cpt. William Ardrey returned from his medical leave, just in time to learn they were going to attack Lincoln's capital.[26]

30th North Carolina Infantry[27]
July 10, 1864

Unit		Strength
Field & Staff	Cpt. Allen, David C. Cpt. Ardrey, William E. 1st Lt. Johnson, Ira J.	4
Co. A	1st Sgt. Crumpler, Robert M.	17
Co. B	Sgt. Davis, Benjamin P.	15
Co. C	Sgt. Wescott, John W.	14
Co. D	3rd Lt. Rodgers, Martin L.	22
Co. E	2nd Lt. Newton, Samuel B.	24
Co. F	2nd Lt. House, James W. 3rd Lt. Moore, Samuel R.	29
Co. G	Sgt. Badgett, Sandy H.	20
Co. H	Sgt. Harrington, Ard A.	16
Co. I	3rd Lt. Perry, Sidney R.	21
Co. K	1st Lt. Downs, John T.	24
		206

Yank troops blocked the pass at Crampton's Gap, but a show of force and a fleeting exchange of musketry scattered the blue coats, opening the highway towards Washington. However, in this brief skirmish, two of Cpt. David Allen's riflemen became separated from the unit in the thick woods and were lost, Pvt. James Rackley (Co. I), and Pvt. Elias

Bailey (Co. K).[28] The brigade hurried down out of South Mountain's heights and made its way to Jefferson, MD, where pickets were deployed to cover the formation's bivouac. The next day, three of Gen. Early's divisions battled against hastily formed Union troops, though, for the Tar Heels, this was someone else's fight. The Tar Heels and the rest of Maj. Gen. Rodes's formation were formed on the Baltimore Pike, east of Frederick with little in front of them besides a light screen of cavalry. Meanwhile the rest of Early's army slugged it out with the main Union force in what would become known as the battle of Monocacy. By nightfall, the Federal forces had been shattered and streamed eastward. The Confederates pursued, though without much vigor. Captain David Allen recorded the loss of one veteran, Pvt. James Eason (Co. H), a Tar Heel who had originally enlisted in 1861 with Company F, but after a year with the regiment, had been discharged because of health reasons. James Eason had recovered and rejoined the Thirtieth, this time with Company H, and served faithfully until getting lost and eventually captured.[29]

Jubal Early ordered his army to chase after the beaten Northerners, and the Tar Heels were up before sunrise, hustling eastward. One excited rifleman crowed, "We privates … want to charge and take the city … [and] especially to get 'Old Abe' in our hands."[30] That evening one writer noted, "July 10–the brigade marched at daylight thirty miles in pursuit of the Yanks and camped four miles from Rockville on the Georgetown Pike."[31] But this trek almost broke the Carolinians; a nearly played-out rifleman scribbled, "The day dazzling hot, dry and dusty. The march distressingly exhausting because of intense heat—suffocating from soil ground into powder finer than the constituents of the atmosphere by rolling wheels and tramping feet of man and beast."[32]

The suffering soldiers were chased from their sleep and forced back on the road, again by sunrise, and they endured a second day of brutal heat and humidity. General Early, knowing there were few Federal troops guarding Washington, pushed his men, wanting them to capture the city before Grant could rush reinforcements into the capital's defense. Unfortunately the heat crushed the men. Jubal Early admitted, "On the morning of the 11th we continued the march, but the day was so excessively hot, even at a very early hour in the morning, and the dust so dense, that many of the men fell by the way, and it became necessary to slacken our pace."[33] One of his staff officers agreed, writing, "The heat of the day was exhausting the men. Long before noon, veterans who had endured some of the hardest marches … were falling out of ranks."[34] A foot-soldier in Cox's brigade noted, "The sun pours down intense heat on the open road—throats parched—thirsty for water—famished for food."[35] Another wrote, "The scorching heat and stifling dust slowed Early's march as surely as iron balls and leaden missiles."[36] And another added, "Our Division … was stretched out almost like skirmishers, and all the men did not get up until night."[37] Captain William Ardrey wrote, "the [Thirtieth's] ranks were greatly thinned out…. Capt. D. C. Allen, Lieuts. Newton and Downs were the only officers in the Reg. and only about seventy-five men for duty."[38]

The exhausted Confederates pushed southward on the Brookville turnpike, stumbling past clusters of houses until reaching a high piece of ground overlooking the Federal capital. A Tar Heel wrote, "About 11 a.m., Washington's Capitol loomed in sight, the great dome unfinished."[39] Another added, "on the eleventh [we] reached [Seventh] Street Pike, which leads into the City of Washington, and advanced to the neighborhood of Fort Stephens."[40] Brigadier General William Cox deployed his heat-shriveled Carolinian regiments into line of battle and sent forward the brigade's sharpshooters, with an officer recording, "Skirmishers were thrown out and moved up to the vicinity of the fortifications."[41]

The Tar Heel skirmish line eased down from the commanding ridge and immediately encountered a thin screen of Union pickets. The two sides began shooting at each other, and this was added to by an occasional cannon shot from the large Federal guns protecting Washington, D.C.'s northern flanks. Chaplain Alexander Betts jotted in his journal, "[We] move on through excessive heat to the 'Blair House,' near fortifications around Washington City. First shell from Federal fort falls in a grove near us about 2 p.m."[42] A Carolinian rifleman added, "[We] met the enemy, formed in line of battle and drove them within their fortifications."[43]

Meanwhile, Gen. Early met with his division commanders, Robert Rodes and Dodson Ramseur, and they examined Washington's defenses. Jubal Early noted, "These we found to be very strong and constructed scientifically. They consist of a circle of enclosed forts connected by breastworks, with ditches, palisades, and abatis in front, and every approach swept by a cross-fire of artillery."[44] The Confederate generals determined the Yank fortifications were impressive and appeared to be heavily defended. One Union soldier described their positions, writing, "[Ft. Stevens had] "375 perimeter yards with 19 guns serviced by 423 officers and men.... It overlooked terrain to its front for several miles, [with] abitis of entwined tree branches at one point surrounding the work." He continued, "weeds and undergrowth covered fields of fire, although the generally cleared terrain sloped northward to a brook and thence to Silver Spring, offered superb ground for her gunners."[45]

Jubal Early ordered his riflemen to advance, writing, "At first I determined to make an assault."[46] Sergeant Aaron DeArmond (Co. K) crept forward, shepherding his Tar Heels in the sharp shooter formation as they rushed from hiding place to hiding place.

Fort Stevens was one of more than sixty forts build to defend Washington, D.C. (Library of Congress).

He later remarked, "[We] sent out our Sharp Shooters and they open fire upon their fortifications."[47] The blue coats resisted the Southerners' advance, slowly giving ground. A Northerner wrote, "Skirmishes broke out against soldiers who were posted in front of the fort." He then bragged, "One of the skirmishers … managed to capture three prisoners."[48]

The Tar Heels pushed forward a couple hundred yards, slogged about in a swampy low area, worked through a section of underbrush, and scrambled across a small creek, firing as they advanced, and receiving musketry from the Union pickets trying to hold them back. Soon though, the veteran Confederates realized to advance any closer to the imposing fortifications would only result in needless casualties. The Southern riflemen hunkered down in an area of felled trees, and only raised themselves up to take an occasional potshot. One Confederate wrote, "Every prominent point at intervals of 800 to 1,000 yards was occupied by an enclosed field, and every approach or depression of ground unseen from the front was swept by artillery and field guns; and the whole connected by rifle trenches." He continued, his morale not optimistic, "Twenty thousands troops were behind these fortifications."[49] The Confederate high command also could see what this rifleman had discovered. Dodson Ramseur recorded, "clouds of dust drifted up from behind the Federal entrenchments and [we] could see Union troops filing into them." He continued, "Rodes' skirmishers, having pushed Union skirmishers to their trenches, could do no more."[50] General Early shook his head in dismay, and wrote, "I became satisfied that the assault, even if successful, would be attended with such great sacrifice as would insure the destruction of my whole force…. I, therefore, reluctantly determined to retire."[51] Jubal Early called off the attack and rotated the sharpshooters out of the danger zone and replaced them with Cpt. David Allen's Thirtieth North Carolina. Sergeant Aaron DeArmond (Co. K) wrote, "that night our Regt. was set out on picket."[52]

Captain David Allen's entire regiment remained on picket duty all night, his weary Carolinians struggling to stay awake, and frustrated by the knowledge they had gotten so near to their opponent's capital, but could get no closer. Allen's riflemen could also

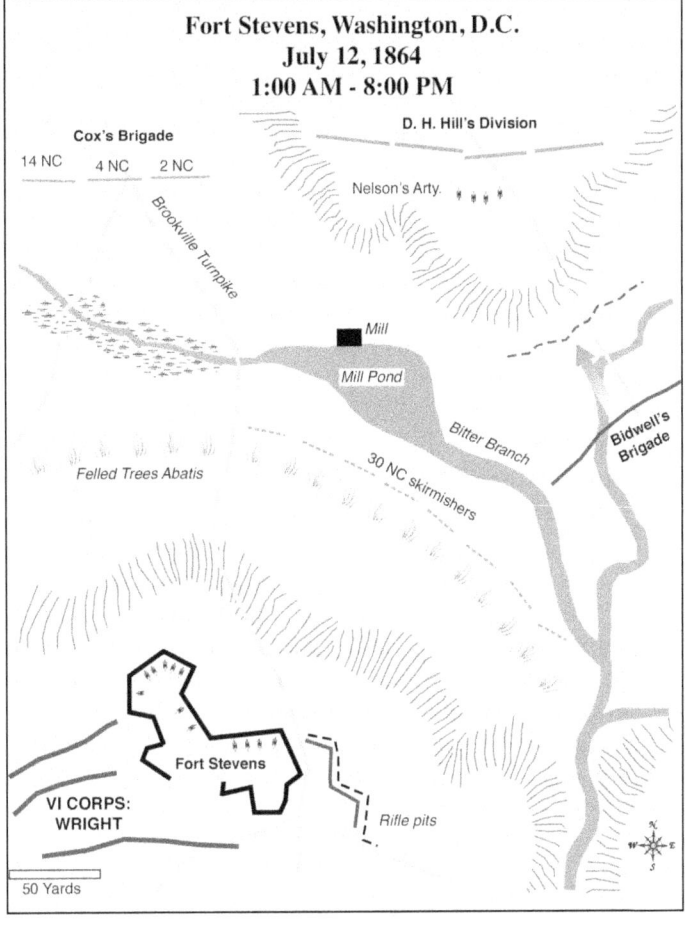

hear the tramp of thousands of boots as Northern reinforcements packed into the Federal fortifications. A Southern officer concluded, "Time was thus given for the enemy to get a sufficient force into his works to prevent our capturing them."[53] When sunrise melted away the darkness, Gen. Early studied the Federal positions and understood his troops would be butchered if he ordered an assault. General Dodson Ramseur agreed with Early as they examined the Northern forts, and noted. "First daylight [12 July] shone on parapets thick with Union soldiers, leaving [us] ... no choice but to give up all hopes of capturing Washington."[54] Jubal Early wrote, "the loss of my force would have had such a depressing effect upon the country."[55] General Early then began making plans to pull his army away from Washington. Meanwhile, Cpt. Allen's riflemen continued at their posts. A Tar Heel recorded, "[We] were under arms at daybreak, being issued 40 rounds, but things were generally quiet along the line of Cox's brigade."[56]

The July sun burned the landscape and began another day of punishing heat. Captain David Allen's Carolinians held their positions beneath this brutal sky, watching enviously as the troop-rich Northerners rotated their tired pickets out of danger and replaced them with fresh ones. These new blue coats were veterans of General Grant's hard-fighting VI Corps. They knew how to protect themselves, and how to fight. Soon, their more aggressive soldiers inched forward and began to fire at the Tar Heels. In the next couple hours of desultory shooting, Pvt. Solomon Penny (Co. D) was killed, and Pvt. Henry Dement (Co. G) wounded.[57] Captain Allen's men were not intimidated and fought back, forcing the Yanks to suspend thoughts of attacking. One blue coat remarked, "The day was spent firing back and forth, with Confederate sharpshooters targeting anyone they could see in the fort."[58] Another Yank wrote, "The enemy was firing lively from the bushes in front of the fort and it was dangerous for any person to look over the parapet."[59]

As morning gave way to afternoon the Tar Heel sharpshooters noticed a tall, darkly dressed individual appearing above Fort Stevens' parapets.[60] The distance for accurate shooting was long, over three hundred yards, however, the better marksmen were intrigued by this unusual target and took aim.[61] A Federal soldier within Fort Stevens recorded, "[President Abraham Lincoln] stood up to look. Now, standing up and supplemented by his high plug hat, Mr. Lincoln was a target of exceptional visibility. From the rebel marksmen came a snarl of musketry fire."[62] The Carolinians blazed away at President Lincoln, who did not flinch. A close-by Union officer wrote, "Lincoln stood, apparently unconscious of danger, watching, with that grave and passive countenance, the progress of the fight amid the whizzing bullets of the sharp-shooters."[63] One Southern minié bullet zipped close to Lincoln and ricocheted off a nearby cannon, causing a Northerner to exclaim, "The ball fired at [Lincoln] struck one of the large guns, glanced back and went through an [officer's] leg."[64] The soldier tumbled to the ground amid cries to Lincoln, to, "Get down, you damned fool!"[65] A shocked Federal added, "[A] sharpshooter in a cherry tree to the right of the road fired the ball passing near Genl. Wright and the President and wounding Surgeon Crawford."[66] Following this, Abraham Lincoln allowed the frightened soldiers to hustle him to safety.

The Union high command in the VI Corps could not let the Confederates remain in such close proximity to Washington, D.C., and immediately moved forces to assault the gray coats. Colonel Daniel Bidwell was ordered to send his thousand-man brigade forward and push the Carolinian riflemen backwards. His division commander recorded, "At 5 p.m. on the 12th.... I was ordered to drive in the enemy's skirmish line and to occupy ... two strong wooded hills in our front, the possession of which gave the enemy great advantage of position near our entrenched line."⁶⁷ Bidwell's brigade formed for the attack behind Fort Stevens, and then moved forward. Brigadier Gen. Frank Wheaton (VI Corps, 2nd Div.) wrote, "Bidwell ... select[ed] three of his best regiments [the 7th ME, 43rd NY, and 49th NY] ... and they dashed forward, surprising and hotly engaging the enemy."⁶⁸ Another Yank officer noted, "Bidwell's attack got off ... in magnificent order and with light steps they ran forward up the ascent thru the orchard, thru the little grove on the right, over the fence rail, up to the road, making straight for their objective point, the frame house 'Carberry' in front."⁶⁹

The Thirtieth's riflemen immediately fired off volleys, forcing a Northerner to complain, "The Rebels at first stood their ground."⁷⁰ However, Cpt. Allen's men could see they would soon be overrun, so the agile Southerners scampered back to the main Confederate, position, and they joined in with their brother Tar Heel regiments who were safely protected within hastily dug entrenchments. Sergeant Aaron DeArmond (Co. K) scribbled, "Still on picket and at 6 o'clock the yankys [*sic.*] advanced in a line of battle and droave [*sic.*] our pickets back for 400 yards."⁷¹ Sadly, before all of Cpt. Allen's Carolinians could safely retire, several of his men were cut off by the rapid Union advance and captured: Pvt. Isham Bobbitt (Co. G), Pvt. James Cheatam (Co. G), and Pvt. Hiram Hagler (Co. H), who was "wounded in the back and left side."⁷² Once the Thirtieth's men took position they began firing volleys at the attackers, adding the weight of their bullets to that of the rest of Cox's brigade. A Federal officer noted, "The enemy's stubborn resistance showed that a farther advance ... would require more troops."⁷³

The Federals advanced three more regiments, the 77th NY, 122nd NY, and the 61st PA. These blue coats joined the battle line, "pouring volleys into the ranks of the [Rebels]."⁷⁴ The two forces blazed away at each other for the next two hours, both sides suffering casualties. First Sergeant Robert Crumpler (Co. A) was wounded, and Sgt. Thomas Shearin (Co. B) killed. Private Francis Hardy (Co. B) had a minié ball slash through both of his forearms, and Pvt. Epinetus Redick (Co. F) was raked by a chunk of lead that ripped his ear and mangled his left eye.⁷⁵ A Northerner also recorded, "The fight had lasted but a few minutes when the stream of mangled and bleeding ones began to come to the rear."⁷⁶ Another blue coat added, "[Our] losses were very severe, the brave Colonel Bidwell losing many of his most valuable commanders."⁷⁷ The Union troops never got closer than two hundred yards of the Confederates and when darkness ended the fighting, over two hundred-fifty Northerners had been wounded or killed. By 10:00 p.m., the battlefield was quiet, save the cries of the hurt. Chaplain Alexander Betts then recorded, "Shelling and sharp shooting. Shearin and Penny killed. Dement mortally wounded."⁷⁸

30th North Carolina Infantry⁷⁹
Fort Stevens Campaign
Casualties
July 8–12, 1864

Unit	Commander	Loss
Field & Staff	Cpt. Allen, David C.	-
Co. A	1st Sgt. Crumpler, Robert M.	1
Co. B	Sgt. Davis, Benjamin P.	2

Unit	Commander	Loss
Co. C	Sgt. Wescott, John W.	-
Co. D	3rd Lt. Rodgers, Martin L.	1
Co. E	2nd Lt. Newton, Samuel B.	-
Co. F	2nd Lt. House, James W.	1
Co. G	Sgt. Badgett, Sandy H.	3
Co. H	Sgt. Harrington, Ard A.	2
Co. I	3rd Lt. Perry, Sidney R.	1
Co. K	1st Lt. Downs, John T.	1
		12

An hour later, at 11:00 p.m., Brig. Gen. William Cox led his weary Tar Heels away from their battle line, directing them northwest; they were the last Confederates to retreat. Captain David Allen's regiment, now numbering less than two hundred men, stumbled forward in the dark. Allen's men were exhausted because of having to endure a second night without sleep, as well as a full day of being deployed as pickets. Chaplain Alexander Betts recorded, "At night we begin to fall back. Tiresome night. Troops halted to rest ten minutes in each hour. Many fell asleep for eight minutes out of ten."[80] Another Tar Heel grumbled, "[I] was never so sleepy in [my] life."[81] The Carolinians were finally allowed to halt just before sunrise. Alexander Betts scribbled, "Just before day-[break] I was so tired and sleepy that I turned aside to rest. I found a little graveyard near the roadside.... I laid down ... [and] was soon asleep."[82]

The weary Southerners were rousted from their short naps and trekked farther eastward, passing through Darnestown, Dawesonville, and Poolesville before bivouacking, having trudged nearly twenty miles. They waited for the last of Gen. Early's wagon train to cross over the Potomac River, before wading through its shallows at White's Ford in the early afternoon of July 14, 1864. The Confederates slopped their way out of the waters and struggled on, reaching Leesburg before stopping. A Southerner recalled, "The hard marching back to Virginia drained [our] already exhausted Valley District army."[83] Another rifleman though, defiantly exclaimed, "we [didn't] take Washington, but we scared Abe Lincoln like hell."[84] The weary soldiers rested on July 15, 1864, waiting for Jubal Early to decide what next to do with them.

The Confederates arose early the next morning and marched westward towards the Blue Ridge Mountains. They climbed up to Snicker's Gap and camped there, among the mountain's forested heights. The next day they descended from Snicker's Gap and splashed across the Shenandoah River at Castleman's Ferry. Then, the Tar Heels tromped a couple more miles to the area near Wickliffe Church. Here, the men were told they could rest. An appreciative rifleman quipped, "It was a relatively easy day when measured against recent standards." Another just noted, "[He] dreamed of wearing—clean linen, white socks and light shoes."[85]

Captain David Allen's men, along with their brothers in Cox's brigade, arose on July 18, 1864, knowing they were going be given a day's rest. They hungry Carolinians immediately set out across the countryside in search of food. One Southerner wrote, "many of the enlisted men had foraged through the nice rich country, obtaining milk and other items that were luxuries to the soldiers," while another remarked, "Snickersville was a great place for honey.... The boys soon ... were busy ... fighting bees."[86] Unfortunately, the Confederates' "flanking" expeditions came to a rude halt just after noon; Gen. Rodes had received news Yankees were crossing the Shenandoah and needed to be stopped.

The 30th NC was formed and Cpt. Allen moved his veterans into the brigade's marching column. Brigadier Gen. William Cox detached the 14th NC as a rear guard, and by 4:00 p.m., started the rest of his Carolina regiments back toward yesterday's river crossing. The Southerners hustled the four miles, hearing the rising sounds of artillery and musketry as they neared the area. Robert Rodes's four brigades reached the field, not far from the Cool Springs farmstead just after 5:30 p.m. General Rodes had about three thousand infantrymen in his organization; his brigade commanders, George Doles, Cullen Battle, Bryan Grimes, and William Cox. Rodes aligned his units sending Battle to the left and Grimes on the right, with Doles behind Battle and Cox following Grimes. He then pushed his sharpshooters out in front and these handpicked riflemen advanced, led by Col. Hamilton Brown (1st NC).[87] They collided with a division of blue coats commanded by Col. Joseph Thoburn, and in a short but fierce exchange of musketry, Battle's men routed the Northerners' right flank, who fled back, into the Shenandoah River. Colonel Thoburn admitted, "the enemy advanced a heavy skirmish line upon my front and [right] flanks ... their sharp enfilading fire ... caused some unsteadiness, and finally [my] first line gave way."[88] Another Northerner added, "they fled shamelessly through the second line, rushed madly down into the river, where many, never looking for the ford ... plunged in to drown."[89]

Meanwhile, Gen. Rodes directed Grimes and Cox to advance their brigades to strike the center and left of the Union position. William Cox's brigade led the way, his Carolinians double-quicked southward, sheltered by a tree-covered ridge. Once Robert Rodes saw there was room for both Grimes and Cox to deploy their men into a battle line, he ordered the two brigades to face to the left, with Grimes on the left and Cox on the right. The Southerners prepared for battle and crept to the hill's crest. The colonel of the 4th NC wrote, "when [we] came in sight of them, the enemy had formed line of battle parallel with and on the [west] side of the river. Our men were in line of battle ...

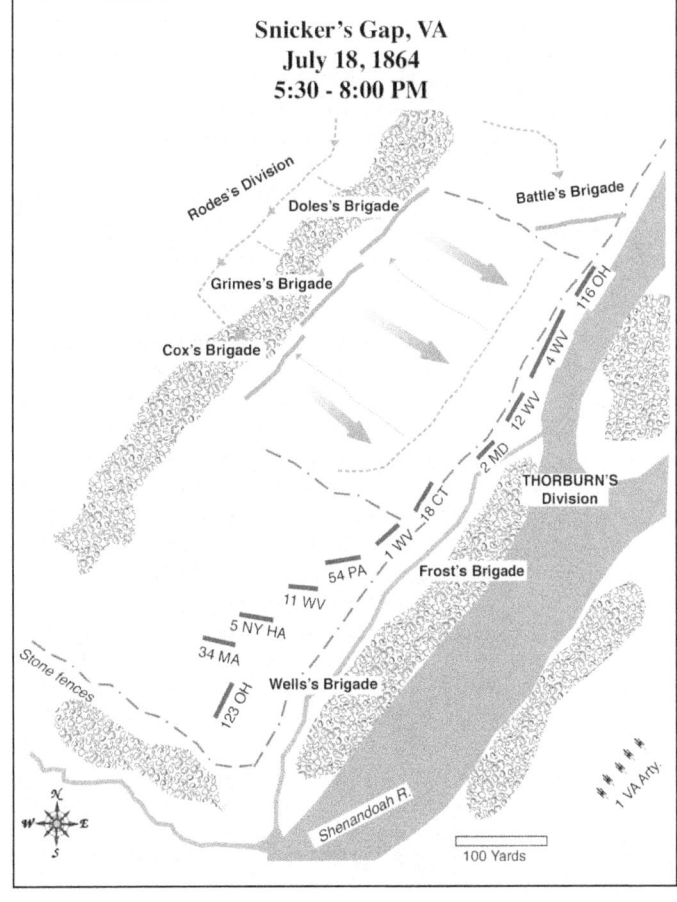

several hundred yards to the [west]." He added, "About half way between the two lines, in the in line of battle ... several hundred yards to the [west]." He added, "About half way between the two lines, in the valley, was a stone fence. As soon as this was seen our men made a dash for it. The Federals seeing this, and knowing the value of such a defense, made a dash for it at the same time." Colonel Osborne continued, "Away went both lines of battle at full speed as fast as their feet could carry them, scarcely taking time to fire a singe shot, both lines running for dear life to gain this coveted prize ... our men had the advantage of down grade, and gained the wall, while the enemy was some fifty or more yards away.... He instantly faced about when he saw that our men would reach the wall first, and beat a hasty retreat."[90] The Union commander conceded, "the Confederates charged out of the woods, and [our men] ... fled in panic without firing shot.... They retreated en masse back toward their comrades waiting behind the stone fence along the river bank."[91] The blue coats took shelter among Thoburn's reserves, knowing they had no place to go. One Yank recalled, "Run we could not.... The river at our back was too deep ... so escape that way was out of the question."[92]

The Federal commanders hurried about, pushing their demoralized men into battle position, but many were incapable of defending themselves. One officer confessed, "Standing behind that wall with the river at their backs, the Union troops stared out at the bluffs, feeling quite besieged. In their front, Rodes's veterans lined the high ground less than one hundred yards away."[93] Brigadier General William Cox realized his Tar Heels could push the demoralized blue coats into the water and destroy the entire force. He ordered the 4th NC to hold the stone wall and direct their fire at the "left-oblique" at exposed Northerner out in the open on their left. Cox then commanded his remaining regiments to attack. The Carolinians pitched forward, hollering the Rebel Yell. A frightened blue coat wrote, "Soon they came charging down on us ... shaking their banners and yelling like demons."[94]

However, just as Cox's riflemen began their charge, a brigade of Ohio infantry commanded by Col. George Wells splashed across the Shenandoah and bolstered the wavering line. An officer in this formation recorded, "five small Ohio companies [rushed] into line behind the wall. The Buckeyes fired a volley and hit Cox's Tar Heels at less than one hundred yards."[95] At this range, their hastily-aimed musketry could not miss, and a Yank crowed, "the air was thick with bullets."[96] Sergeant George Howard (Co. C) fell, a bullet ripping through this right thigh, Cpl. Richard Felton (Co. F) was killed, and Pvt. Louis Wells (Co. F) had a minié bullet punch its way through

Sgt. Maj. Francis M. Fitts, 23 years old, was wounded as Snicker's Gap (Clark, 1901).

14. Campaigning with the Army of the Valley District 199

his chest.[97] The Confederate advance slowed as the Southern riflemen stopped to return fire. Then, Union artillery batteries from the heights of Snicker's Gap, on the eastern side of the Shenandoah, took aim upon the stalled gray-uniformed formation. Their shells ripped into the Carolinians, spewing Tar Heels about, and blasting gaps in their battle line. Sergeant Major Francis Fitts was knocked to the ground, a blast chewing up his left shoulder and burning his scalp. Private John L. Miller's (Co. C) right leg was nearly blown off. Sergeant James Teachey (Co. E) was killed, while his young brother, Pvt. Jacob Teachey (Co. E) took chunks of shrapnel, "though his bowels."[98] Lieutenant Sidney Perry, commanding Company I, tumbled to the ground when, "a shell fragment [having] struck [his] ankle and tibia, shattered both."[99] Private Arkin Bell (Co. I) and Pvt. Thomas Gupton (Co. I) were mangled to death by a direct hit from an artillery round. Sergeant Aaron DeArmond (Co. K) also went down, mutilated by shrapnel.[100] One Tar Heel grumbled, "Like hailstones flew furiously the missiles of death."[101] A triumphant Yank wrote, "heavy cannonading opened from the other side of the river ... the Rebels fell back at this time."[102] More of Cpt. David

Sgt. Aaron DeArmond, 37 years old, was mortally wounded on July 18, 1864. He died the next day (courtesy Martha Brown).

Allen's men went down; Pvt. Lewis King (Co. A) fell, badly hurt; Lt. Martin Rogers (Co. D) dropped, also wounded; and Pvt. Elijah Crotts (Co. H) was killed.[103] The crushed Tar Heel regiment scurried back, retreating to the ridgeline's safety. A relieved blue coat scribbled, "[They] recoiled, broken and shattered." Another added, "[Our artillery] sent the enemy to the cover of the woods."[104]

30th North Carolina Infantry[105]
Snicker's Gap Casualties
July 18, 1864

Unit	Commander	Loss
Field & Staff	Cpt. Allen, David C.	1
Co. A	1st Sgt. Crumpler, Robert M.	1
Co. B	Sgt. Davis, Benjamin P.	-
Co. C	Sgt. Wescott, John W.	2
Co. D	3rd Lt. Rodgers, Martin L.	2

Unit	Commander	Loss
Co. E	2nd Lt. Newton, Samuel B.	3
Co. F	2nd Lt. House, James W.	5
Co. G	Sgt. Badgett, Sandy H.	-
Co. H	Sgt. Harrington, Ard A.	3
Co. I	3rd Lt. Perry, Sidney R.	4
Co. K	1st Lt. Downs, John T.	4
		25

Captain David Allen hurried among his broken companies, trying to reorganize the men into fighting units. Allen knew his sergeant major was down, as well as his left wing commander, 1st Lt. Ira Johnson. A quick head-count produced a casualty number over twenty. The 28-year-old regimental commander shuddered at this loss; a tenth of his force had been slaughtered in less time than it would have taken to complete a company roll call. David Allen's riflemen had nothing left; they lay down behind the hillcrest and did not rejoin the fight. General Cox's brigade was out of the battle. A Federal wrote, "[Our artillery] kept the Rebels discretely under cover."[106] Darkness quieted the field of infantry fire, though the Union cannoneers continued to shell the Confederate positions. A Northerner wrote, "Against the backdrop of the Blue Ridge, the Union guns flashed brilliantly and their shells streaked through the evening sky like 'meteors.'"[107] Later that night, the blue coats slipped back across the river, leaving behind their dead and wounded. The Union commander recorded, "Our loss was 65 killed, 301 wounded, [and] 56 missing; total 422."[108] William Cox's brigade suffered one hundred casualties.[109]

Sunrise on July 19, 1864, found Cpt. David Allen's men still huddled among the trees behind the ridge top. Allen had sent forward a group of hand-picked volunteers during the night and they had covered the battle ground, collecting their regiment's wounded, and burying the killed. Now, with sunlight illuminating the grounds, cautious Union soldiers crossed the river and spent the morning digging graves for their own dead. The Thirtieth's commander also allowed small numbers of his men to travel to nearby farms and gather rations. One officer recorded, "July 19—"no significant military movements occurred ... at Snicker's Gap ... burial parties plied the battlefield.... Confederate details threshed wheat from nearby farms and ground it to flour at local mills to bake bread."[110] But, for the most part, the Thirtieth's men did little; the regiment was shattered. A Confederate groaned, "We had quite a hard fight and lost quite a number of men."[111]

General Early ordered Robert Rodes to pull his men back from the field that evening, once a full moon brightened the night sky. They marched south towards Millwood, and bivouacked not far from Old Church, three miles south of Berryville. The next morning, the Confederates hiked south to Millville and from there, west to the Valley Pike and Newtown, a distance of fifteen miles. Here, Gen. Rodes received word Dodson Ramseur's division had been defeated not far from Rutherford, a dozen miles north of Newton. Robert Rodes turned his brigades north on the Valley Pike and they moved to Kernstown, a couple miles south of Winchester.[112] The tired soldiers scraped out rifle pits and waited for a Yank attack that never came. Then, they bedded down for the night. Next morning, July 21, 1864, the Carolinians were ordered back onto the Valley Pike and they retraced yesterday's steps, hiking south to Middletown, crossing Cedar Creek, and halting to quickly fashion defenses.

On July 22, 1864, Brig. Gen. William Cox shifted his Carolina regiments to Fisher's Hill, a mile south of Strasburg. Captain David Allen's small regiment dug entrenchments not far from Fisher's Mill on Tumbling Run. Captain William Ardrey (Co. K) wrote, "We fell back to Strasburg, and fortified."[113] The Thirtieth's riflemen arose the next morning and were pleased to hear their brigade would not be marching; instead, they would continue to man their posts. One writer noted, "[It was] a cool and pleasant day.... Jubal Early's footsore infantrymen used the respite to rest and nourish their tired, aching bodies. Some Southern soldiers simply relished a day of undisturbed tranquility."[114] Alexander Betts added, "Rest and sleep all day."[115]

Captain David Allen's sergeants had the Thirtieth up before dawn on July 24, 1864. One writer noted, "At four o'clock in the morning ... the Confederate camps around Strasburg buzzed with activity as Early's foot soldiers broke camp and prepared for another offensive."[116] David Allen had re-organized his shrunken regiment into two groups, one led by Cpt. William Ardrey (Co. K) and the other by 1st Lt. John Downs (Co. K), the two remaining, most-senior officers. They left their entrenchments at sunrise, heading north, the Confederates sobered by the news they were going to attack the Northerners. General Jubal Early's leading troops ran into the Federals just outside Kernstown. Early's divisions commanded by John Gordon and Gabriel Wharton pushed against the blue coats while Robert Rodes brought his brigades up in support. The Tar Heel brigade moved into position on the Confederate right and the brigade sharpshooters were sent forward just as Wharton and Gordon attacked. The Carolinians watched as the blue coats' line collapsed and the Yanks fled. Captain William Ardrey wrote, "They retired from our front and we pursued them to Winchester. Gen. Breckinridge and Gordon ... routed them, capturing a portion of their wagon train." He added, "We marched 28 miles ... very tired and camped that night at Winchester."[117]

The foot-sore Confederates hiked another twenty-seven miles in the next two days, reaching Martinsburg. That night, once the regiment had been bivouacked, William Ardrey scribbled in his journal, "Marched to Williamsport, Md. There Gen.

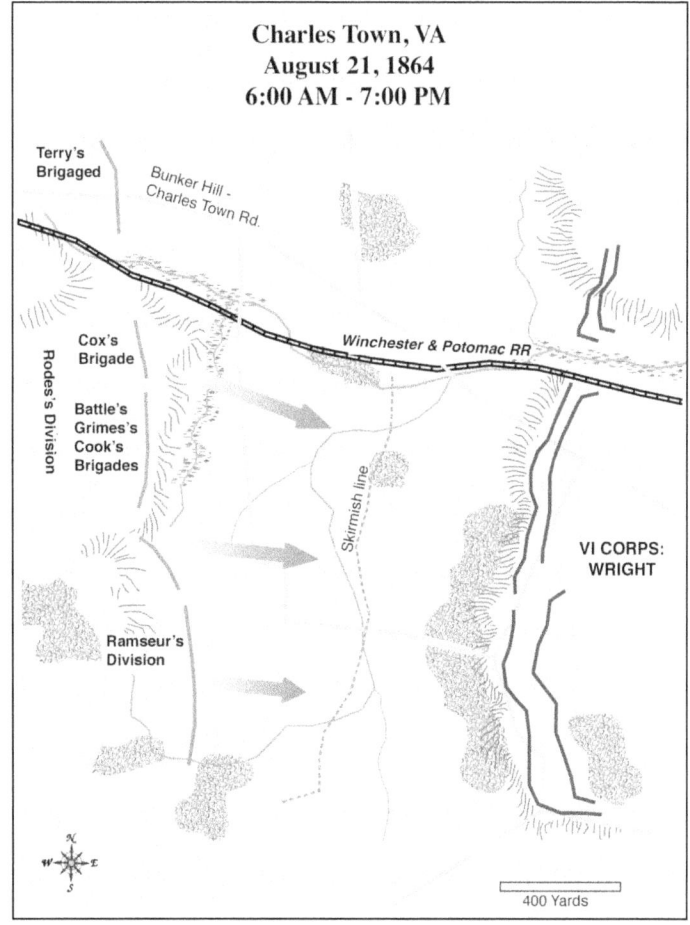

Early pressed all the provisions in the town for his men and we rejoiced to eat them, for we were tired and hungry."[118] The next morning, clouds rolled in and a heavy downpour drenched the tired soldiers. One wrote, "too much exhausted to continue the pursuit,' [we] enjoyed a day of extended rest in [our] wet camps."[119] Later, William Cox's brigade received orders to destroy the nearby railroad tracks, and the Southerners spent the next couple days burning railroad ties and bending rails. On July 27, 1864, Cpt. Allen gathered his men around them and they voted for North Carolina's governor. William Ardrey recorded, "we held elections in the brigade for Governor of North Carolina, Z. B. Vance and W. W. Holden were the candidates ... [the 30th voted] Vance 77, Holden 3."[120]

The next few days proved immensely frustrating for Cpt. Allen's Carolinians; on July 28, 1864, they hiked fifteen miles south to Bunker Hill and went out on picket duty; on July 29 the marched twenty-five miles north to the Potomac River at Williamsport; then on July 30 they trekked a dozen miles south, back to Martinsburg. However, the next morning, when the grumbling Confederates formed, they were told to stand down; they were not going anywhere. The Thirtieth spent the next four days resting. Captain Ardrey wrote, "In camp ... spending the time in bathing in the creek and living on roasted corn and apples."[121]

Newly arrived Federal brigades forced Gen. Early to fall back from his position around Martinsburg. Soon, the Confederates were trudging southward, moving through Winchester and eventually reaching Strasburg. The Carolinians finally ended up near their old positions on Fisher's Hill, overlooking Cedar Creek. William Ardrey recorded, "Marched up the Valley ... camped at Newtown, then through Strasburg and on to Fisher's Hill. Remained there until the tenth." He continued, "The enemy [was] on the opposite side of Cedar Creek and [there was] some skirmishing."[122] Then, once the Tar Heels had settled in and improved their defenses, they received word to march again.

General Robert E. Lee, concerned that Jubal Early's Army of the Valley was being outmaneuvered by a much larger force, sent reinforcements; 5,500 riflemen commanded by Lt. Gen. Richard Anderson. This new force of Confederates crossed the Blue Ridge Mountains at Front Royal and created the potential of coming in behind the Union position. The Federal commander, Maj. Gen. Philip Sheridan, responded quickly. A Yank officer wrote, "This news alarmed Sheridan. His army was now south of Front Royal facing southwest to confront Early on Fisher's Hill. With Anderson on his way to Front Royal, the Southerners could easily threaten the Federal left flank and rear."[123] Sheridan ordered his troops to retreat. When the Union troops back-pedaled northward, the Southerners followed. Captain William Ardrey (Co. K) wrote, "They retired and we pursued them [down] the valley to Bunker Hill."[124]

30th North Carolina Infantry[125]
August 21, 1864

Unit		Strength
Field & Staff	Cpt. Allen, David C. Cpt. Ardrey, William E. 1st Lt. Downs, John T	3
Co. A	1st Sgt. Crumpler, Robert M.	13
Co. B	Cpl. Shearin, Thomas W.	11
Co. C	Sgt. Wescott, John W.	12
Co. D	Cpl. Forsythe, James R.	17

Unit		Strength
Co. E	2nd Lt. Newton, Samuel B.	25
Co. F	2nd Lt. House, James W.	23
Co. G	3rd Lt. Fulford, John T.	18
Co. H	Sgt. Harrington, Ard A.	16
Co. I	1st Sgt. Crowell, Jonas W.	16
Co. K	Sgt. Russell, William D.	25
		179

Heavy summer rains drowned the countryside and made movement difficult. One writer recorded, "Rain, torrents of rain, swept into the Valley during the night of August 17–18, continuing intermittently through to the 20th."[126] The Confederate forces rested, enabling the road-weary Tar Heels time to scrounge for food. A Carolinian noted, "Bunker Hill, Aug. 20th.–We have an admirable camp, but have had nothing but beef and flour, not even hog meat or salt, to help along."[127] Another wrote, "As the second week of August began [our troops were] … 'in all their rags and squalor,' looking 'like wolf-hounds.'"[128]

The next morning, August 21, 1864, the Confederates marched toward Harper's Ferry. One officer recorded, "By 5:00 a.m., Jubal Early had the Second Corps … marching out of their camps at Bunker Hill and following the Smithfield Road."[129] Soon though, they ran into Union troops near Charlestown. Captain William Ardrey recorded, "Marched to Charlestown … our Regt. was deployed as skirmishers."[130] Captain David Allen spread his small regiment out, deploying each rifleman five yards or so between each man, and ordered his troops forward. They advanced cautiously, heading southeast, stumbling through a shallow, muddy brook, and up a gentle incline, shadowed by the rest of the brigade in battle line formation, several hundred yards to their rear. Soon, cavalry rifles began popping and bullets zipped among the Tar Heels, with one projectile striking Pvt. Elijah Wilkins (Co. D), killing him instantly.[131] The Carolinians dropped to the ground while David Allen and William Ardrey surveyed the situation. The Thirtieth's experienced officers shifted squads of riflemen, and in a quick burst, flanked the blue coats. The Federal cavalrymen ran, but not before downing Pvt. James Frazer (Co. G) and David Hunt (Co. G), both wounded.[132] A Northerner wrote of this initial exchange, "An attack was made by the enemy early this morning, about 8 o'clock … [against] our advanced line of cavalry pickets in front of Summit Point, which resulted in our having to abandon that position."[133]

The Confederates pushed forward, gaining several hundred yards, and attained a ridge top. From this vantage point Cpt. Allen's men could see before them a long valley extending nearly half a mile, and beyond that a higher ridge. Even David Allen's poor-visioned riflemen could see dozens of regimental flags flying in the wind on top that hillcrest. They all knew those colors added up to several Yank brigades. Moments later white clouds of smoke billowed out from behind the blue-coated infantry, and soon cannon shells erupted near the Tar Heels. The veteran Carolinians took cover. Captain Allen sent a runner back to brigade, but soon word came back from headquarters—continue the advance. The Tar Heels shuddered, but grimly stood up and crept forward.

Another line of dismounted Union cavalry arose up from their hiding places and fired several quick volleys at the exposed Tar Heels. The range was short, barely a hundred yards; several more Carolina veterans were hit. Private John Pennington (Co. A) was killed; Pvt. John Bland (Co. E) shot through the arm; and Cpl. William McDowell (Co. C) fell, a bullet crashing into his brogans, mangling toes on both of his feet.[134] The Southerners directed their fire against these blue coats, felling many, and forcing them to run. A Federal wrote, "[Our] line retired and slowly moved back toward Berryville pike, and then fell back to within two miles of Charlestown."[135] Captain William Ardrey (Co. K) noted, "[We] pursued the Yankee cavalry."[136] More Union artillery weight was thrown at the Tar Heels and again, the battle-experienced riflemen took cover. David Allen's men could see the Union infantry waiting for them, and they knew there was no way this hill could taken. The Carolinians sought out any protection they could find and began a slow and accurate fire against the Yanks. A Federal complained, "The firing of the Confederate sharpshooters was incredibly accurate.... Although the combat at Charlestown was primarily a high intensity skirmish, the casualty rates among the Federals highlighted the lethal effectiveness of the Confederate sharpshooter battalions."[137]

A reinforced line of skirmishers came up on the Thirtieth's right, infantrymen from Gen. Dodson Ramseur's division. These men pushed against the Union position but were repulsed. One wrote, "Ramseur's division arrived and went into position on Rodes's right flank. His sharpshooters suddenly found themselves engaged in a substantial encounter after they advanced."[138] Meanwhile, though Cpt. David Allen's riflemen tried to keep hidden, the Union fire continued to strike Carolina flesh. Private William A. Williams (Co. B) was killed; Pvt. David Turner (Co. E) was struck in the head; and Pvt. Moses Bentley's (Co. K) right leg was mauled by a chunk of lead.

The next several hours were more of the same; the Tar Heel skirmishers holding their exposed position, firing resolutely, and taking casualties from Northern rifles and artillery. Corporal James Forsyth (Co. D) was killed; Pvt. Jacob Cavenaugh's (Co. E) leg was ripped open; and Pvt. Lemuel Warren (Co. F) was wounded.[139] The Thirtieth's casualties began to cripple the remaining soldiers' fighting spirit. Alexander Betts mourned, "Heavy skirmish most of the day. Five in my Regiment killed."[140]

Later that afternoon the situation changed; several Northern regiments spilled out of their entrenchments and approached the embattled Confederate skirmish line. A Yank recorded, "The Sixth Corps were rapidly thrown into line of battle, and then advanced, steadily driving the enemy's skirmishers into their own line of battle."[141] The Thirtieth's line wavered and then the Tar Heels began to scurry backwards. Sergeant George Newkirk (Co. E) was killed trying to stave off the retreat; Sgt. James Fuller (Co. G) was shot through his left hip, with the minié bullet also ripping into his right leg and fracturing the bone; Cpl. Hilliard Winstead (Co. I) was badly mangled; and William Walston (Co. F) was mortally wounded.[142] The Thirtieth's resistance ended when the men raced back to the safety of the brigade battle line. A brigade officer wrote, "I have had today a good many killed and wounded, we being in advance.... The enemy have a large force ... and are contesting the ground most stubbornly." He continued, "This is a mere feint to frighten them and cover some important move on our part. I have no idea."[143]

General Robert Rodes moved his brigades forward and they engaged the Northerners for several hours, though both sides never closed to within a couple hundred yards of each other. The shooting tapered off once darkness covered the field, however, both sides remained vigilant. A Yankee wrote, "The fighting continued nearly the entire day, and the cannonading lasted until dark ... the losses were ... nearly three hundred." He added, "Toward dark the firing ceased, and our army was busily employed in throwing up breastworks."[144] Robert Rodes' division suffered one hundred sixty casualties.[145]

Sunrise, the next morning, August 22, 1864, revealed to the Confederate pickets a battlefield devoid of Yanks; the Northerners had retreated during the night. Fresh Confederate brigades advanced and chased after the Federals, eventually catching up with them at Harper's Ferry. One Southerner wrote, "Early this morning we pitched into the Yankees and drove them through Charlestown to their position on Boliver heights where they are watching us and occasionally throwing a shell at us."[146] The battle-weary men in Brig. Gen. William Cox's brigade followed behind, remaining close enough to see the action,

30th North Carolina Infantry[147]
Charlestown Casualties
August 21, 1864

Unit	Commander	Loss
Field & Staff	Cpt. Allen, David C.	-
Co. A	1st Sgt. Crumpler, Robert M.	1
Co. B	Sgt. Davis, Benjamin P.	1
Co. C	Sgt. Wescott, John W.	1
Co. D	3rd Lt. Rodgers, Martin L.	2
Co. E	2nd Lt. Newton, Samuel B.	4
Co. F	2nd Lt. House, James W.	2
Co. G	Sgt. Badgett, Sandy H.	3
Co. H	Sgt. Harrington, Ard A.	-
Co. I	3rd Lt. Perry, Sidney R.	1
Co. K	1st Lt. Downs, John T.	1
		16

but never getting into danger. Captain William Ardrey scribbled, "pursued the Yankee[s] ... through Charlestown and all day an exciting engagement, in full view of Harper's Ferry." Alexander Betts added, "Drove enemy through Charlestown and two miles beyond. Heavy rain."[148]

The tired Carolinians remained outside Harper's Ferry until August 25, 1864, when they received orders to march to Leetown, ten miles away. The next day they hiked another ten miles to Shepherdstown, but on August 27, 1864, trudged to Bunker Hill, nearly twenty miles south. William Ardrey noted, "to Bunker Hill, very warm and we suffered for water."[149] Another officer added, once the Confederates had reached Bunker Hill, "we formed line of battle, threw out one Regiment as skirmishers, and advanced upon them, driving them before us. We chased them for upwards of two hours, many of the men fainting from exhaustion."[150] They remained in camp the next day, then on August 29, 1864, splashed across the Opequon River and trekked eastward six miles to Smithfield. Here they stayed for twenty-four hours before returning to Bunker Hill.

The Thirtieth went out on picket duty on September 1, 1864, a duty that proved to be quite advantageous, as the hungry riflemen ended up near an orchard. Captain William Ardrey recorded, "The orchards and the best apples I have ever seen and the greatest abundance." He also noted, "Rained very hard and we had a dreadful night of it."[151] Captain David Allen's regiment remained on picket duty until the afternoon of the next day. Then, they were pulled from that responsibility and joined the march to Stephenson's Depot, ten miles south of Bunker Hill. They arrived in time to learn there had been a skirmish between Yank cavalry and the first of Gen. Rodes's brigades. Therefore, with the danger removed, on September 3, 1864, the Tar Heels turned around and retraced their steps back to Bunker Hill. However, the next morning the frustrated Carolinians followed orders and hiked back to Stephenson's Depot, and from there, to the Berryville area. An exasperated Tar Heel grumbled, "of course the general understands it all, and perhaps [the Lord] does, but nobody else."[152]

The Southern riflemen no longer had much of a military bearing. An officer examined his troops and wrote of their appearance, "[They had] faces browned by exposure and heavily bearded ... begrimed with dust and sweat." They possessed, "A frame tough and sinewy, and trained by hardship to surprising powers of endurance ... [and] above this an old wool hat, worn, and weather beaten ... over a soiled shirt, which is unbuttoned and buttonless at the collar, is a ragged gray jacket that does not reach the hips." This Confederate continued his elaboration, writing, "Below this, trousers of a non-descript color ... are held in place by a leather belt to which is attached the cartridge box ... [and] bayonet scabbard." And finally, "Dirty socks disappear in a pair of badly used and curiously contorted shoes."[153]

Captain David Allen's men looked no different, plus, his Carolinians were used up. The past weeks' continual, and seemingly pointless marching back-and-forth, up-and-down the Valley Turnpike had ground their shoes to nothing. Meanwhile their rations were virtually nonexistent, forcing the men to scrounge for food, and often bed down at night having eaten very little. And finally, the senseless casualties in needless fights completely discouraged the Carolinians. They had been through a lot of adversity since joining in 1861, but what was happening now defied all common sense. A Tar Heel noted, "we reached camp wet, and exhausted, and hungry, without a wagon or tent to shelter us from the rain, spent the night all exposed and woke up next morning drenched to the skin."[154]

Captain John McMillan (Co. E) returned to the Thirtieth on September 8, 1864.[155] Though McMillan was the regiment's senior officer he let Cpt. David Allen continue as temporary regimental commander as the badly depleted formation's surviving veterans were again re-organized. Then, on September 9, 1864, the worn-out Confederates formed on the highway and hiked to Darksville, five miles north of Bunker Hill. The next day, they turned around and trudged back to Stephenson's Depot. General Bryan Grimes wrote to his wife, describing the brigade's condition, which was the situation for all of Rodes's brigade's soldiers: "September 10th, 1864, Stevenson's Depot.–The weather continues very rainy. We are now very much in need of clothes and shoes, there being at least two hundred barefooted and half naked men in my command."[156]

They remained in the Stephenson's Depot area for the next several days, giving the Carolinians a chance to rest and forage for something other than hardtack. The weather turned chilly, forcing the officers to begin planning for the oncoming winter. Brigadier Gen. Grimes, who had the advantage of rank, wrote, "The nights are very cold, I find two or three blankets comfortable."[157] Unfortunately the men did not have this protection, the constant marching had resulting in nearly all the troops losing or throwing away anything that was heavy to carry, including coats, blankets, and tent canvas. Now, they needed those precious items to ward off the weather, and once again, the Confederate supply situation failed.

Chapter 15

September 1864—Disaster in the Shenandoah Valley

The Thirtieth North Carolina, along with the rest of the Tar Heels s in William Cox's brigade, hiked to Stephenson's Depot on September 17, 1864. The veterans with tents set up their shelters while the rest of the men fashioned shebangs and shade covers. The Tar Heels were tired and despondent over the loss of so many comrades. The Thirtieth now numbered around one hundred forty. Captain John McMillan (Co. E) had assumed regimental command, and he re-organized the formation into two amalgamated companies, one led by Cpt. David Allen (Co. C) and the other, Cpt. William Ardrey (Co. K). Each combined company had a first sergeant, two lieutenants, and about sixty riflemen. The men were hungry from paltry rations, poorly supplied in clothing, equipment, and ammunition, and their morale reduced to supporting only those fellows they knew best.

30th North Carolina Infantry[1]
September 19, 1864

Unit		Strength
Field & Staff	Cpt. McMillan, John C. Cpt. Allen, David C. Cpt. Ardrey, William E.	3
Co. A	1st Sgt. Crumpler, Robert M.	11
Co. B	Cpl. Shearin, Thomas W.	9
Co. C	Sgt. Wescott, John W.	9
Co. D	—-	13
Co. E	2nd Lt. Newton, Samuel B.	19
Co. F	2nd Lt. House, James W.	18
Co. G	3rd Lt. Fulford, John T.	12
Co. H	Sgt. Harrington, Ard A.	14
Co. I	1st Sgt. Crowell, Jonas W.	13
Co. K	1st Lt. Downs, John T.	20
		141

The Tar Heels slept past sunrise on September 18, 1864, then Cpt. McMillan's men arose and scrounged for firewood to cook their meager breakfasts. One wrote, "We tarried

... in the morning."[2] But their respite did not last. Brigadier General William Cox received word Union forces were moving to take Bunker Hill, and his Carolinians were to be sent to stop this action. General Cox formed his six, small regiments and hustled them the four miles to the area, only to discover the crisis had passed. The foot-sore riflemen trudged back to their camps, relieved there was no fight, but grumbling at the pointless exercise.

The next morning, September 19, 1864, the Carolinians awoke, hearing the rumble of artillery. This noise, the veterans knew, meant the Yanks had attacked somewhere, and the Tar Heels probably would be headed toward danger. Captain William Ardrey (Co. K) recorded, "In the morning we were aroused from our sleep by the roaring of cannons and the heavy firing of musketry. Soon the long roll was beat."[3] The Tar Heels strapped on their gear and formed to march, rumors quickly informed everyone what was happening. A Carolinian noted, "Sheridan's forces made a heavy assault on Ramseur's lines, which were squarely across the Berryville pike [east of Winchester] ... about daylight."[4] General Jubal Early wrote, "I ordered Rodes, Gordon, and Breckinridge to have their divisions under arms and ready to move to Ramseur's assistance."[5] The order to march arrived sometime after 8:00 a.m. and William Cox's eight hundred veterans moved southward, an important part of Maj. Gen. Robert Rodes's four-brigade division.[6]

The trek to Winchester was about five miles, and the Confederates hustled southward from their morning camps, all knowing from the sounds they could hear, they were going toward something more serious than a minor skirmish. A Carolinians rifleman remarked, "We were immediately and rapidly moved forward [as] the noise of the incipient conflict increasing and deepening as we proceeded."[7] The fighting east of Winchester had begun at sunrise when Federal cavalry and infantry attacked Dodson Ramseur's pickets and quickly drove them backwards. Ramseur reinforced his pickets with infantry brigades and they absorbed the first of several heavy blue-coat onslaughts. The Confederates pulled back to a better defensive position while the Northerners slowly massed brigades of infantry from the VI and XIX Corps. A Federal wrote, "there followed a delay that ... gave the Confederates time to bring up the infantry of Gordon and Rodes."[8]

The Yanks surged forward and crashed into Ramseur's troops, causing one to write, "The Union attack ... hammered back [Ramseur's line]."[9] Robert Rodes's division reached the area and Jubal Early directed his brigades into position, noting, "a little after 10 a.m. ... Rodes was then placed on Gordon's right ... under cover of woods."[10] Captain William Ardrey (Co. K) recorded, "we were formed in line on the Berryville pike road and ordered forward."[11] A Tar Heel rifleman added, "[We] commenced to move forward, the sharpshooters in the advance. We (the sharpshooters) moved forward at a run and to a piece of woods ... when we ran into a strong line of battle of Yankees who were pouring tremendous fire into a Brigade to our left."[12] The Carolinians hunched their shoulders and pressed against the blue coats, shoving them backward. An officer in the 4th NC bragged, "We soon engaged the enemy, who had approached near our position, and who after a short encounter, gave way."[13]

The Thirtieth North Carolina, as well as its brother regiments in Cox's brigade moved through a stand of trees the locals called Second Woods. One of the Confederates exclaimed, "I don't think I ever heard such noise as was made when Rodes started in. It sounded as if every tree in the woods was falling down and that a terrific thunder storm was raging in the woods."[14] Here, within this woodlot with its dense undergrowth, the Carolinians slugged the Northerners with accurate musketry, allowing a gray-coated rifleman to remark, "When their first line gave way we pressed on and their supporting line, about 100 yards to the rear, broke and ran without waiting to receive our fire."[15] A Yankee, punished by the Tar Heels' ferocity, wrote, "The destructiveness of the fire and the falling back of the broken lines in our front caused us to fall back.... The enemy continued to advance and the regiment, with others, fell back slowly, making frequent stands in order to check his advance as much as possible."[16] Captain William Ardrey added, "They fought bravely but we soon repulsed them, with great loss."[17]

The Tar Heels pushed forward nearly a half mile, knocking the Union riflemen out of their way. The commander of the blue coats, Col. Edward Molineux, admitted, "the brigade ... passing through a heavy belt of timber ... [came] under a very heavy fire of musketry ... we

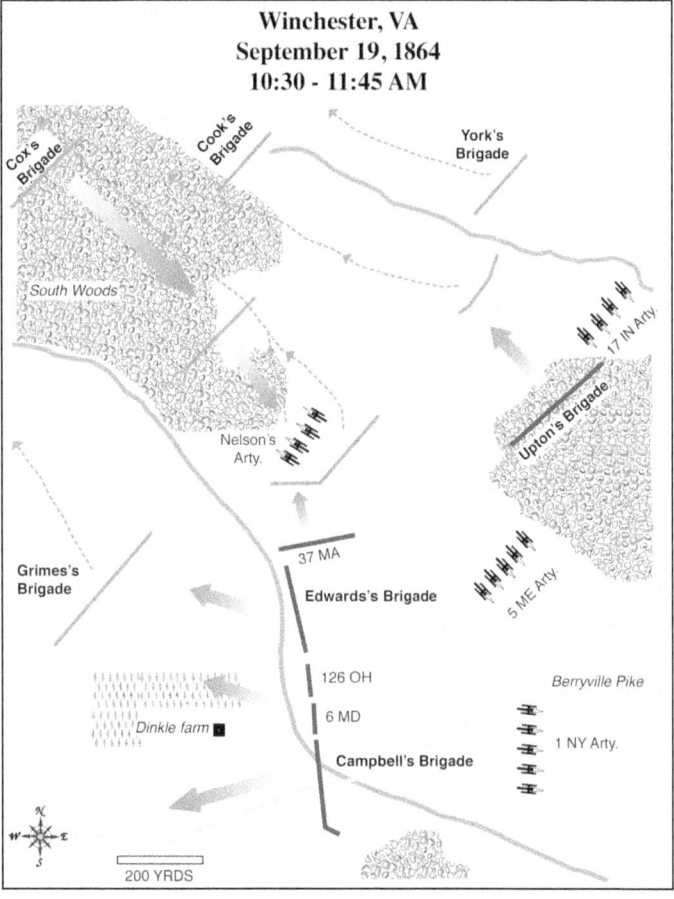

were obliged to fall back some 300 paces to the rear, losing very heavily in killed and wounded."[18] Meanwhile, at the same time, disaster occurred: Maj. Gen. Robert Rodes was killed. An officer nearby when Rodes was struck, described his last moments when a chunk of shrapnel sliced into his skull, just behind his ear: "around 1:00 p.m. ... the general's head was suddenly flung forward and [he] fell off his horse [head first].... He died within a few minutes from severe damage to the brain and loss of blood."[19] Brigadier General Bryan Grimes, whose brigade was not far away, assumed command of the division.

William Cox's riflemen pushed out of the eastern edge of Second Woods, emerging onto an open field extending for nearly a mile, a place the locals called Dinkle's farm. They brushed aside another Yank formation that had taken refuge in one of farmer Dinkle's cornfields; the blue coat's officer remarking, "The enemy at once came upon my right flank in large force; successful resistance was no longer possible ... we were obliged to fall back in some disorder."[20] A Southerner bragged, "The victorious Confederates surged across the Dinkle farm."[21] But now, the Confederates were out in the open, and though they had suffered few casualties, the brigade's riflemen were low on ammunition, winded by their exertions, and their organization jumbled. A Northerner whose regiment was nearby wrote, "The enemy's line was somewhat ragged, both from the opposition it had already received and because in an advance of any troops for a considerable distance the more adventurous or excitable get ahead while those less anxious for close quarters lag behind, and the command becomes broken so that it cannot act ... with its full strength."[22]

A Federal battery, the 5th ME, with its six guns deployed less than a quarter mile away, trained its guns on the Southerners and unleashed a horrid barrage of flame and steel. One of the artillerymen exclaimed, "[We were] literally deluging the enemy ... with canister."[23] Private William Cooper (Co. D) was knocked backwards, wounded in the head; and 1st Lt. John Downs (Co. K) suffered an injury to his wrist.[24] The Union artillery commander wrote, "the battery was ... on the right of the pike ... [and] most hotly engaged for the day, playing mostly upon the enemy's infantry ... some 300 yards [away from] the [Rebels]."[25] Private John Shearin (Co. B) was wounded, as was Cpt. David Allen (Co. C), who fell, his left shoulder ripped open.[26] A rifleman in the 14th NC groaned, "We ran into a masked battery with opened on us with grape and canister."[27]

Then, a blue-coated infantry regiment emerged from out of a ditch and behind a stone fence, and fired a volley into the Tar Heels. This ambush staggered the Southerners, with one rifleman exclaiming, "I never saw Minnie balls and grape shot rain so in all my life."[28] Lieutenant Samuel Moore (Co. F) had a bullet slice through his right side, Pvt. Riol Dickson (Co. E) took a chunk of lead in his thigh, while another punched through his spine; and Cpl. Hardy Matthews (Co. H) fell, his right leg mangled.[29] A Tar Heel rifleman remarked, "We uncovered the enemy behind a rock fence and a battery opened on us with grape and canister."[30] The Confederates were shocked by the severity of the fire shredding their battle line. Though the Union formation was less than a third the size of William Cox's brigade, the blue coats were out-gunning the Southerners. General

Col. Joseph Hamblin's brigade attacked Cox's position in the Second Woods on September 19, 1864 (Johnson & Buel, 1887).

Cox's men had run into the 37th MA, a regiment numbering less than three hundred officers and men, but armed with Spencer repeating rifles. One Tar Heel wrote in dismay, "It was here ... that we ran against the repeating rifle, which was such a surprise to us, having six or eight shots coming from behind each tree when they took to the woods, and we could see only one man."[31] An officer in the 37th MA boasted, "The Spencer could be reloaded with seven bullets in no more time than the placing of a single round in a musket." He continued, recording the fact his men could fire so much faster than a soldier armed with a musket, also noted, "[We] were not long in learning, however, that the repeater required a vastly increased supply of ammunition. The former complement had been 40 rounds, in place of which [we] were now expected to carry 100."[32]

More of Cpt. John McMillan's riflemen went down: Pvt. James Johnston (Co. K), Pvt. James King (Co. G), Pvt. John King, (Co. D), and Pvt. John Howie (Co. K) were all wounded. Two riflemen in Company A who stood side-by-side, Pvt. Robert Cox and Pvt. William Howard, both went down at the same time, one wounded in the right thigh, while the other was injured in the left thigh.[33] The Southerners reeled backward, shrinking away from the constantly banging Spencer rifles, and the devastating canister. A Tar Heel admitted, "Their [fire] caused us to retreat, aye, run to escape."[34] The Northern commander agreed, writing, "The Confederate were astonished at the severity of the fire which opened upon them. The demoralization of the Confederate line was speedy and complete."[35] An officer in the 4th NC conceded, "we fell back in [poor] order."[36] Another cannoneer remarked, "If every man of them had been a Bengal tiger, fighting for his life in his native jungle, they could not have retreated more sullenly ... as they fell back."[37] Unfortunately, not all of William Cox's Tar Heels were able to withdraw; some were so pinned down by rifle fire and canister they could not move. These veterans, including the commander of the 14th NC and a number of his men, plus a collection of veterans from the 30th NC, were captured.

The Tar Heels scurried back into the safety of Second Woods, where regimental leaders corralled their riflemen and halted the retreat. Brigadier General William Cox, once his regiments had steadied themselves, marched his brigade westward, deeper into the woods, and up the sloping terrain to a ridge hidden among the trees. He about-faced his veterans and ordered the men to fashion a defense. Once the Carolinians settled in, Cox sent forward a thick screen of skirmishers to protect the battle line from being surprised. One of these battle-weary riflemen scribbled, "Towards noon there was a pause of several hours in the conflict ... and we all began to fondly hope that the foe was too badly crippled and demoralized to resume."[38]

The Carolinians remained behind their defenses for the next couple hours, waiting, hearing the rumble of artillery and the rattle of infantry going on in other locations, but content to know their small portion of the battlefield was quiet. But there was more fighting to come; around 3:00 p.m., Cox's skirmishers noticed a wall of Union troops approaching through the trees. These Northerners, men from Brig. Gen. Emory Upton's brigade (now led by Col. Joseph Hamblin), advanced cautiously, not knowing where the Confederates were, but once the skirmishers made contact, the blue coats pressed forward. A member of the 2nd CT Heavy Artillery wrote, "Here was the deadliest part of the day ... the regiment [moved forward and] had orders to fire." He continued, "[we] had the privilege of pouring an effective fire into the rebels who were thick in front."[39]

The Carolinian riflemen's fire ripped into Hamblin's men, killing many and wounding scores more. The Northern regiments' formation broke apart as the blue coats sought shelter. But they continued to inch forward, forcing Cox's skirmish line backward. The Confederates retreated back to the main battle line; resolute veterans hunkered down behind rock fences, trees, and make shift defenses, knowing they had to hold. The Northerners slammed into the Tar Heel position and for twenty minutes the two sides fought fiercely at ranges of less than fifty yards. The Southerners, having the advantage of their defenses, savaged the Federals. The commander of the 2nd CTHA would eventually report 138 casualties, while the other regiments in Hamblin's brigade recorded another fifty.[40] The Yank advanced stalled, never-the-less, to the Tar Heels' surprise, the Southerners got orders to abandon their position and fall back to Winchester. A disgusted Cpt. William Ardrey (Co. K) wrote, "About 3:00 p.m. the enemy's cavalry broke our left flank and our lines gave way."[41] Another Confederate added, "In growing confusion, Early fell back to a line of breastworks close to the town … he prepared to stand there."[42] A Federal, not understanding that the Confederates had been ordered to retire, wrote, "The South Woods … [was] cleared when Upton [Hamblin] drove off Cox's brigade."[43]

The Carolinians fell back to a position called the Smithfield Redoubt, where they joined Confederate brigades that were rallying, there having hastily arrived from other abandoned locations. The Smithfield Redoubt had been constructed in 1861 when Gen. Joseph Johnston had gangs of laborers excavate a two-sided set of trenches, one line facing to the east, while the other covered the north. This position, though now eroded by three years of weather, still provided its defenders waist-to-shoulder deep protection. The Tar Heels took shelter and trained their weapons on the woods they had just abandoned.

Soon, Union infantrymen emerged from the trees and massed for an assault. The Confederates watched as at least a half-dozen brigades assembled to attack. The veteran Tar Heels gripped their weapons and waited; they knew their musketry was also supported by a number of cannon; the coming Federal assault would be costly for the blue coats. The Northerners also understood what would happen once the order was given to advance. A dismayed Union officer wrote, "From this point the open ground stretched away to Winchester, the field commanded by the enemy's artillery."[44] Then, the blue coats moved forward, with a Southern rifleman noting, "the enemy came rushing in like an avalanche."[45] Another wrote, "Ramseur's and Battle's remaining troops opened fire at the Northerners from in and around the Redoubt. Southern artillery joined in, adding canister to the ordnance being hurled into the advancing blue ranks."[46] A Yank commented, "The terrible whistle and ping of Minie bullets just above their heads initiated the men into the society of death."[47] Another Federal officer exclaimed, "The fire became unbearable, and [we] ordered the troops to fall back fifty paces and lie down."[48]

Sadly, the Confederates' successful defense from the Smithfield Redoubt was of little value. Union cavalry north of Winchester struck their Confederate counterparts and the Southern horsemen's will to fight collapsed. General Bryan Grimes groused, "Everything up to 4 o'clock in the afternoon looked bright, and promised well for a complete victory … then their Cavalry charged our Cavalry, which was on the left of our Infantry, which gave way in confusion, and their forces came down on the left and rear of our column."[49] Rumors swept through the infantry lines, telling of this disaster, and terrorizing the Confederate riflemen with thoughts of capture. One officer reported, "The spirit of retreat had risen. Some of the troops were close to panic."[50] General Jubal Early wrote, "The enemy's cavalry … charged around my left flank, and the men began to give way … and so demoralized was a larger part of our [army]."[51]

Orders came to withdraw from the Smithfield Redoubt, but little direction followed these commands. The Tar Heels, along with their Confederate brothers, backed away from their position and drifted into the streets of Winchester. By now, frightened soldiers were flooding through the town, running from the north, and carrying with them the disease of panic. They swept the Carolinians southward, out of Winchester. One Southerner wrote, "they turned our left and fell on our rear and made our men give way in great confusion."[52] The Northerners, sensing the lack of Confederate resistance, arose from their positions east of the Smithfield Redoubt and attacked. A Southerner remarked, "About the same time, the heaviest of the Federal attack was delivered."[53]

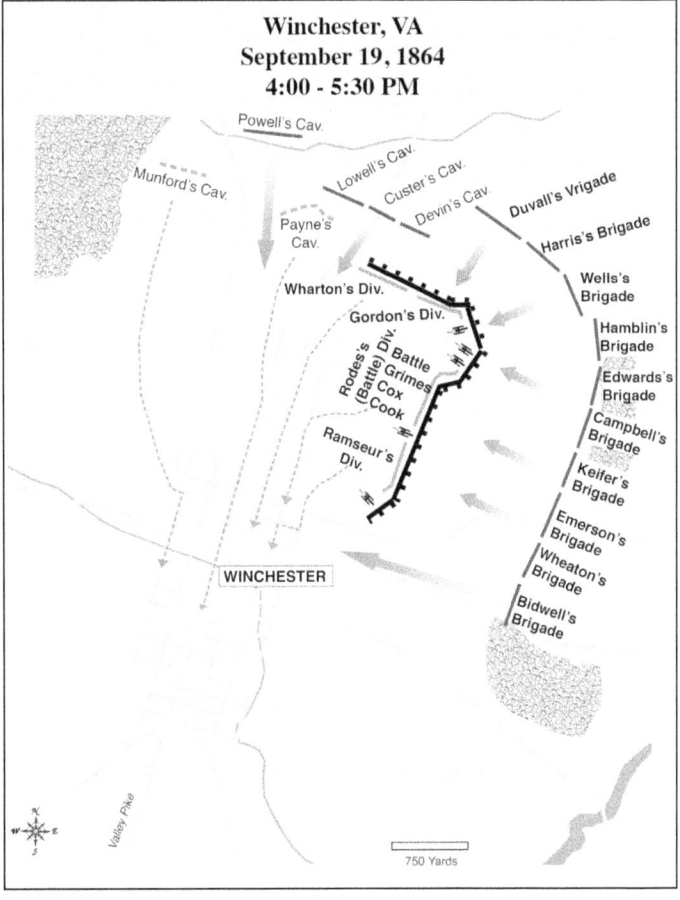

With little to stop the Yanks, they rolled over the Redoubt and crashed into the rear of the retreating Confederates. An exuberant blue coat exclaimed, "We then charged with the balance of the line, completely routing the enemy. My skirmishers passed through Winchester, driving the enemy before them."[54] A Southerner added, "This of course necessitated a rapid falling back upon our part ... [and] almost inevitably engendering confusion, a confusion which was converted into a panic."[55] Another confessed, "As the Confederates fled south out of Winchester ... they threw away rifles, knapsacks, and other perceived impediments, and the streets were littered with the usual debris of a defeated and rapidly retreating army."[56]

The retreat quickly turned into a terrorized frenzy of running Southerners. One Confederate wrote with shame, "We fell back when everything at this moment began to run, wagons, ambulances and everything mixed up together. The whole face of the earth was literally alive with rebels running for their lives."[57] Meanwhile, a Yank officer noted in amazement, "Every damn thing in the shape of a rebel is on the run."[58] Captain John McMillan's veterans skedaddled southward, following the frightened crowd, fleeing the prospects of being scooped up by Federal cavalrymen. One escaping soldier recorded, "I would run a while and stop and laugh at others and think what fools we were making or ourselves, when some shell would come tearing among us and everything would start off again."[59]

Darkness eventually put an end to the Northerners' chase of the routed Confederates. The defeated gray coats continued to stagger southward, putting distance between themselves and danger. One wrote, "Night soon intervened to prevent further pursuit, and we continued to Newtown, near which, we lay the greater portion of the night in line of battle, while through the night, our stragglers were constantly coming in."[60] Another added, "Lucky was the Confederate private on the mournful retreat who knew his own captain ... and most lucky was the commander who knew where to find the main body of his own troops."[61] Brigadier General Bryan Grimes later recorded, "we had a most terrible fight at Winchester, and we were very roughly handled by the enemy. We lost a great many men, and our troops did not behave with their usual valor." He continued, "[I] have been as near exhausted as a man could well be, not slept ten hours in forty-eight."[62] And the 30th's regimental chaplain scribbled in his journal, "We fell back to Strasburg, marching all night. Riding alone and very sad."[63]

30th North Carolina Infantry[64]
Winchester Casualties
September 19, 1864

Unit	Commander	Loss
Field & Staff	Cpt. McMillan, John C.	1
Co. A	1st Sgt. Crumpler, Robert M.	2
Co. B	Cpl. Shearin, Thomas W.	1
Co. C	Sgt. Wescott, John W.	2
Co. D	—-	4
Co. E	2nd Lt. Newton, Samuel B.	2
Co. F	2nd Lt. House, James W.	1
Co. G	3rd Lt. Fulford, John T.	2
Co. H	Sgt. Harrington, Ard A.	2
Co. I	1st Sgt. Crowell, Jonas W.	-
Co. K	1st Lt. Downs, John T.	3
		20

General Jubal Early's staff officers laid out division and brigade positions on Fisher's Hill, just southwest of Strasburg, VA, and passed on their commander's instructions for the men to construct defenses. Major General Dodson Ramseur recalled, "From right to left, roughly a quarter-mile south of a tributary of the North Fork of the Shenandoah called Tumbling Run, Early placed Wharton, Gordon, Pegram, and Ramseur. Ramseur's left rested a mile short of Little North Mountain." The major general continued, "Early extended his line westward [with] ... dismount[ed] ... cavalry [under] Lunsford L. Lomax."[65]

Then, once sunlight enabled everyone to see the landscape, the tired and war-weary Southerners began digging entrenchments. Bryan Grimes wrote, "we erected breastworks, and prepared for the advance of the enemy, and felt very secure of holding the position of the command in front. Were busily engaged day and night up to about one o'clock on the 22nd." Meanwhile, Gen. Early dealt with the loss of Robert Rodes by shifting Maj.

Gen. Dodson Ramseur from command of his division to take over leadership of Rodes' brigades. Brigadier General John Pegram was elevated from his brigade to assume Ramseur's old position. Bryan Grimes, now relieved of temporary division leadership duties, returned to his brigade. He solemnly wrote, "Ramseur has been assigned to this Division and Pegram to Ramseur's old command. Gen. Rodes' place cannot be supplied. He is a serious loss to the Confederacy."[66]

Equipment and rations were delivered to the riflemen, enabling Cpt. William Ardrey (Co. K) to record, "Fisher's Hill, Va. We received a supply of clothing."[67] Once the provisions were distributed, though, the troops resumed their digging. Fisher's Hill was to be a serious defensive position; the Confederates would not be attacking. The Southerners built "bull pens" out in front of the regimental entrenchments, which one soldier described these structures as "structure of rails ... thrown together and covered with earth, scattered along at intervals of ten or twelve yards ... [capable of holding] groups of five or six Rebels."[68] Brigadier General William Cox met with his regimental leaders and they hashed out picket duty rotations and defensive responsibilities. His brigade had suffered two hundred seventy-five losses at Winchester and now barely included five hundred riflemen able to bear arms.[69]

The next morning, September 21, 1864, Union skirmishers crept within the Confederates' danger zone to observe the Southern fortifications. They sent word to their commanders the defenses were formidable. One Federal officer reported, "[The Rebels had] strongly fortified an apparently impregnable position."[70] Another agreed, writing, "The Confederates ... rimmed the entire Union front, utilizing every advantage the terrain provided—knolls, large trees, fences and buildings."[71] Other Union officers surveyed the Confederate line and sought a way to discover its weakness. Later, the Southerners would discover the Northern had developed a strategy. An officer wrote, "Early ... took up a position that was very faulty as a line of defense, in that the right was very strong ... and the left very weak ... and the left was occupied by some of [the army's] less dependable troops."[72] Of course, for the riflemen in Cpt. John McMillan's regiment, they could only fortify their portion of the line, and assume everyone else was also fulfilling their responsibilities. A Tar Heel wrote, "the men cooked what rations they had and those who could, slept."[73]

September 22, 1864, began much as the previous morning, though now Confederate pickets reported to their commanders that more Yankees were hiding in the woods just out of musket range. Captain William Ardrey recorded, "Very quiet in the morning."[74] He and Cpt. McMillan had evaluated their men's battle readiness and came away worried. Their opinion was much like another officer whose men also appeared poorly equipped, and wrote, "A shortage of ammunition added to [our] concern ... [I] felt constrained to limit [our] response lest [the] troops empty their cartridge boxes."[75] McMillan passed his ammunition requirements to brigade headquarters; unfortunately, before the situation could be handled, Northern skirmishers emerged from their hiding spots and began to attack the Confederate picket line. A Southern staff officer noted, "At 9:30 a.m. they engaged our skirmishers quite earnestly ... but did not push forward much ... they only drove in our skirmish line."[76] General Early studied the Federals' tactics and concluded, "After some skirmishing he attained a strong position immediately in my front and fortified it, and I began to think he was satisfied with the advantage he had gained and would not ... press it further."[77]

Other Confederates were confident their defenses were strong enough to discourage the blue coats from making frontal assaults; one rifleman bragged, "Few in the ranks ... believed that the Yankees could take such a strong position from them in a head-on charge."[78] Captain John McMillan and his second-in-command, Cpt. William Ardrey rotated riflemen in and out of the their postings on the picket line. They kept part of their small regiment on duty in their main trench-works, and rested the remainder. The Thirtieth North Carolina now numbered just over one hundred twenty. The injuries to Cpt. David Allen (Co. C) and 1st Lt. John Downs (Co. K) meant there were only junior lieutenants to replace those lost veteran officers. The Tar Heels were tired, battle-weary, and suffering from lack of decent rations. One complained, "he was as sore as a boil all over and could speak barely above a whisper."[79]

Major General Philip Sheridan had studied the Southerners' defenses and concluded a frontal assault would prove disastrous; so he developed a different plan. Sheridan realized Gen. Early had made a serious mistake; the gray coat army's left flank was inadequately protected, and those troops who held that location were some of the Confederates' least effective soldiers. A Federal officer recorded Sheridan's strategy: "On the morning of the 22d, Crook, being still concealed, was marched to the timber near Little North Mountain and massed in it."[80] Philip Sheridan sent Maj. Gen. George Crook with four strong brigades to strike this vulnerable position.

30th North Carolina Infantry[81]
September 22, 1864

Unit		Strength
Field & Staff	Cpt. McMillan, John C. Cpt. Ardrey, William E.	3
Co. A	1st Sgt. Crumpler, Robert M.	9
Co. B	Cpl. Shearin, Thomas W.	8
Co. C	Sgt. Wescott, John W.	7
Co. D	—-	9
Co. E	2nd Lt. Newton, Samuel B.	17
Co. F	2nd Lt. House, James W.	17
Co. G	3rd Lt. Fulford, John T.	10
Co. H	Sgt. Harrington, Ard A.	12
Co. I	1st Sgt. Crowell, Jonas W.	13
Co. K	Sgt. Russell, William D.	19
		124

Major General Lumsford Lomax commanded the cavalry units holding the Confederate's left flank. His troopers were viewed with low regard, as they were believed to the ones who collapsed at Winchester. Lomax's formations were understrength, poorly outfitted, and drastically unsupplied. One of his officers complained, "I have seen my men many a time ... have the hoof of a dead horse strapped to their saddles, which they had cut off at the ankle with their pocket-knives, and would carry them until they could find a smith to take [the horseshoe] off with his nippers, and thus supply their sore-footed mounts." Another grumbled, "Most of the horsemen carried Enfield rifles, a cumbersome, nearly useless weapon in mounted combat."[82]

Major General George Crook's two divisions filed towards the Confederate left flank, heading for the heights of Little North Mountain. The hike was difficult and slow, though his infantrymen's movements were hidden by thick stands of trees. George Crook wrote, "I formed my command in two columns and marched them by the right flank along the mountainside." He continued, "I halted and brought up my rear division alongside of the first, and in this way marched the two by flank, so that when I faced [the Confederates] I would have two lines of battle parallel to each other."[83]

Meanwhile, Sheridan also repositioned the two brigades of Brig. Gen. James Rickett's division, sending them forward against Grimes' and Cox's defenses. The Tar Heels from these two brigades opened fire upon the Yanks, who immediately took cover. Major General Dodson Ramseur watched as the Carolinians stalled the blue coats and recorded, "a sizable body of Federals made its way toward [our] skirmishers posted on a hill half a mile north of the main battle line. Protected by piles of fence rails, the badly outnumbered Confederates stubbornly held their ground ... the attackers halted, wavered, and then retired."[84] But the blue coat riflemen did not retreat completely, instead, as a Federal officer in Ricketts's division wrote, "we moved from our works to the right and advanced along a ravine toward the Rebel left, where we lay in front of a strong earthwork."[85] The battlefield in front of the Tar Heels quieted down, though later in the afternoon, Southern riflemen posted on the far left noticed movement in the woods. They communicated this fact to their officers and the news was passed up the chain of command. Brigade commander, Bryan Grimes, whose men occupied the left flank of the main infantry line, requested reinforcements to counter this surprising development. The Tar Heel recorded, "I then urged upon Ramseur, who commanded our Division, to send a Brigade or two over to their assistance, knowing that the cavalry would run if attacked, but he declined to do so until he could communicate with Gen. Early."[86] Dodson Ramseur did not follow up, believing what Jubal Early had told him: an attack probably would not come at all.

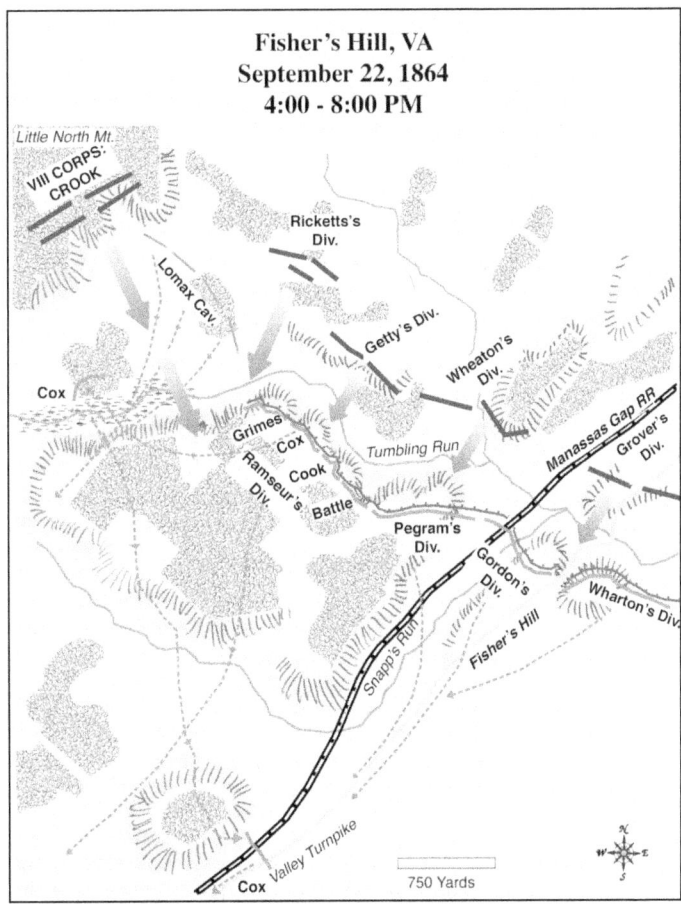

Jubal Early was wrong, and Ramseur's inaction only made the situation worse. Sometime around 5:00 p.m., George Crook had his four brigades positioned themselves on Little North Mountain, and he gave the order to attack. The Northerners, veteran soldiers mainly from Ohio and West Virginia surged downwards onto Lomax's troopers. One writer noted, "at about two hundred yards [we] hit the Confederate skirmishers."[87] General Crook bragged, "had the heavens opened up and we been seen descending from the clouds, no greater consternation would have been created." He added, "unless you have heard my fellows yell once ... you can form no conception of it. It beggars all description."[88] A Confederate officer in Lomax's command described what happened: "the [cavalry] ... was surprised, overlapped, and flanked." He continued, "they gave way ... and just vanished, making their way for the turnpike with all speed."[89]

Crook's men rushed forward, howling their intimidating yell, immediately overwhelming any thought of resistance. One Yank crowed, "The stunned defenders ... scattered at impact."[90] Another recorded, "Within minutes.... Lomax's troopers abandoned their works and the Federals roared down upon the Confederate flank, hitting Grimes' brigade simultaneously in left, front, and rear."[91] Bryan Grimes's Tar Heels resisted, fighting back from any position that offered cover. General Ramseur, seeing the disaster unfolding, sent a frantic order to Brig. Gen. William Cox to pull his men out of their entrenchments and rush to the northwest to counter the Federal onslaught.

William Cox's six small regiments abandoned their position and hurried towards the sounds of fighting. The Carolinians struggled through a dense patch of vegetation, down a slope, and back up onto a tree covered ridge. By now the sounds of shooting echoed though the small valley and seemed to come from everywhere, creating a problem for William Cox; if he was supposed to go to the sounds of the guns, but those sounds were everywhere, which way did he go? Cox halted his men and sent out skirmishers, hoping they could determine their next movement. His riflemen soon reported seeing fighting to the southwest—so Cox redirected his brigade's advance. However, what his lookouts had observed where portions of Lomax's fleeing cavalrymen. One of his Confederates remarked later, "Cox ... marching his six NC regiments towards the sounds of battle ... became confused and then lost in the wooded terrain. He obliqued his command toward the southwest, passed unseen beyond [Crook's] charging troops."[92]

General Philip Sheridan took advantage of the Confederate left flank's collapse by pressing forward his army, all along the front. Most of his blue coats advanced cautiously, as they knew the strength of the Southern lines, though the veterans in James Ricketts's brigade had watched as Grimes's men were being assailed from left and rear, and that Cox's Carolinians had withdrawn from their position. Ricketts's men charged forward, nearly unopposed, slamming into Grimes's riflemen, and spilling through the gap created by Cox's departure. Jubal Early watched in dismay as Bryan Grimes's Tar Heels were overcome and wrote, "After a very brief contest my ... force retired in considerable confusion."[93] Then, when Grimes's men retreated, the entire Confederate line shuddered; this was Winchester all over, the left had been flanked. Each of Early's brigades, one unit at a time, starting in the north and cascading to the south, peeled away from their entrenchments and retreated. A Southerner wrote, "the enemy 'poured in our flank and rear ... [the men were] stampeded and did not keep cool or fight as well as they have heretofore done."[94] Another wrote, "[We had] had enough, scattering pell-mell across the countryside."[95]

Meanwhile, William Cox's brigade floundered around in the trees, searching for the Northerners they were supposed to be fighting. The Tar Heels eventually brushed up against a portion of one of Crook's brigades, Cox's right flank regiments against Crooks' left-most units. In this quick exchange of musketry, Pvt. William Batts (Co. I) suffered, "a gunshot wound to the head," and Sgt. Aley Culp (Co. K) had a bullet punch its way through the flesh of his right leg. Moments later, Pvt. Jonathan Robins (Co. C), Pvt. Richard Phillips (Co. F), and Pvt. Orren Pierce (Co. K) were all wounded, and a handful of tired men captured.[96] William Cox wrote of this fight, "On moving to the left I had a brisk skirmish with a part of Crook's men, but did not encounter his main force." Then the two forces separated and once again Cox's men were by themselves. By now the Carolinian veteran knew the Confederate army was fleeing. General Cox added, "From the firing in the direction of our line it was soon apparent that our army was falling back."[97] One rifleman noted, "Our brigade was marched to the left to intercept them, which we were in the act of accomplishing, when the line to the right became demoralized by an enfilade fire from the enemy and commenced the stampede."[98] One rifleman noted, "Officers and enlisted men ... were all to aware of their own vulnerability."[99]

General Jubal Early's brigades were now all in flight, abandoning much of their equipment and supplies. Early groused, "the infantry got into a panic and gave way in confusion.... I am sorry to say many men threw away their arms."[100] A surprised and amused Federal recorded, "So rapid was his flight that he abandoned shelter-tents, blankets, and a considerable amount of infantry ammunition."[101] General Bryan Grimes added, "the troops on all sides were too much demoralized to make a successful fight, and it was fall back all the time, and I was carried along in the current ... when I found no support."[102] Many other Confederate soldiers no longer cared, and just tossed their muskets aside, sat down, and waited to be captured. A Northerner noted this, writing, "Some even surrendered willingly, telling their captors that they had had enough of poor rations and sound lickings."[103]

Brigadier General William Cox and his lost brigade fumbled its way through the dense vegetation, now heading south, attempting to locate the Valley Turnpike. The veteran riflemen were well aware their army was running away and they were frantic to find a way to escape capture. They reached the turnpike not long after sunset. William Cox recorded, "It was full dusk when we reached the road."[104] Major General Dodson Ramseur was nearby, having collected a handful of staunch defenders around him, and vainly trying to organize the clumps of distraught Confederates streaming past him. A Southerner wrote, "Maj. Gen. Ramseur, who was able to rally a thin line of stragglers ... [ordered Cox] to confront the enemy, which ... we [did].... Thus being reinforced, we made a good line of battle to hold the enemy."[105] William Cox noted, "My brigade [was] thrown across the road to cover the retreat. The brigade was promptly formed, advanced rapidly to a fence."[106]

30th North Carolina Infantry[107]
Fisher's Hill Casualties
September 22, 1864

Unit	Commander	Loss
Field & Staff	Cpt. McMillan, John C.	-
Co. A	1st Sgt. Crumpler, Robert M.	2
Co. B	Cpl. Shearin, Thomas W.	-

Unit	Commander	Loss
Co. C	Sgt. Wescott, John W.	2
Co. D	—	2
Co. E	2nd Lt. Newton, Samuel B.	3
Co. F	2nd Lt. House, James W.	1
Co. G	3rd Lt. Fulford, John T.	3
Co. H	Sgt. Harrington, Ard A.	-
Co. I	1st Sgt. Crowell, Jonas W.	2
Co. K	Sgt. Russell, William D.	3
		18

It was dark now, but the danger remained; the Carolinians could hear the sounds of an approaching body of men, and by the accents of the officers giving orders, the veteran Tar Heels knew these fellows were Yankees. The Confederates opened fire on the advancing shadows, causing one of the Union commanders to record, "About 9:30 p.m. our skirmish line was fired upon ... [by] musketry and artillery.... The enemy was evidently prepared to meet us at this point; wood and other obstacles had been placed to delay [our] ... line."[108] A small portion of the blue coats' skirmish line made contact with the Tar Heels and a brief melee occurred. William Cox remarked, "The brigade [skirmishers] ... met the Federals in a hand-to-hand encounter."[109] The Yanks quickly withdrew, but not before taking with them a few more Carolinians as prisoners. Complete darkness prevented the Northerners from launching a final assault against the beleaguered Confederates and the sounds of war subsided. General Ramseur withdrew his followers and William Cox's Carolinians, ordering them to march southwards, away from Fisher's Hill, and another scene of a Confederate defeat. A gray-coated rifleman wrote, "we had no further trouble with them that night, and enjoyed a quiet march."[110]

Captain John McMillan's veterans trudged up the Valley Turnpike, stunned by this latest debacle. They had fought well, held their ground, and yet had been betrayed by the cavalry again. The Thirtieth's NCOs took a quick head count and come up with the news another eighteen no longer answered when their names were called. Jubal Early's army was haggard and defeated. General Early reported to Robert E. Lee the fight at Fisher's Hill had cost 30 killed, 210 wounded and a 1,000 missing, "a figure he estimated only half [of whom] were captured by the Federals."[111] One Southern officer noted, "I found the morale of the army very bad."[112] The Confederates reached Rude's Hill around 9:00 a.m. on September 23, 1864. By now, aggressive Federal cavalry units had caught up with the tail-end Southern units and skirmished with Early's rear guard. The battered gray coat units formed into a battle line along Rude's Hill's slopes and prepared to stave off a full-fledged Union assault. Brigade General Grimes recorded, "We remained until 12 o'clock, when we found that they were flanking us in the same manner that they had done on the two previous occasions, and Gen. Early then began to withdraw us in line of battle."[113] Then, once a strong rear-guard force was deployed, the Confederates returned to the Valley Turnpike and continued to retreat. Captain William Ardrey (Co. K) noted, "Retreated all day under heavy fire, the hardest day's march we ever had.... I would have been captured if it had not been for Capt. McMillen's horse that I road a while."[114] Jubal Early wrote, "We moved up the valley during the succeeding days ... until we reached New Market."[115]

On September 25, 1864, the Thirtieth hiked another fifteen miles, before halting not far from Port Republic. Alexander Betts noted, "Pass Kernstown, Port Republic, and camp near Brown's Gap."[116] The Yanks continued to crowd behind the retreating Southerners, forcing William Cox's regiments to turn around, form line of battle, and fire volleys to discourage this closeness. The retreat continued; two days later the Tar Heels camped near Weyer's Cave, a formation attracting the interest of many. Alexander Betts, whose duties allowed him more free time than most of the rest of the men in the Thirtieth, wrote, "[We] cross above Weir's Cave, driving cavalry, return and camp near cave. I visit the cave. Grand sight! Eternal night! Many rooms connected by narrow, crooked, rough passages."[117]

The next day, September 28, 1864, they reached Waynesboro, and here, the tired men were allowed to rest. The month of September had been a disaster; Robert Rodes' old division had been reduced to just a little above two thousand; Cox's brigade was less than five hundred; and the 30th NC's final count for the month produced a number of one hundred-twenty, and of those, thirty were absent for various reasons.[118] Captain John McMillan's veterans were weary of war, but they knew the Yankees were not far away and ready to pounce whenever the Southerners let down their guard. They agreed with Brig. Gen. Bryan Grimes, who admitted, "Our men as well as officers [have lost] confidence in Genrl. Early's ability to conduct a campaign."[119]

Chapter 16

Cedar Creek: Jubal Early Is Flanked Again

On October 1, 1864, Jubal Early moved his army to the Mount Sidney area and gave orders for his men to rest. General Early planned no more retreating, and had no ideas of counter attacking. His weary soldiers fashioned shelters and spread out, foraging for food. A cold rain drenched the countryside, turning roads into muddy morasses, and chilling the Southerners. Alexander Betts recorded, "Move through rain and mud [to] camp."[1] The Carolinians rested and listened to rumors. One wrote, "The enemy are reported to be falling back down the Valley, which I hope is so."[2] Then, by October 8, 1864, Gen. Early's scouts had determined Sheridan's forces were withdrawing, enabling the aggressive Southerner to roust his men and commence another advance. Early wrote, "When it was discovered that the enemy was retiring I moved forward at once."[3] The Confederate riflemen sullenly formed up and reluctantly marched, because, as one soldier wrote what many felt, "our army is daily diminishing ... [we] felt and maintained that there was [little] hope for our success."[4] Others added, there was a "strong feeling that few liked and respected Gen. Early."[5]

The Federals slowly back-peddled down the Valley Turnpike with Early's soldiers grudgingly trailing behind them. Brigadier Gen. Bryan Grimes remarked, "Again on the march following the enemy," and by October 13, 1864, the Confederates found themselves, as Cpt. William Ardrey (Co. K) acknowledged, "[on] Fisher's Hill ... in line of battle."[6] The gray-clad forces spread out along Fisher's Hill's defensive positions and stared at the Northerners occupying the ground on the other side of Cedar Creek. Jubal Early wrote, "The enemy was found posted on the north bank of Cedar Creek, in a very strong position and in strong force." The Confederate senior commanded quickly realized his army was faced with a dilemma; his men lacked rations and military supplies. He recorded, "I was now compelled to move back for want of provisions and forage, or attack the enemy in his position with the hope of driving him from it."[7]

30th North Carolina Infantry[8]
October 18, 1864

Unit		Strength
Field & Staff	Cpt. McMillan, John C.	
	Cpt. Ardrey, William E.	4
	Cpt. Moore, Willis B.	
Co. A	1st Sgt. Crumpler, Robert M.	7
Co. B	Cpl. Shearin, Thomas W.	9

Unit		Strength
Co. C	Sgt. Butler, Benjamin C.	7
Co. D	—-	8
Co. E	2nd Lt. Newton, Samuel B.	14
Co. F	2nd Lt. House, James W.	16
Co. G	3rd Lt. Fulford, John T.	8
Co. H	Sgt. Harrington, Ard A.	12
Co. I	1st Sgt. Crowell, Jonas W.	11
Co. K	Sgt. Russell, William D.	18
		114

The Veteran riflemen in the Thirtieth studied the strong Yankee positions and shook their heads. They had seen so many of their brothers-in-arms killed or wounded in the past couple months, and their army had nothing to show for this loss. The Thirtieth remained under the command of Cpt. John McMillan, and its surviving men were clustered together in two amalgamated companies, one led by Cpt. William Ardrey (Co. K) and the other by Cpt. Willis Moore (Co. F). The regiment had been ground down to less than one hundred twenty Tar Heels, and a good number of them were hobbled by exhaustion, poor rations, and illness.

The Thirtieth North Carolina was the largest regiment in William Cox's brigade, as all the units had been reduced to skeletal size, resulting in the entire brigade's fighting force barely reaching six hundred. The 1st and 3rd NC existed as a combined, company-sized formation, while all the rest of the brigade's regiments numbered one hundred, or less riflemen answering their names to roll calls. No regiment was led by a field-grade officer, and the 4th NC was now commanded by a second lieutenant. And nearly every man in the brigade held the thought, "As sensible men, then, why should they sacrifice their limbs or lives for a hopeless cause, however righteous?"[9]

Jubal Early, ignoring the plight of his soldiers, made plans to attack. Captain William Ardrey (Co. K) remarked, "[We were] ordered to prepare two days rations and to leave our canteens and everything that would make a noise in camp."[10] The Carolinians gobbled what food they had, shed the prohibited gear, and formed into marching formation; their order of march—Battle's brigade, then Cook, Cox, and Grimes.[11] Then, once the sun dipped below the western horizon, orders came to move. A rifleman recorded, "We left camp … about twilight."[12] The Southerners trudged through the darkness, stumbling quietly towards the northeast, guided by rumors they were going to sneak around the Federals' flank and strike them from the rear. One soldier wrote, "Silently we moved, sometimes in cow paths and sometimes just through the dense woods."[13] Another added, "the only sound was the continued tread of the men and the oft-repeated command, 'Close up.'"[14] And Pvt. John Bone (Co. I) remarked, "that night we marched down the Creek over muddy hills. The way was so narrow and rough that we had to get in one rank and use our guns against the ground to keep from going down hill too fast."[15]

A moon arose later that night, giving the struggling soldiers slight assistance as they splashed across an icy river. Captain William Ardrey scribbled, "we waded the Shenandoah river and O! but it was cold, for there was a big frost on the ground."[16] Then, once across the Shenandoah, the riflemen bumped to a halt as their leaders worked to maneuver the

Confederate brigades into a battle line. The eastern sky was brightening, but for the Tar Heel riflemen, they could see little. One wrote, "At the break of day ... quite a fog or mist hung over the river."[17] They huddled, shivering, waiting mutely for orders, smelling smoke from camp fires floating down upon them, coming from the nearby Union bivouac. Finally, word came to move, Maj. Gen. John Gordon, commanding this flanking force began shifting his brigades. Jubal Early wrote, "We got in sight of the enemy's fires.... The moon was now shining and we could see the camps."[18] Private John Bone (Co. I) noted, "We were on the Eastside of the enemy. We waded and formed line of battle and moved forward."[19] Brigadier Gen. Bryan Grimes recorded, "[After crossing river] "we were faced to the left and ordered forward, changing direction to the right.... Cook and Cox continued to advance, swinging to the right."[20]

The Confederate's skirmishers quickly overran the blue coats' pickets, shooting or capturing nearly every man within just a couple moments, and then the entire Southern force crashed into the Federal camp. One gray-coated private boasted, "we moved ... quickly ... with the Rebel yell ringing out above all other sounds."[21] Another wrote, "A few flashes of musketry, a few shots of artillery, and we had the works, guns and all, surprising the enemy."[22] One blue coat admitted, "What ensued in the fog along the breastworks ... was a blind, confused, feeble scuffle."[23] A soldier in the 4th NC wrote, "The surprise was complete, and the enemy fled from his tents without arms, and many of the men in their night clothes."[24] Captain William Ardrey agreed, writing, "We captured their pickets and entered their camp before they knew of our approach and they ran like turkeys and in their night clothing and left all their baggage behind."[25]

The Tar Heels milled among the Federal tents, shocked by how easily they had crushed an entire division. Brief skirmishes erupted as small clumps of Northerners resisted, but for the most part, the Confederates just rounded up the distraught Yankees. One jubilant Southerner exclaimed, "I ... captured three Yankees who were scared to death. They had proposed to give up all they had, but I demanded only their guns and cartridge boxes. After emptying their guns at another squad of them near by and filling my cartridge box with cartridges, I ordered them to the rear, keeping one of their new guns."[26] Another added, "Many were still asleep, many came rushing out of tents in all styles of dishabille, without shoes, hats, or coats, and ... nearly all were captured."[27] And another gloated, "It was a complete surprise. Men were captured in bed, not knowing we were nearer than Fisher's Hill."[28] This dramatic success caused concern though, among the Tar Heel leaders; Cpt. William Ardrey noted, "It was a great success for us. We captured their artillery and all their baggage but our troops became demoralized."[29]

The sun had arisen by now, glowing dimly in the thick fog and casting odd shadows throughout the abandoned Union camp. The gray-coated riflemen gawked at what lie before them, eyeing the deserted tents, noticing clean blankets, brand-new uniforms, warm overcoats, and untold collections of personal articles. They also could see stacks of tinned food, boxes of rations, and piles of fresh meat. The hungry soldiers began to fan out among the abandoned company streets, each man hustling in search of what he needed. But Gen. Gordon wanted to crush the Yanks; the spoils could be acquired later, so he ordered his officers to collect their scattered riflemen. The Confederate officers pushed and shoved their frustrated enlisted men back into battle ranks and marched them away from the treasure-trove of prizes.

The fog limited everyone's line of sight, though sounds of musketry told the Southern veterans more blue coats awaited. One Confederate noted, "The sun was now rising, but

The Confederates surprised the Federals on the morning of October 19, 1864 (Johnson & Buel,

in low places fog hung heavily. Smoke drifted and shifted."[30] Another added, "The fog obscured the magnitude of the Union defeat and rout which occurred in the span of less than thirty minutes."[31] This thick mist prevented the Southern infantrymen from seeing two entire Northern corps, the XIX and the VII, retreating. A Federal officer confessed, "[We] scattered and [ran] before the charging Rebels."[32] Later, an officer would report, "Nothing affected the initial three hours of combat more than the fog, which thickened because of the smoke from discharged black powder. The blanket of mist shielded the charging Southerners, reduced their casualties and increased the confusion in Northern ranks as the Federals fashioned patchwork lines against an unseen opponent."[33]

General William Cox's Confederates pushed forward through the fog, feeling for the next blue coat formation, causing one rifleman to write, "We pressed onward and soon struck another brigade … which had been awakened and were a little better prepared, but still were looking more to making an escape than to making a stand."[34] William Cox's Tar Heels advanced across the pastures of the Belle Grove plantation, trampling over any body of blue coats they encountered. Northern resistance was brief and limited, and the Carolinians moved steadily, suffering almost no casualties. Then, to the veterans in the Carolinians' surprise, their battle line was ordered to halt. Captain John McMillan rushed to Brig. Gen. William Cox to find out why their advance had stopped. Staff officers informed him the brigade was advancing too quickly, and was in danger of being flanked. Later, Bryan Grimes recorded, "Cox continued to advance, swinging to the right, driving the enemy in their front with but slight resistance for upward of half a mile ... [then] Gen. Cox report[ed] that he was flanked on the left, [and] a temporary halt was made until reinforcements were sent forward."[35]

By now the sun's heat pushed the mists down into the river's shallows, and as the Confederates moved across the Belle Grove fields they ascended a gentle slope and emerged from the fog's cloaking blindness. General Cox's Tar Heels could see a strong force of blue coats lining the heights before them. These Northerners appeared staunch and ready to repel a frontal assault. One Southern rifleman gazed at the Yanks and remarked, "On [we] rushed to Belle Grove ... where they were in readiness with a fresh division to meet us."[36] Another added, "[we] ran them until we were completely broken down, when we were halted and a line of battle formed. This was about nine or ten o'clock in the morning."[37] Meanwhile, one of these Yanks wrote, "We fell back three miles before we could get a chance to form a line. We done it and checked the rebels."[38]

The riflemen from the two forces glared at each other, both waiting for the other to make a move, but nothing happened. The Carolinians could see more Confederate brigades forming to their right and left, and at the same time, watched as additional Yank troops jammed themselves into a battle line on the heights. Captain John McMillan's veterans knew the next movement would be against soldiers who no longer were surprised and frightened. Then, to their surprise the blue coats about-faced and marched away.

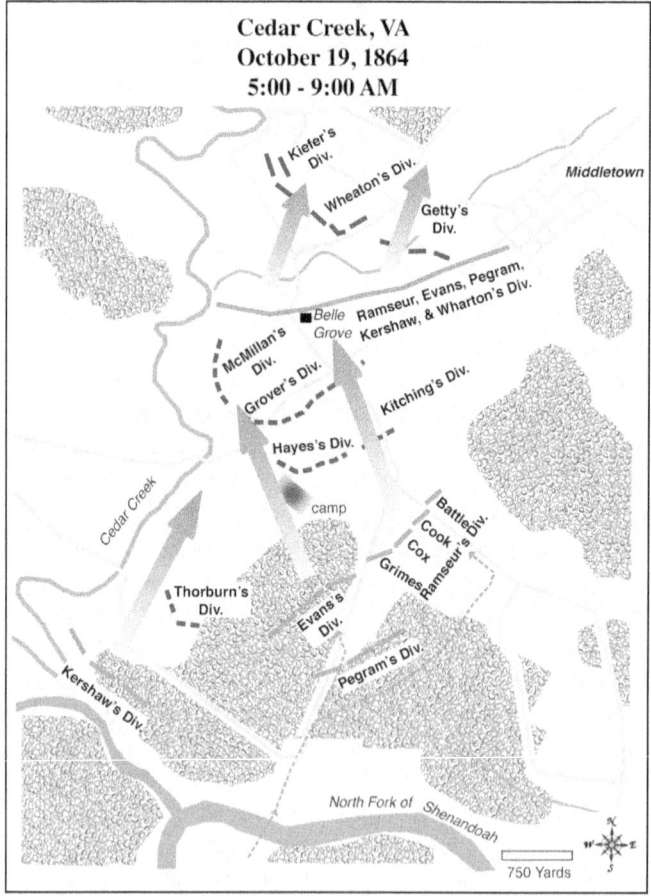

One of these Northerners later wrote, "Between 9 and 10 o'clock, the VI Corps fell back to the 'third position.'"[39] General Gordon, observing the Federals retreating, sent his brigades forward to capture the deserted ridgeline. A Confederate officer recorded, "By 10 a.m. we had formed a new line, extending through Middletown at right angles to the pike and along the Cedarville road on the right.... Gordon was on the left ... then Kershaw came across the ridge, then Ramseur down the slope to Meadow Run; Pegram from that up to the turnpike."[40]

The Confederates halted, dressed their battle lines, and paused. Bryan Grimes wrote, "Upon this hill the division was reformed, cartridge boxes refilled, and [the troops] rested upward of an hour."[41] William Cox's regiments were ordered to the right, and placed a hundred yards behind Battle's brigade. The Carolinians smiled at each other; they were no longer in any danger. A Tar Heel noted, "Cox's brigade [was] in reserve and behind a stone fence."[42] Rumors quickly flooded the Thirtieth; the Yankees were preparing to retreat—they had been badly beaten today. Private Richard Brooks (Co. G) recalled, "it was a stunning victory and [Gen.] Early, believing the enemy beaten, halted his tired troops to eat and rest."[43] Another rifleman added, "[Gen. Early said] 'We have had enough glory for one day.'"[44] However, Gen. Jubal Early's thoughts on his troops' success this morning were tempered by his knowledge of their fragile condition. As he observed the newly forming Union position three-quarters of a mile from his troops, Early knew his men lacked provisions and were poorly supplied. General Early recorded, "It was apparent that it would not do to press my troops further. They had been up all night and were much jaded.... I determined, therefore, to try and hold what had been gained ... and I hoped that the day was finally ours."[45]

Captain John McMillan's riflemen glanced back at the abandoned Union camps, just like all the other Southern enlisted men filling the Confederate ranks that morning. They all were hungry, thirsty, and poorly outfitted, and gazed enviously at the answer to their desperate needs. The soldiers began to sneak away from their defensive position; first, singly, then in twos, and eventually in small groups. One rifleman explained their situation, writing, "The world will never know the extreme poverty of the Confederate soldier at this time. Hundreds of men who were in the charge and who captured the enemy's works were barefooted. Every one of them was ragged.... Many of the tents were open, and in plain sight were rations, shoes, overcoats, and blankets." He continued, "The temptation to stop and eat was too great. Since most of them had had nothing to eat since the evening before, they yielded. While some tried on shoes, others put on warm pants in place of tattered ones. Still others got overcoats and blankets—articles so much needed for the coming cold."[46]

The Thirtieth's riflemen scurried among the captured Yankee company streets, gleefully pillaging the tents, hunting to acquire their urgently needed essentials—food, clothing, blankets, tools, and tent-cloth. One excited Southerner recalled, "Our men, feeling victory was complete, gave way to the disposition to clothe themselves from the enemy's camp.... Fully one third of our army could have been found away from their commands."[47] Another wrote, "We just couldn't resist all them good things we captured."[48] Captain McMillan's NCOs also accompanied the scrounging hordes and made a point of making sure every man obtained a new weapon. The Thirtieth's riflemen went into the fight at Cedar Creek armed with a mixture of .58 caliber Enfields and .69 caliber smoothbores, however, by 3:00 p.m. on October 19, 1864, the entire regiment carried brand new Enfields.[49]

General Jubal Early learned of the mobs absent from his army's battle line and immediately gave commands to drive the men back to their units. Early wrote, "I had discovered a number of men in the enemy's camps plundering, and [I] ordered one of Wharton's battalions to clear the camps and drive the men to their commands." He continued, writing in frustration, "It was reported to me subsequently that a great number [of Wharton's men] were at the same work."[50] The merry looters would not return, instead they sacked the entire camp, and as the hours went by, more and more of them acquired liquor. A Carolinian rifleman admitted, "we were all drunk from 'Old Jube' down to us privates in the rear rank."[51] This pilfered alcohol found its way back to the battle line, causing one officer to record, "As the forenoon passed, the thought of the wreck of his Divisions by absentees began to sap Early's soldierly vigor."[52]

Meanwhile, as the Confederate's combat strength rotted, the Federals' fortunes rose. General Philip Sheridan arrived, accompanied by fresh reinforcements, and immediately worked to improve his soldiers' morale. One blue-coated rifleman acknowledged, "[Sheridan] came to the front, and rode along the lines, telling the boys to fear nothing, stand firm, and he would make the enemy sleep on their own side of the creek that night, if they sleep at all." The Yank added, "The boys cheered all along the line, long and loud."[53] Then, sometime after 3:00 p.m., Sheridan ordered an attack. A wave of blue coats cautiously approached the Confederate line. Bryan Grimes noted, "At half past three P. M, our skirmishers were driven in and the enemy advanced their line of battle. [We] 'double-quicked' upon the line ... to meet this advance on the part of the enemy, and Cox moved up on a line with Cook and to his left." The Tar Heel continued, "[The Yankees'] advance was repulsed most gallantly, the enemy fleeing in disorder and confusion, throwing down their arms and battle flags in their retreat."[54] Another Confederate officer added, "supported by batteries to the rear, [we] scorched the Federals."[55]

The blue coats spilled back towards their main line and moments later, fresh, undefeated troops replaced them. The Confederates shook their heads in dismay; this was their most serious problem—there were so many more Yankees than Southerners. Captain John McMillan's NCOs checked his two amalgamated formations; this brief exchange of musketry had resulted in a couple Thirtieth casualties. The wounded veterans were hauled away for medical care. The last pillagers returned to the Thirtieth's ranks, loaded with treasures, but also driven by the need to stand beside their relatives and friends. One rifleman noted, "What a sight! Here came the stragglers, who looked like half the army, laden with every imaginable kind of plunder—some with an eye for comfort, had loaded themselves with new tent cloths, nice blankets, overcoats, or pants."[56] Moments later, the blue coats appeared to form up for another assault. A Confederate officer wrote, "The enemy having time to rally, had collected in rear of the large body of woods in our front and formed a line of battle and advanced at 4:30 p.m."[57]

Captain John McMillan's riflemen hunkered down behind a stone fence, not far from a mill located along a creek called Meadow Branch. Their field of fire was limited by a stand of trees not more than seventy-five yards away. The veteran riflemen looked behind them and saw a Confederate battery of cannon deploying. When they glanced to their left and right they saw their brothers from the other brigades in the division, all primed to cripple the next Union attack. The open space between the two battle lines grew quiet for a brief span of time as the veterans, both North and South, waited for Sheridan's orders. This strange hush was soon shattered by bugles, causing one soldier to write, "Minutes before [five] o'clock, from one end of the Union infantry line to another, buglers blared the charge—one account placed the number at 200."[58] Three Federal divisions stepped forward as the martial music ebbed away, advancing toward the Confederate battle line. The Carolinians opened fire on the approaching blue coats, quickly knocking down scores. One writer recorded, "Tarheel infantrymen, at the mill and on the ridgeline, flailed at the slow-marching Yankees while Southern batteries, behind the Carolinians and east of the turnpike, shredded [their] ranks."[59] The Northern line shuddered and staggered to a halt. The hard-pressed Yanks leveled their weapons and sent a volley into the Confederate position. A few of Cpt. McMillan's men dropped, including Sgt. Maj. Francis Fitts, who was wounded; Pvt. Jeremiah Bailey (Co. D) with a bullet through his chest; and Cpt. Willis Moore (Co. F), killed.[60]

The Southerners fired as rapidly as they could load their newly acquired Enfields and moments later, the Union line dissolved. A soldier remarked, "The line wavered and then cracked, with the men pouring back into the woods."⁶¹ The Yanks withdrew to the safety of the wood lot, turning and firing as they retreated, injuring a couple more Thirtieth veterans, and killing Pvt. Green Elliott (Co. G).⁶² Once the Northerners were hiding among the trees the two sides exchanged a slow, desultory fire for the next few minutes. Then, unsettling rumors began to flash along the Southern line, sweeping from left to right—the Confederate left had been flanked. A Southern officer grumbled, "At the time our troops [Grimes-Cox-Cook] were cheering for this repulse the enemy ... [attacked] on our left [and] our troops retreated without any organization."⁶³

General Philip Sheridan, along with sending his divisions forward to confront the whole of the Confederate line, also sent cavalry sweeping around his right flank to crash into Jubal Early's left. This flanking maneuver, the same tactic that had worked at Winchester and at Fisher's Hill, proved effective again. Sheridan sent Brig. Gen. George

Cpt. Willis Moore (Co. F), 25 years old, was killed at Cedar Creek on October 19, 1864 (Clark, 1901).

Custer with his division of horseman to strike the Confederate left, and his brigades easily rolled over the unprepared Southerners. George Custer reported, "The skirmishers of the enemy were easily driven from the ridge ... produc[ing] the utmost confusion and great wavering in his ranks."⁶⁴

Custer's cavalry swept aside the Confederate's left flank and galloped towards the Southern infantry line, approaching from the left and from behind. The Southern infantry brigades began to peel away from their battle line, dissolving one regiment at a time, the disaster moving from their left, and proceeding to the right. Jubal Early complained, "the men, under the apprehension of being flanked, commenced falling back in disorder ... the mass of them resisted all appeals [to reform] and continued to go to the rear."⁶⁵ A Yank officer crowed, "A gallant and brilliant charge was made, driving the enemy in scattered and broken squads from [their] positions."⁶⁶ The Confederate line collapsed, much like a line of dominos, as the men of each regiment suddenly found themselves at risk of being attacked from flank and rear. A few staunch units fought back, but they were quickly swept aside. One Confederate officer remarked, "Regiment after regiment, brigade after brigade, in rapid succession was crushed ... and like hard clods of clay under a pelting rain, the superb commands crumbled to pieces."⁶⁷

The Tar Heels in Brig. Gen. William Cox's men convulsed in apprehension, battered by the shouted tattle coming from their left. Bryan Grimes wrote, "Our left wing shamefully gave way, which necessitated the drawing in of our lines, which was done in considerable confusion."⁶⁸ The sounds of disaster crept closer to the Carolinians, eating at their morale, and the less courageous men began to slip away from the battle line. The cry, "we are flanked," now became the only words anyone heard. William Cox ordered his brigade to withdraw, even though his troops had firmly held their portion of the defense. An officer in the 14th NC noted, "The humiliations of defeat fell thick and fast upon the dwindling numbers of our people."⁶⁹ The retreat quickly dissolved into confusion. One Veteran noted, "We did not even see the [Federal] line of battle where I was when we broke."⁷⁰ A member of the 4th NC added, "We were simply overpowered by numbers."⁷¹ And, Bryan Grimes recalled, "The Yankee Cavalry [had] charged and completely routed our men. It was impossible to check the flight, officers and men behaving shamefully."⁷²

Once William Cox's brigade disintegrated, Cpt. John McMillan's veterans raced to the south, each man struggling to escape capture. A number of them encountered a cluster of stalwart Confederates gathered around Maj. Gen. Dodson Ramseur, who was organizing a new defensive line. Ramseur's loyalists created a clot in the panicked soldiers' flight and a few more troopers joined his group, but most of the Southerners just swept on past. A Confederate recalled, "Ramseur heard the cry, 'We are flanked' and saw many of his own men make for the rear. In an effort to keep his brigades in hand, he ordered them back 200 yards to a stone wall on a hill just southwest of Miller's Mill."⁷³ Moments later, Gen. Dodson Ramseur slumped to the ground. A nearby officer described Ramseur's injury, writing, "Ramseur was standing on the ground with his left arm raised to his horse's mane to mount when the ball struck him under the arm, passing entirely through to the right side, lodging just under the skin."⁷⁴ Another officer recalled, "I ran over to him, got some men, and bore him to the rear.... I then went off after an ambulance.... We got him then [in]to the ambu-

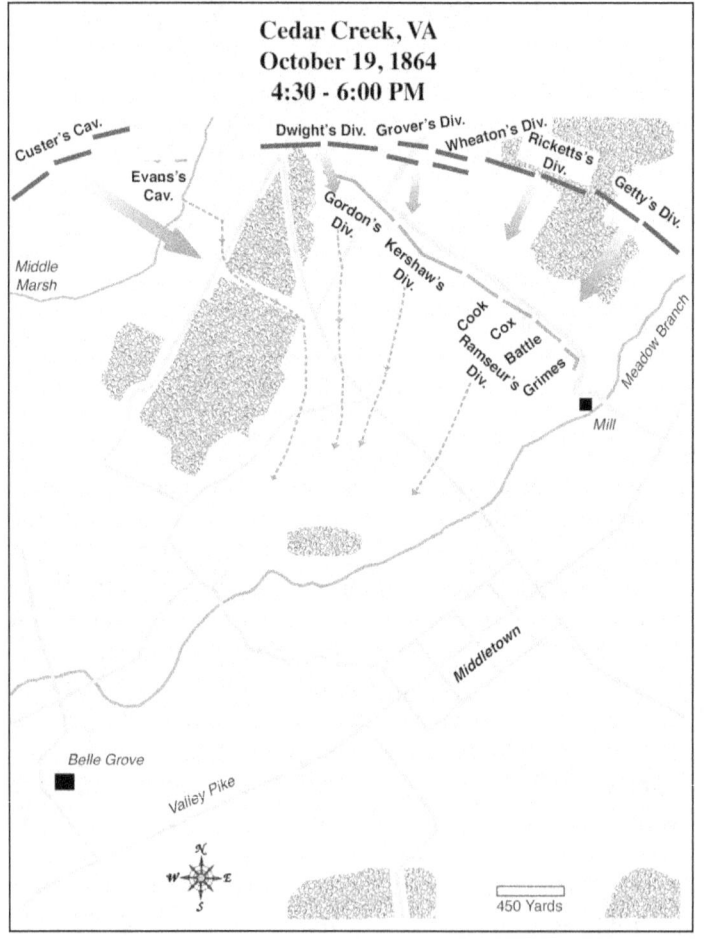

lance I had brought up. I thought he was safe then, not knowing how dangerous was his wound ... [We were] subsequently captured by the enemy's cavalry."[75]

Once Gen. Ramseur fell the remaining infantrymen fled. Private John Bone (Co. I) summed up their disorganized flight: "Our brigade was one of the last to fall back. We were flanked on each side, until we came very near all being captured." He continued, "many of the men got very much confused and in some places fell back in bad order.... When we had to give way we ... had to make the best of it. Every man was looking out for himself."[76] Another Confederate added, "The soldiers were not scared. It was not a panic, it was not fear of the enemy or want of loyalty that caused the rout. [We] were demoralized [and] had lost confidence in the ultimate success of the cause, in each other, and in Gen. Early."[77]

General Custer's troopers flooded the countryside, chasing down the fleeing gray coats. He boasted, "the disorganized masses of the enemy, now completely panic-stricken, threw away their arms, and in a headlong and disgraceful manner sought safety in ignominious flight."[78] A Southern officer sadly agreed, writing, "A terror of the enemy's cavalry had seized [the troops] and there was no holding them."[79] Private John Bone (Co. I) admitted, "I ran until I was very warm and had to stop and walk. The balls and shells were striking all around me. A ball struck between my feet.... I ... passed an old house where a great pile of men were behind for protection, but they were captured."[80] George Custer added, "That which ... had been a pursuit after a broken and routed enemy now resolved itself into an exciting chase after a panic-stricken, uncontrollable mob. It no longer was a question to be decided by force ... it was simply a question of speed between pursuers and pursued; prisoners were taken by the hundreds."[81] Captain William Ardrey remarked, "I was completely exhausted and would have been captured, but for the help of Bill Jack Ross [Co. K]. He carried all my baggage and asked a cavalry man to let me ride behind him across the river and Bill waded the river swinging to the horse's tail.... So we landed safe on the other side."[82]

Darkness put a halt to the Northerners' aggressiveness. Custer noted, "The pursuit was not slackened until the advance ... passed through and beyond Strasburg ... [then] owning to the darkness ... that was only relieved here and there by the light of a burning wagon or ambulance ... detachments of my men soon began returning from the advance."[83] A Tar Heel agreed, "Night, blessed night, and darkness stopped the pursuit."[84] The Carolinians stumbled southward until eventually reaching their old camping grounds, with Bryan Grimes recording, "About seven o'clock arrived at a place on Fisher's Hill, where we halted to endeavor to gather up the stragglers and rearrange our troops ... all was confusion and disorder."[85] Here, as the night's hours slowly ticked by, the broken regiments reformed. Alexander Betts recorded, "Heavy fight ... but our lines are broken in p.m. and we suffer much.... We fall back to Fisher's Hill ...Capt. Moore of Co. F is killed. Mr. Elliot [Co. G] ... killed."

30th North Carolina Infantry[86]
Cedar Creek Casualties
October 19, 1864

Unit	Commander	Loss
Field & Staff	Cpt. McMillan, John C.	2
Co. A	1st Sgt. Crumpler, Robert M.	1

Unit	Commander	Loss
Co. B	Cpl. Shearin, Thomas W.	2
Co. C	Sgt. Butler, Benjamin C.	1
Co. D	—-	2
Co. E	2nd Lt. Newton, Samuel B.	4
Co. F	2nd Lt. House, James W.	2
Co. G	3rd Lt. Fulford, John T.	1
Co. H	Sgt. Harrington, Ard A.	-
Co. I	1st Sgt. Crowell, Jonas W.	1
Co. K	Sgt. Russell, William D.	3
		19

Captain John McMillan's surviving NCOs collected the disheveled men and determined how badly the unit suffered during the retreat. They worked all night and by sunrise on October 20, 1864, Cpt. McMillan knew the names of killed, wounded, and missing, the Thirtieth had lost nineteen. One Tar Heel groaned, "A great victory had been won only to be thrown away."[87] Another wrote, "In the three battles within a month we were much reduced in numbers ... [and] our men were much scattered."[88] Captain William Ardrey scribbled in his journal, "Our army was worse demoralized than ever before and you could scarcely get a corporal's guard in any company."[89] The Northerners, though, triumphantly returned to the camps they had been driven from on the nineteenth. They shuffled among their tents, shocked by the destruction the Confederates had created. One enlisted man wrote, "we found that most of our dead were stripped to the skin ... when they came to one of our men that had good clothes (and there were a great many, because we drew clothing the day before), they just pulled off their lousy clothes and appropriated those that were on the dead."[90]

A few hours after sunrise on October 20, 1864, Union pickets hollered across Cedar Creek and passed the word to their Confederate counterparts; General Dodson Ramseur had died. The wounded general had been captured during the retreat's confusion, and because he was widely known and respected by many Federal officers, Ramseur had been taken to the Belle Grove mansion. A Confederate officer captured with Ramseur who remained with the mortally wounded general wrote, "Several old friends from West Point, now Union officers, visited Ramseur's bedside ... [including] George Custer and Wesley Merritt." He added, "[Philip] Sheridan offered every assistance in his power."[91]

The news about Ramseur, along with the crushing effects caused by more senseless deaths in another pointless defeat smothered the Confederate infantrymen. Captain William Ardrey mourned, "Gen. Ramseur and Capt. Wm. B. Moore were killed.... Two braver officers had never fallen.... We all loved and honored Ramseur. He is a great loss to the army."[92] Ardrey and Cpt. John McMillan reorganized their remaining veterans into one formation and divided it into two platoons, each to be commanded by a second lieutenant. McMillan met with the other captains in the brigade and William Cox instructed them to prepare to move, Gen. Early wanted his army to withdraw. The Confederates stumbled out of the Fisher's Hill defenses and trudged southward, with one Southerner noting, "We retreated up the Valley [that] morning."[93] The morose Southerners took two days to relocate themselves around New Market, a hike of thirty miles. General Jubal

Early commanded his supply division to provide rations and equipment to his dejected troops, but there was little he could do to restore his men's morale. One rifleman summed up how Early's men felt, writing, "The army of the Valley of Virginia never recovered from that defeat."[94]

General Philip Sheridan did not order his army to follow the Confederates; instead, he refitted his battered corps in the area around Cedar Creek. Sheridan sent out patrols to watch the sullen Southerners, but little action occurred; the two armies were fought out. Brigadier General Bryan Grimes was placed in command of Ramseur's division and he assigned the different brigades guard and fatigue duties. The next couple weeks went by very quietly, with neither side making aggressive moves, though one Yank officer did note, "Jubal occasionally came up to the front and barked, but there was no more bite in him."[95] Captain William Ardrey described the Thirtieth's activity, writing, "In camp and on picket."[96] On November 1, 1864, Cpt. John McMillan took leave from the regiment, leaving Ardrey the senior officer. He wrote, "I was in command of the 30th."[97]

On November 12, 1864, Gen. Grimes' small division was sent northward to make sure Sheridan was not preparing to attack. Bryan Grimes reported, "Have again advanced, and are between Middletown and Winchester. Enemy falling back—don't seem disposed to fight."[98] His brigades stomped around the countryside during the cold daylight hours, and struggled to keep warm at night. The men returned to camp two days later, exhausted from their exertions and scant sleep. Private John Bone griped, "We had very few tents, and they were mostly such as we carried with us, and most of the men's clothes were getting very thin from exposure."[99] General Grimes, also unhappy with their situation, wrote, "Have just reached our old camp. Too tired to write. In five days have been eating both meals at night—one before day in the morning, the other after dark."[100] The Thirtieth remained in camp for the next two weeks, and enjoyed the return of a number of comrades who had been away on wounded, or sick leave. Captain Ardrey celebrated when two member of Company K rejoined the regiment, writing, "Lieut. [John] Downs and Sergt. [William] Russell returned to camp. We were mighty glad to see them."[101] Brigadier General William Cox's brigade was inspected on November 30, 1864, with the Thirtieth mustering for roll 152 men and six officers. The report also showed half of Cpt. Ardrey's men needed boots, as well as being short forty-five blankets.[102] A week later, Cpt. David Allen, having recovered sufficiently from his Winchester wound, returned to the Thirtieth and, as the senior captain, resumed command of the Thirtieth on December 9, 1864.[103]

General Robert E. Lee completed his analysis of what had occurred in the Shenandoah Valley and concluded Lt. Gen. Jubal Early was no longer the man he wanted in command. Though the Shenandoah campaign had tied up large numbers of Federal soldiers, Gen. Early had not been able to protect the Confederacy's vital bread basket, and now Lee was receiving reports the Yanks were shifting infantry divisions away from Sheridan and back to the siege at Petersburg. General Lee made plans to return the Second Corps to reinforce his thin lines holding Petersburg. He began by removing Jubal Early from command of the Corps and assigned leadership of this valuable assemblage of veterans to Maj. Gen. John B. Gordon. Lee shunted Early aside by giving him authority over a collection of Confederates who would remain in the Shenandoah Valley. Then, Robert E. Lee ordered John Gordon to bring the Second Corps to Petersburg.

Chapter 17

Winter Near Petersburg, 1864–1865

General Bryan Grimes's division received it orders to march for Richmond on December 14, 1864.[1] He issued instructions to his brigade commanders, who quickly gave the word to their regiments, and soon afterwards, the Confederates began their move. Private John Bone (Co. I) remarked of their journey, "We broke camp, took the turnpike road for the railroad station and Staunton, a distance of forty or forty-five miles.... We marched all day, and that evening we struck camp in a piece of woods. We cut down trees and made log heaps, making a fire and soaking the snow away, we spread our blankets around the heaps and laid down and went to sleep."[2] Captain William Ardrey (Co. K) added, "[We] marched all day through snow. The mountain scenery of the Blue Ridge and Alleghany was peculiarly grand, all covered with snow ... [we] marched through Harrisonburg on the pike, the road was as slick as glass where the snow had been beaten down and the men slipping and falling all the time." Ardrey continued, describing their hardships: "There I saw blood from the soldiers' feet on the snow.... That night we raked the snow away and made a big log heap fire at our feet with a big bank of snow all around us and we slept good. We were so tired that we did not feel the cold."[3]

The cold and tired Southerners reach the railroad depot in Staunton late the next day, with Pvt. Bone noting, "We reached Staunton ... and we were wet, worried and hungry. The cars were not ready for us, so we had to stand on the streets in this condition without fire."[4] Captain Ardrey also recorded, "Arrived at Staunton about 3 o'clock. Bitter cold." Eventually the trains arrived. Ardrey continued, "They put us in old box cars, fifty men to a box car and started us for Richmond, we almost suffocated."[5] However, the chilled rifleman, John Bone experienced the ride differently, writing, "finally [we were] put in a box car and it being closed we got warm by the heat that was produced by us."[6] The Confederates rode in their packed boxcars across Virginia for nearly twenty-four hours before arriving in Richmond in the early afternoon of December 16, 1864. Captain William Ardrey chronicled the next part of their travel, writing, "Arrived at Richmond [at] ... 2 o'clock and marched directly to Petersburg depot. There we were loaded on the cars like cattle and reached Petersburg at 4 o'clock."[7] Guides directed William Cox's brigade out of Petersburg, across the Appomattox River, and three miles north of the city. Here, not far from Dunlap Station, on the rail line running between Petersburg and Richmond, and close to the flowing waters of Swift Creek, the Carolina regiments were ordered to set up their camps.[8]

Brigadier General William Cox called his regimental commanders to his headquarters and gave them their assignments. Cox wrote, "my brigade was detached from the division for [an] important and special duty north of the Appomattox ... only steady troops were trusted to guard the several miles of river front on which we were stationed."[9] He also instructed his officers to tell their men to construct winter quarters. Captain William Ardrey recorded this announcement, writing, "We went into camp and [were] ordered to build winter quarters."[10] Private John Bone described the work that followed, "We were now ordered to build our winter quarters, our tools being a few common axes and shovels. We were to build our quarters 10 by 14 out of poles, rive boards and cover, make a chimney at one end and a door at the other, and chink the cracks with sticks and mud. Ten to twelve men were to occupy a house.... We had very comfortable quarters."[11] Alexander Betts depicted his abode, noting, "G[o]t into my winter quarters—a wall of poles covered with cloth. Chimney of mud and sticks."[12]

30th North Carolina Infantry[13]
December 31, 1864

Unit		Strength
Field & Staff	Cpt. McMillan, John C. Cpt. Allen, David C. Cpt. Ardrey, William E.	4
Co. A	1st Sgt. Crumpler, Robert M.	14
Co. B	1st Sgt. Newsome, John G.	14
Co. C	Sgt. Butler, Benjamin C.	12
Co. D	Sgt. Cousins, John A.	18
Co. E	1st Lt. Johnson, Ira J.	22
Co. F	Cpt. Moore, Samuel R.	30
Co. G	Cpt. Badgett, James W.	16
Co. H	1st Sgt. Harrington, Ard A.	16
Co. I	1st Sgt. Crowell, Jonas W.	25
Co. K	1st Sgt. Smith, William S.	27
		198

The brigade went out on picket duty on December 23, 1864, heading for Chaffin's Bluff.[14] General Cox's brigade was tasked with maintaining some of the Confederate defensive positions linking Richmond with Petersburg. The curves in the Appomattox provided much to the Southerners' security, but there was a critical four-mile stretch north of the Appomattox River, starting at Port Walthall and stretching to a south-bending meander of the James River, at Drury's Bluff and Chaffin's Bluff. The Tar Heels spent Christmas out on this picket line, a duty depressing many of the homesick men. One wrote his wife, "this is the third Christmas that I have been away from you.... I wonder if I shall be spared to see another Christmas morning."[15] And another rifleman mused, "It is the gloomiest Xmas that I ever saw."[16] In time, the gray-clad Carolinians were relieved and they quickly marched back to their winter quarters, where a shipment of clothing and supplies awaited. Private John Bone (Co. I) exclaimed, "We were camped back as a reserve and were subject to go anywhere at any time.... We ... [are] now clothed from head to foot, [and] more rations ... furnished us, and we felt that we were getting along very well."[17] Two days later, on December 29, 1864, the brigade mustered for inspection. The Thirtieth had ten officers and 179 riflemen answering roll call.[18]

The Thirtieth remained in camp for another week before being sent back out for their turn of picket duty; this time Gen. Cox's men were sent farther north than Chaffin's Bluff, to a location where the Northerners' entrenchments were less than a mile away from the Confederates. The two sides' pickets pressed out from the fortifications, often coming within accurate shooting distances from each other. General Bryan Grimes instructed William Cox, "The General desires me to say to you that great caution would have to be observed to prevent the movement of the troops from being seen from 'the Tower,' that it will probably be best to delay relieving the picket until after dark." He also noted, "General Tovey's line [Bermuda Hundred line] at present covers a great deal of ground."[19] The veteran Tar Heels slipped into this dangerous position and quickly accustomed themselves to their new responsibility. This region of the defenses had been under fire since May 1864, when the Yanks had attempted to cut through the lines to Richmond, but their efforts had been stymied. The Carolinians took advantage of this well-used battlefield by scrounging for valuable left over munitions. A rifleman in the 4th NC admitted, "By gathering up unexploded shells, sold shot and lead balls hurled at us by the enemy and selling them to the ordnance official we eked out our rations."[20]

The brigade returned to winter camp near Dunlap Station to discover the Confederate logistical department was failing once again; there was little to eat. Robert E. Lee complained to the high command, "There is nothing within reach of this army to be impressed; the country is swept clear. Our only reliance is upon the railroads. We have but two days supplies."[21] His grievance was seconded by Richmond but little could be done, with a supply officer agreeing, "Without the supplies there, I consider it impossible to keep General Lee's army in the field."[22] Army commissary officers argued with department suppliers, unfortunately though, nothing of substance occurred. The enlisted men were again forced to get by with what little they could scrounge. A Tar Heel grumbled, "cush [fried cornmeal mush] was our standby."[23] Private John Armfield (Co. C) grumbled, "Our rations have been about the same, a little corn meal and pickled pork, or little flour and bacon. We get this about enough for the day to make one good meal for a hungry man."[24]

The famished Confederates went about the business of picket-line duty and camp details, their morale sinking as their hunger grew. Then, rumors swept through the company streets, hinting about a possibility of an end to the war. The war-weary men grasped at the gossip, with many writing home to their families, their words ringing with this hope. One such soldier wrote, "The peace question is all the excitement in camp now.... I do hope peace will be made before spring. The men are getting discouraged, and to tell the truth, they have cause to.... If the men are not fed they will not stay with the army."[25] On January 29, 1865, the troops learned the rumors could actually be true. A Southerner recorded, "three Confederate peace commissioners had appeared with a flag of truce on the front of the IX Federal Corps ... [and] arrangements were made for the commissioners to proceed to Hampton's Roads."[26]

William Cox's brigade was inspected at the end of January 1865, and the Thirtieth, with Cpt. John McMillan commanding, numbered ten officers and 167 men.[27] They all yearned to hear good news coming from the peace conference scheduled for February 3, 1865. However, before the Carolinians could learn what happened, a Federal offensive at the west end of the Petersburg fortifications drew them south of the Appomattox River and into the morass of muddy, trench-bound soldiers. An officer in the 4th NC recorded, "the brigade was moved to Burgess' Mill but arrived too late to take part in the battle of that day."[28] Private John Bone (Co. I) recalled, "the enemy made an attack on the railroad south of Petersburg, and we were ordered to go to the support of the men that had them in check [at Hatcher's Run].... It was raining, hailing and freezing, and we made all the haste we could. We had to go a distance of about ten miles, and had to put a pontoon bridge across the river to cross on, reaching the battle late in the evening." He continued, "As we advanced the enemy fell back and that ended the fight.... We laid on the cold icy ground that night."[29] The riflemen were now stuck out in the open, and since they had hustled to support their Confederate brothers, carrying only light marching order, they had no tents or blankets to protect themselves against the freezing winter night. General Grimes, realizing his Tar Heels would lose more men to the weather than to enemy musketry, immediately notified his troops to do what ever was necessary to survive. Bryan Grimes told William Cox, "[I] wish you to remain where you are, or near, any where near it. Your men can be made comfortable for the night. If they cannot be made comfortable, you will move down the Boydton plank road until you can get to some wood."[30] William Cox sought out the best location he could for his men, though this did not stop his riflemen from griping. One Tar Heel scribbled in his journal,

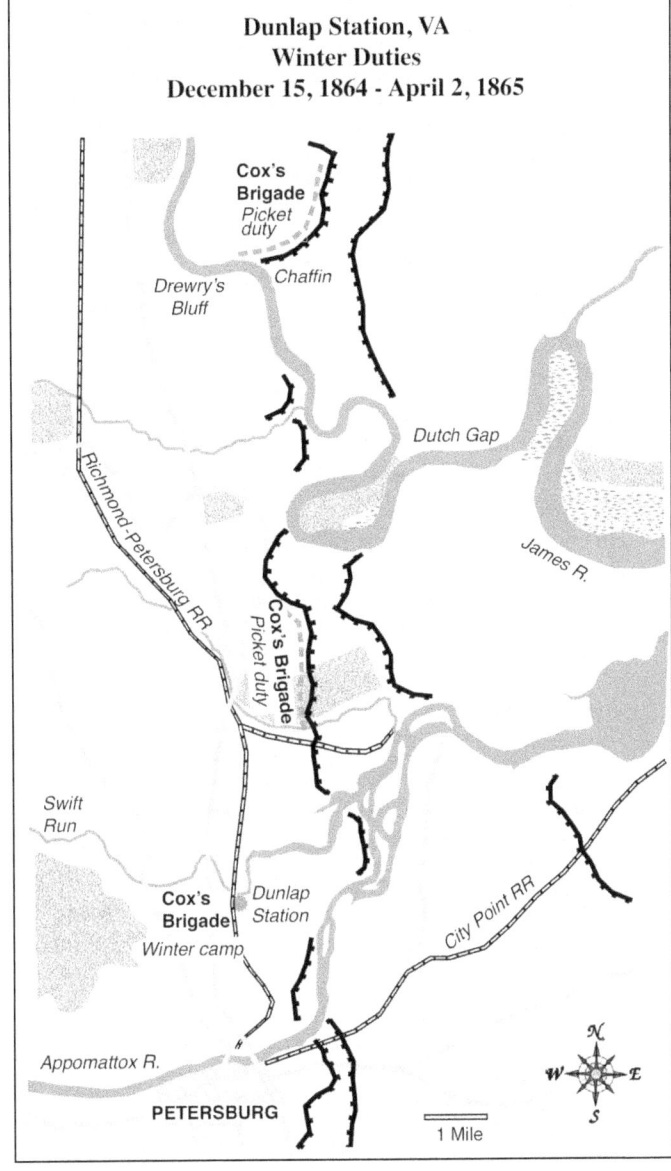

"Three days and nights in line of battle in the cold, hail and sleet, with reduced rations and no meat."[31] The Carolinians endured their privations and on February 7, 1865, returned to the security of their camps near Dunlap Station.

The Thirtieth's men learned the peace commission had failed. A Southerner recorded, "On the morning of February 3, a conference was held between President Lincoln and Secretary of State William H. Seward on one side, and on the other, the Confederate representatives, Vice President Alexander H. Stephens, Senator R. M. T. Hunter and Judge James A. Campbell.... At the close of a single meeting of four hours' duration, the Southerners left, and that same day, started back for Richmond." He continued, "President Davis announced formally that the Hampton Roads conference had failed because Mr. Lincoln had refused to enter into negotiations with the Confederate States ... or to give ... any other terms or guarantee than those which the conqueror may grant, or to permit ... peace on any other basis than ... unconditional submission to [Federal] rule."[32] Alexander Betts voiced what all the heartsick soldiers felt when he wrote, "Peace commission fails." There would no peace unless they surrendered.[33]

Morale plummeted among the Confederate soldiers in the brigades mired in the mud protecting Petersburg. The Carolinians though, fortunate to be camped three miles north of the city and carrying out picket duties far from the fortifications' spirit-crushing conditions, concerned themselves with getting enough to eat and trying to stay warm. Private John Armfield (Co. C) wrote his wife, "Nothing to write about especially but still here in this miserable loathsome business with no bright prospect of getting out of it." He continued, "Pickett is very hard business. We have to go on [the] front line and remain 24 hours then we are relieved and go back to [the] rear lines ... and only get rest of 24 hours. We only have to stand one hour out of every three when we are on the front line, but without any comfortable place to rest or sleep [the] other two hours."[34]

Though the Tar Heels' resolve remained firm, other brigades began to suffer losses through desertion as the cold, dreary weeks of February 1865 ground by. In fact, by mid February, the Federals' knowledge of which Confederate units occupied the lines was maintained solely through interviews of deserting Southerners. On February 17, 1865, a Union intelligence officer notified his division commander, "Deserters ... report no movements. Cooks,' Cox's, and Battle's brigades [of] Grimes' division ... are in reserve at the old factory on Swift Run, three miles this side [northeast] of Petersburg."[35] A week later, another blue-coated officer reported, "Cox's brigade has relieved Grimes' old, now Cowands' brigade, which occupies the camping-ground of the former."[36] On February 23, 1865, a Federal intelligence officer learned the Confederates were making plans and wrote, "Two deserters from Cox's brigade say ... that the three remaining brigades on Swift Run are under marching orders, with four days cooked rations." Then, the next day, another officer also noted that "the three brigades near Swift Creek (Grimes division) left yesterday morning.... Cox's [brigade] was left on picket."[37]

Brigadier General William Cox's brigade, now by itself, carried on with the normal military business of picket duties and winter survival. On February 25, 1865, the Tar Heels mustered for inspection and the Thirtieth, with Cpt. John McMillan still in command, totaled five officers and 176 men. An inventory of the regiment's equipment and clothing revealed a dramatic need for resupply. The report specified, "The regiment suffered from grave clothing deficiencies, particularly pants and underclothing.... Deficiencies included 67 overcoats, 275 coats, 200 trousers, 205 shirts, 120 pairs of shoes, 125 stockings, 46 blankets, 200 knapsacks, 160 canteens, and 50 tents."[38]

The Thirtieth was sent to Chaffin's Bluff on March 2, 1865. The next day the regiment's chaplain, Alexander Betts wrote, "I walk nine miles and preach to my Regiment in picket camp."[39] Captain McMillan's veterans completed another week guarding their posts before trudging back to their Dunlap Station camp. But now disconcerting news from home began to sap at the lonesome Carolinians' resolve. One worried Tar Heel wrote, "I ... hear from the South that Sherman is marching through the state of N. C. I heard this morning that the Yankees had taken Fayetteville and Goldsboro."[40] This veteran, like all the men in the regiment, shuddered when they read a bulletin from North Carolina's Governor, Zebulon Vance that proclaimed, "To delay the advance of the enemy.... I appeal to all good and patriotic citizens to turn out in full force ... with axes, spades and mattocks to destroy and obstruct roads heading towards Charlotte from the South." Governor Vance continued, "They will be protected by.... Home Guards of the State."[41] The anxious Carolinians though, regardless of their concerns, continued to perform their duties; Alexander Betts recorded on March 20, 1865, "Brigade moves to Dunlap's and relieved Thomas' Ga. Brigade."[42]

The morose Tar Heels were shocked out of their doldrums four days later when they received frantic word to put on their battle gear and be ready to march; General Lee had ordered a major Confederate offensive on March 25, 1865. Captain John McMillan's riflemen strapped on their gear and fell into formation, ready to march as the sun set, with Pvt. John Bone (Co. I) writing, "we were ordered to get ready and leave at once for Petersburg. We knew very well that it meant to fight."[43] That evening though, the men of the Thirtieth stood and waited, along with their brothers in William Cox's brigade. The brigade sharpshooters unit, led by Col. Hamilton Brown, 1st NC, marched away, taking among them a number of the Thirtieth's aggressive fighters, but everyone else stood motionlessly, griping at the delay.[44] Eventually the men were told to stack arms and rest, as the guides responsible for leading them to their attack position had not arrived. General Cox remarked, "A courier was sent to me with orders to move at once to the point of the intended assault. This courier lost his way during the night, which lost time ... and delayed my movements until early dawn."[45] Finally, an hour or so before daylight, the guides arrived and the Tar Heels were rousted from their frustration. The brigade hustled southward; Pvt. Bone recalled, "we were soon on the tramp.... We got in about one mile of Petersburg about day break, when the fight was to commence and our presence was wanted."[46]

General Robert E. Lee had gone on the offensive with an assault on the Federal lines east of Petersburg. Lee directed Maj. Gen. John Gordon to mass his divisions for a surprise assault on Ft. Stedman and surrounding gun positions. John Gordon assembled nine brigades and these infantry units slipped out of the entrenchments, quietly following several hand-selected groups of a hundred men each, and struck the Union fortifications just before sunrise.[47] Brigadier General Cox wrote, "my first intimation of the conflict was given by the booming of artillery and the sharp, quick reports of the small arms."[48] He hurried his Tar Heels towards the sounds of the fighting but as the brigade neared the conflict, the noises of war began to diminish; the Confederate attack had failed. William Cox's brigade arrived in time to watch the surviving Southerners flee across the open ground between the two lines. General Cox noted, "the brigade [was ordered] ... to cover the retreat ... and protect the retreat of the army which was rapidly falling back."[49]

Captain John McMillan's veterans filed into a section of trench and manned the rifle mounts, prepared to shoot at any advancing Yanks. The blue coats, though, did not attack; instead, they rounded up hundreds of Confederates who appeared to McMillan's men as just having given up. One Southern officer remarked, "The defeat of the Ft. Stedman attacks, and the number of Confederate soldiers who just surrendered rather than fight, demonstrated that Lee's army had lost hope of final success, and the men were not willing to risk their lives in a hopeless endeavor."[50] Union artillery began to shell the Confederate lines once the gray-coated infantry had been marched away. Private John Bone (Co. I) wrote, "We were under heavy shelling for some time. He added, "the breastworks were about one hundred yards apart, and about three feet high and four feet wide.... Just a few feet from the works were cabin places made with logs doubled, dirt between carried on top with logs, dirt and bags of sand ... they were so arranged that when the enemy got to dropping their mortar shells over in them that the men could run in their holes."[51]

Later, once the Union cannoneers had pounded the Confederate lines sufficiently enough to punish the Southerners for their surprise assault, medical teams crept onto the dangerous space between the two lines, carrying white flags. General Cox wrote, "The opposing lines were then not exceeding two hundred yards apart. Between these lines lay the dead and wounded.... A white flag was now raised on the Federal breastworks, which was responded to on our side, and an agreement for a truce was made in order to removed those who had suffered."[52] A Confederate rifleman recorded what happened next: "We agreed immediately to have the wounded and dead taken off, each by his own people.... Men ran over the field from each side and gathered up their comrades, taking time, when they could, to exchange pipes, tobacco, penknives, hardtacks and anything that was tradable."[53] William Cox remarked, "Isn't it strange? A few hours ago we were endeavoring to kill each other; now we are engaging in hospitalities and in friendly conversation."[54]

General John Gordon sorted out his divisions and assigned positions for each of his brigades. Another formation moved into the trench William Cox's men held. Then, the Tar Heel general led his Carolinians to their new location. They reached their designation position and relieved the Southerners who were there. A departing Confederate who turned the area over to the Tar Heels, wrote, "When [Gordon's troops] came in, they asked a great many questions about the trenches, and it would take a long book to hold all the lies [we] told them."[55] General Cox reported, "I was ... placed on the right of Grimes's Division, where skirmishing and picket firing was kept up day and night and two-thirds of my troops were on constant duty."[56] Captain John McMillan's veterans realized they were not going back to their winter quarters and began to inspect their surroundings. The Carolinians shook their heads in disgust, with one grumbling, "Not the least of the evils encountered was the unavoidable stench."[57] Private John Bone wrote simply, "it was a disagreeable place."[58] The Thirtieth's sharpshooters returned to the Thirtieth, bringing news that Pvt. William Lynn (Co. H) had been seriously wounded in the right thigh in the assault on Ft. Stedman. They did not know if he would live.[59] The Tar Heels stood in ankle-deep mud and gazed across the open ground between the two lines of trenches and shook their heads in dismay. General Bryan Grimes summed up how they all felt, "would to heaven this carnage was over and I permitted to retire from such scenes and live a quiet and domestic life."[60]

The Thirtieth, along with the 1st, 2nd, 3rd, 4th, and 14th NC, remained in position for the next week, the Carolinians alternating between manning the trench's fire-steps, huddling out in front of the fortifications at picket posts, or trying to get some rest while off duty. The spring-like weather soaked the men with repeated, heavy downpours. One soldier groused, "It rained last night.... The rain ... poured down ... one of the heaviest showers of rain I think I ever saw."[61] The men were also plagued by Union artillery, especially mortars. A rifleman recalled, "mortar shells were the most disgusting, low-lived things imaginable.... Old veterans can never forget the noise those missiles made as they went up and came down like an excited bird, their shrieks becoming shriller and shriller, as the time to explode approached."[62] General William Cox, though aware of the hardships his men endured, worried about a Northern attack, especially after returning from a brigade officers' meeting with Maj. Gen. Bryan Grimes, who reported, "On an average throughout the space from man to man was at least eight feet in the line of trenches." He added, "[I knew full] well that the enemy by concentrating a large force on any given point could press their way through the line."[63] A few Tar Heel soldiers slipped away and deserted, enabling the Union leaders to report on March 31, 1865, "Cox's brigade came into the main hue since the 25th and are now on Gordon's left."[64]

Everything changed on April 1, 1865, with the news that Maj. Gen. George Pickett's division had been destroyed in a fight at a place called Five Forks. Rumors swept through the Confederate lines, which one writer recorded, "[US General] Sheridan corralled roughly 2,400 prisoners while another 600 of Pickett's defenders fell killed or wounded."[65] George Pickett's division had occupied a portion of the Confederate entrenchments, but now his troops were gone, creating a massive gap in the Southern line. General Lee inserted what little reserves he had, and stretched his existing forces to cover the area. Bryan Grimes fanned out the men of his four brigades, but he knew they would be hard pressed to hold, when the Yanks attacked. Grimes wrote, "On the night of Saturday, April 1, 1865 ... my left rest[ed] on Otey's Battery, near the memorable Crater, my right extending to the dam on a creek beyond Battery 45." He recorded his brigades' locations, noting that his men "cover[ed] at least three and a half miles of the trenches around Petersburg ... [with] Ramseur's old Brigade of North Carolinians being commanded by Col. W. R. Cox ... on their [left] ... [his] old Brigade of North Carolinians, commanded by Col. D. G. Cowand.... Battle's Brigade of Alabamians, commanded by Col. Hobson ... [and] Cook's Brigade of Georgians commanded by Col. Nash." Grimes reported his division, "number[ed] for duty about 2,200 muskets ... with one third of [the] men constantly on picket duty in our front, one third kept awake at the breastworks during the night, with one third only off duty at a time, and ... required always to sleep with their accoutrements on and upon their arms, ready to repel an attack at a moment's warning."[66]

As darkness settled over the trenches, the Tar Heel riflemen could sense a difference in their situation; Pickett's debacle meant something bad was going to happen, and because the veteran Southerners knew how aggressive General Ulysses S. Grant was, they knew it would be very soon. The Carolinians stood their posts, knowing how far each man stood from the next. One wrote, "Along the line of works we occupied we had but one man to five or six feet, an ordinary skirmish line."[67] They could hear movement arising from the Union lines, and the Confederate picket line relayed messages telling of masses of men preparing to attack. Captain John McMillan worked with his remaining officers and they moved along the thin line of friends and relatives. The Thirtieth numbered just over two hundred, with 184 combat soldiers and twenty-one support troops. His regiment was divided into two groups; one led by Cpt. David Allen, and the other by Cpt. William Ardrey.

30th North Carolina Infantry[68]
April 1, 1865

Unit		Strength
Field & Staff	Cpt. McMillan, John C.	
	Cpt. Allen, David C.	4
	Cpt. Ardrey, William E.	
Co. A	1st Sgt. Crumpler, Robert M.	14

Unit		Strength
Co. B	1st Sgt. Newsome, John G.	14
Co. C	Sgt. Butler, Benjamin C.	12
Co. D	Sgt. Cousins, John A.	17
Co. E	1st Lt. Johnson, Ira J.	21
Co. F	Cpt. Moore, Samuel R.	30
Co. G	Cpt. Badgett, James W.	15
Co. H	1st Sgt. Harrington, Ard A.	15
Co. I	1st Sgt. Crowell, Jonas W.	25
Co. K	1st Sgt. Smith, William S.	27
	Non combat soldiers	21
		205

Disturbing sounds came from the picket lines not long after midnight, and within a few minutes a bunch of wide-eyed Tar Heels scurried into the trenches. The frightened veterans all said the same thing: Yankees were gobbling up their picket posts. Captain McMillan's picket line officer did a count, and four of his men had not come in: Pvt. N. S. Ogburn (Co. A), Pvt. William Rogers (Co. A), Pvt. Gray Armstrong (Co. I), and Pvt. Ruffin Batchelor (Co. I) had been captured. Another Carolinian was brought in, shot through the right shoulder; Pvt. William Moore (Co. D).[69] Captain McMillan reported his losses to brigade headquarters and these numbers were passed on to division. A staff officer summed up the division's losses, writing, "Gordon's pickets had been taken at 11 o'clock on the night of April 1–2."[70]

Union artillery began shelling the Confederate lines, forcing the Southerners to seek shelter, causing one soldier to write, "the firing east of the city had been severe. During the night of the 1st the fire from mortar and guns was incessant."[71] Everyone knew an attack was coming. All of Bryan Grimes' men were standing at their posts, staring out into the darkness, frightened by what they could not see. A Federal officer recorded, "All told, [Maj. Gen. John] Parke [IX Corps] designated eighteen regiments to charge against [Grimes's] ... under strength Confederate brigades."[72] A signal gun was fired at 4:30 a.m. and the blue coats rushed forward. Brigadier General William Cox observed, "the enemy, just before daylight ... [attacked] on the left of Grimes's Division, rushed in, and leaped over our breastworks."[73] Once the sky had lightened enough to enable vision the Carolinians in Cox's brigade could see total confusion on their left. The Northern assault had crushed Battle's and Cook's brigades, but Cowand's and Cox's men were untouched. General Grimes quickly sent Cowand's Carolinians to reinforce the two shattered formations. One writer noted, "General Grimes acted swiftly amidst the crisis sweeping the division. He summoned Cowand's North Carolinians ... and ordered a series of counterattacks designed first to limit the Federal advance and then to regain as much of the lost real estate as possible."[74] William Cox was told to spread his men out and cover Cowand's position. General Cox recorded, "I was [now] covering a mile of our breastworks with my men ten feet apart."[75]

The veterans in Cowand's brigade crashed into the left flank of the Union assault and the two forces mauled each other in a fierce struggle evolving into intimate fights for yards of trench-line at a time. One soldier recalled, "The fight was from traverse to traverse as we slowly drove them back.... The Yankees would get on top of them and shoot down on our men, and as we would re-take them our men did the same thing." He continued, "Adding to the terror of this small-unit combat, huge mortar shells rained down upon the Confederates, exploding in spectacular and often deadly fashion."[76] A Tar Heel in the 4th NC remarked, "The fight ... was very fierce, and the men of our command saw the fall of [part of the line] ... but could afford no assistance, as [our] own front would have been exposed had [we] left [our] position."[77]

General William Cox could see Union troops preparing to advance against his thinly held mile of entrenchments. He knew there would be little his small force could do to hold, once a mass of blue coats attacked, however, a stroke of good fortune came his way. Cox wrote, "there was a long unoccupied traverse on my right, running diagonally to my line.... I discovered an engineer corps composed of 350 negroes under the command of a colonel who were used for strengthening our works." He continued, "I ... placed this corps under my command ... [and] using them as dummies, I extended them on this unoccupied line, and as only their heads were exposed, the enemy naturally supposed they were there to meet any assault that might be made." William Cox boasted, "the enemy were kept at a respectful distance."[78]

The fighting east of Cox's position stabilized and even though there were minor eruptions along small portions of the line, it became clear the Yanks had not punched through Grimes's division. Unfortunately, news from the west completely disturbed the Carolinians. One Southerner wrote, "the enemy ... massed a heavy force against the opposite portion of our line and succeeded in breaking it, and then sweeping down toward the city, capturing a number of men and guns along the line."[79] Another recalled, "By [11:00] a.m., the details of the catastrophe began to take form. The Union VI Corps had delivered at 4:40 a.m. an overpowering attack on Hill's front, had shattered the line held by Heth's and Wilcox's Divisions and had driven the Confederates to right and left."[80] The shocked Tar Heels looked at each other in horror, they all knew what this meant— the Petersburg line had been broken. A veteran summed up their situation: "Neither Gordon nor Lee, nor anyone else believed that more could be accomplished at Petersburg ... the whole of the Richmond-Petersburg front must be abandoned."[81] William Cox wrote, "It was now apparent that the contest was to be continued on our part only to enable us to evacuated our lines, and commence our retreat under cover of night."[82]

The veteran Confederate riflemen knowing what had to be done, waited to hear the official word they would be pulling out of the trenches, but it did not come. As darkness quieted the battlefield, Gen. Cox ordered a force of Tar Heels to once again, occupy the picket posts out in front of their fortifications. Private John Bone (Co. I) wrote, "On Sunday morning, April 2, there was a heavy attack made on our right, and a part of our division was heavily engaged for a short while.... In the evening a number of sharpshooters (I being one of them) were sent out in front, and engaged the enemy's line."[83] Meanwhile, for the soldiers remaining in the trenches, they recognized the signs of retreat. One wrote, "Darkness had gathered over the gory field when I noticed that the artillery was being quietly removed from the works."[84] Then, orders came to prepare to move. John Bone recalled, "After a while our officer had orders to relieve us. He came to us and told each in a whisper to fall in behind him, which we did in a hurry. Those that he did not reach were captured.... We marched to the rear where our men were in the works, but much to our surprise, we did not find anyone."[85]

Major General John Gordon began moving his entire corps out the Petersburg entrenchments as soon as darkness hid his movements from Union observers. He first extracted all the artillery, nearly two hundred-fifty guns, a process that occurred efficiently and quickly. His senior artillery officer recorded, "In obedience to orders from the commanding general, I ordered withdrawal of all the guns at 8 p.m. This was accomplished with great success."[86] Also, at this time, Gordon's wagon trains rolled away from Petersburg, nearly one thousand vehicles, crossing the Appomattox River over the Pocahontas and raidroad bridges linking the city to the north and west.[87] The Second Corps' infantry formations followed next; Brig. Gen. James Walker's division, Brig. Gen. Clement Evans's division, and finally Bryan Grimes's men. General Grimes recalled, "We followed the army, bringing up the rear."[88]

The Confederates of Gordon's Corps moved through Petersburg nearly all night long, and by the time Cpt. John McMillan's Carolinians passed through the darkened streets the sidewalks were filled with crowds of mourning citizens. One rifleman wrote, "he saw the noble women ... weeping as in the agony of despair ... at the passing of the troops.... There was no sleeping in Petersburg that night."[89] Another recorded, "We marched ... through Petersburg for the last time, the old regiment not much more than a company. Our hearts were sad. We knew the end was near, the end of our hopes, perhaps our lives."[90] The Tar Heels crossed the Appomattox River and followed the vast traffic jam of vehicles, artillery, and men. By sunrise, Petersburg was behind them, lost to the massive Union force arrayed outside the city. When Cpt. McMillan asked his sergeant major to take a quick count of the Thirtieth, it was discovered one man was missing, Pvt. J. Cline (Co. F).[91]

The Carolinians stumbled westward, shuffling along, not able to maintain a decent marching pace. Bryan Grimes wrote in frustration, "we ... [were] very much impeded on the march by the wagon train and its most miserable mismanagement, which, as I apprehended, would cause us some disaster."[92] Private John Bone (Co. I) added, "We had to move very slowly, so as to let the artillery and wagon train move on before us. We marched all night and the next day, only stopping at short intervals."[93] The men were exhausted, they had not slept at all during the night of the expected assault, and then, when they slipped away from Petersburg during the dark hours, they had been deprived of rest for a second night. Private Bone noted, "I remember going to sleep at times walking long and would step into a hole or hit my foot against something and wake up. We were so sleepy that we could stand still and go fast asleep."[94] This weariness, along with the despondency caused by war's losses, sapped at the soldiers' morale. A soldier noted this, writing, "every shade of woe and of despair was in the faces of those who had survived nine and a half months of sharpshooting and of desperate combat."[95]

This decay in morale displayed itself as unit discipline began to erode away. Rifleman John Bone observed, "When the men had anything to eat, they had to eat it raw or get a pan or skillet and stop off to one side and cook a bit and then move on and overtake their command."[96] Another Confederate added, "enlisted men ate by the roadside what was left of the rations they had brought with them from the trenches. Little enough it was, of cornpone, and for some, of bacon."[97] And another wrote, "the Confederacy was considered as 'gone up,' and every man felt it his duty, as well as his privilege, to save himself."[98] However, Cpt. John McMillan's men kept together and maintained unit cohesion. Though his riflemen were sleep-deprived and hungry, they had not suffered in the trenches like most of the other regiments. The Tar Heels trudged along at a slow "rout step," not talking much, but not losing men who drifted away at the roadside, like was occurring for many of the Southern units. That evening, the exhausted Tar Heels clustered together in a field not far from the road, the regiment intact, and discipline still in place. Most of McMillan's men figured the end was near, but this was not an excuse to dissolve into disorder. One soldier surmised, "It had not been an easy day, nor a cheerful one, but it had been disastrous."[99]

John McMillan's two hundred men were up by sunrise on April 4, 1865. Nearly all had slept enough to restore their vitality. They had little to eat but had been told there were rations awaiting them at Amelia Court House, some twenty-or-so miles away. A Southerner wrote, "the troops started early. Most were hungry, but not all of those who marched on empty stomachs were without hope. The hungrier they were ... the brighter seemed the prospect of the rations the officers said they would receive at Amelia Court House."[100] The Carolinians shuffled westward, passing clumps of defeated men who had given up. One wrote, "we moved on in disorder, keeping no regular column, no regular pace ... there were not many words spoken."[101] Morning gave way to afternoon, and with each step forward, the Tar Heels shortened the distance between them and the food waiting for them. But then horrible news rippled down the gray-clad column; there were no rations at Amelia Court House. Not long after this paralyzing information crushed the hungry soldiers' expectations, orders came to halt. General William Cox moved his small brigade off the road and instructed his officers to tend to their regiments; they were about five miles from Amelia Court House, close to the railroad station called Scott's Shop.[102] The famished men scattered looking for food. An officer watched his men disperse and wrote, "Many of [the men] wandered off in search of food, with no thought of deserting at all."[103]

General Robert E. Lee had halted his entire army while he sent his commissary and supply officials out to locate food for his men and fodder for the livestock. General Lee recorded, "upon arriving at Amelia Court House on the morning of the 4th ... and not finding the supplies ordered to be placed there, nearly twenty-four hours were lost in endeavoring to collect in the country subsistence for men and horses.... Nothing could be obtained from the adjacent country."[104] Meanwhile, the Federals had marched triumphantly into Petersburg and into Richmond, and then General Grant had his cavalry rushing off in pursuit of the retreating Confederates. The Yanks also pushed several infantry corps to hustle after the Southerners. It now would be a race for survival.

Chapter 18

The End at Appomattox

The Confederates were up before sunrise on April 5, 1865, and found themselves chilled by a cold, spring rain. General Lee, since there were no rations for his men at Amelia Court House, issued orders for supplies to be transported to the rail stop at Jetersville. Then, Lee waited several hours before marching his troops, a delay he could not afford. General Lee admitted, "This delay was fatal, and could not be retrieved."[1] Union commanders, using information received from cavalry reports, as well as railroad messages, determined where Lee planned to go and rushed columns of horsemen to intercept his intentions. Blue-coated horsemen rumbled into Jetersville and prepared defenses. Thus, by the time Lee's famished army moved out and began its trek to Jetersville that avenue of sustenance no longer existed. The Southern army inched toward Jetersville, Longstreet's men leading the way, followed by Anderson's men, Ewell's soldiers, the wagon train, and acting as rear guard, Gordon's troops.

30th North Carolina Infantry[2]
April 6, 1865

Unit		Strength
Field & Staff	Cpt. McMillan, John C. Cpt. Allen, David C. Cpt. Ardrey, William E.	4
Co. A	1st Sgt. Crumpler, Robert M.	12
Co. B	1st Sgt. Newsome, John G.	14
Co. C	Sgt. Butler, Benjamin C.	12
Co. D	Sgt. Cousins, John A.	16
Co. E	1st Lt. Johnson, Ira J.	21
Co. F	Cpt. Moore, Samuel R.	29
Co. G	Cpt. Badgett, James W.	15
Co. H	1st Sgt. Harrington, Ard A.	15
Co. I	1st Sgt. Crowell, Jonas W.	23
Co. K	1st Sgt. Smith, William S.	26
	Non combat soldiers	21
		198

Southern cavalry brushed up against the Yanks at Jetersville and determined there was no way this position could be taken. Word was sent back to General Lee and he halted his force as his staff sought out another route to safety. Robert Lee wrote, "[I] decided to make a night march around the dug-in Union army at Jetersville, and head for Farmville where … [I] was informed that 80,000 rations would be waiting."[3] The Southern leader knew food was now the most critical aspect for his army's survival. He remarked, "Unless the columns reached Farmville and received food there before the arrival of the enemy, the proud Army of Northern Virginia would be helpless."[4] General Lee ordered his men to march and they complied, but the darkness of the night, the muddy roads' poor conditions, and masses of slow-moving wagons bogged down their march. The men staggered forward, shuffling for a few yards and then stopping, to stand needlessly while up ahead, some stuck or broken-down wagon was pushed forward or shunted aside. One road-weary rifleman noted, "I would go to sleep for a second or two, to start up the next second to save myself, an almost agonizing feeling and not restful."[5] Another added, "Drowsiness and nervousness were worse than were hunger and exhaustion. Men staggered as if they were drunk…. Every few minutes, half-dead veterans would leave the column and lie down in dumb despair."[6]

Sunrise on April 6, 1865, revealed to the Confederates how little they had traveled. One officer scribbled in disgust, "We were to march all that night, but, owing to the slow progress of the trains and troops in front, had only reached Amelia Springs, seven miles off."[7] The Carolinians were disheartened by how much effort they had been forced to expend, and how little progress had been made. Captain John McMillan ordered roll taken and learned the Thirtieth continued to maintain its mettle, as well as its numbers; only one man had been lost during the night: Pvt. Eli Church (Co. K), who would eventually be reported as, "captured at Amelia Court House."[8] The Thirtieth totaled near one hundred eighty combat soldiers and another twenty in support. General William Cox called his regimental leaders together and informed them Cowand's brigade, and theirs had been tasked to work together as part of the rear guard. General Bryan Grimes wrote, "I then formed Cox's and Cowand's Brigades in line of battle, with a heavy skirmish line in front to impede [the Federals'] progress and to cover our rear." He continued, "[I] sen[t] Battle's, Cook's and Archer's Brigades [back] for one half mile to form there, across the road, in line of battle, in order to allow Cowand and Cox to retreat safely when the enemy had deployed and prepared to attack."[9]

William Cox's regiments deployed into a battle formation and within minutes, Col. David Cowand's Carolinians moved up on their flank. Both commanders sent out a screen of skirmishers while the riflemen on the line scrounged for fence boards and other materials to fashion a defense. The Tar Heels barely had time to set up before Union skirmishers began popping away at them. William Cox reported, "[Brig. Gen. Gershom Mott's] Division began its attack at daylight."[10] General Gershom Mott, commanding the Third Division of the II Corps had his troops moving in pursuit before sunrise, on orders from his boss, Maj. Gen. Andrew Humphreys, who wrote, "The troops will be ready to move at 5:30 a.m. promptly."[11] Mott's First Brigade, led by Brig. Gen. Regis de Troibriand, began pressing towards the North Carolinians. However, the Yanks were veterans, just as the Tar Heels were, and the blue-coated riflemen realized the conflict was close to finished. None of them wanted to be killed in what might be the final moments of the war. So, the Union skirmishers languished just beyond two hundred yards; within the lethal zone but not into the killing zone. Instead, they just sniped at the Confederate skirmishers, who shot back at them.

Both sets of veterans knew what would happen; Brig. Gen. Mott deployed his second brigade by sending them to the right; they would soon be able to flank the Confederate line. William Cox's riflemen watched the Northerners shifting to the Confederate left, and hoped their brigade commander would give the order to fall back. General Cox waited until the last moment and then gave the word; the Carolinians quickly retreated. They soon passed Bryan Grimes's second formation at their hastily laid out defenses, several miles farther west. William Cox recalled, "Our retreat was conducted in the following manner: One brigade would be formed across the line of retreat, while another brigade was formed in its rear. The front brigade resisted attack as long as it was safe to do so without capture, when it fell back and retired behind the troops in its rear."[12] General Grimes added, "In this manner alternating the Brigades throughout the day we continued to oppose the enemy and retreat, endeavoring to protect the lagging wagon train."[13]

William Cox's and David Cowand's veterans set up their next defensive line at the crossroads village of Deatonsville. The Tar Heel riflemen faced east, hunkered down behind logs, fence rails, and piles of stone, waiting for the retreat of Grimes's other blocking force; men of Battle's, Cook's, and Archer's formations. The sounds of light skirmishing erupted, and following a delay of some time, the Carolinians could see gray coats scampering up the road, toward them. The retreating Confederates hustled past Cox's and Cowand's line and disappeared to the west, beyond Deatonsville. It was now the Tar Heels' turn to hold off the Yankees. Moments later, Federal skirmishers emerged from the distant trees and cautiously approached. The Union commander wrote, "The country

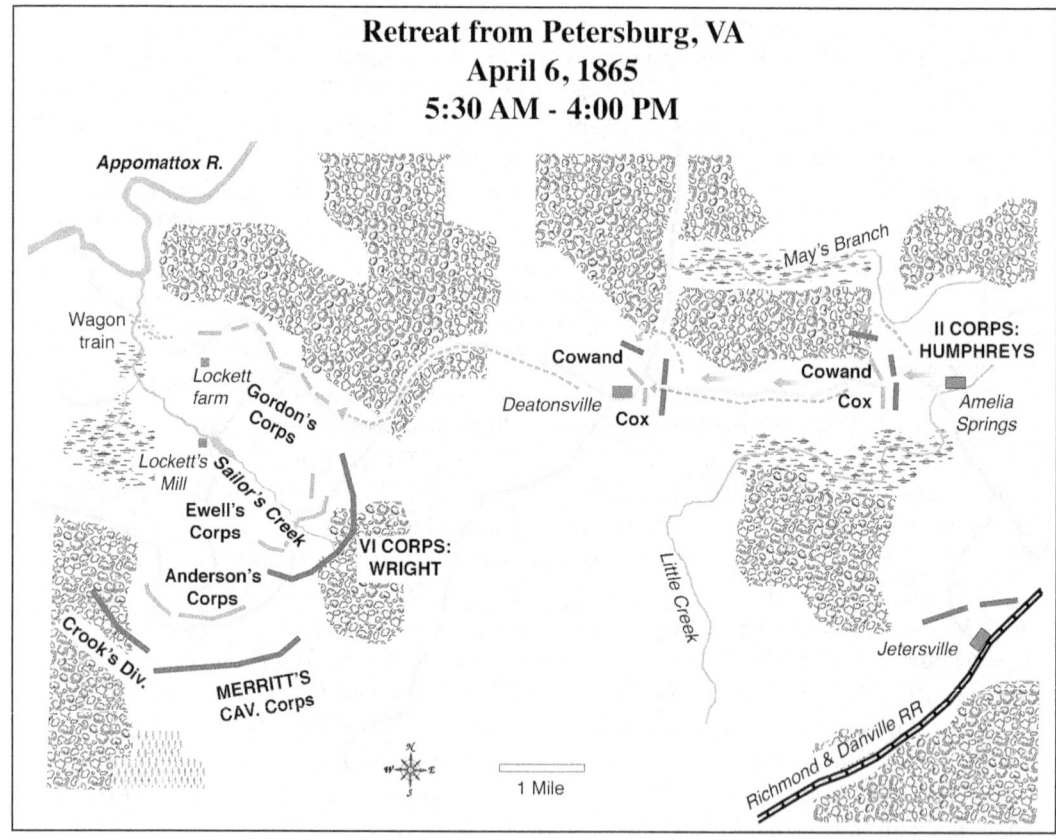

was broken, and consisted of open fields alternating forest with dense growth, and swamps, over and through which the lines of battle followed closely on the skirmish line."[14]

The Federal troops deployed against Cox's and Cowand's line, but this time also brought up a battery of artillery. The Northern gunners began to bombard the Confederate soldiers. Captain William Ardrey (Co. K) scrawled into his journal, "The enemy pressed us very closely and commenced shelling our rear early in the morning. We formed line to the rear and soon the fighting commenced with a fury."[15] The Yanks advanced, pushing in the Southern skirmishers, who fell back to the main battle line. The Tar Heels unleashed volleys into the blue ranks, knocking down many. The Federals fired back, filling the air with minié bullets. Captain John McMillan (Co. E), who calmly walked behind his protected Tar Heels, calling out encouragement and orders, suddenly staggered backwards. A nearby Tar Heel wrote, "he was shot through the body [right side below the shoulder], and with the blood gushing from his nose and mouth, he turned and inquired of one whether the wound was fatal." The soldier noted, "He was placed in an ambulance and taken to the rear."[16] Captain David Allen (Co. C) assumed command of the Thirtieth.

The Northerners backed off from their assault, sent flanking battalions and forced the Tar Heels to withdraw. Private John Bone (Co. I) recorded, "We had a fight ... during the day ... the enemy's infantry would come up with some artillery, and we would fight them awhile, thus giving the wagon train a chance to get ahead. We would leave the enemy after giving them a few rounds, and march on for awhile.[17] Captain Ardrey added, "Soon we were forced to retreat and the enemy pursued hotly."[18] Unfortunately not all of the Thirtieth's veterans were able to fall back; ten Carolinians were captured, including five riflemen from Company K.[19] These men were gathered up by Yank troops and marched down to Burkeville. An hour later a Federal officer recorded, "I am three miles beyond Deatonsville and pushing the enemy. The road is literally lined with their tents, baggage, and cooking utensils."[20] The Carolinians retreated past the next blocking position and hiked another couple miles west. Later, as Maj. Gen. John Gordon watched Grimes's brigades, he wrote, "We turned upon every hilltop to meet them and give our wagon-trains and artillery time to get ahead. Instantly they would strike us; we invariably repulsed them ... but after we had fought for an hour or two, we would find huge masses pressing down our flanks, and to keep from being surrounded I would have to withdraw my men."[21]

John Gordon's troops, slowly retreating behind the unwieldy wagon train, came to a crossroads and turned to the right, heading northwest, unaware they no longer followed the main body of the Confederate army. Robert E. Lee's leading formation, commanded by Lt. Gen. Richard Anderson, which was now two miles southwest of that critical crossroads, had run into a sizeable Yank cavalry force. The Southern infantry units trailing Anderson stacked up behind his column, bumping to a jammed-up halt. Lieutenant General Richard Ewell, who led these stalled troops decided to shunt the wagon train onto another road. A Southerner noted, "[Richard] Ewell ... directed that the wagons remaining between his rear and the front of the Second Corps turn to the right and follow a road to a less exposed crossing of Saylor's Creek, about two and a half miles North and slightly West of the point where the Federals were in front of Anderson." The officer continued, "In diverting the wagon trains, Ewell failed ... to notify the next unit in the column ... to tell Gordon that he must keep straight ahead ... and must close on Ewell, though the wagons had taken the right fork."[22]

Gordon's column covered several miles along this different track before coming to a crossing of a steeply embanked river called Sailor's Creek. The season's rains had turned the dirt approaches to the bridges into a muddy morass that countless wagon wheels churned into a bottomless quagmire. William Cox described the mess: "Our trains had reached Sailor's Creek, a low, muddy stream with high embankments on either side. Our exhausted teams were unable to move forward, but were stalled in the middle of the line of retreat."[23] General Bryan Grimes realized it would take some time to get the hundreds of wagons across the river, so he spread out his five units in a double-line formation on a stretch of high ground, and backed up his infantry with some artillery. Grimes set his far left brigade in a position so its left flank was anchored by the Appomattox River, and the right flank rested on a bluff overlooking a small pond. This was the best he could do to protect his understrength division. Moments later Lt. Gen. Andrew Humphreys's Corps arrived to face off against the Confederates. General Humphreys reported, "The last attempted stand of the enemy was at Sailors Creek [where] … a sharp contest with the enemy commenced at once."[24] Lieutenant General Andrew Humphreys threw seven veteran brigades against Grimes's thin line. Bryan Grimes reported, "The enemy pushed on rapidly, attacking us with great pertinacity. We … repeatedly repulsed their assaults."[25]

Captain David Allen's small force of veterans were fatigued and hungry, and many where low on ammunition. His men, for now, were in the second line, a short distance behind a formation of Georgians, not far from the buildings of the Lockett farmstead. They could see the masses of blue coats maneuvering to attack, and an occasional artillery round exploded nearby, in case anyone had the idea their situation was safe. The Carolinian veterans waited. Their brigade commander, William Cox wrote, "About 5 o'clock p.m., Evan's Georgians were resisting the enemy in the front while my brigade was placed across the road less than a mile from Sailor's Creek, which crossed the line of our retreat."[26] The Tar Heels could hear the rumble of artillery and clatter of musketry to their south, telling them other Confederates were fighting desperately. But then that noise faded away, to be replaced by the sounds of troops approaching. Moments' later terror-stricken gray-coated infantrymen fled towards Cox's formation, bringing with them word that Ewell's divisions had been shattered. And as a testimony of this Confederate debacle, Cpt. Allen's troops noticed many of these retreating men had thrown away their weapons and equipment.

Federal cavalry units appeared behind the fleeing Southerners but veered off from chasing the frantic infantrymen. Instead, the blue coats noticed the massed jumble of stalled wagons and headed for them. The teamsters saw the Yanks approach and panicked, abandoning many of their vehicles. The Northerners swooped in and captured scores of wagons. General Humphreys recalled, "over 200 wagons … several battery forges and limbers were [captured] or destroyed."[27] A Southerner noted, "The column … struck [Gordon's] command while we were endeavoring to push the ponderous wagon trains through the bog, out of which the starved teams were unable to drag them…. Many of these wagons, loaded with ammunition, mired so deep in the mud [were lost]."[28] The Carolinians watched helplessly as their army's supply vehicles fell to the enemy.

The Northerners resumed their assault on Gen. Grimes's position, pinning the Confederates in place. General Humphreys pushed more blue coats forward and they pressed the paltry Southern formation backward. William Cox noted, "The Georgians fell back through my brigade."[29] Meanwhile, Yank infantry brigades arrived from the south, moving against the Confederate right flank and rear. The Thirtieth's veterans could see these new blue-coated formations would soon roll right over them. One Confederate officer recorded, "the enemy, massing heavily on his [Gordon's] front and both flanks, renewed the attack about 6 p.m."[30] Northern minié bullets impacted among the Carolinians, coming from the front and the right. Private George Aycock (Co. B) tumbled to the ground, his left thigh ripped apart by a bullet; Sgt. John Best (Co. E) was knocked down, his right ankle shattered; and Pvt. Edward Beasley's (Co. E) scalp was sliced open. The Carolinians began to drift away from their battle line, melting from right to left. Private William Carroll (Co. B) was hit in the right arm, and Pvt. Eli Felton (Co. F) dropped, a chunk of lead smacking into his body.[31]

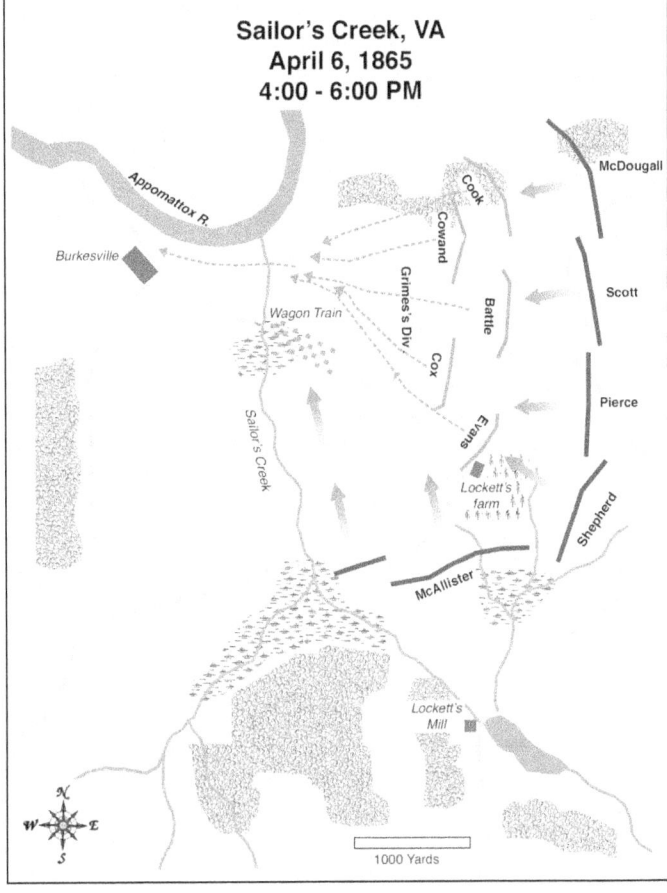

The Union troops, knowing they had flanked the Confederates, inched closer, howling in triumph. The Thirtieth began to disintegrate as more Carolinians gave up their position, shifting to the left, while others simply discarded their weapons and ran. A Tar Heel wrote, "The Federals then moved on Gordon's right. The pressure forced the line to break in confusion."[32] Another added, "After Ewell's troops were captured, Gordon's right was attacked from the south while his front was under heavy pressure.... His line broke in much confusion."[33] Brigadier General Cox, while trying to keep his fragile regiments fighting, worked on a plan to save his formation. He recalled, "the enemy ... advanced in such numbers and impetuosity as to throw our army into confusion and place it beyond control ... it became necessary for me to retire.... I faced the brigade to the left, marched them ... [to] the protection of the woods."[34] But for many of Cpt. David Allen's men, there was no time to retreat, over two dozen, including 2nd Lt. Samuel Newton (Co. E), were forced to drop their rifles and surrender.[35]

The Carolinians stampeded across Sailor's Creek, following the flood of retreating Southerners to the Appomattox River. Here, they joined the uncontrolled disarray of wagons, artillery pieces, and frenzied men fighting to cross the engineering marvel called the High Bridge. This structure, a twenty-one span structure nearly two thousand four hundred feet long and as much as one hundred-sixty-feet high, proved to be a critical choke point for the retreating Confederates. Most of Cpt. Allen's Tar Heels were able to push their way across the bridge; however, another eight were prevented from crossing and captured.[36] Since the men of Gen. Bryan Grimes's division were the last to get across the Appomattox River, those who had crossed earlier in the day, especially the troops led by Lt. Gen. James Longstreet, had been organized into a defensive positions. The Carolinians filtered past Longstreet's men and were eventually corralled together, and William Cox reformed his shrunken band of veterans. Union troops pressed against the Confederate defenses but the blue-coated soldiers were not interested in making a frontal assault and being killed needlessly. A Northern officer recorded, "night put a stop to the pursuit."[37]

Captain David Allen's remaining officers and NCOs gathered their survivors together and tabulated the damage that had occurred to their regiment. The Thirtieth's riflemen, once formed, gazed right and left at the horribly shriveled remnants and shook their heads in dismay; there were less than one hundred forty men remaining, and a number no longer had weapons.[38] They all were hungry, and everyone was exhausted. Few had anything to say, and most just wanted to lie down and sleep. A Carolinian rifleman summed up how they all felt, writing, "We had neither food nor sleep—hollow eyed, sunken cheeked, famished, dead for sleep.... Hunger is bad; lack of sleep is worse."[39]

General Robert E. Lee, once informed of his survivors' numbers, and shocked by the loss of Ewell's divisions exclaimed, "My God! Has the army dissolved?" But when Lee studied the resolute faces of the troops remaining he stated, "there are some true men left."[40] Then, Lee gave the order for his men to march, telling them there were rations at Farmville. General Bryan Grimes wrote, "That night we took the road for Farmville."[41] The weary soldiers shuffled in the darkness, knowing many of their friends and relatives they'd spoken with earlier this day were no longer among them. A riflemen remarked, "The wounded, the sick, the exhausted, the dead, had been left behind."[42] The night sky was dark and the temperature frigid, there were even reports of light snow falling in Burkeville. The regiments possessing cohesion marched as groups while the units with eroded disciple moved in swarms. An officer described the trek, writing, "Disorganized troops and hundreds of men separated from commands wandered hopelessly along, and crowded the road."[43] Private John Bone (Co. I) recalled, "This was a very sad and trying to me."[44]

The tired column of men reached Farmville not long after sunrise on April 7, 1865, and discovered rations awaited them. One soldier remarked, "At Farmville the rebels had some seven trains of supplies which had come down from Lynchburg to meet them."[45] The famished Tar Heels clutched the treasured food and sought a place to prepare their meals. A Southerner noted, "Gordon's Corps received two days' rations, which they undertook to cook in such skillets and frying pans as had survived the long retreat."[46] Others gobbled the food uncooked and then slumped to the ground, asleep. One of these riflemen recalled, "we fell on the ground, with our guns at our sides, from sheer exhaustion, having for four days toiled along the muddy road, fought back the enemy on a little parched corn, and slept the sleep of the weary and exhausted."[47]

But then, Union forces arrived, deployed and moved to drive the hungry Confederates from the railroad station. Major General William Mahone, leading five under-strength brigades in Longstreet's Corps confronted the advancing Federals and was quickly overwhelmed by superior numbers. General Bryan Grimes wrote, "Heavy firing was going on at this point, when Gen. Mahone came rushing up and reported that the enemy had charged, turned his flank, and was driving his men from their guns and the works which he had erected early in the day for the protection of these cross roads."

Grimes continued, "I then ordered my three Brigades, Cook's, Cox's and Cowand's at a doublequick on the line, with Battle and Archer, charging the enemy and driving them well off from Mahone's works, recapturing the artillery taken by them and capturing a large number of prisoners and holding this position."[48] Private John Bone (Co. I) shrugged his shoulders and wrote, "we reached Farmville ... formed line of battle, fought awhile, moved on, and formed line again, made breastworks with fence rails and dirt, and fought again."[49]

General Lee could see more Federal columns approaching the fight and knew his battered troops could not protect the train station; he had to relinquish the depot. A Northerner boasted, "General Lee, not being able to hold Farmville long enough to get the food and clothing off the trains, sent them up to Appomattox."[50] The Confederates broke contact with the Yanks and limped north and west, toward hoped-for salvation. Captain David Allen's formation evolved into two groups; those with weapons and resilience in one, and a mob of unarmed others who drifted behind. General Grimes detailed his troops' condition: "The men were very much jaded and suffering for necessary sustenance, our halts not having been sufficiently long to prepare their food, besides all of our cooking utensils not captured or abandoned were where we could not reach them."[51] Some of the riflemen, their spirit crushed and their morale defeated, fell by the roadside and Yank cavalry gathered them together. One such Tar Heel was described in a story: "A famished, ragged North Carolinian was wandering along a rail fence in the hope of surprising a chicken when a squad of well-fed, warmly clothed Union troops descended on him. 'Surrender, surrender,' they yelled, 'we've got you.' 'Yes,' said the Johnny Reb, as he dropped his gun, 'you've got me, and the hell of a git you've got.'"[52]

The Carolinians awoke near sunrise on April 8, 1865, and soon were on the road, journeying towards the southwest, each soldier moving forward as best as he could. This day though, Gen. Gordon's Corps led the army's march, rather than deal with rear-guard responsibilities. General Lee, as he watched his miserable troops shuffle past, remarked, "The roads were wretched and the progress slow."[53] Private John Bone (Co. I) recalled, "Saturday morning, April 8th, found us tramping on, we marched all day without any engagements."[54] He, like all the survivors in the Thirtieth was relieved to be free of Yank danger. Another gray-clad soldier scribbled, "The enemy left us to a quiet day's march ... nothing disturbing the reargaurd, and our left flank being little annoyed."[55]

General Robert Lee though, had much work to do. A large portion of his infantry had been destroyed, and all that remained of those units were a number of their senior officers. Lee, as he re-organized his understrength army released these leaders from their duties. An officer noted this, writing, "Dick Anderson, George Pickett and Bushrod Johnson ... were relieved and were authorized to return home."[56] One of these commanders, Maj. Gen. Bushrod Johnson, wrote, "my command was assigned to General Gordon's corps [and] marched under orders from that corps commander."[57] General John Gordon took these new troops and assigned many of them to Bryan Grimes's division.[58]

The Southerners hiked until late afternoon, when a halt was called; they were five miles east of Appomattox. Private John Bone wrote, "In the evening we stopped, stacked arms and ... now had a chance to cook and eat a square meal."[59] Another Tar Heel survivor, Cpl. Archy McGill (Co. H) recalled, "We did not take long to prepare supper, for we had nothing to prepare. A few boys had a handful of corn, which they parched and ate, but by far the greater number lay down on the bare ground weary and supperless." McGill added, "I was fortunate in having a tea cup full of corn mean and about an inch square of fat meat, which I had carried through all the toilsome marches and dreadful scenes of that retreat with an opportunity of cooking it. In camp that night, I could not find in our brigade a frying-pan, oven, spider or any other kind of cooking utensil." He continued, "so I thought for a while that I should be constrained to carry my handful of meal and my square inch of fat bacon for a while longer. But at last I found a long handled shovel, in which I made up my dough and baked a little cake of bread about the size of a biscuit, though not nearly so thick. I then fried the bacon, which turned out to be all grease and which I ate out of the shovel."[60]

The exhausted North Carolinians bedded down for the night. John Bone (Co. I) noted, "It was a beautiful evening, but a little cool. After eating, we laid down to sleep, hoping to have one more night's rest."[61] However, even as the tired men drifted off to sleep, their fortunes dissolved. Union troops, though not attacking the Southern line of movement, had aggressively been moving to intercept and surround the Confederates. Cavalry thundered along side roads, paralleling Lee's forces and eventually getting ahead of the gray troops' vanguard. The Northerners had figured out where Lee intended to go—Appomattox Station—and raced to get there before his troops did.

The first soldiers arriving at Appomattox Station were from Maj. Gen. George Custer's cavalry squadrons. They trotted into the small community's center and realized the Confederate supply trains sat there, along with a large portion of the Southern artillery, protected by just three small cavalry units, plus a handful of train workers and guards. George Custer's horsemen attacked and were immediately repulsed by the resolute Southerners, who supported by some of the artillery batteries, forced the Northerners to fall back. But Custer would not quite and ordered more assaults. Captain David Allen's veterans could hear the noise of this conflict. Corporal McGill (Co. H) wrote, "About sunset ... we heard the thunder of artillery in our front. The sound of artillery was familiar to our ears. We heard it unceasingly on the left of our line of march, and as incessantly in our rear, but to hear the sounds of guns in our front plainly indicated that we were being surrounded."[62]

However, as darkness smothered the Virginia countryside, the distant fighting died away. The Carolinians slept, no longer concerned, enabling Cpl. McGill to note, "We were informed ... that we might sleep that night—which was welcome news to men who had scarcely closed their eyes for eight or nine days and nights."[63] But what they did not know, was Custer's men had triumphed. A Northern officer recorded, "Darkness came on, and, guided by the flashed of the enemy's guns, Custer was still pushing and pressing.... [Then] the enemy's position was [taken] and an indiscriminate mass of guns, caissons, and baggage trains captured."[64]

General Robert E. Lee soon learned of this disaster at the train station. Lee now knew there were Union troops in front of him, and that they had taken possession of his army's critical rations and supplies. Lee, again, was forced to improvise. He called in Gen. Gordon and instructed him to attack the Federals as soon as possible on April 9th. John Gordon acknowledged this order and gathered his brigade commanders together to make plans. Gordon now led a dozen brigades, though the largest of these formations numbered less than three hundred effective riflemen. A staff officer put the entire total at, "no more than 1,600 muskets."[65] General Gordon laid out brigade assignments and marching details, and then sent the brigade officers back to their undersized formations. His Corps prepared for one more assault, and within an hour, the Confederates were in motion. Private John Bone (Co. I) grumbled, "Sometime between midnight and day, we were aroused, fell in line, took up our arms, and marched off."[66]

The sullen riflemen hiked the last few miles to Appomattox and halted. One infantryman recalled, "we were aroused from our sleep and marched to the courthouse ... [we] rested in the main street through the town, shivering in the cold until daybreak."[67] Another wrote, "While resting on our arms some of [the] men ... were parching corn on little improvised fires."[68] Unfortunately, those who attempted cooking did not have enough time. John Bone wrote, "About light we ... now at Appomattox Court House ... were soon formed into line of battle."[69] The Carolina riflemen, made their way to the pre-assault position; it was to be on the far right flank, a position it was ordered to hold, due to the Tar Heels' solid organization and staunch morale.

30th North Carolina Infantry[70]
April 9, 1865

Unit		Strength
Field & Staff	Cpt. Allen, David. Cpt. Ardrey, William E. Cpt. Moore, Samuel R.	3
Co. A	1st Sgt. Crumpler, Robert M.	5
Co. B	1st Sgt. Newsome, John G.	9
Co. C	Sgt. Butler, Benjamin C.	4
Co. D	—-	8
Co. E	1st Lt. Johnson, Ira J.	7
Co. F	2nd Lt. House, James W.	14
Co. G	3rd Lt. Fulford, John T.	6
Co. H	—-	14
Co. I	—-	8
Co. K	—-	6
		84

Brigadier General William Cox lined up his small brigade, now numbering less than three hundred riflemen. Each of his five regiments had been stripped down to the last few men still able to carry a musket. The Thirtieth could only muster eighty-four officers and men. Captain David Allen organized his regiment into two units, one commanded by Cpt. William Ardrey and the other by Cpt. Samuel "Rufus" Moore. The Carolinians in this final battle formation gazed at each other and said little. They had been told Yankees surrounded them, and their attack would enable the Confederates to break out and escape.[71] A Southern riflemen summed up how they felt, writing, "and once more, and for the last time, these ragged, foot-sore, and half-starved North Carolinians stood in the strength of their manhood with the men they had met and had driven back on many a bloody field."[72] They waited for the order to advance.

Brigadier General William Cox wrote, "At 5 o'clock a.m., I received an order that on the firing of a cannon the division would move forward." The artillery piece signaled the start and the Confederates advanced, the entire line slowly wheeling to the left, with the inner units supposed to barely move, while the outer formations hustled. The swinging movement did not appear as a wheeling-motion, but rather devolved into a stepped formation. Cox noted, "[we] promptly moved forward in echelon by brigade at intervals of one hundred paces."⁷³ Another officer wrote, "[We] formed a line on the left of the road.... We soon advanced.... Continuing to advance, we seemed to swing more and more to the left, and had left the road a long way to our right, when ordered to halt.... At this point we could see no Yankees."⁷⁴ And a third added, "The quaver of the 'rebel yell' saluted the dawn."⁷⁵

General Gordon's battle line wheeled to the left, heading southward, a mile-long formation composed of separate, en-echelon brigades. William Cox's Tar Heels stomped forward, swinging slowly to the left, with Cook's small brigade of Georgians on their left, and a troop of Virginian and North Carolinian cavalry to their right. A four-gun battery of Napoleons opened upon the Carolinians, firing at a range of less than half a mile. The first salvo struck among the small band of veterans in the 14th NC, causing Cpl. Archy McGill (Co. H) to remark, "On reaching the crest of the first rising ground, the Federal artillery opened upon our advancing line."⁷⁶ A Carolinian in the 14th NC wrote, "the Federal battery ... opened on us with shrapnel, the first one thrown striking right [among us] ... killing and wounding several men. This raised in the Yankee battery a cheer which we plainly heard."⁷⁷ More rounds impacted among the Tar Heels; Maj. Gen. Grimes recorded, "I remember well the appearance of the shell, and how directly they came towards me, exploding, and completely enveloping me in smoke."⁷⁸ William Cox wrote, "The division had not proceeded far before Cooke's and Cox's brigades were exposed to a murderous artillery fire, but [we did not] ... halt ... [or] recoil."⁷⁹

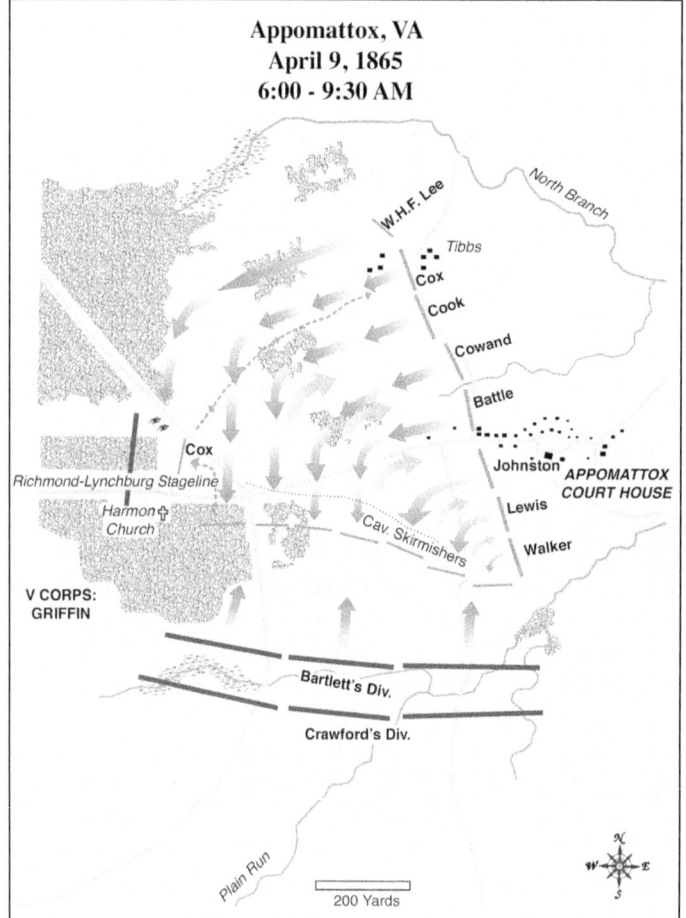

The Carolinian riflemen continued to slowly wheel to the left, trying to ignore the plodding fire from the Yank guns. Fortunately, the artillerymen were not the best, and most of their rounds detonated far beyond the Confederates. Captain David Allen's riflemen could see a thin line of blue-coated Federals a quarter mile away, spread out behind a farmer's fence. Soon, those men would also be shooting at the Tar Heels. Shrieks and yells, off to their right, caused a number of the Carolinians to glance in that direction. They saw Confederate cavalrymen thundering toward the Union guns. The cannoneers were so intent on trying to break up the gray infantry line they did not notice this approaching danger. One of the Tar Heel horsemen recorded, "The enemy's battery of four Napoleon guns ... their shot being directed chiefly at the infantry of Gordon's Corps ... we [75th NC Cav.] approached the battery rapidly and got among them with little loss. They surrendered at once."[80] Another Confederate added, "Two guns were captured from the enemy and a number of prisoners."[81]

General Gordon's fighters pressed forward, crossing the Richmond-Lynchburg Road, and began taking fire from the Union soldiers arrayed behind the fences south of the dirt thoroughfare. The popping from the blue coats' weapons indicated carbines; this line of troops must be dismounted cavalry. Eventually William Cox's men, who had the farthest to go to complete the half-wheel, came within range of the Northerners. Federal bullets zipped among the veteran riflemen. Suddenly, 2nd Lt. James House (Co. F) pitched forward, a bullet ripping through his right foot. Several men in his tiny company carried the wounded officer back to safety.[82] The Southern infantrymen surged forward with a howl and moments later, the Yankees scampered backward. The gray line captured the abandoned Union position moments later; and an officer recorded, "At the crossroads, the breastworks were reached and swept. The uniforms of the first fallen Federals showed to the relief of all ... [they] were dismounted cavalry."[83] General Bryan Grimes wrote, "[we drove] the enemy in confusion for three quarters of a mile beyond a range of hills covered with oak undergrowth."[84]

But then a stupefying sight appeared on a sloping ridge beyond the retreating cavalrymen—a massive wall of Union infantrymen. William Cox recorded what all his Carolinians saw, "At the back side of the field, about one-fourth of a mile away, we saw a heavy line of the enemy in line of battle."[85] The veteran Confederate riflemen stumbled to a halt. They had been told only cavalry separated them from being able to punch a hole through the Union encirclement, but now a vast formation of Yanks before them spoke of untold Federal reinforcements. Robert E. Lee noted, "The enemy was more than five times our numbers."[86] General William Cox's men stared in horror. Cox wrote, "General [Griffin] with ten thousand infantry was on our front." He added, "I ordered a halt when many columns of infantry were seen advancing."[87] Two full-strength Northern divisions were now moving to attack, men of Brig. Gen. Charles Griffins' V Corps. One of the blue-coated officers recorded, "[I] deployed my two [divisions] across the head of the valley just as Lee's advance was pushing out of it, for in spite of Sheridan's attempts to hold him, our cavalry were falling back in confusion before Lee's army." He also added, "We were barely there in time.... I [had] marched my men from daylight on the 8th until 10:00 a.m. on the 9th."[88]

John Gordon conferred with Lee, stating that "[It was] about 8 o'clock.... I have fought my Corps to a frazzle, and I fear I can do nothing unless I am heavily supported by Longstreet's Corps."[89] One of Lee's staff officers noted, "the army ... could not be extricated from its perilous condition surrounded by the immense force of the enemy."[90] General John Gordon and Robert E. Lee concluded an assault by his understrength formation would only result in needless casualties. Lee ordered Gordon to withdraw and then the commanding general sent out messengers holding flags of truce, asking for a cessation of the fighting. Bryan Grimes, not aware of Lee's decision, recorded, "Thereupon I received an order to withdraw, which I declined to do, supposing that Gen. Gordon did not understand the commanding position which my troops occupied.... I received a message from him with an additional one as coming from Gen. Lee to fall back."[91] Grimes sent word to his brigades to slowly withdraw, first the units on the left, and then by echelon, across the battle line towards the right. The formations began to inch away from their position, shuffling towards where their attack had begun, the area around Appomattox Court House.

Bryan Grimes met with William Cox, whose small brigade rested with its far right flank nestled within the safety of a body of trees. Grimes recalled, "I then ordered Cox to maintain his position in line of battle, and not to show himself until our rear was 100 yards distant, and then to fall back in line of battle, so as to protect our rear and right flank from assault."[92] William Cox's two hundred-fifty men held their ground, though the riflemen in the woods could hear Union troops moving through the trees towards them. His Carolinians knew their right flank and rear would soon be crushed. Cox watched as the rest of Gordon's troops fell back and waited as long as he felt his men could do so safely. The Northerners now moved forward to assault his front. General Grimes wrote, "The enemy, upon seeing us move off, rushed out from under cover with a cheer, when Cox's Brigade ... rose and fired a volley into them, which drove them back ... the Brigade then followed their retreating comrades in line of battle unmolested."[93]

Captain David Allen's Thirtieth, along with their brother Carolinians fell back eight hundred yards, slowly pursued by the cautious mass of Northern soldiers. It appeared as if the Yanks were reluctant to put themselves in danger, and though they could have destroyed William Cox's tiny formation, the blue coats just followed along behind. But then, another wall of Federals appeared out of the trees, their battle line coming from the west, aiming to flank Cox's troops. William Cox recorded, "I ordered the regimental commanders ... to meet me.... I directed their attention to a gradually rising hill, between us and the advancing columns of the enemy, and directed that they face their regiments about, and at a double-quick charge to the crest of the hill, and before the enemy should recover from their surprise, halt, fire by brigade, and then with rapid movement, face about and rejoin the division."[94]

William Cox's five regiments shifted their front so their small battle line faced to the west and then, with a holler, they rushed towards the approaching Northerners. Cox wrote, "Raising the 'rebel yell,' the brigade ... promptly and faultlessly executed the order, and having gained the brow of the hill, the enemy anticipating a determined struggle, commenced to deploy and prolong their line as if on parade ... the command rang along the Confederate line ... 'Halt, ready, aim, fire!'"[95] One of Cox's Tar Heel officers added, "the enemy saw us approach, apprehending a hand-to-hand conflict, they commenced to deploy with great alacrity and precision, when the brigade promptly halted and as promptly fired into the deploying line, which fell to the ground as we fired. Without losing seconds, [the] brigade faced about, [and] double-quicked [away] ... before the enemy recovered from the shock."[96] William Cox, as his veterans scurried away from their sudden assault on the Union troops, detached two of his Carolina regiments, along with a collection of brigade sharpshooters to guard the unit's rear. A Tar Heel officer from this small rear-guard wrote, "Gen. Cox then ordered me to take the 14th NC and 4th NC regiments and hold the enemy in check until he could get his command to the rear." He added, "We were soon hotly engaged and pressed back."[97] Corporal Archy McGill (Co. H), who was one of the handpicked sharpshooters, wrote, "The enemy, seeing us moving to the rear, again advanced ... [our] withdrawal being covered by [our] line of sharpshooters."[98]

William Cox's men back-peddled away from the Union onslaught while the handful of men in the 4th NC, 14th NC, and brigade sharpshooters kept up a brisk fire. Strangely, the Yanks quit shooting, though one of their formations moved to attack a Southern artillery battery. Cox called for Cpt. David Allen and, as the Carolinian recorded, "[Cox ordered me] to take my regiment and support a battery then firing, General Cox took the rest of the brigade from the field of action while I remained and fired on the enemy advancing on my flank; [the Yankees] halted and lay down, and immediately another line advanced on my flank, when I changed front and fired another round, the enemy [also] halt[ed] and laying down flat."[99] Private John Bone (Co. I) added, "We were ordered to fire on them by front rank.... We were expecting a heavy fight right here, but as soon as we discharged our guns.... The enemy did not fire on us."[100] Moments later a messenger came to the Thirtieth and, as one Tar Heel remarked, "They ordered us to stop firing, saying that Gen. Lee had surrendered."[101] Captain David Allen recalled later, "Neither line returned my fire. Then I received [the] order to join my command. I think the Federals were informed of the surrender, or they would have wiped us from the earth."[102]

The standoff between Cox's rear guard troops and the Union forces lasted for some time amid a strangely quiet battlefield. Then, William Cox sent word to fall back. The Carolinians made their way back to the brigade and were puzzled by the lack of organization. They, like their division commander, did not know how to interpret the order they received: "General Grimes ... asked General Gordon where he should form his men. The general answered, 'Anywhere you please.'"[103] Private John Bone (Co. I) wrote, "We marched back a piece, ... stacked arms and commenced piling up some fence rails for protection, expecting to be attacked soon. While we were at this somebody passed by and said, 'That Lee had surrendered,' but we did not think it was so."[104] The exhausted men waited, battered by rumors and uncertainty. One veteran observed, "[We laid] on our arms for some time."[105] Noon came and the quiet continued, though interrupted by an occasion outburst of firing.

Northern riders soon appeared and galloped quickly through the throngs of expectant men. A Confederate recalled, "Gen. Custer, bearing a white flag ... came riding up ... saluted, and stated that a surrender had been agreed upon."[106] The Carolinians looked at each other; the gossip was fact— General Lee had surrendered their army. A Southerner remarked, "Everybody, on both lines, stood up and looked in amazement at what was going on."[107] Then, as one writer recorded, "By 3:30 p.m.,

Cpt. James W. Badgett, 20 years old, commanded Co. G at the Appomattox surrender ceremony (Clark, 1901).

the Army of Northern Virginia was no longer a fighting force to be contended with."[108] The shocked Carolinians in the Thirtieth did not know what to do. One Southerner scribbled, "Then followed a scene no pen can describe. Ragged and dirty, gaunt with hunger, and physically exhausted, men went into paroxysms of grief or rage, tears running down grizzly old faces, while others broke up their guns, swords, or drums."[109] Another wrote, stunned by relief, "My God, that I should have lived to see this! ... I did not think I should live till this day."[110] General John Gordon wrote, "The men cried like children."[111] Others stood mutely and gazed towards home, while a few grumbled and whispered about sneaking away and joining Johnson's army in North Carolina. One such soldier remarked, "Oh! But it is a bitter, bitter humiliation. All our hopes of independence blasted! All that a generous people value, gone at one fell blow!"[112]

Regardless of their response, all of the men were war-weary and hungry. One of Lee's staff described the troops, writing, "the men, deprived of food and sleep for many days, were worn out and exhausted."[113] Robert E. Lee immediately made a request for rations to feed his famished men; Grant instantly complied. A Confederate noted, "During the late afternoon, commissary wagons entered the Confederate camps.... Nothing except bread was issued."[114] Corporal Archy McGill (Co. H) recalled, "In a short while after the surrender took place; we had more Yankees than rebels in our midst. There was the utmost consideration and good will. We had nothing to eat; General Grant sent us coffee and crackers in abundance." He added, "There was no demonstration of rejoicing; no firing of salutes; no cheering."[115] And Private John Bone (Co. I) remembered, "Sometime in the evening, we marched off a short distance, each division and brigade camping together as they generally did." He also noted, "The enemy camped near us, and we were soon visiting each other's camps.... I suppose that most of us on both sides took the quietest night rest that we had in many, for we were not dreading and watching for each other."[116]

30th North Carolina Infantry[117]
Surrender Ceremony
April 12, 1865

Unit		Strength
Field & Staff	Cpt. Allen David C	2
Co. A	1st Sgt. Crumpler, Robert M.	11
Co. B	1st Sgt. Newsome, John G.	12
Co. C	Sgt. Butler, Benjamin C.	9
Co. D	—-	14
Co. E	1st Lt. Johnson, Ira J.	12
Co. F	Cpt. Moore, Samuel R.	26
Co. G	Cpt. Badgett, James W.	14
Co. H	Sgt. Cole, Green B.	18
Co. I	Sgt. Crowell, Jonas W.	17
Co. K	Cpt. Ardrey, William E.	15
	Non Combat	2
		152

The next morning, April 10, 1865, the men slept much longer than normal, and then arose to a drippy sky. A Southerner recorded, "The [day] brought rain [and] more food, and refreshment that came from the first long, untroubled sleep that some of the troops had been allowed since April 3."[118] John Bone wrote, "We remained in camp on Monday and Tuesday waiting for our paroles. On Tuesday evening General Lee had us marched out and had all of his men gathered as near as they well could be; then he and others rode in the midst of us, and then setting on his horse, pulled off his hat, and made a speech, tell[ing] of his regrets that we had not succeeded in gaining the cause that we had tried so hard for, but [he] did not put the blame on us." Private Bone continued, "[Lee] compliment[ed] us for the four years of hard services that we had done, and also told us to go home in peace, be good citizens, and try to rebuild our lost fortunes. He sadly bade us all and the army of Northern Virginia adieu, and departed from us for the last time."[119]

On April 12, 1865, the Carolinians formed into regimental and brigade formation for a last time; they were to formally surrender their weapons. The Thirtieth was now larger than it had been since the fighting on April 6, 1865. A number of the stragglers had rejoined the regiment, and even a couple wounded men fell into line, wanting to be a part of this last Thirtieth North Carolina ceremony. They all clung to each other, knowing their extraordinary experience as comrades-in-arms had ended. John Bone described some of these final moments: "We went back to our camps and remained the night.... We spent the night in various ways, some sang and prayed, some sat around the camp fires and told their war jokes, some sang war songs ... others talked of home sweet home that they soon expected to see, and we all slept a little."[120]

Private John Bone recorded the surrender ceremony, writing, "[On April 12, 1865] we received our paroles, and were commanded to fall in with all of our equipment ... and marched out in an open field where there was a line of Yankees.... We fronted them and were commanded by our officer to stack arms, and take off our cartridge boxes, belts, and hang them on their arms. We obeyed the command, and this was the last command that we received."[121] Another Tar Heel commented, depicting a rifleman in the 4th NC, "[The soldier] ... as he places his musket in the stack he spoke his farewell: 'Sit there, Betsy: you've made many of them bite the dust.'"[122] Private John Bone also remarked, "it was a solemn time with us.... We said nothing to those that had been our enemies, neither did they say anything to us. We were marched off some distance, told to break ranks, and go to our homes in peace."[123] And finally, Cpt. William Ardrey (Co. K) recorded simply, "[We] delivered our guns to the enemy and set our [hearts] for our dear homes."[124] Moments later Maj. Gen. Bryan Grimes gathered his men around him and said, "Go home boys ... and act like men, as you always have done during the war."[125]

The Carolinians stockpiled what rations they could scrounge, gathered together their remaining possessions, and began their hike towards home. One Southerner noted, "In a few hours the army scattered, and the men went back to their ruined and dismantled homes ... all of them penniless, worn out, and well-high heart-broken."[126] John Bone recorded, "there were eighteen of us [Co. I] that surrendered. We decided that we would all stay together, and try to make our way home. It was a very solemn time when we began to scatter and start for our homes in different directions."[127] And William Ardrey noted on April 13, 1865, "Marched 21 miles and camped ... [we] made our way homeward with light hearts and weary limbs."[128] The Tar Heels walked towards North Carolina, journeying as far as their feet and stomachs allowed. One anxious-to-get-home fellow wrote, "We left in squads of tens, twenties and fifties with two days' rations in our haversacks, thanks to Grant's thoughtfulness. On the third day these squads were broken into halves and quarters and less, that we might obtain something to eat." He continued, "Day after day we pushed forward, longing to see father, mother, wife and child and the dear 'girl I left behind....' As we wended our weary way, came to forks of the road—the parting of the ways—sad, sad parting, for those who had had all things common for four years."[129]

30th North Carolina Infantry[130]
Prisoners in POW Camps
April 12, 1865

Elmira, NY	30
Point Lookout, MD	26
Ft. Delaware, DE	8
Hart's Island, NY	5
Johnson's Island, OH	3
Ft. McHenry, MD	1
	73

Another group of Thirtieth Tar Heels, the men who had been captured and languished in prisoner of war camps, also set their sights on home. Over seventy 30th NC soldiers languished in Federal prisons in Maryland, Delaware, Ohio, and New York. They soon learned of Lee's surrender, with one soldier remarking, "seems to be settled that Gen. Lee and Army surrendered to Grant. Some seem to rejoice while others lament."[131] Another wrote, "When Lee surrendered ... there was great rejoicing and ringing bells at Elmira."[132] The men waited impatiently to be freed and once the Federals established a procedure, the Southerners signed an oath, were processed for release, and sent towards home. Most gave their oath of allegiance and received their paroles in June 1865. A Confederate prisoner whose turn came for discharge, wrote, "The next morning 300 of us were taken to the cookhouse and while standing together with our right hands raised, the oath of allegiance to the U. S. was administered." He continued, "Then we were given two days rations, our paroles handed to us, and we were ready for our journey.... I will never forget the march from the cookhouse to the big gate. All the prisoners who were left behind congregated near the street as we went out ... many of the fellows left behind waved us farewells." The just-freed prisoner of war added, "The U. S. government gave us free transportation home as far as we could travel by rail."[133] Then, when the trains could go no farther, the Southerners hiked the rest of the way. But the rides were not entirely free; Pvt. James Myers (Co. K), a barefoot rifleman who had been captured at Kelly's Ford in November 1863 and was now a prisoner at Point Lookout, MD, recalled, "he was told if the prisoner did not have shoes, the prison gave them shoes. When released, the shoes were taken back by the prison. He walked all the way home barefoot."[134]

Regardless of how they neared home, these tough Carolinians, and most were young men in the prime of their youth, sloughed off some of the war's misery as they distanced themselves from the battlefields of Virginia, and grew excited about their futures. One such optimistic individual scribbled a note to his girl, "You must prepare for a jolly time when I come home!"[135] The war was over, the boys were coming home.

Appendix 1:
30th North Carolina Infantry Casualties

Gaines' Mill, Virginia
June 27, 1862
74 = 16 Killed, 57 Wounded, 1 Wounded & Missing

Unit	Rank	Name	Remarks
F & S	Lt. Col.	Kell, James T.	Wounded, 6/27/62 at Gaines' Mill
Co. A	1st Sgt.	Crumpler, Robert M.	Wounded (thigh), 6/27/62 at Gaines' Mill (shell fragments)
Co. A	Color Sgt.	Royal, Hardy S.	Wounded, 6/27/62 at Gaines' Mill
Co. A	Pvt.	Goodrich, James T.	Killed, 6/27/62 at Gaines' Mill
Co. A	Pvt.	Royal, Nevil	Wounded, 6/27/62 at Gaines' Mill
Co. A	Pvt.	Tew, Blackman	Killed, 6/27/62 at Gaines' Mill
Co. A	Pvt.	Williamson, James	Wounded (right hip), 6/27/62 at Gaines' Mill
Co. B	2nd Cpl.	Bell, William	Wounded, 6/27/62 at Gaines' Mill
Co. B	Pvt.	Bobbitt, Burwell B.	Wounded, 6/27/62 at Gaines' Mill
Co. B	Pvt.	Hendrick, Alexander W.	Wounded, 6/27/62 at Gaines' Mill
Co. B	Pvt.	Pegram, James B.	Wounded, 6/27/62 at Gaines' Mill
Co. B	Pvt.	Pegram, Robert B.	Wounded (left thigh), 6/26/62 at Mechanicsville
Co. B	Pvt.	Shearin, Richard R.	Killed, 6/27/62 at Gaines' Mill
Co. B	Pvt.	Thompson, John A.	Wounded (arm), 6/27/62 at Gaines' Mill. Died of wounds, 7/30/62
Co. C	Cpl.	Howard, Geo. Washington	Wounded, 6/27/62 at Gaines' Mill
Co. C	Pvt.	Danford, Abram	Wounded (face), 6/27/64 at Gaines' Mill
Co. C	Pvt.	McCall, John W.	Killed, 6/27/62 at Gaines' Mill
Co. C	Pvt.	Russ, Stewart	Wounded, 6/27/62 at Gaines' Mill
Co. C	Pvt.	Stanly, Stewart	Wounded, 6/27/62 at Gaines' Mill.
Co. C	Pvt.	Swain, Benjamin F.	Wounded (left arm), 6/27/62 at Gaines' Mill
Co. D	5th Sgt.	Ray, Zeddock D.	Wounded, 6/27/62 at Gaines' Mill
Co. D	Pvt.	Davis, James T.	Wounded, 6/27/62 at Gaines' Mill
Co. D	Pvt.	Ferrell, John C.	Wounded, 6/27/62 at Gaines' Mill
Co. D	Pvt.	Joyner, John L.	Wounded, 6/27/62 at Gaines' Mill
Co. D	Pvt.	Peed, William C.	Wounded (left side), 6/27/62 at Gaines' Mill
Co. D	Pvt.	Pollard, William H.	Wounded, 6/27/62 at Gaines' Mill. Died of wounds, 12/3/62 at Raleigh, NC
Co. D	Pvt.	Wilkins, James	Wounded, 6/27/62 at Gaines' Mill. Died of wounds, 7/25/62

Appendix 1

Unit	Rank	Name	Remarks
Co. D	Pvt.	Williams, Samuel S	Wounded, 6/27/62 at Gaines' Mill. "Deafness in left ear by explosion of shell"
Co. E	1st Cpl.	Wells, John H.	Wounded, 6/27/62 at Gaines' Mill
Co. E	4th Cpl.	Fursell, Andrew G.	Wounded, 6/27/62 at Gaines' Mill
Co. E	Pvt.	Blanton, Morris	Killed, 6/27/62 at Gaines' Mill
Co. E	Pvt.	Boney, James T.	Killed, 6/27/62 at Gaines' Mill
Co. E	Pvt.	Dickson, James	Wounded (shoulder), 6/27/62 at Gaines' Mill
Co. E	Pvt.	Evans, Adin	Wounded, 6/27/62 at Gaines' Mill
Co. E	Pvt.	Malpass, Carleton	Wounded, 6/27/62 at Gaines' Mill
Co. E	Pvt.	Norris, William W.	Wounded, 6/27/62 at Gaines' Mill
Co. E	Pvt.	Rivenbark, Joseph	Wounded, 7/27/62 at Gaines' Mill. Died of wounds (date unknown)
Co. E	Pvt.	Rouse, Barnet	Wounded, 6/27/62 at Gaines' Mill. Died of wounds (date unknown)
Co. E	Pvt.	Strickland, William W.	Killed, 6/27/62 at Gaines' Mill
Co. F	3rd Lt.	Eagles, Lorenzo Dow	Wounded, 6/27/62 at Gaines' Mill
Co. F	Pvt.	Bryant, John	Killed, 6/27/62 at Gaines' Mill
Co. F	Pvt.	Dew, William	Wounded (head & lungs), 6/27/62 at Gaines' Mill. Died of wounds, 7/3/62
Co. F	Pvt.	Edwards, Montgomery	Wounded ("gunshot wound in side"), 6/27/62 at Gaines' Mill
Co. F	Pvt.	Everett, William	Killed, 6/27/62 at Gaines' Mill
Co. F	Pvt.	Forbes, Arthur	Wounded (side), 6/27/62 at Gaines' Mill
Co. F	Pvt.	Forbes, James	Wounded, 6/27/62 at Gaines' Mill
Co. F	Pvt.	Moore, Thomas J.	Wounded (arm), 6/27/62 at Gaines' Mill
Co. F	Pvt.	Pittman, Reddin E.	Wounded, 6/27/62 at Gaines' Mill
Co. F	Pvt.	Robison, William	Killed, 6/27/62 at Gaines' Mill
Co. F	Pvt.	Wiggins, Martin W.	Wounded (thigh), 6/27/62 at Gaines' Mill
Co. G	1st Cpl.	Hunt, James A.	Wounded (leg), 6/27/62 at Gaines' Mill (leg amputated). Died of wounds, 7/2/62
Co. G	Pvt.	Badgett, John D.	Wounded, 6/27/62 at Gaines' Mill
Co. G	Pvt.	Frazier, Pumfred B.	Wounded (foot), 6/27/62 at Gaines' Mill
Co. G	Pvt.	Hunt, Isaac B.	Wounded, 6/27/62 at Gaines' Mill. Died of wounds, 6/28/62
Co. G	Pvt.	Parrish, Mathew	Killed, 6/27/62 at Gaines' Mill
Co. G	Pvt.	Sizemore, William P.	Wounded, 6/27/62 at Gaines' Mill
Co. H	4th Sgt.	Deaton, James P.	Wounded, 6/27/62 at Gaines' Mill
Co. H	Pvt.	Black, Alfred	Wounded, 6/27/62 at Gaines' Mill
Co. H	Pvt.	Brafford, Eli	Wounded, 6/27/62 at Gaines' Mill
Co. H	Pvt.	Brown, James	Wounded, 6/27/62 at Gaines' Mill
Co. H	Pvt.	Buchanan, Wm. May	Wounded & missing, 6/27/62 at Gaines' Mill
Co. H	Pvt.	Buie, Daniel	Wounded, 6/27/62 at Gaines' Mill. Died of wounds, 7/14/62
Co. H	Pvt.	Carr, Dennis	Wounded, 6/27/62 at Gaines' Mill
Co. H	Pvt.	Graham, Jarratt B.	Wounded, 6/27/62 at Gaines' Mill. Died ("drowned in Cape Fear River"), 7/4/62. "Fell overboard on the passage of the *Hurt* from Wilmington [NC] to Fayetteville [NC]."
Co. H	Pvt.	Knight, Benjamin	Wounded (left hand), 6/27/62 at Gaines' Mill
Co. H	Pvt.	Lawrence, John	Wounded, 6/27/62 at Gaines' Mill
Co. H	Pvt.	Wicker, William M.	Killed, 6/27/62 at Gaines' Mill
Co. I	Pvt.	Bass, Richard H.	Wounded, 6/27/62 at Gaines' Mill. Died of wounds, 6/28/62
Co. K	4th Sgt.	Hood, Abner B.	Killed, 6/27/62 at Gaines' Mill
Co. K	Sgt.	Steel, Andrew F.	Killed, 6/27/62 at Gaines' Mill

Unit	Rank	Name	Remarks
Co. K	Pvt.	Davis, George W.	Killed, 6/27/62 at Gaines' Mill
Co. K	Pvt.	McMullen, James H.	Wounded (shoulder), 6/30/62 at Gaines' Mill. Died of wounds, 7/1/62
Co. K	Pvt.	Tedder, Sidney	Killed, 6/27/64 at Gaines' Mill
Co. K	Pvt.	Thomason, John L.	Wounded, 6/27/62 at Gaines' Mill. Died of wounds, 7/4/62

Malvern Hill, Virginia
July 1, 1862
129 = 20 Killed, 106 Wounded, 2 Wounded & Captured, 1 Missing

Unit	Rank	Name	Remarks
Co. A	2nd Cpl.	Johnson, William H.	Wounded, 7/1/62 at Malvern Hill
Co. A	Cpl.	Pipkin, Lewis H.	Killed, 7/1/62 at Malvern Hill
Co. A	Cpl.	Royal, Sherman	Wounded (head), 7/1/62 at Malvern Hill. Died of wounds, 7/5/62 at Richmond
Co. A	Pvt.	Baggot, James W.	Killed, 7/1/62 at Malvern Hill
Co. A	Pvt.	Boon, Stephen	Wounded & Captured, 7/1/62 at Malvern Hill
Co. A	Pvt.	Brown, George E.	Wounded, 7/1/62 at Malvern Hill
Co. A	Pvt.	Cox, Robert G.	Wounded, 7/1/62 at Malvern Hill
Co. A	Pvt.	Godwin, Nathan H.	Wounded, 7/1/62 at Malvern Hill
Co. A	Pvt.	Howard, Thomas M.	Wounded (head), 7/1/62 at Malvern Hill
Co. A	Pvt.	Pope, Alexander	Wounded (chest), 7/1/62 at Malvern Hill
Co. A	Pvt.	Pope, Wiley	Wounded (head & knee), 7/1/62 at Malvern Hill
Co. A	Pvt.	Register, Edward M.	Wounded, 7/1/62 at Malvern Hill
Co. B	2nd Sgt.	Davis, Burwell P.	Wounded, 7/1/62 at Malvern Hill
Co. B	5th Sgt.	Harriss, John A.	Wounded, 7/1/62 at Malvern Hill
Co. B	1st Cpl.	Newsom, John G.	Wounded (right thigh), 7/1/62 at Malvern Hill
Co. B	Pvt.	Bishop, Alfred	Wounded (right shoulder), 7/1/62 at Malvern Hill
Co. B	Pvt.	Duke, George J.	Wounded, 7/1/62 at Malvern Hill
Co. B	Pvt.	Duke, Robert W.	Wounded, 7/1/63 at Malvern Hill. Died of wounds, 8/1/62
Co. B	Pvt.	Gill, Philip P.	Wounded (face), 7/1/62 at Malvern Hill (shell explosion; "total loss of vision of left eye … impairment of vision of the other."
Co. B	Pvt.	Loughlin, John	Wounded, 7/1/62 at Malvern Hill
Co. B	Pvt.	Neal, Dudley H.	Wounded (leg), 7/1/62 at Malvern Hill
Co. B	Pvt.	Shearin, Nicholas L.	Killed, 7/1/62 at Malvern Hill
Co. B	Pvt.	White, James J.	Wounded, 7/1/62 at Malvern Hill. Died of wounds, 8/1/62
Co. C	1st Lt.	Greer, Ephraim J.	Wounded, 7/1/62 at Malvern Hill. Died of wounds, 7/26/62; "left leg cut off below the knee."
Co. C	4th Sgt.	Tharp, John L.	Wounded (left hand), 7/1/62 at Malvern Hill (3 fingers amputated)
Co. C	5th Sgt.	Butler, Benjamin L.	Wounded (foot), 7/1/62 at Malvern Hill
Co. C	Cpl.	Lambeth, William	Wounded, 7/1/62 at Malvern Hill
Co. C	Cpl.	Leonard, Samuel B.	Wounded (chest), 7/1/62 at Malvern Hill
Co. C	Pvt.	Dew, David C.	Wounded, 7/1/62 at Malvern Hill
Co. C	Pvt.	Flynn, James W.	Wounded, 7/1/62 at Malvern Hill
Co. C	Pvt.	Harris, Geo. Washington	Wounded (knee), 7/1/62 at Malvern Hill. Died of wounds, 7/19/62; "compound fracture of knee joint."

Appendix 1

Unit	Rank	Name	Remarks
Co. C	Pvt.	Hewett, Uriah	Wounded, 7/1/62 at Malvern Hill. Died of wounds, 7/12/62
Co. C	Pvt.	Hickman, Robert	Wounded, 7/1/62 at Malvern Hill
Co. C	Pvt.	Larkins, Robert S.	Wounded, 7/1/62 at Malvern Hill
Co. C	Pvt.	McCall, Paul S.	Wounded, 7/1/62 at Malvern Hill
Co. C	Pvt.	Milliken, Isaac	Wounded (left hand), 7/1/62 at Malvern Hill (one finger amputated)
Co. C	Pvt.	Mott, John	Wounded, 7/1/62 at Malvern Hill
Co. C	Pvt.	Potter, Henry G.	Wounded, 7/1/62 at Malvern Hill
Co. C	Pvt.	Tharp, William H.	Wounded, 7/1/62 at Malvern Hill
Co. C	Pvt.	Wescott, Samuel W.	Wounded, 7/1/62 at Malvern Hill
Co. D	2nd Cpl.	Allen, James P.	Killed, 7/1/62 at Malvern Hill
Co. D	Pvt.	Davis, Arrington J.	Killed, 7/1/62 at Malvern Hill
Co. D	Pvt.	Davis, James R.	Killed, 7/1/62 at Malvern Hill
Co. D	Pvt.	Garner, John T.	Wounded, 7/1/62 at Malvern Hill
Co. D	Pvt.	Jones, Isham F.	Killed, 7/1/62 at Malvern Hill
Co. D	Pvt.	Mangum, Calvin T.	Wounded (left hip & right foot), 7/1/62 at Malvern Hill
Co. D	Pvt.	Mason, Joseph	Wounded, (left leg), 7/1/62 at Malvern Hill. (left leg amputated). Died of wounds, 7/7/62
Co. D	Pvt.	O'Neal, Hardy	Wounded (right arm), 7/1/62 at Malvern Hill
Co. D	Pvt.	Pierce, George W.	Wounded (right knee), 7/1/62 at Malvern Hill
Co. D	Pvt.	Pierce, James T.	Wounded, 7/1/62 at Malvern Hill
Co. D	Pvt.	Piper, Wesley Y.	Wounded, 7/1/62 at Malvern Hill
Co. D	Pvt.	Wheeler, James	Killed, 7/1/62 at Malvern Hill
Co. D	Pvt.	White, Almon W.	Killed, 7/1/62 at Malvern Hill
Co. D	Pvt.	White, James	Wounded (stomach), 7/1/62 at Malvern Hill
Co. D	Pvt.	Wilkins, Elijah	Wounded, 7/1/62 at Malvern Hill
Co. E	2nd Cpl.	Rivenbark, William	Killed, 7/1/62 at Malvern Hill
Co. E	Pvt.	Bland, John J.	Wounded & Captured, 7/1/62 at Malvern Hill
Co. E	Pvt.	Cavenaugh, Jacob W.	Wounded, 7/1/62 at Malvern Hill
Co. E	Pvt.	Cavenaugh, James D.	Wounded (foot), 7/1/62 at Malvern Hill
Co. E	Pvt.	Cavenaugh, Obed E.	Killed, 7/1/62 at Malvern Hill
Co. E	Pvt.	Henderson, Jesse R.	Wounded, 7/1/62 at Malvern Hill
Co. E	Pvt.	Manellis, John	Wounded (ribs), 7/1/62 at Malvern Hill; "fracture of (5) right rib, the ball passing out (7–8) ribs left side near spine."
Co. E	Pvt.	Pickett, William D.	Wounded, 7/1/62 at Malvern Hill
Co. E	Pvt.	Rivenbark, Teachey	Wounded, 7/1/62 at Malvern Hill
Co. E	5th Sgt.	Cherry, Spencer	Wounded, 7/1/62 at Malvern Hill
Co. F	Cpt.	Moore, Willis M.	Wounded, 7/1/62 at Malvern Hill
Co. F	3rd Cpl.	Felton, Richard	Wounded, 7/1/62 at Malvern Hill
Co. F	Pvt.	Boyce, William	Wounded, 7/1/62 at Malvern Hill
Co. F	Pvt.	Crisp, Eason	Wounded, 7/1/62 at Malvern Hill. Died of wounds, 7/27/62
Co. F	Pvt.	Denton, Levi	Wounded (right leg), 7/1/62 at Malvern Hill. "terrible swelling of right leg."
Co. F	Pvt.	Harrell, David	Wounded, 7/1/62 at Malvern Hill
Co. F	Pvt.	Hathaway, Henry	Wounded, 7/1/62 at Malvern Hill
Co. F	Pvt.	Moore, John J.	Wounded, 7/1/62 at Malvern Hill
Co. F	Pvt.	Morgan, James B.	Wounded (shoulder), 7/1/62 at Malvern Hill
Co. F	Pvt.	O'Neal, John	Killed, 7/1/62 at Malvern Hill
Co. F	Pvt.	Phillips, David J.	Killed, 7/1/62 at Malvern Hill
Co. F	Pvt.	Vick, William	Wounded, 7/1/62 at Malvern Hill
Co. F	Pvt.	Walston, James	Killed, 7/1/62 at Malvern Hill

Unit	Rank	Name	Remarks
Co. F	Pvt.	Webb, Hardy	Killed, 7/1/62 at Malvern Hill
Co. F	Pvt.	Williford, Thomas	Killed, 7/1/62 at Malvern Hill
Co. G	2nd Cpl.	Kittrell, William H.	Wounded, 7/1/62 at Malvern Hill
Co. G	Pvt.	Barnett, George P.	Wounded, 7/1/62 at Malvern Hill
Co. G	Pvt.	Blackwell, John	Wounded, 7/1/62 at Malvern Hill. Died of wounds, 7/10/62
Co. G	Pvt.	Chalkley, Ben. Thomas	Killed, 7/1/62 at Malvern Hill
Co. G	Pvt.	Cheatham, William A.	Wounded, 7/1/62 at Malvern Hill
Co. G	Pvt.	Frazier, Alex S.	Wounded (knee), 7/1/62 at Malvern Hill. Died of wounds, 7/6/62
Co. G	Pvt.	Hamme, Richard F.	Wounded, 7/1/62 at Malvern Hill
Co. G	Pvt.	Hobgood, James M.	Wounded, 7/1/62 at Malvern Hill
Co. G	Pvt.	Hunt, John O.	Wounded, 7/1/62 at Malvern Hill
Co. G	Pvt.	Reams, George W.	Wounded, 7/1/62 at Malvern Hill
Co. G	Pvt.	Traylor, A. M.	Wounded, 7/1/62 at Malvern Hill. Died of wounds, 7/22/62
Co. H	2nd Cpl.	Morrison, Horace	Wounded, 7/1/62 at Malvern Hill
Co. H	Pvt.	Blalock, F. Marion	Wounded (left knee), 7/1/62 at Malvern Hill
Co. H	Pvt.	Cole, George C.	Killed, 7/1/62 at Malvern Hill
Co. H	Pvt.	Cox, John Louis	Wounded (right arm), 7/1/62 at Malvern Hill
Co. H	Pvt.	Cox, William O.	Wounded, 7/1/62 at Malvern Hill
Co. H	Pvt.	Hunter, Charles A.	Wounded, 7/1/62 at Malvern Hill
Co. H	Pvt.	Hunter, John R.	Wounded, 7/1/62 at Malvern Hill
Co. H	Pvt.	Hunter, Stanford	Wounded, 7/1/62 at Malvern Hill, Died of wounds, 7/22/62
Co. H	Pvt.	Mashburn, James D.	Wounded, 7/1/62 at Malvern Hill. Died of wounds, 7/3/62
Co. H	Pvt.	McAulay, William	Captured, 7/1/62 at Malvern Hill
Co. H	Pvt.	McCulloch, William	Wounded, 7/1/62 at Malvern Hill. Died of wounds, 7/3/62
Co. H	Pvt.	McFatter, Alexander	Captured, 7/1/62 at Malvern Hill
Co. H	Pvt.	McNeill, Laughlin	Wounded (right arm), 7/1/62 at Malvern Hill (arm amputated)
Co. H	Pvt.	Riddle, George W.	Wounded (left hand & left ankle), 7/1/62 at Malvern Hill
Co. H	Pvt.	Wicker, Kenneth W.	Wounded, 7/1/62 at Malvern Hill. Died of wounds, 7/11/62
Co. H	Pvt.	Yancy, Thomas A.	Wounded, 7/1/62 at Malvern Hill
Co. I	Cpt.	Arrington, William T.	Killed, 7/1/62 at Malvern Hill
Co. I	1st Cpl.	Bryan, James H.	Wounded, 7/1/62 at Malvern Hill
Co. I	2nd Cpl.	Vick, Exum R.	Wounded (right thigh), 7/1/62 at Malvern Hill (leg amputated)
Co. I	Pvt.	Bass, John S.	Wounded, 7/1/62 at Malvern Hill
Co. I	Pvt.	Batchelor, Henry H.	Wounded, 7/1/62 at Malvern Hill
Co. I	Pvt.	Bone, John W.	Wounded (hand), 7/1/62 at Malvern Hill
Co. I	Pvt.	Brantley, Jn. Redmond	Wounded, 7/1/62 at Malvern Hill
Co. I	Pvt.	Langley, Singleton	Wounded (hip), 7/1/62 at Malvern Hill. Died of wounds, 7/7/62
Co. I	Pvt.	Lewis, Arnold L.	Wounded, 7/1/62 at Malvern Hill
Co. I	Pvt.	Price, Joel L.	Wounded (head), 7/1/62 at Malvern Hill
Co. I	Pvt.	Sherwood, George A.	Wounded (shoulder & jaw), 7/1/62 at Malvern Hill
Co. I	Pvt.	Walker, Berryman	Missing, 7/1/62 at Malvern Hill
Co. I	Pvt.	Williams, Henry H.	Wounded, 7/1/62 at Malvern Hill
Co. I	Pvt.	Williams, Micajah T.	Wounded, 7/1/62 at Malvern Hill

Unit	Rank	Name	Remarks
Co. I	Pvt.	Wilbourne, Ruffin F.	Wounded, 7/1/62 at Malvern Hill. Died of wounds, 7/3/62.
Co. I	Pvt.	Winstead, George T.	Wounded, 7/1/62 at Malvern Hill
Co. I	Pvt.	Woodward, John E.	Wounded, 7/1/62 at Malvern Hill
Co. K	3rd Lt.	Downs, John T.	Wounded, 7/1/62 at Malvern Hill
Co. K	Pvt.	Adkins, William H.	Wounded, 7/1/62 at Malvern Hill
Co. K	Pvt.	Bentley, William	Wounded, 7/1/62 at Malvern Hill
Co. K	Pvt.	Black, John H.	Wounded (left arm), 7/1/62 at Malvern Hill
Co. K	Pvt.	Jennings, George W.	Wounded (thigh), 7/1/62 at Malvern Hill. Leg amputated
Co. K	Pvt.	Robinson, James R.	Killed, 7/1/62 at Malvern Hill
Co. K	Pvt.	Younts, John	Wounded, 7/1/62 at Malvern Hill

South Mountain, Maryland
September 14, 1862
15 = 2 Wounded, 1 Wounded & Captured, 12 Captured

Unit	Rank	Name	Remarks
Co. D	Pvt.	Joyner, John L.	Captured, 9/14/62 at South Mountain
Co. D	Pvt.	Pierce, James T.	Captured, 9/14/62 at South Mountain
Co. D	Pvt.	Tilley, John R.	Captured, 9/14/62 at South Mountain
Co. F	Pvt.	Edwards, Elsberry B.	Captured, 9/14/62 at South Mountain
Co. F	Pvt.	Madra, George	Captured, 9/14/62 at South Mountain
Co. F	Pvt.	Morgan, Wm. Gray	Wounded, 9/14/62 at South Mountain
Co. F	Pvt.	Morton, Isaac	Captured, 9/14/62 at South Mountain
Co. F	Pvt.	Walston, William F.	Captured, 9/14/62 at South Mountain
Co. H	Cpt.	Wicker, Jesse J.	Wounded, 9/14/62 at South Mountain
Co. H	Sgt.	Buie, John	Captured, 9/14/62 at South Mountain
Co. H	Pvt.	Baker, Henry C.	Wounded & captured, Captured, 9/14/62 at South Mountain. Died of wounds, 12/17/62
Co. H	Pvt.	Cole, Andrew	Captured, 9/14/62 at South Mountain
Co. H	Pvt.	McDougal, Donald	Captured, 9/14/62 at South Mountain
Co. I	Pvt.	Bissett, Payton	Captured, 9/14/62 at South Mountain
Co. I	Pvt.	Williams, Joseph D.	Captured, 9/14/62 at South Mountain

Sharpsburg, Maryland
September 17, 1862
79 = 9 Killed, 48 Wounded, 2 Wounded & Captured, 20 Captured

Unit	Rank	Name	Remarks
F & S	Col.	Parker, Francis M.	Wounded (head), 9/17/62 at Sharpsburg
F & S	Adj.	Philips, Frederick	Wounded (head), 9/17/62 at Sharpsburg
Co. A	Pvt.	Brown, George E.	Killed, 9/17/62 at Sharpsburg
Co. A	Mus.	Clarkson, Thomas M.	Wounded, 9/17/62 at Sharpsburg
Co. A	Pvt.	Hobbs, Abraham	Wounded, 9/17/62 at Sharpsburg
Co. A	Pvt.	Holland, John R.	Wounded (head), 9/17/62 at Sharpsburg
Co. A	Pvt.	Howard, Fleet H.	Wounded, 9/17/62 at Sharpsburg
Co. A	Pvt.	McLemore, William S.	Captured, 9/17/62 at Sharpsburg
Co. B	Pvt.	Kimball, Nathaniel	Wounded, 9/17/62 at Sharpsburg
Co. B	Pvt.	Myrick, William W.	Wounded, 9/17/62 at Sharpsburg
Co. B	Cpl.	Robertson, Peter E.	Wounded, 9/17/62 at Sharpsburg
Co. B	Pvt.	Shearin, Thomas G.	Wounded, 9/17/62 at Sharpsburg
Co. C	Pvt.	Colman, George W.	Wounded (hip) & Captured, 9/17/62 at Sharpsburg

30th North Carolina Infantry Casualties

Unit	Rank	Name	Remarks
Co. C	Pvt.	Doshier, James H.	Wounded, 9/17/62 at Sharpsburg
Co. C	Sgt.	Edwards, William H.	Killed, 9/17/62 at Sharpsburg
Co. C	Pvt.	Harvell, John V.	Mortally wounded, 9/17/62 at Sharpsburg. Died of wounds, 10/7/62
Co. C	Pvt.	Howard, John J.	Captured, 9/17/62 at Sharpsburg
Co. C	Sgt.	Westcott, John W.	Captured, 9/17/62 at Sharpsburg
Co. D	Pvt.	Allen, Marion F.	Captured, 9/17/62 at Sharpsburg
Co. D	Pvt.	Cooper, William W.	Wounded (right arm), 9/17/62 at Sharpsburg
Co. D	3rd Lt.	Gill, William J.	Mortally wounded, 9/17/62 at Sharpsburg. Died of wounds, 10/13/62
Co. D	Pvt.	Penny, Solomon W.	Wounded, 9/17/62 at Sharpsburg
Co. D	2nd Lt.	Rogers, Charles M.	Killed, 9/17/62 at Sharpsburg
Co. E	Pvt.	Best, John B.	Wounded (leg), 9/17/62 at Sharpsburg
Co. E	Pvt.	Butler, Benjamin A.	Mortally wounded, 9/17/62 at Sharpsburg. Died of wounds, 10/1/62
Co. E	Pvt.	Dickson, Riol	Wounded (flesh, shell fragment), 9/17/62 at Sharpsburg
Co. E	Pvt.	Hanchey, John W.	Wounded, 9/17/62 at Sharpsburg
Co. E	Sgt.	Wells, James W.	Wounded, 9/17/62 at Sharpsburg
Co. F	Cpl.	Brown, William H.	Captured, 9/17/62 at Sharpsburg
Co. F	Pvt.	Bryant, Charles	Captured, 9/17/62 at Sharpsburg
Co. F	Pvt.	Dickens, Ephraim	Wounded (left thigh), 9/17/62 at Sharpsburg
Co. F	Pvt.	Harrell, David	Killed, 9/17/62 at Sharpsburg
Co. F	1st Lt.	Harrell, George K.	Wounded, 9/17/62 at Sharpsburg
Co. F	Pvt.	Hathaway, Augustus	Wounded (shoulder), 9/17/62 at Sharpsburg
Co. F	Pvt.	Jones, Levi	Wounded, 9/17/62 at Sharpsburg
Co. F	Pvt.	Keele, William	Wounded (left shoulder), 9/17/62 at Sharpsburg
Co. F	Pvt.	Lawrence, John J.	Captured, 9/17/62 at Sharpsburg
Co. F	Pvt.	Little, Jesse C.	Wounded, 9/17/62 at Sharpsburg
Co. F	Pvt.	Pittman, George W.	Wounded (right thigh), 9/17/62 at Sharpsburg
Co. F	Pvt.	Vick, Lorenzo	Killed, 9/17/62 at Sharpsburg
Co. F	Cpl.	Walston, Franklin	Wounded, 9/17/62 at Sharpsburg
Co. F	Pvt.	Warren, Lemuel	Wounded (head & left side), 9/17/62 at Sharpsburg
Co. F	Mus.	Webb, Newett	Wounded, 9/17/62 at Sharpsburg
Co. G	Pvt.	Brooks, Henry R.	Captured, 9/17/62 at Sharpsburg
Co. G	Sgt.	Brooks, James L.	Captured, 9/17/62 at Sharpsburg
Co. G	3rd Lt.	Crews, Alexander	Wounded & captured, 9/17/62 at Sharpsburg
Co. G	Pvt.	Daniel, William H.	Captured, 9/17/62 at Sharpsburg
Co. G	Pvt.	Frazier, James H.	Wounded, 9/17/62 at Sharpsburg
Co. H	Pvt.	Brown, James	Killed, 9/17/62 at Sharpsburg
Co. H	Pvt.	Lawrence, Bennett	Mortally wounded & captured, 9/17/62 at Sharpsburg. Died of wounds, 9/24/62
Co. H	Pvt.	McDonald, James S.	Captured, 9/17/62 at Sharpsburg
Co. H	Pvt.	McDonald, Neill	Wounded (shoulder), 9/17/62 at Sharpsburg
Co. H	Pvt.	McFarland, Andrew	Wounded, 9/17/62 at Sharpsburg
Co. H	Pvt.	McFarland, John A.	Captured, 9/17/62 at Sharpsburg
Co. H	Pvt.	Matthews, John B.	Wounded, 9/17/62 at Sharpsburg
Co. H	Pvt.	Mashburn, Alfred I.	Wounded, 9/17/62 at Sharpsburg
Co. H	Pvt.	Monroe, James A.	Wounded, 9/17/62 at Sharpsburg
Co. H	Pvt.	Phillips, John H.	Wounded (left knee), 9/17/62 at Sharpsburg
Co. H	Pvt.	Shaw, Douglas C.	Captured, 9/17/62 at Sharpsburg
Co. H	Pvt.	Sloan, David H.	Wounded, 9/17/62 at Sharpsburg
Co. H	Pvt.	Wicker, Thomas	Wounded, 9/17/62 at Sharpsburg

Unit	Rank	Name	Remarks
Co. H	Pvt.	Wicker, William F.	Wounded (right forearm), 9/17/62 at Sharpsburg
Co. I	Sgt.	Batchelor, Van Buren	Wounded & Captured, 9/17/62 at Sharpsburg
Co. I	Pvt.	Griffin, James D.	Wounded (ankle), 9/17/62 at Sharpsburg
Co. I	Pvt.	Lewis, Edward W.	Killed, 9/17/62 at Sharpsburg
Co. I	Cpl.	Manning, Moses V.	Mortally wounded, 9/17/62 at Sharpsburg. Died of wounds, 9/28/62
Co. I	Sgt.	Renfrow, Perry V.	Wounded, 9/17/62 at Sharpsburg
Co. I	Pvt.	Whitley, Jolley B.	Wounded, 9/17/62 at Sharpsburg
Co. I	Pvt.	Winstead, Hilliard H.	Captured, 9/17/62 at Sharpsburg
Co. K	Pvt.	Baker, Jeptha	Wounded (head), 9/17/62 at Sharpsburg. Died of wounds, 10/23/62
Co. K	Pvt.	Black, James H.	Killed, 9/17/62 at Sharpsburg
Co. K	Pvt.	DeArmond, Aaron L.	Captured, 9/17/62 at Sharpsburg
Co. K	Pvt.	Dunn, Andrew J.	Killed, 9/17/62 at Sharpsburg
Co. K	Pvt.	Culp, Aley A.	Wounded (thigh, shell wound), 9/17/62 at Sharpsburg
Co. K	Pvt.	Howey, John H.	Captured, 9/17/62 at Sharpsburg
Co. K	Pvt.	Johnston, David E.	Wounded, 9/17/62 at Sharpsburg
Co. K	Cpl.	Ezzell, Moses F.	Wounded (back, shell wound), 9/17/62 at Sharpsburg
Co. K	Pvt.	Stephenson, James	Mortally wounded, 9/17/62 at Sharpsburg. Died of wounds, 12/15/62
Co. K	Pvt.	Thompson, Lee	Wounded, 9/17/62 at Sharpsburg
Co. K	Pvt.	Weeks, Rufus B.	Wounded (shoulder), 9/17/62 at Sharpsburg
Co. K	Pvt.	Williamson, William E.	Captured, 9/17/62 at Sharpsburg
Co. K	Pvt.	Wolfe, Thomas D.	Wounded (hand), 9/17/62 at Sharpsburg

Fredericksburg, Virginia
December 13–14, 1862
16 = 15 Wounded, 1 Captured

Unit	Rank	Name	Remarks
Co. A	Pvt.	Taylor, Thomas J.	Wounded, 12/13/62 at Fredericksburg
Co. C	Pvt.	Butler, John C.	Wounded (face), 12/13/62 at Fredericksburg
Co. C	Pvt.	Pilgrim, McGilbert	Captured, 12/13/62 at Fredericksburg
Co. D	Pvt.	Allen, Elias G.	Wounded (both thighs), 12/13/62 at Fredericksburg
Co. D	Pvt.	Lumbley, William L.	Wounded, 12/13/62 at Fredericksburg
Co. D	Pvt.	Wilkins, Elijah	Wounded, 12/13/62 at Fredericksburg
Co. E	Sgt.	Wells, John	Mortally wounded, 12/13/62 at Fredericksburg. Died of wounds, 12/22/62
Co. E	Pvt.	Hanchey, John W.	Wounded, 12/13/62 at Fredericksburg
Co. E	Pvt.	Pickett, John L.	Wounded, 12/13/62 at Fredericksburg
Co. F	Pvt.	Little, Jesse	Wounded, 12/13/62 at Fredericksburg
Co. F	Pvt.	Mayo, James	Wounded, 12/13/62 at Fredericksburg
Co. G	Pvt.	Holbrook, Patterson B.	Wounded, 12/13/62 at Fredericksburg
Co. H	Pvt.	McDougal, Donald	Wounded (both legs), 12/13/62 at Fredericksburg (one leg amputated). Died of wounds, 12/30/62
Co. I	Pvt.	Joyner, Alsey M.	Wounded, 12/13/62 at Fredericksburg
Co. K	Pvt.	DeArmond, Aaron L.	Wounded (arm), 12/13/62 at Fredericksburg
Co. K	Pvt.	Russell, William D.	Wounded, 12/13/62 at Fredericksburg

Chancellorsville, Virginia
May 3, 1862
115 = 24 Killed, 91 Wounded

Unit	Rank	Name	Remarks
Co. A	1st Sgt.	Crumpler, Robert M.	Wounded, 5/3/63 at Chancellorsville
Co. A	2nd Sgt.	Williamson, Henry	Wounded, 5/3/63 at Chancellorsville
Co. A.	Color Sgt.	Royal, Hardy S.	Wounded (knee & thigh), 5/3/63 at Chancellorsville (leg amputated)
Co. A	1st Cpl.	Crumpler, James M.	Wounded (jaw), 5/3/63 at Chancellorsville
Co. A	Pvt.	Butler, Edward N.	Wounded (both thighs), 5/3/64 at Chancellorsville
Co. A	Pvt.	Duncan, Charles W.	Wounded, 5/3/63 at Chancellorsville. Died of wounds, 5/29/63
Co. A.	Pvt.	Holland, John R.	Killed, 5/3/63 at Chancellorsville
Co. A	Pvt.	Kelly, James M	Wounded, 5/3/63 at Chancellorsville
Co. A	Pvt.	Naylor, Ransom	Killed, 5/3/63 at Chancellorsville
Co. A	Pvt.	Parker, James M.	Wounded, 5/3/63 at Chancellorsville
Co. A	Pvt.	Pennington, William	Wounded (head), 5/3/63 at Chancellorsville
Co. A	Pvt.	Rackley, George W.	Wounded, 5/3/63 at Chancellorsville
Co. A	Pvt.	Taylor, William J.	Wounded (back & left shoulder), 5/3/63 at Chancellorsville
Co. A.	Pvt.	Underwood, Daniel R.	Killed, 5/3/63 at Chancellorsville
Co. A	Pvt.	Walker, James C.	Wounded, 5/3/63 at Chancellorsville
Co. A	Pvt.	Weeks, John A.	Wounded, 5/3/63 at Chancellorsville. Died of wounds, 5/11/63 at Richmond
Co. B	1st Sgt.	Newsom, John G.	Wounded (right side), 5/3/63 at Chancellorsville
Co. B	4th Cpl.	Hundley, George W.	Wounded, 5/3/63 at Chancellorsville
Co. B	Pvt.	Arrington, James L.	Wounded (thigh & left hand), 5/3/63
Co. B	Pvt.	Bishop, Samuel D.	Killed, 5/3/63 at Chancellorsville
Co. B	Pvt.	Bobbitt, Burwell B.	Wounded (left hip), 5/3/63 at Chancellorsville (shell wound)
Co. B	Pvt.	Brack, Baker B.	Killed, 5/3/63 at Chancellorsville
Co. B	Pvt.	Brack, George W.	Killed, 5/3/63 at Chancellorsville
Co. B	Pvt.	Buff, Peter	Wounded, 5/3/63 at Chancellorsville
Co. B	Pvt.	Duke, George J.	Wounded (side & arm), 5/3/63 at Chancellorsville
Co. B	Pvt.	Hardy, Francis M.	Wounded, 5/3/63 at Chancellorsville
Co. B	Pvt.	Kimball, Nathaniel	Wounded (right foot), 5/3/63 at Chancellorsville
Co. B	Pvt.	Patterson, Green R.	Wounded, 5/3/63 at Chancellorsville. Died of wounds, 6/4/63
Co. B	Pvt.	Pegram, Robert B.	Wounded (shoulder), 5/3/63 at Chancellorsville
Co. B	Pvt.	Shearin, Thomas G.	Wounded, 5/3/63 at Chancellorsville
Co. B	Pvt.	Thomas, William H.	Wounded, 4/30/63 near Fredericksburg
Co. C	1st Lt.	Bennett, Solomon W.	Wounded (left elbow), 5/3/63 at Chancellorsville
Co. C	Pvt.	Gore, John	Killed, 5/3/63 at Chancellorsville
Co. C	Pvt.	Greer, Lewis T.	Killed, 5/3/63 at Chancellorsville
Co. C	Pvt.	Inscore, James	Wounded, 5/3/63 at Chancellorsville
Co. C	Pvt.	Shew, Jacob W.	Wounded (right leg), 5/3/63 at Chancellorsville
Co. C	Pvt.	Shew, Joel	Wounded, 5/3/63 at Chancellorsville. Died of wounds, 5/5/63

Appendix 1

Unit	Rank	Name	Remarks
Co. C	Pvt.	Simmons, John B.	Killed, 5/3/63 at Chancellorsville
Co. C	Pvt.	Staley, Enoch	Wounded, 5/3/63 at Chancellorsville
Co. C	Pvt.	Stanly, Peter	Wounded, 5/3/63 at Chancellorsville. Died of wounds, 5/7/63.
Co. D	2nd Lt.	Ferrell, James E.	Wounded, 5/3/63 at Chancellorsville
Co. D	4th Sgt.	Allen, Henry C.	Wounded, 5/3/63 at Chancellorsville
Co. D	Pvt.	Bowlin, Willis N.	Wounded (right arm), 5/3/63 at Chancellorsville (right arm amputated). Died of wounds, 5/29/63
Co. D	Pvt.	Branton, Charles E.	Wounded, 5/3/63 at Chancellorsville
Co. D	Pvt.	Davis, Jesse A.	Wounded (right leg), 5/3/63 at Chancellorsville
Co. D	Pvt.	Ferrell, Francis M.	Wounded (arm), 5/3/63 at Chancellorsville (arm amputated)
Co. D	Pvt.	Forsyth, James R.	Wounded, 5/3/63 at Chancellorsville
Co. D	Pvt.	Peed, William C.	Wounded (left hand), 5/3/63 at Chancellorsville
Co. D	Pvt.	Peed, William H.	Wounded, 5/3/63 at Chancellorsville
Co. D	Pvt.	Wheeler, John W.	Killed, 5/3/63 at Chancellorsville
Co. D	Pvt.	Wilkins, Elijah	Wounded, 5/3/63 at Chancellorsville
Co. E	Cpt.	McMillan, John C.	Wounded (wrist), 5/3/63 at Chancellorsville
Co. E	3rd Lt.	Ellis, John W.	Wounded, 5/3/63 at Chancellorsville
Co. E	Pvt.	Bradshaw, Obed	Killed, 5/3/63 at Chancellorsville
Co. E	Pvt.	Jones, James W.	Wounded (shoulder, scapula fractured), 5/3/63 at Chancellorsville
Co. E	Pvt.	Mallard, William W.	Wounded (leg amputated), 5/3/63 at Chancellorsville
Co. E	Pvt.	McNellis, John	Wounded, 5/3/63 at Chancellorsville
Co. E	Pvt.	Wallace, William T.	Killed, 5/3/63 at Chancellorsville
Co. F	Pvt.	Forbes, Arthur	Wounded, 5/3/63 at Chancellorsville
Co. F	Pvt.	Harrell, Peter	Wounded (foot & right leg), 5/3/63 at Chancellorsville
Co. F	Pvt.	Johnson, Ellis	Wounded (head), 5/3/63 at Chancellorsville. Died of wounds, 5/24/63
Co. F	Pvt.	Madra, George	Wounded (face), 5/3/63 at Chancellorsville
Co. F	Pvt.	Mosely, Allen	Killed, 5/3/63 at Chancellorsville
Co. F	Pvt.	Roberson, James	Wounded, 5/3/63 at Chancellorsville
Co. F	Pvt.	Walston, William F.	Wounded, 5/3/63 at Chancellorsville
Co. F	Pvt.	Wiggins, Martin W.	Wounded (right arm), 5/3/63 at Chancellorsville (arm amputated). Died of wounds, 6/8/63
Co. G	3rd Sgt.	Badgett, Wm. Joseph	Wounded, 5/3/63 at Chancellorsville
Co. G	3rd Cpl.	Hobgood, William P.	Wounded, 5/3/63 at Chancellorsville. Died of wounds, 5/14/63.
Co. G	Pvt.	Blevins, Andrew	Wounded (right lung), 5/3/63 at Chancellorsville. Died of wounds, 6/18/62
Co. G	Pvt.	Blevins, Johnathan	Killed, 5/3/63 at Chancellorsville
Co. G	Pvt.	Brooks, Henry R.	Wounded, 5/3/63 at Chancellorsville
Co. G	Pvt.	Brooks, Richard D.	Wounded, 5/3/63 at Chancellorsville; "shell fragments resulting in a broken shoulder."
Co. G	Pvt.	Church, Carlton	Wounded, 5/3/63 at Chancellorsville
Co. G	Pvt.	Hall, James C.	Wounded, 5/3/63 at Chancellorsville
Co. G	Pvt.	Harris, William H.	Wounded, 5/3/63 at Chancellorsville
Co. G	Pvt.	Hobgood, James M.	Wounded, 5/3/63 at Chancellorsville
Co. G	Pvt.	Loftice, William A.	Wounded (right thigh), 5/3/63 at Chancellorsville

30th North Carolina Infantry Casualties

Unit	Rank	Name	Remarks
Co. G	Pvt.	O'Brian, William G.	Killed, 5/3/63 at Chancellorsville
Co. H	1st Sgt.	Cole, Ben. Green	Wounded, 5/3/63 at Chancellorsville
Co. H	Pvt.	Hunter, Charles A.	Wounded, 5/3/63 at Chancellorsville
Co. H	Pvt.	McIver, Kenneth H.	Wounded, 5/3/63 at Chancellorsville. Died of wounds, 6/6/63
Co. H	Pvt.	Shaw, Douglas C.	Wounded (fractured skull), 5/3/63 at Chancellorsville
Co. H	Pvt.	Sloan, David A.	Wounded, 5/3/63 at Chancellorsville
Co. I	1st Lt.	Williford, Burton B.	Wounded (right thigh), 5/3/63 at Chancellorsville; "bullet went through thigh into the pubic region."
Co. I	3rd Lt.	Perry, Sidney R.	Wounded (foot), 5/3/63 at Chancellorsville
Co. I	2nd Sgt.	Renfrow, Perry V.	Wounded, 5/3/63 at Chancellorsville
Co. I	1st Cpl.	Gay, George W.	Wounded, 5/3/63 at Chancellorsville.
Co. I	Pvt.	Bass, John S.	Wounded, 5/3/63 at Chancellorsville. Died of wounds, 5/5/63
Co. I	Pvt.	Batchelor, Andrew J.	Wounded, 5/3/63 at Chancellorsville.
Co. I	Pvt.	Batchelor, Henry H.	Wounded (right arm), 5/3/63 at Chancellorsville (arm amputated)
Co. I	Pvt.	Batchelor, Redmond W.	Wounded, 5/3/63 at Chancellorsville
Co. I	Pvt.	Crickman, Josiah G.	Wounded, 5/3/63 at Chancellorsville
Co. I	Pvt.	Culpepper, John	Wounded, 5/3/63 at Chancellorsville
Co. I	Pvt.	Griffin, John B.	Killed, 5/3/63 at Chancellorsville
Co. I	Pvt.	Joyner, George W.	Wounded, 5/3/63 at Chancellorsville
Co. I	Pvt.	Odom, Jacob E.	Killed, 5/3/63 at Chancellorsville
Co. I	Pvt.	Sherwood, Edwin	Killed, 5/3/63 at Chancellorsville
Co. I	Pvt.	Sherwood, George A.	Wounded (shoulder), 5/3/63 at Chancellorsville
Co. I	Pvt.	Smith, Albert	Killed, 5/3/63 at Chancellorsville
Co. I	Pvt.	Stallings, Franklin	Killed, 5/3/63 at Chancellorsville
Co. I	Pvt.	Winstead, George T.	Killed, 5/3/63 at Chancellorsville
Co. I	Pvt.	Winters, George	Wounded, 5/3/63 at Chancellorsville
Co. I	Pvt.	Wood, William	Wounded, 5/3/63 at Chancellorsville. Died of wounds, 5/10/63
Co. K	Cpl.	Hartis, Wilson L.	Killed, 5/3/63 at Chancellorsville
Co. K	Pvt.	Bailey, James P.	Wounded, 5/3/63 at Chancellorsville
Co. K	Pvt.	Barefoot, N. G.	Wounded, 5/3/63 at Chancellorsville
Co. K	Pvt.	Barnett, Robert	Killed, 5/3/63 at Chancellorsville
Co. K	Pvt.	Glover, Ben. Clint	Wounded ("shell wound of hip, destroying large surface"), 5/3/63 at Chancellorsville
Co. K	Pvt.	Griffith, Aaron E.	Wounded, 5/3/63 at Chancellorsville
Co. K	Pvt.	Johnston, James H.	Wounded, 5/3/63 at Chancellorsville
Co. K	Pvt.	Johnston, S. A.	Wounded, 5/3/63 at Chancellorsville
Co. K	Pvt.	Rea, James M.	Killed, 5/3/63 at Chancellorsville
Co. K	Pvt.	Thompson, Lewis R.	Wounded, 5/3/63 at Chancellorsville
Co. K	Pvt.	Witherspoon, Mitty T.	Wounded, 5/3/63 at Chancellorsville. Died of wounds, 5/7/63
Co. K	Pvt.	Younts, John A.	Wounded, 5/3/63 at Chancellorsville

Gettysburg, Pennsylvania
July 1, 1863
38 = 4 Killed, 34 Wounded

Unit	Rank	Name	Remarks
F & S	Col.	Parker, Francis M.	Wounded (face) 7/1/63 at Gettysburg.

Unit	Rank	Name	Remarks
Co. A	Sgt.	Merritt, Isaac W.	Wounded (side & left arm), 7/1/63 at Gettysburg. Captured, 7/4/63 in retreat from Gettysburg (So. Mountain).
Co. B	Sgt.	Williams, Robert D.	Wounded (scalp), 7/1/63 at Gettysburg.
Co. B	Pvt.	Loughlin, John	Wounded, 7/1/63 at Gettysburg. Deserted, 7/-/63 in retreat from Gettysburg.
Co. C	1st Cpl.	Smith, Benjamin	Wounded (jaw), 7/1/63 at Gettysburg. Captured, 7/4/63 at Gettysburg field hospital.
Co. C	Pvt.	Hewett, Samuel M.	Killed, 7/1/63 at Gettysburg.
Co. C	Pvt.	Robinson, Alexander S.	Wounded (face), 7/1/63 at Gettysburg. Captured, 7/4/63 at Gettysburg field hospital.
Co. C	Pvt.	Swain, George T.	Wounded, 7/1/63 at Gettysburg. Died of wounds, 7/3/63.
Co. C	Pvt.	Williams, Joseph	Wounded (hand), 7/1/63 at Gettysburg. Captured, 7/4/63 at Gettysburg field hospital.
Co. D	Cpt.	Allen, Charles N.	Wounded (left arm amputated just above elbow), 7/1/63 at Gettysburg.
Co. D	5th Sgt.	Cousins, John A.	Wounded, 7/1/63 at Gettysburg.
Co. D	Pvt.	Barker, John W.	Wounded (right arm & hand), 7/1/63 at Gettysburg.
Co. D	Pvt.	Goodin, John C.	Killed, 7/1/63 at Gettysburg.
Co. D	Pvt.	Mason, Israel H.	Wounded, 7/1/63 at Gettysburg. Died of wounds, 7/16/63 in Gettysburg field hospital.
Co. D	Pvt.	Pollard, Willie G.	Wounded, 7/1/63 at Gettysburg.
Co. E	Pvt.	Southerland, James	Wounded, (thigh, flesh wound), 7/1/63 at Gettysburg.
Co. F	Pvt.	Crisp, Levi	Wounded ("badly in the mouth"), 7/1/63 at Gettysburg.
Co. F	Pvt.	Mercer, Jacob J.	Wounded (left arm), 7/1/63 at Gettysburg. Captured, 7/4/63 at Gettysburg field hospital.
Co. G	3rd Cpl.	Cheatham, D. Thomas	Wounded (thigh), 7/1/63 at Gettysburg; "wounded badly through thigh."
Co. H	3rd Lt.	Brown, Alexander H.	Wounded (left thigh; flesh wound), 7/1/63 at Gettysburg.
Co. H	3rd Cpl.	Hight, Joseph J.	Wounded ("flesh wound through thigh"), 7/1/63 at Gettysburg. Captured, 7/4/63 at field hospital
Co. H	Pvt.	Jackson, B. C.	Wounded (right knee dislocated), 7/1/63 at Gettysburg.
Co. H	Pvt.	Lawrence, John	Wounded ("bullet through hip"), 7/1/63 at Gettysburg.
Co. H	Pvt.	McAulay, William	Wounded (neck), 7/1/63 and captured, 7/4/63 at Gettysburg field hospital.
Co. H	Pvt.	Morris, David P.	Wounded (right shoulder & arm—Humerus fractured), 7/1/63 at Gettysburg. Captured, 7/4/63 at Gettysburg field hospital.
Co. H	Pvt.	Phillips, John H.	Wounded (left arm), 7/1/63 at Gettysburg.
Co. H	Pvt.	Wicker, Lewis M.	Killed, 7/1/63 at Gettysburg.
Co. H	Pvt.	Wicker, Thomas	Wounded (left arm & wrist), 7/1/63 at Gettysburg; "arm broken by ball."
Co. I	Pvt.	Jones, John R.	Wounded (foot), 7/1/63 at Gettysburg. Captured, 7/4/63 at Gettysburg field hospital.
Co. I	Pvt.	Joyner, Nelson V.	Wounded (right wrist & fore arm), 7/1/63 at Gettysburg.

Unit	Rank	Name	Remarks
Co. I	Pvt.	Vick, Willie R.	Wounded, 7/1/63 at Gettysburg. Captured, 7/4/63 at Gettysburg field hospital.
Co. I	Pvt.	Westray, Archibald H.	Wounded (right leg), 7/1/63 at Gettysburg. Captured, 7/4/63 at Gettysburg field hospital. (leg amputated below knee)
Co. I	Pvt.	Whitley, Jolley B.	Killed, 7/1/63 at Gettysburg.
Co. I	Pvt.	Winstead, Theophilus T.	Wounded (right leg), 7/1/63 at Gettysburg. Captured, 7/4/63 at Gettysburg field hospital. (leg amputated below knee)
Co. K	4th Cpl.	Russell, William D.	Wounded (slightly), 7/1/63 at Gettysburg. Captured, 7/5/63 at Gettysburg field hospital.
Co. K	Cpl.	Bales, Elijah M.	Wounded (arm; flesh wound), 7/1/63 at Gettysburg.
Co. K	Pvt.	Griffith, Aaron E.	Wounded (hip), 7/1/63 at Gettysburg. Died of wounds, 7/3/63.

Gettysburg
July 2, 1863
2 = 1 Wounded, 1 Missing

Unit	Rank	Name	Remarks
Co. G	Pvt.	Cheatham, James T.	Wounded, 7/2/63 at Gettysburg on skirmish line. Captured at field hospital, 7/4/63.
Co. H	Pvt.	Utley, John Wm.	Missing & Captured, 7/2/63 at Gettysburg on skirmish line. "He skulked off somewhere."

Gettysburg
July 3, 1863
10 = 1 Killed, 7 Wounded, 2 Captured

Unit	Rank	Name	Remarks
Co. A	Pvt.	Brewer, Abraham H.	Wounded (left hand & back), 7/3/63 at Gettysburg. Captured, 7/4/63 in retreat (So. Mountain).
Co. D	Pvt.	Long, Alexander V.	Wounded (both hips), 7/3/63 at Gettysburg. Captured, 7/4/63 at Gettysburg field hospital.
Co. D	Pvt.	Brassfield, James W.	Captured, 7/3/63 at Gettysburg on picket line.
Co. D	Pvt.	Lawrence, William H.	Captured, 7/3/63 at Gettysburg on picket line.
Co. E	Pvt.	Johnson, Major O.	Wounded (head, skull fractured), 7/3/63 at Gettysburg; "caused by artillery shell."
Co. F	Pvt.	Hathaway, Henry	Wounded (jaw & shoulder), 7/3/63 at Gettysburg. Captured at Gettysburg field hospital, 7/4/63. Died of wounds, 7/10/63.
Co. F	Pvt.	Madra, George A.	Wounded (hand & knee), 7/3/63 at Gettysburg.
Co. G	3rd Lt.	Connell, Ira Thomas	Killed, 7/3/63 at Gettysburg.
Co. I	Pvt.	Walker, John Blount	Wounded (right shoulder), 7/3/63 at Gettysburg, "on the skirmish line." Captured, 7/4/63 at Gettysburg field hospital. Died of wounds, 8/13/63.
Co. K	Pvt.	Hood, William L.	Wounded (left hand), 7/3/63 at Gettysburg on skirmish line.

Captured at Gettysburg Field Hospital
July 4–5, 1863
19 Captured

Unit	Rank	Name	Remarks
Co. C	1st Cpl.	Smith, Benjamin	Captured, 7/4/63 at Gettysburg field hospital.
Co. C	Pvt.	Robinson, Alexander S.	Captured, 7/4/63 at Gettysburg field hospital.
Co. C	Pvt.	Williams, Joseph	Captured, 7/4/63 at Gettysburg field hospital.
Co. D	Pvt.	Long, Alexander V.	Captured, 7/4/63 at Gettysburg field hospital.
Co. D	Pvt.	Mason, Israel H.	Captured, 7/4/63 at Gettysburg field hospital. Died of wounds, 7/16/63 at Gettysburg field hospital.
Co. F	Pvt.	Hathaway, Henry	Captured at Gettysburg field hospital, 7/4/63. Died of wounds, 7/10/63 at Gettysburg field hospital.
Co. F	Pvt.	Mercer, Jacob J.	Captured, 7/4/63 at Gettysburg field hospital.
Co. G	Pvt.	Cheatham, James T.	Captured, 7/4/63 at Gettysburg field hospital.
Co. H	3rd Cpl.	Hight, Joseph J.	Captured, 7/4/63 at Gettysburg field hospital.
Co. H	Pvt.	McAulay, William	Captured, 7/4/63 at Gettysburg field hospital.
Co. H	Pvt.	Morris, David P.	Captured, 7/4/63 at Gettysburg field hospital.
Co. I	Pvt.	Jones, John R.	Captured, 7/4/63 at Gettysburg field hospital.
Co. I	Pvt.	Joyner, George W.	Captured, 7/4/63 at Gettysburg field hospital. "He was left to nurse [the] wounded."
Co. I	Pvt.	Vick, Willie R.	Captured, 7/4/63 at Gettysburg field hospital.
Co. I	Pvt.	Walker, John Blount	Captured, 7/4/64 at Gettysburg field hospital. Died of wounds, 8/13/63 at Gettysburg field hospital.
Co. I	Pvt.	Westray, Archibald H.	Captured, 7/4/63 at Gettysburg field hospital.
Co. I	Pvt.	Winstead, Theophilus T.	Captured, 7/4/63 at Gettysburg field hospital.
Co. K	4th Cpl.	Russell, William D.	Captured 7/5/63 at Gettysburg field hospital.

Retreat & Desertion from Gettysburg
July 4–14, 1863
25 Captured/Missing/Deserted

Unit	Rank	Name	Remarks
Co. A	Sgt.	Merritt, Isaac W.	Wounded (side & left arm), 7/1/63. Captured, 7/4/63 in retreat from Gettysburg (So. Mountain).
Co. A	Pvt.	Brewer, Abraham H.	Wounded (left hand & back), 7/3/63 at Gettysburg. Captured, 7/4/63 in retreat (So. Mountain).
Co. B	Pvt.	Loughlin, John	Wounded, 7/1/63 at Gettysburg. Deserted, 7/-/63 in retreat from Gettysburg.
Co. B	Pvt.	Myrick, William W.	Captured, 7/5/63 during retreat from Gettysburg (So. Mountain).
Co. B	Pvt.	Shearin, Landon T.	Captured, 7/4/63 near Gettysburg.
Co. C	Pvt.	Mott, John	Missing, 7/4/63 in retreat from Gettysburg.
Co. C	Pvt.	Everhart, Jacob	Deserted, 7/14/63 at Williamsport, MD.
Co. D	Pvt.	Allen, Marion F.	Captured, 7/4/63 at Gettysburg.
Co. D	Pvt.	Manus, Francis	Captured, 7/7/63 at Williamsport, MD.
Co. D	Pvt.	Wadford, Alexander	Captured, 7/4/63 in retreat from Gettysburg.
Co. D	Pvt.	Ward, Isaac B.	Missing, 7/4/63 in retreat from Gettysburg.
Co. E	Pvt.	Henderson, James W.	Captured, 7/4/63 in retreat from Gettysburg.

Unit	Rank	Name	Remarks
Co. E	Pvt.	Savage, John	Captured, 7/4/63 in retreat from Gettysburg (So. Mountain).
Co. F	Pvt.	Corbett, William W	Captured, 7/4/63 in retreat from Gettysburg.
Co. F	Pvt.	Dew, Frank Lewis	Captured, 7/5/63 in retreat from Gettysburg (Hagerstown).
Co. F	Pvt.	Pittman, George W.	Captured, 7/5/63 in retreat from Gettysburg (Waterloo, MD).
Co. G	Pvt.	Hamme, Richard F.	Sick & Captured, 7/4/63 in retreat from Gettysburg.
Co. H	4th Cpl.	Brown, A. Singa	Missing, 7/10/63 in retreat from Gettysburg. "Listed as a deserter."
Co. H	Pvt.	Campbell, Angus T.	Captured, 7/5/63 in retreat from Gettysburg.
Co. H	Pvt.	Campbell, George W.	Captured, 7/4/63 in retreat from Gettysburg.
Co. H	Pvt.	Kelly, David W.	Captured, 7/5/63 in retreat from Gettysburg (near Chambersburg, PA).
Co. H	Pvt.	Matthews, Nathan	Captured, 7/5/63 in retreat from Gettysburg.
Co. I	3rd Cpl.	Odom, David M.	Deserted, 7/5/63 in retreat from Gettysburg.
Co. I	Pvt.	Joyner, Ira E.	Captured, 7/5/63 in retreat from Gettysburg.
Co. I	Pvt.	Rackley, P. Nicholas	Captured, 7/5/63 in retreat from Gettysburg. "He dropped out on battlefield, sick."

Bristoe Station/Warrenton, Virginia
October 10–19, 1863
9 = 1 Killed, 7 Wounded, 1 Captured

Unit	Rank	Name	Remarks
Co. B	Pvt.	Jackson, Marion J.	Wounded (left foot), 10/12/63 at Bristoe Station (foot amputated)
Co. E	Pvt.	Bradshaw, James B.	Wounded, 10/14/64 at Bristoe Station
Co. E	Pvt.	Cavenaugh, George W.	Captured, 10/14/63 at Bristoe Station
Co. E	Pvt.	Grady, John W.	Wounded (thigh amputated), 10/14/63 at Bristoe Station. Died of wounds, 10/25/63
Co. F	Pvt.	Webb, Morrison	Wounded, 10/11/63 near Warrenton
Co. G	Pvt.	Harris, Richard P.	Wounded (left thigh), 10/12/63 near Warrenton
Co. H	Pvt.	Starnes, Thomas	Wounded, 10/17/63 near Warrenton
Co. H	Pvt.	Underwood, John A.	Wounded, 10/19/63 at Warrenton
Co. I	Pvt.	Ruffin, Charles H.	Killed, 10/14/63 near Warrenton; "in a skirmish."

Kelly's Ford, Virginia
November 11, 1863
43 = 5 Killed, 26 Wounded, 12 Wounded & Captured

Unit	Rank	Name	Remarks
F & S	Lt. Col.	Sillers, William W.	Mortally wounded (lungs), 11/7/63 at Kelly's Ford. Died of wounds, 11/9/63 at Gordonsville
F & S	Adj.	Philips, Frederick	Wounded, (left thigh-'debilitating'), 11/7/63 at Kelly's Ford
Co. A	1st Sgt.	Crumpler, Robert M.	Wounded, 11/7/63 at Kelly's Ford
Co. A	Pvt.	Boswell, William H.	Killed, 11/7/63 at Kelly's Ford
Co. A	Pvt.	Cobb, Obed B.	Wounded, 11/7/63 at Kelly's Ford
Co. A	Pvt.	Dove, Monroe	Wounded (thigh), 11/7/63 at Kelly's Ford
Co. A	Pvt.	Friezland, Jacob	Wounded, 11/7/63 at Kelly's Ford

Appendix 1

Unit	Rank	Name	Remarks
Co. A	Pvt.	Kelly, James M	Wounded, 11/7/63 at Kelly's Ford
Co. A	Pvt.	Warrick, Thomas J.	Wounded, 7/11/63 at Kelly's Ford
Co. A	Pvt.	Williamson, James	Wounded (right arm), 11/7/63 at Kelly's Ford
Co. B	Cpt.	Davis, Weldon E.	Wounded (right leg fractured) and captured, 12/7/63 at Kelly's Ford. Leg amputated at thigh. Died of wounds (tetanus), 12/22/63.
Co. B	1st Sgt.	Newsom, John G.	Wounded (head—flesh wound) & captured, 11/7/63 at Kelly's Ford
Co. B	Pvt.	Aycock, Samuel	Killed, 11/7/63 at Kelly's Ford
Co. C	Pvt.	Patterson, John J.	Wounded (right wrist), 11/7/63 at Kelly's Ford
Co. C	Pvt.	Vuncannon, John P.	Wounded (chest, hip, & hand) and captured, 11/7/63 at Kelly's Ford
Co. D	Color Cpl.	Allen, Elias G.	Wounded (left lung), and captured, 11/7/63 at Kelly's Ford
Co. D	Pvt.	Dickey, Zachariah C.	Wounded (right lung), and captured, 11/7/63 at Kelly's Ford. Died of wounds, 12/9/63.
Co. E	1st Lt.	Johnson, Ira J.	Wounded (right hip), 11/7/63 at Kelly's Ford
Co. E	4th Sgt.	Rivenbark, Teachey	Wounded (thigh fractured), 11/7/63 at Kelly's Ford
Co. E	Pvt.	Thompson, Andrew J.	Killed, 11/7/63 at Kelly's Ford
Co. E	Pvt.	Turner, David W.	Wounded, 11/7/63 at Kelly's Ford
Co. F	2nd Sgt.	House, James W.	Wounded, 11/7/63 at Kelly's Ford
Co. F	Pvt.	Barnes, Wm. Spencer	Wounded, 11/7/63 at Kelly's Ford
Co. F	Pvt.	Forbes, Arthur	Wounded, 11/7/63 at Kelly's Ford
Co. F	Pvt.	Leigh, Theophilus	Wounded, 11/7/63 at Kelly's Ford
Co. F	Pvt.	Lewis, John E.	Wounded (right arm), 11/7/63 at Kelly's Ford. (Arm amputated)
Co. F	Pvt.	Redick, Epinetus	Wounded, 11/7/63 at Kelly's Ford
Co. G	Pvt.	Daniel, William H.	Wounded (left thigh & left side) & captured, 11/7/63 at Kelly's Ford
Co. G	Pvt.	Pruitt, Hampton	Wounded, 11/7/63 at Kelly's Ford. Died of wounds, 12/15/63.
Co. G	Pvt.	Wortman, David D.	Wounded (right eye), 11/7/63 at Kelly's Ford
Co. H	Pvt.	McFatter, Alexander	Wounded (shoulder & back), 11/7/63 at Kelly's Ford. Died of wounds, 11/28/63.
Co. H	Pvt.	Shaw, Douglas C.	Wounded (left foot) & captured, 11/7/63 at Kelly's Ford; "by shell."
Co. I	4th Sgt.	Bryan, James H.	Wounded (neck & scalp) & captured, 11/7/63 at Kelly's Ford
Co. I	2nd Cpl.	Batchelor, Wm. D.	Killed, 11/7/63 at Kelly's Ford
Co. I	Pvt.	Brantley, Jn. Redmond	Wounded (left hip) & captured, 11/7/63 at Kelly's Ford
Co. I	Pvt.	Pender, John	Wounded (left thigh) & captured, 11/7/63 at Kelly's Ford
Co. I	Pvt.	Pridgen, Drewry	Wounded (arm), 11/7/63 at Kelly's Ford. (arm amputated)
Co. K	Cpt.	Witherspoon, John G.	Mortally wounded (breast), 12/7/63 at Kelly's Ford. Captured, died of wounds, 12/8/63.
Co. K	3rd Sgt.	Boyce, Samuel J.	Wounded (right thigh) and captured, 11/7/63 at Kelly's Ford. Right thigh amputated. Died of wounds, 11/11/63; "Thigh fractured."
Co. K	Pvt.	Adkins, William H.	Wounded, 11/7/63 at Kelly's Ford
Co. K	Pvt.	Alexander, Samuel D.	Wounded, 11/7/63 at Kelly's Ford

Unit	Rank	Name	Remarks
Co. K	Pvt.	McLane, Thomas	Wounded (right forearm), 11/7/63 at Kelly's Ford
Co. K	Pvt.	Rayner, Lovett	Killed, 11/7/63 at Kelly's Ford

Kelly's Ford
November 11, 1863
141 Captured

Unit	Rank	Name	Remarks
Co. A	2nd Sgt.	Draughon, Miles S.	Captured, 11/7/63 at Kelly's Ford
Co. A	Pvt.	Alsbrook, S. C.	Captured, 11/7/63 at Kelly's Ford
Co. A	Pvt.	Butler, Hartwell	Captured, 11/7/63 at Kelly's Ford
Co. A	Pvt.	Duncan, James D.	Captured, 11/7/63 at Kelly's Ford
Co. A	Pvt.	Godwin, Nathan H.	Captured, 11/7/63 at Kelly's Ford
Co. A	Pvt.	Hall, William G.	Captured, 11/7/63 at Kelly's Ford
Co. A	Pvt.	Holshouser, Ambrose N.	Captured, 11/7/63 at Kelly's Ford
Co. A	Pvt.	Ivey, W. L.	Captured, 11/7/63 at Kelly's Ford
Co. A	Pvt.	Parting, Henry A.	Captured, 11/7/63 at Kelly's Ford
Co. A	Pvt.	Rogister, James	Captured, 11/7/63 at Kelly's Ford
Co. A	Pvt.	Steele, James H.	Captured, 11/7/63 at Kelly's Ford
Co. A	Pvt.	Williamson, David	Captured, 11/7/63 at Kelly's Ford
Co. A	Pvt.	Winecoff, George W.	Captured, 11/7/63 at Kelly's Ford
Co. B	1st Lt.	Nicholson, John H.	Captured, 11/7/63 at Kelly's Ford
Co. B	4th Sgt.	Harriss, John A.	Captured, 11/7/63 at Kelly's Farm
Co. B	5th Sgt.	Williams, Robert D.	Captured, 11/7/63 at Kelly's Ford
Co. B	2nd Cpl.	Paschall, Samuel A.	Captured, 11/7/63 At Kelly's Ford
Co. B	4th Cpl.	Hundley, George W.	Captured, 11/7/63 at Kelly's Ford
Co. B	Pvt.	Askew, John	Captured, 11/7/63 at Kelly's Ford
Co. B	Pvt.	Borgus, Reuben	Captured, 11/7/63 at Kelly's Ford
Co. B	Pvt.	Carter, William J.	Captured ("deserted to the enemy"), 11/7/63 at Kelly's Ford
Co. B	Pvt.	Collins, David	Captured, 11/7/63 at Kelly's Ford
Co. B	Pvt.	Darnell, James R.	Captured, 11/7/63 at Kelly's Ford
Co. B	Pvt.	Haithcock, Alfred L.	Captured, 11/7/63 at Kelly's Ford
Co. B	Pvt.	Harris, John N.	Captured, 11/7/63 at Kelly's Ford
Co. B	Pvt.	Insco, William	Captured, 11/7/63 at Kelly's Ford
Co. B	Pvt.	Kimball, Nathaniel	Captured, 11/7/63 at Kelly's Ford
Co. B	Pvt.	Kirkland, Stephen H.	Captured, 11/7/63 at Kelly's Ford
Co. B	Pvt.	Shearin, Gardiner E.	Captured, 11/7/63 at Kelly's Ford
Co. B	Pvt.	Williams, William A.	Captured, 11/7/63 at Kelly's Ford
Co. C	3rd Sgt.	Russ, Stewart	Captured, 11/7/63 at Kelly's Ford
Co. C	Pvt.	Balentine, James N.	Deserted, 11/7/63 at Kelly's Ford
Co. C	Pvt.	Blackwelder, Wiley	Captured, 11/7/63 at Kelly's Ford
Co. C	Pvt.	Costner, Jacob B.	Captured, 11/7/63 at Kelly's Ford
Co. C	Pvt.	Danford, John W.	Captured, 11/7/63 at Kelly's Ford
Co. C	Pvt.	Dew, David C.	Captured, 11/7/63 at Kelly's Ford
Co. C	Pvt.	Gallimore, Ransom	Captured, 11/7/63 at Kelly's Ford
Co. C	Pvt.	Harvell, James M.	Captured, 11/7/63 at Kelly's Ford
Co. C	Pvt.	Hewett, Lorenzo D.	Captured, 11/7/63 at Kelly's Ford
Co. C	Pvt.	McCall, Paul S.	Captured, 11/7/63 at Kelly's Ford
Co. C	Pvt.	Pendergrass, J. R.	Captured, 11/7/63 at Kelly's Ford
Co. C	Pvt.	Reidling, William A.	Captured, 11/7/63 at Kelly's Ford
Co. C	Pvt.	White, Eli M.	Captured, 11/7/63 at Kelly's Ford
Co. D	1st Lt.	Abernathy, Sidney S.	Captured, 11/7/63 at Kelly's Ford
Co. D	2nd Lt.	Ferrell, James E.	Captured, 11/7/63 at Kelly's Ford

Appendix 1

Unit	Rank	Name	Remarks
Co. D	2nd Sgt.	Ray, Zeddock D.	Captured, 11/7/63 at Kelly's Ford
Co. D	5th Sgt.	Cousins, John A.	Captured, 11/7/63 at Kelly's Ford
Co. D	2nd Cpl.	Ward, William J.	Captured, 11/7/63 at Kelly's Ford
Co. D	Pvt.	Barker, John W.	Captured, 11/7/63 at Kelly's Ford
Co. D	Pvt.	Branton, Charles E.	Captured, 11/7/63 at Kelly's Ford
Co. D	Pvt.	Champion, Joseph M.	Captured, 11/7/63 at Kelly's Ford
Co. D	Pvt.	Mangum, Calvin T.	Captured, 11/7/63 at Kelly's Ford
Co. D	Pvt.	Marcom, James A.	Captured, 11/7/63 at Kelly's Ford
Co. D	Pvt.	Marcum, William A.	Captured, 11/7/63 at Kelly's Ford
Co. D	Pvt.	O'Neal, Hardy	Captured, 11/7/63 at Kelly's Ford
Co. D	Pvt.	O'Neal, Lofton M.	Captured, 11/7/63 at Kelly's Ford
Co. D	Pvt.	Peed, William H.	Captured, 11/7/63 at Kelly's Ford
Co. D	Pvt.	Pierce, George W.	Captured, 11/7/63 at Kelly's Ford
Co. D	Pvt.	Pollard, Joshua H.	Captured, 11/7/63 at Kelly's Ford
Co. D	Pvt.	Pollard, Samuel R.	Captured, 11/7/63 at Kelly's Ford
Co. D	Pvt.	Pollard, Willie G.	Captured, 11/7/63 at Kelly's Ford
Co. D	Pvt.	Ray, David A.	Captured, 11/7/63 at Kelly's Ford
Co. D	Pvt.	Ray, Henry C.	Captured, 11/7/63 at Kelly's Ford
Co. D	Pvt.	Ray, William B.	Captured, 11/7/63 at Kelly's Ford
Co. D	Pvt.	Smith, Thomas G.	Captured, 11/7/63 at Kelly's Ford
Co. D	Pvt.	Tilley, John R.	Captured, 11/7/63 at Kelly's Ford
Co. D	Pvt.	Tilly, William H.	Captured, 11/7/63 at Kelly's Ford
Co. D	Pvt.	Ward, Wilson	Captured, 11/7/63 at Kelly's Ford
Co. D	Pvt.	Wilkins, William	Captured, 11/7/63 at Kelly's Ford
Co. E	Pvt.	Cavenaugh, James D.	Captured, 11/7/64 at Kelly's Ford
Co. E	Pvt.	Laney, Lewis C.	Captured, 11/7/63 at Kelly's Ford
Co. E	Pvt.	Pickett, John L.	Captured, 11/7/63 at Kelly's Ford
Co. E	Pvt.	Register, Samuel C.	Captured, 11/7/63 at Kelly's Ford
Co. E	Pvt.	Rich, Christopher C.	Captured, 11/7/63 at Kelly's Ford
Co. E	Pvt.	Southerland, James	Captured, 11/7/63 at Kelly's Ford
Co. F	2nd Cpl.	Brown, Wm. Henry	Captured, 11/7/63 at Kelly's Ford
Co. F	3rd Cpl.	Walston, Franklin	Captured, 11/7/63 at Kelly's Ford
Co. F	Pvt.	Dixon, Henry O.	Captured, 11/7/63 at Kelly's Ford
Co. F	Pvt.	Fountain, Almond L	Captured, 11/7/63 at Kelly's Ford
Co. F	Pvt.	Morgan, James B.	Captured, 11/7/63 at Kelly's Ford
Co. F	Pvt.	Pitt, Theophilus	Captured, 11/7/63 at Kelly's Ford
Co. F	Pvt.	Roberson, James	Captured, 11/7/63 at Kelly's Ford
Co. F	Pvt.	Walston, Rufus F.	Captured, 11/7/63 at Kelly's Ford
Co. G	1st Sgt.	O'Brien, Alfred D.	Captured, 11/7/63 at Kelly's Ford
Co. G	1st Cpl.	Knott, George Lawson	Captured, 11/7/63 at Kelly's Ford
Co. G	3rd Cpl.	O'Brian, Alexander P.	Captured, 11/7/63 at Kelly's Ford
Co. G	Music	Morris, John W.	Captured, 11/7/63 at Kelly's Ford
Co. G	Pvt.	Daniel, Robert M.	Captured, 11/7/63 at Kelly's Ford
Co. G	Pvt.	Greenway, Samuel	Captured, 11/7/63 at Kelly's Ford
Co. G	Pvt.	Hester, George W.	Captured, 11/7/63 at Kelly's Ford
Co. G	Pvt.	Holbrook, Patterson B.	Captured, 11/7/63 at Kelly's Ford
Co. G	Pvt.	Howard, Joseph M.	Captured, 11/7/63 at Kelly's Ford
Co. G	Pvt.	King, James D.	Captured, 11/7/63 at Kelly's Ford
Co. G	Pvt.	Ottaway, John	Captured, 11/7/63 at Kelly's Ford
Co. G	Pvt.	Parker, Archibald D.	Captured, 11/7/63 at Kelly's Ford
Co. G	Pvt.	Sollice, Devane	Captured, 11/7/63 at Kelly's Ford
Co. G	Pvt.	Wilkerson, James	Captured, 11/7/63 at Kelly's Ford
Co. H	3rd Lt.	Brown, Alexander H.	Captured, 11/7/63 at Kelly's Ford
Co. H	5th Sgt.	Buie, John	Captured, 11/7/63 at Kelly's Ford
Co. H	Pvt.	Hunter, John R.	Captured, 11/8/63 at Kelly's Ford
Co. H	Pvt.	Kelly, Wm. Alfred	Captured, 11/7/63 at Kelly's Ford

Unit	Rank	Name	Remarks
Co. H	Pvt.	McDonald, James S.	Captured, 11/7/63 at Kelly's Ford
Co. H	Pvt.	Monroe, John E.	Captured, 11/7/63 at Kelly's Ford
Co. H	Pvt.	Monroe, James A.	Captured, 11/7/63 at Kelly's Ford
Co. H	Pvt.	Phillips, John H.	Captured, 11/7/63 at Kelly's Ford
Co. H	Pvt.	Riddle, George W.	Captured, 11/7/63 at Kelly's Ford
Co. H	Pvt.	Sloan, David A.	Captured, 11/7/63 at Kelly's Ford
Co. H	Pvt.	Womack, James R.	Captured, 11/7/63 at Kelly's Ford
Co. H	Pvt.	Yancy, Thomas A.	Captured, 11/7/63 at Kelly's Ford
Co. I	2nd Sgt.	Renfrow, Perry V.	Captured, 11/7/63 at Kelly's Ford
Co. I	5th Sgt.	Batchelor, Van Buren	Captured, 11/7/63 at Kelly's Ford
Co. I	3rd Cpl.	Culpepper, William J.	Captured, 11/7/63 at Kelly's Ford
Co. I	Pvt.	Batchelor, Neverson A.	Captured, 11/7/63 at Kelly's Ford
Co. I	Pvt.	Davis, Miles	Captured, 11/7/63 at Kelly's Ford
Co. I	Pvt.	Deans, William	Captured, 11/7/63 at Kelly's Ford
Co. I	Pvt.	Denson, Alexander	Captured, 11/7/63 at Kelly's Ford
Co. I	Pvt.	Edwards, James	Captured, 11/7/63 at Kelly's Ford
Co. I	Pvt.	Griffin, A. Calhoun	Captured, 11/7/63 at Kelly's Ford
Co. I	Pvt.	Griffin, Jesse R.	Captured, 11/7/63 at Kelly's Ford
Co. I	Pvt.	Hunt, James A.	Captured, 11/7/63 at Kelly's Ford
Co. I	Pvt.	Johnson, Henry	Captured, 11/7/63 at Kelly's Ford
Co. I	Pvt.	Joyner, Jonas A.	Captured, 11/7/63 at Kelly's Ford
Co. I	Pvt.	Lewis, Arnold L.	Captured, 11/7/63 at Kelly's Ford
Co. I	Pvt.	Lindsey, Richard	Captured, 11/7/63 at Kelly's Ford
Co. I	Pvt.	Pridgen, Henry H.	Captured, 11/7/63 at Kelly's Ford
Co. I	Pvt.	Pridgen, Josiah H.	Captured, 11/7/63 at Kelly's Ford
Co. I	Pvt.	Sherwood, George A.	Captured, 11/7/63 at Kelly's Ford
Co. I	Pvt.	Vick, James F.	Captured, 11/7/63 at Kelly's Ford
Co. I	Pvt.	Walker, Richmond D.	Captured, 11/7/63 at Kelly's Ford
Co. I	Pvt.	Walker, Worrell P.	Captured, 11/7/63 at Kelly's Ford
Co. I	Pvt.	Whitfield, John W.	Captured, 11/7/63 at Kelly's Ford
Co. I	Pvt.	Williams, Henry H.	Captured, 11/7/63 at Kelly's Ford
Co. I	Pvt.	Williams, Nathan C.	Captured, 11/7/63 at Kelly's Ford
Co. I	Pvt.	Woodward, John E.	Captured, 11/7/63 at Kelly's Ford
Co. K	5th Sgt.	DeArmond, Aaron L.	Captured, 11/7/63 at Kelly's Ford
Co. K	1st Cpl.	Culp, Aley A.	Captured, 11/7/63 at Kelly's Ford
Co. K	Pvt.	Alexander, J. Lee	Captured, 11/7/63 at Kelly's Ford
Co. K	Pvt.	Bailey, James A.	Captured, 11/7/63 at Kelly's Ford
Co. K	Pvt.	Graham, John W.	Captured, 11/7/63 at Kelly's Ford
Co. K	Pvt.	Myers, James	Captured, 11/7/63 at Kelly's Ford
Co. K	Pvt.	Wolfe, Robert B.	Captured, 11/7/63 at Kelly's Ford

The Wilderness
May 5–6, 1864
7 = 1 Killed, 6 Wounded

Unit	Rank	Name	Remarks
Co. D	Pvt.	Moore, William H.	Wounded, 5/6/64 at The Wilderness
Co. E	Pvt.	Bostick, Bryant W.	Wounded (left thigh—tibia fractured), 5/6/64 at the Wilderness
Co. E	Pvt.	Pickett, William D.	Wounded, 5/6/64 at The Wilderness
Co. G	4th Cpl.	Sizemore, William P.	Killed, 5/6/64 at The Wilderness
Co. H	Pvt.	Cole, George W.	Wounded, (leg) 5/6/64 at The Wilderness
Co. H	Pvt.	Lloyd, Manley C.	Wounded, 5/6/64 at The Wilderness
Co. H	Pvt.	Taylor, Jackson	Wounded, 5/6/64 at The Wilderness

The Wilderness
May 8–11, 1864
23 = 2 Killed, 7 Wounded, 13 Captured, 1 Missing

Unit	Rank	Name	Remarks
Co. A	2nd Cpl.	Bass, William E.	Captured, 5/8/64 near Spotsylvania
Co. A	Pvt.	Butler, Joseph	Wounded (left leg amputated), 5/8/64 at Spotsylvania. Died of wounds, 5/9/64.
Co. B	2nd Sgt.	Shearin, John D.	Captured, 5/8/64 at Spotsylvania
Co. E	Pvt.	Bray, John W.	Captured, 5/8/64 at the Spotsylvania
Co. B	Pvt.	North, Joshua	Wounded, 5/8/64 at Spotsylvania
Co. C	Pvt.	Hickman, Robert	Captured, 5/8/64 at Spotsylvania
Co. D	4th Cpl.	Thomas, Robert H	Captured, 5/8/64 at Spotsylvania
Co. E	Pvt.	Pickett, William D.	Wounded, 5/6/64 at the Wilderness
Co. F	Cpt.	Moore, Willis M. B.	Wounded (left breast), 5/8/64 at Spotsylvania
Co. F	1st Sgt.	Whitehurst, Thomas	Killed, 5/8/64 at Spotsylvania; "shot through the head."
Co. F	Pvt.	Crisp, William S.	Captured, 5/8/64 at Spotsylvania
Co. F	Pvt.	Corbett, William W	Captured, 5/8/64 at Spotsylvania
Co. F	Pvt.	Hathaway, James J.	Captured, 5/8/64 at Spotsylvania
Co. G	Pvt.	Stanton, James R.	Missing, 5/8/64 at Spotsylvania
Co. H	2nd Sgt.	Morrison, Horace	Killed, 5/8/64 at Spotsylvania
Co. H	Pvt.	Cox, William O.	Captured, 5/8/64 at Spotsylvania
Co. I	Pvt.	Griffin, William B.	Captured, 5/8/64 at Spotsylvania
Co. K	Pvt.	Dixon, Solomon L.	Wounded, 5/8/64 at Spotsylvania
Co. K	Pvt.	Dunn, George	Captured, 5/8/64 at Spotsylvania
Co. K	Pvt.	Hall, John G.	Wounded, 5/8/64 at Spotsylvania
Co. K	Pvt.	Johnston, Sandy A.	Wounded, 5/8/64 at Spotsylvania. Died of wounds, 5/18/64.
Co. K	Pvt.	Sample, William	Captured, 5/8/64 at the Wilderness
Co. K	Pvt.	Smith, John S.	Captured, 5/8/64 at Spotsylvania

Spotsylvania, Virginia
May 12, 1864
142 = 22 Killed, 56 Wounded, 3 Wounded & Captured, 61 Captured

Unit	Rank	Name	Remarks
F & S	Col.	Parker, Francis M.	Wounded (slightly), 5/12/64 at Spotsylvania
F & S	Sgt. Maj.	Arrington, Peter W.	Captured, 5/12/64 at Spotsylvania
Co. A	Cpt.	Williams, Gary	Captured, 5/12/64 at Spotsylvania
Co. A	1st Lt.	White, Lallister M.	Killed, 5/12/64 at Spotsylvania
Co. A	3rd Sgt.	Johnson, William H.	Captured, 5/12/64 at Spotsylvania
Co. A	4th Sgt.	Howard, Thomas M.	Killed, 5/12/64 at Spotsylvania
Co. A	5th Sgt.	Rackley, George W.	Captured, 5/12/64 at Spotsylvania
Co. A	Color Sgt.	Pennington, William	Wounded, 5/12/64 at Spotsylvania
Co. A	3rd Cpl.	Boon, Stephen	Captured, 5/12/64 at Spotsylvania
Co. A	Pvt.	Allman, Gideon	Captured, 5/12/64 at Spotsylvania
Co. A	Pvt.	Bell, Robert	Captured, 5/12/64 at Spotsylvania
Co. A	Pvt.	Boon, Nicholas	Captured, 5/12/64 at Spotsylvania
Co. A	Pvt.	Butler, Raiford D.	Captured, 5/12/64 at Spotsylvania
Co. A	Pvt.	Howard, Fleet H.	Captured, 5/12/64 at Spotsylvania
Co. A	Pvt.	Hutchison, Andrew J.	Captured, 5/12/64 at Spotsylvania
Co. A	Pvt.	Jackson, Martin G.	Captured, 5/12/64 at Spotsylvania
Co. A	Pvt.	Johnson, L. W.	Captured, 5/12/64 at Spotsylvania
Co. A	Pvt.	Kelly, James M.	Wounded, 5/12/64 at Spotsylvania
Co. A	Pvt.	McKenzie, Redman	Captured, 5/12/64 at Spotsylvania

Unit	Rank	Name	Remarks
Co. A	Pvt.	McLemore, William S.	Wounded, 5/12/64 at Spotsylvania. Died of wounds, 5/27/64.
Co. A	Pvt.	Miles, John	Wounded, 5/12/64 at Spotsylvania
Co. A	Pvt.	Page, Jacob S.	Killed, 5/12/64 at Spotsylvania
Co. A	Pvt.	Pope, Wiley	Captured, 5/12/64 at Spotsylvania
Co. A	Pvt.	Reynolds, John R.	Captured, 5/12/64 at Spotsylvania
Co. A	Pvt.	Taylor, William J.	Captured, 5/12/64 at Spotsylvania
Co. A	Pvt.	Tindale, Miles S.	Captured, 5/12/64 at Spotsylvania
Co. A	Pvt.	Williamson, James	Captured, 5/12/64 at Spotsylvania
Co. B	3rd Cpl.	Shearin, Thomas W.	Wounded (right thigh), 5/12/64 at Spotsylvania
Co. B	Pvt.	Buff, Peter	Wounded, 5/12/64 at Spotsylvania
Co. B	Pvt.	Pegram, Mitchell S.	Wounded (left foot & right knee), 5/12/64 at Spotsylvania. ("Complete destruction of foot bones.")
Co. B	Pvt.	Riggan, Charles S.	Wounded (shrapnel; right arm), 5/12/64 at Spotsylvania
Co. B	Pvt.	Riggan, Isham S.	Captured, 5/12/64 at Spotsylvania
Co. B	Pvt.	Riggan, Sugar A.	Captured, 5/12/64 at Spotsylvania
Co. B	Pvt.	Saintsing, John A.	Wounded (right shoulder), 5/12/64 at Spotsylvania
Co. C	2nd Lt.	Swain, John R.	Captured, 5/12/64 at Spotsylvania
Co. C	1st Sgt.	Milliken, Isaac	Captured 5/12/64 at Spotsylvania
Co. C	Cpl.	Marshall, William D.	Captured, 5/12/64 at Spotsylvania
Co. C	Pvt.	Butler, John C.	Captured, 5/12/64 at Spotsylvania
Co. C	Pvt.	Coleman, James	Captured, 5/12/64 at Spotsylvania
Co. C	Pvt.	Cress, Wiley	Wounded (right thigh), 5/12/64 at Spotsylvania
Co. C	Pvt.	Dickens, Andrew J.	Wounded, 5/12/64 at Spotsylvania
Co. C	Pvt.	Hendon, Solomon R.	Wounded & captured, 5/12/64 at Spotsylvania
Co. C	Pvt.	Johnson, Alexander L.	Captured, 5/12/64 at Spotsylvania
Co. C	Pvt.	Johnson, A. Marion	Captured, 5/12/64 at Spotsylvania
Co. C	Pvt.	Johnson, John	Captured, 5/12/64 at Spotsylvania
Co. C	Pvt.	Klutts, Tobias	Wounded (mouth), 5/12/64 at Spotsylvania. Died of wounds (gangrene), 6/18/64.
Co. C	Pvt.	Luntzford, James R.	Captured, 5/12/64 at Spotsylvania
Co. C	Pvt.	Miller, Alexander B.	Captured, 5/12/64 at Spotsylvania
Co. C	Pvt.	Moore, Theophilus	Wounded, 5/12/64 at Spotsylvania
Co. C	Pvt.	Pilgreen, William H.	Killed, 5/12/64 at Spotsylvania
Co. C	Pvt.	Skipper, Wesley W.	Wounded (head & neck), 5/12/64 at Spotsylvania. Died of wounds, 5/29/64
Co. C	Pvt.	Smith, Reuben	Captured, 5/12/64 at Spotsylvania
Co. C	Pvt.	Wanett, William A.	Killed, 5/12/64 at Spotsylvania
Co. C	Pvt.	Williamson, Jn. Bailey	Killed, 5/12/64 at Spotsylvania
Co. D	2nd Cpl.	Ferrell, John C.	Captured, 5/12/64 at Spotsylvania
Co. D	Pvt.	Bailey, Young F.	Killed, 5/12/64 at Spotsylvania
Co. D	Pvt.	Edwards, Walter	Captured, 5/12/65 at Spotsylvania
Co. D	Pvt.	King, Caswell	Captured, 5/12/64 at Spotsylvania
Co. D	Pvt.	Rogers, John H.	Captured, 5/12/64 at Spotsylvania
Co. E	Cpt.	McMillan, John C.	Wounded (shoulder & right arm), 5/12/64 at Spotsylvania
Co. E	3rd Sgt.	Henderson, Brantly B.	Killed, 5/12/64 at Spotsylvania
Co. E	1st Cpl.	Pierce, Nixon	Captured, 5/12/64 at Spotsylvania
Co. E	2nd Cpl.	Dempsey, Kinchen H.	Wounded, 5/12/64 at Spotsylvania
Co. E	Pvt.	Beasley, Edward	Wounded, 5/12/64 at Spotsylvania

Appendix 1

Unit	Rank	Name	Remarks
Co. E	Pvt.	Brown, John (2nd)	Wounded (face, fractured jaw), 5/12/64 at Spotsylvania. Died of wounds, 5/24/64.
Co. E	Pvt.	Cavenaugh, Jacob W.	Wounded, 5/12/64 at Spotsylvania
Co. E	Pvt.	Edwards, Isaac N.	Captured, 5/12/64 at Spotsylvania
Co. E	Pvt.	Evans, Adin	Wounded, 5/12/64 at Spotsylvania
Co. E	Pvt.	Hunter, Martin	Captured, 5/12/64 at Spotsylvania
Co. E	Pvt.	Mallard, John W.	Captured, 5/12/64 at Spotsylvania
Co. E	Pvt.	Malpass, Carleton	Wounded (right hip), 5/12/64 at Spotsylvania
Co. E	Pvt.	Murray, Thomas M.	Wounded (hand), 5/12/64 at Spotsylvania
Co. E	Pvt.	Strickland, David R.	Captured, 5/12/64 at Spotsylvania
Co. E	Pvt.	Teachey, Wiley B.	Wounded, 5/12/64 at Spotsylvania
Co. E	Pvt.	Wood, Uzzell T.	Wounded, 5/12/64 at Spotsylvania
Co. F	1st Lt.	Harrell, George K.	Killed (ball passing through head'), 5/12/64 at Spotsylvania
Co. F	2nd Lt.	Eagles, Lorenzo Dow	Wounded (leg shattered), 5/12/64 at Spotsylvania. Died of wounds, 5/24/64.
Co. F	3rd Lt.	Moore, Samuel R.	Wounded (back & abdomen), 5/12/64 at Spotsylvania
Co. F	Sgt.	Watson, John	Wounded (left leg), 5/12/64 at Spotsylvania
Co. F	5th Sgt.	Cherry, Spencer	Wounded (left leg), 5/12/64 at Spotsylvania. Died of wounds, 5/21/64
Co. F	Cpl.	Pittman, Reddin E.	Wounded ("shot in right arm twice, & right breast"), 5/12/64 at Spotsylvania
Co. F	Music	Webb, Newett	Wounded, 5/12/64 at Spotsylvania
Co. F	Pvt.	Brasswell, James B.	Wounded (right shoulder), 5/12/64 at Spotsylvania
Co. F	Pvt.	Burgess, Hardy	Wounded (hand), 5/12/64 at Spotsylvania
Co. F	Pvt.	Crisp, William G.	Wounded (right shoulder), 5/12/64 at Spotsylvania. Died of wounds, 5/20/64.
Co. F	Pvt.	Corbett, Dempsey	Wounded, 5/12/64 at Spotsylvania
Co. F	Pvt.	Eagles, Theodore R.	Wounded (arm), 5/12/64 at Spotsylvania
Co. F	Pvt.	Harrell, Elisha T.	Wounded (head), 5/12/64 at Spotsylvania. Died of wounds, 5/26/64.
Co. F	Pvt.	Johnson, James A.	Wounded (arm), 5/12/64 at Spotsylvania
Co. F	Pvt.	Phillips, Richard	Wounded (arm), 5/12/64 at Spotsylvania
Co. F	Pvt.	Price, Thomas	Killed, ("shot through head") 5/12/64 at Spotsylvania
Co. F	Pvt.	Vick, William	Wounded (neck), 5/12/64 at Spotsylvania
Co. F	Pvt.	Wamack, William D.	Wounded, 5/12/64 at Spotsylvania. Died from wounds, 5/14/64.
Co. F	Pvt.	Watson, Levi	Wounded (right shoulder & neck), 5/12/64 at Spotsylvania
Co. G	3rd Lt.	Fulford, John T.	Wounded (left arm), 5/12/64 at Spotsylvania
Co. G	4th Sgt.	Dean, Simpson	Captured, 5/12/64 at Spotsylvania
Co. G	Pvt.	Dickerson, Martin	Captured, 5/12/64 at Spotsylvania
Co. G	Pvt.	Church, Carlton	Captured, 5/12/64 at Spotsylvania
Co. G	Pvt.	Collins, Samuel A.	Wounded, 5/12/64 at Spotsylvania
Co. G	Pvt.	Connell, Wyatt G.	Wounded (right elbow) & captured, 5/12/64 at Spotsylvania
Co. G	Pvt.	Crawford, James S.	Killed, 5/12/64 at Spotsylvania
Co. G	Pvt.	Dickerson, Martin	Captured, 5/12/64 at Spotsylvania
Co. G	Pvt.	Harris, Richard P.	Captured, 5/12/64 at Spotsylvania
Co. G	Pvt.	Harris, William H.	Killed, 5/12/64 at Spotsylvania
Co. G	Pvt.	Hobgood, James M.	Captured, 5/12/64 at Spotsylvania
Co. G	Pvt.	Merritt, Benjamin H.	Captured, 5/12/64 at Spotsylvania
Co. G	Pvt.	Slaughter, William P.	Killed, 5/12/64 at Spotsylvania

30th North Carolina Infantry Casualties

Unit	Rank	Name	Remarks
Co. G	Pvt.	Wilson, Samuel R.	Killed, 5/12/54 at Spotsylvania
Co. H	Cpt.	Wicker, Jesse J.	Captured, 5/12/64 at Spotsylvania
Co. H	2nd Lt.	Jackson, Archibald J.	Wounded, 5/12/64 at Spotsylvania. Died of wounds, 5/19/64.
Co. H	2nd Cpl.	Matthews, M. Hardy	Wounded (leg & left arm), 5/12/64 at Spotsylvania
Co. H	4th Cpl.	Underwood, John A.	Wounded (right ankle), 5/12/64 at Spotsylvania
Co. H	Pvt.	Black, Alfred	Captured, 5/12/64 at Spotsylvania
Co. H	Pvt.	Burgess, William H.	Killed, 5/12/64 at Spotsylvania
Co. H	Pvt.	Campbell, Angus T.	Captured, 5/12/64 at Spotsylvania
Co. H	Pvt.	Center, Charles H.	Wounded (head) & captured, 5/12/64 at Spotsylvania. Died of wounds, 5/31/64.
Co. H	Pvt.	Green, James L.	Captured, 5/12/64 at Spotsylvania
Co. H	Pvt.	Hornaday, Lewis D.	Captured, 5/12/64 at Spotsylvania
Co. H	Pvt.	Horne, Pleasant	Captured, 5/12/64 at Spotsylvania
Co. H	Pvt.	Jackson, Burgess C.	Killed, 5/12/64 at Spotsylvania
Co. H	Pvt.	King, W. H.	Captured, 5/12/64 at Spotsylvania
Co. H	Pvt.	McFarland, Andrew	Captured, 5/12/64 at Spotsylvania
Co. H	Pvt.	Rogers, James	Captured, 5/12/64 at Spotsylvania
Co. H	Pvt.	Rose, Henry B.	Captured, 5/12/64 at Spotsylvania
Co. H	Pvt.	Starnes, Ephraim	Captured, 5/12/64 at Spotsylvania
Co. I	Cpt.	Harris, James J.	Killed, 5/12/64 at Spotsylvania
Co. I	1st Lt.	Arrington, Kearney W.	Wounded (left calf) & captured, 5/12/64 at Spotsylvania
Co. I	Pvt.	Bone, John W.	Wounded (right breast), 5/12/64 at Spotsylvania
Co. I	Pvt.	Crickman, Josiah G.	Captured, 5/12/64 at Spotsylvania
Co. I	Pvt.	Dortridge, Richard J.	Killed, 5/12/64 at Spotsylvania
Co. I	Pvt.	Jones, Calvin F.	Wounded, 5/12/64 at Spotsylvania
Co. I	Pvt.	Joyner, Alsey M.	Killed, 5/12/64 at Spotsylvania
Co. I	Pvt.	Pitt, James W.	Wounded (left leg), 5/12/64 at Spotsylvania
Co. I	Pvt.	Rigsbee, William C.	Wounded (right lung & shoulder), 5/12/64. Died of wounds, 5/21/64.
Co. K	2nd Sgt.	Lee, James T.	Killed, 5/12/64 at Spotsylvania
Co. K	Pvt.	Alexander, James M.	Killed, 5/12/64 at Spotsylvania
Co. K	Pvt.	Bailey, William	Wounded, 5/12/64 at Spotsylvania
Co. K	Pvt.	Duckworth, Thomas P.	Wounded, 5/12/64 at Spotsylvania. Died of wounds, 7/10/64.
Co. K	Pvt.	Miller, David W.	Wounded, 5/12/64 at Spotsylvania
Co. K	Pvt.	Ross, J. Newell	Wounded, 5/12/64 at Spotsylvania. Died of wounds, 6/5/64.
Co. K	Pvt.	Simpson, Marcus	Captured, 5/12/64 at Spotsylvania
Co. K	Pvt.	Squires, James W.	Killed, 5/12/64 at Spotsylvania

Harris Farm/Spotsylvania, Virginia
May 17–20, 1864
28 = 3 Killed, 9 Wounded, 2 Wounded & Captured, 14 Captured

Unit	Rank	Name	Remarks
F & S	Col.	Parker, Francis M.	Wounded (right side of abdomen), 5/19/64 at Harris Farm
Co. A	Pvt.	Friezland, Jacob	Wounded (head), 5/19/64 at Harris Farm (caused by shell fragment)
Co. B	Pvt.	Arrington, James L.	Captured, 5/20/64 at Spotsylvania

Unit	Rank	Name	Remarks
Co. B	Pvt.	Neal, Dudley H.	Wounded (both legs), 5/16/64 at Harris Farm
Co. D	Pvt.	King, Anderson F.	Captured, 5/19/64 at Harris Farm
Co. D	Pvt.	Lumbley, William L.	Captured, 5/20/64 at Spotsylvania
Co. E	1st Sgt.	Wells, James W.	Killed, 5/19/64 at Harris Farm
Co. E	Pvt.	Hamilton, William S.	Captured, 5/19/64 at Harris Farm
Co. E	Pvt.	Parker, Jacob W.	Captured, 5/19/64 at Harris Farm
Co. E	Pvt.	Piner, James J.	Captured, 5/20/64 at Spotsylvania
Co. E	Pvt.	Tucker, William	Captured, 5/19/64 at Harris Farm
Co. F	Pvt.	Dickens, Ephraim	Killed, 5/19/64 at Harris Farm
Co. F	Pvt.	Madra, George	Captured, 5/19/64 at Harris Farm
Co. F	Pvt.	Summerlin, George	Wounded, 5/19/64 at Harris Farm
Co. G	1st Lt.	Badgett, James W.	Wounded (neck & head), 5/19/64 at Harris Farm; "ball passing through the neck and base of the head, from behind right ear to the mouth."
Co. G	2nd Sgt.	Badgett, Wm. Joseph	Wounded, 5/19/64 at Harris Farm
Co. G	Pvt.	Hamme, Richard F.	Captured, 5/19/64 at Harris Farm
Co. H	1st Lt.	McNeil, Henry J.	Wounded (right leg; tibia shattered), 5/19/64 at Harris Farm
Co. H	4th Sgt.	McIntoch, David J.	Captured, 5/20/64 at Spotsylvania
Co. H	Pvt.	McIver, D. N.	Wounded, 5/19/64 at Harris Farm
Co. H	Pvt.	Thomas Murphy J.	Captured, 5/19/64 at Harris Farm
Co. I	Pvt.	Winters, George	Captured, 5/19/64 at Harris Farm
Co. K	Sgt.	Nichols, Burgess G.	Wounded, 5/19/64 at Harris Farm
Co. K	Sgt.	Weeks, Rufus B.	Killed, 5/19/64 at Harris Farm
Co. K	Pvt.	Adams, William	Wounded and captured, 5/19/64 at Harris Farm
Co. K	Pvt.	Adkins, William H.	Captured, 5/17/64 at Spotsylvania
Co. K	Pvt.	Nichols, J.	Captured, 5/20/64 at Spotsylvania
Co. K	Pvt.	Pierce, James M.	Wounded and captured, 5/19/64 at Harris Farm

North Anna/Cold Harbor, Virginia
May 21—June 30, 1864
27 = 2 Killed, 17 Wounded, 8 Captured

Unit	Rank	Name	Remarks
Co. A	Pvt.	King, Stephen J.	Wounded (right heel), 6/3/64 at Cold Harbor
Co. D	Pvt.	Nichols, John T.	Captured, 6/3/64 at Cold Harbor
Co. D	Pvt.	Pierce, James T.	Wounded (right hand), 6/1/64 at Cold Harbor
Co. E	Pvt.	Brigman, John	Captured, 5/30/64 at Cold Harbor (Old Bethesda Church)
Co. E	Pvt.	Brown, Felix	Captured, 5/30/64 at Cold Harbor (Old Bethesda Church)
Co. E	Pvt.	Butler, Henry G.	Killed, 6/4/64 at Cold Harbor
Co. E	Pvt.	Lanier, Jacob W.	Wounded (bladder & bowels), 6/1/64 at Cold Harbor. Died of wounds, 6/4/64.
Co. E	Pvt.	Rogers, Jobe B.	Captured, 5/31/64 at Cold Harbor (Old Bethesda Church)
Co. E	Pvt.	Steele, Robert	Captured, 5/31/64 at Cold Harbor (Old Bethesda Church)
Co. F	Pvt.	Crisp, Silas E.	Wounded (arm), 6/2/64 at Cold Harbor
Co. F	Pvt.	Langley, Morrison	Killed, 5/31/64 at Cold Harbor (Old Bethesda Church)

Unit	Rank	Name	Remarks
Co. F	Pvt.	Webb, Bennett	Wounded (right leg), 6/1/64 at Cold Harbor
Co. G	2nd Cpl.	Burroughs, William A.	Wounded (hip), 5/31/64 at Cold Harbor (Old Bethesda Church). Died of wounds, 6/8/64.
Co. G	Pvt.	Blevins, Shadrach	Wounded (left arm), 6/2/64 at Cold Harbor
Co. G	Pvt.	Brooks, Henry R.	Wounded (leg), 6/3/64 at Cold Harbor
Co. G	Pvt.	Dean, Jesse	Wounded (head), 6/1/64 at Cold Harbor
Co. H	Pvt.	Dudley, Laban	Captured, 5/24/64 at North Anna
Co. H	Pvt.	Lawrence, John	Wounded (face—jaw), 6/3/64 at Cold Harbor
Co. I	Pvt.	Fryer, Lawrence D.	Wounded (left leg), 6/3/64 at Cold Harbor
Co. I	Pvt.	Sykes, William J.	Wounded (right arm), 6/3/64 at Cold Harbor
Co. I	Pvt.	Williams, Joseph D.	Captured, 5/24/64 at North Anna
Co. K	Cpt.	Ardrey, William	Wounded (head), 6/2/64 at Cold Harbor
Co. K	Pvt.	Hood, William L.	Wounded (right hand), 5/24/64 at Spotsylvania
Co. K	Pvt.	Johnston, James H.	Wounded, 6/3/64 at Cold Harbor
Co. K	Pvt.	Lee, Samuel B.	Wounded (hip & pelvis fractured), 5/24/64 at North Anna. Died of wounds, 6/21/64.
Co. K	Pvt.	Massingil, Robert S.	Captured, 5/30/64 at Cold Harbor
Co. K	Pvt.	McLure, James A.	Wounded (right wrist; arm amputated), 5/30/64 at Cold Harbor; "in a skirmish."

Fort Stevens, Virginia
July 11–12, 1864
10 = 2 Killed, 3 Wounded, 3 Wounded & Captured, 2 Captured

Unit	Rank	Name	Remarks
Co. A	1st Sgt.	Crumpler, Robert M.	Wounded, 7/12/64 at Ft. Stevens
Co. B	3rd Sgt.	Shearin, Thomas G.	Killed, 7/12/64 at Ft. Stevens
Co. B	Pvt.	Hardy, Francis M.	Wounded (both forearms), 7/12/64 at Ft. Stevens
Co. D	Pvt.	Penny, Solomon W.	Killed, 7/12/64 at Fort Stevens.
Co. F	Pvt.	Redick, Epinetus	Wounded (ear & left eye) and captured, 7/12/64 at Ft. Stevens
Co. G	Pvt.	Bobbitt, Isham C.	Missing, 7/13/64 at Ft. Stevens. Captured, 7/12/64 near Washington, D.C.
Co. G	Pvt.	Cheatham, James T.	Captured, 7/12/64 at Ft. Stevens
Co. G	Pvt.	Dement, Henry	Wounded and captured, 7/12/64 at Ft. Stevens. "Left in the enemies [sic] lines"
Co. H	Pvt.	Hagler, Hiram	Wounded (back & left side) and captured, 7/12/64 at Ft. Stevens. Died of gangrene, 8/3/64
Co. K	Pvt.	Robinson, William H.	Wounded, 7/12/64 at Ft. Stevens

Snicker's Gap, Virginia
July 18, 1864
24 = 6 Killed, 18 Wounded

Unit	Rank	Name	Remarks
F&S	Sgt. Maj.	Fitts, Francis M.	Wounded, 7/18/64 at Snicker's Gap
Co. A	Pvt.	King, Lewis D.	Wounded, 7/18/64 at Snicker's Gap
Co. C	4th Sgt.	Howard, Geo. Washington	Wounded (right thigh), 7/18/64 at Snicker's Gap
Co. D	3rd Lt.	Rogers, Martin L.	Wounded, 7/18/64 at Snicker's Gap
Co. D	Pvt.	Harris, Henry	Wounded, 7/18/64 at Snicker's Gap

Unit	Rank	Name	Remarks
Co. E	1st Lt.	Johnson, Ira J.	Wounded, 7/18/64 at Snicker's Gap
Co. E	5th Sgt.	Teachey, James W.	Killed, 7/18/64 at Snicker's Gap
Co. E	Pvt.	Teachey, Jacob T.	Wounded ("through the bowels"), 7/18/64 at Snicker's Gap
Co. F	2nd Cpl.	Felton, Richard	Killed, 7/18/64 at Snicker's Gap
Co. F	Pvt.	Forbes, James	Wounded, 7/18/64 at Snicker's Gap
Co. F	Pvt.	Johnson, A. C. J.	Wounded (right arm), 7/18/64 at Snicker's Gap
Co. F	Pvt.	Morgan, Thomas	Wounded (right leg), 7/18/64 at Snicker's Gap
Co. F	Pvt.	Wells, Louis Redmond	Wounded (breast), 7/18/64 at Snicker's Gap. Died of wounds, 7/21/64.
Co. H	Pvt.	Crotts, Elijah	Killed, 7/18/64 at Snicker's Gap
Co. H	Pvt.	McIntosh, Francis M.	Wounded, 7/18/64 at Snicker's Gap
Co. H	Pvt.	Starnes, D. A.	Wounded (right leg), 7/18/64 at Snicker's Gap
Co. I	3rd Lt.	Perry, Sidney R.	Wounded (right ankle shattered), 7/18/64 at Snicker's Gap; "shell fragment struck ankle and tibia, fracturing both."
Co. I	Pvt.	Batchelor, Ruffin	Wounded, 7/18/64 at Snickers Gap
Co. I	Pvt.	Bell, Arkin B.	Killed, 7/18/64 at Snicker's Gap
Co. I	Pvt.	Gupton, Thomas	Killed, 7/18/64 at Snicker's Gap
Co. K	Sgt.	Black, John N.	Killed, 7/18/64 at Snicker's Gap
Co. K	5th Sgt.	DeArmond, Aaron L.	Wounded, 7/18/64 at Snicker's Gap. Died of wounds, 8/15/64.
Co. K	Pvt.	Bailey, William	Wounded, 7/18/64 at Snicker's Gap
Co. K	Pvt.	Saville, John C.	Wounded, 7/18/64 at Snicker's Gap

Charles Town Virginia
August 21, 1864
16 = 5 Killed, 11 Wounded

Unit	Rank	Name	Remarks
Co. A	Pvt.	Pennington, John	Killed, 8/21/64 at Charles Town
Co. B	Pvt.	Williams, William A.	Killed, 8/21/64 at Charles Town
Co. C	Cpl.	McDowell, William J.	Wounded (both feet), 8/21/64 at Charles Town. (3 toes amputated)
Co. D	Cpl.	Forsyth, James R.	Killed, 8/21/64 at Charles Town
Co. D	Pvt.	Wilkins, Elijah	Killed, 8/21/64 at Charles Town
Co. E	Sgt.	Newkirk, George B.	Killed, 8/21/64 at Charles Town
Co. E	Pvt.	Bland, John J.	Wounded (arm), 8/21/64 at Charles Town
Co. E	Pvt.	Cavenaugh, Jacob W.	Wounded (leg), 8/21/64 at Charles Town
Co. E	Pvt.	Turner, David W.	Wounded (head), 8/21/64 at Charles Town
Co. F	Pvt.	Walston, William F.	Wounded, 8/21/64 at Charles Town. Died of wounds, 3/10/65.
Co. F	Pvt.	Warren, Lemuel	Wounded, 8/21/64 at Charles Town
Co. G	Sgt.	Fuller, James N.	Wounded (left hip & right leg fractured), 8/21/64 at Charles Town
Co. G	Pvt.	Frazer, James H.	Wounded, 8/21/64 at Charles Town
Co. G	Pvt.	Hunt, David Z.	Wounded, 8/21/64 at Charles Town
Co. I	Cpl.	Winstead, Hilliard H.	Wounded, 8/21/64 at Charles Town. Died of wounds, 8/-/64.
Co. K	Pvt.	Bentley, Moses	Wounded (right leg), 8/21/64 at Charles Town

Winchester, Virginia
September 19, 1864
20 = 10 Wounded, 3 Wounded & Captured, 7 Captured

Unit	Rank	Name	Remarks
F & S	Cpt.	Allen, David C.	Wounded (left shoulder), 9/19/64 at Winchester
Co. A	Pvt.	Cox, Robert G.	Wounded (left thigh), 9/19/64 at Winchester. Captured, 9/25/64 at Harrisonburg.
Co. A	Pvt.	Howard, William S.	Wounded (right thigh) and captured, 9/19/64 at Winchester
Co. B	Pvt.	Shearin, John L.	Wounded, 9/19/64 at Winchester
Co. C	Sgt.	Wescott, John W.	Captured, 9/19/64 at Winchester
Co. C	Pvt.	Sprinkle, Hugh	Captured, 9/19/64 at Winchester
Co. D	Pvt.	Cooper, William W.	Wounded (head), 9/19/64 at Winchester
Co. D	Pvt.	Ferrell, Albert L.	Captured, 9/19/64 at Winchester
Co. D	Pvt.	King, John	Wounded, 9/19/64 at Winchester
Co. D	Pvt.	Peed, William C.	Captured, 9/19/64 at Winchester
Co. E	Pvt.	Dickson, Riol	Wounded (spine & thigh), 9/19/64 at Winchester
Co. E	Pvt.	Mobley, William V.	Captured, 9/19/64 at Winchester
Co. F	3rd Lt.	Moore, Samuel R.	Wounded (right side), 9/19/64 at Winchester
Co. G	Pvt.	Critcher, William H.	Captured, 9/19/64 at Winchester
Co. G	Pvt.	King, James D.	Wounded, 9/19/64 at Winchester
Co. H	Cpl.	Matthews, M. Hardy	Wounded (right leg) and captured, 9/19/64 at Winchester
Co. H	Pvt.	Hendricks, Eusileus	Captured, 9/19/64 at Winchester
Co. K	1st Lt.	Downs, John T.	Wounded (wrist), 9/19/64 at Winchester
Co. K.	Pvt.	Howie, John H.	Wounded, 9/19/64 at Winchester
Co. K.	Pvt.	Johnston, James H.	Wounded, 9/19/64 at Winchester

Fisher's Hill, Virginia
September 22, 1864
18 = 3 Wounded, 2 Wounded & Captured, 13 Captured

Unit	Rank	Name	Remarks
Co. A	Pvt.	Honeycutt, Miles C.	Captured, 9/22/64 at Fisher's Hill
Co. A	Pvt.	Pennington, Henry	Captured, 9/22/64 at Fisher's Hill
Co. C	Cpl.	Smith, Benjamin	Captured, 9/22/64 at Fisher's Hill
Co. C	Pvt.	Robins, Jonathan	Wounded, 9/22/64 at Fisher's Hill
Co. D	Pvt.	Canady, Francis R.	Captured, 9/22/64 at Fisher's Hill
Co. D	Pvt.	Davis, James T.	Captured, 9/22/64 at Fisher's Hill
Co. E	Sgt.	Dempsey, Kinchen H.	Captured, 9/22/64 at Fisher's Hill
Co. E	Pvt.	Boney, Hiram S.	Captured, 9/22/64 at Fisher's Hill
Co. E	Pvt.	Bradshaw, James B.	Captured, 9/22/64 at Fisher's Hill
Co. F	Pvt.	Phillips, Richard	Wounded, 9/22/64 at Fisher's Hill
Co. G	Cpl.	Cawthorn, John W.	Captured, 9/22/64 at Fisher's Hill
Co. G	Pvt.	Cheatham, William A.	Captured, 9/22/64 at Fisher's Hill
Co. G	Pvt.	Robertson, Z. R.	Captured, 9/22/64 at Fisher's Hill
Co. I	Pvt.	Batts, William J.	Wounded ("Gunshot wound to the head"), 9/22/64 at Fisher's Hill
Co. I	Pvt.	Vick, Joseph K.	Captured, 9/22/64 at Fisher's Hill
Co. K	Sgt.	Culp, Aley A.	Wounded (right leg, flesh wound) and captured, 9/22/64 at Fisher's Hill
Co. K	Pvt.	Pierce, Orren L.	Wounded and captured, 9/22/64 at Fisher's Hill
Co. K	Pvt.	West, William M.	Captured, 9/22/64 at Fisher's Hill

Cedar Creek, Virginia
October 19, 1864
19 = 2 Killed, 8 Wounded, 1 Wounded & Captured, 8 Captured

Unit	Rank	Name	Remarks
F & S	Sgt. Maj.	Fitts, Francis, M.	Wounded, 10/19/64 at Cedar Creek
Co. A	Sgt.	Hobbs, Judson	Captured, 10/19/64 at Cedar Creek
Co. B	Pvt.	Cloyd, J. M.	Captured, 10/19/64 at Cedar Creek
Co. B	Pvt.	Riggan, Charles S.	Wounded, 10/19/64 at Cedar Creek
Co. C	Pvt.	Simmons, Lewis	Captured, 10/19/64 at Cedar Creek
Co. D	Cpl.	Davis, William E.	Captured, 10/19/64 at Cedar Creek
Co. D	Pvt.	Bailey, Jeremiah	Wounded, 10/19/64 at Cedar Creek. Died of wounds, 10/26/64.
Co. E	Pvt.	Lanier, Brantley	Captured, 10/19/64 at Cedar Creek
Co. E	Pvt.	Pickett, William D.	Wounded, 10/19/64 at Cedar Creek
Co. E	Pvt.	Shute, Henry B.	Captured, 10/19/64 at Cedar Creek
Co. E	Cpl.	Teachey, W. B.	Captured, 10/19/64 at Cedar Creek
Co. F	Cpt.	Moore, Willis D.	Killed, 10/19/64 at Cedar Creek
Co. F	Pvt.	Bell, Bennett	Wounded, 10/19/64 at Cedar Creek
Co. F	Pvt.	Little, Jesse	Wounded, 10/19/64 at Cedar Creek
Co. G	Pvt.	Elliott, Green B.	Killed, 10/19/64 at Cedar Creek
Co. I	Pvt.	Culpepper, John	Captured, 10/19/64 at Cedar Creek
Co. K	Pvt.	Barefoot, Noah G.	Wounded, 10/19/64 at Cedar Creek
Co. K	Pvt.	Hall, John G.	Wounded, 10/19/64 at Cedar Creek
Co. K	Pvt.	Hood, William L.	Wounded and captured, 10/19/64 at Cedar Creek

Near Petersburg, Virginia
Winter 1864—April 3, 1865
9 = 3 Wounded, 5 Captured, 1 Deserted

Unit	Rank	Name	Remarks
Co. A	Pvt.	Ogburn, N. S.	Captured, 4/3/65 at Petersburg
Co. A	Pvt.	Rogers, William	Captured, 4/3/65 at Petersburg
Co. D	Pvt.	King, Anderson F.	Wounded (right thumb), 3/6/65 near Petersburg
Co. D	Pvt.	Moore, William H.	Wounded (left shoulder), 4/2/65 in Petersburg trenches
Co. E	Pvt.	Butler, James C.	Deserted, 1/9/65
Co. F	Pvt.	Cline, J.	Captured, 4/3/65 near Appomattox River
Co. H	Pvt.	Lynn, William	Wounded (right thigh), 3/25/65 near Ft. Stedman
Co. I	Pvt.	Armstrong, Gray R.	Captured, 4/3/65 in Petersburg trenches
Co. I	Pvt.	Batchelor, Ruffin	Captured, 4/3/65 in Petersburg trenches

Sailor's Creek, Virginia
April 6, 1865
8 = 7 Wounded, 1 Captured

Unit	Rank	Name	Remarks
Co. B	Pvt.	Aycock, George G.	Wounded (left thigh) at Sailor's Creek and captured, 4/6/65 at Farmville
Co. B	Pvt.	Carroll, William H.	Wounded (right arm) at Sailor's Creek, 4/6/65. Captured, 4/7/65 at Farmville.
Co. E	Cpt.	McMillan, John C.	Wounded (right side, below shoulder),

30th North Carolina Infantry Casualties

Unit	Rank	Name	Remarks
			4/6/65, near Deatonsville. Captured at Farmville.
Co. E	2nd Lt.	Newton, Samuel B.	Captured, 4/6/65 at Sailor's Creek
Co. E	5th Sgt.	Best, John B.	Wounded (right ankle) at Sailor's Creek and captured, 4/6/65 at Burkesville Jct.
Co. E	Pvt.	Beasley, Edward	Wounded (scalp, flesh), 4/6/65 at Sailor's Creek
Co. F	Pvt.	Corbett, Dempsey	Wounded, 4/6/65 at Sailor's Creek
Co. F	Pvt.	Felton, Eli	Wounded, 4/6/65 at Sailor's Creek

Retreat from Sailor's Creek, Virginia
April 6–8, 1865
48 Captured, 1 Missing

Unit	Rank	Name	Remarks
Co. A	1st Cpl.	Crumpler, James M.	Captured, 4/6/65 at Farmville
Co. A	Pvt.	Friezland, Jacob	Captured, 4/6/65 at Burkeville
Co. B	Pvt.	Aycock, George G.	Wounded (left thigh) at Sailor's Creek and Captured, 4/6/65 at Farmville
Co. B	Pvt.	Carroll, William H.	Wounded (right arm) at Sailor's Creek, 4/6/65. Captured, 4/7/65 at Farmville.
Co. B	Pvt.	Miles, James	Captured, 4/6/65 near High Bridge
Co. B	Pvt.	Shearin, John R.	Missing, 4/8/65 near Appomattox
Co. C	Pvt.	Armfield, John J.	Captured, 4/6/65 at Farmville
Co. C	Pvt.	Haywood, Richard	Captured, 4/6/65 at Farmville
Co. C	Pvt.	Kimmel, Daniel A.	Captured, 4/6/65 at Farmville
Co. D	5th Sgt.	Cousins, John A.	Captured, 4/6/65 at Farmville
Co. D	Pvt.	Cooper, William W.	Captured, 4/6/65 at High Bridge
Co. D	Pvt.	Jones, William H.	Captured, 4/6/65 at Farmville
Co. D	Pvt.	King, John	Captured, 4/6/65 at Farmville
Co. D	Pvt.	Lloyd, George E.	Captured, 4/6/65 at Farmville
Co. D	Pvt.	Vaughan, John G.	Captured, 4/6/65 at High Bridge
Co. D	Pvt.	Ward, Isaac B.	Captured, 4/6/65 at Burkeville
Co. E	Cpt.	McMillan, John C.	Wounded (right side, below shoulder), 4/6/65, near Deatonsville. Captured at Farmville.
Co. E	2nd Lt.	Newton, Samuel B.	Captured, 4/6/65 at Sailor's Creek
Co. E	5th Sgt.	Best, John B.	Wounded (right ankle) at Sailor's Creek and captured, 4/6/65 at Burkesville Jct.
Co. E	3rd Cpl.	Benton, Ellis A.	Captured, 4/6/65 at Burkeville
Co. E	Pvt.	Carr, John James	Captured, 4/6/65 at Farmville
Co. E	Pvt.	Cavenaugh, Jacob W.	Captured, 4/6/65 at High Bridge
Co. E	Pvt.	Helms, Archibald	Captured, 4/6/65 at Burkeville
Co. E	Pvt.	Sholar, James H.	Captured, 4/6/65 at Burkeville
Co. E	Pvt.	Tadlock, Starling D.	Captured, 4/6/65 at Farmville
Co. F	Pvt.	Mathews, Roderick	Captured, 4/6/65 at Farmville
Co. F	Pvt.	Walston, Levi	Captured, 4/6/65 at High Bridge
Co. F	Pvt.	Warren, Lemuel	Captured, 4/6/65 at High Bridge
Co. G	Pvt.	Barnes, Hillmon	Captured, 4/6/65 at Farmville
Co. G	Pvt.	Blevins, Harvey	Captured, 4/6/65 at Farmville
Co. H	Pvt.	Morris, David P.	Captured, 4/6/65 at High Bridge
Co. I	Pvt.	Anderson, Thomas J.	Captured, 4/6/65 at High Bridge
Co. I	Pvt.	Capps, William H.	Captured, 4/6/65 at Farmville
Co. I	Pvt.	Grimmer, Elias G.	Captured, 4/6/65 at Farmville
Co. I	Pvt.	Pitts, William M.	Captured, 4/6/65 at Farmville
Co. K	4th Sgt.	Russell, William D.	Captured, 4/6/65 at Farmville

Unit	Rank	Name	Remarks
Co. K	Pvt.	Bentley, Moses	Captured, 4/6/65 at Burkeville
Co. K	Pvt.	Church, Eli	Captured, 4/6/65 at Amelia Court House
Co. K	Pvt.	Church, Martin	Captured, 4/6/65 at Farmville
Co. K	Pvt.	Fields, Absalom F.	Captured, 4/6/65 at Farmville
Co. K	Pvt.	Graham, John W.	Captured, 4/6/65 at Burkeville
Co. K	Pvt.	Hall, Joseph F.	Captured, 4/6/65 at Farmville
Co. K	Pvt.	Harvey, John F.	Captured, 4/6/65 at Farmville
Co. K	Pvt.	McQuay, Joseph F.	Captured, 4/6/65 at Burkeville
Co. K	Pvt.	Miller, David M.	Captured, 4/6/65 at High Bridge
Co. K	Pvt.	Nelson, John J.	Captured, 4/6/65 at Burkeville
Co. K	Pvt.	Rayl, John F.	Captured, 4/6/65 at Burkeville
Co. K	Pvt.	Richardson, William	Captured, 4/6/65 at Farmville
Co. K	Pvt.	Thomas, Lewis R.	Captured, 4/6/65 at Farmville

Appomattox Surrender, Virginia
April 12, 1865
144 Paroled

Unit	Rank	Name	Remarks
F & S	Surgeon	Briggs, George W.	TDY—Brigade Senior Surgeon. Paroled, 4/9/65 at Appomattox
F & S	Asst. Surgeon	Coke, Lucius	Paroled, 4/9/65 at Appomattox
F & S	QM Sgt.	Stallings, Theophilus	Paroled, 4/9/65 at Appomattox
F & S	Sgt. Maj.	Fitts, Francis M.	Paroled, 4/9/65 at Appomattox
Co. A	1st Sgt.	Crumpler, Robert M.	Paroled, 4/9/65 at Appomattox
Co. A	4th Cpl.	Brewer, Abraham H.	Paroled, 4/9/65 at Appomattox
Co. A	Music	Holland, James F	Paroled, 4/9/65 at Appomattox
Co. A	Pvt.	King, Lewis D.	Paroled, 4/9/65 at Appomattox
Co. A	Pvt.	King, Stephen J.	Paroled, 4/9/65 at Appomattox
Co. A	Pvt.	Parker, James M.	Paroled, 4/9/65 at Appomattox
Co. A	Pvt.	Hall, William G.	Paroled, 4/9/65 at Appomattox
Co. A	Pvt.	Spell, Gaston	Paroled, 4/9/65 at Appomattox
Co. A	Pvt.	Steele, James H.	Paroled, 4/9/65 at Appomattox
Co. A	Pvt.	Williamson, Henry	Paroled, 4/9/65 at Appomattox
Co. B	1st Sgt.	Newsom, John G.	Paroled, 4/9/65 at Appomattox
Co. B	3rd Cpl.	Shearin, Thomas W.	Paroled, 4/9/65 at Appomattox
Co. B	Pvt.	Aycock, Edward S.	Paroled, 4/9/65 at Appomattox
Co. B	Pvt.	North, Joshua	Paroled, 4/9/65 at Appomattox
Co. B	Pvt.	Brown, William E.	TDY—Corps HQ; Provost Guard. Paroled, 4/9/65 at Appomattox
Co. B	Pvt.	Harriss, John W.	Paroled, 4/9/65 at Appomattox
Co. B	Pvt.	Pegram, Robert B.	Paroled, 4/9/65 at Appomattox
Co. B	Pvt.	Riggan, Charles D.	Paroled, 4/9/65 at Appomattox
Co. B	Pvt.	Riggan, Charles S.	Paroled, 4/9/65 at Appomattox
Co. B	Pvt.	Saintsing, John A.	Paroled, 4/9/65 at Appomattox
Co. B	Pvt.	Walker, Christopher N.	Paroled, 4/9/65 at Appomattox
Co. C	Cpt.	Allen, David C.	Paroled, 4/9/65 at Appomattox
Co. C	5th Sgt.	Butler, Benjamin L.	Paroled, 4/9/65 at Appomattox
Co. C	Cpl.	Robinson, Alexander S.	Paroled, 4/9/65 at Appomattox
Co. C	Pvt.	Coleman, Etheldred	Paroled, 4/9/65 at Appomattox
Co. C	Pvt.	Danford, Abram	Paroled, 4/9/65 at Appomattox
Co. C	Pvt.	Lamb, Ithamer	Paroled, 4/9/65 at Appomattox
Co. C	Pvt.	Larkins, Robert S.	Paroled, 4/9/65 at Appomattox
Co. C	Pvt.	Oakley, David	Paroled, 4/9/65 at Appomattox

30th North Carolina Infantry Casualties

Unit	Rank	Name	Remarks
Co. C	Pvt.	Robins, Jonathan	Paroled, 4/9/65 at Appomattox
Co. C	Pvt.	Vines, William T.	Paroled, 4/9/65 at Appomattox
Co. D	Music	Joyner, John L.	Paroled, 4/9/65 at Appomattox
Co. D	Pvt.	Bledsoe, Giles	Paroled, 4/9/65 at Appomattox
Co. D	Pvt.	Dickey, Zachariah C.	Paroled, 4/9/65 at Appomattox
Co. D	Pvt.	Goodin, Joseph J.	Paroled, 4/9/65 at Appomattox
Co. D	Pvt.	Harris, Henry	Paroled, 4/9/65 at Appomattox
Co. D	Pvt.	Harris, Thomas P.	Paroled, 4/9/65 at Appomattox
Co. D	Pvt.	Lloyd, George E.	Paroled, 4/9/65 at Appomattox
Co. D	Pvt.	Mangum, Theophilus P.	Paroled, 4/9/65 at Appomattox
Co. D	Pvt.	Massey, Marion M.	Paroled, 4/9/65 at Appomattox
Co. D	Pvt.	Wadford, Alexander	Paroled, 4/9/65 at Appomattox
Co. E	1st Lt.	Johnson, Ira J.	Paroled, 4/9/65 at Appomattox
Co. E	2nd Sgt.	Hanchey, John W.	Paroled, 4/9/65 at Appomattox
Co. E	4th Sgt.	Jones, James K.	Paroled, 4/9/65 at Appomattox
Co. E	Pvt.	Bradshaw, B. D.	Paroled, 4/9/65 at Appomattox
Co. E	Pvt.	Davis, Simpson	TDY—Teamster. Paroled, 4/9/63 at Appomattox
Co. E	Pvt.	Duff, John T.	Paroled, 4/9/65 at Appomattox
Co. E	Pvt.	Helms, Abel M.	Paroled, 4/9/65 at Appomattox
Co. E	Pvt.	Johnson, Ezra W.	Paroled, 4/9/65 at Appomattox
Co. E	Pvt.	Johnson, Major O.	Paroled, 4/9/65 at Appomattox
Co. E	Pvt.	Norris, William W.	Paroled, 4/9/65 at Appomattox
Co. E	Pvt.	Turner, David W.	Paroled, 4/9/65 at Appomattox
Co. E	Pvt.	Wood, Uzzell T.	Paroled, 4/9/65 at Appomattox
Co. F	Cpt.	Moore, Samuel Rufus	Paroled, 4/9/65 at Appomattox
Co. F	1st Sgt.	Walston, John	Paroled, 4/9/65 at Appomattox
Co. F	Sgt.	Forbes, Arthur	Paroled, 4/9/65 at Appomattox
Co. F	4th Cpl.	Pittman, Reddin E.	Paroled, 4/9/65 at Appomattox
Co. F	Cpl.	Ellis, James	Paroled, 4/9/65 at Appomattox
Co. F	Musician	Webb, Newett	Paroled, 4/9/65 at Appomattox
Co. F	Pvt.	Bailey, Benjamin	Paroled, 4/9/65 at Appomattox
Co. F	Pvt.	Barnes, Wm. Spencer	Paroled, 4/9/65 at Appomattox
Co. F	Pvt.	Brasswell, James B.	Paroled, 4/9/65 at Appomattox
Co. F	Pvt.	Burgess, Hardy	Paroled, 4/9/65 at Appomattox
Co. F	Pvt.	Cobb, John B.	Paroled, 4/9/65 at Appomattox
Co. F	Pvt.	Eagles, Theodore R.	Paroled, 4/9/65 at Appomattox
Co. F	Pvt.	Edwards, Elsberry B.	Paroled, 4/9/65 at Appomattox
Co. F	Pvt.	Felton, Eli	Paroled, 4/9/65 at Appomattox
Co. F	Pvt.	Forbes, James	Paroled, 4/9/65 at Appomattox
Co. F	Pvt.	Harrell, Watson	Paroled, 4/9/65 at Appomattox
Co. F	Pvt.	Hathaway, Richard	TDY—Teamster. Paroled, 4/9/65 at Appomattox
Co. F	Pvt.	Lewis, John D.	TDY—Butcher. Paroled, 4/9/65 at Appomattox
Co. F	Pvt.	Little, Jesse C.	Paroled, 4/9/65 at Appomattox
Co. F	Pvt.	Morgan, Wm. Gray	Paroled, 4/9/65 at Appomattox
Co. F	Pvt.	Norville, James	TDY—Teamster. Paroled, 4/9/65 at Appomattox
Co. F	Pvt.	Phillips, Richard	Paroled, 4/9/65 at Appomattox
Co. F	Pvt.	Stallings, Edwin	Paroled, 4/9/65 at Appomattox
Co. F	Pvt.	Stallings, Rufus	Paroled, 4/9/65 at Appomattox
Co. F	Pvt.	Walston, Ralph	Paroled, 4/9/65 at Appomattox
Co. F	Pvt.	Webb, John	Paroled, 4/9/65 at Appomattox
Co. G	3rd Lt.	Fulford, John T.	Paroled, 4/9/65 at Appomattox
Co. G	2nd Sgt.	Badgett, Sandy H.	Paroled, 4/9/65 at Appomattox

Unit	Rank	Name	Remarks
Co. G	2nd Sgt.	Badgett, Wm. Joseph	Paroled, 4/9/65 at Appomattox
Co. G	Cpl.	Brooks, Richard D.	Paroled, 4/9/65 at Appomattox
Co. G	Pvt.	Badgett, John D.	Paroled, 4/9/65 at Appomattox
Co. G	Pvt.	Barnett, George P.	Paroled, 4/9/65 at Appomattox
Co. G	Pvt.	Collins, Samuel A.	Paroled, 4/9/65 at Appomattox
Co. G	Pvt.	Crews, William F.	Paroled, 4/9/65 at Appomattox
Co. G	Pvt.	Frazer, James H.	Paroled, 4/9/65 at Appomattox
Co. G	Pvt.	Merritt, Benjamin H.	Paroled, 4/9/65 at Appomattox
Co. G	Pvt.	Parham, William A.	TDY—Teamster. Paroled, 4/9/65 at Appomattox
Co. G	Pvt.	Slaughter, Thomas D.	TDY—Ambulance driver. Paroled, 4/9/65 at Appomattox
Co. G	Pvt.	Stanton, James R.	Paroled, 4/9/65 at Appomattox
Co. H	1st Sgt.	Cole, Ben. Green	TDY—Ambulance driver. Paroled at Appomattox, 4/9/65
Co. H	3rd Sgt.	Harrington, Ard A.	Paroled, 4/9/65 at Appomattox
Co. H	1st Cpl.	McGill, Archy D.	Paroled, 4/9/65 at Appomattox
Co. H	Cpl.	Hunter, Charles A.	Paroled, 4/9/65 at Appomattox
Co. H	Cpl.	Lawrence, John	Paroled, 4/9/65 at Appomattox
Co. H	4th Cpl.	Underwood, John A.	Paroled, 4/9/65 at Appomattox
Co. H	Pvt.	Campbell, George W.	Paroled, 4/9/65 at Appomattox
Co. H	Pvt.	Goins, Edward	TDY—Teamster. Paroled, 4/9/65 at Appomattox
Co. H	Pvt.	McFarland, John A.	Paroled, 4/9/65 at Appomattox
Co. H	Pvt.	McIver, John D.	Paroled, 4/9/65 at Appomattox
Co. H	Pvt.	McIver, D. N.	Paroled, 4/9/65 at Appomattox
Co. H	Pvt.	Mason, Albert	Paroled, 4/9/65 at Appomattox
Co. H	Pvt.	Short, William F.	Paroled, 4/9/65 at Appomattox
Co. H	Pvt.	Sinclair, John D.	TDY—Pioneer. Paroled, 4/9/65 at Appomattox
Co. H	Pvt.	Starnes, Thomas	Paroled, 4/9/65 at Appomattox
Co. H	Pvt.	Thomas, Henry	Paroled, 4/9/65 at Appomattox
Co. H	Pvt.	Wicker, Charles B.	TDY—Wheelwright. Paroled, 4/9/65 at Appomattox
Co. I	1st Sgt.	Crowell, Jonas W.	Paroled, 4/9/65 at Appomattox
Co. I	5th Sgt.	Cobb, Jefferson	Paroled, 4/9/65 at Appomattox
Co. I	1st Cpl.	Gay, George W.	Paroled, 4/9/65 at Appomattox
Co. I	Pvt.	Batts, William J.	Paroled, 4/9/65 at Appomattox
Co. I	Pvt.	Bone, John W.	Paroled, 4/9/65 at Appomattox
Co. I	Pvt.	Bryant, James H.	Paroled, 4/9/65 at Appomattox
Co. I	Pvt.	Bunn, James D.	Paroled, 4/9/65 at Appomattox
Co. I	Pvt.	Culpepper, John	Paroled, 4/9/65 at Appomattox
Co. I	Pvt.	Evans, William M.	TDY—Teamster; 2nd Corps Ordnance train. Paroled, 4/9/65 at Appomattox
Co. I	Pvt.	Fox, Reddin P.	Paroled, 4/9/65 at Appomattox
Co. I	Pvt.	Griffin, Mark S.	Paroled, 4/9/65 at Appomattox
Co. I	Pvt.	Joyner, William B.	Paroled, 4/9/65 at Appomattox
Co. I	Pvt.	Lewis, Arnold L.	Paroled, 4/9/65 at Appomattox
Co. I	Pvt.	Manning, Jeremiah D.	Paroled, 4/9/65 at Appomattox
Co. I	Pvt.	Pitt, James W.	Paroled, 4/9/65 at Appomattox
Co. I	Pvt.	Strickland, Henry O.	Paroled, 4/9/65 at Appomattox
Co. K	Cpt.	Ardrey, William E.	Paroled, 4/9/65 at Appomattox
Co. K	1st Sgt.	Smith, Wm. Stewart	Paroled, 4/9/65 at Appomattox
Co. K	Sgt.	Bales, Elijah M.	Paroled, 4/9/65 at Appomattox
Co. K	Sgt.	Nichols, Burgess G.	Paroled, 4/9/65 at Appomattox
Co. K	Cpl.	Hood, William L.	Paroled, 4/9/65 at Appomattox

Unit	Rank	Name	Remarks
Co. K	Pvt.	Bales, James P.	Paroled, 4/9/65 at Appomattox
Co. K	Pvt.	Anderson, M. J.	Paroled, 4/9/65 at Appomattox
Co. K	Pvt.	Burton, J. C.	Paroled, 4/9/65 at Appomattox
Co. K	Pvt.	Dixon, Solomon L.	Paroled, 4/9/65 at Appomattox
Co. K	Pvt.	Howey, John H.	Paroled, 4/9/65 at Appomattox
Co. K	Pvt.	Orr, Thomas J.	Paroled, 4/9/65 at Appomattox
Co. K	Pvt.	Ross, William J.	Paroled, 4/9/65 at Appomattox
Co. K	Pvt.	Saville, John C.	Paroled, 4/9/65 at Appomattox
Co. K	Pvt.	Squires, John Brown	Paroled, 4/9/65 at Appomattox

Appomattox, Virginia
(Surrendered/Captured: Not on Parole List)
April 9, 1865

Unit	Rank	Name	Remarks
Co. A	Pvt.	Currie, John B.	Surrendered, 4/9/65 at Appomattox
Co. F	2nd Lt.	House, James W.	Wounded (right foot) and captured, 4/9/65 at Appomattox
Co. G	2nd Lt.	Crews, Alexander	TDY—in command of wagon train. Surrendered, 4/9/65 at Appomattox
Co. K	Pvt.	Thomas, William B.	TDY—Pioneer. Surrendered, 4/9/65 at Appomattox

Paroled After Surrender, Virginia
April 12–30, 1865
11 Paroled

Unit	Rank	Name	Remarks
Co. C	Pvt.	Moore, Theophilus	Paroled, 4/14/65 at Burkeville Jct.
Co. D	Pvt.	Gilbert, Thaddeus	Paroled, 4/14/65 at Burkeville Jct.
Co. F	Pvt.	Bell, Wm. Bennett	Paroled, 4/11/65 at Farmville
Co. F	Pvt.	Leigh, Theophilus	Paroled, 4/14/65 at Burkeville
Co. G	Pvt.	Forrest, William L.	Paroled, 4/14/65 at Burkeville
Co. G	Pvt.	Frazier, Elisha T.	Paroled, 4/14/65 at Burkeville
Co. H	Pvt.	Watkins, William B.	Paroled, 4/14/65 at Burkeville
Co. I	Pvt.	Batchelor, Andrew J.	Paroled, 4/14/65 at Burkeville Jct.
Co. I	Pvt.	Batchelor, Redmond W.	Paroled, 4/14/65 at Burkeville Jct.
Co. I	Pvt.	Edwards, Willie	Paroled, 4/11/65 at Farmville hospital
Co. I	Pvt.	Johnson, Christopher B.	Paroled, 4/14/65 at Burkeville

30th North Carolina Infantry
Deaths Due to Disease
324 Deaths

Date	Rank	Name	Unit	Death
8/18/61	Pvt.	Sellers, Raymond G.	Co. C	Died of fever at Smithville, NC
9/7/61	Pvt.	Barnett, William S.	Co. G	Died of "diseased lungs" at Oxford, NC
9/7/61	Pvt.	Bradford, William H.	Co. G	Died of typhoid fever at Raleigh, NC
9/29/61	Pvt.	Stalvey, Benjamin L.	Co. C	Died of pneumonia in Brunswick Co., NC
9/-/61	Pvt.	Harper, David	Co. F	Died of typhoid fever at Tarboro, NC
10/11/61	Pvt.	Maltsby, William J.	Co. C	Died of pneumonia at Wilmington, NC
10/11/61	Pvt.	Simmons, John C.	Co. C	Died of pneumonia at Wilmington, NC
10/13/61	Pvt.	Chimis, Michael H.	Co. C	Died of meningitis at Smithville, NC

Date	Rank	Name	Unit	Death
10/28/61	Pvt.	Barnes, Bryant B.	Co. I	Died of typhoid fever in Wilson Co., NC
11/8/61	Pvt.	McIver, John W.	Co. H	Died of measles & pneumonia at Southport, NC
11/10/61	Pvt.	Corbett, James	Co. F	Died of typhoid fever at Smithville, NC
11/13/61	Pvt.	Taylor, Bolen	Co. I	Died of pneumonia at Collins, NC
11/14/61	Pvt.	Lynam, Emelious J.	Co. D	Died of typhoid fever at Camp Wyatt, NC
11/16/61	Pvt.	Carr, Obed	Co. E	Died of disease at Smithville, NC
11/17/61	Pvt.	Cox, William W.	Co. H	Died of pneumonia at Camp Wyatt, NC
11/18/61	Pvt.	Thorn, William E.	Co. I	Died of chronic diarrhea at Arringtons, NC
11/24/61	Pvt.	Stanly, Edward W.	Co. C	Died of pneumonia at Shallotte, NC
11/26/61	Pvt.	Beasly, Calvin	Co. E	Died of disease at Wilmington, NC
11/26/61	Pvt.	Thomas, William A.	Co. H	Died of typhoid fever at Pittsboro, NC
12/1/61	Pvt.	Dunn, Samuel W.	Co. K	Died of typhoid fever at Wilmington, NC
1/1/62	Pvt.	Griffin, John J.	Co. K	Died of typhoid fever at Wilmington, NC
1/4/62	Cpl.	Parker, Josiah	Co. I	Died of pneumonia at Wilmington, NC
1/4/62	Pvt.	Grady, John H.	Co. D	Died of typhoid fever at Wilmington, NC
1/6/62	Pvt.	Patterson, William S.	Co. K	Died of disease at Wilmington, NC
1/15/62	Pvt.	Dudley, Michael	Co. A	Died of typhoid fever at Washington, NC
1/16/62	Pvt.	Williams, James B.	Co. C	Died of meningitis at Guinea Station, VA
1/21/62	Pvt.	Royal, Marshall	Co. A	Died of disease in Sampson Co., NC
1/26/62	Pvt.	Cobb, John R.	Co. F	Died of "bilious fever" at Tarboro, NC
1/28/62	Pvt.	Sellers, Samuel H.	Co. C	Died of mumps at Roberson, NC
1/31/62	Pvt.	Davis, John R.	Co. D	Died of dysentery at Raleigh, NC
2/6/62	Pvt.	Crump, Samuel W.	Co. I	Died of typhoid fever at Camp Wyatt, NC
2/16/62	Pvt.	Thompson, Lee	Co. K	Died of typhoid fever at Richmond, VA
2/25/62	Pvt.	Eller, William W.	Co. C	Died of pneumonia at Richmond, VA
3/2/62	Pvt.	Brown, John (1st)	Co. E	Died of typhoid pneumonia at Camp Wyatt, NC
3/9/62	Pvt.	Stanly, Samuel J.	Co. C	Died of tuberculosis at Shallotte, NC
3/10/62	Pvt.	Goins, Duncan	Co. H	Died of typhoid fever at Wilmington, NC
3/11/62	Pvt.	Bland, David	Co. E	Died of typhoid fever at Wilmington, NC
3/30/62	Pvt.	Whitley, John S.	Co. I	Died of typhoid fever at Wilmington, NC
4/23/62	Pvt.	Brewer, Warren	Co. F	Died of typhoid fever at Wilmington, NC
4/26/62	Pvt.	Leigh, Joseph	Co. F	Died of typhoid fever at Wilmington, NC
5/8/62	Pvt.	Underwood, R. H.	Co. E	Died of disease at Camp Draughon, NC
5/11/62	Pvt.	Vick, William H.	Co. I	Died of disease at Arringtons, NC
5/28/62	Pvt.	Henderson, William T.	Co. K	Died of chronic diarrhea at Charlotte, NC
5/30/62	Pvt.	Incore, James F.	Co. G	Died of disease at Wilmington, NC
6/7/62	Pvt.	Mosely, Elisha	Co. F	Died of typhoid fever at Wilmington, NC
6/10/62	Pvt.	Strange, Albert	Co. G	Died of dysentery at Wilmington, NC
6/11/62	Pvt.	Henderson, Abraham	Co. E	Died of pneumonia at Richmond, VA
6/15/62	Pvt.	Edwards, Thomas	Co. F	Died of typhoid fever at Wilmington, NC
6/22/62	Pvt.	Hearn, Amos	Co. F	Died of disease at Wilmington, NC
6/25/62	Pvt.	Simmons, Daniel F.	Co. C	Died of erysipelas at Wilmington, NC
7/9/62	Pvt.	Duke, John Y.	Co. G	Died of typhoid fever at Richmond, VA
7/13/62	Pvt.	Hunt, Alfred H.	Co. G	Died of acute fever and diarrhea at Wilmington, NC
7/16/62	Pvt.	Morris, John D.	Co. H	Died of disease at Richmond, VA
7/19/62	Pvt.	Wicker, John J.	Co. H	Died of fever at Richmond, VA
7/20/62	Pvt.	Davis, Joseph E.	Co. D	Died of disease at Richmond, VA
7/20/62	Pvt.	Evans, Joseph E.	Co. D	Died of disease at Richmond, VA
7/22/62	Pvt.	Daniel, James R.	Co. G	Died of disease

30th North Carolina Infantry Casualties

Date	Rank	Name	Unit	Death
7/22/62	Pvt.	McPherson, A. Dugall	Co. H	Died of disease at Richmond, VA
7/28/62	Pvt.	Wooten, John S.	Co. F	Died of typhoid fever at Falkland, NC
8/4/62	Pvt.	Gholson, Abraham	Co. B	Died of typhoid fever at Richmond, VA
8/7/62	Pvt.	Harriss, William J.	Co. F	Died of typhoid fever at Richmond, VA
8/7/62	Pvt.	Thomas, John W.	Co. H	Died of typhoid fever at Richmond, VA
8/10/62	Pvt.	Winn, Thomas	Co. G	Died "suddenly" at Richmond, VA
8/10/62	Pvt.	Joyner, Little B.	Co. I	Died of typhoid fever at Richmond, VA
8/12/62	Pvt.	Graham, Samuel W.	Co. H	Died of tuberculosis at Richmond, VA
8/13/62	3rd Lt.	Cain, Lorenzo	Co. C	Died of typhoid fever at Richmond, VA
8/14/62	Sgt.	Teachey, Marshall	Co. E	Died of typhoid fever at Richmond, VA
8/15/62	Pvt.	Bailey, William M.	Co. D	Died of disease at Richmond, VA
8/15/62	Pvt.	Bobbitt, Alexander G.	Co. G	Died of disease at Oxford, NC
8/16/62	Pvt.	Cole, Neill M.	Co. H	Died of typhoid fever as Richmond, VA
8/20/62	Pvt.	Coleman, John C.	Co. C	Died of fever at Richmond, VA
8/21/62	Pvt.	Boney, Joseph K.	Co. E	Died of disease at Richmond, VA
8/25/62	Pvt.	Lewis, Cornelius	Co. A	Died of disease at Richmond, VA
8/25/62	Pvt.	Wainwright, William P.	Co. G	Died of disease at Tar River, NC
8/29/62	Pvt.	Pegram, George W.	Co. B	Died of tonsillitis at Lynchburg, VA
8/30/62	Pvt.	Goodin, William N.	Co. D	Died of typhoid fever at Richmond, VA
8/30/62	Pvt.	Duncan, John B.	Co. G	Died of typhoid fever at Richmond, VA
8/31/62	Mus.	Manning, John E.	Co. I	Died of disease at Richmond, VA
8/31/62	Pvt.	Tilly, William L.	Co. D	Died of disease at Richmond, VA
9/8/62	Pvt.	King, William A.	Co. B	Died of typhoid fever at Richmond, VA
9/13/62	Pvt.	Pollard, James H.	Co. F	Died of typhoid fever at Richmond, VA
9/20/62	Pvt.	Bailey, Jones F.	Co. D	Died of disease at Beaver Dam, NC
9/20/62	Pvt.	Little, William	Co. F	Died of typhoid fever at Richmond, VA
9/22/62	Pvt.	McIver, Murdock A.	Co. H	Died of typhoid fever at Richmond, VA
9/25/62	Pvt.	Thomas, George L.	Co. B	Died of disease at Leesburg, VA
9/27/62	Pvt.	Merritt, Levi	Co. E	Died of disease in Duplin Co., NC
9/28/62	Pvt.	Hart, Obediah	Co. C	Died of typhoid fever at Richmond, VA
10/2/62	Pvt.	Martin, Joseph B.	Co. D	Died of tuberculosis at Brassfields, NC
10/4/62	Pvt.	Wood, James	Co. I	Died of erysipelas at Richmond, VA
10/12/62	Pvt.	Gilbert, William	Co. A	Died of typhoid fever
10/20/62	Sgt.	Savage, Cornelius	Co. E	Died of disease near Winchester, VA
10/23/62	Pvt.	Bobbitt, E. Fletcher	Co. B	Died of typhoid fever at Richmond, VA
10/23/62	Pvt.	Dillard, William	Co. D	Died of disease in Granville Co., NC
11/1/62	Pvt.	Walker, Levi	Co. B	Died of typhoid fever at Petersburg, VA
11/4/62	Pvt.	Shearin, Edwin C.	Co. B	Died of typhoid fever at Richmond, VA
11/4/62	Pvt.	Sloan, John A.	Co. H	Died of pneumonia at Staunton, VA
11/8/62	Sgt.	Kilpatrick, Hugh Y.	Co. K	Died of disease at Strasburg, VA
11/10/62	Pvt.	Potter, Henry G.	Co. C	Died of typhoid fever at Staunton, VA
11/10/62	Pvt.	Manning, Richard M.	Co. I	Died of disease at Winchester, VA
11/13/62	Pvt.	Stallings, John A.	Co. B	Died of typhoid fever at Staunton, VA
11/16/62	Pvt.	Clarkson, Thomas N.	Co. A	Died of pneumonia at Mount Jackson, VA
11/18/62	Pvt.	Wortman, Simeon	Co. G	Died of disease
11/18/62	Pvt.	Bone, Hardy H.	Co. I	Died of pneumonia at Richmond, VA
11/19/62	Pvt.	Milton, Joseph G.	Co. K	Died of chronic diarrhea at Culpepper Court House, VA
11/24/62	Pvt.	Register, Thomas	Co. C	Died of smallpox at Staunton, VA
11/25/62	Pvt.	Harrell, William	Co. F	Died of disease at Tarboro, NC
11/25/62	Pvt.	McPherson, Duncan R.	Co. H	Died of measles at Lynchburg, VA
11/26/62	Pvt.	Tucker, Owen	Co. E	Died of chronic dysentery at Mount Jackson, VA
11/28/62	Pvt.	Absher, Edmund	Co. G	Died of chronic diarrhea at Mount Jackson, VA

Date	Rank	Name	Unit	Death
11/-/62	Pvt.	Parker, G. Washington	Co. C	Died of disease
11/-/62	Pvt.	Pendergrass, Elijah	Co. C	Died of disease at Strasburg, VA
12/1/62	Cpl.	Robertson, Peter E.	Co. B	Died of disease at Lynchburg, VA
12/4/62	Pvt.	Lanier, Lewis W.	Co. E	Died of smallpox in Richmond, VA
12/5/62	Pvt.	Allen, James H.	Co. K	Died of pneumonia at Gordonsville, VA
12/8/62	Pvt.	Buchanan, Thomas	Co. H	Died of scarlet fever at Staunton, VA
12/13/62	Pvt.	McIver, Edward	Co. H	Died of pneumonia at Front Royal, VA
12/13/62	Pvt.	Joyner, Ashley G.	Co. I	Died of "congestion of lungs" at Richmond, VA
12/14/62	Pvt.	Stanly, Stewart	Co. C	Died of meningitis at Port Royal, VA
12/16/62	Cpl.	Bradley, Oliver	Co. F	Died of smallpox at Richmond, VA
12/16/62	Pvt.	Poland, Alford	Co. I	Died of disease at Coopers, NC
12/17/62	Pvt.	Wicker, Alvis	Co. H	Died of disease at Staunton, VA
12/18/62	Pvt.	Autry, William	Co. A	Died of pneumonia at Gordonsville, VA
12/18/62	Pvt.	Aughtry, William A.	Co. E	Died of pneumonia at Gordonsville, VA
12/19/62	Pvt.	Blizzard, William H.	Co. G	Died of disease
12/22/62	Pvt.	Waller, P. H.	Co. D	Died of pneumonia at Richmond, VA
12/24/62	Pvt.	Brown, Wesley	Co. G	Died of measles at Mount Jackson, VA
12/25/62	Pvt.	Davis, Joseph C.	Co. D	Died of heart disease at Richmond, VA
12/25/62	Pvt.	McDonald, Neill	Co. H	Died of disease at Crain's Creek, NC
12/26/62	Pvt.	Draughon, George H.	Co. A	Died of chronic diarrhea at Clinton, NC
12/26/62	Pvt.	Jackson, James W.	Co. A	Died of liver failure
12/29/62	Pvt.	Page, Owen	Co. A	Died of smallpox at Richmond, VA
12/30/62	Pvt.	Morton, Isaac	Co. F	Died of disease as POW at Ft. Delaware, DE
1/2/63	3rd Lt.	Ruark, Edward R	Co. C	Died of smallpox at Smithville, NC
1/2/63	Pvt.	Morris, Alfred J.	Co. D	Died of typhoid pneumonia at Petersburg, VA
1/3/63	Pvt.	Walston, Silas L.	Co. K	Died of disease at Staunton, VA
1/8/63	Pvt.	Abbott, Macon	Co. B	Died of pneumonia at Richmond, VA
1/8/63	Pvt.	George, Presley	Co. K	Died of typhoid fever at Richmond, VA
1/9/63	Pvt.	Holmes, Benjamin	Co. K	Died of disease at Richmond, VA
1/10/63	Pvt.	Cole, Jesse T.	Co. E	Died of disease at Richmond, VA
1/10/63	Pvt.	Black, John N.	Co. K	Died of smallpox at Guineas Station, VA
1/11/63	Pvt.	Reynolds, Charles	Co. A	Died of smallpox at Guinea Station, VA
1/11/63	Pvt.	Brown, Alfred	Co. G	Died of "abscess lung" at Mount Jackson, VA
1/14/63	Pvt.	Mitchell, Henry	Co. A	Died of pneumonia near Fredericksburg, VA
1/14/63	Pvt.	Stiles, John M.	Co. E	Died of "brain fever" at Guinea Station, VA
1/15/63	Pvt.	Faircloth, John L.	Co. A	Died of smallpox at Richmond, VA
1/16/63	Pvt.	Smith, George W.	Co. B	Died of chronic diarrhea at Richmond, VA
1/19/63	Pvt.	Strickland, Walter D.	Co. A	Died of disease at Guinea Station, VA
1/19/63	Pvt.	Tew, Wiley	Co. A	Died of pneumonia at Lynchburg, VA
1/20/63	Pvt.	Bridges, George W.	Co. D	Died of rheumatism at Forestville, NC
1/20/63	Pvt.	Boon, Joseph H.	Co. I	Died of epilepsy at Lynchburg, VA
1/20/63	Pvt.	Joyner, Calvin M.	Co. I	Died of smallpox at Richmond, VA
1/21/63	Pvt.	Wood, Marley	Co. E	Died of pneumonia at Gordonsville, VA
1/29/63	Pvt.	Joplin, William Y.	Co. D	Died of smallpox at Liberty, VA
2/5/63	Pvt.	Marlow, Nathan	Co. F	Died of pneumonia at Richmond, VA
2/7/63	Pvt.	Cottle, Frederick	Co. E	Died of pneumonia at Richmond, VA
2/9/63	Pvt.	Harper, John H.	Co. I	Died of smallpox at Richmond, VA
2/9/63	Pvt.	Brewer, James H.	Co. K	Died of typhoid fever at Staunton, VA

Date	Rank	Name	Unit	Death
2/10/63	Pvt.	Faircloth, John.	Co. A	Died of pneumonia near Fredericksburg, VA
2/11/63	Pvt.	Watson, Andrew J.	Co. H	Died of pneumonia at Rollins Store, NC
2/13/63	Pvt.	Crisp, Amos W.	Co. F	Died of pneumonia near Fredericksburg, VA
2/16/63	Pvt.	Register, Edward M.	Co. A	Died of pneumonia near Fredericksburg, VA
2/16/63	Pvt.	Luntzford, Joel	Co. C	Died of chronic diarrhea at Liberty, VA
2/17/63	Pvt.	Hardy, Henry	Co. B	Died of smallpox at Guinea Station, VA
2/18/63	Pvt.	Hanchey, Bryant W.	Co. E	Died of pneumonia at Richmond, VA
2/21/63	Cpl.	Thraikill, Joseph M.	Co. A	Died of chronic diarrhea near Fredericksburg, VA
2/21/63	Pvt.	Mayo, James	Co. F	Died of typhoid pneumonia at Richmond, VA
2/22/63	Pvt.	Daniell, James W.	Co. G	Died of fever at Grace Church, VA
2/23/63	Pvt.	Talley, Benjamin T.	Co. B	Died of chronic diarrhea at Lynchburg, VA
2/23/63	Pvt.	Gay, Henry	Co. F	Died of typhoid pneumonia at Guinea Station, VA
2/25/63	Pvt.	Morris, William T.	Co. K	Died of disease at Richmond, VA
2/27/63	Pvt.	Lanier, James P.	Co. E	Died of pneumonia in Duplin Co., NC
3/1/63	Pvt.	Wescott, William H.	Co. C	Died of chronic diarrhea at Wilmington, NC
3/4/63	Pvt.	Lovett, Aaron F.	Co. G	Died of measles at Charlottesville, VA
3/6/63	Pvt.	Carter, James	Co. E	Died of pneumonia in Duplin Co., NC
3/8/63	Pvt.	Royal, Martin	Co. A	Died of acute dysentery at Weldon, NC
3/11/63	Pvt.	Wallace, Robert C.	Co. E	Died of pneumonia near Fredericksburg, VA
3/11/63	Pvt.	Cottle, W. Davis	Co. E	Died of chronic bronchitis at Richmond, VA
3/17/63	Pvt.	Bradshaw, Robert M.	Co. A	Died of smallpox at Palmyra, VA
3/18/63	3rd Lt.	McLeod, Louis H.	Co. H	Died of heart failure at Rollins Store, NC
3/18/63	Pvt.	Bass, William	Co. I	Died of pneumonia at Richmond, VA
3/18/63	Pvt.	Webb, William	Co. K	Died of pneumonia at Richmond, VA
3/19/63	Pvt.	Streets, Wimbert	Co. E	Died of pneumonia at Staunton, VA
3/27/63	Pvt.	Wolfe, Thomas D.	Co. K	Died of pneumonia at Richmond, VA
3/28/63	Pvt.	Henderson, Jesse R.	Co. E	Died of pneumonia at Gordonsville, VA
3/28/63	Pvt.	Lee, James A.	Co. K	Died of pneumonia at Richmond, VA
4/2/63	Pvt.	Cole, Andrew	Co. H	Died of pneumonia at Richmond, VA
4/3/63	Pvt.	Wescott, Samuel W.	Co. C	Died of pneumonia at Richmond, VA
4/10/63	Pvt.	Lindsey, William B.	Co. I	Died of "brain fever" at Hamilton's Crossing, VA
4/13/63	Pvt.	Little, Lorenzo	Co. F	Died of pneumonia at Richmond, VA
4/15/63	Pvt.	Stedman, David L.	Co. H	Died of typhoid pneumonia at Richmond, VA
4/18/63	Sgt.	Dozier, James W.	Co. I	Died of pneumonia at Richmond, VA
4/19/63	Pvt.	Edwards, Montgomery	Co. F	Died of typhoid pneumonia at Richmond, VA
4/20/63	Pvt.	Jarvis, Levi	Co. C	Died of pleurisy at Richmond, VA
4/21/63	Pvt.	Byrd, John	Co. C	Died of typhoid pneumonia at Richmond, VA
4/23/63	Pvt.	Cliff, John	Co. C	Died of typhoid pneumonia at Richmond, VA
4/23/63	Pvt.	Johnson, Calvin	Co. C	Died of disease at Richmond, VA
4/25/63	Pvt.	Wilkins, Hinton	Co. D	Died of chronic diarrhea at Granville, NC
5/2/63	Pvt.	Johnson, James C.	Co. E	Died of disease

Appendix 1

Date	Rank	Name	Unit	Death
5/3/63	Pvt.	Tharp, William H.	Co. C	Died of typhoid pneumonia at Richmond, VA
5/9/63	Pvt.	Gaster, John C.	Co. H	Died of typhoid fever at Richmond, VA
5/12/63	Pvt.	Hickman, Benjamin R.	Co. C	Died of pneumonia at Richmond, VA
5/13/63	Pvt.	Hughes, Doctor	Co. H	Died of disease at Hamilton's Crossing, VA
5/18/63	Pvt.	Eason, Haywood	Co. I	Died of disease, in camp, VA
5/19/63	Pvt.	Mobley, Wright W.	Co. E	Died of pneumonia in Duplin Co., NC
5/30/63	Pvt.	Wicker, Oren R.	Co. H	Died of chronic diarrhea at Buffalow, NC
6/3/63	Pvt.	Evans, Isaiah H.	Co. D	Died of disease at Raleigh, NC
6/19/63	Pvt.	Robinson, Harmon R.	Co. A	Died of pneumonia at Martinsburg, VA
6/20/63	Pvt.	Pilgreen, McGilbert	Co. C	Died of disease at Summerville Ford, VA
7/2/63	Pvt.	Norris, James	Co. E	Died of pneumonia in Duplin Co., NC
7/11/63	Cpl.	Smith, Samuel B.	Co. K	Died of disease at Charlotte, NC
7/23/63	Pvt.	Poland, Simeon H.	Co. I	Died of disease at Charlottesville, VA
7/25/63	Pvt.	Jarvis, Wiley	Co. C	Died of disease at Port Royal, VA
8/4/63	2nd Lt.	Pitt, James W.	Co. F	Died of typhoid fever at Richmond, VA
8/11/63	Pvt.	Buchanan, Null	Co. H	Died of fever at Lynchburg, VA
8/12/63	Pvt.	Dail, Benjamin	Co. C	Died of fever at Gordonsville, VA
8/20/63	Pvt.	Rackley, P. Nicholas	Co. I	Died of typhoid fever at Chester, PA
10/31/63	Pvt.	Wilson, John L.	Co. E	Died of typhoid fever at Gordonsville, VA
11/4/63	Pvt.	Potts, Joseph R.	Co. K	Died of typhoid fever at Staunton, VA
11/12/63	Pvt.	Allen, Wyatt M.	Co. D	Died of disease at Morrisville, NC
11/12/63	Pvt.	Dew, Fr. Lewis	Co. F	Died of scurvy as POW at Ft. Delaware, DE
11/12/63	Pvt.	Bell, Nathan	Co. K	Died of typhoid pneumonia at Richmond, VA
11/13/63	Pvt.	Johnson, Josiah	Co. E	Died of disease at Smithville, NC
11/14/63	Pvt.	Hagins, Lewis W.	Co. F	Died of pneumonia at Charlottesville, VA
11/15/63	Pvt.	Slaughter, James H.	Co. G	Died of typhoid fever at Richmond, VA
11/26/63	Pvt.	Pridgen, Josiah H.	Co. I	Died of disease as POW at Point Lookout, MD
11/27/63	Pvt.	Robertson, Robert	Co. I	Died of typhoid fever at Lynchburg, VA
12/12/63	Pvt.	Thompson, James	Co. K	Died of disease at Morton's Ford, VA
12/17/63	Pvt.	Cavenaugh, James H.	Co. E	Died of disease at Orange Court House, VA
12/17/63	Pvt.	Harrell, John O.	Co. E	Died of disease at Orange Court House, VA
12/22/63	Pvt.	Verser, John	Co. B	Died of chronic diarrhea at Richmond, VA
12/25/63	Pvt.	Pegram, James B.	Co. B	Died of hemorrhage of bowels at Orange Court House, VA
12/26/63	Pvt.	Balkum, Lemuel	Co. E	Died of typhoid fever at Richmond, VA
12/28/63	Pvt.	Parting, Henry A.	Co. A	Died of smallpox as POW at Point Lookout, MD
12/28/63	Pvt.	Williams, Nathan C	Co. I	Died of disease as POW at Point Lookout, MD
12/29/63	Pvt.	Cook, Anderson	Co. H	Died of disease at Gordonsville, VA
1/1/64	Pvt.	Greenway, Samuel	Co. G	Died of smallpox as POW at Old Capital Prison, VA
1/8/64	Pvt.	Ragland, William G.	Co. G	Died of measles at Orange Court House, VA
1/11/64	Pvt.	Black, Thomas A.	Co. K	Died of disease at Orange Court House, VA

Date	Rank	Name	Unit	Death
1/14/64	Pvt.	Davis, Burton	Co. D	Died of disease at Orange Court House, VA
1/15/64	Pvt.	Walls, William B.	Co. G	Died of "congestion of the lungs" at Richmond, VA
1/15/64	Pvt.	Anderson, William	Co. K	Died of disease
1/16/64	Pvt.	Lindsey, Richard	Co. I	Died of smallpox as POW at Old Capitol Prison, VA
1/20/64	Pvt.	Gamble, James H.	Co. K	Died of typhoid fever at Richmond, VA
1/23/64	Pvt.	Sollice, Devane	Co. G	Died of disease as POW at Point Lookout, MD
1/24/64	Pvt.	Roach, Archibald D.	Co. C	Died of disease at Orange Court House, VA
1/28/64	Pvt.	Pitt, John W.	Co. I	Died of disease at Richmond, VA
2/2/64	Pvt.	Pitt, Frederick	Co. I	Died of smallpox at Salisbury, NC
2/4/64	Pvt.	Myrick, William W.	Co. B	Died of smallpox as POW at Point Lookout, MD
2/4/64	Pvt.	Hughes, Joseph	Co. C	Died of disease at Orange Court House, VA
2/8/64	Pvt.	Alsbrook, S. C.	Co. A	Died of chronic dysentery as POW at Point Lookout, MD
2/9/64	Pvt.	Pool, Thomas	Co. H	Died of disease at Orange Court House, VA
2/9/64	Pvt.	Batchelor, Neverson A.	Co. I	Died of smallpox as POW at Point Lookout, MD
2/17/64	Pvt.	Clopton, George	Co. G	Died of typhoid fever at Richmond, VA
2/24/64	Pvt.	Pennington, Moses	Co. C	Died of septic pneumonia at Richmond, VA
3/4/64	Pvt.	Piner, James J.	Co. E	Died of smallpox as POW at Elmira, NY
3/13/64	Pvt.	Balentine, James N.	Co. C	Died of smallpox as POW at Old Capital Prison, Washington, D.C.
3/17/64	Pvt.	Williams, Joseph	Co. C	Died of disease at Orange Court House, VA
3/20/64	Pvt.	Hedgepeth, Elias G.	Co. I	Died of disease at Orange Court House, VA
4/1/64	Pvt.	Bailey, James A.	Co. K	Died of disease at Richmond, VA
4/5/64	Pvt.	Dunn, David W.	Co. A	Died of disease at Orange Court House, VA
4/16/64	Pvt.	Blackwelder, Wiley	Co. C	Died of malaria as POW at Point Lookout, MD
5/7/64	Pvt.	Bradshaw, V. B.	Co. K	Died of typhoid fever at Farmville, VA
5/13/64	Pvt.	Hagler, John	Co. A	Died of disease (suddenly)
7/7/64	Pvt.	Warrick, Thomas J.	Co. A	Died of typhoid fever at Richmond, VA
7/13/64	Pvt.	Kelly, David W.	Co. H	Died of disease as POW at Point Lookout, MD
7/18/64	Pvt.	Eason, James S.	Co. H	Died of typhoid fever as POW at Frederick, MD
7/23/64	Pvt.	Everett, Joseph	Co. F	Died of disease at Woodstock, VA
7/28/64	Pvt.	Lewis, John A.	Co. I	Died of chronic diarrhea at Charlottesville, VA
8/11/64	Pvt.	Kirkland, Stephen H.	Co. B	Died of disease as POW at Point Lookout, MD
8/11/64	Pvt.	Blacknail, Thomas B.	Co. G	Died of hernia at Richmond, VA
8/12/64	Pvt.	Harris, John N.	Co. B	Died of disease as POW at Point Lookout, MD
8/25/64	Pvt.	Askew, John	Co. B	Died of disease as POW at Point Lookout, MD

Appendix 1

Date	Rank	Name	Unit	Death
8/29/64	Pvt.	Pendergrass, J. R.	Co. C	Died of disease as POW at Point Lookout, MD
8/-/64	Pvt.	Parker, James C.	Co. C	Died of disease
9/16/64	Pvt.	Matthews, Nathan	Co. H	Died of disease as POW at Point Lookout, MD
9/18/64	Pvt.	Adams, William	Co. K	Died of chronic diarrhea as POW at Point Lookout, MD
9/25/64	Pvt.	Horne, Pleasant	Co. H	Died of scurvy as POW at Elmira, NY
9/27/64	Pvt.	Riggan, Isham S.	Co. B	Died of typhoid fever as POW at Elmira, NY
10/4/64	Pvt.	Green, James L.	Co. H	Died of chronic diarrhea as POW at Elmira, NY
10/4/64	Sgt.	Shearin, John D.	Co. B	Died of chronic diarrhea as POW at Elmira, NY
10/14/64	Pvt.	Edwards, Walter	Co. D	Died of chronic diarrhea as POW at Elmira, NY
10/15/64	Pvt.	Buchanan, Joseph	Co. H	Died of acute diarrhea at Lynchburg, VA
10/16/64	Cpl.	Thomas, Robert H.	Co. D	Died of chronic diarrhea as POW at Elmira, NY
10/24/64	Pvt.	Brigman, John	Co. E	Died of chronic diarrhea as POW at Elmira, NY
11/29/64	Pvt.	Riggan, Sugar A.	Co. B	Died of chronic diarrhea as POW at Elmira, NY
12/1/64	Pvt.	Logan, Philip	Co. H	Died of disease in VA
12/1/64	Pvt.	Dunn, George	Co. K	Died of pneumonia as POW at Point Lookout, MD
12/6/64	Pvt.	Hickman, Robert	Co. C	Died of pneumonia as POW at Elmira, NY
12/9/64	Pvt.	Church, Carlton	Co. G	Died of pneumonia as POW at Elmira, NY
12/15/64	Pvt.	Robertson, Z. R.	Co. G	Died of chronic diarrhea as POW at Baltimore, MD
1/4/65	Pvt.	Butler, John C.	Co. C	Died of smallpox as POW at Elmira, NY
1/8/65	Pvt.	Edwards, Solomon	Co. I	Died of disease at Richmond, VA
1/12/65	Pvt.	Starnes, Ephraim	Co. H	Died of "congestion of the brain" as POW at Elmira, NY
1/15/65	Pvt.	Adkins, William H.	Co. K	Died of chronic diarrhea as POW at Point Lookout, MD
1/22/65	Pvt.	Rogers, John H.	Co. D	Died of smallpox as POW at Elmira, NY
1/25/65	Sgt.	Wescott, John W.	Co. C	Died of disease as POW at Point Lookout, MD
1/26/65	Pvt.	Ivey, W. L.	Co. A	Died of chronic diarrhea as POW at Point Lookout, MD
1/28/65	Pvt.	Rogers, Jobe B.	Co. E	Died of chronic diarrhea as POW at Elmira, NY
1/30/65	Pvt.	Robinson, William H.	Co. K	Died of acute bronchitis as POW at Elmira, NY
2/5/65	Pvt.	Cavenaugh, George W.	Co. E	Died of chronic diarrhea as POW at Point Lookout, MD
2/7/65	Pvt.	Arrington, James L.	Co. B	Died of smallpox as POW at Elmira, NY
2/7/65	Pvt.	Redick, Epinetus	Co. F	Died of pneumonia as POW at Elmira, NY
2/7/65	Pvt.	Smith, John S.	Co. K	Died of chronic diarrhea as POW at Point Lookout, MD

30th North Carolina Infantry Casualties

Date	Rank	Name	Unit	Death
2/8/65	Pvt.	Tilley, John R.	Co. D	Died of chronic diarrhea and scurvy as POW at Point Lookout, MD
2/12/65	Pvt.	Brassfield, James W.	Co. D	Died of chronic diarrhea as POW at Point Lookout, MD
2/12/65	Pvt.	Mobley, William V.	Co. E	Died of consumption as POW at Point Lookout, MD
2/18/65	Pvt.	Howard, Joseph M.	Co. G	Died of chronic diarrhea as POW at Elmira, NY
2/19/65	Pvt.	Bailey, Elias D.	Co. K	Died of chronic diarrhea as POW at Elmira, NY
2/25/65	Pvt.	Shearin, Landon T.	Co. B	Died of pneumonia as POW at Point Lookout, MD
2/28/65	Pvt.	Hutchison, Andrew J.	Co. A	Died of smallpox as POW at Elmira, NY
3/1/65	Pvt.	Wolfe, Robert B.	Co. K	Died of pneumonia as POW at Point Lookout, MD
3/6/65	Pvt.	King, Caswell	Co. D	Died of chronic diarrhea as POW at Elmira, NY
3/14/65	Pvt.	Dickerson, Martin	Co. G	Died of acute gastritis as POW at Elmira, NY
3/22/65	Pvt.	Campbell, Angus T.	Co. H	Died of pneumonia as POW at Elmira, NY
3/29/65	Pvt.	Reynolds, John R.	Co. A	Died of typhoid fever as POW at Elmira, NY
4/12/65	Pvt.	Miller, Alexander B.	Co. C	Died of pneumonia as POW at Elmira, NY
4/25/65	Pvt.	West, William M.	Co. K	Died of pneumonia as POW at Point Lookout, MD
5/3/65	Pvt.	Morris, David P.	Co. H	Died of chronic diarrhea as POW at Point Lookout, MD
5/3/65	Pvt.	Womack, James R.	Co. H	Died of chronic diarrhea as POW at Point Lookout, MD
5/29/65	Pvt.	King, John	Co. D	Died of chronic diarrhea as POW at Point Lookout, MD
6/5/65	Pvt.	Knight, Thomas H.	Co. E	Died of scurvy as POW at Hart's Island, NY
6/8/65	Pvt.	Armfield, John J.	Co. C	Died of chronic diarrhea as POW at Point Lookout, MD
6/14/65	Pvt.	Friezland, Jacob	Co. A	Died of chronic diarrhea as POW at Newport News, VA
6/23/65	Pvt.	Jones, William H.	Co. D	Died of chronic diarrhea as POW at Newport News, VA

Appendix 2:
30th North Carolina Infantry Roster

Field & Staff

Bold lettering indicates a soldier who died. S = Single, M = Married. A blank space means no information was found.

Rank	Name	DOB	M/S	Residence	Occupation	Remarks
Col.	Parker, Francis M. "Frank"	1826	M	Enfield, Halifax Co., NC	Plantation Owner	Elected Col., 10/8/61. Wounded (head), 9/17/62 at Sharpsburg. Wounded (face), 7/1/63 at Gettysburg. Wounded (abdomen—"right side of abdomen wall"), 5/19/64 at Harris Farm. Retired to Invalid Corps due to wounds, 1/17/65.
Lt. Col.	Draughan, Walter F.	1811	M	Fayetteville, Cumberland Co., NC	Sugar Dealer	Appointed, 9/26/61. Defeated in re-organization, 5/1/62.
Major	Kell, James T.	1835	S	Pineville, Mecklenburg Co., NC	Physician's Asst.	Promoted to Maj., 9/27/61. Promoted to Lt. Col., 5/1/62. Severely wounded (compound hip fracture), 6/27/62 at Gaines' Mill. Resigned, 9/3/63, "on the grounds of physical disability from wounds."
Adj.	Carter, Robert M.	1838		Davidson Co., NC	...	Commissioned 1st Lt., 10/8/61. Retired, 5/1/62.
Sgt. Maj.	White, Lallister M.	1833	S	Owensville, Sampson Co., NC	Farm Labor	Promoted to Sgt. Maj., 10/10/61. Elected, 3rd Lt., 5/1/62 (Co. A).
Asst. QM	Stallings, Theophilus	1830	M	Merry Mount, Warren Co., NC	Farmer	Promoted to Qtr. Mstr. Sgt., 10/16/61. Paroled, 4/9/65 at Appomattox.
Asst. Com.	Collins, John	1821	S	Warrenton, Warren Co., NC	Plow Manufacturer	Appointed Cpt., Asst. Commissary, 8/25/61. Dropped from rolls, 8/2/62. Returned to duty, 2/10/63. Dropped from the roles, 8/1/63. ("His office was abolished by an act of the Confederate Congress."
Ord. Sgt.	Ellis, John W.	1828	M	Whiteville, Columbus Co., NC	Lawyer	Promoted to Regimental Ord. Sgt., 10/17/61. Absent, attending the legislature of N.C., 9/1/62–12/31/62. Promoted to 3rd Lt., 2/27/63 (Co. E).
Surg.	Joyner, Henry	1821	M	Enfield, Halifax Co. NC	Physician	Appointed, 10/21/61. Resigned, 5/1/62. ("To serve in the North Carolina House of Commons.")
Asst.	Gregory, Charles G.	1835	S	Arcadia,	Physician	Appointed, 10/25/61.

Rank	Name	DOB	M/S	Residence	Occupation	Remarks
Surg.				Halifax Co., NC		Resigned, 12/31/63.
Chap.	Betts, Alexander D.	1831	M	Elizabeth, Bladen Co., NC	Methodist Minister	Appointed, 11/16/61. No further records after 2/28/65.

Promotions

Rank	Name	DOB	M/S	Residence	Occupation	Remarks
Sgt. Maj.	Arrington, Peter W.	1839	S	North Hampton, Nash Co., NC	Printer	Transferred from 6th VA Inf., 5/28/63. Promoted to Regt. Adj., 4/2/64. Captured, 5/12/64 at Spotsylvania. POW—Ft. Delaware, DE. Released, 6/16/65.
Surg.	Briggs, George W.	1826		Virginia	Physician	Appointed, 4/1/63. Surrendered, 4/9/65 at Appomattox.
Asst. Surg.	Coke, Lucius C.	1837	S	Hamilton, Martin Co., NC	Physician	Assigned to regiment, 8/1/64. Surrendered, 4/9/65 at Appomattox.
Com. Sgt.	Davis, Alexander L.	1823	M	Granville Co., NC	Farmer	Promoted to Commissary Sgt., 1/1/62, from Co. B. Discharged (general disability), 4/20/62.
Sgt. Maj.	Fitts, Francis M. "Frank"	1843	S	Perry, Marion Co., AL	Clerk	Promoted to Sgt. Maj., 4/2/64. Wounded (scalp & left shoulder), 7/18/64 at Snicker's Gap. Wounded (arm), 10/19/64 at Cedar Creek. Absent due to wounds. Surrendered, 4/9/65 at Appomattox.
Surg.	Garrett, Francis M.	1834	M	Tarboro, Edgecombe Co., NC	Physician	Appointed, 9/10/62. Resigned, 4/1/63 "By reason of disability."
Major	Holmes, James C.	1826	M	Clinton, Sampson Co., NC	Merchant	Appointed Maj., 10/3/63, from Co. A. Declared, "Unfit for duty," 4/26/64. Retired to the Invalid Corps, 8/19/64.
Sgt. Maj.	Lawhon, Archibald F.	1837	S	McDaniels, Sampson Co., NC	Teacher	Promoted to Sgt. Maj., 5/1/62, from Co. A. Transferred to 20th NC Inf., 3/12/63.
Adj.	Philips, Frederick	1837	S	Tarboro, Edgecombe Co., NC	Lawyer	Appointed Adjt., 6/5/62. Wounded (head), 9/17/62 at Sharpsburg. Wounded (left thigh, flesh), 11/7/63 at Kelly's Ford. Promoted to Cpt. Quarter Master's, 3/12/64. Assigned as brigade Quarter Master (Cox), 3/8/65. No further records.
Major	**Sillers, William W.**	**1838**	**S**	**Clinton, Sampson Co., NC**	**Lawyer**	**Elected Maj., 5/1/62, from Co. A. Wounded, 7/1/62 at Malvern Hill. Promoted to Lt. Col., 10/3/63. Wounded (lungs), 11/7/63 at Kelly's Ford. Died of wounds, 11/9/63 at Gordonsville, VA.**
Com. Sgt.	Smith, Lemuel H.	1823	S	Charlotte, Mecklenburg Co., NC	Clerk	Promoted to Commissary Sgt., 7/20/63, from Co. F. No further records after 8/23/64.
Regt. QM	Williams, Buckner D.	1833	M	Warrenton, Warren Co., NC	Merchant	Commissioned, Cpt., Regt. QM, 11/1/61, from Co., from Co. B. Promoted to Maj., 11/20/63; transferred to brigade QM.

Company A—Sampson Rangers
Sampson County (Mustered into Regt.—10/8/61)

Rank	Name	DOB	M/S	Residence	Occupation	Remarks
Cpt.	Holmes, James C.	1826	M	Clinton, Sampson Co., NC	Merchant	Enrolled, 4/20/61. Appointed Maj, 9/3/63. On medical leave, 12/1/63–8/19/64. Retired to the Invalid Corps, 8/19/64.
1st Lt.	**Sillers, William W.**	**1838**	**S**	**Clinton, Sampson Co., NC**	**Lawyer**	**Enlisted, 4/20/16. Elected Maj., 5/1/62. Wounded, 7/1/62 at Malvern Hill. Promoted to Lt. Col., 9/3/63. Wounded, 11/7/63 at Kelly's Ford. Died of wounds, 11/9/63 at Gordonsville, VA.**

Appendix 2

Rank	Name	DOB	M/S	Residence	Occupation	Remarks
2nd Lt.	Patrick, Cornelius	1836	S	Clinton, Sampson Co., NC	Merchant	Enlisted, 4/20/61. Lost election, 5/1/62 at reorganization. Left the regiment.
3rd Lt.	Stevens, Charles T.	1829	M	Clinton, Sampson Co., NC	Farmer	Enlisted, 4/20/61. Promoted to 2nd Lt., 5/1/62. Accidently wounded (foot), 1/18/63. TDY—Enrolling Master for Sampson Co., NC, 11/1/63–10/31/64. Did not return to the regiment.
1st Sgt.	Williams, Gary	1840	S	Owensville, Sampson Co., NC	Farm Labor	Elected 1st Lt., 5/1/62. Promoted to Cpt., 10/3/63. Captured, 5/12/64 at Spotsylvania. POW—Ft. Delaware, DE. Released, 6/8/65.
2nd Sgt.	Lawhon, Archibald F.	1837	S	McDaniels, Sampson Co., NC	Teacher	Enlisted, 4/20/61. Promoted to Sgt. Maj., 5/1/62. Transferred to 20th NC Inf.
3rd Sgt.	Draughon, William B.	1840	S	Sampson Co., NC	Farm Labor	Enlisted, 4/20/61. Discharged (provided substitute), 5/1/62.
4th Sgt.	Royal, Hardy S.	1837		Clinton, Sampson Co., NC	Farmer	Enlisted, 4/20/61. Promoted to Color Sgt., 5/1/62. Wounded, 6/27/62 at Gaines' Mill. Wounded (knee & thigh), 5/3/63 at Chancellorsville (leg amputated). Retired to Invalid Corps, 9/21/64.
5th Sgt.	Draughon, Miles S.	1840	S	Clinton, Sampson Co., NC	Farm Labor	Enlisted, 4/20/61. Captured, 11/7/63 at Kelly's Ford. POW—Point Lookout, MD. Exchanged, 2/13/65.
1st Cpl.	**Thrailkill, Joseph M.**	**1828**	**M**	**Clinton, Sampson Co., NC**	**Painter**	**Enlisted, 4/20/61. Promoted to Sgt., 5/1/62. Died of chronic diarrhea, 2/21/63 near Fredericksburg, VA.**
2nd Cpl.	Williams, John C.	1843	S	Owensville, Sampson Co., NC	Farm Labor	TDY—Signal Corps, from 6/1/62–8/31/64. No further records.
3rd Cpl.	Hobbs, Abraham	1835	S	Sampson Co., NC	Farmer	Enlisted, 4/20/61. Wounded, 9/17/62 at Sharpsburg. Promoted to Sgt., 5/1/63. TDY—Carrier for Gen. Ransom, 6/1/63–1/31/64. Reduced to Pvt., 2/1/64. No further records after 10/31/64.
4th Cpl.	Williamson, Henry	1836	S	Taylor's Bridge, Sampson Co., NC	Mechanic	Enlisted, 4/20/61. Promoted to Sgt., 5/1/62. Wounded, 5/3/63 at Chancellorsville. TDY—Provost Guard, from 10/1/63–10/31/64. Paroled, 4/9/65 at Appomattox.
Music	Clarkston, Thomas M.	1811	M	Clinton, Sampson Co., NC	Painter	Enlisted, 9/1/61. Drum major. Wounded, 9/17/62 at Sharpsburg. TDY—General hospital, Goldsboro, NC, 1/1/63–2/28/63. No further records.
Music	Turner, Cicero	1843	S	Clinton, Sampson Co., NC	Painter	Enlisted, 4/20/61. Fifer, 9/1/61–12/31/61. Drummer, 1/1/62–4/30/62. Discharged, 5/1/62.
Pvt.	**Autry, William**	**1839**	**S**	**Clinton, Sampson Co., NC**	**Turpentine Labor**	**Enlisted, 9/1/61. Captured, 9/29/62 at Warrenton. Paroled, 9/30/62. Died of pneumonia, 12/18/62 at Gordonsville, VA.**
Pvt.	**Baggot, James W.**	**1843**	**S**	**Hawley's Store, Sampson Co., NC**	**Farm Labor**	**Enlisted, 9/1/62. Killed, 7/1/62 at Malvern Hill.**
Pvt.	Bass, William E.	1837	S	Bennett's Crossing, Sampson Co., NC	Farmer	Enlisted, 4/20/61. Promoted to Cpl., 1/1/63. Captured, 5/8/64 near Spotsylvania. POW—Elmira, NY. Released, 5/29/65.
Pvt.	Benton, Bradley C.	1838	S	Taylor's Bridge, Sampson Co., NC	Asst. Cabinet Maker	Enlisted, 4/20/61. Wounded, 12/13/62 at Fredericksburg. Discharged (disability), 7/11/63.

30th North Carolina Infantry Roster, Company A

Rank	Name	DOB	M/S	Residence	Occupation	Remarks
Pvt.	Boon, Stephen	1830	M	Calvin Creek, New Hanover Co., NC	Mechanic	Enlisted, 4/14/61. Wounded & Captured, 7/1/62 at Malvern Hill. Paroled, 7/16/62. Returned to duty, 12/1/62. Promoted to Cpl., 1/1/63. Captured, 5/12/64 at Spotsylvania. POW—Elmira, NY. Released, 5/29/65.
Pvt.	Boon, Sylvester	1841	S	Clinton, Sampson Co., NC	Turpentine Labor	Enlisted, 9/27/61. Absent; sick, 5/1/62–4/30/63. No further records.
Pvt.	Boon, Nicholas	1841	S	Taylor's Bridge, Sampson Co., NC	Farm Labor	Enlisted, 9/1/61. Captured, 5/12/64 at Spotsylvania. POW—Elmira, NY. Released, 6/30/65.
Pvt.	Bradshaw, Owen K.	1834	M	Owensville, Sampson Co., NC	Cooper	Enlisted, 9/1/61. Deserted, 4/26/62.
Pvt.	**Bradshaw, Robert M.**	**1841**	**S**	**Sampson Co., NC.**	**Farm Labor**	**Enlisted, 4/20/61. Died of Smallpox, 3/17/63 at Palmyra, VA.**
Pvt.	Bradshaw, William K.	1839	S	Taylor's Bridge, Sampson Co., NC	Farm Labor	Enlisted, 9/1/61. Deserted, 9/12/62.
Pvt.	Brewer, Abraham H.	1826	M	Bennett's Crossroads, Sampson Co., NC	Farmer	Enlisted, 4/20/61. Wounded (left hand & back), 7/3/63 at Gettysburg. Captured, 7/4/63 in retreat (So. Mountain). POW—Point Lookout, MD. Exchanged, 3/6/64. Promoted to Cpl., 6/1/64. Surrendered, 4/9/65 near Appomattox.
Pvt.	Butler, George C.	1841	S	Clinton, Sampson Co., NC	Farm Labor	Enlisted, 4/20/61. Home on sick leave, 3/1/63–8/31/64. No further records.
Pvt.	Butler, Hartwell	1839	S	Clinton, Sampson Co., NC	Farm Labor	Enlisted, 9/1/61. Captured, 11/7/63 at Kelly's Ford. POW—Point Lookout, MD. Exchanged, 9/30/64. No further records.
Pvt.	Butler, James R.	1844	S	Clinton, Sampson Co., NC		Enlisted, 9/1/61. Died of disease, 1/2/63 at Lynchburg, VA.
Pvt.	**Butler, Joseph**	**1834**	**M**	**Clinton, Sampson Co., NC**	**Farm Labor**	**Enlisted, 9/1/61. Wounded (left leg amputated), 5/8/64 at Spotsylvania. Died of wounds, 5/9/64.**
Pvt.	Butler, Raiford D.	1845	S	Clinton, Sampson Co., NC	Farm Labor	Enlisted, 9/1/61. Captured, 5/12/64 at Spotsylvania. POW—Elmira, NY. Released, 6/30/65.
Pvt.	**Clarkson, Thomas N.**	**1838**	**S**	**Clinton, Sampson Co., NC**	**Painter**	**Enlisted, 9/1/61. Died of pneumonia, 11/14/62 at Mount Jackson, VA.**
Pvt.	Cobb, Obed B.	1844	S	Piney Grove, Sampson Co., NC	Turpentine Labor	Enlisted, 4/20/61. Wounded, 11/7/63 at Kelly's Ford. TDY—Light Duty in Sampson Co., NC, 3/1/64–4/9/65.
Pvt.	Cox, Robert G.	1844	S	Clinton, Sampson Co., NC	Farm Labor	Enlisted, 6/21/61. Wounded, 7/1/62 at Malvern Hill. Wounded (left thigh), 9/19/64 at Winchester. Captured, 9/25/64 at Harrisonburg. POW—Point Lookout, MD. Paroled, 11/15/64. In hospital in Richmond. Captured in hospital, 4/3/65.
Pvt.	Crumpler, James M.	1840	S	Clinton, Sampson Co., NC	Farm Labor	Enlisted, 4/20/61. Promoted to Cpl., 5/1/62. Wounded (jaw), 5/3/63 at Chancellorsville. Captured, 4/6/65 at Farmville.
Pvt.	Crumpler, Robert M.	1841	S	Clinton, Sampson Co., NC	Teacher	Enlisted, 9/1/61. Promoted to 1st Sgt., 5/1/62. Wounded (thigh), 6/27/62 at Gaines' Mill. Wounded, 5/3/63 at Chancellorsville. Wounded, 11/7/63 at Kelly's Ford. Wounded, 7/12/64 at Ft. Stevens. Paroled, 4/9/65 at Appomattox.

Appendix 2

Rank	Name	DOB	M/S	Residence	Occupation	Remarks
Pvt.	Currie, John B.	1839	S	Lumberton, Robeson Co., NC	Trader	Enlisted, 4/20/61. TDY–Ambulance driver, 9/1/62–4/31/63. Surrendered, 4/9/65 at Appomattox.
Pvt.	Draughon, George H.	1843	S	Clinton, Sampson Co., NC	Student	Enlisted, 4/20/61. Promoted to Cpl., 5/1/62. Died of chronic diarrhea, 12/26/62 at Clinton, NC.
Pvt.	Dudley, Michael	1842	S	Hawley's Store, Sampson Co., NC	Farm Labor	Enlisted, 9/1/62. Died of typhoid fever, 1/15/62 at Washington, NC.
Pvt.	Dudley, William W.	1843	S	Sampson Co., NC	Farm Labor	Enlisted, 9/1/62. Discharged, 7/–/62.
Pvt.	Duncan, Charles W.	1843	S	Clinton, Sampson Co., NC	Farm Labor	Enlisted, 9/1/62. Wounded, 5/3/63 at Chancellorsville. Died of wounds, 5/29/63.
Pvt.	Duncan, James D.	1839	S	Hawley's Store, Sampson Co., NC	Mechanic	Enlisted, 4/20/61. Captured, 11/7/63 at Kelly's Ford. POW—Point Lookout, MD. Exchanged, 2/25/65.
Pvt.	Faircloth, John L.	1838	S	Owensville, Sampson Co., NC	Farm Labor	Enlisted, 9/1/62. TDY—Shoe maker in Richmond, 9/1/62–11/30/62. Died of smallpox, 1/15/63. "Died at night."
Pvt.	Faircloth, John	1835	S	Owensville, Sampson Co., NC	Farm Labor	Enlisted, 9/1/61. Died of pneumonia, 2/10/63 near Fredericksburg, VA.
Pvt.	Gilbert, Willis	1840	S	Clinton, Sampson Co., NC	Farm Labor	Enlisted, 9/1/61. Died of typhoid fever, 10/12/62.
Pvt.	Godwin, Nathan H.	1842	S	Draughorn's Store, Sampson Co., NC	Farm Labor	Enlisted, 9/1/61. Wounded, 7/1/62 at Malvern Hill. Captured, 11/7/63 at Kelly's Ford. POW—Point Lookout, MD. Exchanged, 2/24/65.
Pvt.	Goodrich, James T.	1843	S	Hawley's Store, Sampson Co., NC	Farm Labor	Enlisted, 9/1/61. Killed, 6/27/62 at Gaines' Mill.
Pvt.	Hall, William G.	1840	S	Owensville, Sampson Co., NC	Farm Labor	Enlisted, 5/22/61. Captured, 11/7/63 at Kelly's Ford. POW—Point Lookout, MD. Exchanged, 11/15/64. Paroled, 4/9/65 at Appomattox.
Pvt.	Herring, Timothy J.	1838	S	Clinton, Sampson Co., NC	Farm Labor	Enlisted, 9/1/61. Promoted to Cpl., 1/1/63. Captured, 5/12/64 at Spotsylvania. No further records.
Pvt.	Hobbs, Judson	1843	S	Clinton, Sampson Co., NC	Farm Labor	Enlisted, 4/20/61. Promoted to Sgt., 6/1/64. "Signed roll commanding the company," 8/64. Captured, 10/19/64 at Cedar Creek. POW—Point Lookout, MD. Released, 6/27/65.
Pvt.	Holland, James F.	1842	S	Owensville, Sampson Co., NC	Farm Labor	Enlisted, 9/1/61. Wounded, 9/11/61 at Ft. Caswell, NC. Promoted to Musician (fifer), 3/1/62. Surrendered, 4/9/65 at Appomattox.
Pvt.	Holland, John R.	1839	S	Owensville, Sampson Co., NC	Farm Labor	Enlisted, 9/1/61. Wounded (head), 9/17/62 at Sharpsburg. Killed, 5/3/63 at Chancellorsville.
Pvt.	Honeycutt, Miles C.	1838	S	Hawley's Store, Sampson Co., NC	Cooper	Enlisted, 9/1/61. Captured, 9/22/64 at Fisher's Hill. POW—Elmira, NY. Released, 5/29/65.
Pvt.	Howard, Fleet H.	1840	S	Clinton, Sampson Co., NC	Farm Labor	Enlisted, 9/1/61. Wounded, 9/17/62 at Sharpsburg. Captured, 5/12/64 at Spotsylvania. POW—Elmira, NY. Exchanged, 10/11/64. No further records.
Pvt.	Howard, Joseph C.	1842	S	Clinton, Sampson Co., NC	Farm Labor	Enlisted, 9/1/61. TDY—Pioneer at Rodes' HQ, 1/1/64–4/9/65. Captured, 4/11/65 at Farmville.

30th North Carolina Infantry Roster, Company A

Rank	Name	DOB	M/S	Residence	Occupation	Remarks
Pvt.	Howard, William S.	1844	S	Clinton, Sampson Co., NC	Farm Labor	Enlisted, 9/1/61. Wounded (right thigh) & captured, 9/19/64 at Winchester. POW—Point Lookout, MD. Exchanged, 2/25/65.
Pvt.	Ingram, William W.	1832	S	Newton Grove, Sampson Co., NC	Farmer	Enlisted, 4/20/61 Discharged (disability), 7/16/62.
Pvt.	**Jackson, James W.**	**1841**	**S**	**Fayetteville, Cumberland Co., NC**	**Turpentine Labor**	**Enlisted, 9/1/61. Died of liver failure, 12/26/62.**
Pvt.	Jackson, Martin G.	1839	S	Hawley's Store, Sampson Co., NC	Farm Labor	Enlisted, 9/1/61. Captured, 5/12/64 at Spotsylvania. POW—Point Lookout, MD. No further records.
Pvt.	Johnson, William H.	1839	S	Clinton, Sampson Co., NC	Mechanic	Enlisted, 4/20/61. Promoted, to Cpl., 5/1/62. Wounded, 7/1/62 at Malvern Hill. Promoted to Sgt., 6/1/63. Captured, 5/12/64 at Spotsylvania. POW—Elmira, NY. Released, 6/19/65.
Pvt.	Kelly, Chester	1843	S	Clinton, Sampson Co., NC	Mechanic	Enlisted, 4/20/61. Colonel's orderly, 11/1/62–12/31/62. Promoted to musician (drummer), 1/1/63. Missing, 10/1/64.
Pvt.	Kelly, James M	1840	S	Clinton, Sampson Co., NC	Farm Labor	Enlisted, 4/20/61. Wounded, 5/3/63 at Chancellorsville. Wounded, 11/7/63 at Kelly's Ford. Wounded, 5/12/64 at Spotsylvania. No further records.
Pvt.	King, Lewis D.	1840	S	Sampson Co., NC	Farm Labor	Enlisted, 4/20/61. Wounded, 7/18/64 at Snicker's Gap. "Acted gallantly at Mine Run as a skirmisher,"11/30/63. Wounded, 7/18/64 at Snicker's Gap. Surrendered, 4/9/65 at Appomattox.
Pvt.	King, Stephen J.	1836	S	Piney Grove, Sampson Co., NC	Farm Labor	Enlisted, 9/1/61. Wounded (right heel), 6/3/64 at Cold Harbor. Surrendered, 4/9/65 at Appomattox.
Pvt.	Lee, Thomas J.	1835	S	Clinton, Sampson Co., NC	Merchant	Enlisted, 4/20/61. Discharged, (disability), 12/26/61.
Pvt.	Lee, Willis	1841	S	Summerville, Harnett Co., NC	Farm Labor	Enlisted, 9/1/61. Deserted, 9/20/62.
Pvt.	Lewis, Archibald A.	1839	S	Sampson Co., NC	Mechanic	Enlisted, 4/20/61. Wounded (arm), 6/21/62, "in a skirmish near Richmond." TDY—Provost Guard at Gordonsville, 9/1/63–8/31/64. No further records.
Pvt.	**Lewis, Cornelius**	**1846**	**S**	**Clinton, Sampson Co., NC**	**Day Labor**	**Enlisted, 9/27/61. Died of disease, 8/25/62 at Richmond, VA.**
Pvt.	McKenzie, Redman	1836	S	Clinton, Sampson Co., NC		Enlisted, 4/20/61. Captured, 5/12/64 at Spotsylvania. POW—Point Lookout, MD. Exchanged, 3/16/65.
Pvt.	**McLemore, Tobias**	**1836**	**S**	**Owensville, Sampson Co., NC**	**Turpentine Labor**	**Enlisted, 9/1/61. Sick in hospital at Lynchburg, VA. "Did not rejoin regiment, supposed to be dead."**
Pvt.	**McLemore, William S.**	**1842**	**S**	**McDaniels, Sampson Co., NC**	**Farm Labor**	**Enlisted, 9/1/61. Captured, 9/17/62 at Sharpsburg. Paroled, 10/2/62. Wounded, 5/12/64 at Spotsylvania. Died of wounds, 5/27/64 at Richmond.**
Pvt.	Merritt, Isaac W.	1834		Sampson Co., NC	Farmer	Enlisted, 4/20/61. Promoted to Cpl., 5/1/62. Promoted to Sgt., 1/1/63. Wounded (side & left arm), 7/1/63. Captured, 7/4/63 in retreat from Gettysburg (So. Mountain). POW—Point Lookout, MD. Exchanged, 2/14/65.

Appendix 2

Rank	Name	DOB	M/S	Residence	Occupation	Remarks
Pvt.	Mitchell, Henry	1820	S	Piney Grove, Sampson Co., NC	Farm Labor	Enlisted, 9/1/61. Died of pneumonia, 1/14/63 near Fredericksburg. "Died at 3 p.m."
Pvt.	Moore, Walter J.	1840	S	Clinton, Sampson Co., NC	Farm Labor	Enlisted, 4/20/61. Discharged (disability—"spinal disease"), 1/30/62.
Pvt.	Naylor, Ransom	1841	S	Hawley's Store, Sampson Co., NC	Turpentine Labor	Enlisted, 9/1/61. Killed, 5/3/63 at Chancellorsville.
Pvt.	Nowles, William R.	1827	M	Mt. Pleasant, Cabarrus Co., NC	Farmer	Enlisted, 9/1/61. Discharged (sickness), 7/16/62.
Pvt.	Page, Jacob S.	1840	S	Owensville, Sampson Co., NC	Farm Labor	Enlisted, 9/1/61. Killed, 5/12/64 at Spotsylvania.
Pvt.	Page, Owen	1838		Sampson Co., NC		Enlisted, 4/20/61. Died of smallpox, 12/29/62 at Richmond, VA.
Pvt.	Parker, James M.	1837	S	Owensville, Sampson Co., NC	Farm Labor	Enlisted, 9/1/61. Wounded, 5/3/63 at Chancellorsville. Surrendered, 4/9/65 at Appomattox.
Pvt.	Pennington, William	1839	S	Piney Grove, Sampson Co., NC	Farm Labor	Enlisted, 4/20/61. Wounded (head), 5/3/63 at Chancellorsville. Promoted to Color Sgt., 7/20/63. Wounded, 5/12/64 at Spotsylvania. Home on wounded furlough. No further records after 9/30/64.
Pvt.	Pipkin, Lewis H.	1832		Crossroads, Wayne Co., NC	Shoe maker	Enlisted, 4/20/61. Killed, 7/1/62 at Malvern Hill.
Pvt.	Pope, Alexander	1827	M	Halls, Sampson Co., NC	Farmer	Enlisted, 9/1/61. Wounded (chest), 7/1/62 at Malvern Hill. Discharged due to wounds, 7/30/62.
Pvt.	Pope, Stephen	1825	M	Clinton, Sampson Co., NC		Enlisted, 9/1/61. Discharged, 7/-/62.
Pvt.	Pope, Wiley	1835	M	Clinton, Sampson Co., NC	Carpenter	Enlisted, 9/1/61. Wounded (head & knee), 7/1/62 at Malvern Hill. "Distinguished for gallantry in the field." Captured, 5/12/64 at Spotsylvania. POW—Point Lookout, MD. Exchanged, 3/14/65.
Pvt.	Pope, William B.	1840		Sampson Co., NC		Enlisted, 9/1/61. Deserted, 9/24/63. "Arrested as a deserter" Returned to Regiment. Captured, 11/28/63 at Mine Run. POW—Point Lookout, MD. Released, 6/17/65.
Pvt.	Pridgen, William E.	1835		Sampson Co., NC		Enlisted, 9/1/61. Discharged (acute rheumatism), 7/-/62.
Pvt.	Rackley, George W.	1839	S	Taylor's Bridge, Sampson Co., NC	Farm Labor	Enlisted, 4/20/61. Wounded, 5/3/63 at Chancellorsville. Promoted to Sgt., 10/-/63. Captured, 5/12/64 at Spotsylvania. POW—Elmira, NY. Released, 6/19/65.
Pvt.	Register, Edward M.	1843	S	Taylor's Bridge, Sampson Co., NC	Farm Labor	Enlisted, 9/27/61. Wounded, 7/1/62 at Malvern Hill. Died of pneumonia, 2/16/63 near Fredericksburg, VA.
Pvt.	Register, Harmon H.	1837	S	Clinton, Sampson Co., NC	Merchant	Enlisted, 4/20/61. Discharged, 11/1/61.
Pvt.	Reynolds, Charles H.	1843	S	Clinton, Sampson Co., NC	Farm Labor	Enlisted, 9/1/61. Died of smallpox, 1/11/63 at Guinea Station, VA.

Rank	Name	DOB	M/S	Residence	Occupation	Remarks
Pvt.	Reynolds, John R.	1839	S	Clinton, Sampson Co., NC	Farm Labor	Enlisted, 9/1/61. Captured, 5/12/64 at Spotsylvania. POW—Elmira, NY. Died of typhoid fever, 3/29/65.
Pvt.	Rich, James O.	1838	S	McDaniels, Sampson Co., NC	Farm Labor	Enlisted, 9/1/61. Discharged, 5/1/62 "by providing a substitute."
Pvt.	Robinson, Harmon R.	1835	S	Taylor's Bridge, Sampson Co., NC	Farm Labor	Enlisted, 4/20/61. Died of pneumonia, 6/19/63 at Martinsburg, VA.
Pvt.	Robinson, Thomas M.	1831	S	Taylor's Bridge, Sampson Co., NC	Cooper	Enlisted, 4/20/61. Discharged, 7/16/62.
Pvt.	Royal, Marshall	1837	S	Owensville, Sampson Co., NC	Farm Labor	Enlisted, 9/1/61. Died of disease, 1/21/62 in Sampson Co., NC.
Pvt.	Royal, Martin	1842	S	Clinton, Sampson Co., NC	Salesman	Enlisted, 9/1/61. Died of acute dysentery, 3/8/63 at Weldon, NC.
Pvt.	Royal, Nevil	1835		Sampson Co., NC		Enlisted, 9/1/61. Wounded, 6/27/62 at Gaines' Mill. Transferred to 35th NC Inf., 1/1/63.
Pvt.	Royal, Sherman	1842	S	Clinton, Sampson Co., NC	Farm Labor	Enlisted, 9/1/61. Promoted to Cpl., 5/1/62. Wounded (head), 7/1/62 at Malvern Hill. Died of wounds, 7/5/62 at Richmond, VA.
Pvt.	Smith, Richard P.	1835		Virginia		Enlisted, 9/27/61. Deserted, 2/7/63.
Pvt.	Spell, Hardy L.	1835	S	Owensville, Sampson Co., NC	Farm Labor	Enlisted, 4/20/61. TDY—hospital steward at Ft. Johnson, NC, 10/1/61–12/31/61. Discharged (sickness), 7/-/62.
Pvt.	Strickland, Walter D.	1837	S	Owensville, Sampson Co., NC	Turpentine Labor	Enlisted, 9/1/61. Died of disease, 1/19/63 at Guinea Station, VA.
Pvt.	Sutton, Michael	1844	S	Sampson Co., NC	Farm Labor	Enlisted, 4/20/61. Discharged (osteoarthritis), 12/20/61.
Pvt.	Taylor, William J.	1844	S	Summerville, Harnett Co., NC	Farm Labor	Enlisted, 9/1/61. Wounded (back & left shoulder), 5/3/63 at Chancellorsville. Captured, 5/12/64 at Spotsylvania. POW—Elmira, NY. Released, 5/29/65.
Pvt.	Tew, Blackman	1839	S	Clinton, Sampson Co., NC	Cooper	Enlisted, 9/1/61. Killed, 6/27/62 at Gaines' Mill.
Pvt.	Tew, Wiley	1838	S	Owensville, Sampson Co., NC	Farm Labor	Enlisted, 9/1/61. Died of pneumonia, 1/19/63 at Lynchburg, VA.
Pvt.	Tindale, David	1836	S	Hawley's Store, Sampson Co., NC	Farm Labor	Enlisted, 9/1/61. Discharged, 1/1/62.
Pvt.	Tindale, Miles S.	1843	S	Hawley's Store, Sampson Co., NC	Farm Labor	Enlisted, 9/1/61. Captured, 5/12/64 at Spotsylvania. POW—Elmira, NY. Exchanged, 3/18/65.
Pvt.	Underwood, Daniel R.	1844	S	Clinton, Sampson Co., NC	Farm Labor	Enlisted, 9/1/61. Killed, 5/3/63 at Chancellorsville.
Pvt.	Walker, James C.	1823		Sampson Co., NC		Enlisted, 9/1/61. Wounded, 5/3/63 at Chancellorsville. No further records after 8/31/64.
Pvt.	Weeks, John A.	1843	S	Piney Grove, Sampson Co., NC	Farm Labor	Enlisted, 4/20/61. Wounded, 5/3/63 at Chancellorsville. Died of wounds, 5/11/63 at Richmond, VA.

Appendix 2

Rank	Name	DOB	M/S	Residence	Occupation	Remarks
Pvt.	Williamson, David	1843	S	Clinton, Sampson Co., NC	Farm Labor	Enlisted, 9/1/61. Captured, 11/7/63 at Kelly's Ford. POW—Point Lookout, MD. Exchanged, 2/24/65.
Pvt.	Williamson, James	1839	S	Clinton, Sampson Co., NC	Farm Labor	Enlisted, 9/1/61. Wounded (right hip), 6/27/62 at Gaines' Mill. Wounded (arm), 4/30/63 near Fredericksburg. Wounded (right arm), 11/7/63 at Kelly's Ford. Captured, 5/12/64 at Spotsylvania. POW—Elmira, NY. Released, 6/23/65.

1862 Recruits

Rank	Name	DOB	M/S	Residence	Occupation	Remarks
Pvt.	Brown, George E.	1836	M	Clinton, Sampson Co., NC	Farmer	**Enlisted, 5/17/62. Wounded, 7/1/62 at Malvern Hill. Killed, 9/1762 at Sharpsburg.**
Pvt.	Butler, Edward N.	1843	S	Clinton, Sampson Co., NC	Farm Labor	Enlisted, 1/1/62. Wounded (both thighs), 5/3/64 at Chancellorsville. Absent sick in hospital. Paroled at Burkeville Jct., 4/17/65.
Pvt.	Howard, Thomas M.	1834	M	Sampson Co., NC	Farmer	**Enlisted, 5/1/62. Wounded (head), 7/1/62 at Malvern Hill. Promoted to Sgt., 9/1/63. Killed, 5/12/64 at Spotsylvania.**
Pvt.	Pennington, John	1844	S	Buck Swamp, Wayne Co., NC	Farm Labor	**Enlisted, 5/1/62. Killed, 8/21/64, at Charles Town, WV.**
Pvt.	Spell, Gaston	1833	M	Owensville, Sampson Co., NC	Sheriff's Deputy	Enlisted, 3/27/62. TDY—Ambulance Corps, 9/1/62–12/31/63. Paroled, 4/9/65 at Appomattox.
Pvt.	Tatom, Love A.	1804	M	Sampson Co., NC	Farmer	Enlisted (substitute), 7/10/62. Discharged (old age), 9/15/62.
3rd Lt.	White, Lallister M.	1833	S	Owensville, Sampson Co., NC	Farm Labor	**Elected, 3rd Lt., 5/1/62 (from Sgt. Maj.). Promoted to 1st Lt., 9/2/63. Killed, 5/12/64 at Spotsylvania.**

1863 Conscripts

Rank	Name	DOB	M/S	Residence	Occupation	Remarks
Pvt.	Allman, Gideon	1819	M	Mt. Pleasant, Cabarrus Co. NC	Day Labor	Conscripted, 9/22/63. Captured, 5/12/64 at Spotsylvania. POW—Elmira, NY. Released, 6/12/65.
Pvt.	Alsbrook, S. C.	1830	S	Weldon, Halifax Co., NC	Farmer	**Conscripted, 6/24/63. Captured, 11/7/63 Kelly's Ford. POW—Point Lookout, MD. Died of chronic dysentery, 2/8/64.**
Pvt.	Bell, Robert	1826	M	Wilmington, New Hanover Co., NC	Day Labor	Conscripted, 7/23/63. Captured, 5/12/64 at Spotsylvania. POW—Elmira, NY. Exchanged, 11/15/64. No further records.
Pvt.	Boswell, William H.	1823	M	Colerain, Bertie Co., NC	Farmer	**Conscripted, 6/24/63. Killed, 11/7/63 at Kelly's Ford.**
Pvt.	Bridges, Joseph	1811	M	Halifax Co., NC	Farmer	Conscripted, 6/23/63 as a substitute. Absent; sick, 11/1/63–8/31/64. No further records.
Pvt.	Dove, Monroe	1821	M	Mt. Pleasant, Cabarrus Co., NC	Farmer	Conscripted, 9/12/63. Wounded (thigh), 11/7/63 at Kelly's Ford. Absent due to wounds. Captured in hospital, 4/3/65 in Richmond.
Pvt.	Dunn, David W	1828	M	Enfield, Halifax Co., NC	Overseer	**Conscripted, 6/24/63. Died of disease, 4/5/64 at Orange Court House, VA.**
Pvt.	Friezland, Jacob	1822	M	Concord, Cabarrus Co., NC	Farmer	**Conscripted, 9/12/63. Wounded, 11/7/63 at Kelly's Ford. Wounded (head), 5/19/64 at Harris Farm. Captured, 4/6/65 at Burkeville. POW—Died of chronic diarrhea, 6/14/65 at Newport News, VA.**

30th North Carolina Infantry Roster, Company A

Rank	Name	DOB	M/S	Residence	Occupation	Remarks
Pvt.	Hagler, John	1819	M	Mt. Pleasant, Cabarrus Co., NC	Farmer	Conscripted, 9/12/63. Died of disease ("suddenly"), 5/13/64.
Pvt.	Holshouser, Ambrose N.	1822	M	Salisbury, Rowan Co., NC	Farmer	Conscripted, 9/12/63. Captured, 11/7/63 at Kelly's Ford. POW—Point Lookout, MD. Exchanged, 2/24/65.
Pvt.	Hutchison, Andrew J.	1820	M	Mt. Pleasant, Cabarrus Co., NC	Agent at gold mine	Conscripted, 9/12/63. Captured, 5/12/64 at Spotsylvania. POW—Elmira, NY. Died of smallpox, 2/28/65.
Pvt.	Ivey, W. L.	1827	M	Weldon, Halifax Co., NC	Farmer	Conscripted, 6/23/63. Captured, 11/7/63 at Kelly's Ford. POW—Point Lookout, MD. Died of chronic diarrhea, 1/26/65.
Pvt.	Johnson, L. W.	1837	M	Arcadia, Halifax Co., NC	Farmer	Conscripted, 6/23/63. Captured, 5/12/64 at Spotsylvania. POW—Point Lookout, MD. Exchanged, 3/16/65.
Pvt.	Mewborn, Parrott	1836		Greene Co., NC		Conscripted, 6/19/63. Sick in hospital since 8/17/64. No further records.
Pvt.	Miles, John	1823		Halifax Co., NC		Conscripted, 6/23/63. Wounded, 5/12/64 at Spotsylvania. Home on wounded furlough. No further records after 8/31/64.
Pvt.	Parting, Henry A.	1845	S	Halifax Co., NC		Conscripted, 6/23/63. Captured, 11/7/63 at Kelly's Ford. POW—Point Lookout, MD. Died of smallpox, 12/28/63.
Pvt.	Reed, M. D.			Halifax Co., NC		Conscripted, 6/23/63. Discharged, 9/3/63.
Pvt.	Rogers, William	1835	S	Scotland Neck, Halifax Co., NC	Farmer	Conscripted, 6/23/63. Captured, 4/3/65 at Petersburg. Released, 6/17/65.
Pvt.	Rogister, James	1835		Halifax Co., NC		Conscripted, 6/23/63. Captured, 11/7/63 at Kelly's Ford. POW—Point Lookout, MD. Exchanged, 2/25/65.
Pvt.	Steele, James H.	1823	M	Concord, Cabarrus Co., NC	Farmer	Conscripted, 9/22/63. Captured, 11/7/63 at Kelly's Ford. POW—Point Lookout, MD. Exchanged, 9/22/64. Paroled, 4/9/65 at Appomattox.
Pvt.	Taylor, Thomas J.	1845	S	Heathsville, Halifax Co., NC	Farm Labor	Enlisted, 6/24/62. Wounded, 12/13/62 at Fredericksburg. Discharged (sickness), 1/20/64.
Pvt.	Wammack, Levi T.			Halifax Co., NC		Conscripted, 6/24/63. TDY—hospital in Richmond, 1/1/64–4/3/65. Captured, 4/3/65 at Richmond.
Pvt.	Warrick, Thomas J.	1845	S	Bennett's Crossroads, Sampson Co., NC	Farm Labor	Conscripted, 7/10/63 at Camp Holmes, NC. Wounded, 7/11/63 at Kelly's Ford. Died of typhoid fever, 7/7/64 at Richmond, VA.
Pvt.	Winecoff, George W.	1825	M	Concord, Cabarrus Co., NC	Farmer	Conscripted, 9/12/63. Captured, 11/7/63 at Kelly's Ford. POW—Point Lookout, MD Exchanged, 2/24/65.

1864 Conscripts

Rank	Name	DOB	M/S	Residence	Occupation	Remarks
Pvt.	Ogburn, N. S.	1847	S	Greensboro, Guilford Co., NC	Farm Labor	Conscripted, 4/1/64. Captured, 4/3/65 at Petersburg. Released, 6/17/65.
Pvt.	Pennington, Henry	1847	S	Wayne Co., NC		Conscripted, 2/17/64. Captured, 9/22/64 at Fisher's Hill. POW—Point Lookout, MD. No further records after 11/30/64.

Company B—Nat Macon Guards
Warren County (Mustered into Regt.—8/16/61)

Rank	Name	DOB	M/S	Residence	Occupation	Remarks
Cpt.	Drake, William C.	1832	M	Warrenton, Warren Co., NC	Clerk	Enrolled, 8/16/61. Wounded, 6/27/62 at Gaines' Mill. Resigned, 1/5/63.
1st Lt.	Williams, Buckner D.	1833	M	Warrenton, Warren Co., NC	Merchant	Enrolled, 8/16/61. Commissioned, Cpt., Regt'l. QM, 11/1/61. Transferred to F & S.
2nd Lt.	Brame, John M.	1835	M	Warrenton, Warren Co., NC	Farmer	Enrolled, 8/16/61. Was not re-elected, 5/1/62.
3rd Lt.	**Davis, Weldon E.**	**1839**	**M**	**Warrenton, Warren Co., NC**	**Farmer**	**Enrolled, 8/16/61. Promoted, to 1st Lt., 5/1/62. Promoted to Cpt., 1/13/63. Wounded (right leg fractured) and captured, 12/7/63 at Kelly's Ford. Leg amputated at thigh. Died of wounds (tetanus), 11/22/63 in hospital at Washington, D.C.**
1st Sgt.	Loughlin, James H.	1839		Warren ., NC		Enrolled, 8/16/61. Promoted to 3rd Lt., 1/13/63. Captured, 7/24/63 in skirmish near Front Royal. POW—Johnson's Island, OH. Released, 6/11/65.
2nd Sgt.	Nicholson, John H.	1832	S	Macon Depot, Warren Co., NC	Farmer	Enrolled, 8/16/61. Promoted to 2nd Lt., 5/1/62. Promoted to 1st Lt., 1/13/63. Captured, 11/7/63 at Kelly's Ford. POW—Johnson's Island, OH. Released, 6/13/65.
3rd Sgt.	Davis, Burwell P.	1833	S	Grove Hill, Warren Co., NC	Farmer	Enrolled, 8/16/61. Wounded, 7/1/62 at Malvern Hill. TDY—Hospital duty in Raleigh, 3/1/63–12/31/63. TDY—Baggage Master in Raleigh, 1/1/64–12/31/64. No further records.
4th Sgt.	**Shearin, John D.**	**1836**	**S**	**Warrenton, Warren Co., NC**	**Overseer**	**Enrolled, 8/16/61. Captured, 5/8/64 at Spotsylvania. POW—Elmira, NY. Died of chronic diarrhea, 10/4/64.**
5th Sgt.	Davis, Benjamin P.	1835	M	Grove Hill, Warren Co., NC	Farmer	Enrolled, 8/16/61. Reduced to Pvt., 5/1/62. Promoted to Sgt., 7/15/64. Sick in hospital since, 9/1/64. No further records after 11/30/64.
1st Cpl.	Harriss, John A.	1843	S	Macon Depot, Warren Co., NC	Rock Mason's Asst.	Enrolled, 8/16/61. Promoted to Sgt., 1/-/62. Wounded, 7/1/62 at Malvern Hill. Captured, 11/7/63 at Kelly's Farm. POW—Point Lookout, MD. Exchanged, 2/10/65.
2nd Cpl.	Williams, Robert D.	1841	S	Warrenton, Warren Co., NC	Farm Labor	Enrolled, 8/16/61. Promoted to Sgt., 5/1/62. Wounded (scalp), 7/1/63 at Gettysburg. Captured, 11/7/63 at Kelly's Ford. POW—Point Lookout, MD. Exchanged, 11/15/64. No further records.
3rd Cpl.	Bell, William	1838	S	Warrenton, Warren Co., NC	Farm Labor	Enrolled, 8/16/61. Wounded, 6/27/62 at Gaines' Mill. No further records after 8/31/64.
4th Cpl.	Hendrick, Alexander W.	1840	M	Warrenton, Warren Co., NC	Overseer	Enrolled, 8/16/61. Reduced to Pvt., 5/1/62. Wounded, 6/27/62 at Gaines' Mill. TDY—hospital duty in Richmond, 7/26/62–8/31/63. TDY—Provost Guard in Raleigh, 8/17/63–12/31/64. No further records.
Music	Loughlin, Charles	1844	S	Warren Co., NC		Enrolled, 8/16/61. (Drummer). Transferred to C.S. Navy, 4/10/62.

30th North Carolina Infantry Roster, Company B

Rank	Name	DOB	M/S	Residence	Occupation	Remarks
Pvt.	Abbott, Macon	1832	S	Warrenton, Warren Co., NC	Farm Labor	Enrolled, 8/16/61. Died of pneumonia, 1/8/63 at Richmond, VA.
Pvt.	Arrington, James L.	1830	M	Exchange, Warren Co., NC	Farm Labor	Enrolled, 8/16/61. Wounded (thigh & left hand), 5/3/63 at Chancellorsville. Captured, 5/20/64 at Spotsylvania. POW—Elmira, NY. Died of smallpox, 2/7/65.
Pvt.	Askew, John	1840	S	Ridgeway, Warren Co., NC	Farm Labor	Enrolled, 8/16/61. Captured, 11/7/63 at Kelly's Ford. POW—Point Lookout, MD. Died of disease, 8/25/64.
Pvt.	Aycock, Edward S.	1839	S	Grove Hill, Warren Co., NC	Farm Labor	Enrolled, 8/16/61. Surrendered, 4/9/65 at Appomattox.
Pvt.	Aycock, George G.	1839	S	Grove Hill, Warren Co., NC	Farm Labor	Enrolled, 8/16/61. Wounded (left thigh) and captured, 4/6/65 at Sailor's Creek. Released, 6/9/65.
Pvt.	Aycock, Samuel	1822	S	Grove Hill, Warren Co., NC	Carpenter	Enrolled, 8/16/61. Killed, 11/7/63 at Kelly's Ford.
Pvt.	Bishop, Alfred	1835	S	Warrenton, Warren Co., NC	Farm Labor	Enrolled, 8/16/61. Wounded (right shoulder), 7/1/62 at Malvern Hill. Transferred to 46th NC Inf., 9/25/62.
Pvt.	Bishop, Samuel D.	1844	S	Warrenton, Warren Co., NC	Farm Labor	Enrolled, 8/16/61. Killed, 5/3/63 at Chancellorsville.
Pvt.	Bobbitt, Burwell B.	1844	S	Warrenton, Warren Co., NC	Student	Enrolled, 8/16/61. Wounded, 6/27/62 at Gaines' Mill. Wounded (left hip), 5/3/63 at Chancellorsville. TDY—Salisbury, NC, since 2/1/64. Paroled, 5/2/65.
Pvt.	Brack, Baker B.	1836	M	Warrenton, Warren Co., NC	Carpenter	Enrolled, 8/16/61. TDY—Nurse in Richmond hospital, 6/1/62-12/31/62. Killed, 5/3/63 at Chancellorsville.
Pvt.	Brack, George W.	1835	M	Warrenton, Warren Co., NC	Farmer	Enrolled, 8/16/61. Killed, 5/3/63 at Chancellorsville.
Pvt.	Carroll, William H.	1842	S	Warrenton, Warren Co., NC	Farm Labor	Enrolled, 8/16/61. Wounded (right arm), 4/6/65 at Sailor's Creek. Captured, 4/7/65 at Farmville.
Pvt.	Carter, John	1837	M	Macon Depot, Warren Co., NC	Farmer	Enrolled, 8/16/61. Discharged (stomach cancer), 3/5/62.
Pvt.	Carter, William J.	1828	M	Warrenton, Warren Co., NC	Farmer	Enrolled, 8/16/61. Captured ("deserted to the enemy"), 11/7/63 at Kelly's Ford. POW—Point Lookout, MD. Released, 1/30/64. Joined 1st U.S. Vol. Inf.
Pvt.	Clanton, Robert K.	1835	M	Ridgeway, Warren Co., NC	Farmer	Enrolled, 8/16/61. Discharged (provided a substitute), 3/5/63.
Pvt.	Darnell, James R.	1842	S	Warrenton, Warren Co., NC	Farm Labor	Enrolled, 8/16/61. Captured, 11/7/63 at Kelly's Ford. POW—Point Lookout, MD. Exchanged, 1/21/65. No further records.
Pvt.	Davis, Isham H.	1832	S	Warrenton, Warren Co., NC		Enlisted, 8/16/61. TDY—Hospital Duty in Raleigh, 3/1/63-12/31/63. Discharged (disability), 3/10/64.
Pvt.	Davis, John S.	1840	S	Warrenton, Warren Co., NC	Farm Labor	Enlisted, 8/16/61. Sent home with Yellow Fever, 3/18/62. Never returned to duty.
Pvt.	Duke, George J.	1836		Warren Co., NC		Enlisted, 8/16/61. Wounded, 7/1/62 at Malvern Hill. Wounded (side & arm), 5/3/63 at Chancellorsville. TDY—hospital duty at Lynchburg, VA, 5/1/64-10/31/64. No further records.

Appendix 2

Rank	Name	DOB	M/S	Residence	Occupation	Remarks
Pvt.	Duke, Robert W.	1835	S	Merry Mount, Warren Co., NC	Teacher	Enlisted, 8/16/61. Wounded, 7/1/63 at Malvern Hill. Died of wounds, 8/1/62 at Richmond, VA.
Pvt.	Floyd, Wyatt A.	1834	S	Ridgeway, Warren Co., NC	Overseer	Enlisted, 8/16/61. Transferred to 12th NC Inf., 3/24/63.
Pvt.	Foote, James S.	1840	S	Warrenton, Warren Co., NC	Farm Labor	Enlisted, 8/16/61. Promoted to 2nd Lt., 1/13/63. Sick after 4/30/63. Discharged due to sickness, 3/8/65.
Pvt.	Gholson, Abraham	1842	S	Warrenton, Warren Co., NC	Farm Labor	Enlisted, 8/16/61. Died of typhoid fever, 8/4/62 at Richmond.
Pvt.	Gill, Philip P.	1832	S	Merry Mount, Warren Co., NC	Farm Labor	Enlisted, 8/16/61. Wounded (face), 7/1/62 at Malvern Hill (shell explosion; "total loss of vision of left eye ... impairment of vision of the other."). Discharged (wounds), 9/20/62.
Pvt.	Goebel, Charles L.	1831		Warren Co., NC		Enlisted, 8/16/61. TDY—Richmond Armory, 3/18/62–6/30/63. Deserted, 7/-/63.
Pvt.	Haithcock, Alfred L.	1839	S	Warrenton, Warren Co., NC	Farm Labor	Enlisted, 8/16/61. Captured, 11/7/63 at Kelly's Ford. POW—Point Lookout, MD. Exchanged, 3/16/65.
Pvt.	Haithcock, William G.	1815	M	Warrenton, Warren Co., NC	Farmer	Enlisted, 8/16/61. Discharged (over age), 12/2/61.
Pvt.	Hardy, Francis M.	1842	S	Merry Mount, Warren Co., NC	Farm Labor	Enlisted, 8/16/61. Captured, 9/13/62 near Frederick, MD. POW—Point Lookout, MD. Exchanged, 12/18/62. Wounded, 5/3/63 at Chancellorsville. Wounded (both forearms), 7/12/64 at Ft. Stevens. Died of wounds, 8/17/64.
Pvt.	Hardy, Henry	1834	M	Merry Mount, Warren Co., NC	Overseer	Enlisted, 8/16/61. Died of smallpox, 2/17/63 at Guinea Station, VA.
Pvt.	Hardy, Thomas W.	1836	M	Grove Hill, Warren Co., NC	Farmer	Enlisted, 8/16/61. Discharged (sickness), 3/19/62. Re-enlisted, 2/20/63. TDY—light duty in Richmond, 6/1/63–3/12//65. Sick in hospital, 3/13/65. Did not return to regiment.
Pvt.	Harris, John N.	1833	M	Grove Hill, Warren Co., NC	Overseer	Enlisted, 8/16/61. Captured, 11/7/63 at Kelly's Ford. POW—Point Lookout, MD. Died of disease, 8/12/64.
Pvt.	Harris, David W.	1811	M	Warrenton, Warren Co., NC	Farmer	Enlisted, 8/16/61. Discharged (disability), 1/14/62.
Pvt.	Harriss, Joseph J. Jr.	1833	M	Warrenton, Warren Co., NC	Overseer	Enlisted, 8/16/61. Discharged (disability), 5/19/62.
Pvt.	Hundley, George W.	1844	S	Warrenton, Warren Co., NC	Farm Labor	Enlisted, 8/16/61. Promoted to Cpl., 1/1/63. Wounded, 5/3/64 at Chancellorsville. Captured, 11/7/63 at Kelly's Ford. POW—Point Lookout, MD. Exchanged, 3/3/65.
Pvt.	Kimball, Nathaniel	1826		Ridgeway, Warren Co., NC	Farmer	Enlisted, 8/16/61. Wounded, 9/17/62 at Sharpsburg. Wounded (right foot), 5/3/63 at Chancellorsville. Captured, 11/7/63 at Kelly's Ford. POW—Point Lookout, MD. Exchanged, 2/18/65.
Pvt.	King, John F.	1840	S	Warrenton, Warren Co., NC	Farm Labor	Enlisted, 8/16/61. Present until 8/31/64. No further records.
Pvt.	King, William A.	1840	S	Macon Depot, Warren Co., NC	Farm Labor	Enlisted, 8/16/61. TDY—Wagon train, 5/1/62–8/-/62. Died of typhoid fever, 9/8/62 at Richmond, VA.

Rank	Name	DOB	M/S	Residence	Occupation	Remarks
Pvt.	Kirkland, Stephen H.	1843	S	Merry Mount, Warren Co., NC	Farm Labor	Enlisted, 8/16/61. Captured, 11/7/63 at Kelly's Ford. POW—Point Lookout, MD. Died of disease, 8/11/64.
Pvt.	Loughlin, John	1834		Warren Co., NC		Enlisted, 8/16/61. Wounded, 7/1/62 at Malvern Hill. Wounded, 7/1/63 at Gettysburg. Deserted, 7/-/63 in retreat from Gettysburg.
Pvt.	Milam, Henry D.	1824	S	Warrenton, Warren Co., NC	Merchant's Asst.	Enlisted, 8/16/61. Discharged, 9/20/61
Pvt.	Neal, Dudley H.	1837	S	Grove Hill, Warren Co., NC	Farmer	Enlisted, 8/16/61. Wounded (leg), 7/1/62 at Malvern Hill. Wounded (both legs), 5/16/64 at Harris Farm. Retired from service due to wounds, 3/14/65.
Pvt.	Newsom, John G.	1845		Warren Co., NC		Enlisted, 8/16/61. Promoted to Cpl., 5/1/62. Wounded (right thigh), 7/1/62 at Malvern Hill. Promoted to 1st Sgt., 1/-/63. Wounded (right side), 5/3/63 at Chancellorsville. Wounded (head) & captured, 11/7/63 at Kelly's Ford. POW—Point Lookout, MD. Exchanged, 11/1/64. Surrendered, 4/9/65 at Appomattox.
Pvt.	Paschall, Samuel A.	1836		Warren Co., NC		Enlisted, 8/16/61. Promoted to Cpl., 5/1/62. Captured, 11/7/63 At Kelly's Ford. POW—Point Lookout, MD. Exchanged, 3/3/65.
Pvt.	**Patterson, Green R.**	**1826**	**S**	**Merry Mount, Warren Co., NC**	**Farm Labor**	**Enlisted, 8/16/61. Wounded, 5/3/63 at Chancellorsville. Died of wounds, 6/4/63 at Richmond.**
Pvt.	Paynter, Thomas P.	1826	M	Warrenton, Warren Co., NC	Farmer	Enlisted, 8/16/61. Discharged (disability), 1/14/62. Re-enlisted, 7/16/63. TDY—Shoemaker in Richmond, 9/17/63-2/28/65. Captured, 4/21/65 in Richmond hospital.
Pvt.	Pegram, Robert B.	1839	S	Warrenton, Warren Co., NC	Farm Labor	Enlisted, 8/16/61. Wounded (left thigh), 6/26/62 at Mechanicsville. Wounded (shoulder), 5/3/63 at Chancellorsville. TDY—Teamster at Ewell's HQ, 2/1/64-12/31/64. Surrendered, 4/9/65 at Appomattox.
Pvt.	Riggan, Charles D.	1832	M	Ridgeway, Warren Co., NC	Overseer	Enlisted, 8/16/61. Surrendered, 4/9/65 at Appomattox.
Pvt.	Riggan, Charles S.	1842	S	Warrenton, Warren Co., NC	Farm Labor	Enlisted, 8/16/61. Wounded (shrapnel; right arm), 5/12/64 at Spotsylvania. Wounded (shoulder), 10/19/64 at Cedar Creek. Surrendered, 4/9/65 at Appomattox.
Pvt.	Riggan, Minga E.	1837	S	Macon Depot, Warren Co., NC	Railroad Labor	Enlisted, 8/16/61. Discharged (fractured arm), 12/14/61.
Pvt.	**Robertson, Peter E.**	**1836**	**S**	**Warrenton, Warren Co., NC**	**Farm Labor**	**Enlisted, 8/16/61. Promoted to Cpl., 5/1/62. Wounded, 9/17/62 at Sharpsburg. TDY—Recruiting detail in Warren Co., 5/1/63 to 7/31/63. Died of disease, 12/1/62 at Lynchburg, VA.**
Pvt.	Rose, Lewis D.	1841	S	Warrenton, Warren Co., NC	Farm Labor	Enlisted, 8/16/61. Discharged (sickness), 5/19/62
Pvt.	Saintsing, John A.	1839	S	Warrenton, Warren Co., NC	Farm Labor	Enlisted, 8/16/61. Wounded (right shoulder), 5/12/64 at Spotsylvania. Surrendered, 4/9/65 at Appomattox.
Pvt.	Salmon, Henry	1815	M	Warrenton, Warren Co., NC	Farm Labor	Enlisted, 8/16/61. Discharged (over age), 12/2/62.

Appendix 2

Rank	Name	DOB	M/S	Residence	Occupation	Remarks
Pvt.	Shearin, Gardiner E.	1838	M	Warrenton, Warren Co., NC	Farmer	Enlisted, 8/16/61. Captured, 11/7/63 at Kelly's Ford. POW—Point Lookout, MD. Exchanged, 2/21/65.
Pvt.	Shearin, Jacob J.	1825	M	Grove Hill, Warren Co., NC	Overseer	Enlisted, 8/16/61. Discharged (disability), 1/22/63.
Pvt.	Shearin, John L.	1842	S	Warren Co., NC		Enlisted, 8/16/61. Discharged (debility), 5/22/62. Re-enlisted, 7/16/63. Captured, 11/7/63 at Kelly's Ford. POW—Point Lookout, MD. Exchanged, 5/8/64. Wounded, 9/19/64 at Winchester. Wounded (face), 4/9/65 at Appomattox.
Pvt.	Shearin, John R.	1831	M	Merry Mount, Warren Co., NC	Carpenter	Enlisted, 8/16/61. Missing, 4/8/65 near Appomattox.
Pvt.	Shearin, Moses T.	1839		Warren Co., NC		Enlisted, 8/16/61. TDY—Provost Guard at Staunton, VA, 3/1/64–4/9/65. Paroled, 4/23/65 at Ashland, VA.
Pvt.	**Shearin, Richard R.**	**1824**	**M**	**Grove Hill, Warren Co., NC**	**Overseer**	**Enlisted, 8/16/61. Killed, 6/27/62 at Gaines' Mill.**
Pvt.	**Shearin, Thomas G.**	**1839**		**Warren Co., NC**		**Enlisted, 8/16/61. Wounded, 9/17/62 at Sharpsburg. Wounded, 5/3/63 at Chancellorsville. Promoted to Sgt., 6/1/64. Killed, 7/12/64 at Ft. Stevens.**
Pvt.	Shearin, Thomas W.	1843		Warren Co., NC		Enlisted, 8/16/61. Promoted to Cpl., 5/1/62. Wounded (right thigh), 5/12/64 at Spotsylvania. Surrendered, 4/9/65 at Appomattox.
Pvt.	**Smith, George W.**	**1817**		**Warren Co., NC**		**Enlisted, 8/16/61. Died of chronic diarrhea, 1/16/63 at Richmond.**
Pvt.	Stallings, Theophilus	1830	M	Merry Mount, Warren Co., NC	Farmer	Enlisted, 9/26/61. Promoted to Qtr. Mstr. Sgt., 10/16/61. Transferred to F & S.
Pvt.	**Talley, Benjamin T.**	**1842**	**S**	**Merry Mount, Warren Co., NC**	**Farm Labor**	**Enlisted, 9/26/61. Died of chronic diarrhea, 2/23/63 at Lynchburg, VA.**
Pvt.	**Thomas, George L.**	**1841**	**S**	**Warrenton, Warren Co., NC**	**Farm Labor**	**Enlisted, 8/16/61. Died of disease, 9/25/62 at Leesburg, VA.**
Pvt.	Thomas, William H.	1839	S	Littleton, Warren Co., NC	Shoe Maker's Asst.	Enlisted, 8/16/61. Wounded, 4/30/63 near Fredericksburg. TDY—Nurse in Richmond hospital, 2/1/64–4/3/65. Captured, 4/3/65 at Richmond.
Pvt.	**Thompson, John A.**	**1832**	**S**	**Warrenton, Warren Co., NC**	**Farm Labor**	**Enlisted, 8/16/61. Wounded (arm), 6/27/62 at Gaines' Mill. Died of wounds, 7/30/62 at Richmond.**
Pvt.	Turner, Henry	1823		Warren Co., NC		Enlisted, 8/16/61. Discharged, 9/28/61.
Pvt.	Walker, Christopher N.	1840		Warren Co., NC		Enlisted, 8/16/61. Surrendered, 4/9/65 at Appomattox.
Pvt.	**Walker, Levi**	**1836**	**S**	**Merry Mount, Warren Co., NC**	**Farm Labor**	**Enlisted, 8/16/61. Died of typhoid fever, 11/1/62 at Petersburg, VA.**
Pvt.	**White, James J.**	**1842**	**S**	**Merry Mount, Warren Co., NC**	**Farm Labor**	**Enlisted, 8/16/61. Wounded, 7/1/62 at Malvern Hill. Died of wounds, 8/1/62 at Richmond,**
Pvt.	Williams, William Al.	1838		Warren Co., NC		Enlisted, 8/16/61. Discharged (sickness), 8/20/62.

1861 Recruits

Rank	Name	DOB	M/S	Residence	Occupation	Remarks
Pvt.	Gregory, Lawrence B.	1845	S	Enfield, Halifax Co., NC	Student	Transferred from 12th NC Inf., 12/19/61. TDY—Ambulance driver, 5/1/62–7/25/62. Discharged (under age), 7/26/62.
Pvt.	Shearin, Nicholas L.	1828	M	Macon Depot, Warren Co., NC	Farmer	Enlisted, 12/6/61. Killed, 7/1/62 at Malvern Hill.

1862 Recruits/Conscripts

Rank	Name	DOB	M/S	Residence	Occupation	Remarks
Pvt.	Bobbitt, E. Fletcher	1829	M	Warrenton, Warren Co., NC	Farmer	Enlisted, 4/28/62. Died of typhoid fever, 10/23/62 at Richmond, VA.
Pvt.	Borgus, Reuben	1834		Wilkes Co., NC		Conscripted, 11/21/61. Captured, 11/7/63 at Kelly's Ford. POW—Point Lookout, MD. Paroled, 5/6/64. No further records.
Pvt.	Buff, Peter	1837	S	Cleveland Co., NC	Farm Labor	Conscripted, 9/21/62. Captured, 11/4/62 near Paris, VA. Paroled, 11/9/62. Wounded, 5/3/63 at Chancellorsville. Wounded, 5/12/64 at Spotsylvania. Home on wounded furlough. No records after 8/31/64.
Pvt.	Buff, William	1832	M	Cleveland Co., NC	Farmer	Conscripted, 9/1/62. Deserted, 6/11/63 near Front Royal, VA. Discharged, 4/1/64.
Pvt.	Cockerham, James B.			Wilkes Co., NC		Conscripted, 9/21/62. Absent, sick, 11/7/62, "sent to hospital ... not heard from again."
Pvt.	Collins, David	1834	S	Warrenton, Warren Co., NC	Plow Maker's Asst.	Transferred from 46th NC Inf., 10/8/62. Captured, 11/7/63 at Kelly's Ford. POW—Point Lookout, MD. Exchanged, 3/15/65.
Pvt.	Harriss, George W.	1833	M	Macon Depot, Warren Co., NC	Carpenter	Enlisted, 1/2/62. Deserted, 5/2/63. Returned to duty, 9/29/63. In Richmond hospital, 5/13/64–4/9/65. Paroled at Richmond, 4/18/65.
Pvt.	Harriss, John W.	1832	M	Warrenton, Warren Co., NC	Farmer	Enlisted, 4/28/62. Surrendered, 4/9/65 at Appomattox.
Pvt.	Harriss, William L.	1847	S	Macon Depot, Warren Co., NC	Farm labor	Enlisted, 4/28/62. Captured, 8/9/64 at Bunker Hill. POW—Elmira, NY. Released, 7/7/65.
Pvt.	Myrick, William W.	1825	M	Grove Hill, Warren Co., NC	Overseer	Enlisted, 4/10/62. Wounded, 9/17/62 at Sharpsburg. Captured, 7/5/63 during retreat from Gettysburg (So. Mountain). POW—Point Lookout, MD. Died of smallpox, 2/4/64.
Pvt.	Pegram, George W.	1832	S	Warrenton, Warren Co., NC	Farm Labor	Enlisted, 4/19/62. Died of tonsillitis, 8/29/62 at Lynchburg, VA.
Pvt.	Pegram, James B.	1838	S	Warrenton, Warren Co., NC	Farm Labor	Enlisted, 1/28/62. Wounded, 6/27/62 at Gaines' Mill. Died of hemorrhage of the bowels, 12/25/63 at Orange Court House, VA.
Pvt.	Pegram, John J.	1844	S	Warrenton, Warren Co., NC	Farm Labor	Enlisted, 3/21/62. Captured, 9/13/62 at Frederick, MD. Exchanged, 10/2/62. Returned to duty, 8/-/63. Captured, 11/7/63 at Kelly's Ford. POW—Point Lookout, MD. Exchanged, 4/30/64. Wounded (left arm), 1/-/65 in Petersburg trenches.
Pvt.	Riggan, Sugar A.	1821	M	Merry Mount, Warren Co., NC	Miller	Enlisted, 4/14/62. Captured, 5/12/64 at Spotsylvania. POW—Elmira, NY. Died of chronic diarrhea, 11/29/64.

Rank	Name	DOB	M/S	Residence	Occupation	Remarks
Pvt.	Shearin, Edwin C.	1838	S	Warrenton, Warren Co., NC	Farm Labor	Enlisted, 4/17/62. Died of typhoid fever, 11/4/62 at Richmond, VA.
Pvt.	Shearin, Landon T.	1843		Warren Co., NC		Enlisted, 1/8/62. Captured, 7/4/63 near Gettysburg. POW—Point Lookout, MD. Died of pneumonia, 2/25/65.
Pvt.	Shearin, Richard E.	1830	M	Grove Hill, Warren Co., NC	Farmer	Enlisted, 4/14/62. Captured, 11/30/62 at Mine Run. POW—Point Lookout, MD. Released, 2/3/65. Joined the U.S. Army.
Pvt.	Stallings, John A.	1834		Warren Co., NC		Enlisted, 4/28/62. Died of typhoid fever, 11/13/62 at Staunton, VA.
Pvt.	Williams, William A.	1845	S	Warrenton, Warren Co., NC	Farm Labor	Enlisted, 11/3/62. Captured, 11/7/63 at Kelly's Ford. POW—Point Lookout, MD. Exchanged, 5/8/64. Killed, 8/21/64 at Charles Town.

1863 Conscripts

Rank	Name	DOB	M/S	Residence	Occupation	Remarks
Pvt.	Bell, Robert M.	1830	S	Piney Grove, Sampson Co., NC	Farmer	Conscripted, 7/28/63. Deserted, 8/1/63.
Pvt.	Brinkley, Thomas H.	1835	S	Raleigh, Wake Co., NC	Farm Labor	Conscripted, 7/1/63. Deserted, 8/1/63.
Pvt.	Brown, William E.	1825	M	Merry Mt., Warren Co., NC	Farmer	Conscripted, 7/16/63. TDY—Corps HQ; Provost Guard, 1/1/64–4/9/65. Surrendered, 4/9/65 at Appomattox.
Pvt.	Collins, Stogdon	1813	S	Warrenton, Warren Co., NC	Farmer	Conscripted, 3/15/63. Died of disease, 6/3/63 at Hamilton's Crossing, VA.
Pvt.	Dickerson, George	1823	S	Louisburg, Franklin Co., NC	Farmer	Conscripted, 9/2/63. Sent to hospital, 11/18/63. Absent, sick until 3/31/64. No further records.
Pvt.	Finch, Ira J.	1827	M	Warrenton, Warren Co., NC	Overseer	Conscripted, 7/16/63. Captured, 8/10/64 near Winchester. POW—Elmira, NY. Exchanged, 3/5/65.
Pvt.	Gladstone, D. S.			Wake Co., NC		Conscripted, 7/11/63. Discharged, 4/26/64.
Pvt.	Hobbs, Monti V.	1830	M	Greensboro, Guilford Co., NC	Farmer	Conscripted, 7/11/63. Sick in hospital in Richmond. Captured, 4/3/65 at Richmond. Released, 6/16/65.
Pvt.	Insco, William	1836	M	Louisburg, Franklin Co., NC	Farmer	Conscripted, 9/30/63. Captured, 11/7/63 at Kelly's Ford. POW—Point Lookout, MD. Exchanged, 3/3/65.
Pvt.	Jackson, Marion J.	1823	S	Louisburg, Franklin Co., NC	Farm Labor	Conscripted, 9/4/63. Wounded (left foot), 10/12/63 at Bristoe Station (foot amputated).
Pvt.	North, Joshua	1826	S	Wentworth, Rockingham Co., NC	Farm Labor	Conscripted, 5/23/63. Wounded, 5/8/64 at Spotsylvania. Surrendered, 4/9/65 at Appomattox.
Pvt.	Pegram, Mitchell S.	1845	S	Warrenton, Warren Co., NC	Stock Clerk	Enlisted, 2/19/63. TDY—Orderly for Gen. Ramseur, 5/1/63–11/30/63. Wounded (left foot & right knee), 5/12/64 at Spotsylvania. Retired (due to wounds), 3/14/65.
Pvt.	Riggan, Isham S.	1822	M	Warrenton, Warren Co., NC	Overseer	Conscripted, 7/16/63. Captured, 5/12/64 at Spotsylvania. POW—Elmira, NY. Died of typhoid fever, 9/27/64.
Pvt.	Shearin, Joseph W.	1846		Warren Co., NC		Conscripted, 4/18/63. Discharged (provided a substitute), 6/1/63.

Rank	Name	DOB	M/S	Residence	Occupation	Remarks
Pvt.	Stallings, Elisha B	1825		Edgecombe Co., NC		Conscripted, 7/1/63. TDY—Hospital nurse in Richmond, 9/1/63–12/31/64. No further records.
Pvt.	**Verser, John**	**1820**	**M**	**Warrenton, Warren Co., NC**	**Farmer**	**Conscripted, 9/1/63. Died of chronic diarrhea, 12/22/63 at Richmond.**
Pvt.	Wimberly, Matthew	1842	S	Morrisville, Wake Co., NC	Farm Labor	Conscripted, 7/23/63. Deserted, 8/15/63.

1864 Conscripts

Rank	Name	DOB	M/S	Residence	Occupation	Remarks
Pvt.	Cloyd, J. M.	1825	M	Lenoir, Caldwell Co., NC	Brick Mason	Conscripted, 7/–/64. Captured, 10/19/64 at hospital in Harrisburg. POW—Point Lookout, MD. Exchanged, 3/30/65.
Pvt.	Miles, James	1830	M	Greensboro, Guilford Co., NC	Day Labor	Conscripted, 9/–/64. Captured, 4/6/65 near High Branch. Released, 6/29/65.

Company C—Brunswick Double Quicks
Brunswick County (Mustered into Regt.—7/18/61)

Rank	Name	DOB	M/S	Residence	Occupation	Remarks
Cpt.	Green, Joseph	1816	M	Northwest, Brunswick Co., NC	Farmer	Enlisted, 7/18/61. Not re-elected at re-organization, 5/1/62.
1st Lt.	Allen, David, C.	1836	S	Black Rock, Brunswick Co., NC	Farmer	Enlisted, 7/17/61. Elected Cpt., 5/1/62. Wounded (left shoulder), 9/19/64 at Winchester. Surrendered, 4/9/65 at Appomattox.
2nd Lt.	Tharp, Samuel P.	1837	S	Smithville, Brunswick Co., NC	Teacher	Enrolled, 7/18/61. Not re-elected, 5/1/62.
3rd Lt.	**Cain, Lorenzo D.**	**1829**	**S**	**Bladen, Brunswick Co., NC**	**Teacher**	**Enrolled, 7/17/61. Died of typhoid fever, 8/13/62 at Richmond.**
1st Sgt.	Swain, John R.	1839	S	Smithville, Brunswick Co., NC	Farm Labor	Enlisted, 9/26/61. Promoted to 2nd Lt., 9/23/62. Captured, 5/12/64 at Spotsylvania. POW—Ft. Delaware, DE. Released, 6/16/65.
2nd Sgt.	**Edwards, William H.**	**1840**	**M**	**Shallotte, Brunswick Co., NC**	**Farmer**	**Enlisted, 7/18/61. Killed, 9/17/62 at Sharpsburg.**
3rd Sgt.	Dosher, James H.	1843	S	Smithville, Brunswick Co., NC	Farm Labor	Enlisted, 7/18/61. Reduced to Pvt., 5/1/62. Wounded, 9/17/62 at Sharpsburg. Promoted to 3rd Lt., 1/13/63. Transferred to 20th NC Inf., 2/5/64.
4th Sgt.	Swain, Benjamin F.	1843	S	Smithville, Brunswick Co., NC	Farm Labor	Enlisted, 7/18/61. Reduced to Pvt., 5/1/62. Wounded (left arm), 6/27/62 at Gaines' Mill. Promoted to Cpl., 1/–/63. Transferred to C.S. Navy, 4/5/64.
5th Sgt.	Butler, Benjamin L.	1836	S	Waccamaw, Brunswick Co, NC	Farm Labor	Enlisted, 7/18/61. Wounded (foot), 7/1/62 at Malvern Hill. TDY—Hospital duty, 10/1/62–6/30/63. Paroled at Appomattox, 4/9/65.
1st Cpl.	Smith, Benjamin	1837	S	Shallotte, Brunswick Co., NC	Overseer	Enlisted, 7/18/61. Wounded (jaw), 7/1/63, and Captured, 7/4/63 at Gettysburg. POW—David's Island, NY. Exchanged, 9/8/63. Captured, 9/22/64 at Fisher's Hill. POW—Point Lookout, MD. Released, 6/3/65.
2nd Cpl.	Wescott, John W.	1834	S	Smithville, Brunswick Co., NC	Overseer	Enlisted, 7/18/61. Promoted to Sgt., 5/1/62. Captured, 9/17/62 at Sharpsburg. POW—Point Lookout, MD. Exchanged, 11/2/62. Captured, 9/19/64 at Winchester. POW—Point Lookout, MD. Died of diease, 1/25/65.

Appendix 2

Rank	Name	DOB	M/S	Residence	Occupation	Remarks
3rd Cpl.	Swain, George T.	1842	S	Smithville, Brunswick Co., NC	Farm Labor	Enlisted, 7/18/61. Reduced to Pvt., 5/1/62. Wounded, 7/1/63 at Gettysburg. Died of wounds, 7/3/63. "Acted very gallantly at Gettysburg."
4th Cpl.	Dew, David C.	1841	S	Lockwood's Folly, Brunswick Co., NC	Merchant's Asst.	Enlisted, 7/18/61. Reduced to Pvt., 12/25/61. Wounded, 7/1/62 at Malvern Hill. Captured, 11/7/63 at Kelly's Ford. POW—Point Lookout, MD. Exchanged, 3/16/65.
Music	Penny, Benjamin F.	1843	S	Brunswick Co., NC		Enlisted (drummer), 7/18/61. Transferred to the C.S. Navy, 9/3/63.
Music	Wescott, Henry A.	1841	S	Smithville, Brunswick Co., NC	Farm Labor	Enlisted, (fifer) 7/18/61. Promoted to Sgt., 3/1/63. Transferred to C.S. Navy, 4/5/64.
Pvt.	Bell, John	1814	M	Smithville, Brunswick Co, NC	Day Labor	Enlisted, 9/2/61. No records after, 8/31/64.
Pvt.	Bennett, Solomon W.	1832		Brunswick Co., NC		Enrolled, 7/18/61. Elected, 2nd Lt., 5/1/62. Promoted to 1st Lt., 8/1/62. Wounded (left elbow), 5/3/63 at Chancellorsville. TDY—Recruiting officer in Brunswick Co., NC, 11/1/63–12/64/64.
Pvt.	Benton, Thomas A.	1839	M	Lockwood's Folly, Brunswick Co, NC	Farmer	Enlisted, 9/2/61. Discharged, 12/-/61 (provided a substitute).
Pvt.	Bowers, John	1817	S	Greenville, Pitt Co, NC	Farmer	Enlisted, 9/2/61. Discharged (for larceny), 3/21/62.
Pvt.	Burns, Ottoway J.	1841	S	Northwest, Brunswick Co, NC	Overseer	Enlisted, 7/20/61. Promoted to Cpl., 12/23/61. Transferred to 41st NC Inf., 6/1/62.
Pvt.	Butler, John C.	1840	S	Maccamaw, Brunswick Co, NC	Farm Labor	Enlisted, 7/18/61. Wounded (face), 12/13/62 at Fredericksburg. Captured, 5/12/64 at Spotsylvania. POW—Elmira, NY. Died of Smallpox, 1/4/65.
Pvt.	Byrd, John	1844	S	Northwest, Brunswick Co., NC	Farm Labor	Enlisted, 9/2/61. Died of Typhoid Fever & Pneumonia, 4/21/63 at Richmond.
Pvt.	Chimis, Michael H.	1844	S	Smithville, Brunswick Co., NC	Farm Labor	Enlisted, 7/18/61. Died of Meningitis, 10/13/61 at Smithville, NC.
Pvt.	Cliff, Edward	1820	M	Town Creek, Brunswick Co., NC	Distiller	Enlisted, 9/2/61. Died of Meningitis, 12/30/61 at Camp Wyatt, NC.
Pvt.	Cliff, John	1846	S	Town Creek, Brunswick Co., NC	Distiller's Asst.	Enlisted, 7/18/61. Died of Typhoid Fever & Pneumonia, 4/23/63 at Richmond.
Pvt.	Coleman, Etheldred "Dred"	1837	S	Town Creek, Brunswick Co, NC	Farm labor	Enlisted, 9/2/61. Paroled, 4/9/65 at Appomattox.
Pvt.	Coleman, John C.	1836		Brunswick Co., NC		Enlisted, 9/2/61. Died of fever, 8/20/62 at Richmond.
Pvt.	Colman, George W.	1834		Brunswick Co, NC		Enlisted, 9/2/61. Wounded (hip) & captured, 9/17/62 at Sharpsburg. No further records.
Pvt.	Colman, James	1830	M	Lockwood's Folly, Brunswick Co., NC	Farmer	Enlisted, 9/2/61. Deserted, 1/1/64. Court Martialed, 2/12/64. Captured, 4/12/64 at Spotsylvania. POW—Point Lookout, MD. Exchanged, 11/15/64.

Rank	Name	DOB	M/S	Residence	Occupation	Remarks
Pvt.	Corbett, Wesley	1842	S	New Hanover Co., NC	Farm Labor	Enlisted, 9/2/61. Discharged (sickness), 2/7/62.
Pvt.	**Dail, Benjamin**	**1843**	**S**	**Smithville, Brunswick Co., NC**	**Farm Labor**	**Enlisted, 9/2/61. TDY—NC artillery, 2/-/62-6/-/62. Died of fever, 8/12/63 at Gordonsville, VA.**
Pvt.	Danford, Abram	1841	S	Smithville, Brunswick Co., NC	Farm Labor	Enlisted, 7/18/61. Wounded (face), 6/27/64 at Gaines' Mill. TDY—Nurse at Weldon hospital, from 2/21/63-12/31/64. Paroled, 4/9/65 at Appomattox.
Pvt.	Danford, John W.	1837	S	Town Creek, Brunswick Co, NC	Farm Labor	Enlisted, 9/2/61. Captured, 11/7/63 at Kelly's Ford. POW—Point Lookout, MD. Exchanged, 2/14/65.
Pvt.	Drew, John T.	1839	S	Town Creek, Brunswick Co, NC	Farm Labor	Enlisted, 9/5/61. Discharged (insanity), 4/-/62.
Pvt.	Flynn, James W.	1843	S	Beaver Island, Stokes Co., NC	Farm Labor	Enlisted, 9/2/61. Wounded, 7/1/62 at Malvern Hill. TDY—Pioneer, 8/1/63-11/30/63. No records after 8/31/64.
Pvt.	**Gore, John**	**1828**	**M**	**Shallotte, Brunswick Co., NC**	**Farmer**	**Enlisted, 7/18/61. Killed, 5/3/63 at Chancellorsville.**
Pvt.	Green, William B.	1842	S	Northwest, Brunswick Co., NC	Farm Labor	Enlisted, 7/18/61. Transferred to 41st NC Inf., 6/1/62.
Pvt.	**Greer, Ephraim J.**	**1833**	**S**	**Lockwood's Folly, Brunswick Co., NC**	**Teacher**	**Enlisted, 9/2/61. Elected, 1st Lt., 5/1/62. Wounded, 7/1/62 at Malvern Hill. Died of wounds, 7/26/62 at Richmond.**
Pvt.	**Greer, Lewis T.**	**1839**	**S**	**Lockwood's Folly,Brunswick Co., NC**	**Farm Labor**	**Enlisted, 9/2/61. Promoted to Cpl., 2/16/63. Killed, 5/3/63 at Chancellorsville.**
Pvt.	**Harris, Geo. Washington**	**1844**	**S**	**Smithville, Brunswick Co., NC**	**Farm Labor**	**Enlisted, 7/18/61. Wounded (knee), 7/1/62 at Malvern Hill. Died of wounds, 7/19/62 at Richmond, VA.**
Pvt.	**Hart, Obediah**	**1823**	**M**	**Smithville, Brunswick Co., NC**	**Steam Mill Labor**	**Enlisted, 7/18/61. Died of typhoid fever, 9/28/62 at Richmond,VA.**
Pvt.	Harvell, James M.	1842	S	Town Creek, Brunswick Co., NC	Farm Labor	Enlisted, 7/18/61. Captured, 11/7/63 at Kelly's Ford. POW—Point Lookout, MD. Exchanged, 3/14/65.
Pvt.	**Harvell, John V.**	**1841**	**S**	**Town Creek, Brunswick Co., NC**	**Farm Labor**	**Enlisted, 9/2/61. Wounded, 9/16/62 at Sharpsburg. Died of wounds, 10/7/62 at Staunton, VA.**
Pvt.	Hewett, Lorenzo D.	1843	S	Shallotte, Brunswick Co., NC	Farm Labor	Enlisted, 9/2/61. Captured, 11/7/63 at Kelly's Ford. POW—Point Lookout, MD. Exchanged, 9/30/64. No further records after 11/30/64.
Pvt.	**Hewett, Samuel M.**	**1840**	**S**	**Lockwood's Folly,Brunswick Co., NC**	**Farm Labor**	**Enlisted, 9/2/61. Killed, 7/1/63 at Gettysburg.**
Pvt.	**Hewett, Uriah**	**1838**	**S**	**Lockwood's Folly,Brunswick Co., NC**	**Farm Labor**	**Enlisted, 9/12/61. Wounded, 7/1/62 at Malvern Hill. Died of wounds, 7/12/62 at Richmond, VA.**
Pvt.	**Hickman, Benjamin R.**	**1831**		**Brunswick Co., NC**		**Enlisted, 7/18/61. Died of pneumonia, 5/12/63 at Richmond,VA.**

Rank	Name	DOB	M/S	Residence	Occupation	Remarks
Pvt.	Hickman, Robert	1828		Brunswick Co., NC		Enlisted, 9/2/61. Wounded, 7/1/62 at Malvern Hill. Captured, 5/8/64 at Spotsylvania. POW—Elmira, NY. Died of pneumonia, 12/6/64.
Pvt.	Howard, Geo. Washington			Smithville, Brunswick Co., NC	Farm Labor	Enlisted, 7/18/61. Promoted to Cpl., 5/1/62. Wounded, 6/27/62 at Gaines' Mill. Promoted to Sgt., 1/-/63. Wounded (right thigh), 7/18/64 at Snicker's Gap. No further records after 8/31/64.
Pvt.	Howard, John J.	1840	S	Smithville, Brunswick Co., NC	Farm Labor	Enlisted, 9/2/61. Captured, 9/17/62 at Sharpsburg. Paroled, 9/21/62. No further records.
Pvt.	Jenkins, Joseph S.	1842	S	Smithville, Brunswick Co., NC	Miller's Asst.	Enlisted, 7/18/61. TDY—Hospital guard at Lynchburg, 5/1/63–3/31/64. Transferred to C.S. Navy, 4/5/64.
Pvt.	Lambeth, William	1828	M	Asheboro, Randolph Co., NC	Farm Labor	Enlisted, 9/2/61. Promoted to Cpl., 5/1/62. Wounded, 7/1/62 at Malvern Hill. Discharged (disability), 2/4/63. Re-enlisted as Pvt., 7/1/63. No records after 8/31/64.
Pvt.	Larkins, Robert S.	1839	S	Northwest, Brunswick Co., NC	Farm Labor	Enlisted, 7/18/61. Wounded, 7/1/62 at Malvern Hill. Surrendered at Appomattox, 4/9/65.
Pvt.	Leonard, Samuel B.	1844	S	Shallotte, Brunswick Co., NC	Farm Labor	Enlisted, 7/18/61. Promoted to Cpl., 5/1/62. Wounded (chest), 7/1/62 at Malvern Hill. Discharged (wounds), 10/-/62.
Pvt.	**McCall, John W.**	**1830**	**S**	**Waccamaw, Brunswick Co., NC**	**Farm Labor**	**Enlisted, 9/2/61. Killed, 6/27/62 at Gaines' Mill.**
Pvt.	McCall, Paul S.	1839	S	Waccamaw, Brunswick Co., NC	Farm Labor	Enlisted, 7/18/61. Wounded, 7/1/62 at Malvern Hill. Captured, 11/7/63 at Kelly's Ford. POW—Point Lookout, MD. Exchanged, 3/3/65.
Pvt.	McDowell, William J.	1843	S	Brunswick Co., NC	Farm Labor	Enlisted, 7/18/61. Promoted to Cpl., 1/-/64. Wounded (both feet), 8/21/64 at Charles Town. Retired due to wounds, 3/14/65. "Nominated for the Badge of Distinction for gallantry at Chancellorsville, 5/3/63."
Pvt.	**Maltsby, William J.**	**1841**	**S**	**West Brook, Bladen Co., NC**	**Student**	**Enlisted, 9/2/61. Died of pneumonia, 10/11/61 at Wilmington, NC.**
Pvt.	Marshall, William D.	1845	S	New Hanover Co., NC	Blacksmith's Asst.	Enlisted, 7/18/61. Promoted to Cpl., 5/1/62. Captured, 5/12/64 at Spotsylvania. POW—Elmira, NY. Released, 6/23/65.
Pvt.	Milliken, Isaac	1837	M	Waccamaw, Brunswick Co., NC	Day Labor	Enlisted, 7/18/61. Wounded (left hand), 7/1/62 at Malvern Hill. Promoted to Sgt., 9/23/62, "for good conduct at Sharpsburg." Promoted to 1st Sgt., 1/-/63. Captured 5/12/64 at Spotsylvania. POW—Elmira, NY. Released, 6/23/65.
Pvt.	Mints, Jesse O.	1836	S	Town Creek, Brunswick Co., NC	Farm Labor	Enlisted, 7/18/61. Discharged (disability), 11/-/61.
Pvt.	**Pilgreen, McGilbert**	**1843**	**S**	**Shallotte, Brunswick Co., NC**	**Farm Labor**	**Enlisted, 7/18/61. Missing, 12/13/62 at Fredericksburg. Died of disease, 6/20/63 at Summerville Ford, VA.**
Pvt.	**Pilgreen, William H.**	**1842**	**S**	**Shallotte, Brunswick Co., NC**	**Farm Labor**	**Enlisted, 9/2/61. Killed, 5/12/64 at Spotsylvania.**

30th North Carolina Infantry Roster, Company C

Rank	Name	DOB	M/S	Residence	Occupation	Remarks
Pvt.	Potter, Henry G.	1846	S	Colvin's Creek, New Hanover Co., NC	Farm Labor	Enlisted, 9/2/61. Wounded, 7/1/62 at Malvern Hill. Died of typhoid fever, 11/10/62 at Staunton, VA.
Pvt.	Potter, William M.	1842	S	Colvin's Creek, New Hanover Co., NC	Farm Labor	Enlisted, 9/2/61. Discharged (disability), 12/-/61.
Pvt.	Pridgeon, Alexander S.	1824	M	Joyner's Depot, Nash Co., NC	Farm Labor	Enlisted, 9/2/61. Deserted, 12/-/61.
Pvt.	Register, Thomas	1832	M	Shallotte, Brunswick Co., NC	Farmer	Enlisted, 7/18/61. Died of smallpox, 11/24/62 at Staunton, VA. "A true man and brave soldier."
Pvt.	Robinson, Alexander S.	1837	M	Wilmington, New Hanover Co., NC	Farmer	Enlisted, 7/18/61. Wounded (face), 7/1/63 & Captured, 7/4/63 at Gettysburg. POW—Point Lookout, MD. Exchanged, 3/6/64. Promoted to Cpl., 6/1/64. Paroled, 4/9/65 at Appomattox.
Pvt.	Ruark, Edward R.	1838	S	Smithville, Brunswick Co., NC	Farm Labor	Enlisted, 7/18/61. Promoted to Sgt., 5/1/62. Promoted to 3rd Lt., 9/23/62. Died of Smallpox, 1/2/63 in Smithville, NC.
Pvt.	Russ, Stewart	1834	M	Waccamaw, Brunswick Co., NC	Day Labor	Enlisted, 9/2/61. Wounded, 6/27/62 at Gaines' Mill. Promoted to Cpl., 12/-/62. Promoted to Sgt., 2/-/63. Captured, 11/7/63 at Kelly's Ford. POW—Point Lookout, MD. Exchanged, 3/3/65.
Pvt.	Sellers, Raymond G.	1843	S	Town Creek, Brunswick Co., NC	Farm Labor	Enlisted, 7/18/61. Died of fever, 10/18/61 at Smithville, NC.
Pvt.	Sellers, Samuel H.	1803	M	Roberson, Brunswick Co., NC	Day Labor	Enlisted, 7/18/61. Died of mumps, 1/28/62 at Roberson, NC.
Pvt.	Simmons, Daniel	1840	S	Shallotte, Brunswick Co., NC	Farm Labor	Enlisted, 7/18/61. No further records after 8/31/64.
Pvt.	Simmons, Daniel F.	1845	S	Shallotte, Brunswick Co., NC	Farm Labor	Enlisted, 7/18/61. Died of erysipelas, 6/25/62 at Wilmington, NC.
Pvt.	Simmons, James A.	1835	M	Shallotte, Brunswick Co., NC	Day Labor	Enlisted, 7/18/61. Deserted from Richmond hospital, 1/-/63.
Pvt.	Simmons, John B.	1835	S	Shallotte, Brunswick Co., NC	Day Labor	Enlisted, 7/18/61. Killed, 5/3/63 at Chancellorsville.
Pvt.	Simmons, John C.	1839	M	Shallotte, Brunswick Co., NC	Day Labor	Enlisted, 7/18/61. Died of pneumonia, 10/11/61 at Wilmington, NC.
Pvt.	Stalvey, Benjamin L.	1843	S	Brunswick Co., NC	Farm Labor	Enlisted, 7/18/61. Died of pneumonia, 9/29/61 in Brunswick Co., NC.
Pvt.	Stanly, Edward W.	1824	M	Shallotte, Brunswick Co., NC	Day labor	Enlisted, 7/18/61. Died of pneumonia, 11/24/61 at Shallotte, NC.
Pvt.	Stanly, Peter	1830	M	Shallotte, Brunswick Co., NC	Day labor	Enlisted, 7/18/61. Wounded, 5/3/63 at Chancellorsville. Died of wounds, 5/7/63.

Rank	Name	DOB	M/S	Residence	Occupation	Remarks
Pvt.	Stanly, Samuel J.	1836	M	Shallotte, Brunswick Co., NC	Day labor	Enlisted, 7/18/61. Died of tuberculosis, 3/9/62 at Shallotte, NC.
Pvt.	Stanly, Stewart	1840	S	Shallotte, Brunswick Co., NC	Day labor	Gaines' Mill. Died of meningitis, 12/14/62 at Port Royal, VA.
Pvt.	Stanly, William F.	1839	S	Shallotte, Brunswick Co., NC	Day labor	Enlisted, 7/18/61. Transferred to 20th NC Inf., 10/-/61.
Pvt.	Tharp, John L.	1839	S	Smithville, Brunswick Co., NC	Teacher	Enlisted, 7/18/61. Promoted to Sgt., 5/1/62. Wounded (left hand), 7/1/62 at Malvern Hill. TDY—Clerk at HQ in Wilmington, NC, 1/1/64–11/30/64. No further records.
Pvt.	Tharp, William H.	1842	S	Smithville, Brunswick Co., NC	Farm Labor	Enlisted, 7/18/61. Wounded, 7/1/62 at Malvern Hill. Died of typhoid pneumonia, 5/3/63 at Richmond, VA.
Pvt.	Vines, William T.	1844	S	Town Creek, Brunswick Co., NC	Day Labor	Enlisted, 7/18/61. Wounded (right hand), 5/3/63 at Chancellorsville. Surrendered, 4/9/65 at Appomattox.
Pvt.	Wanett, William A.	1832	S	Robesons, Brunswick Co., NC	Farmer	Enlisted, 7/18/61. Killed, 5/12/64 at Spotsylvania.
Pvt.	Wescott, Samuel W.	1838	S	Smithville, Brunswick Co., NC	Farm Labor	Enlisted, 7/18/61. Wounded, 7/1/62 at Malvern Hill. Died of pneumonia, 4/3/63 at Richmond, VA.
Pvt.	Wescott, William H.	1841	S	Smithville, Brunswick Co., NC	Merchant's Asst.	Enlisted, 7/18/61. Promoted to 1st Sgt., 9/23/62. Died of chronic diarrhea, 3/1/63 at Wilmington, NC.
Pvt.	White, Eli M.	1843	S	Waccamaw, Brunswick Co., NC	Farm Labor	Enlisted, 9/2/61. Captured, 11/7/63 at Kelly's Ford. POW—Point Lookout, MD. Exchanged, 5/8/64. Did not return to Regiment.
Pvt.	Williams, James B.	1836	S	Colvin's Creek, New Hanover Co., NC	Farm Labor	Enlisted, 7/18/61. Died of meningitis, 1/16/62 at Guinea Station, VA. "[He] died at 6 a.m. … [we] buried him at 6 p.m."
Pvt.	Williams, Joseph	1834	S	Colvin's Creek, New Hanover Co., NC	Farm Labor	Enlisted, 7/18/61. Wounded (hand), 7/1/63 at Gettysburg. Captured, 7/4/63 at Gettysburg. POW—Baltimore, MD. Exchanged, 8/24/63. Died of disease, 3/17/64 at Orange Court House, VA.

1861 Recruits

Rank	Name	DOB	M/S	Residence	Occupation	Remarks
Pvt.	Mott, John	1844	S	Northwest, Brunswick Co., NC	Farm Labor	Enlisted, 10/15/61. Wounded, 7/1/62 at Malvern Hill. Missing, 7/4/63 in Gettysburg retreat.

1862 Recruits/Conscripts

Rank	Name	DOB	M/S	Residence	Occupation	Remarks
Pvt.	Bicknell, Benjamin E.	1828	M	Hendersonville, Henderson Co, NC	Farm Labor	Enlisted, 9/23/62. Wounded, 12/13/62 at Fredericksburg. TDY—Various duties, 1/1/63–12/31/63. Deserted, 1/-/64.
Pvt.	Eller, William W.	1825	S	Purlear's Creek, Wilkes Co., NC	Black-smith's Asst.	Conscripted, 9/23/62. Died of pneumonia, 2/25/62 at Richmond, VA.
Pvt.	Hendon, Solomon R.	1843	S	Wilkesboro, Wilkes Co., NC	Farm Labor	Conscripted, 9/23/62. Wounded & captured, 5/12/64 at Spotsylvania. POW—Point Lookout, MD. Exchanged, 3/16/65.
Pvt.	Jarvis, Levi	1833	S	Lovelace, Wilkes Co., NC	Farm Labor	Conscripted, 9/23/62. Died of pleurisy, 4/20/63 at Richmond, VA.

30th North Carolina Infantry Roster, Company C

Rank	Name	DOB	M/S	Residence	Occupation	Remarks
Pvt.	Jarvis, Wiley	1830	M	Lovelace, Wilkes Co., NC	Farmer	Conscripted, 9/23/62. Died of disease, 7/25/63 at Front Royal, VA.
Pvt.	Johnson, Alexander L.	1827	M	Bald Knob, Wilkes Co., NC	Farm Labor	Conscripted, 9/23/62. Captured, 5/12/64 at Spotsylvania. POW—Elmira, NY. Released, 6/23/65.
Pvt.	Johnson, A. Marion	1835	M	Bald Knob, Wilkes Co., NC	Farm Labor	Conscripted, 9/23/62. Captured, 5/12/64 at Spotsylvania. POW—Elmira, NY. Exchanged, 11/15/64. No further records.
Pvt.	Johnson, Calvin	1838	S	Hunting Creek, Wilkes Co., NC	Shoe Maker	Conscripted, 9/23/62. Died of disease, 4/23/63 at Richmond.
Pvt.	Johnson, John	1837	S	Lovelace, Wilkes Co., NC	Farm Labor	Conscripted, 9/23/62. Captured, 5/12/64 at Spotsylvania. No further records.
Pvt.	Luntzford, James R.	1838	M	Lovelace, Wilkes Co., NC	Day Labor	Conscripted, 9/23/62. Deserted, 3/24/63. Returned to duty, 12/-/63. Captured, 5/12/64 at Spotsylvania. POW—Elmira, NY. Released, 5/29/65.
Pvt.	Luntzford, Joel	1842	S	Lovelace, Wilkes Co., NC	Farm Labor	Conscripted, 9/23/62. Died of chronic diarrhea, 2/16/63 at Liberty, VA.
Pvt.	Miller, Alexander B.	1838	M	Parleer's Creek, Wilkes Co., NC	Farmer	Conscripted, 9/23/62. Deserted, 11/25/62. Returned to duty, 12/-/63. Captured, 5/12/64 at Spotsylvania. POW—Elmira, NY. Died of pneumonia, 4/12/65.
Pvt.	Miller, H. C.	1836		Parleer's Creek, Wilkes Co., NC		Conscripted, 9/23/62. Deserted, 11/25/62.
Pvt.	Miller, John L.	1835		Parleer's Creek, Wilkes Co., NC		Conscripted, 9/23/62. Wounded (right leg) & captured, 7/23/63 at Manassas Gap. POW—Point Lookout, MD. Transferred, 5/8/64. No further records.
Pvt.	Moore, Robert	1825	M	Monroeton, Rockingham Co.,	Mill Wright	Conscripted, 9/23/62. Died of typhoid pneumonia, 5/11/63 at Richmond, VA.
Pvt.	Parker, G. Washington	1828	M	Wilmington, New Hanover Co., NC	Mason	Conscripted, 9/23/62. Died of disease, 11/-/62.
Pvt.	Pendergrass, Elijah	1842	S	Hunting Creek, Wilkes Co., NC	Farm Labor	Conscripted, 9/23/62. Died of disease, 11/-/62 at Strasburg, VA.
Pvt.	Pendergrass, J. R.	1834		Wilkes Co., NC		Conscripted, 9/23/62. Captured, 11/7/63 at Kelly's Ford. POW—Point Lookout, MD. Died of disease, 8/29/64.
Pvt.	Pendergrass, William M	1840	S	Wilkes Co., NC		Conscripted, 9/23/62. Deserted, 1/-/64.
Pvt.	Shew, Jacob W.	1845	S	Wilkesboro, Wilkes Co., NC	Farm Labor	Conscripted, 9/23/62. Wounded (right leg), 5/3/63 at Chancellorsville. TDY—hospital nurse, 6/1/64–11/30/64. No further records.
Pvt.	Shew, Joel	1828	M	Wilkesboro, Wilkes Co., NC	Farmer	Conscripted, 9/23/62. Wounded, 5/3/63 at Chancellorsville. Died of wounds, 5/5/63.
Pvt.	Staley, Enoch	1829	M	Trap Hill, Wilkes Co., NC	Farmer	Conscripted, 9/23/62. Wounded, 5/3/63 at Chancellorsville. Absent due to wounds and AWOL until 2/18/65 when assigned TDY (unspecified duties).

1863 Conscripts

Rank	Name	DOB	M/S	Residence	Occupation	Remarks
Pvt.	Allen, Charles W.	1840	S	Prospect Hill, Bladen Co., NC	Turpentine Labor	Transferred from 18th NC Inf., 7/13/63. No further records after, 8/31/64.
Pvt.	Armfield, John J.	1829	M	Greensboro, Guilford Co., NC	Gunsmith	Conscripted, 9/-/63. Captured, 4/6/65 at Farmville. POW—Point Lookout, MD. Died of chronic diarrhea, 6/8/65.

Appendix 2

Rank	Name	DOB	M/S	Residence	Occupation	Remarks
Pvt.	Balentine, James N.	1821	M	New Hanover Co., NC	Cooper	Conscripted, 6/14/63. Deserted, 11/7/63 at Kelly's Ford. POW—Old Capitol Prison, Washington, D.C. Died of Smallpox, 3/13/64.
Pvt.	Blackwelder, Wiley	1823	M	Mount Pleasant, Cabarrus Co., NC	Farmer	Conscripted, 9/2/63. Captured, 11/7/63 at Kelly's Ford. POW—Point Lookout, MD. Died of malaria, 4/16/64.
Pvt.	Costner, Jacob B.	1822	M	Dallas, Gaston Co., NC	Carpenter	Conscripted, 8/29/63. Captured, 11/7/63 at Kelly's Ford. POW—Point Lookout, MD. Released, 1/25/65. Joined the U.S. Army.
Pvt.	Cress, Wiley	1823	M	Mount Pleasant, Cabarrus Co., NC	Farmer	Conscripted, 9/1/63. Wounded (right thigh), 5/12/64 at Spotsylvania. Absent due to wounds.
Pvt.	Dickens, Andrew J.	1827		Chatham Co., NC		Conscripted, 7/3/63. Wounded, 5/12/64 at Spotsylvania. No records after 8/31/64.
Pvt.	Durden, John M.	1827	M	Mackey's Ferry, Washington Co., NC	Farmer	Conscripted, 8/29/63. Absent, sick, 10/1/63–8/31/64. No further records.
Pvt.	Everhart, Jacob	1844	S	Midway, Davidson Co., NC	Farm Labor	Conscripted, 7/11/63. Deserted, 7/14/63 at Williamsport, MD. POW—Point Lookout, MD. Released, 1/26/64. Joined the U.S. Army.
Pvt.	File, J. N.	1830	M	Mount Pleasant, Cabarrus Co., NC	College Student	Conscripted, 6/30/63. Absent, sick since, 11/25/63. Paroled, 4/13/65 at Lynchburg.
Pvt.	Gallimore, Ransom	1832	M	Asheboro, Randolph Co., NC	Farmer	Conscripted, 7/13/63. Captured, 11/7/63 at Kelly's Ford. POW—Point Lookout, MD. Exchanged, 9/18/64. No further records.
Pvt.	Hughes, Joseph	1820	S	Northwest, Brunswick Co., NC	Shoe maker	Conscripted, 9/23/63. Died of disease, 2/4/64 at Orange Court House, VA.
Pvt.	Inscore, James	1832	M	Wilkesboro, Wilkes Co., NC	Miller	Conscripted, 4/12/63. Wounded, 5/3/63 at Chancellorsville. No records after 8/31/64.
Pvt.	Kimmel, Daniel A.	1845	S	Arcadia, Davidson Co., NC	Farm Labor	Conscripted, 6/20/63. Captured, 4/6/65 at Farmville. Released, 6/27/65.
Pvt.	Klutts, Tobias	1821	M	Mount Pleasant, Cabarrus Co., NC	Farmer	Conscripted, 9/2/63. Wounded (mouth), 5/12/64 at Spotsylvania. Died of wounds (gangrene), 6/18/64 at Richmond.
Pvt.	Moore, Theophilus	1820	M	Pleasantville, Rockingham Co., NC	Farmer	Conscripted, 8/31/63. Wounded, 5/12/64 at Spotsylvania. Paroled, 4/14/65 at Burkeville-Jct.
Pvt.	Parker, Benjamin T.	1845	S	Green Plains, Northampton Co., NC	Farm Labor	Conscripted, 7/11/63. Absent, sick since, 10/-/63 to 8/31/64. No further records.
Pvt.	Parker, James C.	1830	M	Randolph Co., NC	Farmer	Conscripted, 7/1/63. Died of disease, 8/-/64 (location unknown).
Pvt.	Patterson, John J.	1822	M	Mount Pleasant, Cabarrus Co., NC	Farmer	Conscripted, 9/23/63. Wounded (right wrist), 11/7/63 at Kelly's Ford. Discharged (wounds), 3/22/65.
Pvt.	Penninger, Moses	1820	M	Mount Pleasant, Cabarrus Co., NC	Farmer	Conscripted, 9/11/63. Died of septic pneumonia, 2/24/64 at Richmond.
Pvt.	Reidling, William A.	1820	M	Coddle Creek, Cabarrus Co., NC	Tenant Farmer	Conscripted, 9/2/63. Captured, 11/7/63 at Kelly's Ford. POW—Point Lookout, MD. Released, 1/25/64 after joining the Army.

Rank	Name	DOB	M/S	Residence	Occupation	Remarks
Pvt.	Roach, Archibald D.	1826	M	Asheboro, Randolph Co., NC	Mechanic	Conscripted, 9/2/63. Died of disease, 1/24/64 at Orange Court House, VA.
Pvt.	Robins, Jonathan	1825	M	Asheboro, Randolph Co., NC	Farm Labor	Conscripted, 8/30/63. Wounded, 9/22/64 at Fisher's Hill. Surrendered, 4/9/65 at Appomattox.
Pvt.	Simmons, Lewis	1827	M	Lockwood's Folly, Brunswick Co., NC	Day Labor	Conscripted, 9/5/63. Captured, 10/19/64 at Cedar Creek. POW—Point Lookout, MD. Released, 6/20/65.
Pvt.	Smith, Reuben	1834	S	Lumberton, Robeson Co., NC	Farm Labor	Transferred from 12th NC Inf., 7/13/63. Captured, 5/12/64 at Spotsylvania. POW—Elmira, NY. Released, 6/12/65.
Pvt.	Sprinkle, Hugh	1833	M	Yadkin Co., NC	Farmer	Conscripted, 11/22/63. Captured, 9/19/64 at Winchester. POW—Point Lookout, MD. Released, 6/20/65.
Pvt.	Thompson, A. George	1825	M	Albemarle, Stanly Co., NC	Farmer	Conscripted, 8/24/63. No further records after 8/31/64.
Pvt.	Vuncannon, John P.	1829	M	Asheboro, Randolph Co., NC	Shoe Maker	Conscripted, 7/1/63. Wounded (chest, hip, & hand) and Captured, 11/7/63 at Kelly's Ford. POW—Point Lookout, MD. Exchanged, 3/3/64. Returned to duty, 8/-/64. Transferred to Richmond hospital, 1/17/65.

1864 Conscripts / Recruits

Rank	Name	DOB	M/S	Residence	Occupation	Remarks
Pvt.	Haywood, Richard	1823	M	Morrisville, Wake Co., NC	Farmer	Conscripted, 11/-/64. Captured, 4/6/65 at Farmville. POW—Point Lookout, MD. Released, 6/28/65.
Pvt.	Lamb, Ithamer	1831	M	Colvin's Creek, New Hanover Co., NC	Farmer	Conscripted, 9/-/64. Paroled, 4/9/65 at Appomattox.
Pvt.	Oakley, David					Conscripted, 10/-/64. Surrendered, 4/9/65 at Appomattox.
Pvt.	Skipper, Wesley W.	1844	S	Town Creek, Brunswick Co., NC	Farm Labor	Enlisted, 2/2/64. Wounded (head & neck), 5/12/64 at Spotsylvania. Died of wounds, 5/29/64 at Alexandria, VA.
Pvt.	Williamson, Jn. Bailey	1826	M	Brower's Mills, Randolph Co., NC	Farmer	Conscripted, 1/10/64. Killed, 5/12/64 at Spotsylvania.

Company D
Wake and Granville Counties (Mustered into Regt.—8/10/61)

Rank	Name	DOB	M/S	Residence	Occupation	Remarks
Cpt.	Grissom, Eugene	1831	S	Tranquility, Granville Co., NC	Physician	Appointment, 8/10/61. Wounded (clavicle fractured), 6/21/62 on skirmish line near Gaines' Mill. Resigned, 4/3/63, "having been elected a member of the legislature."
1st Lt.	Allen, Solomon J.	1831	M	Roger's Store, Wake Co., NC	Farmer	Enrolled, 8/10/61. Not re-elected at re-organization, 5/1/62.
2nd Lt.	Bailey, Allen	1826	M	New Light, Wake Co., NC	Farmer	Enrolled, 8/10/61. Resigned (disabilities), 12/10/61.
3rd Lt.	Abernathy, Sidney S.	1832	S	New Light, Wake Co., NC	Carpenter	Enrolled, 8/10/61. Resigned, 4/18/62. Appointed 2nd Lt., 9/17/62. Promoted to 1st Lt., 4/12/63. Captured, 11/7/63 at Kelly's Ford. POW—Ft. Delaware, DE. Released, 6/12/65.

Appendix 2

Rank	Name	DOB	M/S	Residence	Occupation	Remarks
1st Sgt.	Allen, Charles N.	1840	S	Forestville, Wake Co., NC	Farm Labor	Enrolled, 8/10/61. Elected, 2nd Lt., 12/5/61. Promoted to 1st Lt., 5/1/62. Promoted to Cpt., 4/12/63. Wounded (left arm amputated just above elbow), 7/1/63 at Gettysburg. TDY—Enlisting Officer, Camp Vance, NC, 1/1/64–11/30/64. Retired, 12/29/64/
2nd Sgt.	**Rogers, Charles M.**	1839	S	Roger's Store, Wake Co., NC	Merchant	**Enlisted, 8/10/61. Promoted to 2nd Lt., 3/10/62. Killed, 9/17/62 at Sharpsburg.Gill, William J.**
3rd Sgt.	**Gill, William J.**	1836	S	Roger's Store, Wake Co., NC	Merchant's Clerk	**Enlisted, 8/10/61. Promoted to 3rd Lt., 3/10/62. Wounded and captured, 9/17/62 at Sharpsburg. Died of wounds, 10/13/62 in U.S. hospital, Frederick, MD.**
4th Sgt.	Nichols, John T.	1835	M	Raleigh, Wake Co., NC	Printer	Enlisted, 8/10/61. Promoted to 1st Sgt., 4/1/62. Reduced to Pvt., 12/1/63. Captured, 6/3/64 at Cold Harbor. No further records.
5th Sgt.	Davis, Alexander L	1823	M	Wilton, Granville Co., NC	Farmer	Enlisted, 8/10/61. Promoted to Commissary Sgt., 1/1/62. Assigned to Regt. staff.
Color Cpl.	Ferrell, James E.	1833	M	Roger's Store, Wake Co., NC	Farmer	Enlisted, 8/10/61. Promoted to 3rd Lt., 9/24/62. Promoted to 2nd Lt., 4/23/62. Wounded, 5/3/63 at Chancellorsville. Captured, 11/7/63 at Kelly's Ford. POW—Johnson's Island. Released, 6/13/65.
1st Cpl.	Ray, David A.	1833	M	New Light, Wake Co., NC	Constable	Enlisted, 8/10/61. Promoted to Sgt., 11/-/61. Reduced to Pvt., 5/1/62. Deserted, 3/28/63. Returned to duty, 10/-/63. Captured, 11/7/63 at Kelly's Ford. POW—Point Lookout, MD. Exchanged, 2/14/65.
2nd Cpl.	Ray, Zeddock D.	1840	S	Roger's Store, Wake Co., NC	Farm Labor	Enlisted, 8/10/61. Promoted to Sgt., 1/-/62. Wounded, 6/27/62 at Gaines' Mill. Captured, 11/7/63 at Kelly's Ford. POW—Point Lookout, MD. Released, 6/17/65.
3rd Cpl.	**White, James D.**	1834	M	**Raleigh, Wake Co., NC**	Engineer	**Enlisted, 8/10/61. Reduced to Pvt., 5/1/62. Deserted, 3/23/63. "Killed while resisting guard in the woods," 1/10/64.**
Music	Davis, Samuel R.	1848	S	Wilton, Granville Co., NC	Farm Labor	Enlisted, 8/10/61 (drummer). Discharged (age), 1/25/62.
Music	Ray, William B.	1841	S	Raleigh, Wake Co., NC	Clerk	Enlisted, 8/10/61. Reduced to Pvt., 11/-/61. Deserted, 3/28/63. Returned to duty, 10/-/63. Captured, 11/7/63 at Kelly's Ford. POW—Point Lookout, MD. Exchanged, 2/14/65.
Pvt.	Allen, James P.	1836	S	Forestville, Wake Co., NC	Farm Labor	Enlisted, 8/10/61. Promoted to Cpl., 5/1/62. Killed, 7/1/62 at Malvern Hill.
Pvt.	Allen, Marion F.	1837		Granville, Co., NC		Enlisted, 8/10/61. Captured, 9/17/62 at Sharpsburg. Paroled, 9/21/62. Captured, 7/4/63 at Gettysburg. POW—Point Lookout, MD. Released, 6/4/65.
Pvt.	**Bailey, Jeremiah "Jerry"**	1843	S	**Beaver Dam, Granville Co., NC**	Tanner	**Enlisted, 8/10/61. Wounded, 10/19/64 at Cedar Creek. Died of wounds, 10/26/64 at Mount Jackson, VA.**
Pvt.	Bailey, Jones F.	1844	S	Beaver Dam, Granville Co., NC	Farm Labor	Enlisted, 8/10/61. Died of disease, 9/20/62 at Beaver Dam, NC.
Pvt.	Bailey, William M.	1843	S	Auburn, Wake Co., NC	Farm Labor	Enlisted, 8/10/61. Died of disease, 8/15/62 at Richmond, VA.
Pvt.	Bailey, Young F.	1822	S	Wilton, Granville Co., NC	Farmer	Enlisted, 8/10/61. Killed, 5/12/64 at Spotsylvania.

30th North Carolina Infantry Roster, Company D

Rank	Name	DOB	M/S	Residence	Occupation	Remarks
Pvt.	Barker, John W.	1836	S	Raleigh, Wake Co., NC	Grocer's Clerk	Enlisted, 8/10/61. Wounded (right arm & hand), 7/1/63 at Gettysburg. Captured, 11/7/63 at Kelly's Ford. POW—Point Lookout, MD. Released, 2/25/65/
Pvt.	**Bridges, George W.**	**1844**	**S**	**New Light, Wake Co., NC**	**Day Labor**	**Enlisted, 8/10/61. Died of rheumatism, 1/20/63 at Forestville, NC.**
Pvt.	Champion, Joseph M. "Jerry"	1835	S	Beaver Dam, Granville Co., NC	Farm Labor	Enlisted, 8/10/61. Captured, 11/7/63 at Kelly's Ford. POW—Point Lookout, MD. Exchanged, 2/15/65.
Pvt.	Clay, Robert L.	1841	S	Tranquility, Granville Co., NC	News Paper Sales	Enlisted, 8/10/61. Promoted to Cpl., 1/-/61. Reduced to Pvt., 5/1/62. Transferred to 3rd NC Cav., 5/28/62.
Pvt.	Cooper, William W. "Willie"	1840	S	Raleigh, Wake Co., NC	Coach Maker's Apprentice	Enlisted, 8/10/61. Wounded (right arm), 9/17/62 at Sharpsburg. Wounded (head), 9/19/64 at Winchester. Captured, 4/6/65 at High Bridge. POW—Point Lookout, MD. Released, 6/26/65
Pvt.	Cousins, John A.	1839	S	Beaver Dam, Granville Co., NC	Farm Labor	Enlisted, 8/10/61. Promoted to Cpl., 5/1/62. Promoted to Sgt., 4/1/63. Wounded, 7/1/63 at Gettysburg. Captured, 11/7/63 at Kelly's Ford. POW—Point Lookout, MD. Exchanged, 2/25/62. Captured, 4/6/65 at Farmville. POW—Point Lookout, MD. Released, 6/26/65.
Pvt.	Crenshaw, Frederick B.	1808	S	NW District, Wake Co., NC	Carpenter	Enlisted, 8/10/61. Discharged (old age), 7/23/62.
Pvt.	**Davis, Arrington J.**	**1843**	**S**	**New Light, Wake Co., NC**	**Farm Labor**	**Enlisted, 8/10/61. Killed, 7/1/62 at Malvern Hill.**
Pvt.	**Davis, James R.**	**1841**	**S**	**Henderson, Granville Co., NC**	**Farm Labor**	**Enlisted, 8/10/61. Killed, 7/1/62 at Malvern Hill.**
Pvt.	Davis, James T.	1844	S	New Light, Wake Co., NC	Farm Labor	Enlisted, 8/10/61. Wounded, 6/27/62 at Gaines' Mill. Deserted, 3/18/63. Returned to duty, 6/-/64. Captured, 9/22/64 at Fisher's Hill. POW—Point Lookout, MD. Released, 6/12/65.
Pvt.	**Davis, John R.**	**1835**	**M**	**Raleigh, Wake Co., NC**	**Day Labor**	**Enlisted, 8/10/61. Died of dysentery, 1/31/62 at Raleigh, NC.**
Pvt.	**Davis, Joseph E.**	**1839**	**S**	**Tranquility, Granville Co., NC**	**Farm Labor**	**Enlisted, 8/10/61. Died of disease, 7/20/62 at Richmond, VA.**
Pvt.	Davis, William E.	1837	S	New Light, Wake Co., NC	Farm Labor	Enlisted, 8/10/61. Deserted, 3/28/63 at Fredericksburg. Returned, 12/-/63. Captured, 10/19/64 at Cedar Creek. POW—Point Lookout, MD. Released, 6/12/65.
Pvt.	**Dillard, William**	**1845**	**S**	**Granville Co., NC**	**Farm Labor**	**Enlisted, 8/10/61. Died of disease, 10/23/62 at home in Granville Co., NC.**
Pvt.	**Ellen, James B.**	**1844**	**S**	**Raleigh, Wake Co., NC**	**Farm Labor**	**Enlisted, 9/2/61. Promoted to Sgt., 8/20/62. Wounded (right lung), and captured, 11/7/63 at Kelly's Ford. Died of wounds, 12/9/63 at Washington, D.C.**
Pvt.	Emery, Simeon	1841	S	Raleigh, Wake Co., NC	Farm Labor	Enlisted, 8/10/61. Discharged (disability), 5/30/62.
Pvt.	Estis, John W.	1818	M	Beaver Dam, Granville Co., NC	Farmer	Enlisted, 8/10/61. Discharged, 8/10/64.

Appendix 2

Rank	Name	DOB	M/S	Residence	Occupation	Remarks
Pvt.	Evans, Absalom R. "Richard"	1818	M	Ragland, Granville Co., NC	Farmer	Enlisted, 8/10/61. Discharged (conscription act), 9/29/62.
Pvt.	**Evans, Isaiah H.**	1832	S	**Raleigh, Wake Co., NC**	Farm Labor	Enlisted, 8/10/61. **Died of disease, 6/3/63 at Raleigh, NC.**
Pvt.	Evans, William A	1838	S	Raleigh, Wake Co., NC	Farm Labor	Enlisted, 8/30/61. TDY—Shoe maker in Richmond, 12/10/62–10/31/64. No further records.
Pvt.	Ferrell, John C.	1840	S	Morrisville, Wake Co., NC	Manager's Asst.	Enlisted, 8/10/61. Wounded, 6/27/62 at Gaines' Mill. Promoted to Cpl., 7/2/62. Wounded, 5/3/63 at Chancellorsville. Promoted to 1st Sgt., 11/12/63. Captured, 5/12/64 at Spotsylvania. POW—Elmira, NY. Exchanged, 2/20/65.
Pvt.	**Goodin, John C.**	1841	S	**Morrisville, Wake Co., NC**	Farm Labor	Enlisted, 9/2/61. **Killed, 7/1/63 at Gettysburg.**
Pvt.	**Goodin, William N. "Willis"**	1837	M	**Morrisville, Wake Co., NC**	Farmer	Enlisted, 9/2/61. **Died of typhoid fever, 8/30/62 at Richmond, VA.**
Pvt.	**Grady, John H.**	1843	S	**Wake Co., NC**	Farm Labor	Enlisted, 8/10/61. **Died of typhoid fever, 1/4/62 at Wilmington, NC.**
Pvt.	Grissom, Lewis T.	1830	S	Cedar Creek, Granville Co., NC	Farmer	Enlisted, 9/25/61. Discharged (disability), 5/29/62.
Pvt.	Harris, Henry	1841	S	Oxford, Granville Co., NC	Day Labor	Enlisted, 8/10/61. Wounded, 7/18/64 at Snicker's Gap. Surrendered, 4/9/65 at Appomattox.
Pvt.	Harris, Thomas P.	1839	S	Cedar Creek, Granville Co., NC	Day Labor	Enlisted, 8/10/61. Surrendered, 4/9/65 at Appomattox.
Pvt.	Holloway, Albert W.	1839	S	Roger's Store, Wake Co., NC	Farm Labor	Enlisted, 8/10/61. Transferred, 9/-/62 to an unknown NC Inf. Regiment.
Pvt.	Husketh, William R.	1820	M	Cedar Creek, Granville Co., NC	Clock Repair	Enlisted, 8/10/61. Discharged (age), 9/30/62.
Pvt.	**Jones, Isham F.**	1839	S	**New Light, Wake Co., NC**	Farm Labor	Enlisted, 8/10/61. **Killed, 7/1/62 at Malvern Hill.**
Pvt.	**Joplin, William Y.**	1835		**Wake Co., NC**		Enlisted, 8/10/61. **Died of smallpox, 1/29/63 at Liberty, VA.**
Pvt.	Joyner, John L.	1841	S	Beaver Dam, Granville Co., NC	Farm Labor	Enlisted, 8/10/61. Wounded, 6/27/62 at Gaines' Mill. Captured, 9/14/62 at South Mountain. Exchanged, 11/10/62. Promoted to Musician, 1/-/63. Surrendered, 4/9/65 at Appomattox.
Pvt.	Lawrence, William H.	1840	S	Cedar Creek, Granville Co., NC	Farm Labor	Enlisted, 8/10/61. Captured, 7/4/63 in Gettysburg retreat. POW—Point Lookout, MD. Exchanged, 2/20/65.
Pvt.	Lloyd, George E.	1840	S	Beaver Dam, Granville Co., NC	Farm Labor	Enlisted, 8/10/61. Wounded, 9/17/62 at Sharpsburg. Surrendered, 4/9/65 at Appomattox.
Pvt.	Long, Alexander V.	1833	S	Beaver Dam, Granville Co., NC	Farm Labor	Enlisted, 8/10/61. Wounded (both hips), 7/1/63, and captured, 7/4/63 at Gettysburg field hospital. POW—Ft. Delaware, DE. Released, 6/19/65.
Pvt.	Lumbley, William L.	1832	S	Raleigh, Wake Co., NC	Day Labor	Enlisted, 8/10/61. Wounded, 12/13/63 at Fredericksburg. Captured, 5/20/64 at Spotsylvania. POW—Elmira, NY. Released, 6/19/65.
Pvt.	**Lynam, Emelious J.**	1842	S	**Granville Co., NC**	Farm Labor	Enlisted, 8/10/61. **Died of typhoid fever, 11/14/61 at Camp Wyatt, NC.**

30th North Carolina Infantry Roster, Company D

Rank	Name	DOB	M/S	Residence	Occupation	Remarks
Pvt.	Lynam, William	1817	M	Granville Co., NC	Mechanic	Enlisted, 8/10/61. Discharged (disability), 2/5/62.
Pvt.	Mangum, Calvin T.	1845	S	New Light, Wake Co., NC	Farm Labor	Enlisted, 8/10/61. Wounded (left hip & right foot), 7/1/62 at Malvern Hill. Captured, 11/7/63 at Kelly's Ford. POW—Point Lookout, MD. Exchanged, 2/21/65.
Pvt.	Mangum, Theophilus P.	1841	M	New Light, Wake Co., NC	Day Labor	Enlisted, 8/10/61. TDY—in Raleigh hospital, 4/1/63–9/1/63. Surrendered, 4/9/65 at Appomattox.
Pvt.	**Martin, Joseph B. "Jesse"**	**1837**	**S**	**Brassfields, Wake Co., NC**	**Teacher**	**Enlisted, 8/10/61. Died of tuberculosis, 10/2/62 at Brassfields, NC.**
Pvt.	Mason, Joseph	1845	S	Beaver Dam, Wake Co., NC	Farm Labor	Enlisted, 8/10/61. Wounded, (left leg), 7/1/62 at Malvern Hill. ("left leg cut off below the knee.") Died of wounds, 7/7/62.
Pvt.	Massey, Marion M.	1823	M	Roger's Store, Wake Co., NC	Farmer	Enlisted, 8/10/61. Promoted to Cpl., 1/–/62. Reduced to Pvt., 12/1/62. Surrendered, 4/9/65 at Appomattox.
Pvt.	Moore, William H.	1839	S	Ledge of Rock, Granville Co., NC	Farm Labor	Enlisted, 8/10/61. Wounded, 5/6/64 at Spotsylvania. Wounded (left shoulder), 4/2/65 in Petersburg trenches.
Pvt.	**Morris, Alfred J.**	**1820**	**M**	**Beaver Dam, Granville Co., NC**	**Grist Mill Labor**	**Enlisted, 8/10/61. Died of typhoid pneumonia, 1/2/63 at Petersburg, VA.**
Pvt.	O'Neal, Hardy	1836	S	Raleigh, Wake Co., NC	Farm Labor	Enlisted, 8/10/61. Wounded (right arm), 7/1/62 at Malvern Hill. Captured, 11/7/63 at Kelly's Ford. POW—Point Lookout, MD. Exchanged, 2/14/65.
Pvt.	O'Neal, Lofton M.	1843	S	Raleigh, Wake Co., NC	Farm Labor	Enlisted, 8/10/61. Captured, 11/7/63 at Kelly's Ford. No further records.
Pvt.	**Penny, Solomon W.**	**1843**	**S**	**Brassfields, Wake Co., NC**	**Farm Labor**	**Enlisted, 8/10/61. Wounded, 9/17/62 at Sharpsburg. Killed, 7/12/64 at Fort Stevens.**
Pvt.	Pierce, James T.	1835	M	New Light, Wake Co., NC	Farmer	Enlisted, 8/10/61. Wounded, 7/1/62 at Malvern Hill. Captured, 9/14/62 at South Mountain. Paroled, 11/8/62. Deserted, 3/28/63. Returned, 12/–/63. Wounded (right hand), 6/1/64 at Cold Harbor. Absent due to wounds, 3/20/65. No further records.
Pvt.	Pollard, Joshua H.	1835	M	Raleigh, Wake Co., NC	Day Labor	Enlisted, 8/23/61. Deserted, 3/28/63. Returned, 8/–/63. Captured, 11/7/63 at Kelly's Ford. POW—Point Lookout, MD. Released, 1/26/64 after joining the U.S. Army.
Pvt.	**Pollard, William H. "Wiley"**	**1842**	**S**	**Brassfields, Wake Co., NC**	**Farm Labor**	**Enlisted, 8/10/61. Wounded, 6/27/62 at Gaines' Mill. Absent due to wounds. Died of wounds, 12/3/62 at Raleigh, NC.**
Pvt.	Pollard, Willie G.	1842	S	Roger's Store, Wake Co., NC	Day Labor	Enlisted, 8/10/61. Wounded, 7/1/63 at Gettysburg. Captured, 11/7/63 at Kelly's Ford. POW—Point Lookout, MD. Exchanged, 3/3/65.
Pvt.	Reavis, Joseph H.	1832	S	Raleigh, Wake Co., NC	Day Labor	Enlisted, 8/10/61. TDY—Shoe maker in Richmond, 6/13/63–12/31/64. No further records.
Pvt.	Rogers, Martin L.	1840	S	Roger's Store, Wake Co., NC	Clerk	Enlisted, 8/10/61. Promoted to Cpl., 11/–/61. Promoted to Sgt., 5/1/62. Promoted to 3rd Lt., 4/12/63. Wounded, 7/18/64 at Snicker's Gap. Home on wounded furlough to 4/9/65.

Rank	Name	DOB	M/S	Residence	Occupation	Remarks
Pvt.	Smith, Thomas G.	1833	M	Roger's Store, Wake Co., NC	Farm Labor	Enlisted, 8/10/61. Captured, 11/7/63 at Kelly's Ford. POW—Point Lookout, MD. Released, 6/19/65.
Pvt.	**Tilly, William L.**	**1840**	**S**	**Brassfields, Wake Co., NC**	**Farm Labor**	**Enlisted, 8/10/61. Died of disease, 8/31/62 at Richmond, VA.**
Pvt.	Vaughan, John G.	1844	S	Granville Co., NC	Farm Labor	Enlisted, 8/10/61. Captured, 4/6/65 at High Bridge. POW—Point Lookout, MD. Released, 6/21/65.
Pvt.	Ward, Isaac B.	1830	M	Roger's Store, Wake Co., NC	Day Labor	Enlisted, 8/10/61. Missing, 7/4/63 in Gettysburg retreat. Captured, 4/6/65 at Burkeville. POW—Point Lookout, MD. Released, 6/21/65.
Pvt.	Ward, Wilson	1844	S	Roger's Store, Wake Co., NC	Day Labor	Enlisted, 8/10/61. Captured, 11/7/63 at Kelly's Ford. POW—Point Lookout, MD. Exchanged, 2/21/65.
Pvt.	Ward, William J.	1842	S	Roger's Store, Wake Co., NC	Farm Labor	Enlisted, 8/10/61. Promoted to Cpl., 5/1/62. Captured, 11/7/63 at Kelly's Ford. POW—Point Lookout, MD. Exchanged, 2/13/65. Captured, 4/6/65 at Burkeville. POW—Point Lookout, MD. Released, 6/21/65.
Pvt.	**Wheeler, John W.**	**1825**	**S**	**Morrisville, Wake Co., NC**	**Day Labor**	**Enlisted, 8/10/61. Killed, 5/3/63 at Chancellorsville.**
Pvt.	**White, Almon W.**	**1832**	**S**	**Beaver Dam, Granville Co., NC**	**Farmer**	**Enlisted, 8/10/61. Killed, 7/1/62 at Malvern Hill.**
Pvt.	White, John E.	1840	S	Morrisville, Wake Co., NC	Day Labor	Enlisted, 8/10/61. Deserted, 3/28/63.
Pvt.	White, Mason	1820	M	Franklinton, Franklin Co., NC	Farmer	Enlisted, 8/10/61. Discharged (disability), 12/26/61.
Pvt.	**Wilkins, Elijah**	**1831**	**S**	**Cedar Creek, Granville Co., NC**	**Farm Labor**	**Enlisted, 9/22/61. Wounded, 7/1/62 at Malvern Hill. Wounded, 12/13/62 at Fredericksburg. Wounded, 5/3/63 at Chancellorsville. Killed, 8/21/64 at Charles Town.**
Pvt.	**Wilkins, James**	**1835**	**M**	**New Light, Wake Co., NC**	**Day Labor**	**Enlisted, 8/10/61. Wounded, 6/27/62 at Gaines' Mill. Died of wounds, 7/25/62 at Camp Winder, VA.**
Pvt.	Williams, Samuel S	1837	S	Oxford, Granville Co., NC	Mechanic	Enlisted, 9/2/62. Wounded, 6/27/62 at Gaines' Mill. Discharged (wounds & disability), 1/16/63 "Deafness in left ear by explosion of shell during the battle near Richmond."
Pvt.	Williams, Simon P.	1831	M	Young's Crossroads, Granville Co., NC	Farmer	Enlisted, 8/10/61. Transferred to 13th NC Inf., 6/20/62.
Pvt.	Yearby, Allen	1811	M	Roger's Store, Wake Co., NC	Farmer	Enlisted, 8/10/61. Deserted, 10/9/61.

1861 Recruits

Rank	Name	DOB	M/S	Residence	Occupation	Remarks
Pvt.	Peed, William C.	1842	S	Ledge of Rock, Granville Co., NC	Farm Labor	Enlisted, 11/1/61. Wounded (left side), 6/27/62 at Gaines' Mill. Wounded (left hand), 5/3/63 at Chancellorsville. Captured, 9/19/64 at Winchester. POW—Point Lookout, MD. Released, 6/16/65.
Pvt.	Peed, William H.	1842	S	Ledge of Rock, Granville Co., NC	Farm Labor	Enlisted, 11/1/61. Wounded, 5/3/63 at Chancellorsville. Captured, 11/7/63 at Kelly's Ford. POW—Point Lookout, MD. Exchanged, 2/20/65.

Rank	Name	DOB	M/S	Residence	Occupation	Remarks
Pvt.	Walker, Jarrett	1836	S	Ledge of Rock, Granville Co., NC	Farm Labor	Enlisted, 11/1/61. Discharged (heart disease), 9/19/62.

1862 Recruits/Conscripts

Rank	Name	DOB	M/S	Residence	Occupation	Remarks
Pvt.	Allen, Elias G.	1843	S	Beaver Dam, Granville Co., NC	Farm Labor	Enlisted, 2/13/62. Wounded (both thighs), 12/13/62 at Fredericksburg. Promoted to Color Cpl., 7/17/63. Wounded (left lung), and captured, 11/7/63 at Kelly's Ford. POW—Point Lookout, MD. Released, 2/9/64 after joining the U.S Army.
Pvt.	Allen, Henry C.	1840	S	Forestville, Wake Co., NC	Farm Labor	Enlisted, 4/20/62. Promoted to Sgt., 4/1/63. Wounded, 5/3/63 at Chancellorsville. TDY—Provost Guard, Raleigh, NC, 11/1/63–4/9/65.
Pvt.	Bledsoe, Giles	1835	M	Durhamsville, Orange Co., NC	Farm Labor	Substitute, 3/30/62. Surrendered, 4/9/65 at Appomattox.
Pvt.	Bowles, David	1833	M	Ledge of Rock, Granville Co., NC	Carpenter	Enlisted, 3/23/62. Absent, sick until Dis-Echarged (disabilities), 7/25/64.
Pvt.	**Bowlin, Willis N.**	1845	S	Orange Co., NC	Farm Labor	**Enlisted, 3/30/62. Hospitalized (gunshot wound), 1/19/63. Wounded (right arm), 5/3/63 at Chancellorsville (right arm amputated) Died of wounds, 5/29/63 at Richmond, VA.**
Pvt.	Branton, Charles E.	1843	S	Raleigh, Wake Co., NC	Farm Labor	Enlisted, 4/18/62. Wounded, 5/3/63 at Chancellorsville. Captured, 11/7/63 at Kelly's Ford. POW—Point Lookout, MD. Released, 2/25/65.
Pvt.	**Brassfield, James W.**	1825	M	Orange Co., NC	Farmer	**Enlisted, 2/13/62. Captured, 7/4/63 in Gettysburg retreat. POW—Point Lookout, MD. Died of chronic diarrhea, 2/12/65.**
Pvt.	Cawthon, Archer L. "Arch"	1818	M	Raleigh, Wake Co., NC	Mechanic	Substitute, 2/13/62. Promoted to Cpl., 5/1/62. Reduced to Pvt., 1/-/63. Absent until 8/31/64. No further records.
Pvt.	**Davis, Joseph C.**	1838	M	Cedar Creek, Granville Co., NC	Farmer	**Transferred, 8/10/62 from 23rd NC Inf. Died of heart disease, 12/25/62 at Richmond, VA.**
Pvt.	**Evans, Joseph E.**	1845	S	**Raleigh, Wake Co., NC**	Farm Labor	**Enlisted, 3/23/62. Died of disease, 7/20/62 at Richmond, VA.**
Pvt.	**Ferrell, Francis M.**	1844	S	Wakefield, Wake Co., NC	Farm Labor	Enlisted, 4/20/62. Wounded (arm), 5/3/63 at Chancellorsville (arm amputated). Retired to Invalid Corps, 12/29/62.
Pvt.	**Forsyth, James R.**	1843	S	**Cedar Creek, Granville Co., NC**	Farm Labor	**Enlisted, 2/13/62. Wounded, 5/3/63 at Chancellorsville. Promoted to Cpl., 6/1/63. Killed, 8/21/64 at Charles Town.**
Pvt.	**Garner, John T.**	1843	S	Forestville, Wake Co., NC	Farm Labor	Enlisted, 2/13/62. Wounded, 7/1/62 at Malvern Hill. No records after 8/31/64.
Pvt.	**Marcom, James A.**	1841	S	Morrisville, Wake Co., NC	Farm Labor	Enlisted, 2/13/62. Captured, 11/7/63 at Kelly's Ford. POW—Point Lookout, MD. Released, 3/3/65.
Pvt.	**Mason, Israel H.**	1837	S	**Beaver Dam, Granville Co., NC**	Farm Labor	**Transferred from 47th NC Inf., 3/-/62. Wounded, 7/1/63 at Gettysburg. Died of wounds, 7/16/63 in Gettysburg field hospital.**
Pvt.	Pierce, George W.	1843	S	New Light, Wake Co., NC	Farm Labor	Enlisted, 2/13/62. Wounded (right knee), 7/1/62 at Malvern Hill. Captured, 11/7/63 at Kelly's Ford. POW—Point Lookout, MD. Exchanged, 9/18/64. No further records.

Appendix 2

Rank	Name	DOB	M/S	Residence	Occupation	Remarks
Pvt.	Piper, Wesley Y.	1835	M	Roger's Store, Wake Co., NC	Mechanic	Enlisted, 4/20/62. Wounded, 7/1/62 at Malvern Hill. TDY—Light Duty, Guard in Raleigh, 5/1/63–8/31/64. Wounded (right leg), 3/15/65 in Petersburg trenches.
Pvt.	Rogers, John H.	1843	S	Brassfields, Wake Co., NC	College Student	Enlisted, 4/20/62. Captured, 5/12/64 at Spotsylvania. POW—Elmira, NY. Died of smallpox, 1/22/65.
Pvt.	Thompson, Solomon	1830	S	Raleigh, Wake Co., NC	Clerk	Substitute, 3/30/62. Deserted, 9/-/62. Returned to duty, 9/28/63. Captured, 4/3/65 in Richmond hospital.
Pvt.	Tilley, John R.	1845	S	Brassfields, Wake Co., NC	Day Labor	Enlisted, 2/10/62. Captured, 9/14/62 at South Mountain. Exchanged, 11/10/62. Captured, 11/7/63 at Kelly's Ford. POW—Point Lookout, MD. Died of chronic diarrhea and scurvy, 2/8/65.
Pvt.	Tilly, William H.	1844	S	Brassfields, Wake Co., NC	Farm labor	Enlisted, 4/20/62. Captured, 11/7/63 at Kelly's Ford. POW—Point Lookout, MD. Exchanged, 4/30/64. Absent, sick until 8/10/64. No further records.
Pvt.	Wadford, Alexander	1835	M	Beaver Dam, Granville Co., NC	Day Labor	Enlisted, 3/21/62. Captured, 7/4/63 in retreat from Gettysburg. POW—Point Lookout, MD. Exchanged, 4/30/64. Surrendered, 4/9/65 at Appomattox.
Pvt.	Walker, Willis S.			Granville Co., NC		Enlisted, 3/13/62. Absent, sick from 7/1/62–8/31/64. No further records.
Pvt.	Waller, P. H.	1839	S	Ledge of Rock, Granville Co., NC	Farm Labor	Enlisted, 2/13/62. Died of pneumonia, 12/22/62 at Richmond, VA.
Pvt.	Wheeler, James "Burl"	1811	M	New Light, Wake Co., NC	Farmer	Killed, 7/1/62 at Malvern Hill. Substitute, 3/21/62.
Pvt.	White, James	1844	S	Beaver Dam, Granville Co., NC	Farm Labor	Enlisted, 5/2/62. Wounded (stomach), 7/1/62 at Malvern Hill. Discharged (disability), 7/23/62.
Pvt.	Wilkins, Hinton	1843		Granville Co., NC		Enlisted, 2/19/62. Died of chronic diarrhea, 4/25/63 at Granville Co., NC.

1863 Conscripts/Recruits

Rank	Name	DOB	M/S	Residence	Occupation	Remarks
Pvt.	Allen, Wyatt M.	1821	M	Morrisville, Wake Co., NC	Farmer	Enlisted, 3/2/63. Died of disease, 11/12/63 at Morrisville, NC.
Pvt.	Canady, Francis R.	1826	S	Roger's Store, Wake Co., NC	Farm Labor	Conscripted, 9/10/63. Captured, 9/22/64 at Fisher's Hill. POW—Point Lookout, MD. Exchanged, 1/21/65.
Pvt.	Daniel, John B.	1818	M	Oaks, Orange Co., NC	Farmer	Conscripted, 7/9/63. TDY—Nurse, Richmond hospital from 9/13/63–8/31/64. No further records.
Pvt.	Davis, Burton	1826		Wake Co., NC		Conscripted, 11/19/63. Died of disease, 1/14/64 at Orange Court House, VA.
Pvt.	Dickey, Zachariah C.	1845	S	Orange Co., NC	Farm Labor	Conscripted, 7/5/63. Surrendered, 4/9/65 at Appomattox.
Pvt.	Edwards, Walter	1835	M	Orange Co., NC	Farmer	Conscripted, 7/30/63. Captured, 4/12/65 at Spotsylvania. POW—Elmira, NY. Died of chronic diarrhea, 10/14/64.
Pvt.	Gilbert, Thaddeus	1845	S	Orange Co., NC	Farm Labor	Conscripted, 7/5/63. Paroled, 4/14/65 at Burkeville Jct.
Pvt.	Hinshaw, Daniel	1836	M	Mud Lick, Chatham Co., NC	Farmer	Conscripted, 7/15/63. Discharged (a Quaker—religious exemption), 11/24/63.

Rank	Name	DOB	M/S	Residence	Occupation	Remarks
Pvt.	Keith, Clement C.	1844	S	Fishdam, Wake Co., NC	Farm Labor	Conscripted, 2/9/63. Deserted, 3/28/63.
Pvt.	Manus, Francis			Moore Co., NC		Conscripted, 4/-/63. Captured, 7/7/63 at Williamsport, MD. POW—Ft. Delaware. Released, 5/3/65.
Pvt.	Marcum, William A.	1848	S	Chapel Hill, Orange Co., NC	Farm Labor	Conscripted, 9/10/63. Captured, 11/7/63 at Kelly's Ford. POW—Point Lookout, MD. Released, 3/3/65.
Pvt.	Pollard, Samuel R.	1834	M	Raleigh, Wake Co., NC	Farm Labor	Conscripted, 8/10/63. Captured, 11/7/63 at Kelly's Ford. POW—Point Lookout, MD. Released, 1/28/64 after joining the U.S. Army.
Pvt.	Ray, Caswell	1836	M	New Light, Wake Co., NC	Farmer	Conscripted, 2/9/63. Deserted, 3/28/63.
Pvt.	Ray, Henry C.	1827	M	Raleigh, Wake Co., NC	Farmer	Conscripted, 2/9/63. Deserted, 3/28/63. Returned to duty, 10/-/63. Captured, 11/7/63 at Kelly's Ford. POW—Point Lookout, MD. Exchanged, 3/16/65.
Pvt.	Ross, Richard S.	1822	M	Brassfields, Wake Co., NC	Farmer	Conscripted, 9/10/63. No further records after 8/31/64.
Pvt.	**Thomas, Robert H.**	**1841**	**S**	**Goshen, Granville Co., NC**	**Farm Labor**	**Conscripted, 3/4/63. Promoted to Cpl., 11/30/63. Captured, 5/8/64 at Spotsylvania. POW—Elmira, NY. Died of chronic diarrhea, 10/16/64.**
Pvt.	Tilly, William B.	1845	S	Orange Co., NC	Farm Labor	Conscripted, 7/30/63. Wounded, 10/12/63 at Bristoe Station. Absent due to wounds, until 8/31/64. Captured, 11/7/63 at Kelly's Ford. No further records.
Pvt.	Wilkins, William	1846	S	Orange Co., NC	Farm Labor	Conscripted, 7/30/63. Captured, 11/7/63 at Kelly's Ford. POW—Point Lookout, MD. Exchanged, 3/3/65.

1864 Conscripts

Rank	Name	DOB	M/S	Residence	Occupation	Remarks
Pvt.	Branton, Lewis O.	1846	S	Raleigh, Wake Co., NC	Farm Labor	Conscripted, 10/-/64. Captured in Richmond hospital, 4/3/65.
Pvt.	Davis, Jesse A.	1839	S	New Light, Wake Co., NC	Farm Labor	Conscripted, 1/28/64. Wounded (right leg), 5/3/63 at Chancellorsville. Absent due to wounds until 8/31/64. No further records.
Pvt.	Ferrell Albert L.	1848	S	Raleigh, Wake Co., NC	Farm Labor	Conscripted, 7/23/64. Captured, 9/19/64 at Winchester. POW—Baltimore, MD. Exchanged, 2/16/65.
Pvt.	Goodin, Joseph J.	1845	S	Summerville, Chatham Co., NC	Farm Labor	Conscripted, 3/20/64. Surrendered, 4/9/65 at Appomattox.
Pvt.	**Jones, William H.**	**1820**	**M**	**Morrisville, Wake Co., NC**	**Day Labor**	**Conscripted, 4/1/64. Captured, 4/6/65 at Farmville. POW—Newport News, VA. Died of chronic dysentery, 6/23/65.**
Pvt.	King, Anderson F.	1839	M	Morrisville, Wake Co., NC	Day Labor	Conscripted, 4/1/64. Captured, 5/18/64 at Harris Farm. POW—Elmira, NY. Exchanged, 11/15/64. Wounded (right thumb), 3/6/65 in Petersburg trenches.
Pvt.	**King, Caswell**	**1825**	**M**	**Roger's Store, Wake Co., NC**	**Day Labor**	**Conscripted, 4/1/64. Captured, 5/12/64 at Spotsylvania. POW—Elmira, NY. Died of chronic diarrhea, 3/6/65.**
Pvt.	King, John	1835	S	Raleigh, Wake Co., NC	Stone Mason	Conscripted, 4/1/64. Wounded, 9/19/64 at Winchester. Captured, 4/6/65 at Farmville. POW—Point Lookout, MD. Died of chronic diarrhea, 5/29/65.

Company E—Duplin Turpentine Boys
Duplin County (Mustered into Regt.—8/28/61)

Rank	Name	DOB	M/S	Residence	Occupation	Remarks
Cpt.	McMillan, John C.	1838	S	Sandy Run, New Hanover Co., NC	Farm Labor	Enrolled, 8/21/61. Court Martial, 10/18/62—found guilty of cowardice at Sharpsburg. Suspended by court martial, 11/1/62–12/31/62. Wounded (wrist), 5/3/63 at Chancellorsville. Wounded (shoulder & right arm), 5/12/64 at Spotsylvania. Wounded (right side, below shoulder), 4/6/65 near Deatonsville. Surrendered, 4/9/65 at Appomattox.
1st Lt.	Johnson, Cornelius	1831		Teachey's Depot, Duplin Co., NC		Enrolled, 8/21/61. Provost Marshall, 3/1/62–4/30/62, in Wilmington, NC. Not re-elected at re-organization, 5/1/62.
2nd Lt.	Boney, William J.	1839	S	Teachey's Depot, Duplin Co., NC	Farmer	Enrolled, 8/21/61. Defeated in election, 3/27/62.
3rd Lt.	Teachey, Daniel	1835	S	Kenansville, Duplin Co., NC	Farm Labor	Enrolled, 8/21/61. Resigned, 1/24/62.
1st Sgt.	Johnson, Ira J.	1840	S	Teachey's Depot, Duplin Co., NC		Enlisted, 8/28/61. Promoted to 3rd Lt., 1/24/62. Promoted to 1st Lt., 3/22/62. Wounded (right hip), 11/7/63 at Kelly's Ford. Wounded, 7/18/64 at Snicker's Gap. Paroled, 4/9/65 at Appomattox.
2nd Sgt.	Carr, Jacob O.	1839	S	Magnolia, Duplin Co., NC	Farm Labor	Enlisted, 8/28/61. Promoted, to 3rd Lt., 3/27/62. Released of command by reason of court martial, 10/28/62."
4th Sgt.	Johnson, James C.	1841	S	Calvin Creek, New Hanover Co., NC	Farm Labor	Enlisted, 8/28/61. Reduced to Pvt., 10/14/61. Died of disease, 5/2/63.
5th Sgt.	Teachey, Marshall	1832	M	Chinquapin, Duplin Co., NC	Farmer	Enlisted, 8/28/61. Died of typhoid fever, 8/14/62 at Richmond.
1st Cpl.	Carter, James	1840	S	Magnolia, Duplin Co., NC	Farm Labor	Enlisted, 8/28/61. Reduced to Pvt.,10/14/61. Died of pneumonia, 3/6/63 in Duplin Co.
2nd Cpl.	Stickland, William H.	1841	S	Wilmington, New Hanover Co., NC	Farm Labor	Enlisted, 8/28/61. Reduced to Pvt. 10/14/61. Discharged (disability—chronic rheumatism), 3/9/62.
3rd Cpl.	**Rivenbark, William**	1841	S	**Chinquapin, Duplin Co., NC**	Farm Labor	**Enlisted, 8/28/61. Killed, 7/1/62 at Malvern Hill.**
4th Cpl.	Newton, Samuel B.	1843	S	Calvin Creek, New Hanover Co., NC	Mechanic's Asst.	Enlisted, 8/28/61. Promoted to Sgt., 10/14/61. Promoted to 1st Sgt., 3/27/62. Promoted to 3rd Lt., 1/24/63. Promoted to 2nd Lt., 3/6/63. Commanded Co's D & E, 7/1/64–8/31/64. Captured, 4/6/65 at Sailor's Creek.
Pvt.	**Aughtry, William A.**	1839	S	Clinton, Sampson Co., NC	Turpentine Labor	**Enlisted, 9/1/61. Died of pneumonia, 12/18/62 at Gordonsville, VA.**
Pvt.	**Beasley, Calvin**	1839	S	**Magnolia, Duplin Co., NC**	Farm Labor	**Enlisted, 8/28/61. Died of disease, 11/26/61 at Wilmington, NC.**
Pvt.	Beasley, Edward	1838	S	Magnolia, Duplin Co., NC	Farm Labor	Enlisted, 8/28/61. Wounded, 5/12/64 at Spotsylvania. Wounded (scalp, flesh), 5/6/65 at Sailor's Creek.
Pvt.	Benton, Ellis A.	1843	S	Magnolia, Duplin Co., NC	Farm Labor	Enlisted, 8/28/61. Promoted to Cpl., 1/1/62. Captured, 5/6/65 at Burkeville.

30th North Carolina Infantry Roster, Company E

Rank	Name	DOB	M/S	Residence	Occupation	Remarks
Pvt.	Best, John B.	1844	S	Mt. Olive, Duplin Co., NC	Farm Labor	Enlisted, 8/28/61. Wounded (leg), 9/17/62 at Sharpsburg. Wounded, 7/1/63 at Gettysburg. Promoted to Sgt., 7/18/64. Wounded (right ankle) at Sailor's Creek, and captured, 4/6/65 at Burkesville Jct.
Pvt.	Best, Rowland J.	1840	S	Kenansville, Duplin Co., NC	Farm Labor	Enlisted, 8/28/61. Discharged due to disability (chronic skin disorder), 3/9/62.
Pvt.	**Bland, David**	**1840**	**S**	**Magnolia, Duplin Co., NC**		**Enlisted, 8/28/61. Died of typhoid fever, 3/11/62 at Wilmington, NC.**
Pvt.	Bland, John J.	1834	S	Magnolia, Duplin Co., NC	Farm Labor	Enlisted, 8/28/61. Wounded & Captured, 7/1/62 at Malvern Hill. Wounded (arm), 8/21/64 at Charles Town.
Pvt.	Blanton, Thomas	1841	S	Magnolia, Duplin Co., NC	Farm Labor	Enlisted, 8/28/61. No further records after 8/31/64.
Pvt.	**Boney, James T.**	**1840**	**S**	**Magnolia, Duplin Co., NC**	**Farm Labor**	**Enlisted, 8/28/61. Killed, 6/27/62 at Gaines Mill.**
Pvt.	**Bowen, John R.**	**1813**	**M**	**Magnolia, Duplin Co., NC**	**Distiller**	Enlisted, 8/28/61. Wounded (side), 7/2/62 at Cold Harbor. Died of wounds, 7/18/62.
Pvt.	Bradshaw, James B.	1844	S	Magnolia, Duplin Co., NC	Farm Labor	Enlisted, 10/8/61. Wounded, 10/14/64 at Bristoe Station. Captured, 9/22/64 at Fisher's Hill. POW—Point Lookout, MD. Exchanged, 3/17/65.
Pvt.	Brown, Jesse	1834	S	Magnolia, Duplin Co., NC	Day Labor	Enlisted, 10/14/61. Absent, sick since, 6/23/64.
Pvt.	**Brown, John (1st)**	**1824**	**M**	**Magnolia, Duplin Co., NC**	**Farmer**	Enlisted, 10/8/61. Died of typhoid pneumonia, 3/2/62 at Camp Wyatt, NC.
Pvt.	**Butler, Benjamin A.**	**1842**	**S**	**Hallsville, Duplin Co., NC**	**Blacksmith**	Enlisted, 10/8/61. Wounded & captured, 9/17/62 at Sharpsburg. Died of wounds, 10/1/62 at Stone House hospital, Sharpsburg, MD.
Pvt.	Carr, John J.	1841	S	Kenansville, Duplin Co., NC	Farm Labor	Enlisted, 10/8/61. Captured, 4/6/65 at Farmville.
Pvt.	**Carr, Obed**	**1817**	**M**	**Magnolia, Duplin Co., NC**	**Farmer**	**Enlisted, 8/28/61. Died of disease, 11/16/61 in Smithville, NC.**
Pvt.	Carter, Linton	1837	S	Magnolia, Duplin Co., NC	Farm Labor	Enlisted, 8/28/61. Wounded (leg), 8/28/64 at Shepherdstown. No further records.
Pvt.	Cavenaugh, Jacob W.	1840	S	Chinquapin, Duplin Co., NC	Farm Labor	Enlisted, 8/28/61. Wounded, 7/1/62 at Malvern Hill. Promoted to Cpl., 9/1/62. Reduced to Pvt., 8/1/63. Wounded, 5/12/64 at Spotsylvania. Wounded, (leg), 8/21/64 at Charles Town, VA. Captured, 4/6/65 at High Bridge. Released, 6/26/65.
Pvt.	**Cottle, Frederick**	**1837**	**M**	**Hallsville, Duplin Co., NC**	**Farmer**	**Enlisted, 8/28/61. Died of pneumonia, 2/7/63 at Richmond, VA.**
Pvt.	Dempsey, Kinchen H.	1842	S	Magnolia, Duplin Co., NC	Farm Labor	Enlisted, 8/28/61. Promoted to Cpl., 7/20/63. Wounded, 5/12/64 at Spotsylvania. Promoted, to Sgt., 8/21/64. Captured, 9/20/64 at Fisher's Hill. POW—Point Lookout, MD. Exchanged, 2/13/65.
Pvt.	Dickson, James G. "German"	1844	S	Mt. Olive, Duplin Co., NC	Farm Labor	Enlisted, 8/28/61. Wounded (shoulder), 6/27/62 at Gaines Mill. Retired, due to wounds, 4/1/64.

Rank	Name	DOB	M/S	Residence	Occupation	Remarks
Pvt.	Dickson, Riol	1843	S	Mt. Olive, Duplin Co., NC	Farm Labor	Enlisted, 8/28/61. Wounded (flesh wound from shell), 9/17/62 at Sharpsburg. Wounded (spine & thigh), and captured, 9/19/64 at Winchester. No further records.
Pvt.	Dickson, Robert L.	1841	S	Chinquapin, Duplin Co., NC	Farm Labor	Enlisted, 8/28/61. Discharged (disability), 2/2/62.
Pvt.	Edwards, Isaac N.	1827	M	Hallsville, Duplin Co., NC	Farmer	Enlisted, 8/28/61. Court Martialed 2/23/63. Captured, 5/12/64 at Spotsylvania. POW—Elmira, NY. Released, 6/25/65.
Pvt.	Ellis, John W.	1828	M	Whiteville, Columbus Co., NC	Lawyer	Enlisted, 8/28/61. Promoted to Ord. Sgt., 10/17/61. "Absent, attending the legislature of N.C," 9/1/62–12/31/62. Promoted to 3rd Lt., 2/27/63. Wounded, 5/3/63 at Chancellorsville. Resigned due to wounds, 9/1/63.
Pvt.	Ezzel, William W.	1828	M	Mt. Olive, Duplin Co., NC	Shoemaker	Enlisted, 8/28/61. Discharged (disability), 1/21/62.
Pvt.	Fursell, Andrew G.	1843	S	Duplin Co., NC	Farm Labor	Enlisted, 8/28/61. Promoted to Cpl., 5/1/62. Wounded, 6/27/62 at Gaines Mill. TDY—hospital duty. Reduced to Pvt., 8/1/63. Retired to Invalid Corps, 12/7/64.
Pvt.	**Grady, John W.**	1840	S	**Mt. Olive, Duplin Co., NC**	**Farm Labor**	**Enlisted, 8/28/61. Wounded (thigh amputated), 10/14/63 at Bristoe Station. Died of wounds, 10/25/63 at Richmond, VA.**
Pvt.	Hanchey, John W.	1839	S	Chinquapin, Duplin Co., NC	Farm Labor	Enlisted, 8/28/61. Wounded, 9/17/62 at Sharpsburg. Wounded, 12/13/62 at Fredericksburg. Promoted to Cpl., 8/1/63. Promoted to Sgt., 5/19/64. Paroled, 4/9/65 at Appomattox.
Pvt.	**Henderson, Abraham**	1833	M	**Chinquapin, Duplin Co., NC**	**Farmer**	**Enlisted, 8/28/61. Died of pneumonia, 6/11/62 at Richmond, VA.**
Pvt.	**Henderson, James W.**	1842	S	**Chinquapin, Duplin Co., NC**	**Farm Labor**	**Enlisted, 8/28/61. Captured, 7/3/63 at Gettysburg. POW—Died of disease, 8/27/63 at Waynesboro, PA.**
Pvt.	Johnson, Ezra W.	1839		Duplin Co., NC		Enlisted, 8/28/61. Paroled, 4/9/65 at Appomattox.
Pvt.	**Johnson, Josiah**	1825	M	**Calvin Creek, New Hanover Co., NC**	**Farmer**	**Enlisted, 8/28/61. Died of disease, 11/13/63 at Smithville, NC.**
Pvt.	Johnson, Major O.	1843	S	Duplin Co., NC		Enlisted, 8/28/61. Wounded ("skull fractured by artillery"), 7/3/63 at Gettysburg. Paroled, 4/9/65 at Appomattox.
Pvt.	Jones, James W.	1842	S	So. Washington, New Hanover Co., NC	Farm Labor	Enlisted, 8/28/61. Wounded (shoulder, scapula fractured), 5/3/63 at Chancellorsville. Discharged due to wounds, 8/20/63.
Pvt.	Jones, John J.	1826	M	Magnolia, Duplin Co., NC	Carpenter	Enlisted, 8/28/61. TDY—carpenter, 11/1/62. TDY—gunboat duty, 3/1/62–4/9/65.
Pvt.	**Lanier, Jacob W.**	1842	S	**Duplin Co., NC**		**Enlisted, 8/28/61. Wounded (head, skull fractured), 7/3/63 at Gettysburg "caused by artillery shell." Wounded (bladder & bowels), 6/1/64 at Cold Harbor. Died of wounds, 6/4/64.**
Pvt.	Mallard, John W.	1843	S	Duplin Co., NC		Enlisted, 8/28/61. TDY—nurse in Richmond hospital, 3/1/62–8/31/63. Captured, 5/12/64 at Spotsylvania. POW—Elmira, NY. Exchanged, 3/14/65.

Rank	Name	DOB	M/S	Residence	Occupation	Remarks
Pvt.	Mallard, William W.	1836	M	Chinquapin, Duplin Co., NC	Farmer	Enlisted, 8/28/61. Wounded (leg amputated), 5/3/63 at Chancellorsville. Retired due to wound, 5/24/64.
Pvt.	Malpass, Carleton	1841	S	Calvin Creek, New Hanover Co., NC	Farm Labor	Enlisted, 8/28/61. Wounded, 6/27/62 at Gainesville. Wounded (right hip), 5/12/64 at Spotsylvania. No further records.
Pvt.	Manellis, John	1835	S	Teachey's Depot, Duplin Co., NC	Farm Labor	Enlisted, 8/28/61. Wounded (ribs & spine), 7/1/62 at Malvern Hill. Absent due to wounds. No further records.
Pvt.	McNellis, John	1833		Duplin Co., NC		Enlisted, 8/28/61. Wounded, 5/3/63 at Chancellorsville. No further records after 8/31/64.
Pvt.	**Merritt, Levi**	**1839**		**Duplin Co., NC**		**Enlisted, 8/28/61. Died of disease, 9/27/62 at home in Duplin Co., NC.**
Pvt.	Murphy, Timothy C.	1814	M	Chinquapin, Duplin Co., NC	Farmer	Enlisted, 8/28/61. Discharged (disability), 12/26/61.
Pvt.	**Newkirk, George B.**	**1840**	**S**	**Magnolia, Duplin Co., NC**	**Farm Labor**	**Enlisted, 8/28/61. Promoted to Sgt., 8/24/62. Killed, 8/21/64 at Charles Town.**
Pvt.	**Newton, James O.**	**1843**	**S**	**Calvin Creek, New Hanover Co., NC**	**Farm Labor**	**Enlisted, 8/28/61. Died, date unknown (late 1862).**
Pvt.	Norris, Joseph	1810	M	Magnolia, Duplin Co., NC	Farmer	Enlisted, 8/28/61. Discharged (chronic rheumatism), 9/27/62.
Pvt.	Pickett, William D.	1836		Duplin Co., NC		Enlisted, 8/28/61. Wounded, 7/1/62 at Malvern Hill. Wounded, 5/6/64 at the Wilderness. Absent due to wounds. No records after 10/31/64.
Pvt.	Rackley, James S.	1841	S	Magnolia, Duplin Co., NC	Farm Labor	Enlisted, 8/28/61. No records after 8/31/64.
Pvt.	Rayner, John C.	1836	M	Chinquapin, Duplin Co., NC	Farm Labor	Enlisted, 8/28/61. Discharged (disability-sickness), 4/26/62.
Pvt.	Register, Samuel C.	1839	S	Magnolia, Duplin Co., NC	Farm Labor	Enlisted, 8/28/61. Captured, 11/7/63 at Kelly's Ford. POW—Point Lookout, MD. Exchanged, 2/24/65.
Pvt.	Rich, Christopher C.	1845	S	Kenansville, Duplin Co., NC	Farm Labor	Enlisted, 8/28/61. Captured, 11/7/63 at Kelly's Ford. POW—Point Lookout, MD. Exchanged, 2/13/65.
Pvt.	Rivenbark, James T.	1843	S	Duplin Co., NC		Enlisted, 8/28/61. Promoted, to Cpl., 10/14/61. Reduced to Pvt., 7/20/63. Captured, 7/24/63 at Manassas Gap, Front Royal. POW—Point Lookout, MD. Exchanged, 2/23/65.
Pvt.	**Rivenbark, Joseph**	**1844**	**S**	**Duplin Co., NC**		**Enlisted, 8/28/61. Wounded, 7627/62 at Gaines Mill. Died of wounds, (date unknown).**
Pvt.	Rivenbark, Teachey	1843	S	Camera, New Hanover Co., NC	Farm Labor	Enlisted, 8/28/61. Wounded, 7/1/62 at Malvern Hill. Promoted to Sgt., 10/24/62. Wounded (thigh fractured), 11/7/63 at Kelly's Ford. Promoted to 1st Sgt., 8/21/64. No records after 10/31/64.
Pvt.	**Rouse, Barnet**	**1836**		**Duplin Co., NC**		**Enlisted, 8/28/61. Wounded, 6/27/62 at Gaines Mill. Died of wounds (date unknown).**
Pvt.	**Savage, Cornelius**	**1841**	**S**	**Magnolia, Duplin Co., NC**	**Farm Labor**	**Enlisted, 8/28/61. Promoted to Sgt., 4/20/62. Died of disease, 10/20/62 near Winchester.**

Rank	Name	DOB	M/S	Residence	Occupation	Remarks
Pvt.	Strickland, Isaac J.	1836	S	Kenansville, Duplin Co., NC	Minister	Enlisted, 8/28/61. Promoted to Cpl., 10/14/61. Promoted to Ord. Sgt., 5/1/64. TDY—Hospital duty in Raleigh since 9/1/64.
Pvt.	Strickland, William W.	1837		Duplin Co., NC		Enlisted, 8/28/61. Killed, 6/27/62 at Gaines Mill.
Pvt.	Stiles, John M.	1833	M	Chinquapin, Duplin Co., NC	Day Labor	Enlisted, 8/28/61. Died of "brain fever," 1/14/63 at Guinea Station, VA.
Pvt.	Teachey, James W.	1838	M	Magnolia, Duplin Co., NC	Day Labor	Enlisted, 8/28/61. Promoted to Sgt., 6/1/63. Killed, 7/18/64 at Snicker's Gap.
Pvt.	Thompson, Andrew J.	1824		Duplin Co., NC		Enlisted, 8/28/61. Killed, 11/7/63 at Kelly's Ford.
Pvt.	Tucker, William	1843	S	Mt. Olive, Duplin Co., NC	Carpenter's Asst.	Enlisted, 8/28/61. Captured, 5/19/64 at Harris Farm. POW—Elmira, NY. Exchanged, 2/21/65.
Pvt.	Wallace, Robert C.	1839	S	Chinquapin, Duplin Co., NC	Teacher	Enlisted, 8/28/61. Promoted to Sgt., 10/14/61. Promoted to 1st Sgt., 3/1/62. Reduced to Pvt., 12/1/62. Died of pneumonia, 3/11/63 near Fredericksburg.
Pvt.	Wallace, William T.	1843	S	Chinquapin, Duplin Co., NC	Farm Labor	Enlisted, 8/28/61. Wounded, 6/27/62 at Gaines Mill. Killed, 5/3/63 at Chancellorsville.
Pvt.	Ward, John F.	1838	S	Magnolia, Duplin Co., NC	Farm Labor	Enlisted, 8/28/61. Promoted to Cpl. 5/19/64. Captured, 10/19/64 at Cedar Creek. POW—Point Lookout, MD. Released, 6/21/65.
Pvt.	Wells, James W.	1839	S	Magnolia, Duplin Co., NC	Farm Labor	Enlisted, 8/28/61. Promoted to Sgt., 5/1/62. Wounded, 9/17/62 at Sharpsburg. Promoted to 1st Sgt., 1/1/64. Killed, 5/19/64 at Harris Farm.
Pvt.	Wells, John H.	1837	S	Magnolia, Duplin Co., NC	Farm Labor	Enlisted, 8/28/61. Promoted to Cpl., 10/14/61. Wounded, 7/27/62 at Gaines Mill. Promoted to Sgt., 10/1/62. Wounded, 12/13/62 at Fredericksburg. Died of wounds, 12/22/62.
Pvt.	Wood, Marley	1825	M	Hallsville, Duplin Co., NC	Farmer	Enlisted, 8/28/61. Died of pneumonia, 1/21/63 at Gordonsville, VA.
Pvt.	Wood, Uzzell T.	1828	M	Hallsville, Duplin Co., NC	Farmer	Enlisted, 8/28/61. Court Martialed, 4/9/63. Wounded, 5/12/64 at Spotsylvania. Paroled, 4/9/65 at Appomattox.

1861 Recruits

Rank	Name	DOB	M/S	Residence	Occupation	Remarks
Pvt.	Bradshaw, Samuel	1843	S	Magnolia, Duplin Co., NC	Farm Labor	Enlisted, 11/10/61. Discharged (disability "paralysis of right foot following fracture," 9/9/62.
Pvt.	Jones, Isaac	1821	M	Mt. Olive, Duplin Co., NC	Farmer	Enlisted, 11/1/61. Discharged (disability), 1/1/62.
Pvt.	Streets, Wimbert	1816	M	Chinquapin, Duplin Co., NC	Carpenter	Enlisted, 11/27/61. Died of pneumonia, 3/19/63 at Staunton, VA.

1862 Recruits

Rank	Name	DOB	M/S	Residence	Occupation	Remarks
Pvt.	Blanton, Morris	1844	S	Magnolia Duplin Co., NC	Farm Labor	Enlisted, 1/1/62. Killed, 6/27/62 at Gaines Mill.
Pvt.	Boney, Hiram S.	1836	M	Magnolia, Duplin Co., NC	Farmer	Enlisted, 3/3/62. Captured, 9/22/64 at Fisher's Hill. POW—Point Lookout, MD. Exchanged, 2/10/65.

30th North Carolina Infantry Roster, Company E

Rank	Name	DOB	M/S	Residence	Occupation	Remarks
Pvt.	Boney, Joseph K.	1834	M	Teachey's Depot, Duplin Co., NC	Farmer	Enlisted, 3/3/62. Died of disease, 8/21/62 at Richmond, VA.
Pvt.	Bostick, Bryant W.	1837	M	Kenansville, Duplin Co., NC	Farmer	Enlisted, 3/3/62. Wounded (left thigh fractured), 5/6/64 at the Wilderness. Discharged due to wounds, 2/18/65.
Pvt.	Bostick, David R.	1845	S	Teachey's Depot, Duplin Co., NC	Student	Enlisted, 3/3/62. Discharged (disability), 9/15/62.
Pvt.	Bradshaw, B. D.	1845	S	Magnolia, Duplin Co., NC	Farm Labor	Enlisted, 4/20/62. Paroled, 4/9/65 at Appomattox.
Pvt.	Bradshaw, Obed	1837	M	Magnolia, Duplin Co., NC	Farmer	Enlisted, 3/3/62. Killed, 5/3/63 at Chancellorsville.
Pvt.	Brown, Felix	1837	M	Chinquapin, Duplin Co., NC	Farmer	Enlisted, 3/3/62 (as a substitute). Captured, 5/30/64 at Cold Harbor. POW—Point Lookout, MD. Exchanged, 10/29/64.
Pvt.	Butler, Henry G.	1832	S	Chinquapin, Duplin Co., NC	Farmer	Enlisted, 3/3/62. Killed, 6/4/64 at Cold Harbor.
Pvt.	Cavenaugh, George W.	1841	S	Chinquapin, Duplin Co., NC	Farm Labor	Enlisted, 3/3/62. Captured, 10/14/63 at Bristoe Station. POW—Point Lookout, MD. Died of chronic diarrhea, 2/5/65.
Pvt.	Cavenaugh, James D.	1837	S	Chinquapin, Duplin Co., NC	Farm Labor	Enlisted, 3/3/62. Wounded (foot), 7/1/62 at Malvern Hill. Captured, 11/7/64 at Kelly's Ford. POW—Point Lookout, MD. Exchanged, 2/24/65.
Pvt.	Cavenaugh, James H.	1844	S	Chinquapin, Duplin Co., NC	Farm Labor	Enlisted, 3/3/62. Died of disease, 12/17/63 at Orange Court House, VA.
Pvt.	Cavenaugh, Obed E.	1828	M	Chinquapin, Duplin Co., NC	Farmer	Enlisted, 3/3/62. Killed, 7/1/62 at Malvern Hill.
Pvt.	Cole, Jesse T.	1844	S	Chinquapin, Duplin Co., NC	Farm Labor	Enlisted, 3/3/62. Died of disease, 1/10/63 at Richmond, VA.
Pvt.	Cole, Jesse	1818	M	Chinquapin, Duplin Co. NC	Farmer	Enlisted, 3/3/62. Discharged (disability-'general neurosis'), 9/29/62.
Pvt.	Dickson, Harrall	1837	S	Mt. Olive, Duplin Co., NC	Farm Labor	Enlisted, 3/3/62. Wounded (head, "severe wound to scalp"), 6/30/62 at Cold Harbor. Retired, 4/1/64 due to wounds.
Pvt.	Evans, Adin	1827	S	Hallsville, Duplin Co., NC	Farm Labor	Enlisted, 3/3/62. Wounded, 6/27/62 at Gaines Mill. Wounded, 5/12/64 at Spotsylvania. Sick at hospital since 6/24/64. No further records.
Pvt.	Hanchey, Bryant W.	1840	S	Chinquapin, Duplin Co., NC	Farm Labor	Enlisted, 3/3/62. Died of pneumonia, 2/18/63 at Richmond, VA.
Pvt.	Harrell, John O.	1827		Magnolia, Duplin Co., NC	Farmer	Enlisted, 3/3/62. Died of disease, 12/17/63 at Orange Court House, VA.
Pvt.	Henderson, Brantly B.	1840	S	Chinquapin, Duplin Co., NC	Farm Labor	Enlisted, 3/3/62. Promoted to Sgt., 3/27/62. Wounded (left leg) & Captured, 9/21/62 near Hagerstown. POW—Ft. Delaware, DE. Exchanged, 12/15/62. Killed, 5/12/64 at Spotsylvania.
Pvt.	Henderson, Jesse R.	1838	M	Cypress Creek, Duplin Co., NC	Farmer	Enlisted, 3/3/62. Wounded, 7/1/62 at Malvern Hill. Died of pneumonia, 3/28/63 at Gordonsville, VA.
Pvt.	Hunter, Martin	1834	M	Chinquapin, Duplin Co., NC	Cooper	Enlisted, 3/3/62. Captured, 5/12/64 at Spotsylvania. POW—Elmira, NY. Released, 6/23/65.

Appendix 2

Rank	Name	DOB	M/S	Residence	Occupation	Remarks
Pvt.	Lanier, Brantly	1827	M	Hallsville, Duplin Co., NC	Farmer	Enlisted, 3/3/62. TDY–Provost Guard, 11/1/63–8/31/64. Captured, 11/19/64 at Cedar Creek (Strasburg). POW—Point Lookout, MD. Exchanged, 2/10/65.
Pvt.	Lanier, James P.	1839		Duplin Co., NC		Enlisted, 3/3/62. Died of pneumonia, 2/27/63 in Duplin Co., NC.
Pvt.	Lanier, Lewis W.	1840	S	Hallsville, Duplin Co., NC	Student	Enlisted, 3/3/62. Died of smallpox, 12/4/62 in Richmond, VA.
2nd Lt.	McMillan, Daniel T.	1838		Duplin Co., NC		Elected to 2nd Lt., 3/27/62. Resigned, 2/14/63 due to disability.
Pvt.	Mobley, William V.	1835	M	Chinquapin, Duplin Co., NC	Day Labor	Enlisted, 3/3/62. Captured, 9/19/64 at Winchester. POW—Point Lookout, MD. Died of consumption, 2/12/65.
Pvt.	Mobley, Wright W.	1838	S	Chinquapin, Duplin Co., NC	Farm Labor	Enlisted, 3/3/62. Died of pneumonia, 5/19/63 at home in Duplin Co., NC.
Pvt.	Murray, Thomas M.	1830	M	Magnolia, Duplin Co., NC	Farmer	Enlisted, 3/3/62. Wounded (hand), 5/12/64 at Spotsylvania. Absent due to wounds. No records after 12/13/64.
Pvt.	Norris, James	1834		Duplin Co., NC		Enlisted, 11/1/62. Died of pneumonia, 7/2/63 at home in Duplin Co., NC.
Pvt.	Norris, Reuben	1819	M	Duplin Co., NC	Farmer	Enlisted, 3/1/62. Discharged (disability), 7/1/63.
Pvt.	Norris, Timothy	1824	M	Chinquapin, Duplin Co., NC	Farmer	Enlisted, 3/6/62. Discharged (Disability-chronic rheumatism), 6/3/63.
Pvt.	Norris, William W.	1842	S	Magnolia, Duplin Co., NC	Farm Labor	Enlisted, 3/3/62. Wounded, 6/27/62 at Gaines Mill. Paroled, 4/9/65 at Appomattox.
Pvt.	Parker, Jacob W.	1837		Duplin Co., NC		Enlisted, 3/3/62. Captured, 5/19/64 at Harris Farm. POW—Elmira, NY. Exchanged, 3/2/65.
Pvt.	Pickett, John L.	1839	S	Hallsville, Duplin Co., NC	Farm Labor	Enlisted, 3/3/62. Wounded, 12/13/63 at Fredericksburg. Captured, 11/7/63 at Kelly's Ford. POW—Point Lookout, MD. Exchanged, 2/25/65.
Pvt.	Pierce, Nixon	1826	M	Magnolia, Duplin Co., NC	Farmer	Enlisted, 3/3/62. Promoted to Cpl., 8/1/63. Captured, 5/12/64 at Spotsylvania. POW—Point Lookout, MD. Paroled, 6/23/65.
Pvt.	Salmon, Kilby	1816	M	Magnolia, Duplin Co., NC	Farmer	Enlisted, 3/3/62. Discharged (disability-old age), 5/29/62.
Pvt.	Savage, John	1843	S	Magnolia, Duplin Co., NC	Farm Labor	Enlisted, 1/2/62. Captured, 7/4/63 at South Mountain (retreat from Gettysburg). POW—Point Lookout, MD. Exchanged, 2/13/65.
Pvt.	Sholar, James H.	1832		Duplin Co., NC		Enlisted, 3/3/62. Deserted & Captured, 9/29/62 near Warrenton. Released, 9/30/62. AWOL until 9/30/64. Captured, 4/6/65 at Burkeville.
Pvt.	Southerland, James	1827		Duplin Co., NC		Enlisted, 3/3/62. Wounded, (thigh, flesh wound), 7/1/63 at Gettysburg. Captured, 11/7/63 at Kelly's Ford. POW—Point Lookout, MD. Joined U.S. forces, 1/25/64.

Rank	Name	DOB	M/S	Residence	Occupation	Remarks
Pvt.	Strickland, David R.	1841	S	New Hanover Co., NC		Enlisted, 3/3/62. Captured, 9/29/62 near Warrenton. Paroled, 9/30/62. AWOL until 4/4/63. Captured, 5/12/64 at Spotsylvania. POW—Elmira, NY. Released, 6/27/65.
Pvt.	Teachey, Atlas	1844	S	Cypress Creek, Duplin Co., NC	Farm Labor	Enlisted, 2/1/62. TDY—light duty at Lynchburg, 1/1/64–4/9/65.
Pvt.	Teachey, Jacob T.	1844	S	Magnolia, Duplin Co., NC	Day Labor	Enlisted, 3/3/62. Wounded ("through the bowels"), 7/18/64 at Snicker's Gap. Retired due to wounds, 1/17/65.
Pvt.	Teachey, Wiley B.	1840	S	Magnolia, Duplin Co., NC	Farm Labor	Enlisted, 3/3/62. Wounded, 5/12/64 at Spotsylvania. Promoted to Cpl., 8/21/64. Captured, 10/19/64 at Cedar Creek. POW—Point Lookout, MD. Exchanged, 2/10/65.
Pvt.	Tucker, Owen	1840	S	Kenansville, Duplin Co., NC	Day Labor	Enlisted, 1/1/62. Died of chronic dysentery, 11/22/62 at Mount Jackson, VA.
Pvt.	Underwood, R. H.			Duplin Co., NC		Enlisted, 3/3/62. Died of disease, 5/8/62 at Camp Draughon, NC

1862 Conscripts

Rank	Name	DOB	M/S	Residence	Occupation	Remarks
Pvt.	Bray, John W.	1844	S	Foust's Mill, Randolph Co., NC	Farm Labor	Conscripted, 7/1/62. Captured, 5/8/64 at the Wilderness. POW—Elmira, NY. Released, 5/29/65.
Pvt.	Cottle, W. Davis	1839	S	Hallsville, Duplin Co., NC	Farm Labor	Substitute, 5/3/62. Died of chronic bronchitis, 3/11/63 at Richmond, VA.

1863 Conscripts

Rank	Name	DOB	M/S	Residence	Occupation	Remarks
Pvt.	Balkum, Lemuel	1821	M	Taylor's Bridge, Sampson Co., NC	Farmer	Conscripted, 9/4/63. Died of typhoid fever, 12/26/63 at Richmond, VA.
Pvt.	Brigman, John	1813	M	Rockingham, Richmond Co., NC	Turpentine Labor	Conscripted, 9/16/63. Captured, 5/30/64 at Cold Harbor ("Old Church"). POW—Elmira, NY. Died of chronic diarrhea, 10/24/64.
Pvt.	Brown, John (2nd)	1820	S	Magnolia, Duplin Co., NC	Farmer	Conscripted, 8/31/63. Wounded (face, fractured jaw), 5/12/64 at Spotsylvania. Died of wounds, 5/24/64.
Pvt.	Davis, Simpson	1820	M	Lane's Creek, Union Co., NC	Farmer	Conscripted, 9/16/63. TDY—Teamster. Paroled, 4/9/63 at Appomattox.
Pvt.	Hamilton, William S.	1819		Union Co., NC		Conscripted, 9/16/63. Captured, 5/19/64 at Harris Farm. POW—Elmira, NY. Exchanged, 10/29/64. No further records.
Pvt.	Hamlet, Charles C.	1844	S	Walkersville, Union Co., NC	Farm Labor	Conscripted, 9/24/63. Absent, sick, 5/1/64. No further records.
Pvt.	Helms, Abel M.	1828	S	Monroe, Union Co., NC	Farmer	Conscripted, 10/3/63. Paroled, 4/9/65 at Appomattox.
Pvt.	Helms, Archibald	1825	M	Monroe, Union Co., NC	Farmer	Conscripted, 9/24/63. Captured, 4/6/65 at Burkeville.
Pvt.	Jones, James K.	1839		Duplin Co., NC		Conscripted, 6/29/63. Promoted to Sgt., 5/19/64. Paroled, 4/9/65 at Appomattox.
Pvt.	Knight, Thomas H.	1845	S	Enfield, Halifax Co., NC	Farm Labor	Conscripted, 6/29/63. TDY—shoe making in Richmond since 8/5/63. Captured, 4/4/65 at Clover Hill. POW—Hart's Island. Died of scurvy, 6/5/65.

Rank	Name	DOB	M/S	Residence	Occupation	Remarks
Pvt.	Laney, Lewis C.	1825	M	Monroe, Union Co., NC	Farmer	Conscripted, 9/24/63. Captured, 11/7/63 at Kelly's Ford. POW—Ft. Delaware, DE. Exchanged, 11/11/64. No further records.
Pvt.	Piner, James J.	1836	S	Calvin Creek, New Hanover Co., NC	Farm Labor	Enlisted, 8/31/63. Captured, 5/20/64 at Spotsylvania. POW—Elmira, NY. Died of smallpox, 3/4/64.
Pvt.	Rogers, Jobe B.	1821	M	Beaver Dam, Union Co., NC	Carpenter	Conscripted, 9/16/63. Captured, 5/31/64 at Old Church. POW—Elmira, NY. Died of chronic diarrhea, 1/28/65.
Pvt.	Shute, Henry B.	1844	S	Beaver Dam, Union Co., NC	Farm Labor	Conscripted, 9/23/63. Captured, 10/19/64 at Cedar Creek. POW—Point Lookout, MD. Released, 6/25/65.
Pvt.	Steele, Robert	1833	M	Walkersville, Union Co., NC	Farmer	Conscripted, 9/24/63. Captured, 5/31/64 at Old Church. POW—Elmira, NY. Exchanged, 3/14/65.
Pvt.	Tadlock, Starling D.	1844	S	Lanes Creek, Union Co., NC	Farm Labor	Conscripted, 9/16/63. Captured, 4/6/65 at Farmville.
Pvt.	Turner, David W.	1836		New Hanover or Duplin Co., NC		Conscripted, 8/31/63. Wounded, 11/7/63 at Kelly's Ford. Wounded (head), 8/21/64 near Charles Town. Paroled, 4/9/65 at Appomattox.

1864 Conscripts

Rank	Name	DOB	M/S	Residence	Occupation	Remarks
Pvt.	Duff, John T.	1846	S	Magnolia, Duplin Co., NC	Day Labor	Enlisted, 2/7/64. Paroled, 4/9/65 at Appomattox.
Pvt.	Wilson, John L.	1834	S	Lumberton, Robeson Co., NC	Railroad Labor	Conscripted, 3/1/64. Died of typhoid fever, 10/31/63 at Gordonsville, VA.

Company F—Sparta Band
Edgecombe County (Mustered into Regt.—8/31/61)

Rank	Name	DOB	M/S	Residence	Occupation	Remarks
Cpt.	Pitt, Franklin G.	1827	M	Tarboro, Edgecombe Co., NC	Physician	Commissioned 9/26/61. Resigned, 3/11/62.
1st Lt.	Moore, Willis M. (Mark)	1839	S	Rocky Mount, Edgecombe Co., NC	Farm Labor	Enlisted, 8/31/61. Elected Cpt., 3/10/62. Wounded (left breast), 5/8/64 at Spotsylvania. Killed, 10/19/64 at Cedar Creek.
2nd Lt.	Pitt, James W.	1841	S	Tarboro, Edgecombe Co., NC	Farm Labor	Enlisted, 8/31/61. Wounded, 6/21/62, on skirmish line. Died of typhoid fever, 8/4/63 at Richmond, VA.
3rd Lt.	Vines, Charles	1843	S	Tarboro, Edgecombe Co., NC	Farm Labor	Enlisted, 8/31/61. Resigned, 3/11/62. Was not re-elected.
1st Sgt.	Harrell, George K.	1842	S		Farm Labor	Enlisted 8/31/61. Elected to 1st Lt., 3/10/62. Wounded, 9/17/62 at Sharpsburg. Killed, 5/12/64 at Spotsylvania ("ball passing through head.")
2nd Sgt.	Cobb, John R.	1838	S	Tarboro, Edgecombe Co., NC	Farm Labor	Enlisted, 8/31/61. Reduced to Pvt., 1/-/62. Died of bilious fever, 1/25/62 at Tarboro, NC.
3rd Sgt.	Eagles, Lorenzo D.	1836	S	Eagles Crossroads, Edgecombe Co., NC	Teacher	Enlisted, 8/31/61. Elected to 3rd Lt., 3/10/62. Wounded, 6/27/62 at Gaines Mill. Promoted to 2nd Lt., 8/3/62. Wounded (above knee), 5/12/64 at Spotsylvania. Leg amputated. Died of wounds, 5/24/64.

30th North Carolina Infantry Roster, Company F

Rank	Name	DOB	M/S	Residence	Occupation	Remarks
4th Sgt.	Cobb, John B.	1841	S	Tarboro, Edgecombe Co., NC	Farm Labor	Enlisted, 8/31/61. Reduced to Pvt., 5/1/62. Paroled, 4/9/65 at Appomattox.
5th Sgt.	Smith, Lemuel H.	1823	S	Charlotte, Mecklenburg Co., NC	Clerk	Promoted to Regt. Commissary Sgt., 7/20/63. Transferred to F & S.
1st Cpl.	**Cherry, Spencer**	**1833**	**S**	**Tarboro, Edgecombe Co., NC**	**Farm Labor**	**Enlisted, 8/31/61. Promoted to Sgt., 5/1/62. Wounded, 7/1/62 at Malvern Hill. Wounded, 5/12/64 at Spotsylvania. Died of wounds, 5/21/64.**
2nd Cpl.	Moore, Thomas J.	1840	S	Tarboro, Edgecombe Co., NC	Farm Labor	Enlisted, 8/31/61. Reduced to Pvt., 3/-/62. Wounded (arm), 6/27/62 at Gaines' Mill. Furloughed from hospital at Danville, VA, 7/16/62. No further records.
3rd Cpl.	Carney, James	1830	M	Greenville, Pitt Co., NC	Farmer	Enlisted, 8/31/61. Discharged (chronic rheumatism), 3/19/62. Re-enlisted, 6/11/63. TDY—Hospital duty at Orange Court House; 12/-/63–8/31/64. No further records.
4th Cpl.	**Wells, Louis Redmond**	**1815**	**M**	**Tarboro, Edgecombe Co., NC**	**Miller**	**Enlisted, 8/31/61. Promoted to Sgt., 3/10/62. Reduced to Pvt., 1/-/64. Wounded (breast), 7/18/64 at Snicker's Gap. Died of wounds, 7/21/64 at Winchester, VA.**
Music	**Harrell, William**	**1843**	**S**	**Tarboro, Edgecombe Co., NC**		**Enlisted, 8/31/61. (Drummer). Reduced to Pvt., 1/-/62, Died of disease, 11/25/62 at Tarboro, NC.**
Pvt.	Bailey, Benjamin	1841	S	Fields, Greene Co., NC	Turpentine Labor	Enlisted, 8/31/61. Paroled, 4/9/65 at Appomattox.
Pvt.	Bell, Wm. Bennett	1822	M	Tarboro, Edgecombe Co., NC	Farmer	Enlisted, 8/31/61. Wounded (left knee), 10/19/64 at Cedar Creek. Paroled, 4/11/65 at Farmville.
Pvt.	Boyce, William	1831	M	Falkland, Pitt Co., NC	Overseer	Enlisted, 8/31/61. Wounded, 7/1/62 at Malvern Hill. Discharged (wounds), 5/15/63.
Pvt.	**Bradley, Oliver**	**1844**	**S**	**Tarboro, Edgecombe Co., NC**	**Farm Labor**	**Enlisted, 8/31/61. Promoted to Cpl., 3/10/62. Died of smallpox, 12/16/62 at Richmond, VA.**
Pvt.	Brasswell, James B.	1843	S	Tarboro, Edgecombe Co., NC	Farm Labor	Enlisted, 8/31/61. Wounded (right shoulder), 5/12/64 at Spotsylvania. Paroled, 4/9/65 at Appomattox.
Pvt.	**Brewer, Warren**	**1832**	**M**	**Bethel, Pitt Co., NC**	**Day Labor**	**Enlisted, 8/31/61. Died of typhoid fever, 4/23/62 at Wilmington, NC.**
Pvt.	Brown, Wm. Henry	1835	S	Tarboro, Edgecombe Co., NC	Farmer	Enlisted, 8/31/61. Promoted to Cpl., 3/10/62. Captured, 9/17/62 at Harper's Ferry. Paroled, 9/30/62. Captured, 11/7/63 at Kelly's Ford. POW—Point Lookout, MD. Exchanged, 3/3/65.
Pvt.	Bryant, Charles	1840	S	Bethel, Pitt Co., NC	Farm Labor	Enlisted, 8/31/61. Missing, 9/17/62 at Sharpsburg. No records after 11/30/62.
Pvt.	Burgess, Hardy	1834	M	Tarboro, Edgecombe Co., NC	Engineer	Enlisted, 8/31/61. TDY—Teamster; 4/1/63–8/31/63. Wounded (hand), 5/12/64 at Spotsylvania. Paroled, 4/9/65 at Appomattox.
Pvt.	Cobb, William	1840	S	Tarboro, Edgecombe Co., NC	Farm Labor	Enlisted, 8/31/61. Discharged (disability), 7/10/62.
Pvt.	Corbett, Dempsey	1833	M	Falkland, Pitt Co., NC	Farmer	Enlisted, 8/31/61. Wounded, 5/12/64 at Spotsylvania. Wounded, 4/6/65 at Sailor's Creek. Paroled, 4/21/65 at Farmville.

Appendix 2

Rank	Name	DOB	M/S	Residence	Occupation	Remarks
Pvt.	Corbett, Henry	1840	S	Tarboro, Edgecombe Co., NC	Farm Labor	Enlisted, 8/31/61. Sick in Hospital; 3/5/63–8/31/64. No further records.
Pvt.	**Corbett, James**	**1845**	**S**	**Tarboro, Edgecombe Co., NC**	**Farm Labor**	**Enlisted, 8/31/61. Died of typhoid fever, 11/10/61 at Smithville, NC.**
Pvt.	Corbett, William W.	1837	M	Falkland, Pitt Co., NC	Day Labor	Enlisted, 8/31/61. Captured, 7/4/63 in retreat from Gettysburg. POW—Ft. Delaware, DE. Exchanged, 8/20/63. Captured, 5/8/64 at Spotsylvania. POW—Elmira, NY. Exchanged, 3/20/65.
Pvt.	**Crisp, Eason**	**1842**	**S**	**Tarboro, Edgecombe Co., NC**	**Farm Labor**	**Enlisted, 8/31/61. Wounded, 7/1/62 at Malvern Hill. Died of wounds, 7/27/62 at Richmond, VA.**
Pvt.	Crisp, Levi	1820	M	Tarboro, Edgecombe Co., NC	Farmer	Enlisted, 8/31/61. Wounded ("badly in the mouth"), 7/1/63 at Gettysburg. Discharged (wounds), 9/8/64.
Pvt.	**Crisp, William G.**	**1841**	**S**	**Tarboro, Edgecombe Co., NC**	**Farm Labor**	**Enlisted, 8/31/61. Wounded (left shoulder), 5/12/64 at Spotsylvania. Died of wounds, 5/20/64.**
Pvt.	Deal, Reuben	1838	S	Rock Cut, Iredell Co., NC	Farm Labor	Enlisted, 8/31/61. Sick in hospital, 6/11/64 in Richmond. No further records.
Pvt.	Denton, Levi	1842	S	Tarboro, Edgecombe Co., NC	Farm Labor	Enlisted, 8/31/61. Wounded (right leg), 7/1/62 at Malvern Hill. Discharged (wounds), 12/28/63.
Pvt.	**Dew, Fr. Lewis**	**1830**	**M**	**Tarboro, Edgecombe Co., NC**	**Brick Mason**	**Enlisted, 8/31/61. Captured, 7/5/63 in retreat from Gettysburg. POW—Ft. Delaware, DE. Died of scurvy, 11/12/63.**
Pvt.	**Dew, William**	**1846**	**S**	**Tarboro, Edgecombe Co., NC**	**Farm Labor**	**Enlisted, 8/31/61. Wounded (head & lungs), 6/27/62 at Gainesville. Died of wounds, 7/3/62 at Richmond, VA.**
Pvt.	**Dickens, Ephraim**	**1841**	**S**	**Tarboro, Edgecombe Co., NC**	**Farm Labor**	**Enlisted, 8/31/61. Wounded (left thigh), 9/17/62 at Sharpsburg. Killed, 5/19/64 at Harris Farm.**
Pvt.	Dixon, Henry O.	1842	S	Tarboro, Edgecombe Co., NC	Farm Labor	Enlisted, 8/31/61. Captured, 11/7/63 at Kelly's Ford. POW—Point Lookout, MD. Released, 6/12/65.
Pvt.	Eason, James S.	1824	M	Tarboro, Edgecombe Co., NC	Farmer	Enlisted, 8/31/61. Discharged (chronic rheumatism), 3/5/62.
Pvt.	Edwards, Elsberry B.	1833	M	Tarboro, Edgecombe Co., NC	Timber Cutter	Enlisted, 8/31/61. Wounded, 9/14/62 at South Mountain. Paroled, 4/9/65 at Appomattox.
Pvt.	**Edwards, Montgomery**	**1840**	**S**	**Tarboro, Edgecombe Co., NC**	**Farm Labor**	**Enlisted, 8/31/61. Wounded ("gunshot wound in side"), 6/27/62 at Gaines' Mill. Died of typhoid pneumonia, 4/19/63 at Richmond, VA.**
Pvt.	**Everett, William**	**1828**	**M**	**Tarboro, Edgecombe Co., NC**	**Farmer**	**Enlisted, 8/31/61. Killed, 6/27/62 at Gaines' Mill.**
Pvt.	Felton, Richard	1834	S	Tarboro, Edgecombe Co., NC	Farmer	Enlisted, 8/31/61. Promoted to Cpl., 3/10/62. Wounded, 7/1/62 at Malvern Hill. Killed, 7/18/64 at Snicker's Gap.

Rank	Name	DOB	M/S	Residence	Occupation	Remarks
Pvt.	Forbes, Arthur	1841	S	Tarboro, Edgecombe Co., NC	Farm Labor	Enlisted, 8/31/61. Wounded (side), 6/27/29 at Gaines' Mill. Wounded, 5/3/63 at Chancellorsville. Wounded, 11/7/63 at Kelly's Ford. Promoted to Sgt., 7/-/64. Paroled, 4/9/65 at Appomattox.
Pvt.	Forbes, James	1842	S	Tarboro, Edgecombe Co., NC	Farm Labor	Enlisted, 8/31/61. Wounded, 6/27/62 at Gaines' Mill. Wounded, 7/18/64 at Snicker's Gap. Surrendered, 4/9/65 at Appomattox.
Pvt.	Fountain, Almond L. "Allen"	1841	S	Tarboro, Edgecombe Co., NC	Farm Labor	Enlisted, 8/31/61. Captured, 11/7/63 at Kelly's Ford. POW—Point Lookout, MD. Exchanged, 2/15/65.
Pvt.	**Harper, David**	**1837**	**S**	**Tarboro, Edgecombe Co., NC**	Farmer	**Enlisted, 8/31/61. Died of typhoid fever, 9/-/61 at Tarboro, NC.**
Pvt.	**Harrell, David**	**1842**	**S**	**Tarboro, Edgecombe Co., NC**	Farm Labor	**Enlisted, 8/31/61. Wounded, 7/1/62 at Malvern Hill. Killed, 9/17/62 at Sharpsburg.**
Pvt.	Harrell, Peter	1839	S	Tarboro, Edgecombe Co., NC	Farm Labor	Enlisted, 8/31/61. Wounded (foot & right leg), 5/3/63 at Chancellorsville. Returned—TDY–Light duty, 4/15/64–12/31/64. No further records.
Pvt.	Harrell, Watson	1842	S	Tarboro, Edgecombe Co., NC	Farm Labor	Enlisted, 8/31/61. Surrendered, 4/9/65 at Appomattox.
Pvt.	**Harriss, William J.**	**1841**	**S**	**Tarboro, Edgecombe Co., NC**	Farm Labor	**Enlisted, 8/31/61. Died of typhoid fever, 8/7/62 at Richmond, VA.**
Pvt.	**Hathaway, Henry**	**1841**	**S**	**Tarboro, Edgecombe Co., NC**	Farmer	**Enlisted, 8/31/61. Wounded, 7/1/62 at Malvern Hill. Wounded (jaw & shoulder), 7/3/63 at Gettysburg. Captured in field hospital, 7/4/63. Died of wounds, 7/10/63 at Gettysburg.**
Pvt.	Hathaway, Richard	1841	S	Tarboro, Edgecombe Co., NC	Farm Labor	Enlisted, 8/31/61. TDY—Teamster; 1/1/64–4/8/65. Surrendered, 4/9/65 at Appomattox.
Pvt.	**Hearn, Amos**	**1837**	**M**	**Tarboro, Edgecombe Co., NC**	Farmer	**Enlisted, 8/31/61. Died of disease, 6/22/62 at Wilmington, NC.**
Pvt.	House, James W.	1835	S	Tarboro, Edgecombe Co., NC	Trader	Enlisted, 8/31/61. Promoted to Sgt., 3/10/62. "Nominated of the Badge of Distinction for gallantry at Chancellorsville." Wounded, 11/7/63 at Kelly's Ford. Elected 2nd Lt., 5/24/64. Wounded (right foot) and captured, 4/9/65 at Appomattox. Released, 6/10/65.
Pvt.	**Johnson, Ellis**	**1844**	**S**	**Tarboro, Edgecombe Co., NC**	Farm Labor	**Enlisted, 8/31/61. Wounded (head), 5/3/63 at Chancellorsville. Died of wounds, 5/24/63 at Petersburg, VA.**
Pvt.	Keele, William	1833	S	Tarboro, Edgecombe Co., NC	Farmer	Enlisted, 8/31/61. Wounded (left shoulder), 9/17/62 at Sharpsburg. TDY—Guards duty at Richmond; 1/-/64–8/31/64.
Pvt.	**Leigh, Joseph**	**1840**	**S**	**Tarboro, Edgecombe Co., NC**	Farm Labor	**Enlisted, 8/31/61. Died of typhoid fever, 4/26/62 at Wilmington, NC.**
Pvt.	Leigh, Theophilus	1838	S	Tarboro, Edgecombe Co., NC	Farm Labor	Enlisted, 8/31/61. Wounded, 11/7/63 at Kelly's Ford. Paroled, 4/14/65 at Burkeville.

Appendix 2

Rank	Name	DOB	M/S	Residence	Occupation	Remarks
Pvt.	Lewis, John E.	1843	S	Tarboro, Edgecombe Co., NC	Farm Labor	Enlisted, 8/31/61. Wounded (right arm), 11/7/63 at Kelly's Ford. (Arm amputated). Retired due to wounds, 4/1/64.
Pvt.	Little, Jesse	1843	S	Tarboro, Edgecombe Co., NC	Farm Labor	Enlisted, 8/31/61. Wounded, 12/13/62 at Fredericksburg. Wounded (left thigh) and captured, 10/19/64 at Cedar Creek. POW—Baltimore, MD. Exchanged, 3/9/65.
Pvt.	Little, Jesse C.	1835	S	Tarboro, Edgecombe Co., NC	Farm Labor	Enlisted, 8/31/61. Wounded, 9/17/62 at Sharpsburg. Surrendered, 4/9/65 at Appomattox.
Pvt.	**Little, Willis**	**1835**	**M**	**Tarboro, Edgecombe Co., NC**	**Farmer**	**Enlisted, 8/31/61. Died of typhoid fever, 9/20/62 at Richmond.**
Pvt.	Madra, George (Alexander)	1842	S	Tarboro, Edgecombe Co., NC	Farm Labor	Enlisted, 8/31/61. Captured, 9/14/62 at South Mountain. POW—Ft. Delaware, DE. Exchanged, 11/10/62. Wounded (face), 5/3/63 at Chancellorsville. Wounded (hand & knee), 7/3/63 at Gettysburg. Captured, 5/19/64 at Harris Farm. POW—Point Lookout, MD. Released, 6/19/65.
Pvt.	**Mayo, James**	**1844**	**S**	**Tarboro, Edgecombe Co., NC**	**Day Labor**	**Enlisted, 8/31/61. Wounded, 12/13/62 at Fredericksburg. Died of typhoid pneumonia, 2/21/63 at Richmond, VA.**
Pvt.	Mercer, Jacob J.	1837	S	Tarboro, Edgecombe Co., NC	Farm Labor	Enlisted, 8/31/61. Wounded (left arm), 7/1/63 at Gettysburg. Captured, 7/4/63 in field hospital. POW—Baltimore, MD. Exchanged, 11/12/63. Retired due to wounds, 1/12/65.
Pvt.	Moore, Samuel R.	1841	S	Tarboro, Edgecombe Co., NC	Farm Labor	Enlisted, 8/31/61. Appointed 1st Sgt., 3/10/62. Elected 3rd Lt., 1/20/63. Wounded (back & abdomen), 5/12/64 at Spotsylvania. Wounded (right side), 9/19/64 at Winchester. Promoted to Cpt., 10/19/64. Surrendered, 4/9/65 at Appomattox.
Pvt.	Morgan, James B.	1842	S	Tarboro, Edgecombe Co., NC	Farm Labor	Enlisted, 8/31/61. Wounded (shoulder), 7/1/62 at Malvern Hill. Captured, 11/7/63 at Kelly's Ford. POW—Point Lookout, MD. Exchanged, 3/3/65.
Pvt.	Morgan, Wm. Gray	1840	S	Tarboro, Edgecombe Co., NC	Farm Labor	Enlisted, 8/31/61. Wounded, 9/14/62 at South Mountain. Surrendered, 4/9/65 at Appomattox.
Pvt.	**Mosely, Elisha**	**1845**	**S**	**Falkland, Pitt Co., NC**		**Enlisted, 8/31/61. Died of typhoid fever, 6/7/62 at Wilmington, NC.**
Pvt.	**O'Neal, John**	**1838**	**S**	**Tarboro, Edgecombe Co., NC**	**Farm Labor**	**Enlisted, 8/31/61. Killed, 7/1/62 at Malvern Hill.**
Pvt.	**Phillips, David J.**	**1840**	**S**	**Tarboro, Edgecombe Co., NC**	**Farm Labor**	**Enlisted, 8/31/61. Killed, 7/1/62 at Malvern Hill.**
Pvt.	Pittman, George W.	1831		Edgecombe or Green Co., NC		Enlisted, 8/31/61. Wounded (right thigh), 9/17/62 at Sharpsburg. Captured, 7/5/63 in retreat from Gettysburg (Waterloo, MD). POW—Point Lookout, MD. Exchanged, 2/23/65.
Pvt.	Pittman, Reddin E.	1839	S	Tarboro, Edgecombe Co., NC	Farmer	Enlisted, 8/31/61. Wounded, 6/27/62 at Gaines' Mill. Promoted to Cpl., 11/1/63. Wounded (right arm & right breast), 5/12/64 at Spotsylvania. Paroled, 4/9/65 at Appomattox.

Rank	Name	DOB	M/S	Residence	Occupation	Remarks
Pvt.	Pollard, James H.	1842	S	Tarboro, Edgecombe Co., NC	Day Labor	Enlisted, 8/31/61. Died of typhoid fever, 9/13/62 at Richmond, VA.
Pvt.	Price, Thomas	1840	S	Tarboro, Edgecombe Co., NC	Farm Labor	Enlisted, 8/31/61. Killed, 5/12/64 at Spotsylvania ("shot through head.")
Pvt.	Redick, Epinetus	1844	S	Tarboro, Edgecombe Co., NC	Farm Labor	Enlisted, 8/31/61. Wounded, 11/7/63 at Kelly's Ford. Wounded (ear & left eye) and captured, 7/12/64 at Ft. Stevens. POW—Elmira, NY. Died of pneumonia, 2/7/65.
Pvt.	Roberson, James	1843	S	Tarboro, Edgecombe Co., NC	Farm Labor	Enlisted, 8/31/61. Wounded, 5/3/63 at Chancellorsville. Captured, 11/7/63 at Kelly's Ford. POW—Point Lookout, MD. Exchanged, 3/3/65.
Pvt.	Robison, William	1838	S	Tarboro, Edgecombe Co., NC	Farm Labor	Enlisted, 8/31/61. Killed, 6/27/62 at Gaines' Mill.
Pvt.	Stallings, Edwin	1843	S	Tarboro, Edgecombe Co., NC	Farm Labor	Enlisted, 8/31/61. Surrendered, 4/9/65 at Appomattox.
Pvt.	Summerlin, George	1832	M	Tarboro, Edgecombe Co., NC	Farmer	Enlisted, 8/31/61. Wounded, 5/19/64 at Harris Farm. No further records after 8/31/64.
Pvt.	Vick, William	1840	S	Tarboro, Edgecombe Co., NC	Farm Labor	Enlisted, 8/31/61. Wounded, 7/1/62 at Malvern Hill. Wounded (neck), 5/12/64 at Spotsylvania. TDY—Teamster; 1/1/64–8/31/64. No further records.
Pvt.	Walston, Franklin	1844	S	Tarboro, Edgecombe Co., NC	Farm Labor	Enlisted, 8/31/61. Appointed, Cpl., 3/10/62. Wounded, 9/17/62 at Sharpsburg. Captured, 11/7/63 at Kelly's Ford. POW—Point Lookout, MD. Exchanged, 2/24/65.
Pvt.	Walston, James	1836	M	Tarboro, Edgecombe Co., NC	Farm Labor	Enlisted, 8/31/61. Killed, 7/1/62 at Malvern Hill.
Pvt.	Walston, Kinchen	1840	S	Wilson, Wilson Co., NC	Day Labor	Enlisted, 8/31/61. Sick in camp, 2/28/62–4/30/62. No further records.
Pvt.	Walston, William F.	1836	M	Tarboro, Edgecombe Co., NC	Farmer	Enlisted, 8/31/61. Captured, 9/14/62 at South Mountain. POW—Ft. Delaware, DE. Exchanged, 11/10/62. Wounded, 5/3/63 at Chancellorsville. Wounded, 8/21/64 at Charles Town. Died of wounds, 3/10/65 at Staunton, VA.
Pvt.	Webb, Morrison	1838	M	Tarboro, Edgecombe Co., NC	Farm Labor	Enlisted, 8/31/61. Wounded, 10/11/63 at Warrenton (Bristoe Station). Died of wounds, 11/2/63.
Pvt.	Webb, Newett	1839	S	Tarboro, Edgecombe Co., NC	Farm Labor	Enlisted, 8/31/61. Wounded, 9/17/62 at Sharpsburg. Promoted to Musician (drummer), 2/1/63. Wounded, 5/12/64 at Spotsylvania. Paroled, 4/9/65 at Appomattox.
Pvt.	Whitehurst, Thomas	1831	S	Tarboro, Edgecombe Co., NC	Farmer	Enlisted, 8/31/61. Promoted to Sgt., 3/10/62. Promoted to 1st Sgt., 4/-/63. Killed, 5/8/64 at Spotsylvania ("shot through head.")
Pvt.	Wiggins, Martin W.	1842	S	Tarboro, Edgecombe Co., NC	Farm Labor	Enlisted, 8/31/61. Wounded (thigh), 6/27/62 at Gaines' Mill. Promoted to Sgt., 1/1/63. Wounded (right arm), 5/3/63 at Chancellorsville. (Arm amputated) Died of wounds, 6/8/63 at Petersburg.

Rank	Name	DOB	M/S	Residence	Occupation	Remarks
Pvt.	Williford, Thomas	1842	M	Tarboro, Edgecombe Co., NC	Farmer	Enlisted, 8/31/61. Promoted to Sgt., 3/10/62. Killed, 7/1/62 at Malvern Hill.
Pvt.	Wooten, John S.	1834	S	Falkland, Pitt Co., NC	Farm Labor	Enlisted, 8/31/61. Died of typhoid fever, 7/28/62 at Falkland, NC.

1861 Recruits

Pvt.	Forbes, Randolph	1845	S	Greensboro, Guilford Co., NC	Farm Labor	Enlisted, 10/10/61. Promoted to Cpl., 1/-/63. Reduced to Pvt., 10/14/63. Wounded, 10/18/64 at Warrenton Springs.

1862 Recruits

Pvt.	Barnes, Wm. Spencer	1843	S	Saratoga, Wilson Co., NC	Farm Labor	Enlisted, 1/20/62. Wounded, 11/7/63 at Kelly's Ford. TDY—guard of ordnance stores; 1/-/64–12/31/64. Paroled, 4/9/65 at Appomattox.
Pvt.	Bryant, John	1846	S	Enfield, Halifax Co., NC	Farm Labor	Enlisted, 3/10/62. Killed, 6/27/62 at Gaines' Mill.
Pvt.	Crisp, Amos W.	1838	S	Speights, Greene Co., NC	Farm Labor	Enlisted, 3/10/62. Died of pneumonia, 2/13/63 near Fredericksburg, VA. ("Died at midnight.")
Pvt.	Crisp, Silas E.	1834	M	Tarboro, Edgecombe Co., NC	Farmer	Enlisted, 5/1/62. Wounded (arm), 6/2/64 at Cold Harbor. No further reports.
Pvt.	Crisp, William S.	1837	M	Tarboro, Edgecombe Co., NC	Farmer	Enlisted, 5/1/62. Captured, 5/8/64 at Spotsylvania. POW—Elmira, NY. Released, 6/30/65.
Pvt.	Eagles, Theodore R.	1842	S	Tarboro, Edgecombe Co., NC	Farm Labor	Enlisted, 5/1/62. Wounded (arm), 5/12/64 at Spotsylvania. Paroled, 4/9/65 at Appomattox.
Pvt.	Edwards, Thomas	1828	M	Tarboro, Edgecombe Co., NC	Farmer	Enlisted, 5/1/62. Died of typhoid fever, 6/15/62 at Wilmington, NC.
Pvt.	Edwards, William B.	1830	S	Tarboro, Edgecombe Co., NC	Farmer	Enlisted, 5/1/62. Discharged (provided substitute), 8/5/62.
Pvt.	Ellis, James	1843	S	Tarboro, Edgecombe Co., NC	Farm Labor	Enlisted, 5/1/62. Promoted to Cpl., 8/-/64. Paroled, 4/9/65 at Appomattox.
Pvt.	Ellis, William "Willie"	1841	S	Tarboro, Edgecombe Co., NC	Farm Labor	Enlisted, 5/1/62. Promoted to Musician, 12/-/62. Reduced to Pvt., 8/-/63. Absent, sick until 3/5/65. No further records.
Pvt.	Everett, Joseph	1837	M	Tarboro, Edgecombe Co., NC	Farmer	Enlisted, 5/1/62. Died of disease, 7/23/64 at Woodstock, VA.
Pvt.	Felton, Eli	1836	M	Gardner, Wilson Co., NC	Farmer	Enlisted, 5/1/62. Wounded, 4/6/65 at Sailor's Creek. Surrendered, 4/9/65 at Appomattox.
Pvt.	Gay, Henry	1842	S	Speight Heights, Greene Co., NC	Day Labor	Enlisted, 5/1/62. Died of typhoid pneumonia, 2/23/63 at Guinea Station, VA.
Pvt.	Hagins, Lewis W.	1842	S	Tarboro, Edgecombe Co., NC	Farm Labor	Enlisted, 5/1/62. Died of pneumonia, 11/14/63 at Charlottesville, VA.
Pvt.	Harrell, Elisha T.	1841	S	Tarboro, Edgecombe Co., NC	Farm Labor	Enlisted, 5/1/62. Wounded (head), 5/12/64 at Spotsylvania. Died of wounds, 5/26/64.

30th North Carolina Infantry Roster, Company F

Rank	Name	DOB	M/S	Residence	Occupation	Remarks
Pvt.	Hathaway, Augustus	1830	M	Tarboro, Edgecombe Co., NC	Cooper	Enlisted, 1/21/62. Wounded (shoulder), 9/17/62 at Sharpsburg. Discharged (disability) caused by wounds, 5/15/63.
Pvt.	Hathaway, James J.	1847	S	Coxville, Pitt Co., NC	Farm Labor	Enlisted, 5/1/62. Captured, 5/8/64 at Spotsylvania. POW—Elmira, NY. Released, 6/27/65.
Pvt.	Johnson, A. C. Jones	1830		Edgecombe Co., NC		Enlisted, 5/1/62. Wounded, 5/12/64 at Spotsylvania. Wounded (right arm), 7/18/64 at Snicker's Gap. No further records.
Pvt.	Jones, Levi	1838	S	Speights, Greene Co., NC	Turpentine Labor	Enlisted, 5/1/62. Wounded, 9/17/62 at Sharpsburg. No records after 8/31/64.
Pvt.	**Langley, Morrison**	**1836**	**S**	**Falkland, Pitt Co., NC**	**Farm Labor**	**Enlisted, 5/1/62. Killed, 5/30/64 at Bethesda Church.**
Pvt.	Lawrence, John J.	1836	S	Enfield, Halifax Co., NC	Printer	Enlisted, 5/1/62. Captured, 9/28/62 at Sharpsburg. POW—Ft. McHenry, MD. Exchanged, 12/1/62. Promoted to Hospital Steward, 11/10/63. Sick in Richmond hospital, 9/1/64–4/9/65.
Pvt.	Lewis, John D.	1833	M	Tarboro, Edgecombe Co., NC	Miller's Asst.	Enlisted, 5/1/62. TDY—Butcher; 6/1/62–4/30/63. TDY—Butcher; 1/1/64–4/9/65. Surrendered, 4/9/65 at Appomattox.
Pvt.	**Little, Lorenzo**	**1832**	**S**	**Falkland, Pitt Co., NC**	**Miller**	**Enlisted, 5/1/62. Died of pneumonia, 4/13/63 at Richmond, VA.**
Pvt.	**Marlow, Nathan**	**1805**	**M**	**Saratoga, Wilson Co., NC**	**Turpentine Labor**	**Enlisted (as substitute), 8/5/62. Died of pneumonia, 2/5/63 at Richmond, VA.**
Pvt.	Moore, John J.	1836	S	Tarboro, Edgecombe Co., NC	Farm Labor	Enlisted, 3/10/62. Wounded, 7/1/62 at Malvern Hill. Discharged (wounds), 3/17/63.
Pvt.	**Morton, Isaac**	**1843**	**S**	**Piney Green, Onslow Co, NC**	**Farm Labor**	**Enlisted, 5/9/62. Captured, 9/14/62 at South Mountain. POW—Ft. Delaware, DE. Exchanged, 11/10/62. Died of disease, 12/30/62 at Richmond, VA.**
Pvt.	Norville, James	1834	M	Tarboro, Edgecombe Co., NC	Farmer	Enlisted, 5/1/62. TDY—Teamster; 11/1/63–4/9/65. Surrendered, 4/9/65 at Appomattox.
Pvt.	Phillips, Richard	1842	S	Tarboro, Edgecombe Co., NC	Farm Labor	Enlisted, 5/1/62. Wounded (arm), 5/12/64 at Spotsylvania. Wounded (right knee), 9/22/64 at Fisher's Hill. Surrendered, 4/9/65 at Appomattox.
Pvt.	Pitt, Theophilus	1838	S	Tarboro, Edgecombe Co., NC	Day Labor	Enlisted, 5/1/62. Captured, 11/7/63 at Kelly's Ford. POW—Point Lookout, MD. Exchanged, 3/3/65.
Pvt.	Stallings, Rufus	1838	S	Ringwood, Halifax Co., NC	Overseer	Enlisted, 5/13/62. Surrendered, 4/9/65 at Appomattox.
Pvt.	Walston, John	1842	S	Tarboro, Edgecombe Co., NC	Farm Labor	Enlisted, 5/1/62. Promoted to Sgt., 1/-/63. Wounded (left leg), 5/12/64 at Spotsylvania. Promoted to 1st Sgt., 8/31/64. Paroled, 4/9/65 at Appomattox.
Pvt.	Walston, Levi	1837	S	Tarboro, Edgecombe Co., NC	Farm Labor	Enlisted, 5/1/62. Wounded (right shoulder & neck), 5/12/64 at Spotsylvania. Captured, 4/6/65 at High Bridge. Released, 6/21/65.
Pvt.	Walston, Rufus F.	1839	S	Maysville, Greene Co., NC	Farm Labor	Enlisted, 5/1/62. Captured, 11/7/63 at Kelly's Ford. POW—Point Lookout, MD. Exchanged, 2/15/65.
Pvt.	Warren, Lemuel	1839	S	Tranter's Creek, Beaufort Co., NC	Farm Labor	Enlisted, 5/1/62. Wounded (head & left side), 9/17/62 at Sharpsburg. Wounded, 8/21/64 at near Charles Town. Captured, 4/6/65 at High Bridge.

Rank	Name	DOB	M/S	Residence	Occupation	Remarks
Pvt.	Webb, Hardy	1826	M	Tarboro, Edgecombe Co., NC	Farmer	Enlisted, 5/1/62. Killed, 7/1/62 at Malvern Hill.

1863 Conscripts

Rank	Name	DOB	M/S	Residence	Occupation	Remarks
Pvt.	Mathews, Roderick	1830	M	Bethel, Pitt Co., NC	Farmer	Conscripted, 8/22/63. Captured, 4/6/65 at Farmville.
Pvt.	**Mosely, Allen**	1844	S	Falkland, Pitt Co., NC	Farm Labor	**Enlisted, 1/20/63. Killed, 5/3/63 at Chancellorsville.**
Pvt.	Owens, James	1836	M	Tarboro, Edgecombe Co., NC	Farmer	Conscripted, 7/11/63. TDY—Hospital duty in Richmond, 8/11/63; 8/11/63–8/31/64. No further records.
Pvt.	**Wamack, William D.**	1833	S	Yanceyville, Caswell Co., NC	Farmer	**Conscripted, 7/11/63. Wounded, 5/12/64 at Spotsylvania. Died from wounds, 5/14/64.**
Pvt.	Wethersby, Joseph	1830	M	Scotland Neck, Halifax Co, NC	Farmer	Conscripted, 6/24/63. Home on medical furlough, 8/3/64. No further records.

1864 Conscripts/Recruits

Rank	Name	DOB	M/S	Residence	Occupation	Remarks
Pvt.	Cline, J.					Conscripted, 11/-/64. Captured, 4/3/65 near Appomattox River.
Pvt.	Morgan, Thomas	1847	S	Tarboro, Edgecombe Co., NC	Farm Labor	Enlisted, 2/10/64. Wounded (right leg), 7/18/64 at Snicker's Gap. Furloughed due to wounds, 12/29/64.
Pvt.	Walston, Ralph	1848	S	Wilson, Wilson Co., NC	Farm Labor	Enlisted, 4/24/64. Surrendered, 4/9/65 at Appomattox.
Pvt.	Webb, Bennett	1847	S	Saratoga, Wilson Co., NC	Farm Labor	Enlisted, 2/20/64. Wounded (right leg), 6/1/64 at Cold Harbor. Home on wounded furlough, 11/4/64. No further records.
Pvt.	Webb, John	1845	S	Saratoga, Wilson Co., NC	Farm Labor	Enlisted, 2/20/64. Surrendered, 4/9/65 at Appomattox.

Company G—Granville Rangers
Granville County (Mustered into Regt.—9/7/61)

Rank	Name	DOB	M/S	Residence	Occupation	Remarks
Cpt.	Taylor, Richard P.	1812	M	Ragland, Granville Co., NC	Farmer	Enrolled, 9/7/61. Defeated in re-election at re-organization, 5/1/62.
1st Lt.	Mitchell, Rush J.	1822	M	Tabs Creek, Granville Co., NC	Farmer	Enrolled, 97/1/61. Defeated in re-organization, 5/1/62.
2nd Lt.	Barnett, James A.	1839	S	Blue Wing, Granville Co., NC	Merchant	Enrolled, 9/7/61. Elected Cpt., 5/1/62. Wounded (left thigh, fracturing femur), 9/17/62 at Sharpsburg. TDY—recruiting service in Granville Co.; 4/1/63–4/9/65.
3rd Lt.	Brooks, William A.	1838	S	Blue Wing, Granville Co., NC	Merchant	Enrolled, 9/7/61. Defeated for re-election, 5/1/62.
1st Sgt.	Barnett, James P.	1824	M	Young's Crossing, Granville Co., NC	Farmer	Enlisted, 9/7/61. Promoted to Sutler, 5/1/62.
2nd Sgt.	Badgett, James W.	1842	S	Tar River, Granville Co., NC	Farm Labor	Enlisted, 9/7/61. Elected 1st Lt., 5/1/62. Wounded (neck & head), 5/19/64 at Harris Farm. Promoted to Cpt., 9/20/64. Surrendered, 4/9/65 at Appomattox.
3rd Sgt.	**Blacknall, Thomas B.**	1842	S	Fairport, Granville Co., NC	Farm Labor	**Enlisted, 9/7/61. Reduced to Pvt., 5/1/62. Died of "hernia right side," 8/11/64 at Richmond.**

30th North Carolina Infantry Roster, Company G

Rank	Name	DOB	M/S	Residence	Occupation	Remarks
4th Sgt.	Crews, Alexander	1841	S	Oxford, Granville Co., NC	Clerk	Enlisted, 9/7/61. Promoted to 3rd Lt., 5/26/62. Wounded ("A minie ball passed through his chest."), 9/17/62 at Sharpsburg. Captured & paroled, 9/30/62 at Shepherdstown, MD. Promoted to 2nd Lt., 5/26/63. TDY—in command of wagon train; 2/1/64–4/9/65. Paroled, 4/9/65 at Appomattox.
5th Sgt.	Hart, James R.	1839	M	Abrams Plains, Granville Co., NC	Farmer	Enlisted, 9/7/61. Discharged (provided a substitute), 4/-/62.
1st Cpl.	**Hunt, James A.**	**1843**	**S**	**Abrams Plains, Granville Co., NC**	**Farm Labor**	**Enlisted, 9/7/61. Wounded (leg), 6/27/62 at Gaines' Mill (leg amputated). Died of wounds, 7/2/62.**
2nd Cpl.	Kittrell, William H.	1825	M	Fishing Creek, Granville Co., NC	Farmer	Enlisted, 9/7/61. Wounded, 7/1/62 at Malvern Hill. Reduced to Pvt., 11/-/62, Dropped from rolls due to wounds, 6/-/63.
3rd Cpl.	Cheatham, D. Thomas	1838	S	Tabs Creek, Granville Co., NC	Farm Labor	Enlisted, 9/7/61. Wounded (thigh), 7/3/63 at Gettysburg. Discharged due to wounds, 8/-/63.
4th Cpl.	Parham, William A.	1838	S	Meherrin, Brunswick Co., VA	Farmer	Enlisted, 9/7/61. Reduced to Pvt., 5/1/62. TDY—Teamster/Ambulance driver, 5/1/62–4/9/65. Surrendered, 4/9/65 at Appomattox.
Music	O'Brian, Alexander P.	1844	S	Tar River, Granville Co., NC	Farm Labor	Enlisted, 9/7/61. (drummer) Promoted to Cpl., 7/1/63. Captured, 11/7/63 at Kelly's Ford. POW—Point Lookout, MD. Exchanged, 2/21/65.
Pvt.	Badgett, Sandy H.	1839	S	Tar River, Granville Co., NC	Farm Labor	Enlisted, 9/7/61. Promoted to Sgt., 5/1/62. Paroled, 4/9/65 at Appomattox.
Pvt.	Badgett, Wm. Joseph	1841	S	Tar River, Granville Co., NC	Farm Labor	Enlisted, 9/7/61. Promoted to Sgt., 5/1/62. Wounded, 5/3/63 at Chancellorsville. Wounded, 5/19/64 at Harris Farm. Paroled, 4/9/65 at Appomattox.
Pvt.	**Barnett, William S.**	**1843**	**S**	**Oxford, Granville Co., NC**	**Farm Labor**	**Enlisted, 9/7/61. Died of "diseased lungs," 12/28/61 at Oxford, NC.**
Pvt.	**Bobbitt, Alexander G.**	**1839**	**S**	**Oxford, Granville Co., NC**	**Farm Labor**	**Enlisted, 9/7/61. Died of disease, 8/15/62 at Oxford, NC.**
Pvt.	Bobbitt, Isham C.	1844	S	Tabs Creek, Granville Co., NC	Farm Labor	Enlisted, 9/7/61. Missing, 7/13/64 at Ft. Stevens. Captured, 7/12/64 near Washington, D.C. POW—Elmira, NY. Exchanged, 3/20/65.
Pvt.	**Bradford, William H.**	**1832**	**M**	**Tabs Creek, Granville Co., NC**	**Farmer**	**Enlisted, 9/7/61. Died of typhoid fever, 10/18/61 at Raleigh, NC.**
Pvt.	Breedlove, John H.	1840	S	Abram Plains, Granville Co., NC	Farm Labor	Enlisted, 9/7/61. Discharged (disability—"broken collar bone"), 9/14/61.
Pvt.	**Burroughs, William A.**	**1846**	**S**	**Island Creek, Granville Co., NC**	**Farm Labor**	**Enlisted, 9/7/61. Promoted to Cpl., 5/20/63. Wounded (hip), 5/31/64 near Bethesda-Church. Died of wounds, 6/8/64 at Richmond.**
Pvt.	Burton, Robert W.	1826	S	Ragland, Granville Co., NC	Farm Labor	Enlisted, 9/7/61. Transferred to 54th NC Inf., 2/15/63 in exchange for Pvt. William D. King (54th NC Inf.).
Pvt.	Cawthorn, John W.	1844	S	Oxford, Granville Co., NC	Farm Labor	Enlisted, 9/7/61. Promoted to Cpl., 7/-/64. Captured, 9/22/64 at Fisher's Hill. POW—Point Lookout, MD. Released, 6/24/65.

Appendix 2

Rank	Name	DOB	M/S	Residence	Occupation	Remarks
Pvt.	Chalkley, Ben. Thomas	1838	S	Young's Crossing, Granville Co., NC	Cooper	Enlisted, 9/7/61. Killed, 7/1/62 at Malvern Hill.
Pvt.	Chalkley, Edward E.	1840	S	Clarksville, Granville Co., NC	Farm Labor	Enlisted, 9/7/61. Discharged (disability—"throat affection"), 3/5/62.
Pvt.	Cheatham, William A.	1836	M	Tabs Creek, Granville Co., NC	Farmer	Enlisted, 9/7/61. Wounded, 7/1/62 at Malvern Hill. Captured, 9/22/64 at Fisher's Hill. POW—Point Lookout, MD. Exchanged, 2/15/65.
Pvt.	Clairborne, Robert F.	1839		Granville Co., NC		Enlisted, 9/7/61. Elected 2nd Lt., 5/1/62. Resigned, 5/26/63.
Pvt.	Collins, Samuel A.	1832		Brinkleyville, Halifax Co., NC		Enlisted, 9/7/61. Wounded, 5/12/64 at Spotsylvania. Paroled, 4/9/65 at Appomattox.
Pvt.	Connell, Ira Thomas	1843	S	Oxford, Granville Co., NC	Farm Labor	Enlisted, 9/7/61. Promoted to Sgt., 5/1/62. Promoted to 3rd Lt., 6/23/63. Killed, 7/3/63 at Gettysburg ("by artillery.")
Pvt.	Connell, Wyatt G.	1835		Oxford, Granville Co., NC		Enlisted, 9/7/61. Wounded (right elbow) & captured, 5/12/64 at Spotsylvania. POW—Elmira, NY. Exchanged, 2/21/65.
Pvt.	Cottrell, Solomon	1820	M	Ragland, Granville Co., NC	Farmer	Enlisted, 9/7/61. Discharged (disability—rheumatism), 9/14/61.
Pvt.	Currin, George W.	1836	S	Tar River, Granville Co., NC	Farm Labor	Enlisted, 9/7/61. Discharged (disability—hernia), 10/22/61.
Pvt.	Daniel, James R.	1844	S	Hester's Store, Person Co., NC	Day Labor	Enlisted, 9/7/61. Died of disease, 7/22/62.
Pvt.	Daniel, William H.	1835	S	Ragland, Granville Co., NC	Farm Labor	Enlisted, 9/7/61. Captured, 9/17/62 at Sharpsburg. Paroled, 9/27/62. Wounded (left thigh & left side) & captured, 11/7/63 at Kelly's Ford. POW—Point Lookout, MD. Exchanged, 3/3/65.
Pvt.	Dean, Simpson	1840	S	Tar River, Granville Co., NC	Farm Labor	Enlisted, 9/7/61. Promoted to Cpl., 5/1/62. Promoted to Sgt., 7/1/63. Captured, 5/12/64 at Spotsylvania. POW—Elmira, NY. Released, 6/21/65.
Pvt.	Dement, Henry	1839	S	Ford Creek, Granville Co., NC	Farm Labor	Enlisted, 9/7/61. Captured, 9/30/62 at Shepherdstown. POW—Ft. McHenry. Exchanged, 4/23/63. Wounded and captured, 7/12/64 at Ft. Stevens. "Left in the enemies [sic] lines" No further records.
Pvt.	Franklin, Thomas F.	1833	M	Tar River, Granville Co., NC	Farmer	Enlisted, 9/7/61. Captured, 5/12/64 at Spotsylvania. POW—Point Lookout, MD. Exchanged, 9/22/64. Paroled, 4/14/65 at Burkeville.
Pvt.	Frazier, Elisha T.	1843	S	Goshen, Granville Co., NC	Farm Labor	Enlisted, 9/7/61. Paroled, 4/14/65 at Burkeville.
Pvt.	Frazier, Ransom P.	1841	S	Goshen, Granville Co., NC	Farm Labor	Enlisted, 9/7/61. TDY—Teamster; 1/1/64–9/30/64. No further records.
Pvt.	Fulford, John T.	1841	S	Ragland, Granville Co., NC	Farm Labor	Enlisted, 9/7/61. Promoted to Cpl., 5/1/62. Promoted to 3rd Lt., 8/23/63. Wounded (left arm), 5/12/64 at Spotsylvania. Surrendered, 4/9/65 at Appomattox.
Pvt.	Fuller, James N.	1843	S	Tar River, Granville Co., NC	Farm Labor	Enlisted, 9/7/61. Promoted to Cpl., 9/22/62. Promoted to Sgt., 8/8/63. Wounded (left hip & right leg fractured), 8/21/64 at Charles Town. Retired to the Invalid Corps, 2/14/65.

30th North Carolina Infantry Roster, Company G

Rank	Name	DOB	M/S	Residence	Occupation	Remarks
Pvt.	Gordon, John W.	1843	S	Oxford, Granville Co., NC	Farm Labor	Enlisted, 9/7/61. Discharged (sickness), 7/22/62.
Pvt.	Hamme, Richard F.	1844	S	Tabs Creek, Granville Co., NC	Farm Labor	Enlisted, 9/7/61. Wounded, 7/1/62 at Malvern Hill. Sick & Captured, 7/4/63 in retreat from Gettysburg. POW—Ft. Delaware, DE. Exchanged, 12/28/63. Captured, 5/19/64 at Harris Farm. POW—Elmira, NY. Released, 6/30/65.
Pvt.	Hancock, Thomas C.					Enlisted, 9/7/61. Transferred to 12th NC Inf., 10/-/61.
Pvt.	Harris, Richard P.	1843	S	Allensville, Person Co., NC	Farm Labor	Enlisted, 9/7/61. Wounded (left thigh), 10/12/63 at Warrenton (Bristoe Station). Captured, 5/12/64 at Spotsylvania. POW—Elmira, NY. Released, 6/19/65.
Pvt.	**Harris, William H.**	**1839**	**S**	**Beaver Dam, Granville Co., NC**	**Farm Labor**	**Enlisted, 9/7/61. Wounded, 5/3/63 at Chancellorsville. Killed, 5/12/64 at Spotsylvania.**
Pvt.	Hart, William H.	1845	S	Young's Crossroads, Granville Co., NC	Farm Labor	Enlisted, 9/7/61. Discharged (disability—"heart disease"), 9/26/61.
Pvt.	Hight, Herbot H.	1829	S	Tabs Creek, Granville Co., NC	Farmer	Enlisted, 9/7/61. Dropped from rolls (sickness), 1/-/64.
Pvt.	Hobgood, James M.	1843	S	Tar River, Granville Co., NC	Farm Labor	Enlisted, 9/7/61. Wounded, 7/1/62 at Malvern Hill. Wounded, 5/3/63 at Chancellorsville. Captured, 5/12/64 at Spotsylvania. No further records.
Pvt.	**Hobgood, William P.**	**1842**	**S**	**Tar River, Granville Co., NC**	**Farm Labor**	**Enlisted, 9/7/61. Promoted to Cpl., 9/22/62. Wounded, 5/3/63 at Chancellorsville. Died of wounds, 5/14/63.**
Pvt.	**Howard, Joseph M.**	**1843**	**S**	**Tar River, Granville Co., NC**	**Farm Labor**	**Enlisted, 9/7/61. Captured, 11/7/63 at Kelly's Ford. POW—Elmira, NY. Died of chronic diarrhea, 2/18/65.**
Pvt.	**Hunt, Alfred H.**	**1843**	**S**	**Tar River, Granville Co., NC**	**Farm Labor**	**Enlisted, 9/7/61. Died of acute diarrhea & fever, 7/13/62 at Wilmington, NC.**
Pvt.	**Hunt, Isaac B.**	**1841**	**S**	**Goshen, Granville Co., NC**	**Farm Labor**	**Enlisted, 9/7/61. Wounded, 6/27/62 at Gaines' Mill. Died of wounds, 6/28/62.**
Pvt.	Hunt, John O.	1839	S	Tabs Creek, Granville Co., NC	Farm Labor	Enlisted, 9/7/61. Wounded (chest), 7/1/62 at Malvern Hill. Discharged due to wounds, 9/9/62.
Pvt.	Jenkins, John T.	1826	M	Island Creek, Granville Co., NC	Farmer	Enlisted, 9/7/61. Discharged (sickness—typhoid fever), 6/3/62.
Pvt.	Jenkins, William T.	1842	S	Abrams Plains, Granville Co., NC	Farm Labor	Enlisted, 9/7/61. Discharged (injury—"dislocation of the arm"), 3/27/62.
Pvt.	Knott, James W.	1840	S	Tar River, Granville Co., NC	Mail Carrier	Enlisted, 9/7/61. Transferred to 12th NC Inf., 11/26/62.
Pvt.	Knott, George Lawson	1835	S	Nutbush, Granville Co., NC	Overseer	Enlisted, 9/7/61. Promoted to Cpl., 4/-/63. Captured, 11/7/63 at Kelly's Ford. POW—Point Lookout, MD. Exchanged, 3/3/65.
Pvt.	Lumpkins, James R.	1838	S	Ragland, Granville Co., NC	Farm Labor	Enlisted, 9/7/61. Discharged (general disability), 2/18/64.
Pvt.	Morris, John W.	1843	S	Woodsdale, Person Co., NC	Farm Labor	Enlisted, 9/7/61. Promoted to Musician (drummer), 5/1/63. Captured, 11/7/63 at Kelly's Ford. POW—Point Lookout, MD. Exchanged, 2/20/65.

Rank	Name	DOB	M/S	Residence	Occupation	Remarks
Pvt.	Moss, Thomas	1825	M	Clarksville, Mecklenburg Co., VA	Farmer	Enlisted, 9/7/61. Discharged (disability—"scrotal hernia"), 3/27/62.
Pvt.	O'Brien, Alfred D.	1842	S	Tar River, Granville Co., NC	Farm Labor	Enlisted, 9/7/61. Promoted to Sgt., 5/1/62. Promoted to 1st Sgt., 6/-/63, Captured, 11/7/63 at Kelly's Ford. POW—Point Lookout, MD. Exchanged, 3/3/65.
Pvt.	**Parrish, Mathew**	**1845**	**S**	**Knap of Reeds, Granville Co., NC**	**Farm Labor**	**Enlisted, 9/7/61. Killed, 6/27/62 at Gaines' Mill.**
Pvt.	Read, David K.	1838	S	Grove Hill, Warren Co., NC	Farm Labor	Enlisted, 9/7/61. Discharged (disability—"epileptic fits"), 3/5/63. Re-enlisted, 6/24/63. Discharged (disability), 9/-/63.
Pvt.	Reams, George W.	1838	S	Oxford, Granville Co., NC	Tobacconist	Enlisted, 9/7/61. Wounded, 7/1/62 at Malvern Hill. Discharged (provided a substitute), 1/1/63.
Pvt.	**Sizemore, William P. "Bill"**	**1837**	**S**	**Cherry Field, Henderson Co., NC**	**Farm Labor**	**Enlisted, 9/7/61. Wounded, 6/27/62 at Gaines' Mill. Wounded, 11/7/63 at Kelly's Ford. Promoted to Cpl., 8/8/63. Killed, 5/6/64 at The Wilderness.**
Pvt.	Slaughter, Thomas D.	1830	S	Tar River, Granville Co., NC	Farmer	Enlisted, 9/7/61. TDY—Ambulance driver; 5/1/63–4/9/65. Surrendered, 4/9/65 at Appomattox.
Pvt.	Stanton, James R.	1849		Granville Co., NC		Enlisted, 9/7/61. Missing, 5/8/64 at Spotsylvania. Returned to duty, 8/-/64. Surrendered, 4/9/65 at Appomattox.
Pvt.	Stone, Daniel B.	1837		Granville Co., NC		Enlisted, 9/7/61. Transferred to 23rd NC Inf., 6/18/62.
Pvt.	Traylor, Charles	1815		Granville Co., NC		Enlisted, 9/7/61. Discharged (disability—"pulmonary disease"), 3/27/62.
Pvt.	**Wainwright, John K.**	**1842**	**S**	**Tar River, Granville Co., NC**	**Farm Labor**	**Enlisted, 9/7/61. Died of disease, 8/25/62 at Tar River, NC.**

1862 Recruits/Conscripts

Rank	Name	DOB	M/S	Residence	Occupation	Remarks
Pvt.	Adams, John P.	1825	M	Dutch, Granville Co., NC	Farmer	Conscripted, 9/21/62. Reported AWOL, 1/-/64. No further records.
Pvt.	**Asher, Edmond**	**1835**	**M**	**Trap Hill, Wilkes Co., NC**	**Farmer**	**Conscripted, 9/21/62. Died of chronic diarrhea, 11/28/62 at Mount Jackson, VA.**
Pvt.	Badgett, John D.	1846	S	Tar River, Granville Co., NC	Farm Labor	Enlisted, 3/4/62. Wounded, 6/27/62 at Gaines' Mill. Paroled, 4/9/65 at Appomattox.
Pvt.	**Blackwell, John**	**1842**	**S**	**Woodsdale, Person Co., NC**	**Farm Labor**	**Enlisted, 5/1/62. Wounded, 7/1/62 at Malvern Hill. Died of wounds, 7/10/62.**
Pvt.	**Blevins, Andrew**	**1841**	**S**	**Trap Hill, Wilkes Co., NC**	**Farm Labor**	**Conscripted, 9/21/62. Wounded (right lung), 5/3/63 at Chancellorsville. Died of wounds, 6/18/62 at Richmond, VA.**
Pvt.	Blevins, Harvey	1842	S	Trap Hill, Wilkes Co., NC	Farm Labor	Conscripted, 9/21/62. Captured, 4/9/65 at Farmville. Released, 6/27/65.
Pvt.	**Blevins, Jonathan**	**1836**	**M**	**Trap Hill, Wilkes Co., NC**	**Farmer**	**Conscripted, 9/21/62/ Killed, 5/3/63 at Chancellorsville.**
Pvt.	**Blizzard, William H.**	**1835**	**M**	**Downingsville, Bladen Co., NC**	**Farmer**	**Enlisted, 3/24/62. Died of disease, 12/19/62.**

30th North Carolina Infantry Roster, Company G

Rank	Name	DOB	M/S	Residence	Occupation	Remarks
Pvt.	Boyd, James A.	1840	S	Abram Plain, Granville Co., NC	Farm Labor	Enlisted, 3/3/62. Deserted, 6/22/62/ Returned to duty, 4/4/64. Discharged, 6/16/64.
Pvt.	Brooks, Henry R.	1830	M	Roxborough, Person Co., NC	Farm Labor	Enlisted, 3/4/62/ Captured, 9/17/62 at Sharpsburg. Paroled, 9/21/62. Wounded, 5/3/63 at Chancellorsville. Wounded (leg), 6/3/64 at Cold Harbor.
Pvt.	Brooks, James L.	1828	S	Woodsdale, Person Co., NC	Farmer	Enlisted, 3/3/62. Promoted to 1st Sgt., 5/1/62. Captured, 9/17/62 at Sharpsburg. Paroled, 9/21/62. Sick in hospital in Richmond since 10/19/62. No further records.
Pvt.	Brooks, Richard D. "RD"	1841	S	Woodsdale, Person Co., NC	Farm Labor	Enlisted, 3/4/62. Wounded ("shoulder broken by shrapnel"), 5/3/63 at Chancellorsville. Promoted to Cpl., 8/-/64. Paroled, 4/9/65 at Appomattox.
Pvt.	**Brown, Alfred**	**1838**	**S**	**Wilkesboro, Wilkes Co., NC**	**Farm Labor**	**Conscripted, 9/27/62. Died of "abscessed lung," 1/11/63 at Mount Jackson, VA.**
Pvt.	**Brown, Wesley**	**1832**	**M**	**Trap Hill, Wilkes Co., NC**	**Day Labor**	**Conscripted, 9/27/62. Died of measles, 12/24/62 at Mount Jackson, VA.**
Pvt.	**Brown, William A.**	**1830**	**S**	**Wilkesboro, Wilkes Co., NC**	**Day Labor**	**Conscripted, 9/27/62. Absent sick, 10/26/62 to 1/1/64. "Supposed to be dead from complications caused by the measles." No further records.**
Pvt.	Cheatham, James T.	1846	S	Tabs Creek, Granville Co., NC	Farm Labor	Enlisted, 7/25/62. Wounded, 7/1/63 at Gettysburg. Captured at field hospital, 7/4/63. POW—David's Island. Exchanged, 9/8/63. Captured, 7/12/64 at Ft. Stevens. POW—Elmira, NY. Released, 6/12/65.
Pvt.	**Church, Carlton**	**1844**	**S**	**Reddies' River, Wilkes Co., NC**	**Farm Labor**	**Conscripted, 9/21/62. Wounded, 5/3/63 at Chancellorsville. Captured, 5/12/64 at Spotsylvania. POW—Elmira, NY. Died of pneumonia, 12/9/64.**
Pvt.	Church, John	1840	S	Reddies' River, Wilkes Co., NC	Farm Labor	Conscripted, 9/21/62. Deserted, 9/-/64. Took Oath of Allegiance, 12/27/64.
Pvt.	Crews, William F.	1843	S	Island Creek, Granville Co., NC	Farm Labor	Enlisted, 5/1/62. Wounded (left leg), 11/14/64 in Petersburg trenches. Surrendered, 4/9/65 at Appomattox.
Pvt.	Currin, Ralph	1842	S	Goshen, Granville Co., NC	Farm Labor	Enlisted, 5/1/62. Deserted, 6/22/62. Returned to duty, 12/13/63. Absent sick from 2/11/64–9/1/64. No further records.
Pvt.	Currin, William R.	1839	S	Goshen, Granville Co., NC	Farm Labor	Enlisted, 5/1/62. Deserted, 6/22/62. Returned to duty, 12/13/63. Paroled, 4/14/65 at Burkeville.
Pvt.	Daniel, Robert M.	1839	S	Blue Wing, Granville Co., NC	Farmer	Enlisted, 3/3/62. Captured, 11/7/63 at Kelly's Ford. POW—Point Lookout, MD. Exchanged, 2/14/65.
Pvt.	**Daniel, James W.**					**Transferred to Co. G, 1/10/62. Died of fever, 2/22/63 at Grace Church, VA.**
Pvt.	Dean, Jess	1840	S	Tar River, Granville Co., NC	Farm Labor	Enlisted, 3/3/62. AWOL, 10/22/63. Returned to duty, 1/-/64. Wounded (head), 6/1/64 at Cold Harbor. Absent due to wounds. No further records after 11/20/64.
Pvt.	**Dickerson, Martin**	**1825**	**M**	**Ragland, Granville Co., NC**	**Farm Labor**	**Enlisted, 8/26/62. Captured, 5/12/64 at Spotsylvania. POW—Elmira, NY. Died of acute gastritis, 3/14/65.**
Pvt.	Duke, John Y.	1805	S	Tar River, Granville Co., NC	Farm Labor	Enlisted, 3/6/62. Died of typhoid fever, 7/9/62 at Richmond, VA.

Appendix 2

Rank	Name	DOB	M/S	Residence	Occupation	Remarks
Pvt.	Duncan, John B.	1828	M	Tar River, Granville Co., NC	Farmer	Enlisted, 3/4/62. Died of typhoid fever, 8/30/62 at Richmond, VA.
Pvt.	Frazier, Alex S.	1840	S	Goshen, Granville Co., NC	Farm Labor	Enlisted, 3/3/62. Wounded (knee), 7/1/62 at Malvern Hill. Died of wounds, 7/6/62 at Richmond, VA.
Pvt.	Frazier, James H.	1847	S	Goshen, Granville Co., NC	Farm Labor	Enlisted, 3/2/62. Wounded, 9/17/62 at Sharpsburg. Wounded, 8/21/64 near Charles Town. Surrendered, 4/9/65 at Appomattox.
Pvt.	Frazier, Pumfred B.	1845	S	Goshen, Granville Co., NC	Farm Labor	Enlisted, 5/1/62. Wounded (foot), 6/27/62 at Gaines' Mill. Died of smallpox, 11/14/62 at Staunton, VA.
Pvt.	Hall, James C.	1840	M	Hay Meadow, Wilkes Co., NC	Farmer	Conscripted, 9/27/62. Wounded, 5/3/63 at Chancellorsville. AWOL since 10/13/63.
Pvt.	Hester, George W.	1842	S	Abrams Plains, Granville Co., NC	Farm Labor	Enlisted, 3/17/62. Captured, 11/7/63 at Kelly's Ford. POW—Point Lookout, MD. Exchanged, 3/3/65.
Pvt.	Hobgood, Isaac	1842	S	Mount Tirzah, Person Co., NC	Farm Labor	Enlisted, 5/1/62. Discharged (sickness), 3/8/64.
Pvt.	Holbrook, Patterson B.	1839	S	Trap Hill, Wilkes Co., NC	Farmer	Conscripted, 9/21/62. Wounded, 12/13/62 at Fredericksburg. Captured, 11/7/63 at Kelly's Ford. POW—Point Lookout, MD. Exchanged, 3/3/65.
Pvt.	Holbrook, William P.	1832	S	Trap Hill, Wilkes Co., NC	Farmer	Conscripted, 9/21/62. Assigned to Co. G, 11/-/63. Absent, sick in Raleigh hospital; 1/1/64–8/31/64. No further records.
Pvt.	Hunt, David Z.	1845	S	Trap Hill, Wilkes Co., NC	Farm Labor	Enlisted, 5/1/62. Wounded, 8/21/64 at Charles Town. No further records.
Pvt.	Incore, James F.	1845	S	Dutch, Granville Co., NC	Farm Labor	Enlisted, 3/4/62. Died of disease, 5/30/62 at Wilmington, NC.
Pvt.	King, James D.	1843	S	Abrams Plains, Granville Co., NC	Farm Labor	Enlisted, 3/4/62. Captured, 11/7/63 at Kelly's Ford. POW—Point Lookout, MD. Exchanged, 3/17/64. Wounded, 9/19/64 at Winchester. Captured in Richmond hospital, 4/3/65. Released, 6/30/65.
Pvt.	Loftice, William A.	1835	S	Halifax Court House, Halifax Co., VA	Farm Labor	Enlisted, 3/8/62. Wounded (right thigh), 5/3/63 at Chancellorsville. Home on wounded furlough, 8/-/63. Did not return.
Pvt.	Lovett, Aaron F.	1834	M	Greensboro, Guilford Co., NC	Farmer	Conscripted, 9/27/62. Died of measles, 3/4/63 at Chancellorsville, VA.
Pvt.	Merritt, Benjamin H.	1842	S	Ledge of Rocks, Granville Co., NC	Farm Labor	Enlisted, 2/4/62. Captured, 5/12/64 at Spotsylvania. POW—Elmira, NY. Exchanged, 11/15/64. Surrendered, 4/9/65 at Appomattox.
Pvt.	Morris, Alexander H.	1837	S	Dutch, Granville Co., NC	Peddler	Transferred from 23rd NC Inf., 6/1/62. Deserted, 6/10/63.
Pvt.	O'Brian, William G.	1846	S	Tar River, Granville Co., NC	Farm Labor	Enlisted, 3/3/62. Killed, 5/3/63 at Chancellorsville.
Pvt.	Pruitt, Hampton	1842	S	Trap Hill, Wilkes Co., NC	Farm Labor	Conscripted, 9/27/62. Wounded, 11/7/63 at Kelly's Ford. Died of wounds, 12/15/63 at Richmond, VA.
Pvt.	Robertson, Charles H.	1845	S	Goshen, Granville Co., NC	Farm Labor	Enlisted, 3/1/62. No records after 8/31/64.

Rank	Name	DOB	M/S	Residence	Occupation	Remarks
Pvt.	Ross, James P.	1835	M	Young's Crossing, Granville Co., NC	Farmer	Enlisted, 3/4/62. Discharged (sickness), 6/-/63.
Pvt.	Slaughter, William P.	1831	S	Tar River, Granville Co., NC	Farmer	Enlisted, 3/3/62. Killed, 5/12/64 at Spotsylvania.
Pvt.	Strange, Albert	1836	S	Clarksville, Mecklenburg Co., NC	Overseer	Enlisted, 3/3/62. Died of dysentery, 6/10/62 at Wilmington, NC.
Pvt.	Taylor, Richard D.	1847	S	Oxford, Granville Co., NC	Farm Labor	Enlisted, 3/2/62. Discharged (under age), 7/17/62.
Pvt.	Traylor, A. M.	1844		Granville Co., NC		Enlisted, 5/1/62. Wounded, 7/1/62 at Malvern Hill. Died of wounds, 7/22/62 at Richmond, Va.
Pvt.	Walls, William B.	1832	M	State Road, Wilkes Co., NC	Farmer	Conscripted, 9/7/62. Deserted, 6/4/63. Returned to duty, 11/10/63. Court martialed, 12/26/62. "Sentenced to work for three years on division fortifications." Died of "congestion of the lungs," 1/15/64 at Richmond, VA.
Pvt.	Watkins, John W.	1835	S	Clarksville, Mecklenburg Co., NC	Farm Labor	Enlisted, 3/10/62. Deserted, 6/4/63. Returned to duty, 12/1/6/63. Transferred to 14th VA Inf., 4/26/64.
Pvt.	Winn, Thomas	1826	M	Ararat, Patrick Co., VA	Farmer	Conscripted, 7/-/62. Died "suddenly," 8/10/62 at Richmond, VA.
Pvt.	Wortman, David D.	1834	M	Cleveland Co., NC	Farmer	Conscripted, 9/21/62. TDY—hospital nurse; 11/1/62–4/30/63. Wounded (right eye), 11/7/63 at Kelly's Ford. Absent due to wounds through 12/31/64. No further records.
Pvt.	Wortman, Simeon	1838	S	Cleveland Co., NC	Farm Labor	Conscripted, 9/22/62. Died of disease, 11/18/62.
Pvt.	Wells, James N.	1837	S	University station, Orange Co., NC	Farm Labor	Conscripted, 9/21/62. Deserted, 12/6/62.
Pvt.	Wilkerson, James	1840	S	Goshen, Granville Co., NC	Farm Labor	Enlisted, 3/5/62. Captured, 11/7/63 at Kelly's Ford. POW—Point Lookout, MD. Exchanged, 2/15/65.

1863 Conscripts

Rank	Name	DOB	M/S	Residence	Occupation	Remarks
Pvt.	Barnes, Hillmon	1822	M	Ragland, Granville Co., NC	Farmer	Conscripted, 10/14/63. Captured, 4/6/54 at Farmville. Released, 6/15/65.
Pvt.	Cliborn, John W.	1844	S	Ragland, Granville Co., NC	Farm Labor	Conscripted, 7/26/63. Dropped from the rolls, 12/31/63.
Pvt.	Crawford, James S.	1819	M	Crowder's Creek, Gaston Co., NC	Farmer	Conscripted, 9/4/63. Killed, 5/12/64 at Spotsylvania.
Pvt.	Critcher, William H.	1827		Granville Co., NC		Conscripted, 6/26/63. Captured, 9/19/64 at Winchester. POW—Point Lookout, MD. Exchanged, 3/18/65.
Pvt.	Daniel, Rufus	1823	M	Tabs Creek, Granville Co., NC	Overseer	Conscripted, 10/14/63. Assigned to Co. G, 6/10/64. No records after 9/1/64.
Pvt.	Elliott, Green B.	1821	M	Goshen, Granville Co., NC	Farmer	Conscripted, 8/18/63. Assigned to Co. G, 6/9/64. Killed, 10/19/64 at Cedar Creek.

Rank	Name	DOB	M/S	Residence	Occupation	Remarks
Pvt.	Greenway, Samuel	1823	M	Ragland, Granville Co., NC	Farm Labor	Conscripted, 8/26/63. Captured, 11/7/63 at Kelly's Ford. POW—Old Capital Prison, Washington, D.C. Died of smallpox, 1/1/64.
Pvt.	Hartwick, Christopher	1827		Mount Pleasant, Cabarrus Co., NC	Farm Labor	Conscripted, 9/30/63. Deserted, 2/25/64.
Pvt.	Hartwick, John	1829	M	Mount Pleasant, Cabarrus Co., NC	Farm Labor	Conscripted, 9/30/63. Deserted, 2/25/64.
Pvt.	King, William D	1841	S	Charlotte, Mecklenburg Co., NC	Day Labor	Transferred from 54th NC Inf., 1/1/63. Listed as a deserted, 7/-/63.
Pvt.	Kittrell, Harvey W.	1822	M	Fishing Creek, Granville Co., NC	Farmer	Conscripted, 10/4/63. Assigned to Co. G, 6/10/64. No records after 8/31/64.
Pvt.	Oakley, William	1845	S	Tar River, Granville Co., NC	Farm Labor	Conscripted, 6/10/63. Captured, 9/2/64 near Martinsburg, WV. POW—Ft. Delaware, DE. Released, 6/19/65.
Pvt.	Ottaway, John	1828	M	Wilmington, New Hanover Co., NC	Carpenter	Conscripted, 8/22/63. Captured, 11/7/63 at Kelly's Ford. POW—Point Lookout, MD. Released, 5/14/65.
Pvt.	Parker, Archibald D.	1826	M	Deep Well, Iredell Co., NC	Day Labor	Conscripted, 6/3/63. Captured, 11/7/63 at Kelly's Ford. POW—Point Lookout, MD. Exchanged, 9/22/64. No further records.
Pvt.	Ragland, William G.	1811	M	Oxford, Granville Co., NC	Farmer	Enlisted (substitute), 4/4/63. Died of measles, 1/8/64 at Orange Court House, VA.
Pvt.	Slaughter, James H.	1820	M	Tar River, Granville Co., NC	Farmer	Conscripted, 9/4/63. Discharged (sickness), 10/21/63. Died of typhoid fever, 11/15/63 at Richmond, VA.
Pvt.	Sollice, Devane	1833	M	Piney Grove, Sampson Co., NC	Turpentine Labor	Conscripted, 9/4/63. Captured, 11/7/63 at Kelly's Ford. POW—Point Lookout, MD. Died of disease, 1/23/64.
Pvt.	Wilson, Samuel R.	1806	S	Yanceyville, Caswell Co., NC	Day Labor	Conscripted, 2/23/63. Killed, 5/12/64 at Spotsylvania.

1864 Conscripts/Recruits

Rank	Name	DOB	M/S	Residence	Occupation	Remarks
Pvt.	Blevins, Shadrach	1847	S	Seven Mile Ford, Smyth Co., VA	Farm Labor	Enlisted, 3/17/64. Wounded (left arm), 6/2/64 at Cold Harbor. Absent due to wounds until 8/31/64. No further records.
Pvt.	Clopton, George	1830	M	Hanover, Norfolk Co., VA	Day Labor	Enlisted, 1/15/64. Died of typhoid fever, 2/17/64 at Richmond, VA.
Pvt.	Forrest, William L.	1846	S	York Co., VA	Day Labor	Enlisted, 3/11/64. Missing, 10/19/64 at Cedar Creek. POW—Libby Prison, VA.
Pvt.	Robertson, Z. R.	1834	M	Tabs Creek, Granville Co., NC	Farmer	Conscripted, 6/10/64. Captured, 9/22/64 at Fisher's Hill. POW—Baltimore, MD. Died of chronic diarrhea, 12/15/64.

Company H
Moore County (Mustered into Regt.—8/15/61)

Rank	Name	DOB	M/S	Residence	Occupation	Remarks
Cpt.	Swann, William M.	1834	S	Sloan, Moore Co., NC	Accountant	Enrolled, 9/10/61. Defeated in re-organization, 5/1/62.
1st Lt.	McIntosh, Archibald A.	1837	S	Moore Co., NC	Farm Labor	Enrolled, 9/10/61. Defeated in re-organization, 5/1/62.
2nd Lt.	McIntosh, Daniel W.	1835	S	Crain's Creek, Moore Co., NC	Clerk	Enrolled, 9/10/61. Defeated in re-organization, 5/1/62.

30th North Carolina Infantry Roster, Company H

Rank	Name	DOB	M/S	Residence	Occupation	Remarks
3rd Lt.	Moore, Francis M.	1840	S	Robesons, Brunswick Co., NC	Farm Labor	Enrolled, 9/10/61. Defeated in re-organization 5/1/62.
1st Sgt.	Cole, Benjamin Green	1820	S	Buffalow, Moore Co., NC	Farmer	Enlisted, 8/15/61. Wounded, 5/3/63 at Chancellorsville. TDY—Ambulance driver; 1/-/64–4/9/65. Surrendered at Appomattox.
2nd Sgt.	McIntosh, David J.	1835	S	Crain's Creek, Moore Co., NC	Clerk	Enlisted, 8/15/61. Reduced to Pvt., 5/1/62. Promoted to Cpl., 7/-/62. Promoted to Sgt., 4/-/63. Captured, 5/20/64 at Spotsylvania. POW—Elmira, NY. Release, 6/30/65.
3rd Sgt.	Wicker, Jesse J.	1838	S	Buffalow, Moore Co., NC	Student	Enlisted, 8/15/61. Promoted to 2nd Lt., 2/-/62. Elected to Cpt., 5/1/62. Wounded, 9/14/62 at South Mountain. Captured, 5/12/64 at Spotsylvania. POW—Ft. Delaware, DE. Released, 6/6/65.
4th Sgt.	Cox, John Louis	1841	S	Rollins Store, Moore Co., NC	Farm Labor	Enlisted, 8/15/61. Reduced to Pvt., 5/1/62. Wounded (right arm), 7/1/62 at Malvern Hill. TDY—Collecting conscripts in NC; 2/-/63–6/21/64. Retired to Invalid Corps, 6/21/64.
5th Sgt.	**Wicker, Lewis M.**	**1832**	**S**	**Long Street, Moore Co., NC**	**Farm Labor**	**Enlisted, 8/15/61. Reduced to Pvt., 5/1/62/ Killed, 7/1/63 at Gettysburg.**
1st Cpl.	McNeil, Henry J.	1839	S	Crain's Creek, Moore Co., NC	Merchant	Enlisted, 8/15/61. Elected to 1st Lt., 5/1/62. Wounded (right leg—tibia shattered), 5/19/64 at Harris Farm. Resigned due to wounds, 2/25/65.
3rd Cpl.	**McLeod, Louis H.**	**1830**	**M**	**Rollins Store, Moore Co., NC**	**Farmer**	**Enlisted, 8/15/61. Elected to 3rd Lt., 5/1/62. Died of heart failure, 3/18/63 at Rollins Store, NC.**
4th Cpl.	**Jackson, Archibald J.**	**1834**	**S**	**Crain's Creek, Moore Co., NC**	**Turpentine Distiller**	**Enlisted, 8/15/61. Promoted to Sgt., 2/1/62. Promoted to 2nd Lt., 5/1/62. Wounded, 5/12/64 at Spotsylvania. Died of wounds, 5/19/64.**
Pvt.	Baker, James	1838	S	Crain's Creek Moore Co., NC	Farm Labor	Enlisted, 8/15/61. Discharged (provided a substitute), 2/15/62.
Pvt.	Black, Alfred	1830	S	Fayetteville, Cumberland Co., NC	Cooper's Asst.	Enlisted, 8/15/61. Wounded, 6/27/62 at Gaines' Mill. AWOL—9/1/62 to 11/3/63. Transferred to 13th NC Light Arty., 11/4/63. Transferred back to Co. H, 2/26/64. Captured, 5/12/64 at Spotsylvania. POW—Point Lookout, MD. Released, 5/19/64.
Pvt.	Blalock, F. Marion	1838	S	Orange Co., NC	Day Labor	Enlisted, 8/15/61. Wounded (left knee), 7/1/62 at Malvern Hill. TDY—shoemaker in Richmond; 12/28/63 to 8/1/64. Deserted, 8/2/64.
Pvt.	Brafford, Eli	1843	S	Chatham Co., NC	Farm Labor	Enlisted, 8/15/61. Wounded, 6/27/62 at Gaines' Mill. TDY—Recruiting conscripts in NC; 2/9/63–2/13/65. Retired to Invalid Corps, 2/14/65.
Pvt.	Brown, A. Singa	1842	S	Carthage, Moore Co., NC	Farm Labor	Enlisted, 8/15/61. Promoted to Cpl., 4/-/63/ Missing, 7/10/63 in retreat from Gettysburg. "Listed as a deserted."
Pvt.	Brown, Alexander	1842	S	Pittsboro, Chatham Co., NC	Farm Labor	Enlisted, 8/15/61. Promoted to Sgt., 5/1/62. Promoted to 3rd Lt., 3/19/63. Wounded (left thigh—flesh wound), 7/1/63 at Gettysburg. Captured, 11/7/63 at Kelly's Ford. POW—Johnson's Island, OH. Released, 6/12/65.

Appendix 2

Rank	Name	DOB	M/S	Residence	Occupation	Remarks
Pvt.	Brown, James	1835	S	Gold Region, Moore Co., NC	Farm Labor	Enlisted, 8/15/61. Wounded, 6/27/62 at Gaines' Mill. Killed, 9/17/62 at Sharpsburg.
Pvt.	Buchanan, Null	1840	S	Summerville, Harnett Co., NC	Farm Labor	Enlisted, 8/15/61. Died of fever, 8/11/63 at Lynchburg, VA.
Pvt.	Buchanan, Thomas	1842	S	Pittsboro, Chatham Co., NC	Farm Labor	Enlisted, 8/15/61. Died of scarlet fever, 12/8/62 at Staunton, VA.
Pvt.	Buchanan, Wm. May	1844	S	Pittsboro, Chatham Co., NC	Farm Labor	Enlisted, 8/15/61. Wounded & missing, 6/27/62 at Gaines' Mill. AWOL—7/1/62-8/-/63. Dropped from rolls, 8/-/63.
Pvt.	Buie, Daniel	1837	S	Crain's Creek, Moore Co., NC	Farm Labor	Enlisted, 8/15/61. Wounded, 6/27/62 at Gaines' Mill. Died of Wounds, 7/14/62 at Drewry's Bluff, VA.
Pvt.	Buie, John	1827	S	Rollins Store, Moore Co., NC	Farmer	Enlisted, 8/15/61. Promoted to Sgt., 5/1/62. Captured, 9/14/62 at South Mountain. POW—Ft. Delaware, DE. Exchanged, 11/10/62. Captured, 11/7/63 at Kelly's Ford. POW—Point Lookout, MD. Exchanged, 3/18/65.
Pvt.	Campbell, Angus T.	1827	M	Jackson Springs, Moore Co., NC	Farm Labor	Enlisted, 8/15/61. Captured, 7/5/63 in retreat from Gettysburg. POW—David's Island, NY. Exchanged, 8/28/63. Captured, 5/12/64 at Spotsylvania. POW—Elmira, NY. Died of pneumonia, 3/22/65.
Pvt.	Campbell, Daniel	1838	S	Crain's Creek, Moore Co., NC	Farm Labor	Enlisted, 8/15/61. Missing ("left on the march into Maryland."), 9/6/62 near Leesburg, VA. Dropped from the rolls, 8/-/63.
Pvt.	Campbell, George W.	1841	S	Carthage, Moore Co., NC	Farm Labor	Enlisted, 8/15/61. Captured, 7/4/63 in retreat from Gettysburg. POW—Point Lookout, MD. Exchanged, 3/20/64. Surrendered, 4/9/65 at Appomattox.
Pvt.	Campbell, John M.	1835	S	Buffalow, Moore Co., NC	Physician	Enlisted, 8/15/61. Discharged (provided a substitute), 8/16/62.
Pvt.	Carr, Dennis	1825	S	Buffalow, Moore Co., NC	Railroad Labor	Enlisted, 8/15/61. Wounded, 6/27/62 at Gaines' Mill. Discharged ("being an alien from Ireland.'). 9/22/62.
Pvt.	Cole, George C.	1836	S	Pocket, Moore Co., NC	Farm Labor	Enlisted, 8/15/61. Killed, 7/1/62 at Malvern Hill.
Pvt.	Cole, George W.	1842S	S	Buffalow, Moore Co., NC	Farm Labor	Enlisted, 8/15/61. Wounded (leg), 5/6/64 at The Wilderness. Absent due to wounds until 8/31/64. No further records.
Pvt.	Cole, Neill M.	1839	S	Pocket, Moore Co., NC	Farm Labor	Enlisted, 8/15/61. Died of typhoid fever, 8/16/62 at Richmond, VA.
Pvt.	Cox, William W.	1842	S	Eastern Chatham, Co., NC	Farm Labor	Enlisted, 8/15/61. Died of pneumonia, 11/17/61 at Camp Wyatt, NC.
Pvt.	Deaton, James P.	1842	S	Pittsboro, Chatham Co., NC	Well digger	Enlisted, 8/15/61. Promoted to Musician, 11/1/61. Promoted to Sgt., 5/1/62. Wounded, 6/27/62 at Gaines' Mill. Reduced to Pvt., 2/9/63. TDY—Gathering stragglers in NC; 2/9/63-8/31/64. No further records.
Pvt.	Freeman, William M.	1838		Moore Co., NC		Enlisted, 8/15/61. No further records after 8/31/64.
Pvt.	Goins, Duncan	1838	S	Pittsboro, Chatham Co., NC	Farm Labor	Enlisted, 8/15/61. Died of typhoid fever, 3/10/62 at Wilmington, NC.

30th North Carolina Infantry Roster, Company H

Rank	Name	DOB	M/S	Residence	Occupation	Remarks
Pvt.	Goins, Edward	1840	S	Pittsboro, Chatham Co., NC	Farm Labor	Enlisted, 8/15/61. TDY—Teamster; 7/-/62–4/9/65. Surrendered, 4/9/65 at Appomattox.
Pvt.	**Graham, Jarrett B.**	**1827**	**S**	**Carthage, Moore Co., NC**	**Day Labor**	**Enlisted, 8/15/61. Wounded, 6/27/62 at Gaines' Mill. Died ("Drowned in Cape Fear River"), 7/4/62. "Fell overboard on the passage of the *Hurt* from Wilmington [NC] to Fayetteville [NC]."**
Pvt.	**Graham, Samuel**			**Chatham Co., NC**		**Enlisted, 8/15/61. Died of tuberculosis, 8/12/62 at Richmond, VA.**
Pvt.	Harrington, Ard A.	1820	M	Sloan, Moore Co., NC	Farmer	Enlisted, 8/15/61. Promoted to Sgt., 5/1/62/ Paroled, 4/9/65 at Appomattox.
Pvt.	Hight, Joseph J.	1839	S	Long Street, Moore Co., NC	Farm Labor	Enlisted, 8/15/61. Promoted to Cpl., 5/1/62. Wounded ("flesh wound through thigh"), 7/1/63 at Gettysburg. Captured at field hospital, 7/4/63. POW—David's Island, NY. Exchanged, 8/28/63. Returned to duty, 12/-/63. No further records after 8/31/64.
Pvt.	**Hughes, Doctor**	**1839**	**S**	**Pittsboro, Chatham Co., NC**	**Farm Labor**	**Enlisted, 8/15/61. Died of disease, 5/13/63 at Hamilton's Crossing, Va.**
Pvt.	Hunter, Charles A.	1842	S	Moore Co., NC	Farm Labor	Enlisted, 8/15/61. Wounded, 7/1/62 at Malvern Hill. Wounded, 5/3/63 at Chancellorsville. Promoted to Cpl. 8/31/64. Surrendered, 4/9/65 at Appomattox.
Pvt.	Hunter, John R.	1842	S	Pittsboro, Chatham Co., NC	Farm Labor	Enlisted, 8/15/61. Wounded, 7/1/62 at Malvern Hill. Captured, 11/7/63 at Kelly's Ford. POW—Old Capital Prison, Washington, D.C. Took Oath of Allegiance, 3/18/64.
Pvt.	**Hunter, Stanford**	**1841**	**S**	**Pittsboro, Chatham Co., NC**	**Carpenter**	**Enlisted, 8/15/61. Wounded, 7/1/62 at Malvern Hill. Died of wounds, 7/22/62 at Richmond, VA.**
Pvt.	Johnson, John	1840	S	Crain's Creek, Moore Co., NC	Farm Labor	Enlisted, 8/15/61. Discharged (disability—"dropsy palsy"), 8/3/63.
Pvt.	Kelly, Alex David	1842	S	Pittsboro, Chatham Co., NC	Farm Labor	Enlisted, 8/15/61. TDY—Teamster; 5/1/62–8/31/64. No further records.
Pvt.	Kelly, Archibald, Jr.	1842	S	Pittsboro, Chatham Co., NC	Farm Labor	Enlisted, 8/15/61. Discharged ("Exchanged for another man"), 7/30/62.
Pvt.	Kelly, Archibald, Sr.	1819	M	Long Street, Moore Co., NC	Wheelwright	Enlisted, 8/15/61. Discharged (Disability—ruptured hernia), 7/25/62.
Pvt.	Kelly, Wm. Alfred	1829	M	Long Street, Moore Co., NC	Blacksmith	Enlisted, 8/15/61. Captured, 11/7/63 at Kelly's Ford. POW—Old Capital Prison, Washington, D.C. Took Oath of Allegiance, 3/15/64.
Pvt.	Knight, Benjamin	1830		Long Street, Moore Co., NC		Enlisted, 8/15/61. Wounded (left hand), 6/27/62 at Gaines' Mill. TDY—Arresting stragglers & deserters in NC; 2/9/63–8/31/64. No further records.
Pvt.	McAulay, William	1835	M	Long Street, Moore Co., NC	Farmer	Enlisted, 8/15/61. Captured, 7/1/62 at Malvern Hill. Exchanged, 8/5/62. "Nominated for the Badge of Distinction for Gallantry at Chancellorsville," 5/3/63. Wounded (neck), 7/1/63 at Gettysburg. Captured at field hospital, 7/4/63. POW—David's Island, NY. Exchanged, 9/27/63. Retired to Invalid Corps, 5/15/64.

Appendix 2

Rank	Name	DOB	M/S	Residence	Occupation	Remarks
Pvt.	McDonald, James S.	1838	S	Crain's Creek, Moore Co., NC	Farm Labor	Enlisted, 8/15/61. Captured, 9/17/62 at Sharpsburg. Exchanged, 11/25/62. Captured, 11/7/63 at Kelly's Ford. POW—Point Lookout, MD. Exchanged, 3/3/65.
Pvt.	McDonald, Neill	1833	S	Crain's Creek, Moore Co., NC	Farmer	Enlisted, 8/15/61. Wounded (shoulder), 9/17/62 at Sharpsburg. Died of disease, 12/25/62 at Crain's Creek, NC.
Pvt.	McDonald, Donald	1837	S	Rollins Store, Moore Co., NC	Farm Labor	Enlisted, 8/15/61. Captured, 9/14/62 at South Mountain. POW—Ft. Delaware, DE. Exchanged, 11/10/62. Wounded (both legs), 12/13/62 at Fredericksburg. (One leg amputated). Died of wounds, 12/30/62.
Pvt.	McFarland, Andrew	1830	S	Buffalow, Moore Co., NC	Railroad Labor	Enlisted, 8/15/61. Wounded, 9/17/62 at Sharpsburg. Captured, 5/12/64 at Spotsylvania. No further records.
Pvt.	McFarland, John A.	1843	S	Rollins Store, Moore Co., NC	Farm Labor	Enlisted, 8/15/61. Captured, 9/17/62 at Sharpsburg. POW—Ft. Delaware, DE. Exchanged, 11/10/62. Surrendered, 4/9/64 at Appomattox.
Pvt.	McFatter, Alexander	1810	M	Buffalow, Moore Co., NC	Railroad Labor	Enlisted, 8/15/61. Captured, 7/1/62 at Malvern Hill. POW—Ft. Delaware, DE. Exchanged, 8/5/62. Wounded (shoulder & neck), 11/7/63 at Kelly's Ford. Died of wounds, 11/28/63 at Richmond, VA.
Pvt.	McIntosh, Francis M.			Crain's Creek, Moore Co., NC		Transferred from 26th NC Inf., 8/20/61. Wounded, 7/18/64 at Snicker's Gap. Absent, sick after 2/25/65. No further records.
Pvt.	McIver, John W.	1837	S	Buffalow, Moore Co., NC	Farm Labor	Enlisted, 8/15/61. Died of measles and pneumonia, 11/8/61 at Southport, NC.
Pvt.	McIver, Murdock A.	1842	S	Buffalow, Moore Co., NC	Farm Labor	Enlisted, 8/15/61. Died of typhoid fever, 9/22/62 at Richmond, VA.
Pvt.	McNeill, Laughlin	1825	M	Long Street, Moore Co., NC	Carpenter	Enlisted, 8/15/61. Wounded (right arm), 7/1/62 at Malvern Hill. (Arm amputated). Discharged (wounds), 8/3/62.
Pvt.	McPherson, A. Dugall	1840	S	Buffalow, Moore Co., NC	Railroad Labor	Enlisted, 8/15/61. Died of disease, 7/22/62 at Richmond, VA.
Pvt.	Mashburn, Alfred I.	1840	S	Rollins Store, Moore Co., NC	Farm Labor	Enlisted, 8/15/61. Wounded, 9/17/62 at Sharpsburg. TDY—Light assignment at Richmond hospital; 3/16/64–12/31/64. No further records.
Pvt.	Mashburn, James D.	1836	S	Rollins Store, Moore Co., NC	Farm Labor	Enlisted, 8/15/61. Wounded, 7/1/62 at Malvern Hill. Died of wounds, 7/3/62.
Pvt.	Matthews, M. Hardy	1840	S	Long Street, Moore Co., NC	Farm Labor	Enlisted, 8/15/61. Promoted, to Cpl., 5/1/62. Wounded (leg & left arm), 5/12/64 at Spotsylvania. Wounded (right leg) and captured, 9/19/64 at Winchester. POW—Point Lookout, MD. Exchanged, 3/4/65.
Pvt.	Matthews, Nathan	1842	S	Long Street, Moore Co., NC	Farm Labor	Enlisted, 8/15/61. Captured, 7/5/63 in retreat from Gettysburg. POW—Point Lookout, MD. Died of disease, 9/16/64.
Pvt.	Monroe, James A.	1842	S	Gold Region, Moore Co., NC	Farm Labor	Enlisted, 8/15/61. Wounded, 9/17/62 at Sharpsburg. Captured, 11/7/63 at Kelly's Farm. POW—Point Lookout, MD. Exchanged, 2/24/65.

Rank	Name	DOB	M/S	Residence	Occupation	Remarks
Pvt.	Morris, David P.	1822	M	Summerville, Harnett Co., NC	Farmer	Enlisted, 8/15/61. Wounded (right shoulder & arm—humerus fractured), 7/1/63 at Gettysburg. Captured in field hospital, 7/4/63. POW—Baltimore, MD. Exchanged, 9/27/63. Captured, 4/6/65 at High Bridge. POW—Point Lookout, MD. Died of chronic diarrhea, 5/3/65.
Pvt.	Morris, John D.	1838	S	Pocket, Moore Co., NC	Farmer	Enlisted, 8/15/61. Died of disease, 7/16/62 at Richmond, VA.
Pvt.	Morrison, Horace	1838	S	Crain's Creek, Moore Co., NC	Farm Labor	Enlisted, 8/15/61. Promoted to Cpl., 10/1/61. Wounded, 7/1/62 at Malvern Hill. Promoted to Sgt., 4/1/63. Killed, 5/8/64 at Spotsylvania.
Pvt.	Nason, Albert	1833	M	Rollins Store, Moore Co., NC	Railroad Labor	Enlisted, 8/15/61. Surrendered, 4/9/65 at Appomattox.
Pvt.	Phillips, John H.	1843	S	Buffalow, Moore Co., NC	Farm Labor	Enlisted, 8/15/61. Wounded (left knee), 9/17/62 at Sharpsburg. Wounded (left arm), 7/1/63 at Gettysburg. Captured 11/7/63 at Kelly's Ford. POW—Point Lookout, MD. Exchanged, 3/3/65.
Pvt.	Riddle, George W.	1836	S	Pocket, Moore Co., NC	Turpentine Labor	Enlisted, 8/15/61. Wounded (left hand & left ankle), 7/1/62 at Malvern Hill. Captured, 11/7/63 at Kelly's Ford. POW—Point Lookout, MD. Exchanged, 11/15/64. No further records.
Pvt.	Rogers, James	18391	S	Carbonton, Chatham Co., NC	Miner	Enlisted, 8/15/61. Captured, 5/12/64 at Spotsylvania. POW—Point Lookout, MD. Joined the 1st Regt. U.S. Vol., 6/18/64.
Pvt.	Shaw, Douglas C.	1839		Moore Co., NC		Enlisted, 8/15/61. Captured, 9/17/62 at Sharpsburg. POW—Ft. McHenry, MD. Exchanged, 11/10/62. Wounded (fractured skull), 5/3/63 at Chancellorsville. Wounded (left foot) and captured, 11/7/63 at Kelly's Ford. POW—Ft. Delaware, DE. Released, 6/7/65.
Pvt.	Stedman, David L.	1839	S	Pittsboro, Chatham Co., NC	Farm Labor	Enlisted, 8/15/61. Died of typhoid pneumonia, 4/15/63 at Richmond, VA.
Pvt.	Taylor, Jackson	1825		Harnett Co., NC		Enlisted, 8/15/61. Wounded, 5/6/64 at The Wilderness. Absent due to wounds. No records after 10/9/64.
Pvt.	Thomas, Jefferson	1835	M	Long Street, Moore Co., NC	Shoe maker	Enlisted, 8/15/61. Wounded, 10/31/61 at Wilmington, NC. Discharged (disability—dislocated left arm and fracture of the clavicle), 2/15/62.
Pvt.	Thomas, John W.	1838	S	Rollins Store, Moore Co., NC	Cooper	Enlisted, 8/15/61. Died of typhoid fever, 8/7/62 at Richmond, VA.
Pvt.	Thomas, Marshall G.	1836	S	Pittsboro, Chatham Co., NC	Farm Labor	Enlisted, 8/15/61. Discharged (provided a substitute), 2/15/62.
Pvt.	Thomas, Murphy J.	1843	S	Pittsboro, Chatham Co., NC	Farm Labor	Enlisted, 8/15/61. Captured, 5/19/64 at Harris Farm. No further records.
Pvt.	Thomas, William A.	1842	M	Pittsboro, Chatham Co., NC	Farm Labor	Enlisted, 8/15/61. Died of typhoid fever, 11/26/61 at Pittsboro, NC.
Pvt.	Underwood, John A.	1842	S	Long Street, Moore Co., NC	Farm Labor	Enlisted, 8/15/61. Wounded, 10/19/63 at Warrenton (Bristoe Station). Promoted to Cpl., 12/1/63. Wounded (right ankle), 5/12/64 at Spotsylvania. Surrendered, 4/9/65.

Rank	Name	DOB	M/S	Residence	Occupation	Remarks
Pvt.	Walker, Sandy	1836	S	Rollins Store, Moore Co., NC	Farm Labor	Enlisted, 8/15/61. TDY—Hospital service at Raleigh; 3/13/63–4/9/65. Paroled, 4/20/65 at Raleigh, NC.
Pvt.	Watson, Andrew J.	1832	S	Rollins Store, Moore Co., NC	Farm Labor	Enlisted, 8/15/61. Died of pneumonia, 2/11/63 at Rollins Store, NC.
Pvt.	Wicker, John J.	1837	S	Buffalow, Moore Co., NC	Farm Labor	Enlisted, 8/15/61. Died of fever, 7/19/62 at Richmond, VA.
Pvt.	Wicker, Oren R.	1839	S	Buffalow, Moore Co., NC	Farm Labor	Enlisted, 8/15/61. Died of chronic diarrhea, 5/30/63 at Buffalow, NC.
Pvt.	Wicker, Thomas	1824	M	Buffalo, Moore Co., NC	Farmer	Enlisted, 8/15/61. Wounded, 9/17/62 at Sharpsburg. Wounded (left arm & wrist—"arm broken by ball"). 7/1/63 at Gettysburg. Absent due to wounds through 2/-/65. No further records.
Pvt.	Wicker, William M.	1835	S	Pittsboro, Chatham Co., NC	Cooper	Enlisted, 8/15/61. Killed, 6/27/62 at Gaines' Mill.
Pvt.	Womack, James R.	1843	S	Pittsboro, Chatham Co., NC	Farm Labor	Enlisted, 8/15/61. Captured, 11/7/63 at Kelly's Ford. POW—Point Lookout, MD. Died of chronic diarrhea, 5/3/65.
Pvt.	Yancy, Thomas A.	1845	S	Summerville, Harnett Co., NC	Day Labor	Enlisted, 8/15/61. Wounded, 7/1/62 at Malvern Hill. Captured, 11/7/63 at Kelly's Ford. POW—Point Lookout, MD. Exchanged, 3/3/65. Sick and captured in Richmond hospital, 4/3/65. Released, 4/22/65.
Pvt.	Yarborough, W. T.	1836	S	Long Street, Moore Co., NC	Turpentine Labor	Enlisted, 8/15/61. Discharged (provided a substitute), 3/1/62.

1861 Recruits

Rank	Name	DOB	M/S	Residence	Occupation	Remarks
Pvt.	McCulloch, William	1826	M	Bushy Fork, Person Co., NC	Farmer	Enlisted, 10/20/61. Wounded, 7/1/62 at Malvern Hill. Died of wounds, 7/3/62.

1862 Recruits/Conscripts

Rank	Name	DOB	M/S	Residence	Occupation	Remarks
Pvt.	Baker, Henry C.	1844	S	Rollins Store, Moore Co., NC	Day Labor	Enlisted, 4/26/62. Wounded and captured, 9/14/62 at South Mountain. Died of wounds, 12/17/62 at Frederick, MD.
Pvt.	Buchanan, Joseph	1825	M	Rollins Store, Moore Co., NC	Farmer	Enlisted, 3/1/62 (as a substitute). Died of acute diarrhea, 10/15/64 at Lynchburg, VA.
Pvt.	Cole, Andrew	1842	S	Pocket, Moore Co., NC	Farm Labor	Enlisted, 4/24/62. Captured, 9/14/62 at South Mountain. Exchanged, 10/2/62. Died of pneumonia, 4/2/63 at Richmond, VA.
Pvt.	Cox, William O.	1832		Moore Co., NC		Enlisted, 4/24/62. Wounded, 7/1/62 at Malvern Hill. Captured, 5/8/64 at Spotsylvania. POW—Point Lookout, MD. No further records after 5/17/64.
Pvt.	Gaster, John C.	1841	S	Rollins Store, Moore Co., NC	Farm Labor	Enlisted, 10/3/62. Died of typhoid fever, 5/9/63 at Richmond, VA.
Pvt.	Hornaday, Lewis D.	1832	M	Buffalow, Moore Co., NC	Farmer	Enlisted, 8/2/8/62, Captured, 5
Pvt.	Jackson, Burgess C.	1840	S	Crain's Creek, Moore Co., NC	Turpentine Salesman	Enlisted, 5/10/62. TDY—Richmond: 8/1/62–12/31/62. Wounded (right knee dislocated), 7/1/63 at Gettysburg. Killed, 5/12/64 at Spotsylvania.
Pvt.	Kelly, David W.	1842	S	Pittsboro, Chatham Co., NC	Farm Labor	Enlisted, 3/1/62 (substitute for Archibald Kelly). Captured, 7/5/63 near Chambersburg, PA. POW—Point Lookout, MD. Died of disease, 7/13/64.

30th North Carolina Infantry Roster, Company H

Rank	Name	DOB	M/S	Residence	Occupation	Remarks
Pvt.	Lawrence, Bennett	1842	S	Long Street, Moore Co., NC	Farm Labor	Enlisted, 2/15/62 (substitute for Marshall Thomas). Wounded and captured, 9/17/62 at Sharpsburg. Died of wounds, 9/24/62 at Stone House hospital, Sharpsburg, MD.
Pvt.	Lawrence, John	1839	S	Long Street, Moore Co., NC	Farm Labor	Enlisted, 2/15/62 (substitute for James Baker). Wounded, 6/27/62 at Gaines' Mill. Wounded ("bullet through hip"), 7/1/63 at Gettysburg. Wounded (face & jaw), 7/3/64 at Cold Harbor. Promoted to Cpl., 8/31/64. Surrendered, 4/9/65 at Appomattox.
Pvt.	McGill, Archy D.	1842	S	Fayetteville, Cumberland Co., NC	Day Labor	Enlisted, 1/16/62. Promoted to Cpl., 1/-/63. Paroled, 4/9/65 at Appomattox.
Pvt.	McIver, D. N.	1834	M	Buffalow, Moore Co., NC	Farmer	Enlisted, 4/24/62. Wounded, 5/19/64 at Harris Farm. Surrendered, 4/9/65 at Appomattox.
Pvt.	McIver, Dan W.	1830	S	Buffalow, Moore Co., NC	Farm Labor	Enlisted, 1/9/62. Discharged (disability), 7/22/62.
Pvt.	**McIver, Edward**	1832	S	**Buffalow, Moore Co., NC**	**Farm Labor**	**Enlisted, 4/24/62. Died of pneumonia, 12/13/62 at Front Royal, VA.**
Pvt.	McIver, John D. M.	1836	S	Buffalow, Moore Co., NC	Farmer	Enlisted, 4/26/62. TDY—Nurse at Orange Court House hospital, 5/1/63–10/31/63. Surrendered, 4/9/65 at Appomattox.
Pvt.	**McIver, Kenneth H.**	1844	S	**Buffalow, Moore Co., NC**	**Farm Labor**	**Enlisted, 4/24/62. Wounded, 5/3/63 at Chancellorsville. Died of wounds, 6/6/63 at Richmond, VA.**
Pvt.	**McPherson, Duncan R.**	1843	S	**Buffalow, Moore Co., NC**	**Farm Labor**	**Enlisted, 4/28/62. Died of Measles, 11/25/62 at Lynchburg, VA.**
Pvt.	Matthews, John B.	1836	M	Buffalow, Moore Co., NC	Farmer	Enlisted, 4/20/62 (as drummer). Wounded and captured, 9/17/62 at Sharpsburg. Exchanged, 9/30/62. TDY—Hospital nurse; 3/1/63–7/31/63. Placed in Invalid Corps, 4/25/64.
Pvt.	Monroe, John E.	1845	S	Gold Region, Moore Co., NC	Farm Labor	Enlisted, 4/26/62. Captured, 11/7/63 at Kelly's Ford. POW—Point Lookout, MD. Exchanged, 2/14/65.
Pvt.	O'Neal, Daniel	1814	M	Philippi, Barbour Co., VA	Farm Labor	Enlisted, 8/16/62 (as substitute). Deserted, 8/16/62. "Deserted same day."
Pvt.	Sinclair, John D.	1844	S	Buffalow, Moore Co., NC	Farm Labor	Enlisted, 1/16/62. TDY—Pioneer Corps; 2/1/62–4/9/64. Surrendered, 4/9/65 at Appomattox.
Pvt.	Sloan, David A.	1843	S	Long Street, Moore Co., NC	Farm Labor	Enlisted, 1/9/62. Wounded, 9/17/62 at Sharpsburg. Wounded, 5/3/63 at Chancellorsville. Captured, 11/7/63 at Kelly's Ford. POW—Ft. Delaware, DE. Released, 6/8/65.
Pvt.	**Sloan, John A.**	1844	S	**Long Street, Moore Co., NC**	**Farm Labor**	**Enlisted, 1/9/62. Died of pneumonia, 11/4/62 at Staunton, VA.**
Pvt.	Thomas, Henry T.	1845	S	Hadley's Mill, Chatham Co., NC	Farm Labor	Enlisted, 2/12/62. Surrendered, 4/9/65 at Appomattox.
Pvt.	Utley, John Wm.	1844	S	Pittsboro, Chatham Co., NC	Farm Labor	Enlisted, 1/26/62. Missing and captured, 7/2/63 at Gettysburg. "He skulked off somewhere." POW—Point Lookout, MD. Joined the 1st Regt. U.S. Vol., 2/9/64.
Pvt.	**Wicker, Alvis**	1846	S	**Buffalow, Moore Co., NC**	**Farm Labor**	**Enlisted, 7/12/62. Died of disease, 12/17/62 at Staunton, VA.**

Rank	Name	DOB	M/S	Residence	Occupation	Remarks
Pvt.	Wicker, Charles B.	1812	M	Buffalow, Moore Co., NC	Farmer	Enlisted, 10/9/62 (as a substitute). TDY—Wheelwright; 1/1/64–4/9/65. Surrendered, 4/9/65 at Appomattox.
Pvt.	Wicker, Kenneth W.	1831	M	Pocket, Moore Co., NC	Farmer	Enlisted, 4/26/62. Wounded, 7/1/62 at Malvern Hill. Died of wounds, 7/11/62 at Richmond, VA.
Pvt.	Wicker, William F.	1843	S	Long Street, Moore Co., NC	Farm Labor	Enlisted, 4/24/62. Wounded (right forearm), 9/17/62 at Sharpsburg. Discharged due to wounds, 12/25/63.

1863 Recruits/Conscripts

Rank	Name	DOB	M/S	Residence	Occupation	Remarks
Pvt.	Branch, Everett L.	1815	M	Summerville, Harnett Co., NC		Conscripted, 9/28/63. Deserted, 2/25/64.
Pvt.	Burgess, William H.	1829	M	Fayetteville, Cumberland Co., NC	Carpenter	Conscripted, 10/27/63. Killed, 5/12/64 at Spotsylvania.
Pvt.	Center, Charles H.	1819	M	Summerville, Harnett Co., NC	Day Labor	Conscripted, 9/28/63. Wounded (head) and captured, 5/12/64 at Spotsylvania. Died of wounds, 5/31/64 at Washington, D.C.
Pvt.	Cook, Anderson	1825	M	Graham, Alamance Co., NC	Farmer	Conscripted, 9/19/63. Died of disease, 11/29/63 at Gordonsville, VA.
Pvt.	Crotts, Elijah	1822		Cleveland Co., NC		Conscripted, 8/27/63. Killed, 7/18/64 at Snicker's Gap.
Pvt.	Dudley, Laban	1824	M	Summerville, Harnett Co., NC	Cooper	Conscripted, 9/28/63. Captured, 5/24/64 at North Anna. POW—Point Lookout, MD. Exchanged, 3/16/65.
Pvt.	Eason, James S.	1824	M	Tarboro, Edgecombe Co., NC	Farmer	Conscripted, 10/5/63. Previously served in Co. F. Captured 6/10/64, "in Maryland." Died of typhoid fever, 7/18/64 at Frederick, MD.
Pvt.	Fields, Absalom	1832	M	Greensboro, Guilford Co., NC	Farmer	Conscripted, 9/12/63. Deserted, 11/20/63.
Pvt.	Green, James L.	1820	M	Cleveland Co., NC	Farmer	Conscripted, 8/23/63. Captured, 5/12/64 at Spotsylvania. POW—Elmira, NY. Died of chronic diarrhea, 10/4/64.
Pvt.	Hagler, Hiram	1824	M	Morgan's Mill, Union Co., NC	Farmer	Conscripted, 9/24/63. Wounded (back & left side) and captured, 7/12/64 at Ft. Stevens. Died of gangrene, 8/3/64 at Washington, D.C.
Pvt.	Hendricks, Eusileus	1821	M	Cleveland Co., NC	Farmer	Conscripted, 8/25/63. Captured, 9/19/64 at Winchester. POW—Point Lookout, MD. Exchanged, 1/21/65.
Pvt.	Horne, Pleasant	1824	M	Fort Gaines, Clay Co., GA	Farmer	Conscripted, 9/13/63. Captured, 5/12/64 at Spotsylvania. POW—Elmira, NY. Died of scurvy, 9/25/64.
Pvt.	Hoyle, Nicholas	1821	M	Cleveland Co., NC	Farmer	Conscripted, 9/22/63. Absent, sick; 6/12/64–10/27/64. No further records.
Pvt.	Hughes, Henry	1826	M	Salem, Forsythe Co., NC	Farmer	Conscripted, 9/24/63. No further records after 10/1/64.
Pvt.	Hunter, John S.	1821	M	Monroe, Union Co., NC	Farmer	Conscripted, 9/24/63. Deserted, 2/28/64.
Pvt.	King, W. H.	1822	M	Morrisville, Wake Co., NC	Farmer	Conscripted, 9/14/63. Captured, 5/12/64 at Spotsylvania. POW—Point Lookout, MD. Died of disease, 6/30/64.

Rank	Name	DOB	M/S	Residence	Occupation	Remarks
Pvt.	Lloyd, Manley C.	1824	M	White Cross, Orange Co., NC	Farmer	Conscripted, 9/6/63. Wounded, 5/6/64 at The Wilderness. Absent due to wounds through 8/31/64. No further records.
Pvt.	Logan, Philip	1822	M	Cleveland Co., NC	Farmer	Conscripted, 9/22/63. Died of disease, 12/1/64 in VA.
Pvt.	Lynn, William	1820	M	Durhamsville, Orange Co., NC	Farmer	Conscripted, 9/16/63. Wounded (right thigh), 3/25/65 near Ft. Stedman. No further records.
Pvt.	McDonald, John A.	1823	M	Summerville, Harnett Co., NC	Farmer	Conscripted, 9/28/63. Absent, sick; 5/4/64–4/3/65. Captured, 4/3/65 in Richmond hospital.
Pvt.	Pool, Thomas	1846	S	Orange Co., NC	Farm Labor	Enlisted, 9/4/63. Died of disease, 2/9/64 in camp near Orange Court House, VA.
Pvt.	Rape, Isaac S.	1820	M	Monroe, Union Co., NC	Farm Labor	Conscripted, 9/21/63. Sick in hospital at Farmville; 5/1/64–8/31/64. No further records.
Pvt.	Rhodes, Wiley	1823	M	Orange Co., NC	Farmer	Conscripted, 9/4/63. TDY—Nurse in Raleigh hospital; 11/1/63–4/9/65. Paroled, 5/3/65 in Greensboro, NC.
Pvt.	Rose, Henry B.			Fayetteville, Cumberland Co., NC		Conscripted, 3/-/63. Captured, 5/12/64 at Spotsylvania. POW—Elmira, NY. Released, 5/29/65.
Pvt.	Shore, William F.	1841	S	Wadesboro, Anson Co., NC	Farm Labor	Conscripted, 9/24/63. Surrendered, 4/9/65 at Appomattox.
Pvt.	Starnes, D. A.	1821		Union Co., NC		Conscripted, 9/24/63. Wounded (right leg), 7/18/64 at Snicker's Gap. No further records.
Pvt.	Starnes, Ephraim	1825	M	Monroe, Union Co., NC	Farm Labor	Conscripted, 9/24/63. Captured, 5/12/64 at Spotsylvania. POW—Elmira, NY. Died of "congestion of the brain," 1/12/65.
Pvt.	Starnes, Thomas	1822	M	Wolfsville, Union Co., NC	Farmer	Conscripted, 9/24/63. Wounded, 10/17/63 near Warrenton (Bristoe Station). Surrendered, 4/9/65 at Appomattox.

1864 Conscripts

Rank	Name	DOB	M/S	Residence	Occupation	Remarks
Pvt.	Watkins, William B.	1846	S	Salisbury, Rowan Co., NC	Farm Labor	Conscripted, 8/1/64. Paroled, 4/14/65 at Burkesville, VA.

Company I
Nash County (Mustered into Regt.,—9/10/61)

Rank	Name	DOB	M/S	Residence	Occupation	Remarks
Cpt.	Arrington, William T.	1822	M	Dortches, Nash Co., NC	Farmer	Enrolled, 9/10/61. Killed, 7/1/62 at Malvern Hill.
1st Lt.	Bunn, Elias	1842	S	Rocky Mount, Nash Co., NC	Farm Labor	Enrolled, 9/10/61. Defeated in re-election, 5/1/62.
2nd Lt.	Harris, James I.	1835	S	Nashville, Nash Co., NC	Public Registrar	Enrolled, 9/10/61. Promoted to 1st Lt., 3/27/62. Promoted to Cpt. 7/2/62. Injury ankle dislocated), 9/17/62 at Sharpsburg. (Killed, 5/12/64 at Spotsylvania.
3rd Lt.	Woodward, Coleman W.	1827	S	Castalia, Nash Co., NC	Farmer	Enrolled, 9/10/61. Resigned, 4/1/62.
1st Cpl.	Barkley, James H.	1840	S	Arringtons, Nash Co., NC	Day Labor	Enlisted, 9/10/61. Reduced to Pvt., 4/1/62. Promoted to Cpl., 6/1/63. Captured, 11/7/63 at Kelly's Ford. POW—Point Lookout, MD. Exchanged, 3/3/65.

Appendix 2

Rank	Name	DOB	M/S	Residence	Occupation	Remarks
3rd Cpl.	Batchelor, Van Buren	1834	M	Dortches, Nash Co., NC	Farmer	Enlisted, 9/10/61. Promoted to Sgt., 4/1/62. Wounded & captured, 9/17/62 at Sharpsburg. Paroled, 9/20/62. Captured, 11/7/63 at Kelly's Ford. POW—Point Lookout, MD. Exchanged, 3/3/65.
4th Cpl.	Robbins, Willie H.	1835	M	Ricks, Nash Co., NC	Farmer	Enlisted, 9/10/61. Reduced to Pvt., 12/14/61. Absent on furlough and never returned. Dropped from rolls, 12/31/62.
Pvt.	Barnes, Bryant B.	1840	S	Arringtons, Nash Co., NC	Farm Labor	Enlisted, 9/10/61. Died of typhoid fever, 10/28/61 in Wilson Co., NC.
Pvt.	Bass, John S.	1843		Madison Co., C		Enlisted, 9/10/61. Wounded, 7/1/62 at Malvern Hill. Wounded, 5/3/63 at Chancellorsville. Died of wounds, 5/5/63.
Pvt.	Bass, Richard H.	1843	S	Dortches, Nash Co., NC	Farm Labor	Enlisted, 9/10/61. Wounded, 6/27/62 at Gaines' Mill. Died of wounds, 6/28/62.
Pvt.	Batchelor, Elkanah	1830	S	Mannings, Nash Co., NC	Teacher	Enlisted, 9/10/61. TDY—Nurse at Kittrell Springs, NC; 10/-/64–4/9/65. Paroled, 5/1/65 at Greensboro, NC.
Pvt.	Batchelor, Neverson A.	1839	M	Ricks, Nash Co., NC	Farm Labor	Enlisted, 9/10/61. Captured, 11/7/63 at Kelly's Ford. POW—Point Lookout, MD. Died of smallpox, 2/9/64.
Pvt.	Batchelor, William D. "Willie"	1840	S	Coopers, Nash Co., NC	Farm Labor	Enlisted, 9/10/61. Promoted to Cpl., 5/1/63. Killed, 11/7/63 at Kelly's Ford.
Pvt.	Bone, Hardy H.	1833	M	Winsteads, Nash Co., NC	Farmer	Enlisted, 9/10/61. Died of pneumonia, 11/18/62 at Richmond, VA.
Pvt.	Bone, John Wesley	1842	S	Dortches, Nash Co., NC	Farm Labor	Enlisted, 9/10/61. Wounded (hand), 7/1/62 at Malvern Hill. Wounded (right breast), 5/12/64 at Spotsylvania. Paroled, 4/9/65 at Appomattox.
Pvt.	Brantley, Jn. Redmond	1838	S	Coopers, Nash Co., NC	Farm Labor	Enlisted, 9/10/61. Wounded, 7/1/62 at Malvern Hill. Wounded (left hip) and captured, 11/7/63 at Kelly's Ford. POW—Elmira, NY. Exchanged, 2/21/65.
Pvt.	Bryan, James H.	1843	S	Ricks, Nash Co., NC	Farm Labor	Enlisted, 9/10/61. Promoted to Cpl., 4/1/62/ Wounded, 7/1/62 at Malvern Hill. Promoted to Sgt., 5/1/63. Wounded (neck & scalp) and captured, 11/7/63 at Kelly's Ford. POW—Point Lookout, MD. Exchanged, 10/25/64. Reduced to Pvt., 12/-/64. Paroled, 4/9/65 at Appomattox.
Pvt.	Bunn, Benjamin	1844	S	Rocky Mount, Nash Co., NC	Student	Enlisted, 9/10/61. Promoted to 1st Sgt., 11/1/61. Reduced to Pvt., 4/1/62. Transferred to 47th NC Inf., 9/24/62.
Pvt.	Capps, William H.	1830	M	Louisburg, Franklin Co., NC	Farmer	Enlisted, 9/10/61. Absent, sick much of the time with regt. "Dropped out of the march [into PA]," 6/6/63. Captured, 4/6/65 at Farmville. Confined at Newport News, VA. Released, 6/27/65.
Pvt.	Coley, James J.	1837	S	Dortches, Nash Co.,	Farm Labor	Enlisted, 9/10/61. Discharged (disability), 4/18/62.
Pvt.	Cook, Ransom L.	1840	S	Coopers, Nash Co., NC	Farm Labor	Enlisted, 9/10/61. Discharged (disability—general anemic condition), 12/14/61.
Pvt.	Crickman, Josiah G.	1844	S	Arringtons, Nash Co., NC	Farm Labor	Enlisted, 9/10/61. Wounded, 5/3/63 at Chancellorsville. Captured, 5/12/64 at Spotsylvania. POW—Elmira, NY. Released, 6/27/65.

30th North Carolina Infantry Roster, Company I

Rank	Name	DOB	M/S	Residence	Occupation	Remarks
Pvt.	Crump, Samuel W.	1835	S	Collins, Nash Co., NC	Farm Labor	Enlisted, 9/10/61. Died of typhoid fever, 2/6/62 at Camp Wyatt, NC.
Pvt.	Denson, Alexander	1842	S	Dortches, Nash Co., NC	Farm Labor	Enlisted, 9/10/61. Captured, 11/7/63 at Kelly's Ford. POW—Point Lookout, MD. Exchanged, 3/3/65.
Pvt.	Denson, Benjamin E.	1839	S	Dortches, Nash Co., NC	Farm Labor	Enlisted, 9/10/61. Discharged (disability), 3/14/62.
Pvt.	Dozier, James W.	1837	S	Bailey, Nash Co. NC	Teacher	**Enlisted, 9/10/61. Promoted, to Cpl., 10/-/61. Promoted to Sgt., 5/1/62. Died of typhoid fever, 4/18/63 at Richmond, VA.**
Pvt.	Edwards, James	1840	S	Dortches, Nash Co., NC	Farm Labor	Enlisted, 9/10/61. Captured 11/7/63 at Kelly's Ford. No further records.
Pvt.	Edwards, Robert C.	1839	S	Dortches, Nash Co., NC	Farm Labor	Enlisted, 9/10/61. Discharged (disability), 2/14/62.
Pvt.	Fox, Reddin P.	1847	S	Collins, Nash Co., NC	Farm Labor	Enlisted, 9/10/61. Surrendered, 4/9/65 at Appomattox.
Pvt.	Fryer, Lawrence D.	1843	S	Collins, Nash Co., NC	Farm Labor	Enlisted, 9/10/61. Wounded (left leg), 6/3/64 at Cold Harbor. Absent due to wounds until 8/31/64. No further records.
Pvt.	Griffin, James D.	1839	S	Ricks, Nash Co., NC	Farm Labor	Enlisted, 9/10/61. Wounded (ankle), 9/17/62 at Sharpsburg. TDY—Nurse in Richmond hospital; 5/1/63–4/9/65. Paroled, 4/21/65 at Richmond.
Pvt.	Griffin, Jesse R.	1838	S	Ricks, Nash Co., NC	Farm Labor	Enlisted, 9/10/61. Promoted to Sgt., 4/1/62. Reduced to Pvt., 1/-/63. Deserted, 6/4/63. Returned to duty, 10/-/63. Captured, 11/7/63 at Kelly's Ford. POW—Point Lookout, MD. Exchanged, 2/20/65.
Pvt.	Gupton, Thomas	1840	S	Louisburg, Franklin Co.,NC	Farm Labor	**Enlisted, 9/10/61. Killed, 7/18/64 at Snicker's Gap.**
Pvt.	Harris, Elbert H.	1820	M	Warrenton, Warren Co., NC	Carpenter	Enlisted, 9/10/61. Dropped from rolls, 6/25/62.
Pvt.	Hedgepeth, Elias G.	1833	M	Collins, Nash Co., NC	Farm Labor	**Enlisted, 9/10/61. Died of disease, 3/20/64 at Orange Court House, VA.**
Pvt.	Hunt, James A.	1833		Nash Co., NC	Farmer	Enlisted, 9/10/61. Captured, 11/7/63 at Kelly's Ford. POW—Point Lookout, MD. Joined the 1st U.S. Vol., 1/30/64.
Pvt.	Jones, John R.	1845	S	Dortches, Nash Co., NC	Factory Labor	Enlisted, 9/10/61. Wounded (foot), 7/1/63 at Gettysburg. Captured, 7/4/63 in field hospital. POW—Point Lookout, MD. Exchanged, 2/20/65.
Pvt.	Joyner, Alsey M.	1839	S	Franklinton, Franklin Co., NC	Teacher	**Enlisted, 9/10/61. Wounded, 12/13/62 at Fredericksburg. Killed, 5/12/64 at Spotsylvania.**
Pvt.	Joyner, Ashley G.	1844	S	Ricks, Nash Co., NC	Farm Labor	Enlisted, 9/10/61. Died of congestion of lungs, 12/13/62 at Richmond, VA.
Pvt.	Joyner, James A.	1837	M	Ricks, Nash Co., NC	Turpentine Labor	Enlisted, 9/10/61. Deserted, 11/-/62.
Pvt.	Joyner, Jonas A.	1840	S	Ricks, Nash Co., NC	Turpentine Labor	Enlisted, 9/10/61. Captured, 11/7/63 at Kelly's Ford. POW—Point Lookout, MD. Exchanged, 3/3/65.
Pvt.	Joyner, Nathan T.	1837	M	Coopers, Nash Co., NC	Turpentine Labor	Enlisted, 9/10/61. Discharged (disability—mental & physical debility), 4/25/62.

Appendix 2

Rank	Name	DOB	M/S	Residence	Occupation	Remarks
Pvt.	Joyner, Nelson V.	1841		Nash Co., NC	Farm Labor	Enlisted, 9/10/61. Wounded (right wrist & forearm), 7/1/63 at Gettysburg. Transferred to Invalid Corps, 2/17/65.
Pvt.	Joyner, William B.	1818	S	Ricks, Nash Co., NC	Farm Labor	Enlisted, 9/10/61. Surrendered, 4/9/65 at Appomattox.
Pvt.	Langley, Singleton	1821	M	Coopers, Nash Co., NC	Farm Labor	Enlisted, 9/10/61. Wounded (hip & thigh), 7/1/62 at Malvern Hill. Died of wounds, 7/7/72 at Richmond, VA.
Pvt.	Lewis, Edward W.	1843	S	Mannings, Nash Co., NC	Farm Labor	Enlisted, 9/10/61. Killed, 9/17/62 at Sharpsburg.
Pvt.	Lindsey, Neverson A.	1844	S	Winsteads, Nash Co., NC	Farm Labor	Enlisted, 9/10/61. Discharged, 2/14/62.
Pvt.	Lindsey, Richard	1841	S	Ricks, Nash Co., NC	Farm Labor	Enlisted, 9/10/61. Captured, 11/7/63 at Kelly's Ford. POW—Old Capital Prison, Washington, D.C. Died of smallpox, 1/16/64.
Pvt.	Manning, John E.	1838	S	Dortches, Nash Co., NC	Farm Labor	Enlisted, 9/10/61. Appointed Musician, 11/1/61. Died of disease, 8/31/62 at Richmond, VA.
Pvt.	Morgan, Moses B.	1825	S	Stanhope, Nash Co., NC	Farm Labor	Enlisted, 9/10/61. Died of disease, 12/2/61 at Camp Wyatt, NC.
Pvt.	Odom, David M.	1835		Nash Co., NC		Enlisted, 9/10/61. Promoted to Cpl., 4/1/62. Deserted, 7/5/63 on retreat from Gettysburg. Returned to duty, 11/-/63. Transferred to the 32nd NC Inf., 2/16/64.
Pvt.	Odom, Jacob E.	1842	S	Dortches, Nash Co., NC	Farm Labor	Enlisted, 9/10/61. Killed, 5/3/63 at Chancellorsville.
Pvt.	Parker, Josiah	1830	M	Winsteads, Nash Co., NC	Farmer	Enlisted, 9/10/61. Promoted to Cpl., 11/14/61. Died of pneumonia, 1/4/62 at Wilmington, NC.
Pvt.	Perry, Sidney R.	1843	S	Dortches, Nash Co., NC	Turpentine Labor	Enlisted, 9/10/61. Promoted to 1st Sgt., 4/1/62. Promoted to 3rd Lt., 3/17/63. Wounded (foot), 5/3/63 at Chancellorsville. Wounded (right ankle shattered), 7/18/64 at Snicker's Gap. "Shell fragment struck ankle and tibia, fracturing both." Did not return to Regt.
Pvt.	Pitt, Frederick "Buck"	1841	S	Dortches, Nash Co., NC	Farm Labor	Enlisted, 9/10/61. TDY—Working on Richmond fortifications; 11/1/63–12/31/63. Died of smallpox, 2/2/64 at Salisbury, NC.
Pvt.	Pitt, James W.	1844	S	Dortches, Nash Co., NC	Farm Labor	Enlisted, 9/10/61. Wounded (left leg), 5/12/64 at Spotsylvania. Surrendered, 4/9/65 at Appomattox.
Pvt.	Poland, Alfred	1821	M	Coopers, Nash Co., NC	Butcher	Enlisted, 9/10/61. Died of disease, 12/16/62 at Coopers, NC.
Pvt.	Price, Joel L.	1836	S	Collins, Nash Co., NC	Farm Labor	Enlisted, 9/10/61. Wounded (head), 7/1/62 at Malvern Hill. TDY—Working on Richmond fortifications; 11/1/63–12/25/63. Court martialed, 12/26/63.
Pvt.	Pridgen, Alexander	1824	M	Winsteads, Nash Co. NC	Farm Labor	Enlisted, 9/10/61. Deserted, 11/15/62.
Pvt.	Rackley, James M.	1835	S	Stanhope, Nash Co., NC	Carpenter	Enlisted, 9/10/61. Captured, 7/9/64 neat the Monocacy R. POW—Ft. McHenry, MD. Released, 5/13/65.

30th North Carolina Infantry Roster, Company I

Rank	Name	DOB	M/S	Residence	Occupation	Remarks
Pvt.	Renfrow, Perry V.	1840	S	Arringtons, Nash Co., NC	Farm Labor	Enlisted, 9/10/61. Promoted, to Cpl., 1/6/62. Promoted to Sgt., 4/1/62. Wounded, 9/17/62 at Sharpsburg. Wounded, 5/3/63 at Chancellorsville. Captured, 11/7/63 at Kelly's Ford. POW—Point Lookout, MD. Exchanged, 2/24/65.
Pvt.	Ricks, John A.	1839	S	Collins, Nash Co., NC	Farm Labor	Enlisted, 9/10/61. Promoted to Sgt., 11/1/61. Reduced to Sgt., 4/1/62. Discharged (provided a substitute), 7/-/62.
Pvt.	Robbins, Edward J.	1825		Nash Co., NC		Enlisted, 9/10/61. Absent, sick since 3/9/62. Did not return to Regt.
Pvt.	**Ruffin, Charles H. "Charlie"**	**1844**	**S**	**Tarboro, Edgecombe Co., NC**	**Farm Labor**	**Enlisted, 9/10/61. Wounded, 10/14/63 near Warrenton (Bristoe Station), "in a skirmish." Died of wounds, 10/15/63.**
Pvt.	Sykes, William J.	1841	S	Mannings, Nash Co., NC	Farm Labor	Enlisted, 9/10/61. Wounded (right arm), 7/3/64 at Cold Harbor. No records after 8/31/64.
Pvt.	**Taylor, Bolen**	**1842**	**S**	**Collins, Nash Co., NC**	**Farm Labor**	**Enlisted, 9/10/61. Died of pneumonia, 11/13/61 at Collins, NC.**
Pvt.	Taylor, Calvin C.	1836	M	Collins, Nash Co., NC	Carpenter	Enlisted, 9/10/61. Discharged (disability—"chest disease of a pulmonary character"), 5/18/62.
Pvt.	Taylor, Egbert H.	1824	M	Ricks, Nash Co., NC	Farmer	Enlisted, 9/10/61. Deserted, 2/10/63.
Pvt.	**Thorn, William E.**	**1841**	**S**	**Arringtons, Nash Co., NC**	**Farm Labor**	**Enlisted, 9/10/61. Died of chronic diarrhea, 11/18/61 at Arringtons, NC.**
Pvt.	Tidsale, Thomas B.	1835	S	Dortches, Nash Co., NC	Farm Labor	Enlisted, 9/10/61. Promoted to Sgt., 11/-/61 Promoted to 3rd Lt., 3/27/62. Absent, sick; 8/1/62–3/17/63. Dropped from rolls, 3/17/63.
Pvt.	Turner, Walter S.	1848	S	Tarboro, Edgecombe Co., NC	Clerk	Enlisted, 9/10/61. Promoted to Musician, 11/1/61. TDY—Orderly for Col. Parker; 5/1/62–5/31/62. Discharged (under age), 9/29/62.
Pvt.	Vick, Benjamin S.	1833	M	Collins, Nash Co., NC	Farmer	Enlisted, 9/10/61. Discharged (disability), 2/-/62.
Pvt.	Vick, Exum R.	1839	S	Dortches, Nash Co., NC	Farm Labor	Enlisted, 9/10/61. Promoted to Cpl., 4/1/62. Wounded (right thigh), 7/1/62 at Malvern Hill (leg amputated). Reduced to Pvt., 5/1/63. Retired to Invalid Corps, 4/27/64.
Pvt.	Vick, James F.	1825	M	Dortches, Nash Co., NC	Farm Labor	Enlisted, 9/10/61. Captured, 11/7/63 at Kelly's Ford. POW—Point Lookout, MD. Joined the 1st U.S. Inf., 1/30/64.
Pvt.	Vick, Joseph J.	1829	M	Collins, Nash Co., NC	Farmer	Enlisted, 9/10/61. Deserted, 6/20/63 on march to Gettysburg. Returned, 8/-/64. Captured, 9/22/64 near Fisher's Hill. POW—Point Lookout, MD. Exchanged, 3/19/65.
Pvt.	Walker, Richmond D.	1840		Nash Co., NC		Enlisted, 9/10/61. Captured, 11/7/63 at Kelly's Ford. POW—Point Lookout, MD. Joined the 1st U.S. Inf., 1/30/64.
Pvt.	Walker, Worrell P.	1828	M	Collins, Nash Co., NC	Overseer	Enlisted, 9/10/61. Promoted to Sgt., 10/-/61. Reduced to Pvt., 3/6/62. Promoted to Cpl., 5/1/62. Reduced to Pvt., 6/1/63. Deserted, 6/4/63. Returned to duty, 10/-/63. Captured, 11/7/63 at Kelly's Ford. POW—Point Lookout, MD. Paroled, 3/20/64. Captured, 4/6/65 at Farmville. Confined at Newport News, VA. Released, 6/15/65.

Appendix 2

Rank	Name	DOB	M/S	Residence	Occupation	Remarks
Pvt.	Whitley, John S.	1832	M	Dortches, Nash Co., NC	Farm Labor	Enlisted, 9/10/61. Died of typhoid fever, 3/30/62 at Wilmington, NC.
Pvt.	Williams, Henry H.	1833	M	Mannings, Nash Co., NC	Turpentine Labor	Enlisted, 9/10/61. Wounded, 7/1/62 at Malvern Hill. Captured, 11/7/63 at Kelly's Ford. POW—Point Lookout, MD. Joined the 1st U.S. Inf., 1/30/64.
Pvt.	Williams, Joseph D.	1830	M	Dortches, Nash Co., NC	Clerk	Enlisted, 9/10/61. Captured, 9/14/62 at South Mountain. POW—Ft. Delaware, DE. Exchanged, 11/10/62. Captured, 5/24/64 at North Anna. POW—Point Lookout, MD. Exchanged, 3/18/65.
Pvt.	Williford, Burton B.	1844	S	Arringtons, Nash Co., NC	Merchant's Asst.	Enlisted, 9/10/61. Promoted to Sgt., 11/-/61. Promoted to 2nd Lt., 3/27/62. Promoted to 1st Lt., 7/1/62. Wounded (right thigh), 5/3/63 at Chancellorsville, "bullet went through thigh into the pubic region." Resigned due to wounds, 9/14/63.
Pvt.	Wilbourne, Ruffin F	1833	M	Dortches, Nash Co., NC	Farmer	Enlisted, 9/10/61. Wounded, 7/1/62 at Malvern Hill. Died of wounds, 7/3/62.
Pvt.	Winstead, George T.	1844	S	Mannings, Nash Co., NC	Farm Labor	Enlisted, 9/10/61. Wounded, 7/1/62 at Malvern Hill. Killed, 5/3/63 at Chancellorsville.
Pvt.	Winters, George	1843	S	Nash Co., NC	Farm Labor	Enlisted, 9/10/61. Wounded, 5/3/63 at Chancellorsville. TDY—Nurse at Richmond hospital; 11/1/63–2/28/64. Captured, 5/19/64 at Harris Farm. POW—Elmira, NY. Released, 6/30/65.
Pvt.	Wood, James	1840	S	Mannings, Nash Co., NC	Farm Labor	Enlisted, 9/10/61. Died of erysipelas, 10/4/62 at Richmond, VA.
Pvt.	Wood, William	1840	S	Mannings, Nash Co., NC	Farm Labor	Enlisted, 9/10/61. Wounded, 5/3/63 at Chancellorsville. Died of wounds, 5/10/63.
Pvt.	Woodward, John E.	1836		Nash Co., NC		Enlisted, 9/10/61. Wounded, 7/1/62 at Malvern Hill. Captured, 11/7/63 at Kelly's Ford. POW—Point Lookout, MD. Exchanged, 3/3/65.

1861 Recruits

Rank	Name	DOB	M/S	Residence	Occupation	Remarks
Pvt.	Cobb, Jefferson	1840	S	Mannings, Nash Co., NC	Farm Labor	Enlisted, 12/19/61. Promoted to Cpl., 4/1/62. Captured, 9/12/62 at Frederick, MD. POW—Ft. Delaware, DE. Paroled, 11/10/62. Promoted to Sgt., 6/1/63. Paroled, 4/9/65 at Appomattox.
Pvt.	Winstead, Hilliard H.	1843	S	Mannings, Nash Co., NC	Farm Labor	Enlisted, 11/20/61. Captured, 9/17/62 at Sharpsburg. Paroled, 9/24/62. Promoted to Cpl., 11/7/63. Wounded, 8/21/64 at Charles Town. Died of wounds, 8/-/64.

1862 Recruits/Conscripts

Rank	Name	DOB	M/S	Residence	Occupation	Remarks
Pvt.	Bass, William	1812	M	Collins, Nash Co., NC	Farm Labor	Enlisted, 12/4/62 (as a substitute). Died of pneumonia, 3/18/63 at Richmond, VA.
Pvt.	Batchelor, Andrew J.	1837	S	Dortches, Nash Co., NC	Farm Labor	Enlisted, 1/28/62. Wounded, 5/3/63 at Chancellorsville. "He was noted for coolness in battle." Paroled, 4/14/65 at Burkeville Jct.
Pvt.	Batchelor, John W.	1840	S	Mannings, Nash Co., NC	Farm Labor	Enlisted, 3/4/62. Absent, sick or AWOL most of service. No records after 8/31/64.
Pvt.	Batchelor, Redmond W.	1846	S	Winsteads, Nash Co., NC	Farm Labor	Enlisted, 5/1/62. Wounded, 5/3/63 at Chancellorsville. Paroled, 4/14/65 at Burkeville Jct.

30th North Carolina Infantry Roster, Company I

Rank	Name	DOB	M/S	Residence	Occupation	Remarks
Pvt.	Batchelor, Samuel M.	1843	S	Mannings, Nash Co., NC	Farm Labor	Enlisted, 3/4/62. Died of chronic diarrhea, 9/22/62 at Richmond, VA.
Pvt.	Batchelor, Thomas R.	1833	M	Ricks, Nash Co., NC	Farmer	Enlisted, 3/4/62. Deserted, 6/28/63 in Perry Co., PA on road to Gettysburg. "Deserted to the enemy." POW—Ft. Mifflin, PA. Took Oath of Allegiance, 1/1/64.
Pvt.	Battle, Lawrence F.	1838	S	Collins, Nash Co., NC	Farmer	Enlisted, 5/1/62. Discharged (provided a substitute), 9/1/62.
Pvt.	Batts, William J.	1833	M	Coopers, Nash Co., NC	Farmer	Enlisted, 5/1/62. Wounded ("Gunshot wound to the head."), 9/22/64 at Fisher's Hill. Paroled, 4/9/65 at Appomattox.
Pvt.	**Bell, Arkin B.**	**1835**	**S**	**Black Creek, Wilson Co., NC**	**Carpenter**	**Enlisted, 3/10/62. TDY—Hospital at Wilson, NC; 4/1/62–4/30/63. Killed, 7/18/64 at Snicker's Gap.**
Pvt.	Bissett, Payton	1825	M	Stanhope, Nash Co., NC	Farmer	Conscripted, 8/5/62. Captured, 9/14/62 at South Mountain. POW—Ft. Monroe, VA. Paroled, 12/18/62. Transferred to 47th NC Inf., 1/22/64.
Pvt.	**Boon, Joseph H.**	**1832**	**M**	**Winsteads, Nash Co., NC**	**Farmer**	**Enlisted, 3/4/62. Died of epilepsy, 1/20/63 at Lynchburg, VA.**
Pvt.	Bunn, James D.	1845	S	Dortches, Nash Co., NC	Farm Labor	Enlisted, 3/4/62 Paroled, 4/9/65 at Appomattox.
Pvt.	Crumpler, Bennett	1825	M	Gardner, Wilson Co., NC	Farmer	Enlisted, 5/1/62. "Left on the road to Maryland," 9/-/62. Apprehended, 10/29/63, and "held in division headquarters." Deserted, 12/22/63.
Pvt.	Culpepper, John	1838	S	Dortches, Nash Co., NC	Farm Labor	Enlisted, 5/1/62. Wounded, 5/3/63 at Chancellorsville. Captured, 10/19/64 at Cedar Creek. POW—Point Lookout, MD. Exchanged, 3/17/65. Surrendered, 4/9/65 at Appomattox.
Pvt.	Davis, Miles	1844	S	Coopers, Nash Co., NC	Farm Labor	Enlisted, 5/1/62. Captured, 11/7/63 at Kelly's Ford. No further records.
Pvt.	**Eason, Haywood**	**1835**	**S**	**Dortches, Nash Co., NC**	**Carpenter**	**Enlisted, 5/1/62. Died of disease, 5/18/63, "in camp."**
Pvt.	Eason, William	1844	S	Dortches, Nash Co., NC	Carpenter's Asst.	Enlisted, 5/1/62. Presented until 8/31/64. No further records.
Pvt.	Evans, William M	1837	S	Collins, Nash Co., NC	Engineer	Enlisted, 5/1/62. TDY—Teamster, 2nd Corps Ordnance train; 11/1/63–4/9/65. Paroled, 4/9/65 at Appomattox.
Pvt.	Gay, George W.	1839	S	Dortches, Nash Co., NC	Farm Labor	Enlisted, 3/4/62. Promoted, to Cpl., 5/1/63. Wounded, 5/3/63 at Chancellorsville. Paroled, 4/9/65 at Appomattox.
Pvt.	Griffin, A. Calhoun	1843	S	Ricks, Nash Co., NC	Farm Labor	Enlisted, 3/4/62. Captured, 11/7/63 at Kelly's Ford. POW—Point Lookout, MD. Exchanged, 2/20/65.
Pvt.	**Harper, John H.**	**1839**	**S**	**Nashville, Nash Co., NC**	**Wheelwright Asst.**	**Enlisted, 3/4/63. Died of smallpox, 2/9/63 at Richmond VA.**
Pvt.	Jones, Calvin F.	1813	M	Arringtons, Nash Co., NC	Farmer	Enlisted, 3/15/62. Wounded, 5/12/64 at Spotsylvania. No further records.
Pvt.	**Joyner, Calving M.**	**1833**	**M**	**Winsteads, Nash Co., NC**	**Farmer**	**Enlisted, 5/1/62. Died of smallpox, 1/10/63 at Richmond, VA.**
Pvt.	Joyner, Ira E.	1832	M	Coopers, Nash Co., NC	Farmer	Enlisted, 5/1/62. Captured, 7/5/63 in retreat from Gettysburg. POW—Point Lookout, MD. Exchanged, 11/1/64. No further records.

Appendix 2

Rank	Name	DOB	M/S	Residence	Occupation	Remarks
Pvt.	Joyner, Little B.	1829	M	Coopers, Nash Co., NC	Farmer	Enlisted, 5/12/62. Died of typhoid fever, 8/10/62 at Richmond, VA.
Pvt.	Lewis, Arnold L.	1844	S	Mannings, Nash Co., NC	Farm Labor	Enlisted, 3/15/62. Wounded, 7/1/62 at Malvern Hill. Captured, 11/7/63 at Kelly's Ford. POW—Point Lookout, MD. Exchanged, 2/25/65. Surrendered, 4/9/65 at Appomattox.
Pvt.	Manning, Jeremiah D.	1842	S	Dortches, Nash Co., NC	Farm Labor	Enlisted, 5/1/62. Surrendered, 4/9/65 at Appomattox.
Pvt.	Manning, Moses V.	1839	S	Mannings, Nash Co., NC	Turpentine Labor	Enlisted, 5/1/62. Wounded, 9/17/62 at Sharpsburg. Died of wounds, 9/28/62 at Mannings, NC.
Pvt.	Manning, Richard M.	1833	S	Dortches, Nash Co., NC	Farm Labor	Enlisted, 5/1/62. Died of disease, 11/10/62 at Winchester, VA.
Pvt.	Pitt, John W. "Jack"	1835	S	Dortches, Nash Co., NC	Overseer	Transferred from 15th NC Inf., 6/21/62. TDY—Working on Richmond fortifications; 11/1/63–12/31/63. Died of disease, 1/28/64 at Richmond, VA.
Pvt.	Pitts, William M.	1841	S	Dortches, Nash Co., NC	Farm Labor	Transferred from 15th NC Inf., 6/21/62. Captured, 4/6/65 at Farmville. Confined at Newport News, VA. Released, 6/15/65.
Pvt.	Pittman, William B.	1827	M	Winsteads, Nash Co., NC	Farm Labor	Enlisted, 3/4/62. Absent, sick; 5/-/63–8/31/64. No further records.
Pvt.	Poland, Simeon H.	1832	M	Coopers, Nash Co., NC	Farmer	Enlisted, 5/1/62. Died of disease, 7/23/63 at Charlottesville, VA.
Pvt.	Pridgen, Drewry	1830	M	Coopers, Nash Co., NC	Farmer	Enlisted, 5/1/62. Wounded (arm), 11/7/63 at Kelly's Ford. (Arm amputated) retired to Invalid Corps, 4/16/64.
Pvt.	Pridgen, Henry H.	1834	M	Coopers, Nash Co., NC	Overseer	Enlisted, 5/1/62. Captured, 11/7/63 at Kelly's Ford. POW—Point Lookout, MD. Joined, 1st U.S. Inf., 1/30/64.
Pvt.	Pridgen, Josiah H.	1839	S	Winsteads, Nash Co., NC	Farm Labor	Enlisted, 5/1/62. Captured, 11/7/63 at Kelly's Ford. POW—Point Lookout, MD. Died of disease, 11/26/63.
Pvt.	Rackley, P. Nicholas	1839	S	Mannings, Nash Co., NC	Farm Labor	Enlisted, 5/1/62. Captured, 7/5/63 in retreat from Gettysburg. "He dropped out on the battlefield." Died of typhoid fever, 8/20/63 at Chester, PA.
Pvt.	Sherwood, Edwin	1839		Nash Co., NC		Enlisted, 5/1/62. Killed, 5/3/63 at Chancellorsville.
Pvt.	Sherwood, George A.	1841	S	Coopers, Nash Co., NC	Farm Labor	Enlisted, 5/1/62. Wounded (shoulder & jaw), 7/1/62 at Malvern Hill. Wounded (shoulder), 5/3/63 at Chancellorsville. Captured, 11/7/63 at Kelly's Ford. POW—Point Lookout, MD. Exchanged, 3/3/65.
Pvt.	Smith, Albert			Nash Co., NC		Enlisted, 5/1/62 Killed, 5/3/63 at Chancellorsville.
Pvt.	Stallings, Franklin	1831	M	Winsteads, Nash Co., NC	Farmer	Enlisted, 5/1/62 Killed, 5/3/63 at Chancellorsville.
Pvt.	Stallings, Willie	1835	M	Winsteads, Nash Co., NC	Farmer	Enlisted, 5/1/62. Absent, sick since 9/1/63. Retired to the Invalid Corps, 1/9/65.
Pvt.	Vick, William H.	1835	S	Arringtons, Nash Co., NC	Farm Labor	Enlisted, 3/10/62. Died of disease, 5/11/62 in Arringtons, NC.
Pvt.	Walker, Berryman	1843	S	Mannings, Nash Co., NC	Farm Labor	Enlisted, 3/4/62. Missing, 7/1/62 at Malvern Hill. No further records.

Rank	Name	DOB	M/S	Residence	Occupation	Remarks
Pvt.	Walker, Jn. Blount	1838	S	Collins, Nash Co., NC	Farm Labor	Enlisted, 4/25/62. Wounded (right shoulder), 7/3/63 at Gettysburg, "on the skirmish line." Captured, 7/4/63 in field hospital. Died of wounds, 8/13/63 at Camp Letterman, Gettysburg, PA.
Pvt.	Westray, Archibald H. "Baldy"	1839	S	Franklin Co., NC	Farm Labor	Enlisted, 3/1/62. Wounded (right leg), 7/3/63 at Gettysburg. Captured, 7/4/63 in field hospital. (Leg amputated below knee.) POW—Baltimore, MD. Paroled, 9/25/63. Retired to the Invalid Corps, 7/12/64.
Pvt.	Whitfield, John W.	1834	M	Warrenton, Warren Co., NC	Overseer	Enlisted, 5/1/62. Captured, 11/7/63 at Kelly's Ford. POW—Point Lookout, MD. Exchanged, 11/15/64. No further records.
Pvt.	Whitfield, Patrick L.	1828	M	Dortches, Nash Co., NC	Farm Labor	Enlisted, 3/4/62. Absent, 6/-/63. "Dropped out on the march [to Gettysburg]." TDY—Nurse at Wilson, NC; 3/1/64–12/31/64. No further records.
Pvt.	**Whitley, Jolley B.**	**1840**	**S**	**Dortches, Nash Co., NC**	**Farmer**	**Enlisted, 3/4/62. Wounded & captured, 9/17/62 at Sharpsburg. Exchanged, 9/21/62. Killed, 7/1/63 at Gettysburg.**
Pvt.	Williams, Micajah T.	1845	S	Winsteads, Nash Co., NC	Farm Labor	Enlisted, 5/1/62. Wounded, 7/1/62 at Malvern Hill. Promoted to Cpl., 6/1/63. No records after 6/30/63.
Pvt.	Williams, Wright J.	1835	S	Whiteville, Columbus Co., NC	Cooper	Enlisted, 3/13/62. Discharged (disability—inguinal hernia), 7/23/62.
Pvt.	Winstead, G. J.	1833	M	Coopers, Nash Co., NC	Farmer	Enlisted, 11/-/62. Wounded (leg), 7/1/63 at Gettysburg. (Leg amputated) No further records.
Pvt.	Winstead, Theophilus T.	1845	S	Mannings, Nash Co., NC	Cooper's Asst.	Enlisted, 3/4/62. Captured, 9/12/62 near Frederick, MD. Exchanged, 11/10/62. Wounded (right leg shattered), 7/1/63 at Gettysburg. Captured, 7/4/63 in field hospital. (Leg amputated below knee.) POW—Baltimore, MD. Exchanged, 11/17/63. Retired to Invalid Corps, 7/8/64.

1863 Recruits/Conscripts

Rank	Name	DOB	M/S	Residence	Occupation	Remarks
Pvt.	Addison, Quincy Edward	1844	S	Brassfields, Wake Co., NC	Day Labor	Conscripted, 9/1/63. TDY—Provost Guard in Gordonsville; 11/-/63–4/30/64. Discharged (disability), 5/3/64.
Pvt.	Anderson, Thomas J.	1840	S	Tarboro, Edgecombe Co., NC	Farm Labor	Conscripted, 7/8/63. Captured, 4/6/65 at High Bridge. Released, 6/28/65.
Pvt.	Armstrong, Gray Robert	1839	S	Dortches, Nash Co., NC	Overseer	Conscripted, 9/1/63. Captured, 4/3/65 in Petersburg trenches. POW—Hart's Island, NY. Released, 6/17/65.
2nd Lt.	Arrington, Kearney W.	1843	S	Nash Co., NC		Transferred from 2nd NC Cav., 2/17/63. Promoted to 1st Lt., 12/14/63. Wounded (left calf) and captured, 5/12/64 at Spotsylvania. POW—Ft. Delaware, DE. Exchanged, 2/27/65.
Pvt.	Borrows, James B.	1821	M	Pittards, Halifax Co., NC	Farmer	Conscripted, 7/30/63. Deserted, 8/7/63.
Pvt.	Crowell, Jonas W.	1838	S	Hamleton, Martin Co., NC	Merchant's Clerk	Transferred from 5th AL Inf., 4/5/63. Promoted to 1st Sgt., 5/1/63. Wounded (left thigh), 6/3/64 at Cold Harbor. Paroled, 4/9/65 at Appomattox.

Appendix 2

Rank	Name	DOB	M/S	Residence	Occupation	Remarks
Cpl.	Culpepper, William J.	1837	S	Dortches, Nash Co., NC	Farm Labor	Transferred from 12th NC Inf., 10/1/63. Captured, 11/7/63 at Kelly's Ford. No further records.
Pvt.	**Dartridge, Richard J.**	1845	S	Nash Co., NC	Farm Labor	**Conscripted, 3/2/63. Killed, 5/12/64 at Spotsylvania.**
Pvt.	Deans, William	1822	M	Mannings, Nash Co., NC	Day Labor	Conscripted, 9/1/63. Captured, 11/7/63 at Kelly's Ford. POW—Point Lookout, MD. Exchanged, 4/27/64. Did not return to Regt.
Pvt.	Edwards, Edwin	1823	M	Dortches, Nash Co., NC	Farmer	Conscripted, 9/20/63. TDY—Teamster; 1/1/64–8/31/63. No further records.
Pvt.	**Edwards, Solomon**	1846	S	**Dortches, Nash Co., NC**	**Farm Labor**	**Conscripted, 11/10/63. Died of disease, 1/8/65 at Richmond, VA.**
Pvt.	**Griffin, John B.**	1832	M	**Arringtons, Nash Co., NC**	**Farmer**	**Conscripted, 3/1/63. Killed, 5/3/63 at Chancellorsville.**
Pvt.	Griffin, William B.	1836	S	Ricks, Nash Co., NC	Farm Labor	Conscripted, 3/1/63. Captured, 5/8/64 at Spotsylvania. POW—Point Lookout, MD. Exchanged, 3/18/65.
Pvt.	Grimmer, Elias G	1830	M	Tarboro, Edgecombe Co., NC	Engineer	Conscripted, 7/8/63. TDY—Second Corps HQ Provost Guard; 1/1/64–3/6/65. Captured, 4/2/65 in Petersburg trenches. Confined, at Newport News, VA. Released, 6/27/65.
Pvt.	Johnson, Christopher B.	1825	M	Collins, Nash Co., NC	Farmer	Conscripted, 9/1/63. TDY—Provost Guard at Gordonsville; 11/1/63–12/31/64. Absent, sick most of 1864. Paroled, 4/14/65 at Burkeville.
Pvt.	Johnson, Henry	1823	M	Wake Co., NC		Conscripted, 9/1/63. Captured, 11/7/63 at Kelly's Ford. POW—Point Lookout, MD. Exchanged, 3/18/65.
Pvt.	Joyner, George W.	1845	S	Coopers, Nash Co., NC	Farm Labor	Conscripted, 3/10/63. Wounded, 5/3/63 at Chancellorsville. Captured, 7/4/63 at Gettysburg field hospital. "He was left to nurse [the] wounded." POW—Point Lookout, MD. Exchanged, 11/15/64. No further records.
Pvt.	**Lindsey, William B**	1843	S	**Winsteads, Nash Co., NC**	**Farm Labor**	**Conscripted, 3/15/63. Died of brain fever, 4/10/63 at Hamilton's Crossing, VA.**
Pvt.	Pender, John	1844	S	Tarboro, Edgecombe Co., NC	Hat maker's Apprentice	Conscripted, 7/8/63. Wounded (left thigh) and captured, 11/7/63 at Kelly's Ford. POW—Point Lookout, MD. Exchanged, 3/3/65.
Pvt.	**Rigsbee, William C.**	1819	M	**Morrisville, Wake Co., NC**	**Manager**	**Conscripted, 9/1/63. Wounded (right lung & shoulder), 5/12/64 at Spotsylvania. Died of wounds, 5/21/64 at Richmond, VA.**
Pvt.	**Robertson, Robert**	1824		**Caswell Co., NC**		**Conscripted, 9/1/63. Died of typhoid fever, 11/27/63 at Lynchburg, VA.**
Pvt.	Strickland, Henry O.	1830	M	Nash Co., NC	Farmer	Conscripted, 7/8/63. Surrendered, 4/9/65 at Appomattox.
Pvt.	**Williams, Nathan C. "Nat"**	1824	M	**Chapel Hill, Orange Co., NC**	**Wheelwright**	**Conscripted, 9/1/63. Captured, 11/7/63 at Kelly's Ford. POW—Point Lookout, MD. Died of disease, 12/28/63.**

1864 Conscripts

Rank	Name	DOB	M/S	Residence	Occupation	Remarks
Pvt.	Batchelor, Ruffin	1830		Nash Co., NC		Transferred from 47th NC Inf., 1/22/64. Wounded, 7/18/64 at Snicker's Gap. Captured, 4/3/65 in Petersburg trenches. POW—Hart's Island, NY. Released, 6/17/65.
Pvt.	Edwards, Willie	1847	S	Dortches, Nash Co., NC	Farm Labor	Conscripted, 3/18/64. Paroled, 4/11/65 at Farmville hospital.

Rank	Name	DOB	M/S	Residence	Occupation	Remarks
Pvt.	Griffin, Mark S.	1846	S	Ricks, Nash Co., NC	Farm Labor	Conscripted, 2/15/64. Surrendered, 4/9/65 at Appomattox.
Pvt.	Lewis, John A.	1825	M	Winsteads, Nash Co., NC	Farmer	Conscripted, 2/23/64. Died of chronic diarrhea, 7/28/64 at Charlottesville, VA.
Pvt.	Matthews, Hilliard	1843	S	Dortches, Nash Co., NC	Farm Labor	Conscripted, 3/10/64. No records after 9/26/64.

Company K
Mecklenburg County (Mustered into Regt.—9/13/1861)

Rank	Name	DOB	M/S	Residence	Occupation	Remarks
Cpt.	Kell, James T.	1835		Pineville, Mecklenburg Co., NC	Physician's assistant	Appointed, Cpt., 913/61. Promoted to Maj., and transferred to F & S, 9/26/61.
1st Lt.	Morrow, Benjamin F.	1833	M	East Charlotte, Mecklenburg Co., NC	Farmer	Elected Cpt., 9/27/61. Lost election for Cpt., 5/1/62. Leaves regiment.
2nd Lt.	Bell, Charles E.	1828	M	East Charlotte, Mecklenburg Co., NC	Farmer	Commissioned, 1st Lt., 9/28/61. Resigned, 3/14/62.
3rd Lt.	Witherspoon, John G.	1838	M	Coddle Creek, Cabarrus Co., NC	Farmer	Enlisted, 9/13/61 as 1st Sgt. Elected 3rd Lt., 9/27/61. Elected Cpt., 5/1/62. Wounded, 7/1/63 at Gettysburg. Killed, 12/7/63 at Kelly's Ford.
1st Sgt.	Orr, Nathan D.	1839	S	Pineville, Mecklenburg Co., NC	Merchant	Transferred from 10th NC Arty., 9/13/61. Promoted 1st Sgt., 9/27/61. Elected to 3rd Lt., 4/8/62. Promoted to 1st Lt., 5/1/62. Resigned, 9/1/63 because of disability.
2nd Sgt.	Lee, James T.	1838	S	East Charlotte, Mecklenburg Co., NC	Merchant	Enlisted, 9/13/61. Killed, 5/12/64 at Spotsylvania.
4th Sgt.	DeArmond, Aaron L.	1827	M	East Charlotte, Mecklenburg Co., NC	Farmer	Enlisted, 9/13/61. Promoted to 3rd Sgt., 9/27/61. Reduced to Pvt., 8/2/62. Captured, 9/17/62 at Sharpsburg. Paroled, 9/21/62 at Sharpsburg. Wounded, (arm), 12/13/62 at Fredericksburg. Promoted to 5th Sgt., 4/1/63. Captured, 11/7/63 at Kelly's Ford. Exchanged, 3/17/64. Wounded, 7/18/64 at Snicker's Gap. Died of wounds, 8/19/64.
1st Cpl.	McKinney, John W. "Wesley"	1821	M	East Charlotte, Mecklenburg Co., NC	Overseer	Enlisted, 9/13/61. Promoted to Sgt., 11/1/61. Reduced to Pvt., 2/26/62. Discharged (Conscript law), 11/21/62.
3rd Cpl.	Coltharp, Henry T.	1826	M	Pleasant Valley, Lancaster Co., SC	Farm Manager	Enlisted, 9/13/61. Reduced in rank, 4/8/62. Discharged (disability), 9/1/62.
4th Cpl.	Dunn, Andrew J.	1828	M	West Charlotte, Mecklenburg Co., NC	Farmer	Enlisted, 9/13/61. Reduced to Pvt., 5/1/62. Killed, 9/17/62 at Sharpsburg.
Pvt.	Adkins, William H.	1843	S	Ft. Mills, SC	Farm labor	Enlisted, 9/13/61. Wounded, 7/1/62 at Malvern Hill. Wounded, 11/7/63 at Kelly's Ford. Captured, 5/17/64 at Spotsylvania. POW—Point Lookout, NY. Died of chronic diarrhea, 1/15/65.
Pvt.	Alexander, Samuel D. "Sam"	1840	S	East Charlotte, Mecklenburg Co., NC	Farm labor	Enlisted, 9/13/61. Wounded, 11/7/63 at Kelly's Ford.
Pvt.	Ardrey, William E.	1839	S	East Charlotte, Mecklenburg Co., NC	Student	Enlisted, 9/13/61. Elected 2nd Lt., 5/1/62. Elected 1st Lt., 9/1/63. Promoted to Cpt., 2/28/64. Wounded (head), 6/2/64 at Cold Harbor. Paroled at Appomattox, 4/9/65.

Appendix 2

Rank	Name	DOB	M/S	Residence	Occupation	Remarks
Pvt.	Bales, Elijah M.	1842	S	Gatesville, Gates Co. NC	Farm labor	Enlisted, 9/13/61. Promoted to Cpl., 5/3/63. "Received the medal of honor for bravery at Chancellorsville." Wounded (arm; flesh wound), 7/1/63 at Gettysburg. Promoted, 3rd Sgt., 8/1/64. Paroled, 4/9/65 at Appomattox.
Pvt.	**Baker, Jeptha K. "Jeff"**	**1834**	**S**	**East Charlotte, Mecklenburg Co., NC**	**House carpenter**	**Enlisted, 9/13/61. Wounded (head; left ear)), 9/17/62 at Sharpsburg. Died of wounds, 10/23/63.**
Pvt.	Bentley, Moses W. H.	1842	S	Swannanoa, Buncombe Co., NC	Farm labor	Enlisted, 9/13/61. Wounded, 7/1/62 at Malvern Hill. Wounded (right leg), 8/21/64 at Charles Town, WV. Captured, 4/6/65 at Farmville, VA.
Pvt.	Black, James. H.	1844	S	West Charlotte, Mecklenburg Co., NC	Farm labor	Enlisted, 9/13/61. Wounded (left arm), 7/1/62 at Malvern Hill. Killed, 9/17/62 at Sharpsburg. "Very gallant."
Pvt.	Black, John N.	1832	S	West Charlotte, Mecklenburg Co., NC	Farm labor	Enlisted, 9/13/61. Died of smallpox, 1/10/63 at Guineas Station, VA.
Pvt.	Boyce, Samuel J.	1843	S	Winnsboro, Fairfield Co., SC	Student	Enlisted, 9/13/61. Promoted to 1st Cpl., 5/1/62. "Noted for coolness in battle" at Sharpsburg. Promoted to Sgt., 1/1/63, Wounded (right thigh) and captured, 11/7/63 at Kelly's Ford. Right thigh amputated. Died of wounds, 11/11/63.
Pvt.	Coffey, Andrew S.	1826		Bellair, Lancaster Co., SC	Farm Manager	Enlisted, 9/13/61. "With company until 8/64—no further records"
Pvt.	Crowell, Israel	1830	M	East Charlotte, Mecklenburg Co., NC	Carpenter	Enlisted, 9/13/61. TDY—Gunboat service, Wilmington, NC, until 8/64—no further records.
Pvt.	Culp, Aley A.	1836	S	Charlotte, Mecklenburg Co., NC	Farmer	Enlisted, 9/13/61. Wounded (thigh & chest burnt by explosion), 9/17/62. Promoted to Cpl., 1/1/63. Captured, 11/7/63 at Kelly's Ford. Exchanged, 3/17/64. Promoted to Sgt., 7/1/64. Wounded (both thighs, flesh wound) and captured, 9/22/64 at Fisher's Hill.
Pvt.	**Davis, George W.**	**1844**	**S**	**Charlotte, Mecklenburg Co., NC**		**Enlisted, 9/13/61. Killed, 6/27/62 at Gaines' Mill.**
Pvt.	Downs, John Thomas	1839	M	West Charlotte, Mecklenburg Co., NC	Clerk	Enlisted, 9/13/61. Elected 3rd Lt., 5/1/62. Promoted 2nd Lt., 9/30/62. Promoted to 1st Lt., 11/7/63. Wounded (wrist), 9/19/64 at Winchester. No further records after 2/65.
Pvt.	Downs, William H.	1844	S	West Charlotte, Mecklenburg Co., NC	Student	Enlisted, 9/13/61. Discharged (disability), 1/1/62.
Pvt.	Dunn, Andrew S.	1838	M	Charlotte, Mecklenburg Co., NC	Farmer	Enlisted, 9/13/61. Discharged (disability), 11/24/61.
Pvt.	**Dunn, Samuel W.**	**1844**	**S**	**Charlotte, Mecklenburg Co., NC**	**Farm labor**	**Enlisted, 9/13/61. Died of typhoid fever, 12/1/61 at Wilmington, NC.**
Pvt.	George, Ed Payson	1840	S	West Charlotte, Mecklenburg Co. NC	Carpenter's Asst.	Enlisted, 9/13/61. Appointed 2nd Sgt., 1/1/62. Promoted to drill master, 3/1/62. Transferred to 49th NC Inf., 5/1/62.
Pvt.	Glover, Benjamin C.	1845	S	Pineville, Mecklenburg Co., NC	Farm labor	Enlisted, 9/13/61. Wounded ("shell wound of hip, destroying large surface"), 5/3/63 at Chancellorsville. Transferred to the Invalid Corps, 12/17/64.

Rank	Name	DOB	M/S	Residence	Occupation	Remarks
Pvt.	Griffin, John J.	1845	S	Charlotte, Mecklenburg Co., NC	Farm labor	Enlisted, 9/13/61. Died of typhoid fever, 1/1/62 at Wilmington, NC.
Pvt.	Hall, John G.	1827	M	Charlotte, Mecklenburg Co., NC	Farmer	Enlisted, 9/13/61. Wounded, 5/8/64 at Spotsylvania. Wounded (left hand), 10/19/64 at Cedar Creek.
Pvt.	Hall, Robert B. "Bob"	1831	M	West Charlotte, Mecklenburg Co., NC	Farmer	Enlisted, 9/13/61. Discharged (disability), 1/6/63.
Pvt.	Hartis, John H.	1826	M	East Charlotte, Mecklenburg Co., NC	Farmer	Enlisted, 9/13/61. Deserted, 9/62.
Pvt.	Henderson, William T. "Taylor"	1839	S	Charlotte, Mecklenburg Co., NC	Farm labor	Enlisted, 9/13/61. Died of chronic diarrhea, 5/28/62 at Charlotte.
Pvt.	Hood, Abner B.	1838	S	East Charlotte, Mecklenburg Co., NC	Farm labor	Enlisted, 9/13/61. Promoted to Sgt., 10/1/61. Killed, 6/27/62 at Gaines' Mill.
Pvt.	Hood, William L.	1844	S	East Charlotte, Mecklenburg Co., NC	Farm labor	Enlisted, 9/13/61. Wounded (left hand), 7/3/63 at Gettysburg. Wounded (right hand), 5/24/64 at North Anna. Wounded (arm broken) and Captured, 10/19/64 at Cedar Creek. Exchanged, 10/30/63. Paroled, 4/9/65 at Appomattox.
Pvt.	Howey, John H.	1844	S	East Charlotte, Mecklenburg Co., NC	Farm labor	Enlisted, 9/13/61. Captured, 9/17/62 at Sharpsburg. Paroled, 9/27/62. Wounded, 9/19/64 at Winchester. Paroled, 4/9/65 at Appomattox.
Pvt.	Howey, William	1819	M	East Charlotte, Mecklenburg Co., NC	Farm labor	Enlisted, 9/13/61. Discharged (disability), 2/13/62.
Pvt.	Jennings, George W.	1837	S	Fort Mill, York Co., SC	Millwright	Enlisted, 9/13/61. Wounded (thigh), 7/1/62 at Malvern Hill. Leg amputated. Discharged due to wounds, 9/28/62.
Pvt.	Johnston, David E.	1819	M	Pleasant Valley, Lancaster Co., SC	Farm labor	Enlisted, 9/13/61. Discharged (Conscript law), 10/25/62.
Pvt.	Lee, James A.	1842	S	Charlotte, Mecklenburg Co., NC	Farm labor	Enlisted, 9/13/61. Died of pneumonia, 3/28/63 at Richmond, VA.
Pvt.	Lee, Samuel B. "Sam"	1842	S	East Charlotte, Mecklenburg Co., NC	Farm labor	Enlisted, 9/13/61. Wounded (hip & pelvis fractured), 5/24/64 at North Anna. Died of wounds, 6/21/64.
Pvt.	McKinney, R. Munroe	1833	S	West Charlotte, Mecklenburg Co., NC	French Professor	Enlisted, 9/13/61. TDY—Teamster from 9/1/62 to 12/31/64. No further records.
Pvt.	McMullen, James H.	1837	M	Greensboro, Guilford Co., NC	Farmer	Enlisted, 9/13/61. Wounded (shoulder), 6/30/62 at Gaines' Mill. Died of wounds, 7/1/62.
Pvt.	Milton, Joseph G.	1844	S	West Charlotte, Mecklenburg Co., NC	Brick making labor	Enlisted, 9/13/61. Died of chronic diarrhea, 10/19/62 at Culpepper Court House, VA.
Pvt.	Morris, James T.	1843	S	East Charlotte, Mecklenburg Co., NC	Farm labor	Enlisted, 9/13/61. Missing, 9/3/63, "on march to Maryland." Unaccounted for, "supposed dead."
Pvt.	Patterson, William S.	1844	S	Yorkville, York Co., SC	Student	Enlisted, 9/13/61. Died of disease, 1/6/62 at Wilmington, NC.

Appendix 2

Rank	Name	DOB	M/S	Residence	Occupation	Remarks
Pvt.	Pierce, James M.	1839	S	Mecklenburg Co., NC	Farm labor	Enlisted, 9/13/61. Wounded and captured, 5/19/64 at Harris Farm. No further records.
Pvt.	Pierce, Orren L.	1841	S	Mecklenburg Co., NC	Farm labor	Enlisted, 9/13/61. Captured, 9/17/62 at Sharpsburg. POW—Ft. Delaware, DE. Exchanged, 11/10/62. Wounded and captured, 9/22/64 at Fisher's Hill. POW—Point Lookout, MD. Exchanged, 3/17/65.
Pvt.	**Rea, James M. "Milton"**	**1837**	**S**	**East Charlotte, Mecklenburg Co., NC**	**Farm labor**	**Enlisted, 9/13/61. Killed ("shot in left eye"), 5/3/63 at Chancellorsville.**
Pvt.	Richardson, William W.	1844	S	Charlotte, Mecklenburg Co., NC	Farm labor	Enlisted, 9/13/61. Captured, 4/6/65 at Farmville.
Pvt.	**Robinson, James R. "Jimmy"**	**1845**	**S**	**Stevens Mill, Union Co., NC**	**Farm labor**	**Enlisted, 9/13/61. Killed, 7/1/62 at Malvern Hill.**
Pvt.	**Robinson, William H.**	**1827**	**M**	**Clark's Fork, York Co., SC**	**Farmer**	**Enlisted, 9/13/61. TDY—hospital duty, 1/1/63-12/31/63. TDY—hospital duty at smallpox hospital, Richmond, 1/1/64-4/30/64, Captured, 7/12/64 at Ft. Stevens. POW—Elmira, NY. Died of acute bronchitis, 1/30/65.**
Pvt.	Ross, William J. "Bill Jack"	1828	M	East Charlotte, Mecklenburg Co., NC	Farmer	Enlisted, 9/13/61. Paroled, 4/9/65 at Appomattox.
Pvt.	Russell, William D.	1842	S	Charlotte, Mecklenburg Co., NC	Farm labor	Enlisted, 9/13/61. Appointed to Cpl., 5/4/62. Wounded, 12/13/62 at Fredericksburg. Wounded (slightly), 7/1/63 and captured at field hospital, 7/5/63 at Gettysburg. Exchanged, 7/31/63. Wounded, 5/12/64 at Spotsylvania. Promoted to Sgt., 8/1/64. Captured, 4/6/65 at Farmville, VA.
Pvt.	Shaw, Alexander D.	1838	M	East Charlotte, Mecklenburg Co., NC	Wagon Maker	Enlisted, 9/13/61. TDY—Gunboat duty; 5/62-9/64. No further records.
Pvt.	Simpson, Jefferson	1818	M	Mecklenburg Co., NC	Farmer	Enlisted, 9/13/61. Discharged (Conscript law), 10/15/62.
Pvt.	Smith, William S.	1837	S	West Charlotte, Mecklenburg Co., NC	Railroad Conductor	Enlisted, 9/13/61. Promoted to 1st Sgt., 5/1/62. Paroled, 4/9/65 at Appomattox.
Pvt.	**Squires, James W.**	**1836**	**S**	**East Charlotte, Mecklenburg Co., NC**	**Farm labor**	**Enlisted, 9/13/61. Killed, 5/12/64 at Spotsylvania.**
Pvt.	Stancil, Arthur G.	1841	S	East Charlotte, Mecklenburg Co., NC	Farm labor	Enlisted, 9/13/61. Discharged (disability), 2/12/63.
Pvt.	Stanford, Moses T.	1816	M	East Charlotte, Mecklenburg Co., NC	Farmer	Enlisted, 9/13/61. Discharged (Conscript Law), 10/12/62.
Pvt.	**Steel, Andrew F.**	**1830**	**M**	**West Charlotte, Mecklenburg Co., NC**	**Farmer**	**Enlisted, 9/13/61. Promoted to Cpl., 11/1/61. Promoted to Sgt., 5/1/62. Killed, 6/27/62 at Gaines' Mill.**
Pvt.	**Stephenson, James Robert "Bob"**	**1842**	**S**	**Providence, Mecklenburg Co., NC**	**Farm labor**	**Enlisted, 9/13/61. Wounded, 9/17/62 at Sharpsburg. Died of wounds, 12/15/62.**
Pvt.	**Tedder, Sidney**	**1830**	**M**	**East Charlotte, Mecklenburg Co., NC**	**Boot maker**	**Enlisted, 9/13/61. Killed, 6/27/64 at Gaines' Mill.**

Rank	Name	DOB	M/S	Residence	Occupation	Remarks
Pvt.	Thomason, John L.	1843	S	Charlotte, Mecklenburg Co, NC	Farm labor	Enlisted, 9/13/61. Wounded, 6/27/62 at Gaines' Mill. Died of wounds, 7/4/62.
Pvt.	Thompson, Lee	1833	S	East Charlotte, Mecklenburg Co., NC	Farm labor	Enlisted, 9/13/61. Wounded, 9/17/62 at Sharpsburg. Died of typhoid fever, 2/16/62 at Richmond.
Pvt.	Thompson, Lewis R.	1827	M	East Charlotte, Mecklenburg Co., NC	Farmer	Enlisted, 9/13/61. Wounded, 5/3/63 at Chancellorsville. TDY—light duty at Charlotte; 11/63–9/64. No further records.
Pvt.	Thrower, Thomas J	1844	S	East Charlotte, Mecklenburg Co., NC	Farm labor	Enlisted, 9/13/61. Discharged (disability), 3/1/62.
Pvt.	Williamson, William E.	1845	S	West Charlotte, Mecklenburg Co., NC	Farm labor	Enlisted, 9/13/61. Captured, 9/17/62 at Sharpsburg. Exchanged, 8/2/62. Discharged (Conscript law), 10/1/62.
Pvt.	Wolfe, John N.	1845	S	East Charlotte, Mecklenburg Co., NC	Farm labor	Enlisted, 9/13/61. Discharged (Conscript law), 8/1/62.
Pvt.	Wolfe, Robert B. "Bob"	1841	S	East Charlotte, Mecklenburg Co., NC	Farm labor	Enlisted, 9/13/61. Deserted, 5/1/62. Returned to duty, 8/8/62. Captured, 11/7/63 at Kelly's Ford. POW—Point Lookout, MD. Died of pneumonia, 3/1/65.
Pvt.	Younts, John A.	1845		Leaksville, Rockingham Co., NC	Wool carding	Enlisted, 9/13/61. Wounded, 7/1/62 at Malvern Hill. Wounded, 5/3/63 at Chancellorsville. Discharged (Conscript Law), 8/1/63.

1861 Recruits

Rank	Name	DOB	M/S	Residence	Occupation	Remarks
Pvt.	Griffith, Aaron E. "Eli"	1843	S	East Charlotte, Mecklenburg Co., NC	Farm labor	Enlisted, 10/5/61. Wounded, 5/3/63 at Chancellorsville. Wounded (hip), 7/1/63 at Gettysburg. Died of wounds, 7/3/63 at Gettysburg.

1862 Recruits

Rank	Name	DOB	M/S	Residence	Occupation	Remarks
Pvt.	Alexander, J. Lee	1838	S	West Charlotte, Mecklenburg Co., NC	Farm labor	Transferred from 6th NC Inf., 9/13/62. Captured at Kelly's Ford, 11/7/63. POW—Point Lookout, MD. Exchanged, 2/24/65. On medical furlough, 3/1/65.
Pvt.	Barnett, Robert (Bob) C.	1840	S	West Charlotte, Mecklenburg Co., NC	Farm labor	Enlisted, 2/10/62. Killed, 5/3/63 at Chancellorsville. "Shot by grapeshot in the bowels."
Pvt.	Ezzell, Moses F.	1844	S	East Charlotte, Mecklenburg Co., NC	Farm labor	Enlisted, 2/10/62. Promoted to Cpl., 4/8/62. Wounded (back bruised by explosion), 9/17/62 at Sharpsburg. No further records.
Pvt.	Hartis, Wilson L. "Willie"	1833	M	Charlotte, Mecklenburg Co., NC	Farmer	Enlisted, 1/18/62. Promoted to Cpl., 1/1/63. Killed, 5/3/63 at Chancellorsville. "Shot between the eyes."
Pvt.	Kirkpatrick, Hugh Y.	1841	S	East Charlotte, Mecklenburg Co., NC	Farm labor	Enlisted, 2/1/62. Appointed 4th Sgt., 4/8/62. Died of disease, 11/8/62 at Strasburg, VA. "Died in the house of Mrs. Davis, 10:30 p.m.—Buried by candle light."
Pvt.	Nichols, Burgess G.	1840	S	Orange Co.	Day laborer	Enlisted, 2/10/62. Promoted to Cpl., 11/1/63. Promoted to Sgt., 4/1/64. Wounded, 5/19/64 at Harris Farm. Paroled, 4/9/65, at Appomattox.
Pvt.	Orr, Thomas J.	1840	S	East Charlotte, Mecklenburg Co., NC	Physician's assistant	Enlisted, 2/2/62. TDY—at Camp Holmes in charge of the sick, 3/1/62. Paroled, 4/9/65 at Appomattox.

Rank	Name	DOB	M/S	Residence	Occupation	Remarks
Pvt.	Simpson, Marcus	1837	S	Mecklenburg Co., NC	Farm labor	Enlisted, 10/5/61. Captured, 5/12/64 at Spotsylvania. Joined U.S. Service, 5/27/64.
Pvt.	Squires, John B.	1838	S	East Charlotte, Mecklenburg Co., NC	Farm labor	Enlisted, 1/25/62. Promoted to Sgt., 2/26/62. Reduced to Pvt., 5/1/62. Promoted to Ord. Sgt., 5/10/64. Reduced to Pvt., 9/1/64. Paroled, 4/9/65 at Appomattox.
Pvt.	Thomas, William B.	1838	S	West Charlotte, Mecklenburg Co., NC	Day laborer	Enlisted, 1/1/62. TDY—Pioneer; 6/63–4/65. Surrendered, 4/9/65 at Appomattox.
Pvt.	Weeks, Rufus B.	1844	S	East Charlotte, Mecklenburg Co., NC	Farm labor	Enlisted, 2/10/62. Wounded (shoulder bruised), 9/17/62 at Sharpsburg. Promoted to Sgt., 1/1/64. Killed, 5/19/64 at Harris Farm. "Struck in the head and killed instantly."
Pvt.	Witherspoon, Mitty J. "Jake"	1844	S	Concord, Cabarrus Co., NC	Farm labor	Enlisted, 5/26/62. Wounded (thigh & bowels), 5/3/63 at Chancellorsville. Died of wounds, 5/7/63. "Wounded in thigh from grapeshot through the bowels."
Pvt.	Wolfe, Thomas D.	1842	S	East Charlotte, Mecklenburg Co., NC	Farm labor	Enlisted, 2/10/62. Wounded (palm of hand), 9/17/62 at Sharpsburg. Died of pneumonia, 3/27/63 at Richmond.

1862 Conscripts

Rank	Name	DOB	M/S	Residence	Occupation	Remarks
Pvt.	Alexander, Thomas P.	1835	S	Pineville, Mecklenburg Co., NC	Mill labor	Conscripted, 3/25/62. TDY—Hospital Duty, Richmond. Captured, 4/3/65 at hospital.
Pvt.	Allen, James H.	1828	M	West of Neuse River, Johnson Co., NC	Farmer	Conscripted, 9/17/62. Died of pneumonia, 12/5/62 at Gordonsville, VA
Pvt.	Anderson, William	1833	M	Monroe, Union Co., NC	Farmer	Conscripted, 9/17/62. Died of disease, 1/15/64.
Pvt.	Bailey, Elias D.	1841	S	Roger's Store, Wake Co.	Farm labor	Conscripted, 9/17/62. Captured, 7/8/64, near Harper's Ferry. POW—Elmira, NY. Died of chronic diarrhea, 2/19/65.
Pvt.	Bailey, James A.	1840	S	West Charlotte, Mecklenburg Co., NC	Farm labor	Conscripted, 9/17/62. Wounded, 5/3/63 at Chancellorsville. Captured, 11/7/63 at Kelly's Ford. Exchanged, 3/16/64. Died of disease, 4/1/64, General Hospital #4 at Richmond.
Pvt.	Barefoot, Noah G.	1827	M	Droughorn's Store, Sampson Co., NC	Farmer	Conscripted, 9/17/62. Wounded, 5/3/63 at Chancellorsville. TDY—Div. HQ Provost Guard until 8/-/64. Wounded (hand), 10/19/64 at Winchester. No further records.
Pvt.	Brewer, James H.	1832	S	Charlotte, Mecklenburg Co., NC	Farm labor	Conscripted, 9/17/62. Died of typhoid fever, 2/9/63 at Staunton, VA.
Pvt.	Church, Eli	1841	S	Laurel Springs, Ashe Co., NC	Farm labor	Conscripted, 9/17/62. Captured, 4/6/65 at Amelia Court House. Confined at Point Lookout, MD. Released, 6/24/65.
Pvt.	Church, Martin	1840	S	Laurel Springs, Ashe Co., NC	Farm labor	Conscripted, 9/17/62. Captured, 4/6/65 at Farmville. Confined at Point Lookout, MD. Released, 6/24/65.
Pvt.	George, Presley	1832	M	Morrisville, Wake Co., NC	Farmer	Conscripted, 9/17/62. Died of pneumonia and typhoid fever, 1/8/63 at Richmond, VA.
Pvt.	Henderson, William M.	1829	S	Johnston Co., NC	Farmer	Conscripted, 9/17/62. In hospital at Richmond until 8/64. No further records.

Rank	Name	DOB	M/S	Residence	Occupation	Remarks
Pvt.	Holmes, Benjamin	1830	M	Newton Grove, Johnston Co., NC	Farmer	Conscripted, 9/17/62. Died of disease, 1/9/63 at Richmond, VA.
Pvt.	Johnson, George W.	1839	S	Trap Hill, Wilkes Co., NC	Farm labor	Conscripted, 9/17/62. Deserted, 4/15/63.
Pvt.	Johnston, James H.	1834	M	Yanceyville, Caswell Co. NC	Tailor	Conscripted, 9/17/62. Wounded, 5/3/63 at Chancellorsville. Wounded, 6/3/64 at Cold Harbor. Wounded (side), 10/19/64 at Winchester. No further records.
Pvt.	Johnston, Sandy A.	1838	S	Wilkes Co., NC	Farm labor	Conscripted, 9/17/62. Wounded, 5/3/63 at Chancellorsville. Wounded, 5/8/64 at Spotsylvania. Died of wounds, 5/18/64.
Pvt.	Massingil, Robert S.	1829	M	Newton Grove, Johnston Co., NC	Farmer	Conscripted, 9/17/62. Captured, 5/30/64 at Cold Harbor. POW—Elmira, NY.
Pvt.	McLane, Thomas	1834		Johnston Co., NC		Conscripted, 9/17/62. Wounded (eye), 11/7/63 at Kelly's Ford. Did not return to company. "Ball still in head, giving great pain and swelling."
Pvt.	Pierce, James W.	1837	S	Wake Co., NC	Farm labor	Conscripted, 9/17/62. Deserted, 3/29/63.
Pvt.	Rayner, Lovet	1829	M	Newton Grove, Johnston Co., NC	Farmer	Conscripted, 9/17/62. Killed, 11/7/63 at Kelly's Ford.
Pvt.	Smith, Samuel B.	1836	S	East Charlotte, Mecklenburg Co., NC	Farm labor	Conscripted, 7/2/62. Promoted to Cpl., 3/1/64. Died of disease, 7/11/63 at Charlotte, NC.
Pvt.	Walston, Silas L.	1834	S	Elevation, Johnston Co., NC	Farm labor	Conscripted, 9/17/62. Died of disease, 1/3/63 at Staunton, VA.
Pvt.	Webb, William	1825	M	Elevation, Johnston Co., NC	Farmer	Conscripted, 9/17/62. Died of pneumonia, 3/18/63 at Richmond.
Pvt.	Yeargen, Wyatt	1834	M	Mecklenburg Co., NC	Farmer	Conscripted, 9/17/62. Transferred to 6th N.C. Infantry, 4/10/63.

1863 Conscripts

Rank	Name	DOB	M/S	Residence	Occupation	Remarks
Pvt.	Adams, William	1828	M	Newton Grove, Johnston Co., NC	Cooper	Conscripted, 5/18/63. Wounded & captured, 5/19/64 at Harris Farm. POW–Point Lookout, MD. Died of chronic diarrhea, 9/18/64.
Pvt.	Alexander, James M.	1819	M	West Charlotte, Mecklenburg Co., NC	Mill labor	Conscripted, 8/20/63. Killed, 5/12/64 at Spotsylvania.
Pvt.	Bailey, William	1820	M	Chapel Hill, Orange Co., NC	Farmer	Conscripted, 10/20/63. Wounded, 5/12/64 at Spotsylvania. Wounded, 7/18/64 at Snicker's Gap. Paroled, 4/14/65 at Burkeville.
Pvt.	Bell, Nathan J.	1823	M	Fayetteville, Cumberland Co., NC	Farmer	Conscripted, 6/12/63. Died, typhoid pneumonia, 11/12/63 at General Hospital #9, Richmond, VA.
Pvt.	Black, Thomas A.	1820	M	East Charlotte, Mecklenburg Co., NC	Farmer	Conscripted, 10/1/63. Died of disease, 1/11/64 at Orange Court House, VA.
Pvt.	Bowman, Riley	1830	M	New Salem, Randolph Co., NC	Farmer	Conscripted, 7/1/63. Deserted, 12/21/63 at Mohn's Ford, VA.

Appendix 2

Rank	Name	DOB	M/S	Residence	Occupation	Remarks
Pvt.	Bradshaw, V. B.	1824	M	Mountain Island, Gaston Co., NC	Farm labor	Conscripted, 10/20/63. Died of typhoid fever, 5/7/64 at Farmville, VA.
Pvt.	Brinkley, Henry	1841	S	Raleigh, Wake Co., NC	Farm labor	Conscripted, 7/1/63. TDY—hospital duty (nurse) at Richmond. Captured, 4/3/65, at Richmond hospital.
Pvt.	Burton, J. C.	1823	M	Olin, Iredell Co., NC	Farmer	Conscripted, 7/1/63. Paroled, 4/9/65 at Appomattox.
Pvt.	Dixon, Solomon L.	1823	M	Mount Lawrence, Chatham Co., NC	Millwright	Conscripted, 11/3/63. Wounded, 5/8/64 at Spotsylvania. Paroled, 4/9/65 at Appomattox.
Pvt.	Duckworth, Thomas P.	1821	M	West Charlotte, Mecklenburg Co., NC	Farmer	Conscripted, 10/1/63. Wounded, 5/12/64 at Spotsylvania. Died of wounds, 7/10/64.
Pvt.	Dunn, George	1823	M	Salisbury, Rowan Co., NC	Farmer	Conscripted, 7/1/63. Captured, 5/8/64 at Spotsylvania. POW—Point Lookout, MD. Died of pneumonia, 12/1/64.
Pvt.	Gamble, James H.	1822	M	West Charlotte, Mecklenburg Co., NC	Farmer	Conscripted, 8/20/63. Died of typhoid fever, 1/20/64 at Richmond, VA.
Pvt.	Graham, John W.	1834	S	Lumberton, Robison Co., NC	Day laborer	Conscripted, 5/15/63. Captured, 11/7/63 at Kelly's Ford. POW—Point Lookout, MD. Exchanged, 3/17/64. Captured, 4/6/65 at Farmville, VA.
Pvt.	Hall, Joseph F.	1835		Mecklenburg Co.,		Conscripted, 8/10/63. Captured, 4/6/65 at Farmville.
Pvt.	Lewis, William H.	1821	S	Ringwood, Halifax Co., NC	Farmer	Conscripted, 10/2/63. Deserted, 10/1/64.
Pvt.	McLure, James A.	1837	S	West Charlotte, Mecklenburg Co., NC	Day laborer	Conscripted, 6/4/63. Wounded (right wrist; arm amputated), 5/30/64 at Cold Harbor, "in a skirmish." Discharged due to wounds, 12/1/64.
Pvt.	McQuay, Joseph F.	1834	M	West Charlotte, Mecklenburg Co., NC	Day laborer	Conscripted, 8/20/63. Captured, 4/6/65 at Farmville.
Pvt.	Miller, David M.	1821	M	East Charlotte, Mecklenburg Co., NC	Farmer	Conscripted, 8/20/63. Wounded, 5/12/64 at Spotsylvania. Captured, 4/6/65 at Farmville.
Pvt.	Morris, William T.	1846	S	Charlotte, Mecklenburg Co., NC	Farm labor	Conscripted, 1/12/63. Died of disease, 2/25/63 at Richmond, VA.
Pvt.	Myers, James	1823	M	Advance, Davie Co., NC	Weaver	Conscripted, 7/9/63. Captured, 11/7/63 at Kelly's Ford. POW—Point Lookout, MD. Exchanged, 2/24/65.
Pvt.	Nelson, John J.	1836	S	Bethel, Pitt Co., NC	Farm labor	Conscripted, 7/1/63. Wounded (left foot), 10/19/64 at Cedar Creek. Captured, 4/6/65 at Burkeville.
Pvt.	Potts, Joseph R.	1823	M	West Charlotte, Mecklenburg Co., NC	Farmer	Conscripted, 8/20/63. Died of typhoid fever, 11/4/63 at Staunton, VA.
Pvt.	Ross, J. Newell	1835		East Charlotte, Mecklenburg Co., NC	Farmer	Conscripted, 11/3/63. Wounded, 5/12/64 at Spotsylvania. Died of wounds, 6/5/64.
Pvt.	Sample, William	1824	M	East Charlotte, Mecklenburg Co., NC	Farmer	Conscripted, 10/3/63. Captured, 5/8/64 at the Wilderness. POW—Point Lookout, MD. Exchanged, 10/11/64. In hospital at Richmond. No further records.

Rank	Name	DOB	M/S	Residence	Occupation	Remarks
Pvt.	Saville, John C.	1844	S	West Charlotte, Mecklenburg Co., NC	Day laborer	Conscripted, 8/20/63. Wounded, 7/8/64, at Snicker's Gap. Paroled, 4/9/65 at Appomattox.
Pvt.	Shelby, David H.	1819	M	Charlotte, Mecklenburg Co., NC	Farmer	Conscripted, 8/20/63. Sick at hospital; 12/63–3/65. No further records.
Pvt.	Simmons, Elisha	1817	M	Yanceyville, Caswell Co., NC	Farmer	Conscripted, 9/10/63. Sick in hospital. Captured in hospital, 4/3/65 at Richmond.
Pvt.	Smith, J. D.	1822	M	Cabarrus Co., NC	Farmer	Conscripted, 6/2/63. TDY—hospital nurse in Raleigh; 12/64–4/65.
Pvt.	**Smith, John S.**	**1826**		**Anson Co., NC**	**Farmer**	**Conscripted, 4/2/63. Captured, 5/8/64 at Spotsylvania. POW—Point Lookout, MD. Died of chronic diarrhea, 2/7/65.**
Pvt.	Tart, Henry	1845	S	Newton Grove, Johnston Co., NC	Farm labor	Conscripted, 6/1/63. Deserted, 9/1/64.
Pvt.	**Thompson, James**	**1830**	**M**	**Rowan Mills, Rowan Co., NC**	**Carpenter**	**Conscripted, 6/16/63. Died of disease, 12/12/63 at Morton's Ford, VA.**
Pvt.	**West, William M.**	**1823**	**M**	**Salisbury, Rowan Co., NC**	**Farmer**	**Conscripted, 7/1/63. Captured, 9/22/64 at Fisher's Hill. POW—Point Lookout, MD. Died of pneumonia, 4/26/65.**

1864 Conscripts

Rank	Name	DOB	M/S	Residence	Occupation	Remarks
Pvt.	Anderson, M. J.					Conscripted, 12/20/65. Paroled, 4/9/65 at Appomattox.
Pvt.	Fields, Absalom F.	1832	M	Greensboro, Guilford Co., NC	Farmer	Conscripted, 12/31/65. Captured, 4/6/65 at Farmville.
Pvt.	Harvey, John F.	1825	M	Greensboro, Guilford Co., NC	Farmer	Conscripted, 12/1/64. Captured, 4/6/65 at Farmville.
Pvt.	Nichols, J.					Conscripted, 1/1/64. Captured, 5/20/64 at Spotsylvania. POW—Elmira, NY. Exchanged, 3/14/65.
Pvt.	Rayl, John F.	1846	S	Greensboro, Guilford Co., NC		Conscripted, 12/1/64. Captured, 4/6/65 at Burkeville.

Chapter Notes

Chapter 1

1. Parker, Francis M., letter, 18 March 1862, in Taylor, Michael W., *To Drive the Enemy from Southern Soil: The Letters of Col. Francis Marion Parker and the History of the 30th Regiment North Carolina Troops* (Dayton, OH: Morningside House, Inc., 1998). Hereafter referred to Parker, Francis M., letter.
2. 30th North Carolina Infantry Regiment, *Compiled Service Records of Confederate Soldiers Who Served in Organizations from the State of North Carolina,* hereafter referred to as *CSRC.*
3. Parker, Francis M., letter, 17 May 1862.
4. Philips, Frederick, *CSRC.*
5. Bone, John W., in Mehegan, Julianne, and David Mehegan (ed.), *Record of a Soldier in the Late War: The Confederate Memoir of John Wesley Bone* (Hingham, MA: Chinquapin, 2014), 20.
6. Parker, Francis M., letter, 11 June 1861, and 23 June 1861.
7. *The Weekly Raleigh Register*, 10 July 1861.
8. Taylor, Michael W., *To Drive the Enemy from Southern Soil*, 16.
9. Taylor, Michael W., *To Drive the Enemy from Southern Soil*, 17–8.
10. Taylor, Michael W., *To Drive the Enemy from Southern Soil*, 18.
11. *1850 United States Census*, Edgecombe County, North Carolina, Agricultural Schedule.
12. Taylor, Michael W., *To Drive the Enemy from Southern Soil*, 18.
13. *1860 United States Census*, Halifax County, North Carolina, Agricultural Schedule.
14. Musik, Michael P., "To Drive the Enemy from Southern Soil: The Letters of Col. Francis Marion Parker," (Book Review). *Civil War History*, Vol. 47, No. 2, June 2001.
15. Jordan, Weymouth T., (comp.), *North Carolina Troops: 1861–1865: A Roster* (Raleigh, NC: North Carolina Office of Archives and History, 1981), Vol. 8: 314.
16. *1860 United States Census*, Cumberland County, and Mecklenburg County, North Carolina.
17. Parker, Francis M., letter, 29 October 1861.
18. Parker, Francis M., letter, 5 November 1861.
19. Parker, Francis M., letter, 5 November 1861.
20. 30th North Carolina Infantry Regiment, *CSRC.*
21. Parker, Francis M., letter, 5 November 1861.
22. *1860 United States Census*, Sampson County, North Carolina.
23. 30th North Carolina Infantry Regiment, *CSRC.*
24. 30th North Carolina Infantry Regiment, *CSRC.*
25. Smith, William A., *The Anson Guards: Company C, Fourteenth Regiment North Carolina Volunteers, 1861–1865* (Charlotte, NC: Stone, 1914), 2.
26. Bone, John W., *Record of a Soldier in the Late War,* 6.
27. Warlick, Lewis, letter, 12 May 1861. In Lawing, Mike, and Carolyn Lawing, eds., *My Dearest Friend: The Civil War Correspondence of Carnelia McGrimsey and Lewis Warlick* (Durham, NC: Carolina Academic, 2000).
28. Smith, William A., *The Anson Guards*, 4.
29. Witherspoon, John G., letter, 21 September 1861. Thirtieth North Carolina Troops; The Living History Association of North Carolina, Concord, NC.
30. Day, William A., *A True History of Company I, 49th Regiment, North Carolina Troops in the Great Civil War Between the North and the South* (Newton, NC: Enterprise Job Office, 1898), 11.
31. Day, William A., *A True History of Company I*, 10–11.
32. Parker, Francis M., letter, 29 October 1861.
33. Smith, William A., *The Anson Guards*, 70–1.
34. Bone, John W., *Record of a Soldier in the Late War,* 6.
35. Jordan, Weymouth, T., *North Carolina Troops*, Vol. 8: 314.
36. Bone, John W., *Record of a Soldier in the Late War,* 6.
37. Jordan, Weymouth, T., *North Carolina Troops*, Vol. 8: 314.
38. Parker, Francis M., letter, 26 October 1861.
39. Bone, John W., *Record of a Soldier in the Late War,* 7.
40. Parker, Francis M., letter, 26 October 1861.
41. Smith, William A., *The Anson Guards*, 20.
42. Fraley, Ashbel, "The Purposes for Brigade Drill," in Warford, Christopher, ed., *The Civil War in North Carolina: Soldiers and Civilians' Letters and Diaries, 1861–1865* (Jefferson, NC: McFarland, 2003).
43. Bone, John W., *Record of a Soldier in the Late War,* 7.
44. Witherspoon, John G., letter, 17 November 1861.
45. Chapman, Craig S., *More Terrible Than Victory: North Carolina's Bloody Bethel Regiment, 1861–1865* (Dulles, VA: Brassey's, 1998), 57.
46. Parker, Francis M., letter, 26 October 1861.
47. Parker, Francis M., letter, 26 October 1861.
48. Bone, John W., *Record of a Soldier in the Late War,* 7–8.
49. Maltsby, William J.; Chimis, Michael H.; Simmons, John C., *CSRC.*
50. Witherspoon, John G., letter, 17 November 1861. Witherspoon, John G., *CSRC.*
51. Parker, Francis M., letter, 5 November 1861.
52. Bone, John W., *Record of a Soldier in the Late War,* 7–8.
53. Cooke, R. J., "Confederate Military Hospital #4—Wilmington, NC," *Old New Hanover Genealogical Society*, Wilmington, NC, 2005.
54. Parker, Francis M., letter, 8 November 1861.
55. Bone, John W., *Record of a Soldier in the Late War,* 9.
56. Parker, Francis M., letter, 5 November 1861.

57. Smith, William A., *The Anson Guards*, 316.
58. Smith, William A., *The Anson Guards*, 68.
59. Parker, Francis M., letter, 14 November 1861.
60. Venner, William Thomas, *The 11th North Carolina Infantry in the Civil War* (Jefferson, NC: McFarland, 2015), 28.
61. Bone, John W., *Record of a Soldier in the Late War*, 10.
62. Witherspoon, John G., letter, 18 November 1861.
63. Smith, William A., *The Anson Guards*, 67.
64. Bone, John W., *Record of a Soldier in the Late War*, 10.
65. Parker, Francis M., letter, 15 November 1861.
66. Smith, William A., *The Anson Guards*, 71.
67. Parker, Francis M., letter, 5 November 1861.
68. Williams, Buckner D., *CSRC*.
69. Parker, Francis M., letter, 15 December 1861.
70. Venner, William Thomas, *The 11th North Carolina Infantry in the Civil War*, 72.
71. Jordan, Weymouth, T., *North Carolina Troops*, Vol. 8, 314.
72. Bone, John W., *Record of a Soldier in the Late War*, 11.
73. Parker, Francis M., letter, 14 December 1861.
74. Parker, Francis M., letter, 17 December 1861.
75. Ardrey, William E., *Diary*, 20 April 1862. Davidson College Archives, Davidson, NC
76. Witherspoon, John G., letter, 20 February 1862
77. Parker, Francis M., letter, 17 December 1861.
78. Witherspoon, John G., letter, 29 March 1862.
79. Venner, William Thomas, *The 11th North Carolina Infantry in the Civil War*, 29.
80. Tuther, Jr., T., compiler, *Kelley's Wilmington Directory, Business Directory for 1860-61* (Wilmington, NC: Geo. H. Kelley Bookseller and Stationer, 1860), 72.
81. Wellman, Manly, W., "Tar Heel Lover," *Raleigh News and Observer*, 16 September 1861.
82. Smith, William A., *The Anson Guards*, 21.
83. Buel, Clarence C., and Robert U. Johnson, *Battles and Leaders of the Civil War* (New York, NY: Century, 1914), Vol. 1, 643.
84. Branch, Lawrence, in Buel, Clarence C., and Robert U. Johnson, *Battles and Leaders*, Vol. 1, 651.
85. Jordan, Weymouth, T., *North Carolina Troops*, Vol. 8, 314.
86. Parker, Francis M., letter, 2 April 1862.
87. Ardrey, William E., *Diary*, 8 April 1862.
88. Parker, Francis M., letter, 20 April 1862.
89. Bone, John W., *Record of a Soldier in the Late War*, 13.
90. Ardrey, William E., *Diary*, 24 April 1862.
91. Witherspoon, John G., letter, 3 March 1862.
92. Bone, John W., *Record of a Soldier in the Late War*, 13.
93. Freeman, Douglas S., *Lee's Lieutenants: Manassas to Malvern Hill* (New York, NY: Scribner's, 1942), Vol. 1, 130.
94. Witherspoon, John G., letter, 3 March 1862.
95. Bone, John W., *Record of a Soldier in the Late War*, 11–12.
96. Green, James L., letter, 16 May 1862, in "Family letters of Mary G. Green, 1859–1866," *A Broad River Digest*, 1990.
97. Freeman, Douglas S., *Lee's Lieutenants*, Vol. 1, 130.
98. Bone, John W., *Record of a Soldier in the Late War*, 11–12.
99. Parker, Francis M., letter, 6 April 1862.
100. Parker, Francis M., letter, 1 May 1862.
101. Clark, Walter (ed.). *Histories of the Several Regiments and Battalions from North Carolina in the Great War, 1861-65* (Raleigh, NC: E.M. Uzzell, 1901), Vol. 1, 221.
102. Greer, Ephraim; Claireborn, Robert; Downs, J. Thomas; Ardrey, William E., *CSRC*.
103. Witherspoon, John G., letter, 2 May 1862.
104. Jordan, Weymouth, T., *North Carolina Troops*, Vol. 8, 314.
105. Parker, Francis M., letter, 22 May 1862.
106. Witherspoon, John G., letter, 29 May 1862.
107. Ardrey, William E., *Diary*, 29 May 1862.
108. Ardrey, William E., *Diary*, 26 May 1862.
109. Turner, Walter, *CSRC*.
110. Witherspoon, John G., letter, 5 June 1862.
111. Jordan, Weymouth, T., *North Carolina Troops*, Vol. 8, 314.
112. Parker, Francis M., letter, 14 June 1862.
113. Taylor, Michael W., *To Drive the Enemy from Southern Soil*, 182.
114. Ardrey, William E., *Diary*, 13–14 June 1862.
115. 30th North Carolina Infantry Regiment, *CSRC*.

Chapter 2

1. Gallagher, Gary W. (ed.), *Fighting for the Confederacy: The Personal Recollections of General Edward Porter Alexander* (Chapel Hill: University of North Carolina Press, 1989), 154.
2. Warner, Ezra J. *Generals in Gray: Lives of the Confederate Commanders* (Baton Rouge: Louisiana State University Press, 1959), 5–6.
3. Manly, Matt., "Second Regiment," in Clark, Walter (ed.), *Histories of the Several Regiments*, Vol. 1: 165.
4. Osborne, E. A., "Fourth Regiment," in Clark, Walter (ed.), *Histories of the Several Regiments*, Vol. 1: 235.
5. 30th North Carolina Infantry Regiment, *CSRC*.
6. Bennett, Risden Tyler, "Fourteenth Regiment," in Clark, Walter (ed.), *Histories of the Several Regiments*, Vol. 1: 710.
7. Bone, John W., *Record of a Soldier in the Late War*, 21.
8. Ardrey, William E., *Diary*, 18 June 1862.
9. Bone, John W., *Record of a Soldier in the Late War*, 21.
10. Ardrey, William E., *Diary*, 21 June 1862.
11. Bone, John W., *Record of a Soldier in the Late War*, 21-2.
12. Ardrey, William E., *Diary*, 21 June 1862.
13. Ardrey, William E., *Diary*, 21 June 1862.
14. Grissom, Eugene, *CSRC*.
15. Bone, John W., *Record of a Soldier in the Late War*, 21-2.
16. Lewis, Archibald A., *CSRC*.
17. Parker, Francis M., "Thirtieth Regiment," in Clark, Walter (ed.), *Histories of the Several Regiments*, Vol. 2: 498.
18. Betts, Alexander, *Experience of a Confederate Chaplain, 1861-1864* (Greenville, SC: n. p., 1907), 23 June 1862.
19. Betts, Alexander, *Experience of a Confederate Chaplain*, 23 June 1862.
20. Parker, Francis M., letter, 14 November 1861.
21. Ardrey, William E., *Diary*, 22 June 1862.
22. Bone, John W., *Record of a Soldier in the Late War*, 22.
23. Bone, John W., *Record of a Soldier in the Late War*, 22.
24. Betts, Alexander, *Experience of a Confederate Chaplain*, 26 June 1862.
25. Jordan, Weymouth T., *North Carolina Troops*, Vol. 8, 314.
26. Taylor, Michael W., *To Drive the Enemy from Southern Soil: The Letters of Col. Francis Marion Parker and the History of the 30th North Carolina Troops* (Dayton, OH: Morningside, 1998), 184.
27. Ardrey, William E., *Diary*, 26 June 1862.
28. Ardrey, William E., *Diary*, 26 June 1862.
29. Smith, William A., *The Anson Guards*, 82.

30. Ardrey, William E., *Diary,* 26 June 1862.
31. Ardrey, William E., *Diary,* 24–6 June 1862.
32. Manly, Matt., "Second Regiment," in Clark, Walter (ed.), *Histories of the Several Regiments,* 1: 165.
33. Ardrey, William E., *Diary,* 26 June 1862.
34. Bone, John W., *Record of a Soldier in the Late War,* 23.
35. Pegram, Robert B., *CSRC.*
36. Taylor, Michael W., *To Drive the Enemy from Southern Soil,* 187.
37. Bone, John W., *Record of a Soldier in the Late War,* 26.
38. Ardrey, William E., *Diary,* 26 June 1862.
39. Ardrey, William E., *Diary,* 27 June 1862.
40. Jordan, Weymouth T., *North Carolina Troops,* Vol. 3, 372.
41. Ardrey, William E., *Diary,* 27 June 1862.
42. Freeman, Douglas, S., *Lee's Lieutenants,* Vol. 1, 520.
43. Smith, William A., *The Anson Guards,* 100.
44. Jordan, Weymouth T., *North Carolina Troops,* Vol. 8, 314
45. Green, Samuel J., letter, 29 June 1862.
46. Ardrey, William E., *Diary,* 27 June 1862. Steel, Andrew F., *CSRC.*
47. Bone, John W., *Record of a Soldier in the Late War,* 26.
48. Freeman, Douglas, S., *Lee's Lieutenants,* Vol. 1, 531.
49. Ardrey, William E., *Diary,* 27 June 1862.
50. Freeman, Douglas, S., *Lee's Lieutenants,* Vol. 1, 526.
51. Jordan, Weymouth T., *North Carolina Troops,* Vol. 3, 372–3.
52. Freeman, Douglas, S., *Lee's Lieutenants,* Vol. 1, 520.
53. Crumpler, Robert M.; Williams, Samuel S., *CSRC.*
54. Everett, William; Dew, William, *CSRC.*
55. Ardrey, William E., *Diary,* 27 June 1862. Hood, Abner B.; Kell, James T., *CSRC.*
56. Parker, Francis M., "Thirtieth Regiment," in Clark, Walter (ed.), *Histories of the Several Regiments,* Vol. 2, 499.
57. Bone, John W., *Record of a Soldier in the Late War,* 24.
58. Osborne, E. A., "Fourth Regiment," in Clark, Walter (ed.), *Histories of the Several,* Vol. 1, 242.
59. Tidball, Eugene C., *No Disgrace to My Country: The Life of John C. Tidball* (Kent, OH: Kent State University Press, 2002), 235.
60. Strickland, William W.; Hunt, Isaac B.; Boney, James T. *CSRC.*
61. Bone, John W., *Record of a Soldier in the Late War,* 24.
62. Buchanan, Robert C., *The War of the Rebellion: A Compilation of the Official Records of the Union and Confederate Armies* (Washington D.C.: Government Printing Office, 1880–1901), Vol. 11, Pt. 2, 359. Hereafter referred to as *Official Records.*
63. Bone, John W., *Record of a Soldier in the Late War,* 24.
64. Walker, Thomas W., *Official Records,* Vol. 11, Part 2, 362.
65. Goodrich, James T.; McCall, John W.; Parrish, Mathew, *CSRC.*
66. McMullen, James H.; Edwards, Montgomery, *CSRC.*
67. Ardrey, William E., *Diary,* 27 June 1862.
68. Bone, John W., *Record of a Soldier in the Late War,* 25.
69. Royal, Hardy S., *CSRC.*
70. Ardrey, William E., *Diary,* 27 June 1862.
71. Bone, John W., *Record of a Soldier in the Late War,* 25.
72. Buchanan, Robert C., *Official Records,* Vol. 11, Pt. 2, 359.
73. Tew, Blackman; Thompson, John A.; Hunt, James A.; Peed, William C.; Eagles, Lorenzo D., *CSRC.*
74. Ardrey, William E., *Diary,* 27 June 1862.
75. Collins, Joseph B., *Official Records,* Vol. 11, Pt. 2, 365.
76. Walker, Thomas W., *Official Records,* Vol. 11, Pt. 2, 362.
77. Williamson, James; Danford, Abram; Wiggins, Martin W., *CSRC*
78. Ridgeway, Matt, Personal communication, 13 September 2015.
79. Tidball, Eugene C., *No Disgrace to My Country,* 236.
80. Ardrey, William E., *Diary,* 27 June 1862.
81. 30th North Carolina Infantry Regiment, *CSRC.*
82. Ardrey, William E., *Diary,* 27 June 1862.
83. Ardrey, William E., *Diary,* 27 June 1862.
84. Ardrey, William E., *Diary,* 26 June 1862.
85. 30th North Carolina Infantry Regiment, *CSRC.*
86. Smith, William A., *The Anson Guards,* 101.
87. Smith, William A., *The Anson Guards,* 106.
88. Ardrey, William E., *Diary,* 28 June 1862.
89. Smith, William A., *The Anson Guards,* 107.
90. Ardrey, William E., *Diary,* 28 June 1862.
91. Smith, William A., *The Anson Guards,* 105.
92. Freeman, Douglas, S., *Lee's Lieutenants,* Vol. 1, 568.
93. Ardrey, William E., *Diary,* 29 June 1862.

Chapter 3

1. 30th North Carolina Infantry Regiment, *CSRC.*
2. Freeman, Douglas S., *Lee's Lieutenants,* Vol. 1, 571.
3. 30th North Carolina Infantry Regiment, *CSRC.*
4. Green, Samuel, letter 27 June 1862.
5. Betts, Alexander, *Experience of a Confederate Chaplain,* 29 June 1862.
6. Bennett, Risden T., "Fourteenth Regiment," in Clark, Walter (ed.), *Histories of the Several Regiments,* Vol. 1, 712.
7. Ardrey, William E., *Diary,* 30 June 1862.
8. Smith, William A., *The Anson Guards,* 110.
9. Osborne, E. A., "Fourth Regiment," in Clark, Walter (ed.), *Histories of the Several Regiments,* Vol. 4, 2.
10. Ardrey, William E., *Diary,* 30 June 1862.
11. Bone, John W., *Record of a Soldier in the Late War,* 26.
12. Betts, Alexander, *Experience of a Confederate Chaplain,* 3 July 1862.
13. Taylor, Michael W., *To Drive the Enemy from Southern Soil,* 190.
14. Hill, Daniel H., *Official Records,* Vol. 11, pt. 2, 627.
15. Phillips, Charles, letter 12 July 1862.
16. Parker, Francis M., letter, 3 July 1862.
17. Hill, Daniel H., *Official Records,* Vol. 11, pt. 2, 627.
18. Freeman, Douglas S., *Lee's Lieutenants,* Vol. 1, 576.
19. Bone, John W., *Record of a Soldier in the Late War,* 26.
20. Freeman, Douglas S., *Lee's Lieutenants,* Vol. 1, 593.
21. Hill, Daniel H., *Official Records,* Vol. 11, pt. 2, 627.
22. Freeman, Douglas S., *Lee's Lieutenants,* Vol. 1, 594.
23. Hill, Daniel H., *Official Records,* Vol. 11, pt. 2, 628.
24. Snow, Alonzo, *Official Records,* Vol. 11, Pt. 2, 267.
25. Smith, William A., *The Anson Guards,* 115.
26. Bone, John W., *Record of a Soldier in the Late War,* 28.
27. Howe, Albion P., *Official Records,* Vol. 11, Pt. 2, 208.
28. Snow, Alonzo, *Official Records,* Vol. 11, Pt. 2, 267.
29. Howe, Albion P., *Official Records,* Vol. 11, Pt. 2, 208.
30. Snow, Alonzo, *Official Records,* Vol. 11, Pt. 2, 267.
31. Hill, Daniel H., *Official Records,* Vol. 11, pt. 2, 628.
32. Freeman, Douglas S., *Lee's Lieutenants,* Vol. 1, 596.
33. Freeman, Douglas S., *Lee's Lieutenants,* Vol. 1, 597.

34. Armistead, Lewis A., *Official Records*, Vol. 11, Pt. 2, 819.
35. Manly, Matt., "Second Regiment, in Clark, Walter (ed.), *Histories of the Several Regiments*, Vol. 1, 165.
36. Hill, Daniel H., *Official Records*, Vol. 11, pt. 2, 628.
37. Calder, William, letter, 4 July 1862. Southern Historical Collection, in Sears, Stephen W. *To the Gates of Richmond* (New York: Ticknor and Fields, 1992), 326.
38. Smith, William A., *The Anson Guards*, 115.
39. Taylor, Michael W., *To Drive the Enemy from Southern Soil*, 193.
40. McWhiney, Grady, and Perry D. Johnson, *Attack and Die: Civil War Military Tactics and the Southern Heritage* (Tuscaloosa: University of Alabama Press, 1982), 50.
41. Howe, Albion P., *Official Records*, Vol. 11, Pt. 2, 208.
42. Bone, John W., *Record of a Soldier in the Late War*, 27.
43. Manarian, Louis H. (comp.), *North Carolina Troops 1861–1865: A Roster*, Vol. 3, 373.
44. Clarence P. Puckett, "Richard David Brooks—The Young Man at War." Brantley, Steven, personal communication, 19 June 2015.
45. Roe, Alfred S., *The Tenth Regiment, Massachusetts Infantry, 1861–1864* (Springfield, MA: Tenth Regiment Veteran Association, 1909), 120.
46. Baggot, James W.; Howard, Thomas M.; Pope, Alexander; Pope, Wiley; Allen, James P.; Davis, Arrington J.; Davis, James R.; Mangun, Calvin T.; Mason, Joseph; Arrington, William T.; Price, Joel L.; Sherwood, George A., *CSRC*.
47. Roe, Alfred S., *The Tenth Regiment, Massachusetts Infantry, 1861–1864*, 120.
48. Smith, William A., *The Anson Guards*, 115.
49. Bone, John W., *Record of a Soldier in the Late War*, 28.
50. Langley, Singleton, CSRC. Vick, Robert, personal communication, 3 June 2015.
51. Manly, Matt., "Second Regiment, in Clark, Walter (ed.), *Histories of the Several Regiments*, Vol. 1, 165.
52. Garland, Samuel, *Official Records*, Vol.11, Pt. 2, 643.
53. Black, James H.; Jennings, George W.; Robinson, James R.; Greer, Ephraim J.; Tharp, John L.; Harris, George Washington, *CSRC*.
54. Roe, Alfred S., *The Tenth Regiment, Massachusetts Infantry, 1861–1864*, 120.
55. Smith, William A., *The Anson Guards*, 86.
56. Shearin, Nicholas L.; Neal, Dudley H.; Duke, Robert W.; Newsom, John G.; Gill, Philip P., *CSRC*.
57. Smith, William A., *The Anson Guards*, 131.
58. Calder, William, letter, 4 July 1862. Southern Historical Collection, in Sears, Stephen W., *To the Gates of Richmond*.
59. Roe, Alfred S., *The Tenth Regiment, Massachusetts Infantry, 1861–1864*, 120.
60. Bates, Samuel P., *History of Pennsylvania Volunteers, 1861–1865* (Harrisburg, PA: State Printer, 1869–71), 582.
61. Howe, Albion P., *Official Records*, Vol. 11, Pt. 2, 208.
62. Pipkin, Lewis H.; Jones, Isham F.; Rivenbark, William; Moore, Willis M.; Kittrell, H.; Younts, John A.; Woodard, John E., *CSRC*.
63. Smith, William A., *The Anson Guards*, 116.
64. Roe, Alfred S., *The Tenth Regiment, Massachusetts Infantry, 1861–1864*, 120.
65. McWhiney, Grady, and Perry D. Johnson, *Attack and Die*, 97.
66. Royal, Sherman; Cox, John L.; Morgan, James B.; Leonard, Samuel B.; Manellis, John, *CSRC*.
67. Witherspoon, John G., letter, 3 July 1862.
68. Bone, John W., *Record of a Soldier in the Late War*, 27.
69. Manarian, Louis H. (compiler), *North Carolina Troops 1861–1865: A Roster*, Vol. 3, 373.
70. Garland, Samuel, *Official Records*, Vol. 11, Pt. 2, 643.
71. Bone, John W., *Record of a Soldier in the Late War*, 27.
72. Howe, Albion P., *Official Records*, Vol. 11, Pt. 2, 208.
73. Freeman, Douglas S., *Lee's Lieutenants*, Vol. 1, 602.
74. Bone, John W., *Record of a Soldier in the Late War*, 27.
75. Prank, John D., *Official Records*, Vol. 11, Pt. 2, 53.
76. Wheeler, James; White, Almond W.; O'Neal, Hardy; Pierce, George W.; White, James, *CSRC*.
77. Ardrey, William E., *Diary*, 1 July 1862.
78. Bone, John W., *Record of a Soldier in the Late War*, 27.
79. Parker, Francis M., letter, 3 July 1862.
80. Smith, William A., *The Anson Guards*, 86.
81. Garland, Samuel, *Official Records*, Vol. 11, Pt. 2, 643.
82. Bone, John W., *Record of a Soldier in the Late War*, 28.
83. Freeman, Douglas S., *Lee's Lieutenants*, Vol. 1, 602
84. Palmer, Innis N., *Official Records*, Vol. 11, Pt. 2, 213–4.
85. Roe, Alfred S., *The Tenth Regiment, Massachusetts Infantry, 1861–1864*, 120.
86. Palmer, Innis N., *Official Records*, Vol. 11, Pt. 2, 213–4.
87. Newell, Joseph K., *Annals of the 10th Regiment Massachusetts Volunteers* (Springfield, MA: C. A. Nichols & Co., 1875), 126.
88. Parker, Francis M., letter, 3 July 1862.
89. Bone, John W., *Record of a Soldier in the Late War*, 28.
90. Manly, Matt., "Second Regiment, in Clark, Walter (ed.), *Histories of the Several Regiments*, Vol. 1, 166.
91. Garland, Samuel, *Official Records*, Vol. 11, Pt. 2, 643.
92. Smith, William A., *The Anson Guards*, 118.
93. Witherspoon, John G., letter, 3 July 1862.
94. Newell, Joseph K., *Annals of the 10th Regiment Massachusetts Volunteers*, 126–7.
95. Kingsbury, Henry W., *Official Records*, Vol. 11, Pt. 2, 287.
96. Newell, Joseph K., *Annals of the 10th Regiment Massachusetts Volunteers*, 126–7.
97. Ardrey, William E., *Diary*, 1 July 1862.
98. Bone, John W., *Record of a Soldier in the Late War*, 28.
99. Parker, Francis M., letter, 3 July 1862.
100. 30th North Carolina Infantry Regiment, *CSRC*.
101. Bone, John W., *Record of a Soldier in the Late War*, 28.
102. Witherspoon, John G., letter, 3 July 1862.
103. Ardrey, William E., *Diary*, 2 July 1862.
104. Bone, John W., *Record of a Soldier in the Late War*, 29.
105. Taylor, Michael W., *To Drive the Enemy from Southern Soil*, 195.
106. Hill, Daniel H., *Official Records*, Vol. 11, pt. 2, 628.
107. Witherspoon, John G., letter, 3 July 1862.
108. Ardrey, William E., *Diary*, 2 July 1862.
109. Parker, Francis M., letter, 3 July 1862.

Chapter 4

1. 30th North Carolina Infantry Regiment, *CSRC*.
2. Ardrey, William E., *Diary*, 4 July 1862, 8 July 1862.
3. Ardrey, William E., *Diary*, 4 July 1862, 8 July 1862.
4. Taylor, Michael W., *To Drive the Enemy from Southern Soil*, 199. Manarian, Louis H. (comp.), *North Carolina Troops 1861–1865*, Vol. 3, 373.
5. Ardrey, William E., *Diary*, 4 July 1862, 10 July 1862.
6. Jordan, Weymouth T. (comp.), *North Carolina Troops 1861–1865*, Vol. 4, 3.
7. Ardrey, William E., *Diary*, 11–12 July 1862.

8. Ardrey, William E., *Diary*, 14 July 1862.
9. Witherspoon, William E., letter, 16 July 1862.
10. Parker, Francis M., letter, 24 July 1862.
11. 30th North Carolina Infantry Regiment, *CSRC*. Cain, Lorenzo D., *CSRC*.
12. 30th North Carolina Infantry Regiment, *CSRC*. Cain, Lorenzo D.; Pegram, George W.; Graham, Samuel W., *CSRC*.
13. Sewell, George, letter, 10 August 1862, *CSRC*.
14. Ardrey, William E., *Diary*, 27–29 July 1862.
15. Witherspoon, William E., letter, 16 July 1862.
16. Hill, Daniel H., *Official Records*, Vol. 11, pt. 1, 646.
17. Venner, William Thomas, *The 11th North Carolina in the Civil War*, 35.
18. Hardy, Michael C., *Civil War Charlotte: Last Capital of the Confederacy* (Charleston, SC: History, 2012), 32–4.
19. Ardrey, William E., *Diary*, 31 July 1862.
20. Barnett, John G., *The Civil War in North Carolina* (Chapel Hill: University of North Carolina Press, 1963), 182–3.
21. Parker, Francis M., letter, 2 August 1862.
22. Ardrey, William E., *Diary*, 5 August 1862.
23. Manarin, Louis, H. (comp.), *North Carolina Troops*, Vol. 3, 373. Ardrey, William E., *Diary*, 6 August 1862.
24. Parker, Francis M., letter, 8 August 1862.
25. Orr, Nathan D., letter 17 August 1862, *CSRC*.
26. Kell, James T., letter 18 August 1862, *CSRC*.
27. Parker, Francis M., "Thirtieth Regiment," in Clark, Walter (ed.), *Histories of the Several Regiments*, Vol. 2, 499.
28. Ardrey, William E., *Diary*, 18 August 1862.
29. Ardrey, William E., *Diary*, 19–20 August 1862.
30. Parker, Francis M., letter, 22 August 1862.
31. Betts, Alexander, *Experience of a Confederate Chaplain*, 26 August 1862. Ardrey, William E., *Diary*, 27 August 1862.
32. Taylor, Michael W., *To Drive the Enemy from Southern Soil*, 210.
33. Betts, Alexander, *Experience of a Confederate Chaplain*, 29 August 1862.
34. Taylor, Michael W., *To Drive the Enemy from Southern Soil*, 210.
35. Betts, Alexander, *Experience of a Confederate Chaplain*, 31 August 1862.
36. 30th North Carolina Infantry Regiment, *CSRC*.
37. Ardrey, William E., *Diary*, 31 August–1 September 1862.
38. Bone, John W., *Record of a Soldier in the Late War*, 39. Ardrey, William E., *Diary*, 2 September 1862. Betts, Alexander, *Experience of a Confederate Chaplain*, 2 September 1862.
39. Betts, Alexander, *Experience of a Confederate Chaplain*, 3–4 September 1862.
40. Taylor, Michael W., *To Drive the Enemy from Southern Soil*, 210.
41. Ardrey, William E., *Diary*, 5 September 1862.
42. Freeman, Douglas S., *Lee's Lieutenants*, Vol. 2, 152.
43. Ardrey, William E., *Diary*, 7 September 1862. Freeman, Douglas S., *Lee's Lieutenants*, Vol. 2, 153.
44. Bone, John W., *Record of a Soldier in the Late War*, 37.
45. Ardrey, William E., *Diary*, 9 September 1862.
46. Parker, Francis M., letter, 9 September 1862.
47. Freeman, Douglas S., *Lee's Lieutenants*, Vol. 2, 149.
48. Bone, John W., *Record of a Soldier in the Late War*, 39.
49. Griffin, James D., letter, ? September 1862.
50. Smith, William A., *The Anson Guards*, 156.
51. Ardrey, William E., *Diary*, 10 September 1862.
52. Ardrey, William E., *Diary*, 11 September 1862. Freeman, Douglas S., *Lee's Lieutenants*, Vol. 2, 85.
53. Freeman, Douglas S., *Lee's Lieutenants*, Vol. 2, 150–1.
54. Smith, William A., *The Anson Guards*, 161.
55. Ardrey, William E., *Diary*, 12 September 1862.
56. Taylor, Michael W., *To Drive the Enemy from Southern Soil*, 213.
57. Hill, Daniel H., "The Battle of South Mountain, or Boonsboro," in Johnson, Robert U., and Clarence C. Buel, *Battles and Leaders of the Civil War*, Vol. 2, 565.
58. Hill, Daniel H., *Official Records*, Vol. 19, pt. 1, 1019.
59. Hill, Daniel H., "The Battle of South Mountain," *Battles and Leaders of the Civil War*, Vol. 2, 566.
60. Hill, Daniel H., "The Battle of South Mountain," *Battles and Leaders of the Civil War*, Vol. 2, 568.
61. Grimes, Bryan, *Official Records*, Vol. 19, Pt. 1, 1049.
62. Hill, Daniel H., "The Battle of South Mountain," *Battles and Leaders of the Civil War*, Vol. 2, 572.
63. Edwards, Elsberry B.; Morgan, William G.; Wicker, Jesse J., *CSRC*.
64. Baker, Henry C., *CSRC*.
65. Freeman, Douglas S., *Lee's Lieutenants*, Vol. 2, 180–1.
66. Hill, Daniel H., "The Battle of South Mountain," *Battles and Leaders of the Civil War*, Vol. 2, 579–80.
67. Manly, Matthew, "Second Regiment," in Clark, Walter (ed.) *Histories of the Several Regiments*, Vol. 1, 166.
68. Grimes, Bryan, *Official Records*, Vol. 19, Pt. 1, 1049.
69. Hill, Daniel H., "The Battle of South Mountain," *Battles and Leaders of the Civil War*, Vol. 2, 579–80.
70. 30th North Carolina Infantry Regiment, *CSRC*.
71. Hill, Daniel H., "The Battle of South Mountain," *Battles and Leaders of the Civil War*, Vol. 2, 570, 573.
72. Sillers, William J., *Official Records*, Vol. 19, Pt. 1, 1050–1.
73. 30th North Carolina Infantry Regiment, *CSRC*.

Chapter 5

1. Witherspoon, John, letter, 22 September 1862. John Witherspoon family collection.
2. Taylor, Michael W., *To Drive the Enemy from Southern Soil*, 219.
3. Ardrey, William, *Diary*, 17 September 1862.
4. 30th North Carolina Regiment. *CSRC*.
5. 30th North Carolina Regiment, *CSRC*.
6. Priest, John M., *Antietam: The Soldiers' Battle* (Shippensburg, PA: White Mane, 1989), 329.
7. Hill, Daniel H., *Official Records*, Vol. 19, Pt. 1, 1018–30.
8. Shepard, Henry E., *Confederate Veteran*, Vol. 26 (1918), 72.
9. Ardrey, William, *Diary*, 26 May 1862.
10. Priest, John M., *Antietam: The Soldiers' Battle*, 329.
11. Rodes, Robert E., *Official Records*. Vol. 19, Pt.1, 1033–39.
12. Sillers, William W., *Official Records*. Vol. 19, Pt. 1, 1050–52.
13. Ardrey, William, *Diary*, 26 May 1862.
14. Rodes, Robert E., *Official Records*. Vol. 19, Pt. 1, 1033–39.
15. Sillers, William W., *Official Records*. Vol. 19, Pt. 1, 1050–52.
16. Priest, John M., *Antietam: The Soldiers' Battle*, 137.
17. Gordon, John B., *Reminiscences of the Civil War* (New York: Charles Scribners' Sons, 1903), 84.
18. Taylor, Michael W., *To Drive the Enemy from Southern Soil*, 220.
19. Sillers, William W., *Official Records*. Vol. 19, Pt. 1, 1050–52.
20. Taylor, Michael W., *To Drive the Enemy from Southern Soil*, 220.
21. Priest, John M., *Antietam: The Soldiers' Battle*, 139.
22. Priest, John M., *Antietam: The Soldiers' Battle*, 139.
23. Andrews, John W., *Official Rec-*

ords, Vol. 19, Pt. 1, 336–7. Priest, John M., *Antietam: The Soldiers' Battle*, 142.
24. Gordon, John B., *Reminiscences of the Civil War*, 6.
25. Ardrey, William, *Diary*, 26 May 1862.
26. Parker, Francis, M., "Thirtieth North Carolina," in Clark, Walter (ed.) *Histories of the Several Regiments*, Vol. 2, 500.
27. Gordon, John B., *Reminiscences of the Civil War*, 6.
28. Parker, Francis, M., "Thirtieth North Carolina," in Clark, Walter (ed.) *Histories of the Several Regiments*, Vol. 2, 500.
29. Serville, William P., *History of the First Regiment, Delaware Volunteers: From the Commencement of the Three Months Service to the Final Muster-Out at the Close of the Rebellion* (Wilmington: Historical Society of Delaware, 1913), 48.
30. Hitchcock, Frederick, L., *War From the Inside: The Story of the 132nd Regiment Pennsylvania Volunteer Infantry in the War for the Suppression of the Rebellion, 1862–1863* (Philadelphia, PA: J. B. Lippincott, 1904). [Project Gutenberg ebook.]
31. Serville, William P., *History of the First Regiment, Delaware Volunteers*, 48.
32. Wilmer, L. Allison, Jarrett, J. H., Vernon, George W., *History and Roster of Maryland Volunteers, War of 1861–5* (Baltimore, MD: Guggenheim, Weil, and Co., 1899), 180.
33. Wells, James W.; Dunn, Andrew J., *CSRC*.
34. Priest, John M., *Antietam: The Soldiers' Battle*, 336.
35. Phisterer, Frederick, *New York in the War of the Rebellion, 1861–1865* (Albany, NY: J. B. Lyon, 1912), 377.
36. Serville, William P., *History of the First Regiment, Delaware Volunteers*, 48.
37. Foote, Shelby, *The Civil war: A Narrative* (New York: Vintage, 1958), 377.
38. Priest, John M., *Antietam: The Soldiers' Battle*, 336.
39. Page, Charles, *History of the Fourteenth Regiment Connecticut Vol. Infantry* (Meriden, CT: Horton, 1907), 37.
40. Washburn, George H., *A Complete Military History of the 108th Regiment N.Y. Vol., From 1862 to 1894* (Rochester, NY: Press of E. R. Andrews, 1984), 10–6.
41. Washburn, George H., *A Complete Military History of the 108th Regiment N.Y.*, 24.
42. Washburn, George H., *A Complete Military History of the 108th Regiment N.Y.*, 24.
43. Page, Charles. *History of the Fourteenth Regiment Connecticut Vol. Infantry*, 32–3.

44. Washburn, George H., *A Complete Military History of the 108th Regiment N.Y.*, 24–5.
45. Washburn, George H., *A Complete Military History of the 108th Regiment N.Y.*, 25.
46. Sillers, William, *Official Records*, Vol. 19, Pt. 1, 1051.
47. Holland, John; Warren, Lemuel; Lewis, Edward, *CSRC*.
48. Morris, Dwight, *Official Records*, Vol. 19, Pt. 1, 333. Palmer, Oliver, *Official Records*, Vol. 2, pt. 1, 335.
49. Kimball, Nathan, *Official Records*, Vol. 19, Pt. 1, 326–8.
50. Priest, John M., *Antietam: The Soldiers' Battle*, 156.
51. Kimball, Nathan, *Official Records*, Vol. 19, Pt. 1, 326–8.
52. Mellott, David. Personal Correspondence, 24 January 2015.
53. Snider, Joseph, *Official Records*, Vol. 19, Pt. 1, 332.
54. Snider, Joseph, *Official Records*, Vol. 19, Pt. 1, 332.
55. Cooper, William; Brown, James; Hathaway, Augustus; Baker, Jeptha. *CSRC*.
56. Priest, John M., *Antietam: The Soldiers' Battle*, 157.
57. Atkinson, Matt, "We were now complete masters of the field," in *Papers of the 2006 Gettysburg National Military Park Seminar* (Gettysburg, PA: National Park Service, 2008), 211.
58. Edwards, William; McDonald, Neill; Vick, Lorenzo, *CSRC*.
59. Wintermyre, James P., "Confederates Buried at Shepherdstown," *Confederate Veteran*, Vol. 19 (1911), 75.
60. Taylor, Michael W., *To Drive the Enemy from Southern Soil*, 223.
61. Philips, Frederick, letter, 25 Aug 1894. In John M. Gould Papers, Courtesy of Dartmouth College Library.
62. Taylor, Michael W., *To Drive the Enemy from Southern Soil*, 223.
63. Feltus, Abram M., *Official Records*, Vol. 19, Pt. 1, 884–5.
64. Priest, John M., *Antietam: The Soldiers' Battle*, 336.
65. Snider, Joseph, *Official Records*, Vol. 19, Pt. 1, 332.
66. Kimball, Nathan, *Official Records*, Vol. 19, Pt. 1, 327.
67. Priest, John M., *Antietam: The Soldiers' Battle*, 336.
68. Meagher, Thomas F., *Official Records*, Vol. 19, Pt. 1, 293–5.
69. Meagher, Thomas F., *Official Records*, Vol. 19, Pt. 1, 293–5.
70. Priest, John M., *Antietam: The Soldiers' Battle*, 160.
71. Feltus, Abram M., *Official Records*, Vol. 19, Pt. 1, 884–5.
72. Meagher, Thomas F., *Official Records*, Vol. 19, Pt. 1, 293–5.
73. McCormick, John, "The Irish Brigade: Never Were Men So Brave," *Civil War Times Illustrated*, Vol. 8, #1, April 1969, 39.

74. Meagher, Thomas F., *Official Records*, Vol. 19, Pt. 1, 293–5.
75. Catton, Bruce, *Mr. Lincoln's Army* (Garden City, NY: Doubleday,1965), 296.
76. Meagher, Thomas F., *Official Records*, Vol. 19, Pt. 1, 293–5.
77. Priest, John M., *Antietam: The Soldiers' Battle*, 160.
78. Black, James H.; Wicker, William F.; Dickens, Ephraim, *CSRC*.
79. Hill, Daniel H., *Official Records*, Vol. 19, Pt. 1, 018–30.
80. Kelly, Patrick, *Official Records*, Vol. 19, Pt. 1, 298.
81. Meagher, Thomas F., *Official Records*, Vol. 19, Pt. 1, 293–5.
82. Caldwell, John C., *Official Records*, Vol. 19, Pt. 1, 284–7.
83. Caldwell, John C., *Official Records*, Vol. 19, Pt. 1, 284–7.
84. Priest, John M., *Antietam: The Soldiers' Battle*, 180.
85. Priest, John M., *Antietam: The Soldiers' Battle*, 182.
86. Sillers, William, *Official Records*, Vol. 19, Pt. 1, 1051.
87. Sillers, William, *Official Records*, Vol. 19, Pt. 1, 1051.
88. Betts, Alexander D., *Experience of a Confederate Chaplain*, 14 September 1862.
89. Sillers, William, *Official Records*, Vol. 19, Pt. 1, 1051.
90. Rodes, Robert E., *Official Records*. Vol. 19, Pt. 1, 1033–39.
91. Barlow, Francis C., *Official Records*, Vol. 19, Pt. 1, 289–90.
92. Manly, Matt, "Second Regiment," in Clark, Walter (ed.) *Histories of the Several Regiments*, Vol. 1; 167.
93. Miles, Nelson A., *Official Records*, Vol. 19, Pt. 1, 291–2.
94. Barlow, Francis C., *Official Records*, Vol. 19, Pt. 1, 289–90.
95. Livermore, Thomas L., *Days and Events: 1860–1866* (Boston, MA: Houghton Mifflin, 1900), 135.
96. Livermore, Thomas L., *Days and Events: 1860–1866*, 138.
97. Beall, Thomas D., "Reminiscences About Sharpsburg," *Confederate Veteran*, Vol. 1 (1893), 246.
98. Harrell, George; Gill, William; Crews, Alexander; Rogers, Charles, *CSRC*.
99. Sillers, William, *Official Records*, Vol. 19, Pt. 1, 1051.
100. Griffin, Loren, letter, 6 October 1862, in Delpino, Irene, R., *A Broad River Digest; For Family and Friends* (Philadelphia, PA: Omega, 1991).
101. "General Court Martial of Captain J. C. McMillan," General Orders No. 123, 28 October 1862, *CSRC*.
102. 30th North Carolina Regiment. *CSRC*.
103. Best, John; Culp, Aley; Griffin, James D.; Weeks, Rufus, *CSRC*.
104. Sillers, William, *Official Records*, Vol. 19, Pt. 1, 1051.

105. Taylor, Michael W., *To Drive the Enemy from Southern Soil*, 226.
106. Sillers, William, *Official Records*, Vol. 19, Pt. 1, 1051.
107. Livermore, Thomas L., *Days and Events: 1860–1866*, 140.
108. Bennett, Robert, *Official Records*, Vol. 19, Pt. 1, 1048.
109. Miles, Nelson A., *Official Records*, Vol. 19, Pt. 1, 291–2.
110. Sillers, William, *Official Records*, Vol. 19, Pt. 1, 1051.
111. Ardrey, William, *Diary*, 17 September 1862.
112. Livermore, Thomas L., *Days and Events: 1860–1866*, 140.
113. Priest, John M., *Antietam: The Soldiers' Battle*, 334–6.
114. Priest, John M., *Antietam: The Soldiers' Battle*, 329.
115. Page, Charles. *History of the Fourteenth Regiment Connecticut Vol. Infantry*, 48.

Chapter 6

1. Taylor, Michael W., *To Drive the Enemy from Southern Soil*, 227–8.
2. Betts, Alexander, *Experience of a Confederate Chaplain*, 18 September 1862.
3. Ardrey, William E., *Diary*, 18 September 1862.
4. Betts, Alexander, *Experience of a Confederate Chaplain*, 19 September 1862.
5. Ardrey, William E., *Diary*, 20 September 1862.
6. Bone, John W., *Record of a Soldier in the Late War*, 40.
7. Sillers, William W., Letter, 1 October 1862. Sillers-Holmes Family Correspondence. University of Notre Dame Rare Books and Special Collections.
8. Ardrey, William E., *Diary*, 22 September 1862, 25 September 1862.
9. Ardrey, William E., *Diary*, 27–8 September 1862
10. Ardrey, William E., *Diary*, 28 September 1862
11. Ardrey, William E., *Diary*, 30 September 1862
12. Bunn, Benjamin H., *CSRC*.
13. Ardrey, William E., *Diary*, 14 October 1862
14. Warner, Ezra J., *Generals in Gray*, 6.
15. Grimes, Bryan, in Cowper, Pulaski, *Extracts of Letters of Bryan Grimes to His Wife, Written While in Active Service in the Army of Northern Virginia* (Raleigh, NC: Edwards, Broughton & Co., 1883), 10–1.
16. Grimes, Bryan, in Cowper, Pulaski, *Extracts of Letters of Bryan Grimes to His Wife*, 19, 21.
17. Betts, Alexander, *Experience of a Confederate Chaplain*, 25 October 1862.
18. Witherspoon, John G., letter, 26 October 1862.
19. Grimes, Bryan, in Cowper, Pulaski, *Extracts of Letters of Bryan Grimes to His Wife*, 22–3.
20. Betts, Alexander, *Experience of a Confederate Chaplain*, 27 October 1862.
21. Grimes, Bryan, in Cowper, Pulaski, *Extracts of Letters of Bryan Grimes to His Wife*, 22.
22. Ardrey, William E., *Diary*, 31 October 1862
23. Ardrey, William E., *Diary*, 4 November 1862
24. Sillers, William W., Letter, 6 November 1862.
25. Betts, Alexander, *Experience of a Confederate Chaplain*, 6 November 1862.
26. Grimes, Bryan, in Cowper, Pulaski, *Extracts of Letters of Bryan Grimes to His Wife*, 24.
27. Witherspoon, John G., letter, 5 November 1862.
28. Betts, Alexander, *Experience of a Confederate Chaplain*, 9 November 1862.
29. Witherspoon, John G., letter, 10 November 1862.
30. 30th North Carolina Regiment. *CSRC*.
31. Venner, William Thomas, *The 7th Tennessee Infantry in the Civil War* (Jefferson, NC: McFarland, 2013), 64.
32. Betts, Alexander, *Experience of a Confederate Chaplain*, 7 November 1862.
33. Bone, John W., *Record of a Soldier in the Late War*, 41.
34. Witherspoon, John G., letter, 10 November 1862.
35. Gallagher, Gary W., *Stephen Dodson Ramseur: Lee's Gallant General* (Chapel Hill: University of North Carolina Press, 1985), 7.
36. Cox, William R., "Address on the Life and Character of Maj. Gen. Stephen D. Ramseur" (Raleigh, NC: E. M. Uzzell; Steam Printers and Binder, 1891).
37. Betts, Alexander, *Experience of a Confederate Chaplain*, 15 November 1862.
38. Manly, Matt, "Second Regiment," in Clark, Walter (ed.), *Histories of the Several Regiments*, Vol. 1, 168.
39. Sillers, William W., Letter, 15 November 1862.
40. Bone, John W., *Record of a Soldier in the Late War*, 41.
41. Manly, Matt, "Second Regiment," in Clark, Walter (ed.), *Histories of the Several Regiments*, Vol. 1, 168.
42. 30th North Carolina Regiment. *CSRC*.
43. Freeman, Douglas S., *Lee's Lieutenants*, Vol. 2, 340.
44. Hill, Daniel H., *Official Records*, Vol. 21, Pt. 1, 643.
45. Venner, William Thomas, *The 7th Tennessee Infantry in the Civil War*, 65.
46. Hill, Daniel H., *Official Records*, Vol. 21, Pt. 1, 643.
47. Grimes, Bryan, in Cowper, Pulaski, *Extracts of Letters of Bryan Grimes to His Wife*, 26.
48. Freeman, Douglas S., *Lee's Lieutenants*, Vol. 2, 345.
49. Moore, J. H., "Fredericksburg," *The Southern Bivouac*, August 1886, 181.
50. Bennett, R. T., "Fourteenth Regiment," Clark, Walter (ed.), *Histories of the Several Regiments*, Vol. 1, 713.
51. Reynolds, John F., "The Report of General John F. Reynolds," in Johnson, Robert U., and Clarence C. Buel, *Battles and Leaders of the Civil War*, Vol. 3, 141.
52. Moore, J. H., "Fredericksburg," *The Southern Bivouac*, 182.
53. Reynolds, John F., "The Report of General John F. Reynolds," in Johnson, Robert U., and Clarence C. Buel, *Battles and Leaders of the Civil War*, Vol. 3, 141.
54. Hill, Daniel H., *Official Records*, Vol. 21, Pt. 1, 643.
55. Reynolds, John F., "The Report of General John F. Reynolds," in Johnson, Robert U., and Clarence C. Buel, *Battles and Leaders of the Civil War*, Vol. 3, 141.
56. Hanchey, John W.; Pickett, John L.; Wells, John; Allen, Elias G.; Lumbley, William L.; Wilkins, Elijah, *CSRC*.
57. Hill, Daniel H., *Official Records*, Vol. 21, Pt. 1, 643.
58. McDougald, Donald; Little, Jesse; Mayo, James, *CSRC*.
59. Taylor, Michael W., *To Drive the Enemy from Southern Soil*, 316.
60. Bone, John W., *Record of a Soldier in the Late War*, 41.
61. Wells, John H.; MacDougald, Donald, *CSRC*.
62. Wood, Rob. Personal communication, 3 June 2015.
63. 30th North Carolina Regiment. *CSRC*.
64. Crowder, J. A. letter, 21 December 1862, in Green family collection.
65. Grimes, Bryan, in Cowper, Pulaski, *Extracts of Letters of Bryan Grimes to His Wife*, 26.
66. Grimes, Bryan, in Cowper, Pulaski, *Extracts of Letters of Bryan Grimes to His Wife*, 27.
67. Hill, Daniel H., *Official Records*, Vol. 21, Pt. 1, 644.
68. Smith, George B., "In the Ranks at Fredericksburg," in Johnson, Robert U., and Clarence C. Buel, *Battles and Leaders of the Civil War*, Vol. 3, 142.
69. DeArmond, Aaron L., letter, 12 January 1863, in Brown, Martha R., *Holding Sweet Communion: Civil War Letters Home* (Winston-Salem, NC: Briarpatch, 2012).

70. Butler, John C., *CSRC*.
71. Venner, William Thomas, *Hoosiers' Honor: The Iron Brigade's 19th Indiana Regiment* (Shippensburg, PA: Burd Street, 1998), 140.
72. Hill, Daniel H., *Official Records*, Vol. 21, Pt. 1, 643–4.
73. 30th North Carolina Regiment. *CSRC*.
74. Bone, John W., "Visiting Virginia Battlefields," *Confederate Veteran*, Vol. 34 (1926), 10.
75. Witherspoon, John G., letter, 22 December 1862.
76. Smith, William A., *Anson Guards*, 173.
77. Freeman, Douglas S., *Lee's Lieutenants*, Vol. 2, 430.
78. DeArmond, Aaron L., letter, 12 January 1863.
79. Smith, William A., *Anson Guards*, 162.
80. Witherspoon, John G., letter, 6 January 1863.
81. Bone, John W., *Record of a Soldier in the Late War*, 42.
82. Smith, William A., *Anson Guards*, 174.
83. Freeman, Douglas S., *Lee's Lieutenants*, Vol. 2, 430.
84. DeArmond, Aaron L., letter, 3 January 1863.
85. Sillers, William W., Letter, 13–4 January 1863.
86. DeArmond, Aaron L., letter, 3 January 1863.
87. Smith, William A., *Anson Guards*, 175.
88. Venner, William Thomas, *The 7th Tennessee Infantry in the Civil War*, 70.
89. Witherspoon, John G., letter, 15 February 1863.
90. DeArmond, Aaron L., letter, 12 January 1863.
91. Betts, Alexander, *Experience of a Confederate Chaplain*, 7 October 1862.
92. Ardrey, William E., *Diary*, 11 February 1863.
93. Smith, William A., *Anson Guards*, 173.
94. Witherspoon, John G., letter, 3 January 1863.
95. Witherspoon, John G., letter, 3 January 1863.
96. Betts, Alexander, *Experience of a Confederate Chaplain*, 25 November 1862.
97. Witherspoon, John G., letter, 6 January 1863.
98. 30th North Carolina Regiment. *CSRC*.
99. Sillers, William W., Letter, 9 February 1863.
100. Witherspoon, John G., letter, 15 February 1863.
101. Witherspoon, John G., letter, 3 January 1863.
102. Puckett, Clarence P., "Richard David Brooks; The Young Man at War," 5.
103. Sillers, William W., Letter, 22 March 1863.
104. Ardrey, William E., *Diary*, 11 January 1863, 27 January 1863.
105. Covington, W., letter, ? January 1863, in Green family collection.
106. Sillers, William W., Letter, 28 January 1863.
107. Betts, Alexander, *Experience of a Confederate Chaplain*, 29 January 1863–4 February 1863.
108. Griffin, L., letter 23 March 1863, in Green family collection.
109. Watford, Christopher (ed.), *The Civil War in North Carolina: Soldiers and Civilians' Letters and Diaries*, Vol. 2, 97.
110. Sillers, William W., 26 February 1863.
111. Bone, John W., *Record of a Soldier in the Late War*, 43.
112. Venner, William Thomas, *The 7th Tennessee Infantry in the Civil War*, 69.
113. Venner, William Thomas, *The 7th Tennessee Infantry in the Civil War*, 70.
114. Witherspoon, John G., letter, 15 February 1863.
115. Witherspoon, John G., letter, 8 March 1863.
116. Witherspoon, John G., letter, 14 March 1863.
117. Witherspoon, John G., letter, 14 March 1863.
118. Gallagher, Gary W., *Stephen Dodson Ramseur: Lee's Gallant General*, 50.
119. Witherspoon, John G., letter, 14 March 1863.
120. Manly, Matt, "Second Regiment," in Clark, Walter (ed.), *Histories of the Several Regiments*, Vol. 1, 169.
121. Ardrey, William E., *Diary*, 11 April 1863.
122. Taylor, Michael W., *To Drive the Enemy from Southern Soil*, 233.
123. Parker, Francis M., letter, 11 April 1863.
124. Parker, Francis M., letter, 12 April 1863.
125. Whirley, Vonda, and Mitrovich, Jean, personal communication, 10 June 2015.
126. Parker, Francis M., letter, 12 April 1863.
127. Freeman, Douglas S., *Lee's Lieutenants*, Vol. 2, 519.
128. Gallagher, Gary W., *Stephen Dodson Ramseur: Lee's Gallant General*, 51.
129. Ardrey, William E., *Diary*, 24 April 1863.
130. Parker, Francis M., letter, 25 April 1863.
131. Rodes, Robert E., *Official Records*, Vol. 25, Pt. 1, 939.
132. Ramseur, Stephen D., *Official Records*, Vol. 25, Pt. 1, 995.
133. Ramseur, Stephen D., *Official Records*, Vol. 25, Pt. 1, 995.
134. Taylor, Michael W., *To Drive the Enemy from Southern Soil*, 245.
135. Ardrey, William E., *Diary*, 30 April 1863.

Chapter 7

1. Ardrey, William E., Diary, 30 April 1863.
2. Taylor, Michael W. *To Drive the Enemy*, 245.
3. 30th North Carolina Regiment. *CSRC*.
4. Freeman, Douglas S., *Lee's Lieutenants*, Vol. 2, 528.
5. Gallagher, Gary W., *Stephen Dodson Ramseur: Lee's Gallant General*, 53.
6. Gallagher, Gary W., *Stephen Dodson Ramseur: Lee's Gallant General*, 54.
7. Ardrey, William E., Diary, 1 May 1863.
8. Schaub, J. L., "Gen. Robert E. Rodes," *Confederate Veteran*, Vol. 16 (1908), 269.
9. Rodes, Robert E., *Official Records*, Vol. 25, Pt. 1, 940.
10. Norman, William, *A Portion of My Life: Being A Short and Imperfect History Written While a Prisoner of War on Johnson's Island*, 1864 (Winston-Salem, NC: John F. Blair, 1959).
11. Grimes, Bryan, in Cowper, Pulaski, *Extracts of Letters of Bryan Grimes to His Wife*, 29.
12. Ramseur, Stephen D., *Official Records*, Vol. 25, Pt. 1, 997.
13. Rodes, Robert E., *Official Records*, Vol. 25, Pt. 1, 940.
14. Taylor, Michael W. *To Drive the Enemy*, 245.
15. Bone, John W., "Visiting Virginia Battlefields," *Confederate Veteran*, Vol. 34 (1926), 10.
16. Freeman, Douglas S., *Lee's Lieutenants*, Vol. 2, 534.
17. Doubleday, Abner, *Chancellorsville and Gettysburg: Campaigns of the Civil War—VI* (New York: Charles Scribner's Sons, 1882), 13.
18. Steadman, Charles M., "Gen. Stephen Dodson Ramseur," *Confederate Veteran*, Vol. 28 (1920), 454.
19. Bone, John W., *Record of a Soldier in the Late War*, 47.
20. Doubleday, Abner, *Chancellorsville and Gettysburg*, 13.
21. Ramseur, Stephen D., *Official Records*, Vol. 25, Pt. 1, 995.
22. Bone, John W., *Record of a Soldier in the Late War*, 47.
23. Grimes, Bryan, in Cowper, Pulaski, *Extracts of Letters of Bryan Grimes to His Wife*, 30.
24. Bone, John W., *Record of a Soldier in the Late War*, 47.
25. Ramseur, Stephen D., *Official Records*, Vol. 25, Pt. 1, 995.
26. Taylor, Michael W. *To Drive the Enemy*, 246.

27. Gallagher, Gary W., *Stephen Dodson Ramseur: Lee's Gallant General*, 57.
28. Gallagher, Gary W., *Stephen Dodson Ramseur: Lee's Gallant General*, 57.
29. Bone, John W., *Record of a Soldier in the Late War*, 47, 49.
30. Ramseur, Stephen D., *Official Records*, Vol. 25, Pt. 1, 995.
31. Rodes, Robert E., *Official Records*, Vol. 25, Pt. 1, 940.
32. Bone, John W., "Visiting Virginia Battlefields," *Confederate Veteran*, Vol. 34 (1926), 10.
33. Freeman, Douglas S., *Lee's Lieutenants*, Vol. 2, 548.
34. Bennett, R. T., "Fourteenth Regiment," in Clark, Walter (ed.), *Histories of the Several Regiments*, Vol. 1, 715.
35. Gallagher, Gary W., *Stephen Dodson Ramseur: Lee's Gallant General*, 58.
36. Steadman, Charles M., "Gen. Stephen Dodson Ramseur," *Confederate Veteran*, Vol. 28 (1920), 454.
37. Freeman, Douglas S., *Lee's Lieutenants*, Vol. 2, 555.
38. Freeman, Douglas S., *Lee's Lieutenants*, Vol. 2, 558.
39. Howard, Oliver O., *Official Records*, Vol. 25, Pt. 1, 630.
40. Howard, Oliver O., *Official Records*, Vol. 25, Pt. 1, 630.
41. Freeman, Douglas S., *Lee's Lieutenants*, Vol. 2, 557.
42. Ramseur, Stephen D., *Official Records*, Vol. 25, Pt. 1, 995.
43. Ramseur, Stephen D., *Official Records*, Vol. 25, Pt. 1, 995.
44. Bennett, R. T., "Fourteenth Regiment," in Clark, Walter (ed.), *Histories of the Several Regiments*, Vol. 1, 715.
45. Ramseur, Stephen D., *Official Records*, Vol. 25, Pt. 1, 995.
46. Rodes, Robert E., *Official Records*, Vol. 25, Pt. 1, 941.
47. Bennett, R. T., "Fourteenth Regiment," in Clark, Walter (ed.), *Histories of the Several Regiments*, Vol. 1, 715.
48. Taylor, Michael W. *To Drive the Enemy*, 249.
49. Bauer, K. Jack (ed.), *Soldiering: The Civil War Diary of Rice C. Bull* (Novato, CA: Presidio, 1977), 52–3.
50. Grimes, Bryan, in Cowper, Pulaski, *Extracts of Letters of Bryan Grimes to His Wife*, 31.
51. Bone, John W., "Visiting Virginia Battlefields," *Confederate Veteran*, Vol. 34 (1926), 10.
52. Ardrey, William E., Diary, 2 May 1863.
53. Venner, William Thomas, *The Seventh Tennessee Infantry*, 71.
54. Ross, Samuel, *Official Records*, Vol. 25, Pt. 1, 699.
55. Freeman, Douglas S., *Lee's Lieutenants*, Vol. 2, 586.
56. Goolrick, William K., *Rebels Resurgent: Fredericksburg to Chancellorsville* (Alexandria, VA: Time-Life, 1985), 142.
57. Sears, Stephen W., *Chancellorsville* (Boston, MA: Houghlin Mifflin, 1996), 336.
58. Steadman, Charles M., "Gen. Stephen Dodson Ramseur," *Confederate Veteran*, Vol. 28 (1920), 454.
59. Rodes, Robert E., *Official Records*, Vol. 25, Pt. 1, 943.
60. Ramseur, Stephen D., *Official Records*, Vol. 25, Pt. 1, 995.
61. Bone, John W., *Record of a Soldier in the Late War*, 50.
62. Rodes, Robert E., *Official Records*, Vol. 25, Pt. 1, 944.
63. Terry, William, "The Stonewall Brigade at Chancellorsville," *Southern Historical Society Papers*, 1886, Vol. 14.
64. Osborne, E. A., "Fourth Regiment," in Clark, Walter (ed.), *Histories of the Several Regiments*, Vol. 1, 125.
65. Freeman, Douglas S., *Lee's Lieutenants*, Vol. 2, 595.
66. Ramseur, Stephen D., *Official Reeords*, Vol. 25, Pt. 1, 995.
67. Grimes, Bryan, in Cowper, Pulaski, *Extracts of Letters of Bryan Grimes to His Wife*, 33.
68. Ramseur, Stephen D., *Official Records*, Vol. 25, Pt. 1, 996.
69. Gallagher, Gary W., *Stephen Dodson Ramseur: Lee's Gallant General*, 62.
70. Bennett, R. T., "Fourteenth Regiment," in Clark, Walter (ed.), *Histories of the Several Regiments*, Vol. 1, 716.
71. Ardrey, William E., Diary, 3 May 1863.
72. Smith, William A., *Anson Guards*, 182.
73. Wiley, H. O., "Army Correspondence; 123rd Regt. N. Y. S. Vols.," *Salem Press*, 3 May 1863.
74. Rodes, Robert E., *Official Records*, Vol. 25, Pt. 1, 944.
75. Bennett, R. T., "Fourteenth Regiment," in Clark, Walter (ed.), *Histories of the Several Regiments*, Vol. 1, 716.
76. Ramseur, Stephen D., *Official Records*, Vol. 25, Pt. 1, 996.
77. Francine, Louis R., *Official Records*, Vol. 25, Pt. 1, 478.
78. Bennett, R. T., "Fourteenth Regiment," in Clark, Walter (ed.), *Histories of the Several Regiments*, Vol. 1, 716.
79. Ramseur, Stephen D., *Official Records*, Vol. 25, Pt. 1, 996.
80. Putnam, S., letter, 3 May 1863, in Green family collection.
81. Harding, E. H., "Sketch of Major General S. D. Ramseur," in Schenck, David, *Sketches of Maj. Gen. Stephen Dodson Ramseur* (self-published, 1892), 35.
82. Stuart, J. E. B., *Official Records*, Vol. 25, Pt. 1, 889.
83. Ramseur, Stephen D., *Official Records*, Vol. 25, Pt. 1, 996.
84. Manly, Matt, "Second Regiment, "in Clark, Walter (ed.), *Histories of the Several Regiments*, Vol. 1, 170.
85. Sears, Stephen W., *Chancellorsville*, 336.
86. Putnam, S., letter, 3 May 1863, in Green family collection.
87. Gales, Seaton, *Official Records*, Vol. 25, Pt. 1, 998.
88. Francine, Louis R., *Official Records*, Vol. 25, Pt. 1, 478.
89. Bone, John W., *Record of a Soldier in the Late War*, 50.
90. Taylor, Michael W., *To Drive the Enemy*, 263.
91. Parker, Francis M., "Thirtieth Regiment," in Clark, Walter (ed.), *Histories of the Several Regiments*, Vol. 2, 501.
92. Bone, John W., *Record of a Soldier in the Late War*, 50.
93. Stewart, George R., *Pickett's Charge: A Microhistory of the Final Attack at Gettysburg, July 3, 1863* (Boston, MA: Houghton Mifflin, 1959), 168.
94. Parker, Francis M., "Thirtieth Regiment," in Clark, Walter (ed.), *Histories of the Several Regiments*, Vol. 2, 501.
95. Gibbon, John, *The Artilleryist Manual* (New York: D. Van Nostrand, 1860), 540–5.
96. Odom, Jacob; Griffin, John B.; Winstead, George T.; Hartis, Wilson L.; Barnett, Robert; Glover, Benjamin C., *CSCR*.
97. Bishop, Samuel D.; Brack, Baker B.; Brack, George W.; Newsom, John G.; Duke, George J.; Bobbitt, Burwell B., *CSCR*.
98. Royal, Hardy S.; Crumpler, James M.; Butler, Edward N.; Naylor, Ransom; Taylor, William J., *CSRC*.
99. Bone, John W., *Record of a Soldier in the Late War*, 50.
100. Ardrey, William E., Diary, 3 May 1863.
101. Hobgood, James M.; Brantley, Steve, personal communication, 3 June 2015.
102. Gallagher, Gary W., *Stephen Dodson Ramseur: Lee's Gallant General*, 62.
103. Doubleday, Abner, *Chancellorsville and Gettysburg*, 48.
104. Bigelow, John, Jr., *The Campaign of Chancellorsville: A Strategic and Tactical Study* (New Haven, CT: Yale University Press, 1910), 361.
105. Greer, Lewis T.; Wallace, William T.; Crumpler, Robert M.; Hundley, George W.; Ferrell, James E., Johnson, Ellis; Batchelor, Henry H.; Witherspoon, Mitty T., *CSRC*.
106. Bone, John W., *Record of a Soldier in the Late War*, 50.
107. Smith, William A., *Anson Guards*, 178.

108. Parker, Francis M., "Thirtieth Regiment," in Clark, Walter (ed.), *Histories of the Several Regiments*, Vol. 2, 501.
109. Ramseur, Stephen D., *Official Records*, Vol. 25, Pt. 1, 996.
110. Ramseur, Stephen D., *Official Records*, Vol. 25, Pt. 1, 997.
111. Gallagher, Gary W., *Stephen Dodson Ramseur: Lee's Gallant General*, 63.
112. Parker, Francis M., "Thirtieth Regiment," in Clark, Walter (ed.), *Histories of the Several Regiments*, Vol. 2, 501.
113. Parker, Francis M., letter, 9 May 1863.
114. Shew, Jacob W.; Pegram, Robert B.; Wheeler, John W.; Bennett, Solomon W.; Wiggins, Martin W.; Shaw, Douglas C., *CSRC*.
115. Williford, Burton B., letter, 11 May 1863, *CSRC*.
116. Ardrey, William E., Diary, 3 May 1863.
117. Ardrey, William E., Diary, 3 May 1863.
118. Jackson, Archibald A., letter, 15 May 1863, in Taylor, Michael W., *To Drive the Enemy*, 266.
119. Gallagher, Gary W., *Stephen Dodson Ramseur: Lee's Gallant General*, 62–3.
120. 30th North Carolina Regiment. *CSRC*.
121. Johnson, Robert U., and Clarence C. Buel, *Battles and Leaders of the Civil War*, Vol. 3, 238.
122. Ramseur, Stephen D., *Official Records*, Vol. 25, Pt. 1, 997.
123. Bone, John W., *Record of a Soldier in the Late War*, 51.
124. Collins, Darrell L., *Major General Robert E. Rodes of the Army of Northern Virginia: A Biography* (New York: Savas Beatie, 2008), 229.
125. Ardrey, William E., Diary, 3 May 1863.
126. Smith, William A., *Anson Guards*, 183.
127. Collins, Darrell L., *Major General Robert E. Rodes*, 230.
128. Freeman, Douglas S., *Lee's Lieutenants*, Vol. 2, 598.
129. Bone, John W., *Record of a Soldier in the Late War*, 51.
130. Parker, Francis M., letter, 9 May 1863.
131. Witherspoon, John G., letter, 4 May 1863.
132. Bone, John W., *Record of a Soldier in the Late War*, 56.
133. Collins, Darrell L., *Major General Robert E. Rodes*, 228.

Chapter 8

1. Ardrey, William E., Diary, 4 May 1863.
2. Ardrey, William E., Diary, 4 May 1863.
3. Ardrey, William E., Diary, 5 May 1863.
4. Rodes, Robert E., *Official Records*, Vol. 25, Pt. 1, 945.
5. Ardrey, William E., Diary, 7 May 1863.
6. Rodes, Robert E., *Official Records*, Vol. 25, Pt. 1, 946.
7. Freeman, Douglas S., *Lee's Lieutenants*, Vol. 2, 674.
8. Ardrey, William E., Diary, 8 May 1863.
9. Betts, Alexander, *Experience of a Confederate Chaplain*, 8–10 May 1863.
10. Ardrey, William E., Diary, 8 May 1863.
11. Betts, Alexander, *Experience of a Confederate Chaplain*, 10 May 1863.
12. Ardrey, William E., Diary, 11 May 1863.
13. Grimes, Bryan, in Cowper, Pulaski, *Extracts of Letters of Bryan Grimes to His Wife*, 37.
14. Taylor, Michael W., *To Drive the Enemy*, 270.
15. Griffin, L., letter, 17 May 1863, in Green family collection.
16. Ardrey, William E., Diary, 12 May 1863.
17. Claireborne, Robert F., letter, 11 May 1863, *CSRC*.
18. Griffin, L., letter, 17 May 1863, in Green family collection.
19. Ardrey, William E., Diary, 20 May 1863.
20. Parker, Francis M., letter, 21 May 1863.
21. Parker, Francis M., letter, 21 May 1863.
22. Witherspoon, John, G., letter, 21 May 1863.
23. Ardrey, William E., Diary, 20 May 1863.
24. Freeman, Douglas S., *Lee's Lieutenants*, Vol. 2, 695–6.
25. Johnson, Robert U., and Clarence C. Buel, *Battles and Leaders of the Civil War*, Vol. 3, 438.
26. Ardrey, William E., Diary, 25 May 1863.
27. Harris, James, letter 24 August 1863, in Taylor, Michael W., *To Drive the Enemy from Southern Soil*, 397–416.
28. Parker, Francis M., letter, 31 May 1863.
29. Jones, Terry L. (ed.), *Campbell Brown's Civil War: With Ewell and the Army of Northern Virginia* (Baton Rouge: Louisiana State University Press, 2001), 186.
30. Harris, James, letter 24 August 1863, in Taylor, Michael W., *To Drive the Enemy from Southern Soil*, 397–416.
31. Ardrey, William E., Diary, 3 June 1863.
32. Ardrey, William E., Diary, 4 June 1863.
33. Ardrey, William E., Diary, 5 June 1863.
34. Betts, Alexander, *Experience of a Confederate Chaplain*, 6 June 1863.
35. Rodes, Robert E., *Official Records*, Vol. 27, Pt. 2, 546.
36. Rodes, Robert E., *Official Records*, Vol. 27, Pt. 2, 547.
37. Ardrey, William E., Diary, 11 June 1863.
38. Ardrey, William E., Diary, 12 June 1863.
39. Rodes, Robert E., *Official Records*, Vol. 27, Pt. 2, 547.
40. Harris, James, letter 24 August 1863, in Taylor, Michael W., *To Drive the Enemy from Southern Soil*, 397–416.
41. Ardrey, William E., Diary, 13 June 1863.
42. Harris, James, letter 24 August 1863, in Taylor, Michael W., *To Drive the Enemy from Southern Soil*, 397–416.
43. Ardrey, William E., Diary, 14 June 1863.
44. Bennett, R. T., "Fourteenth Regiment," in Clark, Walter (ed.), *Histories of the Several Regiments*, Vol. 1, 718.
45. Rodes, Robert E., *Official Records*, Vol. 27, Pt. 2, 549.
46. Harris, James, letter 24 August 1863, in Taylor, Michael W., *To Drive the Enemy from Southern Soil*, 397–416.
47. Smith, William A., *Anson Guards*, 198–9.
48. Harris, James, letter 24 August 1863, in Taylor, Michael W., *To Drive the Enemy from Southern Soil*, 397–416.
49. Gorman, George (ed.), "Memoirs of a Rebel being the Narratives of John Calvin Gorman, Captain, Company B, 2nd North Carolina Regiment, 1861–1865: Part II; Chancellorsville and Gettysburg," *Military Images*, Vol. 3, no. 6 (May-June, 1982), 24.
50. Smith, William A., *Anson Guards*, 198–9.
51. Rodes, Robert E., *Official Records*, Vol. 27, Pt. 2, 550.
52. Rodes, Robert E., *Official Records*, Vol. 27, Pt. 2, 550.
53. Rodes, Robert E., *Official Records*, Vol. 27, Pt. 2, 550.
54. Harris, James, letter 24 August 1863, in Taylor, Michael W., *To Drive the Enemy from Southern Soil*, 397–416.
55. Venner, William Thomas, *The 11th North Carolina Infantry in the Civil War*, 67.
56. Lineback, Julius, letter, 25 June 1863, in Venner, William Thomas, *The 11th North Carolina Infantry in the Civil War*, 67.
57. Harris, James, letter 24 August 1863, in Taylor, Michael W., *To Drive the Enemy from Southern Soil*, 397–416.

58. Ardrey, William E., Diary, 15 June 1863.
59. Ardrey, William E., Diary, 17–8 June 1863.
60. Bennett, R. T., "Fourteenth Regiment," in Clark, Walter (ed.), *Histories of the Several Regiments*, Vol. 1, 718.
61. Ardrey, William E., Diary, 18 June 1863.
62. Ardrey, William E., Diary, 17 June 1863.
63. Betts, Alexander, *Experience of a Confederate Chaplain*, 22 June 1863.
64. Davis, Archie K., *Boy Colonel of the Confederacy: The Life and Times of Henry King Burgwyn, Jr.* (Chapel Hill: University of North Carolina Press, 1985), 272.
65. Betts, Alexander, *Experience of a Confederate Chaplain*, 20 June 1863.
66. Rodes, Robert E., *Official Records*, Vol. 27, Pt. 2, 551.
67. Rodes, Robert E., *Official Records*, Vol. 27, Pt. 2, 551.
68. Freeman, Douglas S., *Lee's Lieutenants*, Vol. 3, 30.
69. Hess, Earl J., *Lee's Tar Heels: The Pettigrew-Kirkland-MacRae Brigade* (Chapel Hill: University of North Carolina Press, 2002), 114.
70. Ardrey, William E., Diary, 22 June 1863.
71. Rodes, Robert E., *Official Records*, Vol. 27, Pt. 2, 551.
72. Smith, William A., *Anson Guards*, 200.
73. Gragg, Rod, *Covered with Glory: The 26th North Carolina Infantry at the Battle of Gettysburg* (New York: HarperCollins, 2000), 65.
74. Hotchkins, Jedediah, *Make Me a Map of the Valley: The Civil War Journal of Stonewall Jackson's Topographer* (Dallas, TX: Southern Methodist University Press, 1973), 155.
75. Parker, Francis M., letter, 23 June 1863.
76. Lineback, Julius, letter, 27 June 1863, in Venner, William Thomas, *The 11th North Carolina Infantry in the Civil War*, 67.
77. Venner, William Thomas, *The 7th Tennessee Infantry in the Civil War*, 78.
78. Freeman, Douglas S., *Lee's Lieutenants*, Vol. 3, 36.
79. Harris, James, letter 24 August 1863, in Taylor, Michael W., *To Drive the Enemy from Southern Soil*, 397–416.
80. Smith, William A., *Anson Guards*, 200.
81. Freeman, Douglas S., *Lee's Lieutenants*, Vol. 3, 36.
82. Ardrey, William E., Diary, 24–5 June 1863.
83. Ardrey, William E., Diary, 27 June 1863.
84. Betts, Alexander, *Experience of a Confederate Chaplain*, 27 June 1863.
85. Parker, Francis M., "Thirtieth Regiment," in Clark, Walter (ed.), *Histories of the Several Regiments*, Vol. 2, 502.
86. Ardrey, William E., Diary, 28 June 1863.
87. Harris, James, letter 24 August 1863, in Taylor, Michael W., *To Drive the Enemy from Southern Soil*, 397–416.
88. Sillers, William, letter, 7 August 1863.
89. Ardrey, William E., Diary, 28 June 1863.
90. Ardrey, William E., Diary, 29 June 1863.
91. Parker, Francis M., letter, 23 June 1863.
92. Rodes, Robert E., *Official Records*, Vol. 27, Pt. 2, 551.
93. Harris, James, letter 24 August 1863, in Taylor, Michael W., *To Drive the Enemy from Southern Soil*, 397–416.
94. Harris, James, letter 24 August 1863, in Taylor, Michael W., *To Drive the Enemy from Southern Soil*, 397–416.
95. Freeman, Douglas S., *Lee's Lieutenants*, Vol. 3, 38.
96. Betts, Alexander, *Experience of a Confederate Chaplain*, 30 June 1863.

Chapter 9

1. 30th North Carolina Regiment. CSRC.
2. 30th North Carolina Regiment. CSRC.
3. Welch, Spencer, *A Confederate Surgeon's Letters to His Wife* (New York: Neale, 1911), 57.
4. Grimes, Bryan, in Cowper, Pulaski, *Extracts of Letters of Bryan Grimes to His Wife*, 37.
5. Gallagher, Gary W., *Stephen Dodson Ramseur: Lee's Gallant General*, 76.
6. Ramseur, Stephen D., *Official Records*, Vol. 27, Pt. 2, 587.
7. Freeman, Douglas, *Lee's Lieutenants*, Vol. 3, 78.
8. Rodes, Robert E., *Official Records*, Vol. 27, Pt. 2, 553.
9. Harris, James, letter 24 August 1863, in Taylor, Michael W., *To Drive the Enemy from Southern Soil*, 397–416.
10. Smith, William A., *Anson Guards*, 201.
11. Murdock, Alexander, letter, 10 August 1863.
12. Harris, James, letter 24 August 1863, in Taylor, Michael W., *To Drive the Enemy from Southern Soil*, 397–416.
13. Harris, James, letter 24 August 1863, in Taylor, Michael W., *To Drive the Enemy from Southern Soil*, 397–416.
14. Osborne, E. A., "Fourth Regiment," in Clark, Walter (ed.), *Histories of the Several Regiments*, Vol. 1, 253. Ramseur, Stephen D., *Official Records*, Vol. 27, Pt. 2, 587.
15. Murdock, Alexander, letter, 10 August 1863.
16. Steadman, Charles M., "Gen. Stephen Dodson Ramseur," *Confederate Veteran*, Vol. 28 (1920), 454.
17. Murdock, Alexander, letter, 10 August 1863.
18. Ramseur, Stephen D., *Official Records*, Vol. 27, Pt. 2, 587.
19. Murdock, Alexander, letter, 10 August 1863.
20. Freeman, Douglas, *Lee's Lieutenants*, Vol. 3, 83.
21. Freeman, Douglas, *Lee's Lieutenants*, Vol. 3, 86.
22. Rodes, Robert E., *Official Records*, Vol. 27, Pt. 2, 553.
23. Runge, William H. (ed.), *Four Years in the Confederate Artillery: The Diary of Pvt. H. R. Berkeley* (Chapel Hill: University of North Carolina Press, 1961), 50.
24. Osborne, E. A., "Fourth Regiment," in Clark, Walter (ed.), *Histories of Several Regiments*, Vol. 1, 253.
25. Ramseur, Stephen D., *Official Records*, Vol. 27, Pt. 2, 587.
26. Murdock, Alexander, letter, 10 August 1863.
27. Vick, Robert, personal communication, 3 June 2015.
28. Harris, James, letter, 24 August 1863, in Taylor, Michael W., *To Drive the Enemy from Southern Soil*, 397–416.
29. Ardrey, William E., *Diary*, 1 July 1863.
30. Harris, James, letter, 24 August 1863, in Taylor, Michael W., *To Drive the Enemy from Southern Soil*, 397–416.
31. Davis, Charles E., *Three Years in the Army: The Story of the Thirteenth Massachusetts Volunteers* (Boston, MA: Estes and Lauriat, 1894), 227.
32. Smith, William A., *Anson Guards*, 206.
33. Lambeth, J. H., *Official Records*, Vol. 27, Pt. 2, 590.
34. Davis, Charles E., *Three Years in the Army*, 227.
35. Wicker, Lewis M.; Wicker, Thomas, CSRC.
36. Merritt, Isaac W.; Southerland, James; Westray, Archibald H., CSRC.
37. Betts, Alexander, *Experience of a Confederate Chaplain*, 39–40. Allen, Charles N.; Cheatham, Thomas; McAulay, William; Hewett, Samuel M., CSRC.
38. Williams, Robert D.; Barker, John W.; Crisp, Levi, CSRC.
39. Parker, Francis M, "Thirtieth Regiment, in Clark, Walter (ed.), *Histories of the Several Regiments*, Vol. 2, 502.
40. Fisher, J. B., "From the 104th

Regiment," *New York Herald*, 2 July 1863.
41. Taylor, Michael W., *To Drive the Enemy*, 291.
42. Bennett, Risden T., "Fourteenth Regiment," in Clark, Walter (ed.), *Histories of the Several Regiments*, Vol. 1, 719.
43. Smith, William A., *Anson Guards*, 207.
44. Harris, James, letter, 24 August 1863, in Taylor, Michael W., *To Drive the Enemy from Southern Soil*, 397–416.
45. Smith, Benjamin; Hight, Joseph J.; Whitley, Jolley B.; Brown, Alexander H., *CSRC*.
46. DeArmond, Aaron, letter 5 July 1863, in Brown, Martha R., *Holding Sweet Communion*.
47. Betts, Alexander, *Experience of a Confederate Chaplain*, 39–40.
48. Ramseur, Stephen D., *Official Records*, Vol. 27, Pt. 2, 587.
49. Davis, Charles E., *Three Years in the Army*, 228.
50. Rucker, E., *CSRC*. Ardrey, William, *Diary*, 1 July 1863.
51. Harris, James, letter, 24 August 1863, in Taylor, Michael W., *To Drive the Enemy from Southern Soil*, 397–416.
52. Davis, Charles E., *Three Years in the Army*, 228.
53. Prey, Gilbert, "Our Army Correspondence," *New Yorker*, 9 July 1863.
54. "Correspondence of the Union," *New York Herald*, 12 August 1863.
55. Ramseur, Stephen D., *Official Records*, Vol. 27, Pt. 2, 587.
56. Harris, James, letter, 24 August 1863, in Taylor, Michael W., *To Drive the Enemy from Southern Soil*, 397–416.
57. Harris, James, letter, 24 August 1863, in Taylor, Michael W., *To Drive the Enemy from Southern Soil*, 397–416.
58. Bennett, Risden T., "Fourteenth Regiment," in Clark, Walter (ed.), *Histories of the Several Regiments*, Vol. 1, 719.
59. Freeman, Douglas, *Lee's Lieutenants*, Vol. 3, 88.
60. Smith, William A., *Anson Guards*, 207.
61. Williams, Orren, *Official Records*, Vol. 27, Pt. 2, 589.
62. McCardell, Paul, "The Weather during the Battle of Gettysburg," *The Baltimore Sun*, 29 June 2013.
63. Grimes, Bryan, *Official Records*, Vol. 27, Pt. 2, 589.
64. Ramseur, Stephen D., *Official Records*, Vol. 27, Pt. 2, 587.
65. Bates, Samuel P., *History of the Pennsylvania Volunteers* (Harrisburg, PA: State Printer, 1869–71), Vol. 4, 652.
66. Harris, James, letter, 24 August 1863, in Taylor, Michael W., *To Drive the Enemy from Southern Soil*, 397–416.
67. Bennett, Risden T., "Fourteenth Regiment," in Clark, Walter (ed.), *Histories of the Several Regiments*, Vol. 1, 719.
68. Rodes, Robert E., *Official Records*, Vol. 27, Pt. 2, 553.
69. Steadman, Charles M, "Gen. Stephen Dodson Ramseur," *Confederate Veteran*, Vol. 28 (1920), 454.
70. Ramseur, Stephen D., *Official Records*, Vol. 27, Pt. 2, 587.
71. Grimes, Bryan, *Official Records*, Vol. 27, Pt. 2, 589.
72. Murdock, Alexander, letter, 10 August 63.
73. Rodes, Robert E., *Official Records*, Vol. 27, Pt. 2, 553.
74. Lambeth, J. H., *Official Records*, Vol. 27, Pt. 2, 590.
75. Rodes, Robert E., *Official Records*, Vol. 27, Pt. 2, 553.
76. Murdock, Alexander, letter, 10 August 63.
77. Harris, James, letter, 24 August 1863, in Taylor, Michael W., *To Drive the Enemy from Southern Soil*, 397–416.
78. Smith, William A., *Anson Guards*, 207.
79. Rodes, Robert E., *Official Records*, Vol. 27, Pt. 2, 555.
80. Bennett, Risden T., "Fourteenth Regiment," in Clark, Walter (ed.), *Histories of the Several Regiments*, Vol. 1, 720.
81. Ramseur, Stephen D., *Official Records*, Vol. 27, Pt. 2, 587.
82. Harris, James, letter, 24 August 1863, in Taylor, Michael W., *To Drive the Enemy from Southern Soil*, 397–416.
83. Harris, James, letter, 24 August 1863, in Taylor, Michael W., *To Drive the Enemy from Southern Soil*, 397–416.
84. Harris, James, letter, 24 August 1863, in Taylor, Michael W., *To Drive the Enemy from Southern Soil*, 397–416.
85. Harris, James, letter, 24 August 1863, in Taylor, Michael W., *To Drive the Enemy from Southern Soil*, 397–416.
86. Ramseur, Stephen D., *Official Records*, Vol. 27, Pt. 2, 587.
87. Cheatham, James T., *CSRC*.
88. Rodes, Robert E., *Official Records*, Vol. 27, Pt. 2, 556.
89. Harris, James, letter, 24 August 1863, in Taylor, Michael W., *To Drive the Enemy from Southern Soil*, 397–416.
90. Harris, James, letter, 24 August 1863, in Taylor, Michael W., *To Drive the Enemy from Southern Soil*, 397–416.
91. Harris, James, letter, 24 August 1863, in Taylor, Michael W., *To Drive the Enemy from Southern Soil*, 397–416.
92. Ramseur, Stephen D., *Official Records*, Vol. 27, Pt. 2, 587.
93. Rodes, Robert E., *Official Records*, Vol. 27, Pt. 2, 556.
94. Harris, James, letter, 24 August 1863, in Taylor, Michael W., *To Drive the Enemy from Southern Soil*, 397–416.
95. Harris, James, letter, 24 August 1863, in Taylor, Michael W., *To Drive the Enemy from Southern Soil*, 397–416.
96. Rodes, Robert E., *Official Records*, Vol. 27, Pt. 2, 556.
97. Harris, James, letter, 24 August 1863, in Taylor, Michael W., *To Drive the Enemy from Southern Soil*, 397–416.
98. Utley, John W., *CRCS*.
99. Philips, Frederick, letter, 27 October 1891, in Taylor, Michael, *To Drive the Enemy from Southern Soil*, 410.
100. Harris, James, letter, 24 August 1863, in Taylor, Michael W., *To Drive the Enemy from Southern Soil*, 397–416.
101. Harris, James, letter, 24 August 1863, in Taylor, Michael W., *To Drive the Enemy from Southern Soil*, 397–416.
102. Hood, William L., *CSRC*.
103. Sillers, William, *Official Records*, Vol. 27, Pt. 2, 591.
104. Bennett, Risden T., "Fourteenth Regiment," in Clark, Walter (ed.), *Histories of the Several Regiments*, Vol. 1, 720.
105. Stewart, George W., *Pickett's Charge*, 127.
106. Harris, James, letter, 24 August 1863, in Taylor, Michael W., *To Drive the Enemy from Southern Soil*, 397–416.
107. Chapman, Craig, S, *More Terrible Than Victory*, 107.
108. Rodes, Robert E., *Official Records*, Vol. 27, Pt. 2, 557.
109. *North Carolina Standard*, 29 July 1863.
110. Harris, James, letter, 24 August 1863, in Taylor, Michael W., *To Drive the Enemy from Southern Soil*, 397–416.
111. McConnel, Ira T.; Hathaway, Henry; Johnson, Major O., *CSRC*.
112. Ramseur, Stephen D., *Official Records*, Vol. 27, Pt. 2, 588.
113. Stewart, George W., *Pickett's Charge*, 138.
114. Brewer, Abramam H.; Madra, George A., *CSRC*.
115. Harris, James, letter, 24 August 1863, in Taylor, Michael W., *To Drive the Enemy from Southern Soil*, 397–416.
116. Stewart, George W., *Pickett's Charge*, 185.
117. Harris, James, letter, 24 August 1863, in Taylor, Michael W., *To Drive the Enemy from Southern Soil*, 397–416.

118. Venner, William Thomas, *The 7th Tennessee Infantry*, 106–7.
119. Priest, John M., *Into the Fight: Pickett's Charge at Gettysburg* (Shippensburg, PA: White Mane, 1998), 199.
120. Young, Joseph J., *Official Records*, Vol. 27, Pt. 2, 645. *Weekly Standard*, 29 July 1863.
121. Hartwig, D. Scott, *Gettysburg Magazine*, Vol. 4, January 1991, 89–100.
122. Alleman, Tillie Pierce, *At Gettysburg: What a Girl Saw and Heard of the Battle* (New York: W. Lake Borland, 1889), 44.
123. Parker, Francis M.; Swain, George T.; Southerland, James; Bales, Elijah M., *CSRC*.
124. Rodes, Robert E., *Official Records*, Vol. 27, Pt. 2, 557.
125. Harris, James, letter, 24 August 1863, in Taylor, Michael W., *To Drive the Enemy from Southern Soil*, 397–416.
126. Venner, William Thomas, *The 7th Tennessee Infantry*, 113.
127. Betts, Alexander, *Experience of a Confederate Chaplain*, 40.
128. Harris, James, letter, 24 August 1863, in Taylor, Michael W., *To Drive the Enemy from Southern Soil*, 397–416.
129. Lambeth, J. H., *Official Records*, Vol. 27, Pt. 2, 590.
130. Rodes, Robert E., *Official Records*, Vol. 27, Pt. 2, 557.
131. Gragg, Rod, *Covered with Glory*, 209.
132. Freeman, Douglas, *Lee's Lieutenants*, Vol. 3, 165.
133. Peake, Heather, "General John D. Imboden and the Confederate Retreat from Gettysburg," *Civil War Interactive*, http://www.civilwarinteractive.com/ArticleGeneralJohnDImboden.htm.
134. Imboden, John, in Johnson, Robert U., and Clarence C. Buel, *Battles and Leaders*, Vol. 3, 420.
135. Smith, William A., *Anson Guards*, 209.
136. Rodes, Robert E., *Official Records*, Vol. 27, Pt. 2, 558.
137. Harris, James, letter, 24 August 1863, in Taylor, Michael W., *To Drive the Enemy from Southern Soil*, 397–416.
138. Rodes, Robert E., *Official Records*, Vol. 27, Pt. 2, 558.
139. Manarin, Louis H., "Second Regiment N.C. Troops," *North Carolina Troops*, Vol. 3, 376.
140. Rodes, Robert E., *Official Records*, Vol. 27, Pt. 2, 558.
141. Smith, William A., *Anson Guards*, 211.
142. 30th North Carolina Regiment, *CSRC*.
143. Merritt, Isaac W.; Brewer, Abraham H., *CSRC*.
144. Sillers, William, letter, 16 July 1863.
145. Harris, James, letter, 24 August 1863, in Taylor, Michael W., *To Drive the Enemy from Southern Soil*, 397–416.
146. Taylor, Michael W., *To Drive the Enemy*, 295.
147. Betts, Alexander, *Experience of a Confederate Chaplain*, 41.
148. Rodes, Robert E., *Official Records*, Vol. 27, Pt. 2, 558.
149. Harris, James, letter, 24 August 1863, in Taylor, Michael W., *To Drive the Enemy from Southern Soil*, 397–416.
150. Rodes, Robert E., *Official Records*, Vol. 27, Pt. 2, 559.
151. Harris, James, letter, 24 August 1863, in Taylor, Michael W., *To Drive the Enemy from Southern Soil*, 397–416.
152. Rodes, Robert E., *Official Records*, Vol. 27, Pt. 2, 561.
153. Sillers, William, letter, 16 July 1863.
154. Putnam, Samuel, letter, 7 July 1863, in Green family collection.
155. Sillers, William, letter, 16 July 1863.
156. 30th North Carolina Regiment. *CSRC*.

Chapter 10

1. Rodes, Robert E., *Official Records*, Vol. 27, pt. 2: 560–1.
2. DeArmond, Aaron L., letter, 23 July 63, in Brown, Martha R., *Holding Sweet Communion*.
3. Betts, Alexander, *Experience of a Confederate Chaplain*, 27 July 1863.
4. Sillers, William, W., letter, 29 July 1863.
5. Jackson, Archibald A., letter, 30 July 1863, in Taylor, Michael W., *To Drive the Enemy from Southern Soil*, 296.
6. Betts, Alexander, *Experience of a Confederate Chaplain*, 30 July 1863.
7. DeArmond, Aaron L., letter, 31 July 1863, in Brown, Martha R., *Holding Sweet Communion*.
8. 30th North Carolina Regiment, *CSRC*.
9. Ardrey, William E., *Diary*, 21 August 1863.
10. Sillers, William W., letter 7 August 1863.
11. Harris, James I., letter, 24 August 1863, in Walter J. Bone collection.
12. Freeman, Douglas, *Lee's Lieutenants*, Vol. 3, 218.
13. Harris, James I., letter, 24 August 1863, in Walter J. Bone collection.
14. DeArmond, Aaron L., letter, 17 August 1863, in Brown, Martha R., *Holding Sweet Communion*.
15. 30th North Carolina Regiment, *CSRC*.
16. Gallagher, Gary W., *Stephen Dodson Ramseur: Lee's Gallant General*, 76.
17. Ardrey, William E., *Diary*, 22 August 1863.
18. Sillers, William W.; Ardrey, William E.; Holmes, James C., *CSRC*.
19. Ardrey, William E., *Diary*, 1 September 1863.
20. Harris, James I., letter, 24 August 1863, in Walter J. Bone collection.
21. Ardrey, William E., *Diary*, 3–12 September 1863, 14 September 1863.
22. Sillers, William W., letter, 28 September 1863.
23. 30th North Carolina Regiment, *CSRC*.
24. Ardrey, William E., *Diary*, 3 October 1863.
25. Hinshaw, Daniel, *CSRC*.
26. Smith, William A., *Anson Guards*, 216.
27. Webb, Morrison, *CSRC*.
28. Taylor, Michael W., *To Drive the Enemy from Southern Soil*, 299.
29. Smith, William A., *Anson Guards*, 216.
30. Jackson, Marion, J.; Harris, Richard P., *CSRC*.
31. Freeman, Douglas, *Lee's Lieutenants*, Vol. 3, 241.
32. Ardrey, William E., *Diary*, 13 October 1863.
33. *North Carolina Standard*, 27 October 1863.
34. Manarin, Louis H., "Second Regiment N. C. Troops," *North Carolina Troops*, Vol. 3, 376.
35. Freeman, Douglas, *Lee's Lieutenants*, Vol. 3, 247.
36. Ardrey, William E., *Diary*, 14 October 1863.
37. Bradshaw, James B.; Grady, John W.; Ruffin, Charles H., *CSRC*.
38. Betts, Alexander, *Experience of a Confederate Chaplain*, 15 October 1863.
39. Hanes, J. H., letter, 30 October 1863. Catherine Harris papers, Southern Historical Collection, Wilson Library, UNC-Chapel Hill.
40. Grimes, Bryan, in Cowper, Pulaski, *Extracts of Letters of Bryan Grimes to His Wife*, 41.
41. Smith, William A., *Anson Guards*, 217.
42. Ardrey, William E., *Diary*, 17 October 1863.
43. Ardrey, William E., *Diary*, 18 October 1863.
44. Betts, Alexander, *Experience of a Confederate Chaplain*, 28 October 1863.
45. Gallagher, Gary W., *Stephen Dodson Ramseur: Lee's Gallant General*, 84.
46. Welling, Edgar P., "On the Picket Line at Kelly's Ford," Diary of 1st Lieut. Edgar P. Welling, Co. C., 150th New York Volunteers. 150th Regiment NY Infantry website.
47. Welling, Edgar P., "On the Picket Line at Kelly's Ford."

48. Freeman, Douglas, *Lee's Lieutenants*, Vol. 3, 264.
49. Rodes, Robert E., *Official Records*, Vol. 29, Pt. 1, 631.
50. 30th North Carolina Regiment. CSRC.
51. Rodes, Robert E., *Official Records*, Vol. 29, Pt. 1, 631.
52. Sneden, Robert K., in Bryan, Charles F., Kelly, James C., et. al. (ed.). *Images from the Storm: Private Robert Know Sneden* (New York: Free, 2001), 176.
53. Hanes, J. H., letter, 30 October 1863.
54. Randoph, George E., *Official Records*, Vol. 29, Pt. 1, 566.
55. Stevens, Charles A., *Berdan's United States Sharpshooters in the Army of the Potomac, 1861–1865* (St. Paul, MN: The Price-McGill Co., 1892), 367.
56. Manarin, Louis H., "Second Regiment N. C. Troops," *North Carolina Troops*, Vol. 3, 377.
57. Early, Gerald L., *The Second United States Sharpshooters in the Civil War: A History and Roster* (Jefferson, NC: McFarland, 2009), 143.
58. Stevens, Charles A., *Berdan's United States Sharpshooters in the Army of the Potomac*, 367.
59. Arrington, Peter W., "Record of Events," in Taylor, Michael T., *To Drive the Enemy from Southern Soil*, 303–4.
60. Rodes, Robert E., *Official Records*, Vol. 29, Pt. 1, 631.
61. Stevens, Charles A., *Berdan's United States Sharpshooters in the Army of the Potomac*, 367.
62. Randoph, George E., *Official Records*, Vol. 29, Pt. 1, 566.
63. Stevens, Charles A., *Berdan's United States Sharpshooters in the Army of the Potomac*, 367.
64. French, William H., *Official Records*, Vol. 29, Pt. 1, 555.
65. Bone, John W., *Record of a Soldier in the Late War*, 63.
66. Batchelor, William D.; Pridgen, Drewry; McLane, Thomas; Philips, Frederick; Rivenbark, Teachy, CSRC.
67. Boswell, William H.; Dove, Monroe; Williamson, James; Kelly, James M.; David D.; Pruitt, Hampton, CSRC.
68. Stevens, Charles A., *Berdan's United States Sharpshooters in the Army of the Potomac*, 368.
69. Rodes, Robert E., *Official Records*, Vol. 29, Pt. 1, 632.
70. Arrington, Peter W., "Record of Events," in Taylor, Michael T., *To Drive the Enemy from Southern Soil*, 303–4.
71. McFatter, Alexander; Aycock, Samuel; Lewis, John, E.; Johnson, Ira J., CSRC.
72. Randoph, George E., *Official Records*, Vol. 29, Pt. 1, 567.
73. Arrington, Peter W., "Record of Events," in Taylor, Michael T., *To Drive the Enemy from Southern Soil*, 303–4.
74. Parker, Francis, "Thirtieth Regiment, "Clark, Walter (ed.), *Histories of the Several Regiments*," Vol. 2, 503.
75. Rodes, Robert E., *Official Records*, Vol. 29, Pt. 1, 631.
76. Williams, Gary F., letter, 11 November 1863, Sillers collection.
77. Thompson, Andrew J.; Patterson, John J., CSRC.
78. Puckett, Clarence P., "Richard David Brooks—The Young Man at War."
79. House, James W.; Barnes, William S.; Forbes, Arthur, CSRC.
80. Randolph, George E., *Official Records*, Vol. 29, Pt. 1, 567.
81. Vuncannon, John P.; Daniel, William, H., CSRC.
82. Kelly, John P., letter, 4 July 1866, in Witherspoon collection.
83. Stevens, Charles A., *Berdan's United States Sharpshooters in the Army of the Potomac*, 367.
84. Sleeper, J. Henry, *Official Records*, Vol. 29, Pt. 1, 573.
85. Stevens, Charles A., *Berdan's United States Sharpshooters in the Army of the Potomac*, 369.
86. Stevens, Charles A., *Berdan's United States Sharpshooters in the Army of the Potomac*, 369.
87. Early, Gerald L., *The Second United States Sharpshooters in the Civil War*, 143.
88. DeArmond, Aaron L., letter, 17 August 1863, in Brown, Martha R., *Holding Sweet Communion*.
89. Kelly, John P., letter, 4 July 1866, in Witherspoon collection. Davis, Weldon E.; Allen, Elias G.; Boyce, Samuel J., CSRC.
90. DeArmond, Aaron L., letter, 17 August 1863, in Brown, Martha R., *Holding Sweet Communion*.
91. Stevens, Charles A., *Berdan's United States Sharpshooters in the Army of the Potomac*, 369.
92. Stevens, Charles A., *Berdan's United States Sharpshooters in the Army of the Potomac*, 370.
93. Newsom, John G.; Dickey, Zachariah C.; Pender, John, CSRC.
94. Bone, John W., *Record of a Soldier in the Late War*, 63.
95. Gallagher, Gary W., *Stephen Dodson Ramseur: Lee's Gallant General*, 86.
96. Parker, Francis, "Thirtieth Regiment, "Clark, Walter (ed.), *Histories of the Several Regiments*," Vol. 2, 503.
97. Betts, Alexander, *Experience of a Confederate Chaplain*, 7 November 1863.
98. Arrington, Peter W., "Record of Events," in Taylor, Michael T., *To Drive the Enemy from Southern Soil*, 303–4.
99. Smith, William A., *Anson Guards*, 221.
100. Randolph, George E., *Official Records*, Vol. 29, Pt. 1, 568.
101. Bucklyn, John K., *Official Records*, Vol. 29, Pt. 1, 568.
102. 30th North Carolina Regiment. CSRC.
103. 30th North Carolina Regiment. CSRC.
104. Manly, Matt., "Second Regiment," in Clark, Walter (ed.), *Histories of the Several Regiments*, Vol. 1, 171.
105. Parker, Francis, "Thirtieth Regiment, "Clark, Walter (ed.), *Histories of the Several Regiments*," Vol. 2, 503.
106. Ardrey, William E., *Diary*, 7 November 1863.
107. Williams, Gary F., letter 11/11/63, Sillers collection.
108. Kelly, John P., letter 4 July 1866, in Witherspoon collection.
109. Witherspoon, John G.; Davis, Weldon E., CSRC.
110. Stevens, Charles A., *Berdan's United States Sharpshooters in the Army of the Potomac*, 373.
111. Gallagher, Gary W., *Stephen Dodson Ramseur: Lee's Gallant General*, 86.
112. Betts, Alexander, *Experience of a Confederate Chaplain*, 7 November 1863.
113. Arrington, Peter W., "Record of Events," in Taylor, Michael T., *To Drive the Enemy from Southern Soil*, 303–4.
114. Ardrey, William E., *Diary*, 25 December 1863.

Chapter 11

1. Bennett, Risden; Cox, William; Grimes, Bryan, CSRC.
2. Betts, Alexander, *Experience of a Confederate Chaplain*, 10 November 1863.
3. Betts, Alexander, *Experience of a Confederate Chaplain*, 11 November 1863.
4. Ardrey, William E., *Diary*, 16 November 1863.
5. Bone, John W., *Record of a Soldier in the Late War*, 67.
6. Betts, Alexander, *Experience of a Confederate Chaplain*, 23 November 1863.
7. Ardrey, William E., *Diary*, 26 November 1863.
8. Gallagher, Gary W., *Stephen Dodson Ramseur: Lee's Gallant General*, 87.
9. Ardrey, William E., *Diary*, 27 November 1863.
10. Gallagher, Gary W., *Stephen Dodson Ramseur: Lee's Gallant General*, 86.
11. Early, Jubal A., *Official Records*, Vol. 29, Pt. 1, 830.
12. Rodes, Robert F., *Official Records*, Vol. 29, Pt. 1, 877.

13. Meade, George W., *Official Records*, Vol. 29, Pt. 1, 15.
14. Early, Jubal A., *Official Records*, Vol. 29, Pt. 1, 832.
15. Ardrey, William E., *Diary*, 27 November 1863.
16. Ramseur, Stephen D., *Official Records*, Vol. 29, Pt. 1, 886.
17. Pope, William B., *CSRC*.
18. Early, Jubal A., *Official Records*, Vol. 29, Pt. 1, 834.
19. Rodes, Robert F., *Official Records*, Vol. 29, Pt. 1, 878.
20. Meade, George W., *Official Records*, Vol. 29, Pt. 1, 15.
21. Rodes, Robert F., *Official Records*, Vol. 29, Pt. 1, 878.
22. Ramseur, Stephen D., *Official Records*, Vol. 29, Pt. 1, 886.
23. Meade, George W., *Official Records*, Vol. 29, Pt. 1, 15.
24. Gallagher, Gary W., *Stephen Dodson Ramseur: Lee's Gallant General*, 87.
25. Early, Jubal A., *Official Records*, Vol. 29, Pt. 1, 834.
26. Shearin, Richard E., *CSRC*.
27. Grimes, Bryan, in Cowper, Pulaski, *Extracts of Letters of Bryan Grimes to His Wife*, 44.
28. Ent, Uzal W., *The Pennsylvania Reserves in the Civil War: A Comprehensive History* (Jefferson, NC: McFarland, 2014), 233.
29. Grimes, Bryan, in Cowper, Pulaski, *Extracts of Letters of Bryan Grimes to His Wife*, 44.
30. Meade, George W., *Official Records*, Vol. 29, Pt. 1, 16.
31. Ramseur, Stephen D., *Official Records*, Vol. 29, Pt. 1, 887.
32. Ardrey, William E., *Diary*, 2 December 1863.
33. Gallagher, Gary W., *Stephen Dodson Ramseur: Lee's Gallant General*, 89.
34. 30th North Carolina Infantry, *CSRC*.
35. Ardrey, William E., *Diary*, 10 December 1863.
36. 30th North Carolina Infantry, *CSRC*.
37. Ardrey, William E., *Diary*, 11 December 1863.
38. Mitchell, W. S., letter, 26 April 1864, *CSRC*.
39. Ardrey, William E., *Diary*, 11 December 1863.
40. Ardrey, William E., *Diary*, 20 December 1863.
41. Betts, Alexander, *Experience of a Confederate Chaplain*, 23–34 December 1863.
42. Ardrey, William E., *Diary*, 25 December 1863.
43. Betts, Alexander, *Experience of a Confederate Chaplain*, 31 December 1863.
44. Ardrey, William E., *Diary*, 1 January 1864.
45. Ardrey, William E., *Diary*, 2 January 1864.
46. Moore, Willis B., *CSRC*.
47. Betts, Alexander, *Experience of a Confederate Chaplain*, 4 January 1864.
48. Ardrey, William E., *Diary*, 3 January 1864.
49. Battle, Walter, letter, 12 March 1864, in Craig, Joel and Baker, Charlene (ed.), *As You May Never See Us Again: The Civil War Letters of George and Walter Battle, 4th North Carolina Infantry* (Wake Forest, NC: Scuppernong, 2010).
50. Smith, William A., *Anson Guards*, 222–3.
51. Gallagher, Gary W., *Stephen Dodson Ramseur: Lee's Gallant General*, 89.
52. Ardrey, William E., *Diary*, 10 January 1864.
53. Black, Thomas A., *CSRC*.
54. White, James D., *CSRC*.
55. Ardrey, William E., *Diary*, 12 January 1864.
56. Ardrey, William E., *Diary*, 21 January 1864.
57. Parker, Francis M., letter, 26 January 1864.
58. Ardrey, William E., *Diary*, 24 January 1864.
59. Parker, Francis M., letter, 26 January 1864.
60. 30th North Carolina Regiment. *CSRC*.
61. Betts, Alexander, *Experience of a Confederate Chaplain*, 17 January 1864, 13–4 March 1864.
62. Harmon, Troy D., *The Great Revival of 1863: The Effects Upon Lee's Army of Northern Virginia* (Damascus, MD: Penny Hill, 2013), 105.
63. Parker, Francis M., letter, 26 January 1864.
64. Betts, Alexander, *Experience of a Confederate Chaplain*, 30 December 1863.
65. Parker, Francis M., letter, 26 January 1864.
66. Ardrey, William E., *Diary*, 1 February 1864, 5 February 1864.
67. Smith, William A., *Anson Guards*, 67.
68. Isaac, Will L., *Official Records*, Vol. 33, Pt. 1, 136.
69. Owen, Joshua T., *Official Records*, Vol. 33, Pt. 1, 133.
70. Cabell, Henry C., *Official Records*, Vol. 33, Pt. 1, 142.
71. Owen, Joshua T., *Official Records*, Vol. 33, Pt. 1, 133.
72. Ardrey, William E., *Diary*, 6 February 1864.
73. Ardrey, William E., *Diary*, 7 February 1864.
74. Ardrey, William E., *Diary*, 7 February 1864.
75. Betts, Alexander, *Experience of a Confederate Chaplain*, 16–18 February 1864.
76. Penninger, Moses, *CSRC*.
77. Green, James L., letters, 4 March 1864, in Delpino, Irene R., *A Broad River Digest* (Philadelphia, PA: Omega, 1990), 272.
78. Green, James L.; Hunter, John S.; Branch, Everett L., *CSRC*.
79. Ardrey, William E., *Diary*, 18 February 1864.
80. Ardrey, William E., *Diary*, 19 February 1864.
81. Ardrey, William E., *Diary*, 27 February 1864.
82. Green, James L., letters, 4 March 1864.
83. Ardrey, William E., *Diary*, 28 February 1864.
84. Ardrey, William E., *Diary*, 28 February 1864.
85. Battle, Walter, letter, 21 March 1864.
86. Betts, Alexander, *Experience of a Confederate Chaplain*, 22 March 1864.
87. Gallagher, Gary W., *Stephen Dodson Ramseur: Lee's Gallant General*, 94.
88. Parker, Francis M., letter, 22 March 1864.
89. Taylor, Michael W., *To Drive the Enemy*, 319–20.
90. Ramseur, Stephen D., letter, 28 April 1864.
91. Gallagher, Gary W., *Stephen Dodson Ramseur: Lee's Gallant General*, 92.
92. Mitchell, W. S., letter, 26 April 1864, *CSRC*.
93. Green, James L., letter 28 April 1864, in Taylor, Michael W., *To Drive the Enemy*, 320.
94. Taylor, Michael W., *To Drive the Enemy*, 321.
95. Freeman, Douglas, *Lee's Lieutenants*, Vol. 3, 344.
96. Bone, John W., *Record of a Soldier in the Late War*, 67.
97. Freeman, Douglas, *Lee's Lieutenants*, Vol. 3, 345.

Chapter 12

1. Ardrey, William E., *Diary*, 4 May 1864.
2. Ramseur, Stephen D., *Official Records*, Vol. 36, Pt. 1, 1081.
3. 30th North Carolina Regiment. *CSRC*.
4. Smith, William A., *Anson Guards*, 133–4.
5. Freeman, Douglas, *Lee's Lieutenants*, Vol. 3, 349.
6. Gallagher, Gary W., *Stephen Dodson Ramseur: Lee's Gallant General*, 99.
7. Gallagher, Gary W., *Stephen Dodson Ramseur: Lee's Gallant General*, 99.
8. Taylor, Michael W., *To Drive the Enemy from Southern Soil*, 322.
9. Bone, John W., *Records of a Soldier in the Late War*, 72.
10. Bostick, Bryant W.; Sizemore, William P., *CSRC*.

11. Cole, George W.; Pickett, William D., *CSRC*.
12. Dawes, Rufus R., *Service With the Sixth Wisconsin Volunteers* (Marietta, OH: E. R. Alderman and Sons, 1890), 265.
13. Bennet, Risden T., "Fourteenth Regiment," in Clark, Walter (ed.), *Histories of the Several Regiments*, Vol. 1, 721-2.
14. Gallagher, Gary W., *Stephen Dodson Ramseur: Lee's Gallant General*, 100.
15. Grimes, Bryan, in Cowper, Pulaski, *Extracts of Letters of Bryan Grimes to His Wife*, 52.
16. Ramseur, Stephen D., *Official Records*, Vol. 36, Pt. 1, 1082.
17. Ardrey, William E., *Diary*, 6 May 1864.
18. Bennet, Risden T., "Fourteenth Regiment," in Clark, Walter (ed.), *Histories of the Several Regiments*, Vol. 1, 721-2.
19. Puckett, Clarence, "Richard David Brooks: The Young Man at War."
20. Brantley, Steve. Personal Communication, 3 June 2015.
21. Grimes, Bryan, in Cowper, Pulaski, *Extracts of Letters of Bryan Grimes to His Wife*, 53.
22. Gallagher, Gary W., *Stephen Dodson Ramseur: Lee's Gallant General*, 103.
23. Grimes, Bryan, in Cowper, Pulaski, *Extracts of Letters of Bryan Grimes to His Wife*, 53.
24. Ardrey, William E., *Diary*, 7 May 1864.
25. Ramseur, Stephen D., *Official Records*, Vol. 36, Pt. 1, 1082.
26. Gallagher, Gary W., *Stephen Dodson Ramseur: Lee's Gallant General*, 104.
27. Ewell, Richard S., *Official Records*, Vol. 36, Pt. 1, 1071.
28. Battle, Walter, letter, 14 May 1864.
29. Bone, John W., *Records of a Soldier in the Late War*, 73.
30. Gallagher, Gary W., *Stephen Dodson Ramseur: Lee's Gallant General*, 104.
31. Gallagher, Gary W., *Stephen Dodson Ramseur: Lee's Gallant General*, 104.
32. Ardrey, William E., *Diary*, 8 May 1864.
33. Bone, John W., *Records of a Soldier in the Late War*, 73.
34. Osborne, E. A., "Fourth Regiment," in Clark, Walter (ed.), *Histories of the Several Regiments*, Vol. 1, 255.
35. Whitehurst, Thomas; Butler, Joseph; Johnston, Sandy A., *CSRC*.
36. Osborne, E. A., "Fourth Regiment," in Clark, Walter (ed.), *Histories of the Several Regiments*, Vol. 1, 255.
37. Moore, Willis; Morrison, Horace,; North, Joshua, *CSRC*.
38. Ramseur, Stephen D., *Official Records*, Vol. 36, Pt. 1, 1081.
39. Ramseur, Stephen D., *Official Records*, Vol. 36, Pt. 1, 1082.
40. Smith, William A., *Anson Guards*, 235.
41. Ramseur, Stephen D., *Official Records*, Vol. 36, Pt. 1, 1081.
42. Bennett, Risden T., "Fourteenth Regiment," in Clark, Walter (ed.), *Histories of the Several Regiments* Vol. 1, 722.
43. 30th North Carolina Regiment. *CSRC*.
44. Taylor, Michael W., *To Drive the Enemy from Southern Soil*, 322.
45. Bone, John W., *Records of a Soldier in the Late War*, 73.
46. Gallagher, Gary W., *Stephen Dodson Ramseur: Lee's Gallant General*, 105.
47. Ardrey, William E., *Diary*, 9 May 1864.
48. Gallagher, Gary W., *Stephen Dodson Ramseur: Lee's Gallant General*, 105.
49. Gallagher, Gary W., *Stephen Dodson Ramseur: Lee's Gallant General*, 105.
50. Bennett, Risden T., "Fourteenth Regiment," in Clark, Walter (ed.), *Histories of the Several Regiments* Vol. 1, 722.
51. Keiser, Henry, Diary, 10 May 1864. In Wynn, Jake, "The 96th Pennsylvania on May 10, 1864." winninghistory.blogspot.com.
52. Bennett, Risden T., "Fourteenth Regiment," in Clark, Walter (ed.), *Histories of the Several Regiments* Vol. 1, 722.
53. Keiser, Henry, Diary, 10 May 1864.
54. Keiser, Henry, Diary, 10 May 1864.
55. Ardrey, William E., *Diary*, 11 May 1864.
56. Grimes, Bryan, in Cowper, Pulaski, *Extracts of Letters of Bryan Grimes to His Wife*, 53.
57. Osborne, E. A., "Fourth Regiment," in Clark, Walter (ed.), *Histories of the Several Regiments*, Vol. 1, 255.
58. Ewell, Richard S., *Official Records*, Vol. 36, Pt. 1, 1071.
59. Venner, William Thomas, *The 11th North Carolina Infantry*, 146.
60. Freeman, Douglas, *Lee's Lieutenants*, Vol. 3, 398.
61. Gallagher, Gary W., *Stephen Dodson Ramseur: Lee's Gallant General*, 107.
62. Bone, John W., *Records of a Soldier in the Late War*, 74.
63. Bone, John W., *Records of a Soldier in the Late War*, 74.
64. Ewell, Richard S., *Official Records*, Vol. 36, Pt. 1, 1071.
65. Gallagher, Gary W., *Stephen Dodson Ramseur: Lee's Gallant General*, 107.
66. Ramseur, Stephen D., *Official Records*, Vol. 36, Pt. 1, 1082.
67. Ardrey, William E., *Diary*, 12 May 1864.
68. Gallagher, Gary W., *Stephen Dodson Ramseur: Lee's Gallant General*, 107.
69. Hancock, Winfield S., *Official Records*, Vol. 36, Pt. 1, 335.
70. Burns, Michael W., *Official Records*, Vol. 36, Pt. 1, 505.
71. McAllister, Robert, *Official Records*, Vol. 36, Pt. 1, 491.
72. Ardrey, William E., *Diary*, 12 May 1864.
73. Bone, John W., *Records of a Soldier in the Late War*, 74.
74. Ewell, Richard S., *Official Records*, Vol. 36, Pt. 1, 1072.
75. Ramseur, Stephen D., *Official Records*, Vol. 36, Pt. 1, 1082.
76. Ramseur, Stephen D., *Official Records*, Vol. 36, Pt. 1, 1082.
77. Taylor, Michael W., *To Drive the Enemy from Southern Soil*, 322.
78. Hancock, Winfield S., *Official Records*, Vol. 36, Pt. 1, 335-6.
79. Jackson, Archibald J., *CSRC*.
80. Matter, William D., *If It Takes All Summer: The Battle of Spotsylvania* (Chapel Hill: University of North Carolina Press, 1998), 205.
81. Ardrey, William E., *Diary*, 12 May 1864.
82. Bone, John W., *Records of a Soldier in the Late War*, 74.
83. Ramseur, Stephen D., *Official Records*, Vol. 36, Pt. 1, 1082.
84. Gallagher, Gary W., *Stephen Dodson Ramseur: Lee's Gallant General*, 108.
85. Bone, John W., *Records of a Soldier in the Late War*, 74.
86. Bone, John W., *Records of a Soldier in the Late War*, 131.
87. Gallagher, Gary W., *Stephen Dodson Ramseur: Lee's Gallant General*, 108.
88. Smith, William A., *Anson Guards*, 247.
89. Matter, William D., *If It Takes All Summer*, 205.
90. Howard, Thomas M.; Buff, Peter; Cornell, Wyatt G.; Burgess, Hardy, *CSRC*.
91. Gallagher, Gary W., *Stephen Dodson Ramseur: Lee's Gallant General*, 108.
92. Ardrey, William E., *Diary*, 12 May 1864.
93. Gallagher, Gary W., *Stephen Dodson Ramseur: Lee's Gallant General*, 107.
94. Gordon, John B., *Official Records*, Vol. 36, Pt. 1, 336.
95. Gallagher, Gary W., *Stephen Dodson Ramseur: Lee's Gallant General*, 108.
96. Cress, Wiley; Saintsing, John A.; Fulford, John T.; Henderson, Brantley B., *CSRC*.

97. Schoonover, John, *Official Records*, Vol. 36, Pt. 1, 494.
98. Manarin, Louis H., "Second Regiment N. C. Troops," *North Carolina Troops*, Vol. 3, 377.
99. Hancock, Winfield S., *Official Records*, Vol. 36, Pt. 1, 336.
100. Burns, Michael W., *Official Records*, Vol. 36, Pt. 1, 505.
101. McAllister, Robert, *Official Records*, Vol. 36, Pt. 1, 491.
102. Burns, Michael W., *Official Records*, Vol. 36, Pt. 1, 505.
103. Grimes, Bryan, in Cowper, Pulaski, *Extracts of Letters of Bryan Grimes to His Wife*, 54.
104. Grimes, Bryan, in Cowper, Pulaski, *Extracts of Letters of Bryan Grimes to His Wife*, 54.
105. Smith, William A., *Anson Guards*, 247.
106. Bone, John W., *Records of a Soldier in the Late War*, 74.
107. Squires, James W.; Jackson, Burgess C.; Lee, James T.; Pitts, James W.; Underwood, John A.; Bone, John W., *CSRC*.
108. Bone, John W., *Records of a Soldier in the Late War*, 74.
109. Bennett, Risden T., "Fourteenth Regiment," in Clark, Walter (ed.), *Histories of the Several Regiments* Vol. 1, 723.
110. Gallagher, Gary W., *Stephen Dodson Ramseur: Lee's Gallant General*, 108.
111. Schoonover, John, *Official Records*, Vol. 36, Pt. 1, 494.
112. Osborne, E. A., "Fourth Regiment," in Clark, Walter (ed.), *Histories of the Several Regiments*, Vol. 1, 256.
113. Riggan, Charles S.; Shearin, Thomas W.; White, Lallister M.; Burgess, William H.; Wanett, William A., *CSRC*.
114. Ardrey, William E., *Diary*, 12 May 1864.
115. Steadman, Charles M., *Confederate Veteran*, Vol. 28 (1920), 455.
116. Gallagher, Gary W., *Stephen Dodson Ramseur: Lee's Gallant General*, 110.
117. Taylor, Michael W., *To Drive the Enemy from Southern Soil*, 325.
118. Gallagher, Gary W., *Stephen Dodson Ramseur: Lee's Gallant General*, 110.
119. Bennett, Risden T., "Fourteenth Regiment," in Clark, Walter (ed.), *Histories of the Several Regiments* Vol. 1, 724.
120. Hancock, Winfield S., *Official Records*, Vol. 36, Pt. 1, 335.
121. Schoonover, John, *Official Records*, Vol. 36, Pt. 1, 494.
122. Gallagher, Gary W. (ed.), *The Spotsylvania Campaign* (Chapel Hill: University of North Carolina Press, 1998), 105.
123. Osborne, E. A., "Fourth Regiment," in Clark, Walter (ed.), *Histories of the Several Regiments*, Vol. 1, 257.
124. McAllister, Robert, *Official Records*, Vol. 36, Pt. 1, 491.
125. Ramseur, Stephen D., *Official Records*, Vol. 36, Pt. 1, 1082.
126. Taylor, Michael W., *To Drive the Enemy*, 325.
127. McLemore, William S.; Pilgreen, William H.; Williamson, John Bailey; Eagles Lorenzo D.; Eagles, Theodore R., *CSRC*.
128. Ramseur, Stephen D., *Official Records*, Vol. 36, Pt. 1, 1082.
129. Smith, William A., *Anson Guards*, 247.
130. Williams, Gary; Swain, John R.; Wicker, Jesse J., *CSRC*.
131. Ardrey, William E., *Diary*, 12 May 1864.
132. Bone, John W., *Records of a Soldier in the Late War*, 76.
133. Bennet, Risden T., "Fourteenth Regiment," in Clark, Walter (ed.), *Histories of the Several Regiments*, Vol. 1, 723.
134. "Medals of Honor Awarded for Distinguished Services," *Official Records*, Vol. 36, Pt. 1, 1020.
135. Bennett, Risden T., "Fourteenth Regiment," in Clark, Walter (ed.), *Histories of the Several Regiments* Vol. 1, 724.
136. Smith, William A., *Anson Guards*, 247.
137. Smith, William A., *Anson Guards*, 247.
138. Ramseur, Stephen D., *Official Records*, Vol. 36, Pt. 1, 1082.
139. Smith, William A., *Anson Guards*, 247.
140. Osborne, E. A., "Fourth Regiment," in Clark, Walter (ed.), *Histories of the Several Regiments*, Vol. 1, 257.
141. McAllister, Robert, *Official Records*, Vol. 36, Pt. 1, 491.
142. Osborne, E. A., "Fourth Regiment," in Clark, Walter (ed.), *Histories of the Several Regiments*, Vol. 1, 256.
143. Bone, John W., *Records of a Soldier in the Late War*, 75.
144. Dawes, Rufus R., *Service with the Sixth Wisconsin Volunteers*, 268.
145. Taylor, Michael W., *To Drive the Enemy from Southern Soil*, 328.
146. Hendrix, D. I., "That Bloody Angle Battle," *Confederate Veteran*, Vol. 17 (1909), 438.
147. Ewell, Richard S., *Official Records*, Vol. 36, Pt. 1, 1073.
148. Grimes, Bryan, in Cowper, Pulaski, *Extracts of Letters of Bryan Grimes to His Wife*, 54.
149. Bennett, Risden T., "Fourteenth Regiment," in Clark, Walter (ed.), *Histories of the Several Regiments* Vol. 1, 724.
150. Burnside, Ambrose E., *Official Records*, Vol. 36, Pt. 1, 910.
151. Bennett, Risden T., "Fourteenth Regiment," in Clark, Walter (ed.), *Histories of the Several Regiments* Vol. 1, 724.
152. Gallagher, Gary W. (ed.), *The Spotsylvania Campaign*, 105.
153. Smith, William A., *Anson Guards*, 247.
154. Bennett, Risden T., "Fourteenth Regiment," in Clark, Walter (ed.), *Histories of the Several Regiments* Vol. 1, 725.
155. Smith, William A., *Anson Guards*, 241.
156. Harrell, George K.; Price, Thomas, *CSRC*.
157. Gallagher, Gary W., *Stephen Dodson Ramseur: Lee's Gallant General*, 110.
158. Bailey, Young F.; Malpass, Carleton, *CSRC*.
159. Osborne, E. A., "Fourth Regiment," in Clark, Walter (ed.), *Histories of the Several Regiments*, Vol. 1, 257.
160. Thompson, Thomas C., *Official Records*, Vol. 36, Pt. 1, 500.
161. McMillan, John C.; Harris, William H.; Center, Charles H., *CSRC*.
162. Bone, John W., *Records of a Soldier in the Late War*, 77–8.
163. Gallagher, Gary W. (ed.), *The Spotsylvania Campaign*, 104.
164. Brown, John (2nd); Skipper, Wesley W.; Moore, Samuel R., *CSRC*.
165. Gallagher, Gary W., *Stephen Dodson Ramseur: Lee's Gallant General*, 111.
166. McAllister, Robert, *Official Records*, Vol. 36, Pt. 1, 491.
167. Battle, Walter, letter, 17 May 1864.
168. Bennett, Risden T., "Fourteenth Regiment," in Clark, Walter (ed.), *Histories of the Several Regiments* Vol. 1, 724.
169. Schenck, David, *Sketches of Ramseur*, 33.
170. Osborne, E. A., "Fourth Regiment," in Clark, Walter (ed.), *Histories of the Several Regiments*, Vol. 1, 258.
171. Bennett, Risden T., "Fourteenth Regiment," in Clark, Walter (ed.), *Histories of the Several Regiments* Vol. 1, 724.
172. McAllister, Robert, *Official Records*, Vol. 36, Pt. 1, 491.
173. Gallagher, Gary W., *Stephen Dodson Ramseur: Lee's Gallant General*, 111.
174. Crisp, William G.; Harris, James J., *CSRC*.
175. Gallagher, Gary W. (ed.), *The Spotsylvania Campaign*, 105.
176. Ewell, Richard S., *Official Records*, Vol. 36, Pt. 1, 1073.
177. 30th North Carolina Regiment. *CSRC*.
178. Taylor, Michael W., *To Drive the Enemy from Southern Soil*, 329.
179. Grimes, Bryan, in Cowper, Pulaski, *Extracts of Letters of Bryan Grimes to His Wife*, 54.

180. Hancock, Winfield S., *Official Records*, Vol. 36, Pt. 1, 337.
181. Bennett, Risden T., "Fourteenth Regiment," in Clark, Walter (ed.), *Histories of the Several Regiments* Vol. 1, 724.
182. Ardrey, William E., *Diary*, 12 May 1864.
183. Battle, Walter, letter, 17 May 1864.

Chapter 13

1. Freeman, Douglas, *Lee's Lieutenants*, Vol. 3, 407.
2. Taylor, Michael W., *To Drive the Enemy from Southern Soil*, 329.
3. Fuller, Ted, 12 September 2015. Personal Communication.
4. Gallagher, Gary W., *Stephen Dodson Ramseur: Lee's Gallant General*, 111.
5. Freeman, Douglas, *Lee's Lieutenants*, Vol. 3, 408.
6. Ardrey, William E., *Diary*, 13 May 1864.
7. Bone, John W., *Records of a Soldier in the Late War*, 82.
8. Bone, John W., *Records of a Soldier in the Late War*, 82.
9. 30th North Carolina Regiment, CSRC.
10. Bone, John W., *Records of a Soldier in the Late War*, 80.
11. Freeman, Douglas, *Lee's Lieutenants*, Vol. 3, 434.
12. Grimes, Bryan, in Cowper, Pulaski, *Extracts of Letters of Bryan Grimes to His Wife*, 54.
13. Ardrey, William E., *Diary*, 15 May 1864.
14. Bone, John W., *Records of a Soldier in the Late War*, 82.
15. Brown Hamilton A., "First Regiment," in Clark, Walter (ed.), *Histories of the Several Regiments*, Vol. 1, 153.
16. Jordan, Weymouth T., *North Carolina Troops*, Vol. 4, 7.
17. Venner, William Thomas, *The 11th North Carolina Infantry*, 148.
18. Gallagher, Gary W., *Stephen Dodson Ramseur: Lee's Gallant General*, 113.
19. Freeman, Douglas, *Lee's Lieutenants*, Vol. 3, 437.
20. Freeman, Douglas, *Lee's Lieutenants*, Vol. 3, 437.
21. Cutshaw, W. E., "The battle near Spotsylvania Court-House on May 18, 1864," *Southern Historical Society Papers*, Vol. 33, 320.
22. Jaynes, Gregory, *The Killing Ground: Wilderness to Cold Harbor* (Alexandria, VA: Time-Life, 1986), 125.
23. Ramseur, Stephen D., letter, 19 May 1864.
24. Rhea, Gordon C., *To The North Anna: Grant and Lee, May 13–25, 1864* (Baton Rouge: Louisiana State University Press, 2000), 168.
25. Rhea, Gordon C., *To The North Anna: Grant and Lee*, 168.
26. Ramseur, Stephen D., *Official Records*, Vol. 36, Pt. 1, 1083.
27. Kirk, Hyland C., *Heavy Guns and Light: History of the 4th New York Heavy Artillery* (New York: C.T. Dillingham, 1890), 217–8.
28. Ardrey, William E., *Diary*, 19 May 1864.
29. Roe, Alfred S., and Nutt, Charles, *History of the First Regiment of Heavy Artillery Massachusetts Volunteers* (Boston, MA: Commonwealth, 1917), 152.
30. Kirk, Hyland C., *Heavy Guns and Light*, 218.
31. Correspondent, "In Line of Battle in Woods," *Ontario County Times*, 20 May 1864.
32. Rhea, Gordon C., *To The North Anna: Grant and Lee*, 171.
33. Kirk, Hyland C., *Heavy Guns and Light*, 220.
34. 30th North Carolina Regiment. CSRC.
35. Ramseur, Stephen D., *Official Records*, Vol. 36, Pt. 1, 1082.
36. Kirk, Hyland C., *Heavy Guns and Light*, 220.
37. Correspondent, "Camp in Front of Hanover Junction," *Ontario County Times*, 25 May 1864.
38. Correspondent, "Camp in Front of Hanover Junction," *Ontario County Times*, 25 May 1864.
39. Hancock, Winfield S., *Official Records*, Vol. 36, Pt. 1, 337–8.
40. Rhea, Gordon C., *To The North Anna: Grant and Lee*, 172.
41. *Richmond Examiner*, 20 May 1864.
42. Kirk, Hyland C., *Heavy Guns and Light*, 221.
43. Badgett, James W., CSRC.
44. Badgett, James W.; McIver, John D. M.; Wells, James W.; CSRC.
45. Osborne, E. A., "Fourth Regiment," in Clark, Walter (ed.), *Histories of the Several Regiments*, Vol. 1, 258
46. Kirk, Hyland C., *Heavy Guns and Light*, 222.
47. Kirk, Hyland C., *Heavy Guns and Light*, 221–2.
48. Kirk, Hyland C., *Heavy Guns and Light*, 224.
49. Ardrey, William E., *Diary*, 19 May 1864.
50. Dickens, Ephraim; McNeil, Henry J., CSRC.
51. Adams, William; Parker, Francis M.; Burroughs, William A.; Pierce, James M., CSRC.
52. Kirk, Hyland C., *Heavy Guns and Light*, 225.
53. Roe, Alfred S., and Nutt, Charles, *History of the First Regiment of Heavy Artillery Massachusetts Volunteers*, 164.
54. Kirk, Hyland C., *Heavy Guns and Light*, 224.
55. Roe, Alfred S., and Nutt, Charles, *History of the First Regiment of Heavy Artillery Massachusetts Volunteers*, 155.
56. Roe, Alfred S., and Nutt, Charles, *History of the First Regiment of Heavy Artillery Massachusetts Volunteers*, 153.
57. Roe, Alfred S., and Nutt, Charles, *History of the First Regiment of Heavy Artillery Massachusetts Volunteers*, 164.
58. Nichols, Burgess G., CSRC.
59. Roe, Alfred S., and Nutt, Charles, *History of the First Regiment of Heavy Artillery Massachusetts Volunteers*, 157.
60. Kirk, Hyland C., *Heavy Guns and Light*, 228.
61. Roe, Alfred S., and Nutt, Charles, *History of the First Regiment of Heavy Artillery Massachusetts Volunteers*, 155.
62. Ramseur, Stephen D., *Official Records*, Vol. 36, Pt. 1, 1083.
63. Roe, Alfred S., and Nutt, Charles, *History of the First Regiment of Heavy Artillery Massachusetts Volunteers*, 161.
64. Bennett, Risden, "Fourteenth Regiment," in Clark, Walter (ed.), Histories of the Several Regiments, Vol. 1, 726.
65. Kirk, Hyland C., *Heavy Guns and Light*, 225, 231.
66. Ramseur, Stephen D., *Official Records*, Vol. 36, Pt. 1, 1083.
67. Rhea, Gordon C., *To The North Anna: Grant and Lee*, 185.
68. Venable, Charles S., "The Campaign from the Wilderness to Petersburg," *Southern Historical Society Papers*, Vol. 14, 533.
69. Ramseur, Stephen D., *Official Records*, Vol. 36, Pt. 1, 1083.
70. Hancock, Winfield S., *Official Records*, Vol. 36, Pt. 1, 337–8.
71. Rhea, Gordon C., *To The North Anna: Grant and Lee*, 185–6
72. Correspondent, "In Line of Battle in Woods," *Ontario County Times*, 20 May 1864. Roe, Alfred S., and Nutt, Charles, *History of the First Regiment of Heavy Artillery Massachusetts Volunteers*, 155.
73. Rhea, Gordon C., *To The North Anna: Grant and Lee*, 187.
74. Grimes, Bryan, in Cowper, Pulaski, *Extracts of Letters of Bryan Grimes to His Wife*, 55.
75. 30th North Carolina Regiment. CSRC.
76. Osborne, E. A., "Fourth Regiment," in Clark, Walter (ed.), *Histories of the Several Regiments*, Vol. 1, 274.
77. Parker, Francis M, "Thirtieth Regiment," in Clark, Walter (ed.), *Histories of Several Regiments*, Vol. 2, 502–3.
78. Gallagher, Gary W., *Stephen Dodson Ramseur: Lee's Gallant General*, 115.
79. Ardrey, William E., *Diary*, 21 May 1864.
80. Grimes, Bryan, in Cowper, Pulaski, *Extracts of Letters of Bryan Grimes to His Wife*, 56.

81. Ardrey, William E., *Diary*, 23–24 May 1864.
82. Smythe, Thomas A., *Official Records*, Vol. 36, Pt. 1, 450.
83. Cowan, Charles W., *Service of the Tenth New York Volunteers National Zouaves, in the War of the Rebellion* (New York: Charles H. Ludwig, Publisher, 1882), 277.
84. Smythe, Thomas A., *Official Records*, Vol. 36, Pt. 1, 450.
85. Smythe, Thomas A., *Official Records*, Vol. 36, Pt. 1, 450.
86. Smythe, Thomas A., *Official Records*, Vol. 36, Pt. 1, 450.
87. Dudley, Laban; Williams, Joseph D., *CSRC*.
88. Page, Charles D., *History of the Fourteenth Regiment Connecticut*, 282.
89. Grimes, Bryan, in Cowper, Pulaski, *Extracts of Letters of Bryan Grimes to His Wife*, 56.
90. Ellis, Theodore G., *Official Records*, Vol. 36, Pt. 1, 457.
91. Ardrey, William E., *Diary*, 24 May 1864.
92. Lee, Samuel B., *CSRC*.
93. McLure, James A., *CSRC*.
94. Hood, William L., *CSRC*.
95. Smith, John D., *The History of the Nineteenth Regiment of Maine Volunteer Infantry, 1862–1865* (Minneapolis, MN: John Day Smith, 1909), 177–8.
96. Smythe, Thomas A., *Official Records*, Vol. 36, Pt. 1, 451.
97. Grimes, Bryan, in Cowper, Pulaski, *Extracts of Letters of Bryan Grimes to His Wife*, 56.
98. Rhea, Gordon C., *To the North Anna: Grant and Lee*, 348.
99. Rhea, Gordon C., *To the North Anna: Grant and Lee*, 349.
100. Gallagher, Gary W., *Stephen Dodson Ramseur: Lee's Gallant General*, 115.
101. Warner, Ezra J., *Generals in Gray*, 64–5.
102. Taylor, Michael W., *To Drive the Enemy from Southern Soil*, 331.
103. Smith, William A., *Anson Guards*, 244–5.
104. Ardrey, William E., *Diary*, 28 May 1864.
105. Ardrey, William E., *Diary*, 29 May 1864.
106. Thompson, Thomas C., *Official Records*, Vol. 36, Pt. 1, 501.
107. Ramseur, Stephen D., Report, 3 August 1864.
108. Tilton, William S., *Official Records*, Vol. 36, Pt. 1, 564.
109. Langley, Morrison, *CSRC*.
110. Gallagher, Gary W., *Stephen Dodson Ramseur: Lee's Gallant General*, 115.
111. Bennett, Risden, "Fourteenth Regiment," in Clark, Walter (ed.), *Histories of the Several Regiments*, Vol. 1, 727.
112. Brigman, John; Brown, Felix; Massingil, Robert, *CSRC*.
113. Ardrey, William E., *Diary*, 1 June 1864.
114. Ardrey, William E., *Diary*, 2 June 1864.
115. Meservey, Benjamin F., *Official Records*, Vol. 36, Pt. 1, 579.
116. Leentz, John D., *Official Records*, Vol. 36, Pt. 1, 556–7.
117. Ardrey, William E., *Diary*, 2 June 1864.
118. Harney, George, *Official Records*, Vol. 36, Pt. 1, 635.
119. Ardrey, William E., *Diary*, 2 June 1864.
120. Johnston, James H.; Crisp, Silas E., *CSRC*.
121. Webb, Bennett; Blevins, Shadrach, *CSRC*.
122. Butler, Henry G.; Dean, Jesse, *CSRC*. Ardrey, William E., *Diary*, 2 June 1864.
123. Dana, C. A., *Official Records*, Vol. 36, Pt. 1, 86.
124. 30th North Carolina Regiment. *CSRC*.
125. John Lawrence, John; Burroughs, William A.; Brooks, Henry R.; Lanier, Jacob W., *CSRC*.
126. Smith, William A., *Anson Guards*, 244–5.
127. Hofmann, J. William, *Official Records*, Vol. 36, Pt. 1, 627.
128. Ardrey, William E., *Diary*, 2 June 1864.
129. Osborne, E. A., "Fourth Regiment," in Clark, Walter (ed.), *Histories of the Several Regiments*, Vol. 1, 258.
130. Smith, William A., *Anson Guards*, 257.
131. Freeman, Douglas, *Lee's Lieutenants*, Vol. 3, 558–9.

Chapter 14

1. Taylor, Michael W., *To Drive the Enemy from Southern Soil*, 335.
2. Betts, Alexander, *Experience of a Confederate Chaplain*, 13 June 1864.
3. Smith, William A., *The Anson Guards*, 264.
4. Grimes, Bryan, in Cowper, Pulaski, *Extracts of Letters of Bryan Grimes to His Wife*, 58.
5. Puckett, Clarence P., "Richard David Brooks—The Young Man at War."
6. Smith, William A., *The Anson Guards*, 264.
7. Patchan, Scott C., *The Last Battle of Winchester* (El Dorado Hills, CA: Savas Beatie, 2013), 27.
8. Patchan, Scott C., *The Last Battle of Winchester*, 27–31.
9. Patchan, Scott C., *The Last Battle of Winchester*, 25.
10. Patchan, Scott C., *The Last Battle of Winchester*, 24.
11. 30th North Carolina Regiment. *CSRC*.
12. Taylor, Michael W., *To Drive the Enemy from Southern Soil*, 335.
13. Smith, William A., *The Anson Guards*, 264.
14. Smith, William A., *The Anson Guards*, 265.
15. Taylor, Michael W., *To Drive the Enemy from Southern Soil*, 336.
16. Grimes, Bryan, in Cowper, Pulaski, *Extracts of Letters of Bryan Grimes to His Wife*, 58.
17. Smith, William A., *The Anson Guards*, 266.
18. De Armond, Aaron L., "Diary," in Brown, Martha R., *Holding Sweet Communion*.
19. Davis, George B., Perry, Leslie J., Kirkley, Joseph W., *The Official Military Atlas of the Civil War* (New York: Fairfield, 1983), 81.
20. Patchan, Scott C., *Shenandoah Summer: The 1864 Valley Campaign* (Lincoln: University of Nebraska Press, 2007), 19.
21. Smith, William A., *The Anson Guards*, 268.
22. Smith, William A., *The Anson Guards*, 266-8.
23. Osborne, E. A., "Fourth Regiment," in Clark, Walter (ed.), *Histories of the Several Regiments*, Vol. 1, 259.
24. Freeman, Douglas, *Lee's Lieutenants*, Vol. 3, 560.
25. Patchan, Scott C., *Shenandoah Summer: The 1864 Valley Campaign*, 20.
26. Ardrey, William E., *CSRC*.
27. 30th North Carolina Regiment. *CSRC*.
28. Rackley, James M.; Bailey, Elias D., *CSRC*.
29. Eason, James S., *CSRC*.
30. Patchan, Scott C., *Shenandoah Summer: The 1864 Valley Campaign*, 21.
31. Taylor, Michael W., *To Drive the Enemy from Southern Soil*, 338. Early, Jubal A., *Official Records*, Vol. 37, Pt. 1, 348.
32. Smith, William A., *The Anson Guards*, 268.
33. Early, Jubal A., *Official Records*, Vol. 37, Pt. 1, 348.
34. Freeman, Douglas, *Lee's Lieutenants*, Vol. 3, 561.
35. Smith, William A., *The Anson Guards*, 268.
36. Patchan, Scott C., *Shenandoah Summer: The 1864 Valley Campaign*, 20.
37. Freeman, Douglas, *Lee's Lieutenants*, Vol. 3, 561.
38. Ardrey, William E., *Diary*, 21 July 1864.
39. Smith, William A., *The Anson Guards*, 269.
40. Osborne, E. A., "Fourth Regiment," in Clark, Walter (ed.), *Histories of the Several Regiments*, Vol. 1, 259.
41. Early, Jubal A., *Official Records*, Vol. 37, Pt. 1, 348.

42. Betts, Alexander, *Experience of a Confederate Chaplain*, 11 July 1864.
43. Smith, William A., *The Anson Guards*, 269.
44. Early, Jubal A., *Official Records*, Vol. 37, Pt. 1, 348.
45. Cooling, Benjamin F., *The Day Lincoln Was Almost Shot: The Fort Stevens Story* (Lanham, MD: Scarecrow, 2013), 145.
46. Early, Jubal A., *Official Records*, Vol. 37, Pt. 1, 348.
47. De Armond, Aaron L., "Diary," in Brown, Martha R., *Holding Sweet Communion*, 214.
48. Pohl, Robert S., *Urban Legends and Historic Lore of Washington* (Charleston, SC: History, 2013), 63.
49. Smith, William A., *The Anson Guards*, 269.
50. Gallagher, Gary, *Stephen Dodson Ramseur—Lee's Gallant General*, 129.
51. Early, Jubal A., *Official Records*, Vol. 37, Pt. 1, 348.
52. De Armond, Aaron L., "Diary," in Brown, Martha R., *Holding Sweet Communion*, 214.
53. Freeman, Douglas, *Lee's Lieutenants*, Vol. 3, 567.
54. Gallagher, Gary, *Stephen Dodson Ramseur—Lee's Gallant General*, 130.
55. Early, Jubal A., *Official Records*, Vol. 37, Pt. 1, 348.
56. Taylor, Michael W., *To Drive the Enemy from Southern Soil*, 339.
57. Penny, Solomon W.; Dement, Henry, *CSRC*.
58. Pohl, Robert S., *Urban Legends and Historic Lore of Washington*, 64.
59. Welles, Gideon, *Diary of Gideon Wells, Secretary of the Navy Under Lincoln and Johnson* (Boston, MA: Houghton Mifflin, 1911), Vol. 2, 74–5.
60. Cooling, Benjamin F., *The Day Lincoln Was Almost Shot*, 117–24.
61. Cramer, John H., *Lincoln Under Fire: The Complete Account of His Experiences During Early's Attack on Washington* (Knoxville: University of Tennessee Press, 2009), 43–4.
62. Woolcott, Alexander, "Get Down, You Fool!" *Atlantic Monthly*, February 1938, 170–3.
63. Welles, Gideon, *Diary of Gideon Wells*, Vol. 2, 74–5.
64. Welles, Gideon, *Diary of Gideon Wells*, Vol. 2, 74–5.
65. Woolcott, Alexander, "Get Down, You Fool!"
66. Cooling, Benjamin F., *The Day Lincoln Was Almost Shot*, 117–24.
67. Wheaton, Frank, *Official Records*, Vol. 37, Pt. 1, 277.
68. Wheaton, Frank, *Official Records*, Vol. 37, Pt. 1, 277.
69. Cooling, Benjamin F., *The Day Lincoln Was Almost Shot*, 185.
70. Cooling, Benjamin F., *The Day Lincoln Was Almost Shot*, 185.
71. De Armond, Aaron L., "Diary," in Brown, Martha R., *Holding Sweet Communion*, 215.
72. Bobbitt, Isham C.; Cheatam, James T.; Hagler, Hiram, *CSRC*.
73. Wheaton, Frank, *Official Records*, Vol. 37, Pt. 1, 277.
74. Cooling, Benjamin F., *The Day Lincoln Was Almost Shot*, 185.
75. Crumpler, Robert M.; Shearin, Thomas G.; Hardy, Francis M.; Redick, Epinetus, *CSRC*.
76. Cooling, Benjamin F., *The Day Lincoln Was Almost Shot*, 185.
77. Wheaton, Frank, *Official Records*, Vol. 37, Pt. 1, 277.
78. Betts, Alexander, *Experience of a Confederate Chaplain*, 12 July 1864.
79. 30th North Carolina Regiment. *CSRC*.
80. Betts, Alexander, *Experience of a Confederate Chaplain*, 12 July 1864.
81. Taylor, Michael W., *To Drive the Enemy from Southern Soil*, 339.
82. Betts, Alexander, *Experience of a Confederate Chaplain*, 13 July 1864.
83. Patchan, Scott C., *Shenandoah Summer: The 1864 Valley Campaign*, 23.
84. Davis, Daniel T., and Greenwalt, Phillip S., *Bloody Autumn: The Shenandoah Valley Campaign of 1864* (El Dorado Hills, CA: Savas Beatie, 2013), 1.
85. Patchan, Scott C., *Shenandoah Summer: The 1864 Valley Campaign*, 54.
86. Patchan, Scott C., *Shenandoah Summer: The 1864 Valley Campaign*, 70, 60–1.
87. Patchan, Scott C., *Shenandoah Summer: The 1864 Valley Campaign*, 72.
88. Thoburn, Joseph, *Official Records*, Vol. 37, Pt. 1, 291.
89. Patchan, Scott C., *Shenandoah Summer: The 1864 Valley Campaign*, 74.
90. Osborne, E. A., "Fourth Regiment," in Clark, Walter (ed.), *Histories of the Several Regiments*, Vol. 1, 260.
91. Patchan, Scott C., *Shenandoah Summer: The 1864 Valley Campaign*, 74.
92. Wildes, Thomas F., *Record of the One Hundred and Sixteenth Ohio Infantry Volunteers in the War of the Rebellion* (Sandusky, OH: I. F. Mack and Bros., 1884), 130.
93. Patchan, Scott C., *Shenandoah Summer: The 1864 Valley Campaign*, 79.
94. Keyes, C. M., *The Military History of the 123rd Regiment Ohio Volunteer Infantry* (Sandusky, OH: Register Steam Press, 1874), 79.
95. Patchan, Scott C., *Shenandoah Summer: The 1864 Valley Campaign*, 83.
96. Keyes, C. M., *The Military History of the 123rd Regiment*, 78.
97. George Howard W.; Felton, Richard; Wells, Louis R., *CSRC*.
98. Fitts, Francis M.; Miller, John L.; Teachey, James W.; Teachey, Jacob T., *CSRC*.
99. Perry, Sidney R., *CSRC*.
100. Bell, Arkin B.; Gupton, Thomas; DeArmond, Aaron L., *CSRC*.
101. Patchan, Scott C., *Shenandoah Summer: The 1864 Valley Campaign*, 84.
102. Wildes, Thomas F., *Record of the One Hundred and Sixteenth Ohio*, 131.
103. King, Lewis D.; Rogers, Martin L.; Crotts, Elijah, *CSRC*.
104. Keyes, C. M., *The Military History of the 123rd Regiment*, 79. Lincoln, William S., *Life With the Thirty-Fourth Massachusetts Infantry in the War of the Rebellion* (Worcester, MA: Press of Noyes, Snow, and Co., 1879), 333.
105. 30th North Carolina Regiment. *CSRC*.
106. Wildes, Thomas F., *Record of the One Hundred and Sixteenth Ohio*, 131.
107. Patchan, Scott C., *Shenandoah Summer: The 1864 Valley Campaign*, 89.
108. Thoburn, Joseph, *Official Records*, Vol. 37, Pt. 1, 292.
109. Patchan, Scott C., *Shenandoah Summer: The 1864 Valley Campaign*, 98.
110. Patchan, Scott C., *Shenandoah Summer: The 1864 Valley Campaign*, 97.
111. Hotchkins, Jedediah, *Make Me A Map of the Valley*, 19 July 1864.
112. Patchan, Scott C., *Shenandoah Summer: The 1864 Valley Campaign*, 150.
113. Ardrey, William E., *Diary*, 22 July 1864.
114. Patchan, Scott C., *Shenandoah Summer: The 1864 Valley Campaign*, 170.
115. Betts, Alexander, *Experience of a Confederate Chaplain*, 23 July 1864.
116. Patchan, Scott C., *Shenandoah Summer: The 1864 Valley Campaign*, 182.
117. Ardrey, William E., *Diary*, 24 July 1864.
118. Ardrey, William E., *Diary*, 26 July 1864.
119. Patchan, Scott C., *Shenandoah Summer: The 1864 Valley Campaign*, 255.
120. Ardrey, William E., *Diary*, 27 July 1864.
121. Ardrey, William E., *Diary*, 4 August 1864.
122. Ardrey, William E., *Diary*, 8–10 August 1864.
123. Patchan, Scott C., *The Last Battle of Winchester*, 72.
124. Ardrey, William E., *Diary*, 20 August 1864.
125. 30th North Carolina Regiment. *CSRC*.

126. Wert, Jeffry D., *From Winchester to Cedar Creek: The Shenandoah Campaign of 1864* (New York: Simon & Schuster, 1987), 35.
127. Grimes, Bryan, in Cowper, Pulaski, *Extracts of Letters of Bryan Grimes to His Wife*, 61.
128. Wert, Jeffry D., *From Winchester to Cedar Creek*, 26.
129. Patchan, Scott C., *The Last Battle of Winchester*, 112.
130. Ardrey, William E., *Diary*, 21 August 1864.
131. Wilkins, Elijah, *CSRC*.
132. Frazer, James H.; Hunt, David Z., *CSRC*.
133. "The Battle at Summit Point—Severe Fighting," *New York Times*, 21 Aug 1864.
134. John Pennington, John; Bland, John J.; McDowell, William J., *CSRC*.
135. "The Battle at Summit Point—Severe Fighting," *New York Times*, 21 Aug 1864.
136. Ardrey, William E., *Diary*, 22 August 1864.
137. "The Battle at Summit Point—Severe Fighting," *New York Times*, 21 Aug 1864.
138. Patchan, Scott C., *The Last Battle of Winchester*, 118.
139. Williams, William A.; Turner, David W.; Bentley, Moses; Forsyth, James R.; Cavenaugh, Jacob W.; Warren, Lemuel, *CSRC*.
140. Betts, Alexander, *Experience of a Confederate Chaplain*, 21 August 1864.
141. "The Battle at Summit Point—Severe Fighting," *New York Times*, 21 Aug 1864.
142. Newkirk, George B.; Fuller, James N.; Winstead, Hilliard H.; Walston, William F., *CSRC*.
143. Grimes, Bryan, in Cowper, Pulaski, *Extracts of Letters of Bryan Grimes to His Wife*, 62.
144. "The Battle at Summit Point—Severe Fighting," *New York Times*, 21 Aug 1864.
145. Wert, Jeffry D., *From Winchester to Cedar Creek*, 35.
146. Grimes, Bryan, in Cowper, Pulaski, *Extracts of Letters of Bryan Grimes to His Wife*, 62.
147. 30th North Carolina Regiment. *CSRC*.
148. Ardrey, William E., *Diary*, 22 August 1864. Betts, Alexander, *Experience of a Confederate Chaplain*, 21 August 1864.
149. Ardrey, William E., *Diary*, 27 August 1864.
150. Grimes, Bryan, in Cowper, Pulaski, *Extracts of Letters of Bryan Grimes to His Wife*, 63.
151. Ardrey, William E., *Diary*, 1 September 1864.
152. Wert, Jeffry D., *From Winchester to Cedar Creek*, 35.
153. Davis, Daniel T., and Greenwalt, Phillip S., *Bloody Autumn: The Shenandoah Valley Campaign of 1864*, 12.
154. Grimes, Bryan, in Cowper, Pulaski, *Extracts of Letters of Bryan Grimes to His Wife*, 65.
155. McMillan, John C., *CSRC*.
156. Grimes, Bryan, in Cowper, Pulaski, *Extracts of Letters of Bryan Grimes to His Wife*, 66.
157. Grimes, Bryan, in Cowper, Pulaski, *Extracts of Letters of Bryan Grimes to His Wife*, 67.

Chapter 15

1. 30th North Carolina Regiment. *CSRC*.
2. Gales, Seaton, *Our Living and Our Dead*, Newbern, N.C., 4 March 1874.
3. Ardrey, William E. *Diary*, 19 September 1864.
4. Hatton, C. R., "The Valley Campaign of 1864," *Confederate Veteran*, Vol. 27 (1919), 169.
5. Early, Jubal A. *Official Records*, Vol. 43, Pt. 1, 554.
6. Patchan, Scott C., *The Last Battle of Winchester*, 279.
7. Gales, Seaton, *Our Living and Our Dead*, Newbern, N.C., 4 March 1874.
8. Merritt, Wesley, "Sheridan in the Shenandoah Valley," in Buel and Johnson, *Battles and Leaders*, Vol. 4, 507.
9. Patchan, Scott C., *The Last Battle of Winchester*, 279.
10. Early, Jubal A. *Official Records*, Vol. 43, Pt. 1, 553.
11. Ardrey, William E. *Diary*, 19 September 1864.
12. Collier, Samuel, letter, 21, September 1864, in Patchan, Scott C., *The Last Battle of Winchester*, 509.
13. Osborne, "Fourth Regiment, in Clark, Walter (ed.), *Histories of the Several Regiments*, Vol. 1, 262.
14. Patchan, Scott C., *The Last Battle of Winchester*, 293.
15. Smith, William A., *The Anson Guards*, 279.
16. Bradshaw, J. E.; *Official Records*, Vol. 43, Pt.1, 259.
17. Ardrey, William E. *Diary*, 19 September 1864.
18. Molineux, Edward L., *Official Records*, Vol. 43, Pt.1, 330.
19. Trout, Kristen, "Their Brave and Beloved Commander: Maj. Gen. Robert E. Rodes at Third Winchester," *Noble Deed of the Civil War Blog*, November 3, 2015.
20. Keifer, Warren, *Official Records*, Vol. 43, Pt.1, 247.
21. Patchan, Scott C., *The Last Battle of Winchester*, 296.
22. Bowen, James L., *History of the Thirty-Seventh Regiment Mass. Volunteers in the Civil War of 1861–1865* (Holyoke, MA: Clark W. Bryan & Co., 1884), 376.
23. Buell, Augustus C., *The Cannoneer: Recollections of Service in the Army of the Potomac* (Washington, D.C.: The National Tribune, 1890), 292.
24. Cooper, William W.; Downs, John T., *CSRC*.
25. Stevens, Greenleaf T.; *Official Records*, Vol. 43, Pt.1, 273.
26. Shearin, John L.; Allen, David C., *CSRC*.
27. Schaub, Julius L., letter, in Patchan, Scott C., *The Last Battle of Winchester*, 302.
28. Collier, Samuel, letter, 21, September 1864, in Patchan, Scott C., *The Last Battle of Winchester*, 509–10.
29. Moore, Samuel R.; Dickson, Riol; Matthews, M. Hardy, *CSRC*.
30. Smith, William A., *The Anson Guards*, 279.
31. Hatton, C. R., "The Valley Campaign of 1864," *Confederate Veteran*, Vol. 27 (1919), 169.
32. Bowen, James L., *History of the Thirty-Seventh Regiment*, 355.
33. Johnston, James H.; King, James D.; King, John; Howie, John H.; Cox, Robert G.; Howard, William S., *CSRC*.
34. Smith, William A., *The Anson Guards*, 279.
35. Bowen, James L., *History of the Thirty-Seventh Regiment*, 377.
36. Osborne, "Fourth Regiment, in Clark, Walter (ed.), *Histories of the Several Regiments*, Vol. 1, 262.
37. Buell, Augustus C., *The Cannoneer*, 293.
38. Gales, Seaton, *Our Living and Our Dead*, Newbern, N.C., 4 March 1874.
39. Vaill, Theodore F., *History of the Second Connecticut Volunteer Heavy Artillery, Originally the Nineteenth Connecticut Vols.* (Winsted, CT: Winsted Printing Co., 1868), 96.
40. Patchan, Scott C., *The Last Battle of Winchester*, 487.
41. Ardrey, William E. *Diary*, 19 September 1864.
42. Freeman, Douglas, *Lee's Lieutenants*, Vol. 3, 580.
43. Patchan, Scott C., *The Last Battle of Winchester*, 381.
44. Hamblin, Joseph B.; *Official Records*, Vol. 43, Pt.1, 177.
45. Gales, Seaton, *Our Living and Our Dead*, Newbern, N.C., 4 March 1874.
46. Patchan, Scott C., *The Last Battle of Winchester*, 403.
47. Wert, Jeffry D., *From Winchester to Cedar Creek*, 57.
48. Arnold, John C., *Official Records*, Vol. 43, Pt. 1, 189.
49. Grimes, Bryan, in Cowper, Pulaski, *Extracts of Letters of Bryan Grimes to His Wife*, 69.
50. Freeman, Douglas, *Lee's Lieutenants*, Vol. 3, 580.

51. Early, Jubal A. *Official Records*, Vol. 43, Pt. 1, 555.
52. Hotchkiss, Jedediah, *Official Records*, Vol. 43, Pt.1, 574.
53. Freeman, Douglas, *Lee's Lieutenants*, Vol. 3, 580.
54. Binkley, Otho H., *Official Records*, Vol. 43, Pt. 1, 258.
55. Gales, Seaton, *Our Living and Our Dead*, Newbern, N.C., 4 March 1874.
56. Patchan, Scott C., *The Last Battle of Winchester*, 417.
57. Collier, Samuel, letter, 21 September 1864, in Patchan, Scott C., *The Last Battle of Winchester*, 510.
58. "The John Beech Story," *Newark Sunday News Magazine*, 29 January 1961.
59. Collier, Samuel, letter, 21 September 1864, in Patchan, Scott C., *The Last Battle of Winchester*, 510.
60. Gales, Seaton, *Our Living and Our Dead*, Newbern, N.C., 4 March 1874.
61. Gordon, John B., in Wert, Jeffry D., From Winchester to Cedar Creek, 108.
62. Grimes, Bryan, in Cowper, Pulaski, *Extracts of Letters of Bryan Grimes to His Wife*, 67–8.
63. Betts, Alexander, *Experience of a Confederate Chaplain*, 19 September 1864.
64. 30th North Carolina Regiment. CSRC.
65. Gallagher, Gary, *Stephen Dodson Ramseur—Lee's Gallant General*, 147
66. Grimes, Bryan, in Cowper, Pulaski, *Extracts of Letters of Bryan Grimes to His Wife*, 71.
67. Ardrey, William E. *Diary*, 20 September 1864.
68. Wert, Jeffry D., *From Winchester to Cedar Creek*, 118.
69. Patchan, Scott C., *The Last Battle of Winchester*, 495.
70. Keifer, Warren, *Official Records*, Vol. 43, Pt.1, 248.
71. Wert, Jeffry D., "First Fair Chance: The Battle of Fisher's Hill," *Civil War Times Illustrated*, Vol. 18 (August 1979), 41.
72. Hatton, C. R., "The Valley Campaign of 1864," *Confederate Veteran*, Vol. 27 (1919), 170.
73. Grimes, Bryan, in Cowper, Pulaski, *Extracts of Letters of Bryan Grimes to His Wife*, 71.
74. Ardrey, William E. *Diary*, 22 September 1864.
75. Gallagher, Gary, *Stephen Dodson Ramseur—Lee's Gallant General*, 148.
76. Hotchkiss, Jedediah, *Official Records*, Vol. 43, Pt.1, 575.
77. Early, Jubal A., "Winchester, Fisher's Hill, and Cedar Creek," in Buel and Johnson, *Battles and Leaders*, Vol. 4, 524.
78. Wert, Jeffry D., *From Winchester to Cedar Creek*, 119.
79. Grimes, Bryan, in Cowper, Pulaski, *Extracts of Letters of Bryan Grimes to His Wife*, 71.
80. Merritt, Wesley, "Sheridan in the Shenandoah Valley," in Buel and Johnson, *Battles and Leaders*, Vol. 4, 510.
81. 30th North Carolina Regiment. CSRC.
82. Munford, Thomas, letter, in Wert, Jeffry D., *From Winchester to Cedar Creek*, 25.
83. Crook, George, *Official Records*, Vol. 43, Pt. 1, 363–4.
84. Gallagher, Gary, *Stephen Dodson Ramseur—Lee's Gallant General*, 148.
85. Young, John F., *Official Records*, Vol. 43, Pt. 1, 269.
86. Grimes, Bryan, in Cowper, Pulaski, *Extracts of Letters of Bryan Grimes to His Wife*, 71.
87. Robinson, Charles, M., *General Crook and the Western Frontier* (Norman: University of Oklahoma Press, 2001), 65.
88. Crook, George, *Official Records*, Vol. 43, Pt. 1, 363–4.
89. Hatton, C. R., "The Valley Campaign of 1864," *Confederate Veteran*, Vol. 27 (1919), 170.
90. Wert, Jeffry D., *From Winchester to Cedar Creek*, 121.
91. Gallagher, Gary, *Stephen Dodson Ramseur—Lee's Gallant General*, 148–9.
92. Wert, Jeffry D., *From Winchester to Cedar Creek*, 122–3.
93. Early, Jubal A., "Winchester, Fisher's Hill, and Cedar Creek," in Buel and Johnson, *Battles and Leaders*, Vol. 4, 524.
94. Gallagher, Gary, *Stephen Dodson Ramseur—Lee's Gallant General*, 151.
95. Wert, Jeffry D., *From Winchester to Cedar Creek*, 123.
96. Batts, William J.; Culp, Aley, A.; Robins, Jonathan; Phillips, Richard; Pierce, Orren L., CSRC.
97. Cox, William R., letter, in Taylor, Michael W., *To Drive the Enemy from Southern Soil*, 346–7.
98. Beall, T. B., "That Stampede at Fisher's Hill," *Confederate Veteran*, Vol. 5 (1897), 26.
99. Gallagher, Gary, *Stephen Dodson Ramseur—Lee's Gallant General*, 148.
100. Early, Jubal A., *Official Records*, Vol. 43, Pt. 1, 556.
101. Keifer, Warren, *Official Records*, Vol. 43, Pt.1, 248.
102. Grimes, Bryan, in Cowper, Pulaski, *Extracts of Letters of Bryan Grimes to His Wife*, 73.
103. Wert, Jeffry D., *From Winchester to Cedar Creek*, 126.
104. Cox, William R., letter, in Taylor, Michael W., *To Drive the Enemy from Southern Soil*, 346–7.
105. Beall, T. B., "That Stampede at Fisher's Hill," *Confederate Veteran*, Vol. 5 (1897), 26.
106. Cox, William R., letter, in Taylor, Michael W., *To Drive the Enemy from Southern Soil*, 346–7.
107. 30th North Carolina Regiment. CSRC.
108. Molineux, Edward L., *Official Records*, Vol. 43, Pt.1, 332.
109. Cox, William R., letter, in Taylor, Michael W., *To Drive the Enemy from Southern Soil*, 346–7.
110. Beall, T. B., "That Stampede at Fisher's Hill," *Confederate Veteran*, Vol. 5 (1897), 26.
111. Wert, Jeffry D., *From Winchester to Cedar Creek*, 128.
112. "Fisher's Hill and 'Sheridan's Ride,'" *Confederate Veteran*, Vol. 10 (1902), 165.
113. Grimes, Bryan, in Cowper, Pulaski, *Extracts of Letters of Bryan Grimes to His Wife*, 73–4.
114. Ardrey, William E. *Diary*, 24 September 1864.
115. Early, Jubal A., "Winchester, Fisher's Hill, and Cedar Creek," in Buel and Johnson, *Battles and Leaders*, Vol. 4, 524.
116. Betts, Alexander, *Experience of a Confederate Chaplain*, 25 September 1864.
117. Betts, Alexander, *Experience of a Confederate Chaplain*, 27 September 1864.
118. Gallagher, Gary, *Stephen Dodson Ramseur—Lee's Gallant General*, 148. Taylor, Michael W., *To Drive the Enemy from Southern Soil*, 348.
119. Grimes, Bryan., letter, 4 October 1864, in Taylor, Michael W., *To Drive the Enemy from Southern Soil*, 349–50.

Chapter 16

1. Betts, Alexander, *Experience of a Confederate Chaplain*, 1 October 1864.
2. Grimes, Bryan, in Cowper, Pulaski, *Extracts of Letters of Bryan Grimes to His Wife*, 75.
3. Early, Jubal A., "Winchester, Fisher's Hill, and Cedar Creek," in Buel and Johnson, *Battles and Leaders*, Vol. 4, 525.
4. "Fisher's Hill and 'Sheridan's Ride,'" *Confederate Veteran*, Vol. 10 (1902), 165.
5. Freeman, Douglas, *Lee's Lieutenants*, Vol. 3, 595–9.
6. Grimes, Bryan, in Cowper, Pulaski, *Extracts of Letters of Bryan Grimes to His Wife*, 76. Ardrey, William E. *Diary*, 14 October 1864.
7. Early, Jubal A., "Winchester, Fisher's Hill, and Cedar Creek," in Buel and Johnson, *Battles and Leaders*, Vol. 4, 526.

8. 30th North Carolina Regiment. *CSRC*.
9. "Fisher's Hill and 'Sheridan's Ride,'" *Confederate Veteran*, Vol. 10 (1902), 165.
10. Ardrey, William E., *Diary*, 18 October 1864.
11. Grimes, Bryan, *Official Records*, Vol. 43, Pt. 1, 598.
12. Harris, E. Ruffin, "Battle Near Cedar Creek, Va.," *Confederate Veteran*, Vol. 9 (1901), 390.
13. Hatton, C. R., "The Valley Campaign of 1864," *Confederate Veteran*, Vol. 27 (1919), 170.
14. Buck, S. D., "Battle of Cedar Creek—Tribute to Early," *Confederate Veteran*, Vol. 2 (1894), 75.
15. Bone, John W., *Records of a Soldier in the Late War*, 93-4.
16. Ardrey, William E., *Diary*, 19 October 1864.
17. Hatton, C. R., "The Valley Campaign of 1864," *Confederate Veteran*, Vol. 27 (1919), 170.
18. Early, Jubal A., "Winchester, Fisher's Hill, and Cedar Creek," in Buel and Johnson, *Battles and Leaders*, Vol. 4, 526.
19. Bone, John W., *Records of a Soldier in the Late War*, 94.
20. Grimes, Bryan, *Official Records*, Vol. 43, Pt. 1, 598.
21. Hatton, C. R., "The Valley Campaign of 1864," *Confederate Veteran*, Vol. 27 (1919), 171.
22. Hotchkiss, Jedediah, *Official Records*, Vol. 43, Pt.1, 581.
23. Wert, Jeffry D., *From Winchester to Cedar Creek*, 179.
24. Osborne, E. A., "Fourth Regiment, in Clark, Walter, *Histories of the Several Regiments*, Vol. 1, 263.
25. Ardrey, William E., *Diary*, 19 October 1864.
26. Harris, E. Ruffin, "Battle Near Cedar Creek, Va.," *Confederate Veteran*, Vol. 9 (1901), 390.
27. Hatton, C. R., "The Valley Campaign of 1864," *Confederate Veteran*, Vol. 27 (1919), 171.
28. Buck, S. D., "Battle of Cedar Creek—Tribute to Early," *Confederate Veteran*, Vol. 2 (1894), 76.
29. Ardrey, William E., *Diary*, 19 October 1864.
30. Freeman, Douglas, *Lee's Lieutenants*, Vol. 3, 601.
31. Wert, Jeffry D., *From Winchester to Cedar Creek*, 187.
32. Wert, Jeffry D., *From Winchester to Cedar Creek*, 186.
33. Wert, Jeffry D., *From Winchester to Cedar Creek*, 203.
34. Hatton, C. R., "The Valley Campaign of 1864," *Confederate Veteran*, Vol. 27 (1919), 171.
35. Grimes, Bryan, in Cowper, Pulaski, *Extracts of Letters of Bryan Grimes to His Wife*, 81.
36. Buck, S. D., "Battle of Cedar Creek—Tribute to Early," *Confederate Veteran*, Vol. 2 (1894), 76.
37. Harris, E. Ruffin, "Battle Near Cedar Creek, Va.," *Confederate Veteran*, Vol. 9 (1902), 390.
38. Langley, A. W., "Camp near Cedar Creek, Va., Oct. 21, 1864," *The Gallipolis Journal*, 10 November 1864.
39. Keifer, Warren, *Official Records*, Vol. 43, Pt. 1, 226-7.
40. Hotchkiss, Jedediah, *Official Records*, Vol. 43, Pt.1, 581.
41. Grimes, Bryan, *Official Records*, Vol. 43, Pt. 1, 599.
42. Grimes, Bryan, *Official Records*, Vol. 43, Pt. 1, 599.
43. Puckett, Clarence P., "Richard David Brooks—The Young Man at War."
44. Hatton, C. R., "The Valley Campaign of 1864," *Confederate Veteran*, Vol. 27 (1919), 172.
45. Early, Jubal A., "Winchester, Fisher's Hill, and Cedar Creek," in Buel and Johnson, *Battles and Leaders*, Vol. 4, 528.
46. Wert, Jeffry D., *From Winchester to Cedar Creek*, 218.
47. Buck, S. D., "Battle of Cedar Creek—Tribute to Early," *Confederate Veteran*, Vol. 2 (1894), 76.
48. Smith, William A., *The Anson Guards*, 285.
49. Taylor, Michael W., *To Drive the Enemy from Southern Soil*, 348.
50. Early, Jubal A., "Winchester, Fisher's Hill, and Cedar Creek," in Buel and Johnson, *Battles and Leaders*, Vol. 4, 528.
51. Smith, William A., *The Anson Guards*, 285.
52. Freeman, Douglas, *Lee's Lieutenants*, Vol. 3, 605.
53. Langley, A. W., "Camp near Cedar Creek, Va., Oct. 21, 1864," *The Gallipolis Journal*, 10 November 1864.
54. Grimes, Bryan, in Cowper, Pulaski, *Extracts of Letters of Bryan Grimes to His Wife*, 84.
55. Wert, Jeffry D., *From Winchester to Cedar Creek*, 218.
56. Wert, Jeffry D., *From Winchester to Cedar Creek*, 217.
57. Hotchkiss, Jedediah, *Official Records*, Vol. 43, Pt.1, 581.
58. Wert, Jeffry D., *From Winchester to Cedar Creek*, 230.
59. Wert, Jeffry D., *From Winchester to Cedar Creek*, 233.
60. Fitts, Francis M.; Bailey, Jeremiah; Moore, Willis D., *CSRC*.
61. Wert, Jeffry D., *From Winchester to Cedar Creek*, 233.
62. Elliott, Green B., *CSRC*.
63. Grimes, Bryan, *Official Records*, Vol. 43, Pt. 1, 599.
64. Custer, George A., *Official Records*, Vol. 43, Pt. 1, 524.
65. Early, Jubal A., "Winchester, Fisher's Hill, and Cedar Creek," in Buel and Johnson, *Battles and Leaders*, Vol. 4, 528.
66. Molineux, Edward L., *Official Records*, Vol. 43, Pt. 1, 334-5.
67. Wert, Jeffry D., *From Winchester to Cedar Creek*, 234.
68. Grimes, Bryan, in Cowper, Pulaski, *Extracts of Letters of Bryan Grimes to His Wife*, 77.
69. Bennett, Risden T., "Fourteenth Regiment," in Clark, Walter, *Histories of the Several Regiments*, Vol. 1, 728.
70. "Fisher's Hill and 'Sheridan's Ride,'" *Confederate Veteran*, Vol. 10 (1902), 165.
71. Osborne, E. A., "Fourth Regiment, in Clark, Walter, *Histories of the Several Regiments*, Vol. 1, 263.
72. Grimes, Bryan, in Cowper, Pulaski, *Extracts of Letters of Bryan Grimes to His Wife*, 77.
73. Gallagher, Gary, *Stephen Dodson Ramseur—Lee's Gallant General*, 161.
74. Schenck, David, *Sketches of Maj. Gen. Stephen Dodson Ramseur*, 22.
75. Hutchison, R. R., "Major-General Stephen D. Ramseur: His Life and Character," *Southern Historical Society Papers*, Vol. 18 (1891), 257-8.
76. Bone, John W., *Records of a Soldier in the Late War*, 94.
77. "Fisher's Hill and 'Sheridan's Ride,'" *Confederate Veteran*, Vol. 10 (1902), 165.
78. Custer, George A., *Official Records*, Vol. 43, Pt. 1, 524.
79. Freeman, Douglas, *Lee's Lieutenants*, Vol. 3, 607.
80. Bone, John W., *Records of a Soldier in the Late War*, 94.
81. Custer, George A., *Official Records*, Vol. 43, Pt. 1, 525.
82. Ardrey, William E., *Diary*, 19 October 1864.
83. Custer, George A., *Official Records*, Vol. 43, Pt. 1, 525-6.
84. Smith, William A., *The Anson Guards*, 284.
85. Grimes, Bryan, in Cowper, Pulaski, *Extracts of Letters of Bryan Grimes to His Wife*, 86.
86. 30th North Carolina Regiment. *CSRC*.
87. Buck, S. D., "Battle of Cedar Creek—Tribute to Early," *Confederate Veteran*, Vol. 2 (1894), 76.
88. Manly, Matt, "Second Regiment, in Clark, Walter, *Histories of the Several Regiments*, Vol. 1, 174.
89. Ardrey, William E., *Diary*, 19 October 1864.
90. Langley, A. W., "Camp near Cedar Creek, Va., Oct. 21, 1864," *The Gallipolis Journal*, 10 November 1864.
91. Hutchison, R. R., "Major-General Stephen D. Ramseur: His Life and Character," *Southern Historical Society Papers*, Vol. 18 (1891), 258.
92. Ardrey, William E., *Diary*, 20 October 1864.
93. Buck, S. D., "Battle of Cedar

Creek—Tribute to Early," *Confederate Veteran*, Vol. 2 (1894), 76.
94. Harris, E. Ruffin, "Battle Near Cedar Creek, Va.," *Confederate Veteran*, Vol. 9 (1901), 390.
95. Vaill, Theodore F., *History of the Second Connecticut*, 131.
96. Ardrey, William E., *Diary*, 1 November 1864.
97. Ardrey, William E., *Diary*, 8 November 1864.
98. Grimes, Bryan, in Cowper, Pulaski, *Extracts of Letters of Bryan Grimes to His Wife*, 89.
99. Bone, John W., *Records of a Soldier in the Late War*, 98.
100. Grimes, Bryan, in Cowper, Pulaski, *Extracts of Letters of Bryan Grimes to His Wife*, 89.
101. Ardrey, William E., *Diary*, 23 November 1864.
102. Taylor, Michael W., *To Drive the Enemy from Southern Soil*, 354.
103. Ardrey, William E., *Diary*, 9 December 1864.

Chapter 17

1. Hotchkiss, Jedediah, *Official Records*, Vol. 43, Pt. 1, 587.
2. Bone, John W., *Records of a Soldier in the Late War*, 98.
3. Ardrey, William E., *Diary*, 14 December 1864.
4. Bone, John W., *Records of a Soldier in the Late War*, 98.
5. Ardrey, William E., *Diary*, 15 December 1864.
6. Bone, John W., *Records of a Soldier in the Late War*, 98.
7. Ardrey, William E., *Diary*, 16 December 1864.
8. Jordan, Weymouth T., "4th Regiment," *North Carolina Troops*, Vol. 4, 8.
9. Cox, William R., "The Anderson-Ramseur-Cox Brigade," in Clark, Walter, *Histories of the Several Regiments*, Vol. 4, 450.
10. Ardrey, William E., *Diary*, 16 December 1864.
11. Bone, John W., *Records of a Soldier in the Late War*, 99.
12. Betts, Alexander D., *Experience of a Confederate Chaplain*, 29 December 1864.
13. 30th North Carolina Regiment. CSRC.
14. Ardrey, William E., *Diary*, 23 December 1864.
15. Kendrick, Thomas L., letter, 25 December 1864. Thomas L. Kendrick Family Collection. Lincolnton Library, NC.
16. Craig, Joel, and Baker, Sharlene, *As You May Never See Us Again*, 83.
17. Bone, John W., *Records of a Soldier in the Late War*, 99.
18. Taylor, Michael W., *To Drive the Enemy from Southern Soil*, 355.
19. Grimes, Bryan, in Cowper, Pulaski, *Extracts of Letters of Bryan Grimes to His Wife*, 95.
20. Smith, William A., *The Anson Guards*, 291.
21. Lee, Robert E., *Official Records*, Vol. 46, Pt. 2, 1035.
22. Seddon, J. A., *Official Records*, Vol. 46, Pt. 2, 1035.
23. Smith, William A., *The Anson Guards*, 291.
24. Armfield, John J., letter, 17 February 1865, in Watford, Christopher (ed.), *The Civil War in North Carolina*, 195.
25. Craig, Joel, and Baker, Sharlene, *As You May Never See Us Again*, 85.
26. Freeman, Douglas S., *Lee's Lieutenants*, Vol. 3, 640.
27. Taylor, Michael W., *To Drive the Enemy from Southern Soil*, 361.
28. Jordan, Weymouth T., "4th Regiment," *North Carolina Troops*, Vol. 4, 8.
29. Bone, John W., *Records of a Soldier in the Late War*, 100.
30. Grimes, Bryan, in Cowper, Pulaski, *Extracts of Letters of Bryan Grimes to His Wife*, 98.
31. Smith, William A., *The Anson Guards*, 292.
32. Freeman, Douglas S., *Lee's Lieutenants*, Vol. 3, 640–1.
33. Betts, Alexander D., *Experience of a Confederate Chaplain*, 8 February 1865.
34. Armfield, John J., letter, 17 February 1865, in Watford, Christopher (ed.), *The Civil War in North Carolina*, 195.
35. Manning, Fred L., *Official Records*, Vol. 46, Pt. 2, 581.
36. Sharpe, George H., *Official Records*, Vol. 46, Pt. 2, 657.
37. Manning, Fred, L., *Official Records*, Vol. 46, Pt. 2, 664. Ord, O. C., *Official Records*, Vol. 46, Pt. 2, 678.
38. Taylor, Michael W., *To Drive the Enemy from Southern Soil*, 361.
39. Betts, Alexander D., *Experience of a Confederate Chaplain*, 3 March 1865.
40. Wright, Stuart T., *The Confederate Letters of Benjamin H. Freeman* (Hicksville, NY: Exposition, 1974), 60–1.
41. Vance, Zebulon B., "Important Appeal: Headquarters Division of the West, Feb. 23d, 1865," in the Zebulon Baird Vance Papers #3952, Southern Historical Collection, The Wilson Library, University of North Carolina at Chapel Hill.
42. Betts, Alexander D., *Experience of a Confederate Chaplain*, 20 March 1865.
43. Bone, John W., *Record of a Soldier in the Late War*, 101.
44. Jordan, Weymouth T., "4th Regiment," *North Carolina Troops*, Vol. 4, 8.
45. Cox, William R., "The Anderson-Ramseur-Cox Brigade," in Clark, Walter, *Histories of the Several Regiments*, Vol. 4, 450.
46. Bone, John W., *Record of a Soldier in the Late War*, 101.
47. Bearrs, Edwin C., *The Petersburg Campaign: The Western Front Battles, September 1864–April 1865* (El Dorado Hills, CA: Savas Beatie, 2014), 263.
48. Cox, William R., "The Anderson-Ramseur-Cox Brigade," in Clark, Walter, *Histories of the Several Regiments*, Vol. 4, 450.
49. Cox, William R., "The Anderson-Ramseur-Cox Brigade," in Clark, Walter, *Histories of the Several Regiments*, Vol. 4, 451.
50. Freeman, Douglas S., *Lee's Lieutenants*, Vol. 3, 652.
51. Bone, John W., *Record of a Soldier in the Late War*, 102.
52. Cox, William R., "The Anderson-Ramseur-Cox Brigade," in Clark, Walter, *Histories of the Several Regiments*, Vol. 4, 451.
53. Trudeau, Noah A., *The Last Citadel: Petersburg, Virginia, June 1864–April 1865* (Baton Rouge: Louisiana State University Press, 1991), 352.
54. Cox, William R., "The Anderson-Ramseur-Cox Brigade," in Clark, Walter, *Histories of the Several Regiments*, Vol. 4, 451.
55. Day, William A., "Life Among Bullets—In The Rifle Pits," *Confederate Veteran*, Vol. 29 (1921), 218.
56. Cox, William R., "The Anderson-Ramseur-Cox Brigade," in Clark, Walter, *Histories of the Several Regiments*, Vol. 4, 451–2.
57. Trudeau, Noah A., *The Last Citadel*, 289.
58. Bone, John W., *Record of a Soldier in the Late War*, 103.
59. Lynn, William, CSRC.
60. Grimes, Bryan, in Cowper, Pulaski, *Extracts of Letters of Bryan Grimes to His Wife*, 101.
61. Pearce, T. H. (ed.), *Diary of Captain Henry A. Chambers* (Wendell, NC: Broadfoot's Bookmark, 1983), 255.
62. Trudeau, Noah A., *The Last Citadel*, 291.
63. Grimes, Bryan, in Cowper, Pulaski, *Extracts of Letters of Bryan Grimes to His Wife*, 112.
64. Parke, John G., *Official Records*, Vol. 46, Pt. 3, 373.
65. Greene, A. Wilson, *The Petersburg Campaign: The Final Battles* (Mason City, IA: Savas, 2000), 241.
66. Grimes, Bryan, in Cowper, Pulaski, *Extracts of Letters of Bryan Grimes to His Wife*, 107–8.
67. Greene, A. Wilson, *The Petersburg Campaign: The Final Battles*, 443.
68. 30th North Carolina Regiment. CSRC.

69. Ogburn, N. S.; Rogers, William; Armstrong, Gray; Batchelor, Ruffin; Moore, William H., *CSRC*.
70. Freeman, Douglas S., *Lee's Lieutenants*, Vol. 3, 680.
71. Pendleton, William N., *Official Records*, Vo. 46, Pt. 1, 1281.
72. Greene, A. Wilson, *The Petersburg Campaign: The Final Battles*, 443.
73. Cox, William R., "The Anderson-Ramseur-Cox Brigade," in Clark, Walter, *Histories of the Several Regiments*, Vol. 4, 453.
74. Greene, A. Wilson, *The Petersburg Campaign: The Final Battles*, 443.
75. Cox, William R., "The Anderson-Ramseur-Cox Brigade," in Clark, Walter, *Histories of the Several Regiments*, Vol. 4, 453.
76. Greene, A. Wilson, *The Petersburg Campaign: The Final Battles*, 448.
77. Osborne, E. A., "Fourth Regiment," in Clark, Walter, *Histories of the Several Regiments*, Vol. 1, 264.
78. Cox, William R., "The Anderson-Ramseur-Cox Brigade," in Clark, Walter, *Histories of the Several Regiments*, Vol. 4, 453.
79. Pendleton, William N., *Official Records*, Vo. 46, Pt. 1, 1281.
80. Freeman, Douglas S., *Lee's Lieutenants*, Vol. 3, 680, 683.
81. Freeman, Douglas S., *Lee's Lieutenants*, Vol. 3, 680.
82. Cox, William R., "The Anderson-Ramseur-Cox Brigade," in Clark, Walter, *Histories of the Several Regiments*, Vol. 4, 452–3.
83. Bone, John W., *Record of a Soldier in the Late War*, 104.
84. Greene, A. Wilson, *The Petersburg Campaign: The Final Battles*, 464.
85. Bone, John W., *Record of a Soldier in the Late War*, 104.
86. Pendleton, William N., *Official Records*, Vo. 46, Pt. 1, 1281.
87. Trudeau, Noah A., *The Last Citadel*, 401.
88. Grimes, Bryan, in Cowper, Pulaski, *Extracts of Letters of Bryan Grimes to His Wife*, 113.
89. Greene, A. Wilson, *The Petersburg Campaign: The Final Battles*, 464.
90. Day, William A., "Life Among Bullets—In The Rifle Pits," *Confederate Veteran*, Vol. 29 (1921), 218.
91. Cline, J., *CSRC*.
92. Grimes, Bryan, in Cowper, Pulaski, *Extracts of Letters of Bryan Grimes to His Wife*, 113.
93. Bone, John W., *Record of a Soldier in the Late War*, 110.
94. Bone, John W., *Record of a Soldier in the Late War*, 110.
95. Freeman, Douglas S., *Lee's Lieutenants*, Vol. 3, 686.
96. Bone, John W., *Record of a Soldier in the Late War*, 110.
97. Freeman, Douglas S., *Lee's Lieutenants*, Vol. 3, 687.
98. Freeman, Douglas S., *Lee's Lieutenants*, Vol. 3, 688.
99. Freeman, Douglas S., *Lee's Lieutenants*, Vol. 3, 688.
100. Freeman, Douglas S., *Lee's Lieutenants*, Vol. 3, 689.
101. Freeman, Douglas S., *Lee's Lieutenants*, Vol. 3, 689.
102. Lee, Robert E., *Official Records*, Vol. 46, Pt. 3, 1385.
103. Freeman, Douglas S., *Lee's Lieutenants*, Vol. 3, 690.
104. Lee, Robert E., *Official Records*, Vol. 46, Pt. 1, 1266.

Chapter 18

1. Lee, Robert E., "Lee's Report of the Surrender at Appomattox," in Buel, Clarence C., and Johnson, Robert U., *Battles and Leaders of the Civil War*, Vol. 4, 724.
2. 30th North Carolina Regiment. *CSRC*.
3. Bearss, Edwin C., *The Petersburg Campaign*, Vol. 1, 550.
4. Freeman, Douglas S., *Lee's Lieutenants*, Vol. 3, 694.
5. Haskell, John C. (ed.), *The Haskell Memoirs* (New York: G. P. Putnam's Sons, 1960), 91.
6. Freeman, Douglas S., *Lee's Lieutenants*, Vol. 3, 694, 696.
7. Ewell, Richard S., *Official Records*, Vol. 46, Pt. 1, 1294.
8. Church, Eli, *CSRC*.
9. Grimes, Bryan, in Cowper, Pulaski, *Extracts of Letters of Bryan Grimes to His Wife*, 113.
10. Cox, William R., "The Anderson-Ramseur-Cox Brigade," in Clark, Walter, *Histories of the Several Regiments*, Vol. 4, 454.
11. Brown, Richard A., *Official Records*, Vol. 46, Pt. 3, 602.
12. Cox, William R., "The Anderson-Ramseur-Cox Brigade," in Clark, Walter, *Histories of the Several Regiments*, Vol. 4, 454.
13. Grimes, Bryan, in Cowper, Pulaski, *Extracts of Letters of Bryan Grimes to His Wife*, 113.
14. Humphreys, Andrew A., *Official Records*, Vol. 46, Pt. 1, 682.
15. Ardrey, William E., *Diary*, 6 April 1865.
16. Cox, William R., "The Anderson-Ramseur-Cox Brigade," in Clark, Walter, *Histories of the Several Regiments*, Vol. 4, 454.
17. Bone, John W., *Record of a Soldier in the Late War*, 111.
18. Ardrey, William E., *Diary*, 6 April 1865.
19. 30th North Carolina Infantry, *CSRC*.
20. Humphreys, Anderson A., *Official Records*, Vol. 46 Pt. 3, 600.
21. Gordon, John B., in LaBree, Ben, *Campfires of the Confederacy* (Louisville, KY: Courier-Journal, 1898), 459.
22. Freeman, Douglas S., *Lee's Lieutenants*, Vol. 3, 701–2.
23. Cox, William R., "The Anderson-Ramseur-Cox Brigade," in Clark, Walter, *Histories of the Several Regiments*, Vol. 4, 455.
24. Humphreys, Andrew A., *Official Records*, Vol. 46, Pt. 1, 682.
25. Grimes, Bryan, in Cowper, Pulaski, *Extracts of Letters of Bryan Grimes to His Wife*, 114.
26. Cox, William R., "The Anderson-Ramseur-Cox Brigade," in Clark, Walter, *Histories of the Several Regiments*, Vol. 4, 454–5.
27. Humphreys, A. A., *Official Records*, Vol. 46, Pt. 1, 682.
28. Freeman, Douglas S., *Lee's Lieutenants*, Vol. 3, 710.
29. Cox, William R., "The Anderson-Ramseur-Cox Brigade," in Clark, Walter, *Histories of the Several Regiments*, Vol. 4, 454–5.
30. Lee, Robert E., "Lee's Report of the Surrender at Appomattox," in Buel, Clarence C., and Johnson, Robert U., *Battles and Leaders of the Civil War*, Vol. 4, 724.
31. Aycock, George G.; Best, John B.; Beasley, Edward; Carroll, William H.; Felton, Eli, *CSRC*.
32. Jordan, Weymouth T., "4th Regiment," *North Carolina Troops*, Vol. 4, 8.
33. Freeman, Douglas S., *Lee's Lieutenants*, Vol. 3, 710.
34. Cox, William R., "The Anderson-Ramseur-Cox Brigade," in Clark, Walter, *Histories of the Several Regiments*, Vol. 4, 454–5.
35. Newton, Samuel B., 30th North Carolina Infantry, *CSRC*.
36. 30th North Carolina Infantry, *CSRC*.
37. Humphreys, A. A., *Official Records*, Vol. 46, Pt. 1, 682.
38. 30th North Carolina Infantry, *CSRC*.
39. Smith, William A., *The Anson Guards*, 294.
40. Freeman, Douglas S., *Lee's Lieutenants*, Vol. 3, 711.
41. Grimes, Bryan, in Cowper, Pulaski, *Extracts of Letters of Bryan Grimes to His Wife*, 115.
42. Smith, William A., *The Anson Guards*, 294.
43. Freeman, Douglas S., *Lee's Lieutenants*, Vol. 3, 712–3.
44. Bone, John W., *Record of a Soldier in the Late War*, 111.
45. Rawlings, John A., *Official Records*, Vol. 46, Pt. 1, 1162.
46. Freeman, Douglas S., *Lee's Lieutenants*, Vol. 3, 715.
47. Smith, William A., *The Anson Guards*, 294.
48. Grimes, Bryan, in Cowper, Pu-

laski, *Extracts of Letters of Bryan Grimes to His Wife*, 115–6.
49. Bone, John W., *Record of a Soldier in the Late War*, 112.
50. Rawlings, John A., *Official Records*, Vol. 46, Pt. 1, 1162.
51. Grimes, Bryan, in Cowper, Pulaski, *Extracts of Letters of Bryan Grimes to His Wife*, 116–7.
52. Freeman, Douglas S., *Lee's Lieutenants*, Vol. 3, 718.
53. Lee, Robert E., *Official Records*, Vol. 46, Pt. 1, 1266.
54. Bone, John W., *Record of a Soldier in the Late War*, 113–4.
55. Freeman, Douglas S., *Lee's Lieutenants*, Vol. 3, 722.
56. Freeman, Douglas S., *Lee's Lieutenants*, Vol. 3, 721.
57. Johnson, Bushrod B., *Official Records*, Vol. 46, Pt. 1, 1291.
58. Freeman, Douglas S., *Lee's Lieutenants*, Vol. 3, 721.
59. Bone, John W., *Record of a Soldier in the Late War*, 113–4.
60. McGill, Archy D., *Daily News and Observer, Raleigh*, 11 April 1865, in Taylor, Michael W., *To Drive the Enemy from Southern Soil*, 367–8.
61. Bone, John W., *Record of a Soldier in the Late War*, 113–4.
62. McGill, Archy D., *Daily News and Observer, Raleigh*, 11 April 1865.
63. McGill, Archy D., *Daily News and Observer, Raleigh*, 11 April 1865.
64. Tremain, Henry E., *Last Hours of Sheridan's Cavalry: A Reprint of War Memoranda* (New York: Bonnell, Silver & Bowers, 1904), 227–8.
65. Freeman, Douglas S., *Lee's Lieutenants*, Vol. 3, 726.
66. Bone, John W., *Record of a Soldier in the Late War*, 113–4.
67. Schwab, Julius L., "Some Closing Events at Appomattox," *Confederate Veteran*, Vol. 8 (1900), 71.
68. Metts, James I., "Last Shot Fired at Appomattox," *Confederate Veteran*, Vol. 7 (1899), 52.
69. Bone, John W., *Record of a Soldier in the Late War*, 113–4.
70. 30th North Carolina Regiment. CSRC.
71. Bearss, Edwin C., *The Petersburg Campaign*, Vol. 1, 554.
72. Metts, James I., "Last Shot Fired at Appomattox," *Confederate Veteran*, Vol. 7 (1899), 52.
73. Cox, William R., "The Anderson-Ramseur-Cox Brigade," in Clark, Walter, *Histories of the Several Regiments*, Vol. 4, 457.
74. Jenkins, N. E., letter, 9 April 1906, in Taylor, Michael W., *To Drive the Enemy from Southern Soil*, 65.
75. Freeman, Douglas S., *Lee's Lieutenants*, Vol. 3, 728.
76. McGill, Archy D., *Daily News and Observer, Raleigh*, 11 April 1865.
77. Schwab, Julius L., "Some Closing Events at Appomattox," *Confederate Veteran*, Vol. 8 (1900), 71.
78. Grimes, Bryan, in Cowper, Pulaski, *Extracts of Letters of Bryan Grimes to His Wife*, 119.
79. Cox, William R., "The Anderson-Ramseur-Cox Brigade," in Clark, Walter, *Histories of the Several Regiments*, Vol. 4, 458.
80. Report of the Committee Appointed by the North Carolina Literary and Historical Society, *Five Points in the Record of North Carolina in the Great War, 1861–65* (Goldsboro, NC: Nash Brothers, 1904), 67.
81. Pendleton, William N., *Official Records*, Vol. 46, pt. 1, 1282.
82. House, James W., CSRC.
83. Freeman, Douglas S., *Lee's Lieutenants*, Vol. 3, 728.
84. Grimes, Bryan, in Cowper, Pulaski, *Extracts of Letters of Bryan Grimes to His Wife*, 119.
85. Cox, William R., "The Anderson-Ramseur-Cox Brigade," in Clark, Walter, *Histories of the Several Regiments*, Vol. 4, 458.
86. Lee, Robert E., Lee's Report of the Surrender at Appomattox," in Buel, Clarence C., and Johnson, Robert U., *Battles and Leaders of the Civil War*, Vol. 4, 724.
87. Cox, William R., "The Anderson-Ramseur-Cox Brigade," in Clark, Walter, *Histories of the Several Regiments*, Vol. 4, 458.
88. Rawlings, John A., *Official Records*, Vol. 46, Pt. 1, 1162.
89. Freeman, Douglas S., *Lee's Lieutenants*, Vol. 3, 729.
90. Pendleton, William N., *Official Records*, Vol. 46, pt. 1, 1282.
91. Grimes, Bryan, in Cowper, Pulaski, *Extracts of Letters of Bryan Grimes to His Wife*, 120–1.
92. Grimes, Bryan, in Cowper, Pulaski, *Extracts of Letters of Bryan Grimes to His Wife*, 121.
93. Grimes, Bryan, in Cowper, Pulaski, *Extracts of Letters of Bryan Grimes to His Wife*, 121.
94. Cox, William R., "The Anderson-Ramseur-Cox Brigade," in Clark, Walter, *Histories of the Several Regiments*, Vol. 4, 458–9.
95. Cox, William R., "The Anderson-Ramseur-Cox Brigade," in Clark, Walter, *Histories of the Several Regiments*, Vol. 4, 458–9.
96. Metts, James I., "Last Shot Fired at Appomattox," *Confederate Veteran*, Vol. 7 (1899), 53.
97. Report of the Committee, *Five Points in the Record of North Carolina in the Great War, 1861–65*, 65.
98. McGill, Archy D., *Daily News and Observer, Raleigh*, 11 April 1865.
99. Allen, David C., letter, in Clark, Walter, *Histories of the Several Regiments*, Vol. 4, 505.
100. Bone, John W., *Record of a Soldier in the Late War*, 114.
101. Report of the Committee, *Five Points in the Record of North Carolina in the Great War, 1861–65*, 66.
102. Allen, David C., letter, in Clark, Walter, *Histories of the Several Regiments*, Vol. 4, 505.
103. Osborne, E. A., "Fourth Regiment," Clark, Walter, *Histories of the Several Regiments*, Vol. 1, 265.
104. Bone, John W., *Record of a Soldier in the Late War*, 114.
105. Schwab, Julius L., "Some Closing Events at Appomattox," *Confederate Veteran*, Vol. 8 (1900), 71.
106. Kaigler, William, "Concerning Last Charge At Appomattox," *Confederate Veteran*, Vol. 6 (1898), 524.
107. Schwab, Julius L., "Some Closing Events at Appomattox," *Confederate Veteran*, Vol. 8 (1900), 71.
108. Bearss, Edwin C., *The Petersburg Campaign*, Vol. 1, 555.
109. Schwab, Julius L., "Some Closing Events at Appomattox," *Confederate Veteran*, Vol. 8 (1900), 71.
110. Freeman, Douglas S., *Lee's Lieutenants*, Vol. 3, 740.
111. Gordon, John B., in LaBree, Ben, *Campfires of the Confederacy*, 462.
112. Pearce, T. H. (ed.), *Diary of Captain Henry A. Chambers*, 262.
113. Lee, Robert E., Lee's Report of the Surrender at Appomattox," in Buel, Clarence C., and Johnson, Robert U., *Battles and Leaders of the Civil War*, Vol. 4, 724.
114. Freeman, Douglas S., *Lee's Lieutenants*, Vol. 3, 741.
115. McGill, Archy D., *Daily News and Observer, Raleigh*, 11 April 1865.
116. Bone, John W., *Record of a Soldier in the Late War*, 115.
117. 30th North Carolina Infantry, CSRC.
118. Brock, R. A., *Paroles of the Army of Northern Virginia, R. E. Lee, Gen., C. S. A., Commanding, Surrendered at Appomattox C. H., VA, April 9, 1865, Southern Historical Society Papers*, Vol. XV (Richmond, VA: Wm. Ellis Jones Printer, 1887), 253–60.
119. Bone, John W., *Record of a Soldier in the Late War*, 116.
120. Bone, John W., *Record of a Soldier in the Late War*, 116.
121. Bone, John W., *Record of a Soldier in the Late War*, 116.
122. Freeman, Douglas S., *Lee's Lieutenants*, Vol. 3, 748.
123. Bone, John W., *Record of a Soldier in the Late War*, 117.
124. Ardrey, William E., *Diary*, 12 April 1865.
125. Freeman, Douglas S., *Lee's Lieutenants*, Vol. 3, 752.
126. Gordon, John B., in LaBree, Ben, *Campfires of the Confederacy*, 463.

127. Bone, John W., *Record of a Soldier in the Late War*, 120.
128. Ardrey, William E., *Diary*, 13 April 1865.
129. Smith, William A., *The Anson Guards*, 306–7.
130. 30th North Carolina Regiment. CSRC.
131. Horigan, Michael, *Elmira: Death Camp of the North* (Mechanicsburg, PA: Stackpole, 2002).
132. King, John R., *My Experience in the Confederate Army and in Northern Prisons* (Clarksburg, WV: United Daughters of the Confederacy, 1917), 48.
133. King, John R., *My Experience in the Confederate Army and in Northern Prisons*, 50–1.
134. Myers, Jimmy. Personal communication, 1 August 2015.
135. Venner, William Thomas, *The 11th North Carolina Infantry*, 219.

Bibliography

Books

Alleman, Tillie Pierce. *At Gettysburg: What a Girl Saw and Heard of the Battle.* New York: W. Lake Borland, 1889.

Barnett, John G. *The Civil War in North Carolina.* Chapel Hill: University of North Carolina Press, 1963.

Bates, Samuel P. *History of Pennsylvania Volunteers, 1861-1865.* Harrisburg, PA: State Printer, 1869-71.

Bauer, K. Jack, (ed.). *Soldiering: The Civil War Diary of Rice C. Bull.* Novato, CA: Presidio, 1977.

Bearrs, Edwin C. *The Petersburg Campaign: The Western Front Battles, September 1864—April 1865.* El Dorado Hills, CA: Savas Beatie, 2014.

Betts, Alexander. *Experience of a Confederate Chaplain, 1861-1864.* Greenville, SC: n. p., 1907.

Bigelow, John, Jr. *The Campaign of Chancellorsville: A Strategic and Tactical Study.* New Haven, CT: Yale University Press, 1910.

Bowen, James L. *History of the Thirty-Seventh Regiment Mass. Volunteers in the Civil War of 1861-1865.* Holyoke, MA: Clark W. Bryan & Co., 1884.

Brock, R. A. *Paroles of the Army of Northern Virginia, R. E. Lee, Gen., C. S. A., Commanding, Surrendered at Appomattox C. H., VA. April 9, 1865, Southern Historical Society Papers,* Vol. XV. Richmond, VA: Wm. Ellis Jones Printer, 1887.

Brown, Martha R. *Holding Sweet Communion: Civil War Letters Home.* Winston-Salem, NC: Briarpatch, 2012.

Bryan, Charles F., James C. Kelly, et al., (ed.). *Images From the Storm: Private Robert Know Sneden.* New York: Free, 2001.

Buell, Augustus C. *The Cannoneer: Recollections of Service in the Army of the Potomac.* Washington, D.C.: The National Tribune, 1890.

Catton, Bruce. *Mr. Lincoln's Army.* Garden City, NY: Doubleday, 1965.

Chapman, Craig S. *More Terrible Than Victory: North Carolina's Bloody Bethel Regiment, 1861-1865.* Dulles, VA: Brassey's, 1998.

Clark, Walter, (ed.). *Histories of the Several Regiments and Battalions from North Carolina in the Great War, 1861-65.* Raleigh, NC: E.M. Uzzell, 1901.

Collins, Darrell L. *Major General Robert E. Rodes of the Army of Northern Virginia: A Biography.* New York: Savas Beatie, 2008.

Cooling, Benjamin F. *The Day Lincoln Was Almost Shot: The Fort Stevens Story.* Lanham, MD: Scarecrow, 2013.

Cowan, Charles W. *Service of the Tenth New York Volunteers National Zouaves, in the War of the Rebellion.* New York: Charles H. Ludwig, 1882.

Cowper, Pulaski. *Extracts of Letters of Bryan Grimes to His Wife, Written While in Active Service in the Army of Northern Virginia.* Raleigh, NC: Edwards, Broughton & Co., 1883.

Cox, William R. "Address on the Life and Character of Maj. Gen. Stephen D. Ramseur." Raleigh, NC: E. M. Uzzell; Steam Printers and Binder, 1891.

Craig, Joel, and Charlene Baker, (ed.). *As You May Never See Us Again: The Civil War Letters of George and Walter Battle, 4th North Carolina Infantry.* Wake Forest, NC: Scuppernong, 2010.

Cramer, John H. *Lincoln Under Fire: The Complete Account of His Experiences During Early's Attack on Washington.* Knoxville: University of Tennessee Press, 2009.

Davis, Archie K. *Boy Colonel of the Confederacy: The Life and Times of Henry King Burgwyn, Jr.* Chapel Hill: University of North Carolina Press, 1985.

Davis, Charles E. *Three Years in the Army: The Story of the Thirteenth Massachusetts Volunteers.* Boston, MA: Estes and Lauriat, 1894.

Davis, Daniel T., and Phillip S. Greenwalt. *Bloody Autumn: The Shenandoah Valley Campaign of 1864.* El Dorado Hills, CA: Savas Beatie, 2013.

Davis, George B., Leslie J. Perry and Joseph W. Kirkley. *The Official Military Atlas of the Civil War.* New York: Fairfield, 1983.

Dawes, Rufus R. *Service with the Sixth Wisconsin Volunteers.* Marietta, OH: E. R. Alderman and Sons, 1890.

Day, William A. *A True History of Company I, 49th Regiment, North Carolina Troops in the Great Civil War Between the North and the South.* Newton, NC: Enterprise Job Office, 1898.

Delpino, Irene R. *A Broad River Digest.* Philadelphia, PA: Omega, 1990.

Doubleday, Abner. *Chancellorsville and Gettysburg: Campaigns of the Civil War—VI.* New York: Charles Scribner's Sons, 1882.

Early, Gerald L. *The Second United States Sharpshooters in the Civil War: A History and Roster.* Jefferson, NC: McFarland, 2009.

Ent, Uzal W. *The Pennsylvania Reserves in the Civil*

War: A Comprehensive History. Jefferson, NC: McFarland, 2014.
Foote, Shelby. *The Civil War: A Narrative.* New York: Vintage, 1958.
Freeman, Douglas S. *Lee's Lieutenants: Manassas to Malvern Hill.* New York: Scribner's, 1942.
Gallagher, Gary W. *Stephen Dodson Ramseur: Lee's Gallant General.* Chapel Hill: University of North Carolina Press, 1985.
Gallagher, Gary W., (ed.). *Fighting for the Confederacy: The Personal Recollections of General Edward Porter Alexander.* Chapel Hill: University of North Carolina Press, 1989.
Gallagher, Gary W., (ed.). *The Spotsylvania Campaign.* Chapel Hill: University of North Carolina Press, 1998.
Gibbon, John. *The Artilleryist Manual.* New York: D. Van Nostrand, 1860.
Goolrick, William K. *Rebels Resurgent: Fredericksburg to Chancellorsville.* Alexandria, VA: Time-Life, 1985.
Gordon, John B. *Reminiscences of the Civil War.* New York: Charles Scribner's Sons, 1903.
Gragg, Rod. *Covered With Glory: The 26th North Carolina Infantry at the Battle of Gettysburg.* New York: HarperCollins, 2000.
Greene, A. Wilson. *The Petersburg Campaign: The Final Battles.* Mason City, IA: Savas, 2000.
Hardy, Michael C. *Civil War Charlotte: Last Capital of the Confederacy.* Charleston, SC: History, 2012.
Harmon, Troy D. *The Great Revival of 1863: The Effects Upon Lee's Army of Northern Virginia.* Damascus, MD: Penny Hill, 2013.
Haskell, John C., (ed.). *The Haskell Memoirs.* New York, NY: G. P. Putnam's Sons, 1960.
Hess, Earl J. *Lee's Tar Heels: The Pettigrew-Kirkland-MacRae Brigade.* Chapel Hill: University of North Carolina Press, 2002.
Hitchcock, Frederick, L. *War from the Inside: The Story of the 132nd Regiment Pennsylvania Volunteer Infantry in the War for the Suppression of the Rebellion, 1862-1863.* Philadelphia, PA: J. B. Lippincott, 1904.
Horigan, Michael. *Elmira: Death Camp of the North.* Mechanicsburg, PA: Stackpole, 2002.
Hotchkins, Jedediah. *Make Me a Map of the Valley: The Civil War Journal of Stonewall Jackson's Topographer.* Dallas, TX: Southern Methodist University Press, 1973.
Jaynes, Gregory. *The Killing Ground: Wilderness to Cold Harbor.* Alexandria, VA: Time-Life, 1986.
Johnson, Robert U., and Clarence C. Buel. *Battles and Leaders of the Civil War.* New York: Century, 1887.
Jones, Terry L., (ed.). *Campbell Brown's Civil War: With Ewell and the Army of Northern Virginia.* Baton Rouge: Louisiana State University Press, 2001.
Jordan, Weymouth T., (comp.). *North Carolina Troops, 1861-1865: A Roster.* Raleigh: North Carolina Office of Archives and History, 1981.
Keyes, C. M. *The Military History of the 123rd Regiment Ohio Volunteer Infantry.* Sandusky, OH: Register Steam Press, 1874.
King, John R. *My Experience in the Confederate Army and in Northern Prisons.* Clarksburg, WV: United Daughters of the Confederacy, 1917.
Kirk, Hyland C. *Heavy Guns and Light: History of the 4th New York Heavy Artillery.* New York: C.T. Dillingham, 1890.

LaBree, Ben. *Campfires of the Confederacy.* Louisville, KY: Courier-Journal, 1898.
Lawing, Mike, and Carolyn Lawing, (eds.). *My Dearest Friend: The Civil War Correspondence of Carnelia McGrimsey and Lewis Warlick.* Durham, NC: Carolina Academic, 2000.
Lincoln, William S. *Life with the Thirty-Fourth Massachusetts Infantry in the War of the Rebellion.* Worchester, MA: Press of Noyes, Snow, and Co., 1879.
Livermore, Thomas L. *Days and Events: 1860-1866.* Boston, MA: Houghton Mifflin, 1900.
Matter, William D. *If It Takes All Summer: The Battle of Spotsylvania.* Chapel Hill: University of North Carolina Press, 1998.
McWhiney, Grady, and Perry D. Johnson. *Attack and Die: Civil War Military Tactics and the Southern Heritage.* Tuscaloosa: University of Alabama Press, 1982.
Mehegan, Julianne, and David Mehegan, (ed.). *Record of a Soldier in the Late War: The Confederate Memoir of John Wesley Bone.* Hingham, MA: Chinquapin, 2014.
Newell, Joseph K. *Annals of the 10th Regiment Massachusetts Volunteers.* Springfield, MA: C. A. Nichols & Co., 1875.
Norman, William. *A Portion of My Life: Being a Short and Imperfect History Written While a Prisoner of War on Johnson's Island, 1864.* Winston-Salem, NC: John F. Blair, 1959.
Page, Charles. *History of the Fourteenth Regiment Connecticut Vol. Infantry.* Meriden, CT: Horton, 1907.
Patchan, Scott C. *The Last Battle of Winchester.* El Dorado Hills, CA: Savas Beatie, 2013.
Patchan, Scott C. *Shenandoah Summer: The 1864 Valley Campaign.* Lincoln: University of Nebraska Press, 2007.
Pearce, T. H., (ed.). *Diary of Captain Henry A. Chambers.* Wendell, NC: Broadfoot's Bookmark, 1983.
Phisterer, Frederick. *New York in the War of the Rebellion, 1861-1865.* Albany, NY: J. B. Lyon, 1912.
Photographic History of the Civil War in Ten Volumes. New York: Review of Reviews, 1911.
Pohl, Robert S. *Urban Legends and Historic Lore of Washington.* Charleston, SC: History Press, 2013.
Priest, John M. *Antietam: The Soldiers' Battle.* Shippensburg, PA: White Mane, 1989.
Priest, John Michael. *Into the Fight: Pickett's Charge at Gettysburg.* Shippensburg, PA: White Mane, 1998.
Report of the Committee Appointed by the North Carolina Literary and Historical Society. *Five Points in the Record of North Carolina in the Great War, 1861-65.* Goldsboro, NC: Nash Brothers, 1904.
Rhea, Gordon C. *To the North Anna: Grant and Lee, May 13-25, 1864.* Baton Rouge: Louisiana State University Press, 2000.
Robinson, Charles, M. *General Crook and the Western Frontier.* Norman: University of Oklahoma Press, 2001.
Roe, Alfred S. *The Tenth Regiment, Massachusetts Infantry, 1861-1864.* Springfield, MA: Tenth Regiment Veteran Association, 1909.
Roe, Alfred S., and Charles Nutt. *History of the First Regiment of Heavy Artillery Massachusetts Volunteers.* Boston, MA: Commonwealth, 1917.
Runge, William H., (ed.), *Four Years in the Confederate Artillery: The Diary of Pvt. H. R. Berkeley.* Chapel Hill: University of North Carolina Press, 1961.

Sears, Stephen W. *Chancellorsville.* Boston, MA: Houghlin Mifflin, 1996.
Sears, Stephen W. *To the Gates of Richmond.* New York: Ticknor and Fields, 1992.
Serville, William P. *History of the First Regiment, Delaware Volunteers: From the Commencement of the Three Months Service to the Final Muster-Out at the Close of the Rebellion.* Wilmington: Historical Society of Delaware, 1913.
Smith, John D. *The History of the Nineteenth Regiment of Maine Volunteer Infantry, 1862–1865.* Minneapolis, MN: John Day Smith, 1909.
Smith, William A. *The Anson Guards: Company C, Fourteenth Regiment North Carolina Volunteers, 1861–1865.* Charlotte, NC: Stone, 1914.
Stevens, Charles A. *Berdan's United States Sharpshooters in the Army of the Potomac, 1861–1865.* St. Paul, MN: The Price-McGill Co., 1892.
Stewart, George R. *Pickett's Charge: A Microhistory of the Final Attack at Gettysburg, July 3, 1863.* Boston, MA: Houghton Mifflin, 1959.
Taylor, Michael W. *To Drive the Enemy from Southern Soil: The Letters of Col. Francis Marion Parker and the History of the 30th Regiment North Carolina Troops.* Dayton, OH: Morningside House, 1998.
Tidball, Eugene C. *No Disgrace to My Country: The Life of John C. Tidball.* Kent, OH: Kent State University Press, 2002.
Tremain, Henry E. *Last Hours of Sheridan's Cavalry: A Reprint of War Memoranda.* New York: Bonnell, Silver & Bowers, 1904.
Trudeau, Noah A. *The Last Citadel: Petersburg, Virginia, June 1864—April 1865.* Baton Rouge: Louisiana State University Press, 1991.
Tuther, T., Jr. (comp.). *Kelley's Wilmington Directory, Business Directory for 1860–61.* Wilmington, NC: Geo. H. Kelley Bookseller and Stationer, 1860.
Vaill, Theodore F. *History of the Second Connecticut Volunteer Heavy Artillery, Originally the Nineteenth Connecticut Vols.* Winsted, CT: Winsted Printing Co., 1868.
Venner, William Thomas. *The 11th North Carolina Infantry in the Civil War.* Jefferson, NC: McFarland, 2015.
Venner, William Thomas. *Hoosiers' Honor: The Iron Brigade's 19th Indiana Regiment.* Shippensburg, PA: Burd Street, 1998.
Venner, William Thomas. *The 7th Tennessee Infantry in the Civil War.* Jefferson, NC: McFarland, 2013.
The War of the Rebellion: A Compilation of the Official Records of the Union and Confederate Armies. Washington, D.C.: Government Printing Office, 1880–1901.
Warford, Christopher, (ed.). *The Civil War in North Carolina: Soldiers and Civilians' Letters and Diaries, 1861–1865.* Jefferson, NC: McFarland, 2003.
Warner, Ezra J. *Generals in Gray: Lives of the Confederate Commanders.* Baton Rouge: Louisiana State University Press, 1959.
Washburn, George H. *A Complete Military History of the 108th Regiment N.Y. Vol., from 1862 to 1894.* Rochester, NY: Press of E. R. Andrews, 1984.
Welch, Spencer. *A Confederate Surgeon's letters to His Wife.* New York: Neale, 1911.
Welles, Gideon. *Diary of Gideon Wells, Secretary of the Navy Under Lincoln and Johnson.* Boston, MA: Houghton, Mifflin, 1911.
Wert, Jeffry D. *From Winchester to Cedar Creek: The Shenandoah Campaign of 1864.* New York: Simon & Schuster, 1987.
Wildes, Thomas F. *Record of the One Hundred and Sixteenth Ohio Infantry Volunteers in the War of the Rebellion.* Sandusky, OH: I. F. Mack and Bros., 1884.
Wilmer, L. Allison, J. H. Jarrett and George W. Vernon. *History and Roster of Maryland Volunteers, War of 1861–5.* Baltimore, MD: Guggenheim, Well, and Co., 1899.
Wright, Stuart T. *The Confederate Letters of Benjamin H. Freeman.* Hicksville, NY: Exposition, 1974.

Diaries and Journals

Family History Collection

Ardrey, William E. Diary. Davidson College Archives, Davidson, NC.
Bone, Walter J., Collection. North Carolina Department of Archives and History (Digital Collection), Raleigh, NC.
Gould, John M., Papers. Dartmouth College Library, Hanover, NH.
Harris, Catherine. Papers, Southern Historical Collection, Wilson Library, UNC-Chapel Hill, NC.
Sillers-Holmes Family Correspondence. University of Notre Dame Rare Books and Special Collections, IN.
Thirtieth North Carolina Troops. The Living History Association of North Carolina, Concord.
Vance, Zebulon Baird. Papers #3952, Southern Historical Collection, Wilson Library, UNC-Chapel Hill, NC.

Manuscripts

Compiled Service Records of Confederate Soldiers Who Served in Organizations from the State of North Carolina. Washington, D.C.
1850 United States Census, Agricultural Schedule, North Carolina.
1860 United States Census, Agricultural Schedule, North Carolina.
1860 United States Census, North Carolina.
Puckett, Clarence P. "Richard David Brooks—The Young Man at War."
Schenck, David. *Sketches of Maj. Gen. Stephen Dodson Ramseur.* Self-published, 1892.

Newspapers and Periodicals

Atlantic Monthly (Washington, D.C.), 1838.
Baltimore Sun (MD), 29 June 2013.
A Broad River Digest (NC), 1990–1991.
Civil War History (OH), Vol. 47, No. 2, June 2001.
Civil War Times Illustrated (VA), 1969, 1979.
Confederate Veteran (GA), 1890–1923.
Daily News and Observer, Raleigh (NC), April 1865.
Gallipolis Journal (OH), 10 November 1864.
Gettysburg Magazine (PA), Vol. 4 (January 1991).
Military Images (VA), Vol. 3, No. 6 (May-June), 1982.
New York Herald, 2 July 1863, 12 August 1863.
New York Times, 21 August 1864.
New Yorker, 9 July 1863.
Newark Sunday News Magazine (NJ), 29 January 1961.
North Carolina Standard, 29 July 1863.
Old New Hanover (NC) *Genealogical Society,* 2005.

Ontario County Times (NY), 20 May 1864.
Our Living and Our Dead (NC), 4 March 1874.
Papers of the 2006 Gettysburg National Military Park Seminar (PA), 2008.
Raleigh (NC) *News and Observer*, 16 September 1861.
Salem Press (NY), 1863.
Southern Bivouac (KY), August 1886.
Southern Historical Society Papers (VA), 1886, 1891.
Weekly Raleigh (NC) *Register*. 10 July 1861.

Personal Communications

Brantley, Steven. Personal communication, 3 June 2015, 19 June 2015.
Fuller, Ted. Personal communication, 12 September 2015.
Mellott, David. Personal communication, 24 January 2015.
Myers, Jimmy. Personal communication, 1 August 2015.
Ridgeway, Matt. Personal communication, 13 September 2015.
Vick, Robert. Personal communication, 3 June 2015.
Whirley, Vonda, and Jean Mitrovich. Personal communication, 10 June 2015.
Wood, Rob. Personal communication, 3 June 2015.

Websites

Peake, Heather. "General John D. Imboden and the Confederate Retreat from Gettysburg," *Civil War Interactive*, http://www.civilwarinteractive.com/ArticleGeneralJohnDImboden.htm.
Trout, Kristen. "Their Brave and Beloved Commander: Maj. Gen. Robert E. Rodes at Third Winchester," *Noble Deed of the Civil War Blog*, November 3, 2015.
Welling, Edgar P. "On the Picket Line at Kelly's Ford," Diary of 1st Lieut. Edgar P. Welling, Co. C., 150th New York Volunteers. 150th Regiment NY Infantry website. http://www.150thpvibucktails.com/about.html.
Wynn, Jake. "The 96th Pennsylvania on May 10, 1864." website—winninghistory.blogspot.com.

Index

Abbott, Macon, Pvt. (Co. B) 298, 315
Abernathy, Sidney, Lt. (Co. D) 71, 83, 108, 130, 137, 279, 329
Absher, Edmund, Pvt. (Co. G) 297
Adams, John P., Pvt. (Co. G) 358
Adams, William, Pvt. (Co. K) 176, 286, 302, 387
Addison, Quincy E., Pvt. (Co. I) 379
Adkins, William H., Pvt. (Co. K) 268, 278, 286, 302, 381
Alabama Inf.: 3rd 111, 112; 6th 53, 62
Alexander, J. Lee, Pvt. (Co. K) 281, 385
Alexander, James M., Pvt. (Co. K) 285, 387
Alexander, Samuel D., Pvt. (Co. K) 278, 381
Alexander, Thomas P., Pvt. (Co. K) 386
Allen, Charles N., Lt. (Co. D) 16, 19, 21, 28, 30, 39, 45, 49, 51, 52, 63, 71, 74, 78, 83, 96, 108, 112, 124, 274, 330
Allen, Charles W., Pvt. (Co. C) 327
Allen, David C., Lt.-Cpt. (Co. C) 5, 16, 19, 28, 30, 39, 45, 49, 51, 63, 71, 74, 78, 83, 96, 108, 117, 118, 124, 130, 137, 145, 151, 152, 160, 162, 172, 175, 177, 179, 180, 181, 183, 185, 186, 187, 188, 189, 190, 191, 194, 195, 196, 199, 200, 201, 202, 203, 205, 206, 207, 210, 216, 233, 235, 241, 246, 249, 255, 259, 260, 289, 292, 321
Allen, Elias G., Pvt.-Cpl. (Co. D) 74, 135, 270, 278, 335
Allen, Francis R. Pvt. (Co. D) 336
Allen, Henry C., Sgt. (Co. D) 272, 335
Allen, James P., Cpl. (Co. D) 35, 266, 330
Allen, James H., Pvt. (Co. K) 298, 386
Allen, Marion F., Pvt. (Co. D) 269, 276, 330
Allen, Solomon J., Lt. (Co. D) 5, 329
Allen, Wyatt M., Pvt. (Co. D) 300
Allman, Gideon, Pvt. (Co. A) 282, 312

Alsbrook, S.C., Pvt. (Co. A) 279, 301, 312
Alsop farm, Virginia 155
Amelia Court House, Virginia 245, 246, 247
Ammerman, Robert W., U.S., Pvt. 165
Anderson, George B., CS, Gen. 18, 20, 22, 25, 28, 31, 32, 47, 48, 49, 52, 58, 59, 68
Anderson, M.J., Pvt. (Co. K) 295, 389
Anderson, Richard, CS, Gen. 84, 202, 249
Anderson, Thomas J., Pvt. (Co. I) 291, 379
Anderson, William, Pvt. (Co. K) 301, 386
Appomattox Court House, Virginia 253, 255, 256
Appomattox River 234, 235, 244, 250, 251, 252
Archer, James, CS, Gen. 73, 89
Ardrey, William E., Pvt.-Lt.-Cpt. (Co. K) 1, 2, 6, 12, 13, 14, 15, 16, 17, 19, 20, 21, 22, 23, 24, 25, 26, 27, 28, 29, 30, 31, 32, 37, 38, 39, 40, 41, 42, 43, 44, 45, 46, 47, 50, 51, 52, 54, 63, 64, 66, 67, 69, 77, 79, 80, 81, 82, 83, 84, 88, 91, 94, 95, 97, 98, 99, 100, 101, 102, 104, 105, 111, 112, 123, 126, 127, 128, 129, 137, 138, 139, 140, 142, 143, 144, 145, 146, 147, 148, 151, 152, 153, 154, 155, 156, 157, 158, 160, 161, 163, 165, 169, 170, 171, 172, 174, 175, 176, 177, 180, 181, 182, 183, 184, 185, 186, 188, 190, 191, 201, 202, 203, 204, 205, 207, 208, 209, 212, 215, 216, 220, 222, 223, 224, 231, 232, 233, 234, 235, 241, 246, 249, 255, 260, 261, 287, 294, 381
Armfield, John J., Pvt. (Co. C) 236, 238, 291
Armistead, Lewis, CS, Gen. 34
Armstrong, Gray R., Pvt. (Co. I) 242, 290, 379
Arrington, James L., Pvt. (Co. B) 271, 285, 302, 315
Arrington, Kearny, Lt. (Co. I) 81, 108, 130, 145, 151, 172, 285, 379

Arrington, Peter, Sgt. Maj.-Lt. 133, 134, 136, 138, 145, 151, 152, 165, 282, 305
Arrington, William T., Cpt. (Co. I) 5, 14, 17, 19, 28, 30, 35, 39, 43, 267, 371
Armfield, John J., Pvt. (Co. C) 303, 327
Asher, Edmond, Pvt. (Co. G) 358
Askew, John, Pvt. (Co. B) 279, 301, 315
Aughtry, William A., Pvt. (Co. E) 298, 338
Autry, William, Pvt. (Co. A) 298, 306
Aycock, Edward S., Pvt. (Co. B) 292, 315
Aycock, George G., Pvt. (Co. B) 251, 290, 291, 315
Aycock, Samuel, Pvt. (Co. B) 134, 278, 315

Badgett, James W., Lt.-Cpt. (Co. G) 17, 71, 74, 78, 83, 96, 108, 124, 130, 137, 145, 151, 169, 175, 176, 180, 235, 242, 246, 259, 260, 286
Badgett, John D., Pvt. (Co. G) 264, 294, 358
Badgett, Sandy, Sgt. (Co. G) 180, 185, 190, 196, 200, 205, 293, 355
Badgett, William J., Sgt. (Co. G) 272, 286, 294, 355
Baggot, James W., Pvt. (Co. A) 35, 265, 306, 354
Bailey, Elias D., Pvt. (Co. K) 190, 303
Bailey, Allen, Lt. (Co. D) 5, 329
Bailey, Benjamin, Pvt. (Co. F) 293, 347
Bailey, Elias D., Pvt. (Co. F) 386
Bailey, James A., Pvt. (Co. K) 301, 386
Bailey, James P., Pvt. (Co. K) 273, 281
Bailey, Jeremiah, Pvt. (Co. D) 228, 290, 330
Bailey, Jones F., Pvt. (Co. D) 297, 330
Bailey, William, Pvt. (Co. K) 285, 288, 387
Bailey, William M., Pvt. (Co. D) 297, 330

Index

Bailey, Young F., Pvt. (Co. D) 168, 283, 330
Baker, Henry C., Pvt. (Co. H) 49, 268
Baker, James, Pvt. (Co. H) 363
Baker, Henry H., Pvt. (Co. H) 368
Baker, James H., Pvt. (Co. K) 260
Baker, Jeptha, Pvt. (Co. K) 58, 270, 382
Balentine, James N., Pvt. (Co. C) 301
Bales, Elijah M., Cpl.-Sgt. (Co. K) 120, 275, 294, 382
Bales, James P., Pvt. (Co. K) 295
Balentine, James N., Pvt. (Co. C) 279, 328
Balkum, Lemuel, Pvt. (Co. E) 300, 345
balloons 20
Barefoot, Noah G., Pvt. (Co. K) 273, 290, 386
Barker, John W., Pvt. (Co. D) 112, 274, 280, 330
Barkley, James H., Cpl. (Co. I) 371
Barlow, Francis, U.S., Col. 62
Barnes, Bryant B., Pvt. (Co. I) 296, 372
Barnes, Hilmon, Pvt. (Co. G) 291, 361
Barnes, William S., Pvt. (Co. F) 135, 278, 293
Barnett, George P., Pvt. (Co. G) 267, 294
Barnett, Robert, Pvt. (Co. K) 93, 273
Barnett, James A., Lt.-Cpt. (Co. G) 5, 17, 30, 39, 45, 49, 51, 63, 354
Barnett, James P., 1st Sgt. (Co. G) 354
Barnett, Robert C., Pvt. (Co. K) 385
Barnett, William S., Pvt. (Co. G) 295, 352, 355
Bass, John S., Pvt. (Co. I) 267, 273, 372
Bass, Richard H., Pvt. (Co. I) 264, 372
Bass, William, Pvt. (Co. I) 299, 376
Bass, William E., Pvt.-Cpl. (Co. A) 282, 306
Batchelor, Andrew J., Pvt. (Co. I) 273, 295, 376
Batchelor, Elkahah, Pvt. (Co. I) 372
Batchelor, Henry H., Pvt. (Co. I) 95, 267, 273
Batchelor, John W., Pvt. (Co. I) 376
Batchelor, Neverson A., Pvt. (Co. I) 281, 301, 372
Batchelor, Redmond W., Pvt. (Co. I) 273, 295, 376
Batchelor, Ruffin, Pvt. (Co. I) 242, 288, 290, 380
Batchelor, Samuel M., Pvt. (Co. I) 377
Batchelor, Thomas R., Pvt. (Co. I) 377
Batchelor, Van Buren, Sgt. (Co. I) 270, 281, 372
Batchelor, William D., Cpl. (Co. I) 133, 278, 372
Battle, Cullen, CS, Gen. 143, 147, 156, 184, 197

Battle, Lawrence F., Pvt. (Co. I) 377
Batts, William J., Pvt. (Co. I) 219, 289, 294, 377
Baxter, Henry, U.S., Gen. 110
Beasley, Calvin, Pvt. (Co. E) 296, 338
Beasley, Edward, Pvt. (Co. E) 251, 283, 291, 338
Beaver Creek Dam, Virginia 22, 23, 183
Bell, Arkin, Pvt. (Co. I) 199, 288, 377
Bell, Bennett, Pvt. (Co. F) 290
Bell, Charles E., Lt. (Co. K) 5, 381
Bell, John, Pvt. (Co. C) 322
Bell, Nathan, Pvt. (Co. K) 300, 387
Bell, Robert, Pvt. (Co. A) 282, 312
Bell, Robert, Pvt. (Co. B) 320
Bell, William, Cpl. (Co. B) 175, 180, 185, 263, 314
Bell, William B., Pvt. (Co. F) 295, 347
Belle Grove plantation, Virginia 225, 226, 232
Bennett, James A., Cpt. (Co. G) 19, 27
Bennett, Risden, CS, Col. 52, 66, 95, 113, 129, 133, 136, 137, 139, 153, 156, 165, 166, 167, 168, 170, 183, 184
Bennett, Solomon W., Lt. (Co. C) 16, 19, 30, 45, 51, 71, 83, 95, 106, 164, 271, 322
Bentley, Moses, Pvt. (Co. K) 204, 288, 292, 382
Bentley, William, Pvt. (Co. K) 268
Benton, Bradley C., Pvt. (Co. A) 306
Benton, Ellis A., Cpl. (Co. E) 291, 338
Benton, Thomas A., Pvt. (Co. C) 322
Berryville, Virginia 200
Best, John B., Pvt.-Sgt. (Co. E) 63, 251, 269, 291, 339
Best, Rowland H., Pvt. (Co. E) 339
Betts, Alexander, Chaplain 21, 22, 23, 31, 32, 44, 61, 66, 68, 69, 70, 77, 79, 99, 101, 104, 107, 112, 120, 122, 125, 126, 128, 129, 136, 138, 139, 143, 145, 148, 187, 192, 196, 201, 204, 205, 221, 222, 235, 238, 239, 305
Bicknell, Benjamin E., Pvt. (Co. C) 326
Bidwell, Daniel, U.S., Col. 194, 195
Big Bethel, battle 3
Bishop, Alfred, Pvt. (Co. B) 265, 315
Bishop, Samuel D., Pvt. (Co. B) 93, 271, 315
Bissett, Payton, Pvt. (Co. I) 268, 377
Black, Alfred, Pvt. (Co. H) 264, 285, 363
Black, Baker B., Pvt. (Co. B) 93
Black, George W., Pvt. (Co. B) 93
Black, James, Pvt.-Sgt. (Co. K) 60, 143, 382
Black, John, Pvt. (Co. K) 36, 78
Black, John H., Pvt. (Co. K) 268

Black, John N., Pvt. (Co. K) 298, 382
Black, John N., Sgt. (Co. K) 288
Black, T.A., Pvt. (Co. K) 144
Black, Thomas A., Pvt. (Co. K) 300, 387
Blacknail, Thomas B., Pvt. (Co. G) 301, 354
Blackwelder, Wiley, Pvt. (Co. C) 279, 301, 328
Blackwell, John, Pvt. (Co. G) 267, 358
Blalock, F. Marion, Pvt. (Co. H) 267, 363
Bland, David, Pvt. (Co. E) 296, 339
Bland, John J., Pvt. (Co. E) 204, 266, 288, 339
Blanton, Morris, Pvt. (Co. E) 264, 342
Blanton, Thomas, Pvt. (Co. E) 339
Bledsoe, Giles, Pvt. (Co. D) 293, 335
Blevins, Andrew, Pvt. (Co. G) 272, 358
Blevins, Harvey, Pvt. (Co. G) 291, 358
Blevins, Johnathan, Pvt. (Co. G) 272, 358
Blevins, Shadrach, Pvt. (Co. G) 185, 287, 362
Blizzard, William H., (Co. G) 298, 358
Bobbitt, Alexander G., Pvt. (Co. G) 297, 355
Bobbitt, Burwell B., Pvt. (Co. B) 93, 263, 271, 315
Bobbitt, E. Fletcher, Pvt. (Co. B) 297, 319
Bobbitt, Isham C., Pvt. (Co. G) 195, 287, 355
Bone, Hardy H., Pvt. (Co. I) 297, 372
Bone, John W., Pvt. (Co. I) 3, 6, 7, 8, 9, 10, 12, 13, 14, 20, 21, 22, 23, 24, 25, 26, 27, 32, 33, 34, 35, 37, 38, 39, 45, 46, 47, 66, 70, 71, 74, 76, 79, 85, 86, 88, 90, 93, 94, 95, 96, 97, 132, 136, 139, 150, 153, 155, 156, 157, 158, 160, 162, 165, 166, 168, 171, 223, 224, 231, 233, 234, 235, 237, 239, 240, 243, 244, 249, 252, 253, 254, 255, 259, 260, 261, 267, 285, 294, 372
Boney, Hiram S., Pvt. (Co. E) 289, 342
Boney, James T., Pvt. (Co. E) 26, 264, 339
Boney, Joseph K., Pvt. (Co. E) 297, 343
Boney, William J., Lt. (Co. E) 5, 338
Boon, Joseph H., Pvt. (Co. I) 298, 377
Boon, Nicholas, Pvt. (Co. A) 282, 307
Boon, Stephen, Pvt. (Co. A) 265, 282, 307
Boon, Sylvester, Pvt. (Co. A) 307
Borgus, Reuben, Pvt. (Co. B) 279, 319
Borrows, James B., Pvt. (Co. I) 126, 379

Index

Bostick, Bryant W., Pvt. (Co. E) 153, 281, 343
Bostick, David R., Pvt. (Co. E) 343
Boswell, William H., Pvt. (Co. A) 133, 277, 312
Bowen, John R., Pvt. (Co. E) 339
Bowers, John, Pvt. (Co. C) 322
Bowles, David, Pvt. (Co. D) 335
Bowlin, Charles E., Pvt. (Co. D) 272
Bowlin, Willis N., Pvt. (Co. D) 335
Bowman, Riley, Pvt. (Co. K) 387
Boyce, Samuel, Pvt.-Sgt. (Co. K) 97, 134, 135, 278, 382
Boyce, William, Pvt. (Co. F) 266, 347
Boyd, James A., Pvt. (Co. G) 359
Brack, Baker B., Pvt. (Co. B) 271, 315
Brack, George W., Pvt. (Co. B) 271, 315
Bradford, William H., Pvt. (Co. G) 295, 355
Bradley, Oliver, Cpl. (Co. F) 298, 347
Bradshaw, B.D., Pvt. (Co. E) 293, 343
Bradshaw, James B., Pvt. (Co. E) 128, 277, 289, 339
Bradshaw, Obed, Pvt. (Co. E) 272, 343
Bradshaw, Owen K., Pvt. (Co. A) 307
Bradshaw, Robert M., Pvt. (Co. A) 299, 307
Bradshaw, Samuel, Pvt. (Co. E) 342
Bradshaw, V.B., Pvt. (Co. K) 301, 388
Bradshaw, William K., Pvt. (Co. A) 307
Brafford, Eli, Pvt. (Co. H) 264, 363
Brame, John M., Lt. (Co. B) 5, 314
Branch, Everett, Pvt. (Co. H) 147, 370
Branch, Lawrence, CSA-Gen. 12, 13
Brantley, John R., Pvt. (Co. I) 267, 278, 372
Branton, Charles E., Pvt. (Co. D) 272, 280, 335
Branton, Lewis O., Pvt. (Co D) 337
Brassfield, James W., Pvt. (Co. D) 275, 303, 335
Brasswell, James B., Pvt. (Co. F) 284, 293, 347
Bray, John W., Pvt. (Co. E) 282, 345
Breedlove, John H., Pvt. (Co. G) 355
Brewer, Abraham H., Pvt.-Cpl. (Co. A) 119, 122, 275, 276, 292, 307
Brewer, James H., Pvt. (Co. K) 386
Brewer, Warren, Pvt. (Co. F) 296, 347
Bridges, George W., Pvt. (Co. D) 298, 331
Bridges, Joseph, Pvt. (Co. A) 312
Brewer, James H., Pvt. (Co. K) 298
Brigman, John, Pvt. (Co. E) 302, 345
Briggs, George W., Dr. (F & S) 120, 128, 153, 156, 292, 305
Brigman, John, Pvt. (Co. E) 184, 286

Brinkley, Henry, Pvt. (Co. K) 388
Brinkley, Thomas H., Pvt. (Co. B) 320
Brooks, Henry R., Pvt. (Co. G) 94, 185, 269, 272, 287, 359
Brookes, James L., Sgt. (Co. G) 269, 359
Brooks, Richard D., Pvt.-Cpl. (Co. G) 35, 79, 94, 134, 154, 187, 227, 272, 294, 359
Brooks, William A., Lt, (Co. G) 354
Brown, A. Singa, Cpl. (Co. H) 277, 363
Brown, Alexander, Lt., (Co. H) 112, 274, 280, 363
Brown, Alfred, Pvt. (Co. G) 298, 359
Brown, Felix, Pvt. (Co. E) 184, 286, 343
Brown, George E., Pvt. (Co. A) 265, 268, 312
Brown, Hamilton, CS, Col. 197, 239
Brown, James, Pvt. (Co. H) 58, 264, 269, 364
Brown, Jesse, Pvt. (Co. E) 339
Brown, John 69
Brown, John (1st), Pvt. (Co. E) 168, 296, 339
Brown, John (2nd), Pvt. (Co. E) 284, 345
Brown, Wesley, Pvt. (Co. G) 298, 359
Brown, William A., Pvt. (Co. G) 359
Brown, William E., Pvt. (Co. B) 292, 320
Brown, William H., Cpl. (Co. F) 280, 347
Brown, William W., Cpl. (Co. F) 269
Brunswick Double-Quicks 5, 321
Bryan, James H., Cpl.-Sgt. (Co. I) 267, 278, 372
Bryant, Charles, Pvt. (Co. F) 269, 347
Bryant, James H., Pvt. (Co. I) 294
Bryant, John, Pvt. (Co. F) 264, 352
Buchanan, Joseph, Pvt. (Co. H) 302, 368
Buchanan, Null, Pvt. (Co. H) 300, 364
Buchanan, Robert, U.S., Lt. Col. 27
Buchanan, Thomas, Pvt. (Co. H) 298, 364
Buchanan, William M., Pvt. (Co. H) 264, 364
Buff, Peter, Pvt. (Co. B) 161, 271, 283, 319
Buff, William, Pvt. (Co. B) 319
Buie, Daniel, Pvt. (Co. H) 264, 364
Buie, John, Sgt. (Co. H) 268, 280, 364
Bunn, Benjamin, Pvt. (Co. I) 67, 372
Bunn, Elias, Lt. (Co. I) 5, 371
Bunn, James D., Pvt. (Co. I) 294, 377
Burgess, Hardy, Pvt. (Co. F) 161, 284, 293, 347
Burgess, William H., Pvt. (Co. H) 163, 285, 370

Burns, Ottoway J., Pvt. (Co. C) 322
Burnside, Ambrose, USA-Gen. 12
Burroughs, William A., Cpl. (Co. G) 177, 185, 287, 355
Burton, J.C., Pvt. (Co. K) 295, 388
Burton, Robert W., Pvt. (Co. G) 355
Butler, Benjamin A., Pvt. (Co. E) 269, 339
Butler, Benjamin C., Sgt. (Co. C) 223, 232, 235, 242, 246, 255, 260
Butler, Benjamin L., Sgt. (Co. C) 265, 292, 321
Butler, Benjamin, Pvt. (Co. E) 6
Butler, Edward N., Pvt. (Co. A) 94, 271, 312
Butler, George C., Pvt. (Co. A) 307
Butler, Hartwell, Pvt. (Co. A) 279, 307
Butler, Henry G., Pvt. (Co. E) 185, 286, 343
Butler, James C., Pvt. (Co. E) 290
Butler, James R., Pvt. (Co. A) 307
Butler, John C., Pvt. (Co. C) 75, 270, 283, 302, 322
Butler, Joseph, Pvt. (Co. A) 155, 282, 307
Butler, Railford D., Pvt. (Co. A) 282, 307
Byrd, John, Pvt. (Co. C) 299, 322

Cain, Lorenzo, Lt. (Co. C) 6, 42, 297, 321
Caldwell, John, U.S., Gen. 61
Camp Holmes, North Carolina 13
Camp Lamb, North Carolina 7, 12, 13, 15
Camp Mangum, North Carolina 5, 6, 7
Camp Walker, North Carolina 7
Camp Wyatt, North Carolina 9, 10, 18
Campbell, Angus T., Pvt. (Co. H) 277, 285, 303, 364
Campbell, Daniel, Pvt. (Co. H) 364
Campbell, George W., Pvt. (Co. H) 277, 294, 364
Campbell, John M., Pvt. (Co. H) 364
Canady, Francis R., Pvt. (Co. D) 289, 336
Capps, William H., Pvt. (Co. I) 291, 372
Carlisle, Pennsylvania 106
Carlisle Barracks, Pennsylvania 106
Carney, James, Cpl. (Co. F) 347
Carr, Dennis, Pvt. (Co. H) 264, 364
Carr, Jacob O., Lt. (Co. E) 45, 338
Carr, John J., Pvt. (Co. E) 291, 339
Carr, Obed, Pvt. (Co. E) 296, 339
Carroll, William H., Pvt. (Co. B) 251, 290, 291, 315
Carter, James, Cpl.-Pvt. (Co. E) 299, 338
Carter, John, Pvt. (Co. B) 315
Carter, Linton, Pvt. (Co. E) 339
Carter, Robert M., Adj. (F & S) 304
Carter, William J., Pvt. (Co. B) 279, 315
Cashtown, Pennsylvania 109
Catoctin Mountains, Maryland 47

Index

Cavenaugh, George W., Pvt. (Co. E) 277, 302, 343
Cavenaugh, Jacob W., Pvt. (Co. E) 204, 266, 284, 288, 291, 339
Cavenaugh, James D., Pvt. (Co. E) 266, 280, 343
Cavenaugh, James H., Pvt. (Co. E) 300, 343
Cavenaugh, Obed E., Pvt. (Co. E) 266, 343
Cawthon, Archer L., Pvt. (Co. D) 335
Cawthorn, John W., Cpl. (Co. G) 289, 355
Cedar Creek 200, 202, 222
Cedar Creek, battle 220, 221, 233
Cemetery Hill, Pennsylvania 116
Center, Charles H., Pvt. (Co. H) 168, 285, 370
Chaffin's Bluff, Virginia 235, 236, 238
Chalkley, Benjamin T., Pvt. (Co. G) 267, 356
Chalkley, Edward E., Pvt. (Co. G) 356
Chambersburg, Pennsylvania 105
Champion, Joseph M., Pvt. (Co. D) 280, 331
Chancellorsville, battle 83–97
Chancellor House, Virginia 85, 87, 93
Charlottesville, Virginia 187
Cheatham, D. Thomas, Cpl. (Co. G) 112, 274, 355
Cheatham, James, Pvt. (Co. B) 116
Cheatham, James T., Pvt. (Co. G) 195, 275, 276, 287, 359
Cheatham, William A., Pvt. (Co. G) 267, 289, 356
Cherry, Spencer, Sgt. (Co. F) 266, 284, 347
Chickahominy River 22, 23, 28, 31
Chickahominy Swamp 24, 29
Chimis, Michael H., Pvt. (Co. C) 9, 295, 322
Church, Carlton, Pvt. (Co. G) 272, 284, 302, 359
Church, Eli, Pvt. (Co. K) 247, 292, 386
Church, John, Pvt. (Co. G) 359
Church, Martin, Pvt. (Co. K) 292, 386
Clairborne, Robert, F., Lt. (Co. G) 14, 17, 19, 30, 45, 51, 99, 356
Clanton, Robert K., Pvt. (Co. B) 315
Clark, Henry T., North Carolina Governor 4, 42
Clarkson, Thomas M., Mus., (Co. A) 268, 306
Clarkson, Thomas N., Pvt. (Co. A) 297, 307
Clay, Robert L., Pvt. (Co. D) 331
Cliborn, John W., Pvt. (Co. G) 361
Cliff, Edward, Pvt. (Co. C) 322
Cliff, John, Pvt. (Co. C) 299, 322
Cline, J., Pvt. (Co. F) 244, 290, 354
Clopton, George, Pvt. (Co. G) 301, 362
Cloyd, J.M., Pvt. (Co. B) 290, 321
Cobb, Jefferson, Sgt. (Co. I) 294, 376

Cobb, Obed B., Pvt. (Co. A) 277, 307
Cobb, John B., Pvt. (Co. F) 293, 347
Cobb, John R., Sgt.–Pvt. (Co. F) 296, 346
Cobb, William, Pvt. (Co. F) 347
Cockerham, James B., Pvt. (Co. B) 319
Coffee, Andrew S., Pvt. (Co. K) 382
Coke, Lucius, Asst. Surgeon (F & S) 292, 305
Cole, Andrew, Pvt. (Co. H) 268, 299, 368
Cole, Benjamin G., 1st Sgt. (Co. H) 273, 294, 363
Cole, George C., Pvt. (Co. H) 153, 267, 364
Cole, George W., Pvt. (Co. H) 281, 364
Cole, Jesse, Pvt. (Co. E) 343
Cole, Jesse T., Pvt. (Co. E) 298, 343
Cole, Neill M., Pvt. (Co. H) 297, 364
Coleman, Etheldred, Pvt. (Co. C) 292, 322
Coleman, James, Pvt. (Co. C) 283
Coleman, John C., Pvt. (Co. C) 297, 322
Coley, James H., Pvt. (Co. I) 372
Collins, John, Asst. Com. (F & S) 304
Collins, Samuel A., Pvt. (Co. G) 356
Collins, Stogdon, Pvt. (Co. B) 320
Collins, David, Pvt. (Co. B) 279, 319
Collins, Samuel A., Pvt. (Co. G) 284, 294
Colman, George W., Pvt. (Co. C) 268, 322
Colman, James, Pvt. (Co. C) 322
Colquitt, Alfred, CS, Col. 52, 86
Coltharp, Henry T., Cpl. (Co. K) 381
Connecticut H. Arty.: 2nd 211, 212
Connecticut Inf.: 14th 55, 56
Connell, Ira T., Lt., (Co. G) 108, 119, 275, 356
Connell, Wyatt G., Pvt. (Co. G) 284, 356
Cook, Anderson, Pvt. (Co. H) 300, 370
Cook, Ransom, L., Pvt. (Co. I) 372
Cooper, William W., Pvt. (Co. D) 58, 210, 269, 289, 291, 331
Corbett, Dempsey, Pvt. (Co. F) 284, 291, 347
Corbett, Henry, Pvt. (Co. F0) 348
Corbett, James, Pvt. (Co. F) 296, 348
Corbett, Wesley, Pvt. (Co. C) 323
Corbett, William W., Pvt. (Co. F) 277, 282, 348
Cornell, Wyatt, Pvt. (Co. G) 161
Costner, Jacob B., Pvt. (Co. C) 279, 328
Cottle, Frederick, Pvt. (Co. E) 298, 339
Cottle, W. Davis, Pvt. (Co. E) 299, 345

Cottrell, Solomon, Pvt. (Co. G) 356
Cousins, John A., Sgt. (Co. D) 235, 242, 246, 274, 280, 291, 331
Cowand, David, CS, Col. 247
Cox, John, Pvt. (Co. H) 36
Cox, John Louis, Pvt. (Co. H) 267, 363
Cox, Robert G., Pvt. (Co. A) 211, 265, 289, 307
Cox, William, CS, Col. 139, 159, 162, 182, 183, 187, 190, 191, 196, 197, 198, 201, 205, 208, 211, 212, 215, 218, 219, 220, 221, 223, 225, 226, 227, 232, 234, 235, 237, 239, 240, 242, 243, 247, 248, 250, 251, 252, 255, 256, 257, 258, 259
Cox, William O., Pvt. (Co. H) 267, 282, 368
Cox, William W., Pvt. (Co. H) 296, 364
Crawford, James S., Pvt. (Co. G) 284, 361
Crenshaw, Frederick, Pvt. (Co. D) 6
Cress, Wiley, Pvt. (Co. C) 161, 283, 328
Crews, Alexander, Lt., (Co. G) 19, 30, 45, 62, 63, 130 151, 269, 295, 355
Crews, William F., Pvt. (Co. G) 294, 359
Crickman, Josiah G., Pvt. (Co. I) 273, 285, 372
Crisp, Amos W., Pvt. (Co. F) 299, 352
Crisp, Eason, Pvt. (Co. F) 266, 348
Crisp, Levi, Pvt. (Co. F) 112, 274, 348
Crisp, Silas E, Pvt. (Co. F) 185, 286, 352
Crisp, William G., Pvt. (Co. F) 284, 348
Crisp, William S., Pvt. (Co. F) 169, 282, 352
Critcher, William H., Pvt. (Co. G) 289, 361
Crook, George, U.S., Gen. 216, 217, 218, 219
Cross, Edward, U.S., Col. 62
Crotts, Elijah, Pvt. (Co. H) 199, 288, 370
Crowell, Israel, Pvt. (Co. K) 382
Crowell, Jonas W., 1st Sgt. (Co. I) 203, 207, 214, 216, 220, 223, 232, 235, 242, 246, 260, 294, 379
Crump, Samuel W., Pvt. (Co. I) 296, 373
Crumpler, Bennett, Pvt. (Co. I) 377
Crumpler, James M., Cpl. (Co. A) 94, 271, 291, 307
Crumpler, Robert, 1st Sgt. (Co. A) 25, 95, 175, 180 185, 190, 195, 199, 202, 205, 207, 214, 216, 219, 222 231, 235, 241, 246, 255, 260, 263, 271, 277, 287, 292 307
Culp, Aley A., Pvt.–Cpl. (Co. K) 63, 219, 270, 281, 289382
Culpepper, John, Pvt. (Co. I) 273, 290, 294, 377

Index

Culpepper, William J., Cpl. (Co. I) 281, 380
Culpepper Court House, Virginia 44, 101, 127, 128
Cumberland University, Tennessee 129
Currie, John B., Pvt. (Co. A) 295, 308
Currin, George W., Pvt (Co G) 356
Currin, Ralph, Pvt. (Co. G) 359
Currin, William R., Pvt. (Co. G) 359
Custer, George, U.S., Gen. 229, 231, 232, 254, 259

Dail, Benjamin, Pvt. (Co. C) 300, 323
Danford, Abram, Pvt. (Co. C) 27, 263, 292, 323
Danford, John W., Pvt. (Co. C) 279, 323
Daniel, James R., Pvt. (Co. G) 296, 356
Daniel, James W., Pvt. (Co G) 359
Daniel, John B., Pvt. (Co. D) 336
Daniel, Junius, CS, Gen. 110, 156, 182
Daniel, Robert M., Pvt. (Co. G) 280, 359
Daniel, Rufus, Pvt. (Co. G) 361
Daniel, William H., Pvt. (Co. G) 135, 269, 278, 356
Darnell, James R., Pvt. (Co. B) 279, 315
Daniell, James W., Pvt. (Co. G) 299
Dartridge, Richard J., Pvt. (Co. I) 380
Davidson College, North Carolina 1, 6, 70, 129
Davis, Alexander L., Com. Sgt. (F & S) 305, 330
Davis, Arrington J., Pvt. (Co. D) 35, 266, 331
Davis, Benjamin P., Sgt. (Co. B) 190, 195, 199, 205, 314
Davis, Burton, Pvt. (Co. D) 301, 336
Davis, Burwell P., Sgt., (Co. B) 265, 314
Davis, George W., Pvt. (Co. K) 265, 382
Davis, Isham H., Pvt. (Co. B) 315
Davis, James R., Pvt. (Co. D) 35, 266, 331
Davis, James T., Pvt. (Co. D) 263, 289, 331
Davis, Jefferson, CS President 18, 22, 42, 100
Davis, Jesse A., Pvt. (Co. D) 272, 337
Davis, John R., Pvt. (Co. D) 296, 331
Davis, John S., Pvt. (Co. B) 315
Davis, Joseph C., Pvt. (Co. D) 298, 335
Davis, Joseph E., Pvt. (Co. D) 296, 331
Davis, Miles, Pvt. (Co. I) 281, 377
Davis, Samuel, Pvt. (Co. D) 6
Davis, Samuel R., Mus. (Co. D) 330
Davis, Simpson, Pvt. (Co. E) 293, 345
Davis, Weldon E., Lt.-Cpt. (Co. B) 16, 19, 30, 39, 45, 49, 51, 63, 71, 74, 78, 83, 96, 108, 124, 130, 134, 135, 137, 278, 314
Davis, William E., Cpl. (Co. D) 290, 331
Deal, Reuben, Pvt. (Co. F) 348
Dean, Jess, Pvt. (Co. G) 359
Dean, Jesse, Pvt. (Co. G) 185, 287
Dean, Simpson, Sgt. (Co. G) 284, 356
Deans, William, Pvt. (Co. I) 281, 380
Deaton, James, Pvt. (Co. H) 6, 364
Deaton, James P., Sgt. (Co. H) 264
DeArmond, Aaron L., Pvt.-Sgt. (Co. K) 75, 76, 77, 112, 125, 126, 135, 189, 192, 193, 195, 199, 270, 281, 288, 381
Delaware Inf.: 1st 181; 51st 4
Dement, Henry, Pvt. (Co. G) 194, 287, 356
Democratic Party 4, 42
Dempsey, Kinchen H., Cpl. (Co. E) 283, 289, 339
Denson, Benjamin E., Pvt. (Co. I) 373
Denson, Alexander, Pvt. (Co. I) 281, 373
Denton, Levi, Pvt. (Co. F) 266
desertion 79, 144, 147, 238, 348
Dew, David C., Pvt. (Co. C) 265, 279, 322
Dew, Frank L., Pvt. (Co. F) 277, 300, 348
Dew, William, Pvt. (Co. F) 25, 264, 348
Dickey, Zachariah, Pvt. (Co. I) 136
Dickey, Zachariah C., Pvt. (Co. D) 278, 293, 336
Dickens, Andrew J., Pvt. (Co. C) 283, 328
Dickens, Ephraim, Pvt. (Co. F) 348
Dickerson, George, Pvt. (Co. B) 320
Dickerson, Martin, Pvt. (Co. G) 284, 303, 359
Dickins, Ephraim, Pvt. (Co. F) 60, 177, 269, 286
Dickson, Harrall, Pvt. (Co. E) 343
Dickson, James G., Pvt. (Co. E) 27, 264, 339
Dickson, Riol, Pvt. (Co. E) 210, 269, 289, 340
Dickson, Robert L., (Co. E) 340
Dillard, William, Pvt. (Co. D) 297, 331
Dixon, Henry O., Pvt. (Co. F) 280, 348
Dixon, Solomon L., Pvt. (Co. K) 282, 295, 388
Dole, George, CS, Gen. 148, 157
Doles, George, CS, Gen. 197
Dortridge, Richard J., Pvt. (Co. I) 285
Dosher, James H., Sgt. (Co. C) 321
Doshier, James H., Pvt. (Co. C) 269
Dove, Monroe, Pvt. (Co. A) 133, 277, 312
Downs, John T., Lt. (Co. K) 19, 30, 45, 52, 67, 72, 100, 108, 130, 144, 145, 147, 152, 175, 180, 185, 190, 191, 196, 200, 201, 205, 207, 210, 214, 216, 233, 268, 289, 382
Downs, Thomas J., Lt. (Co. K) 14
Downs, William H., Pvt. (Co. K) 382
Dozier, James W., Sgt. (Co. I) 299, 373
Drake, William C., Cpt. (Co. B) 5, 16, 19, 27, 77, 79, 314
Draughon, George H., Pvt. (Co. A) 298, 308
Draughon, Miles S., Sgt. (Co. A) 279, 306
Draughon, Walter, Lt. Col. 4, 5, 13, 14, 304
Draughon, William B., Sgt. (Co. A) 306
Drew, John T., Pvt. (Co. C) 323
Duckworth, Thomas P., Pvt. (Co. K) 285, 388
Dudley, Laban, Pvt. (Co. H) 181, 287, 370
Dudley, Michael, Pvt. (Co. A) 296, 308
Dudley, William W., Pvt. (Co. A) 308
Duff, John T., Pvt. (Co. E) 293, 346
Duke, Robert, Pvt. (Co. B) 36
Duke, George J., Pvt. (Co. B) 93, 265, 271, 315
Duke, John Y., Pvt. (Co. G) 296, 359
Duke, Robert W., Pvt. (Co. B) 265, 316
Duncan, Charles W., Pvt. (Co. A) 271, 308
Duncan, James D., Pvt. (Co. A) 279, 308
Duncan, John B., Pvt. (Co. G) 297, 360
Dunker Church, Maryland 52
Dunlap Station, Virginia 234, 236, 237, 238
Dunn, Andrew J., Pvt. (Co. K) 55, 270, 381
Dunn, Andrew S., Pvt. (Co. K) 382
Dunn, David W., Pvt. (Co. A) 301, 312
Dunn, George, Pvt. (Co. K) 282, 302, 388
Dunn, Samuel W., Pvt. (Co. K) 296, 382
Duplin Turpentine Boys 5, 338
Durden, John M., Pvt. (Co. C) 328

Eagles, Lorenzo D., Lt. (Co. F) 27, 130, 145, 164, 165, 264, 284, 346
Eagles, Theodore, Pvt. (Co. F) 164, 284, 293, 352
Early, Jubal, CS, Gen 73, 139, 141, 183, 187, 188, 189, 191, 192, 193, 194, 196, 200, 208, 212, 214, 215, 216, 217, 218, 219, 220, 221, 222, 224, 227, 229, 231, 232, 233
Eason, Haywood, Pvt. (Co. I) 300, 377
Eason, James S., Pvt. (Co. H) 191, 301, 348, 370
Eason, William, Pvt. (Co. I) 377

Edwards, Edwin, Pvt. (Co. I) 380
Edwards, Elsberry B., Pvt. (Co. F) 49, 268, 293, 348
Edwards, Isaac N., Pvt. (Co. E) 284, 340
Edwards, James, Pvt. (Co. I) 281, 373
Edwards, Montgomery, Pvt. (Co. F) 26, 264, 299, 348
Edwards, Robert C., Pvt. (Co. I) 373
Edwards, Solomon, Pvt. (Co. I) 302, 380
Edwards, Thomas, Pvt. (Co. F) 296, 352
Edwards, Walker, Pvt. (Co. D) 283
Edwards, Walter, Pvt. (Co. D) 302, 336
Edwards, William B., Pvt. (Co. F) 352
Edwards, William H, Sgt. (Co. C) 58, 268, 321
Edward, Willie, Pvt. (Co. I) 295, 380
Ellen, James B., Pvt. (Co. D) 331
Eller, William W., Pvt. (Co. C) 296, 326
Elliott, Green B., Pvt. (Co. G) 229, 231, 290, 361
Ellis, James, Cpl. (Co. F) 293, 351
Ellis, John, North Carolina Governor 3, 4, 42
Ellis, John W., Lt. (Co. E) 272, 340
Ellis, John W., Ord. Sgt. (F & S) 304
Ellis, William, Pvt. (Co. F) 352
Elmira Prison, New York 262
Emery, Simeon, Pvt. (Co. D) 331
Enfield Blues 3, 4
Enfield Rifles 20, 38, 72, 131, 136, 216, 227
Estis, John W., Pvt. (Co. D) 331
Evans, Absalom R., Pvt. (Co. D) 332
Evans, Adin, Pvt. (Co. E) 264, 284, 343
Evans, Isiah H., Pvt. (Co. D) 300, 332
Evans, Joseph E., Pvt. (Co. D) 296, 335
Evans, William A., Pvt. (Co. D) 332
Evans, William M., Pvt. (Co. I) 294, 377
Everett, Joseph, Pvt. (Co. I) 301, 352
Everett, William, Pvt. (Co. F) 25, 264, 348
Everhart, Jacob, Pvt. (Co. C) 276, 328
Ewell, Richard S., CS, Gen. 100, 101, 114, 115, 157, 166, 182, 183, 188, 249
Ezzel, William W., Pvt. (Co. E) 340
Ezzell, Moses F., Cpl. (Co. K) 270, 385

Faircloth, John, Pvt. (Co. A) 308
Faircloth, John L., Pvt. (Co. A) 298, 299, 308
Falling Waters, Maryland 122, 123
Farmville, Virginia 247, 252, 253

Felton, Eli, Pvt. (Co. F) 251, 291, 293, 352
Felton, Richard, Cpl. (Co. F) 198, 266, 288, 348
Ferrell, Albert L., Pvt. (Co. D) 289, 337
Ferrell, Francis M., Pvt. (Co. D) 272, 335
Ferrell, James C., Pvt.-Cpl. (Co. D) 263, 283
Ferrell, James E., Lt., (Co. D) 95, 130, 272, 279, 330
Ferrell, John C., Pvt. (Co. D) 332
Fields, Absalom, Pvt. (Co. H) 370
Fields, Absalom F., Pvt. (Co. K) 291, 389
File, J.N., Pvt. (Co. C) 328
Finch, Ira J., Pvt. (Co. B) 320
Fisher's Hill, Virginia 202, 215, 222
Fisher's Hill, battle 216-220
Fitts, Francis M., Sgt. Maj. 188, 198, 199, 228, 287, 290, 292, 305
Floyd, Wyatt A., Pvt. (Co. B) 316
Flynn, James W., Pvt. (Co. C) 265, 323
Foote, James S., Pvt. (Co. B) 316
Forbes, Arthur, Pvt.-Sgt. (Co. F) 135, 264, 272, 278, 293, 349
Forbes, James, Pvt. (Co. F) 264, 288, 293, 349
Forbes, Randolph, Pvt. (Co. F) 352
Forrest, William L., Pvt. (Co. G) 295, 362
Forsythe, James R., Pvt.-Cpl. (Co. D) 202, 204, 272, 288, 335
Fort Delaware Prison, Delaware 262
Fort Fisher, North Carolina 9, 10, 11
Fort Stedman, Virginia 239, 240
Fort Stevens, Washington D. C. 191, 192, 193, 194
Fountain, Almond L., Pvt. (Co. F) 280, 349
Fox, Reddin P., Pvt. (Co. I) 294, 373
Francine, Louis, U.S., Col. 92
Franklin, Thomas F., Pvt. (Co. G) 356
Fraser's Farm, battle 31
Frazer, James H., Pvt. (Co. G) 203, 269, 288, 294
Frazier, Alex S., Pvt. (Co. G) 267, 360
Frazier, Elisha T., Pvt. (Co. G) 295, 356
Frazier, James H., Pvt. (Co. G) 360
Frazier, Pumfred B., Pvt. (Co. G) 264, 360
Frazier, Ransom P., Pvt. (Co. G) 356
Frederick, Maryland 47
Fredericksburg, battle 72-75
Freeman, William M., Pvt. (Co. H) 364
Friezland, Jacob, Pvt. (Co. A) 277, 285, 291, 303, 312
Front Royal, Virginia 101, 125, 202
Fryer, Lawrence D., Pvt. (Co. I) 287, 373
Fulford, John T., Lt. (Co. G) 145, 161, 172, 203, 207, 214, 220, 223, 232, 255, 284, 293, 356

Fuller, James N., Sgt. (Co. G) 171, 204, 288, 356
Furlough and Bounty Act 13
Fursell, Andrew G., Cpl. (Co. E) 264, 340

Gaines Mill, battle 3, 24-28
Gallimore, Ransom, Pvt. (Co. C) 279, 328
Gamble, James H., Pvt. (Co. K) 301, 388
Garland, Samuel, CS, Gen. 18, 23, 48
Garner, John T., Pvt. (Co. D) 266, 335
Garret, Francis M., Dr. (F & S) 44, 74, 305
Gaster, John C., Pvt. (Co. H) 300, 368
Gay, George W., Cpl. (Co. I) 273, 294, 377
Gay, Henry, Pvt. (Co. F) 299, 352
George, Ed Payson, Pvt. (Co. K) 382
George, Presley, Pvt. (Co. K) 298, 386
Gettysburg, Pennsylvania 113, 114
Gettysburg, battle 108-120
Gholson, Abraham, Pvt. (Co. B) 297, 316
Gibbon, John, U.S., Gen. 181
Gilbert, Thaddeus, Pvt. (Co. D) 295, 336
Gilbert, William, Pvt. (Co. A) 297
Gilbert, Willis, Pvt. (Co. A) 308
Gill, Philip P., Pvt. (Co. B) 36, 265, 316
Gill, William J., Lt. (Co. D) 30, 45, 63, 269, 330
Gladstone, D.S., Pvt. (Co. B) 320
Glover, Benjamin C., Pvt. (Co. K) 93, 273, 382
Godwin, Nathan H., Pvt. (Co. A) 265, 279, 308
Goebel, Charles L., Pvt. (Co. B) 316
Goins, Duncan, Pvt. (Co. H) 296, 364
Goins, Edward, Pvt. (Co. H) 294, 365
Goldsboro, North Carolina 16
Goodin, John C., Pvt. (Co. D) 274, 332
Goodin, Joseph J., Pvt. (Co. D) 293, 337
Goodin, William N., Pvt. (Co. D) 297, 332
Goodrich, James, Pvt. (Co. A) 26, 263, 308
Gordon, John, CS, Col.-Gen 53, 54, 157, 161, 201, 208, 224, 226, 233, 239, 240, 243, 244, 253, 254, 257, 259, 260
Gordon, John W., Pvt. (Co. G) 357
Gordonsville, Virginia 139
Gore, John, Pvt. (Co. C) 271, 323
Grady, John H., Pvt. (Co. D) 296, 332
Grady, John W., Pvt. (Co. E) 128, 277, 340
Graham, Jarratt B., Pvt. (Co. H) 264, 365

Graham, John W., Pvt. (Co. K) 281, 292, 388
Graham, Samuel W., Pvt. (Co. H) 42, 297, 365
Granville Rangers 5, 354
Grant, Ulysses, U.S., Gen. 154, 175, 241, 260, 261
Green, James L., Pvt. (Co. H) 147, 149, 285, 302, 370
Green, Joseph, Cpt. (Co. C) 5, 9, 321
Green, William B., Pvt. (Co. C) 323
Greencastle, Pennsylvania 104, 105
Greenway, Samuel, Pvt. (Co. G) 280, 300, 362
Greer, Ephraim, J., Lt. (Co. C) 14, 16, 19, 30, 32, 36, 265, 323
Greer, Lewis Y., Pvt. (Co. C) 95, 271, 323
Gregory, Charles G., Dr. (F & S) 9, 21, 28, 74, 77, 78, 120, 304
Gregory, Lawrence B., Pvt. (Co. B) 319
Griffin, A. Calhoun, Pvt. (Co. I) 281, 377
Griffith, Aaron E., Pvt. (Co. K) 275, 385
Griffin, James D., Pvt. (Co. I) 47, 63, 270, 373
Griffin, Jesse R., Pvt. (Co. I) 281, 373
Griffin, John B., Pvt. (Co. I) 93, 273, 380
Griffin, John J., Pvt. (Co. K) 296, 383
Griffin, Loren, Sgt. (Co. I) 63
Griffin, Mark S., Pvt. (Co. I) 294, 381
Griffin, William B., Pvt. (Co. I) 282, 380
Griffins, Charles, U.S., Gen. 257
Griffith, Aaron E. Pvt. (Co. K) 120, 273
Griffith, Ely, Pvt. (Col. K) 112
Grimes, Bryan, CS, Maj.-Col. 18, 25, 32, 48, 68, 69, 72, 73, 74, 84, 88, 90, 99, 114, 139, 154, 159, 162, 167, 179, 180, 181, 182, 189, 197, 206, 209, 212, 214, 215, 217, 218, 219, 220, 221, 222, 224, 225, 226, 228, 229, 230, 231, 233, 236, 237, 241, 244, 247, 248, 250, 252, 256, 257, 258, 259, 261
Grimmer, Elias G., Pvt. (Co. I) 291, 380
Grissom, Eugene, Cpt. (Co. D) 5, 6, 15, 16, 19, 21, 54, 329
Grissom, Lewis T., Pvt. (Co. D) 332
Guinea Station, Virginia 75, 81
Gutpton, Thomas, Pvt. (Co. I) 199, 288, 373
Gutelius, Joseph, U.S., Cpl. 114

Hagerstown, Maryland 47, 104, 121
Hagins, Lewis W., Pvt. (Co. F) 300, 352
Hagler, Hiram, Pvt. (Co. H) 195, 287, 370
Hagler, John, Pvt. (Co. A) 301, 313
Haithcock, Alfred L., Pvt. (Co. B) 279, 316

Haithcock, William G., Pvt. (Co. B) 316
Hall, James C., Pvt. (Co. G) 272, 360
Hall, John G., Pvt. (Co. K) 47, 282, 290, 382
Hall, Joseph F., Pvt. (Co. K) 292, 388
Hall, Robert B., Pvt. (Co. K) 382
Hall, William G., Pvt. (Co. A) 279, 292, 308
Hamblin, Joseph, U.S., Col. 210, 211, 212
Hamilton, William S., Pvt. (Co. E) 286, 345
Hamlet, Charles C., Pvt. (Co. E) 345
Hamme, Richard F., Pvt. (Co. G) 267, 277, 286, 357
Hanchey, Bryant W., Pvt. (Co. E) 299, 343
Hanchey, John W., Pvt.-Sgt. (Co. E) 74, 269, 270, 293, 340
Hancock, Thomas C., Pvt. (Co. G) 357
Hancock, Winfield, U.S., Gen. 85, 179
Hanover Junction, Virginia 44, 180, 181
Hardy, Francis M., Pvt. (Co. B) 195, 271, 287, 316
Hardy, Henry, Pvt. (Co. B) 299, 316
Hardy, Thomas W., Pvt. (Co. B) 316
Harney, Frank, CS, Lt. 113, 114
Harper, David, Pvt. (Co. F) 295, 349
Harper, John H., Pvt. (Co. I) 298, 377
Harper's Ferry, Virginia 190, 203, 205
Harrell, David, Pvt. (Co. F) 266, 269, 349
Harrell, Elisha T., Pvt. (Co. F) 284, 352
Harrell, George K., Lt. (Co. F) 17, 19, 30, 45, 51, 63, 71, 83, 108, 130, 137, 145, 151, 167, 172, 269, 284, 346
Harrell, John O., Pvt. (Co. E) 300, 343
Harrell, Peter, Pvt. (Co. F) 272, 349
Harrell, Watson, Pvt. (Co. F) 293, 349
Harrell, William, Mus.-Pvt. (Co. F) 297, 347
Harrington, Ard, Sgt. (Co. H) 180, 190, 196, 200, 203, 205, 207, 214, 216, 220, 223, 232, 235, 242, 246, 285, 294, 365
Harris Farm, battle 173-180
Harris farm, Virginia 174, 174, 175
Harris, David W., Pvt. (Co. B) 316
Harris Elbert H., Pvt. (Co. I) 373
Harris, George W., Pvt. (Co. C) 36, 265, 323
Harris, Henry, Pvt. (Co. D) 287, 293, 332
Harris, James J., Lt.-Cpt. (Co. I) 5, 17, 19, 30, 45, 50, 51, 63, 71, 74, 78, 84, 96, 100, 101, 102, 103, 104, 105, 106, 107, 108, 109, 111, 112, 113, 114, 115, 116, 117, 118, 119, 120, 121, 122, 123, 124, 126, 127, 137, 145, 151, 169, 172, 285, 371
Harris, John N., Pvt. (Co. B) 279, 301, 316
Harris, John W., Pvt. (Co. B) 292
Harris, Richard P., Pvt. (Co. G) 128, 277, 284, 357
Harris, Thomas P., Pvt. (Co. D) 293, 332
Harris, William H., Pvt. (Co. G) 168, 272, 273, 284, 357
Harriss, George W., Pvt. (Co. B) 319
Harriss, John A., Sgt. (Co. B) 265, 279, 314
Harriss, John W., Pvt. (Co. B) 319
Harriss, Joseph J. Jr., Pvt. (Co. B) 316
Harriss, William J., Pvt. (Co. F) 297, 349
Harriss, William L., Pvt. (Co. B) 319
Hart, James R., Sgt. (Co. G) 355
Hart, Obediah, Pvt. (Co. C) 297, 323
Hart, William H., Pvt. (Co. G) 357
Hart's Island Prison, New York 262
Hartis, John H., Pvt. (Co. K) 383
Hartis, Wilson L., Cpl. (Co. K) 93, 385
Hartwick, Christopher, Pvt. (Co. G) 362
Hartwick, John, Pvt. (Co. G) 362
Harvell, James M., Pvt. (Co. C) 279, 323
Harvell, John V., Pvt. (Co. C) 269, 323
Harvey, John F., Pvt. (Co. K) 292, 389
Hatcher Mills, North Carolina 13
Hathaway, Augustus, Pvt. (Co. F) 58, 269, 353
Hathaway, Henry Pvt. (Co. F) 119, 266, 275, 276, 349
Hathaway, James J., Pvt. (Co. F) 282, 353
Hathaway, Richard, Pvt. (Co. F) 293, 349
Haywood, Richard, Pvt. (Co. C) 291, 329
Hazel Grove, Virginia 89, 90, 94
Hearn, Amos, Pvt. (Co. F) 296, 349
Hedgepeth, Elias G., Pvt. (Co. I) 301, 373
Helms, Abel M., Pvt. (Co. E) 293, 345
Helms, Archibald, Pvt. (Co. E) 291, 345
Henderson, Abraham, Pvt. (Co. E) 296, 340
Henderson, Brantly B., Sgt. (Co. E) 161, 283, 343
Henderson James W., Pvt. (Co. E) 276, 340
Henderson, Jesse R., Pvt. (Co E) 266, 299, 343
Henderson, William M., Pvt. (Co. K) 386
Henderson, William T., Pvt. (Co. K) 296, 383

Index

Hendon, Solomon R., Pvt. (Co. C) 283, 326
Hendrick, Alexander W., Pvt.-Cpl. (Co. B) 263, 314
Hendricks, Eusileus, Pvt. (Co. H) 289, 370
Herring, Timothy J., Pvt. (Co. A) 308
Hester, George W., Pvt. (Co. G) 280, 360
Hewett, Lorenzo D., Pvt. (Co. C) 279, 323
Hewett, Samuel M., Pvt. (Co. C) 112, 274, 323
Hewett, Uriah, Pvt. (Co. C) 266, 323
Hickman, Benjamin R., Pvt. (Co. C) 300, 323
Hickman, Robert, Pvt. (Co. C) 266, 282, 302, 324
High Bridge 251
Hight, Herbot H., Pvt. (Co. G) 357
Hight, Joseph J., Cpl. (Co. H) 112, 274, 276, 365
Hill, Ambrose P., CS, Gen. 100, 188
Hill, Daniel H., CS, Gen. 22, 24, 32, 33, 34, 39, 42, 44, 47, 48, 50, 52, 53, 60, 66, 71, 73, 74, 82, 100
Hinshaw, Daniel, Pvt. (Co. D) 127, 336
Hobgood, Isaac, Pvt. (Co. G) 360
Hobgood, James M., Pvt. (Co. G) 94, 267, 272, 284, 357
Hobgood, William P., Cpl. (Co. G) 272, 357
Hobbs, Abraham, Pvt.-Cpl. (Co. A) 268, 306
Hobbs, Judson, Sgt. (Co. A) 290, 308
Hobbs, Monti V., Pvt. (Co. B) 320
Hoffman, John, CS, Gen. 182
Holbrook, Patterson B., Pvt. (Co. G) 270, 280, 360
Holbrook, William P., Pvt. (Co. G) 360
Holland, James, Mus. (Co. A) 292, 308
Holland, John R., Pvt. (Co. A) 56, 268, 271, 308
Holloway, Albert W., Pvt. (Co. D) 332
Holmes, Benjamin, Pvt. (Co. K) 298, 387
Holmes, James C. Cpt.-Maj. (Co. A) 5, 16, 19, 27, 30, 31, 45, 49, 51, 63, 71, 72, 74, 78, 83, 88, 93, 108, 110, 121, 127, 130, 134, 136, 137, 139, 140, 141, 142, 143, 144, 149, 305
Holshouser, Ambrose N., Pvt. (Co. A) 279, 313
Honeycutt, Miles C., Pvt. (Co. A) 289, 308
Hood, Abner B., Pvt.-Sgt. (Co. K) 25, 31, 264, 383
Hood, William L., Pvt.-Cpl. (Co. K) 118, 144, 182, 275, 287, 290, 294, 383
Hornaday, Lewis D., Pvt. (Co. H) 285, 368
Horne, Pleasant, Pvt. (Co. H) 285, 302, 370
House, James W., Sgt.-Lt. (Co. F) 135, 175, 180, 185, 190, 196, 200, 203, 205, 207, 214, 216, 220, 223, 232, 255, 257, 278, 295, 349
Howard, Fleet H., Pvt. (Co. A) 268, 282, 308
Howard, George W., Cpl.-Sgt. (Co. C) 198, 263, 287, 324
Howard, John J., Pvt. (Co. C) 269, 324
Howard, Joseph C., Pvt. (Co. A) 308
Howard, Joseph M., Pvt. (Co. G) 280, 303, 357
Howard, Oliver, U.S., Gen. 87
Howard, Thomas, Pvt.-Sgt. (Co. A) 35, 161, 282
Howard, William M., Pvt. (Co. A) 211, 265, 312
Howard, William S., Pvt. (Co. A) 289, 309
Howey, John H., Pvt. (Co. K) 6, 7, 47, 211, 270, 289, 295, 383
Howey, William, Pvt. (Co. K) 6, 7, 383
Howie, Mary 1
Hoyle, Nicholas, Pvt. (Co. H) 370
Hughes, Doctor, Pvt. (Co. H) 300, 365
Hughes, Henry, Pvt. (Co. H) 370
Hughes, Joseph, Pvt. (Co. C) 301, 328
Humphreys, Andrew, U.S., Gen. 247, 250
Hundley, George W., Cpl. (Co. B) 95, 271, 279, 316
Hunt, Alfred H., Pvt. (Co. G) 296, 357
Hunt, David Z., Pvt. (Co. G) 203, 288, 360
Hunt, Isaac B., Pvt. (Co. G) 26, 264, 357
Hunt, James A., Cpl. (Co. G) 26, 264, 355
Hunt, James A., Pvt. (Co. I) 281, 373
Hunt, John O., Pvt. (Co. G) 267, 357
Hunter, Charles A., Pvt.-Cpl. (Co. H) 267, 273, 294, 365
Hunter, John R., Pvt. (Co. H) 267, 280, 365
Hunter, John S., Pvt. (Co. H) 147, 370
Hunter, Martin, Pvt. (Co. E) 284, 343
Hunter, Stanford, Pvt. (Co. H) 267, 365
Hurrt, Daniel, CS, Maj. 98
Husketh, William R., Pvt. (Co. D) 332
Hutchison, Andrew J., Pvt. (Co. A) 282, 303, 313

Imboden, John, CS, Gen. 121
Incore, James F., Pvt. (Co. G) 296, 360
Indiana Inf.: 14th 57
Ingram, William W., Pvt. (Co. A) 309
Insco, William, Pvt. (Co. B) 279, 320
Inscore, James, Pvt. (Co. C) 271, 328
Irish Brigade 60
Iron Brigade 75
Iverson, Alfred, CS, Gen. 86, 87, 110
Ivey, W.L., Pvt. (Co. A) 279, 302, 313

Jackson, Archibald J., Lt. (Co. H) 17, 19, 30, 45, 51, 96, 125, 160, 172, 285, 363
Jackson, B.C., Pvt. (Co. H) 274
Jackson, Burgess, Pvt. (Co. F) 162
Jackson, Burgess C., Pvt. (Co. H) 285, 368
Jackson, James W., Pvt. (Co. A) 298, 309
Jackson, Marion J., Pvt. (Co. B) 128, 277, 320
Jackson, Martin G., Pvt. (Co. A) 282, 309
Jackson, Thomas "Stonewall," CS, Gen. 31, 34, 67, 72, 81, 84, 86, 88, 99
James River, Virginia 43
Jarvis, Levi, Pvt. (Co. C) 299, 326
Jarvis, Wiley, Pvt. (Co. C) 300, 327
Jefferson, Maryland 191
Jenkins, John T., Pvt. (Co. G) 357
Jenkins, Joseph S., Pvt. (Co. C) 324
Jenkins, William T., Pvt. (Co. G) 357
Jennings, George W., Pvt. (Co. K) 36, 268, 383
Jetersville, Virginia 246, 247
Johnson, A.C., Pvt. (Co. F) 288, 353
Johnson, A. Marion, Pvt. (Co. C) 283, 327
Johnson, Alexander L., Pvt. (Co. C) 283, 327
Johnson, Bushrod, CS, Gen. 253
Johnson, Calvin, Pvt. (Co. C) 299, 327
Johnson, Cornelius, Lt. (Co. E) 5, 338
Johnson, Christopher B., Pvt. (Co. I) 295, 380
Johnson, Edward, CS, Gen. 105, 117, 172
Johnson, Ellis, Pvt. (Co. F) 95, 272, 349
Johnson, Ezra W., Pvt. (Co. E) 293, 340
Johnson, Henry, Pvt. (Co. I) 281, 380
Johnson, Ira J., Lt. (Co. E) 17, 19, 71, 74, 78, 83, 108, 130, 134, 137, 145, 151, 175, 180, 190, 200, 235, 242, 246, 255, 260, 278, 288, 293, 338
Johnson, James A., Pvt. (Co. F) 284
Johnson, James C., Sgt.-Pvt. (Co. E) 299, 338
Johnson, John, Pvt. (Co. C) 283, 327
Johnson, John, Pvt. (Co. H) 365
Johnson, Josiah, Pvt. (Co. E) 300, 340
Johnson, L.W., Pvt. (Co. A) 282, 313

Johnson, Major O., Pvt. (Co. E) 119, 275, 293, 340
Johnson, William H., Cpl.-Sgt. (Co. A) 265, 282, 309
Johnson's Island Prison, Ohio 262
Johnston, David E., Pvt. (Co. K) 270, 383
Johnston, George W., Pvt. (Co. K) 387
Johnston, James H., Pvt. (Co. K) 185, 211, 273, 287, 289, 387
Johnston, S.A., Pvt. (Co. K) 273
Johnston, Sandy A., Pvt. (Co. K) 155, 282, 387
Johnston, William A., CS, Lt. Col. 19, 43
Johnston, William J. 42
Jones, Calvin F., Pvt. (Co. I) 285, 377
Jones, David R., CS, Gen. 50
Jones, Isham F., Pvt. (Co. D) 36, 266, 332
Jones, Isaac, Pvt. (Co. E) 342
Jones, James K., Sgt. (Co. E) 293, 345
Jones, James W., Pvt. (Co. E) 272, 340
Jones, John J., Pvt. (Co. E) 340
Jones, John R., Pvt. (Co. I) 274, 276, 373
Jones, Joseph, CS, Cpt. 183
Jones, Levi, Pvt. (Co. F) 269, 353
Jones, William H., Pvt. (Co. D) 291, 303, 337
Joplin, William Y., Pvt. (Co. D) 298, 332
Joyner, Alsey M., Pvt. (Co. I) 270, 285, 373
Joyner, Ashley G., Pvt. (Co. I) 298, 373
Joyner, Calvin M., Pvt. (Co. I) 298, 377
Joyner, George W., Pvt. (Co. I) 273, 276, 380
Joyner, Henry, Dr. (F & S) 9, 2, 28, 44, 304
Joyner, Ira E., Pvt. (Co. I) 277, 377
Joyner, James, Pvt. (Co. I) 6, 373
Joyner, John L., Mus. (Co. D) 293
Joyner, John L., Pvt. (Co. D) 263, 268, 332
Joyner, Jonas A., Pvt. (Co. I) 281, 373
Joyner, Little B., Pvt. (Co. I) 297, 378
Joyner, Nathan T., Pvt. (Co. I) 373
Joyner, Nelson V., Pvt. (Co. I) 274, 374
Joyner, William B., Pvt. (Co. I) 294, 374

Keele, William, Pvt. (Co. F) 269, 349
Keith, Clement C., Pvt. (Co. D) 337
Kell, James, Maj.-Lt. Col. 4, 5, 6, 8, 14, 15, 16, 18, 19, 25, 31, 44, 81, 84, 127, 263, 304, 381
Kelly, Alex D., Pvt. (Co. H) 365
Kelly, Archibald, Jr., Pvt. (Co. H) 6, 365
Kelly, Archibald, Sr., Pvt. (Co. H) 6, 365

Kelly, Chester, Pvt. (Co. A) 309
Kelly, David W., Pvt. (Co. H) 277, 301, 368
Kelly, James M., Pvt. (Co. A) 133, 271, 278, 282, 309
Kelly, William Alfred, Pvt. (Co. H) 280, 365
Kelly's Ford, Virginia 129, 139
Kelly's Ford, battle 130-137
Kellysville, Virginia 129, 132, 134, 136, 137
Kilpatrick, Hugh Y., Sgt. (Co. K) 297, 385
Kimball, Nathan, U.S., Gen. 57
Kimball, Nathaniel, Pvt. (Co. B) 268, 271, 279, 316
Kimmel, Daniel A., Pvt. (Co. C) 291, 328
King, Anderson F., Pvt. (Co. D) 286, 290, 337
King, Caswell, Pvt. (Co. D) 283, 303, 337
King, James D., Pvt. (Co. G) 211, 280, 289, 360
King, John, Pvt. (Co. D) 211, 289, 291, 303, 337
King, John F., Pvt. (Co. B) 316
King, Lewis D., Pvt. (Co. A) 199, 287, 292, 309
King, Stephen J., Pvt. (Co. A) 286, 292, 309
King, W.H., Pvt. (Co. H) 285, 370
King, William A., Pvt. (Co. B) 46, 297, 316
King, William D., Pvt. (Co. G) 362
Kirkland, Stephen H., Pvt. (Co. B) 279, 301, 317
Kirkpatrick, Hugh, Pvt. (Co. K) 69
Kittrel, Harvey W., Pvt. (Co. G) 362
Kittrel, William H., Cpl. (Co. G) 36, 267, 355
Klutts, Tobias, Pvt. (Co. C) 283, 328
Knight, Benjamin, Pvt. (Co. H) 264, 365
Knight, Thomas H., Pvt. (Co. E) 303, 345
Knott, George Lawson, Cpl. (Co. G) 136, 280, 357
Knott, James W., Pvt. (Co. G) 357

Ladies' Guards 5
Lamb, Ithamer, Pvt. (Co. C) 292, 329
Lambeth, William, Cpl. (Co. C) 265, 324
Laney, Lewis C., Pvt. (Co. E) 280, 346
Langley, Morrison, Pvt. (Co. F) 184, 286, 353
Langley, Singleton, Pvt. (Co. I) 35, 267, 374
Lanier, Brantley, Pvt. (Co. E) 290, 344
Lanier, Jacob W., Pvt. (Co. E) 185, 286, 340
Lanier, James P., Pvt. (Co. E) 299, 344
Lanier, Lewis W., Pvt. (Co. E) 298, 344

Larkins, Robert S., Pvt. (Co. C) 266, 292, 324
Lawhorn, Archibald, Sgt.-Sgt. Maj. (Co. A) 6, 16, 305, 306
Lawrence, Bennett, Pvt. (Co. H) 269, 369
Lawrence, John, Pvt. (Co. H) 185, 264, 274, 294, 369
Lawrence, John J., Pvt. (Co. F) 269, 353
Lawrence William H., Pvt. (Co. D) 275, 287, 332
Lawson, Dr. 146
Lee, James, Lt. (Co. K) 162
Lee, James A., Pvt. (Co. K) 299, 383
Lee, James T., Sgt. (Co. K) 285, 381
Lee, Robert E., CS, Gen. 22, 53, 100, 106, 120, 122, 124, 126, 127, 128, 166, 188, 202, 220, 233, 236, 241, 243, 244, 246, 247, 252, 253, 254, 257, 259, 260, 261, 262
Lee, Samuel B., Pvt. (Co. K) 182, 287, 383
Lee, Taylor, Sgt. (Co. K) 143
Lee, Thomas J., Pvt. (Co. A) 309
Lee, Willis, Pvt. (Co. A) 309
Leesburg, Virginia 196
Leigh, Joseph, Pvt. (Co. F) 296, 349
Leigh, Theophilus, Pvt. (Co. F) 278, 295, 349
Leonard, Samuel B., Cpl. (Co. C) 36, 265, 324
Leventhorpe, Collett, CS, Col. 122
Lewis, Archibald, Pvt. (Co. A) 21, 309
Lewis, Arnold L., Pvt. (Co. I) 267, 281, 294, 378
Lewis Cornelius, Pvt. (Co. A) 297, 309
Lewis, Edward W., Pvt. (Co. I) 56, 270, 374
Lewis, John A., Pvt. (Co. I) 301, 381
Lewis, John D., Pvt. (Co. F) 293, 353
Lewis, John E., Pvt. (Co. F) 134, 278, 350
Lewis, William H., Pvt. (Co. K) 388
Lexington, Virginia 189
lice 10
Lincoln, Abraham, President 13, 21, 194, 196, 238
Lindsey, Neverson A., Pvt. (Co. I) 374
Lindsey, Richard, Pvt. (Co. I) 281, 301, 374
Lindsey, William B., Pvt. (Co. I) 299, 380
Little Jesse, Pvt. (Co. F) 350
Little, Jesse C., Pvt. (Co. F) 74, 269, 270, 290, 293, 350
Little, Lorenzo, Pvt. (Co. F) 299, 353
Little, William, Pvt. (Co. F) 297
Little, Willis, Pvt. (Co. F) 350
Lloyd, George E., Pvt. (Co. D) 291, 293, 332
Lloyd, Manley C., Pvt. (Co. H) 281, 371
Loftice, William A., Pvt. (Co. G) 272, 360

Index

Logan, Philip, Pvt. (Co. H) 302, 371
Lomax, Lunsford L., CS, Gen. 214, 216, 218
Long, Alexander V., Pvt. (Co. D) 275, 276, 332
Longstreet, James, CS, Gen. 100, 252
Loughlin, Charles, Mus. (Co. A) 314
Loughlin, James H., Lt. (Co. B) 30, 314
Loughlin, John, Pvt. (Co. B) 265, 274, 276, 317
Lovett, Aaron F., Pvt. (Co. G) 299, 360
Lumbley, William L., Pvt. (Co. D) 74, 270, 286, 332
Lumpkins, James R., Pvt. (Co. G) 357
Luntzford, James R., Pvt. (Co. C) 283, 327
Luntzford, Joel, Pvt. (Co. C) 299, 327
Lynam, Emelious J., Pvt. (Co. D) 296, 332
Lynam, William, Pvt. (Co. D) 333
Lynchburg, Virginia 187, 189
Lynn, William, Pvt. (Co. H) 240, 290, 371

Madra, George A., Pvt. (Co. F) 119, 268, 272, 275, 286, 350
Mahone, William, CS, Gen. 166, 252
Maine Inf.: 5th 210; 7th 195; 19th 182
Mallard, John W., Pvt. (Co. E) 284, 340
Mallard, William W., Pvt. (Co. E) 272, 341
Malpass, Carleton, Pvt. (Co. E) 168, 264, 284, 341
Maltsby, William, Pvt. (Co. C) 9
Maltsby, William J., Pvt. (Co. C) 295, 324
Malvern Hill, battle 32–40
Manellis, James, Pvt. (Co. E) 36
Manellis, John, Pvt. (Co. E) 266, 341
Mangum, Calvin T., Pvt. (Co. D) 35, 266, 280, 333
Mangum, Theophilus P., Pvt. (Co. D) 293, 333
Manly, Matt, CS, Cpt. 71
Manning, Jeremiah D., Pvt. (Co. I) 294, 378
Manning, John E., Mus. (Co. I) 297, 374
Manning, Moses V., Cpl. (Co. I) 270, 378
Manning, Richard M., Pvt. (Co. I) 297, 378
Manus, Francis, Pvt. (Co. D) 276, 337
Marcom, James A., Pvt. (Co. D) 280, 335
Marcom, William A., Pvt. (Co. D) 280, 337
Marlow, Nathan, Pvt. (Co. F) 298, 353
Marsh, William CS, Cpt. 52

Marshall, William D., Cpl. (Co. C) 283, 324
Martin, Joseph B., Pvt. (Co. D) 297, 333
Martinsburg, Virginia 102, 201
Maryland Inf.: 5th 54
Mashburn, Alfred I., Pvt. (Co. H) 269, 366
Mashburn, James D., Pvt. (Co. H) 267, 366
Masingal, Robert S., Pvt. (Co. K) 184, 287, 387
Mason, Albert, Pvt. (Co. H) 294
Mason, Israel H., Pvt. (Co. D) 274, 276, 335
Mason, Joseph, Pvt. (Co. D) 35, 266, 333
Massachusetts Arty.: 10th 131
Massachusetts H. Arty.: 1st 177
Massachusetts Inf.: 13th 111, 113; 29th 60; 37th 211
Massaponax Creek 82
Massey, Marion M., Pvt. (Co. D) 293, 333
Mathews, Roderick, Pvt. (Co. F) 291, 354
Matthews, Hilliard, Pvt. (Co. I) 381
Matthews, John B., Pvt. (Co. H) 269, 369
Matthews, M. Hardy, Cpl. (Co. H) 210, 285, 289, 366
Matthews, Nathan, Pvt. (Co. H) 277, 302, 366
Mayo, James, Pvt. (Co. F) 74, 270, 299, 350
McAulay, William, Pvt. (Co. H) 112, 267, 274, 276, 365
McCall, John W., Pvt. (Co. C) 26, 263, 324
McCall, Paul S., Pvt. (Co. C) 266, 279, 324
McCoull farm, Virginia 159, 160, 161
McCulloch, William, Pvt. (Co. H) 267, 368
McDonald, Donald, Pvt. (Co. H) 74, 366
McDonald, James S., Pvt. (Co. H) 269, 281, 366
McDonald, John A., Pvt. (Co. H) 371
McDonald, Neill, Pvt. (Co. H) 58, 269, 298, 366
McDougal, Donald, Pvt. (Co. H) 268, 270
McDowell, William J., Cpl. (Co. C) 204, 288, 324
McFarland, Andrew, Pvt. (Co. H) 269, 285, 366
McFarland, John A., Pvt. (Co. H) 269, 294, 366
McFatter, Alexander, Pvt. (Co. H) 134, 267, 278, 366
McGill, Archy D., Cpl. (Co. H) 253, 254, 256, 258, 260, 294, 369
McGowan, Samuel, CS, Gen. 167
McIntosh, Archibald A., Lt. (Co. H) 5, 362
McIntosh, Daniel W. Lt. (Co. H) 5, 362

McIntosh, David J., Sgt. (Co. H) 286, 363
McIntosh, Francis M., Pvt. (Co. H) 288, 366
McIver, D.N., Pvt. (Co. H) 286, 294, 369
McIver, Dan W., Pvt. (Co. H) 369
McIver, Edward, Pvt. (Co. H) 298, 369
McIver, John D., Pvt. (Co. H) 176, 294, 369
McIver, John W., Pvt. (Co. H) 296, 366
McIver, Kenneth H., Pvt. (Co. H) 273, 369
McIver, Murdock A., Pvt. (Co. H) 297, 366
McKenzie, Redman, Pvt. (Co. A) 282, 309
McKinney, John W., Cpl. (Co. K) 381
McKinney, R. Monroe, Pvt. (Co. K) 6, 383
McLane, Thomas, Pvt. (Co. K) 133, 279, 387
McLemore, Tobias, Pvt. (Co. A) 309
McLemore, William S., Pvt. (Co. A) 164, 268, 283, 309
McLeod, Louis H., Lt. (Co. H) 299, 363
McLure, James A., Pvt. (Co. K) 182, 287, 388
McMillan, Daniel T., Lt. (Co. E) 17, 19, 45, 51, 344
McMillan, John C., Cpt. (Co. E) 5, 17, 19, 27, 30, 39, 45, 49, 51, 63, 83, 96, 108, 121, 124, 139, 143, 144, 145, 146, 151, 152, 168, 169, 206, 207, 211, 214, 216, 219, 220, 221, 222, 223, 225, 227, 231, 232, 233, 235, 236, 238, 239, 241, 242, 244, 246, 247, 249, 272, 283, 290, 291, 338
McMullen, James H., Pvt. (Co. K) 26, 265, 383
McNeil, Henry J., Lt. (Co. H) 17, 19, 30, 45, 51, 52, 54, 63, 71, 84, 108, 130, 145, 151, 175, 177, 180, 286, 363
McNeill, Laughlin, Pvt. (Co. H) 267, 366
McNellis, John, Pvt. (Co. E) 272, 341
McPherson, A. Dugall, Pvt. (Co. H) 297, 366
McPherson, Duncan R., Pvt. (Co. H) 297, 369
McQuay, Joseph F., Pvt. (Co. K) 292, 388
Meagher, Thomas, U.S., Gen. 60
measles 8
Mechanicsville, Virginia 22
Mecklenburg Beauregards 5
Mercer, Jacob J., Pvt. (Co. F) 274, 276, 350
Merritt, Benjamin H., Pvt. (Co. G) 284, 294, 360
Merritt, Isaac W., Sgt. (Co. A) 111, 122, 274, 276, 309
Merritt, Levi, Pvt. (Co. E) 297, 341

Index

Merritt, Wesley, U.S., Gen. 232
Mewborn, Parrott, Pvt. (Co. A) 313
Mexican War 100, 187
Middletown, Virginia 226, 233
Milam, Henry D., Pvt. (Co. B) 317
Miles, James, Pvt. (Co. B) 291, 321
Miles, John, Pvt. (Co. A) 283, 313
Miller, Alexander B., Pvt. (Co. C) 283, 303, 327
Miller, David W., Pvt. (Co. K) 285, 292, 388
Miller, H.C., Pvt. (Co. C) 327
Miller, John L., Pvt. (Co. C) 199, 327
Milliken, Isaac, Pvt.-Cpl. (Co. C) 266, 283, 324
Milton, Joseph G., Pvt. (Co. K) 297, 383
Mine Run, Virginia 140, 141
Mints, Jesse O., Pvt. (Co. C) 324
Mississippi Inf.: 12th 85; 16th 60
Mitchell, Henry, Pvt. (Co. A) 298, 310
Mitchell, Rush J., Lt. (Co. G) 5, 354
Mobley, William V., Pvt. (Co. E) 289, 303, 344
Mobley, Wright W., Pvt. (Co. E) 300, 344
Molineux, Edward, U.S., Co. 209
Monaghan, William, CS, Gen. 158
Monroe, James A., Pvt. (Co. H) 269, 281, 366
Monroe, James E., Pvt. (Co. H) 281
Monroe, John E, Pvt. (Co. H) 369
Moore County rifles 5
Moore, Francis M., Lt. (Co. H) 363
Moore, John J., Pvt. (Co. F) 266, 353
Moore, Robert, Pvt. (Co. C) 327
Moore, Samuel R., Lt.-Cpt. (Co. F) 190, 210, 235, 242, 246, 255, 260, 284, 289, 293, 350
Moore, Theophilus, Pvt. (Co. C) 283, 295, 328
Moore, Thomas J., Pvt. (Co. F) 264, 347
Moore, Walter J., Pvt. (Co. A) 310
Moore, William H., Pvt. (Co. D) 242, 281, 290, 333
Moore, Willis M., Lt.-Cpt. (Co. F) 5, 17, 19 27, 36, 39, 45, 49, 51, 63, 71, 72, 74, 78, 83, 96, 108, 121, 124, 130, 133, 134, 143, 144, 145, 151, 155, 168, 169, 175, 222, 223, 228, 229, 231, 232, 266, 282, 290, 346
Morgan, Isaac, Pvt. (Co. F) 268
Morgan, James B., Pvt. (Co. F) 36, 266, 280, 350
Morgan, Moses B., Pvt. (Vo. I) 374
Morgan, Thomas, Pvt. (Co. F) 288, 354
Morgan, William, Pvt. (Co. H) 49
Morgan, William G., (Co. F) 268, 293, 350
Morris, Alexander H., Pvt. (Co. G) 360
Morris, Alfred J., Pvt. (Co. D) 298, 333
Morris, David P., Pvt. (Co. H) 274, 276, 291, 303, 367
Morris, Dwight, U.S., Col. 55, 57

Morris, James P., Pvt. (Co. K) 299, 383
Morris, John D., Pvt. (Co. H) 296, 367
Morris, John W., Mus., (Co. G) 280, 357
Morris, William T., Pvt. (Co. K) 388
Morrison, Horace, Cpl.-Sgt. (Co. H) 155, 267, 282, 367
Morrow, Benjamin E., Cpt. (Co. K) 5, 10, 13, 381
Morton, Isaac, Pvt. (Co. F) 298, 353
Morton's Ford, Virginia 142, 143, 146
Mosely, Allen, Pvt. (Co. F) 272, 354
Mosely, Elisha, Pvt. (Co. F) 296, 350
Moss, Thomas, Pvt. (Co F) 358
Mott, Gershom, U.S., Gen. 247, 248
Mott, John, Pvt. (Co. C) 266, 276, 326
Murphy, Timothy C., Pvt. (Co. E) 341
Murray, Thomas M., Pvt. (Co. E) 284, 344
Myers, James, Pvt. (Co. K) 262, 281, 388
Myrick, William W., Pvt. (Co. B) 268, 276, 301, 319

Nason, Albert, Pvt. (Co. H) 367
Nat Macon Guards 5, 314
Naylor, Ransom, Pvt. (Co. A) 94, 271, 310
Neal, Dudley H., Pvt. (Co. B) 36, 265, 286, 317
Nelson, John J., Pvt. (Co. K) 292, 388
New Hampshire Inf.: 5th 61, 62, 63
New Jersey Inf.: 7th 91, 92
New York Inf.: 12th 181
Newkirk, George B., Sgt. (Co. E) 204, 288, 341
Newsom, John G., Cpl. (Co. B) 36, 265, 317
Newsom, John G., 1st Sgt. (Co. B) 93, 136, 235, 242, 246, 255, 260, 271, 278, 292
Newton, James O., Pvt. (Co. E) 341
Newton, Samuel B., Lt. (Co. E) 71, 130, 175, 185, 190, 191, 196, 200, 203, 205, 207, 214, 216, 220, 223, 232, 251, 291, 338
Neuse River Guards 5, 21
New Bern, North Carolina 12, 13, 18
New York Arty.: 12th 131
New York H. Arty: 4th 175, 176, 179
New York Inf.: 4th 54, 55, 56; 7th 61; 43rd 195; 49th 195; 61st 61; 63rd 60; 64th 61; 69th 60, 182; 72nd 195; 88th 60; 104th 111, 112, 113; 108th 55, 56, 57, 181; 122nd 195; 170th 182
New York University 6
Nichols, Burgess, Sgt. (Co. K) 177, 286, 294, 385
Nichols, J., Pvt. (Co. K) 286, 389
Nichols, John T., Sgt.-Pvt. (Co. D) 286, 330

Nicholson, John H., Lt., (Co. B) 16, 19, 30, 45, 51, 71, 83, 108, 130, 279, 314
Norris, James, Pvt. (Co. E) 300, 344
Norris, Joseph, Pvt. (Co. E) 6, 341
Norris, Reuben, Pvt. (Co. E) 344
Norris, Timothy, Pvt. (Co. E) 344
Norris, William W., Pvt. (Co. E) 264, 293, 344
North Anna River 181
North, Joshua, Pvt. (Co. B) 155, 282, 292, 320
North Carolina Cav.: 75th 256
North Carolina Inf.: 1st 3, 173, 182, 223, 240; 2nd 18, 22, 32, 34, 35, 39, 41, 47, 48, 49, 50, 56, 59, 62, 80, 84, 85, 86, 89, 90, 91, 92, 96, 109, 110, 114, 115, 121, 130, 131, 132, 133, 135, 137, 146, 158, 159, 160, 164, 182, 240; 3rd 173, 182, 223, 240; 4th 18, 22, 25, 32, 39, 41, 48, 49, 50, 52, 56, 58, 59, 63, 84, 85, 86, 89, 90, 91, 92, 96, 109, 110, 113, 115, 126, 128, 141, 153, 162, 164, 168, 198, 208, 211, 223, 230, 236, 237, 240, 243; 7th 13; 14th 18, 19, 21, 22, 32, 35, 38, 41, 48, 49, 52, 56, 59, 62, 84, 86, 89, 90, 91, 92, 96, 109, 110, 111, 112, 113, 115, 121, 147, 161, 162, 164, 166, 197, 210, 211, 224, 230, 240, 256, 258; 12th 48; 18th 9, 88; 26th 42; 30th 22, 32, 35, 38, 39, 41, 48, 49, 54, 56, 58, 60, 84, 86, 89, 94, 95, 96, 109, 110, 112, 115, 132, 135, 137, 140, 147, 149, 162, 165, 170, 178, 186, 188, 197, 204, 208, 211, 216, 220, 223, 228, 232, 233, 236, 238, 240, 249, 253, 261; 35th 13; 47th 67; 49th 70
North Carolina Military Institute, Charlotte, North Carolina 6
Norville, James, Pvt. (Co. F) 293, 353
Nowles, William R., Pvt. (Co. A) 310

Oakley, David, Pvt. (Co. C) 292, 329
Oakley, William, Pvt. (Co. G) 362
O'Brian, Alexander P., Cpl. (Co. G) 280, 355
O'Brien, Alfred, 1st Sgt. (Co. G) 71, 83, 280, 358
O'Brien, William G., Pvt. (Co. G) 273, 360
Ohio Inf.: 8th 57, 181
O'Neal, Daniel, Pvt. (Co. H) 369
O'Neal, Edward, CS, Col. 110
O'Neal, Hardy, Pvt. (Co. D) 37, 266, 280, 333
O'Neal, John, Pvt. (Co. F) 266, 333, 350
O'Neal, Lofton M., Pvt. (Co. D) 280
Odom, David M., Cpl. (Co. I) 277, 374
Odom, Jacob E., Pvt. (Co. I) 93, 273, 374
Ogburn, N.S., Pvt. (Co. A) 242, 290, 313

Index

Ojibwa Indians 153
Orange Court House, Virginia 44, 125, 143
Orange Plank Road, Virginia 84, 86, 88, 98
Orr, Nathan, D., Pvt.-Lt. (Co. K) 12, 17, 19, 28, 30, 39, 43, 127, 381
Orr, Thomas J., Pvt. (Co. K) 295, 385
Osborne, Edwin, CS, Lt. Col. 155, 179, 180, 198
Ottaway, John, Pvt. (Co. G) 280, 362
Owen, Joshua, U.S., Gen. 146
Owens, James, Pvt. (Co. F) 354

Page, Jacob S., Pvt. (Co. A) 283, 310
Page, Owen, Pvt. (Co. A) 298, 310
Palmer, Oliver, U.S., Col. 56, 57
Parham, William A., Pvt. (Co. G) 294, 355
Parke, John, U.S., Gen. 242
Parker, Archibald D., Pvt. (Co. G) 280, 362
Parker, Benjamin T., Pvt. (Co. C) 328
Parker, Francis, Col. 3, 4, 5, 7, 8, 9, 10, 11, 12, 13, 14, 15, 16, 18, 19, 21, 22, 24, 25, 26, 27, 28, 29, 30, 31, 32, 33, 37, 38, 39, 40, 41, 42, 43, 44, 45, 46, 48, 49, 51, 52, 54, 59, 61, 62, 63, 67, 80, 81, 83, 85, 88, 89, 90, 93, 94, 95, 96, 97, 98, 99, 100, 101, 105, 108, 109, 112, 120, 124, 136, 137, 144, 145, 146, 147, 149, 150, 151, 152, 153, 156, 159, 160, 162, 165, 169, 172, 173, 174, 175, 176, 180, 189, 268, 273, 282, 285, 304
Parker, G. Washington, Pvt. (Co. C) 298, 327
Parker, Jacob W., Pvt. (Co. E) 286, 344
Parker, James C., Pvt. (Co. C) 302, 328
Parker, James M., Pvt. (Co. A) 271, 292, 310
Parker, Josiah, Cpl. (Co. I) 296, 374
Parrish, Mathew, Pvt. (Co. G) 26, 264, 358
Parting, Henry A., Pvt. (Co. A) 279, 300, 313
Paschall, Samuel A., Cpl. (Co. B) 279, 317
Patrick, Cornelius, Lt. (Co. A) 5, 306
Patterson, Green R., Pvt. (Co. B) 271, 317
Patterson, John J., Pvt. (Co. C) 134, 278, 328
Patterson, William S., Pvt. (Co. K) 296, 383
Paul, Gabriel, U.S., Gen. 111
Paxton, Elisha, CS, Gen. 73
Paynter, Thomas P., Pvt. (Co. B) 317
Peed, William C., Pvt. (Co. D) 27, 263, 272, 289, 334
Peed, William H., Pvt. (Co. D) 272, 280, 334
Pegram, George W., Pvt. (Co. B) 42, 297, 319

Pegram, James B., Pvt. (Co. B) 263, 300, 319
Pegram, John, CS, Gen. 215
Pegram, John J., Pvt. (Co. B) 319
Pegram, Robert B., Pvt. (Co. B) 23, 95, 263, 271, 292, 317
Pegram, Mitchell S., Pvt. (Co. B) 142, 283, 320
Pegram, William, CS, Maj. 89, 92, 93
Pender, John, Pvt. (Co. I) 136, 278, 380
Pendergrass, Elijah, Pvt. (Co. C) 297, 327
Pendergrass, J.R., Pvt. (Co. C) 279, 302, 327
Pendergrass, William M., Pvt. (Co. C) 327
Penninger, Moses, Pvt. (Co. C) 328
Pennington, Henry, Pvt. (Co. A) 289, 313
Pennington, John, Pvt. (Co. A) 203, 288, 312
Pennington, Moses, Pvt. (Co. C) 147, 301, 328
Pennington, William, Pvt.-Sgt. (Co. A) 95, 271, 282, 310
Pennsylvania Inf.: 14th 165; 61st 195; 81st 61; 96th 157; 130th 55, 56, 57; 132nd 57; 150th 114
Penny, Benjamin, Mus. (Co. C) 322
Penny, Solomon W., Pvt. (Co. D) 194, 269, 287, 333
Perkins, Sanford, U.S., Lt. Col. 55
Perry, Sidney R., Lt. (Co. I) 175, 180, 185, 190, 196, 199, 200, 205, 273, 288, 374
Petersburg, Virginia 16, 233, 234, 235, 237, 238, 244
Pettigrew, James, CS, Gen. 121, 123
Phillips, David J., Pvt. (Co. F) 266, 350
Philips, Frederick, Lt.-Cpt. 3, 31, 50, 51, 52, 54, 59, 71, 108, 115, 117, 133, 144, 150, 268, 277, 305
Phillips, John H., Pvt. (Co. H) 269, 274, 281, 367
Phillips, Richard, Pvt. (Co. F) 219, 284, 289, 293, 353
Philips, Sarah "Sally" Tartt 4
Pickett, George, CS, Gen. 241
Pickett, John L., Pvt. (Co. E) 74, 270, 280, 344
Pickett, William D., Pvt. (Co. E) 153, 266, 281, 282, 290, 341
Pierce, George W., Pvt. (Co. D) 37, 266, 280, 335
Pierce, James M., Pvt. (Co. K) 286, 384
Pierce, James T., Pvt. (Co. D) 268, 286, 333
Pierce, James T., Pvt. (Co. K) 177, 266
Pierce, James W., Pvt. (Co. K) 387
Pierce, Nixon, Cpl. (Co. E) 283, 344
Pierce, Orren L., Pvt. (Co. K) 47, 219, 289, 384
Pilgreen, McGilbert, Pvt. (Co. C) 300, 324
Pilgreen, William H., Pvt. (Co. C) 164, 283, 324

Pilgrim, McGilbert, Pvt. (Co. C) 270
Piner, James J., Pvt. (Co. E) 286, 301, 346
Piper, Wesley Y., Pvt. (Co. D) 266, 336
Pipkin, Lewis H., Cpl. (Co. A) 36, 265, 310
Pitt, Franklin G., Cpt. (Co. F) 5, 346
Pitt, Frederick, Pvt. (Co. I) 146, 301, 374
Pitt, James W., Pvt. (Co. I) 162, 285, 294, 374
Pitt, James W., Lt. (Co. F) 5, 17, 19, 30, 300, 346
Pitt, John W., Pvt. (Co. I) 146, 301, 378
Pitt, Theophilus, Pvt. (Co. F) 280, 353
Pitt, William M., Pvt. (Co. I) 378
Pittman, George W., Pvt. (Co. F) 269, 277, 350
Pittman, Reddin E., Pvt.-Cpl. (Co. F) 264, 284, 293, 350
Pittman, William B., Pvt. (Co. I) 378
Pitts, William M., Pvt. (Co. I) 291
Point Lookout Prison, Maryland 137, 262
Poland, Alford, Pvt. (Co. I) 298
Poland, Alfred, Pvt. (Co. I) 6, 374
Poland, Simeon H., Pvt. (Co. I) 300, 374
Pollard, James H., Pvt. (Co. F) 297, 351
Pollard, Joshua H., Pvt. (Co. D) 280, 333
Pollard, Samuel R., Pvt. (Co. D) 280, 337
Pollard, William H., Pvt. (Co. D) 263, 333
Pollard, Willie G., Pvt. (Co. D) 274, 280, 333
Pool, Thomas, Pvt. (Co. H) 301, 371
Pope, Alexander, Pvt. (Co. A) 35, 265, 310
Pope, Stephen, Pvt. (Co. A) 310
Pope, Wiley, Pvt. (Co. A) 35, 265, 283, 310
Pope, William B., Pvt. (Co. A) 140, 310
Posey, Carnot, CS, Col.-Gen. 59, 84
Potomac River 46, 47, 52, 66, 103, 104, 122, 123, 190, 196, 202
Potter, Henry G., Pvt. (Co. C) 266, 297, 325
Potter, William M., Pvt. (Co. C) 325
Potts, Joseph R., Pvt. (Co. K) 300, 388
Price, Joel L., Pvt. (Co. I) 35, 146, 267, 374
Price, Thomas, Pvt. (Co. F) 167, 284, 351
Pridgen, Alexander, Pvt. (Co. I) 374
Pridgen, Alexander S., Pvt. (Co. C) 325
Pridgen, Drewry, Pvt. (Co. I) 133, 278, 378

Index

Pridgen, Henry H., Pvt. (Co. I) 281, 378
Pridgen, Josiah H., Pvt. (Co. I) 281, 300, 378
Pridgen, William E., Pvt. (Co. A) 310
Prince, Henry, U.S., Gen. 140
Pruitt, Hampton, Pvt. (Co. G) 133, 278, 360

Raccoon Ford, Virginia 151
Rackley, George W., Pvt.-Sgt. (Co. A) 271, 282, 310
Rackley, James, Pvt. (Co. I) 190, 374
Rackley, James S., Pvt. (Co. E) 341
Rackley, P. Nicholas, Pvt. (Co. I) 122, 277, 300, 378
Ragland, William G., Pvt. (Co. G) 80, 81, 300, 362
Ramseur, Stephen D., CS, Gen 70, 80, 81, 83, 84, 85, 86, 87, 88, 89, 90, 91, 92, 94, 95, 96, 98, 99, 100, 101, 104, 109, 110, 111, 112, 113, 114, 115, 116, 117, 119, 125, 126, 129, 137, 139, 140, 142, 147, 148, 149, 151, 153, 154, 155, 156, 157, 158, 159, 160, 161, 162, 164, 171, 172, 173, 174, 176, 178, 179, 182, 183, 184, 192, 193, 194, 208, 214, 215, 217, 218, 219, 220, 230, 231
Rape, Isaac S., Pvt. (Co. H) 371
Rapidan River 44, 101, 146, 150
Rappahannock River 81, 82, 84, 127, 129
Ray, Caswell, Pvt. (Co. D) 337
Ray, David A., Pvt. (Co. D) 280, 330
Ray, Henry C., Pvt. (Co. D) 280, 337
Ray, John F., Pvt. (Co. K) 292
Ray, William B., Pvt. (Co. D) 280, 330
Ray, Zeddock D., Sgt. (Co. D) 263, 280, 330
Rayl, John F., Pvt. (Co. K) 389
Raynor, John C., Pvt. (Co. D) 341
Rayner, Lovett, Pvt. (Co. K) 133, 279, 387
Rea, James M., Pvt. (Co. K) 273, 384
Read, David K., Pvt. (Co. G) 358
Reams, George W., Pvt. (Co. G) 6, 267, 358
Reavis, Joseph H., Pvt. (Co. D) 333
Redick, Epinetus, Pvt. (Co. F) 195, 278, 287, 302, 351
Reed, M.D., Pvt. (Co. A) 313
Register, Edward M., Pvt. (Co. A) 265, 299, 310
Register, Harmon H., Pvt. (Co. A) 310
Register, Samuel C., Pvt. (Co. E) 280, 341
Register, Thomas, Pvt. (Co. C) 297, 325
Reidling, William A., Pvt. (Co. C) 279, 328
Renfrow, Perry V., Sgt. (Co. I) 270, 273, 281, 375
Reynolds, Charles H., Pvt. (Co. A) 298, 310

Reynolds, John R., Pvt. (Co. A) 283, 303, 311
Rhodes, Wiley, Pvt. (Co. H) 371
Rich, Christopher C., Pvt. (Co. E) 280, 341
Rich, James O., Pvt. (Co. A) 311
Richardson, William W., Pvt. (Co. K) 292, 384
Richmond, Virginia 20, 41, 42, 44, 172, 180, 183, 186, 234 235, 236
Ricketts, James, U.S., Gen. 152, 217, 218
Ricks, John A., Pvt. (Co. I) 375
Riddle, George W., Pvt. (Co. H) 267, 281, 367
Riggan, Charles, D., Pvt. (Co. B) 292, 317
Riggan, Charles S., Pvt.-Cpl. (Co B) 163, 283, 290, 292, 317
Riggan, Isham S., Pvt. (Co. B) 283, 302, 320
Riggan, Minga E., Pvt. (Co. B) 317
Riggan, Sugar A., Pvt. (Co. B) 283, 302, 319
Rigsbee, William C., Pvt. (Co. I) 285, 380
Rivenbark, James T., Pvt. (Co. E) 341
Rivenbark, Joseph, Pvt. (Co. E) 264, 341
Rivenbark, Teachy, Pvt.-Sgt. (Co. E) 133, 266, 278, 341
Rivenbark, William, Cpl. (Co. E) 36, 266, 338
Roach, Archibald D., Pvt. (Co. C) 301, 329
Roanoke, North Carolina 12
Robbins, Edward J., Pvt. (Co. I) 375
Robbins, Willie H., Cpl. (Co. I) 372
Roberson, James, Pvt. (Co. F) 280
Robertson, Charles H., Pvt. (Co. G) 360
Robertson, James, Pvt. (Co. F) 272, 350
Robertson, Peter E., Pvt.-Cpl. (Co. B) 268, 298, 317
Robertson, Robert, Pvt. (Co. I) 300, 380
Robertson, Z.R., Pvt. (Co. G) 289, 302, 362
Robins, Jonathan, Pvt. (Co. C) 289, 293, 329
Robinson, Alexander S., Pvt.-Cpl. (Co. C) 274, 276, 292, 325
Robinson, Harmon R., Pvt. (Co. A) 300, 311
Robinson, James R., Pvt. (Co. K) 36, 268, 384
Robinson, Margaret "Maggie" 1
Robinson, Thomas M., Pvt. (Co. A) 311
Robinson, William H., Pvt. (Co. K) 287, 302, 384
Robison, William, Pvt. (Co. F) 264, 351
Rodes, Robert, CS, Gen. 52, 62, 82, 84, 86, 88, 90, 99, 100, 101, 102, 103, 104, 105, 106, 109, 110, 114, 115, 116, 117, 118, 120, 121, 122, 123, 125, 129, 130, 132, 133, 138, 140,
142, 154, 159, 172, 184, 189, 192, 200, 201, 204, 208, 209, 214, 215, 221
Rogers, Charles M., Lt. (Co. D) 16, 19, 30, 45, 51, 63, 269, 330
Rogers, James, Pvt. (Co. H) 285, 367
Rogers, Jobe B., Pvt. (Co. E) 286, 302, 346
Rogers, John H., Pvt. (Co. D) 283, 302, 336
Rogers, Martin L., Lt. (Co. D) 145, 151, 169, 175, 180, 185, 190, 196, 197, 199, 205, 287, 333
Rogers, William, Pvt. (Co. A) 242, 290, 313
Rogister, James, Pvt. (Co. A) 279, 313
Rose, Henry B., Pvt. (Co. H) 285, 371
Rose, Lewis D., Pvt. (Co. B) 317
Ross, J. Newell, Pvt. (Co. K) 285, 388
Ross, James P., Pvt. (Co. G) 361
Ross, Richard S., Pvt. (Co. D) 337
Ross, William J., Pvt. (Co. K) 231, 295, 384
Rouse, Barnet, Pvt. (Co. E) 264, 341
Royal, Hardy S., Sgt. (Co. A) 26, 93, 263, 271, 306
Royal, Marshall, Pvt. (Co. A) 296, 311
Royal, Martin, Pvt. (Co. A) 299, 311
Royal, Nevin, Pvt. (Co. A) 263, 311
Royal, Sherman, Cpl. (Co. A) 36, 265, 311
Ruark, Edward, Lt. (Co. K) 78
Ruark, Edward R., Lt. (Co. C) 298, 325
Ruffin, Charles H., Pvt. (Co. I) 128, 277, 375
Rugar, Thomas, U.S., Gen. 85
Russ, Stewart, Pvt.-Sgt. (Co. C) 263, 279, 325
Russell, William D., Pvt.-Sgt. (Co. K) 203, 216, 220, 223, 232, 233, 270, 275, 276, 291, 384

Saintsing, John A., Pvt. (Co. B) 161, 283, 292, 317
Salmon, Henry, Pvt. (Co. B) 317
Salmon, Kilby, Pvt. (Co. E) 344
Sample, William, Pvt. (Co. K) 282, 388
Sampson Rangers 5, 305
Savage, Cornelius, Sgt. (Co. E) 297, 341
Savage, John, Pvt. (Co. E) 277, 344
Saville, John C., Pvt. (Co. K) 288, 295, 389
Saylor's Creek 249, 250, 251
Sellers, Raymond G., Pvt. (Co. C) 295, 325
Sellers, Samuel H., Pvt. (Co. C) 296, 325
Seward, William H., Sec. of State 238
Sharps Rifles 131, 135, 136
Sharpsburg, battle 51–65
Sharpshooter Corps 80, 82, 85, 98,

Index

113, 116, 117, 118, 125, 128, 140, 155, 175, 192, 201, 239, 243
Shaw, Alexander D., Pvt. (Co. K) 384
Shaw, Douglas C., Pvt. (Co. H) 95, 269, 273, 278, 367
Shearin, Edwin C., Pvt. (Co. B) 297, 320
Shearin, Gardiner E., Pvt. (Co. B) 6, 279, 318
Shearin, Jacob, Pvt. (Co. B) 6, 318
Shearin, John, Pvt. (Co. B) 210
Shearin, John D., Sgt. (Co. B) 145, 151, 169, 282, 302, 314
Shearin, John L., Pvt. (Co. B) 6, 289, 318
Shearin, John R., Pvt. (Co. B) 6, 291, 318
Shearin, Joseph W., Pvt. (Co. B) 320
Shearin, Landon T., Pvt. (Co. B) 276, 303, 320
Shearin, Moses, Pvt. (Co. B) 6, 318
Shearin, Nicholas L., Pvt. (Co. B) 36, 265, 319
Shearin, Richard E., Pvt. (Co. B) 320
Shearin, Richard R., Pvt. (Co. B) 6, 141, 263, 318
Shearin, Thomas G., Pvt.-Cpl.-Sgt. (Co. B) 6, 163, 195, 202, 207, 214, 216, 219, 222, 232, 268, 271, 287, 318
Shearin, Thomas W., Cpl. (Co. B) 283, 292, 318
Shelby, David H., Pvt. (Co. K) 389
Shenandoah River 69, 102, 196, 197, 223
Shenandoah Valley, Virginia 102, 186, 187, 188, 189, 233
Shepherdstown, Virginia 66, 190, 205
Sheridan, Philip, U.S., Gen. 202, 216, 217, 218, 222, 228, 229, 232, 233, 241
Sherwood, Edwin, Pvt. (Co. I) 273, 378
Sherwood, George A., Pvt. (Co. I) 35, 267, 273, 281, 378
Shew, Jacob W., Pvt. (Co. C) 95, 271, 327
Shew, Joel, Pvt. (Co. C) 271, 327
Sholar, James H., Pvt. (Co. E) 291, 344
Shore, William F., Pvt. (Co. H) 371
Short, William F., Pvt. (Co. H) 294
Shute, Henry B., Pvt. (Co. E) 290, 346
Sillers, William W. Lt.-Maj.-Lt. Col. (Co. A) 5, 14, 15, 16, 19, 30, 31, 45, 51, 52, 53, 56, 61, 62, 63, 64, 66, 67, 69, 71, 72, 74, 76, 78, 79, 81, 83, 88, 93, 96, 99, 106, 108, 110, 112, 113, 114, 115, 117, 118, 121, 122, 123, 124, 125, 126, 127, 130, 131, 132, 133, 134, 136, 137, 139, 277, 305
Simmons, Daniel, Pvt. (Co. C) 325
Simmons, Daniel F., Pvt. (Co. C) 296, 325
Simmons, Elisha, Pvt. (Co. K) 389

Simmons, James A., Pvt. (Co. C) 325
Simmons, John B., Pvt. (Co. C) 272, 325
Simmons, John C., Pvt. (Co. C) 9, 295, 325
Simmons, Lewis, Pvt. (Co. C) 290, 329
Simpson, Jefferson, Pvt. (Co. K) 384
Simpson, Marcus, Pvt. (Co. K) 285, 386
Sinclair, John D., Pvt. (Co. H) 294, 369
Sizemore, William P., Pvt.-Cpl. (Co. G) 153, 264, 281, 358
Skipper, Wesley W., Pvt. (Co. C) 168, 283, 329
Slaughter, James H., Pvt. (Co. G) 300, 362
Slaughter, Thomas D., Pvt. (Co. G) 294, 358
Slaughter, William P., Pvt. (Co. G) 284, 361
Sloan, David A., Pvt. (Co. H) 273, 281, 369
Sloan, David H., Pvt. (Co. H) 269
Sloan, John A., Pvt. (Co. H) 297, 369
Smallpox 77, 78
Smith, Albert, Pvt. (Co. I) 273, 378
Smith, Benjamin, Cpl. (Co. C) 112, 274, 276, 289, 321
Smith, George W. Pvt. (Co. B) 298, 318
Smith, J.D., Pvt. (Co. K) 389
Smith, John S., Pvt. (Co. K) 282, 302, 389
Smith, Lemuel H., Com. Sgt. (F & S) 305, 347
Smith, Reuben, Pvt. (Co. C) 283, 329
Smith, Richard P., Pvt. (Co. A) 311
Smith, Samuel B., Cpl. (Co. K) 300, 387
Smith, Thomas G., Pvt. (Co. D) 280, 334
Smith, William S., 1st Sgt. (Co. K) 235, 242, 246, 294, 384
Smithfield Redoubt, Virginia 212, 212
Smithville, North Carolina 7, 8, 9
Smythe, Thomas, U.S., Col. 181, 182
Snicker's Gap, Virginia 196, 197, 200
Snider, Joseph, U.S., Col. 57, 60
Sollice, Devane, Pvt. (Co. G) 280, 301, 362
South Anna River 44
South Mountain, Maryland 47, 51, 191
South Mountain, battle 48–50
Southerland, James, Pvt. (Co. E) 111, 120, 274, 280, 344
Sparta Band 5, 346
Spell, Gaston, Pvt. (Co. A) 292, 312
Spell, Hardy L., Pvt. (Co. A) 311
Spencer rifles 211
Spotsylvania Court House, Virginia 101, 155
Sprinkle, Hugh, Pvt. (Co. C) 289, 329

Squires, James W., Pvt. (Co. K) 162, 285, 384
Squires, John B., Pvt. (Co. K) 47, 295, 386
Staley, Enoch, Pvt. (Co. C) 272, 327
Staley, Peter, Pvt. (Co. C) 272
Stallings, Edwin, Pvt. (Co. F) 293, 351
Stallings, Elisha B., Pvt. (Co. B) 321
Stallings, Franklin, Pvt. (Co. I) 273, 378
Stallings, John A., Pvt. (Co. B) 297, 320
Stallings, Rufus, Pvt. (Co. F) 293, 353
Stallings, Theophilus, QM Sgt. (F & S) 144, 292, 304, 318
Stallings, Walter, CS, Lt. Col. 183
Stallings, Willie, Pvt. (Co. I) 378
Stalvey, Benjamin L., Pvt. (Co. C) 295, 325
Stancil, Arthur G., Pvt. (Co. K) 384
Stanford, Moses T., Pvt. (Co. K) 384
Stanley, Stewart, Pvt. (Co. C) 263
Stanly, Edward W., Pvt. (Co. C) 296, 325
Stanly, Samuel J., Pvt. (Co. C) 296, 326
Stanly, Stewart, Pvt. (Co. C) 298, 326
Stanly, William F., Pvt. (Co. C) 326
Stanton, James R., Pvt. (Co. G) 282, 294, 358
Starnes, D.A., Pvt. (Co. H) 288, 371
Starnes, Ephraim, Pvt. (Co. H) 285, 302, 371
Starnes, Thomas, Pvt. (Co. H) 277, 294, 371
Staunton, Virginia 234
Stedman, David L., Pvt. (Co. H) 299, 367
Steel, Andrew F., Sgt. (Co. K) 24, 264, 384
Steele, James H., Pvt. (Co. A) 279, 292, 313
Steele, Robert, Pvt. (Co. E) 286, 346
Stephens, Alexander H., CS Vice Pres. 238
Stephenson, James, Pvt. (Co. K) 270
Steuart, George, CS, Gen. 146, 158
Stevens, Charles T., Lt. (Co. A) 16, 19, 30, 45, 306
Stevenson, James R., Pvt. (Co. K) 384
Stiles, John M., Pvt. (Co. E) 298, 342
Stone, Daniel B., Pvt. (Co. G) 358
Strange, Albert, Pvt. (Co. G) 296, 361
Strasburg, Virginia 201, 202, 214, 231
Streets, Wimbert, Pvt. (Co. E) 299, 342
Strickland, David R., Pvt. (Co. E) 284, 345
Strickland, Henry O., Pvt. (Co. I) 294, 380
Strickland, Isaac J., Pvt. (Co. E) 342

Index

Strickland, Walter D., Pvt. (Co. A) 298, 311
Strickland, William H., Cpl. (Co. E) 338
Strickland, William W., Pvt. (Co. E) 26, 264, 342
Stuart, J.E.B., CS, Gen. 89, 90, 92, 172
Summerlin, George, Pvt. (Co. F) 286, 351
Summerville Ford, Virginia 101
Sunken Road, Maryland 53, 64
Sutton, Michael, Pvt. (Co. A) 311
Swain, Benjamin F., Pvt. (Co. C) 263, 321
Swain, George T., Pvt. (Co. C) 120, 274, 322
Swain, John R., Lt. (Co. C) 108, 130, 145, 151, 165, 283, 321
Swann, William M., Cpt. (Co. H) 5, 362
Swift Creek 234, 238
Sykes, William J., Pvt. (Co. I) 287, 375

Tadlock, Starling D., Pvt. (Co. E) 291, 346
Talley, Benjamin T., Pvt. (Co. B) 299, 318
Tart, Henry, Pvt. (Co. K) 389
Tatom, Love A., Pvt. (Co. A) 312
Taylor, Bolen, Pvt. (Co. I) 296, 375
Taylor, Calvin C., Pvt. (Co. I) 375
Taylor, Egbert H., Pvt. (Co. I) 375
Taylor, Jackson, Pvt. (Co. H) 281, 367
Taylor, Richard, D., Pvt. (Co. G) 361
Taylor, Richard P., Cpt. (Co. G) 5, 354
Taylor, Thomas J., Pvt. (Co. A) 270, 313
Taylor, William J., Pvt. (Co. A) 271, 283, 311
Teachey, Atlas, Pvt. (Co. E) 345
Teachey, Daniel, Lt. (Co. E) 338
Teachey, Jacob T., Pvt. (Co. E) 199, 288, 345
Teachey, James W., Sgt. (Co. E) 199, 288, 342
Teachey, Marchal, Sgt. (Co. E) 297, 338
Teachey, Wiley B., Pvt.–Cpl. (Co. E) 284, 290, 345
Tedder, Sidney, Pvt. (Co. K) 31, 265, 384
Tennessee Inf.: 7th 89
Tew, Blackman, Pvt. (Co. A) 27, 263, 311
Tew, Charles, CS, Col. 18, 32, 33, 35, 38, 39, 41, 42, 47, 52, 54, 59, 62, 131
Tew, Wiley, Pvt. (Co. D) 298, 311
Tharp, John L., Sgt. (Co. C) 36, 265, 326
Tharp, Samuel P., Lt. (Co. C) 5, 321
Tharp, William H., Pvt. (Co. C) 266, 300, 326
Thomas, George L., Pvt. (Co. B) 297, 318
Thomas, Henry, Pvt. (Co. H) 294, 369
Thomas, Jefferson, Pvt. (Co. H) 6, 367
Thomas John W., Pvt. (Co. H) 297, 367
Thomas, Lee, Pvt. (Co. A) 6
Thomas, Lewis R., Pvt. (Co. K) 292
Thomas, Marshall G., Pvt. (Co. H) 367
Thomas, Murphy J., Pvt. (Co. H) 286, 367
Thomas, Robert H., Cpl. (Co. D) 282, 302, 337
Thomas, William A., Pvt. (Co. H) 296, 367
Thomas, William B., Pvt. (Co. K) 295, 386
Thomas, William H., Pvt. (Co. B) 271, 318
Thomason, John L., Pvt. (Co. K) 265, 385
Thompson, A. George, Pvt. (Co. C) 329
Thompson, Andrew, Pvt. (Co. C) 134
Thompson, Andrew J., Pvt. (Co. E) 278, 342
Thompson, James, Pvt. (Co. K) 142, 300, 389
Thompson, John A., Pvt. (Co. B) 27, 263, 318
Thompson, Lee, Pvt. (Co. K) 270, 296, 385
Thompson, Lewis R., Pvt. (Co. K) 273, 385
Thompson, Solomon, Pvt. (Co. D) 336
Thompson, William, CS, Cpt. 183
Thorburn, Joseph, U.S., Col. 197, 198
Thorn, William E., Pvt. (Co. I) 296, 375
Thraikill, Joseph M., Cpl. (Co. A) 299, 306
Thrower, Thomas J., Pvt. (Co. K) 385
Tidball, John, U.S., Cpt. 25, 26, 27
Tidsale, Thomas B., Pvt. (Co. I) 375
Tilley, William H., Pvt. (Co. D) 280
Tilly, John R., Pvt. (Co. D) 268, 280, 303, 336
Tilly, William B., Pvt. (Co. D) 337
Tilly, William H., Pvt. (Co. D) 336
Tilly, William L., Pvt. (Co. D) 297, 334
Tindale, David, Pvt. (Co. A) 311
Tindale, Miles S., Pvt. (Co. A) 283, 311
Traylor, A.M., Pvt. (Co. G) 267, 361
Traylor, Charles, Pvt. (Co. G) 358
Tucker, Owen, Pvt. (Co. E) 297, 345
Tucker, William, Pvt. (Co. E) 286, 342
Turner, Cicero, Mus. (Co. A) 306
Turner, David W., Pvt. (Co. E) 204, 278, 288, 293, 346
Turner, Henry, Pvt. (Co. B) 318
Turner, Walter, Pvt. (Co. I) 15, 375

Typhoid fever 9, 46

Underwood, Daniel R., Pvt. (Co. A) 271, 311
Underwood, John A., Pvt.–Cpl. (Co. H) 162, 277, 285, 294, 367
Underwood, R.H., Pvt. (Co. E) 296, 345
United States Regulars 3rd 26, 27
United States Regulars 4th 26, 27
United States Regulars 12th 26
United States Sharpshooters 1st 131, 135
United States Sharpshooters, 2nd 131, 135
Upton, Emory, U.S., Col.–Gen. 156, 211, 212
Utley, John W., Pvt. (Co. H) 117, 275, 369

Vance, Zebulon, North Carolina Governor 42, 43, 149, 202, 239
Vaughan, John G., Pvt. (Co. D) 291, 334
Verser, John, Pvt. (Co. B) 300, 321
Vick, Benjamin S., Pvt. (Co. I) 375
Vick, Exum R., Cpl. (Co. I) 35, 267, 375
Vick, James F., Pvt. (Co. I) 281, 375
Vick, Joseph J., Pvt. (Co. I) 375
Vick, Joseph K., Pvt. (Co. I) 289
Vick, Lorenzo, Pvt. (Co. F) 58, 269
Vick, William, Pvt. (Co. F) 266, 284, 351
Vick, William H., Pvt. (Co. I) 296, 378
Vick, Wylie R., Pvt. (Co. I) 111, 275, 276
Vines, Charles, Lt., (Co. F) 346
Vines, William T., Pvt. (Co. C) 293, 326
Vuncannon, John P., Pvt. (Co. C) 135, 278, 329

Wadford, Alexander, Pvt. (Co. D) 276, 293, 336
Wainwright, John K., Pvt. (Co. G) 358
Wainwright, William P., Pvt. (Co. G) 297
Walker, Berryman, Pvt. (Co. I) 267, 378
Walker, Christopher N., Pvt. (Co. B) 292, 318
Walker, James, CS, Gen. 158
Walker, James C., Pvt. (Co. A) 271, 311
Walker, Jarrett, Pvt. (Co. D) 335
Walker, John Blount, Pvt. (Co. I) 118, 275, 276, 379
Walker, Levi, Pvt. (Co. B) 297, 318
Walker, Richmond D., Pvt. (Co. I) 281, 375
Walker, Sandy, Pvt. (Co. H) 368
Walker, Willis S., Pvt. (Co. D) 336
Walker, Worrell P., Pvt. (Co. I) 281, 375
Wallace, Robert C., Pvt. (Co. E) 299, 342
Wallace, William T., Pvt. (Co. E) 95, 272, 342

438 Index

Waller, P.H., Pvt. (Co. D) 298, 336
Walls, William B., Pvt. (Co. G) 301, 361
Walston, Franklin, Cpl. (Co. F) 269, 280, 351
Walston, James, Pvt. (Co. F) 266, 351
Walston, John, Sgt.–1st Sgt. (Co. F) 284, 293, 353
Walston, Kinchen, Pvt. (Co. F) 351
Waltson, Levi, Pvt. (Co. F) 291, 353
Walston, Ralph, Pvt. (Co. F) 354
Walston, Rufus F., Pvt. (Co. F) 280, 353
Walston, Silas L., Pvt. (Co. K) 298, 387
Walston, William F., Pvt. (Co. F) 204, 268, 272, 288, 351
Wamack, William D., Pvt. (Co. F) 284, 354
Wammack, Levi T., Pvt. (Co. A) 313
Wanett, William A., Pvt. (Co. C) 163, 283, 326
Ward, Isaac B., Pvt. (Co. D) 276, 291, 334
Ward, John F., Pvt. (Co. E) 342
Ward, William J., Cpl. (Co. D) 280, 334
Ward, Wilson, Pvt. (Co. D) 280, 334
Warren, Lemuel, Pvt. (Co. F) 56, 204, 269, 288, 291, 353
Warrick, Thomas J., Pvt. (Co. A) 278, 301, 313
Washington D. C. 191, 192, 194
Watkins, John W., Pvt. (Co. G) 361
Watkins, William B., Pvt. (Co. H) 295, 371
Watson, Andrew J., Pvt. (Co. H) 299, 368
Watson, Levi, Pvt. (Co. F) 284
Watson, Ralph, Pvt. (Co. F) 293
Webb, Bennett, Pvt. (Co. F) 185, 287, 354
Webb, Hardy, Pvt. (Co. F) 267, 354
Webb, John, Pvt. (Co. F) 293, 354
Webb, Morrison, Pvt. (Co. F) 128, 277, 351
Webb, Newett, Mus., (Co. F) 269, 284, 293, 351
Webb, William, Pvt. (Co. K) 299, 387
Weber, Max, U.S., Gen. 54
Weeks, John A., Pvt. (Co. A) 271, 311
Weeks, Rufus, Pvt.–Sgt. (Co. K) 63, 176, 270, 286, 386
Wells, George, U.S., Col. 198
Wells, James N., Pvt. (Co. G) 361
Wells, James W., Sgt.–1st Sgt. (Co. E) 55, 56, 73, 74, 176, 269, 286, 342
Wells, John, Sgt. (Co. E) 270
Wells, John H., Cpl. (Co. E) 264, 342
Wells, Louis R., Pvt.–Cpl. (Co. F) 6, 198, 288, 347
West Point 18, 68, 70, 100, 187
West, William M., Pvt. (Co. K) 289, 303, 389

Westcott, Henry A., Mus. (Co. C) 322
Westcott, John W., Cpl.–Sgt. (Co. C) 6, 175, 180, 185, 190, 196, 199, 202, 205, 207, 214, 216, 220, 269, 289, 302, 321
Westcott, Samuel W., Pvt. (Co. C) 266, 299, 326
Westcott, William H., Pvt. (Co. C) 299, 326
Westray, Archibald H., Pvt. (Co. I) 112, 275, 276, 379
Wethersby, Joseph, Pvt. (Co. F) 354
Wharton, Gabriel, CS, Gen. 201
Wheeler, James, Pvt. (Co. D) 37, 266, 336
Wheeler, John W., Pvt. (Co. D) 95, 272, 334
Whitley, Jolley B., Pvt. (Co. I) 112
White Oak Bridge, Virginia 31
White, Almond, Pvt. (Co. D) 37, 266, 334
White, Eli M., Pvt. (Co. C) 279, 326
White, James, Pvt. (Co. D) 266, 336
White, James D., Cpl. (Co. D) 330
White, James J., Pvt. (Co. B) 37, 265, 318
White, John E., Pvt. (Co. D) 334
White, Lassiter, Sgt. Maj.–Lt. (Co. A) 83, 108, 130, 145, 151, 163, 172, 282, 304, 312
White, Mason, Pvt. (Co. D) 334
Whitehurst, Thomas, Sgt. (Co. F) 155
Whitfield, John W., Pvt. (Co. I) 281, 379
Whitfield, Patrick L., Pvt. (Co. I) 379
Whitley, John S., Pvt. (Co. I) 296, 376
Whitley, Jolley B., Pvt. (Co. I) 270, 275, 379
Whitehurst, Thomas, 1st Sgt. (Co. F) 282, 351
Wicker, Alvis, Pvt. (Co. H) 298, 369
Wicker, Charles B., Pvt. (Co. H) 294, 370
Wicker, Jesse J., Cpt. (Co. H) 15, 17, 19, 28, 30, 39, 45, 48, 49, 50, 71, 74, 78, 84, 96, 108, 124, 130, 144, 145, 151, 152, 160, 165, 169, 172, 268, 285, 363
Wicker, John J., Pvt. (Co. H) 296, 368
Wicker, Kenneth W., Pvt. (Co. H) 267, 370
Wicker, Lewis M., Pvt. (Co. H) 111, 274, 363
Wicker, Oren R., Pvt. (Co. H) 300, 368
Wicker, Thomas, Pvt. (Co. H) 111, 269, 274, 368
Wicker, William F., Pvt. (Co. H) 270, 370
Wicker, William M., Pvt. (Co. H) 60, 264, 368
Wiggins, Martin W., Pvt. (Co. F) 27, 95, 264, 272, 351
Wilbourne, Ruffin F., Pvt. (Co. I) 268, 376

Wilcox, Cadmus, CS, Gen. 158
Wilkerson, James, Pvt. (Co. G) 280, 361
Wilkins, Elijah, Pvt. (Co. D) 74, 203, 266, 270, 272, 288, 334
Wilkins, Hinton, Pvt. (Co. D) 299, 336
Wilkins, James, Pvt. (Co. D) 263, 334
Wilkins, William, Pvt. (Co. D) 280, 337
Williams, Buckner D., Lt. (Co. B) 5, 314
Williams, Buckner, QM-Cpt. (F & S) 11, 305
Williams, Gary, Lt.–Cpt. (Co. A) 16, 19, 30, 31, 39, 71, 83, 96, 108, 124, 130, 134, 136, 137, 145, 151, 165, 169, 172, 282, 306
Williams, Henry H., Pvt. (Co. I) 267, 281, 376
Williams, James B., Pvt. (Co. C) 296, 326
Williams, John C., Cpl. (Co. A0) 306
Williams, Joseph, Pvt. (Co. C) 274, 276, 301, 326
Williams, Joseph D., Pvt. (Co. I) 181, 268, 287, 376
Williams, Micajah T., Pvt. (Co. I) 267, 379
Williams, Nathan C., Pvt. (Co. I) 281, 300, 380
Williams, Robert D., Sgt. (Co. B) 112, 274, 279, 314
Williams, Samuel S., Pvt. (Co. D) 25, 264, 334
Williams, Simon P., Pvt. (Co. D) 334
Williams, William A., Pvt. (Co. B) 204, 279, 288, 318, 320
Williams, Wright J., Pvt. (Co. I) 379
Williamson, David, Pvt. (Co. A) 279, 312
Williamson, Henry, Cpl.–Sgt. (Co. A) 271, 292, 306
Williamson, James, Pvt. (Co. A) 27, 133, 263, 278, 283, 312
Williamson, John B., Pvt. (Co. C) 164, 283, 329
Williamson, William E., Pvt. (Co. K) 12, 270, 385
Williamsport, Maryland 104, 123, 201, 202
Williford, Burton B., Lt., (Co. I) 17, 19, 30, 45, 52, 71, 84, 95, 273, 376
Williford, Thomas, Pvt. (Co. F) 267, 352
Wilmington, North Carolina 7, 8, 9, 11, 12, 13, 15, 16
Wilson, John L., Pvt. (Co. E) 300, 346
Wilson, Samuel R., Pvt. (Co. G) 285, 362
Wimberly, Matthew, Pvt. (Co. B) 321
Winchester, Virginia 208, 212, 213, 233
Winchester, battle 208–214
Winecoff, George W., Pvt. (Co. A) 279, 313

Index

Winn, Thomas, Pvt. (Co. G) 297, 361
Winstead G. J., Pvt. (Co. I) 379
Winstead, George T., Pvt. (Co. I) 93, 268, 273, 376
Winstead, Hilliard H., Pvt.-Cpl. (Co. I) 204, 270, 288, 376
Winstead, Robert T., Pvt. (Co. I) 112
Winstead, Theophilus T., Pvt. (Co. I) 275, 276, 379
Winn, Thomas, Pvt. (Co. G) 42
Winters, George, Pvt. (Co. I) 273, 286, 376
Wisconsin Inf.: 6th 75; 7th 153
Witcher, William, CS, Col. 158
Witherspoon, John G., 1st Sgt.-Lt.-Cpt. (Co. K) 5, 6, 8, 9, 10, 12, 13, 14, 15, 17, 37, 38, 39, 42, 51, 67, 68, 69, 70, 72, 74, 76, 77, 78, 79, 80, 84, 96, 97, 100, 108, 124, 130, 134, 135, 137, 138, 278, 381
Witherspoon, Mitty J., Pvt. (Co. K) 80, 94, 95, 97, 273, 386
Wolfe, Robert B., Pvt. (Co. K) 281, 303
Wolfe, John N., Pvt. (Co. K) 385
Wolfe, Robert B., Pvt. (Co. K) 385
Wolfe, Thomas D., Pvt. (Co. K) 270, 299, 386
Womack, James R., Pvt. (Co. H) 281, 303, 368
Wood, James, Pvt. (Co. I) 297, 376
Wood, Marley, Pvt. (Co. E) 298, 342
Wood, Uzzell T., Pvt. (Co. E) 284, 293, 342
Wood, William, Pvt. (Co. I) 273, 376
Woods, James, Pvt. (Co. D) 144
Woods, James, CS, Col. 183
Woods, Marley, Pvt. (Co. E) 74
Woodward, Coleman W., Lt. (Co. I) 371
Woodward, John E., Pvt. (Co. I) 36, 268, 281, 376
Wooten, John S., Pvt. (Co. F) 297, 352
Wortman, David D., Pvt. (Co. G) 133, 278, 361
Wortman, Simeon, Pvt. (Co. G) 297, 361
Wright, Ambrose, CS, Gen. 58, 125
West Virginia Inf.: 7th 57, 59, 60
Wyatt, Henry 3, 9

Yancy, Thomas A., Pvt. (Co. H) 267, 281, 368
Yarborough, W.T., Pvt. (Co. H) 368
Yearby, Allen, Pvt. (Co. D) 334
Yeargen, Wyatt, Pvt. (Co. K) 387
Younts, John A., Pvt. (Co. K) 36, 268, 273, 385

www.ingramcontent.com/pod-product-compliance
Lightning Source LLC
Chambersburg PA
CBHW080753300426
44114CB00020B/2721